SIXTH EDITION

WOMEN'S HEALTH

Readings on Social, Economic, and Political Issues

Dawna Marie Thomas

Kendall Hunt
publishing company

Cover image © Shutterstock.com

Kendall Hunt
publishing company

www.kendallhunt.com
Send all inquiries to:
4050 Westmark Drive
Dubuque, IA 52004-1840

TABLE OF CONTENTS

CHAPTER 3:   Sex, Gender Roles, and Image 209

PREFACE

This edition of the book builds on the success of the previous five editions and includes articles that highlight cutting-edge issues and innovative approaches to women's health and responds to reviewers' comments regarding women's health, wellness, and activism—all to ensure that women are informed and empowered in their decision-making process about health.

The edition of the book:

- Includes eighty-six articles with over fifty new and *classic* readings that are important to understand the history and progress of women's health and the women's health movements.

- Includes traditional chapters that have been in previous five editions, redesign of previous chapters, and new chapters: Disability and Society; Menstruation and the Politics of Sex Education; Fertility, Childbirth, and Reproductive Justice; Aging, Ageism, and Older Women's Issues; and Politics of Disease and Alternative Approaches to Health Care.

- Provides a history of the women's health movements with both *classic* articles and the latest information, inspiring women to get involved in today's movement.

- Introduces readers to the organizations, publications, and resources that provide scientific and culturally relevant information on women's health needs.

- Includes both *classic* and new articles from the National Women's Health Network, which will inspire readers to get involved in the women's health movement.

- Provides readers diverse perspectives with information on global women's health, and on race, ethnicity, class, culture, and gender in the United States.

- Includes chapter introductions that highlight sociocultural, political, and economic themes that impact women's health and access to services.

- Includes essay questions to each chapter to analyze and develop new inquiries regarding women's health as well as to prepare for exams and essay papers.

- Inspires consumer literacy with a new directory of women's health resources.

ACKNOWLEDGMENTS

Nancy Worcester, Ph.D. and Mariamne H. Whately first developed this book in 1988. Their book provided important information about the lack of knowledge and disparities in the healthcare system and health education regarding women's bodies and their health needs. Their book highlighted the activism of the Women's Health Movements across the globe. Their book was dedicated to all the people who participated in the Women's Health Movements and those who wanted to change the world of health care and information for women. Their book continues to change the world by teaching practitioners, activists, leaders, and anyone interested in women's health to reflect on women's social, economic, and political status, which has a direct impact on women's ability to access health services, which advocated for themselves, and live an empowered life. I began using this book in 2003 in my Race, Gender, and Health class at Simmons College in Massachusetts. The book continues to provide a unique opportunity for students to learn about science, activism, and leadership. I am honored to continue the traditions of Nancy Worcester and Mairamne H. Whately. I thank them for their vision, philosophy, dedication, and compassion for wanting to change the world for women.

The National Women's Health Network (www.nwhn.org) continues to be a valuable partner in developing this edition of the book. A percentage of royalties go to the NWHN as a vote of thanks for their dedication to women's health and activism.

A very special thank you to Bob Largent, editor at Kendall Hunt, who had the faith in me to develop this edition. In addition, a thank you to Michelle Bahr for guiding me through the process.

Thanks to the Book Project Team—Mary Morrissey, Marissa Knaak, and Tiffany Souza-Sibulkin. Mary and Marissa are students in the Gender and Cultural Studies graduate program at Simmons College. Mary has a background in critical theory, feminist theory, and queer studies. Marissa has a background in public history and women's history. Mary and Marissa were instrumental in completing this book. Tiffany has a background in graphic art and an ability to design my thoughts into reality. I could not have accomplished this book without their dedication and efficiency. A special thank you to Simmons College for The Presidential Grant for Faculty Excellence. Thank you to Ms. Valerie Beaudrault, Mr. Jon Kimball, and Dr. Jo Trigilio for always supporting me.

For
Elizabeth, Deborah, and Tiffany
They are the women who support, inspire, and empower me.

PASSING THE BATON

By Nancy Worcester & Marianne H. Whatley

We have enjoyed editing/writing five editions *of Women's Health: Readings on Social, Economic, and Political Issues* (Edition 1: 1988; Edition 5: 2009). We have loved the challenge of pulling together articles representing a wide diversity of sources and voices, reflecting the best in critical thinking in the science and politics of women's health, drawing on research and activism, and exploring cutting-edge issues. Originally, the book was specifically designed as a text for the 400 students per semester in Gender and Women's Studies 103: *Women and Their Bodies in Health and Disease* at the University of Wisconsin-Madison. Then, over the years, we were delighted to find the book used in more and more women's health courses throughout the country and we enjoyed meeting many course instructors at various conferences (National Women's Studies Association, American Public Health Association, the Society for Menstrual Cycle Research, etc.). Each edition reflected the rapidly changing area of women's health, the tremendous interest shown in women's health by both healthcare providers and consumers, the ever-changing national and international debates, and the evolution of many women's health movements.

As our lives demonstrate, activists never retire! However, when we retired from our positions as professors at the University of Wisconsin-Madison, we decided to pass this baton. In all editions of the book, we worked toward emphasizing anti-racist, cross-cultural perspectives on topics, and looked for articles that make the connections among social, economic, and political issues and women's mental and physical health. There are still cutting-edge issues to be explored and important articles to be written. We hope new editions will continue to dig deeply in examining health ramifications related to poverty, age, race, religion, sexuality, gender, disability, size, and their intersections. As we hand over this project to others, we also hope readers/students will be actively engaged in this ongoing process. Do new researches, write your own articles and books, teach in a range of settings, and change the world. This project is now yours.

Nancy Worcester and Mariamne Whatley
Professors Emeritae
Department of Gender and Women's Studies
University of Wisconsin-Madison

ABOUT THE AUTHOR

Dawna Marie Thomas, Ph.D. is an Associate Professor in the Sociology and Women's and Gender Studies departments at Simmons College. She teaches a cross section of courses that relate to women, gender, race, culture, family violence, and health and disability. Dr. Thomas' research interests include health and disability policy, racial/ethnic and gender disparities in health, and family violence. Her study *Understanding Disability in the Cape Verdean Community: An Analysis of Race and Disability in Massachusetts* was the first research conducted on disability in the Cape Verdean Community. The latest study *The Cape Verdean Women's Project* includes four generations of Cape Verdean women throughout New England where she explores their experiences with family life, marriage, domestic violence, health care and disability, and concepts of womanhood. Dr. Thomas remains committed to culturally relevant pedagogy that integrates theory and practice to reduce health care and disability service disparities. She is dedicated to a philosophy that empowers those who are marginalized in our society—women, women of color, and people with disabilities.

INTRODUCTION

Women cannot have control over our lives until we have control over our bodies: thus, understanding and gaining control over our bodies and our health are essential to taking control of our lives (Worcester & Whatley, 2009, p. xvii). Since the inception of this book's first edition, women have made great strides in society, advancing in many ways educationally, economically, and socially. Although there has been more attention paid to understanding women's health needs, women continue to experience social oppression and discrimination based on sex, gender, race, ethnicity, and class. Women professionals and patients continue to experience sexism in the healthcare industry. Women of color, patients and professionals, experience multilayered oppression and discrimination. The lesbian, gay, bisexual, transgender, and plus community continue to be misunderstood and underserved within the healthcare system. While progress has been made, the struggle continues; thus, a book dedicated to women's health needs is essential for women to gain true control over their bodies and lives.

This edition of this book reflects changing perspectives and ongoing interest in women's health. In the twenty-first century, the chapters and collection of readings are very different than those in previous editions. Yet, staying true to the book's mission and philosophy, this edition continues the tradition with eighty-seven articles in ten chapters that include classic and new readings. The classic readings not only provide a historical context about women, their environment, and health needs, but also offer a yardstick to measure progress. They allow us to see how far we have come, where we have stalled, and how much more needs to be done. The new selection of readings introduces innovative approaches around women's health and alternative methods in health care, addresses reasons why inequalities persist, offers updated information about gender and sex, and supports women's healthcare advocacy. The chapter topics include women and the healthcare system; inequalities in health, sex, gender roles, and image; politics of sex education; disability and society; violence against women; childbirth and reproductive justice; aging and older women; and, finally, the politics of disease and alternative modalities.

This book was designed for a women's health course and has been used by others across the country to learn about women, their health, and the system that, at times, has ignored and neglected their health needs, which puts them in jeopardy. This book continues to provide important information for advocates to organize and support health equality for all women. The collection of readings, chapter essay questions, and resources listed at the back of the book were selected to cross borders and create bridges. For example, the readings in the book complement other courses across the humanities, science, and management.

Women's health and well-being cannot be addressed without understanding where we come from, our culture, family life, and dreams for the future. Thus, the collection of readings in this book represents interdisciplinary and multidisciplinary perspectives of women's worldviews, understanding the differences between sex and gender, as

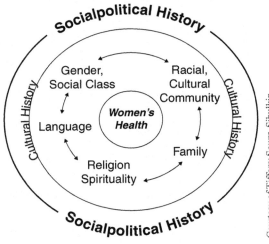

well as how socioeconomic, racial, and cultural differences play a role in why some women have better access to health resources—giving them better health outcomes even when they become ill—compared to other women. The readings emphasize racial justice and cross-cultural and gender-oriented perspectives of the topics. The goal is that readers will make connections across social, economic, and political issues supporting women's physical, mental, and emotional health. Readers are encouraged to think about how health ramifications related to poverty, ageism, racism, anti-Semitism, heterosexism, homophobia, fatphobia, violence, and disability impact women's lives. ***Readers are encouraged to write their own articles or books and change the world.***

Women and the Healthcare System

The role of women in the healthcare system and the priority given to good mental and physical health for all women reflects much of the values of a society. Studying the changing and non-changing roles of women in the healthcare system, women's grassroots activism, and professional organizing to improve women's health illustrates the societal changes in the twentieth and early twenty-first centuries. This chapter provides historical and contemporary perspectives of women in the healthcare system as both patients and practitioners. The chapter includes fourteen articles offering an overview of the women's health movement as well as how sexism continues today in the healthcare system for both patients and practitioners.

The chapter begins with the classic article *Diagnosing Gender Disparities in Health Care* by Andrea Irwin that explores the many ways women receive unequal treatment in healthcare. Irwin notes "Until I became a women's health advocate immersed in the nuances of Medicaid, health insurance, and other complicated policy issues, I never appreciated the numerous disparities that exist between the ways men and women access the health care system." Despite the progress and advancements toward better care for women, disparities persist.

The next set of articles chronicles the Women's Health Movements. These movements were instrumental in changing how women viewed their bodies, increasing the inclusion of female subjects in health research, and influencing the healthcare system to serve them better. Francine Nichols' classic article, *History of the Women's Health Movement in the 20th Century,* shows how the movement created changes in policies, clinical practices, and futures for women.

Next, a historical account of the collective movement around *Our Bodies, Ourselves* demonstrates how grassroots activism changed healthcare for women. Known as OBOS, *Our Bodies, Ourselves* has been described as one of the most influential books ever published, having a decisive impact on how generations of women felt about their bodies, their sexuality, and their health. We could not study women's health without OBOS and how it continues to be significant in changing how women and society view their bodies as well as medicine and the healthcare industry. Today, the book has been published in thirty languages and plays an important role in the Global Women's Health Movement. The article *The Spiral of Women's Health Activism* by Amy Allina offers a brief overview of *Our Bodies, Ourselves'* impact on women. The next article, *The Making of Our Bodies Ourselves: Transnational Knowledge, Transnational Politics,* outlines the history of the book and its impact on women's health, sexuality, and grassroots organizational beginnings. *The Boston Women's Health Book Collective and Our Bodies, Ourselves: A Brief History and Reflection,* also provides a historical perspective on the grassroots organizing around women's bodies, health, and well-being.

The next set of classic articles focuses on women's gynecological health and pelvic examinations. *The Gynecologic Exam and the Training of Medical Students: An Opportunity for Health Education* by Judith Schmidt offers an example of a medical program that consciously aims to educate physicians to be "patient-oriented" so that they can communicate appropriately with their patients. In a more theoretical approach to the same issue, Terri Kapsalis in *Cadavers, Dolls, and Prostitutes: Medical Pedagogy and the Pelvic Rehearsal* explores how medical practices reveal and promote specific ideas about bodies and sexuality that are held by medical institutions. Molly Kenefick, in *Spreading My Legs for Womankind,* shares reasons why it is important to teach medical students how to conduct pelvic exams for women. She worked for a number of years as a "pelvic educator" at a medical school and offers a unique perspective based on her personal experience.

The last articles show how, even as more women are becoming physicians, sexual harassment and gender bias in medicine persist. *Balancing It All: Women and Medicine* by Khendi White highlights the struggles and obstacles women physicians endure as they navigate the competitive environment of medicine. Unlike their male counterparts, female physicians face harsh criticism when they decide to have children and play an active role in raising their children. *The Making of the "Women's Physician" in American Obstetrics and Gynecology: Re-Forging an Occupational Identity and a Division of Labor* and *"I'm too Used to It": A Longitudinal Qualitative Study of Third Year Female Medical Students' Experiences of Gendered Encounters in Medical Education* are studies that followed women in various points of the medical

educational experience. The studies showed how female medical students experience sexual harassment and gender bias not only from supervisors but also patients. For example, study participants reported being routinely referred to as "honey" or "sweetie." Despite the progress that women have made in medicine, they have become acculturated to the negative experiences in medical training.

The chapter ends with *The Little Brown Woman: Gender Discrimination in American Medicine* by Wasudha Bhatt. Bhatt's article provides an intersectional perspective on sexism and racism in medicine. Bhatt's qualitative research study is based on 121 in-depth interviews with first- and second-generation women and men physicians of Indian origin in the U.S. Southwest. She suggests that many physicians—women and men—continue to perceive sexist and patriarchal attitudes in American medicine. Gendered racism is not a static phenomenon, but subject to change and transformation: "While twenty-first century racial practices in the United States may now be less overt, and more informal, my research suggests that Indian women physicians continue to face racialized gender discrimination."

 # Diagnosing Gender Disparities in Health Care

by Andrea Irwin

Until I became a women's health advocate immersed in the nuances of Medicaid, health insurance, and other complicated policy issues, I never truly appreciated the numerous disparities that exist between the ways men and women access the healthcare system. Most of my female friends are now in their mid-to-late twenties and I am constantly amazed at the myriad medical concerns that are unique to the female anatomy. For starters, research shows that women's reproductive systems are just so much more complex than men's and women are more likely than men to need healthcare throughout their lifetimes. Our ovaries, uteruses, breasts, cervixes, and fallopian tubes are all subject to various cancers, infections and other complications making routine monitoring a necessity, in addition to women's overarching need for safe, effective and affordable birth control. Among my circle of friends we have experienced breast biopsies, vaginal ultrasounds, and colposcopies galore.

At a minimum, a young woman is advised to visit her gynecologist once a year to have a pelvic exam and Pap test, but she may require further and additional visits to receive contraception and STI/HIV testing, or to follow-up on any abnormalities discovered through these preventive screenings. For women with comprehensive health insurance, most of these preventive services are covered benefits—but, unfortunately, not all. Moreover, some of these services are not covered in a way that makes sense. For instance, I just learned that many insurance plans will not cover STI/HIV tests at a woman's annual physical visit, which forces a woman to make an additional appointment for these tests and adds an extra layer of stress and burden to an already anxiety-producing procedure. Luckily, my provider pointed this out to me, but most women are not likely to be aware of such hidden costs. Instead of creating disincentives for women to be smart, efficient consumers of healthcare, insurers should end this policy that may increase a woman's health expenses or lead her to avoid care altogether.

Even worse, some insurance plans do not cover contraceptives despite the fact that the plans usually cover other prescription drugs. And, even when plans do cover contraceptives, they may not cover Emergency Contraception (EC) now that it's sold over-the-counter. EC costs around $45, which impedes access for many young women. Some insurance plans (notably the federal government employees' plan) also refuse to pay for abortion services, despite the fact that abortion is a safe and legal procedure, and that plans cover all prenatal care and pregnancy-related services.[1] The typical first trimester abortion costs, on average, around $468, which is extremely expensive for many women, particularly young and low-income women.[1]

Beyond the reproductive health disparities between men and women in terms of needed services and covered benefits, young women are more likely than men to suffer from chronic conditions like rheumatoid arthritis, lupus, or asthma.[2] Over one-third (38%) of women suffer from chronic conditions that require ongoing treatment, compared with 30% of men.[2] I've seen my peers struggle with all of these illnesses first-hand, as well as with the on-going treatment and medications they necessitate.

Young women are also more prone to be diagnosed with anxiety, depression, eating disorders, and other mental health conditions that may require extensive therapy and/or medications, and which may also result in increased physical health problems if left untreated.[2] Twice as many women as men are diagnosed with certain mental health problems such as anxiety and depression.[2] Even for women who have health insurance, the costs of these services can add up and co-pays and deductibles can become very expensive.

Moreover, because most health insurance plans are not required to cover mental health services, many insurers refuse to cover treatment for some or all mental health conditions, or may set very low limits on the number of mental health visits an individual can receive. These practices leave many young women with no ability to seek needed treatment. The high prevalence of violence against women—and the media's negative influences on women's body image that have largely shaped our generation's tormented relationships with our bodies (and driven us to seek out carcinogenic cigarettes to stay thin, and cancer-causing tanning beds to improve our appearance)—also exacerbate women's need for comprehensive healthcare.[3] We need to advocate for policies that reduce the powerful, negative, influence of these harmful external forces on our health and promote universal healthcare for all.

While these insurance practices are bad for women, more than one-third of all young women between the ages of 19 and 24 aren't insured at all.[4] For these women, the situation is far more dire because, without health insurance, women are more likely to avoid needed healthcare. Women in this age group are also more likely than men to have high medical debts or to experience bankruptcy because of medical expenses.[2] This is due to both women's lower incomes on average (thanks to the gender gap in pay) and their greater healthcare needs.[4] Proposals that expand healthcare coverage to more people—including individuals who work part-time, run their own businesses, or stay at home to raise families—are essential to ensuring women's autonomy and full equality with men.

One major lesson I've learned is that young women tend to underestimate the value of healthcare to our lives and well-being. We constantly sacrifice our mental and physical health so that we can nurture our careers, and build financial nest eggs for our futures. Like the importance of setting up a 401(k) at work or pursuing higher education to ensure access to better employment opportunities, accessing quality healthcare when we are young is an investment women must learn to make in order to ensure our health throughout our lives. Young women need to share our stories and encourage our peers to empower and educate themselves about the importance of preventive care. Most importantly, we must demand that lawmakers develop and implement healthcare reform proposals that meet young women's unique healthcare needs.

I am fortunate to have comprehensive health insurance through my employer. I was also raised by a strong feminist mother with more than 30 years of nursing experience who helps me to navigate the increasingly convoluted healthcare system. My hope is that my generation will continue to advocate for improved healthcare services and access for all so that everyone can enjoy a brighter, healthier future and better quality of life than our grandmothers experienced.

References

1. National Network of Abortion Funds. *Policy Report—Abortion Funding: A Matter of Justice.* Amherst, MA: NNAF. 2005, 2, 6.

2. The Commonwealth Fund and The National Women's Law Center. *Issue Brief—Women and Health Coverage: The Affordability Gap.* Washington, DC: CF. April, 2007, p. 4.

3. Charlie Guild Melanoma Foundation (CGMF) Website. "10 Facts About Melanoma." Richmond, CA: CGMF. No date. Accessed June 6, 2007 from http://www.charlie.org/melanoma_facts.html.

4. The National Women's Law Center (NWLC). *Issue Brief—Women and Health Coverage: A Framework for Moving Forward.* Washington, DC: NWLC. April, 2007, p. 2.

JOGNN

History of the
Women's Health Movement
in the 20th Century

by Francine H. Nichols, RNC, PhD, FAAN

The Women's Health Movement (WHM) emerged during the 1960s and the 1970s with the primary goal to improve health care for all women. Despite setbacks in the area of reproductive rights during the 1980s, the WHM made significant gains in women's health at the federal policy level during the 1980s and 1990s. The WHM became a powerful political force. The achievements of the movement in improving women's health during the 20th century were numerous and significant. *JOGNN, 29,* 56–64; 2000.

Key words: Women's health history—Women's health care movement—Women's health care policy

Accepted: June 1999

The Women's Health Movement (WHM) emerged during the 1960s and the 1970s during the second wave of feminism in the United States. It has striking similarities to the first wave of feminism that occurred in the 1830s and 1840s. During that time in the mid-1800s, women who were consumer health activists demanded changes in health care (the Popular

Health Movement) and women's rights activists demanded equal rights for women (the Women's Liberation Movement) (Marieskind, 1975).

The Early Women's Health Movement

One can argue that the Women's Health Movement started in the early 1900s with Margaret Sanger's fight for women's rights to birth control (Wardell, 1980). However, the literature reveals that it is commonly thought the WHM began in the 1960s (Marieskind, 1975). The focus of the woman activists during the 1960s and 1970s was fighting to gain control of their own reproductive rights (Ruzek, 1978). During the 1960s, abortion was illegal in all states except to save the life of the woman. Although there were approximately 8,000 therapeutic abortions done annually, there were more than 1 million illegal abortions annually. Approximately one-third of the women who had illegal abortion experienced complications requiring hospital admittance. Between 500 and 1,000 women died annually as a result of an illegal abortion (Geary, 1995). Activists in the WHM and other feminists groups formed a powerful force that culminated in the Supreme Court decision of Roe *v* Wade in 1973, which legalized abortion. Although reproductive rights continued to be a major focus, the WHM moved rapidly into many other areas that affected women's health. In a short time, the WHM had developed a comprehensive approach to women's health. Individuals within the WHM had widely divergent goals. However, one common goal united them all: "a demand for improved health care for all women and an end to sexism in the health system" (Marieskind, 1975, p. 219).

The first women's self-help health group in the United States is thought to have been formed in 1970. After that, new groups organized at phenomenal speed, and by 1973, there were more than 1,200 women's self-help health groups across the country (Schneir, 1994). The common theme of these groups was the dissatisfaction with health care. The common goals were women reclaiming power from the paternalistic and condescending medical community and assuming control of their own health (Geary, 1995).

Changing childbirth practices became a major effort of the WHM movement in the 1960s and

1970s as women sought to give birth without medical intervention and with their husbands present. During this time, women spearheaded the formation of two childbirth organizations, Lamaze International (formerly ASPO/Lamaze) and the International Childbirth Educational Association. The goals of these organizations were to change childbirth practices by advocating choice for expectant parents during childbirth and by preparing expectant parents for birth through childbirth education. In 1972, Doris Haire's expose *The Cultural Warping of Childbirth* described the negative effects of medical intervention during childbirth. In the book, medicalized birth in the United States was compared with humanistic birth conducted by midwives in other developed countries. The childbirth movement peaked in the 1980s when many hospitals began to change from traditional maternity care to family-centered care and when most hospitals began to offer prepared childbirth classes. Through the efforts of the WHM and concerned professionals, childbirth was changed for millions of women who wanted to give birth without medical intervention, be awake during birth, and have their husbands present.

> Changing childbirth practices became a major effort of the WHM movement in the 1960s and 1970s as women sought to give birth without medical intervention and with their husbands present.

The WHM of the 1960s and 1970s was a grassroots advocacy movement that quickly swelled in numbers, thus gaining strength and power. It was fueled by the passion of women who experienced injustice and were fighting for their rights. The WHM became even more powerful because of its participants' commitment to the cause and their tireless activist efforts. Significant events in the WHM during the 20th century that were pivotal in creating awareness of problems and promoting needed changes are shown in Table 1.

The 1980s: An Era of Setbacks and Gains

The WHM flourished during the liberal political environment of the 1960s and 1970s. Ronald Reagan's election as president in 1980 heralded the beginning of an increasingly conservative political environment. The New Right became firmly entrenched in American politics during the 1980s and wielded increasing power in political decisions. Legalized abortions were under attack from antiabortion activists. Feminist's health clinics became the targets of violence, and many clinics closed. In 1989, the Webster *v* Reproductive Health Services decision by the Supreme Court placed increased restrictions on abortion (Butler & Walbert, 1992; Geary, 1995). During the same time the WHM was experiencing setbacks in the area of reproductive rights, definite progress occurred with the establishment of federal task forces and agencies that were charged with the responsibility of ensuring that women's health needs were met.

Women's Health and Health Policy

During the 1980s and 1990s, significant gains were made in women's health at the federal policy level (see Table 1). The Congressional Caucus for Women's Issues was formed in 1977 as a Legislative Service Organization with an active bipartisan voice in the House of Representatives on the behalf of women (Remarks by the President at the Congressional Caucus for Women's Issues, 1997; Update—The Congressional Caucus for Women's Issues, 1999). When the Caucus was forced to reorganize as a Congressional Members Organization in the late 1990s, it had to close its office. However, the Caucus still provides a strong bipartisan voice for women at the federal level. The Caucus' Statement on Women's Health is shown in Table 2.

The first formal federal action was the establishment of the Task Force on Women's Health Issues in 1983 by the U. S. Public Health Service (USPHS). The Task Force was charged with the responsibility of ensuring that women's needs were being met and making recommendations (Kirschstein, 1987; Women's Health, 1985). The Task Force's first report, in 1985, was based only on data from women who were federal employees. To correct this deficiency, 11 regional meetings were held across the country to gather additional data from women in communities. The major finding from the original study and the additional meetings was women's dissatisfaction with access to information

and medical care. The Task Force recommended research on women's health problems and research on contraceptive devices and approaches for both women and men (Geary, 1995).

In 1986, the National Institutes of Health (NIH) adopted a policy requiring the inclusion of women in clinical research. Women leaders, in 1989, voiced their concern to the Congressional Caucus for Women's Issues that research on women's health was still being neglected. A formal General Accounting Office (GAO) investigation of NIH research on women's health was requested by the Congressional Caucus and Henry Waxman (D-California). The findings of the investigation confirmed that only 13.5% of NIH monies went for women's health research and that women were still being excluded from clinical studies (Congressional Research Report, 1993). Angell (1993) summarized three ways that women were discriminated against in clinical research: diseases that affect women disproportionately were less likely to be studied, women were less likely to be included in clinical trials, and women were less likely to be senior investigators conducting trials. LaRosa (1994) in an article on the Office of Research on Women's Health said the evidence did not indicate that women were being systematically excluded from biomedical research, but rather that the numbers of women included were not sufficient to detect gender differences or that they had been excluded from some studies.

In response to the GAO report, the NIH adopted a number of strategies to resolve the problem. In 1990, the Office of Research on Women's Health (ORWH) was established within NIH with the charge of ensuring that NIH research addressed women's health needs and that women were included in clinical trials. As a part of its mandate, the ORWH developed a women's health research agenda and designed a 14-year, $625 million Women's Health Initiative study that has been implemented in 45 clinical centers across the United States and includes 160,000 postmenopausal women. The study examines the effect of hormone replacement therapy and diet and exercise on coronary heart disease, breast and colon cancers, and osteoporosis (Congressional Research Report, 1994).

Table 1.	Significant Events in the Women's Health Movement
1969	*The Doctors' Case Against the Pill* was published. Written by Barbara Seaman, a health columnist, this exposé on the birth control pill described deadly side effects of the pill, including stroke, heart disease, depression. The controversy generated by the book cost Seaman her job but led to the 1970 federal hearing on the safety of the birth control pill.
1973	*Our Bodies, Ourselves* published by the Boston Women's Health Collective; cost 30 cents per copy.
1974	The National Women's Health Network, an advocacy clearinghouse was founded by Seaman and four other woman activists. There were nearly 2000 women's self-help medical projects across the United States.
1975	The first International Conference on Women was held.
1977	The Food and Drug Administration (FDA) banned the inclusion of women of childbearing years in Phase 1 and 2 drug trials.
1983	First comprehensive national survey of women's health by The Commonwealth Fund, New York city.
1984	Boogaard's article "Rehabilitation of the female patient after myocardial infarction" (Boogaard, 1984) was significant because it stimulated nurse researchers to explore women's experiences with cardiac disease. In the mid-1980s, women began to be viewed as a unique group in the investigations of cardiac patients, "rather than as a subgroup of the larger male-dominated paradigm (King & Paul, 1996).
1989	The Congressional Caucus for Women's Issues (CCWI) exposed the National Institutes of Health (NIH) lack of research on women and demanded change.
	The Jacobs Institute of Women's Health was founded to "advance the understanding and practice of women's health care."
1990	The Office of Research on Women's Health (ORWH) of NIH was established by Bernadine Healy, MD, the first female director of the NIH. The Society for the Advancement of Women's Health Research was established to bring public attention to the lack of research on women's health and to garner support for creating permanent change.
	Congresswomen Patricia Schroeder and Olympia Snow introduced the first Women's Health Equity Act (WHEA), which included bills covering provisions for research and programs to improve the status of women's health. It did not pass in 1990 but was reintroduced and passed in 1991. The Act brought increased awareness to women's health issues.
1991	The first issue of the *Journal of Women's Health* was published by the Society for the Advancement of Women's Health Research.
	The Health of Women: A Global Perspective, a report of the 1991 National Council for International Health (NCIH) Conference, was published.
1992	The Women's Health Initiative, a $625 million, 14-year randomized controlled trial, the largest study ever of women's diseases, began by NIH. The study examines the use of preventive measures, such as diet, behavior, and drug treatment, against cardiovascular disease, cancer, and osteoporosis in postmenopausal women.
1993	FDA withdrew the 1977 federal ban on the inclusion of women in early drug trials and developed its new gender guideline, which recognized the need for adequate representation of women in drug trials and left decisions about including women of childbearing age in drug trials to the internal review boards, the women who were potential subjects, and their physicians. The US NIH Revitalization Act of 1993 required that any clinical trial involving the treatment of a disease be designed in a manner that would provide a valid analysis of if the variables being studied affect women or members of minority groups.

(Continued)

Table 1. Significant Events in the Women's Health Movement *(Continued)*	
1994 to 1995	Women's health issues were the focus of the International Year of the Family; The International Conference on Population and Development in Cario, Egypt; the World Summit on Social Development in Copenhagen, Denmark; and the United Nations Fourth World Conference on Women, Beijing, PRC.
1998	The New Mothers' Breastfeeding Promotion and Protection Act (H.R. 3531) was introduced by Representative Carolyn Maloney. The Act protects breastfeeding under the civil rights acts and provides provisions for unpaid time for breast-feeding mothers to express milk in the workplace.

Based on data from Meinert, C.L. (1995). The inclusion of women in clinical trials. *Science, 269,* 795–796; Sharp, N. (1993). Women's health: A powerful public issues. *Nursing Management,* 24(6), 17–19.

Table 2. The Congressional Caucus for Women's Issues Statement on Women's Health
Healthcare coverage should be available to all regardless of income or eligibility.
All basic health benefits packages must include essential preventive, diagnostic and treatment services.
Access to full information must be available about all treatment options and alternatives to treatment, so that women can make informed decisions.
Health care services should be available in a variety of settings, including an array of outpatient settings.
Health care services should be provided by a variety of providers, such as physicians, nurse-practitioners, and nurse midwives.
Individualized care should be the basis for health care to each woman.
Primary health care services should be community based.
Research on the most effective ways of promoting health and preventing illness in women should be included in health care reform.

Update—The Congressional Caucus for Women's Issues. (1999, March 15). [Online]. Available: http://www.house.gov/lowey/caucus.htm.

Two other federal agencies were actively involved in women's health research. In 1993, the Food and Drug Administration eliminated the 1977 restriction excluding women of childbearing potential from participating in the early phases of drug testing and published revised guidelines that required sex-specific analyses of safety and efficacy be a part of all new drug applications (Merkatz & Junod, 1994). The Centers for Disease Control (CDC) 1994 budget appropriations from Congress included an additional $2 million to initiate a screening program for chlamydia in women and their partners and $51 million designated for Papanicolaou smears and mammography screening for low-income women (Congressional Research Report, 1994). The CDC also established an Office of Women's Health which, provides leadership, guidance, and coordination on policy, programs, and activities related to women's health (CDC, 1999). A federal infrastructure for addressing women's health developed and expanded during the 1980s and 1990s, and there were substantial gains in federal funding for women's health research during this time.

Advocacy Organizations

Activists in the Women's Health Movement formed a powerful lobby that has brought the inequities in women's health care to the attention of legislators and the public. Through their efforts, women's health has become an important public and political issue that commands responses from individuals in public policy, medicine, research, and government. For example, the Older Women's League (OWL) worked hard to bring women's health issues to the attention of the public and to improve health care for women. The OWL coordinated the Campaign for Women's Health that consisted of more than 40 national organizations all working to create the changes needed to improve health care for women (Sharp, 1993). The WHM probably is one of the finest examples of grass-roots advocacy efforts that have resulted in widespread, needed changes from the community level to the level of the federal government.

Women's Health and Women's Health Nursing

Literature on issues and topics related to women's health is plentiful. However, the term women's health is rarely defined. In 1997, the Expert Panel on Women's Health of the American Academy of Nursing (AAN Expert Panel, 1997) defined women's health as health promotion, maintenance and restoration throughout the entire life span. The Panel (p. 7) emphasized that "Understanding women's health requires more than a biomedical view; it requires awareness of the context of women's lives." School of Nursing faculty at the University of Michigan (1999) describes women's health as pertaining "to the physical, psychological and social well-being of women," which includes the "diversity and heterogeneity of women as well as the variety of concerns that affect their well-being." The feminist perspective that "acknowledges the socio-political context which in many ways, determines the health of women" is an integral part of the definition (University of Michigan, 1999). The most comprehensive medical definition of women's health is one that was developed for the Women's Health Medical Education Program (Donoghue, 1996):

> Women's health is devoted to facilitating the preservation of wellness and prevention of illness in women and includes

screening, diagnosing and managing conditions which are *unique* to women, are *more common* in women, are *more serious* in women, have *manifestations, risk factors* or *interventions* which are different for women.

There is general agreement on core concepts related to women's health: recognition of the diversity of women's health needs throughout the life span (Donoghue, 1996; Fogel & Woods, 1995); emphasis on the empowerment of women as informed participants in their own health care (Donoghue; Fogel & Woods); the importance of research of gender differences in diseases and responses to drugs (Donoghue; Fogel & Woods); and the need for a multidisciplinary team approach (Donoghue; Fogel & Woods). Andrist (1997) declared that the goal of women's health care should be social transformation, which includes symmetry in provider–patient relationships, access to information, shared decision making, and striving for change in the larger social structure.

The Association of Women's Health, Obstetric and Neonatal Nurses (AWHONN) has been a leader in providing legislative testimony on women's health issues and pushing for needed changes in health care for women. Highly regarded by individuals in the political arena, government officials, and health care professionals throughout the years, AWHONN has contributed significantly to ensuring the passage of important legislation to improve women's health. For example, in 1998, AWHONN provided testimony to the Congressional Caucus for Women's Issues in support of H.R. 3531 bill, the New Mothers' Breastfeeding Promotion and Protection Act. The bill clarified that breastfeeding was protected under the civil rights act and provided as much as 1 hour per day of unpaid time in the workplace for as long as 1 year for breastfeeding mothers to express milk (Harris, 1998). Although the bill was not passed that year, it was reintroduced the following year, and AWHONN's efforts to promote passage of the bill continues.

> Highly regarded by individuals in the political arena, government officials, and health care professionals throughout

the years, AWHONN has contributed significantly to ensuring the passage of important legislation to improve women's health.

Two other women's health organizations have made significant contributions to improving women's health: the National Association of Women's Health Professionals, which was formed in 1987, and the Jacobs Institute of Women's Health, which was founded in 1989. By the 1990s, the WHM had a strong voice that commanded the attention of health policy makers through the combined efforts of professional organizations and grass-roots advocacy organizations.

Development of Nursing and Medical Specialties in Women's Health

The number of women's health nurse practitioner programs expanded quickly in response to the need, and these practitioners were readily accepted by the women for whom they provided care and by many health care professionals (Chang et al., 1999; Myers, Lenci, & Sheldon, 1997; Ryan, 1999).

In an effort to end the discrimination against women in health care and to educate practitioners about women's health and the diseases that affect them, the medical profession established a new medical specialty in women's health. However, in contrast to the acceptance of the women's health nurse practitioner programs, this approach has met with opposition from some leaders in the WHM. Harrison (1992) argued that a new women's health specialty would "marginalize" the care of women, and mainstream medical and health care would cease to focus on women and become exclusively for men. She suggests a medical specialty in men's health with mainstream health care being for women. Others have described a medical specialty in women's health as co-optation of the WHM. Surprisingly, this conflict appears to be a common theme when the goals of grass-roots advocacy organizations become an integral part of mainstream health care. This opposition to the incorporation of women's health as an integral part of medicine and health care and the view of

cooptation parallels the responses of some childbirth advocacy leaders to the movement of childbirth education from the community and into the health care agency setting.

Achievements of the Women's Health Movement

The WHM confronted many problems and blatant discrimination against women that plagued women's health care. Undaunted, by the 1980s the WHM had attracted the attention of the media, government agencies, and researchers at the local, state, and federal levels. From that time forward, the WHM became a powerful political force to be reckoned with, from reproductive rights to prenatal care to hazards in the workplace (Sechzer, Griffin, & Pfafflin, 1994).

The WHM achievements were numerous and significant.

Women gained more control over their reproductive rights. Abortion was legalized, although restrictions remain, and new contraceptive technology became available.

Gender-based research emerged as an important area of biomedicine. Today, women are no longer automatically excluded from early drug trials. Research on conditions that affect women as well as men must adequately include women as subjects. Woods (1994) cautioned that merely adding a cohort of women to a study would not necessarily render appropriate findings that can be used to improve health care for women.

Significant progress has been made in research on cardiovascular diseases of women (King & Paul, 1996). The literature on cardiovascular disease during the 1960s and 1970s did not include gender-specific conclusions, even when women were included in the studies. It was not until the mid-1980s that there was interest in exploring the impact of cardiac disease and surgery on women. Significant progress was made since that time.

Violence and discrimination against women have been recognized as a significant problem worldwide, and numerous programs have been implemented to address these issues (Varkevisser, 1995). The WHM is fighting to gain support for breastfeeding mothers in the workplace. The passion of the women involved in response to the discrimination against breastfeeding mothers in the workplace parallels that of the participants in the early WHM.

The Future of the Women's Health Movement

After a long, hard-fought battle, women's health has finally become an integral and important part of the health care system. Great strides have been made in understanding how diseases uniquely affect women and developing effective health promotion programs for women. However, there is still much to be accomplished. The recognition of the significant role that sex and gender play in scientific and medical practice will continue to be a major emphasis (Sechzer et al., 1994). Hormonal differences between women and men, women's unique responses to diseases and drugs, and gender equity in research programs will continue to be areas of important interest in the 21st century (Pinn, 1992). Nursing has always led in the development of needed and effective programs for women's health during the 20th century. Morse (1995) asserts that this will continue and that nursing "is likely to emerge as the profession that is the most responsive to women's health" (p. 273) because of its emphasis of active involvement of the individual in her own health care and the emphasis on health promotion and health maintenance and because nurses have viewed women's health care from feminist perspectives and have challenged patriarchal, paternalistic values.

Women's Health Centers

The development of women's health centers is emerging as a new model for the provision of women's health care at a rapid pace (Budoff, 1994; Levison, 1996). These centers provide primary care to women, including reproductive care, pregnancy and childbirth care, breast care programs, and other essential services, with easy access to specialists when they are needed. Women's health became an area of primary interest for medicine and health care agencies in the mid-1990s. By 1997, approximately one-third of hospitals in the United States had some kind of women's health center, compared with 19% in 1990 (Day, 1997).

An Integrative Science of Women's Health

Walker and Tinkle (1996) point out that women's health has been fragmented, with childbearing separated from general health promotion activities and the treatment of chronic diseases. These researchers provide a solid case for an integrative science of women's health that would provide a knowledge base that "brings together phenomena relevant to women" (Walker & Tinkle, p. 379). This integrative science of women's health has two significant dimensions:

- the incorporation of all of the sciences that study women's health issues so that the woman is viewed as a "whole woman"; and

- linking childbearing with other women's health needs and problems throughout life, with emphasis on health promotion, disease prevention, and management of chronic illness.

This would provide a basis for a comprehensive seamless approach to women's health care that would promote improved health and well-being (Walker & Tinkle).

Women's Health in Developing Countries

The WHM that started in the developed world is now a significant force in developing countries, and a global agenda for women's health has emerged (Doyal, 1996). The political, economic, and social forces that affect all women's health are of even greater significance in developing countries (Dyches & Rushing, 1993). The concerns of women in the developing world are different from those in industrialized countries. Many women still die of reproductive problems and diseases and childbirth-related problems that could be easily prevented or cured (Mann, 1995). Third World health care programs have focused primarily on Third World children, and the problems of their mothers are often ignored.

During the 1960s, 1970s, and 1980s, while the deaths of children younger than 5 years were cut in half, pregnancy and childbirth-related problems continued to be the leading cause of maternal mortality (Nowak, 1995). The World Health Organization (WHO), the World Bank, and the United Nations Population Fund (UNFPA) launched the Safe Motherhood Initiative with the goal to decrease maternal mortality rates by the year 2000 by one-half. It is clear the goal for the year 2000 will not be reached, but progress has been made. In addition, the WHO goal of Health for All by the year 2000 has drawn the world's attention to women's lack of access and equity in health care.

Implications for Clinical Practice

Although there have been many gains in the area of women's health in the United States during the 20th century, the goals of the WHM have been only partly achieved (Ruzek, 1993). Activism still is needed against potentially dangerous drugs and treatments, to gain health care services for women who are not being served, and probably most importantly, to help women gain power "over their own bodies and their own lives" (Mann, 1995). Continued progress will be made only as women demand attention to their concerns and problems, and vigilance will be essential after changes are evoked.

Normal life transitions in a woman's life, such as childbearing and menopause, are still "medicalized" (Taylor & Woods, 1996). Greater emphasis is needed on cultural diversity, effective means to decrease violence against women, and increasing the link between research and effective health care for women (Sechzer et al., 1994). Raftos, Mannix, and Jackson (1997), in a review of women's health articles indexed by CINAHL between 1993 and 1995, concluded that although holism is claimed to be the key feature of women's health, the articles approached women's health "from a narrow and stereotypical perspective with a bio-medical focus" on reproductive, maternal, neonatal, family, and sexual health. Another concern is the quality and philosophy of some family-centered care maternity programs. Most birthing environments have changed to warmer, more home-like rooms where women labor and give birth, but the traditional medicalized approach to birth remains the same in many birthing agency settings (Nichols & Gennaro, in press). Clancy and Massion (1992) called American women's health care a "patchwork quilt with gaps." Although progress has been made in achieving more comprehensive and coordinated women's health care, many gaps still remain in women's health care in the early 21st century. Andrist (1997) voiced concern about the commercialization of women's health, which has created a profitable industry for pharmaceutical companies, hospitals that use women's health as a marketing tool, and other corporations that market products and services to women.

Nurses play an important role as political activists in promoting the WHM and gender equity and empowering women to take charge and assume an active role in their own health care (Taylor & Woods, 1996). Taylor and Woods cite the need for a "woman-centered health care delivery system" (p. 797) that would provide comprehensive women's health care. Ruzek (1993) advocates using a more inclusive social model of health and well-being, as opposed to the current biomedical model, for women's health. The social model requires consideration of the total context of women's lives, such as economics, women's perceptions of their health risks, and the diversity of women's health needs across the life span. This implies that use of different health resources at various times in a woman's life are needed to improve women's health. In summary, LaRosa (1994) wrote that the success of women's health initiatives depends on the collaboration and cooperation of all concerned—the scientific community, health care providers, and the women who seek care. This remains true today in the 21st century.

> Nurses play an important role as political activists in promoting the WHM and gender equity and empowering women to take charge and assume an active role in their own health care.

References

AAN Expert Panel on Women's Health. (1997). Women's health and women's health care: Recommendations of the 1996 AAN Expert Panel on Women's Health. *Nursing Outlook, 45*(1), 7–15.

Andrist, L. (1997). A feminist model for women's health care. *Nursing Inquiry, 4*, 268–274.

Angell, M. (1993). Caring for women's health: What is the problem? *New England Journal of Medicine, 329*, 271–272.

Boogaard, M. A. (1984). Rehabilitation of the female patient after myocardial infarction. *Nursing Clinics of North America, 19*, 433–440.

Budoff, P. W. (1994). Women's centers: A model for future health care. *Annals of the New York Academy of Sciences, 30*, 165–170.

Butler, J. D., & Walbert, D. F. (1992). *Abortion, medicine and the law* (4th ed.). New York: Facts on File, Inc.

Centers for Disease Control (CDC). (1999, May 28). Office of Women's Health. [Online]. Available: http://www.cdc.gov/maso/owhfs.htm.

Chang, E., Daly, J., Hawkins, A., McGirr, J., Fielding, K., Hemmings, L., O'Donoghue, A., & Dennis M. (1999). An evaluation of the nurse practitioner role in a major rural emergency department. *Journal of Advanced Nursing, 30*(1), 260–268.

Clancy, C. M., & Massion, C. T. (1992). American women's health care. A patchwork quilt with gaps. *Journal of the American Medical Association, 268*, 1918–1920.

Congressional Research Report. (1993, Spring). Selected women's health conditions: Federal spending and prevalence. Washington, DC: US Congress Publication No. 93–670.

Congressional Research Report. (1994, Spring). Women's health research. Washington, DC: US Congress Publication No. 94–495.

Day, K. (1997, June 26). A fever for women's health care. *Washington Post*, p. CO1.

Donoghue, D. F. (ed.) (1996). *Women's health in the curriculum: A resource guide for faculty*. Philadelphia: National Academy on Women's Health Medical Education.

Doyal, L. (1996). The politics of women's health: Setting a global agenda. *International Journal of Health Services, 26*, 47–65.

Dyches, H., & Rushing, B. (1993). The health status of women in the world-system. *International Journal of Health Services, 23*, 359–371.

Fogel, C. I., & Woods N. F. (1995). *Women's health care: A comprehensive handbook*. Thousand Oaks, CA: Sage.

Geary, M.S. (1995). An analysis of the women's health movement and its impact on the delivery of health care within the United States. *Nurse Practitioner, 20*(11), 24, 27–28, 30–31.

Haire, D. (1972). *The cultural warping of childbirth*. Seattle, WA: International Childbirth Education Association.

Harris, J. (1998, July). Lactation in the workplace: What happens when a breastfeeding mother returns to work? Testimony of the Association of Women's Health, Obstetrics and Neonatal Nurses to The Bipartisan Congressional Caucus for Women's Issues. [Online]. Available: http://www.awhonn.org/advocacy/testimony7-98.htm.

Harrison, M. (1992). Women's health as a specialty: A deceptive solution. *Journal of Women's Health, 1*, 101–106.

King, K. M., & Paul, P. (1996). A historical review of the depiction of women in cardiovascular literature. *Western Journal of Nursing Research, 18*(1), 89–101.

Kirschstein, R. (1987). Women's health: A course of action. *Public Health Reports, July/August* (Suppl), 7–8.

LaRosa, J. H. (1994). Office of Research on Women's Health. National Institutes of Health and the women's health agenda. *Annals of the New York Academy of Sciences, 30*, 196–204.

Levison, S. P. (1996). Multidisciplinary women's health centers: A viable option? *International Journal of Fertility and Menopausal Studies, 41*(2), 132–135.

Mann, C. (1995). Women's health research blossoms. *Science, 267* (5225), 766–770.

Marieskind, H. (1975). The women's health movement. *International Journal of Health Services, 5*(2), 217–223.

Meinert, C. L. (1995). The inclusion of women in clinical trials. *Science, 269* (5225), 795–796.

Merkatz, R. B., & Junod, S. W. (1994). Historical background of changes in FDA policy on the study and evaluation of drugs in women. *Academic Medicine, 69*(9), 703–707.

Morse, G. G. (1995). Reframing women's health in nursing education: A feminist approach. *Nursing Outlook, 43*, 273–277.

Myers, P. C., Lenci, B., & Sheldon, M. G. (1997). A nurse practitioner as the first point of contact for urgent medical problems in a general practice setting. *Family Practice, 14*, 492–497.

Nichols, F., & Gennaro, S. (2000). The childbirth experience. In F. Nichols & S. Humenick (Eds.), *Childbirth birth education: Practice, research and theory* (2nd ed. [pp. 66–83]). Philadelphia: W. B. Saunders.

Nowak, R. (1995). New push to reduce maternal mortality in poor countries. *Science, 269* (5225), 780–782.

Pinn, V. (1992, October 14). Women's health research. *Journal of the American Medical Association, 268*, 1921–1922.

Raftos, M., Mannix, J., & Jackson, D. (1997). More than motherhood? A feminist exploration of 'women's health' in papers indexed by CINAHL 1993–1995. *Journal of Advanced Nursing, 26*, 1142–1149.

Remarks by the President at Congressional Caucus for Women's Issues. Speech presented by President Clinton, Mellon Auditorium, Department of Commerce, Washington, DC, October 21, 1997 [Online]. Available: http://www.usia.gov/usa/womenusa/speech5.htmn [1999, March 22].

Ruzek, S. B. (1978). *The women's health movement: Feminist alternatives to medical control.* New York: Praeger.

Ruzek, S. B. (1993). Towards a more inclusive model of women's health. *American Journal of Public Health, 83*(1), 6–8.

Ryan, J. W. (1999). Collaboration of the nurse practitioner and physician in long-term care. *Lippincott's Primary Care Practice, 3*(2), 127–134.

Schneir, M. (1994). *Feminism in our time.* New York: Vintage.

Sechzer, J. A., Griffin, A., & Pfafflin, S. M. (1994). Women's health and paradigm change. *Annals of the New York Academy of Sciences, 30,* 2–20.

Sharp, N. (1993). Women's health: A powerful public issue. *Nursing Management, 24,* 17–19.

Taylor, D. L., & Woods, N. F. (1996). Changing women's health, changing nursing practice. *JOGNN, 25,* 791–802.

University of Michigan School of Nursing (1999, March 15). Women's health. [Online]. Available: http://www.umich.edu/~nursing/academics/phd/womenshlt.html.

Update—The Congressional Caucus for Women's Issues. (1999, March 15). [Online]. Available: http://www.house.gov/lowey/caucus.htm.

Varkevisser, C. M. (1995). Women's health in a changing world. A continuous challenge. *Tropical and Geographical Medicine, 47*(5), 186–192.

Walker, L. O., & Tinkle, M. B. (1996). Toward an integrative science of women's health. *JOGNN, 25,* 379–382.

Wardell, D. (1980). Margaret Sanger: Birth control's successful revolutionary. *American Journal of Public Health, 70,* 736–742.

Women's Health. (1985). Report of the Public Health Service Task Force on Women's Health Issues. *Public Health Reports, 100*(1), 73–106.

Woods, N. R. (1994). The United States women's health research agenda analysis and critique. *Western Journal of Nursing Research, 16,* 467–479.

Francine H. Nichols is Professor and Coordinator of Women's Health in the School of Nursing at Georgetown University in Washington, DC.

Address for correspondence: Francine H. Nichols, RNC, PhD, FAAN, 2138 California Street, NW 203, Washington, DC 20008.

The Spiral of Women's Health Activism

by Amy Allina

A report from the Global Symposium Celebrating 40 Years of Our Bodies, Ourselves

When 14 women got together around a kitchen table in Boston in 1970 to write Women and Their Bodies (which would later become Our Bodies, Ourselves), they had grand ambitions. They knew their newsprint creation was much more than a book, and asked readers to view it instead "as a tool which stimulates discussion and action, which allows for new ideas and for change." Through writing the book, the authors explained that they learned "how we could act together on our collective knowledge [about our bodies] to change the health care system for women and for all people."

But they could not have imagined the impact their work would have, for women not only in the United States but also around the world. On the 40th anniversary of the publication of the first edition of OBOS, men and women gathered in Boston for a global symposium. The day's program included a welcome by Massachusetts Governor Deval Patrick (D), in which he thanked the OBOS founders, saying, "This book has made me a better person," as well as presentations by women from

11 of the more than 30 countries where OBOS has been translated and adapted.

Through its global initiative, the OBOS women's health activist approach has supported publication and use of materials in more than 25 languages, in print, Braille, audio, digital, and social interactive formats. The latest edition of the book—the ninth, published in the fall of 2011—includes a chapter on relationships that grew out of a month-long on-line dialogue between women who engaged with each other on a broad range of intimate topics.

A legacy of Challenging Shame, Stigma and Repression

Sally Whelan, Program Director at OBOS, told the crowd assembled in Boston that she views the legacy of the original OBOS work to be the global transformations that have been produced. The book now belongs, she said, to all the women around the world who have culturally adapted it to meet their communities' needs. The anniversary symposium was an opportunity to learn about the legacy through the voices and experiences of the book's new owners.

Women from the United States, Turkey, Japan and Tanzania shared their perspectives during a panel on how the OBOS creation process was similar and different in various places. In every case, for example, the project was collaborative and used the experiences of individual women as a guide for presenting evidence-based information.

And, virtually every woman who had been involved in an OBOS creation spoke about the shift from the beginning, when the anatomy and vocabulary of women's bodies were unfamiliar and uncomfortable, to the end, when it felt more natural to talk openly about bodies and sexuality and to see images of what women actually look like. One audience member spoke of learning about her own body and menstruation by reading OBOS when she first came to the United States from Uganda and of wanting to call her sisters at home to tell them "You have vaginas!"

Some experiences were unique to each country, however, such as the dilemma facing the Japanese women, who decided not to use the kanji characters for women's genitalia, because they connote dark and shady meanings.

During a panel on challenges to autonomy and activism, a co-author of the Serbian OBOS,

explained how the experiences of Bosnian refugees who had been raped during the war shaped their book's approach to sexual violence and drove home the knowledge that women's health and lives are tightly linked to the social and political context in which we live. The project coordinator for the Indian Bengali language version—My Health, My Self—said that their book defied "the complete obliteration of sexuality from the common language" by publishing the first health information in Bengali on safer sex practices in same sex relationships. The panelists agreed that, when OBOS projects are created in a post-colonial context, it's very important that the content be community-specific to avoid the trap of being dismissed as part of the Western/colonial model.

In the final panel, presenters discussed how their countries' OBOS projects have fueled movement-building and political change. In Senegal, this meant confronting the nation's health care provider shortage and the increased infant and maternal mortality that have resulted from structural adjustment policies that cut women's health services. In Israel, it produced a challenge to ageist language and cultural constructions affecting older women in a society where the state invests substantial resources in fertility promotion. The Israeli project also bridged the fundamental divisions which affect the lives of every woman in the country by bringing Jewish and Arab women together to publish two books—one in Hebrew and one in Arabic—despite of the publishing industry's objections that a book published in Arabic will not be profitable.

Early in the day, Jaclyn Friedman, the symposium's mistress of ceremonies, explained her belief that women's health activism moves in a spiral, not a circle, because while we are connected to our beginnings, we are also continually moving forward. The day's discussions provided a perfect demonstration of that concept.

Changing Lives and the World

The opening and closing keynotes of the day also mirrored the panel discussions' themes. Loretta Ross, National Coordinator of SisterSong, noted that while OBOS "masquerades as just a health manual," in fact, it is "one of the most subversive books out there, creating space for women to talk about issues not discussed in any other way in our societies." And Byllye Avery of the Black Women's Health Imperative reminded the audience that the anniversary is not just about history but also about celebrating sustained activism. It can't stop with us, Avery said, ending with a call to action: "There's still a woman's health movement, and if you don't know it, get in it!" (Videos

of the event are at:http://www.youtube.com/user/ourbodiesourselves#p/c/21193CA7E013C735 (http://www.youtube.com/user/ourbodiesourselves#p/c/21193CA7E013C735))

This Article Was Written by: Amy Allina

Amy Allina is the NWHN Program & Policy Director

The Making of Our Bodies Ourselves:
How Feminism Travels across Borders

by Kathy Davis

This is a book about a book: the feminist classic on women's health, *Our Bodies, Ourselves (OBOS)*, and how it "traveled." The story begins in 1969. The country was in turmoil over the Vietnam War. Richard "Tricky Dick" Nixon had just been elected president after the riots at the Democratic National Convention in Chicago. Radical activism was everywhere: the civil rights movement and its offshoots—Black Power, La Raza, and the American Indian movement; antiwar demonstrations and draft resistance; radical student activism of the Marxist, socialist, or anarchist persuasion; hippies, yippies, and the "sexual revolution"; and, last but not least, a burgeoning women's movement. It was in this context that a small group of young women met at a workshop called Women and Their Bodies, held at one of the first feminist conferences in the United States, which took place in Boston. Some of the women had already been active in the civil rights movement or had helped draft resisters during the Vietnam War, but this was for many of them their first encounter with feminism. They talked about their sexuality (which was still, despite the sexual revolution, very much taboo), abortion (which was illegal—*Roe v. Wade* wasn't decided until 1973), their experiences with pregnancy and childbirth (several were young mothers), and their frustrations

with physicians and healthcare. The group, which later evolved into the Boston Women's Health Book Collective (BWHBC), began to meet regularly. Its members collected information about health issues (which was, unlike today, scarce and hard to find) and wrote papers, which they discussed in meetings attended by increasing numbers of local women. These meetings were electrifying, leaving many of the participants irrevocably changed.

A year later the group assembled the discussion papers, and the first version of *OBOS* was born. Originally printed on newsprint by an underground publisher and selling for seventy-five cents, *OBOS* was a lively and accessible manual on women's bodies and health. It was full of personal experiences and contained useful information on issues ranging from masturbation (how to do it) to birth control (which methods were available and how to use them) to vaginal infections, pregnancy, and nursing. It combined a scathing critique of patriarchal medicine and the medicalization of women's bodies with an analysis of the political economics of the health and pharmaceutical industries. But, above all, *OBOS* validated women's embodied experiences as a resource for challenging medical dogmas about women's bodies and, consequently, as a strategy for personal and collective empowerment.

The book was an overnight success, and the group—to its surprise—found itself being wooed by commercial publishers. Since the first commercial edition was published in 1973, *OBOS* has sold over four million copies and gone through six major updates. The latest edition appeared in 2005. It occupied the *New York Times* best seller list for several years, was voted the best young adult book of 1976 by the American Library Association, and has received worldwide critical acclaim for its candid and accessible approach to women's health.

Often called the "bible of women's health," *OBOS* shaped how generations of women have felt about their bodies, their sexuality and relationships, and their reproduction and health. It has not only enjoyed a wide-spread popularity, unique for a feminist book, but has also transformed the provision of healthcare, helped shape healthcare policies, and stimulated research on women's health in the United States.[1] No family practice is complete without a copy of *OBOS* in the waiting room. Gynecological examinations have become more responsive to the patient's needs (e.g., by abandoning cold metal speculums in favor of more comfortable plastic ones), and hospitals have allowed women more control over the process of giving birth. As a result of *OBOS*, many women have been encouraged to enter medicine and midwives and nurse practitioners have been rehabilitated as respectable professionals in the U.S. healthcare system. The book has been a catalyst for myriad consumer and patient advocate organizations and campaigns for women's reproductive rights. It was instrumental in getting patient information inserts packaged with medications and has played an advocacy role in congressional hearings and scientific conferences on the safety of medications, medical devices, and procedures ranging from silicone breast implants to the injectable contraceptive Depo-Provera and the new genetic technologies. It has inspired research on women's health within the health sciences and medicine. Research protocols on—for example—heart disease no longer leave women out, and diseases that specifically effect women (such as breast cancer) have been given considerably more attention since the publication of *OBOS*. The recent study on the dangers of hormone replacement therapy (HRT), which exposed the negligence of the pharmaceutical industry and medical profession in indiscriminately promoting estrogen supplements for menopausal women, owes a debt to the pioneering work of *OBOS*.[2]

REFERENCES

A list of references is available in the original source.

The Boston Women's Health Book Collective and Our Bodies, Ourselves: A Brief History and Reflection

by Judy Norsigian, Vilunya Diskin,
Paula Doress-Worters, Jane Pincus, Wendy Sanford,
and Norma Swenson.

Originally published in the Winter 1999 edition of Journal of the American Medical Women's Association.

This article offers a brief history of Our Bodies, Ourselves, the landmark book about women's health and sexuality first published in 1970, as well as the Boston Women's Health Book Collective, its author and sponsor of numerous women's health initiatives. The organization's transition from a small, grassroots collective to a non-profit organization working at both the domestic and international levels is briefly discussed, including the development of a more diverse board and staff. Past accomplishments and current concerns of the global women's health movements are described, including some of the larger advocacy organizations now active in the women's health field. Collaboration with feminist physicians over the past two decades is also noted.

Our Early History

The history of Our Bodies, Ourselves (OBOS) and the Boston Women's Health Book Collective (BWHBC) began in the spring of 1969 at a women's liberation conference held in Boston. At a workshop on "Women and Their Bodies," we discovered that every one of us had a "doctor story," that we had all experienced feelings of frustration and anger toward the medical maze in general, and toward those doctors who were condescending, paternalistic, judgmental, and uninformative in particular. As we talked and shared our experiences, we realized just how much we had to learn about our bodies, that simply finding a "good doctor" was not the solution to whatever problems we might have. So we decided on a summer project: we would research our questions, share what we learned in our group, and then present the information in the fall as a course "by and for women." We envisioned an ongoing process that would involve other women who would then go on to teach such a course in other settings.

In creating the course, we learned that we were capable of collecting, understanding, and evaluating medical information; that we could open up to one another and find strength and comfort through sharing some of our most private experiences; that what we learned from one another was every bit as important as what we read in medical texts; and that our experiences frequently contradicted medical pronouncements. Over time these facts, feelings, and controversies were intertwined in the various editions of OBOS.

When we began this work, our ages ranged from 23 to 39, and we focused heavily on reproductive health and sexuality, new issues in the second wave of feminism. As we revised subsequent editions of OBOS, we included more material on such topics as environmental and occupational health, menopause and aging, often at the behest of readers and

with outside help. At this writing, those of us in the original group range in age from our late 40s to our mid-60s, and one of our original members, Esther Rome, has died of breast cancer.

In the 1970s, we worked together in "cottage industry" mode at home or in libraries, often meeting together around our kitchen tables. In 1980 we consolidated our books, articles, and correspondence in a rented office and began to hire women not part of the original Collective to do cataloging and to help with other tasks. This effort marked the beginning of our Women's Health Information Center (WHIC) and two decades of networking and information sharing that has extended beyond the publication of OBOS to a number of women's health education, activist, and advocacy projects involving us locally, nationally, and internationally. We supported the founding of the National Women's Health Network—the first national women's health advocacy membership organization. We were also among the few women's organizations calling for universal health care in the 1970s, and we supported Congressman Ron Dellums' National Health Services Act, a visionary bill that included provisions for contraceptive, sexually transmitted disease, and abortion services, and access to midwives and out-of-hospital childbearing options. Internationally, we served on the Advisory Board of ISIS (an information and communication service focused on women in developing countries), distributed packets and books to health workers and groups overseas, attended global women's health meetings, and ensured, when possible, that women's groups translating OBOS would be able to reap royalties to support their work.

The founders of the BWHBC were all college educated, but a significant number of us were from working class backgrounds and were the first in our families to attend college. Some of us had professional degrees, but none of us were in health fields. Many of us had been active in the social protest movements of the 1960s, particularly the civil rights movement, the antiwar movement, movements for women-centered childbirth and legal abortion. Some of us came from families with histories of struggle for social justice. Others of us came of age during a time of social change and found our own way to political activism. When we came together as part of a larger women's liberation movement, we were thrilled by the realization that working for social justice could affect the conditions of our lives as women. We believed that with our newfound freedom and solidarity as feminists, we could be more effective advocates on behalf of ourselves and other women, as well as other progressive causes.

Recent Growth and Development

Over the nearly three decades since the first edition of OBOS, we have continued to develop our awareness of the injustices that prevent women from experiencing full and healthy lives. As we approach the millennium, such causes of poor health as poverty, racism, hunger, and homelessness continue to disproportionately affect black and brown populations in this country and around the world. We continue to believe that effective strategies for mitigating these problems require all of us to reject the assumptions that so often hurt women of color and women who are poor. Over the years we have collaborated with women's groups both in the United States and abroad to ensure that the priorities for the women's health movement reflect the needs and concerns of all women. We also recognize the importance of supporting the leadership of women of color and low-income women within our own organization as well as in the larger women's health movements. Although this is a difficult challenge for many groups founded originally by white women, we believe that our ultimate success as a movement depends on respectful collaboration at many levels.

BWHBC's own structure has evolved over the years. We began as a collective, a circle of 12 women who met weekly and grew together both personally and politically, raising our own consciousness about health and sexuality as we reached out to inform others. We took no profits from sales of the books, using the royalties to support women's health projects and eventually to start our own WHIC and advocacy work. As soon as we hired staff who were not authors of the book, the BWHBC was not formally a collective anymore, although the board (mostly original authors for many years) and the paid staff each worked in a largely collaborative manner.

As the staff grew, so did organizational tensions and the need to develop a different model of management. For the past four years, the board of directors—now a more diverse group than it was originally—worked closely with a variety of consultants to shape a structure for the BWHBC that would introduce mechanisms of accountability that are consistent, dependable, and consonant with feminist principles. The organization now has a unionized staff (including a signed union contract) and formally designated leadership positions that operate in quite a different manner from the earlier years.

During the past few years a major revision of OBOS was also produced, Our Bodies, Ourselves for the New Century (May 1998). For this edition we expanded even more our efforts to include other women whose backgrounds and experiences are different from the original co-authors in terms of race, class, ethnicity, geographic origin, and sexual/gender identity. This experience helped us to develop an even greater appreciation for the challenges facing any organization working across differences, many of which have the potential to separate us.

BWHBC's Role in the Global Women's Health Movement

Within five years of its first publication, OBOS became a bestseller first in the United States, and then internationally (more than 4 million copies have been sold to date). Almost 20 foreign-language editions have been produced, including Japanese, Russian, Chinese, Spanish, French, Italian and German versions. Women in Egypt produced an Arabic book modeled after OBOS, as women are now doing in French-speaking Africa. More projects are underway today in Asia, Eastern Europe, and Armenia. At the 1995 NGO Women's Forum in Beijing, many of the women working on these translation/adaptation projects came together to compare notes and to share strategies for dealing with problems such as government censorship and fundraising.

In all editions of OBOS, we have encouraged women to meet, talk, and listen to each other as a first step toward bringing about needed change. Over the years, we have developed a number of fruitful collaborations with women's groups in different countries and have attended almost all the international women and health meetings that have been convened since the first "International Conference on Woman and Health" held in Rome in 1977. The activism of women's health groups across the globe has been spurred by the advent of email and the Internet, and we are excited to be part of a growing web of organizations working on such issues as breastfeeding, maternal mortality, and environmental health hazards.

One continuing concern of the current global women's health movement has been the growing trend, especially among environmental groups, to label population growth as a primary cause of environmental degradation. It would be a serious step back if this trend were to lead to more overly zealous family planning programs1 driven by demographic goals rather than by women's reproductive health needs. We believe that the unethical and growing use of quinacrine, a sclerosing agent, and a means of nonsurgical sterilization in countries such as Indonesia, India, Pakistan, and Vietnam, represents the very "population control" mentality that has so often been destructive to women's health. Thus, we have joined activists around the globe in protesting the use of quinacrine.[2]

We also collaborated with such other groups as the Women's Global Network for Reproductive Rights (Amsterdam), the International Reproductive Rights and Research Action Group (IRRRAG), and WomanHealth Philippines to sponsor "The Double Challenge," a well-attended workshop series at the Beijing NGO Forum in September 1995. The brochure for this series stated:

> Women from around the world face a formidable challenge. On one side are the fundamentalists led by the Vatican; on the other is the population establishment. Both are vying for control over women's sexual and reproductive lives. While the fundamentalists outlaw contraception and abortion, the populationists push new reproductive and contraceptive technologies.

The Continued Need for a Women's Health Movement[3,4]

The concerns that brought women together several decades ago to form women-controlled health centers, advocacy groups, and other educational and activist organizations largely remain. Women are still the major users of health and medical services, for example, seeking care for themselves even when essentially healthy (birth control, pregnancy and childbearing, and menopausal discomforts).[5]; Because women live longer than men, they have more problems with chronic diseases and functional impairment, and thus require more community- and home-based services. Women usually act as the family "health broker": arranging care for children, the elderly, spouses, or relatives, and are also the major unpaid caregivers for those around them.[6]

Although women represent the great majority of health workers, they still have a relatively small role in policy making in all arenas. Despite increases in the number of women physicians, they also have a limited leadership role in US medical schools, where women represent less than 10% of all tenured faculty.[7]; Women face discrimination on the basis of sex, class, race, age, sexual orientation, and disability in most medical settings. Many continue to experience condescending, paternalistic and culturally insensitive treatment. Older women, women of color, fat women, women with disabilities, and lesbians routinely confront discriminatory attitudes and practices, and even outright abuse.[8]

Women usually find it difficult to obtain the good health and medical information necessary to ensure informed decision making, especially for alternatives to conventional forms of treatment. This problem is intensified for poor women and for those who do not speak English, in part because their class, race, and culture increasingly differ markedly from those of their health care providers.[9]

Many women are subjected to inappropriate medical interventions, such as overmedication with psychotropic drugs (especially tranquilizers and antidepressants), questionable hormone therapy, and unnecessary cesarean sections and hysterectomies, although managed care has reduced the rates of unnecessary surgery in some places. The medical care system has been slow to recognize the importance of preventive and routine care, as well as the need for more rigorous study of alternative (nonallopathic) approaches to women's health problems that have not responded well to conventional forms of treatment.[10]

Despite enormous advances for women over the past two decades, ongoing gender bias in public and private settings continues to relegate women to a separate and unequal place in society. We must have a strong community of women's organizations to assist women individually, to articulate women's needs, to advocate for policy reform, and to resist the more destructive aspects of corporate medicine. Organizations such as the National Women's Health Network, the National Black Women's Health Project, the National Latino Health Organization, the National Asian Women's Health Organization, and the Native American Women's Health Education Resource Center, to name just a few, could play a key role in insuring that lay and consumer voices are part of any larger women's health debate. The inclusion of such groups by the office of Women's Health Research at the National Institutes of Health already has enriched discussions concerning research affecting women.

Ironically, except in a handful of states, poor women on Medicaid can obtain a federally funded sterilization but not a federally funded abortion. This limitation has led some women to "choose" sterilization because they have so few options. As the women's health movement continues to emphasize, without access to all reproductive health services, there can be no real choice in matters of childbearing.

Over the years, the BWHBC has collaborated with physicians who have shared the feminist perspective represented in OBOS. One such colleague, Mary Howell, MD, (more recently known as Mary Raugust), died from breast cancer in February 1998. The author of a popular 1972 book entitled Why Would a Girl Go into Medicine? and the first woman dean at Harvard Medical School, Mary contributed to the research that resulted in a legal ruling forcing medical schools to eliminate female quotas. These informal quotas had kept the female presence in medical schools well below 20 percent of the total number of students since the turn of the century. She remains for us one of the finest role models for women in medicine, and we hope that her speeches and writings will be published to inspire the younger generations of female physicians. Another physician, Alice Rothchild, MD, has written and spoken eloquently about her experience as a feminist obstetrician-gynecologist, and we have made her 1997 AMWA speech available at our website.[11]

Members of the media often ask us if we think that progress has been made in addressing the concerns women have had about medicine. We believe that physician awareness of condescending and paternalistic behaviors that are now generally regarded as disrespectful elsewhere in society has been heightened. It also appears that more women feel that their physicians take their concerns seriously, rather than dismissing their complaints with "it's all in your head." But other problems have been exacerbated, and although not unique to women, women's more frequent contact with the medical care system means that women confront these issues much more regularly than men do.

Many managed care plans have contributed to reductions in access to care, especially good quality care, for some women. They have, for example, not allowed some physicians to provide needed treatments. Sometimes, physicians have not had the time to adequately assess the plethora of new drugs and medical technologies that they regularly recommend to patients. Cutbacks in local community services and public health programs make it harder to sustain an emphasis on preventive health care. The BWHBC has a special interest in such problems as the increasing influence of right-wing organizations over public policies affecting women's health, the explosion of health and medical technologies marketed primarily to women, the objectification of women's bodies in the media, the exclusion of consumers from policy setting and oversight functions in many managed care plans, and the relatively few sources of noncommercial information about women and health, especially with a well-informed consumer perspective. We recognize institutional racism as a continuing problem exacerbated by the fact that most caregivers and health care administrators come from economic, social, racial and ethnic backgrounds quite different from those of the people they are serving. Finally, we believe it is critical to challenge the tendency to over-"medicalize"[12] women's lives and turn normal events such as childbearing and menopause into disabling conditions requiring medical intervention.

As the women's health movement moves into the next century, the ability to build broad coalitions will largely determine the political effectiveness of women's health care advocates. We can learn much, for example, from the passage of the

Americans with Disabilities Act, which succeeded in large part because the disability rights community reached out to form broad alliances with other groups not initially aware of the universal impact of this legislation. Finding common ground and ways to bridge racial, ethnic, and class difference in particular, will be among the great challenges we face.

Early Accomplishments of the Women's Health Movement

Here are just a few snapshots:

In the early 1970s, lack of information about birth control polls and a growing awareness among women about problems associated with their use led to organized protests, including disruption of special hearings in Congress conducted by Senator Gaylord Nelson. Fortuitously, Barbara Seaman, author of The Doctor's Case Against the Pill,[13] and Alice Wolfson met at the Nelson hearings; several years later they co-founded the National Women's Health Network with Dr. Mary Howell, Belita Cowan, and Phyllis Chesler, Ph.D. One important result of women's efforts to obtain more and better information about oral contraceptives (as well as other drugs) was the introduction of the Patient Package Insert (PPI) program at the FDA (Food and Drug Administration). A related struggle involved the provision of PPIs for so-called estrogen replacement therapy. Not long after PPIs appeared for estrogen products, the Pharmaceutical Manufacturers Association joined the American College of Obstetricians and Gynecologists to sue the FDA in an effort to block the distribution of PPIs for estrogen products. In response, four women's and consumer organizations, led by the National Women's Health Network, entered the case as co-defendants and filed an amicus brief cogently arguing for the right to such basic information. And we won. PPIs for estrogen products were retained through the late 1970s, although later suspended by the Reagan Administration. The Clinton Administration has reinstated them in a different form.[14]

Sterilization abuse, a longstanding problem for poor women in the United States, became the focus of a government inquiry after activists, journalists, and community organizations documented and publicized the degree to which certain women, especially women of color and Native American women, were sterilized without informed consent.[15] This happened in a variety of ways: some women agreed to be sterilized without fully understanding what it meant, especially when information was given in terminology they did not understand; others were told that their public welfare benefits would be denied unless they agreed to sterilization; some were told that the procedure was reversible, when, of course, that was not true. Special hearings resulted in regulations, written in part by both consumer and physician health activists, designed to curb the incidence of abuse among federally funded sterilizations. These regulation included a 30-day waiting period, the provision of information in a language clearly understood by the woman, and prohibition of hysterectomy solely for the purpose of sterilization. Though far from perfect, these regulation have been somewhat effective.

As early as the mid-1970s, the women's health movement addressed controversies surrounding breast cancer. For many years the standard practice of US doctors, in doing a breast biopsy and finding malignant tissue, was to proceed immediately with a mastectomy. Several years of hard work during the 1970s, especially on the part of activist and journalist Rose Kushner, who has since died from breast cancer, resulted in a landmark recommendation by the National Cancer Institute that breast biopsies be performed as part of a two-step procedure in most cases. The panel advised that a diagnostic biopsy specimen be studied with permanent histologic sections before offering various treatment options to a patient with breast cancer. This recommendation represented an important step forward in the treatment of breast cancer and also increased general awareness of the importance of nonsurgical treatments.

During the 1970s dozens of women-controlled health centers emerged as alternatives to the conventional delivery of health and medical care. Many were organized nonhierarchically with physicians having little or no policy-making roles. Most offered self-help groups that taught cervical self-exam, abortion services that were often the only ones in the region, and support groups for dealing with such experiences as premenstrual problems; infertility, and menopause. They also pioneered a more thorough, client-centered approach to informed consent. Several women among the founders of the Feminist Women's Health Centers pioneered the development of a menstrual extraction technique that has since been used by women in other countries. In large part because of these women-controlled health centers, abortion became firmly established as an outpatient service. In 1992 only 7% of abortions were performed in hospitals, while in 1973 more than half of all abortions had been performed in hospitals.[16] This assured that first-trimester abortions in this country would be appropriately demedicalized.

The authors wish to thank interns Tricia Collins and Jennifer Stetzer.

Endnotes

1 Hartmann B. To vanquish the hydra. Political Environments. Spring 1994.

2 Berer M. The quinacrine controversy one year on. Reproductive Health Matters. November 1994:10.5

3 Swenson N. Women's health movement. In: Mankiller W, et al, eds. Reader's Companion to U.S. Women's History. New York, NY: Houghton-Mifflin; 1998:648.

4 Norsigian J. Women and national health care reform: A progressive feminist agenda. J Women's Health. 1993;2:91.

5 Managed Care Consumer Protections and Women's Health: The Balanced Budget Act. Washington DC: Women's Legal Defense Fund; 1997:1.

6 Horton J. ed. The Women's Health Data Book: A Profile of Women's Health in the United States. Washington, DC: Jacobs Institute of Women's Health; 1992:93.

7 The Blue Sheet. Washington, DC: F-D-C-Reports; 1996:5.

8 Scully D. Men Who Control Women's Health: The Miseducation of Obstetrician/Gynecologists. New York, NY: Teacher's College Press; 1994.

9 Health Care Reform: What Is at Stake for Women? New York, NY: The Commonwealth Fund Commission of Women's Health; 1994:13.

10 Ruzek S. Access, cost and quality medical care: where are we heading? In: Ruzek S, Oleson V, Clarke A, eds. Women's Health Complexities and Differences. Columbus, Ohio: Ohio State University Press; 1997:197.

11 Rothchild A. From both ends of the speculum: A feminist analysis of health care. Paper presented at the American Medical Women's Association meeting, New York City, March 8, 1998.

12 Zola IK. Medicine as an institution of social control. In Zola IK. Socio-Medical Inquiries. Philadelphia, Pa: Temple University Press; 1983.

13 Seaman B. The Doctor's Case Against the Pill. New York, NY: Doubleday; 1969.

14 The phoenix rises: Patient package inserts reborn (if you help!). Network News. November/December 1994:3.

15 Chase A. Sterilization: The legacy and the lack of watch dogs. Medical Tribune. September 7, 1977:1,22.

16 Henshaw SK, Van Vort J. Abortion services in the United States, 1991 and 1992. Fam Plann Perspect. 1994;26:104.

Special thanks to the American Medical Women's Association for generously giving us permission to reprint the following article. The article was originally published in the Winter 1999 edition of Journal of the American Medical Women's Association.

http://www.ourbodiesourselves.org/about/jamwa.asp

The Gynecologic Exam and the Training of Medical Students: An Opportunity for Health Education

by Judith Schmidt

This article is a personal account written by a senior health education major about her experience as a teaching associate (TA) in training medical students for the gynecological examination. This method of using teaching associates who "teach on their own bodies" has evolved in medical schools across the country in recent years. It is an attempt to counter inadequate medical school preparation in this important area of women's health and to improve the physician-patient relationship in gynecological medicine. Lack of sensitivity to female patients has taken the form of high rates of malpractice litigation in gynecology, a situation which might well be reversed given the improved communication between physician and patient. Medical school teaching staff across the country have now widely accepted the use of teaching associates as the most effective teaching method for this part of the complete physical examination.

One of the ideas emphasized in this approach is that of the "activated patient." An activated patient is one who is fully and equally involved as a participant in the examination process. One projected outcome of this approach is greater personal responsibility for one's health such as doing self-breast exams. But the potential of using this approach goes beyond mere "disease prevention" of traditional medical care. It gives female patients a sense of control over what happens to them—both inside and out of a gynecologist's office—and enters a psychological and social health dimension that makes the concept known as "high-level wellness" accessible. In the context of medical intervention by physicians during the gynecological exam, the potential exists to take steps toward the goal of optimal wellness. This article attempts to explore that potential.

"What's it like doing that sort of thing?" curious and sometimes incredulous friends ask. I have just told them about my job. I am a teaching associate (TA) for the instruction of the gynecological examination to first and second-year medical students. As such, I am a "professional patient." I give feedback to these students about their technique and attitude, and most important, about the way they communicate with me as a patient during the gynecological exam.

I respond to my friends' questions by telling them my job is demanding. I experience the same feelings that any woman facing a breast and pelvic exam does, including anxiety and nervousness. But overall, I feel good about doing it. I feel that what I am doing is important.

The next question, "Does it pay well?" The implication is that the only reason for my engaging in such an occupation must be money. "Yes, it does," is my answer. "And well it should! My job takes a good deal of knowledge and ability." Not only does it require knowledge of female sexual and reproductive anatomy, but it means that I must be comfortable discussing my own anatomy with others. It requires good teaching and interpersonal skills, plus a lot of sensitivity about a topic that is emotionally loaded for students and patient alike.

"But money isn't the main reason I do it," I explain. My own experiences with gynecologists have for the most part not been satisfactory. The opportunity to improve this area of women's health through my input into the training of medical students appeals to me. Also, as a student majoring in health education at the same university, I see the potential for patient education and the role

physicians might play in this process. As a TA, I feel I have some influence in this direction.

"Does your job take training?"

"Yes it does," I respond, as I visualize our initial training sessions. In these first sessions, we learn right along with the medical students. We all become part of a "learning team" which I can now see is beneficial for reducing anxiety and developing a comfortable working relationship with the students prior to the actual examination.

Just as the medical students do, we watch the Bates videotape, "Female Pelvic Examination." And just as they do, we practice inserting the speculum and examining internal anatomy manually on the plastic Gynny model. As I practice using the speculum on the Gynny model, the idea then seems less scary to me. I wonder, as a health educator, whether offering other women this experience on a Gynny model prior to a pelvic exam might lessen their anxiety, as it has mine.

In these initial training sessions my actual teaching role begins. I am called upon to recall my own feelings during the gynecological exam. The medical students are also encouraged to explore the kinds of feelings that they, as physicians, might experience. How should the physician, for example, handle a situation in the best interests of the patient and him or herself if sexually attracted to the patient prior to the examination? Issues such as these are dealt with in these sessions.

Emphasis in these training sessions is put on the importance of involving the patient during the process of the exam itself. An activated patient who is involved in such a way has some sense of control over what is happening to her during her exam. Again, as a teaching associate I am called upon to describe how being "activated" in this way as a patient allows me to feel less victimized during the gynecological exam.

Part of this initial discussion focuses on empathy. To learn to empathize with female patients, all the students are required to disrobe, drape, and get into the lithotomy position—or into the stirrups, as it is commonly called. Through this first-hand experience, medical students can vividly relate to the feelings of vulnerability shared by their female patients as they lie naked, legs suspended, waiting to be examined—covered only by a thin piece of paper that fails to intercept the cool flow of air over one's usually concealed private anatomy.

After these preliminary training sessions, my difficult work begins. I find that my anxiety soon disappears as I get actively involved in teaching. The students are much more nervous than I am so that relating to them in a calm and confident way has the effect of putting us both at ease.

The nature of the suggestions that I give during the actual examination stresses technique. I might suggest that a student flatten his or her hand while palpating my abdomen. I might help a student identify that fleeting moment when my ovaries roll past. But I do not emphasize the mechanics, as I know these will improve with practice.

The general feedback I give each student in turn afterward about how well he or she communicated with me and attended to my emotional needs is far more important. I begin by reinforcing those things which I like. This might include confirming that the student maintained eye contact with me and watched my face for nonverbal signals indicating discomfort. Or it might mean commending a student's effective use of firm and reassuring touch. Then, I follow with a suggestion for improvement. This might include suggesting to the student that he or she replace specialized medical jargon with common conversational language that the patient can more easily understand.

Occasionally, my job demands that I be assertive. For example, I had to tell a male student that I was uneasy having his groin against my knee, while having my breast examined—under ordinary circumstances a female patient might interpret this in a sexual way. We were both embarrassed, but he expressed appreciation for telling him this.

Only once did I find it necessary to tell a student about poor attitude. "I am uncomfortable with the way you treated me—as if I were a plastic model," I had to say. Fortunately, this is rare as most students are respectful and caring to the extreme.

I am proud of the student who is able to include me actively and equally as a participant. I keep a mental checklist during the exam of the various ways the student might accomplish this. Does the student remember to offer me a mirror? Does he or she offer it in such a way that is *not* just an off-hand question? ("Do you want a mirror?") But rather in a way so that I, as patient, understand that it is important and acceptable to know about my own female anatomy. "Would you like to hold a mirror while I examine your pelvic area? That way I can better explain to you what I see, and you can see everything for yourself?"

There are other check-offs on my mental list. Does the student offer me the option of having my head raised during the pelvic part of the examination to facilitate communication between us? Does the student actively solicit my verbal input; not just telling and explaining, but questioning and encouraging any questions I, as patient, might have regarding my anatomy or sexual functioning?

Finally, I consider certain non-verbal aspects of our communication exchange. I consider the student's attitude. Is it flippant or overbearing in any way? Does the student display appropriate respect and a willingness to share power in the interaction that goes on between us? What clues do I get from facial expression, body position and movement that support my assessment?

By assessing the answers to all these questions, I am able to evaluate how well I was activated as an involved and equal participant during the examination. When done effectively, this process allows me to feel in control—not as a passive bystander whose body is "being done to."

At this point, relating the notion of the activated patient to the idea of wellness begins. By actively engaging female patients in the gynecological exam itself, the physician can play an important role in aiding the female patient in knowing and being comfortable with her body. Not only might this have a spin-off effect of encouraging women to practice self-examination and prevention at home (I am an example of one who only began doing regular self-breast exams since beginning this job even though I had long known the appalling statistics about breast cancer), but it might help overcome those culturally programmed negative feelings that many women still have about their bodies and lead to a greater degree of sexual satisfaction.

At the end of the teaching session, it is my time for reinforcement. The students all express their gratitude. They are relieved that doing a procedure that had worried them has turned into a positive learning experience; they give me credit. I accept their thanks and express my hope that they will use what they have learned here to make the experience of the gynecological exam a better one for their patients.

One of my fears when I took this job was how the students would react when we would meet in public after the training sessions. I knew this was inevitable as I am a student on the same campus in a small city. Contrary to my worries, I have not felt the slightest embarrassment. Rather I sense a mutual respect between us resulting from the difficult task we shared together.

This feeling of mutual respect might not be something peculiar to my own particular experience. Perhaps it is a reflection of this kind of interaction between a patient-oriented physician and an activated, involved patient. It is an interaction that is designed to allow the patient to feel more in control and, in so doing, to enhance her self-esteem.

The positive effect of this interaction for the patient and its contribution to her overall health status should not be minimized. Replacing negative feelings that many women still have regarding their sexual-reproductive anatomy with positive ones can enhance a woman's sense of well-being and personal fulfillment. Satisfying such a psychological health need represents a step on that continuum toward that elusive concept known as high level wellness. Entering this psychological and social health dimension goes beyond the purely physical realm of traditional medical care.

Medical intervention by a physician which attempts to accomplish such a task is a concrete way to lessen the gap between disease prevention and that lofty goal of optimal wellness. It is an intervention mutually rewarding to patient and physician alike.

Bibliography

1. DiMatteo R M, Friedman HS: *Social Psychology and Medicine.* Oelgeschlager, West Germany, Gum and Hain, Publishers, Inc., 1982.

2. Miller G D: The gynecological examination as a learning experience. *Journal of the American College Health Association* 1974; 23(2).

Cadavers, Dolls, and Prostitutes: Medical Pedagogy and the Pelvic Rehearsal

by Terri Kapsalis

My first question, as I suspect yours may be, was, "what *kind* of woman lets four or five novice medical students examine her?"—James G. Blythe, M.D.

Fearing the Unknown

In a paper entitled "The First Pelvic Examination: Helping Students Cope with Their Emotional Responses," printed in the *Journal of Medical Education* in 1979, Julius Buchwald, M.D., a psychiatrist, shares his findings after ten years of conducting seminars with medical students starting their training in OB/GYN. He locates six primary fears associated with a first pelvic examination: (1) "hurting the patient"; (2) "being judged inept"; (3) the "inability to recognize pathology"; (4) "sexual arousal"; (5) "finding the examination unpleasant"; and (6) the "disturbance of the doctor-patient relationship" (when a patient reminded them of somebody they knew, e.g., mother or sister).

Because the pelvic exam produces fear and anxiety in medical students, numerous methods have been used to offer them a pelvic exam "rehearsal." This practice performance is meant to help soothe or disavow student fears while allowing them to practice manual skills. The types of practice performances adopted reveal and promote specific ideas about female bodies and sexuality held by the medical institution. The use of gynecology teaching associates (GTAS), trained lay women who teach students using their own bodies, is a relatively new addition to pelvic exam pedagogy that will be examined at length. Previous to and contemporaneous with this practice, medical schools have cast a variety of characters as subjects of this pelvic exam rehearsal, including actual patients, cadavers, anesthetized women, prostitutes, and plastic manikins such as "Gynny," "Betsi," and "Eva". The ways medical students have been taught to perform pelvic exams illustrate the predicament of the gynecological scenario, a situation in which a practitioner must, by definition, examine women's genitals in a clinical and necessarily nonsexual manner. The array of pedagogical methods used to teach pelvic exams reveals how the medical institution views female bodies, female sexuality, and the treatment of women.

In pelvic exams, physicians-to-be are confronted with both female genital display and manipulation, two highly charged cultural acts. If students have previously engaged in gazing at or touching female genitals, most likely they have done so as a private sexual act (e.g., male students engaging in heterosexual activities and female students masturbating or engaging in lesbian activities). Occasionally there are male or female students who, for a variety of reasons, have had little or no exposure to naked female bodies, and their fears often revolve around a fear of the "unknown," which in the case of women's genitals takes the form of a particularly stigmatized mystery.

Students seem to find it very difficult to consider female genital display and manipulation in the medical context as entirely separate from sexual acts and their accompanying fears. Buchwald's list of fears makes explicit the perceived connection between a pelvic examination and a sexual act. "A fear of the inability to recognize pathology" also reflects a fear of contracting a sexually transmitted disease, an actual worry expressed by some of Buchwald's student doctors. Likewise, "a fear of sexual arousal" makes explicit the connection between the pelvic exam and various sexual acts. Buchwald notes that both men and women are subject to this fear of sexual arousal. "A fear of being judged inept" signals a kind of "performance anxiety," a feeling common in both inexperienced and experienced clinical and sexual performers. "A fear of the disturbance of the doctor-patient relationship" recognizes the existence of a type of "incest taboo" within the pelvic exam scenario. Buchwald shares anecdotes of students feeling sick or uncomfortable if the patient being examined reminded them of their mother or sister. Buchwald's work deviates from most publications dealing with the topic of medical students and pelvic exams. Largely, any acknowledgment of this precarious relationship between pelvic exams and sex acts is relatively private and informal, taking place in conversations between students, residents, and doctors, sometimes leaking into private patient interactions. For example, as a student in the 1960s, a male physician was told by the male OB/GYN resident in charge, "During your first 70 pelvic exams, the only anatomy you'll feel is your own." Cultural attitudes about women and their bodies are not checked at the hospital door. If women are largely marketed as sexualized objects of the gaze, why should a gynecological scenario necessarily produce different meanings?

Rehearsing Pelvics

Teaching medical practices is the act of constructing medical realities. In other words, the student is continuously learning by lecture and example what is right and acceptable and, conversely, what is wrong and unacceptable in medical practice. The intractability of medical teaching from medical practice is built into the very title of Foucault's *Birth of the Clinic*. The translator's note recognizes the importance of the choice of the word "clinic": "When Foucault speaks of *la clinique*, he is thinking of both clinical medicine and of the teaching hospital so if one wishes to retain the unity of the concept, one is obliged to use the rather odd-sounding clinic." Medical pedagogy, including textbooks (the focus of the following chapter) and experiential learning, is symbiotic with medical practice; the two work together in the formation, transferal, and perpetuation of medical knowledge. With regard to pelvic exams, this medical knowledge has been acquired in a number of ways.

Many medical students have encountered their first performance of a pelvic exam on an actual patient. Oftentimes a group of students on rounds would repeat pelvic exams one after another on a chosen patient while the attending physician watched. If we consider that the pelvic exam is often sexualized by novice practitioners, this pedagogical situation resembles a "gang rape." Many times there is little communication with the woman being examined, nor is her explicit consent necessarily requested. Due to the intimidation of the medical institution, a woman may not resist repeated examination, even if she is adamantly against the use of her body for pedagogical purposes. This actual patient situation is one that Buchwald locates as anxiety provoking for the medical student (he fails to mention the anxiety this may cause the woman being examined). This situation adds to what Buchwald refers to as the student's "fear of being judged inept": "a frequent remark was, 'if the resident sees the way I'm going about it, he'll think I'm stupid.' In some respects what began to evolve was the image of the experienced, wise, worldly, and sexually competent adult (the resident or attending physician) sneering at the floundering explorations of an adolescent (the medical student) who is striving to become a 'man.'" Buchwald's reading of this situation is gendered inasmuch as he compares the pelvic exam to an adolescent male rite of passage. This gendered reading is telling. The medical apparatus, particularly this 1970s version, incorporates specifically gendered male positions of physician and medical student. Even though there are increasing numbers of women medical students, physicians, and medical educators, the structures of this apparatus, specifically the structures of medical pedagogy, are

in many instances unchanged or slow in changing and require a female medical student to fit into this masculinized subject position. Her relationship to this ascribed subject position, particularly as a medical student, may be uncomfortable, as she may be split between identifying with the woman pelvic patient (as she herself has most likely undergone such exams) and with her newly forming role as masculinized spectator. As a medical educator, I frequently witness such a split in female medical students. As Laura Mulvey describes, "trans-sex identification is a *habit* that very easily becomes *second nature*. However, this Nature does not sit easily and shifts restlessly in its borrowed transvestite clothes." Although Mulvey is discussing female cinematic spectatorship, her words are applicable to female medical spectatorship as well. While the anxieties located and described by Buchwald as very "male" in nature may be the very same anxieties experienced by a female medical student, these anxieties take on different twists and meanings with female physicians-in-training.

Other than the attending physician, one person within the pelvic equation who might also judge the student as inept or whose presence might distract the student from performing a proper first exam and therefore cause the student anxiety, is the patient herself. Cadavers, anesthetized women, and anthropomorphic pelvic models like the plastic manikins "Gynny," "Betsi," and "Eva" are pelvic exam subjects who, for a variety of reasons, are rendered absent and therefore cannot talk back or have an opinion about the medical student's performance. These female models alleviate anxiety regarding inappropriate patient performance since they cannot possibly act out. The pedagogical use of these models may also have been developed in order to avert other student fears. If the woman's body is anesthetized, dead, or replaced altogether by a plastic model certainly there can be no fear of causing her pain. However, this logic is questionable in the case of the anesthetized patient: How might repeated pelvic exams under anesthetic affect how a woman "feels" both psychologically and physically when she wakens?

More importantly, the legality of this practice is extremely questionable. How many women would actually consent to this practice? Many women are anxious at the thought of a single pelvic exam, let alone multiple exams. Furthermore, the fear of a pelvic exam is often associated with feeling vulnerable and out of control; under anesthetic, a woman is particularly vulnerable and out of control. And yet teaching medical students how to do pelvic exams on anesthetized women appears to be widely practiced, although public discussion of this method outside (and inside) the medical community is relatively scarce. At a 1979 conference sponsored by the Women's Medical Associations of New York City and State, New Jersey, and Connecticut held at Cornell University Medical College, this issue was discussed and found its way into the *New York Times*, where the conference recommendation was quoted: "If examined in the operating room, patients must be told prior to anesthesia that they will be examined by the members of the operating team, including the medical student." Decades later this recommendation is often unheeded. For example, a surgical nurse I interviewed provided a common scenario: "While doing an exam on a woman who is sedated for a urological procedure, a physician may discover that she has a prolapsed uterus. The student or students observing the procedure will then be invited to perform a bi-manual exam on the woman [inserting two fingers in her vagina while pressing on her abdomen] in order to feel her uterus." I have overheard physicians at a prestigious Chicago medical school encouraging students to "get in surgery as much as possible to get pelvic exam practice." The assumption is that students will not be intimidated by an unconscious woman and that the patient will, in addition, have relaxed abdominal muscles, thus permitting easy palpation of her ovaries and uterus. Many physicians have not heard about such "practicing" and are outraged at the suggestion, maintaining that this is medically sanctioned sexual assault. Some physicians who are aware of the practice dodge the questionable issues, maintaining that for some students it is the only way they will learn.

But what *are* students learning in this scenario? By using anesthetized women, cadavers, or plastic models as pelvic exam subjects students are being taught that a model patient (or patient model) is one who is essentially unconscious or backstage to the performance of the pelvic exam; she should be numb to the exam, providing no feedback and offering no opinions. In the tradition of Sims's experiments, passive and powerless female patients are considered ideal "participants" in the learning process. In addition, students practicing on essentially silent and lifeless models are learning that the manual skills associated with completing a pelvic exam are more important than the fundamental skills needed to interact with the patient—skills that ideally would help the patient relax and participate in the exam.

Perhaps these rehearsal methods are used under the assumption that an anesthetized, dead, or plastic model is unerotic and will thus relieve students of Buchwald's fear #4, "a fear of sexual arousal." And yet the rendering of the object of manipulation or the gaze as passive simply heightens the power differential between examiner and examined that can in effect tap into an altogether different system of erotics. Necrophilia may be coded into a pelvic examination on a cadaver. Similarly, there have been noted cases of sexual abuse when patients are under anesthetic. Likewise, the anthropomorphically named pelvic manikins "Gynny," "Betsi," and "Eva," with their custom orifices for medical penetration, could be recognized as the medical correlates to inflatable sex dolls.

In the late 1970s, numerous medical pedagogues were reexamining what one physician referred to as "the time-honored methods" of pelvic exam pedagogy: students examining anesthetized women, conscious patients, cadavers, or plastic models. The problems with these methods were discussed in a number of articles. The authors of the 1977 article "Professional Patients: An Improved Method of Teaching Breast and Pelvic Examination" in the *Journal of Reproductive Medicine* found that training medical students on actual patients "has many disadvantages, including infringement of patients' rights, inadequate feedback and moral and ethical concerns. Another approach that is widely used is the anesthetized preoperative patient. Again, problems include informed consent, increased cost and/or risk and lack of an interpersonal exchange. The introduction of the 'Gynny' and 'Betsi' models has been an attempt at improvement, but not without drawbacks, which include a lack of personal communication, unreal exposure and difficulty with 'live' correlation." Where was the medical community to find these living models? Some went to what must have seemed a very natural source. In the early 1970s a number of schools, including the University of Washington Medical School and the University of Oklahoma Physician's Associate Program, hired prostitutes to serve as "patient simulators." What other women would accept payment for spreading their legs? Logically, these educators felt that a prostitute would be the most fitting *kind* of woman for the job. In a sense, the patriarchal medical establishment took the position of a rich uncle, paying for his nephew, the medical student, to have his first sexual experience with a prostitute. This gendered suggestion assumes that female medical students are structurally positioned as masculinized "nephew" subjects as well.

Although lip service has been paid to the supposed importance of desexualizing the pelvic patient, in choosing prostitute patient models, medical educators inadvertently situated the exam as a sexualized act. They must have thought that only a prostitute would voluntarily submit to exams repeatedly and for nondiagnostic purposes. Or perhaps the underlying assumption was that a lady *pays* to get examined whereas a whore *gets paid* for the same exam. It may have also been assumed that prostitutes are more accustomed to and have a higher tolerance for vaginal pain than other women and would thus be more fitting practice models for novice students. In choosing to hire prostitutes as patients the boundaries of pornographic and medical practice were collapsed. Within this scenario of a hired prostitute, the student physician was put in the position of a medicalized lover or "john." Certainly Buchwald's fear #3, "a fear of sexual arousal," was confirmed and even encouraged by hiring prostitutes. Buchwald notes that certain students "appeared to project their anxiety by asking, 'what should I do if the patient starts responding sexually?'" By hiring prostitutes as pelvic patients, the medical establishment not only enforced the trope of the "seductive patient," but also paid for it. "Playing doctor" in this pelvic rehearsal cast with patient prostitutes threatened to translate the pelvic exam into an act of sexualized penetration and bodily consumption.

In many cases when prostitutes were hired, the medical student was led to believe that the woman being examined was a clinical outpatient rather than a prostitute. Thus the prostitute still had a relatively passive position in the training of medical students. In order to properly perform her role as clinical outpatient, she could offer the student little feedback. In addition, the working logic of the medical educators remained relatively opaque inasmuch as the student was not directly learning about the medical establishment's opinion of model patients. And yet these attitudes undoubtedly found their way into medical practice. Years later, students are still told by certain unaware medical faculty that GTAS are prostitutes. Today certain faculty still conclude that no other *kind* of woman would submit her body to multiple exams in exchange for a fee. This points to the importance of understanding the recent history of pelvic pedagogy. Those physicians trained in the 1970s are the same physicians practicing and educating today.

Some physicians found fault with the use of prostitutes as pelvic models. According to the authors of "Utilization of Simulated Patients to Teach the Routine Pelvic Examination," "the employment of prostitute patient simulators is not satisfactory. The prostitutes employed by the PA (Physician's Associate) program were not articulate enough to provide the quality of instructive feedback necessary for an optimal educational experience. Their employment was costly at $25 per hour, and that expense prohibited their extensive and long-term use. Also, and more importantly prostitutes had abnormal findings on examination prior to their utilization." Pathology was not desirable in these model patients: in the pelvic rehearsal, students were not to be distracted by abnormal findings. Rather, the patient simulator needed to be standardized as normal like the plastic model. In addition, the prostitute was expensive. She received market value for her bodily consumption, unlike the income-free corpse, indebted actual patient, and the cut-rate graduate students that the authors of the article hired at $10 per hour. And although prostitutes did offer some student critique (comments such as "poor introduction," "too serious," "too rough," and "forgot to warm the speculum") their language skills were not medically acceptable. What the medical establishment needed was a model who could engage in medicalese, was more cost efficient, and had normal, healthy anatomy. The GTA would be the answer.

The GTA Program

In 1968 at the University of Iowa Medical School's Department of Obstetrics and Gynecology, Dr. Robert Kretzschmar instituted a new method for teaching junior medical students how to perform the pelvic exam. For the pelvic model he used a "simulated patient," first defined in the medical literature as a "person who has been trained to completely simulate a patient or any aspect of a patient's illness depending upon the educational need." Many simulated patients were actresses and actors hired by the medical establishment to realistically portray a patient. Their critical feedback was not traditionally requested. They simply served as a warm body for the practicing student. This stage of Kretzschmar's program was not dissimilar to the other programs that hired prostitutes. Initially, Kretzschmar adhered to this simulated patient model. He hired a nurse for the role of patient. She agreed to repeated exams by medical students; "however, it was necessary to compromise open communication with her, as she was draped at her request in such a way as to remain anonymous." The curtain rose but the nurse's knowledge, thoughts, feelings, and face remained backstage. All that was revealed was the object of the exam: the woman's pelvic region. The logic behind draping the simulated patient presumed that if "only a whore gets paid" for a nondiagnostic exam, perhaps the nurse could avoid whore status by becoming faceless and silent.

In many gynecology textbooks, as will be examined in the following chapter, a similar logic prevails. Photographs picturing women are cropped so that faces are not shown or bands are placed across eyes to maintain the model's anonymity. If the woman's face and eyes are pictured, the photo could enter the realm of pornography; the woman imaged cannot be soliciting or meeting the medical practitioner's gaze, a potentially sexualized act. If the nurse who served as simulated patient was draped to maintain her anonymity she was in effect attempting to desexualize her body for the medical gaze. But is this an effective strategy for the desexualization of the exam? Is a faceless, vulnerable female body less erotic? In addition, although this professional patient model rehearsal did save actual patients from the task of performing the role

of pelvic model, it did little to encourage communication between student and patient. Maintaining such anonymity taught the students that it was acceptable and even preferable for them to ignore the woman backstage behind the drape. They were also shown that a modest woman, unlike a prostitute, would need to disassociate her face from her body. And therefore, a modest woman preferred to be treated as though she were anonymous and invisible.

In 1972, Kretzschmar instituted a different program. The new simulated patient, now named the gynecology teaching associate (GTA), would serve as both patient and instructor, stressing the importance of communication skills in addition to teaching the manual skills required to perform a proper pelvic exam. Unlike the nurse clinician who was first hired as a simulated patient in 1968, the GTA would actively teach and offer feedback to medical students, forsaking any anonymity through draping. The GTAS first hired by Kretzschmar were women who were working on or had received advanced degrees in the behavioral sciences but who had no formal medical training. The women had normal, healthy anatomy and were willing to undergo multiple exams. They then received elaborate instruction in female anatomy and physiology, pelvic and breast examination, self-breast-examination and abdominal examination, with an emphasis on normal anatomy. They worked in pairs, one GTA serving as "patient" TA, one as "instructor" TA. They were assigned a small group of medical students and conducted the educational session in an exam room. The "patient" TA received the exam, role-playing as patient and co-instructor, while the "instructor" TA remained alongside the students, helping and instructing them during the exam. After receiving two exams the "patient" TA changed from gown to street clothes and became "instructor" TA, and the "instructor" TA changed from street clothes to gown to become the "patient" TA. The teaching session was then repeated with a new group of medical students, thus assuring that one TA of each pair would not receive all the exams.

Kretzschmar's GTA model provided a radically new way of teaching medical students how to do pelvic and breast exams. No longer was the simulated patient a teaching tool; now she was both teacher and patient. The women's movement undoubtedly influenced this model. In the 1960s and 70s women were demanding better healthcare and some took matters into their own hands by establishing self-help groups and feminist clinics. In fact, many early GTAS were directly associated with these groups and clinics and believed their new position within the medical establishment as GTA could allow them to bring their alternative knowledge to the heart of the beast.

Kretzschmar received a variety of critical responses from the medical community for his new GTA program. Some were positive, applauding him for his innovative method and his success in avoiding a "men's club" attitude by hiring women as teachers. Some, however, were skeptical at best. They were particularly cautious regarding the GTAS' motives for participating in such a perverse endeavor. The epigraph to this chapter—"What *kind* of woman lets four or five novice medical students examine her?"—was a question asked by many physicians, according to Kretzschmar. Some human subjects committee members who reviewed the GTA concept "felt that women who were willing to participate must be motivated by one or more of several questionable needs, such as desperate financial circumstances (in which case exploiting their need would be unethical). Others fear the women would be exhibitionists or that they would use the pelvic exam to serve some perverse internal sexual gratification (in which case portraying them as normal to medical students would be irresponsible)." Once again, the pelvic exam was compared to a sexual act by the medical establishment. Cultural fears regarding female sexuality and its perversions surface in these objections to the GTA program. Only a nymphomaniac would seek out multiple exams, enjoying repeated penetration with speculums and fingers. Also, poor women might lower themselves to such embodied work out of desperation, thereby aligning the GTA with the prostitute in an explanatory narrative. Furthermore, the committee questioned the psychological stability of the GTA, with the assumption "that women who are emotionally unstable might be attracted to the program, or that undergoing repeated examination might be psychologically harmful." These human subject committee members reveal their nineteenth-century ideas about (white) women: frail female psychological health and sexual health are

seen as mutually dependent and delicate partners. If their equilibrium is tipped by the "pleasure" or pain incurred by the excessive sexualized act of multiple pelvic exams, then who knows what horrors will take place.

Unquestionably, teaching female genital display and manipulation has been the cause of a great deal of anxiety. These fears are much more reflective of the medical institution's constructions of the female psyche and female sexuality than of any actual threat to women posed by the role of GTA. One reason the role of GTA could seem threatening to these critics is that they were faced with a new and potentially powerful position for women in the predominantly male medical establishment. Their attempt at pathologizing the GTA could have been propelled by a desire to maintain the status quo: that *normal* women are passive, quiet, disembodied recipients of a hopelessly unpleasant but necessary pelvic exam. For them, perhaps this was the least threatening alternative.

Despite its early critics, Kretzschmar's model has become the pedagogical norm in the vast majority of institutions. Over 90 percent of North American medical schools employ this instructional method, recognized as "excellent" by the Association of Professors of Gynecology and Obstetrics Undergraduate Education Committee. Many GTA programs throughout the country maintain the same basic form as Kretzschmar's 1972 incarnation, though there is some variation. For example, some schools have GTAS working alone, rather than in pairs; a few schools still hire the more passive live pelvic model or "professional patient" to be used in conjunction with an instructing physician. The use of pelvic manikins, anesthetized women, cadavers, and actual patients continues to supplement some student learning.

Beginning in 1988, I was employed as a GTA by the University of Illinois at Chicago (UIC) medical school. Periodically, I also taught at two other Chicago-area medical schools and in one physician's assistant program. Excepting one institution, all my teaching experiences have followed Kretzschmar's GTA model. For the institution that had not adopted Kretzschmar's model, I worked as a "professional patient." A physician or nurse-midwife served as instructor, and I was hired primarily to model the exam for three students and the instructor. Whenever a clinician-instructor was unable to attend, I volunteered to work as both instructor and model, adopting a variation of Kretzschmar's model.

In discussing the GTA, I will collapse the roles of instructor and patient GTA into a single role. While this is reductive of the complexity of the partner relationship assumed by the instructor and patient GTAS, it may help clarify their common mission. And indeed many schools have collapsed the roles of the two GTAS into a single GTA who is paired with three or four students. After years of teaching, I find this to be a better model. It is impossible for students to position the instructor as silent patient if she is the only educator in the room. When there is a single teacher who also serves as "patient" students are faced with the jarring experience of examining a woman who knows more about gynecological exams than they do.

The Teaching Session

The students enter the exam room, where the GTA wears a patient gown. She is both their teacher and the object of their examination. The GTA explains the purpose of the teaching session. She is a healthy woman with normal anatomy who is there to help the students learn how to perform a proper breast and pelvic exam. Medical students, however, have been indoctrinated into a system that privileges pathology. They have learned that what is normal and healthy is not as interesting as what is abnormal and unhealthy. Some students seem disappointed when they are told that the GTA session is one part of their medical education in which they will not be presented with pathology.

The GTA explains that the patient, performed by herself, is there for a yearly exam. She has no complaints. Rather, they are there to have the experience of examining a normal, healthy woman and thus should offer the "patient" feedback after each part of the exam, letting her know that "everything appears healthy and normal." The GTA emphasizes that no woman can hear the phrase "healthy and normal" too much. For many medical students "healthy" and "normal" are new additions to their medical script. Often, these second- and third-year medical students admit that the GTA session is the first time they have been encouraged to use these words. In a moment that struck

me as simultaneously encouraging and tragicomic, one student, upon hearing me discuss the phrase "healthy and normal," pulled a 3 × 5 notecard and pen out of his pocket. He then said, "Tell me those words again. I want to write them down so I can remember them." In medical pedagogy, pathology is the norm, and normalcy is often viewed as mundane or unremarkable. For a woman in need of her yearly pap smear, the clinician's preoccupation with pathology can have sad consequences, both adding to the woman's anxiety about the possibility of the clinician finding that something is wrong and leaving her with the feeling that something is wrong regardless of actual clinical findings.

During the GTA session, other aspects of the students' scripts are rewritten and relearned. They are taught to use words that are less sexually connotative or awkward. For example, "I am going to *examine* your breasts now" as opposed to "I'm going to *feel* your breasts now." A number of script adjustments are made: "insert" or "place" the speculum as opposed to "stick in"; "healthy and normal" as opposed to "looks great." Changes are encouraged with regard to tool names: "footrests" as opposed to "stirrups"; "bills" rather than "blades" of the speculum.

When I was working as a "professional patient" with a young white woman physician as instructor, she kept referring to the "blades" of the speculum while teaching the students. I explained to her that many people within the medical community were replacing the term "blades" with "bills" because of the obvious violent connotations of the term, especially given that it refers to that part of the speculum placed inside the woman's body. The physician replied, agitated, "Well, we don't say it to the *patient*." Her assumption was that words that circulate within the medical community do not affect patient care or physician attitudes toward patients as long as those words do not reach the patient's ears. This is naive and faulty thinking, resistant to change, disabling the idea that language does indeed help structure attitudes and practice.

Furthermore, in that scenario *I* was the patient and the word "blade" was being used to refer to the part of an instrument that was to be placed inside *my* body. My thoughts were largely ignored even though I was hired to perform the role of patient. For the rest of the session, the physician begrudgingly used the word "bills," looking at me and punching the word each time she used it. Weeks later I worked at the same institution with a young white male physician whose language was considerate and carefully chosen and who continually encouraged my feedback and participation within the session. He consistently referred to the "bills" of the speculum of his own accord. By seeking out a patient's opinion and input within both a teaching situation and an actual exam, the clinician is relinquishing a portion of control and offering the patient more power within the exam scenario. As is evident in these two examples, gender does not necessarily determine a clinician's attitudes toward patients or the patient model.

The GTA offers many tips on how the clinician may help the patient feel more powerful and less frightened during an exam. "Talk before touch" is a technique used in the pelvic exam by which the clinician lets the patient know that she or he is about to examine the patient: with the phrase "You'll feel my hand now," the clinician applies the back of her or his hand to the more neutral space of the insides of a patient's thighs. Since the patient cannot *see* where the clinician's hands are, this technique offers her important information about where and when she will be touched.

Eye contact is another important and often ignored part of the pelvic exam. The GTA reminds the student to maintain eye contact with her throughout most parts of the exam. Many women complain that oftentimes clinicians have spoken at their genitals or breasts rather than to them. Eye contact not only offers the clinician another diagnostic tool, since discomfort and pain are often expressed in a patient's face, but it also makes the patient feel as though she is being treated as a person rather than as fragmented parts. In order to facilitate eye contact, the students are taught to raise the table to a 45-degree angle rather than leaving it flat. This has the added benefit of relaxing the woman's abdominal muscles. Specific draping techniques are taught so that the student-clinician cannot hide in front of the drape, ignoring the parts of the woman that reside backstage behind the curtain.

Given that the medical institution routinely segments and dissects bodies for examination, maintaining eye contact with the patient is often difficult

for students. Considering the sexual overtones of this particular exam, many students (and practitioners) find it very difficult to meet their patient's gaze. Likewise, there are patients who will not look into their examiner's eyes due to shame or embarrassment or a desire to be "invisible." While this is always a possibility, the GTA asserts that the practitioner must initiate eye contact even if the patient declines the offer, so that the patient at least has a choice of whether to "look back" at the clinician.

Similarly, the GTA encourages students to continuously communicate with the patient, informing her as to what they are doing, how they are doing it, and why they are doing it. For example, the student must show the woman the speculum, holding it high enough so that she can see it (without aiming it at her like a gun), while explaining, "This is a speculum. I will insert this part, the bills, into your vagina, opening them so that I can see your cervix, the neck of your uterus. I do this so that I can take a pap smear, which is a screening test for cervical cancer." Many women have had dozens of pelvic exams without ever having had the opportunity to see a speculum. More often, they hear the clanking of metal as the speculum is snuck out of its drawer and into their vagina.

Clinicians should not use words that patients will not understand, nor should they patronize patients; rather, they should piggyback medical terms with simpler phrases. In addition, students are taught that women should be given verbal instruction when they need to move or undress. For example, the woman should not be handled like a limp doll as a clinician removes her gown for the breast exam; instead the woman should be asked to remove her own gown. This helps her feel a little more in control of her own body and space. Ideally, the pelvic exam can become an educational session and the patient a partner in her own exam.

Lilla Wallis, M.D., an OB/GYN professor at Cornell University Medical School and a strong advocate of the GTA program, promotes this idea of "the patient as partner in the pelvic exam," and in addition encourages the use of many techniques popular within the women's health movement. Wallis adopts what some institutions might consider radical techniques. For instance, she urges clinicians to offer patients a hand mirror so that they might see what is being done to them. The patient is encouraged to look at her own genitals and not feel as though this were a view limited to the practitioner. Wallis also questions the draping of the patient: "This separates the patient from her own body. It suggests that the genitals are a forbidden part of her body that she should modestly ignore. It also isolates the doctor." Instead, she believes that patients should have the choice of whether to be draped or not. She refers to the use of GTAS as "a quiet revolution" in American medical schools, believing that GTA programs will lead to better, more thoughtful care by physicians.

Is the rehearsal with GTAS enough to change medical attitudes about women, female sexuality, and women's bodies? Can the use of GTAS actually affect these attitudes? While I was working as a "professional patient" or "model" at an esteemed Chicago-area medical school, an interesting sequence of events happened that pointed out to me the vast difference between teaching students as a GTA and serving as a "model." The physician I was to be working with was delayed at a meeting, so I started working with the four medical students. I stressed patient communication, helping the woman relax, "talk before touch," and educating the woman during the exam. The students were responsive, as the vast majority of students are, understanding my explanations for why these techniques were important and making an effort to adopt them as they made their way through the breast and pelvic exam.

I had finished teaching all four students how to do a breast exam and two students had completed pelvic exams, when the physician, a young white man, rushed in, apologizing for being late. He then proceeded to contradict much of what I had taught the students. I argued my points, but he insisted that many women were not interested in explanations or education but just "wanted it to be over with." He taught students a one-handed technique so that only one hand ever got "dirty," leaving the other hand free. He basically ignored my presence, so much so that at one point I had to dislodge his elbow, which was digging into my thigh as he leaned over, bracing himself on me, to see if my cervix was in view. The two remaining students were visibly more nervous than the students who had already had their

turns. They were rushed and forgot "talk before touch" in an attempt to incorporate the shortcuts that the physician had taught them.

At the end of the session, he encouraged the students to get into surgery to examine as much pathology as possible: "I have an 18cm uterus I'll be working on. Come by." I pictured this enlarged uterus alone on a surgical table without it's woman-encasement. He assured the students, "The only way you're going to learn what is normal is to see a lot of pathology." I had emphasized the wide variety of what is normal, how vulvas were all different and that students would need to see a lot of normal anatomy to understand what was not normal. After this physician's intrusion, the lone female medical student in the group kept looking at me at each point the physician contradicted me. She smiled at me empathetically, understanding the severity of the emotional and political sabotage I must have been feeling as both an educator and a naked woman "patient." Before the students left, three of the four shook my hand, genuinely thanking me for helping them. The one student who had been resistant to some of the techniques I had taught them was more suspicious. He said to me sternly, "Can I ask you, what are your motivations for doing this?"

The View from the Table

Implicit in the role of the GTA is a fundamental contradiction. On the one hand, she is an educator, more knowledgeable than medical students about pelvic and breast exams although she holds no medical degree. In this sense she is in a position of power, disseminating various truths about the female body and its examination. On the other hand, the GTA is bound to a traditionally vulnerable and powerless lithotomy position: lying on her back, heels in footrests. Oftentimes, her body is viewed as the true learning tool, with her words taking a back seat to this "hands-on" educational experience. In an interview, one GTA expressed her frustration: "Sometimes I feel like it's strange being nice, being like an airline hostess of the body. For example [she points two fingers as stewardesses do at cabin exits], 'Now we're coming to the *mons pubis*.' You have to be nice. I've seen some GTAs who were strong and businesslike about it, and I don't feel comfortable doing that but it's a strain having to be nice." This is a beautiful metaphor for describing the GTA's predicament: She is there to make medical students comfortable as they journey across the female body. Comparing the GTA to an airline hostess highlights the pink-collar service role she performs: she is working for the medical school in a position that only women can fill and she is there to make the students feel less apprehensive and more knowledgeable. The fact that she needs to be "nice" while presenting her own body points to one of the performative aspects of the GTA's role as educator. Like the stewardess, the GTA is costumed with a smile, a well-defined script, and a uniform.

In her book *The Managed Heart: Commercialization of Human Feeling*, Arlie Russell Hochschild connects Marx's factory worker to the flight attendant; both must "mentally detach themselves—the factory worker from his own body and physical labor, and the flight attendant from her own feelings and emotional labor." The case of the GTA becomes an interesting blend of these two types of alienation. She is like the flight attendant in that she manages her own feelings, what the GTA above calls "being nice." She must learn how to deal with the occasional hostile or overtly sexual medical student customer. She is there to make the student's trip through the female body comfortable, safe, and enjoyable. But it is her own body, not the meal tray or the fuselage of the airplane, that she is presenting to the paying customer. In this sense, the GTA is like Marx's factory laborer who uses his own body. She is getting paid for her body's use-value in the production of a trained medical student.

Structurally, with regard to physical labor and the management of feelings, the GTA resides in a position similar to that of a prostitute. Both GTAs and prostitutes sell the use of their body for what may be loosely termed "educational purposes." Both must manage their feelings, acting the part of willing recipient to probing instruments. Medical school history aside, GTAs and prostitutes have a good deal in common. This is perhaps why numerous GTAs have remarked on their husband's or partner's discomfort with their work. Certainly not all GTAs have partners who consider their teaching to be a sexual act and so object to or are threatened by it. But partner discontent is not uncommon. One GTA explains, "My boyfriend had problems with my teaching when I first moved in with him. It didn't bother him before I was living with him. I moved in only a couple of months before we got married and then he started voicing his complaints . . . I think they [significant others] are afraid it's sexual and I think the students are afraid it's sexual. They're afraid about how they're going to react, whether they're going to be aroused, but it's so clinical." Another GTA present at this interview said she had a similar problem in that her boyfriend was "concerned" and "uneasy": "I said to him if you're going to give me $150 to sit with you or have sex with you or whatever, fine, otherwise I'm going to make my money."

GTAs' partners are not the only ones who have been distressed by the GTA role. Some early women's health activists expressed a different kind of uneasiness as they quickly realized the pink-collar nature of the job. When the GTA program was first starting in the 1970S, these feminist health activists participating in the project sensed that they were still expected to mimic a patriarchal medical performance, employing language, techniques, and attitudes that reinforced the established power differential between pelvic exam clinician and female patient. These groups felt that working for a medical school did not allow them enough autonomy to teach what were, for them, important exam techniques. They believed that change within the medical establishment was virtually impossible and encouraged women not to participate in pelvic teaching within medical schools. Of these GTAs, some simply discontinued their work with medical students. Others continued teaching self-motivated medical students who would voluntarily visit feminist self-help clinics for continuing education. These feminist teachers regarded this new experience as highly valuable. As one activist notes: "The rapport experienced by the program participants and the [feminist teaching] nurses had been astounding . . . The result was an exploration with students of such topics as sexuality, abortion, contraception and ambivalent feelings regarding their roles." After refusing the medical institution's version of a proper pelvic exam rehearsal, these health activists composed their own.

In his article about medical students' six fears of pelvic exams, Buchwald accepted student fears without either questioning why young physicians-to-be would have such fears or searching for the cultural attitudes underlying them. Indeed, he might have been employing a Freudian psychoanalytic model that would entirely justify such fears: faced with the abject, castrated vulva, medical students *would* be terrified by the exam. These feminist teachers who rejected the GTA program, however, confronted and questioned student fears, realizing the importance of helping these future caregivers shed deep anxieties and ambivalences regarding female bodies. For years, medical pedagogues blatantly sidestepped these issues by employing teaching methods that would simply ignore or Band-aid student fears: hiring prostitutes would confirm student ideas regarding promiscuous female sexuality and its relationship to the pelvic exam; the use of plastic manikins would soothe student fears of touching real female genitals; while the use of anesthetized women and cadavers would present an unconscious "model" patient. Only with the use of GTAS have medical schools attempted to incorporate women patients' thoughts, feelings, and ideas into pelvic exam teaching. And yet, as these feminist teachers pointed out decades ago and as my experiences have occasionally confirmed, it may be impossible to educate students properly within the medical institution given unacknowledged cultural attitudes about female bodies and female sexuality.

. . .

The pelvic exam is in itself a pedagogical scenario. The woman receiving the exam, despite the political or philosophical orientation of the clinician, is taught attitudes about female bodies. In this respect, the physician is as much a pedagogue as a healer, if the two roles can be separated. In teaching medical students, one is therefore teaching teachers, transferring knowledge, methods, and attitudes to those practitioners who will in turn conduct private tutorials with individual women who seek their care. Thus the methods used to teach medical students how to do pelvic exams significantly structure how these physicians-to-be will educate their future patients. The various ways medical students have been taught to do pelvic exams are intimately related to the medical institution's attitudes toward women and in turn structure how future practitioners perceive and treat their women patients.

The use of GTAS alters the normal pelvic scenario to some degree. Here the "doctor" is being educated by the "patient," a potentially powerful role for the GTA. As an educator, she may critique the student from the patient's perspective (e.g., "Use less pressure," "you're not palpating the ovary there"). One would think that the medical student would not argue with the woman who is experiencing the exam. And yet, because the GTA is not a physician, the student is sometimes skeptical of her expertise, doubting her advice even if it is based on her bodily experience. The very fact that her experience is bodily may serve to deny the importance of her role. Her embodiment of the exam makes her a curious and suspect educator in the eyes of many since she is being *paid* for the use of her body in addition to her teaching skills. Her role continually elicits questions about what *kind* of woman she must be to undergo multiple exams.

In the GTA's educational performance there is no hypothetical signified, no abstract female body; rather the GTA is a fleshy referent with her own shape, anatomical variation, and secretions. At the site of the GTA, medicine, pornography, and prostitution mingle, highlighting medical attitudes regarding female sexuality, vulvar display, and genital manipulation. The teaching session may be a "representation" of a "real" exam, but for the GTA, as well as the medical student, it is simultaneously representation *and* practice.

It is curious, but not surprising, that the medical institution has focused so much attention on the GTA's role. Instead of focusing on what *kind* of woman would allow multiple exams to be performed on her, physicians might be more justified in asking how the medical establishment perceives the proper pelvic model or model patient. Or to turn the question back onto the medical institution itself, one might ask what *kind* of man or woman will *give* multiple exams. Unless there is a continued investigation of the medical structures that construct and reflect attitudes about female bodies and sexuality, the answer to this question might indeed be something to really fear.

References

A list of references is available in the original source.

Spreading My Legs for Womankind

by Molly Kenefick

Ever wonder how doctors learn to do pelvic exams? Well, I can answer that question for more than six hundred medical students: I taught them—on my body.

At some medical schools, students learn to do the exam on cadavers, women under anesthesia, or with "pelvic models" (women who function simply as bodies for professors to demonstrate on). Students on the campuses where I teach learn from "pelvic educators," women who instruct students in anatomy, physiology, palpation techniques, and various emotional and cultural issues that arise in a clinical setting.

When I first heard about the job, it sounded amazing. I'd already been working to overcome negative feelings about my body (the same body-image crap most women internalize growing up in our culture), and this seemed like a good next step. More important, I felt that teaching future doctors to do sensitive, thorough pelvic exams could positively impact the lives of many female patients down the line. I thought of Joan Rivers's joke that there should be a commemorative stamp of a woman on an examining table, feet in the footrests, to honor those who keep their annual appointments. I remember thinking at the time, *Joan is right: Many women do dread the exam. But it shouldn't* have *to be horrible.* Now, years later, I take pride in teaching my students the many details that can make an exam a positive, comforting experience.

I was scared at first. I'd take the hospital gown into the bathroom to change, and then climb onto the table, holding the johnny tight to make sure nothing extra was exposed. I felt shy about opening my legs to strangers (especially without any foreplay!), so as I did this, I avoided looking students in the eyes. I steeled myself by acting nonchalant and businesslike, and held onto the idea that this was important to women. Now, after six years, I simply turn my back to change (yes, in front of students), wrap a sheet around me, and casually hop onto the table.

Working with two to four students at a time, I first go over psychosocial issues. I tell them that though their patient may be an adult, it could be her first exam. I suggest they offer her a hand mirror so she can see what they are doing, and that they explain what they're doing as they do it. We discuss asking questions without making assumptions about a patient's sexual orientation or practices; looking for signs of sexual abuse, and, if they suspect it, how to handle it; words patients use to describe their anatomy; and culturally specific sexual customs.

Then it's time for the physical exam. I undress from the waist down and sit on the exam table, feet in the footrests ("Not stirrups; it's not a saddle"). I teach draping technique ("Expose only the area you will be examining"), the physician's first touch ("Put your hands by the outside of her knees, and ask her to bring her knees to meet your hands—that way she touches you first"), and subsequent touch techniques ("Clinical touch should feel as different from sexual touch as possible"). We start with the external exam, checking beneath the pubic hair for redness, lice, and scabies ("Don't mention lice and scabies unless she has them"). The external exam includes inspecting the vulva, perineum, and anus ("Always avoid touching the clitoris").

The internal exam is next. I teach them to insert an index finger to find my cervix and check my glands for infection and my vaginal walls for laxity. I demonstrate how to put in and open the speculum ("Warm it first, for patient comfort"). Then we view the cervix (a first sighting and a thrill for most students) and practice the Pap smear.

Next, the bimanual exam. With two fingers inside me, a student checks for cervical tenderness and feels for the uterus. The outside hand palpates the abdomen, pushing down toward the inside fingers. The most rewarding part for students is finding an ovary (yet another first), which feels like an almond hidden under layers of pastry dough ("The number of layers depends on how much pastry I've eaten"). Lastly, a student inserts one finger in my rectum, another in my vagina. They are often surprised at how much better they can feel my uterus from two angles.

In separate sessions with students, I also teach breast exams. The first time I did this, I looked at my 38-C breasts (heavy and pendulous: nipples soft, not pert) and wished they were perkier. Then I thought, *Who the hell looks like a centerfold in real life? I'm a real woman, and this is what women look like.* More important, this is what their patients will look like. My self pep talk ended with: *You're healthy. Get over it. Focus on the work.*

With up to eight students, we first practice on a silicone-filled model (with quite lumpy breasts). I show them the palpation technique: Fingers make circles of light, medium, and deep pressure as they move in a vertical stripe pattern (lawnmower versus zigzag). Then I take off my shirt and bra and we look for rashes, dimpling, and changes in the nipples (such as spontaneous discharge or inversion). I teach them to palpate my nodes along the clavicle and under the armpit ("No tickling!"). Then, one at a time, they practice the vertical stripe technique on my breast.

Most students have been a pleasure to teach. A few had terrible palpation skills (I can only hope they've gone into research). Two got noticeable erections (I sympathized, as they seemed mortified at this betrayal of their body). A couple were inappropriate (one kept asking if my parents and boyfriend knew I did this work), and one asked me out (though I thought, *Wouldn't this be a story to tell our grandkids?* I said *no*, of course). The majority of my students, however, have been respectful and grateful for the opportunity to learn from, and on, me.

I'm amazed by all the ways this job has impacted my life. As hoped (and as strange as it may sound), undressing in front of strangers has made me more comfortable with my body. Now, years into the job, I take off my shirt and bra, drop my pants, and often feel like a superhero. I'm not a "perfect 10," just a healthy, strong woman, unashamed of her body. I feel students' admiration and respect, and I deserve it because I am doing important work for women and women's health. In addition, I've become knowledgeable about my reproductive health. Knowing where my uterus is and what my cervix looks like makes me more in touch with being a woman. On the downside, as "party talk" goes, telling people I'm a pelvic educator can be a conversation starter—or stopper. And at times, no amount of kisses could summon my libido because it got lost earlier in the day during the third pelvic exam. In general, however, I've found this to be rewarding work, both because of the immediate positive changes I see in my students and because of the ripple effect I know my work will have on their future patients. Finally, a nice benefit is that every day when I go to work, I'm reminded that *Hey, I've got ovaries.*

Balancing It All:
Women and Medicine

by Khendi White

As a female physician-to-be, I know that I will face some tough decisions. Medicine is a competitive and demanding field that requires unwavering devotion and constant sacrifices. On the one hand, I want to be a top-notch clinician who puts her patients first; on the other hand, I want to be a mother who plays an active role in raising her children. Although many women have navigated this territory, it remains challenging because of the tremendous pressure and time demands on women working in medicine, particularly in the competitive, male-dominated specialties like surgery and cardiology.

For women like me who want both a medical career and children, the options are limited. I expect to be at least 30 before I finish my medical training. During the four years of medical school, there is precious little time to have children and doing so requires diligent planning and preparation. Medical students usually have the summer after their first year off, and this is the best time to have a child without the risk of dropping out. The second year is more intense than the first and culminates in the first exam for the boards (which helps determine residents' fates). Since the third year consists of an intense series of clinical rotations that begin immediately after completion of the second year, it's a terrible time to try to have a baby. The next viable opportunity doesn't really present itself until Spring of the fourth, and last, year of medical school. By then, students have completed their residency interviews and required electives and there is more flexibility with schedules, and even a few weeks of vacation time.

After medical school, the next stage of training is a residency program that varies in length, depending upon the physician's specialty, from 3–7 years. Half of all female medical students who get pregnant have their first child during their residency, according to the American Medical Women's Association (AMWA). This seems like the best time for me to do so, as well. However, I am concerned by the lack of maternity leave policies at the majority of medical schools and residency programs. According to AMWA, it is common for pregnant residents to conceal their condition until it becomes unambiguous, due to their fear that they would be dismissed or harassed.

Female physicians who are just starting out in their careers often face harsh criticism when they decide to have children. When a woman takes time off during her residency, her fellow residents often have to cover her shifts, and may resent or harass her because of it. Attending physicians, who tend to be male, are not likely to empathize. Since coveted positions such as Chief Resident are based on performance during the residencies' early years, a woman who has kids during this time may be disadvantaged against receiving such promotions.

This struggle does not ease up once a woman completes her residency, either. Equal number of men and women currently graduate from medical schools, but there is still a severe shortage of female physicians in academic positions. Women comprise only about 12% of professorships in academic settings, a number that has remained stable over the past three decades, despite the increase in the female physician workforce.[1] To obtain academic tenure and advancement, a physician must invest a significant amount of time in conducting research, treating patients, and teaching students–leaving little time for much else. Female doctors frequently state that their interest in academic medicine is reduced due to concerns about balancing their multiple work and family responsibilities.[2] One study found that, when considering numbers of papers published, levels of research funding, career satisfaction, and self-reported career progress, female physicians who have children have far less success in academic medicine compared to men and childless women.[3]

There are other, less obvious, obstacles for childbearing women who choose to enter certain medical specialties. I am interested in the specialty of cardiology. On a networking site for health professionals (www.studentdoctor.net (http://www.studentdoctor.net/)), I found a post about being pregnant during this specialties' catheter rotation. The blogger commented that, "Having cath rotations doesn't mean you absolutely can't be pregnant" but there is a danger that as a fellow, "you are often right up front [during procedures] most of the time, which makes your radiation exposure risk higher." You would not want to be pregnant and subject your fetus to the potentially hazardous risks of radiation exposure. These risks apply to other medical specialties as well, such as radiology and oncology.

I am afraid that my own guilt will become an additional, albeit less quantifiable, obstacle. If I have a child during residency, for example, and decide to continue with the grueling schedule of 80-120 hours per week, I would have to put my child into daycare or with a spouse, if that's possible. I would inevitably feel guilty about not being able to spend quality time with my kid. I would much rather have my fellow residents resent me than my own children do so years later. At the same time, I am highly ambitious and resent having to compromise my dreams for anyone. I disagree with the situation—deeply engrained in our society to this day–in which working women are not supported to continue their careers, and that women are forced to sacrifice their careers for the children's sake before men do.

Becoming a doctor—just like being a mother—requires sacrifice and there's no perfect way to get there. There are steps that the medical field can take, however, to make this juggling act less difficult for women. Efforts should be made to decrease the stigmatization, and increase advancement opportunities, for doctors who select part-time or slower progression tracks. To attract and retain more female physicians in academic positions and clinical specialties, one expert recommends that women receive "stronger support from the medical community, including increased availability of childcare in academic settings, flexibility at work, strong mentors, and decreased 'good old boy' cronyism." As I anticipate entering this difficult arena, I hope to achieve a work-life balance that is fulfilling to both my roles as a physician and mother. Perhaps I will not be able to pick my children up from school, but I will be there to read them a bedtime story and tuck them in at night. I may not be able to cook my children dinner most evenings, but I will be there at their baseball games. It really comes down to setting priorities and knowing that you can't have everything, but with a lot of effort, you can have everything that matters.

By Khendi White

Khendi White is an admitted medical student for the Class of 2012. She graduated from Swarthmore College with a double major in biology and psychology in 2007. A native of Silver Spring, MD, her career interest includes serving the medically underserved in hospital settings.

References

1. Verlander, G. 2004. "Female physicians: Balancing career and family." Acad Psychiatry 28(4):331-6.

2. Carr PL, Ash AS, Friedman RH, et al. 1998. "Relation of family responsibilities and gender to the productivity and career satisfaction of medical faculty." Ann Intern Med 129:532-538.

3. See http://forums.studentdoctor.net/showthread.php?t=462211 (http://%20%20http//forums.studentdoctor.net/showthread.php?t=462211). "Women in cardiology." Anonymous blog postings. Accessed May 6, 2008.

The Making of the "Women's Physician" in American Obstetrics and Gynecology: Re-Forging an Occupational Identity and a Division of Labor[*]

by James R. Zetka, Jr.

After struggling as a surgical specialty, obstetrics and gynecology initiated its "women's physician" program in the 1970s. This program officially defined the mostly male obstetricians and gynecologists at that time as women's primary care physicians. Using archival data, this article explains this development as a response to the specialty's dishonored position within the medical division of labor. Whatever else it was intended to be, the women's physician program, in its most developed form, aimed to galvanize the various interests within obstetrics and gynecology behind a strategy to restructure the medical division of labor serving women so that obstetricians and gynecologists controlled both the upstream positions responsible for their own case referrals and the downstream positions to which they referred their difficult cases. The article illustrates the importance of integrating insights from both macro-institutional and intra-occupational explanatory frameworks in accounting for significant developments in medicine.

After World War II, increasing numbers of U.S. physicians entered specialty practice. In 1940, only 24 percent of physicians were full-time specialists (Starr 1982:358–59). By the late 1960s, almost 90 percent of U.S. medical graduates entered specialty residencies (LeRoy and Lee 1977:145). As specialization increased, the ratio of primary care physicians to people in the population declined. There were 94 primary care physicians per 100,000 people in 1931; there were only 55 per 100,000 in 1974 (LeRoy and Lee 1977:146). Policy-makers defined the primary care shortage as a serious problem and enacted innovative responses to correct it during the 1970s.

One of the more fascinating of these responses was that of obstetrics and gynecology (ob/gyn). After fighting to establish itself as a consultant/specialty, ob/gyn embraced the role of "the women's physician" in the 1970s.[1] In this new role, ob/gyns were to deliver comprehensive primary care to women for ob/gyn and non-ob/gyn conditions. They were to provide checkups and routine care, keep medical histories and, when appropriate, refer patients to other specialists. Historically, general practitioners provided primary care after finishing their internships. Medical specialists, after three or more additional years of residency training, defined primary care as ill suited to their hard-won expertise (see Halpern 1990:32–33). Why, then, did ob/gyns embrace the primary care role?

While scholars have associated feminine values of caring and empathy with primary care (see Riska 2001, chapter 2), female ob/gyns did not play a significant role in either formulating or

* I would like to thank Janet M. Feldgaier for comments on earlier drafts of this article, as well as the editors and reviewers for *JHSB*. Address correspondence to Jim Zetka, Department of Sociology, The University at Albany, Albany, NY 12222 (e-mail: j.zetka@albany.edu).

The Making of the 'Women's Physician' in American Obstetrics and Genecology: Re-Forging an Occupational Identity and a Division of Labor from *Journal of Health and Social Behavior, Vol. 49, No. 3 (Sept., 2008), pp. 335–351* by James R. Zetka, Jr. Reprinted by permission.

initiating ob/gyn's women's physician program during the 1970s. Historically, ob/gyn had discriminated against female physicians, defining work in ob/gyn as men's work (see Willson 1972). During the 1970s, ob/gyn was still, like the rest of medicine, overwhelmingly male—only 7.1 percent of ob/gyns were women in 1970, compared to 7.7 percent for all physicians (figures from American Medical Association Council on Long Range Planning and Development, 1987:3548).[2] While the numbers of women in ob/gyn increased during the 1970s—reaching 12.3 percent in 1980—it was not until the 1990s that ob/gyn became disproportionately female. In the 1970s, female ob/gyns lacked the numbers, resources, and power to shape ob/gyn's occupational policies and programs. Thus, male physicians developed ob/gyn's initial women's physician program.

This article employs a multi-level theoretical framework to explain this puzzling development. This framework integrates insights from theories of the U.S. medical profession's institutional development, particularly the professional dominance and "countervailing powers" theories, with insights from an intra-occupational perspective drawing heavily from Everett C. Hughes' essays (1971). The article shows that ob/gyn leaders initiated their women's physician program in the 1970s in response to intense inter-specialty competition, dishonoring, and structural dependency. Whatever else it was intended to be, ob/gyn leaders used this program as a resource for changing the specialty's dishonored position in the medical division of labor.

Institutional Developments Fueling the Primary Care Crisis

Expressing the central theme of the professional dominance perspective, Magali Sarfatti Larson (1977) argues that physicians reshaped the U.S. health care system during the early twentieth century with a "professional project" aiming to create a monopoly market. This professional project defined physicians' service as a commodity, standardized this commodity through the routinization of training, and won state backing to exclude competitors from the market (see, also, Starr 1982). This professional project legitimated physicians' control over their work with an institutional logic

asserting that, in order to produce the highest quality care, physicians' work judgments had to be free from market and administrative controls. This logic favored, and presumed, fee-for-service, private practice (see Scott et al. 2000; Freidson 2001; Light 2004; Mechanic 2004). Scholars have singled out a number of factors in explaining this development, including technical efficacy (see Freidson [1970] 1988:21; Mechanic 2004:12–13; Scott et al. 2000: 21–22), work organization that maximizes private responsibility and isolates physicians' work processes from scrutiny (Freidson [1970] 1988), and physicians' use of their cultural authority to block the development of "countervailing powers" in civil society and the state (Starr 1982, chapter 3; see, also, Hafferty and Light 1995; Light 2004).

While national governments elsewhere cultivated strong countervailing powers and mobilized them to counter physicians' dominance, in the United States the federal government accommodated its policies to the interests of a medical profession committed to private, fee-for-service practice (Hafferty and Light 1995; Light 2004; Starr 1982). Donald W. Light (2004; see, also, Hafferty and Light 1995) has argued that this failure to develop strong countervailing powers is behind many of the current pathologies of the U.S. health care system. Indeed, this failure played a role in creating the primary care shortage of interest here.

In the post-World War II decades, as Paul Starr (1982) documents, the federal government committed itself to liberal activism with regard to medicine, in essence, restructuring the system with massive investments in hospital construction and medical research. Total national expenditures for medical research, for example, increased from 18 million dollars in 1941 to 181 million in 1951; average medical school income increased from 1.5 million at the end of the 1940s to 15 million by 1968–1969 (Starr 1982:342–43). This massive centralized investment occurred without centralized controls, as the federal government respected physician dominance over medical institutions (Light 2004; Scott et al. 2000; Starr 1982). Furthermore, because the National Institutes of Health distributed research funds to researchers through separate institutes, federal research investments encouraged specialization (Starr 1982; see, also,

Hafferty and Light 1995; Light 2004). Medical researchers met their labor demands not with general interns but with residents who had specialty training (Ginsberg et al. 1981:511–12; Hiestand 1984; LeRoy and Lee 1977:145–46). While the number of candidates for medical degrees (M.D.) increased 31 percent from 1950 to 1967, the number of residents training in specialties increased 311 percent (Fein and Weber 1971:54).

These research investments did not break the medical profession's tenacious grip over the numbers admitted to medical school—the entrée port into the physicians' labor market. The number of students entering medical school did not increase substantially above general population increases, even as opportunities for post-graduate residency and fellowship training increased (Starr 1982). Indeed, the ratio of physicians to population, even in the face of a serious physician shortage, changed little from the end of World War II until federal policies were enacted, beginning in 1963, to increase physician supply (Starr 1982:364). Medical school graduates, who in the past entered quickly into general practice, entered residencies supported by research and training grants. This development fueled the primary care crisis (Starr 1982:337–38). As we argue below, ob/gyn leaders, through their women's physician program, attempted to appropriate this crisis as a resource in pursuit of their own occupational ends.

Re-Embracing Everett C. Hughes' Occupational Perspective

While useful for understanding how the primary care crisis developed, the macro-institutional perspectives cannot really explain why ob/gyn embraced a primary care role. There is good reason for this. At the institutional level, the medical profession must represent itself ideally—as a unified, standardized commodity (Larson 1977). Organized medicine, as represented by the American Medical Association, speaks with one voice, as if all physicians held a common identity and set of interests. However, institutionalists realize that professional reality in medicine no longer conforms to this ideal (see Scott et al. 2000). Frederick W. Hafferty and Donald W. Light (1995), for example, refer to this ideal as "medicine's public façade of internal equanimity" (p. 136).

With increasing specialization, a complex division of labor with splintered occupational ideologies, identities, and interests has largely replaced organized medicine as a unified profession (see Ginzberg et al. 1981:525–26; Hafferty and Light 1995; Light 2004; Scott et al. 2000:185–86; Zola and Miller 1971). Thus, we must supplement our theorizing at the institutional level with theorizing about developments at this splintered intra-occupational level to better understand developments like ob/gyn's initiation of its women's physician program (Zetka 2003, 2008; see, also, Berman 2006). To do this, medical sociology would do well to re-embrace Everett C. Hughes' (1971) occupational sociology. The historical analysis of ob/gyn's embrace of the primary care role presented below draws from the basic tenets of Hughes' occupational perspective.

Hughes encourages us, first, to specify the definitional frames within which occupational groups assign meaning and significance to their work tasks, and from which they develop their senses of identity and worth (1971, chapters 28, 30, 33). These definitional frames are referred to here and elsewhere as core-skill definitional frames (see Zetka 2001, 2008; Zetka and Walsh 1994). They orient action and provide the foundation for each medical specialty's distinctive occupational program. In medicine's splintered intra-occupational division of labor, many core-skill definitional frames coexist, compete, and contradict one another (Hughes 1971:295–98; see, also, Bucher and Strauss 1961; Bucher [1962] 1972; Bucher 1988).

Hughes also encourages us to recognize that the programs emanating from occupational groups' core-skill definitional frames unfold in complex divisions of labor (1971, chapters 30, 35). Macro-institutional developments, like those fueling the primary care shortage discussed above, partially structure these divisions of labor, providing both constraints and opportunities. Occupational groups also pursue the programs emanating from their core-skill definitional frames within these divisions of labor in the face of significant others who themselves have vested interests in their outcomes. Indeed, such programs are often directed toward these significant others in sometimes subtle, and sometimes not so subtle, ways. For Hughes, understanding these interactions and relationships at the inter- and intra-occupational level are critical to understanding how occupational groups mobilize themselves and act collectively.

Professional Divisions of Labor and Their Coordination and Control Dynamics

The professional division of labor within which these occupational programs unfold contain a structural contradiction. At the most basic level, the professional division of labor consists of two types of workers: (1) generalists who screen work-flow, handle routine cases, and refer complex cases to others, and (2) consultant/specialists who limit their workload to complex cases requiring a level of expertise beyond that possessed by generalists.[3] While research suggests that structural positions that control the work flow of many task units gain power and status (see Hickson et al. 1971; Wallace, Griffin, and Rubin 1989), generalist positions in professional divisions of labor often are devalued. Professionals view the work of the specialist as important, skilled, even heroic, and that of the gatekeeper/generalist as routine. However, since generalists control market access (see Hafferty and Light 1995:136–37; Hughes 1971:382–83), positional power and status honor stand inversely to one another. This, as discussed in the case narrative presented below, can be problematic.

Historically, because of the institutional developments discussed above, the U.S. medical division of labor has lacked effective structures for regulating specialty developments and relationships (see De Santis 1980; Gritzer 1982; Stevens 1971). Over time, normative scripts have emerged to direct workflow between generalists/gatekeepers and specialists. These scripts define which specialist should get which case, when they should get it, and why. They carry moral authority over the market spaces they regulate (see Zetka 2001, 2003).

Securing specialized turf in this division of labor usually required that those in gatekeeper positions accepted specialists' core-skill definitions and "turf logics" as legitimate scripts for processing cases. Turf logics are the arguments specialists use to persuade others in the division of labor that their core-skills, rather than those of competitors, are

most critical for servicing a particular market. Turf logics define the skills of the specialists they favor as superior to others. They direct gatekeepers to send relevant cases to these specialists (see Zetka 2008). Gatekeepers/generalists have used these normative scripts to perform screening functions. Specialists typically have worked downstream and have received their new cases from these gatekeepers. They have stood structurally in a dependency relationship with them.[4]

Having one's core-skill definition and turf logic incorporated into a legitimated script for directing workflow within this division of labor has been problematic, for this development restricts market opportunities for others within the profession (Stevens 1971; Zetka 2003). Ob/gyn belongs to the first wave of surgical specialties achieving independence from general surgery. Ob/gyn's traditional core-skill definition challenged surgeons' control over pelvic turf by promising superior treatment outcomes. With a formidable competitor antagonized, ob/gyn had to deliver the superior outcomes it promised to secure its legitimacy. To understand ob/gyn's women's physician program, we must first understand the core-skill definition and turf logic ob/gyn used historically to justify its turf claims. We must then extend our focus outward to the medical division of labor and examine how important groups, acting within its web of institutionally-structured opportunities and constraints, responded to ob/gyn's claims.

The argument developed in the historical narrative presented below is this: In the face of ob/gyn's historic failure to legitimate its traditional core-skill definition, ob/gyn leaders initiated their women's physician program as a tool for restructuring the medical division of labor and ob/gyn's position within it. With this tool, ob/gyn leaders aimed to secure better access to ob/gyn's coveted market turf. Ob/gyn leaders, thus, appropriated the primary care crisis fueled by a medical care system structured by both a logic of professional dominance and weak "countervailing powers" so as to serve their own occupational ends. The information used below to support this argument was collected from medical and ob/gyn specialty journals, including editorials, presidential addresses, commentaries, letters to the editor, and published study results (on methodology, see Zetka 2008).

Ob/Gyn's Historic Core-Skill Definition and Turf Logic

Ob/gyn formed in 1930 as a specialty combining obstetrics and gynecology. Ob/gyn allied itself to a new order of medicine that opposed the traditional division of labor between medicine and surgery. This new order based its divisions not on specific task skills but on comprehensive care in diagnosing and treating anatomical regions. Ob/gyns claimed superior expertise to care for all aspects of women's reproductive and sexual lives (Hodgkinson 1961; Sturgis 1957). They embraced a broad skill set, including diagnosis, endocrinology, medicine, surgery, and later even psychological counseling (Beecham 1969; Mengert 1959; Reid 1961; see, also, Zetka 2008). Ob/gyn's core-skill definition held that ob/gyn's comprehensive knowledge of women's gynecological and reproductive organs made their skills in diagnosing and treating these organs superior to other physicians.

The foil in ob/gyn's core-skill definition—that which ob/gyn defined itself against—was typified as "the mechanical surgeon," a one-dimensional cutter rather than a true doctor (see Perdue 1952:77). Such a surgeon diagnosed through the open incision, subjecting patients to surgical trauma unnecessarily (see Ellison and Thornton 1955; Perdue 1952). In contrast, ob/gyns, with their broad comprehensive knowledge, claimed to be better able to diagnose accurately the true nature of patients' gynecological and reproductive troubles. Whether the problem proved to be medical or surgical, the greater diagnostic skill, afforded through ob/gyn's comprehensive understanding of the pathology of female genital and reproductive systems, enabled better treatment outcomes (Beecham 1969; Bloss 1950; Sturgis 1957). While ob/gyns performed surgery, surgery was but one of their many treatment options. And, rather than simply remove organs from the pelvis, ob/gyn's procedures aimed, whenever possible, to preserve organ functioning (Riva 1965:645). The anticipated successes promised in ob/gyn's core-skill definitional frame—improvements in diagnostic accuracy, reductions in unnecessary surgeries, and better preservation of organ functioning—were to establish and secure its turf jurisdiction.

Ob/Gyn's Turf Logic and Medicine's Intra-Occupational Division of Labor

As documented below, ob/gyn's experience in winning legitimacy as a consultant/specialty was dismal. This experience contrasted starkly with that of other specialties. For example, urology and otolaryngology, like ob/gyn, claimed jurisdiction over all functions involved in servicing their anatomical regions. Each specialty mastered endoscopic technologies early on that combined diagnostic and treatment functions. These technologies enabled each specialty to claim impressive improvements in its diagnostic and surgical outcomes. Once these specialties became associated with their endoscopic technologies, surgical competitors, without endoscopic experience, could not easily encroach upon their turf.

While ob/gyn tried various endoscopic technologies, none became widely embraced, or particularly successful until fiberoptic laparoscopy in the 1970s. It was not until the late 1970s, in fact, that this technology began to improve results. For the period of interest, ob/gyn shared the diagnostic, medical, and surgical techniques used by others and, as recognized in commentary (Mengert 1959; Taylor 1958), this made ob/gyn's turf vulnerable to encroachment.

During the period of focus, ob/gyn had failed to achieve the diagnostic and treatment successes anticipated in its core-skill definition (see Zetka 2008) and, according to its own commentary (discussed below), ob/gyn's reputation in the medical division of labor had tarnished considerably. The failure to improve diagnostic and treatment outcomes threatened ob/gyn's hold on its surgical turf. The poor reputation resulting from this failure blocked the referrals coveted in ob/gyn's consultant/specialty role, and it hindered recruitment efforts as well. By the 1970s, commentators were questioning ob/gyn's survival as a specialty.

"Baby Catchers"

Ob/gyn made considerable progress in obstetrics after 1930. Maternal and infant mortality showed impressive continuing declines, as did morbidity, obstetric injuries, and complications. Despite its accomplishments, however, obstetrics was dishonored in the medical division of labor (Bloss 1950; Simard 1957). Ob/gyns accomplished their improvements as much through public health campaigns as from any innovation they developed. Ob/gyns also took advantage of innovations in other fields that they had no hand in developing themselves. Basic obstetric deliveries, in fact, held little mystery for physicians. All were trained to perform them, and, historically, family practitioners and general surgeons did so early in their careers. Because the hours were long and unpredictable, and because the process was both routine and stressful, most abandoned this work as soon as possible (see Brewer 1953; Simard 1957). As one very frank ob/gyn commentary suggested (Brewer 1953), obstetricians established their independence only because surgeons did not generally value deliveries and no one else wanted to claim this turf as their own.

Ob/gyn commentators spoke of obstetrics' image as being that of a "humble art" involving the work of "skilled laborers" (see Simard 1957). Others looked upon obstetricians as "baby catchers" overseeing a natural process. This role lacked the glory associated with, say, saving lives through surgical intervention, or with relieving misery medically after a successful, complex diagnosis. One ob/gyn commentary made this point well:

> Obstetrics . . . still remains, in the minds of many, a poor relation of medicine and surgery. Sometimes a good friend will repeat the sally: "If your son is intelligent, let him be a physician; if he is clever, let him be a surgeon; if he is neither, let him be an accoucheur [obstetrician]!" (Simard 1957:1163)

"Womb Snatchers"

Surgical residencies traditionally trained residents to perform all tasks necessary to treat patients' surgical problems regardless of which organ systems were involved. Attaining this level of skill required that all surgical specialists undergo training in general surgery, usually for one year or more. Ob/gyn, however, split obstetrics and gynecology into two 18-month stints. Thus, a typical ob/gyn had no general surgery training, and no more than 18 months

of total training in gynecological surgery, far less than other surgical specialists. Ob/gyn leaders held that, because of impressive developments in anesthesia, blood and electrolyte monitoring, aseptic and antiseptic techniques, etc., any ob/gyn resident during a relatively short stint could learn to perform gynecological surgeries effectively (Mengert 1949: 207–208). This position presumed that ob/gyns needed only basic proficiency to manage cases on their own, so long as a viable referral system existed that could match quickly the demands of the more difficult cases to more accomplished surgeons with requisite skills. One commentator explains it in this way:

> The type of surgeon visualized by this school will be a relatively standardized product, capable of carrying out effectively the accepted procedures in the area in which he has been trained and indoctrinated with the ideal that he must not undertake procedures beyond his capabilities. This school proposes to solve the problem of surgical care through organization and the interrelationship of one surgeon with another, rather than by what it believes to be the futile task of attaining and maintaining versatility and virtuosity in a sufficient number of 'ideal surgeons.' (Taylor 1965:36)

However, as its treatment outcomes paled in comparison to others, many began to challenge the viability of ob/gyn's alternative approach. The general belief voiced in numerous ob/gyn commentaries was that gynecological surgery's glory years were behind it (see Brunschwig 1968; Mengert 1959; Willson 1972). Ob/gyn's surgical record continued to draw consternation well into the 1970s. Ob/gyns, for example, were responsible for most of the ureteral injuries and genitourinary fistulas treated by urologists on referral (see Symmonds 1976). In studies of second opinions for elective surgeries, moreover, ob/gyns had higher rates of non-agreement between physicians providing initial and second opinions than other specialties (McCarthy and Finkel 1980). One commentary (Barter 1975) went so far as to state that "the specialty of Ob-Gyn as a surgical entity may be doomed to indistinction and to ultimate death" (p. 814).

General surgeons held a low opinion of ob/gyn's surgical abilities, and this opinion spread throughout the medical division of labor (Hodgkinson 1968; Mengert 1959). General surgeons refused to cede to ob/gyn's jurisdiction over the uterus and ovaries. General surgeons performed the majority of gynecological surgery in the United States long after ob/gyn incorporated. General surgeons, who trained long and hard in surgical residencies, felt they were far more competent in performing operations on the gynecological organs through the abdominal incision than were ob/gyns (see Taylor 1965). Apparently many gatekeeping physicians agreed, since the bulk of the gynecological cases general surgeons treated came to them in this way.[5]

Recruitment into a Dishonored Specialty

Ob/gyn leaders realized that the specialty's future lay in its ability to attract talent. Improving the quality of the ob/gyn recruit became a preoccupation. Yet efforts here were stymied. Why would successful medical graduates enter ob/gyn when others generally viewed this specialty as a routinized field, a view reinforced with a barrage of demeaning nicknames like "glorified midwives" (Willson 1972) and "baby catchers and uterus snatchers" (Tyson 1973)? Top medical students, in fact, were not attracted to this field. Ob/gyn drew its residents from the bottom third of the academic barrel (Tyson 1971; Willson 1962, 1972).

This situation was not acceptable to ob/gyn's leaders and efforts were made to improve it. At the 1953 American Gynecological Society (AGS) meeting, Dr. Howard C. Taylor, Jr. presented a statement critical of the caliber of graduates choosing ob/gyn. The AGS then appointed a committee, chaired by Taylor, to study the issue. The Taylor committee surveyed eighty ob/gyn departments and reported findings to the AGS in 1954 that documented Taylor's claims. These results led to more committees and further efforts (see Barnes 1971). However, even with these efforts, neither the numbers entering ob/gyn residencies, nor the residents' academic quality, improved greatly during the period of focus. A 1971 commentary proclaimed such efforts "pathetic failures" (Lund 1971:464).

Dishonor and Its Outcomes

Figure 1 illustrates case-flow relationships in the medical division of labor. The simple relationship depicted in row A illustrates the ideal relationship coveted by surgical specialties. Only one arrow depicts case flow from the primary care screeners to the specialty. Here, screeners accept as legitimate the specialty's normative scripts for processing cases. They refer such cases to the specialist and do not contemplate other options. The specialty's core skill definition has cognitive and moral authority over this space in the division of labor.

The relationships depicted in row B in Figure 1 illustrate the case-flow relationships ob/gyns experienced in the postwar period in their role as surgical consultants/specialists. Dual arrows depict case flow from primary care screeners: one to ob/gyns, one to general surgeons. Screeners, in essence, had a choice as to where they sent cases. Ob/gyns failed to legitimate their normative scripts for processing their cases, and the competition ob/gyns experienced with general surgeons shifted power to screeners. This situation made ob/gyn's case flow vulnerable. A second arrow in row B extends from ob/gyn to other surgical specialists, depicting ob/gyn's dependency upon others to manage their surgical complications. This dependency opened up ob/gyn to external criticism. This criticism fed back to the screeners and reinforced ob/gyn's difficulties in receiving referrals. The dual dependency did not bode well for ob/gyn's fate.

In fact, it is reasonable to expect failure, even death, as the likely fate of a specialty that (1) fails to establish superior work outcomes, (2) fails to secure control over its market turf, (3) fails to improve its reputation and status in the division of labor from which it draws referrals, and (4) fails to attract recruits. Compared to specialties such as urology and otolaryngology, ob/gyn performed very poorly in all areas, producing the very difficult, perhaps unworkable, case flow relationships depicted in row B. Yet ob/gyn did not die.

The institutional system characterized by professional dominance and weak countervailing powers discussed above actually abetted ob/gyn's survival. This system, by encouraging specialization (Ginsberg et al. 1981:511–12; Hiestand 1984), created a rather large structural vacancy for primary care

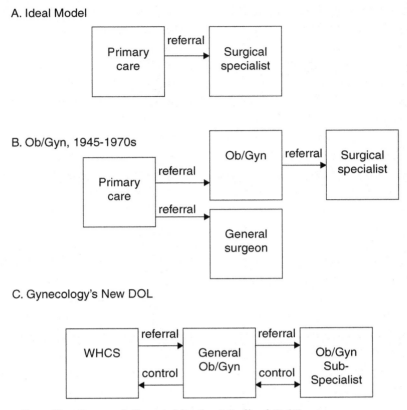

A. Ideal Model

B. Ob/Gyn, 1945-1970s

C. Gynecology's New DOL

Figure 1. Workflow Coordination and Control in the Medical DOL

services (see Abbott 1988, chapter 4). Unintentionally, this structural vacancy became a "mop-up" market open to those physicians inclined to move into it. This development provided opportunity and protection to those experiencing increasing competition. Since this space was not a downstream position in the medical division of labor, its occupants were not dependent upon referrals. Whether they were honored or dishonored in the medical division of labor made little difference. This space was one demanding more physicians. Without official guidance, many ob/gyns moved to this mop-up space and provided primary care to women, long before federal legislation favored primary care specialties (Gardner 1966).

The Women's Physician Program Revisited

Ob/gyn's failure to win legitimation for its core-skill definition conditioned its responses to policy initiatives. In general, academic ob/gyns desired more support for their residency programs and research; community practitioners wanted better

access to their surgical markets. Ob/gyn leaders championing the women's physician program, in essence, appropriated the primary care initiatives to serve the market interests of both segments of the specialty.

Academic Interests and Ob/Gyn's Women's Physician Program

By the 1970s health policymakers had recognized the decline in the numbers of primary care practitioners as a serious problem. The 1976 Health Professions Educational Assistance Act, renewing earlier legislation providing capitation grants to medical schools, stipulated that medical schools should insure that by 1980 50 percent of their graduates were entering primary care (Ginzberg 1986:3; LeRoy and Lee 1977). Ob/gyn leaders realized that their number of residency programs, their number of residents, and their research funds all hinged upon the specialty's recognition as a primary care provider (McElin 1977). In 1972, the American College of Obstetricians and Gynecologists produced a policy statement proclaiming that ob/gyns should be equipped to serve as primary care physicians. In 1979, the American College of Obstetricians and Gynecologists sponsored a "task force committee" to study the issue, and in 1980 it formally defined ob/gyns as both consultants and women's primary care physicians.

Ob/gyn leaders directed several large studies documenting ob/gyns' contributions to primary care. Lo and behold, such studies found that ob/gyns spent much of their time providing routine periodic services to well women: cancer screenings, physicals, and medical histories. Ob/gyns also were found to treat non-ob/gyn conditions and served as entry ports to the medical system, making referrals to other specialists (Ranney et al. 1976; Willson and Burkons 1976a, 1976b). In a large representative study, 40 percent of practicing ob/gyns reported that half or more of their patients came to them for primary care (Yankauer et al. 1971). A survey of 1,000 ob/gyn patients in Michigan found that 44 percent had no primary care physician and 86 percent only saw their ob/gyns for regular checkups (Burkons and Willson 1975). A study conducted by the Medical Foundation of Massachusetts found that ob/gyns gave more hours to primary care than internists (Wechsler, Dorsey, and Bovey 1978).

Ob/gyn leaders proffered a demand-driven explanation for these patterns. Their explanation favored, and drew heavily from, the definitional frame of conservative obstetricians, who had contributed actively to ob/gyn commentary since the founding of the specialty. According to the conservative obstetricians' definitional frame, a special bond existed between a woman and her ob/gyn. This bond developed naturally during first pregnancy, with the ob/gyn at the young mother's bedside during one of her most intimate life experiences. Here, the ob/gyn gained the mother's trust and devotion (see Craig 1959). Afterwards, the ob/gyn nurtured this "special relationship" through periodic examinations throughout the woman's reproductive years. The ob/gyn, in this definitional frame, was the true woman's physician because of this bond and, according to one commentary, "the true woman's physician [was] actually, other than her husband, the most intimate man in her life" (Burman 1968:393). Women preferred to see their ob/gyns for routine care, according to this

frame, because they learned to trust them over an extended period. It was just natural that women chose to rely upon their ob/gyns for medical guidance and referrals (Ranney 1976:287).[6]

Influential health planners did not buy ob/gyn's claims, however (Pearson 1975). Ob/gyn was not listed in 1971 legislation linking medical school scholarships to the promise of practicing primary care in needy areas. After intense lobbying, The Department of Health, Education, and Welfare recognized ob/gyn as a primary care specialty in 1974. However, ob/gyn was removed from the list of primary care specialties in the 1976 Health Professions Education Assistance Act (McElin 1977; Pearse and Trabin 1977). The stickler in ob/gyn's efforts to have its primary care role recognized by policy makers was Dr. Robert Knouss, heading the Federal Bureau of Health Manpower Committee. Dr. Knouss, an internist, did not accept the practice data supporting ob/gyn's primary care role as evidence that ob/gyn was a true primary care specialty. He demanded data indicating that a primary care emphasis played a prominent role in the training of ob/gyns (Pearse 1980). Ob/gyn's leadership was hard pressed to provide this.

Many within the discipline felt that the ob/gyn residency poorly trained ob/gyns for primary care (Dunn 1993; Willson and Burkons 1976b). Efforts were made to address this shortcoming. On the basis of findings from a series of studies he conducted with David Burkons, Dr. J. Robert Willson proposed reforms for residency training to better prepare ob/gyns as primary care providers in his presidential address before a joint meeting of the American Gynecological Society and the American Association of Obstetricians and Gynecologists in 1974. Willson, drawing from a number of earlier proposals, argued for expanding the length of general training to four years to provide better training in primary care and counseling, including weekly stints in outpatient clinics and more training in general and internal medicine (Willson and Burkons 1976b).

The fourth year requirement that Willson and others proposed was reinstated in 1976. In addition, the American Board of Obstetrics and Gynecology recommended in its 1979, 1980, and 1981 statements regarding residency training that ob/gyn residencies provide "a significant portion of graduate education in a broadly oriented approach to patient care" (quoted in Dunn 1993:1053). These statements, however, did not come with real requirements, and they were not repeated after 1981 when the Reagan Administration ended federal funding for enrollment increases. Then, the advantages that academic medicine reaped from being officially recognized as a primary care specialty evaporated (see Dunn 1993).

The Interests of Surgical Gynecologists and Ob/Gyn's Women's Physician Program

Traditionally, ob/gyn trained its residents to become surgically-oriented consultants/specialists. Most ob/gyns embraced the surgical role as at least part of their occupational identity; some considered themselves as primarily surgeons and worked throughout their careers to establish exclusive surgical practices. And, while practicing obstetrics and providing primary care services enabled most ob/gyns to establish busy practices and good incomes, these were not the practices for which they were trained. Many commentators defined primary care work as boring and addressed the issue of the resulting alienation inherent to such a role (Willson 1972; Willson and Burkons 1976b; see, also, Halpern 1990). Some ob/gyn leaders felt that something had to be done to reconcile the consultant/specialty role emphasized in residency training with the primary care role most ob/gyns played out of necessity (Willson and Burkons 1976b).

Dr. J. Robert Willson's proposals for incorporating the primary care role into the specialty, and his associated proposals for reforming residency training discussed above, spoke to this contradiction. Willson was an academic ob/gyn who held a keen interest in reforming residency training. He held high offices in ob/gyn's elite associations throughout his career. Willson, for example, was elected President of the American College of Obstetricians and Gynecologists in 1970. He presented his famous presidential address in 1974, where he spelled out the features of his version of the women's physician program before a joint annual meeting of the American Gynecological Society and the American Association of Obstetricians and Gynecologists.

Recently, Neil Fligstein (2001) has championed a "social skills" framework for analyzing how significant actors create and modify institutional fields. Elizabeth Popp Berman's (forthcoming) recent work employs Fligstein's social skills framework effectively to account for the mobilization of a network of occupational actors across federal government and university positions in support of a standardized "institutional patent agreement." Willson was the type of leader that the social skills framework singles out for intensive analysis. Willson defined his version of the women's physician program as hegemonic, serving the interests of all of ob/gyn's diverse constituencies. He attempted to use his position and its resources to mobilize these constituencies in support of the program.

Willson fully recognized ob/gyns' dishonored position within the medical division of labor and spoke for the interests of the surgically-oriented ob/gyns. Willson's women's physician program, while responding to federal initiatives designed to alleviate the primary care shortage, also contained an occupational agenda. Willson's program ultimately aimed to re-structure the medical division of labor serving women so that ob/gyns controlled both the upstream positions responsible for their own case referrals and the downstream positions to which they referred cases. Willson's program was consistent with the views of ob/gyn's academic leadership, and it incorporated into a coherent structure a variety of innovations championed and implemented within ob/gyn, such as subspecialties and the use of paraprofessional physicians' assistants.

Here, we examine the logic behind Willson's program and how this logic linked to the interests of surgical ob/gyns. While the major features of the program were accepted, Willson's program generated opposition. The focus here is on the program's logic and how it spoke to ob/gyn's surgically-oriented rank and file. The contentious processes that this program set in motion will be examined in future papers.

The New Division of Labor Within Ob/Gyn

A key pillar in Willson's program, a pillar widely accepted within ob/gyn's leadership, involved tracking ob/gyns into generalist and subspecialist roles. General ob/gyns would make up perhaps 90 percent of all ob/gyns. They would provide primary care, general obstetrics, and perform surgical procedures, such as hysterectomies and cesarean sections. The advocacy of primary care for the role was new, at least officially. The surgical content of the role, as Willson envisioned, would not change. Ob/gyn subspecialists in reproductive endocrinology, maternal-fetal medicine, and gynecological oncology would make up a small proportion of ob/gyns. They would be tracked for special training during residency and would undergo additional fellowship training for subspecialty certification. Through the creation of referral systems, subspecialists would serve as consultants to general ob/gyns on their complex cases (see Burkons and Willson 1975).

Willson's proposal was controversial. Early commentaries tended to see Willson as splitting the ob/gyn role into two parts: the ob/gyn subspecialist as a true consultant/specialist, and essentially an ob/gyn general practitioner overwhelmed by primary care. Since only about 10 percent of ob/gyns would serve as subspecialists, some saw this as demeaning. One critic proclaimed that most ob/gyns were dissatisfied with a primary care role that underutilized their skills (Hester 1975). For such critics, ob/gyn was, is, and always should be a consultant/specialty. The solution to the primary care shortage for women was not to saddle ob/gyns with this role but to train others for it.

But this was precisely Willson's goal for routine primary care. Willson's aim was to restore the general ob/gyn to a consultant/specialist role. However, because of the expansion of ob/gyn residencies, this could not be done by simply abandoning the general services most ob/gyns provided, for doing so would so reduce the ob/gyn market that drastic cuts to residency programs would be inevitable (see Burkons and Willson 1975). Willson aimed not to displace but to preserve the traditional role. Willson articulated his own vision:

> . . . a role for obstetrician-gynecologists of the future which relieved them of most of the routine care of normal women in order that they might add interesting and challenging medical responsibilities to the specific diagnostic, therapeutic, and surgical services they now supply.

We believe the major question generated by our suggestion was whether acceptance of a role of primary physician for women might represent a giant step toward transforming obstetrician-gynecologists from specialists to general practitioners. Nothing could have been further from our minds. (Willson and Burkons 1976a:631)

Placing "Women's Health Care Specialists" in the Screening/Gatekeeping Role

The lynchpin in Willson's system was the use of paraprofessional "women's health care specialists" (WHCS) for routine primary care, a position also supported by presidents of the American College of Obstetricians and Gynecologists in their inaugural addresses in 1971 and 1973 (see Ostergard, Gunning, and Marshall 1975). These women's health care specialists would hold the status of nurse and would serve as physicians' assistants in ob/gyn practices, under the authority of the ob/gyns employing them. The women's health care specialists would provide periodic checkups, medical histories, consultations for minor problems and complaints, advice and counseling on routine health matters, etc. In addition, the women's health care specialists would screen cases, referring those cases that might require expert diagnosis and/or surgery to the general ob/gyns employing them. The general ob/gyns would become managers of the women's health care specialists. The purpose of the women's health care specialists in Willson's system was to minimize the alienation ob/gyns allegedly experienced in routine primary care, freeing them to concentrate on their more complex and interesting cases (Burkons and Willson 1975; Willson and Burkons 1976a, 1976b).

Row C of Figure 1 specifies case-flow relationships in Willson's reorganized division of labor. Ob/gyns' downstream, referral-dependent relationship with screeners changes fundamentally from that depicted in row B, since the general ob/gyn now employs, controls, and regulates the women's health care specialists serving in this position. This is represented in row C by the lower (control) arrow moving from the general ob/gyn to the women's health care specialists. While screening cases, the women's health care specialists do not have the choice of sending them to other specialists without permission. This system enables general ob/gyns to do structurally what they could not do normatively within the medical division of labor: establish market closure over cases requiring gynecological surgery.

Generalists and Subspecialists Within Ob/Gyn

The dependency relationship between general ob/gyns and other surgical specialists also changes in row C. While general ob/gyns must still seek referral for their difficult surgical cases, the latter become, in the Willson system, ob/gyn subspecialists, who share residency training, identification, and allegiance with general ob/gyns. This keeps knowledge, recognition, and consternation regarding general ob/gyns' surgical skills in house. It enables ob/gyn's alternative surgical model to operate covertly, without damaging ob/gyn's reputation within the medical division of labor. The common bond cementing this relationship is demonstrated in the model by the double-headed control arrow beneath the arrow representing case flow in row C.

Subspecialties were established in ob/gyn during the 1970s. Afterwards, subspecialists in gynecological oncology, reproductive endocrinology, and maternal/fetal medicine stood downstream from general ob/gyns to service their complex, troubling cases. Gynecological oncologists, with two additional years of surgically-oriented fellowship training after residency, usually assisted on surgical complications. They had the requisite skills to repair bowels, ureters, etc., thereby keeping ob/gyn's surgical complications out of the hands of competitors outside the specialty.

Thus, under the banner of the women's physician program, the system Willson and other ob/gyn leaders envisioned addressed the interests of the surgically-oriented ob/gyn. Willson's system removed the upstream positions supplying ob/gyns with referrals, and the downstream positions correcting ob/gyns' surgical mistakes, from the general medical division of labor. Willson's system placed these positions under the sole control and purview of ob/gyn. Whatever else it was intended to do, Willson's system was designed to reduce ob/gyns' dependence upon other physicians. Willson's reorganized division of labor was to help ob/gyns

secure better access to their surgical markets than when they were dependent in a medical division of labor that dishonored them.

Theoretical Discussion

Ironically, American physicians' successful professional project set in motion forces in the post-World War II decades that undermined the project's signal creation—the physician as an idealized commodity. State investments in health care, coupled with the absence of strong countervailing powers, fueled rapid specialization and the primary care crisis of focus. As more physicians specialized, the commonalities thought to unite, and "standardize," physicians weakened. The ideal of the solo, multi-skilled practitioner was replaced by a complex, splintered, intra-occupational division of labor. While medical sociologists have recognized this, our theoretical frameworks have not adjusted well to this change.

This article works within Everett C. Hughes' (1971) general theoretical framework to address why ob/gyn initiated the women's physician program during the 1970s, a program that, in essence, redefined the specialty as a primary care provider to women in response to policy initiatives. Ob/gyn's historic struggle to legitimate its core-skill definition greatly influenced its women's physician program. Ob/gyn defined itself as a comprehensive organ specialty. Its turf logic held that ob/gyns would produce better results, because of their broad focus and training, than would others treating women's genital and reproductive systems. General surgeons, in fact, held a central position in ob/gyn's definitional frame; they became a foil to what ob/gyns claimed to be. Ob/gyn's history was a struggle to claim their surgical turf from general surgeons, and to make good on the claim. For much of the postwar era, however, ob/gyn failed to do so.

This failure affected ob/gyn's quest to establish itself as a true surgically-oriented consultant/specialty. Gatekeepers had the option of referring their suspected gynecological surgical cases to either ob/gyns or general surgeons. These gatekeepers chose general surgeons frequently. Ob/gyns never completely won legitimation as a proper consultant/specialty as a result. This historical context shaped ob/gyn's women's physician program. Savvy ob/gyn leaders structured their women's physician program to free the specialty from its disadvantaged and dishonored position within medicine by recasting a new division of labor for women who they themselves defined and could better control. Understanding the historical context within which this struggle unfolded also enables us to understand better the actual influences of macro-institutional and gender variables on this and related outcomes.

Ob/Gyns' Struggle for Legitimation and the Institutional Field

Ob/gyn's historic struggle to legitimate its core-skill definition unfolded within a macro-institutional structure characterized generally by professional dominance and weak countervailing powers. The larger system influenced this struggle in two ways. First, this structure generated a mop-up market space open to those willing to provide basic primary care in the early postwar period. This market space allowed ob/gyns to prosper, even in practices with increasingly low surgical content. Second, federal policies initiated to alleviate the systemic shortage of primary care physicians in the 1970s created a resource for ob/gyns to appropriate in their struggle. Skillful ob/gyn leaders such as Willson articulated programs specifying a central role for ob/gyns in primary care that, at the same time, addressed the specialty's pressing occupational concerns. The state's primary care initiatives became a kind of legitimating cloak for these programs, masking their more basic occupational designs. The U.S. health care system's weak regulatory powers at the inter-specialty level have functioned generally to encourage this type of development. We should look for it in the implementation of every policy initiative in health care, whether the initiative concerns increasing the physician supply, integrating women into the profession, or negotiating managed care. Distinctive specialties react strategically to such initiatives in ways reflecting their particular definitional frames, market interests, and place within the existing intra-occupational division of labor.

Ob/Gyns' Struggle for Legitimation and Gender

Understanding ob/gyn's historic struggle to legitimate its core-skill definition also gives us insight into how gender dynamics can work in the medical division of labor. Ob/gyn's women's physician program was a bit of a paradox. On the one hand, its rhetoric did suggest a type of medical orientation that Elianne Riska (2001) and others have linked to feminine gender, that of holistic, comprehensive health care provided by physicians in tune with their patients' personal histories, troubles, and needs. However, a male leadership created the 1970s program, as it responded to a threat from male surgeons. This program appealed to male rank and file ob/gyns desiring a larger role as surgeons. The program's rhetoric was also sexist. It spoke of women as being childlike in their relationship with ob/gyns; it presumed as natural the gender roles of male-dominated society; and it defined ob/gyn's function as adjusting women to these roles.

This peculiar women's physician program was not insignificant to the later struggles of female physicians, however. Ob/gyn leaders rapidly increased the proportion of women accepted into ob/gyn residencies during the 1980s and 1990s. Ob/gyn commentators singled out women medical graduates' alleged preference for a primary care orientation as one of their attractive features (see Hayashi and McIntyre-Seltman 1987). As their numbers rose in later decades, women activists within ob/gyn could draw upon the women's physician ideal introduced in the 1970s, strip it of its sexist rhetoric and intent, and then use it to legitimate the more feminist agendas developing in medicine during the 1990s (on these agendas, see Riska 2001, chapter 8). This article addresses how and why male ob/gyns carried this peculiar resource into ob/gyn's occupational culture in the first place. The historical processes involved in the appropriation of this program to serve a more feminist-oriented agenda should be explored in future work. It may well be the case, generally, that intra-occupational struggles and developments, like those documented above for ob/gyn, often create, quite unintentionally, significant resources for supporting such movements.

Conclusion

When we begin our analyses of health care system developments with the basic recognition that "the doctor" of the medical profession of the past has been replaced with a splintered occupational division of labor, new insights may be forthcoming. This article suggests that, at a fundamental level, this splintered medical division of labor may contain a serious yet largely unrecognized structural contradiction. To achieve high status and prestige, medical graduates must specialize. In specializing, however, they must enter into dependency relationships with generalists, who play a screening/gatekeeping role vital to their market access. When confronted by viable competitors in the medical division of labor, this market access can become jeopardized, as in the case of post-war ob/gyns. This simple structural contradiction may well lie at the root of many of the pathologies and paradoxes of the contemporary health care system. Consider how an appreciation of this structural contradiction may allow us to address two paradoxes.

Paradox 1

How did a health care system, famous for its extraordinary levels of professional dominance in the early decades after World War II, so quickly become threatened by managed care and the specter of market controls during the 1980s and 1990s? While scholars have proffered many explanations for this development, the status/dependency contradiction discussed here may well be the most robust. Perhaps the natural tendency in systems of pure professional dominance is to increase specialization, and the resources supporting it, thereby creating a chronic shortage of devalued screening/gatekeeping positions. An unintended consequence of this shortage is a system quite vulnerable to rationalization and external control by third parties. When the profession itself delegates the screening/gatekeeping role to other less prestigious occupations outside the profession—a likely occurrence when everybody specializes—those in the screening/gatekeeping role become much less capable of resisting routinization and rationalization. Those in the screening/gatekeeping roles, for instance, cannot employ the classic professional logic discussed by Eliot Freidson (2001) to defend their autonomy and control. Then, as Hafferty and Light (1995:136–37) suggest, external agents are in position to control specialists, not by dictating work contents, but by controlling patient access through their control over the screening/gatekeeping positions. Ironically, systems with well developed countervailing powers may not be so vulnerable to this contradiction, since they are less likely to develop severe imbalances between generalist and specialist roles. Strong countervailing powers may protect such professional systems from their natural tendency to overspecialize. The impact of this structural contradiction within different types of systems should be further developed theoretically and further explored empirically.

Paradox 2

Why do specialists, investing extra years and resources in residency training, willfully embrace primary care roles? This paper addresses this paradox in examining the case of the women's physician program ob/gyn leaders initiated in the 1970s. This response may have little to do with gender. Rather, the move to the primary care position, as in the case of ob/gyn, may well be a market strategy designed to gain, or retake, control over positions regulating a specialty's access to valued markets. Organized medicine's contemporary movement to increase greatly the number of primary care physicians—a move sponsored by the American Medical Association and the American Association of Medical Colleges—may well have a similar motivation, after a failed but threatening bout with managed care in the 1990s. Retaking the screening/gatekeeping positions within the medical division of labor may well be necessary for securing professional dominance in the future.[7] While all of this is speculative, it does suggest the potential importance of the theoretical framework employed here in generating insight into contemporary, as well as historical, developments.

Notes

1. The "women's physician" concept became popularized with Burman's 1968 article titled, "The Gynecologist—The Woman's Physician." Other commentators used different labels for the same role, such as "the primary physician to women" or women's "principal physician." This article refers to ob/gyn leaders' campaign to win official legitimation for their claim to be primary care physicians to women as the "women's physician program."

2. The actual percentages used to indicate numbers in the specialties depend on the source used. The American Medical Association data bank categorizes physicians into specialties on the basis of physicians' self-reports. Sources restricting their categories to only board-certified physicians report fewer absolute numbers and smaller percentages.

3. A third category might include auxiliary workers, who provide services for those in either the screener or specialist roles. Halpern (1992) provides the best account of these types of roles and how they relate to others in the medical division of labor.

4. As Freidson ([1970] 1988:93) and others have long noted, the power of the individual in the "feeder/gatekeeper" role to control work flow within a local network of specialists has declined. This does not suggest, however, that those in surgical specialties are no longer dependent upon physicians working upstream from them for initially diagnosing a surgical condition. This categorical dependency has not changed fundamentally for elective surgery. Patients with recurring stomach pain do not typically make appointments with surgeons on their own to have their gallbladders removed; those with severe headaches do not contact neurosurgeons prior to an initial diagnosis from a non-surgeon. Once patients have been diagnosed, they are much more likely than in the past to shop around, consult their lay networks, etc. The self-referred category does not typically mean self-diagnosed.

5. Surgeons were much less likely than ob/gyns to serve in a primary care capacity in the medical division of labor. They worked downstream from those serving in screening/gatekeeping roles and received the bulk of their cases from referrals, including their ob/gyn cases.

6. As is evident in its rhetoric, ob/gyn's women's physician program presumed a patriarchal relationship between young females and their male ob/gyns. This rhetoric accepted women's traditional roles in male-dominated society. The patient thought to demand ob/gyns' primary care services was not a feminist but a rather traditional woman. Some commentaries sympathetic to this definitional frame even seemed to equate women's health and well-being to the state of their genital and reproductive organs (see Burman 1968). For these reasons, it is very doubtful that feminism generally, or the feminist health care center movement of the 1970s in particular, had much of an impact upon ob/gyn's women's physician program.

7. A *JHSB* reviewer suggested this possibility on an earlier draft of the manuscript.

References

Abbott, Andrew D. 1988. *The System of Professions: An Essay on the Division of Expert Labor*. Chicago, IL: University of Chicago Press.

American Medical Association, Council on Long Range Planning and Development. 1987. "The Future of Obstetrics and Gynecology." *Journal of the American Medical Association* 258:3547–53.

Barnes, Allan G. 1971. "Quality and Quantity in the Specialty of Obstetrics and Gynecology." *American Journal of Obstetrics and Gynecology* 109:203–205.

Barter, Robert H. 1975. "Discussion." *American Journal of Obstetrics and Gynecology* 121:814.

Beecham, Clayton T. 1969. "Self-Purification: Presidential Address." *American Journal of Obstetrics and Gynecology* 103:605–608.

Berman, Elizabeth Popp. 2006. "Before the Professional Project: Success and Failure at Creating an Organizational Representative for English Doctors." *Theory and Society* 35:157–91.

———. Forthcoming. "Why Did Universities Start Patenting? Institution-Building and the Road to the Bayh-Dole Act." *Social Studies of Science* 38.

Bloss, James R. 1950. "Presidential Address: The Ideals, Responsibilities, and Reward of the Obstetrician." *American Journal of Obstetrics and Gynecology* 59:1183–88.

Brewer, John I. 1953. "From Little Acorns: Presidential Address." *American Journal of Obstetrics and Gynecology* 65:465–71.

Brunschwig, Alexander. 1968. "Whither Gynecology?" *American Journal of Obstetrics and Gynecology* 100:122–27.

Bucher, Rue. [1962] 1972. "Pathology: A Study of Social Movements within a Profession." Pp. 113–27 in *Medical Men and Their Work*, edited by Eliot Freidson and Judith Lorber. Chicago, IL: Aldine-Atherton.

———. 1988. "On the Natural History of Health Care Occupations." *Work and Occupations* 15:131–47.

Bucher, Rue and Anselm L. Strauss. 1961. "Professions in Process." *American Journal of Sociology* 66:325–34.

Burkons, David M. and J. Robert Willson. 1975. "Is the Obstetrician-Gynecologist a Specialist or Primary Physician to Women?" *American Journal of Obstetrics and Gynecology* 121:808–16.

Burman, Richard G. 1968. "The Gynecologist—The Woman's Physician." *Southern Medical Journal* 61:391–94.

Craig, R. Glenn, 1959. "Presidential Address: Our Opportunities." *Obstetrics and Gynecology* 14:811–14.

De Santis, Grace. 1980. "Realms of Expertise: A View from within the Medical Profession." *Research in the Sociology of Health Care* 1:179–236.

Dunn, Leo J. 1993. "Not to Decide is to Decide: Presidential Address." *American Journal of Obstetrics and Gynecology* 168:1053–62.

Ellison, Eugene T. and W. D. Thornton. 1955. "Late Results of Pelvic Surgery." *Southern Medical Journal* 47:913–18.

Fein, Rashi and Gerald I. Weber. 1971. *Financing Medical Education: An Analysis of Alternative Policies and Mechanisms*. New York: McGraw-Hill.

Fligstein, Neil. 2001. "Social Skill and the Theory of Fields." *Sociological Theory* 19:105–25.

Freidson, Eliot. [1970] 1988. *Profession of Medicine: A Study of the Sociology of Applied Knowledge*. Chicago, IL: University of Chicago Press.

———. 2001. *Professionalism: The Third Logic*. Chicago, IL: University of Chicago Press.

Gardner, Herman L. 1966. "The Gynecologist and the Periodic Checkup: Presidential Address." *American Journal of Obstetrics and Gynecology* 95:1–4.

Ginzberg, Eli, ed. 1986. *From Physician Shortage to Patient Shortage: The Uncertain Future of Medical Practice*. Boulder, CO: Westview Press.

Ginzberg, Eli, Edward Brann, Dale Hiestand, and Miriam Ostow. 1981. "The Expanding Physician Supply and Health Policy: The Clouded Outlook." *Milbank Quarterly* 59:508–41.

Gritzer, Glenn. 1982. "Occupational Specialization in Medicine: Knowledge and Market Explanations." *Research in the Sociology of Health Care* 2:251–83.

Hafferty, Frederic W. and Donald W. Light. 1995. "Professional Dynamics and the Changing Nature of Medical Work." *Journal of Health and Social Behavior* 35:132–53.

Halpern, Sydney A. 1990. "Medicalization as Professional Process: Postwar Trends in Pediatrics." *Journal of Health and Social Behavior* 31:28–42.

———. 1992. "Dynamics of Professional Control: Internal Coalitions and Crossprofessional Boundaries." *American Journal of Sociology* 97:994–1021.

Hayashi, T. Terry and Kathleen McIntyre-Seltman. 1987. "The Role of Gender in an Obstetrics and Gynecology Residency Program: Presidential Address." *American Journal of Obstetrics and Gynecology* 156:769–77.

Hester, Lawrence L. 1975. "Discussion." *American Journal of Obstetrics and Gynecology* 121: 812–13.

Hickson, D. J. C. R. Hinings, C. A. Lee, R. E. Schneck, and J. M. Pennings. 1971. "A Strategic Contingencies' Theory of Intraorganizational Power." *Administrative Science Quarterly* 16:216–29.

Hiestand, Dale L. 1984. "Medical Residencies in a Period of Expanding Physician Supply." Pp. 69–82 in *The Coming Physician Surplus: In Search of a Policy*, edited by Eli Ginzberg and Miriam Ostow. Totawa, NJ: Rowman and Allanheld.

Hodgkinson, C. Paul. 1961. "Continuing Education in Gynecology-Obstetrics." *Obstetrics and Gynecology* 18:243–50.

———. 1968. "Challenge and Response: Presidential Address." *American Journal of Obstetrics and Gynecology* 101:1–7.

Hughes, Everett C. 1971. *The Sociological Eye: Selected Papers*. Chicago, IL: Aldine-Atherton.

Larson, Magali Sarfatti. 1977. *The Rise of Professionalism: A Sociological Analysis*. Berkeley: University of California Press.

LeRoy, Lauren and Philip R. Lee, eds. 1977. *Deliberations and Compromise: The Health Professions Education Assistance Act of 1976*. Cambridge, MA: Ballinger.

Light, Donald W. 1995. "Countervailing Powers: A Framework for Professions in Transition." Pp. 25–41 in *Health Professions and the State in Europe*, edited by Terry Johnson, Gerry Larkin, and Mike Saks. London: Routledge.

———. 2004. "Introduction: Ironies of Success: A New History of the American Health Care 'System.'" *Journal of Health and Social Behavior* 45:1–24.

Lund, Curtis J. 1971. "Their Shadows Are Cast: Coming Events in the Education of the Obstetrician-Gynecologist." *American Journal of Obstetrics and Gynecology* 111:463–68.

McCarthy, Eugene G. and Madelon Lubin Finkel. 1980. "Second Consultant Opinion for Elective Gynecologic Surgery." *Obstetrics and Gynecology* 56:403–10.

McElin, Thomas W. 1977. "Discussion." *American Journal of Obstetrics and Gynecology* 128:306–307.

Mechanic, David. 2004. "The Rise and Fall of Managed Care." *Journal of Health and Social Behavior* 45:76–86.

Mengert, William F. 1949. "President's Address: The Organization and Relationship of a Department of Obstetrics and Gynecology." *American Journal of Obstetrics and Gynecology* 58:207–14.

———. 1959. "Obstetrics and Gynecology Today: President's Address." *American Journal of Obstetrics and Gynecology* 77:697–705.

Ostergard, Donald R., John E. Gunning, and John R. Marshall. 1975. "Training and Function of a Women's Health-Care Specialist, a Physician's Assistant, or Nurse Practitioner in Obstetrics and Gynecology." *American Journal of Obstetrics and Gynecology* 121:1029–37.

Pearse, Warren H. 1980. "Closing." *American Journal of Obstetrics and Gynecology* 137:326.

Pearse, Warren H. and Jay R. Trabin. 1977. "Subspecialization in Obstetrics and Gynecology." *American Journal of Obstetrics and Gynecology* 128:303–307.

Pearson, Jack W. 1975. "The Obstetrician and Gynecologist: Primary Physician for Women." *Journal of the American Medical Association* 231:815–16.

Perdue, J. Randolph. 1952. "The Future in Gynecology." *Southern Medical Journal* 45:77–79.

Ranney, Brooks. 1976. "Shadows or Light?: Presidential Address." *American Journal of Obstetrics and Gynecology* 125:283–89.

Ranney, Brooks, David Holzwarth, Richard Thornton, and Marjorie MacNeil. 1976. "The Practice of Gynecology and Obstetrics: An Analysis." *Obstetrics and Gynecology* 47:725–29.

Reid, Duncan E. 1961. "The Obstetric and Gynecologic Discipline: Potentials and Responsibilities." *Obstetrics and Gynecology* 17:263–68.

Riska, Elianne. 2001. *Medical Careers and Feminist Agendas: American, Scandinavian, and Russian Women Physicians*. New York: Aldine de Gruyter.

Riva, H. L. 1965. "Hysterectomy: Indications and Technics." *Postgraduate Medicine* 39:645–49.

Scott, W. Richard, Martin Ruef, Peter J. Mendel, and Carol A. Caronna. 2000. *Institutional Change and Healthcare Organizations: From Professional Dominance to Managed Care*. Chicago, IL: University of Chicago Press.

Simard, J. A. René. 1957. "Considerations on Obstetrics and Obstetricians: Presidential Address." *American Journal of Obstetrics and Gynecology* 73:1163–68.

Starr, Paul. 1982. *The Social Transformation of American Medicine: The Rise of a Sovereign Profession and the Making of a Vast Industry*. New York: Basic Books.

Stevens, Rosemary. 1971. *American Medicine and the Public Interest: A History of Specialization*. New Haven, CT: Yale University Press.

Sturgis, Somers H. 1957. "The Challenge of Comprehensive Gynecology." *American Journal of Obstetrics and Gynecology* 73:180–89.

Symmonds, Richard E. 1976. "Ureteral Injuries Associated with Gynecologic Surgery: Prevention and Management." *Clinical Obstetrics and Gynecology* 19:623–44.

Taylor, Howard C., Jr. 1958. "Competition and Cooperation: Presidential Address." *American Journal of Obstetrics and Gynecology* 76: 931–38.

———. 1965. "Objectives and Principles in the Training of the Obstetrician-Gynecologist: Training for Surgical Virtuosity and Versatility or for Public Service." *American Journal of Surgery* 110:35–42.

Tyson, John E. 1971. "A Contemporary Approach to Recruitment in Obstetrics and Gynecology." *American Journal of Obstetrics and Gynecology* 111:711–17.

———. 1973. "The Attractiveness of Obstetrics and Gynecology as a Professional Career." *American Journal of Obstetrics and Gynecology* 117:130–35.

Wallace, Michael, Larry J. Griffin, and Beth A. Rubin. 1989. "The Positional Power of American Labor, 1963–1977." *American Sociological Review* 54:197–214.

Wechsler, Henry, Joseph L. Dorsey, and Joanne D. Bovey. 1978. "A Follow-Up Study of Residents in Internal-Medicine, Pediatrics and Obstetrics-Gynecology Training Programs in Massachusetts: Implications for the Supply of Primary-Care Physicians." *New England Journal of Medicine* 298:15–21.

Willson, J. Robert. 1962. "Undergraduate Education in Obstetrics and Gynecology." *Obstetrics and Gynecology* 20:929–36.

———. 1972. "Recruitment into Obstetrics-Gynecology." *Obstetrics and Gynecology* 40:432–37.

Willson, J. Robert and David M. Burkons. 1976a. "Obstetrician-Gynecologists Are Primary Physicians to Women. I. Practice Patterns of Michigan Obstetrician-Gynecologists." *American Journal of Obstetrics and Gynecology* 126:627–32.

———. 1976b. "Obstetrician-Gynecologists Are Primary Physicians to Women: II. Education for a New Role." *American Journal of Obstetrics and Gynecology* 126:744–54.

Yankauer, Alfred, Jan Schneider, Sally H. Jones, Louis M. Hellman, and Jacob J. Feldman. 1971. "Practice of Obstetrics and Gynecology in the United States." *Obstetrics and Gynecology* 38:800–808."

Zetka, James R., Jr. 2001. "Occupational Divisions of Labor and Their Technology Politics: The Case of Surgical Scopes and Gastrointestinal Medicine." *Social Forces* 79:1495–1520.

———. 2003. *Surgeons and the Scope*. Ithaca, NY: Industrial and Labor Relations Press.

———. 2008. "Radical Logics and Their Carriers in Medicine: The Case of Psychopathology and American Obstetricians and Gynecologists." *Social Problems* 55:95–116.

Zetka, James R., Jr. and John P. Walsh. 1994. "A Qualitative Protocol for Studying Technological Change in the Labor Process." *Bulletin de Methodologie Sociologique* 45:37–73.

Zola, Irving K. and Stephen J. Miller. 1971. "The Erosion of Medicine from Within." Pp. 153–172 in *Professions and their Prospects*, edited by Eliot Freidson. Chicago, IL: Aldine Atherton.

James R. Zetka, Jr. is an associate professor of sociology at the University of Albany. He is author of *Militancy, Market Dynamics, and Workplace Authority* (SUNY Press, 1995) and *Surgeons and the Scope* (ILR Press, 2003). Professor Zetka's current research interests concern how and why actors introduce radical innovations—both new technologies and new cultural definitions—into occupational and professional divisions of labor.

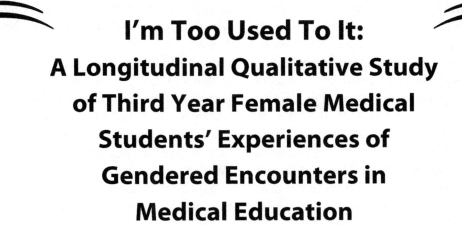

I'm Too Used To It:
A Longitudinal Qualitative Study of Third Year Female Medical Students' Experiences of Gendered Encounters in Medical Education

by Palav Barbaria, Sakena Abedin, David Berg, Marcella Nunez-Smith

Abstract Although the number of women entering medical school has been steadily rising in the USA, female medical students continue to report instances of sexual harassment and gender discrimination. The full spectrum of such experiences and their effect on the professional identity formation of female students over time remains largely unknown. To investigate these experiences, we interviewed 12 third year female medical students at a private New England medical school over several points during the 2006–2007 academic year. Using theoretical frameworks of gender performance and the centrality of student–patient and student–supervisor relationships, we were better able to understand how female medical students interpret the role of 'woman doctor' and the effect of negative and positive gendered interactions on the evolution of their professional identity. We found that participants quickly learned how to confront and respond to inappropriate behavior from male patients and found interactions with female patients and supervisors particularly rewarding. However, they did not feel equipped to respond to the unprofessional behavior of male supervisors, resulting in feelings of guilt and resignation over time that such events would be a part of their professional identity. The rapid acculturation to unprofessional behavior and resignation described by participants has implications for not only professional identity formation of female students but specialty choices and issues of future physician workforce.

© 2012 Elsevier Ltd. All rights reserved.

Introduction

The number of women in medicine has risen steadily over the past three decades, with females now comprising almost 50% of all American medical school matriculates (Barzansky & Etzel, 2008). Despite this relatively rapid rise in the number of women within this once all-male profession, studies have shown that female medical students

From *Social Science & Medicine, Volume 74, Number 7, April 2012* by Palav Barbaria, Sakena Abedin, David Berg, and Marcella Nunez-Smith. Copyright © 2012 Elsevier. Reprinted by permission.

in the U.S. continue to experience high rates of gender discrimination (Nora et al., 2002; Stratton, McLaughlin, Witte, Fosson, & Nora, 2005; Wear, Aultman, & Borges, 2007). More recent work has attempted to clarify how male and female students differentially view their own professional identity formation as physicians (Blanch, Hall, Roter, & Frankel, 2008; Gude et al., 2005). However, little work has been done to localize the professional identity formation of female students within the larger framework of a largely masculine medical hierarchy and constantly evolving professional relationships. We therefore utilize a dual theoretical framework of gender performance and the centrality of relationships to analyze the longitudinal gendered experiences of third year female medical students and their effect on professional identity formation.

Early sociological work such as Becker's "Boys in White" provides a useful starting point for understanding the process of American medical socialization. As Becker pointed out that "science and skill do not make a physician; one must also be initiated into the status of physician; to be accepted, one must have learned to play the part of a physician in the drama of medicine" (Becker, Geer, Hughes, & Strauss, 1961, p.4). Numerous studies have described the socialization process that occurs during medical training as students learn how to be "initiated" into their profession (Beagan, 2000; Becker et al., 1961; Shapiro, 1987), conforming to the dominant culture and becoming more homogenized over time (Shapiro, 1987). The transition from pre-clinical to clinical years of medical training is an important period in the socialization process (Beagan, 2000) and largely signifies the beginning of professional identity formation for physician trainees. In this new learning environment, a complex series of clinical encounters with peers, patients and supervisors, medical students first experience the "hidden" and "informal curriculum" (Hafferty & Franks, 1994), which has a substantial and profound effect on medical education (Karnieli-Miller, Vu, Holtman, Clyman, & Inui, 2010). It is during this time that students subtly learn "what medicine values," (Delvecchio Good, 1998, chap. 6 & 7; Karnieli-Miller et al., 2010). The clinical years of medical education are almost entirely based upon hierarchical team dynamics and interpersonal relationships that can either enhance

or impair learning (Conrad, 1988; Daugherty, Baldwin, & Rowley, 1998; Dyrbye et al., 2009; Richman, Flaherty, Rospenda, & Christensen, 1992). Unlike other professions, *both* male and female medical students in the U.S. routinely report experiences of harassment and belittlement (Richman et al., 1992; Sheehan, Sheehan, White, Leibowitz, & Baldwin, 1990), and complacency is seen as a crucial component of both learning and professional advancement (Wear & Aultman, 2005).

Much of the earlier work on medical socialization, however, largely ignores gender and "talk[s] mainly of boys becoming medical men" (Becker et al., 1961, p.3), reflecting an outdated white male demographic of medical students. More recent work has shown that women report greater levels of abuse than men, and that for both genders, experiences of mistreatment and harassment have been shown to have profound implications on student wellbeing and learning (Dyrbye, Thomas, & Shanafelt, 2006; Richman et al., 1992). Yet, mistreatment and harassment are only a small fraction of the types of gendered experiences that female medical students encounter during their clinical training (Babaria, Abedin, & Nunez-Smith, 2009) and little is known about the process of socialization in medical school as it occurs for female medical students. Beagen's study of Canadian medical students and the effect of gender, class and race on their experiences is one of the few that touches upon how female students are socialized, describing how students adopt the prevailing [male] culture and learn to neutralize their gender in mannerisms, behavior and dress (Beagan, 2000).

Prior work focusing specifically on gender and professional identity has been centered around differential attributes between male and female students. Multiple studies have documented that although female students tend to perform equally to their male peers on objective assessments of their clinical skills, they consistently report less confidence in their abilities and significant anxiety over their performance (Blanch et al., 2008; Kilminster, Downes, Gough, Murdoch-Eaton, & Roberts, 2007; Whittle & Eaton, 2001). Similarly, male medical students are more likely than female students to feel like they are "doctors" by the end of medical school (Gude et al., 2005). Interestingly, in some studies, although male and female students enter medical school with similar levels of stress and anxiety, females report increased anxiety about their skills compared with males by the third year, suggesting the milieu of medical education may be differentially affecting confidence levels (Blanch et al., 2008). These gender differences are often perpetuated by external bias, with female students being rated consistently as 'less confident' than their male peers (Kilminster et al., 2007) and or referred to as "nurses" rather than "doctors" by other staff and patients (Houry, Shockley, & Markovchick, 2000).

Other scholars have examined gender differences in professional identity formation by examining what attributes are valued within medical culture. As one historian of women in medicine states, "Indeed a central theme in the story of women in medicine has been the tension between 'femininity,' 'feminism' and 'morality,' on the one hand; and 'masculinity,' 'professionalism,' and 'science,' on the other" (Morantz-Sanchez, 2000, p. 200). Hinze's 1999 sociological study of the gendered hierarchy of medical specialties exemplifies the complex gender performance that underlies individual attributes of 'confidence' or 'toughness' in medicine. Participants defined the most "prestigious" specialties, such as surgery, as having "hands-on" experiences and "balls," (Hinze, 1999, p. 12). What becomes valued then, in terms of professional identity, is defined by male attributes and a male-defined system of behavior.

There is a gap between these two literatures, one on medical student socialization and the other on gender and professional identity, with neither addressing the question of how female medical students develop a professional identity that takes into account the gendered aspects of medical culture. We set out to understand how these problems of gender and professional identity manifest themselves and are addressed by female students during the third year of medical school. Our analysis is organized around two main concerns. The first, borrowed from gender theory, is the idea of gender performance. As Judith Butler describes, "what is called gender identity is a performative accomplishment compelled by social sanction and taboo," (Butler, 1988, p. 520). We contend that professional identity, like gender identity, is being constantly made and re-made. As third year medical students get drawn into the culture of medicine, they learn how to perform the role of doctor; for female

medical students, this learning process includes learning how to perform or enact the role of 'woman doctor,' (Butler, 1988). We posit that "woman doctor" is not a fixed construct, but a dynamic identity that represents female students' reconciliation of their identities as females and physicians-to-be. This identity is constantly evolving based upon student experiences, but is informed by institutional culture and stereotypical gender roles.

Our second analytic mainstay is the centrality of relationships to the formation of professional identity in medicine, notably the student–patient and student–supervisor relationships. As Haidet et al. have concluded, "Students proceed through medical school embedded in complex webs of relationships that exert a powerful influence (both positive and negative) on their formation as physicians," (Haidet et al., 2008, p. 382) and it is likely these relationships that enact much of the hidden curriculum that has been previously described (Hafferty & Franks, 1994). Through our participants' accounts of these relationships, we are able to see in which contexts they develop a coherent identity and at what points their attempts at becoming female physicians falter. Issues of power become central in the analysis of these relationships. The student–patient and student–supervisor relationship exhibit parallel power differentials (Ekstein & Wallerstein, 1958), such that the student's power in the student–patient relationship parallels the supervisor's power in the student–supervisor relationship. Position in the hierarchy and the associated power over those lower in the hierarchy shape the educational experience and the associated process of identity formation. Utilizing theories of the performance of gender and the centrality of relationships, we sought to characterize how gender effected the professional identity formation of third year female medical students.

Methods

Study design and sample

We conducted a longitudinal study of 12 female third year medical students, using serial in-depth interviews at regular intervals over an entire academic year (Murray et al., 2009). Given that little was known about the longitudinal experiences of female medical students, we chose a qualitative approach in order to characterize participants' perceptions regarding the influence of gender on their clinical training experiences. We used grounded theory to inform data collection and did not form any *a priori* hypotheses about what would emerge as thematic content. The initial code structure reflected ideas raised by participants in early interviews and evolved over subsequent interviews (Glaser & Strauss, 1967; Miles & Huberman, 1994).

We used a purposive sampling technique with attention to recruiting students that would represent diversity across several participant characteristics such as age, self-identified racial/ethnic background, childhood experiences, type of undergraduate education, work experience, and relationship status (Patton, 2002). An *N* of 12 was chosen as a feasible cohort for one interviewer to follow, and represented almost 25% of females in that class at a private U.S. medical school. Two invited students declined to participate in the study; one student cited time constraints and the other student expressed concern about the potential for study participation to negatively affect her career. Participants' clinical experiences took place across three large hospitals, over twelve specialties and sub-specialties, and over fifteen community-based training sites representing academic and private settings. This research protocol was approved by the Institutional Review Board and signed consent was obtained from all participants (Table 1).

Data collection

We conducted in-depth, in-person interviews with all participants from June 2006–June 2007. We interviewed participants at the end of every 4- or 6-week clinical clerkship; we also conducted baseline interviews prior to the start of the third year and exit interviews within 3 months of completion of their third year. All interviews were conducted by one member of the research team (PB), who was also a third year female medical student at the time of the interviews. A gender- and role-concordant interviewer was chosen to facilitate a comfortable relationship with participants (Edwards, 1990; Wilde, 1992). Although the interviewer's previous experiences suggested gender had an effect on medical education, she was aware of this bias prior to the start of the study, and

took precautions to minimize its influence on data collection and analysis. Members of the research team had differing degrees of gender attribution to professional experiences in medicine, allowing for skepticism in the analytic process. Caution was taken to ensure that the interview guide and all follow-up questions were neutral and open-ended. Initial interview transcripts were reviewed by other members of the coding team to ensure that leading questions were not being used and to provide feedback to the interviewer.

Interviews averaged 35 min and were conducted with only the interviewer and participant present. Interviews were audiotaped, transcribed, and verified by the interviewer. Interval interviews were conducted using a standardized interview guide and started with the general question, "What do you think the impact of gender has been, if any, on your experiences on the wards during the past rotation?" Specific probes regarding participants' perceptions of interactions with patients, medical staff and other students followed.

Table 1. Participant characteristics.

Characteristics of 12 study participants	N(%)
Median age (range), y	25 (23–30)
Race	
White	9 (75)
Black	2 (17)
Asian	1 (8)
Religion	
Christian	7 (58)
None	5 (42)
Marital status	
Single	5 (42)
In a relationship	5 (42)
Married	2 (17)
Parent	1 (8)
Undergraduate education completed at a single-sex institution	2 (17)
Took time off before coming to medical school	7 (58)
Median gap in years (range), y	2 (1–6)

Data analysis

We used qualitative principles of inductive reasoning to guide our data analysis and interpretation (Bradley, Curry, & Devers, 2007). A coding team composed of three women–a medical student, an internist and a pediatrician (PB, MNS, SA)–developed an initial code list based on three randomly chosen transcripts from interviews from the first month of clinical clerkships. This code list was then revised using the constant comparative method of data analysis. Because we were interested in each participant's individual journey over the year, each code team member assumed responsibility for four participants, whom she then followed closely forward in time. In order to identify recurrent themes across participants, each coding team member was responsible for the line-by-line coding of all transcripts for these four participants. Code team members created a summary document based upon standardized analytic questions (Fig. 1) to provide an overview of the longitudinal experience for each study participant. In addition, the coding team maintained an electronic document of ideas that emerged from ongoing analysis of the transcripts using the scientific software, ATLAS.ti 5.0 (Berlin). Once all of the transcripts were analyzed, the entire research team (including DB) met regularly to develop a construct for the research findings.

Findings

We found that the contrast between participants' interactions with patients and supervisors, as well as their evolving reactions to these interactions were salient to their ideas of what it meant to be a "woman doctor," our primary phenomenon of interest. Participants began their clerkships with expectations of professional learning environments; subsequent gendered experiences that were deemed inappropriate and unprofessional challenged their self-views as women doctors. Although each of our participants' experiences was unique, all reported that they were ill equipped to respond to most inappropriate workplace experiences. Almost all participants also concluded by the end of their year that gender would play a substantial role in their future careers, but had accepted the inevitability of inappropriate gendered behavior in their medical training.

> 1. How are the subject's views/experiences the same or different from last month?
> 2. How are the subject's views/experiences the same or different from the other 3 subjects you are following?
> 3. Choose a salient quotation that is representative of this participant's experience over the past month.

Figure 1. Summary document questions.

The Student–Patient Relationship

All participants described numerous workplace interactions with male patients that involved flirting or sexual innuendo. Most participants described being routinely called "honey" or "sweetie" by male patients. One participant on a surgical rotation described male patients that "were very excited . . . one guy wanted me to change his underwear." Sexualized encounters with patients were more explicit in some cases, such as one patient who began masturbating while a participant was obtaining a history. Participants were typically very tolerant of sexualized comments and behaviors from male patients, often minimizing or denying any subsequent emotional impact. As one participant explained "[The flirting from patients'] didn't really bother me deeply. I just thought . . . this is just . . . where he's coming from and, and then I'll have him for a few days and then we'll move on."

By the second and third months of third year, as participants' comfort level increased, they developed ways of addressing exposure to inappropriate patient behavior. As one participant described, "Men always have sexual . . . comments and stuff . . . I'm getting more comfortable with it as in I just dismiss it or just talk back if I feel that it's more than I find acceptable." Despite learning how to navigate such encounters, repeated exposure to inappropriate behavior from male patients affected participants' self-image as women doctors, sometimes affecting their ability to function effectively as medical students. Several participants described becoming "a little more distant from [male patients]" and altering their dress in an attempt to "hide [their] womanhood." As one participant described, "I didn't want to be perceived as sort of a feminine kind of role. And I didn't want my body to ever be noticed . . . I sort of used my coat as a cover sometimes."

Participants often reported being more upset by administrators and clinical team members who reinforced inappropriate patient encounters rather than addressing them. Responses of team members to inappropriate patient behavior ranged from silence, where the "attending didn't say anything, [the] resident didn't say anything," to laughing and actively teasing a student who was kissed good-bye on rounds by a patient. There was only one instance reported all year of a male supervisor addressing an inappropriate situation, when a male resident commented, "Wow . . . that was really inappropriate and he shouldn't have said that to you . . . we can get you another patient." The participant described her response "It was really amazing to me because . . . I don't remember another time in the year when somebody else, and a *man* noticed something like that and, and took the time to say something about it." Participants also reported being "disappointed" that female residents and attendings, whom they often idealized as role models, recommended responding to sexualized encounters by "just dealing with it."

In contrast to the student–male patient relationship, participants felt that they were "able to establish a rapport rather easily" with female patients and felt "more comfortable with them." Several participants attributed their increased comfort with female patients as a direct result of inappropriate encounters with male patients. As one participant described:

> With women I'm *much* more prone to . . . making a lot of eye contact, holding their hand . . . giving them a hug after the visit sometimes if it's been very tough on them . . . whereas with men I tend to stand, be a lot more distant with them . . . it's been a response to some of these situations that have come up in the outpatient clinic, and me trying to deter any further situations. Um, kind of trying to put on a more androgynous front.

Participants' positive encounters with female patients served to reaffirm their identities as women doctors. As one participant described:

> [The male OB/Gyn residents] didn't go that step further beyond knowing how to do the *treatment* . . . they didn't acknowledge that it was happening to another

human . . . but I felt that a lot of times, as a *woman*, I felt that I was filling in that gap for them. And like I said I was more vocal and assertive than I'd ever been in the whole rotation because of that."

Student–Supervisor Relationship

Participants also consistently reported inappropriate encounters with male attendings, ranging from sexist comments and sexual innuendo to inappropriate touching and solicitation throughout the year. These experiences spanned a range of clinical settings and degrees of familiarity between student and attending. One participant described an outpatient clinic attending who would "put his arms around you and be *very very* touchy with you and *in* your personal space, with all the females." Another participant described an encounter with a married attending who had a primary teaching role on the clerkship who started massaging her:

> "[He] started saying, '[You're] just such a good medical student. You're always just so interested. I can't tell you, like, how gratifying it is for me to have you here,' and he didn't say anything that was outrageously inappropriate but it was also *clearly* inappropriate for him to be like rubbing my *neck* while we're alone walking through this hallway at eight p.m."

A few male attendings were responsible for repeatedly harassing students every month, such that every single participant rotating through two particular services apparently had inappropriate encounters with the same male attendings. In some cases, the egregious behavior of specific attendings seemed to escalate over the year. A participant who encountered one of these "notorious" attendings later in the year described his behavior:

> I heard about [this attending] before I started this particular rotation . . . and he was supposed to be one of these head people to actually make us feel comfortable and to facilitate our learning on the clerkship but yet he was probably the one being the most invasive and definitely inappropriate towards women specifically. And then when *I* got on the clerkship he did

that to me even to a greater extent . . . And now a good friend of mine is on that same clerkship and she's gotten the same sort of harassment but *vastly* worse.

In contrast to inappropriate patient encounters, participants did not report finding satisfactory mechanisms of addressing inappropriate attendings, even at the end of their third year. As one participant reflected in her exit interview about several of these experiences, "I had no idea what to do and frankly didn't tell anyone about it. I mean it's only been recorded in these interviews because . . . I didn't *know* like what to do." Another participant described attempts to mitigate inappropriate touching, "I would sort of keep my elbow between my hip and [the attending] so it wasn't easy to grab [my waist]." However, such measures did not alleviate her discomfort. As she concluded her description of the encounter, "[It made me feel] just kind of dirty. Like is this what I'm doing to get a good education."

Participants thought that reporting inappropriate encounters with attendings would only "make things worse," and resigned themselves that it "was just going to be an uncomfortable situation." For some, the transient nature of clinical clerkships made it easier to endure such behavior rather than report it, because, as one participant described: "We wouldn't have to be in the same place at the same time basically at all anymore . . . If it went on for yesterday and then was over, then it was fine." Several participants "recognized the power dynamic" that prevented them from reporting inappropriate behavior. As one participant reflected in her exit interview months later, "[The attending who wanted] me to date his son had *all* the power, *all* the power in the relationship . . . and I felt pretty much helpless in the situation." In several instances, participants reported that attendings contributed to non-reporting by actively mocking students' ability to report them; one particular attending was described by several participants throughout the year:

A: Every time [the male surgeons] said a misogynistic thing, after three or four misogynistic comments in like one hour, they would say, 'Oh, what are you going to do? Tell [the dean]? What're you going to

do, tell [the ombudsman]?' Or they would say something offensive and then say, "Oh, it's ok if you tell [the dean], she knows I'm an asshole" . . . being in that kind of situation made me feel totally silenced and disempowered . . . it reminded me of the stories of women that I read about, who were raped. This has kind of heightened that sense, because it's like-an abuser is always saying, 'What are you going to do about it?' . . . I know if they ever heard this, they'd be like, you're overreacting, you're being over-sensitive, we didn't mean it-we wouldn't have done it if you'd said it was making you uncomfortable. All this crap that's meaningless, if you're going to do it anyway, again and again. And you do it to the student before me and the student after me. And the nurses, and the staff that you work with everyday.

Q: How did you deal with those situations?

A: Zoned out. I just stopped listening to them. So it'd be twelve hours of standing there retracting, and not listening. You know, but, I mean-I'm paying a lot of money for this. Paying a lot of money to be silent and not listen.

As described previously, participants rarely reported inappropriate experiences to anyone; when they did, they perceived that administrators usually did not take action. One student described the clerkship coordinator's reaction to student complaints about one of the "notorious" male attendings: "When students told-when *numerous* students told the course directors about this, the course directors were like, 'yeah, there's not so much we can do." In some cases, clerkship coordinators appeared to be aware of the reputation of some male faculty members and warned students in advance of rotations. However, such warnings seemed to place the onus of addressing inappropriate attending behavior on the student. As one participant described, "We were warned actually by [program administrator]. He said, "Doctor [Y] sort of has a reputation for being inappropriate. It's part of his personality. We try to keep him in line, every now and then he slips back out of line . . . Just let him know if he's going out of bounds." This participant then proceeded to recount inappropriate and sexist jokes that this attending engaged in throughout the rotation. When asked in their exit interviews to provide advice to clerkship directors, almost all participants wished that directors were "more honest about what goes on," enforced a "very little tolerance policy for things that are grossly out of proportion," and "communicate[d] . . . that there are resources [and] support."

Of import, negative gendered interactions also directly influenced the future sub-specialty choice of some participants. As one student described of her decision to not apply in urology after completing her sub-internship:

> I heard a lot, just a fair bit of trash talking in particular of, of a female surgeon . . . it just seemed like it could conceivably be a pathway to like a really unhappy future. And I don't think it's a coincidence that she's a woman . . . I just had several [female emergency medicine] mentors . . . that were completely confident and, and competent and great teachers and seemed happy in what they're doing.

Another participant who decided to apply in OB-Gyn felt that medicine was "an old boy's club" and jokingly described how she was "going to run away to a field that has fewer men."

Unlike the student–patient relationship in which participants evolved methods of dealing with inappropriate behavior, participants did not evolve methods by which to address inappropriate supervisor behavior. Over the course of the year, participants did develop progressive feelings of guilt and isolation, as well as desensitization and resignation to continued inappropriate behavior by attendings. These feelings appeared to be reinforced by the responses of clinical team members and perceived lack of institutional response, and undermined participants' perceived professional identities. Many participants described a tension between viewing themselves as the type of individuals who would "take action in response to things that were inappropriate" and resigning themselves to the barriers of reporting and saying "well that wasn't *so* bad." Participants often blamed themselves when they did not know how to respond effectively. As one participant

described, "I would never stand for that kind of talk in my life, and I was often silent, and so it was feeling bad twice. It was feeling bad being in that situation, hearing that kind of stuff and then it was feeling bad for not saying anything and for feeling totally silenced and powerless." In many cases, participants felt vulnerable and isolated by what they had experienced and might have acted differently if they had had support from other students. One participant felt she "wouldn't react the same way now" in her exit interview because of, "hearing accounts of people who went through *very* similar situations with the same attending . . . I no longer have this tendency to just compartmentalize it as this isolated incident that was probably just me." However, even when asked in exit interviews to reflect upon how they reacted in such situations, most participants reiterated that they were unsure how they should have acted. Some stated that they wished they had been more vocal at the time, but none identified any systemic channels through which they felt comfortable reporting such experiences.

Moreover, as the year progressed, many participants described a process of desensitization that occurred and felt that they were "much more live and let live" and "impervious" to gendered encounters by the end of the year. When one participant was asked if she had told anyone about the attending who always put his arms around her, she responded, "No. No . . . it's too late in the year. I'm too used to it." This desensitization was evident in participants' exit interviews, in which participants largely dismissed the importance of uncomfortable situations with attendings, a stark contrast from their prior interviews throughout the year. Even when confronted with the discrepancy between earlier interviews where participants were very upset by inappropriate gendered experiences and their seeming acceptance of such behavior at the end of the year, participants reiterated that "it's probably a lot better than it used to be . . . there're going to be bad situations where you feel like you can't say anything without causing problems . . . that's awful and it's unfair and um, you know, I guess just know that it happens to other people too; you're not alone." Another participant who described learning how to ignore egregious behavior over the course of the year and to not "trouble yourself too much" cast her experiences as a learning opportunity: "So like what this highlighted to me, all these experiences was I'm not, this is not the place that I want to be. And I'm not going to be able to change the world so why should I put myself in these situations." Only one participant directly acknowledged her discrepant reaction:

> Just me hearing myself talk and recognizing just the absurdity for how I would so passively let things occur and recognizing how illogical it is for me to let certain things have just passed by . . . hearing how much it sort of contradicts some of the other things that I say that I stand for has allowed me to . . . want to be strong in those situations.

Some participants felt that much of this desensitization was related to fatigue from repeatedly dealing with inappropriate behavior and that they were "just too tired to care."

Toward the end of the year, some participants also identified how gendered encounters were part of the system of medical education. As one participant explained, "This is the way a system has been set up. This is the way things go and you either adapt . . . or you revolutionize and at least at this point in the time I don't think I can revolutionize." Another participant shared similar views:

> I think it's tiresome to always be the person who's speaking up . . . And so at some point I definitely made a decision that one out of ten times I was going to say something and the rest of the times I wasn't and that's at an emotional price. I mean, it takes an emotional toll to *not* speak up when you feel like you should.

For other participants, desensitization was a means by which to actively avoid dealing with inappropriate experiences. As one participant recounted in her last interview, "I don't want to record [gendered experiences] in my mind because I don't want to remember them." Another student who remained optimistic about women finding a way to enter male-dominated fields such as surgery explained, "I just I *have* to believe that because it's the only way I can go through life without going insane."

In contrast to the inappropriate experiences described, participants provided numerous examples of interactions in which they felt either valued as female physicians-in-training or gender-neutral interactions with equal aspirations for both male and female students.

These experiences almost universally involved interactions with female supervisors. Interestingly, all participants at the beginning of the year felt that their female attendings were "really disappointing," or "poor teachers" or "mean." However, by halfway through the year, many participants began describing how the culture of medicine affected the behavior of female physicians. As one participant explained, "I ended up bonding with most [male supervisors] and clashing with all of my female superiors . . . I think it speaks to what women have to go through in order to get to the positions that they're in."

By the end of the year, several participants commented upon how their "expectations of women are *higher*." One participant described being disturbed by a female intern who "wasn't caring and loving at the bedside" but barely noticing when a male resident enacted the same behavior. As she reflected, "It's interesting how the standards are so different and I don't think that that's necessarily fair. *Especially* in a field where women are expected to excel in all these areas that are categorized for quote unquote men only and we're supposed to transition ourselves *into* those expectations."

Despite participants' complicated and evolving relationships with female attendings, participants reported that "gender lines" were "obscured, or more unnoticeable," on all-female and female-led clinical teams. Participants also felt that interactions with female supervisors allowed them to be 'women doctors.' One participant described how she enjoyed working with women because, "I feel like I can be more of myself and there doesn't have to be this attitude of no fear, no emotion." Often, participants' affirmation of their professional identity was intimately tied to their negative experiences with male attendings, as evidenced by four participants who independently used the word "refreshing" to describe their experiences with all-female clinical teams or female attendings. Even on surgery, a "very male-dominated" and "uncomfortable" rotation, gendered experiences were mitigated by all-female teams, as one participant described:

If I wasn't retracting properly, it wasn't like, "come on, pull like a man" it was "come on, pull like a woman!" . . . people acknowledged me like a human being-and so people would ask me questions about my life, and what I was interested in and sort of the reasons for such. It was just a completely different world and one that I really appreciated.

Discussion

Utilizing the differences between student–patient and student–supervisor relationships, we were better able to understand how female medical students enact (and continuously reinterpret) the role of 'woman doctor' and the effect of negative and positive gendered interactions on their professional identity development. In the former relationship, participants were able to confront and respond to inappropriate behavior from male patients and derive positive reinforcement from their connections with female patients. In the latter relationship, participants did not feel equipped to respond to the unprofessional behavior of male supervisors, resulting in feelings of guilt and resignation over time that such events would be a part of their professional identity.

Using Butler's concept of gender identity as a performance (Butler, 1988), it becomes apparent that much of the "hidden curriculum" (Hafferty & Franks, 1994) for third year female medical students lies in understanding and performing what it means to be a "woman doctor," often with conflicting messages. Participants' interpretations of "woman doctor" were constantly shifting based upon their clinical experiences, ranging from adopting stereotypically female attributes to erasing their sexuality and adopting masculine behavior to challenging their own expectations of female doctors. Within the student–male patient relationship, participants were able to identify their own power within the medical hierarchy in terms of medical knowledge and the role of caregiver and address inappropriate behavior. However, participants still felt they had to adapt their identity to inappropriate messages from patients, and tried to "hide their femininity" or appear more "androgynous," thus erasing their gender in order to play the role of physician. In male-dominated clinical teams, participants reported having to adopt a "no

emotion, no fear" attitude, and found it "refreshing" when all-female clinical teams offered a respite from such performance. Numerous inappropriate interactions with male supervisors reaffirmed the female medical student identity as one of a sexualized token, and less valued in the hierarchy of medicine. At other times, participants felt internal and external expectations to adopt a more stereotypical gender role based on views that female students are more nurturing (Clack & Head, 1999; Lempp & Seale, 2006). Patients and peers often expect female physicians to be "more sympathetic, approachable and empathetic," and are disappointed when their encounters deviate from such perceptions (Kilminster et al., 2007). As the author points out, "These attributes were viewed as an optional extra and not integral to male physician's work identity" (Kilminster et al., 2007). And in fact, many of our participants described having similar expectations of female supervisors at the beginning of their third year, and it was only as they underwent their own gendered encounters with patients and supervisors that they were able to objectively appreciate their own unrealistic expectations of female supervisors. Participants' experiences of becoming "women doctors" were not always negative. In appropriate and professional learning environments, usually with female patients and supervisors, participants' enactment of the role of "woman doctor" was seen as a positive, reaffirming experience.

The difficulty, however, with gender performance, as Butler describes, lies in the fact that, "In the theatre, one can say, 'this is just an act,' and de-realize the act, make acting into something quite distinct from what is real . . . on the street or in the bus, there is no presumption that the act is distinct from a reality; the disquieting effect of the act is that there are no conventions that facilitate making this separation," (Butler, 1988, p. 527). Such blurring of reality was echoed in Hinze's analysis of sub-specialty hierarchies. As one female surgeon explained, "I didn't want to be a man. I didn't want to be like real tough and have to chew people out and play hardball with them, that wasn't the goal . . . [crying harder now] You know, if this is what, you know, if everyone hates working with me then it wasn't worth it at all. Toughness, being macho, having balls, suffering," (Hinze, 1999, p. 230). As the author concluded, "for women to survive in the highest prestige specialty and sub-specialties asks them to 'exchange major aspects of their gender identity for a masculine version without prescribing a similar 'degendering' process for men,'" (Hinze, 1999, p. 233). Such descriptions parallel the experiences of our participants who described the "emotional toll" and guilt of enacting institutionally prescribed gendered identities. Ironically, despite stating repeatedly in exit interviews that they would advocate "just dealing with it" or that they were "too used to it," when asked what advice they had for incoming female medical students participants universally advocated that they "be themselves."

Perhaps the most salient effect of gendered experiences on participants' professional identity was the progressive desensitization toward inappropriate behavior that occurred throughout the year. Even when participants were confronted with individual experiences that they had found distressing earlier in the year, they tended to minimize their importance in their exit interviews, stating that they were "just too tired to care" or "impervious to [gendered situations]." When asked to explain such contradictions, most participants recognized the prevalence of gendered encounters but advocated for "just dealing with it" and resigned themselves to the fact that "they're going to be bad situations." Such responses exemplify a stark learning point that was universally internalized by all of our participants—that medicine itself is gendered and inappropriate encounters would continue to be a part of their medical training.

Importantly, the messages of tolerating inappropriate behavior voiced in the exit interviews closely mirrored teachings by senior female residents and attendings who advised female students to "just deal with it." Through the course of their third year education, participants experienced the contradictory roles of female supervisors, and came to their own realizations of what it means to be a female attending. The adoption of cultural norms expressed by female supervisors in their exit interviews can thus be seen as simply another manifestation of gender performance. Prior qualitative studies have shown that female students are often advocates of just "sucking it up" (Wear et al., 2007). Although previous studies have documented how medical students are acculturated over time (Hafferty & Franks, 1994), and that higher rates of gender discrimination have been reported during the clinical years of medical education (Baldwin, Daugherty, & Eckenfels, 1991; Richman et al., 1992), our study adds to the existing literature by characterizing how female students systematically learn to tolerate gender discrimination through the course of their medical education.

The above findings should be considered in the context of some important limitations. This study was conducted with 12 participants of the same graduating class at a single, private, New England medical school because we purposefully wanted all study participants to have been exposed to the identical formal curriculum and classroom environments. Still, we purposefully sampled a diverse group of students representing a variety of backgrounds, ages, and race/ethnicities. We also employed rigorous qualitative methods such as consistent use of a structured code sheet, audiotaped interviews, transcript verification, and the use of a single interviewer. No participants were lost to follow-up, and the longitudinal nature of the study allowed us to capture experiences over multiple points in time. In addition, the utilization of a mixed gender, racial and hierarchical research team (involving a medical student, fellow and faculty from different specialties, and socio-demographic groups) enhanced the diversity of perspectives in the analytic process. Future work is needed to include the perspective of male medical students.

Our findings have several important implications for research and policy related to gender discrimination in medical education. Acculturation to inappropriate behavior is influenced by the institutional culture and structures in place to address gendered experiences. Given that the majority of students never report experiences of gender discrimination, the lack of institutional response experienced by our participants to reported complaints likely will contribute to future non-reporting (Komaromy, Bindman, Haber, & Sande, 1993; Wear et al., 2007).

Participants in our study identified a number of barriers to reporting gendered experiences, including the incident being not serious enough, the transient nature of clinical clerkships, affect of reporting on future career, and lack of institutional response, consistent with previous studies (Komaromy et al., 1993; Wear et al., 2007). The differential participant response to inappropriate student–patient and student–supervisor also underscores the continued hierarchy and power dynamics within medicine. Participants repeatedly did not feel that they had adequate power to challenge inappropriate supervisor behavior.

Notably, none of the participants referred to the instances described as "sexual harassment" although many situations would likely be appropriately termed as such, a phenomenon that has been described in similar populations previously (Wear et al., 2007). Institutions that explicitly seek reports of "sexual harassment" may be missing the true spectrum of inappropriate gendered behavior. Additionally, our findings that female students become progressively acculturated over time and deny the effect of previous gendered experiences suggest that surveys conducted at the end of medical school may grossly underestimate the true prevalence of gender discrimination amongst medical students.

Comments by our participants regarding the effect of gendered experiences on sub-specialty choice suggest that in addition to guiding their professional identities, such experiences may also influence future career choices as physicians. Such preliminary findings are consistent with studies with female faculty illustrating women in medicine continue to experience lower rates of job-satisfaction, inequitable remuneration, and higher rates of sexual harassment (SH) and gender discrimination (GD) compared with their male peers (Bickel, 1997; Carr et al., 2000; Corbie-Smith, Frank, Nickens, & Elon, 1999; Nonnemaker, 2000). Some studies have also suggested that experiences of gender discrimination have an effect on the specialty choices of female medical students (Lambert & Holmboe, 2005; Stratton et al., 2005). This is an increasingly salient issue for medical education in an era with increasing numbers of female medical school graduates.

Conclusion

Third year female medical students are educated on what it means to be a woman doctor throughout the course of their third year through student–patient and student–physician relationships. Positive and negative experiences value and devalue, respectively, their identities as women doctors. Female medical students most commonly use a strategy of denial and minimization in the face of these negative experiences. They become

rapidly acculturated to inappropriate experiences over the course of their third year clinical clerkships, and come to emulate their female supervisors in resigning themselves to the inevitability of negative gendered experiences in their clinical training. Perhaps what is most distressing is such acculturation is actively advocated by superiors and promoted by the institutional silence surrounding issues of gender. The resultant desensitization and fatigue have implications not only for students' identities as female physicians, but also for specialty choices and issues of future physician workforce.

Acknowledgments

The authors received funding from the Yale University School of Medicine Office of Student Research and the Yale University School of Medicine Office of Education.

References

Babaria, P., Abedin, S., & Nunez-Smith, M. (2009). The effect of gender on the clinical clerkship experiences of female medical students: results from a qualitative study. *Academic Medicine, 84*(7), 859–866.

Baldwin, D. C., Jr., Daugherty, S. R., & Eckenfels, E. J. (1991). Student perceptions of mistreatment and harassment during medical school. A survey of ten United States schools. *Western Journal of Medicine, 155*(2), 140–145.

Barzansky, B., & Etzel, S. I. (2008). Medical schools in the United States, 2007–2008. *Journal of the American Medical Association, 300*(10), 1221–1227.

Beagan, B. L. (2000). Neutralizing differences: producing neutral doctors for (almost) neutral patients. *Social Science & Medicine, 51*(8), 1253–1265.

Becker, H., Geer, B., Hughes, E., & Strauss, A. (1961). *Boys in White: Medical student culture.* Chicago: University of Chicago Press.

Bickel, J. (1997). Gender stereotypes and misconceptions: unresolved issues in physicians' professional development. *Journal of the American Medical Association, 277*(17), 1405–1407.

Blanch, D. C., Hall, J. A., Roter, D. L., & Frankel, R. M. (2008). Medical student gender and issues of confidence. *Patient Education and Counseling, 72*(3), 374–381.

Bradley, E. H., Curry, L. A., & Devers, K. J. (2007). Qualitative data analysis for health services research:

developing taxonomy, themes, and theory. *Health Services Research, 42*(4), 1758–1772.

Butler, J. (1988). Performative acts and gender constitution: an essay in phenomenology and feminist theory. *Theatre Journal, 40*(4), 519–531.

Carr, P. L., Ash, A. S., Friedman, R. H., Szalacha, L., Barnett, R. C., Palepu, A., et al. (2000). Faculty perceptions of gender discrimination and sexual harassment in academic medicine. *Annals of Internal Medicine, 132*(11), 889–896.

Clack, G. B., & Head, J. O. (1999). Gender differences in medical graduates' assessment of their personal attributes. *Medical Education, 33*(2), 101–105.

Conrad, P. (1988). Learning to doctor: reflections on recent accounts of the medical school years. *Journal of Health and Social Behavior, 29*(4), 323–332.

Corbie-Smith, G., Frank, E., Nickens, H. W., & Elon, L. (1999). Prevalences and correlates of ethnic harassment in the U.S. Women Physicians' Health Study. *Academic Medicine, 74*(6), 695–701.

Daugherty, S. R., Baldwin, D. C., Jr., & Rowley, B. D. (1998). Learning, satisfaction, and mistreatment during medical internship: a national survey of working conditions. *Journal of the American Medical Association, 279*(15), 1194–1199.

Delvecchio Good, M.-J. (1998). *American medicine: The quest for competence.* Berkeley: University of California Press.

Dyrbye, L. N., Thomas, M. R., Harper, W., Massie, F. S., Jr., Power, D. V., Eacker, A., et al. (2009). The learning environment and medical student burnout: a multi-centre study. *Medical Education, 43*(3), 274–282.

Dyrbye, L. N., Thomas, M. R., & Shanafelt, T. D. (2006). Systematic review of depression, anxiety and other indicators of psychological distress among U.S. and Canadian medical students. *Academic Medicine, 81*(4), 354–373.

Edwards, R. (1990). Connecting method and epistemology–a white woman interviewing Black women. *Women's Studies International Forum, 13*(5), 477– 490.

Ekstein, R., & Wallerstein, R. S. (1958). *The teaching and learning of psychotherapy.* New York: International Universities Press.

Glaser, B., & Strauss, A. (1967). *The discovery of grounded theory: Strategies for qualitative research.* Chicago: Aldine Publishing.

Gude, T., Vaglum, P., Tyssen, R., Ekeberg, O., Hem, E., Rovik, J. O., et al. (2005). Identification with the role of doctor at the end of medical school: a nationwide longitudinal study. *Medical Education, 39*(1), 66–74.

Hafferty, F. W., & Franks, R. (1994). The hidden curriculum, ethics teaching, and the structure of medical education. *Academic Medicine, 69*(11), 861–871.

Haidet, P., Hatem, D. S., Fecile, M. L., Stein, H. F., Haley, H. L., Kimmel, B., et al. (2008). The role of relationships in the professional formation of physicians: case report and illustration of an elicitation technique. *Patient Education and Counseling, 72*(3), 382–387.

Hinze, S. (1999). Gender and the body of medicine or at least some body parts: (re) constructing the prestige hierarchy of medical specialties. *Sociological Quarterly, 40*(2), 217–239.

Houry, D., Shockley, L. W., & Markovchick, V. (2000). Wellness issues and the emergency medicine resident. *Annals of Emergency Medicine, 35*(4), 394–397.

Karnieli-Miller, O., Vu, T. R., Holtman, M. C., Clyman, S. G., & Inui, T. S. (2010). Medical students' professionalism narratives: a window on the informal and hidden curriculum. *Academic Medicine, 85*(1), 124–133.

Kilminster, S., Downes, J., Gough, B., Murdoch-Eaton, D., & Roberts, T. (2007). Women in medicine–is there a problem? A literature review of the changing gender composition, structures and occupational cultures in medicine. *Medical Education, 41*(1), 39–49.

Komaromy, M., Bindman, A. B., Haber, R. J., & Sande, M. A. (1993). Sexual harassment in medical training. *The New England Journal of Medicine, 328*(5), 322–326.

Lambert, E. M., & Holmboe, E. S. (2005). The relationship between specialty choice and gender of U.S. medical students, 1990–2003. *Academic Medicine, 80*(9), 797–802.

Lempp, H., & Seale, C. (2006). Medical students' perceptions in relation to ethnicity and gender: a qualitative study. *BMC Medical Education, 6,* 17.

Miles, M. B., & Huberman, A. M. (1994). *Qualitative data analysis: An expanded sourcebook.* Thousand Oaks: Sage Publications.

Morantz-Sanchez, R. M. (2000). *Sympathy & science: Women physicians in American medicine.* UNC Press Books.

Murray, S. A., Kendall, M., Carduff, E., Worth, A., Harris, F. M., Lloyd, A., et al. (2009). Use of serial qualitative interviews to understand patients' evolving experiences and needs. *British Medical Journal, 339,* b3702.

Nonnemaker, L. (2000). Women physicians in academic medicine: new insights from cohort studies. *The New England Journal of Medicine, 342*(6), 399–405.

Nora, L. M., McLaughlin, M. A., Fosson, S. E., Stratton, T. D., Murphy-Spencer, A., Fincher, R. M., et al. (2002).

Gender discrimination and sexual harassment in medical education: perspectives gained by a 14-school study. *Academic Medicine, 77*(12 Pt 1), 1226–1234.

Patton, M. Q. (2002). *Qualitative research & evaluation methods.* Thousand Oaks, Calif.: Sage Publications.

Richman, J. A., Flaherty, J. A., Rospenda, K. M., & Christensen, M. L. (1992). Mental health consequences and correlates of reported medical student abuse. *Journal of the American Medical Association, 267*(5), 692–694.

Shapiro, M. (1987). *Getting doctored: Critical reflections on becoming a physician.* Toronto, Ontario: Between The Lines.

Sheehan, K. H., Sheehan, D. V., White, K., Leibowitz, A., & Baldwin, D. C., Jr. (1990). A pilot study of medical student 'abuse'. Student perceptions of mistreatment and misconduct in medical school. *Journal of the American Medical Association, 263*(4), 533–537.

Stratton, T. D., McLaughlin, M. A., Witte, F. M., Fosson, S. E., & Nora, L. M. (2005). Does students' exposure to gender discrimination and sexual harassment in medical school affect specialty choice and residency program selection? *Academic Medicine, 80*(4), 400–408.

Wear, D., & Aultman, J. (2005). Sexual harassment in academic medicine: persistence, non-reporting, and institutional response. *Medical Education Online, 10,* 1–11.

Wear, D., Aultman, J., & Borges, N. (2007). Retheorizing sexual harassment in medical education: women students' perceptions at five US medical schools. *Teaching and Learning in Medicine, 19*(1), 20–29.

Whittle, S. R., & Eaton, D. G. (2001). Attitudes towards transferable skills in medical undergraduates. *Medical Education, 35*(2), 148–153.

Wilde, V. (1992). Controversial hypotheses on the relationship between researcher and informant in qualitative research. *Journal of Advanced Nursing, 17*(2), 234–242.

The Little Brown Woman: Gender Discrimination in American Medicine

by Wasudha Bhatt

University of Texas at Austin

Drawing on 121 in-depth interviews with first- and second-generation women and men physicians of Indian origin in the U.S. Southwest, I examine the incidence and nature of gender-based discrimination in American medicine. I focus on two aspects: (1) gender discrimination by employers and colleagues against women physicians of Indian origin and (2) the interaction of gender discrimination with race in the professional lives of first- and second-generation physicians. U.S. healthcare has become increasingly dependent on immigrants, in particular women physicians, from the developing world. I document the significant impact gender and race can have in molding the professional trajectories of Indian women physicians. The experiences of these physicians help clarify the interaction of skilled migrant workers with racial/ethnic and gender relations in U.S. workplaces.

Keywords: race; class; gender; race/ethnicity; migration

There is almost a racial hierarchy that exists. If for the same job there are four-five options available, and it's not just the race, it's also gender. So if there is a white male available, that will always be the number one choice.

So if you have to go and make a rank order list, in general white male gets preference, and then black male second, then white female, then Indian male, then black females, and then everybody else. And Indian female comes, really, at the bottom.

And sometimes equal to or even below the Hispanic. This is just the way they work. And it does not matter whether the person making decision up top necessarily is black or white or Indian. (Piya Jaiswal, first-generation woman)

This study examines how race/ethnicity, gender, and nationality shape the experience of Indian physicians in the United States, and how in the environments of racially different foreign-born medical professionals, gendered and racial dynamics create complex conditions of inequality and disadvantage for women of color. I explore how workplaces are gendered, but also racialized. I further consider how discrimination based on nationality and country of medical training impacts these experiences.

Gender constitutes "an emergent feature of social situations: both as an outcome of and a rationale for various social arrangements and as a means of legitimating one of the most fundamental divisions of society," often tailoring the limits and the choices of women in the United States (West and Zimmerman 1987, 126). A gendered hierarchy that privileges hegemonic masculinity and subordinates or excludes women is embedded within the assumptions and practices that comprise most contemporary work organizations (Acker 1990). This is achieved by the reproduction of complex inequalities within organizations through gendered relations at work that pattern "advantage and disadvantage, exploitation and control, meaning and identity" in terms of a distinction between men and women (Acker 1990, 146). In fact, professional women of color are at an added disadvantage, being differentially situated in workplaces (Crenshaw 1991). They often find themselves as the sole representative of their demographic group, and more vulnerable to stereotyping because of their extreme visibility as tokens (Browne and Misra 2003; Kanter 1977).

The differential treatment they receive because of their gender and race culminates in second-class citizenship for them (Collins 2001), multiplying the disadvantages of race and gender (Browne and Misra 2003; King 1989). Particularly for first-generation women, the social categories of race and gender merge with nationality to create intersecting systems of oppression that mutually constitute, maintain, and transform each other rather than functioning as independent structures of inequality. This results in a matrix of domination that interlocks privilege and disadvantage (Collins 2000), playing a critical role in shaping the experiences of women physicians of Indian origin in the United States.

Drawing on more than 100 interviews with Indian physicians—both first- and second-generation—as well as interviews with some non-Indian administrators, I explore how gender, race, and nationality intersect in the experiences and perceptions of Indian physicians in the United States. This allows me to paint a rich portrait of how Indian women physicians continue to experience discrimination in the United States in the twenty-first century.

Literature Review

Acker (2006) describes inequality in organizations as differential access between men and women in power in their control over goals, available resources, and their outcome. Organizational practices, in turn, reinforce the segregation of work by gender, widen status and income disparity between men and women, and replicate cultural stereotypes of gender. Gender stereotypes portray women as less competent and better at less valued communal tasks when compared to men, who are viewed as status worthy, instrumental, and agentic. In professional fields that have been culturally perceived as masculine, like management, defense, or medicine, men are evaluated more favorably than women (Ridgeway and Correll 2004). Therefore, even when women perform comparably to men, men are regarded as being more capable at a given task than women, who may have to accomplish more than men to be rated equally (Correll 2004).

For instance, women-dominated occupations and whole subsections of U.S. medicine with a high rate of female physicians have less standing in terms of income, prestige, and career opportunities (Heath 2004). Research shows that women in academic medicine earn less than men with similar productivity (Ash et al. 2004). Women are also passed over in rank advancements (Dobson 1997). The glass ceiling in U.S. academic medicine is often seen as hindering the advancement of women into leadership positions despite any tangible barriers (Carnes, Morrissey, and Geller 2008). The present academic structure perceives women as less competitive and with fewer leadership abilities, underrepresenting women in positions of management and leadership (Eagly and Karau 2002).

Academic medicine in particular mirrors the dichotomy between the numerical strength of women in the field versus their underrepresentation in leadership positions and among tenured faculty. Studies show how systematic disadvantages, like the absence of effective mentorship, harsh and sexist work environments, and inadequate job opportunities, limit the career advancement of women in U.S. academic medicine (Carnes, Morrissey, and Geller 2008; Carr et al. 2003). Besides, women are more apt to engage in "institutional housekeeping" and be educators and clinicians instead of being on research-based faculty tracks that lead to management positions (Bird, Litt, and Wang 2004). For instance, in 2005 only 11 percent of department chairs, 15 percent of full professors, and 32 percent of U.S. medical school faculty were women; in academic surgery, women comprised only 2 percent of department chairs, 6 percent of full professors, and 16 percent of the faculty (Kass, Souba, and Thorndyke 2006, 179). Moreover, women comprise 10 percent or fewer of department chairs in psychiatry and pediatrics, fields in which women have constituted at least 50 percent of those workforces for the past two decades (Carnes, Morrissey, and Geller 2008, 6). Women headed only 20 percent of the National Institutes of Health (NIH) in 2006, receiving lesser budget increases than units headed by men (Carnes, Morrissey, and Geller 2008, 6). Even when women attain management positions, research shows that they are closely scrutinized (Bendl and Schmidt 2010). But given the already troubled waters for women physicians in the United States, there is strangely little research investigating how women physicians from ethnic minorities fare in an essentially white male–dominated medical environment.

With race and gender as a foundation for exclusion or for hiring still persisting in many organizations (Acker 2006), gender and racial inequalities are often re-created by interaction practices that are unspoken, subtle, and difficult to document (Acker 2006). Collins (2001) shows that racial/ethnic minority groups encounter a politics of containment, ridden with exploitation of less powerful racial groups for the benefit of more powerful racial groups (Collins 2001). Existing intersectional research on gender and race shows that ethnic minority women unlike their white female counterparts contend additional burdens of gender and race, their achievements are undervalued, and they are assigned less responsibility than they can handle (García-López 2008). Women of color report higher occurrences of being denied opportunities for advancement than did white women (Shrier et al. 2007). Earning differentials still persist across ethnic groups even after controlling for other factors like level of education, region, and occupation (Kim and Sakamoto 2010). Structural arrangements following a racial hierarchy further provide social and economic advantages to whites by offering them better opportunities in terms of "enhanced college admissions, favored job interviews, improved career opportunities, and higher labor market rewards" (Kim and Sakamoto 2010, 935), whereas Asian Americans, despite their professional attainments in the United States, are required to be more educated to receive a similar income to whites (Waters and Eschbach 1995).

Research also shows that Asians are unable to achieve full equality in the U.S. labor market in lieu of fewer economic returns for their level of education when compared to their white counterparts and the glass ceiling that accounts for their absence in top executive positions despite their considerable numbers in such occupations (Espiritu 1997; Kibria 1998; Purkayastha 2005). Despite controlling for individual-level characteristics, substantial differences in the earnings between Asian Indian women and white women persist (Stone, Purkayastha, and Berdahl 2006). Purkayastha (2005) in her research shows that experiences of racialization make even second-generation South Asian Americans who are economically incorporated into U.S. mainstream view themselves as distinct from white Americans and other Asian American groups. More so, when accompanied by discrimination and prejudice, their physical features act as a barrier at the workplace (Portes and Zhou 1993). In fact, Murti (2012) finds that Indian male physicians find greater social acceptance in public on revealing their occupational status, whereas Indian female physicians become more intimidating socially and risk greater social marginalization for seizing high social status reserved for white men.

Gender and racial discrimination thus act as a double bind for minority women in medicine, who, when compared to men, report higher levels of discrimination (Carr et al. 2007). Gray, Gallagher, and Masters (1996) report substantial differences in perceptions for women and minority graduates compared to white male graduates regarding experiences at medical school and the professional medical environment in the United States. Minority faculty members report lower levels of satisfaction (Palepu et al. 2000) and are more likely to leave their academic careers (Hadley et al. 1992). This dissatisfaction can be traced to lower returns on education for first-generation Indians, who are paid well but less than whites in medical and other professions in the United States (Barringer and Kassebaum 1989), and a lower rate of promotion of minority faculties compared to their white counterparts in medicine (Fang et al. 2000; Palepu et al. 1998).

Labor market opportunities and incorporation are further impacted by nationality and citizenship status along with gender, race, and ethnicity (Browne and Misra 2003). However, the interlinked impact of gender, race, and nationality in shaping the career trajectories of Asian American women doctors has largely remained unexamined (Xu and Leffler 1992). Purkayastha (2005) argues that compared to their counterparts with credentials from the developed world, immigrants from former colonies are often held back. Foreign medical degrees act as a "major liability," enhancing the "difficulty" of "breaking in" even for women who have better access to networks of Indian physicians (Purkayastha 2005, 188). These women also encounter "subtle forms of gender and race marginalization" (Purkayastha 2005, 191). In fact, first-generation immigrant women from ethnic minorities face a triple bind in American medicine, with the addition of bias against foreign medical graduates.

Research shows that foreign medical graduates who are largely first-generation immigrants face added prejudice and are discriminated against very or somewhat significantly (Coombs and King 2005), either overtly or in subtle ways, on the basis of their country of origin, xenophobia, and chauvinistic attitudes (Desbiens and Vidaillet 2010). In fact Coombs and King (2005) in their survey of 445 licensed physicians in Massachusetts found more than 60 percent of their respondents to have reported that discrimination against foreign medical graduates was very or somewhat significant. While 44 percent of U.S. medical graduates reported that discrimination against foreign medical graduates in

their present organization was significant. Moreover, there are relatively fewer foreign medical graduates than American graduates in competitive, financially lucrative specialties (Brotherton and Etzel 2010; Ebell 2008). Surgery in particular is infamous for discriminating against foreign medical graduates, with some surgical directors acknowledging external pressure to rank a U.S. medical graduate over a better-qualified foreign medical graduate (Desbiens and Vidaillet 2010).

Focusing on any one category ignores the internal divisions of races along gender and nationality lines, and precludes an understanding of how these categories have a complex, mutually reinforcing or contradicting interaction. I focus on discrimination by race and gender, along with nationality, which has introduced another facet of discrimination through a new visa category (H-1B and J-1)[1] for high-skilled nonimmigrant (temporary) workers in the United States. I argue that workspaces of Indian physicians in the United States are significant social spaces for the perpetuation of gendered, racialized, and ethnicized norms. My primary research question is "How does gender discrimination in U.S. medical workplaces manifest itself in the professional lives of women physicians of Indian origin?" To explore this, I focus on (1) gender discrimination by employers and colleagues against women physicians of Indian origin and (2) how gender discrimination interacts with race and manifests itself in the professional lives of first- and second-generation physicians. Lastly, I explain how analyzing these physicians' experiences can help us understand the operation of gender and race in the medical workplace in new and important ways.

Method

The racial experiences of Indian physicians in the United States have been studied in a few works (Sethi 2003), and limited primarily to third-person narratives, while there is very limited research on the experiences of Indian women physicians in U.S. workplaces (Murti 2012). My study draws extensively on in-depth interviews addressing the general and specific attitudes of Indian physicians and some administrators toward gender and racial discrimination in the workplace. I used semi-structured interviews,[2] where "two individuals come together to try to create meaning about a particular topic" (Esterberg 2002).

I identified 108 physicians, 43 women and 65 men,[3] whom I interviewed in the summer and fall of 2009 and 2010.[4] Thirteen of these 108 physicians were reinterviewed in 2010,[5] leading to a total of 121 interviews with 108 physicians. Of the total sample size, 55 interviews were carried out with first-generation Indian physicians, 59 with second-generation Indian physicians, and seven with senior faculty in higher administrative positions.[6] The criteria of eligibility for the participants included self-identifying as physicians of Indian origin, being over the age of 18, and engaged in training (residency or fellowship) or employed at the time of the interview. To be categorized as second-generation, participating physicians had to have been born in the United States and have one or two immigrant parents, or have migrated to the United States when they were 10 years old or younger.[7]

I conducted my research in a large metropolitan area housing a major biomedical research center, making it a common location for Indian physicians in U.S. Southwest. I established my initial round of participants using a snowball sampling technique by contacting Indian physicians employed or in training, through emails listed on the medical center department websites. Once I established my initial round of participants, I requested referrals to other physicians who might be interested in participating in this study, indicating that I was interested in how Indian physicians experience gender and race relations in the workplace, and racial and gender discrimination, if any, in particular.

Being a first-generation Indian woman, I was unsure if I would be able to inspire the trust needed of second-generation physicians to be candid about their emotions, dilemmas, and fears about discrimination in and out of American medicine. Yet, I found the second-generation physicians to be much more enthusiastic, articulate, and forthcoming participants. However, I did face greater difficulty in securing interviews with first-generation Indians vis-à-vis their second-generation counterparts, which might have less to do with my identity and more to do with their unwillingness "to face the reality of racism," as Ritika, a first-generation female, put it.

After obtaining the consent of my research participants I audio-recorded each interview. I transcribed every interview verbatim myself. Finally, I coded each of the interviews by organizing all the material thematically and cross-listing pieces that were relevant to more than one area. Given the sensitivity of the subject, and the extent to which the physicians were self-selected, I was able to interview only women and men who were forthcoming about revealing how they experience race and gender relations at work. I have attempted to portray their experiences in this research with the same sincerity and honesty. Table 1 summarizes the characteristics of physicians of Indian origin enrolled in the study.

The following sections address findings of the three major issues that emerged in my interviews.

Gender Discrimination in American Medicine

A majority of the Indian women physicians who were interviewed for this research experienced gender-based discrimination at all levels in the medical workplace—as residents and faculty, and in promotions to positions of power.[8] Most women physicians reported experiencing gender-based discrimination (see Table 2), with almost one-third reporting "absolute" or "definite" bias against women physicians who were in positions of power. Several examples of these reports are given in this section to illustrate and elaborate on these cases.

Gender discrimination was visible even in the recruitment process, when women were asked questions about their families unlike their male colleagues, despite such questions being illegal. Shweta, a second-generation female, noting that the same was not true for her male colleagues, recounts about her residency interviews:

> I was asked whether I was single, whether I was seeing somebody, whether or not I was serious or married, and if there was any possibility of me having children. These are personal. And in fact the ACGME [Accreditation Council for Graduate Medical Education], ERAS [Electronic Residency Application Service], and all of those institutions will flat out tell you these are illegal questions that are not supposed to be asked during an interview.

The women in my sample also reported that women residents were reprimanded more severely than men residents for the same mistakes.

Table 1. Characteristics of Physicians of Indian Origin Enrolled in the Study

	First-Generation	1.5-Generation[a]	Second-Generation
	(*n = 50*)	(*n = 21*)	(*n = 30*)
Age group, n (%)			
18-30 years	9 (18)	6 (29)	10 (33)
31-40 years	21 (42)	11 (52)	18 (60)
>40 years	20 (40)	4 (19)	2 (7)
Men, n (%)	33 (66)	10 (48)	19 (63)
Marital status, n (%)			
Single	2 (4)	5 (24)	7 (23)
Married	46 (92)	14 (67)	23 (77)
Divorced	1 (2)	2 (10)	0 (0)
Widowed	1 (2)	0 (0)	0 (0)
Duration of stay in the U.S., n (%)			
<5 years	3 (6)	–	–
5-10 years	13 (26)	–	–
11-20 years	28 (56)	–	–
20 years	6 (12)	–	–
Citizenship/visa status at the time of immigration, n (%)			
B-1	3 (6)	–	–
F-1	10 (20)	–	–
J-1	12 (24)	–	–
H-1B	13 (26)	–	–
Dependent (H-4, J-2)	8 (16)	–	–
Permanent resident	4 (8)	–	–
Specialty, n (%)			
Dermatology	–	1 (5)	–
Family medicine	1 (2)	–	–
Internal medicine	19 (38)	6 (29)	14 (47)
Neurology	3 (6)	–	1 (3)
Pathology	4 (8)	1 (5)	1 (3)
Pediatrics	8 (16)	7 (33)	7 (23)
Physical medicine and rehabilitation	–	2 (10)	–
Psychiatry	10 (20)	2 (10)	4 (13)
Radiology	1 (2)	–	–
Surgical specialties	4 (8)	2 (10)	4 (13)
Current professional status, n (%)			
In training[b]	15 (30)	6 (29)	10 (33)
Academic practice[c]	33 (66)	15 (71)	19 (63)
Private practice	2 (4)	–	1 (3)

[a] Immigrants who immigrated at a young age and underwent most of their childhood and adolescent socialization in the United States.
[b] Residents and fellows in training at a university hospital setting.
[c] Academic medical faculty at a university hospital setting.

Both men and women physicians argued that competitive procedure-oriented specialties and subspecialties like general surgery and orthopedics were fields where women physicians faced discrimination. Women noted that both attending physicians and fellow colleagues tried to steer women away from opting for these specialties, suggesting that probable family commitments might impede them from committing the requisite time in these subfields. Women physicians instead reported being steered more towards "less time and labor-intensive specialties" like psychiatry, pediatrics, and family medicine. These branches were also both less remunerative and less competitive. Women residents perceived discrimination from women attending physicians and the nursing staff. Tanuja felt that because women attendings "had a hard time" in medicine and "had more hoops to jump through" they took out their "frustration" on their female residents.

Question	Percentage of Women Responding "Yes"	Percentage of Men Responding "Yes"
Being a woman physician, do you feel that you have to overcome extra hurdles at work?	78	N/A
Is there a gender bias in positions of power?	75	74
There is "absolute" or "definite" bias against women physicians in positions of power	33	14
Is there a racial bias in positions of power?	63	74
Is there bias against foreign medical graduates in the United States?	100	97
Is the bias against foreign medical graduates unjustified?	70	68

Table 2 Physicians in Sample Reporting Discrimination

Women also perceived greater challenges for women in being promoted in academic medicine. Lata, a second-generation female, revealed, "Men much more often get promoted than women and get promoted to higher positions more quickly than women. ... I feel like their [men's] accomplishments get recognized more often." When it came to hiring women in leadership positions or promoting them to positions of power, a number of first- (Hemant, David) and second-generation (Mahesh) men faculty voiced similar points to Shweta, who voiced:

> it's kind of an old boys club [in medicine], so if you are a white Caucasian male it's easier for you than if you are a woman or of color. ... I mean, you can look at our institution, the head of medicine has been a male for years, I don't think there's ever been a female head of medicine.

Previous research has shown that women in traditionally male professions, like medicine, face stereotyping and negative judgments (Williams 1992). Successful women in these jobs may face a double-bind, as they are viewed as "hostile" (Heilman 2001, 667-68) and less "nurturing" (Benard and Correll 2010, 620). Jennifer, a white senior faculty member, revealed that "if a woman is really strong, then people are kind of angry and bitter about that, but if a man is really strong, then he is viewed as a strong leader. ... I think that sort of perception that a woman is a man-hater, or they use that phrase 'ball-buster.'" These adverse reactions augment the challenges that women in managerial positions face and also perpetuate the glass ceilings they encounter (Ridgeway and Correll 2004). Sheila, a first-generation female, similarly commented:

> One of my attendings [an African American female] in residency told me, "You have to wear balls around your neck. You have to think like a man, and you have to act like a man, otherwise you can't survive in academics or anywhere."

Moreover, Shaurya, a first-generation man, argued:

> Women physicians [in positions of power] have a harder time than male physicians. ... [A] lot of women physicians feel like they need to work twice as hard than [*sic*] their male counterparts to get the same respect. And on the same side, if a male physician is abrasive and authoritative, people are kind of more scared of him and they will get more respect than if the female is the same way and the female will be regarded more as just a bitch.

Overall, both men and women in my sample reflected their perceptions that women physicians faced significant challenges in being seen as leaders or being promoted to upper ranks.

For women physicians, perceptions of possible motherhood, and motherhood itself, exacerbated their discriminatory experiences in the workplace at all levels of their medical training and career (Duffy 2007; Glauber 2007). Status-based discrimination by employers stereotype mothers as "less competent and committed to paid work than non-mothers" (Benard and Correll 2010), and decreases their chances of getting training, winning promotions, or engaging in networking when they work part time (Dick and Hyde 2006; Lawrence and Corwin 2003).

These experiences are reflected in medical training, as well as in jobs and opportunities for promotion. For example, Shweta recollected:

> There was one [Indian] girl who was pregnant when she started internship with us. ... She had kind of planned it so that her vacation would be right around the time of delivery anyway, but they [faculty and administration] were like, "Why can't you just get induced 'cause you are so close? That way you won't mess up the call schedule or any of that other stuff."

Priyanka, a second-generation female, similarly felt that women are "shamed for having a baby [in residency] ... it's really a very hostile environment to try to have a baby ... it's awful." Harish, a second-generation male, senior male faculty in dermatology, revealed:

> And what I see is that many of them [women faculty] are moms, so if they miss a few things, then instead of giving them support ... what they do is they penalize them for that, by not giving them certain rank advancements or pay and things like that ... we only have now two women left on all of our faculty ... which is bad.

Similarly, Shaurya, a first-generation man noted, "I think there's more of a stigma of being a woman, there's a stigma of taking time off to have babies." Lindsay, a white senior faculty in administration, noted that women physicians who "get on the mommy track ... lose years of recruitment of seniority or on your promotion track." With pervasive reservations and discouragement against motherhood in the medical environment, mothers who work part time faced even lower wages and fewer chances of promotions in the workplace.

Overall, both women and men physicians in my sample report fairly substantial gender discrimination from supervisors and coworkers in the workplace. This discrimination shapes each step of their careers, from applying for residencies, to jobs, to promotions. A part of this discrimination seems focused around the potential for motherhood to derail or slow women's career progress. However, a large part of this discrimination as my findings reveal, is centered on the assumption that women are inherently less capable and hard working than men, and are more "obsessive" about details, hence more suitable for secretarial jobs than leadership positions in academic medicine.

Gender, Race, and Foreign Medical Graduates

> Whenever I start a new job, or when I was training for my residency and fellowship, it's a man's profession. So number one, being a female you have to jump through extra hoops to establish yourself. And then, when you look like me and when you talk like me you stand out ... if you are a new member of the team nobody is going to accept you ... I have to prove myself, right? I have to prove that I am capable of taking care of the 20 patients that I am supposed to take care of. So when you are a female

physician, and then you are a female "not Caucasian," then you are definitely made to prove yourself twice over, before they accept you as one of them. (Deepti, first-generation female)

Gender, when combined with race, acted as a "double hit" for Indian women physicians in the workplace. The additional influence of foreign medical graduate bias in American medicine cumulates in a "triple bind" for first-generation Indian women physicians. All of the women respondents in this study perceived bias against foreign medical graduates in the United States (see Table 2). Jennifer, a white senior administrative faculty, acknowledged, "There is a lot of prejudice against people who trained elsewhere [in South Asia and Africa, unlike foreign graduates who trained in England or other Western European countries]." She explained, "Anytime somebody hears an accent you are immediately, I think, going to be treated differently. I think you are treated with less respect . . . people expect you not to be very good and they are surprised if you are . . . most people by nature are pretty xenophobic, unfortunately." Likewise, Surbhi, a second-generation female, said, "Even in foreign medical graduates there is a different classification. So if you are from Canada or if you are from Europe you are considered okay on some level, but then if you are from Asia, and I don't know why that bias is there."

Ameena, a second-generation female, explained how, in her residency training program (internal medicine), the people who are selected as being chief residents are usually white men, reflecting how race and gender intersect in this selection process:

> And if you go back the last five or ten years, there's very few nonwhite women, or even nonwhite people, selected [as chief] residents. Yet the demographics of the residency class is not white men. White men are actually the minority . . . people [other students] have said, "You know, it's funny that our chiefs are always white guys when most of the residents are not white guys."

Harish, a senior faculty in dermatology, noted a similar pattern of selection of chief residents over the years.

Foreign medical graduate Indian women fellows and faculty members reported similar biases when it came to hiring, salary structure, and social incorporation in the workplace. Two-thirds of the women respondents in this study felt discriminated against because of their race/ethnicity at their place of work at some time during their career. An overwhelming proportion (90 percent) of these respondents reported racial bias in positions of power while one-third reported "absolute" or "definite" racial bias in positions of power. Aparna, a second-generation female, agreed with Ameena that "I think that's across the board, male Caucasian, tall, the demographics of certain people who are more likely to look like [a] professional and be more likely to be hired than the others."

Lindsay, a white administrator, affirmed that

> if you are a black woman or an Indian woman, if you are diminutive, if you are short and slender, you don't have an imposing physical force, you have the disadvantage of being viewed as someone who would not be in a leadership position and it requires extra effort and artful communication to get people to respect you. It's a harder job to get them to respect you, to listen to you, do what you say . . . I think it's harder to get people to cooperate with you.

Lindsay further noted, "It's not typical, they think, for a woman of color to be in the position of power, that's not the prototype powerful person in the United States. It's like I said, a white man in his fifties or sixties." Second-generation Indian women like Lata also felt that

> sometimes achievements are minimized [from Caucasian and African American colleagues, fellow students, fellow students' parents] because there are so many Indian doctors anyway and of course you are gonna be a doctor . . . there's almost an anger, like all you Indian people become doctors and kind of take away the spots of everybody else, 'cause you spend all your time studying.

Such sentiments often echo the model minority thesis that is applied to Asian Americans in the United States. Critics argue that the model minority stereotype is not really an indication of increased acceptance of Asians into the U.S. mainstream, but an ideological apparatus to actually create and sustain the racial marginalization of Asians in the U.S. mainstream and brew resentment against Asian achievements (Kibria 1998).

This "Indianness" acts as a barrier in the professional advancements of Indian women. Lata vividly remembered how, during medical school "there was this one professor I remember, this old white guy who was an OBGYN attending . . . one of the things that he specifically said was, 'You know, you were fine once you got over your natural cultural tendencies of not talking very much and of not being open.'" Rather than being judged on her medical competence, Lata felt that she was judged on racialized and gendered grounds.

Moreover, the stigma of being a foreign medical graduate multiplies the discriminatory experiences of first-generation Indian women physicians in the workplace. Ameena explained that accents lead to differential treatment of foreign medical graduate physicians in the workplace. Foreign graduates like Sheila, a first-generation female, reported having to work harder to gain access into competitive fellowship spots; Sheila was refused a gastroenterology fellowship at an Ivy League U.S. medical university because she was a foreign medical graduate, despite support from the chair of the department. When it came to rank advancement, Nidhi, a first-generation female faculty, felt that it

is very hard to get promoted in the workplace "if you are Indian or if you are a foreign graduate."

Neeraj, a first-generation male faculty, who has sponsored the visas of some first-generation Indian women who were discriminated against in their medical programs yet chose to fight the system, elaborated, "One of the people who were [sic] fired had to leave the country in two weeks. And then they had a provision of hearing, so they put the hearing four weeks later, knowing very well that she is not going to able to attend the hearing . . . that is how their careers are being spoilt."

In comparing experiences of second-generation versus first-generation physicians, interesting differences as well as similarities were observed (see Table 3). Because of the small sample size, statistical analyses to test for significance were not performed. Second-generation physicians were more likely to perceive discrimination due to their race/ethnicity and gender, and believe that there is gender-based discrimination against women in positions of power. However, a greater proportion of first-generation physicians reported that they had to work harder or prove themselves more at work because of their race/ethnicity. Although all first- and second-generation physicians reported that there is foreign medical graduate bias in the U.S. medical system, first-generation physicians were more likely to feel that it was unjustified, suggesting that second-generation physicians may share some of these biases again foreign medical training.

Table 3. Comparing Discriminatory Experiences of Second-Generation versus First-Generation Physicians

Discriminatory Experience	First-Generation, %	Second-Generation, %
Gender based		
Women physicians have to overcome extra hurdles at work	61	85
Gender-based discrimination against women physicians in positions of power	60	88
Race/ethnicity based		
Discriminated against because of race/ethnicity	50	71
Discriminated against by patients because of race/ethnicity	65	57
Had to work harder or prove themselves at work because of their race/ethnicity	50	35

(Continued)

Table 3. Comparing Discriminatory Experiences of Second-Generation versus First-Generation Physicians *(Continued)*		
Negative influence of race/ethnicity in positions of power	90	87
Foreign medical graduate bias		
There is bias against foreign medical graduates in the United States	100	100
Bias against foreign medical graduates is unjustified	45	10

Discussion and Conclusion

Gender is a fundamental constituent of workplaces, "present in [its] processes, practices, images and ideologies, and distributions of power" (Acker 1992, 567). While feminist scholarship has recognized the gendered nature of workplaces (Acker 1990, 1992, 2006; Britton 2000), it is also important to explore how race and nationality figure into the gendering of workplaces.

My research suggests that many physicians—both women and men—continue to perceive sexist and patriarchal attitudes in American medicine. My women respondents felt that they worked harder to gain the respect of their supervisors and coworkers, while they were also more likely to be steered into less prestigious subfields (Dresler et al. 1996). For example, Raghav, a second-generation male, who is a faculty member in geriatrics, admitted that they "do occasionally hear about older physicians who may have differing expectations of male and female students or may be biased in their evaluations of students and those sorts of things, based on gender."

Despite the entrenchment of gendered and racialized assumptions and expectations within the practices of these organizations, most research ignores how the gender category is deeply complicated by racial and ethnic differences (Acker 2006). Except for Neeraj, a first-generation man in my sample, who filed and won a racial discrimination lawsuit against an Ivy League U.S. medical school, both the first- and second-generation participants in my sample did not make an active effort to resist discrimination; instead, most were spectators or victims of discrimination. Combating institutionalized discrimination can be mentally taxing and financially draining for individual

physicians, as illustrated by Neeraj's description of the case of a second-generation Indian female physician who won a gender discrimination lawsuit for 1.6 million dollars against a prestigious university hospital in Massachusetts: "After that judge went, they fired her chair and then they [the university] appealed that their [judge's] judgment is wrong . . . and it is going to go on for a couple of years. And they [the university] have a lot of money. They [lawsuits] cost a lot of money." Hemant, a second-generation male faculty, aptly summarized the prevalent belief among physicians of Indian origin:

> Why would you [complain to the administration if discriminated]? If you were trying to move forward, why would you go and talk to the administration? That would just be counterproductive. You try to work within the system or you leave, go somewhere else, and that's why some people have left [in his program].

Gendered racism, of course, is not a static phenomenon, but subject to change and transformation. While twenty-first century racial practices in the United States may now be less overt, and more informal (Bonilla-Silva 2000), my research suggests that Indian women physicians continue to face racialized gender discrimination. My findings confirm that, compared to second-generation Indian women physicians, first-generation women who are also foreign medical graduates face particularly troubling racial discrimination by their colleagues, senior faculty, and the medical system at large. Second-generation Indian physicians, who are unaffected by the foreign medical graduate stigma, rigid visa regulations, and accent discrimination, may offer more promise to prospective employers. Yet even this group reports very high levels of gender and racial discrimination, even as they themselves may see discrimination against foreign-trained physicians as justified.

With the health care workforce becoming increasingly dependent on women immigrants from the developing world, more research is needed to understand the interaction of the recent migration of skilled personnel with developing racial/ethnic and gender relations in U.S. workplaces. Such studies will also have policy implications for the flow of professional immigrants between the developing and the developed world. Moreover, given the significant impact gender, race, and nationality can have in molding and restricting the career/migration trajectories of Indian women physicians in the United States, conceptualizations that recognize and inform the impact of discrimination against skilled professionals are imperative.

Notes

1. The H-1B visa is issued to people in specialty occupations requiring the application of highly specialized knowledge in their field of work. The J-1 visa is issued to people who wish to participate in work and study based educational and cultural exchange programs.

2. The semistructured interviews contained a similar set of questions asked of each participant, though I let the interview take its own course depending on the participant's experiences. Some responses required intensive and extensive probing, shedding new light on the subject, thus generating an impromptu new set of queries that were also explored in the interviews.

3. Men physicians outnumber women physicians in this study. This is due to the snowball sampling approach, as well as my focus on racial discrimination broadly, including the intersection of gender and racial discrimination. The views of men participants on gender discrimination in U.S. medicine are useful as they resonate, enhance, and lend support to the perceptions and reported experiences of female physicians.

4. I use pseudonyms for my study participants in order to protect their confidentiality and privacy.

5. The first sets of pilot interviews for this study were conducted with 30 physicians in 2009; these helped frame the larger interview study. Based on the findings that emerged when the 108 interviews were completed in 2010, I reinterviewed 13 of the 30

physicians whose interviews helped lay the foundations of this study. These reinterviews revealed new insights from the respondents, who felt more comfortable and had acquired more trust since the first interview.

6. The seven senior faculty in higher administrative positions were composed of three Caucasian females (Christine, Jennifer, and Lindsay), one second-generation Sri-Lankan male (Shiva), one Caucasian male (Ronald), one African American female (Andrea), and one first-generation Iranian male (Ramin).

7. This criterion is consistent with Rumbaut and Portes's (2001) definition of the "1.5 generation," which refers to immigrants who immigrated at a young age and underwent most of their childhood and adolescent socialization in the United States. Moreover, all of the physicians belonging to the 1.5-generation category identified themselves as second-generation and did not recognize commonalities with first-generation Indians.

8. In U.S. academic medicine, an "attending" is a physician who has completed his residency and practices medicine in a clinical or hospital setting and oversees both residents and fellows. "Resident" is the term used to address students who are in the graduate medical training stage called "residency." Residents are supervised by attending physicians who may have an academic title such as "associate professor" or "professor," and also by postdoctoral "fellows," who are training in a particular subspecialty after having completed their residency.

References

Acker, J. 1990. Hierarchies, jobs, bodies: A theory of gendered organizations. *Gender & Society* 4:139-58.

Acker, J. 1992. Gendered institutions: From sex roles to gendered institutions. *Contemporary Sociology* 21:565-69.

Acker, J. 2006. Inequality regimes: Gender, class, and race in organizations. *Gender & Society* 20:441-64.

Ash, A. S., P. L. Carr, R. Goldstein, and R. H. Friedman. 2004. Compensation and advancement of women in academic medicine: Is there equity? *Annals of Internal Medicine* 141:205-12.

Barringer, H., and G. Kassebaum. 1989. Asian Indians as a minority in the United States: The effect of education, occupations and gender on income. *Sociological Perspectives* 32:501-20.

Benard, S., and S. J. Correll. 2010. Normative discrimination and the motherhood penalty. *Gender & Society* 24:616-46.

Bendl, R., and A. Schmidt. 2010. From "glass ceilings" to "firewalls": Different metaphors for describing discrimination. *Gender, Work & Organization* 17:612-34.

Bonilla-Silva, E. 2000. "This is a white country": The racial ideology of the Western nations of the world-system. *Sociological Inquiry* 70:188-214.

Britton, D. M. 2000. The epistemology of the gendered organization. *Gender & Society* 14:418-34.

Brotherton, S. E., and S. I. Etzel. 2010. Graduate medical education, 2009-2010. *Journal of the American Medical Association* 304:1255.

Browne, I., and J. Misra. 2003. The intersection of gender and race in the labor market. *Annual Review of Sociology* 29:487-513.

Carnes, M., C. Morrissey, and S. E. Geller. 2008. Women's health and women's leadership in academic medicine: Hitting the same glass ceiling? *Journal of Women's Health* 17:1453-62.

Carr, P. L., A. Palepu, L. Szalacha, C. Caswell, and T. Inui. 2007. "Flying below the radar": A qualitative study of minority experience and management of discrimination in academic medicine. *Medical Education* 41:601-9.

Carr, P. L., L. Szalacha, R. Barnett, C. Caswell, and T. Inui. 2003. A "ton of feathers": Gender discrimination in academic medical careers and how to manage it. *Journal of Women's Health* 12:1009-18.

Collins, P. 2000. *Black feminist thought: Knowledge, consciousness, and the politics of empowerment.* 2nd ed. New York: Routledge.

Collins, P. 2001. Like one of the family: Race, ethnicity, and the paradox of U.S. national identity. *Ethnic and Racial Studies* 24:3-28.

Coombs, A. A., and R. K. King. 2005. Workplace discrimination: Experiences of practicing physicians. *Journal of the National Medical Association* 97:467-77.

Correll, S. J. 2004. Constraints into preferences: Gender, status, and emerging career aspirations. *American Sociological Review* 69:93-113.

Crenshaw, K. 1991. Mapping the margins: Intersectionality, identity politics, and violence against women of color. *Stanford Law Review* 43:1241-99.

Desbiens, N. A., and H. J. Vidaillet Jr. 2010. Discrimination against international medical graduates in the United States residency program selection process. *BMC Medical Education* 10 (5).

Dick, P., and R. Hyde. 2006. Consent as resistance, resistance as consent: Re-reading part-time professionals' acceptance of their marginal positions. *Gender, Work & Organization* 13:543-64.

Dobson, R. 1997. Women doctors believe medicine is male dominated. *British Medical Journal* 315:80.

Dresler, C. M., D. L. Padgett, S. E. MacKinnon, and G. A. Patterson. 1996. Experiences of women in cardiothoracic surgery: A gender comparison. *Archives of Surgery* 131:1128-34.

Duffy, M. 2007. Doing the dirty work: Gender, race, and reproductive labor in historical perspective. *Gender & Society* 21:313-36.

Eagly, A. H., and S. J. Karau. 2002. Role congruity theory of prejudice toward female leaders. *Psychological Review* 109:573-98.

Ebell, M. H. 2008. Future salary and U.S. residency fill rate revisited. *Journal of the American Medical Association* 300:1131-32.

Espiritu, Y. 1997. *Asian American women and men: Love, labor, laws.* Thousand Oaks, CA: Sage.

Esterberg, K. 2002. *Qualitative methods in social research.* New York: McGraw Hill.

Fang, D., E. Moy, L. Colburn, and J. Hurley. 2000. Racial and ethnic disparities in faculty promotion in academic medicine. *Journal of the American Medical Association* 284:1085-92.

García-López, Gladys. 2008. ''Nunca Te Toman En Cuenta [They never take you into account]'': The challenges of inclusion and strategies for success of Chicana attorneys. *Gender & Society* 22:590.

Glauber, R. 2007. Marriage and the motherhood penalty among African Americans, Hispanics, and whites. *Journal of Marriage and Family* 69: 951-61.

Gray, G. M., T. C. Gallagher, and M. S. Masters. 1996. Contrasting experiences and perceptions of women and men physician graduates of Stanford University School of Medicine. *Transactions of the American Clinical and Climatological Association* 107:159-71.

Hadley, J., J. C. Cantor, R. J. Willke, J. Feder, and A. B. Cohen. 1992. Young physicians most and least likely to have second thoughts about a career in medicine. *Academic Medicine* 67:180-90.

Heath, I. 2004. Women in medicine. *British Medical Journal* 329:412-13.

Heilman, M. E. 2001. Description and prescription: How gender stereotypes prevent women's ascent up the organizational ladder. *Journal of Social Issues* 57:657-74.

Kanter, R. M. 1977. *Men and women of the corporation.* New York: Basic Books.

Kass, R. B., W. W. Souba, and L. E. Thorndyke. 2006. Challenges confronting female surgical leaders: Overcoming the barriers. *Journal of Surgical Research* 132:179-87.

Kibria, N. 1998. The contested meanings of Asian American: Racial dilemmas in the contemporary U.S. *Ethnic and Racial Studies* 21:939-58.

Kim, Chang Hwan, and Arthur Sakamoto. 2010. Have Asian American men achieved labor market parity with white men? *American Sociological Review* 75:934.

King, D. 1989. Multiple jeopardy, multiple consciousness: The context of a black feminist ideology. *Signs* 14:42-72.

Lawrence, T., and V. Corwin. 2003. Being there: The acceptance and marginalization of part-time professional employees. *Journal of Organizational Behaviour* 24:923-43.

Murti, L. 2012. Who benefits from the white coat? Gender differences in occupational citizenship among Asian-Indian doctors. *Ethnic and Racial Studies* 35 (12): 2035-53.

Palepu, A., P. L. Carr, R. H. Friedman, H. Amos, A. S. Ash, and M. A. Moskowitz. 1998. Minority faculty and academic rank in medicine. *Journal of the American Medical Association* 280:767-71.

Palepu, A., P. L. Carr, R. H. Friedman, H. Amos, A. S. Ash, and M. A. Moskowitz. 2000. Specialty choices, compensation, and career satisfaction of underrepresented minority faculty in academic medicine. *Academic Medicine* 75:157-60.

Portes, A., and M. Zhou. 1993. The new second generation: Segmented assimilation and its variants. *Annals of the American Academy of Political and Social Science* 530:74-96.

Purkayastha, B. 2005. Skilled migration and cumulative disadvantage: The case of highly qualified Asian Indian immigrant women in the U.S. *Geoforum* 36:181-96.

Ridgeway, C. L., and S. J. Correll. 2004. Unpacking the gender system: A theoretical perspective on gender beliefs and social relations. *Gender & Society* 18:510-31.

Rumbaut, R., and A. Portes. 2001. *Ethnicities: Children of Immigrants in America.* Russell Sage Foundation. Berkeley: University of California Press.

Sethi, R. C. 2003. Smells like racism. In *Race, class, and gender in the United States: An integrated study*, edited by Paula S. Rothenberg. New York: Worth.

Shrier, D. K., A. N. Zucker, A. E. Mercurio, L. J. Landry, M. Rich, and L. A. Shrier. 2007. Generation to generation: Discrimination and harassment experiences of physician mothers and their physician daughters. *Journal of Women's Health* 16:883-94.

Stone, R. T., B. Purkayastha, and T. A. Berdahl. 2006. Beyond Asian American: Examining conditions and mechanisms of earnings inequality for Filipina and Asian Indian women. *Sociological Perspectives* 49:261-81.

Waters, Mary C., and Karl Eschbach. 1995. Immigration and ethnic and racial inequality in the United States. *Annual Review of Sociology* 21:419-46.

West, C., and D. H. Zimmerman. 1987. Doing gender. *Gender & Society* 1:125-51.

Williams, C. L. 1992. The glass escalator: Hidden advantages for men in the "female" professions. *Social Problems* 39:253-67.

Xu, W., and A. Leffler. 1992. Gender and race effects on occupational prestige, segregation, and earnings. *Gender & Society* 6:376-92.

Wasudha Bhatt is a PhD candidate in the department of sociology at the University of Texas at Austin. Her research interests include international migration, gender, and race and ethnicity.

Women and the Healthcare System

1. This chapter begins with describing the Women's Health Movements. Describe today's movements surrounding women's health. Provide three examples of activism that improve women's healthcare.

2. Building on information in several articles, describe how the gynecological exam is symbolic of the consumer–health practitioner relationship. Identify things every woman should be able to expect as part of a good gynecological exam.

3. *Our Bodies, Ourselves* has been instrumental in changing women's healthcare experience. This book has been translated into thirty languages and sociocultural environments. Discuss examples of how this book has changed and has not changed the healthcare experience for women around the world.

4. Describe the "best" and "worst" healthcare experiences. Briefly, identify the behaviors (or characteristics) that were different for you and the health providers in the two situations. Describe some examples as to how the experience should have been different.

5. Women in medicine continue to face barriers, such as sexism, challenges to family life, and male-centered research practices. What policy changes would you recommend to combat these challenges?

Inequalities and Health

2

Any analysis of women's health must include an understanding of the social structural factors that contribute to why and how health disparities persist. It also requires an understanding of why some women have better health outcomes than others when they do fall ill. This understanding involves learning how social discrimination, oppression, environment, and socioeconomic factors impact women's health in general and their ability to heal. Students and practitioners must consider how racism, sexism, culturalism, anti-Semitism, ableism, poverty, homophobia, ageism, body image shaming, and other forms of oppression hurt women's ability to access safe and healthy environments in which to live and work. Similarly, women's ability to be healthy is improved when they have access to services, those who conduct research do so in respectful ways, and finally, knowledge and wisdom is shared. Culturally and linguistically appropriate services are aimed at offering a holistic and inclusive approach to women's health needs by having an understanding of women, their culture and social status, and environments they live and work in. The articles in this chapter were selected to stimulate dialogue about how social structural oppression impacts women's health. The section also is designed to address inequalities, create bridges, and build a collaborative understanding between the practitioner and patient/client.

The first set of articles begins the conversation about disparities in the healthcare system. *Disparities in Health and Health Care: Five Key Questions and Answers* by Petry Ubri and Samantha Artiga from The Henry J. Kaiser Family Foundation offers important questions and answers about health disparities in healthcare. They provide information on the initiatives designed to address health disparities. In the article, *Systemic Racism and U.S. Health Care* by Joe Feagin and Zinobia Bennefield, systemic racism theory is discussed to show how racism has prevailed from generation to generation in the healthcare and the public health systems. Their article illustrates that racism is so deeply embedded systematically and culturally due, in part, to a lack of cultural appropriateness in education and an administrative level staffed primarily by Whites. They suggest real reform involves calling out administrators' and practitioners' racial biases and practices and developing inclusive education for them. *Differences in Belief About the Causes of Health Disparities in Black and White Nurses* by Susan Roberts-Dobie, Elana Joram, Michele Devin, DeAnn Ambroson, and Joyce Chen provides valuable insights into providers' perceptions and causes as to why health disparities persist. They show differences in beliefs about disparities between White and Black nurses. "Black nurses gave more weight to external factors than White nurses, where White nurses considered genetic differences between racial groups to be more important when accounting for disparities." This study demonstrates how providers' beliefs about disparities are important to developing effective cultural competency training. It requires providers to think about their beliefs and examine how external and internal factors play a role in the ways in which they understand and treat their patients. *Health Disparities between Rural and Urban Women in Minnesota* by Kim Tjaden examines the differences in rural and urban locations for women. Where one lives is a major factor in women's access to quality health services and how those services may be designed and distributed.

Vanessa Northington Gamble's classic article, *Under the Shadow of Tuskegee: African Americans and Health Care* chronicles the long history of racism in public health that Blacks have experienced. This infamous government-funded research study demonstrated how Black men were targeted subjects for studies on syphilis for thirty years and were denied effective treatment when it became available. The Tuskegee study left a legacy of mistrust of the healthcare system for generations. Twenty-five years later, Carol Kaesuk Yoon's *New York Times* article, *Families Emerge as Silent Victims of Tuskegee Syphilis Experiment* describes a news conference and interviews with some of the surviving participants of the study, including Dr. Gamble, as they request an apology from the government.

The next set of articles provides examples of challenges faced by specific cultural groups, such as oppression, discrimination, and barriers to quality services. While there may be some commonality between each group, they all deserve practitioners, researchers, and policy makers who understand diversity within each group and work to develop policies, research methods, and services that will address their unique needs.

Bodies Don't Just Tell Stories, They Tell Histories: Embodiment of Historical Trauma among American Indians and Alaska Natives, by Karina L. Walters, Selina A. Mohammed, Teresa Evans-Campbell, Ramona E. Beltrán, David H. Chae, and Bonnie Duran highlights the importance of historical trauma in present-day health disparities. There is a link between historical trauma and Native Americans' overall health, health outcomes, and wellness. Kim & Keefe's article, *Barriers to Healthcare Among Asian Americans* addresses the myth that Asian Americans are one of the best adjusted, physically healthier, and socioeconomically successful groups compared to other immigrant populations in the United States. The reality is that Asian Americans are culturally diverse in all aspects, including their ethnicity, language, religion, socioeconomic status, and health. There are groups that have an underutilization of health services due to a number of barriers, including language and culture, health literacy, access to insurance, and immigrant status. Recommendations include policy changes that address their underutilization of healthcare services; consider

patient characteristics, language, and ethnicity; and support their ability to trust healthcare providers. *Women Finding the Way: American Indian Women Leading Intervention Research in Native Communities* by Maria Yellow Horse Brave Heart, Josephine Chase, Jennifer Elkins, Jennifer Martin, Jennifer S. Nanez, and Jennifer J. Moots offers a comprehensive literature summary of community-engaged research conducted in Native communities. The authors describe the process and experiences of researchers working in Native communities and the tools necessary to conduct culturally relevant and respectful research. Community-engaged research involves understanding the importance of women in the community and how they are the carriers of the culture. It also involves understanding Native communities' historical trauma in order to develop and practice cultural humility.

In *Rumors and Realities: Making sense of HIV/AIDS Conspiracy Narratives and Contemporary Legends,* Jacob Heller argues that rumors reveal a trust gap between African Americans and predominantly White physicians. This lack of trust of White physicians stems from African Americans' history of abuse, a lack of funding to address their medical needs, and the persistence of HIV/AIDS. While this article does not focus on women, it importantly recognizes the social and racialized context of HIV/AIDS and the historical relationship between the Black community and medical institutions.

The lack of information regarding the LGBTQ+ community is a major barrier to quality service delivery. Patti Rager Zuzelo, in *Improving Nursing Care for Lesbian, Bisexual, and Transgender Women* suggests that nurses are not well educated on issues within the lesbian, bisexual, queer, and transgender community, which contributes to inadequate service delivery. She highlights a number for resources to help nursing staff develop respectful protocols.

This chapter ends with articles that focus on developing cultural competency protocols. Cultural competency has become a standard in most healthcare institutions. It involves reducing disparities by developing language-appropriate services, hiring staff who reflect the patient population, outreach to culturally diverse communities, and ongoing research about community changes to ensure equitable services. The following articles provide an overview of the challenges and recommendations for developing the best practices and policies.

Community Participation for Transformative Action on Women's, Children's, and Adolescents' Health by Cicely Marston, Rachel Hinton, Stuart Kean, Sushil Baral, Arti Ahuja, Anthony Costello, and Anayda Portela suggests that women and adolescents are the most powerful agents for improving their own health and achieving prosperous societies. They describe a system that is more collaborative, involving community participation and people-centered services.

Finally, *Cultural Humility versus Cultural Competence: A Critical Distinction in Defining Physician Training Outcomes in Multicultural Education* by Melanie Tervalon and Jann Murray-Garcia is a classic article that proposes an anti-oppression approach to cultural competency training for all providers. Their article is just as important today as it was yesterday. In order to promote positive patient outcomes, reduce disparities, and provide equitable service delivery, they propose changing much of the traditional philosophy that is embedded in healthcare practitioners' training, which often creates the imbalances that contribute to health disparities. Cultural humility incorporates a life-long commitment to self-evaluation, self-critique, readdressing the inherent power imbalances throughout the healthcare system, and developing mutually beneficial and non-paternalistic partnership whenever and wherever possible on behalf of individuals.

Disparities in Health and Health Care: Five Key Questions and Answers

by Petry Ubri and Samantha Artiga

Executive Summary

1. What are Health and Health Care Disparities?
Health and health care disparities refer to differences in health and health care between population groups. Disparities occur across many dimensions, including race/ethnicity, socioeconomic status, age, location, gender, disability status, and sexual orientation.

2. Why do Health and Health Care Disparities Matter?
Disparities in health and health care not only affect the groups facing disparities, but also limit overall improvements in quality of care and health for the broader population and result in unnecessary costs. As the population becomes more diverse, with people of color projected to account for over half of the population in 2045, it is increasingly important to address health disparities.

3. What is the Status of Disparities Today?
Many groups are at disproportionate risk of being uninsured, lacking access to care, and experiencing worse health outcomes, including people of color and low-income individuals. Hispanics, Blacks, American Indians/Alaska Natives, and low-income individuals are more likely to be uninsured relative to Whites and those with higher incomes. Low-income individuals and people of color also face increased barriers to accessing care, receive poorer quality care, and experience worse health outcomes.

4. What are Key Initiatives to Address Disparities?

The 2011 Department of Health and Human Services (HHS) Disparities Action Plan and the Affordable Care Act (ACA) advance efforts to reduce health disparities. The HHS Disparities Action Plan sets out a series of priorities, strategies, actions, and goals to achieve a vision of "a nation free of disparities in health and health care." The ACA increases coverage options for low- and moderate-income populations and includes other provisions to address disparities. States, local communities, private organizations, and providers are also engaged in efforts to reduce health disparities.

5. How has the ACA affected Health Coverage Disparities?

The ACA sharply reduced uninsured rates for people of color and low-income populations, but coverage disparities remain. Continued enrollment efforts may further narrow disparities, but eligibility for coverage under the ACA among the remaining nonelderly uninsured varies by race and ethnicity.

Introduction

Disparities in health and health care in the United States have been a longstanding challenge resulting in some groups receiving less and lower quality health care than others and experiencing poorer health outcomes. This brief provides an introductory overview of health and health care disparities, including what disparities are and why they matter, the status of disparities today, and key efforts to address disparities, including provisions in the Affordable Care Act (ACA) and their impact on health coverage disparities.

1. What are Health and Health Care Disparities?

Health and health care disparities refer to differences in health and health care between populations. Disparities in "health" and "health care" are related, but not synonymous, concepts. A "health disparity" refers to a higher burden of illness, injury, disability, or mortality experienced by one population group relative to another.[1] A "health care disparity" typically refers to differences between groups in health insurance coverage, access to and use of care, and quality of care. More specifically, health and health care disparities often refer to differences that cannot be explained by variations in health care needs, patient preferences, or treatment recommendations. Several related terms, such as health inequality and health inequity, are also often used interchangeably[2] to describe differences that are socially-determined and/or deemed to be unnecessary, avoidable, or unjust.[3]

A complex and interrelated set of individual, provider, health system, societal, and environmental factors contribute to disparities in health and health care. Individual factors include a variety of health behaviors from maintaining a healthy weight to following medical advice. Provider factors encompass issues such as provider bias and cultural and linguistic barriers to patient-provider communication. How health care is organized, financed, and delivered also shapes disparities as do social and environmental factors, such as poverty, education, proximity to care, and neighborhood safety.

Health and health care disparities are commonly viewed through the lens of race and ethnicity, but they occur across a broad range of dimensions. Examples of characteristics across which disparities occur include socioeconomic status, age, geography, language, gender, disability status, citizenship status, and sexual identity and orientation. Federal efforts to reduce disparities include a focus on designated priority populations who are particularly vulnerable to health and health care disparities.[4,5] These priority populations include people of color, low-income groups, women, children, older adults, individuals with special health care needs, and individuals living in rural and inner-city areas.[6] These groups are not mutually exclusive and often interact in important ways. Disparities also occur within subgroups of populations. For example, there are differences among Hispanics in health and health care based on length of time in the country, primary language, and immigration status.[7,8]

Health and health care disparities in the United States are a long-standing and persistent

issue. Disparities have been documented for many decades and, despite overall improvements in population health over time, many disparities have persisted and, in some cases, widened.[9] Research also suggests that disparities occur across the life course, from birth, through mid-life, and among older adults.[10,11]

2. Why do Health and Health Care Disparities Matter?

Disparities in health and health care not only affect the groups facing disparities, but also limit overall improvements in quality of care and health for the broader population and result in unnecessary costs. Addressing disparities in health and health care is not only important from a social justice standpoint, but also for improving the health of all Americans by achieving improvements in overall quality of care and population health. Moreover, health disparities are costly. One analysis estimates that approximately 30% of total direct medical expenditures for Blacks, Hispanics, and Asians are excess costs

due to health inequities.[12] Disparities also result in economic losses due to indirect costs associated with lost work productivity and premature death.[13]

As the population becomes more diverse, it is increasingly important to address health disparities. Over time the population is becoming increasingly heterogeneous. In 2015, nearly four in ten (38%) individuals living in the United States were people of color. It is projected that people of color will account for over half of the population in 2045, with the largest growth occurring among Hispanics (Figure 1). Moreover, the gaps between the richest households and poor and middle income households are wide and growing in most states. As of 2014, the richest 20% of households have an average income of $194,053, nearly 17 times the average income of $11,676 for the bottom 20% of households (Figure 2).[14] Given that people of color make up a disproportionate share of the low-income[15] and the uninsured[16] relative to their size in the population, the growth of communities of color and widening of income gaps amplify the importance of addressing health and health care disparities.

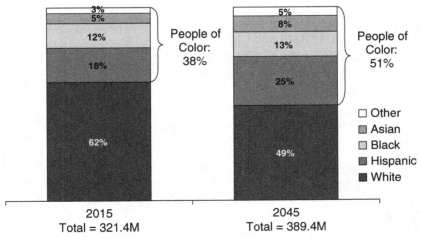

Figure 1 Distribution of U.S. Population by Race/Ethnicity, 2015 and 2045

NOTES: All racial groups are non-Hispanic. Other includes Native Hawaiians and Pacific Islanders, Native Americans/Alaska Natives, and individuals with two or more races. Data do not include residents of Puerto Rico, Guam, the U.S. Virgin Islands, or the Northern Mariana Islands.

SOURCE: U.S. Census Bureau, Projections of the Population by Sex, Hispanic Origin, and Race for the United States 2015 to 2060. http://www.census.gov/population/projections/data/national/2014/summarytables.html

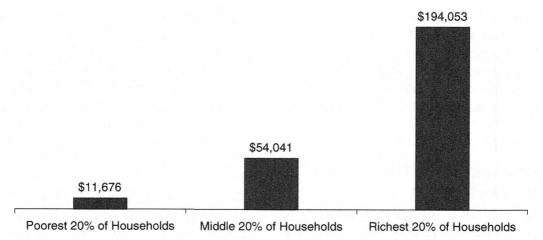

Figure 2 Gaps Between Average Annual Income of Richest and Poorest Households in the United States, 2014

SOURCE: Carmen DeNavas-Walt and Bernadette Proctor, Income and Poverty in the United States: 2014 Current Population Reports, (Washington, DC: United States Census Bureau, September 2015), http://www.census.gov/content/dam/Census/library/publications/2015/demo/p60-252.pdf.

3. What is the Status of Disparities Today?

Today, many groups face significant disparities in access to and utilization of care. People of color generally face more access barriers and utilize less care than Whites. For example, among nonelderly adults, Hispanics, Blacks, and American Indians and Alaska Natives are more likely than Whites to delay or go without needed care (Figure 3).[17] Moreover, nonelderly Black and Hispanic adults are less likely than their White counterparts to have a usual source of care or to have

had a health or dental visit in the previous year.[18] Low-income individuals also experience more barriers to care and receive poorer quality care than high-income individuals[19], and lesbian, gay, bisexual, and transgender (LGBT) individuals are more likely to experience challenges obtaining care than heterosexuals.[20] In addition, individuals with limited English proficiency are less likely than those who are English proficient to seek care even when insured.[21] Patient experiences and satisfaction levels also differ by race, gender, education levels, and language.[22,23,24]

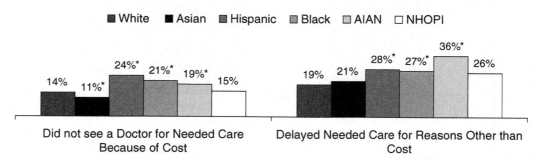

Figure 3 Percent of Nonelderly Adults who did not Receive or Delayed Care in the Past 12 Months by Race/Ethnicity, 2014

* Indicates statistically significant difference from the White population at the $p < 0.05$ level.

NOTE: AIAN refers to American Indians and Alaska Natives. NHOPI refers to Native Hawaiians and Other Pacific Islanders. Persons of Hispanic origin may be of any race but are categorized as Hispanic for this analysis; other groups are non-Hispanic. Includes nonelderly individuals 18-64 years of age.

SOURCE: Kaiser Family Foundation analysis of CDC, Behavioral Risk Factor Surveillance System, 2014.

Additionally, some groups have high rates of certain health conditions and experience poor health outcomes. Blacks and American Indians and Alaska Natives fare worse than Whites on many measures of health status and health outcomes. For example, among nonelderly adults, Blacks and American Indians and Alaska Natives have a higher prevalence of asthma, diabetes, and cardiovascular disease (Figure 4). Health disparities are particularly striking in the burden of AIDS and HIV diagnoses and death rates, with Blacks experiencing over eight and ten times higher rates of HIV and AIDS diagnoses than Whites (Figure 5).[25] Infant mortality rates are significantly higher for Blacks and American Indians and Alaska Natives compared to Whites[26], and Black males have the shortest life expectancy compared to other groups.[27] Low-income people

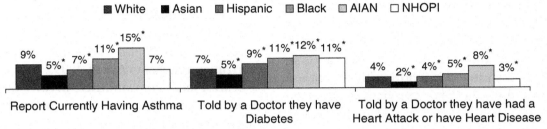

Figure 4 Percent of Nonelderly Adults with Selected Health Conditions by Race/Ethnicity, 2014

* Indicates statistically significant difference from the White population at the p<0.05 level.

NOTE: AIAN refers to American Indians and Alaska Natives. NHOPI refers to Native Hawaiians and Other Pacific Islanders. Persons of Hispanic origin may be of any race but are categorized as Hispanic for this analysis; other groups are non-Hispanic. Includes nonelderly individuals 18-64 years of age.

SOURCE: Kaiser Family Foundation analysis of CDC, Behavioral Risk Factor Surveillance System, 2014.

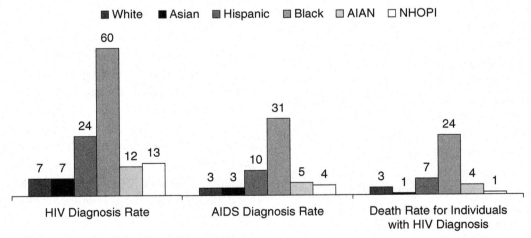

Figure 5 Age-Adjusted HIV or AIDS Diagnosis and Death Rate per 100,000 Among Teens and Adults by Race/Ethnicity

Rates are not subject to sampling error variation; therefore, significance testing is not needed to detect differences.

NOTE: AIAN refers to American Indians and Alaska Natives. NHOPI refers to Native Hawaiians and Other Pacific Islanders. Persons categorized by race were not Hispanic or Latino. Individuals in each race category may, however, include persons whose ethnicity was not reported. Includes individuals age 13 and older. Data for HIV and AIDS diagnoses are as of 2014; death rate is as of 2013.

SOURCE: Centers for Disease Control and Prevention, National Center for HIV/AIDS, Viral Hepatitis, STD, and TB Prevention (NCHHSTP) Atlas, 2014.

of all races report worse health status than higher income individuals.[28] Further, research suggests that some subgroups of the LGBT community have more chronic conditions as well as higher prevalence and earlier onset of disabilities than heterosexuals.[29]

4. What are Key Initiatives to Eliminate Disparities?

Significant recognition of health and health care disparities began over a decade ago with several landmark reports and the first major legislation focused on reduction of disparities. The release of two Surgeon General's reports in the early 2000s showed disparities in tobacco use and access to mental health services by race and ethnicity.[30,31] The first major legislation focused on reduction of disparities, the Minority Health and Health Disparities Research and Education Act of 2000,[32] created the National Center for Minority Health and Health Disparities, and authorized the Agency for Healthcare Research and Quality (AHRQ) to regularly measure progress on reduction of disparities. Soon after, the Institute of Medicine released two seminal reports documenting racial and ethnic disparities in access to and quality of care.[33,34]

In 2011, the Department of Health and Human Services (HHS) developed an action plan for eliminating racial and ethnic health disparities. The HHS Disparities Action Plan sets out a series of priorities, strategies, actions, and goals to achieve its vision of, "a nation free of disparities in health and health care."[35] Since the release of the report, HHS has undertaken various efforts to implement the Disparities Action Plan, including coordinating programmatic and policy efforts to advance health equity, expanding access and quality of coverage and care, and strengthening the health care infrastructure and workforce.[36] In 2013, HHS also updated the national standards for Culturally and Linguistically Appropriate Services (CLAS), which seek to ensure that people receive care in a culturally and linguistically appropriate manner.

The ACA advances efforts to improve health and health care and reduce disparities.[37] Some provisions explicitly focus on disparities, including creating Offices of Minority Health within key

HHS agencies to coordinate disparity reduction efforts. Others have broader goals that will benefit groups facing disparities, such as the major health coverage expansions and increased funding for community health centers. The ACA also promotes workforce diversity and cultural competence, increasing funding for health care professional and cultural competence training and education materials, and strengthens data collection and research efforts. Lastly, the ACA includes prevention and public health initiatives, like a national oral health education campaign with an emphasis on racial and ethnic disparities, and permanently reauthorizes the Indian Health Care Improvement Reauthorization Extension Act of 2009.

States, local communities, private organizations, and providers also are engaged in efforts to reduce health disparities. Through Racial and Ethnic Approaches to Community Health (REACH) grants funded by the Centers for Disease Control and Prevention, a number of states, local health departments, universities and non-profit groups implemented community-focused interventions to reduce specific neighborhood-based disparities.[38] These interventions vary in scope and focus on outreach, cultural competency training, and education.[39] Private foundations have also developed significant initiatives aimed at reducing disparities and providers are increasingly undertaking disparities-focused efforts.[40]

Growing efforts to integrate social and environmental needs into the health care system may support continued reductions in disparities. A number of states are engaged in payment and delivery system reforms that focus on population health and recognize the role of social determinants of health. The Centers for Medicare & Medicaid Services also launched a new Accountable Health Communities initiative to test delivery approaches that address health-related social needs through clinical-community linkages.[41]

5. How has the ACA Affected Health Coverage Disparities?

The ACA sharply reduced the uninsured rate for low-income groups and people of color, but coverage disparities remain. The ACA significantly increased coverage options for low- and moderate-income populations. Under the ACA, Medicaid coverage is extended to low-income adults with incomes up to 138% of the federal poverty level (FPL) ($27,724 for a family of three in 2016) in the 32 states that have implemented the Medicaid expansion to date, and tax credits are available for middle-income people who purchase coverage through health insurance Marketplaces established under the ACA. Since these coverage provisions took effect in 2014, uninsured rates for the nonelderly population have decreased, falling from 17% in 2013 to 11% in 2015.[42] Uninsured rates declined most sharply among the poor or near-poor and among Hispanics, Blacks, and Asians (Figures 6 and 7). Although these reductions have

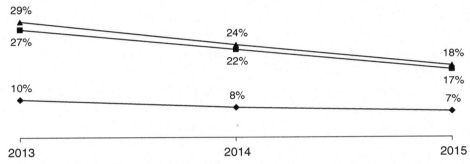

Figure 6 Uninsured Rates for the Nonelderly Population by Income, 2013–2015

NOTE: Includes individuals ages 0 to 64. Insurance coverage is based on coverage level at time of interview. FPL refers to the Federal Poverty Level. As of 2015, the FPL was $20,090 for a family of three.

SOURCE: Robin Cohen, Michael Martinez, and Emily Zammitti, Health insurance coverage: Early release of estimates from the National Health Interview Survey, 2015, (Rockville, MD: National Center for Health Statistics, May 2016), http://www.cdc.gov/nchs/nhis/releases.htm.

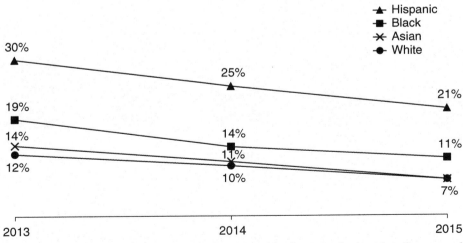

Figure 7 Uninsured Rates for the Nonelderly Population by Race and Ethnicity, 2013–2015

NOTE: Other includes non-Hispanic other races and multiple races. Includes individuals ages 0 to 64. Uninsured rate based on coverage level at time of interview.

SOURCE: Robin Cohen, Michael Martinez, and Emily Zammitti, Health insurance coverage: Early release of estimates from the National Health Interview Survey, 2015, (Rockville, MD: National Center for Health Statistics, May 2016), http://www.cdc.gov/nchs/nhis/releases.htm.

narrowed disparities for these groups, they remain more likely to be uninsured compared to higher income people and Whites.

Continued efforts to enroll eligible individuals into coverage will contribute to ongoing coverage gains and narrowing of disparities, but eligibility for coverage under the ACA among the remaining nonelderly uninsured varies by race and ethnicity. American Indians and Alaska Natives have the highest share of nonelderly uninsured who are eligible for Medicaid or tax credits at 70%, followed by Blacks at 55% (Figure 8). However, Blacks are twice as likely as Whites to falls into the coverage gap that exists in the 19 states that have not expanded Medicaid. Consistent with immigrants accounting for large shares of uninsured Asians and Hispanics, over half of these groups remain ineligible for coverage options.

Conclusion

In conclusion, health and health care disparities persist in the United States, leading to certain groups being at higher risk of being uninsured, having more limited access to care, experiencing poorer quality of care, and ultimately experiencing worse health outcomes. While health and health care disparities are commonly viewed through the lens of race and ethnicity, they occur across a broad range of dimensions and reflect a complex set of individual, social, and environmental factors. Disparities not only affect the groups facing disparities but also limit continued improvement in overall quality of care and health for the broader population and result in unnecessary costs. It is increasingly important to address disparities as the population becomes more diverse. For over the past decade, there has been increased focus on reducing disparities and a growing set of initiatives to address disparities at the federal, state, community, and provider level. In addition, the ACA includes provisions that advance efforts to eliminate disparities. The ACA's coverage expansions have resulted in notable coverage gains for low- and moderate-income populations and people of color that have helped narrow differences in coverage rates, but disparities in coverage for these groups remain. As the population becomes increasingly diverse, broad

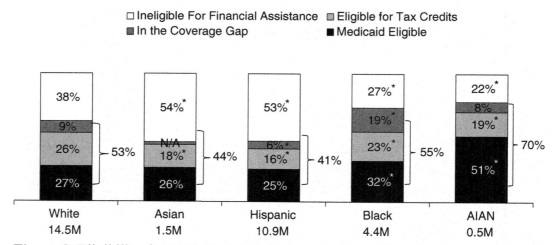

Figure 8 Eligibility for ACA Coverage Among the Nonelderly Uninsured by Race/Ethnicity as of 2015

* Indicates statistically significant difference from the White population at the p<0.05 level.

NOTE: AIAN refers to American Indians and Alaska Natives. NHOPI refers to Native Hawaiians and Other Pacific Islanders. Persons of Hispanic origin may be of any race but are categorized as Hispanic; other groups are non-Hispanic. Includes nonelderly individuals age 0-64 years. Totals may not sum to 100% due to rounding. N/A: Point estimates do not meet minimum standards for statistical reliability. Ineligible for financial assistance includes those ineligible due to ESI, income, or immigration status.

SOURCE: Kaiser Family Foundation analysis based on the March 2015 Current Population Survey, Annual Social and Economic Supplement and the 2015 Medicaid eligibility levels updated to reflect Medicaid expansion decisions as of January 2016.

and integrated efforts to address the wide range of factors that contribute to disparities, including social and environmental factors that extend beyond the health care system, will be important.

Endnotes

[1] Definitions of health disparity differ. For example, the Department of Health and Human Services describes health disparities as "differences in health outcomes that are closely linked with social, economic, and environmental disadvantage" while the National Institutes of Health defines a health disparity as a "difference in the incidence, prevalence, mortality, and burden of disease and other adverse health conditions that exist among specific population groups in the United States." United States Department of Health and Human Services, *HHS Action Plan to Reduce Racial and Ethnic Health Disparities*, (Washington, DC: Department of Health and Human Services, April 2011), http://minorityhealth.hhs.gov/npa/files/plans/hhs/hhs_plan_complete.pdf. "NIH Announces Institute on Minority Health and Health Disparities," National Institutes of Health, published September 2010, https://www.nih.gov/news-events/news-releases/nih-announces-institute-minority-health-health-disparities.

[2] However, they may have nuanced distinctions. For example, a health disparity, which typically refers to differences caused by social, environmental attributes, is sometimes distinguished from a health inequality, used more often in scientific literature to describe differences associated with specific attributes such as income, or race. A health inequity implies that a difference is unfair or unethical. Centers for Disease Control and Prevention, "CDC Health Disparities and Inequalities Report – United States 2011," *Morbidity and Mortality Weekly Report* 60 (Jan 2011):55–114. Olivia Carter-Pokras and Claudia Baquet. "What is a Health Disparity?" *Public Health Reports* 117 (Sep-Oct 2002):426–434.

[3] "Social Determinants of Health: Definitions," Centers for Disease Control and Prevention, accessed published March 2014, http://www.cdc.gov/socialdeterminants/Definitions.html.

[4] Agency for Healthcare Research and Quality, *Agency for Healthcare Research and Quality: Division of Priority Populations*, (Rockville, MD: Agency for Healthcare Research and Quality, April 2016), http://www.ahrq.gov/sites/default/files/wysiwyg/research/findings/factsheets/priority-populations/priority-populations_factsheet.pdf.

[5] "Chapter Eight: Focusing on Vulnerable Populations," Agency for Healthcare Research and Quality, published March 1998, http://archive.ahrq.gov/hcqual/meetings/mar12/chap08.html.

[6] Agency for Healthcare Research and Quality, *Agency for Healthcare Research and Quality: Division of Priority Populations*, (Rockville, MD: Agency for Healthcare Research and Quality, 2016), http://www.ahrq.gov/sites/default/files/wysiwyg/research/findings/factsheets/priority-populations/prioritypopulations_factsheet.pdf.

[7] Kaiser Commission on Medicaid and the Uninsured, *Key Facts on Health Coverage for Low-Income Immigrants Today and Under the Affordable Care Act*, (Washington, DC: Kaiser Commission on Medicaid and the Uninsured, March 2013), http://www.kff.org/uninsured/8279.cfm.

[8] Kaiser Commission on Medicaid and the Uninsured, *Overview of Health Coverage for Individuals with Limited English Proficiency*, (Washington, DC: Kaiser Commission on Medicaid and the Uninsured, August 2012), http://www.kff.org/uninsured/8343.cfm.

[9] Gopal Singh and Mohammad Siahpush, "Widening Socioeconomic Inequalities in US Life Expectancy 1980–2000," *International Journal of Epidemiology* 35 (May 2006):969–979, doi:10.1093/ije/dyl083.

[10] Ibid.

[11] David Williams, "A Time for Action: the Enigma of Social Disparities in Health and How to Effectively Address Them," PowerPoint Presentation.

[12] Thomas LaVeist, Darrell Gaskin, and Patrick Richard, *The Economic Burden of Health Inequalities in the United States*, (Washington, DC: Joint Center for Political and Economic Studies, September 2009), http://www.hhnmag.com/ext/resources/inc-hhn/pdfs/resources/Burden_Of_Health_FINAL_o.pdf.

[13] Ibid.

[14] Carmen DeNavas-Walt and Bernadette Proctor, *Income and Poverty in the United States: 2014 Current Population Reports*, (Washington, DC: US Census Bureau, September 2015), http://www.census.gov/content/dam/Census/library/publications/2015/demo/p60-252.pdf.

[15] The Kaiser Family Foundation State Health Facts. Data Source: Census Bureau's March 2015 Current Population Survey, "Poverty Rate by Race/Ethnicity. (2014)," accessed July 20, 2016, http://www.statehealthfacts.org/comparemaptable.jsp?ind=14&cat=1&sub=2&yr=274&typ=2.

[16] Kaiser Commission on Medicaid and the Uninsured, *The Uninsured: A Primer – Key Facts about Health Insurance and the Uninsured in the Era of Health Reform*, (Washington, DC: Kaiser Commission on Medicaid and the Uninsured, November 2015), http://files.kff.org/attachment/primer-the-uninsured-a-primer-key-facts-about-health-insurance-and-the-uninsured-in-the-era-of-health-reform.

[17] Kaiser Family Foundation, *Key Facts on Health and Health Care by Race and Ethnicity*, (Washington, DC: Kaiser Family Foundation, June 2016), http://files.kff.org/attachment/Chartpack-Key-Facts-on-Health-and-Health-Care-by-Race-and-Ethnicity.

[18] Ibid.

[19] Agency for Healthcare Research and Quality, *2014 National Healthcare Quality and Disparities Report*, (Rockville, MD: Agency for Healthcare Research and Quality, May 2015), http://www.ahrq.gov/sites/default/files/wysiwyg/research/findings/nhqrdr/nhqdr14/2014nhqdr.pdf.

[20] Kaiser Family Foundation, *Health And Access to Care and Coverage for Lesbian, Gay, Bisexual, and Transgender Individuals in the U.S.*, (Washington, DC: Kaiser Family Foundation, June 2016), http://kff.org/disparities-policy/issue-brief/health-and-access-to-care-and-coverage-for-lesbian-gay-bisexual-and-transgender-individuals-in-the-u-s/.

[21] Kaiser Commission on Medicaid and the Uninsured, *Overview of Health Coverage for Individuals with Limited English Proficiency*, (Washington, DC: Kaiser Commission on Medicaid and the Uninsured, August 2012), http://www.kff.org/uninsured/8343.cfm.

[22] Mitchell Peck and Meredith Denney, "Disparities in the Conduct of the Medical Encounter: The Effect of Physician and Patient Race and Gender," *SAGE Open* (Jul–Sep 2012):1-14, doi:10.1177/2158244012459193.

[23] Agency for Healthcare Research and Quality, *National Healthcare Disparities Report 2011*, (Rockville, MD: Agency for Healthcare Research and Quality, 2011), http://archive.ahrq.gov/research/findings/nhqrdr/nhdr11/nhdr11.pdf.

[24] Diane Smith, "Health Care Disparities for Person with Limited English Proficiency: Relationships from the 2006 Medical Expenditure Panel Survey," *Journal of Health Disparities Research and Practice 3(3)* (Spring 2012): 57–67.

[25] Kaiser Family Foundation, *Key Facts on Health and Health Care by Race and Ethnicity*, (Washington, DC: Kaiser Family Foundation, June 2016), http://files.kff.org/attachment/Chartpack-Key-Facts-on-Health-and-Health-Care-by-Race-and-Ethnicity.

[26] Ibid.

[27] Elizabeth Arias, "United States Life Tables, 2011," *National Vital Statistics Reports* 64(11) (Sep 2015).

[28] Paula Braverman et al., "Socioeconomic Disparities in Health in the United States: What the Patterns Tell Us," *American Journal of Public Health* 100(1) (April 2010):186–196.

[29] Kaiser Family Foundation, *Health And Access to Care and Coverage for Lesbian, Gay, Bisexual, and Transgender Individuals in the U.S.*, (Washington, DC: Kaiser Family Foundation, June 2016), http://kff.org/disparities-policy/issue-brief/health-and-access-to-care-and-coverage-for-lesbian-gay-bisexual-and-transgender-individuals-in-the-u-s/.

[30] U.S. Department of Health and Human Services, *Reducing Tobacco Use: A Report of the Surgeon General*, (Atlanta, Georgia: Centers for Disease Control and Prevention, 2000), http://www.cdc.gov/tobacco/data_statistics/sgr/2000/index.htm.

[31] U.S. Department of Health and Human Services, *Mental Health: Culture, Race, and Ethnicity. A Supplement to Mental Health: A Report of the Surgeon General*, (Rockville, MD: National Institute of Mental Health, August 2001), http://www.ncbi.nlm.nih.gov/books/NBK44243/.

[32] Pub. L. 106–525, Nov. 22, 2000, 114 Stat. 2495.

[33] U.S. Department of Health and Human Services, *Unequal Treatment: Confronting Racial and Ethnic Disparities in Health Care*, (Washington, DC: Institute of Medicine, March 2002), http://www.nationalacademies.org/hmd/Reports/2002/Unequal-Treatment-Confronting-Racial-and-Ethnic-Disparities-in-Health-Care.aspx.

[34] U.S. Department of Health and Human Services, *Unequal Treatment: What Healthcare Providers Need to Know about Racial and Ethnic Disparities in Healthcare*, (Washington, DC: Institute of Medicine, March 2002), http://www.nationalacademies.org/hmd/~/media/Files/Report%20Files/2003/Unequal-Treatment-Confronting-Racial-and-Ethnic-Disparities-in-Health-Care/Disparitieshcproviders8pgFINAL.pdf.

35 "Frequently Asked Question," National Partnership for Action to Health Disparities, revised March 25, 2016, http://www.minorityhealth.hhs.gov/npa/templates/browse.aspx?lvl=1&lvlid=5.

36 U.S. Department of Health and Human Services, *HHS Action Plan to Reduce Racial and Ethnic Disparities: Implementation Progress Report 2011-2014*, (Washington, DC: U.S. Department of Health and Human Services, November 2015), http://minorityhealth.hhs.gov/assets/pdf/FINAL_HHS_Action_Plan_Progress_Report_11_2_2015.pdf.

37 See Dennis Andrulis et al., *Patient Protection and Affordable Care Act of 2010: Advancing Health Equity for Racially and Ethnically Diverse Populations*, (Washington, DC: Joint Center for Political and Economic Studies, July 2010), http://www.jointcenter.org/research/patient-protection-and-affordable-care-act-of-2010-advancing-health-equity-for-racially-and for a comprehensive and detailed overview of these provisions.

38 U.S. Department of Health and Human Services, *The Power to Reduce Health Disparities: Voices from Reach Communities*, (Atlanta, GA: Centers for Disease Control and Prevention, 2007), https://stacks.cdc.gov/view/cdc/12109/.

39 Ibid.

40 See for example, the Cultural-Quality-Collaborative http://www.jhsph.edu/research/centers-and-institutes/johns-hopkins-center-for-health-disparities-solutions/Projects/culture_quality_collaborative.html, which is a network of leading healthcare organizations that is working to share ideas, experiences, and solutions to real world problems that arise as a result of cross-cultural interactions that hinder the elimination of disparities in healthcare settings.

41 "Accountable Health Communities Model," Centers for Medicare & Medicaid Services, revised May 18, 2016, https://innovation.cms.gov/initiatives/AHCM.

42 Robin Cohen, Michael Martinez, and Emily Zammitti, *Health Insurance Coverage: Early Release of Estimates from the National Health Interview Survey, 2015*, (Hyattsville, MD: National Center for Health Statistics, May 2016), http://www.cdc.gov/nchs/nhis/releases.htm.

Systemic Racism and U.S. Health Care

by Joe Feagin*, Zinobia Bennefield
Department of Sociology, Texas A&M University, College Station, TX 77845, USA

Abstract This article draws upon a major social science theoretical approach–systemic racism theory–to assess decades of empirical research on racial dimensions of U.S. health care and public health institutions. From the 1600s, the oppression of Americans of color has been systemic and rationalized using a white racial framing–with its constituent racist stereotypes, ideologies, images, narratives, and emotions. We review historical literature on racially exploitative medical and public health practices that helped generate and sustain this racial framing and related structural discrimination targeting Americans of color. We examine contemporary research on racial differentials in medical practices, white clinicians' racial framing, and views of patients and physicians of color to demonstrate the continuing reality of systemic racism throughout health care and public health institutions. We conclude from research that institutionalized white socioeconomic resources, discrimination, and racialized framing from centuries of slavery, segregation, and contemporary white oppression severely limit and restrict access of many Americans of color to adequate socioeconomic resources–and to adequate health care and health outcomes. Dealing justly with continuing racial "disparities" in health and health care requires a conceptual paradigm that realistically assesses U.S. society's white-racist roots and contemporary racist realities. We conclude briefly with examples of successful public policies that have brought structural changes in racial and class differentials in health care and public health in the U.S. and other countries.

Introduction

Decades of research indicate that a serious U.S. public health problem involves *systemic* white racism and its negative effects on minds and bodies in all racial groups, most especially Americans of color. Dealing justly with racial inequalities in health requires a conceptual analysis realistically assessing society's white-racist roots and contemporary structural-racist realities. We draw on the black counter-framed tradition and social science research in that tradition by Joe Feagin (2006; 2010) and other analysts (Bonilla-Silva, 1997; Feagin & Feagin, 1978; Feagin & Vera, 1995). Systemic racism theory is firmly grounded in the race-critical literature created since the 1960s black civil rights movement and first articulated for the health care system by Kwame Ture and Charles Hamilton (1967: 3–4). They argued that "racism" involves "predication of decisions and policies on considerations of race for the purpose of subordinating a racial group." While recognizing individual racism, they accented institutional (what we term systemic) racism that is "less overt" and "less identifiable in terms of specific individuals committing the acts. But it is no less destructive of human life."

We use important concepts from this analytical tradition–which has more fully illuminated key aspects of systemic racism than previous work on U.S. racial matters–and use that lens to assess the extensive impact of systemic racism in the medical and public health world. Absent an adoption of systemic racism concepts, which go beyond the "structural stigma" paradigm, that world is unlikely to seriously address racist realities and, thus, is likely to perpetuate them.

Systemic racism theory (Feagin, 2006; 2010) details these major dimensions of U.S. racism: the (1) dominant racial hierarchy, (2) comprehensive white racial framing, (3) individual and collective discrimination, (4) social reproduction of racial-material inequalities, and (5) racist institutions integral to white domination of Americans of color. The U.S. is a country with systemic oppression—centuries of genocide, 336 years of slavery and legal segregation, about 85 percent of U.S. history. Since the 17th century a white elite has played the central role in maintaining racialized institutions and a rationalizing white framing, while ordinary whites have usually supported oppression because of white privilege. Over about *20 generations*, whites have inherited socioeconomic resources from ancestors who benefitted unjustly from slavery, segregation, and other racial oppression. Unjust enrichment of whites from this oppression brought unjust impoverishment for people of color. To the present, Americans of color have been economically impoverished and unhealthy because white Americans have long used extensive discrimination and resistance to change to insure they as a group are economically much better off and generally healthier.

Today, unjustly inherited white resources and continuing discrimination restrict access of many Americans of color to better jobs, quality education, healthy neighborhoods, quality health care, and political power. From the beginning a white racial framing with its major elements—not only racial bias, but also *racial ideologies, images, narratives, emotions, and inclinations to discriminate*—has aggressively defended this unequal and unjust society.

Powerful white actors and racial framing

The conceptual language of most contemporary health researchers regarding racial matters is euphemistic or white-concealing—for example, vague white-framed language such as "racial disparities." Research on disparities typically focuses on health problems faced by people of color and neglects the white perpetuators of racist practices and institutions creating these problems. As researchers concerned with accuracy, we focus here on the roles, framing, and institutionalized actions of influential whites and problematize them as responsible for many health-related problems. In the literature we observe little attention to powerful, mostly white decisionmakers whose racial framing and racialized actions have created, shaped, or maintained these health inequalities—and the health-related institutions imbedding racial framing and inequalities.

The majority-white decisionmakers include public health researchers and policymakers, medical educators and officials, hospital administrators, and insurance and pharmaceutical executives, as well as important medical personnel. A substantial majority are white. According to an Association of American Medical Colleges report (2010), three quarters of those practicing medicine are white. Incomplete data suggest that whites are more dominant in prestigious specialties and heading up major medical practices, associations, hospital systems, and public health institutions. Some 77 percent of AMA delegates are white, as are 85 percent of AMA board members. At NIH, the director and six deputy directors are white, as are 23 of 27 directors of NIH agencies. The decision-making top of this complex is overwhelmingly white. Some 90 per cent of NIH branch and lab chiefs are white, as are 83 percent of senior investigators (Gottesman 2011, 2).

Over the last century, mainstream researchers working on inequality have developed relatively weak individualistic concepts such as "bias," "prejudice," and "cultural competence." Stronger analytical concepts are necessary—such as systemic racism, white discriminators, white racial framing—to make better sense of society's racist realities.

Significant data strongly suggest the majority of white health care and public health personnel and researchers operate from this white framing, with its pro-white and anti-racial-others orientations. This framing includes normalized notions (e.g., stereotypes, images, narratives, ideologies) of biologically and culturally distinct racial groups, and it links to discriminatory practices accounting for institutionalized inequalities in health care and health.

The structural approach: an important research shift

An increasing number of articles in the research literature have begun to locate racism in the health care context and health disparities (Gee & Ford, 2011; Paradies, 2006; Walters et al., 2011). We offer our theoretical insights to assist in substantially expanding their conceptual implications in the direction of a much more institutional and systemic racism direction. Generally, these articles fail to situate analysis of racism in pivotal research by those working in the tradition of the racial-realism founders of critical race theory. Assessing U.S. racism without drawing on the institutional racism research of critical researchers such as Ture and Hamilton, Derrick Bell, Joe Feagin, and Eduardo Bonilla Silva leads to recurring major oversights and errors, such as unreflectively equating individual prejudice with "racism."

For example, an article by Camara P. Jones (2000) briefly and insightfully lists three types of racism, including institutional racism, but has no references to this extensive critical race research; it theorizes a category of "personally mediated racism" in a way that accents individual prejudice without adequately contextualizing that in institutionalized racism. In 2003 Krieger noted that racism was coming out of the "closet" and being named as a determinant of population health, but that one still had to defend racism research. Health disparities involve both individual and institutional actions generating "oppressive systems" (Krieger, 2003). She categorized structural pathways by which racism harms health but did not develop the concept of institutional racism drawing on critical race research. Recently, Gee and Ford (2011) have accented "structural racism" as a concept needing integration into disparities research and do, briefly, cite some critical race research. Yet, they only begin to take the steps necessary for analyzing well the impact of *white-controlled* systemic racism on health care.

Numerous empirical studies have studied individual discrimination by medical professionals (e.g., Williams & Mohammed, 2009). However, as Ture and Hamilton (1967) long ago argued, while such individual acts are important, they constitute a tiny snapshot of the larger institutional racism picture. Other micro- and meso-level research, such as that on residential segregation (Acevedo-Garcia, 2003; LaVeist, 1989, 1993; Massey, 1988; Williams & Collins, 2001), identifies aspects of inequality in U.S. institutions and some health consequences, but typically fails to draw on the critical literature on systemic racism and to assess directly how the racist actions of specific white actors regularly shape those institutions and their health consequences.

We recognize the importance of this relatively new emphasis on certain structural determinants of health. However, using historical and contemporary data, we emphasize white-created systemic racism as it operates at the micro-individual level and also at the meso and macro levels of the health care system. Studies of individual discrimination and residential segregation are evidence at the micro and meso levels, respectively, that a theory of systemic racism at the broader macro level is accurate and necessary for a full explanation of U.S. racism and health inequalities.

Phelan and Link (2004) have pioneered in a fundamental-cause-of-disease theory seeking to explain socioeconomic and racial disparities. Phelan, Link, Diez-Roux, Kawachi, and Levin (2004: 268) argue the "fundamental cause explanation posits that the use of resources to benefit heath, by groups and individuals, is purposeful." Link and Phelan (1995) and Phelan, Link, and Tehranifar (2010) accent racial disparities in health, but do not examine how racial and socioeconomic status are closely interwoven. Many generations of unjust enrichment from oppression have resulted in whites having superior resources. People with high socioeconomic status utilize superior resources for better health, while individuals with low status have historically been denied such resources. Health researchers need to better specify the racially advantaged identities and advantages of privileged whites who control the differential allocation of relevant resources. This accent on resource inequality along socioeconomic and racial lines marks an important shift, but draws little on the critical-race tradition and does not

explicitly articulate the ongoing racist realities of the institutionalized *white* racial framing and practices of the health care system.

Individual experiences of health care and broader public health issues should be considered together when examining racism and health. Socioeconomic fundamentals, many generated by racist practices in institutions other than health care, significantly shape public health, but so do practices of medical and other health decision-makers. Although health care providers care for individuals, their racial views are not just individualized, but are part of the shared white racial frame learned in society (Feagin, 2010). Provider-patient relationships that are racialized affect the health of populations. Americans of color get much health information and treatment from white or white-oriented professionals. Among other analysts (e.g., Williams, 2012), Roberts (1996: 117–122) argues that (mostly white) doctors' treatment decisions about women of color involving ethical dilemmas are not just individual decisions, but are shaped by the power most such practitioners secure from society's gender/racial hierarchies. All physician-patient relationships, especially those involving white (or white-oriented) physicians and patients of color, are relationships shaped by societal-power imbalances, and thus are matters of public health. Medical decisions are not isolated from contextual constraints, but centrally involve groups of white or white-oriented physicians and large publics of color. Consider that black women are less likely to contract breast cancer than whites, yet, if they contract it, they are much more likely to die. Black women with white physicians are often not educated as well about preventive care, are not screened as effectively, or are not as often referred to state-of-the-art treatments as white women with white physicians (Ginty, 2005; Roberts, 2011; loc. 2540–48). As a result, morbidity rates associated with breast cancer are affected by patient–physician interaction, as well as by unjust distribution of health care resources from generations of systemic racism.

Historically, medical and other health organizations, such as the American Medical Association, have contributed significantly to white bio-racist framing of Americans of color –and have done little to counter continuing bio-racist framing in white (and white-oriented) practitioners', officials', and researchers' minds. Consider the explosion of genome science and "race." Roberts (2011, loc. 5589-96) summarizes: Biologized "race is central to every aspect of the new science and technology that is emerging from genomic research." Pseudo-scientific, biological-race categories are thereby reinforced (Daniels & Schulz, 2006).

Important historical background: persisting systemic racism

Generally, the medical and public health communities, including their mostly white leadership and leading medical schools, seem unwilling to examine the current impacts of past racial oppression on U.S. medical and public health institutions. Systemic racism and medical/biological science, including the latter's medical and public health practices, evolved together in society. Medical treatments and public health practices were frequently matters involving a white-racist framing. For example, in the 18th-19th centuries prominent white physicians, medical professors, and biological scientists played a central role in creating the conception of "race" at the heart of the still-dominant white racial framing (Feagin, 2010).

Roberts (1996: 123) argues contemporary dehumanizing medical treatments of black women are grounded in a racist history of medical experimentation. In the 19th century, profit-driven growth of the scientific medical system pressed white physicians and scientists to discover technologies and treatments to serve whites. In the South medical experiments were carried out on black women that no white physician would try on whites. This resulted in death for many enslaved women and set the model for continued use of African Americans as guinea pigs for medical progress, as well as for white physicians' provision of inadequate care for them (Washington, 2006). Black women were often denied treatment for real ailments, resulting in excruciatingly painful deaths for many (Roberts, 1996; Washington, 2006). The racialized abuse endured today by black patients frequently replicates the racialized abuse their ancestors suffered.

Medical historians and reporters often exalt white physicians and medical scientists who committed *atrocities*. For example, James Marion Sims

is venerated as the father of gynecology. Rarely do mainstream accounts assess his sadistic treatment of blacks. In the mid-1800s black children died from a neuromuscular disease caused by mineral/vitamin deficiencies. Convinced it was caused by misplaced skull bones, Sims conducted surgical experiments without anesthesia (Sims, 1884). He "took a black baby from its mother, made incisions in its scalp, then wielded a cobbler's tool to pry the skull bones into new positions" (Washington, 2006: 62). Sims (1884) forced Anarcha, an enslaved girl suffering from fistulas, to kneel in agony while he inserted a speculum into her vagina and attempted to close ravaged openings by abrading their edges before suturing (Sims, 1884; Washington, 2006). Other whites held Anarcha as she screamed. Only when perfected did he perform this surgery on whites, with anesthesia (Sims, 1884).

Collaborative actions of abusive experimentation and malpractice by early medical scientists and physicians often set a white model for later discriminatory experimentation and treatment. Throughout the first half of the 20th century, black women were recurring victims of involuntary sterilization and hysterectomies (Hartmann, 1995). One was Fannie Lou Hamer, later a civil rights leader. In 1961 she was hospitalized to have a uterine tumor removed; the white doctor performed a hysterectomy instead. "I went to the doctor who did that to me and I asked him, 'Why? Why had he done that to me?' He didn't have to say nothing—and he didn't." (DeMuth, 1964: 538, 549). Hamer was silenced by powerful white agents of a systemically racist system. Hundreds of black women have reported a similar story; thousands more probably remain undocumented (Hartmann, 1995).

Black women suffered at the hands of physicians and scientists involved in early 20th century "eugenics." According to Washington (2006: 191), "Eugenics was appropriated to label Black women as sexually indiscriminate and as bad mothers who were constrained by biology to give birth to defective children. The demonization of Black parents, particularly mothers, as medically and behaviorally unfit has a long history, but twentieth century eugenicists provided the necessary biological underpinnings to scientifically validate these beliefs." Margaret Sanger, birth control pioneer, helped to devise a 1939 "Negro Project," which sought to reduce the black population through negative eugenics (Sanger, 1922). Partly due to Sanger's lobbying, numerous forms of birth control were tested in black communities. Because of high levels of hormones in early pills, black women were placed at high risk of hypertension and stroke; early IUDs were silent killers in African American communities because of the high rate of infection associated with them (Washington, 2006). White women were mostly sheltered from these effects. White government officials supported birth-control-eugenics and forced sterilization by funding experimentation. Thousands suffered and died in this highly racist medical system (Darity & Turner, 1972, 1973).

In 1932 the U.S. Public Health Service joined with Tuskegee Institute in its "Study of Syphilis in the Untreated Male." White study directors sought a cure for the disease and to study how it manifested, positing that it affected neurological systems of white men but only sexual organs of black men—because in these directors' racist framing blacks had primitive brains and sexual desires. After a good treatment for syphilis was discovered, white physicians withheld it to examine how syphilis ravaged black bodies. Many died or passed on the disease (Jones & Tuskegee Institute, 1981). Moreover, in 1951 Henrietta Lacks, a black woman, went to John Hopkins hospital for a lump in her abdomen. Diagnosed with cancer, she was treated with radiation. Blood samples were taken without her knowledge. Doctors abandoned radiation for antibiotics because they believed her condition to be caused by venereal disease. She died, and her stolen blood cells were given to George Grey. He discovered they survived exponentially longer than other cell samples and mass-produced them for profit. Her cells have been used to help develop a polio vaccine and research cancer. Not until the 1970s did the public learn her cells had started a multi-billion dollar industry. Lacks got posthumous credit for her "donation" to science, but her children have not been given any money generated, nor has anyone been sanctioned for cell theft (Skloot, 2010).

Much of this historical white-racist framing of black patient inferiority and white medical superiority remains operative in health-related institutions. Key elements of age-old racism are evident in institutionalized discrimination targeting patients of color–and white insistence on white authority, norms, and framing as medically and organizationally correct. There are great similarities to this racist past in commonplace white condescension and the institutionalized practice of ignoring black patients' and physicians' perspectives on barriers in health-related organizations. The contemporary neglect of this racist history is also related to systemic racism, for it is rarely taught in historically white medical schools and schools of public health (Hoberman, 2012).

Differential racial treatments today: health care providers

Much research demonstrates the systemically racist character of contemporary health patterns, medical framing and practices, and health care institutions. Numerous disparities reports demonstrate that Americans of color "continue to suffer from greater health problems than their white counterparts . . . . African-American women are more likely to die of breast cancer than women of any other racial or ethnic group. American Indians are nearly three times as likely to be diagnosed with diabetes as White Americans. Eighty-two percent of the pediatric AIDS cases . . . . consisted of African-American and Latino children" (Association of American Medical Colleges, 2010: 11.) Such inequalities do not result from something inherent in Americans of color, but are health consequences of systemic racism's pathways of negative impact.

Numerous studies demonstrate African Americans, Latinos, Native Americans, and Asian Americans receive a poorer quality of health care (Chin, Walters, Cook, & Huang, 2007; Smedley, Stith, & Nelson, 2003). One review noted that researchers have "repeatedly documented racial and ethnic differences in access to invasive diagnostic and therapeutic interventions for heart disease and stroke. Study findings have consistently indicated that African Americans are less likely to receive pharmacological therapy, diagnostic angiography and catheterization, and invasive surgical treatments for heart disease and stroke relative to white Americans with similar clinical disease characteristics" (Mayberry, Mili, & Ofili,

2000: 122). In one study actors portrayed black and white patients with coronary disease symptoms. Some 720 physicians were asked to look at these recorded interviews and other patient data, assess the probability of disease, and suggest treatments. Blacks were less likely to be recommended for standard catheterization, compared to whites with similar occupations and medical histories. Another study found black patients with lung cancer were less likely to receive the best surgical treatment than white patients (Bach et al., 1999; Fincher et al., 2004; Schulman et al, 1999).

Researchers have found barriers for blacks and the poor in getting kidney transplants, and that black patients are less likely to receive transplants than whites. The reasons suggested by one group of researchers included physicians' "subconscious bias" and "financial disincentives" (Alexander & Sehgal, 1998). Another study found most black patients with end-stage renal disease wanted transplants, yet large differences in proportions of black and white patients referred by physicians for transplantation were not explained by control variables (Ayanian et al., 1999). Implied or explicit in some of these studies is blaming patients of color for being too passive, in contrast to white patients who have better health because they "actively" seek it. One study reported in the *New England Journal of Medicine* (Anonymous, 1996) showed that among Medicare patients blacks with circulatory problems were much more likely to have a leg amputated than otherwise comparable whites, and blacks with prostate cancer were much more likely than others to have testicles removed. Black patients with problems comparable to whites got less attention from nurses, fewer tests, and less sophisticated or no heart treatments. Other researchers have found significant racial differences in access to best therapies for HIV/AIDS, prenatal care, and child health services (e.g., Mayberry et al., 2000).

Another study (Gemson, Linson, & Messeri, 1988) found physicians with 50 percent or more black and Hispanic patients differed greatly in treatments of patients compared to physicians with 50 percent or more white patients. The former were less likely to recommend mammography screening, influenza immunization for older patients, and smoking cessation programs.

Physicians with more patients of color often failed to recommend best treatments and seemed to be highly influenced by a racial framing of health behaviors of patients of color. A study of emergency room care found that (predominantly black) children with sickle-cell disease got less attention to pain than nonblack (apparently mostly white) children with bone fractures (Zempsky, Corsi, & McKay, 2011). One overview study (Cintron & Morrison, 2006) examined medical articles on pain and found patients of color were more likely to have their pain taken too lightly and less likely to have it medically recorded accurately than white patients. In a majority of studies patients of color were less likely than whites to get best quality pain management.

In addition, researchers have found that for decades African Americans have frequently been misdiagnosed by (mostly white) mental health professionals. Beginning in the 1960s, black men seen by clinicians as anti-establishment protestors were frequently diagnosed as "schizophrenic" or otherwise mentally ill (Metzl, 2010). African Americans in some areas are today at a greater risk than whites "of being conscripted into [health care] research without giving their consent, because Blacks are more likely than Whites to receive their health care from emergency rooms" (Washington, 2006: 397). One scandal involving medical research since the 1940s is the heavy use of people of color as "guinea pigs." Their health is often negatively affected, yet they are frequently abandoned once research is completed. In 1945, white doctors, working with the Atomic Energy Commission, injected plutonium into patients of color without consent to observe effects of radiation, without follow-up care (Washington, 2006; Welsome, 1999). Recently, prisoners of color have been used for drug trials, including for drugs too toxic for use on the general population (Mitford, 1973; Washington, 2006).

In some research areas the needs of Americans of color get little attention. In spite of high rates of certain cancers (Ginty, 2005), black women are less likely than whites to be prescribed innovative cancer treatments or combination therapy or to be included in important research on these cancers (Dressler, 1993; Ginty, 2005). Karen Jackson of the Sisters Network has criticized foundation-funded research: "Some clinical trials are set up to automatically exclude women of color. In breast cancer studies, for instance, most research is done on the estrogen-positive form of the disease and not on the estrogen-negative form common among African American women" (Ginty, 2005: 1). This lack of inclusion may be one reason African Americans die from such cancers at higher rates.

One problem with much research on differential medical treatment is that researchers focus on the "trees" and neglect "forest" issues. For example, in 2003 the Institute of Medicine published an important report on differential treatment (Smedley et al., 2003). It provides an excellent overview of research at the time, but tiptoes around the contextual issue of institutional and systemic racism. The term "institutional racism" does not appear in the report, "institutional discrimination" appears once in passing, and there is no analysis in the main body of the report on the elite, mostly white, administrators and professionals who control major decisionmaking at the top of the racially inegalitarian health care institutions.

Implicit bias: only *one* aspect of the white racial frame

Mainstream researchers have attempted to explain health care differentials. Some focus on patients of color as having problems communicating with or distrusting physicians, yet do not systematically examine why. Others reference the medical system as less responsive to patients of color, but such commentaries are usually underdeveloped or written in the passive voice with hidden causal agents. Researchers speak of "unknown" or "complex" causes. In no article that we have seen are the systemic discrimination and associated white racial framing in health care and public health institutions systematically analyzed in regard to health disparities.

Some research demonstrates one aspect of racial framing by health professionals. Several studies examine the "implicit" or "unconscious" bias of providers and make use of the implicit association test (IAT). When given this test of supposedly unconscious stereotyping, most whites associate images of black faces with negative words and

traits (e.g., negative character traits). Most have more difficulty in linking photos of black faces to pleasant words and positive traits than they do for white faces. Analyses of thousands of face-reaction tests show the overwhelming majority of whites reveal an antiblack, pro-white bias (Dasgupta, McGhee, Greenwald, & Banaji, 2000). Other research shows that IAT scores predict interracial behaviors better than explicitly measured attitudes (Greenwald et al., 2009).

One study using the IAT online examined responses of 2535 self-identified physicians. Seventy percent revealed they implicitly preferred whites to blacks. White physicians, most of this sample, revealed the strongest implicit white preference, Black physicians showed no implicit preference for white or black Americans (Sabin, Nosek, Greenwald, & Rivara, 2009). Another study of mostly white pediatricians found that they revealed an implicit preference for whites over blacks, but the preference was not as great as that found for other whites. These pediatricians also revealed a stereotype of black patients as more compliant than whites (Sabin, Rivara, & Greenwald, 2008). A related study (Sabin & Greenwald, 2012) found that pediatricians' IAT scores were correlated with differentials in recommended pain treatments favoring white patients. One review of five studies found that four studies documented an implicit antiblack bias among clinicians, but only one of two that examined the impact of implicit bias on treatments found a connection (Blair, Steiner, & Havranek, 2011).

In the few studies faulting practitioners for racial bias, analysts speak of "well-intentioned" or "fatigued" practitioners who exhibit *unconscious* bias. One research group suggests that "Even well-intentioned providers who are motivated to be non-prejudiced may stereotype racial/ethnic minority members, particularly under . . . time pressure, fatigue, and information overload—are frequently found in health care settings" (Burgess, Fu, & Van Ryn, 2004: 1154). John Hoberman (2012) cites numerous medical literature examples of similar health professionals and researchers tiptoeing around realities of "medical racism" with such an accent on unconscious bias.

Beyond implicit bias: more extensive racial framing

Understanding systemic racism and how it shapes health and health care requires going beyond a conceptualization of individual racial biases disconnected from a broad white racial framing and associated structural power inequalities. Systemic discrimination has long been reproduced by a well-institutionalized white framing—through recurring racial stereotypes and prejudices ("biases"), but also through racist ideologies, images, narratives, emotions, and inclinations to discriminate in practice. Much research (Feagin, 2006, 2010) demonstrates that an age-old, white racial framing remains central to most white minds.

A slowly growing research literature indicates many white health care providers harbor a broad racial framing of Americans of color, one that can be causative in their not providing equitable health care. Such framing involves not only implicit bias but also more overt racial perspectives that shape white (and white-oriented) physicians' interactions with patients of color. One study found that (mostly white) physicians tend to view black patients and those with low incomes less favorably than white patients and those with higher incomes. White patients were viewed as more intelligent and likely to follow professional advice (Van Ryn & Burke, 2000). Research has shown that many white physicians automatically assume that black women lack the drive to follow medical instructions or the income necessary to afford medication (Dressler 1993; Ginty 2005). One rare study (Malat, Clark-Hitt, Burgess, Friedemann-Sanchez, & Van Ryn, 2010) conducted interviews with white doctors and nurses about how they explain racial inequalities. They most often blamed patients themselves—black patients for being passive and failing to make medical requests of practitioners. They rarely implicated white practitioners' discrimination in explaining inequality in care.

One survey of physicians found most whites agreed with a statement that patients rarely suffer racial discrimination in medical treatments, while only a small minority of black physicians also agreed (Clark-Hitt et al.. 2010). Another study (Snipes et al., 2011) found white and black physicians hold similar beliefs that medical information is most important for decision-making. Focus groups with white and black physicians revealed that most whites (the majority had few patients of color) consciously expressed the view that patients' race (apparently including racial experience) was unimportant in treatment decision-making and that medical history should drive decision-making. Whites exhibited discomfort in talking about race. Most black physicians (a substantial majority with many patients of color) had no difficulty in discussing racial matters, and many reported patients' racial backgrounds, experience, and cultural understandings were relevant to treatments.

These limited studies suggest important elements of deep racial framing beyond "bias," such as racially framed interpretations, as revealed by white or white-oriented decisionmakers in key roles in health-related institutions. Venturing beyond implicit bias, they point strongly to systemic racism at the heart of health inequalities. Researchers assessing racial inequalities in health outcomes usually ignore the central importance of white decisionmakers in significant institutional roles who operate out of this white frame in shaping or sabotaging the health of people of color. Structural explanations of disparities that accent differentials in socioeconomic resources or housing segregation are important for moving away from biological-race, blame-the-victim approaches, but do not offer a sufficient explanation for persisting racial differentials (Daniels & Schulz, 2006).

Linking racial framing to treatment

White-oriented health practitioners typically bring to interactions with patients of color the broad racial framing that whites have long used. Only a few studies show more explicitly that physicians' racial framing includes views of how suitable black patients are for important procedures or how likely black patients are to follow a physician's directions (Anonymous, 2001; Feagin & McKinney, 2003). One study found that physicians were less trusting of nonwhite HIV patients. Researchers suggested this distrustful view might explain why patients of color got inadequate pain management compared to whites (Moskowitz et al., 2011).

One Harvard study examined the connection between explicit and unconscious racial bias of 287 Boston and Atlanta physicians and their thrombolysis recommendations for white and black patients. These mostly white physicians showed no overt bias for white or black patients when asked explicit questions, yet showed a prowhite, antiblack bias on the IAT. As prowhite bias increased, so did their likelihood of treating white and black patients differently in regard to procedures like "thrombolysis for myocardial infarction" (Green et al., 2007). Another recent study (Cooper et al., 2012) of mostly white and Asian inner-city physicians found those with greater implicit racial bias and stereotyping in regard to patient compliance were more likely to dominate dialogs with black patients, have less positive patient responses during the visit, and get more negative patient ratings on trust and confidence. Another study of Johns Hopkins' medical students found that a substantial majority exhibited an implicit preference for whites, but this preference did not translate into discrimination in judgments about vignette-based clinical assessments (Haider et al., 2011).

The importance of listening to patients and physicians of color

Another issue is the lack of detailed attention paid by white health decisionmakers to views of black patients, physicians, and community representatives about health issues. A growing number of studies (Burgess et al. 2008; Hausmann, Jeong, Bost, & Ibrahim, 2008; Krieger, 1990; Ryan, Gee, & Grith, 2008) have reported on the important, often revealing views of patients of color. One Seattle survey (Seattle and King County Department of Public Health, 2001) found that African Americans and Native Americans were 3–4 times as likely as whites to report discrimination in health care.

Researchers have found that white physicians who accept, consciously or unconsciously, the white frame's old racial stereotypes are likely to communicate negative feelings in verbal or nonverbal treatment behavior, sometimes causing patients of color to withhold the health self-disclosure necessary for effective treatment (Ridley, 1984). While concordance studies indicate many patients prefer

practitioners from their racial-ethnic group (Saha, Komaromy, Koepsell, & Bindman, 1999), this situation is especially difficult for African Americans facing a mostly nonblack health care system. Given their personal and collective history of experiencing medical racism, many African American women and men feel uncomfortable expressing medical concerns to professionals who are disproportionately white men. Because many white physicians treat patients of color inadequately, the latter often prefer physicians of color or physicians from their racial group (Saha, Arbelaez, & Cooper, 2003). Patients of color often rate them as superior to white physicians in decision making and providing information, treating patients with respect, or being available (Cooper-Patrick et al., 2009; Saha, Taggart, Komaromy, & Bindman, 2000). Assessing the literature, Sabin et al. (2009) have summarized the consequences stemming from experiences of people of color with recurring discrimination by health care personnel–added stress, distrust of health care practitioners, delays in seeking medical care and returning for follow-ups, and not adhering to prescribed treatments or screening recommendations. These studies thus link well-institutionalized, discriminatory medical practices to likely effects on morbidity and mortality rates for populations of color. A survey (Peterson, Friedman, Ash, Franco, & Carr, 2004) of faculty at two dozen medical schools found a substantial majority of underrepresented minority (mostly black) faculty reported racial barriers, while only 29 percent of white faculty agreed there were racial barriers.

Conclusion: seeking systemic solutions

Racism in health care and public health institutions is multidimensional and systemic. We recognize that generations of white-imposed racism in other institutions—including employment, housing, and education–have contributed greatly to racial inequalities in health. We accent here the racial character and impact of health care institutions and their practitioners on these significant health inequalities. Importantly, we emphasize that even much race-critical literature does not call out specifically and analyze *who* controls these major institutions. Racialized health and health care inequalities are centrally generated by the direct and indirect discriminatory actions of powerful white decision-makers and other key decisionmakers operating out of a white racial framing. Over centuries racial framing and consequent discrimination by health-related decisionmakers have produced and institutionalized health care inequalities for Americans of color and have also reinforced racist decisions in other major institutions. Operating jointly, these decisions have had significant negative impacts on morbidity and mortality for Americans of color. White racism is systemic and involves far more than individual racial bias.

Some analysts say "you can't change structural inequalities" and "let's focus on what we can change." However, numerous countries have made progress in reducing health inequalities. Research on Canada and European countries shows that shifting health care framing and structuring to accent well-run nationalized health care has positive systemic impacts. Countries with nationalized systems not so linked to race and class usually have less health inequality than the U.S. (Olafsdottir, 2007; Wilson, 2009). In the U.S., the white-black mortality gap lessened during the 1960s-1980s era of anti-poverty programs—which era significantly reduced segregation in health-related institutions and racial-socioeconomic differences (Krieger et al., 2008; Roberts, 2011, Kindle loc. 2900–2912). That mortality gap increased in the 1980s with conservative efforts rolling back government programs substantially benefiting Americans of color.

Our leading public health institutions, the 30-billion-dollar National Institutes of Health, have done much to improve health research, yet remain substantially white-run and white-oriented. Only recently (2010) was the NIH minority health center redesignated the National Institute on Minority Health and Health Disparities–with expanded, if modest, funding for minority health initiatives (National Institute on Minority Health and Health Disparities, 2012). Additionally, disparities research efforts at numerous other NIH institutes and centers are ongoing, but overall remain seriously underfunded (Thomson, Mitchell, & Williams, 2006). Public agencies' and private foundations' periodic studies of health inequalities are moving in the correct direction, yet have usually brought modest positive health policy results

for Americans of color. Major, publicly discussed research on systemic health-related racism and its mostly white decisionmakers has barely begun (see Lukachko, Hatzenbuehler, & Keyes, 2014; Williams, 2012), yet this seems the minimum national effort necessary to move the white majority's political will to back significant health policy changes.

We need to press influential white (and white-oriented) administrators, researchers, and politicians who structure and control health-related institutions to step away from dominant white racial framing and learn counter-framing from Americans of color. Comprehensive research and other educational efforts to *publicly voice* experiences of people of color with institutionalized racism in health-related institutions–and their policy solutions–constitute one step. These voices will likely say that tier-generated health care inequalities (see Golub et al., 2011) should be eliminated and that all populations must have access to the best medical facilities and staffing.

Another educational effort should involve calling out and teaching about the commonplace racist framing and structured-in practices of white (and white-oriented) administrators and professionals who still mostly control historically white medical, public health, and research-funding institutions. They too need to listen to the important voices and counter-framing of people of color. One recent study (Ginther et al., 2011) found that black NIH applicants were significantly less likely than comparable whites to receive research funding. Consider also condescending public health efforts that take the form of apparently benevolent whites seeking to free people of color from "destructive health habits." These "white savior" efforts are similar to those of Western missionaries who have tried to convert people overseas to "better" western folkways (Warwick, 2006). Instead, we need to forthrightly problematize the unhealthy racist framing and damaging discrimination of white public health officials and health care personnel.

Beyond education, those concerned about structural reform in health-related institutions need to organize for change. One goal would be an accent on aggressive enforcement of existing civil rights laws. Title VI of the 1964 Civil Rights Act bans discrimination in health-related institutions: "No person in the United States shall, on the grounds of race, color, or national origin, be excluded from participation in, be denied the benefits of, or be subjected to discrimination under any program or activity receiving Federal financial assistance." Yet this law has rarely been assertively enforced in our health-related institutions (Fauci, 2001).

In sum, while the current efforts of some health-related researchers and public health organizations to research racial disparities in health do advance the country in the direction of equity in health and health care, no lasting changes for all Americans will occur until systemic racism is more directly conceptualized, focused upon, and eradicated.

Acknowledgment

We are indebted to Jessie Daniels and Verna Keith for comments on earlier drafts.

References

Acevedo-Garcia, D., et al. (2003). Future directions in residential segregation and health research: a multilevel approach. *American Journal of Public Health, 93*(2), 215–221.

Alexander, G. C., & Sehgal, A. R. (1998). Barriers to cadaveric renal transplantation among blacks, women, and the poor. *Journal of the American Medical Association, 280*, 1148–1152.

Anonymous. (1996). The New England Journal of Medicine produces flat-out proof of racism in medicare-funded medicine. *Journal of Blacks in Higher Education, 13*, 39.

Anonymous. (2001). Racial disparities in medical care. *The New England Journal of Medicine, 344*(19), 1471–1473.

Association of American Medical Colleges. (2010). *Diversity in the physician workforce: Facts & figures 2010* (pp. 11). Washington, D.C.: Association of American Medical Colleges.

Ayanian, J. Z., et al. (1999). The effect of patients' preferences on racial differences in access to transplantation. *New England Journal of Medicine, 341*, 1661–1669.

Bach, P. B., et al. (1999). Racial differences in the treatment of early-stage lung cancer. *New England Journal of Medicine, 341*, 1198–1205.

Blair, I. V., Steiner, J. F., & Havranek, E. P. (2011). Unconscious (implicit) bias and health disparities: where do we go from here? *Permanente Journal, 15*(2), 71–78.

Bonilla-Silva, E. (1997). Rethinking racism: toward a structural interpretation. *American Sociological Review, 62*(3), 465–480.

Burgess, D. J., Ding, Y., Hargreaves, M., et al. (2008). The association between perceived discrimination and underutilization of needed medical and mental health care in a multi-ethnic community sample. *Journal of Health Care for the Poor and Underserved, 3*, 894–911.

Burgess, D. J., Fu, S. S., & Van Ryn, M. (2004). Why do providers contribute to disparities and what can be done about it? *Journal of General Internal Medicine, 19*, 1154–1159.

Chin, M. H., Walters, A. E., Cook, S. C., & Huang, E. S. (2007). Interventions to reduce racial and ethnic disparities in health care. *Medical Care Research and Review, 64*(5), 7S–28S.

Cintron, A., & Morrison, C. A. (2006). Pain and ethnicity in the United States: a systematic review. *Journal of Palliative Medicine, 9*(6), 1454–1473.

Clark-Hitt, R., et al. (2010). Doctors' and nurses' explanations for racial disparities in medical treatment. *Journal of Health Care for the Poor and Underserved, 21*, 387–390.

Cooper-Patrick, L., Gallo, J., Gonzales, J., et al. (2009). Race, gender, and partnership in the patient-physician relationship. *The Journal of the American Medical Association, 282*(6), 583–589.

Cooper, L. A., Roter, D. L., Carson, K. A., Beach, M. C., Sabin, J. A., Greenwald, A. G., et al. (2012). The associations of clinicians' implicit attitudes about race with medical visit communication and patient ratings of interpersonal care. *American Journal of Public Health, 102*, 979–987.

Daniels, J., & Schulz, A. J. (2006). Whiteness and the construction of health disparities. In Leith Mullings, & Amy J. Schulz (Eds.), *Gender, race, class, and health* (pp. 89–127). San Francisco, CA.: Jossey-Bass.

Darity, W. A., & Turner, C. B. (1972). Family planning, race consciousness and the fear of race genocide. *American Journal of Public Health, 62*, 1454–1459.

Darity, W. A., & Turner, C. B. (1973). Fears of genocide among black Americans as related to age, sex, and region. *American Journal of Public Health, 63*, 1029–1034.

Dasgupta, N., McGhee, D. E., Greenwald, A. G., & Banaji, M. R. (2000). Automatic preference for white Americans: eliminating the familiarity explanation. *Journal of Experimental Social Psychology, 36*, 316–328.

DeMuth, J. (1964). Sick and tired of being sick and tired. *The Nation, 538,* 549.

Dressler, W. W. (1993). Health in the African American community: accounting for health inequalities. *Medical Anthropology Quarterly, 7*(4), 321–416.

Fauci, C. A. (2001). Racism and health care in America: legal responses to racial disparities in the allocation of kidneys. *Boston College Third World Law Journal, 21,* 35–68.

Feagin, J. R. (2006). *Systemic racism: A theory of oppression.* New York: Routledge.

Feagin, J. R. (2010). *Racist America.* Revised ed. New York: Routledge

Feagin, J. R., & Feagin, C. (1978). *Discrimination American style: Institutional racism and sexism.* Englewood Cliffs, N.J.: Prentice-Hall.

Feagin, J. R., & McKinney, K. (2003). *The many costs of racism.* Lanham, MD: Rowman and Littlefield.

Feagin, J. R., & Vera, H. (1995). *White racism: The basics.* New York: Routledge.

Fincher, C., et al. (2004). Racial disparities in coronary heart disease: sociological view of the medical literature on physician bias. *Ethnicity & Disease, 14,* 360–371.

Gee, G., & Ford, C. (2011). Structural racism and health Inequities: old issues, new directions. *Du Bois Review, 8*(1), 115–132.

Gemson, D. H., Linson, J., & Messeri, P. (1988). Differences in physician prevention practice patterns for white and minority patients. *Journal of Community Health, 15*(1), 53–64.

Ginther, D. K., Schaffer, W. T., Schnell, J., Masimore, B., Liu, F., Haak, L. L., et al. (2011). Race, ethnicity, and NIH research awards. *Science, 333,* 1015–1019.

Ginty, M. M. (2005). Black women at higher risk for major diseases. *We News.* Available at http://womensenews.org/story/health/050225/black-women-at-higher-risk-major-diseases Accessed 13.10.09.

Golub, M., et al. (2011). Community mobilizes to end medical apartheid. *Progress in Community Health Partnerships: Research, Education, and Action, 5*(3), 317–325.

Gottesman, M. (2011). Valuing diversity at NIH. *NIH Catalyst, 19,* 2.

Green, A. R., et al. (2007). Implicit bias among physicians and its prediction of thrombolysis decisions for black and white patients. *Journal of General and Internal Medicine, 22,* 1231–1238.

Greenwald, A. G., Poehlman, A. T., Ulhman, E., et al. (2009). Understanding and using the implicit association test: III. meta-analysis of predictive validity. *Journal of Personality and Social Psychology, 97,* 17–41.

Haider, A. H., et al. (2011). Association of unconscious race and social class bias with vignette-based clinical assessments by medical students. *The Journal of the American Medical Association, 306*(9), 942–951.

Hartmann, B. (1995). *Reproductive rights and wrongs: The global politics of population control.* Boston: South End Press.

Hausmann, L. R. M., Jeong, K., Bost, J. E., & Ibrahim, S. A. (2008). Perceived discrimination in health care and health status in a racially diverse sample medical care. *Medical Care, 46*(9), 905–914.

Hoberman, J. (2012). *Black and blue: The origins and consequences of medical racism.* Berkeley, California: University of California Press.

Jones, C. (2000). Levels of racism: a theoretic framework and a Gardener's tale. *American Journal of Public Health, 90*(8), 1212–1215.

Jones, J. H., & Tuskegee Institute. (1981). *Bad blood: The Tuskegee syphilis experiment.* New York and London: Free Press.

Krieger, N. (1990). Racial and gender discrimination: risk factors for high blood pressure? *Social Science & Medicine, 30,* 1273–1281.

Krieger, N. (2003). Does racism harm health? Did child abuse exist before 1962? On explicit questions, critical science, and current controversies: an ecosocial perspective. *American Journal of Public Health, 93*(2), 194–199.

Krieger, N., Rehkopf, D. H., Chen, J. T., Waterman, P. D., Marcelli, E., & Kennedy, M. (2008). The fall and rise of US inequities in premature mortality: 1960–2002. *PLoS Medicine, 5*(2), 227–241.

LaVeist, T. (1989). Linking residential segregation to the infant mortality race disparity in U.S. cities. *Sociology and Social Research, 73*(2), 90–94.

LaVeist, T. (1993). Segregation, poverty, and empowerment: health consequences for African Americans. *The Milbank Quarterly, 71*(1), 41–64.

Link, B. G., & Phelan, J. (1995). Social conditions as fundamental causes of disease. *Journal of Health and Social Behavior, 35,* 80–94.

Lukachko, A., Hatzenbuehler, M. L., & Keyes, K. M. (2014). Structural racism and myocardial infarction.

Social Science & Medicine, 103, 42–50. http://dx.doi.org/10.1016/j.socscimed.2013.07.021.

Malat, J., Clark-Hitt, R., Burgess, D. J., Friedemann-Sanchez, G., & Van Ryn, M. (2010). White doctors and nurses on racial inequality in health care in the USA: whiteness and colour-blind racial ideology. *Ethnic and Racial Studies, 33*, 1431–1450.

Massey, D. (1988). The dimensions of residential segregation. *Social Forces, 67*(2), 281–315.

Mayberry, R., Mili, F., & Ofili, E. (2000). Racial and ethnic differences in access to medical care. *Medical Care Research and Review, 57*, 108–145.

Metzl, J. (2010). *The protest psychosis: How schizophrenia became a black disease.* Boston: Beacon.

Mitford, J. (1973). *Kind and unusual punishment: The prison business.* New York: Alfred A. Knopf.

Moskowitz, D., Thom, D. H., Guzman, D., Penko, J., Miaskowski, C., & Kushel, M. (2011). Is primary care providers' trust in socially marginalized patients affected by race? *Journal of General Internal Medicine, 26*(8), 846–851.

National Institute on Minority Health and Health Disparities. (2012). *Important events in NIMHD history.* Retrieved 10.15.12, from http://www.nih.gov/about/almanac/organization/NIMHD.htm.

Olafsdottir, A. (2007). Fundamental causes of health disparities: stratification, the welfare state, and health in the United States and Iceland. *Journal of Health and Social Behavior, 48*, 239–253.

Paradies, Y. (2006). A systematic review of empirical research on self-reported racism and health. *International Journal of Epidemiology, 35*, 888–901.

Peterson, N., Friedman, R., Ash, A., Franco, S., & Carr, P. (2004). Faculty self-reported experience with racial and ethnic discrimination in academic medicine. *Journal of General Internal Medicine, 19*(3), 259–265.

Phelan, J. C., Link, B. G., Diez-Roux, A., Kawachi, I., & Levin, B. (2004). Fundamental causes' of social inequalities in mortality: a test of the theory. *Journal of Health and Social Behavior, 45*(3), 265–285.

Phelan, J. C., Link, B. G., & Tehranifar, P. (2010). Social conditions as fundamental causes of health inequalities theory, evidence, and policy implications. *Journal of Health and Social Behavior, 51*(1), S28–S40.

Ridley, C. R. (1984). Clinical treatment of the non-disclosing black client. *American Psychologist, 39*, 1234–1244.

Roberts, D. (1996). Reconstructing the patient: starting with women of color. In S. M. Wolf (Ed.), *Feminism and bioethics: Beyond reproduction* (pp. 124). New York: Oxford University Press.

Roberts, D. (2011). *Fatal invention.* New York: The New Press. Kindle electronic edition.

Ryan, A. M., Gee, G. C., & Grith, D. (2008). Effects of perceived discrimination on diabetes management. *Journal of Health Care for the Poor and Underserved, 19*(1), 149–163.

Sabin, J. A., & Greenwald, A. G. (2012). The influence of implicit bias on treatment recommendations for 4 common pediatric conditions: pain, urinary tract infection, attention deficit hyperactivity disorder, and asthma. *American Journal of Public Health, 102*(5), 988–995.

Sabin, J., Nosek, B. A., Greenwald, A., & Rivara, F. P. (2009). Physicians' implicit and explicit attitudes about race by MD race, ethnicity, and gender. *Journal of Health Care for the Poor and Underserved, 20*(3), 896–913.

Sabin, J. A., Rivara, F. P., & Greenwald, A. G. (2008). Physician implicit attitudes and stereotypes about race and quality of medical care. *Medical Care, 46*(7), 678–685.

Saha, S., Arbelaez, J., & Cooper, L. (2003). Patient-physician relationships and racial disparities in the quality of health care. *American Journal of Public Health, 93*(10), 1713–1719.

Saha, S., Komaromy, M., Koepsell, T. D., & Bindman, A. B. (1999). Patient-physician racial concordance and the perceived quality and use of health care. *Archives of Internal Medicine, 159*(9), 997.

Saha, S., Taggart, S. H., Komaromy, M., & Bindman, A. B. (2000). Do patients choose physicians of their own race. *Health Affairs, 19*(4), 76–83.

Sanger, M. (1922). *The pivot of civilization.* New York: Brentano's Publishers.

Schulman, K., et al. (1999). The effect of race and sex on physicians' recommendations for cardiac catheterization. *The New England Journal of Medicine, 340*(8), 618–626.

Seattle and King County Department of Public Health. (2001). *Racial and ethnic discrimination in healthcare settings.* Seattle, WA: Seattle and King County Department of Public Health.

Sims, J. M. (1884). *The story of my life.* New York: D. Appleton.

Skloot, R. (2010). *The immortal life of Henrietta Lacks.* New York: Crown Publishing Group.

Smedley, B. D., Stith, A. Y., & Nelson, A. R. (2003). *Unequal treatment: confronting racial and ethnic disparities in health care*. Washington, D.C.: National Academies Press.

Snipes, S., et al. (2011). Is race medically relevant? A qualitative study of physicians' attitudes about the role of race in treatment decision-making. *BMC Health Services Research, 11*, 183.

Thomson, G. E., Mitchell, F., & Williams, M. (2006). *Examining the health disparities research plan of the National Institutes of Health: Unfinished business*. Washington, D.C: National Academies Press.

Ture, K., & Hamilton, C. (1967). *Black power*. New York: Random House.

Van Ryn, M., & Burke, J. (2000). The effect of race and socio-economic status on physicians' perceptions of patients. *Social Science & Medicine, 50*, 813–828.

Walters, K. (2011). Bodies don't just tell stories, they tell histories embodiment of historical trauma among American Indians and Alaska Natives. *Du Bois Review, 8*(1), 179–189.

Warwick, A. (2006). *Colonial pathologies: American tropical medicine, race, and hygiene in the Philippines*. Durham, NC: Duke University Press.

Washington, H. A. (2006). *Medical apartheid: The dark history of medical experimentation on black Americans from colonial times to the present*. New York, New York: Harlem Moon.

Welsome, E. (1999). *The plutonium files*. New York: The Dial Press.

Williams, D. R. (2012). Miles to go before we sleep: racial inequities in health. *Journal of Health and Social Behavior, 53*(3), 279–295.

Williams, D. R., & Collins, C. (2001). Racial residential segregation: a fundamental cause of racial disparities in health. *Public Health Reports, 116*(5), 404–416 (Washington, D.C.: 1974).

Williams, D., & Mohammed, S. (2009). Discrimination and racial disparities in health: evidence and needed research. *Journal of Behavioral Medicine, 32*(1), 20–47.

Wilson, A. E. (2009). Fundamental causes of health disparities: a comparative analysis of Canada and the United States. *International Sociology, 24*, 93–113.

Zempsky, W. T., Corsi, J. M., & McKay, K. (2011). Pain scores: are they used in sickle cell pain? *Pediatric Emergency Care, 27*(1), 27–28.

Differences in Beliefs About the Causes of Health Disparities in Black and White Nurses

by Susan Roberts-Dobie, PhD, Elana Joram, PhD, Michele Devlin, DPH, DeAnn Ambroson, PhD, MSN, MA, RN, LMSW, COI, CNE, and Joyce Chen, PhD

One of the central challenges in health care today is determining the causes of health disparities and identifying methods to reduce them. Despite recent gains in the health of the U.S. population as a whole, gaps in health status and life expectancy associated with income, race/ethnicity, education, sex, and other social characteristics persist (CDC, 2011). Research reveals disparities in care received by Blacks, Latinos, and other ethnic minority groups "independent of clinical appropriateness, insurance status, treatment site, and other clinical and socioeconomic status (SES) correlates" (van Ryn & Fu, 2003, p. 248). This raises the possibility that in addition to other known contributors to health disparities such as housing, stress, and environmental exposures (Williams & Jackson, 2005), the perceptions, attitudes, and actions of healthcare providers may also contribute to health disparities. In this study, we investigate a relatively unexplored yet potentially significant contributor to health disparities: nurses' attitudes toward the causes of racial health disparities.

Literature Review

A growing body of literature describes the status of health disparities and the strategies for their reduction (Adler & Rehkopf, 2008; Smedley, Stith, & Nelson, 2002), but few studies have examined healthcare providers' perceptions of the source of these disparities. Providers in these studies often acknowledge that there are disparities in treatment based on race; however, they reject the possibility that there are significant disparities within their own practice. For example, Sequist, Ayanian, Marshall, Fitzmaurice, and Safran (2008) reported that while 88% of primary care physicians acknowledged racial disparities in diabetes care in the United States, only 40% reported health disparities within their own patients. Lurie et al. (2005) reported a similar trend; although 34% of cardiologists agreed that disparities existed overall in the healthcare system, only 12% reported disparities in their own hospital, and only 5% reported disparities in their own practices. Similarly, 13% of thoracic surgeons reported disparities in cardiac care, but only 2% reported it was likely in their own patients (Taylor et al., 2006).

The concept of "unintentional bias" may help explain the discrepancy between physicians' acknowledgment of health disparities in general and their lack of acknowledgment of disparities within their own patients. Unintentional biases are unconscious stereotypes that influence clinical decisions "outside conscious awareness," in contrast to overt biases against groups (Burgess, van Ryn, Dovidio, & Saha, 2007, p. 882). van Ryn and Fu (2003) identify these biases as a possible factor that contributes to racial/ethnic disparities

in many studies related to clinical decision making, including selection for cardiac procedures, types of psychiatric care, adequate pain management, and access to kidney transplants. This type of bias, within one's practice or self, can be difficult to identify. Unintentional bias, or "aversive racism" as Dovidio et al. (2008) label it, is subtle, and "aversive racists consciously endorse the principle of racial equality and regard themselves as not prejudiced . . . [but] possess unconscious negative feelings and beliefs about particular minority groups" (p. 479). Acknowledging these feelings and accepting that they may negatively impact the health care of some patients can be particularly difficult in a profession dedicated to helping others. In a focus group on the causes of racial disparities in medical treatment, one participant described the idea of a different type of treatment ordered based on a patient's race as "a horrifying thought" (Clark-Hill, Malat, Burgess, & Friedemann-Sanchez, 2010, p. 392).

Another central belief that emerged in the literature on providers' perceived causes of health disparities is that they are caused by factors related to the patient rather than to providers or the healthcare system. Among diabetes care providers, for example, patient behaviors were the most frequently reported explanation for racial health disparities (73%), taking precedence over system factors, such as lack of time to address patient resources (39%) or differential prescribing of medications ("rarely") (Sequist et al., 2008). Similarly, cardiovascular surgeons reported that patient factors, such as adherence to treatment and attitudes toward providers, contributed more to health disparities than system or provider factors (Taylor et al., 2006). Even cardiologists who agreed that minority patients receive dissimilar diagnoses and procedures still identified patient behaviors as equal or stronger contributors to disparities than provider or system factors (Lurie et al., 2005).

The responses of medical students, however, were inconsistent with those of the physicians in the studies described above. First-year medical students, when surveyed about the causes of health disparities, were more likely to place the locus of contribution on system factors. Wilson, Grumbach, Huebner, Agrawal, and Bindman (2004) compared first-year and fourth-year medical students' perceptions with those of practicing physicians using the results of a Kaiser Family Foundation survey of practicing physicians regarding unfair treatment in the healthcare system. First-year students were "consistently more likely to perceive unfair treatments than the fourth-year students, although the fourth-year students were still much more likely than physicians to perceive unfairness in all categories" (p. 717). The authors suggested that "the process of acculturation affects perception of unequal treatment" (p. 715), and that over time acculturation reduces medical students' and physicians' willingness to assign blame to a system to which they belong.

Two studies have considered perceptions of the causes of health disparities among non-healthcare providers. Taylor-Clark, Mebane, SteelFisher, and Blendon (2007) attempted to identify the public's perceptions of the causes of health disparities by examining the prominence and content of newspaper coverage of inequalities in health care over a 10-year period in three major national and 12 regional newspapers. These researchers found that in all three time periods, when the stories mentioned a causal factor related to a disparity in health, the largest number of stories attributed the cause to the patient (35–43%), followed by the healthcare system (24–25%), and then the physician (16–21%). Despite the slant of the news toward personal factors, people not employed in the medical field identified system factors as the major causes of health disparities in a study by Zekeri and Habtemariam (2006). Utilizing a mixed-methods design with 50 African American college students, Zekeri and Habtemariam investigated perceptions of the causes of racial health disparities. A factor analysis identified racism in the healthcare system, lack of trust in medical professionals, and poverty/lack of health insurance as the factors perceived to be the most responsible for health disparities, all of which are system factors.

Perceptions of the causes of health disparities, whether internal (related to patient factors) or external (related to provider or system factors), are important to identify because providers who view the causes of disparities as related to internal factors, such as choice of diet or compliance with medication regimens, may believe that reducing health disparities is contingent upon changes in patient behaviors. They may also believe that disparities simply cannot be changed if they consider that genetics play a primary role. In contrast, providers who view the causes of disparities as being related to external factors, such as provider attitudes, may believe that health disparities can be reduced through changes within the healthcare system or provider behavior. If those beliefs translate into behavior, they could then play a critical role in mediating both the maintenance and the reduction of health disparities.

Despite the importance of examining healthcare providers' perceptions of the causes of health disparities, we were unable to locate any studies specific to nurses' perceptions; additionally, we were interested what role, if any, a nurse's race may play in the perception in the "locus of contribution," which we define as the perception of the relative influence of internal and external factors on health disparities. Therefore, our study was designed to address this gap in the literature. Specifically, the research questions posed in this study were as follows:

1. Are there differences in the extent to which Black and White nurses attribute health disparities to internal (patient) versus external (healthcare worker, system) causes?

2. Do Black and White nurses view specific contributors to health disparities differently?

Methods

Sample and Procedure

To obtain a stratified random sample for this study, the names and addresses of 100 native-born African American or African immigrant registered nurses (RNs) (referred to as "Black nurses") and 100 non-Hispanic White registered nurses (referred to as "White nurses") were drawn from the Iowa Board of Nursing's registry. A stratified sampling method was utilized to ensure a sufficiently large sample of both groups as, at the time of data collection, 97.6% of 37,372 registered nurses were White and 0.6% were Black, in a state that is 91.3% White and 2.9% Black (U.S. Census Bureau, 2011).

Methodologically, Iowa is a particularly interesting setting to study issues related to culture and health as the diversification that many states experienced decades ago is happening there and in other rural states today. Iowa, in particular, is currently experiencing some of the most significant demographic changes in the United States as many meatpacking and agricultural processing companies are recruiting thousands of refugees and immigrants from Latin America, Eastern Europe, Southeast Asia, and Africa (Iowa Center on Health Disparities, n.d.). This "rapid ethnic diversification" (Grey, 2000) allows for a natural experiment-like situation, where attitudes can be measured as populations undergo demographic shifts.

Following approval by the institutional review board, the 200 nurses were mailed a consent form, survey, and return envelope in March 2009. Following the Dillman method (Salant & Dillman, 1994), a postcard reminder was sent out after 2 weeks to thank those who had responded and to encourage non-respondents to return their questionnaires. Two weeks after the postcard was mailed, a second copy of the survey was sent to all nonrespondents. Several months later, the process was repeated in order to recruit more participants. A total of 226 Black nurses (all Black RNs in Iowa) and 200 White nurses were contacted. All participants who returned a survey were mailed a $10 gift card to a convenience store as compensation for their time.

Survey Instrument

Consistent with previous research (Zekeri & Habtemariam, 2006), and in order to ensure that participants' responses were based on a shared understanding of "health disparities," a definition was included at the beginning of the survey ("gaps in the quality of health and health care among racial, ethnic, and socioeconomic groups") based on the *Healthy People 2010* definition. The directions indicated that the researchers were interested in what participants thought to be the most important causes of health disparities, particularly with respect to disparities between African American and White patients. Participants were asked to broadly consider the term *healthcare provider* to include physicians, nurse practitioners, pharmacists, and others involved in the provision of health care.

Participants were to rate the extent to which 24 psychosocial factors contributed to health disparities using a 4-point Likert-type scale, where "1"

was equal to "no contribution to health disparities in the U.S.," through "4," which designated "a large contribution to health disparities in the U.S." The psychosocial questions were developed based on factors that have been previously identified as relevant to individuals' perceptions of the causes of health disparities (Taylor-Clark et al., 2007; Zekeri & Habtemariam, 2006). We based our classification of questions as reflecting "internal" or "external" factors on previous work by Taylor-Clark et al. (2007). Questions intentionally represented internal factors, for example "patients' distrust of the healthcare system" or "limited proficiency in English of patients," or external factors (healthcare workers, healthcare system, or societal factors), for example "poor communication skills on the part of the providers" or "a lack of translation services." Face and content validity were established via consultation by two experts in the field who regularly provide cultural competency training to healthcare providers. A pilot test was conducted on the survey with 33 nursing students to ensure clarity and consistency in the interpretation of wording. Modifications to the questions were made on the basis of participants' responses. Information regarding five demographic variables was also collected on the survey, namely race, sex, age, years of experience, and highest level of education.

Analyses

Statistical analyses were performed using SPSS 19 to assess group differences. Differences were considered statistically significant at $p < .05$, unless otherwise stated.

Results

Of the surveys sent to 426 nurses, 152 usable surveys from 57 Black (37.5%) and 95 White (62.5%) nurses were returned, yielding an overall response rate of 35.7% (25.2% Black, 47.5% White). Demographic information beyond race and sex was not reported by four participants. As in the distribution of nurses in Iowa, the majority of the sample was female, with only seven male participants (4.6%). The mean age of the sample overall was 47.91 (*SD* = 11.62) years, with a mean of 46.82 (*SD* = 11.17) years for Black nurses and 48.55 (*SD* = 11.88) years for White nurses. The majority of nurses held an associate's degree (40%), followed by a 3-year diploma (21%), or a BSN (30%). An additional 8%

identified MSN as their highest level of nursing degree, although they were most recently licensed as RNs, not advanced practice registered nurses. Both the median and modal range of time that nurses had practiced was 20+ years, with 54.1% of the participants selecting that response category.

A Pearson chi-square analysis on the category *years of experience* indicated a significant difference between Black and White nurses (χ^2 [3,148] = 10.85, p = .013). As shown in Table 1, this difference reflects a greater proportion of White nurses who had 20+ years of experience, and a greater proportion of Black nurses who had 9 years or less of experience. Analyses of the other demographic variables, including age and type of degree, did not yield significant results.

To address the first research question, whether Black and White nurses differ in their perception of the contribution of internal and external factors to health disparities, separate mean scores were created for each internal and external question. Cronbach's alpha for the 11 external questions and 13 internal questions were .89 and .77, respectively, indicating a sufficient level of internal consistency for both. A mixed analysis of variance was then performed, with one between-group variable (*participant race*) and one repeated measures variable (*locus of contribution*), where *locus of contribution* consisted of participants' mean internal scores and their mean external scores. Results indicate a main effect for *locus of contribution* (F [1,150] = 42.84, p < .000, partial η^2 = .22), as well as a significant interaction between *locus of contribution* and *participant race* (F [1,150]) = 19.98, p < .000, partial η^2 = .118). Follow-up

Table 2. Mean (SD) Internal and External Scores by Participant Race

| Factors | Race | | |
	Black nurses (n = 57)	White nurses (n = 95)	All nurses (n = 152)
Internal	2.99 (.44)	3.08 (.37)	3.04 (.40)
External	2.89 (.58)	2.58 (.59)	2.70 (.60)

independent samples *t*-tests reveal that although both Black and White nurses assign internal factors roughly the same degree of contribution (t [1,150] = 1.48, n.s.), Black nurses report that external factors are significantly more important contributors to health disparities than White nurses (t [1,150] = 3.14, p = .002) (see Table 2). There was no main effect for *participant race* (F [1,150] = 2.22, n.s.).

To address the second research question regarding participants' perceptions about specific contributors to health disparities, independent sample *t*-tests were performed on all 24 questions. In order to keep the number of participants the same for each *t*-test that was run, the analyses do not include six nurses whose data for some questions were incomplete. Given the large number of variables, a Bonferroni correction was applied to reduce the likelihood of a type I error (Glass & Hopkins, 1996), resulting in a stringent alpha level of .002.

Significant differences between Black and White nurses were found on one internal and four external variables. The one internal item, which significantly differed between race groups, was "genetic differences between racial groups" (see Table 3), with White nurses reporting that they considered genetic differences to be a more important contributor to health disparities than did Black nurses. Four items related to external factors differed significantly between the groups of nurses: "provision of different quality medical treatment to different racial groups," "lack of programs that are tailored for high risk populations like minorities," "discrimination in society," and "lack of research specific to ethnicity and other factors." As shown in Table 4, Black nurses considered all four of these external factors to be significantly greater contributors to health disparities than did White nurses.

Table 1. Frequencies (Percentage) of Participants' Number of Years of Experience by Race

| Years of experience | Race | | |
	Black nurses (n = 54)	White nurses (n = 94)	All nurses (n = 148)
0–4	10 (19%)	4 (4%)	14 (10%)
5–9	11 (20%)	12 (13%)	23 (15%)
10–19	9 (17%)	22 (23%)	31 (21%)
20+	24 (44%)	56 (60%)	80 (54%)

Table 3. Mean (SD) Internal Question Scores and t-Test Values as a Function of Participant Race

Survey questions	Ethnicity			τ	ρ
	Black nurses (v = 54)	White nurses (v = 92)	All nurses (v = 146)		
African American patients' eating habits	3.32 (.67)	2.98 (.72)	3.11 (.72)	2.71	.007
African American patients' exercise habits	3.04 (.85)	2.82 (.76)	2.90 (.79)	1.63	.103
Many African American patients are poor	2.98 (.90)	3.15 (.77)	3.09 (.82)	1.21	.227
Genetic differences between race groups	2.57 (.66)	3.01 (.82)	2.85 (.79)	3.33	.001[a]
Limited proficiency in English of patients	2.68 (.23)	2.99 (.73)	2.88 (.82)	2.19	.030
Lack of initiative to improve one's health	3.00 (.73)	3.27 (.76)	3.17 (.76)	2.12	.035
Limited education or reading level of patients	3.04 (.80)	3.11 (.72)	3.08 (.75)	.56	.578
Use of herbal/traditional/alternative practices or medicines by patients	2.17 (.75)	2.22 (.66)	2.20 (.69)	.43	.670
Patients' distrust of the healthcare system	3.04 (.82)	2.97 (.86)	2.99 (.84)	.48	.631
Patients waiting too long to seek care	3.57 (.63)	3.51 (.66)	3.53 (.65)	.57	.569
Patients not following doctors' recommendations	3.20 (.74)	3.44 (.72)	3.35 (.73)	1.86	.064
Patients' lack of knowledge of how to prevent disease	3.28 (.69)	3.20 (.72)	3.23 (.70)	.68	.497
Patients' improper use of medications: not taken at all or not taken as directed	3.33 (.78)	3.33 (.70)	3.33 (.73)	.06	.954

[a]Significant at the .002 alpha level.

Table 4. Mean (SD) External Question Scores and t-Test Values as a Function of Participant Race

Survey questions	Ethnicity			τ	ρ
	Black nurses (v = 54)	White nurses (v = 92)	All nurses (v = 146)		
Limited numbers of African American health providers	2.70 (.94)	2.29 (.79)	2.45 (.87)	2.81	.006
Lack of political will to address inequalities in health care	3.07 (.80)	2.64 (.87)	2.80 (.87)	2.98	.003
Not enough doctors and nurses located in many African American communities	2.74 (1.00)	2.78 (.88)	2.75 (.92)	.50	.619
Physicians provide different quality medical treatment to different racial groups	2.67 (.99)	2.00 (.94)	2.25 (1.01)	4.06	.000[a]
Lack of programs that are tailored for high-risk populations like minorities	3.37 (.71)	2.92 (.84)	3.09 (.82)	3.27	.001[a]
Poor communication skills on the part of the providers	3.07 (.77)	2.84 (.83)	2.93 (.81)	1.71	.089
Discrimination in society	3.06 (.86)	2.38 (.78)	2.63 (.87)	4.86	.000[a]
Lack of minority healthcare providers	2.72 (.98)	2.35 (.98)	2.49 (.99)	2.23	.027
Lack of consistent relationships between patient and provider	3.00 (.80)	3.12 (.72)	3.08 (.75)	.93	.356
Lack of translation services	2.65 (.81)	2.66 (.87)	2.66 (.84)	.10	.918
Lack of research specific to ethnicity and other factors	3.07 (.86)	2.45 (.86)	2.68 (.91)	4.26	.000[a]

[a]Significant at the .002 alpha level.

Discussion

The nurses in this study provide valuable insights into healthcare providers' perceptions of the causes of health disparities, specifically the perceptions of Black and White nurses. We found that the groups differed in significant ways: Black nurses gave more weight to external factors than White nurses, whereas White nurses considered genetic differences between racial groups to be more important when accounting for health disparities. Our findings, that Black and White nurses perceive the causes of health disparities differently, may contribute to underlying perceptions that impact practice. For example, if providers believe health disparities are more related to system or provider factors, they may subconsciously alter their behavior, perhaps offering more information, support, or empathy. Thus, the finding that Black nurses are more likely to perceive external factors as contributors to health disparities is important, as their perceptions may influence their practice. On the other hand, if providers consider health disparities to be more related to internal factors that cannot be altered, as the White nurses did in this study, then they may subconsciously feel less compelled to extend additional supports, work to change their own beliefs/behaviors, or work to change the healthcare system itself.

It is plausible then that a provider's belief that health disparities are due to internal factors that cannot be controlled, such as genetic differences between races, rather than to external factors that can be ameliorated, could contribute to bias, and in turn to health disparities. Exactly how the interaction between a doctor or nurse and patient might contribute to health disparities is not yet fully explained, but the impact of underlying beliefs on behavior has been repeatedly demonstrated (Balsa & McGuire, 2003). For example, Bogart, Catz, Kelly, and Benotsch (2001) found that physicians who perceived patients to be less likely to adhere to HIV treatment were less likely to prescribe advanced treatment options.

The most immediate application of these findings to practice relates to the design and delivery of cultural competency trainings. Findings indicate that as cultural competency trainings are designed for healthcare providers, it may be important to include information about the interaction of internal and external factors. Clearly, both internal and external factors play a role in health disparities, and the weight of that role differs in every situation, but that a healthcare provider's perception of the role could influence interactions with patients is a topic that cultural competency trainings need to address. Case study analysis or situation analysis, in which cases are presented with similar symptoms but with patients of different races/ethnicities, could be used to accomplish this.

The results of this study also suggest that developers of cultural competency trainings should consider including information on the role that unconscious beliefs may have on practice behaviors. While our findings relate to the underlying beliefs about the sources of health disparities, others' works related to the underlying beliefs about race are similar in nature. For example, Sequist et al. (2008) recommends the use of "community visits" to sensitize clinicians to the many social issues and system factors that can interfere with a patient's chronic disease management. Dovidio et al. (2008) recommend that since negative stereotypes are unconscious and usually unrecognized within a person's self, the first step in behavior change is to help providers identify the existence of these beliefs through the use of software such as the Implicit Association Test (Project Implicit, 2008). Dovidio et al. then suggest that the guilt produced when majority individuals find that their behavior may be prejudiced provides great motivation to alter their behaviors in order to respond without prejudice in the future, and "over time, these individuals learn to reduce prejudicial responses and to respond in ways that are consistent with their nonprejudiced personal standards" (2008, p. 483).

Additionally, based on our findings, cultural competency trainings should specifically address the limited role that genetics play in most diseases. Research that directly compares the DNA of individuals from different race groups indicates that there is more genetic variation within race groups than between them (Barbujani, Maggini, Minch, & Cavalli-Sforza, 1997). Thus, outside of diseases with known genetic causes, we suggest that patients may benefit from a reduced assumption by their providers of the contribution of genetics to health disparities, and a sharper focus on the social determinants that contribute to the disease.

Lastly, in rural states in the United States that are currently experiencing rapid ethnic diversification, it may be important to tailor any widely available cultural competency materials to explicitly address the impact of external factors on health status. In areas experiencing expanding minority populations, where few existed before, early work with healthcare providers to analyze and address any weaknesses in the local healthcare system may help improve short- and long-term health status for immigrating populations.

The results of our study reveal patterns in the perceptions of Black and White nurses, yet several limitations should be noted. Despite efforts to include a stratified random sample in the study, the sample included more White than Black nurses. This was due to an uneven response rate from Black and White nurses. Additionally, the sample was relatively small, and consisted of nurses from a rural state with a growing but limited minority population; thus, generalizations to nurses in geographical areas with more diverse populations must be made with caution.

Despite these limitations, this paper is the first, to our knowledge, to specifically consider nurses' perceptions of the causes of health disparities, and to compare the views of Black and White nurses. The findings of this study suggest that there are many other issues to be explored. We recommend that future researchers investigate whether practice behaviors differ between groups that differently attribute health disparities, and if practice differs between groups that differently attribute health disparities when patient–provider pairs are race-concordant or race-discordant.

According to Jones, Cason, and Bond (2004), the "singular challenge facing health care institutions in this century will be assisting an essentially homogeneous group of health care professionals to meet the special needs of a culturally diverse society" (p. 283). There is much work yet to be done to achieve equity in health outcomes. The findings of this study contribute to efforts to understand and address provider perceptions of the causes of health disparities, particularly in states experiencing rapid ethnic diversification, as we work toward meeting the needs of our continuously more diverse society.

References

Adler, N. E., & Rehkopf, D. H. (2008). U.S. disparities in health: Descriptions, causes, and mechanisms. *Annual Review of Public Health, 29*, 235–252. doi:10.1146/annurev.publhealth.29.020907.090852

Balsa, A. I., & McGuire, T. G. (2003). Prejudice, clinical uncertainly and stereotyping as sources of health disparities. *Journal of Health Economics, 22*, 89–116. doi:10.1016/S0167-6296(02)00098-X

Barbujani, G., Maggini, A., Minch, E., & Cavalli-Sforza, L. L. (1997). An apportionment of human DNA diversity. *Proceedings of the National Academy of Sciences of the United States of America, 94*(9), 4516–4519.

Bogart, L. M., Catz, S. L., Kelly, J. A., & Benotsch, E. G. (2001). Factors influencing physicians' judgments of adherence and treatment decisions for patients with HIV disease. *Medical Decision Making, 21*, 28–36. doi:10.1177/0272989X0102100104

Burgess, D., van Ryn, M., Dovidio, J., & Saha, S. (2007). Reducing racial bias among health care providers: Lessons from social-cognitive psychology. *Journal of General Internal Medicine, 22*, 882–887. doi:10.1007/s11606-007-0160-1

Centers for Disease Control and Prevention. (2011). CDC health disparities and inequality report—United States, 2011. *Morbidity and Mortality Weekly Report, 60*(82), 1–114. Retrieved from http://www.cdc.gov/mmwr/pdf/other/su6001.pdf

Clark-Hill, R., Malat, J., Burgess, D., & Friedemann-Sanchez, G. (2010). Doctors' and nurses' explanations for racial disparities in medical treatment. *Journal of Health Care for the Poor and Underserved, 21*, 386–400. doi:10.1353.hpu.0.0275

Dovidio, J. F., Penner, L. A., Albrecht, T. L., Norton, W. E., Gaertner, S. L., & Shelton, J. N. (2008). Disparities and distrust: The implication of psychological processes for understanding racial disparities in health and health care. *Social Science and Medicine, 67*, 478–486. doi:10.1016/j.socscimed.2008.03.019

Glass, G. V., & Hopkins, K. D. (1996). *Statistical methods in education and psychology* (3rd ed.). Needham Heights, MA: Allyn & Bacon.

Grey, M. A. (2000). New immigrants in old Iowa. *Anthropology News, 41*(8), 9. doi:10.1111/an.2000.41.8.9.1

Iowa Center on Health Disparities. (n.d.). *About the center*. Retrieved from http://www.iowahealthdisparities.org/about.php

Jones, M. E., Cason, C. L., & Bond, M. L. (2004). Cultural attitudes, knowledge, and skills of a health workforce. *Journal of Transcultural Nursing, 15*(4), 283–290.

Lurie, N., Fremont, A., Jain, A. K., Taylor, S. L., McLaughlinn, R., Peterson, E., . . . Ferguson, T. B. Jr. (2005). Racial and ethnic disparities in care: The perspectives of cardiologists. *Circulation, 111*, 1264–1269. doi:10.1161/01.cir.0000157738.12783.71

Project Implicit. (2008). *Exploring the unconscious*. Retrieved from http://www.projectimplicit.net/index.php

Salant, P., & Dillman, D. A. (1994). *How to conduct your own survey*. New York: John Wiley & Sons.

Sequist, T. D., Ayanian, J. Z., Marshall, R., Fitzmaurice, G. M., & Safran, D. G. (2008). Primary-care clinician perceptions of racial disparities in diabetes care. *Journal of General Internal Medicine, 23*, 678–684. doi:10.1007/s11606-008-0510-7

Smedley, B. D., Stith, A. Y., & Nelson, A. R. (Eds.) (2002). *Unequal treatment: Confronting racial and ethnic disparities in health care*. Washington, DC: Institute of Medicine.

Taylor, S. L., Fremont, A., Jain, A. K., McLaughlin, R., Peterson, T. B. Jr., & Lurie, N. (2006). Racial and ethnic disparities in care: The perspectives of cardiovascular surgeons. *Annals of Thoracic Surgery, 81*, 531–536. doi:10.1016/j.athoracsur.2005.08.004

Taylor-Clark, K. A., Mebane, F. E., SteelFisher, G. K., & Blendon, R. J. (2007). News of disparity: Content analysis of news coverage of African American healthcare inequities in the USA, 1994–2004. *Social Science and Medicine, 65*, 405–417. doi:10.1016/j.socscimed.2007.03.039

U.S. Census Bureau. (2011). *Iowa. State and county quick facts*. Retrieved from http://quickfacts.census.gov/qfd/states/19000.html

van Ryn, M., & Fu, S. S. (2003). Paved with good intentions: Do public health and human service providers contribute to racial/ethnic disparities in health? *American Journal of Public Health, 93*, 248–255. doi:10.2105/ajph.93.2.248

Williams, D. R., & Jackson, P. B. (2005). Social sources of racial disparities in health. *Health Affairs, 24*, 325–334. doi:10.1377/hlthaff.24.2.325

Wilson, E., Grumbach, K., Huebner, J., Agrawal, J., & Bindman, A. B. (2004). Medical student, physician, and public perceptions of health care disparities. *Medical Student Education, 36*(10), 715–721.

Zekeri, A. A., & Habtemariam, T. (2006). African American college students' perceptions of psychosocial factors influencing racial disparities in health. *College Student Journal, 40*(4), 901–915.

Health Disparities between Rural and Urban Women in Minnesota

by Kim Tjaden, Md

With much discussion about health disparities in Minnesota in recent years, there has been growing awareness about the inequities between rich and poor and between majority and minority groups. Attention also needs to be paid to the disparities between women who live in rural areas and those who live in urban parts of the state. Rural women are poorer, older and less likely to have adequate health insurance than their urban counterparts, which can compromise their health status. They also fare worse on a number of health indicators and face barriers to adequate health care that can exacerbate disparities. This article describes the root causes of health disparities between women living in rural and urban parts of the state and explores strategies to mitigate them that include increasing the rural physician workforce, improving access to primary and specialty care through telehealth services, and expanding health insurance options.

In the United States, women face poorer health outcomes and have a greater incidence of illness than men. Heart disease and stroke, for example, are responsible for a greater percentage of deaths in women than men. In addition, women are more likely than men to suffer the physical and emotional limitations of chronic disease.[1] Disparities also exist between women in rural* and urban areas. Contributing to those disparities are the facts that women living in rural areas have access to fewer health care providers and have higher levels of poverty than women in urban areas. Women in rural areas also have less education, more transportation challenges and lower levels of adequate health insurance coverage than women living in urban areas.[1] Poor health in women affects more than just individuals. It often translates into poor health for families, as women are frequently the ones who are responsible for making sure their family members receive needed care.[2] This article examines some of the reasons why women living in rural parts of Minnesota have poorer health indicators than women in urban parts of the state and offers suggestions for eliminating health disparities between these two groups.

Women in Rural Minnesota

Demographics

According to Women's Health USA 2013, 16.7% of all women in the United States reside in rural areas.[3] The mean age of women living in rural parts of the country is 50 years compared with 46 years for those living in urban areas.[3] In Minnesota, 18% of women in rural areas are age 65 and older, compared with 12% of women in urban areas.[4] In addition, women living in rural Minnesota are less ethnically diverse than women living in the state's urban communities.[4]

Women in rural areas also are less affluent than their urban counterparts. Women's Health 2013 found 18% of women in rural parts of the United States live below the poverty threshold compared with 15% of women in urban areas.[3] In Minnesota, the household poverty rate for women over age 18 is 9.7%, while the poverty rate for males over 18 is just 7.1%.[5] Twelve percent of women in rural Minnesota live below the poverty line, while only 10% of women in the state's urban areas do so.[4] In addition, 33% of rural women in the state live below 200% of the poverty line compared with 22% of urban Minnesota women.[4]

Men and women in rural Minnesota are also less likely to have at least some college education than those living in metro areas (just over 50% in rural regions compared with 67% statewide).[6] Although rural women have similar high school graduation rates to those of their urban counterparts, they have lower college graduation rates. In 2006, the high school graduation rates for rural and urban Minnesota women were 94.3% and 94.9%, respectively, while their respective college graduation rates were 25% and 40%.[4]

Health indicators

Women living in rural areas fare worse than those in urban areas on a number of health indicators. The greatest differences can be seen in terms of cervical cancer, sexually transmitted infections and teen pregnancy.[7] Cervical cancer is quite rare in Minnesota, but rural women have a 30% higher risk of being diagnosed with invasive disease than urban women. Sexually transmitted infections (STIs) are increasingly diagnosed among women in rural Minnesota.[7] Although STI rates are higher in metro areas, the rate of increase has been higher in rural areas. For example, the rates of chlamydia and gonorrhea among women in rural parts of the state increased 10% and 14%, respectively, in

From *Minnesota Medicine Journal, Volume 98, Number 10, October 2015* by Kim Tjaden. Copyright © 2015 by Minnesota Medical Association. Reprinted by permission

For the purposes of this article, rural is defined as the population living outside of a metropolitan area of 50,000 people. It is further defined as large rural, small rural and isolated rural based on the distance to a major town or city.

2008.[7] Rural areas experience higher-than-average teen pregnancy rates. In 2010, the teen birth rate in rural counties in the United States was nearly one-third higher than in the rest of the country (43 versus 33 births per 1,000 females 15 to 19 years of age).[8] In Minnesota, 43 counties have teen birth rates higher than the state average of 16.8 live births per 1,000 females 15 to 19 years of age, with the highest rates being in the most rural counties (Mahnomen, 64.7; Cass, 40.1; and Pennington, 39.8 per 1,000).[9]

In addition, women in rural areas have higher rates of obesity, cancer, heart disease and diabetes than women in urban areas.[10] In Minnesota, 28% of rural women are obese compared with 21% of urban women. Furthermore, this percentage has increased since 2004, when 23% of rural and 20% of urban women in the state were obese.[6] Mortality or death rates from heart disease and diabetes are significantly lower among individuals living in Minnesota's urban communities than in its rural areas.[6]

Root Causes of Health Disparities

Poverty

Nationwide, nonmetro areas have higher rates of poverty than metro areas (Figure). In Minnesota, 27% of people in rural areas live in poverty, which is defined as having an income lower than the federal guideline ($24,250 for a family of four in 2015), as opposed to 12% in metropolitan areas.[11] Reasons for this include a lack of high-paying jobs in rural areas, a population with less education, and a prevalence of part-time or seasonal agricultural jobs. In addition, people in rural areas tend to pay more for goods and services than people in urban areas.[11]

In general, women are more likely than men to be poor, and households headed by single women are more likely to be poor than those headed by men.[2] Lack of financial stability negatively affects access to health services and decreases health status. People who live in poverty have a higher incidence of chronic diseases, including mental illnesses such as depression and anxiety.[12] Additionally, poor women in rural Minnesota have higher rates of tobacco and substance use than their urban counterparts, contributing to poorer overall health.[6]

Lack of access to health care

Rural areas have fewer physicians per population than urban areas, making access to care a challenge for individuals living in rural parts of the state. A Minnesota Department of Health summary found isolated rural parts of Minnesota have only one primary care physician for every 3,191 residents, whereas urban areas have one for every

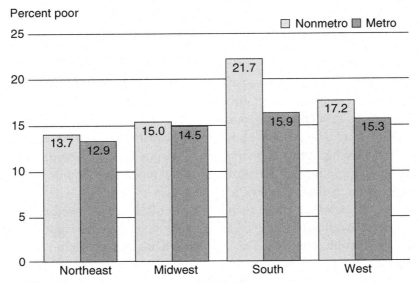

Figure Poverty rates by region and metro/nonmetro status— United States, 2009–13

Source: USDA Economic Research Service

1,098 residents.[13] In addition, data from a Minnesota Office of Rural Health and Primary Care workforce survey show a 48% decline in physicians providing obstetrical care in rural areas between 2003 and 2007.[7]

The future does not bode well, as it is difficult to attract young physicians to work in rural areas. This may be because there are fewer primary care residency positions in rural communities and because positions pay more in urban areas.[14] Adding to these challenges is the fact that the primary care workforce in rural Minnesota is older than that in metropolitan areas. In isolated rural parts of the state, 51% of the physicians are older than 55 years of age; in urban areas only 34% are 55 or older.[15]

Other factors expected to make it more difficult to access care in the future are the aging of the population and the increase in the number of people covered by insurance, both of which increase demand for services. It is estimated that Minnesota will need 1,187 primary care physicians in addition to its current 4,215 by the year 2030.[14]

The shortage of physicians in rural areas affects women in a number of ways. For example, having fewer doctors providing obstetrical care in rural areas results in decreased access to prenatal care, which leads to poor maternal and infant outcomes.[7] It also forces women to travel greater distances for pregnancy care.

Inadequate health insurance

Lack of or inadequate health insurance coverage are additional barriers to care faced by women in rural areas.[16] Rural women who hold low-paying agricultural jobs or who only have part-time employment are less likely to have employer-sponsored health insurance.[17] Those who purchase coverage on their own often have higher copayments, larger deductibles and higher premiums than those who receive coverage through their employer.[18] These higher out-of-pocket expenses cause many women to forgo preventive health screenings[16] as well as ongoing care for chronic conditions such as diabetes, hypertension, depression and anxiety.[1] It has been shown that individuals with insurance are more likely than those without it to establish and maintain a relationship with a primary care provider, which decreases costs and improves health outcomes.[17]

Recommendations

The following may help reduce, if not eliminate, the health disparities between women in rural and urban parts of the state.

Expand the rural health care workforce

In order to increase the number of rural primary care physicians, medical and premed students must be exposed to primary care practices in rural communities. Efforts must be made to provide more experiences such as that offered through the Rural Physician Associate Program (RPAP) at the University of Minnesota Medical School, through which third-year medical students spend nine months living and training in rural Minnesota settings.[19] A similar program should be created to expose undergraduate premedical students to the benefits of rural medical practice.

Because medical school debt is one reason graduates choose higher-paying nonprimary care specialties, we need more loan-repayment programs for those entering primary care in rural areas.[20] In 2015, the Minnesota Legislature voted to increase funding by $5.2 million for loan forgiveness programs in 2016 and 2017 for physicians and other health care providers who serve in rural and underserved urban settings. Lawmakers also allocated $1.5 million for additional residency slots and included funding to better utilize the skills of foreign-trained immigrant physicians in hope of increasing the primary care workforce.[21] These are good first steps, but the burden of medical school debt is greater now than ever. We also need to promote real payment reform at the national and state level to bring primary care salaries in line with those for specialty care, which would encourage more medical students to pursue primary care careers.[22]

In addition, we need to increase efforts to promote job satisfaction among doctors who currently practice rural medicine so that they will be less like to retire early or leave their practices. One way to do that is to decrease paperwork and other administrative burdens that consume their time. Another is to allow physician extenders such as nurse practitioners and physician assistants to do as much as they are allowed to do within the scope of their licensure so physicians can concentrate on their more challenging cases.

Improve access to care through telehealth services

Electronic or virtual medical visits (e-visits) can be used in conjunction with office visits for monitoring chronic conditions such as diabetes and high blood pressure as well as addressing straightforward acute issues such as sinus infections. E-visits also would be extremely effective for contraceptive counseling and reproductive care for younger women who may not have access to such services in their communities. Using telehealth technologies in this way would enable women with complicated pregnancies to remain at home longer and avoid having to travel to a city for late-term pregnancy care. Electronic consultations also could be used to provide specialty care in rural areas where specialists are not as available as they are in urban areas. A number of barriers limit the use of such consultations. For one thing, they are poorly reimbursed by insurance companies. In addition, many rural areas lack broadband Internet service, and hospitals and clinics do not have the technical infrastructure needed to engage in such activities.[23] Better payment models for teleheath services and expanded Internet capabilities in rural areas would greatly improve access to care, thereby decreasing disparities.

Expand health insurance options to women in rural Minnesota

One of the goals of the Affordable Care Act (ACA) is to reduce the number of uninsured people in the United States. Under the ACA, states could expand access to Medicaid to individuals with incomes less than 138% of the federal poverty level.[24] Minnesota was one of the states that expanded access to Medicaid. As a result, the number of people who were uninsured declined by 40.6% during the first year of implementation.[25] In addition, individuals and families with incomes between 100% and 400% of the federal poverty level who purchase private coverage through an insurance exchange now receive tax credits. About 75% of rural residents in the state who were once without insurance are now eligible to receive coverage through one of these options.[25] Although data on the numbers of rural women who are still uninsured and underinsured are not yet available, we know that not all have coverage. Anecdotally, we now know that many individuals who gained health insurance through the ACA have been unable to pay the high deductibles and copays associated with the lower-cost products, leading to delays in care.

Conclusion

Public health officials, rural physicians and rural community leaders must all work together if we are to improve the health status of women in rural Minnesota. Achieving health equity among rural and urban women is important to improving the health of the state's population in general and to controlling rising health care costs. Bringing awareness to the problem of health disparities between rural and urban women in the state is the first step toward solving the problem. With the continued hard work on the part of the public health and medical communities, health equity is attainable for women in rural parts of the state. **MM**

Kim Tjaden is a family physician practicing in St. Cloud. She is currently pursuing a master's in public health at the University of Minnesota.

References

1. Shi L, Singh D. Delivering Health Care in America: A Systems Approach 6th Edition. Burlington, MA: Jones and Bartlett; 2015: 433

2. Cawthorne A. The Straight Facts on Women in Poverty. Center for American Progress. October 8, 2008. Available at: www.americanprogress.org/issues/women/report/2008/10/08/5103/the-straight-facts-on-women-in-poverty/. Accessed September 16, 2015.

3. U.S. Department of Health and Human Services, Health Resources and Services Administration, Maternal and Child Health Bureau. Women's Health USA 2013. Rockville, MD. Available at: http://mchb.hrsa.gov/whusa13/. Accessed September 16, 2015.

4. McMurray M, Gillaspy T. The demographics of rural women: now and the future. RMJ. 2008;3(1):1–9.

5. Scheffert D. Strengthening social capital to tackle poverty. RMJ. 2008;3(1):36.

6. Minnesota Department of Health. Rural Health Advisory Committee. Office of Rural Health and Primary Care. Health Status of Rural Minnesotans. Updated November 2011. Available at: www.health.state.mn.us/divs/orhpc/pubs/workforce/status.pdf/. Accessed September 16, 2015.

7. Tharaldson K, Sechler A. Reproductive health services in rural Minnesota. RMJ. 2008; 3(1):101–26.

8. Centers for Disease Control and Prevention. Teen Birth Rates Drop, But Disparities Persist. Available at: www.cdc.gov/features/dsteenpregnancy. Accessed September 15, 2015.

9. Teenwise Minnesota. Minnesota Adolescent Birth and Pregnancy Rate Ranked by County. Available at: http://teenwisemn.org/adolescent-sexual-health-reports. Accessed September 16, 2015.

10. Bennett K, Lopes Jr J, Spencer K, van Hecke S. Rural Women's Health. National Rural Health Association Policy Brief. 2013.

11. Henry J. Kaiser Family Foundation. Poverty Rate by Metropolitan Status. Available at: http://kff.org/other/state-indicator/poverty-rate-by-metropolitan-status/. Accessed September 16, 2015.

12. Brown A. With poverty comes depression, more than other illnesses. Available at: www.gallup.com/poll/158417/poverty-comes-depression-illness.aspx. Accessed September 16, 2015.

13. Minnesota Department of Health. Overview of Minnesota's Physician Workforce, 2013-2014. Available at: www.health.state.mn.us/divs/orhpc/workforce/phy/phys2013.pdf. Accessed September 16, 2015.

14. Petterson SM, Cai A, Moore M, Bazemore A. State-level projections of primary care workforce, 2010-2030. September 2013, Robert Graham Center, Washington, D.C. Available at: www.graham-center.org/online/etc/medialib/graham/documents/tools-resources/minnesotapdf.Par.0001.File.dat/Minnesota_final.pdf. Accessed September 15, 2015.

15. Minnesota Department of Health. Office of Rural Health and Primary Care. Minnesota's Primary Care Workforce 2011-2012. September 2013. www.health.state.mn.us/divs/orhpc/pubs/workforce/primary.pdf. Accessed September 16, 2015.

16. Rustgi S, Doty M, Collins S. Women at Risk: Why Many Women are Forgoing Needed Health Care. The Commonwealth Fund. May 2009. Available at: www.commonwealthfund.org/~/media/Files/Publications/Issue%20Brief/2009/May/Women%20at%20Risk/PDF_1262_Rustgi_women_at_risk_issue_brief_Final.pdf. Accessed September 16, 2015.

17. Newkirk V, Damico A. The Affordable Care Act and Insurance Coverage in Rural Areas. Kaiser Family Foundation. Available at: http://kff.org/uninsured/issue-brief/the-affordable-care-act-and-insurance-coverage-in-rural-areas/. Accessed September 16, 2015.

18. Minnesota Department of Health. Office of Rural Health and Primary Care. Health Care Reform: Addressing the Needs of Rural Minnesotans. October 2007. Available at: www.health.state.mn.us/divs/orhpc/pubs/hcreform.pdf. Accessed September 16, 2015.

19. Rural Physician Associate Program. University of Minnesota Medical School. Available at: www.rpap.umn.edu/about/home.html. Accessed September 16, 2015.

20. Minnesota Department of Health. Office of Rural Health and Primary Care. Minnesota's Rural Health Plan. November 2008. Available at: www.health.state.mn.us/divs/orhpc/flex/studies/rhplan.pdf. Accessed September 15, 2015.

21. MMA Legislative Wrap up. Available at: www.minnesotamedicine.com/Portals/mnmed/June%202015/oilandwater_hauser_1506.pdf. Accessed September 16, 2015.

22. Minnesota Medical Association. MMA Primary Care Physician Workforce Expansion Advisory Task Force Final Report. May 3, 2014. Available at: www.mnmed.org/Portals/MMA/PDFs/MMA_Primary_Care_Physician_Workforce_Expansion_Advisory_Task_Force-FINAL_Task_Force_Report-May_2014.pdf. Accessed September 16, 2015.

23. Minnesota Rural Health Association. State of Minnesota Rural Health 2015. Presentation February 3, 2015.

24. Obamacare facts. Medicaid Expansion. Available at: http://obamacarefacts.com/obamacares-medicaid-expansion. Accessed September 16, 2015.

25. Early Impacts of the Affordable Care Act on Health Insurance Coverage in Minnesota. State Health Access Data Assistance Center. June 2014. Available at: www.shadac.org/MinnesotaCoverageReport. Accessed September 16, 2015.

Under the Shadow
of Tuskegee:
African American
and Health Care

by Vanessa Northington Gamble

ABSTRACT   The Tuskegee Syphilis Study continues to cast its long shadow on the contemporary relationship between African Americans and the biomedical community. Numerous reports have argued that the Tuskegee Syphilis Study is the most important reason why many African Americans distrust the institutions of medicine and public health. Such an interpretation neglects a critical historical point: the mistrust predated public revelations about the Tuskegee study. This paper places the syphilis study within a broader historical and social context to demonstrate that several factors have influenced—and continue to influence—African Americans' attitudes toward the biomedical community. (*Am J Public Health.* 1997;87:1773–1778)

Introduction

On May 16, 1997, in a White House ceremony, President Bill Clinton apologized for the Tuskegee Syphilis Study, the 40-year government study (1932 to 1972) in which 399 Black men from Macon County, Alabama, were deliberately denied effective treatment for syphilis in order to document the natural history of the disease. "The legacy of the study at Tuskegee," the president remarked, "has reached far and deep, in ways that hurt our progress and divide our nation. We cannot be one America when a whole segment of our nation has no trust in America." The president's comments underscore that in the 25 years since its public disclosure, the study has moved from being a singular historical event to a powerful metaphor. It has come to symbolize racism in medicine, misconduct in human research, the arrogance of physicians, and government abuse of Black people.

The continuing shadow cast by the Tuskegee Syphilis Study on efforts to improve the health status of Black Americans provided an impetus for the campaign for a presidential apology. Numerous articles, in both the professional and popular press, have pointed out that the study predisposed many African Americans to distrust medical and public health authorities and has led to critically low Black participation in clinical trials and organ donation.

The specter of Tuskegee has also been raised with respect to HIV/AIDS prevention and treatment programs. Health education researchers Dr Stephen B. Thomas and Dr Sandra Crouse Quinn have written extensively on the impact of the Tuskegee Syphilis Study on these programs. They argue that "the legacy of this experiment, with its failure to educate the study participants and treat them adequately, laid the foundation for today's pervasive sense of black distrust of public health authorities." The syphilis study has also been used to explain why many African Americans oppose needle exchange programs.

"Under the Shadow of Tuskegee: African Americans and Health Care," by Vanessa Northington Gamble, *American Journal of Public Health*, Vol. 87, No. 11, November 1997, pp. 1773–1778. Reprinted with permission from the American Public Health Association.

Needle exchange programs provoke the image of the syphilis study and Black fears about genocide. These programs are not viewed as mechanisms to stop the spread of HIV/AIDS but rather as fodder for the drug epidemic that has devastated so many Black neighborhoods. Fears that they will be used as guinea pigs like the men in the syphilis study have also led some African Americans with AIDS to refuse treatment with protease inhibitors.

The Tuskegee Syphilis Study is frequently described as the singular reason behind African-American distrust of the institutions of medicine and public health. Such an interpretation neglects a critic historical point: the mistrust predated public revelations about the Tuskegee study. Furthermore, the narrowness of such a representation places emphasis on a single historical event to explain deeply entrenched and complex attitudes within the Black community. An examination of the syphilis study within a broader historical and social context makes plain that several factors have influenced, and continue to influence, African Americans' attitudes toward the biomedical community.

Black Americans' fears about exploitation by the medical profession date back to the antebellum period and the use of slaves and free Black people as subjects for dissection and medical experimentation. Although physicians also used poor Whites as subjects, they used Black people far more often. During an 1835 trip to the United States, French visitor Harriet Martineau found that Black people lacked the power even to protect the graves of their dead. "In Baltimore the bodies of coloured people exclusively are taken for dissection," she remarked, "because the Whites do not like it, and the coloured people cannot resist." Four years later, abolitionist Theodore Dwight Weld echoed Martineau's sentiment. "Public opinion," he wrote, "would tolerate surgical experiments, operations, processes, performed upon them [slaves], which it would execrate if performed upon their master or other whites." Slaves found themselves as subjects of medical experiments because physicians needed bodies and because the state considered them property and denied them the legal right to refuse to participate.

Two antebellum experiments, one carried out in Georgia and the other in Alabama, illustrate the abuse that some slaves encountered at the hands of physicians. In the first, Georgia physician Thomas Hamilton conducted a series of brutal experiments on a slave to test remedies for heatstroke. The subject of these investigations, Fed, had been loaned to Hamilton as repayment for a debt owed by his owner. Hamilton forced Fed to sit naked on a stool placed on a platform in a pit that had been heated to a high temperature. Only the man's head was above ground. Over a period of 2 to 3 weeks, Hamilton placed Fed in the pit five or six times and gave him various medications to determine which enabled him best to withstand the heat. Each ordeal ended when Fed fainted and had to be revived. But note that Fed was not the only victim in this experiment; its whole purpose was to make it possible for masters to force slaves to work still longer hours on the hottest of days.

In the second experiment, Dr J. Marion Sims, the so-called father of modern gynecology, used three Alabama slave women to develop an operation to repair vesico-vaginal fistulas. Between 1845 and 1849, the three slave women on whom Sims operated each underwent up to 30 painful operations. The physician himself described the agony associated with some of the experiments: "The first patient I operated on was Lucy. . . . That was before the days of anesthetics, and the poor girl, on her knees, bore the operation with great heroism and bravery." This operation was not successful, and Sims later attempted to repair the defect by placing a sponge in the bladder. This experiment, too, ended in failure. He noted:

> The whole urethra and the neck of the bladder were in a high state of inflammation, which came from the foreign substance. It had to come away, and there was nothing to do but to pull it away by main force. Lucy's agony was extreme. She was much prostrated, and I thought that she was going to die; but by irrigating the parts of the bladder she recovered with great rapidity.

Sims finally did perfect his technique and ultimately repaired the fistulas. Only after his experimentation with the slave women proved successful did the physician attempt the procedure, with anesthesia, on White women volunteers.

Exploitation after the Civil War

It is not known to what extent African Americans continued to be used as unwilling subjects for experimentation and dissection in the years after emancipation. However, an examination of African-American folklore at the turn of the century makes it clear that Black people believed that such practices persisted. Folktales are replete with references to night doctors, also called student doctors and Ku Klux doctors. In her book, *Night Riders in Black Folk History*, anthropologist Gladys-Marie Fry writes, "The term 'night doctor' (derived from the fact that victims were sought only at night) applies both to students of medicine, who supposedly stole cadavers from which to learn about body processes, and [to] professional thieves, who sold stolen bodies—living and dead—to physicians for medical research." According to folk belief, these sinister characters would kidnap Black people, usually at night and in urban areas, and take them to hospitals to be killed and used in experiments. An 1889 *Boston Herald* article vividly captured the fears that African Americans in South Carolina had of night doctors. The report read, in part:

> The negroes of Clarendon, Williamsburg, and Sumter counties have for several weeks past been in a state of fear and trembling. They claim that there is a white man, a doctor, who at will can make himself invisible and who then approaches some unsuspecting darkey, and having rendered him or her insensible with chloroform, proceeds to fill up a bucket with the victim's blood, for the purpose of making medicine. After having drained the last drop of blood from the victim, the body is dumped into some secret place where it is impossible for any person to find it. The colored women are so worked up over this phantom that they will not venture out at night, or in the daytime in any sequestered place.

Fry did not find any documented evidence of the existence of night riders. However, she demonstrated through extensive interviews that many African Americans expressed genuine fears that they would be kidnapped by night doctors and used for medical experimentation. Fry concludes that two factors explain this paradox. She argues that Whites, especially those in the rural South, deliberately spread rumors about night doctors in order to maintain psychological control over Blacks and to discourage their migration to the North so as to maintain a source of cheap labor. In addition, Fry asserts that the experiences of many African Americans as victims of medical experiments during slavery fostered their belief in the existence of night doctors. It should also be added that, given the nation's racial and political climate, Black people recognized their inability to refuse to participate in medical experiments.

Reports about the medical exploitation of Black people in the name of medicine after the end of the Civil War were not restricted to the realm of folklore. Until it was exposed in 1882, a grave robbing ring operated in Philadelphia and provided bodies for the city's medical schools by plundering the graves at a Black cemetery. According to historian David C. Humphrey, southern grave robbers regularly sent bodies of southern Blacks to northern medical schools for use as anatomy cadavers.

During the early 20th century, African-American medical leaders protested the abuse of Black people by the White-dominated medical profession and used their concerns about experimentation to press for the establishment of Black controlled hospitals. Dr Daniel Hale Williams, the founder of Chicago's Provident Hospital (1891), the nation's first Black-controlled hospital, contended that White physicians, especially in the South, frequently used Black patients as guinea pigs. Dr Nathan Francis Mossell, the founder of Philadelphia's Frederick Douglass Memorial Hospital (1895), described the "fears and prejudices" of Black people, especially those from the South, as "almost proverbial." He attributed such attitudes to southern medicine practices in which Black people, "when forced to accept hospital attention, got only the poorest care, being placed in inferior wards set apart for them, suffering the brunt of all that is experimental in treatment, and all this is the sequence of their race variety and abject helplessness." The founders of Black hospitals claimed that only Black physicians possessed the skills required to treat Black patients optimally and that Black hospitals provided these patients with the best possible care.

Fears about the exploitation of African Americans by White physicians played a role in the establishment of a Black veterans hospital in Tuskegee, Ala. In 1923, 9 years before the initiation of the Tuskegee Syphilis Study, racial tensions had erupted in the town over control of the hospital. The federal government had pledged that the facility, an institution designed exclusively for Black patients, would be run by a Black professional staff. But many Whites in the area, including members of the Ku Klux Klan, did not want a Black-operated federal facility in the heart of Dixie, even though it would serve only Black people.

Black Americans sought control of the veterans hospital, in part because they believed that the ex-soldiers would receive the best possible care from Black physicians and nurses, who would be more caring and sympathetic to the veterans' needs. Some Black newspapers even warned that White southerners wanted command of the hospital as part of a racist plot to kill and sterilize African-American men and to establish an "experiment station" for mediocre White physicians. Black physicians did eventually gain the right to operate the hospital, yet this did not stop the hospital from becoming an experiment station for Black men. The veterans hospital was one of the facilities used by the United States Public Health Service in the syphilis study.

During the 1920s and 1930s, Black physicians pushed for additional measures that would battle medical racism and advance their professional needs. Dr Charles Garvin, a prominent Cleveland physician and a member of the editorial board of the Black medical publication *The Journal of the National Medical Association*, urged his colleagues to engage in research in order to protect Black patients. He called for more research on diseases such as tuberculosis and pellagra that allegedly affected African Americans disproportionately or idiosyncratically. Garvin insisted that Black physicians investigate these racial diseases because "heretofore in literature, as in medicine, the Negro has been written about, exploited and experimented upon sometimes not to his physical betterment or to the advancement of science, but the advancement of the Nordic investigator." Moreover, he charged that "in the past, men of other races have for the large part interpreted our diseases, often tinctured with inborn prejudices."

Fears of Genocide

These historical examples clearly demonstrate that African Americans' distrust of the medical profession has a longer history than the public revelations of the Tuskegee Syphilis Study. There is a collective memory among African Americans about their exploitation by the medical establishment. The Tuskegee Syphilis Study has emerged as the most prominent example of medical racism because it confirms, if not authenticates, long-held and deeply entrenched beliefs within the Black community. To be sure, the Tuskegee Syphilis Study does cast a long shadow. After the study had been exposed, charges surfaced that the experiment was part of a governmental plot to exterminate Black people. Many Black people agreed with the charge that the study represented "nothing less than an official, premeditated policy of genocide." Furthermore, this was not the first or last time that allegations of genocide have been launched against the government and the medical profession. The sickle cell anemia screening programs of the 1970s and birth control programs have also provoked such allegations.

In recent years, links have been made between Tuskegee, AIDS, and genocide. In September 1990, the article "AIDS: Is It Genocide?" appeared in *Essence*, a Black woman's magazine. The author noted "As an increasing number of African-Americans continue to sicken and die and as no cure for AIDS has been found some of us are beginning to think the unthinkable: Could AIDS be a virus that was manufactured to erase large numbers of us? Are they trying to kill us with this disease?" In other words, some members of the Black community see AIDS as part of a conspiracy to exterminate African Americans.

Beliefs about the connection between AIDS and the purposeful destruction of African Americans should not be cavalierly dismissed as bizarre and paranoid. They are held by a significant number of Black people. For example, a 1990 survey conducted by the Southern Christian Leadership Conference found that 35% of the 1056 Black church members who responded believed that AIDS was a form of genocide. A *New York Times/WCBS* TV News poll conducted the same year found that 10% of Black Americans thought that the AIDS virus had been created in a laboratory in order to infect Black people. Another 20% believed that it could be true.

African Americans frequently point to the Tuskegee Syphilis Study as evidence to support their views about genocide, perhaps, in part, because many believe that the men in the study were actually injected with syphilis. Harlon Dalton, a Yale Law School professor and a former member of the National Commission on AIDS, wrote, in a 1989 article titled, "AIDS in Black Face," that "the government [had] purposefully exposed Black men to syphilis." Six years later, Dr Eleanor Walker, a Detroit radiation oncologist, offered an explanation as to why few African Americans become bone marrow donors. "The biggest fear, she claimed, is that they will become victims of some misfeasance, like the Tuskegee incident where Black men were infected with syphilis and left untreated to die from the disease." The January 25, 1996, episode of *New York Undercover*, a Fox Network police drama that is one of the top shows in Black households, also reinforced the rumor that the U.S. Public Health Service physicians injected the men with syphilis. The myth about deliberate infection is not limited to the Black community. On April 8, 1997, news anchor Tom Brokaw, on "NBC Nightly News," announced that the men had been infected by the government.

Folklorist Patricia A. Turner, in her book *I Heard It through the Grapevine: Rumor and Resistance in African-American Culture*, underscores why it is important not to ridicule but to pay attention to these strongly held theories about genocide. She argues that these rumors reveal much about what African Americans believe to be the state of their lives in this country. She contends that such views reflect Black beliefs that White Americans have historically been, and continue to be, ambivalent and perhaps hostile to the existence of Black people. Consequently, African-American attitudes toward biomedical research are not influenced solely by the Tuskegee Syphilis Study. African Americans' opinions about the value White

society has attached to their lives should not be discounted. As Reverend Floyd Tompkins of Stanford University Memorial Church has said, "There is a sense in our community, and I think it shall be proved out, that if you are poor or you're a person of color, you were the guinea pig, and you continue to be the guinea pigs, and there is the fundamental belief that Black life is not valued like White life or like any other life in America."

Not Just Paranoia

Lorene Cary, in a cogent essay in *Newsweek*, expands on Reverend Tompkins' point. In an essay titled "Why It's Not Just Paranoia," she writes:

> We Americans continue to value the lives and humanity of some groups more than the lives and humanity of others. That is not paranoia. It is our historical legacy and a present fact; it influences domestic and foreign policy and the daily interaction of millions of Americans. It influences the way we spend our public money and explains how we can read the staggering statistics on Black Americans' infant mortality, youth mortality, mortality in middle and old age, and not be moved to action.

African Americans' beliefs that their lives are devalued by White society also influence their relationships with the medical profession. They perceive, at times correctly, that they are treated differently in the healthcare system solely because of their race, and such perceptions fuel mistrust of the medical profession. For example, a national telephone survey conducted in 1986 revealed that African Americans were more likely than Whites to report that their physicians did not inquire sufficiently about their pain, did not tell them how long it would take for prescribed medicine to work, did not explain the seriousness of their illness or injury, and did not discuss test and examination findings. A 1994 study published in the *American Journal of Public Health* found that physicians were less likely to give pregnant Black women information about the hazards of smoking and drinking during pregnancy.

The powerful legacy of the Tuskegee Syphilis Study endures, in part, because the racism and disrespect for Black lives that it entailed mirror Black people's contemporary experiences with the medical profession. The anger and frustration that many African Americans feel when they encounter the healthcare system can be heard in the words of Alicia Georges, a professor of nursing at Lehman College and a former president of the National Black Nurses Association, as she recalled an emergency room experience. "Back a few years ago, I was having excruciating abdominal pain, and I wound up at a hospital in my area," she recalled. "The first thing that they began to ask me was how many sexual partners I'd had. I was married and owned my own house. But immediately, in looking at me, they said, 'Oh, she just has pelvic inflammatory disease.'" Perhaps because of her nursing background, Georges recognized the implications of the questioning. She had come face to face with the stereotype of Black women as sexually promiscuous. Similarly, the following story from the *Los Angeles Times* shows how racism can affect the practice of medicine:

> When Althea Alexander broke her arm, the attending resident at Los Angeles County-USC Medical Center told her to "hold your arm like you usually hold your can of beer on Saturday night." Alexander who is Black, exploded. "What are you talking about? Do you think I'm a welfare mother?" The White resident shrugged: "Well aren't you?" Turned out she was an administrator at USC medical school.

This example graphically illustrates that healthcare providers are not immune to the beliefs and misconceptions of the wider community. They carry with them stereotypes about various groups of people.

Beyond Tuskegee

There is also a growing body of medical research that vividly illustrates why discussions of the relationship of African Americans and the medical profession must go beyond the Tuskegee Syphilis Study. These studies demonstrate racial inequities in access to particular technologies and raise critical questions about the role of racism in medical decision making. For example, in 1989 *The Journal of the American Medical Association*

published a report that demonstrated racial inequities in the treatment of heart disease. In this study, White and Black patients had similar rates of hospitalization for chest pain, but the White patients were one third more likely to undergo coronary angiography and more than twice as likely to be treated with bypass surgery or angioplasty. The racial disparities persisted even after adjustments were made for differences in income. Three years later, another study appearing in that journal reinforced these findings. It revealed that older Black patients on Medicare received coronary artery bypass grafts only about a fourth as often as comparable White patients. Disparities were greatest in the rural South, where White patients had the surgery seven times as often as Black patients. Medical factors did not fully explain the differences. This study suggests that an already-existing national health insurance program does not solve the access problems of African Americans. Additional studies have confirmed the persistence of such inequities.

Why the racial disparities? Possible explanations include health problems that precluded the use of procedures, patient unwillingness to accept medical advice or to undergo surgery, and differences in severity of illness. However, the role of racial bias cannot be discounted, as the American Medical Association's Council on Ethical and Judicial Affairs has recognized. In a 1990 report on Black-White disparities in healthcare, the council asserted:

> Because racial disparities may be occurring despite the lack of any intent or purposeful efforts to treat patients differently on the basis of race, physicians should examine their own practices to ensure that inappropriate considerations do not affect their clinical judgment. In addition, the profession should help increase the awareness of its members of racial disparities in medical treatment decisions by engaging in open and broad discussions about the issue. Such discussions should take place as part of the medical school curriculum, in medical journals, at professional conferences, and as part of professional peer review activities.

The council's recommendation is a strong acknowledgment that racism can influence the practice of medicine.

After the public disclosures of the Tuskegee Syphilis Study, Congress passed the National Research Act of 1974. This act, established to protect subjects in human experimentation, mandates institutional review board approval of all federally funded research with human subjects. However, recent revelations about a measles vaccine study financed by the Centers for Disease Control and Prevention (CDC) demonstrate the inadequacies of these safeguards and illustrate why African Americans' historically based fears of medical research persist. In 1989, in the midst of a measles epidemic in Los Angeles, the CDC, in collaboration with Kaiser Permanente and the Los Angeles County Health Department, began a study to test whether the experimental Edmonston-Zagreb vaccine could be used to immunize children too young for the standard Moraten vaccine. By 1991, approximately 900 infants, mostly Black and Latino, had received the vaccine without difficulties. (Apparently, one infant died for reasons not related to the inoculations.) But the infants' parents had not been informed that the vaccine was not licensed in the United States or that it had been associated with an increase in death rates in Africa. The 1996 disclosure of the study prompted charges of medical racism and of the continued exploitation of minority communities by medical professionals.

The Tuskegee Syphilis Study continues to cast its shadow over the lives of African Americans. For many Black people, it has come to represent the racism that pervades American institutions and the disdain in which Black lives are often held. But despite its significance, it cannot be the only prism we use to examine the relationship of African Americans with the medical and public health communities. The problem we must face is not just the shadow of Tuskegee but the shadow of racism that so profoundly affects the lives and beliefs of all people in this country.

References

A list of references is available in the original source.

 # Families Emerge as Silent Victims of Tuskegee Syphilis Experiment

by Carol Kaesuk Yoon

TUSKEGEE, Ala., May 9— It has been 25 years since the nation learned that more than 400 black men infected with syphilis went untreated for decades in a federally financed experiment in this rural Southern town laced with sandy roads and pine forests.

These men, who are expected to receive a Presidential apology on Friday in Washington, have been the subject of countless academic studies, news articles and books, as well as a play and a made-for-television movie.

Yet their families -- the wives and children they may have unwittingly exposed to the disease -- have remained largely unseen and unheard, bearing in silence a legacy of anger and shame as well as possible damage to their health. In an acknowledgment of the harm that may have been done, the Federal Government, since 1975, has been quietly running a small program that provides medical benefits to family members infected with syphilis. "You get treated like lepers," said Albert Julkes Jr., 55, whose father was a participant in the project the Government called the Tuskegee Study of Untreated Syphilis in the Negro Male. "People think it's the scourge of the earth to have it in your family."

Mr. Julkes, a retired customer service supervisor for a gas and electric utility, recounted his father's ordeal as he sat in the kitchen of his home just across the border in Columbus, Ga. "It was one of the worst atrocities ever reaped on people by the Government," he said. "You don't treat dogs that way."

In 1974 the Federal Government began making well-publicized reparations to the men who participated in the experiment, in which they were led to believe they were receiving free medical care, when its actual purpose was to study the long-term effects of untreated syphilis on black men. But since 1975, the Government has also been making amends to some of the families, providing lifetime medical benefits to the 22 wives, 17 children and 2 grandchildren with syphilis they may have contracted as a direct result of the lack of treatment accorded the men in the study.

"What they deserve is the best medical care we can provide," said Dr. Bill Jenkins, who in 1969, while a statistician with the National Center for Health Statistics in Washington, was among several people who unsuccessfully tried to end the experiment. Dr. Jenkins, who said he was appalled by the experiment and haunted by his unsuccessful effort to halt it, is now an epidemiologist and devotes himself to running the Government's program to provide medical benefits to the men and eligible family members. "I try to give them the care that I would want to give to my mother," Dr. Jenkins said.

In addition to providing care to the family members, the program, at the Federal Centers for Disease Control and Prevention, called the Participants Health Benefits Program, also serves the eight surviving men. The program, formerly known as the Tuskegee Health Benefits Program, cost the Federal Government $2.1 million last year, Dr. Jenkins said.

But while the program treats physical ills, the family members' emotional wounds have gone largely unrecognized, some relatives say. The pain of Tuskegee is still very real even among grandchildren of the study participants, some of whom

had not even been born when the study was officially ended after its existence was widely reported in the press in 1972.

"I'm angry about it, very, very angry about it," said Carmen Head, whose grandfather, Freddie Lee Tyson, participated in the study. Miss Head, who is 22 and lives in Fairfax, Va., said family members had told her very little about her grandfather's participation. The subject is taboo, particularly with her grandmother, she said, adding, "It's a painful issue in my family."

Miss Head's mother, Lillie Head of Waterbury, Conn., is one of many family members no longer living in the South. Mrs. Head said she had never learned whether her father was one of the more than 400 participants with syphilis or if he was one of some 200 men without syphilis who were in a control group.

"It was something to be ashamed of, so it wasn't talked about," said Mrs. Head, 52, a high school physical education and health education teacher. "We were really very disturbed after we found out my father was a part of it."

Martha Jernigan, 49, a home health aide in Tuskegee, said she has two cousins who are descendants of men in the experiment and knows many other relatives of participants who are living in the area. "They thought we were animals, stupid, that we didn't know better," she said. "Times haven't changed when it comes to blacks."

Herman Shaw, 94, a survivor of the study still living on his family farm in Tuskegee, sat on his front porch on Thursday sifting through photographs of his late wife, Fannie Mae. Mr. Shaw was able to offer one of the few memories of a wife's reaction to learning the truth about the study. "She was somewhat shocked, may I say," he said, "because it was a disease. It wasn't anything that we'd heard about and nobody seemed to know about."

Dr. Vanessa Northington Gamble, a medical historian and physician who directs the Center for the Study of Race and Ethnicity in Medicine at the University of Wisconsin medical school, said such reactions are common among family members.

"There is a lot of pain that people still express and feel about what the Government has done to them and their family members, their community," said Dr. Gamble, who has studied the experiment for years and is chairwoman of the Tuskegee Syphilis Study Legacy Committee, a group of experts formed last year to press for an official apology.

"I talked to a woman in Wisconsin who knew that I'd been studying this," she recalled. "All of a sudden she started crying, saying her uncle was also in the study."

The lingering shame and a distrust of the Government may be one reason that the number of family members in the Participants Health Benefits Program has never been high. Originally, 106 men who were in the experiment began receiving benefits in 1974, Dr. Jenkins said, but the number of wives appears never to have been very large. He said that in 1975, at what was probably the peak of participation by wives, only 50 had been tested. Of those, 27 were found to be positive for syphilis and eligible for the program.

In the study, which began in 1932, more than 600 men were recruited by Government health workers, who led them to believe they were receiving free medical treatment. Throughout the 40-year study, the men were never told of the experiment and those with syphilis were never told they were infected. They never received any treatment for the disease, even when the use of penicillin became routine in the 1940's. When participants died, researchers offered their families free burials in exchange for the rights to do autopsies so they could gather their final data for the study, which researchers say was scientifically flawed from the start.

Dr. Jenkins said that when the true nature of the study became known, some family members became so distrustful of the Government that they refused to be tested for syphilis. No effort was ever made to track down sexual partners of the men, other than their wives.

When the study was under way, some wives tried to enroll, believing the project was a reliable source of medical care. When they were turned away, many were upset, according to Dr. Jim Jones, a historian at the University of Houston and the author of "Bad Blood" (Free Press, 1993), which historians regard as the definitive account of the experiment.

Dr. Jenkins said another reason the number of wives in the program might be low is that the men chosen for the study were supposedly in a latent, non-infectious stage of syphilis, unable to transmit the disease to their wives. That point, however, is still being debated.

"It's unclear what stage of the disease the men were at," Dr. Gamble said. "So that brings the issues around to the women and children."

Nowadays, the Tuskegee experiment is so notorious that scientists resist doing anything that could be construed as continuing the so-called research. "No one has ever studied the health consequences to the families, not to my knowledge," Dr. Jenkins said. "We will not compile the data in any way to make an assessment of them as a group. It would seem too much like another study." If such an effort is organized, he added, "I don't want to have anything to do with it."

But Dr. Jenkins said even if researchers knew how many family members were infected with syphilis, there is no way to be certain whether the syphilis was contracted from the men in the study. The test for syphilis is a blood test for antibodies to the disease. A positive result indicates only that a person had syphilis at some point in their lives, with no indication of when or from where the infection arose.

Fred David Gray, a lawyer who has represented the participants in the study since 1972, winning them an out-of-court settlement totaling $10 million, said that in 1974, as part of that agreement, the Government was ordered to provide lifetime health care for participants as well as some family members.

"I hope to see and I think what the men would like to see is some final closure," Mr. Gray said in an interview on Thursday in his Tuskegee office. He said in the last 23 years, he has given out settlement payments to some 6,000 heirs and participants. Despite the fact that the apology is expected this Friday, and Mr. Gray as well as four of the elderly survivors are planning to attend, Mr. Gray said he is continuing to press for the President to change the site of his apology to Tuskegee.

It was soon after Mr. Gray and some of the survivors of the experiment held a news conference here in April to request the Government apology that the White House said one would be forthcoming. Dr. Gamble said the study legacy committee she heads had been pressing for months for an official apology.

But Dr. Jenkins said any form of apology should be seen not as an end but as a beginning.

"There's a tendency to believe that African-Americans are reluctant to participate in research because of this one study and I think that belittles the concerns of African-Americans," Dr. Jenkins said. "They are concerned about public health research because they're alienated from American society in any number of ways and this study is the bellwether. It's much bigger than just this study and we're going to have to do a lot more work than just apologize for this."

Photos: Dr. Bill Jenkins, who in 1969 tried unsuccessfully to end the Tuskegee experiments, now runs a program that provides medical care to the men who participated in the study and to survivors of the participants. (Associated Press for The New York Times); Albert Julkes Jr. said of the Tuskegee experiments on his father and more than 400 other black men, "You don't treat dogs that way." (Chuck Rogers for The New York Times) (pg. B8)

Bodies Don't Just Tell Stories, They Tell Histories: Embodiment of Historical Trauma among American Indians and Alaska Natives[1]

by Karina L. Walters, Selina A. Mohammed, Teresa Evans-Campbell, Ramona E. Beltrán, David H. Chae, and Bonnie Duran

Abstract Increasingly, understanding how the role of historical events and context affect present-day health inequities has become a dominant narrative among Native American communities. Historical trauma, which consists of traumatic events targeting a community (e.g., forced relocation) that cause catastrophic upheaval, has been posited by Native communities and some researchers to have pernicious effects that persist across generations through a myriad of mechanisms from biological to behavioral. Consistent with contemporary societal determinants of health approaches, the impact of historical trauma calls upon researchers to explicitly examine theoretically and empirically how historical processes and contexts become embodied. Scholarship that theoretically engages how historically traumatic events become embodied and affect the magnitude and distribution of health inequities is clearly needed. However, the scholarship on historical trauma is limited. Some scholars have focused on these events as etiological agents to social and psychological distress; others have focused on events as an outcome (e.g., historical trauma response); others still have focused on these events as mechanisms or pathways by which historical trauma is transmitted; and others have focused on

---

historical trauma-related factors (e.g., collective loss) that interact with proximal stressors. These varied conceptualizations of historical trauma have hindered the ability to cogently theorize it and its impact on Native health. The purpose of this article is to explicate the link between historical trauma and the concept of embodiment. After an interdisciplinary review of the "state of the discipline," we utilize ecosocial theory and the indigenist stress-coping model to argue that contemporary physical health reflects, in part, the embodiment of historical trauma. Future research directions are discussed.

Keywords Historical Trauma, Embodiment, Stress, American Indian, Alaska Native, Native American, First Nations, Indigenous

Introduction

American Indians and Alaska Natives (AIANs) throughout North America suffer devastatingly high rates of health disparities, many of which are linked to land loss, cultural devastation, and a lack of access to healthy environments (Walters et al., 2011). AIAN poor health is manifested in disproportionately high rates of chronic and communicable diseases coupled with inadequate living conditions, insufficient nutrition, and exposure to high levels of environmental contaminants (Barnes et al., 2010).

Health disparities among AIANs have been theoretically and empirically linked to social, economic, cultural, or political inequalities and not to any inherent Native trait or gene (Adelson 2005). Moreover, the complex political histories between AIANs and the federal government have limited the ability of AIAN communities to adequately address their own health needs. Ecosocial theory (Krieger 1999) has been put forth as an epidemiological framework integrating social and biologic conceptualizations of health and articulating how social inequalities become embodied in human beings. According to Krieger (1999), ecosocial theory posits

> . . . that how we develop, grow, age, ail, and die necessarily reflects a constant interplay, within our bodies, of our intertwined and inseparable social and biological history . . . Taking literally the notion of 'embodiment,' this theory asks how we literally incorporate biologically—from conception to death—our social experiences and express this embodiment in population patterns of health, disease, and well-being (p. 296).

Although classic social determinants of health (e.g., low socioeconomic status) contribute to poor health among AIANs, these factors do not sufficiently explain the high rates of poor health and mental health, particularly with respect to Post Traumatic Stress Disorder (PTSD), anxiety, depression, diabetes, cardiovascular disease (CVD), and pain reactions among AIANs (Walters and Simoni, 2002). As a result, scholars have turned their attention to examining how historical and societal determinants of health—and in particular historically traumatic events (e.g., forced relocation and boarding schools), microaggressions, and disproportionate exposures to lifetime trauma—impact not only contemporary AIAN health, but may persist for generations (Chae and Walters, 2009; Evans-Campbell 2008). Utilizing an ecosocial framework, one can examine health disparities among AIANs and question how social experiences, such as historical trauma (HT), have shaped health status.

AIANs have suffered numerous historical experiences of European colonization and the ongoing contemporary effects of colonization (e.g., oppression). The amassing of HT-related cumulative emotional and psychological wounding has been a key discourse among AIAN communities as it relates to various health conditions, and an area of bourgeoning empirical study in the last decade among Native scholars. Yet, while scholars have theoretically engaged how HT events have shaped societal and biophysical outcomes, little HT research has actually focused on the physical health impact of HT. An understanding of how HT events are embodied and how these embodied events affect the magnitude and distribution of health inequities among AIANs is clearly needed.

The purpose of this article is to explicate the link between HT and the concept of embodiment. Specifically, we will review the "state of the discipline" with respect to theoretical and empirical scholarship on historical trauma, intergenerational trauma, and embodiment across disciplines. Additionally, we will locate the "state of the discipline" in terms of AIAN theory development and empirical scholarship related to HT. Finally, building upon an expansive view of Indigenous health frameworks, such as the indigenist stress-coping model (Walters and Simoni, 2002), we argue that contemporary health and health risk behaviors are, in part, the embodiment of HT.

State of the Discipline: Historical and Intergenerational Trauma

Historical Trauma: Key Components

Historical trauma can be conceptualized as an event or set of events perpetrated on a group of people (including their environment) who share a specific group identity (e.g., nationality, tribal affiliation, ethnicity, religious affiliation) with genocidal or ethnocidal intent (i.e., annihilation or disruption to traditional lifeways, culture, and identity) (Walters et al., 2011). Such events include direct attacks on the community, as in the case of massacres, as well as indirect attacks, as in the case of destroying buffalo to near extinction. Individually, each event is profoundly traumatic; taken together they constitute a history of sustained cultural disruption and destruction directed at AIAN tribal communities. The resulting trauma is often conceptualized as collective, in that it impacts a significant portion of a community, and compounding, as multiple historically traumatic events occurring over generations join in an overarching legacy of assaults. For AIANs, cumulative HT events are coupled with high rates of contemporary lifetime trauma and interpersonal violence, as well as high rates of chronic stressors such as microaggressions and daily discriminatory events (Chae and Walters, 2009). Together, these historical and contemporary events undermine AIAN physical, spiritual, and psychological health and well-being in complex and multifaceted ways.

Historically Traumatic Events

The last 500 years of AIAN history has largely been a history of trauma and resistance. Beginning with the first contact between European "explorers" and AIAN communities and lasting into the present, AIAN people have been devastated by disease, warfare, forced migration, cultural genocide, racism, and poverty. Likewise, cultural practices, including languages, educational systems, spirituality, and the daily practices of everyday life were systematically attacked, oppressed or outlawed. HT is not a historical anecdote for contemporary AIAN peoples. The parents and grandparents of many AIAN people faced rapid social change and cultural destruction wrought by HT-based policies designed to "kill the Indian to save the man." Specifically, by the mid-nineteenth century, American expansionist attitudes laid the foundation for massive American Indian removal policies. On the heels of the removal and reservation efforts, the U.S. government also instituted a boarding-school campaign with the express purpose of assimilation by removing AIAN children from their tribal communities and placing them in non-Indian run residential schools. Torn from family, land, and ancestors, children were forbidden to practice any form of their traditional ways of life and, instead, were forced to learn Western mannerisms and speak English (Evans-Campbell 2008). Physical abuse and neglect were commonplace, and high numbers of children were also sexually abused. Simultaneously, during this time period, the Court of Indian Offense legally mandated the prohibition of cultural and spiritual practices under threat of imprisonment or withholding of rations. The collective cultural disruption that resulted from these initiatives was profound.

Historical trauma also includes the systematic destruction of environment. Today, tribal lands are subject to some of the most invasive, toxic, and destructive environmental practices. Perhaps the best contemporary example of this can be seen in the rapid rise of diabetes among the Pimas and Maricopas when, after their water was diverted from their traditional lands for non-Native community and commercial consumption, the diabetes rate increased 500% (Bennett 1999).

Historical Trauma and Intergenerational Trauma: Empirical Support

Currently, the scholarship on "historical trauma" is limited, in part because the term itself has been used interchangeably with other terms such as *soul wound, collective unresolved grief, collective trauma, intergenerational trauma, transgenerational trauma, intergenerational post traumatic stress, and multigenerational trauma* (Palacios and Portillo, 2009), and also because the term has been used differentially across a number of studies. For example, some scholarship has focused on HT events as etiological agents to social and psychological distress (Palacios and Portillo, 2009; Walters et al., 2011), whereas others have focused on HT as an outcome—also known as either historical trauma response (Brave Heart 1999) or colonial trauma response (Evans-Campbell 2008)—which includes clustering of Native-specific expressions of distress. Others have focused on HT as a potential mechanism or pathway by which it is transmitted (e.g., storytelling or secondary traumatization (Palacios and Portillo, 2009)); and others still have focused on HT-related factors (e.g., collective loss or pain) that interact with proximal stressors (Whitbeck et al., 2004). The simultaneous use of the term "historical trauma" to encapsulate four different HT processes (as an etiological factor; as a particular type of trauma response and syndrome; as a pathway or mechanism to transfer trauma across generations; and as an HT-related stressor interacting with other proximal stressors) has hindered the ability to cogently theorize historical trauma and its impact on indigenous health across disciplines.

Despite these divergent conceptualizations, HT scholars have noted individual-and communal-level impacts of HT events on AIAN health. At the individual level, the impact includes impairments in family communication (Evans-Campbell 2008); mental health symptoms of PTSD survivor guilt, anxiety, depression and substance abuse (Whitbeck et al., 2004). At the community level, collective responses include the disruption of traditional customs, languages, and practices. Notably, despite exposure to historical and cumulative traumatic stressors, many Native people do not manifest psychopathology. Indeed, emerging research indicates that the very areas of Native culture that have been targeted for destruction (e.g., identity, spirituality, traditional practices) may, in fact, be sites of resistance (Walters et al., 2011). Moreover, some communities commemorate HT events to signify and celebrate the ability of subsequent generations to thrive and survive after such events (e.g., the Trail of Tears commemorative annual walk among the Choctaw).

"A related field, intergenerational trauma, also recognizes collective traumatic events but is inclusive of natural disasters and other traumatic events (e.g., famine) that are man-made but not targeted with intention upon a particular group for social, cultural, ethnic, or political decimation or annihilation" (Walters et al., 2011, p. 10). As Walters et al. (2011) note, intergenerational trauma and HT research indicates that the impact of these massive traumatic events that target a collective may persist over generations (Nagata et al., 1999); that the trauma may have a greater effect on descendant survivors if both parents were exposed to the event (Yehuda 1999); that the trauma may be differentially experienced by men and women (Brave Heart 1999); and that the trauma can literally become embodied, manifesting as poor mental and physical health outcomes in descendant generations (e.g., Kuzawa and Sweet, 2009). Although descendants of survivors are not more likely than others to have poor mental health, they may be predisposed to higher stress vulnerability. Thus, when descendant survivors experience high levels of contemporary traumatic stress, they may be more likely than others to exhibit PTSD or related symptomology (e.g., Yehuda et al., 2005). Despite emerging research on HT and intergenerational trauma, few studies have focused on HT-related issues specific to AIAN populations. For example, recovery from historically traumatic events is compounded by the fact that AIANs remain living in the places where historically traumatic events occurred and experience constant reminders of these events. Additionally, there has been little articulation of how the *chronicity* of certain HT events (e.g., boarding school) might produce different mental and physical health outcomes over generations compared to acute but discrete HT events (e.g., massacre). It also appears that diverse types of HT events might yield very different trauma reactions—psychological and physiological. Our preliminary research, for example, indicates that HT events that *disrupt ties* to family, community, or place (e.g., boarding school, forced relocation) may be associated with depressive symptoms, whereas HT events that cause *direct physical harm* to community, body, land, or sacred sites are more likely to be associated with anxiety or PTSD symptoms (Walters et al., 2011). Finally, though we know that many people exposed to HT remain healthy, research has not explored factors related to maintaining health in the face of HT events.

Embodiment and Historical Trauma

Embodiment Overview

Recently, the body has emerged as a key focus in the social and behavioral sciences. In particular, researchers have begun to examine the impact of social and economic inequities on physical health and how embodiment of these inequities is multifaceted and influenced by social, cultural, economic, and biological processes. As Krieger and Davey Smith (2004) note, recognition of the link between the body and social inequities first gained attention in the 1840s when social scientists found that the impact of abhorrent working conditions, poor access to food, and inadequate health care in childhood led to premature mortality. However, it was not until the Depression Era that American researchers began to move away from "faulty gene" research to explore how social, economic, and political forces were expressed in bodies. Recently, research has attempted to examine gene-environment interactions as a way to explore environmental impact on health outcomes. However, as Krieger and Davey Smith (2004; p. 94) state, shifting from gene-frequency concerns to determinants of gene expression, researchers called "into question the popular notion of "gene-environment interaction," since "genes" do not interact with environments—only organisms do, with consequences for gene regulation and expression."

Additionally, embodiment acknowledges that while bodies tell [his]stories, they reveal stories that are also not conscious, hidden, forbidden, or even denied by individuals or groups. Studying the embodiment of HT and corresponding health consequences allows us to determine the forces driving intergenerational patterns of health and disease among AIANs (Krieger 1999). Moreover, such knowledge will likely yield important directions for developing culturally relevant policies and practices to reduce AIAN health inequities and ultimately grow AIAN health and wellness for future generations.

AIAN Relational Worldviews and Embodiment

The concept of embodiment is consistent with AIAN spatial and relational world-views that recognize the interdependency between humans and nature, the physical and spiritual worlds, the ancestors and the future generations (Walters et al., 2011). According to AIAN worldviews, environment, mind, body, and emotional health are inextricably linked to human behavior, practices, wholeness, and hence, wellness (Walters et al., 2011).

In recent years, a wholistic orientation that incorporates the interconnectedness of the mind, body, and spirit has gained acceptance, particularly in the fields of psychoneuroimmunology (Lyons and Chamberlain, 2006), epigenetics (Holliday 2006), cardiovascular disease (Kuzawa and Sweet, 2009), inflammation disorders (Jessop et al., 2004), and neuroendocrine and immune functions (Seeman et al., 2003).

Epigenetics and Historical Trauma

There is strong evidence that poor health outcomes are linked to genetic, environmental, and behavioral risk factors (Matthews and Phillips, 2010), yet the actual pathways and mechanisms, particularly biological and sociological mechanisms, for the intergenerational transmission of HT events among humans are hotly contested and remain open to debate. Specifically, the relative impact of HT on descendant physical and mental health is a point of contention, particularly among behavioral scientists. While some scholars have argued that the intergenerational effects of historical trauma (i.e., distal causes) are likely negligible once lifetime trauma exposures (i.e., proximal causes) are accounted for; other scholars point to preliminary evidence indicating that extreme environmental stress in one generation can alter health outcomes for descendant generations (Walters et al., 2011). Specifically, as Walters et al. (2011) note "these scholars point to the amassing of evidence at the cellular level that powerful stressful environmental conditions can leave an imprint or "mark" on the epigenome (cellular genetic material) that can be carried into future generations with devastating consequences" (p. 11). For example, inadequate prenatal maternal nutrition at key gestational developmental periods can lead to descendant offspring developing CVD in adulthood (Kuzawa and Sweet, 2009). The debate about which has the strongest or combined net effect on poor health outcomes and the persistence of health disparities remains open to ongoing empirical verification; however, the preliminary evidence for intergenerational transmission of stress has critical implications for the study of HT among AIANs.

Several animal and, more recently, human studies have demonstrated pervasive and enduring effects of the neurobiological toll of stress on neurodevelopmental delays, hypothalamic-pituitary-adrenal (HPA) axis dysfunction, metabolic syndrome, CVD, immune system dysfunction, major depressive disorder, PTSD, compromised reproductive health and transgenerational effects of stress exposure on the health of offspring generations (Brand et al., 2010; Yehuda and Bierer, 2009). Moreover, different changes in HPA axis and related neuroendocrine systems are linked with different disease outcomes (Matthews and Phillips, 2010). For example, hypercortisolemia (abnormally high levels of cortisol) increases susceptibility to depression, hypertension, and diabetes whereas hypocortisolemia (abnormally low levels of cortisol) increases susceptibility to chronic fatigue syndrome, fibromyalgia, and PTSD (Matthews and Phillips, 2010). Emerging epigenetic and neurobiological research is beginning to provide evidence that neuroendocrine response to stress can be transmitted to future generations by means of nongenomic mechanisms—having major implications for how environmental stressors in one generation can influence the disease risk of subsequent generations (Matthews and Phillips, 2010). For example, maternal stress exposure studies indicate that maternal psychological and nutritional stress during pregnancy can lead to

biological changes that predispose their offspring to diabetes, CVD, and other diseases (Kuzawa and Sweet, 2009). Finally, overfeeding and overeating during critical developmental periods following periods of poor nutrition could lead to metabolic adaptations over generations—particularly high CVD- and diabetes-related mortality in subsequent generations (interestingly, transmitted through the male line (Kaati et al., 2002)). Clearly, there is growing consensus that environmental influences contribute to health disparities by influencing biological processes and responses at key developmental periods throughout the life course and across generations.

In terms of AIANs, our own work has shown that a high proportion of AIANs have high levels of historical-trauma loss manifesting in thinking about the impact of land-based trauma, on a weekly, and in some cases, daily basis. Moreover, after controlling for contemporary trauma, we found that HT land-based events continued to have a significant effect on mental and physical health (Walters et al., 2011). These findings provide preliminary support that HT related to land losses may persist and also become embodied. Although we cannot conclude directionality given the cross-sectional nature of the survey data from this study, the findings illuminate some of the HT factors that may lead to poor health.

Although embodiment reminds us that we cannot exclude social, historical, or cumulative experiences and their corresponding impact on our health and wellness, and ultimately on population health disparities, parsing out these processes is difficult in HT research and requires a multilevel, integrated approach (Krieger 2005). However, this should not preclude our delving into the intricacies and complexities of HT research nor should we assume that HT is irrelevant because of the difficulties involved in disentangling its effect on health inequities from other traumatic stressors.

Pathways to Embodying HT

Biological expressions of HT may, in part, produce health disparities in a wide spectrum of outcomes—from chronic and persistent illnesses (e.g., diabetes) to poor mental health (e.g., PTSD, depression). From an ecosocial perspective, certain pathways to embodiment of HT are clearer given that some HT events are tied to exposures to noxious physical, chemical, biological, and psychosocial insults—all of which can affect biological integrity at numerous interacting levels (Krieger 2005). Other pathways are much more challenging to investigate, but no less important. The net effect of these multiple, intersecting pathways leads to health inequities not only in the life course of an individual, but over generations.

Another relevant factor is the varied responses AIAN people have to HT, ranging from internalized oppression and substance use to community organizing around HT as a social movement strategy. From a theoretical viewpoint, the utility of an ecosocial framework and embodiment encourages the identification of potential testable hypotheses by systematically tracing pathways between HT events and their potential embodied expressions. Additionally, resistance, positive coping, and resiliency can be mapped by utilizing an indigenist stress-coping framework (Walters and Simoni, 2002) to identify how HT events not only have direct effects on wellness outcomes, but also how cultural protective factors (e.g., identity) can buffer the impact of these events on wellness outcomes. Importantly, pathways could also be traced across generations to examine how the cumulative effect of HT events, or perhaps type of events, continue to impact the health of the present generation.

Future Directions: Measurement and Methodological Issues

Measuring the pernicious health effects of HT is daunting. Because HT is so difficult to measure, indirect methods (Krieger 1999) might be one way to infer the impact of HT on AIAN health. For example, with AIAN populations, exceedingly high rates of psychological and physiological distress and disparities have been identified as indirect indicators of not only structural and economic inequalities, but also of successive exposures to HT over generations. Although indirect approaches do not allow for investigation of issues related to intensity, duration, time period of exposure to HT—particularly generational cohort effects to HT events; indirect strategies could address whether HT-related losses or other factors presumed to be

related to HT account for observed differences in health between dominant and subordinate groups (Krieger 1999) and in some cases between tribal members who experienced an HT event compared to tribal members who did not (e.g., Cherokees who were not removed in the 1830s vs. the ones who were relocated on the infamous Trail of Tears).

Slightly more direct routes would involve specifically measuring HT events, as well as their intensity, duration, and time period of exposure (Krieger 1999) for particular tribal populations. In some cases, there are opportunities to observe how an HT event within a particular tribe had differential impact on tribal members who either directly or indirectly experienced the event or descended from someone who directly or indirectly experienced the event. Additionally, depending on health outcomes under study, chronic and acute HT exposures (e.g., one day massacre) may matter, as will the intensity of the HT event, its duration, and the frequency of exposure to HT events in a particular generation or across generations. Moreover, the daily wear and tear of HT-event exposure (e.g., boarding school living; experimental bombing on traditional homelands) may pose health hazards distinct from those resulting in major acute HT events (e.g., massacre) (Krieger 1999). Finally, chronicity of events over one's lifetime and over generations may have health consequences different from those ensuing from one or two events over generations. All of these factors have to be considered when measuring HT. Moreover, future research should work with tribal communities to identify resiliency responses, resistance strategies, positive coping and other factors that buffered the impact of HT on tribal, communal, familial, and individual wellness.

Epidemiologic principles can provide useful guidance for measuring and analyzing self-reported experiences of HT and its effects on health and wellness (Krieger 1999). Drawing on Krieger's (1999) tenets for measurement of the health effects of discrimination, to examine the health effects of HT, researchers would need to do the following: assess the variability in the time period since exposure to the HT within a tribal community, the family, and for the individual; determine: (1) the domain or level of specificity for examination (global HT as a variable or specific HT events that could be examined individually or collectively); (2) the intensity and frequency of exposure (e.g., boarding school vs. massacre survival); (3) the relevant etiologic historical period; (4) the variability of targets of HT (land, objects, body, mind, spirituality) and whether descendancy is direct from HT survivors or indirect (e.g., individual has an aunt who attended boarding school vs. a parent); (5) the developmental age and time for the person or ancestor/s who experienced the event; and (6) the destructive or disruptive valence of the HT event (e.g., near-death experience, direct attacks on person, place, object, culture vs. indirect via disruptions in relationships to persons, place, culture).

Developing culturally valid and reliable measures is a major concern in HT research. Measures should include questions on specific HT events and be separate from HT sociopsychological responses (e.g., historical trauma response). Moreover, the HT-event questions should be clear and direct and address multiple facets of an HT event for measures that study the health consequences of a particular HT event. This is an easier approach when working with a particular tribal community, more challenging when working in urban settings where many different tribes live and AIANs tend to descend from multiple tribes. In the case of urban HT research, it may be necessary to develop HT-event items that cut across tribes, where members of different tribes (each with its own different specific HT history) who share similar cross-cutting HT events could say "yes" to an item that they could plug themselves into (e.g., been forcefully relocated)—although the cultural and tribal specificity of that particular event would be lost with such a measure. Global HT event indexes could be developed (e.g., Walters et al., 2011) that measure different types of HT events within an individual's lifetime and across generations. In other words, the respondent may be asked if he/she experienced a particular HT event or set of events and then would be given follow-up stem questions asking if his/her parents, grandparents, etc. also experienced the same event (e.g., forced relocation or boarding school attendance). We have successfully used this approach, albeit with limitations, in urban AIAN samples. It is important to note that global indexes or a summary HT event measure would likely yield underestimates of HT exposure. Moreover, HT events that are tied to specific generational cohorts (e.g., massacres in the grandparent generation) may require the respondent to have "knowledge" or consciousness of the HT event itself, as well as their own familial experience of that event. This approach will likely yield an underestimate of HT transgenerational experiences, in part because survivors and descendant offspring of HT experiences tend not to want to "talk" about the event, thus the respondent may not have specific knowledge of the event from their family of origin. Thus, it is important to identify qualitative and archival methods that will supplement some of this information to better interpret HT data.

Conclusion

This article has provided conceptual links among HT and overall health and well-being among AIANs. Future research is needed to further discern the relationship among proximal and distal HT factors on specific health outcomes and to identify important factors, such as identity, that buffer against the impact of such potentially traumatic losses. These protective factors may play a significant role in regulating biological mechanisms. Future research will need to better elucidate the biological pathways and mechanisms associated with HT effects on physical health. Moreover, even if HT makes only a moderate contribution to our understanding of population health in future studies, modest findings indicate the importance of examining further potential nongenomic biological mechanisms and pathways that might allow AIAN bodies to reveal their histories even as AIAN communities are beginning to find the words and [re] generating the practices to heal.

Corresponding author: Karina L. Walters, School of Social Work, University of Washington, Box 354900, 4101 Fifteenth Avenue NE, Seattle, WA 98105. E-mail: kw5@uw.edu

Note

1. The theoretical development of this work was supported in part by the Network for Multicultural Research on Health and Healthcare, Dept. of Family Medicine, David Geffen School of Medicine, UCLA, funded by the Robert Wood Johnson Foundation;

as well as supported in part by the National Heart, Lung, and Blood Institute (5U01HL087322-05), National Institute of Mental Health (MH65821), the Office of Research on Women's Health, The Office of AIDS Research, and the National Center on Minority Health and Health Disparities.

References

Adelson, Naomi (2005). The Embodiment of Inequity: Health Disparities in Aboriginal Canada. *Canadian Journal of Public Health*, 96: S45–S61.

Barnes, Patricia M., Patricia F. Adams, and Eve Powell-Griner (2010). Health Characteristics of the American Indian or Alaska Native Adult Population: United States, 2004–2008. *National Health Statistics Reports*, (20): 1–22.

Bennett, Peter (1999). Type 2 Diabetes Among the Pima Indians of Arizona: An Epidemic Attributable to Environmental Change? *Nutrition Reviews*, 57(5): S51–S54.

Brand, Sarah R., Patricia A. Brennan, D. Jeffrey Newport, Alicia K. Smith, Tamara Weiss, and Zachary N. Stowe (2010). The Impact of Maternal Childhood Abuse on Maternal and Infant HPA Axis Function in the Postpartum Period. *Psychoneuroendocrinology*, 35(5): 686–693.

Brave Heart, Maria Yellow Horse (1999). Oyate Ptayela: Rebuilding the Lakota Nation Through Addressing Historical Trauma Among Lakota parents. *Journal of Human Behavior in the Social Environment*, 2 (1): 109–126.

Chae, David H. and Karina L. Walters (2009). Racial Discrimination and Racial Identity Attitudes in Relation to Self-Rated Health and Physical Pain and Impairment Among Two-Spirit American Indians/Alaska Natives. *American Journal of Public Health*, 99 (S1): S144–S151.

Evans-Campbell, Teresa (2008). Historical Trauma in American Indian/Native Alaska Communities: A Multilevel Framework for Exploring Impacts on Individuals, Families, and Communities. *Journal of Interpersonal Violence*, 23 (3): 316–338.

Holliday, Robin (2006). Epigenetics: A Historical Overview. *Epigenetics*, 1(2): 76–80.

Jessop, D. S., L. J. Richards, and M. S. Harbuz (2004). Effects of Stress on Inflammatory Autoimmune Disease: Destructive or Protective? *Stress*, 7(4): 261–266.

Kaati, G., L. O. Bygren, and S. Edvinsson (2002). Cardiovascular And Diabetes Mortality Determined by Nutrition During Parents' And Grandparents' Slow Growth Period. *European Journal of Human Genetics*, 10(11): 682–688.

Krieger, Nancy (1999). Embodying Inequality: A Review of Concepts, Measures, and Methods for Studying Health Consequences of Discrimination. *International Journal of Health Services*, 29(2): 295–352.

Krieger, Nancy (2005). Embodiment: A Conceptual Glossary For Epidemiology. *Journal of Epidemiological Community Health*, 59(5): 350–355.

Krieger, Nancy and George Davey Smith (2004). "Bodies Count," and Body Counts: Social Epidemiology and Embodying Inequality. *Epidemiologic Reviews*, 26: 92–103.

Kuzawa, Christopher W. and Elizabeth Sweet (2009). Epigenetics and the Embodiment of Race: Developmental Origins of US Racial Disparities In Cardiovascular Health. *American Journal of Human Biology*, 21(1): 2–15.

Lyons, A. C. and K. Chamberlain (2006). *Health Psychology: A Critical Introduction*. Cambridge, MA: Cambridge University Press.

Matthews, Stephen G. and David I. W. Phillips (2010). Minireview: Transgenerational Inheritance of the Stress Response: A New Frontier in Stress Research. *Endocrinology*, 151(1): 7–13.

Nagata, Donna K., Steven J. Trierweiler, and Rebecca Talbot (1999). Long-Term Effects Of Internment During Early Childhood In Third Generation Japanese Americans. *American Journal of Orthopsychiatry*, 69(1): 19–29.

Palacios, Janelle F. and Carmen J. Portillo (2009). Understanding Native Women's Health: Historical Legacies. *Journal of Transcultural Nursing*, 20(1): 15–27.

Seeman, T. E., L. F. Dubin, and M. Seeman (2003). Religiosity/Spirituality and Health: A Critical Review of the Evidence for Biological Pathways. *American Psychologist*, 58(1): 53–63.

Walters, Karina L., Ramona E. Beltran, David Huh, and Teresa Evans-Campbell (2011). Dis-placement and Dis-ease: Land, Place and Health among American Indians and Alaska Natives. In Linda M. Burton, Susan P. Kemp, ManChui Leung, Stephen A. Matthews, and David T. Takeuchi (Eds.), *Communities, Neighborhood, and Health: Expanding the Boundaries of Place*, pp. 163–199. Philadephia, PA: Springer Science + Business Media, LLC.

Walters, Karina L. and Jane M. Simoni (2002). Reconceptualizing Native Women's Health: An "Indigenist" Stress-Coping Model. *American Journal of Public Health*, 92 (4): 520–524.

Whitbeck, Les B., Gary W. Adams, Dan R. Hoyt, and Xiaojin Chen (2004). Conceptualizing and Measuring Historical Trauma Among American Indian People. *American Journal of Community Psychology*, 33 (3–4): 119–130.

Yehuda, Rachel (1999). *Risk Factors for Posttraumatic Stress Disorder.* Washington, DC: American Psychiatric Press.

Yehuda, Rachel and Linda M. Bierer (2009). The Relevance of Epigenetics to PTSD: Implications for the DSM-V. *Journal of Traumatic Stress,* 22(5): 427–434.

Yehuda, Rachel, Stephanie Mulherin Engel, Sarah R. Brand, Jonathan Seckl, Sue M. Marcus, and Gertrud S. Berkowitz (2005). Transgenerational Effects of Posttraumatic Stress Disorder in Babies of Mothers Exposed to the World Trade Center Attacks during Pregnancy. *Journal of Clinical Endocrinology & Metabolism,* 90(7): 4115–4118.

Barriers to Healthcare Among Asian Americans

by Wooksoo Kim and Robert H. Keefe

School of Social Work, University at Buffalo, State University of New York, Buffalo, New York, USA

The myth of the well-adjusted Asian American resulted from sample-biased research studies that concluded that Asian Americans are physically healthier and financially better off than Caucasians. The myth has been perpetuated by researchers who have often categorized Asian Americans as a single, undifferentiated group rather than as distinct ethnic groups. Consequently, data analysis techniques do not reveal distinctions that may exist had the researchers controlled for ethnic group variation. The authors discussed four major barriers—language and culture, health literacy, health insurance, and immigrant status—to healthcare that may influence within-group disparities among Asian Americans that may go unreported. The authors argue that healthcare policy makers and researchers should consider Asian Americans as members of discrete ethnic groups with unique healthcare needs. Recommendations for health policies and future research are provided.

Keywords Asian Americans, access to healthcare, health literacy, immigrant health, health disparities

The utilization of healthcare services by any group is determined by calculating the ratio of the number of group members who receive healthcare services against the number of group members within the population at large (Snowden, Collinge, & Runkle, 1982). Parity of service use is achieved when the ratio of the group receiving the service is the same as the ratio for the members within the population at large. In the past few decades, research has documented the disparities in healthcare service use by race, whereby Caucasians consistently have greater access to healthcare and enjoy better health than their non-Caucasian counterparts. Although there are many racial and ethnic minority groups, much of the research has focused on differences between Caucasian Americans and African and Hispanic Americans.

Address correspondence to Robert H. Keefe, PhD, ACSW, School of Social Work, 685 Baldy Hall, University at Buffalo, State University of New York, Buffalo, NY 14260-1050, USA. E-mail: rhkeefe@buffalo.edu

Although research studies have explored important aspects of racial and ethnic health disparities, many of the studies categorized diverse subgroups under one racial category, thus ignoring important within–race group and–ethnic group variation. Asian Americans comprise multiple ethnic groups that have been found to underutilize healthcare services compared to their Caucasian counterparts (Snowden et al., 1982; Takada, Fort, & Lloyd, 1998). Existing research, however, has largely considered Asian Americans as one monolithic group that has been faring better than the general population, rather than as separate and unique groups with their own healthcare needs. Within-group diversity is not an exclusive characteristic of Asian Americans. In recent years, many researchers have begun to investigate the diversity within racial/ethnic groups that historically have been treated as homogeneous groups, such as Hispanic and African Americans.

The purpose of this article is to discuss barriers to healthcare for Asian Americans and to provide policy and research recommendations that will benefit people of all Asian American ethnic groups. The discussion will focus on major barriers to healthcare among Asian Americans groups, including language and culture, health literacy, insurance, and immigrant status. These barriers will be discussed against the backdrop of the Asian American myth, which puts forth that all people from Asian backgrounds are better off than are other groups with respect to their healthcare.

Diversity Among Asian Americans and its Research Implications

Asian Americans are among of the fastest growing ethnic groups in the United States. According to the 2000 U.S. Census, approximately 13.1 million individuals (4.2% of the American population) self-identify as Asian American. The number of Asian Americans is expected to increase to 33.4 million (8% of the American population) by 2050 (U.S. Census Bureau, 2004a). Despite the rapid increase, there is a dearth of knowledge on the issues related to healthcare use among various Asian American ethnic groups.

Language has been a continuing issue in conducting research on Asian Americans. Due to their limited English-speaking skills, recent Asian immigrants may not be able to adequately answer survey questions and thus either refuse or are considered ineligible to participate in health research studies. As a result, much of the research on Asian Americans includes English-speaking and well-acculturated individuals, who have more education, better insurance, and higher incomes than the nonrespondents. Consequently, the existing national data sets are unrepresentative of all Asian Americans (Takada et al., 1998). The sampling bias, in turn, perpetuates the myth of the well-adjusted Asian American.

Due in part to the limitations of existing research, many Asian Americans ethnic groups have not been represented in existing research and have thus been deprived of potential help from the U.S. government (Fong & Mokuau, 1994). A bimodal pattern has emerged in which several ethnic Asian American groups are faring better than others. With respect to poverty, Japanese and Filipino Americans have much lower poverty rates than their Caucasian counterparts, while other Asian American groups such as Cambodians, Hmongs, Laotians, and Vietnamese Americans have much higher poverty rates (Niedzwiecki & Duong, 2004).

Other problems in carrying out research on Asian Americans are the methodological difficulties inherent in studying them. Included with these difficulties is the relatively small number of Asian Americans in some ethnic groups. Although they form one of the fastest growing populations in the United States, there are only small numbers of different ethnic Asian American groups who have been living in the United States for more than one or two generations. As such, it can be difficult for researchers to find ethnic enclaves of Asian Americans. Another reason for the limited knowledge of Asian American health is the diversity within each Asian American ethnic group. Researchers have identified between 27 and 32 unique Asian American groups in the United States that fall under the umbrella of "Asian/Pacific Islanders." Consequently, due to the relatively small number of people in some of the other ethnic groups, differences in their language, and their wide geographic dispersion, it is extremely difficult to come up with a representative sample.

Because of the sampling issues, most of the help-seeking behavior and health service use studies on Asian Americans have been limited to either small and regional samples or service use data (Cheung & Snowden, 1990). To overcome the difficulties in sampling and recruitment, researchers often choose samples from one Asian American group (Kim, 2002). In turn, researchers may extrapolate from their findings to form a model they believe is representative of all Asian Americans. This limitation not only fails to flush out differences among the Asian American groups not being studied, but the one group under study is unlikely to be representative of its own ethnic Asian American population. Moreover, the extant studies on the health of Asian Americans have been limited unless the researchers intentionally invest in bilingual interviewers. While considering the fact that language proficiency is a proxy measure for acculturation, Asian Americans whose English skills are sufficient for research may have biased the results, thus indicating that all Asian Americans are better off than Caucasians and other racial and ethnic groups. Considering the above limitations, researchers who review Asian American healthcare issues need to exercise caution when pointing out the implications and limitations of the research.

Barriers to Healthcare

Language/Culture

Language has been identified as the most formidable barrier for Asian American immigrants in accessing healthcare (Mayeno & Hirota, 1994). Language is not only a measure of adjustment but also a means to adjust to a new environment. Many Asian Americans who are not proficient in English experience barriers in help-seeking, including making an appointment, locating a health facility, communicating with health professionals, and acquiring knowledge on illness. The language barrier is a particular obstacle for elderly Asian Americans, who are the least likely to be proficient in English (Jones, Chow, & Gatz, 2006).

The lack of language proficiency may bring about role disruptions in Asian American families. Children of recent immigrants tend to speak, read, and understand English better than their parents do and, as such, are often burdened

with the duty of being the family translator when dealing with family illnesses (Lauderdale, Wen, Jacobs, & Kandula, 2006). This temporarily reversed family role creates awkward situations in the healthcare setting: no matter how fluent the children are in English, their role as children predominates and as such they may feel uncomfortable facilitating their elder family members' healthcare decisions.

Moreover, although interpreter services may be available and helpful, people with limited English-speaking skills tend to refrain from asking questions about their health. In fact, Green et al. (2005) found that Chinese and Vietnamese patients with limited English-speaking skills appeared to refrain from asking questions about their health, compared to their counterparts with better skills. Interpreter services do not necessarily mean that the immigrant patient will procure quality care, as many individuals who must rely on interpreters fear that the interpreter will not respect their confidentiality within the larger Asian American community.

The presence of an expert who understands Asian American culture and expressions of illness can help remove the barriers to healthcare. In fact, Asian Americans' perceptions of cultural, gender, and linguistic sensitivity have been found to predict more help-seeking behavior, even when controlling for insurance coverage (Fung & Wong, 2002). However, culturally responsive service can be a double-edged sword and, as such, cultural understanding is not a panacea for improving healthcare for Asian Americans. In an HIV/AIDS project in New York City, providers' cultural literacy ensured that they were being understood even without speaking. This comfort, however, can come with a fear of lack of confidentiality due to the tight social networks of Asian communities (Chin, Kang, Kim, Martinez, & Eckholdt, 2006).

Health Literacy

A related issue to language and culture is health literacy, which includes the ability not only to read health content but also to understand the content in the context of specific health situations. Such situations include understanding instructions on prescription drug labels, appointment slips, health education fliers, physician's directions and consent forms, and complex healthcare systems. The National Library of Medicine reports that the definition of health literacy is not simply the ability to read health literature but also the ability to use analytic and decision-making skills in healthcare situations (Sullivan & Glassman, 2007).

Asian Americans have been found to have limited health literacy and often to have erroneous beliefs regarding disease that in turn can prevent them from seeking healthcare services, thus leading to poorer health outcomes (Jones et al., 2006; Juon, Kim, Shankar, & Han, 2004). Additionally, if the prevalent belief based on studies with nonrepresentative samples is that Asians rarely have breast cancer, Asian immigrant women might not seek regular screenings. In the case of Korean Americans, Juon et al. (2004) found that only 14.8% of Korean immigrant women aged 65 and older had heard of mammography screenings, compared to 40.9% of Caucasian women of the same age. The first generation of Asian Americans, especially the elderly, tends to hold different beliefs on healthcare. For example, many seek healthcare only when their symptoms are severe enough as not to be resolved with standard preventive care (Han, Kang, Kim, Ryu, & Kim, 2007).

Health Insurance

Health insurance serves as a major gatekeeper to accessing care. Most industrialized countries place a high value on equality in their healthcare system, with cultural sensitivity being an important issue (Donnelly, 2006). In the United States, however, there is not as great a focus on parity in healthcare among all groups, as in other countries, thus leading to health disparities regarding which individuals and groups receive healthcare. Despite the public's view of Asian Americans as the financially well-to-do "model minority," the poverty rate for Asian Americans as a group is actually higher than that of Caucasians (U.S. Census Bureau, 2004b).

Moreover, employment is not the best predictor of health insurance for Asian Americans. Although unemployment rates among Asian Americans are relatively low, many Asian Americans do not have health insurance. This is because many Asian Americans work for small businesses or have multiple low-wage jobs, which typically do not offer health insurance (Takada et al., 1998). In fact, whereas approximately 26% of all Americans are covered by employer-sponsored health insurance, only 6% of Asian Americans are covered by employer-sponsored health insurance (U.S. Census Bureau, 2007). Further, there is an insurance loophole into which many self-employed Asian Americans fall: they earn too much money to qualify for government-sponsored health insurance programs and yet too little to purchase private insurance. As such, Asian Americans from the lowest socioeconomic strata may have a better chance of being insured than do those with higher incomes. For example, Southeast Asian refugees who are relatively less well off than other Asian ethnic groups had greater access to health insurance coverage because, as refugees, they qualify for government-sponsored insurance (Mayeno & Hirota, 1994). Additionally, Asian Americans with certain demographic characteristics, specifically young, unmarried, non–English-speaking Chinese American females, were found to have healthcare access problems (Ying & Miller, 1992). In a recent national survey of Asian Americans, Alegría et al. (2006) found that 8.3% of Asian Americans received public health insurance, whereas the U.S. Census data demonstrated that 18.6% of Asian Americans received public health insurance (U.S. Census Bureau, 2007). The source of this discrepancy is not clear and requires further investigation.

There are also discrepancies between the national data set and local surveys. The National Latino and Asian American Survey, the most comprehensive and recent national study, concluded that 14.4% of Asian Americans are uninsured, with Vietnamese having the highest rate at 20.2% (Alegría et al., 2006). However, local surveys present a different picture. For instance, more than 50% of Korean Americans in Los Angeles and 41% in Chicago, 35% of Chinese Americans in Oakland, 37% of Southeast Asians in San Diego, 15% of Vietnamese Americans in San Francisco (Alegría et al., 2006), and 21% of Asian women in Southern

California (Mayeno & Hirota, 1994) indicated that they did not have any health insurance.

Uninsured or inadequately insured Asian Americans may resort to less costly alternative medicine. Asian Americans are likely to be knowledgeable about alternative medicine as an option, substitute, or complementary treatment, and many have found it to be effective. For example, acupuncture and herbal medicine are still considered the best means to treat certain types of illnesses such as sprained ankles, nerve problems, or mental illnesses not recognized by Western medicine (Donnelly, 2006). Most forms of alternative medicine have been used for thousands years and have been found to relieve pain, treat illness, and save lives. Because alternative medicine can produce undesirable side effects or complications when combined with other treatments, the use of alternative medicine can become problematic when patients and their families use alternative medicine without telling their physicians. Further, research has not sufficiently addressed the interactions between alternative and Western medicine. Because some forms of alternative medicine are underregulated in the United States, the quality of treatment is potentially dubious. Accordingly, comprehensive community health education is needed for Asian American ethnic communities to understand that alternative medicine is not a substitute; rather, it should be used with caution. Overall, health insurance information on Asian Americans is not conclusive. Considering the significance of health insurance in healthcare access, these issues need to be investigated further to enhance access to healthcare for Asian Americans.

Immigrant Status

Asian Americans comprise three distinct immigration groups: those who voluntarily chose to come to the new country, refugees who were forced to leave their homeland because of war or political persecution, and decedents of immigrants (Mayeno & Hirota, 1994). The data on actual health service use provide evidence of factors that impede Asian American immigrants from receiving healthcare. Moreover, immigration status has been an important criterion for many healthcare benefits, whereby undocumented immigrants encounter significantly more barriers than documented immigrants in receiving healthcare.

The Immigration Act of 1965 is considered a tipping point that led to the influx of Asian Americans into the United States (Reimers, 1985). Under the act, 170,000 immigrants from countries in the Eastern Hemisphere (for example, people from Asian countries) are granted residence, with no more than 20,000 per country. Prior to the immigration act, the McCarran-Walter Act of 1952 granted residence to only 2,990 Asian immigrants per year (Kutler, 2003). This dramatic change led to the influx of Asian Americans into the United States.

Many researchers found an inverse relationship between years of residence and health status among foreign-born Americans (Frisbie, Cho, & Hummer, 2001; Uretsky & Mathiesen, 2007). Two other hypotheses have been proposed to explain the effect of immigration on health. The "selective immigration hypothesis" holds that those who decided to embark on the adventure of immigrating to the United States aspire to be successful and as such are strongly motivated and mentally and physically in better shape than those who have been living in the country to which they immigrated. Consequently, the immigrant group does not use services because the members do not need them. This hypothesis argues that although the majority of Asian Americans come from economically less privileged countries, their health is much better than those who remained in their homeland. However, as they live longer in the host country, the positive effects wear off and the differences between immigrants and those who are native to the new country disappear. Empirical evidence suggests that Asian Americans, like other immigrant ethnic/racial groups, tend to have poorer health and frequent hospitalizations (Frisbie et al., 2001). In comparison, the "salmon bias hypothesis" focuses on the differences between returning and remaining immigrants. It argues that unhealthy, unemployed, and unsuccessful immigrants may choose to return to their country of origin (Uretsky & Mathiesen, 2007), thus leaving their healthier expatriates in the host country.

Illegal Asian immigrants experience other health access problems. Due to their illegal immigrant status, most of them are not allowed to hold jobs that offer health insurance or purchase health insurance policies and do not qualify for government-sponsored insurance. To date, most of the studies on health insurance coverage focus on Asian Americans who have legal residence, thus limiting our understanding of healthcare for Asian Americans residing in the United States illegally.

Recommendations for Health and Social Policy and Future Research

In order to develop health and social policies that address the issue of underutilization of healthcare services among Asian Americans, health and social policy analysts must make a significant effort to take into account patient characteristics such as primary language, ethnicity (Ray-Mazumder, 2001), culture, health literacy, insurance coverage, and immigrant status. Policy analysts and health researchers need to familiarize themselves with the emotional, psychological, and physical aspects of Asian American cultures including the vast diversity between groups. Without knowing the origin and nature of health behavior, it is impossible to develop health policies that are relevant to the needs of the various Asian American groups. It is also imperative for health policy analysts to pay extra attention to the social and political environments of the immigrants' homeland and the changes in immigration laws. The legal status of an individual directly affects her or his employment opportunities, insurance coverage, and therefore health options. Developing greater sensitivity in these areas will lead to richer foundations on which to build research and health policy agendas to enhance healthcare for Asian Americans.

The presence of healthcare experts who are knowledgeable about Asian American culture and social conditions can help remove, or mitigate, the effects of the barriers to healthcare for Asian Americans. Asian Americans' perceptions of a health provider's cultural, gender, and linguistic sensitivity have been found to predict greater help-seeking behavior, even when controlling for insurance coverage (Fung & Wong, 2002). This example can be expanded to the societal level so that Asian Americans' perception of society's cultural and linguistic responsiveness would increase the opportunity and eventually the quality of healthcare for Asian Americans.

Healthcare issues for Asian Americans cannot be conceptualized without considering healthcare for all Americans. Legislative bodies in the United States have historically avoided addressing equal access to healthcare. Consequently, the United States has remained the only industrialized country without universal healthcare for its citizens. Healthcare has been left in the hands of others, which in turn results in unequal access to healthcare services. Providing culturally competent healthcare services and conducting comprehensive research studies on Asian American ethnic group members and healthcare programs that reach out to people with limited health literacy and resources will eliminate the myth of the well-adjusted Asian American and warrant equal access to healthcare. In the long run, "healthy Asian Americans" is a necessary condition to build a stronger healthcare system in the United States.

References

Alegría, M., Cao, Z., McGuire, T. G., Ojeda, V. D., Sribney, B., Woo, M., et al. (2006). Health insurance coverage for vulnerable populations: Contrasting Asian Americans and Latinos in the United States. *Inquiry, 43*(3), 231–254.

Cheung, F. K., & Snowden, L. R. (1990). Community mental health and ethnic minority population. *Community Mental Health Journal, 26*(3), 277–291.

Chin, J. J., Kang, E., Kim, J. H., Martinez, J., & Eckholdt, H. (2006). Serving Asians and Pacific Islanders with HIV/AIDS: Challenges and lessons learned. *Journal of Health Care for the Poor and Underserved, 17*(4), 910–927.

Donnelly, T. T. (2006). Living 'in-between'—Vietnamese Canadian women's experiences: Implications for health care practice. *Health Care for Women International, 27*(8), 695–708.

Fong, R., & Mokuau, N. (1994). Not simply "Asian Americans": Periodical literature review on Asians and Pacific Islanders. *Social Work, 39*(3), 298–305.

Frisbie, W. P., Cho, Y., & Hummer, R. A. (2001). Immigration and the health of Asian and Pacific Islander adults in the United States. *American Journal of Epidemiology, 153*(4), 372–380.

Fung, K., & Wong, Y. L. R. (2007). Factors influencing attitudes towards seeking professional help among East and Southeast Asian immigrant and refugee women. *International Journal of Social Psychiatry, 53*(3), 216–231.

Green, A. R., Ngo-Metzger, Q., Legedza, A. T. R., Massagli, M. P., Phillips, R. S., & Iezzoni, L. I. (2005). Interpreter services, language concordance, and health care quality. Experiences of Asian Americans with limited English proficiency. *Journal of General Internal Medicine, 20*(11), 1050–1056.

Han, H. R., Kang, J., Kim, K. B., Ryu, J. P., & Kim, M. T. (2007). Barriers to and strategies for recruiting Korean Americans for community-partnered health promotion research. *Journal of Immigrant and Minority Health, 9*(2), 137–146.

Jones, R. S., Chow, T. W., & Gatz, M. (2006). Asian Americans and Alzheimer's disease: Assimilation, culture, and beliefs. *Journal of Aging Studies, 20*(1), 11–25.

Juon, H. S., Kim, M., Shankar, S., & Han, W. (2004). Predictors of adherence to screening mammography among Korean American women. *Preventive Medicine, 39*(3), 474–481.

Kim, W. (2002). Ethnic variations in mental health symptoms and functioning among Asian Americans. Doctoral dissertation, University of Washington, 2002. *Dissertation Abstracts International, 63*, 3004.

Kutler, S. (2003). Immigration Act of 1965. In S. L. Kutler (Ed.), *Dictionary of American history* (3rd ed.). Farmington, MI: Thompson/Gale.

Lauderdale, D. S., Wen, M., Jacobs, E. A., & Kandula, N. R. (2006). Immigrant perceptions of discrimination in health care: The California Health Interview Survey 2003. *Medical Care, 44*(10), 914–920.

Mayeno, L., & Hirota, S. M. (1994). Access to health care. In N. W. S. Zane, D. T. Takeuchi, & K. N. J. Young (Eds.), *Confronting critical health issues of Asian and Pacific Islander Americans* (pp. 347–375). Thousand Oaks, CA: Sage Publications.

Niedzwiecki, M., & Duong, T. C. (2004). *Southeast Asian American statistical profile*. Washington, DC: Southeast Asian Resource Action Center (SEARAC).

Ray-Mazumder, S. (2001). Role of gender, insurance status and culture in attitudes and health behavior in a US Chinese student population. *Ethnicity and Health, 6*(3/4), 197–209.

Reimers, D. M. (1985). *Still the golden door: The third world comes to America.* (3rd ed.). New York: Columbia University Press.

Snowden, L. R., Collinge, W. B., & Runkle, M. C. (1982). Help seeking and underservice. In L. R. Snowden (Ed.), *Reaching the underserved* (pp. 281–297). Beverly Hills, CA: Sage.

Sullivan, E., & Glassman, P. (2007). *Health literacy, consumer health manual national network of libraries of medicine.* Retrieved September 19, 2007, from http://nnlm.gov/outreach/consumer/hlthlit.html.

Takada, E., Fort, J. M., & Lloyd, L. S. (1998). Asian Pacific Islander Health. In S. Loue (Ed.), *Handbook of immigrant health* (pp. 303–327). New York: Plenum.

U.S. Census Bureau. (2004a). *Facts for features: Asian American heritage month: May 2004.* Retrieved August 20, 2007, from http://www.census.gov/Press-Release/www/releases/archives/facts_for_features_special_editions/001738.html.

U.S. Census Bureau. (2004b). *Poverty status of population in 2003 by sex and age, by Asian alone or combination or White alone not Hispanic: March 2004.* Retrieved August 8, 2007, from http://www.census.gov/population/socdemo/race/api/ppl-184/tab16ic.pdf.

U.S. Census Bureau. (2007). *Health insurance coverage status and type of coverage by selected characteristics: 2005.* Retrieved August 8, 2007, from http://pubdb3.census.gov/macro/032006/health/h01_000.htm.

Uehara, E. S., Takeuchi, D. T., & Smukler, M. (1994). Effects of combining disparate groups in the analysis of ethnic differences: Variations among Asian American mental health service consumers in level of community functioning. *American Journal of Community Psychology, 22*(1), 83–99.

Uretsky, M. C., & Mathiesen, S. G. (2007). The effects of years lived in the United States on the general health status of California's foreign-born populations. *Journal of Immigrant Health, 9*, 125–136.

Ying, Y. W., & Miller, L. S. (1992). Help-seeking behavior and attitude of Chinese Americans regarding psychological problems. *American Journal of Community Psychology, 20*(4), 549–556.

Women Finding the Way: American Indian Leading Intervention Research in Native Communities

by Maria Yellow Horse Brave Heart, PhD,
Josephine Chase, MSW, PhD, Jennifer
Elkins, PhD, MSSW, Jennifer Martin, BSW,
Jennifer S. Nanez, MSW, LMSW, and
Jennifer J. Mootz, PhD

Abstract Although there is literature concentrating on cross-cultural approaches to academic and community partnerships with Native communities, few address the process and experiences of American Indian women leading federally funded and culturally grounded behavioral health intervention research in Native communities. This paper summarizes relevant literature on community-engaged research with Native communities, examines traditional roles and modern challenges for American Indian women, describes the culturally grounded collaborative process for the authors' behavioral health intervention development with Native communities, and considers emergent themes from our own research experiences navigating competing demands from mainstream and Native communities. It concludes with recommendations for supporting and enhancing resilience.

Despite the need for effective behavioral health interventions within American Indian and Alaska Native (AI/AN) treatment settings, few empirically supported or evidence-based treatments (EBTs) exist for AI/ANs (Gone & Alcantara, 2007; Gone & Trimble, 2012; Indian Health Services [IHS] National Tribal Advisory Committee on Behavioral Health & Behavioral Health Work Group, 2011). The high level of need among AI/ANs is reflected in the lifetime prevalence of any mental health disorder, ranging from 35% to 54% (Beals, Manson, et al., 2005; Beals, Novins, et al., 2005; Oetzel, Duran, Jiang, & Lucero, 2007). Mental health disorders rank in the top 10 leading causes of hospitalization and outpatient treatment within IHS (IHS, 2015). Disparities between AI/ANs and the general U.S. population across the lifespan in behavioral health persist, though much variability

exists based on geographic region, cultural group, and gender (Allen, Levintova, & Mohatt, 2011; Denny, Holtzman, & Cobb, 2003; Espey et al., 2014; Gone & Trimble, 2012; Wexler, Silveira, & Bertone-Johnson, 2012).

AI/ANs also experience significant levels of historical trauma. Historical trauma is understood as the collective trauma exposure within and across generations, including interpersonal losses and unresolved grief (Brave Heart, 2003; Brave Heart, Chase, Elkins, & Altschul, 2011; Whitbeck, Adams, Hoyt, & Chen, 2004; Whitbeck, Chen, Hoyt, & Adams, 2004); as well, AI/ANs are at high risk for post-traumatic stress disorder (PTSD; Beals et al., 2013; Manson, Beals, Klein, Croy, & the AI-SUPERPFP Team, 2005; Tsosie et al., 2011). Many have emphasized that AI/AN mental health must be understood within the context of AI/AN histories of collective traumas and the damages those and subsequent traumas have caused in terms of culture, identity, and spirituality (Brave Heart, 1998, 1999a, 1999b; Gone & Alcantara, 2007; Walls & Whitbeck, 2012). Increasing consensus exists that historical trauma is an important part of AI/AN emotional, mental, and psychological experience (Brave Heart, Elkins, Tafoya, Bird, & Salvador, 2012; Evans-Campbell, 2008; Gone & Trimble, 2012; Mohatt, Thompson, Thai, & Tebes, 2014; Walters & Simoni, 2002; Whitbeck, Adams et al., 2004). While AI/ANs think often about such historically traumatic events and losses (Whitbeck, Adams et al., 2004; Whitbeck, Chen et al., 2004), current EBTs do not specifically target this reality.

Although there is literature addressing cross-cultural approaches to academic and community partnerships in research with Native communities (Dickerson & Johnson, 2011; Hartmann & Gone, 2012; Holkup et al., 2009; Katz, Martinez, & Paul, 2011; Thomas, Rosa, Forcehimes, & Donovan, 2011; Wallerstein & Duran, 2010), few articles address the experiences of AI/AN women leading behavioral health intervention research as Principal Investigators (PIs). This paper describes our process and experiences as AI/AN women and non-AI/AN women allies engaging Native communities in developing culturally grounded intervention research to address depression, PTSD, and the impact of collective generational traumatic events. The remaining sections of this article 1) summarize relevant literature on community-engaged approaches for participatory research with Native communities; 2) examine traditional roles and modern challenges for AI/AN women; 3) describe the collaborative process for the authors' behavioral health intervention development with Native communities; and 4) consider emergent themes from our research experiences. Themes include our individual responses to AI/AN multigenerational trauma; navigating multiple identities as AI/AN women (or allies), clinicians, and researchers; traditional Native cultures as protective factors in prevention of and early intervention with behavioral health challenges; and the role of AI/AN women and non-AI/AN women as allies in this process. It concludes with recommendations for other AI/AN intervention research projects and for supporting and enhancing resilience in

Native communities to address behavioral health issues.

Community-Engaged Approaches with AI/ANs

There is limited empirical information regarding EBTs for AI/ANs. AI/ANs are absent or under-represented in behavioral health outcome studies and clinical trials. Moreover, the necessary translational research where common EBTs are culturally adapted for AI/AN settings, is rare (Gone & Alcantara, 2007; Miranda, 2011; Miranda et al., 2005). Engagement and retention of AI/ANs in treatment is complicated by underutilization, mistrust, barriers in establishing a therapeutic alliance, suspicion of government-sponsored treatment, concerns about the lack of cultural sensitivity of providers, and limited IHS funding for mental health services (Gone, 2004, 2008, 2010; Novins et al., 2004). The unique relationship of AI/AN communities with the federal government as sovereign nations facing a history of colonization also may impact the view AI/ANs have of EBTs as based in Western medical practices that are foreign to the traditional practices and Indigenous interventions they view as appropriate and helpful (Gone, 2009). AI/ANs may regard standard mental health treatment, even in IHS facilities, as an arm of colonization and, as a result, often are reluctant to seek care (Gone, 2008).

Numerous researchers have recommended developing community-based and culturally informed interventions to treat AI/AN behavioral health problems (Croff, Rieckmann, & Spence, 2014; Dickerson & Johnson, 2011; Gone & Trimble, 2012; Yuan, Bartgis, & Demers, 2014). Community-engaged approaches, often beneficial in intervention development, vary in design and by name. Some examples include community-based participatory research (CBPR), involved research, collaborative research, community-based research, action research, participatory action research (PAR), participatory research, mutual inquiry, action/science inquiry, cooperative inquiry, critical action research, empowerment evaluation, feminist participatory research, and community-partnered participatory research (Israel et al., 2005; Minkler & Wallerstein, 2008). However all of these methods share the following common principles: they are cooperative, involve co-learning and local community capacity building, are empowering, and balance research and action (Israel et al., 2005; Minkler & Wallerstein, 2008; Montoya & Kent, 2011; Wallerstein & Duran, 2010). Ideally, these participatory approaches share power and benefit the communities involved through action and information dissemination (Israel et al., 2005).

Community-engaged approaches that are common in research focusing on AI/AN populations include CBPR (Katz, Martinez, & Paul, 2011; Wallerstein & Duran, 2010), PAR (Mohatt et al. 2004; Wexler, 2006), and other AI/AN-specific community engagement strategies (Fisher & Ball, 2003; Hartmann & Gone, 2012; Holkup et al., 2008; Salois, Holkup, Tripp-Reimer, & Weinert, 2006; Thurman, Allen, & Deters, 2004). Wallerstein and Duran (2010) asserted that CBPR can be utilized for translational implementation research. While participatory strategies are preferential to research that does not involve community input, academic researchers are frequently the ones to initiate projects with Native communities (Chino & DeBruyn, 2006). Here, we focus on research strategies that transcend the approaches used to date and assert that AI/ANs have our own models of intervention and implementation that can—and should—play a primary role in the development and testing of EBTs for behavioral health treatment in AI/AN settings. Rather than simply seeking to translate the Western research strategies, we actively incorporate traditional AI/AN knowledge and practice (Chino & DeBruyn, 2006; Gone, 2012). Collaboration with traditional healers and use of sanctioned traditional cultural approaches is common among AI/ANs (Beals, Manson, et al., 2005; Beals, Novins, et al., 2005; Novins et al., 2004) and likely plays a critical role in ensuring appropriate engagement and retention in clinical care.

AI/AN Women: Traditional Roles and Modern Challenges

In a number of Native communities, women have been the culture carriers and political advisors, either informally through consultation with male relatives (Brave Heart, 1999a) or more formally, as in the selection and advising of AI/AN leaders. For some tribes where multiple wives traditionally were permitted, these were non-sexual unions, typically with the wife's widowed or single sisters needing a home until they were married to other men. Federal government policies limited the power of AI/AN women, as treaties were only negotiated with AI/AN men and imposed the use of a family surname, with implicit male ownership of women and children. Moreover, the predominant European influence included the legacy of legalized domestic abuse such as the "rule of thumb," referring to English law permitting a man to beat his wife with a board no thicker than the width of his thumb (U.S. Commission on Civil Rights, 1982). Over time, with the introduction of alcohol, changing cultural influences, and the impact of warfare on the frontier, these relationships with multiple wives became sexual unions, but still, for the most part, had the agreement of the first wife. Reservations were established, confiscating AI/AN land, with the emphasis on individual land ownership rather than collective land caretaking. Beginning in 1879, the Carlisle Indian School became the standard for enacting the policy of "the removal of children from all tribal influence . . . and the employment of officers of the army as teachers" (U.S. House of Representatives, Committee on Indian Affairs, 1879) and the early location of the boarding schools far away from traditional homelands. With the inception of the boarding schools, the European American culture prevailed, including the legacy of oppressing women and children. Testimonies of boarding school trauma abound in many Native communities through the 1970s, including physical and sexual abuse, as well as prohibitions against speaking AI/AN languages and practicing AI/AN spirituality (Chase, 2011). The trauma experienced in the boarding school system undermined the traditional roles and power of AI/AN women and contributed to the learned behavior of physical and sexual abuse of AI/AN women and children in many Native communities. Boarding school trauma also has undermined the status of AI/AN men as the warriors and protectors of the tribe. Traditionally, in many AI/AN cultures, women and children were sacred and were never considered the property of men, and domestic violence was not tolerated (Brave Heart, 1999a, Brave Heart et al., 2012). Although AI/AN women have made significant contributions to AI/

AN leadership in modern times as elected officials and have asserted traditional strengths in many ways across generations, currently AI/AN women also have the highest rates of violent and interpersonal trauma risk of any racial or ethnic group. AI/AN women experience higher prevalence of interpersonal violence (Bachman, Zaykowski, Lanier, Poteyeva, & Kallmyer, 2010; Beals et al., 2013; Oetzel & Duran, 2004; Yuan, Belcourt-Dittloff, Schultz, Packard, & Duran, 2015) and are at least twice as likely to be a victim of rape, sexual assault, or other violent crime (Evans-Campbell, Lindhorst, Huang, & Walters, 2006; Oetzel & Duran, 2004).

AI/AN women have obligations to their respective Native communities while simultaneously navigating often competing and culturally antithetical expectations from the academic research environment and funders. This conflict leads to unique challenges in developing, designing, and executing research projects in Native communities. As a group of AI/AN women and non-AI/AN women allies, our team's journey on the path to leading the development of behavioral health intervention research is consonant with a modern fulfillment of our traditional roles as women: nurturers, caretakers, and culture carriers, with the capacity to be *winyan was'aka* ("strong women" in Lakota) for the survival of our nations in the face of overwhelming odds.

The Context: the *Iwankapiya* (Healing) Study

The Iwankapiya study seeks to address a gap in the availability of culturally grounded EBTs for AI/ANs; further, it includes AI/ANs in development, design, and delivery of treatments. Evaluation is done in a manner consonant with traditional AI/AN cultural values. In this National Institute of Mental Health-funded pilot study, eligible AI/ANs in two different communities, one rural reservation and one urban, are randomly assigned to two distinct and promising evidence-based interventions targeting depression, grief, and PTSD symptoms: 1) group Interpersonal Psychotherapy (IPT) only; and 2) group IPT combined with the Historical Trauma and Unresolved Grief intervention

(HTUG). The following sections briefly describe these two interventions.

IPT, which focuses on the interpersonal context for depression and the relationship of current life events to mood, has demonstrated clinical efficacy (Weissman, Markowitz, & Klerman, 2000) among various groups, including Latino and African American adults (Miranda et al., 2005), low-income women with PTSD (Krupnick et al., 2008), and tribal villagers in Uganda (Bolton et al., 2007; Verdeli, 2008; Verdeli et al., 2003). Although the etiology of depression is complex, psychosocial contexts contribute to triggers for depressive episodes. Those triggers typically fall into one of four categories: grief, social role transition (e.g., marriage), role dispute (e.g., marital conflict), or interpersonal deficits. IPT connects mood and life events, "diagnosing" the primary focal interpersonal problem area related to the depression (Markowitz et al., 2009). There also is increasing evidence that IPT is an effective treatment for PTSD (Bleiberg & Markowitz, 2005; Krupnick et al., 2008; Markowitz et al., 2015).

Selected as a Tribal Best Practice (Echo Hawk et al., 2011), HTUG is based upon the historical trauma paradigm, which includes the historical trauma response. The historical trauma response refers to a constellation of features that have been observed among massively traumatized populations, including depressive symptoms, psychic numbing, self-destructive behavior, and identification with the dead (Brave Heart, 1998; Brave Heart et al., 2012). Historical trauma has been operationalized in measures of historical loss (i.e., thoughts about historical losses in AI/AN history) and historical loss-associated symptoms (i.e., anxiety, PTSD, depression, anger, and other symptoms prompted by those thoughts; Whitbeck, Adams, et al., 2004; Whitbeck, Chen, et al., 2004). Historical trauma provides a context for current trauma, grief, and loss across the lifespan by rooting them in the collective psychosocial suffering across generations. Ideally, this collective suffering is addressed in a group milieu. In an AI/AN traditional cultural worldview, time is fluid and the past is present. Contemporary individual suffering is rooted in the ancestral legacy and continues into the present. Traditionally, one cannot separate oneself from the influences of the ancestral suffering. There is an interrelationship with all of creation. Time is non-linear, circular, and simultaneous. If one heals in the present, one can go back in time and heal the suffering of the ancestors (Brave Heart, 2001a, 2001b; Brave Heart, 2003).

The initial version of HTUG was delivered to a small group of primarily Lakota adults (Brave Heart, 1998). It incorporated traditional culture, language, and ceremonies as well as clinical trauma and grief intervention strategies in a 4-day psychoeducational group experience in the Black Hills of South Dakota. It included four major components: 1) didactic and videotape stimulus material on Lakota trauma (*confronting the history*), 2) a review of the dynamics of unresolved grief and trauma (*education about trauma and grief*), 3) small-group exercises and sharing (*cathartic release of emotional pain*), and 4) the *oinikage/ inipi* (Lakota purification) ceremony and a traditional grief resolution Wiping of the Tears ceremony (*transcending the trauma*). HTUG has the advantage of being adaptable to specific AI/AN history and culture. For the current Iwankapiya study, HTUG has been adapted to address the histories and healing traditions of multiple AI/AN groups.

Themes Emerging from our Process

Similar to the process of acculturation, AI/AN women researchers often navigate competing demands and priorities from AI/AN communities and from mainstream academic environments. Themes emerging from our research experience that will be discussed in this section center around the emotional responses of the research team to their own multigenerational and lifespan trauma; multiple identities as AI/AN women, clinicians, and researchers; the impact of historical trauma in Native communities; the importance of traditional AI/AN culture as a protective factor for prevention and early intervention with behavioral health challenges; and the role of non-AI/AN women as allies.

Voices of AI/AN Women Leading the Research

Congruent with Salois et al. (2006), our research is a "sacred covenant" as it arose from our own

grounding and immersion in our traditional AI/AN cultures and ceremonies. This traditional foundation to our approach, including clinical practice in AIAN communities, culminated in the development of HTUG and a Native collective to advance healing for AI/ANs—the Takini Network. *Takini* is a Lakota word meaning "to come back to life or be reborn." In 1992, we formed the Takini Network and also delivered the first HTUG as a 4-day intensive immersion intervention (Brave Heart, 1998). Our HTUG model and research are grounded in the Lakota *Woope Sakowin*—Seven Laws—which are guiding principles for how we are to live our lives. These laws include generosity; compassion; humility; respect; courage; development of a great mind, including the capacity for patience, silence, and tolerance; and wisdom. We began as AI/AN women first, grounded in our own AI/AN cultures, becoming clinicians. Our work evolved into conducting clinical intervention research that sought to maximize its helpfulness to our communities. We began collaborating with compassionate non-AI/AN women allies who were committed to advancing our work, which they believe will help Native communities as well as other oppressed populations.

Some of us began providing direct clinical behavioral health services to our Native communities over 35 years ago. We have sought to enact traditional values such as generosity. We have further incorporated reciprocity in research, with a cornerstone being the provision of some benefit to community members who would participate in the process. The Iwankapiya study includes the same principles by providing treatment at no cost to participants, providing opportunity for healing, and training community providers to help sustain the work. An integral part of conducting research in AI/AN communities is relationship building and collaboration with other service providers in the community (i.e., tribal school parent advisory committees and school staff; tribal, federal, and state behavioral health programs; elders; local culture informants and traditional healers; tribal colleges; and urban health providers). Networking with local providers and community members has been a key factor in implementing successful interventions and supports sustainability post-intervention. Ongoing presence and involvement fosters receptivity and supports relationships in Native communities, enhancing sustainability. For example, the initial development of HTUG included ceremonies to guide us in the process and to ensure, on a traditional cultural level, the sacredness of our work. Our initial HTUG interventions were held in sacred places in the Black Hills, and one of our traditional healers gave us a closing piece of the intervention based upon a Lakota grief resolution ceremony. Participants formed a kinship network, building upon the importance of relationship and connection in Native communities. As AI/AN women, we have found that nurturing professional as well as personal relationships is essential for creating authentic services and interventions.

As AI/AN women we bring to our research our experiences of being culturally and spiritually immersed in our own Native communities. Researching and writing about AI/AN historical legacy can be overwhelmingly painful, as well as cathartic and healing. Commitment to this work can keep us immersed in the pain and traumatic past, but for a greater good—to help the *Oyate* (the People) to heal. Writing and developing manuscripts and research proposals often means revisiting a history that is simultaneously collective, generational, familial, and idiosyncratic, and that spans the past as well as the present. In our loyalty to our ancestors, we unconsciously remain loyal to their suffering through internalization of generational trauma, enacted as the need to suffer as a memorial; vitality is a betrayal to ancestors who suffered so much (Brave Heart, 1998). However, part of the healing process is to let go of this guilt for being joyful. We recognize as Takini that we are *wakiksuyapi* (memorial people; Brave Heart, 2000), and still healing as we are helping others to heal.

As AI/AN women and AI/AN researchers, our work is both a professional and a spiritual commitment. We are not immune to trauma in our own families and communities, to experiencing and witnessing the suffering, and to carrying the trauma of our ancestors. We bring this to our clinical work and to our research. Being AI/AN women, we experience racial and gender discrimination, ongoing oppression and exclusion; in academic and professional settings, we are underrepresented, particularly at higher academic

ranks. It is common for AI/ANs to be challenged to adhere to academic expectations while encountering marginalization and a glass ceiling in work settings (Walters & Simoni, 2009). We struggle with allowing for personal care and personal time; we often experience guilt at taking time away for enjoyment, given the degree of suffering in AI/AN communities. Additionally, our process of writing may be different from that of mainstream colleagues due to cultural differences in thinking and organizing; AI/ANs typically exhibit more circular thought processes and communicate using traditional AI/AN storytelling and metaphor. Questions frequently are answered by sharing a story. Clarification or interpretation of that sharing then is often met with another story, particularly with older AI/AN adults (Brave Heart, 2001a, 2001b; Chase, 2011). Our processing style often follows a cultural norm of deliberation, looking at everything that could be even remotely related to the topic at hand, writing in a narrative, storytelling format first; and then, once we feel that no stone is left unturned, we begin to narrow and edit. This process results in a very rich, thoughtful, and comprehensive product, often with the eloquence of our ancestors, who carefully deliberated before making decisions so that all decisions would be wise ones. However, in the climate of academia with its demand for rapid production of manuscripts, the traditional AI/AN process may run counter to expectations for advancement. Further, because we are writing about collective AI/AN traumatic experiences to which we have a personal relationship, manuscript development requires time for our own emotional processing, empathic attunement to our AI/AN relatives with whom we work, and working through our own personal pain in order to be of the highest service to our communities as well as our commitment to excellence in all aspects of our work.

In addition to our own personal and family trauma, we are frequently exposed to secondary trauma through stories shared by individuals in workshops and interventions of their past and ongoing abuse, grief, loss, and tragedy. Also, due to our knowledge of historical trauma, we may be hypervigilant to historical trauma responses and carry extra concern for participants, so that it is sometimes difficult to maintain objectivity. We carry the People in our hearts and make decisions with the People in mind, including the future seven generations. Such commitments derive from the traditional teachings and values that we embrace and that guide us in our lives and in our work. We are educating our non-AI/AN colleagues in academia about these concerns, which our non-AI/AN allies understand. Being an AI/AN PI on a study is uncommon. In the past, some of us have been discouraged and told we could never fulfill the role of PI as AI/AN women. However, our traditional healers have continued to encourage and motivate us, and our traditional ceremonies sustain us. In more recent years, we have developed non-AI/AN allies—both women and men—who are interested in mentoring and facilitating the development of female researchers, including AI/ANs.

Navigating the Landscape

Carrying out the study is akin to whitewater rafting, given the multiple challenges. We have to negotiate multiple Institutional and Research Review Boards (IRBs/RRBs), including university and AI/AN sites as well as IHS. Despite enthusiastic and supportive IRB/RRBs, navigating multiple deadlines can be challenging, as every change requires approval from each entity. Limited resources in Native communities also can be a challenge. Capacity for carrying out research in terms of infrastructure and financial resources is limited. Despite research incentives, people still have transportation barriers (i.e., bad roads, long travel distances, old vehicles that break down), and communication challenges due to unreliable and intermittent cell phone coverage. Because of the poverty on many reservations, cell phones are sometimes cut off due to lack of payment, or people run out of gas money. Often people are in crisis and must focus on basic survival needs. These realities, combined with the lack of community services (e.g., child care), complicate participation in interventions or consistency in attendance. Transportation, poverty, and child care issues are still prevalent for urban AI/ANs as well. Many have personal and family health challenges and familial deaths, which may impact participation and attendance. We have witnessed the determination and resilience of AI/ANs who have persevered and maintained their commitment to participate in healing interventions despite overwhelming challenges such as personal loss, trauma, homelessness, and extreme poverty.

Voices of Non-AI/AN Women Allies Supporting the Research

For those of us who are non-AI/AN women, our pathways to this work are inextricably linked to a lifelong commitment to social justice and sociopolitical advocacy rooted in our own personal and professional experiences. For some of us, this commitment stems from our Jewish heritage; a religion with a longstanding emphasis on social justice and social action through the values of *tzedakah* (righteousness), *gemilut chasidim* (acts of loving kindness), and *tikkun olam* (repairing the world; Accomazzo, Moore, & Sirojudin, 2014). For others, this commitment stems from growing up in states such as South Dakota and bearing witness to the discrimination, inequalities, and trauma AI/ANs experience both on and off reservations. We recognize the disjuncture between AI/AN culture and the predominant present-based, individualistic, and meritocratic (i.e., "pulling yourself up by your bootstraps") models and explanations for the behavioral health disparities among AI/ANs and the general U.S. population. Supporting research that advances treatment approaches that are Indigenous, contextual, and systemically informed may help shift discourse away from individualistic and pathologizing explanations for disparities.

Non-AI/AN collaborators can enrich AI/AN-led intervention research projects by contributing diverse perspectives and interpretations regarding methodological design, clinical processes, and study outcomes. Being outside of the culture allows distance and provides multiple perspectives, which, in turn, balances any blind spots AI/AN women may carry, especially given the toll that immersion in the trauma can take on inside researchers. The more objective, removed, and fresh outsider perspectives that allies bring also offer empathy and validation of AI/AN experiences. In addition to providing background, instrumental, and logistical support, this kind of emotional support from allies can be motivating and empowering for AI/AN researchers navigating the challenges of upholding scientific rigor and cultural responsiveness in settings with limited resources.

Women Finding the Way: Recommendations and Future Directions

This paper describes the process and experiences of AI/AN researchers and non-AI/AN women allies engaging AI/AN communities in developing culturally grounded clinical intervention research to address depression, PTSD, and the impact of collective generational traumatic as well as ongoing events. Below are recommended strategies for successful engagement with AI/AN communities to support healing and enhance resilience:

- *Start with the theoretical and practice wisdom, your own cultural experience and grounding.* Traditional AI/AN cultural factors can be sources for renewal and healing (Walters & Simoni, 2002); for example, recognizing the value of ceremonies and culture to guide the healing work, connecting with AI/AN elders and traditional leaders to ask for help and blessings. Developing relationships with other AI/AN women researchers and non-AI/AN allies as mentors and collaborators can be invaluable for guidance in balancing multiple roles.

- *Practice cultural humility.* Cultural humility, recommended for education and training of medical practitioners and researchers, incorporates ongoing self-evaluation of knowledge, skills, and interactions with diverse cultures, cognizance of power imbalances, and a commitment to respectful collaborations with communities (Tervalon & Murray-Garcia, 1998). It is critical for outside researchers to be conscious of biases and privilege and be willing to take a "not-knowing" stance, which may include becoming more familiarized with community-engaged, critical, and decolonizing research strategies. It also may include being a non-participant observer ahead of time as part of project planning and preparation. Trust can be developed by being consistent, humble, and sincere—including honesty about our limitations and strengths as well as a willingness to admit when we do not have an answer. For example, while non-AI/AN allies were culturally competent and aware of differences in communication style prior to the beginning of this project, they developed a greater understanding by observing early planning phase meetings and trainings. It is through these experiences that they learned to become more comfortable with listening and taking a step back from the agenda to allow the time and space for the telling of stories and talking in metaphors. Cultural humility also includes recognition of our privilege as heterosexual AI/AN and non-AI/AN women writing this paper.

- *Recognize and respect AI/AN wisdom, knowledge, and intelligence.* Facilitate healing from within the community by using culturally based community engagement that gives equal weight to local knowledge and Western scientific rigor. In this approach, cultural wisdom informs and leads research design and community engagement. One way to achieve this balance is by seeking collaboration with local AI/AN experts who may not be formally identified as such by academic researchers, but may be regarded as wisdom-keepers in terms of AI/AN knowledge (i.e., AI/AN history, language, and culture). Also, someone may hold Western credentials, but still defer to cultural experts for guidance. The ideal approach is to have access to both Western-trained and culturally oriented expertise, along with reading and studying AI/AN history from the perspective of AI/ANs, and valuing oral tribal historical accounts.

- *Be prepared to have contingency plans.* A project may not unfold according to one's original plan, requiring perseverance and ingenuity. In resource-poor settings, researchers must be able to leverage available resources in creative ways to adapt when problems or disruptions occur. In these cases, knowledge of local programs and resources is important. Collaborators, particularly a study monitoring team, can be instrumental in implementing alternate plans that also maintain fidelity to the original proposed model. Research costs (i.e., transportation, outreach, refreshments— which often are culturally expected) likely will be higher in rural reservation settings. Due to poverty and limited phone access, outreach home visits may be necessary, requiring extra time, fuel, and expense. In addition to the cultural significance of sharing food, participants traveling long distances to get to the study site in rural reservation settings may need to be fed upon arrival, particularly given conditions like diabetes and malnourishment. In urban settings, participants who lack a permanent address due to homelessness and housing instability may be difficult to locate, may lack transportation, and also may be malnourished.

- *Be prepared to play multiple roles.* On any given day, a research team member's role may include conducting outreach, providing supplies, setting up equipment, interviewing research candidates or participants, co-facilitating interventions, making copies of data collection forms, and so on. Researchers also may need to be creative in finding suitable space. Typically there are no facilities set up for research on the reservation. In urban settings, meeting outside of academic institutions is often preferable for AI/AN participants. Research team members need to find locations to conduct interviews that ensure confidentiality. Research at crowded IHS facilities is challenging, and use of confidential space has to be negotiated clearly. An alternative may be identifying use of other tribal program space where confidentiality can be maintained. However, this approach also can be challenging due to limited availability of such locations.

- *Be patient and flexible.* Inclement weather, community crises, and illness are all challenges, particularly for remote rural reservation sites with high rates of trauma exposure related to the prevalence of life-threatening health conditions, elevated accident rates, and consequent frequent deaths. Creative adaptation to these conditions may require rescheduling, outreach, crisis intervention skills, compassion, and sensitivity. At times, these crises may impact the researchers' own families directly. Having research teams where

coverage and support is available is important and can enhance flexibility. Being prepared to contribute long hours devoted to engaging community members and providers as well as establishing trust and reliability will facilitate increased resources. Having credibility can save a project that might otherwise be vulnerable to noncompletion. If people in the community recognize researchers' sincerity and dedication they will be willing to go the extra mile to assist and support a project, and possibly advocate on your behalf with others to see it succeed.

- *Recognize that ongoing community trauma and loss will impact your research.* Incorporate a trauma-informed care framework into the planning, programming, and implementation of research projects.

[A] program . . . that is trauma informed realizes the widespread impact of trauma and understands potential paths for recovery; recognizes the signs and symptoms of trauma in clients, families, staff and others involved in the system; and responds by fully integrating knowledge about trauma into policies, procedures and practices, and seeks to actively resist re-traumatization (Substance Abuse and Mental Health Services Administration [SAMHSA], 2014, p. 9).

- Trauma-informed principles include safety; trustworthiness and transparency; peer support; collaboration and mutuality; empowerment; and cultural, historical, and gender issues (for more details see SAMSHA, 2014). For example, knowing that crises and/or losses frequently occur for participants requires research team members to be consistent and reliable. We avoid changing meeting dates, times or locations. We maintain communication with participants, especially those who seem more vulnerable. When possible, plan for backup support in terms of consultants who are considered experts in trauma and loss in AI/AN communities.

● *Make the best effort to implement some form of sustainability.* Although continuation of a service or project at full capacity may prove infeasible, it is crucial to ensure some sense of continuity and hope. In communities with such limited services, it can be devastating if participants are left without any supportive base after the program. Fostering peer support as part of behavioral interventions is one strategy to increase a supportive environment. For example, some sites start peer support groups so that participants will be able to continue meeting periodically once a study ends, in addition to being linked to existing professional services. Traditional cultural resources in the community, or church groups for those who practice other faiths, are important resources to facilitate sustainability of gains made in behavioral health interventions. Booster sessions or reunions after the study can be incorporated into the design as funding permits; also, volunteers and supervised behavioral health student interns may be available to assist. A number of colleges and universities increasingly have students interested in working with tribal communities.

Traditionally, AI/ANs have Indigenous practices to address behavioral health, including primary preventive measures. For example, culturally congruent mourning processes first permitted emotional cathartic release, followed by a limited period of mourning and cognitive reframing to enhance acceptance of deaths, and utilized coping strategies such as self-soothing and calming through prayer, song, and smudging, which served to facilitate mourning resolution. Conditions that are now viewed as behavioral health disorders were addressed through ceremonies to restore balance and interpret symptoms within a culturally congruent context, typically resulting in their resolution. People with unusual behaviors often were seen as special individuals with gifts, rather than being stigmatized and isolated. Through HTUG, we emphasize this traditional and strength-based approach to healing, normalizing, and destigmatizing trauma responses and unresolved grief, and focus on restoring traditional strengths and culturally congruent practices for enhancing coping

strategies. In our experience, framing modern behavioral health symptoms within the historical collective context gives participants an empowering foundation for addressing both collective and individual manifestations of behavioral health issues such as depression, trauma response features, and interpersonal conflicts. As women leading the way in this healing behavioral health intervention research, we are restoring the role of AI/AN women as the culture carriers and caretakers for our families and extended kinship networks. We carry the People in our hearts; contribute to healing the current, past, and future seven generations; restore joy and hope to our communities; and facilitate resilience and transcendence of the trauma. We are contributing to the mending of the Sacred Hoop in fulfillment of the prophecy (Black Elk & Neihardt, 1972) and return to the sacred path of healing—*Iwankapiya.*

References

Accomazzo, S., Moore, M., & Sirojudin, S. (2014). Social justice and religion. In M. Austin (Ed.), *Social justice and social work: Rediscovering a core value of the profession* (pp. 65–82). Thousand Oaks, CA: Sage.

Allen, J., Levintova, M., & Mohatt, G. (2011). Suicide and alcohol related disorders in the US Arctic: Boosting research to address a primary determinant of health disparities. *International Journal of Circumpolar Health, 70*(5), 473. http://dx.doi.org/10.3402/ijch.v70i5.17847

Bachman, R., Zaykowski, H., Lanier, C., Poteyeva, M., & Kallmyer, R. (2010). Estimating the magnitude of rape and sexual assault against American Indian and Alaska Native women. *Australian & New Zealand Journal of Criminology, 43*(2), 199–222. http://dx.doi.org/10.1375/acri.43.2.199

Beals, J., Belcourt-Dittloff, A., Garroutte, E. M., Croy, C., Jervis, L., Whitesell, N., . . . AI-SUPERPFP Team (2013). Trauma and conditional risk of posttraumatic stress disorder in two American Indian reservation communities. *Social Psychiatry and Psychiatric Epidemiology, 48*, 895-905. http://dx.doi.org/10.1007/s00127-012-0615-5

Beals J., Manson, S.M., Croy, C., Klein, S., Whitesell, N., Mitchell, C. (2013). Lifetime prevalence of posttraumatic stress disorder in two American Indian reservation populations. *Journal of Traumatic Stress, 26*, 512–520. http://dx.doi.org/10.1002/jts.21835

Beals, J., Manson, S. M., Whitesell, N. R., Spicer, P., Novins, D., Mitchell, C., & the AI-SUPERPFP Team (2005). Prevalence of DSM-IV disorders and attendant help-seeking in two American Indian reservation populations. *Archives of General Psychiatry, 62*, 99–108. http://dx.doi.org/10.1001/archpsyc.62.1.99

Beals, J., Novins, D. K., Whitesell, N. R., Spicer, P., Mitchell, C. M., & Manson, S. M. (2005). Prevalence of mental disorders and utilization of mental health services in two American Indian reservation populations: Mental health disparities in a national context. *American Journal of Psychiatry, 162*, 1723–1732. http://dx.doi.org/10.1176/appi.ajp.162.9.1723

Black Elk & Neihardt, J.G. (1972). *Black Elk speaks*. NY: Pocket Books.

Bleiberg, K. L., & Markowitz, J. C. (2005). A pilot study of interpersonal psychotherapy for posttraumatic stress disorder. *American Journal of Psychiatry, 162*, 181–183. http://dx.doi.org/10.1176/appi.ajp.162.1.181

Bolton, P., Bass, J., Betancourt, T., Speelman, L., Onyango, G., Clougherty, K., . . . Verdeli, H. (2007). Interventions for depression symptoms among adolescent survivors of war and displacement in Northern Uganda: A randomized controlled trial. *Journal of the American Medical Association, 298*(5), 519–527. http://dx.doi.org/10.1001/jama.298.5.519

Brave Heart, M. Y. H. (1998). The return to the sacred path: Healing the historical trauma response among the Lakota. *Smith College Studies in Social Work, 68*, 287–305. http://dx.doi.org/10.1080/00377319809517532

Brave Heart, M.Y.H. (1999a) Gender differences in the historical trauma response among the Lakota. *Journal of Health and Social Policy, 10*(4), 1–21. http://dx.doi.org/10.1300/J045v10n04_01

Brave Heart, M.Y.H. (1999b). Oyate Ptayela: Rebuilding the Lakota Nation through addressing historical trauma among Lakota parents. *Journal of Human Behavior and the Social Environment, 2*(1/2), 109–126. http://dx.doi.org/10.1300/J137v02n01_08

Brave Heart, M. Y. H. (2000). *Wakiksuyapi:* Carrying the historical trauma of the Lakota. *Tulane Studies in Social Welfare, 21–22*, 245–266. Retrieved from http://citeseerx.ist.psu.edu/viewdoc/download?doi=10.1.1.452.6309&rep=rep1&type=pdf

Brave Heart, M. Y. H. (2001a). Clinical assessment with American Indians. In R. Fong & S. Furuto (Eds.), *Culturally competent social work practice: Practice skills, interventions, and evaluation* (pp. 163–177). Reading, MA: Longman Publishers.

Brave Heart, M. Y. H. (2001b). Clinical interventions with American Indians. In R. Fong & S. Furuto (Eds.), *Culturally competent social work practice: Practice skills, interventions, and evaluation* (pp. 285–298). Reading, MA: Longman Publishers.

Brave Heart, M.Y.H. (2003). The historical trauma response among Natives and its relationship with substance abuse: A Lakota illustration. *Journal of Psychoactive Drugs, 35*, 7–13. http://dx.doi.org/10.1080/02791072.2003.10399988

Brave Heart, M.Y.H., Chase, J., Elkins, J., & Altschul, D.B. (2011). Historical trauma among Indigenous peoples of the Americas: Concepts, research, and clinical considerations. *Journal of Psychoactive Drugs, 43*, 282–290. http://dx.doi.org/10.1080/02791072.2011.628913

Brave Heart, M.Y.H., Elkins, J., Tafoya, G., Bird, D., & Salvador, M. (2012). *Wicasa Was'aka:* Restoring the traditional strength of American Indian males. *American Journal of Public Health, 102*(S2), 177–183. http://dx.doi.org/10.2105/AJPH.2011.300511

Chase, J. (2011). *Native American elders' perceptions of the boarding school experience on Native American parenting: An exploratory study.* Unpublished doctoral dissertation, Smith College, Northampton, MA.

Chino, M., & DeBruyn, L. (2006). Building true capacity: Indigenous models for indigenous communities. *American Journal of Public Health, 96*(4), 596. http://dx.doi.org/10.2105/AJPH.2004.053801

Croff, R. L., Rieckmann, T. R., & Spence, J. D. (2014). Provider and state perspectives on implementing cultural-based models of care for American Indian and Alaska Native patients with substance use disorders. *The Journal of Behavioral Health Services and Research, 41*(1), 64–79. http://dx.doi.org/10.1007/s11414-013-9322-6

Denny, C. H., Holtzman, D., & Cobb, N. (2003). Surveillance for health behaviors of American Indians and Alaska Natives: Findings from the Behavioral Risk Factor Surveillance System, 1997-2000. *Morbidity and Mortality Weekly Report: Surveillance Summaries, 52*(7), 1–13. Retrieved from http://www.cdc.gov/mmwr/preview/mmwrhtml/ss5207a1.htm

Dickerson, D. L., & Johnson, C. L. (2011). Design of a behavioral health program for urban American Indian/Alaska Native youths: A community informed approach. *Journal of Psychoactive Drugs, 43*, 337–342. http://dx.doi.org/10.1080/02791072.2011.629152

Echo-Hawk, H., Erickson, J., Naquin, V., Ganju, V., McCutchan-Tupua, K., Benavente, B., . . . Alonzo, D. (2011). *Compendium of best practices for American Indian/Alaska Native and Pacific Island indigenous populations: A description of selected best practices and cultural analysis of local evidence-building, summary report.* Portland, OR: First Nations Behavioral Health Association.

Espey, D. K., Jim, M. A., Cobb, N., Bartholomew, M., Becker, T., Haverkamp, D., & Plescia, M. (2014). Leading causes of death and all-cause mortality in American Indians and Alaska Natives. *American Journal of Public Health, 104*(S3), S303–S311. http://dx.doi.org/10.2105/AJPH.2013.301798

Evans-Campbell, T. (2008). Historical trauma in American Indian/Alaska Native communities: A multilevel framework for exploring impacts on individuals, families, and communities. *Journal of Interpersonal Violence, 23*, 316–338. http://dx.doi.org/10.1177/0886260507312290

Evans-Campbell, T., Lindhorst, T., Huang, B., & Walters, K. L. (2006). Interpersonal violence in the lives of urban American Indian and Alaska Native women: Implications for health, mental health, and help-seeking. *American Journal of Public Health, 96*, 1416–1422. http://dx.doi.org/10.2105/AJPH.2004.054213

Fisher, P. A., & Ball, T. J. (2003). Tribal participatory research: Mechanisms of a collaborative model. *American Journal of Community Psychology, 32*(3-4), 207-216. http://dx.doi.org/10.1023/b:ajcp.0000004742.39858.c5

Gone, J. P. (2004). Mental health services for Native Americans in the 21st century United States. *Professional Psychology Research and Practice, 35*, 10–18. http://dx.doi.org/10.1037/0735-7028.35.1.10

Gone, J. P. (2008). 'So I can be like a Whiteman': The cultural psychology of space and place in American Indian mental health. *Culture and Psychology, 14*, 369–399. http://dx.doi.org/10.1177/1354067X08092639

Gone, J. P. (2009). A community-based treatment for Native American historical trauma: Prospects for evidence-based practice. *Journal of Consulting and Clinical Psychology, 77*, 751–762. http://dx.doi.org/10.1037/a0015390

Gone, J. P. (2010). Psychotherapy and traditional healing for American Indians: Exploring the prospects for therapeutic integration. *The Counseling Psychologist, 38*, 166–235. http://dx.doi.org/10.1177/0011000008330831

Gone, J. P. (2012). Indigenous traditional knowledge and substance abuse treatment outcomes: The problem of efficacy evaluation. *The American Journal of Drug and Alcohol Abuse, 38*, 493–497. http://dx.doi.org/10.3109/00952990.2012.694528

Gone, J. P., & Alcantara, C. (2007). Identifying effective mental health interventions for American Indians and Alaska Natives: A review of the literature. *Cultural Diversity and Ethnic Minority Psychology, 13*, 356–363. http://dx.doi.org/10.1037/1099-9809.13.4.356

Gone, J. P., & Trimble, J. E. (2012). American Indian and Alaska Native mental health: Diverse perspectives on enduring disparities. *Annual Review of Clinical Psychology, 8*, 131–160. http://dx.doi.org/10.1146/annurev-clinpsy-032511-143127

Hartmann, W. E., & Gone, J. P. (2012). Incorporating traditional healing into an urban American Indian health organization: A case study of community member perspectives. *Journal of Counseling Psychology, 59*, 542–554. http://dx.doi.org/10.1037/a0029067

Holkup, P. A., Rodehorst, T. K., Wilhelm, S. L., Kuntz, S. W., Weinert, C., Stepans, M. B. F., . . . Hill, W. (2009). Negotiating three worlds: Academia, nursing science, and tribal communities. *Journal of Transcultural Nursing, 20*(2), 164–175. http://dx.doi.org/10.1177/1043659608325845

Indian Health Services (2015). *Trends in Indian Health: 2014 edition.* Washington, DC: U.S. Department of Health and Human Services.

Indian Health Service National Tribal Advisory Committee on Behavioral Health, & Behavioral Health Work Group. (2011). *American Indian/Alaskan Native behavioral health briefing book.* Rockville, MD: U.S. Department of Health and Human Services.

Israel, B. A., Parker, E. A., Rowe, Z., Salvatore, A., Minkler, M., López, J., . . . Halstead, S. (2005). Community-based participatory research: Lessons learned from the Centers for Children's Environmental Health and Disease Prevention Research. *Environmental Health Perspectives, 113*(10), 1463–1471. http://dx.doi.org/10.1289/ehp.7675

Katz, J. R., Martinez, T., & Paul, R. (2011). Community-based participatory research and American Indian/Alaska Native nurse practitioners: A partnership to promote adolescent health. *Journal of the American Academy of Nurse Practitioners, 23*, 298–304. http://dx.doi.org/10.1111/j.1745-7599.2011.00613.x

Krupnick, J., Green, B., Stockton, P., Miranda, J., Krause, E., & Mete, M. (2008). Group interpersonal psychotherapy for low-income women with posttraumatic stress disorder. *Psychotherapy Research, 18*, 497–507. http://dx.doi.org/10.1080/10503300802183678

Manson, S.M., Beals, J., Klein, S.A., Croy, C.D., & the AI-SUPERPFP Team. (2005). Social epidemiology of trauma among 2 American Indian reservation populations. *American Journal of Public Health, 95*(5), 851–859. http://dx.doi.org/10.2105/AJPH.2004.054171

Markowitz, J., Patel, S., Balan, I., Bell, M., Blanco, C., Brave Heart, M.Y.H., . . . Lewis-Fernandez, R. (2009). Toward an adaptation of interpersonal psychotherapy for Hispanic patients with DSM-IV major depressive disorder. *Journal of Clinical Psychiatry, 70*, 214–222. http://dx.doi.org/10.4088/JCP.08m04100

Markowitz, J. C., Petkova, E., Neria, Y., Van Meter, P. E., Zhao, Y., Hembree, E., . . . Marshall, R. (2015). Is exposure necessary? A randomized clinical trial of interpersonal psychotherapy for PTSD. *American Journal of Psychiatry, 172*(5), 430–440. http://dx.doi.org/10.1176/appi.ajp.2014.14070908

Minkler M, & Wallerstein N, (2008). *Community-based participatory research for health: From process to outcomes.* San Francisco: Jossey-Bass.

Miranda, J. (2011, July). *Disparities in mental health: Past, present, and future.* Paper presented at the 21st NIMH Conference on Mental Health Services Research, Washington, DC.

Miranda, J., Bernal., G., Lau, A., Kohn, L., Wei-Chin, H., & LaFromboise, T. (2005). State of the science on psychological interventions for ethnic minorities. *Annual Review of Clinical Psychology, 1*, 113–142. http://dx.doi.org/10.1146/annurev.clinpsy.1.102803.143822

Mohatt, G. V., Hazel, K. L., Allen, J., Stachelrodt, M., Hensel, C., & Fath, R. (2004). Unheard Alaska: Culturally anchored participatory action research on sobriety with Alaska Natives. *American Journal of Community Psychology, 33*(3–4), 263–273. http://dx.doi.org/10.1023/B:AJCP.0000027011.12346.70

Mohatt, N. V., Thompson, A. B., Thai, N. D., & Tebes, J. K. (2014). Historical trauma aspublic narrative: A conceptual review of how history impacts present-day health. *Social Science and Medicine, 106*, 128–136. http://dx.doi.org/10.1016/j.socscimed.2014.01.043

Montoya, M. J., & Kent, E. E. (2011). Dialogical action: Moving from community-based to community-driven participatory research. *Qualitative*

Health Research, 21(7), 1000–1011. http://dx.doi.org/10.1177/1049732311403500

Novins, D., Beals, J., Moore, L., Spicer, P., Manson, S., & the AI-SUPERPFP Team. (2004). Use of biomedical services and traditional healing options among American Indians: Sociodemographic correlates, spirituality, and ethnic identity. *Medical Care, 42*, 670–679. http://dx.doi.org/10.1097/01.mlr.0000129902.29132.a6

Oetzel, J., & Duran, B. (2004). Intimate partner violence in American Indian and/or Alaska Native communities: A social ecological framework of determinants and interventions. *American Indian and Alaska Native Mental Health Research, 11*(3), 49–68. http://dx.doi.org/10.5820/aian.1103.2004.49

Oetzel, J., Duran, B., Jiang, Y. & Lucero, J. (2007). Social support and social undermining as correlates for alcohol, drug, and mental disorders in American Indian women presenting for primary care at an Indian Health Service Hospital. *Journal of Health Communication, 12*(2), 187–206. http://dx.doi.org/10.1080/10810730601152771

Salois, E., Holkup, P., Tripp-Reimer, T. & Weinert, C. (2006). Research as a spiritual covenant. *Western Journal of Nursing Research, 28*(5), 505–524. http://dx.doi.org/10.1177/0193945 906286809

Substance Abuse and Mental Health Services Administration (2014). *SAMHSA's concept of trauma and guidance for a trauma-informed approach.* HHS Publication No. (SMA) 14-4884. Rockville, MD: Author.

Tervalon, M., & Murray-Garcia, J. (1998). Cultural humility versus cultural competence: A critical distinction in defining physician training outcomes in multicultural education. *Journal of Health Care for the Poor and Underserved, 9*(2), 117–125. http://dx.doi.org/10.1353/hpu.2010.0233

Thomas, L. R., Rosa, C., Forcehimes, A., & Donovan, D. M. (2011). Research partnerships between academic institutions and American Indian and Alaska Native tribes and organizations: Effective strategies and lessons learned in a multisite CTN study. *The American Journal of Drug and Alcohol Abuse, 37*(5), 333–338. http://dx.doi.org/10.3109/00952990.2011.596976

Thurman, P. J., Allen, J., & Deters, P. B. (2004). The Circles of Care evaluation: Doing participatory evaluation with American Indian and Alaska Native communities. *American Indian and Alaska Native Mental Health Research, 11*(2), 139–154. http://dx.doi.org/10.5820/aian.1102.2004.139

Tsosie, U., Nannauck, S., Buchwald, D., Russo, J., Trusz, S., Foy, H., & Zatzick, D. (2011). Staying connected: A feasibility study linking American Indian and Alaska Native trauma survivors to their tribal communities. *Psychiatry, 74*, 374–359. http://dx.doi.org/10.1521/psyc.2011.74.4.349

U.S. Commission on Civil Rights. (1982). *Under the rule of thumb: Battered women and the administration of justice.* Washington, DC: Author.

U.S. House of Representatives Committee on Indian Affairs (1879). *Industrial training schools for Indian youths, U.S. House of Representatives, 46th Congress.* (Report No. 29, Vol. 1, Nos. 1–36). Washington, DC: Government Printing Office.

Verdeli, H. (2008). Towards building feasible, efficacious, and sustainable treatments for depression in developing countries. *Depression and Anxiety, 25*, 899–902. http://dx.doi.org/10.1002/da.20536

Verdeli, H., Clougherty, K., Bolton, P., Speelman, L., Lincoln, N., Bass, J., . . . Weissman, M. (2003). Adapting group interpersonal psychotherapy for a developing country: Experience in rural Uganda. *World Psychiatry, 2*, 114–120. Retrieved from http://www.ncbi.nlm.nih.gov/pmc/articles/PMC1525093/

Wallerstein, N. B., & Duran, B. (2006). Using community-based participatory research to address health disparities. *Health Promotion Practice, 7*(3), 312–323. http://dx.doi.org/10.1177/1524839906289376

Wallerstein, N., & Duran, B. (2010). Community-based participatory research contributions to intervention research: The intersection of science and practice to improve health equity. *American Journal of Public Health, 100*(S1), S40–S46. http://dx.doi.org/10.2105/AJPH.2009. 184036

Walls, M. L., & Whitbeck, L. B. (2012). The intergenerational effects of relocation policies on indigenous families. *Journal of Family Issues, 33*(9), 1272–1293. http://dx.doi.org/10.1177/0192513X12447178

Walters, K. L., & Simoni, J. M. (2002). Reconceptualizing Native women's health: An "Indigenist" stress-coping model. *American Journal of Public Health, 92*(4), 520–524. http://dx.doi.org/10.2105/AJPH.92.4.520

Walters, K. L., & Simoni, J. M. (2009). Decolonizing strategies for mentoring American Indians and Alaska Natives in HIV and mental health research. *American Journal of Public Health, 99*, S71. http://dx.doi.org/10.2105/AJPH.2008.136127

Weissman, M. M., Markowitz, J. C., & Klerman, G. L. (2000). *Comprehensive guide to interpersonal psychotherapy.* NY: Oxford University Press.

Wexler, L. M. (2006). Inupiat youth suicide and culture loss: Changing community conversations for prevention. *Social Science and Medicine, 63*(11), 2938–2948. http://dx.doi.org/10.1016/j.socscimed.2006.07.022

Wexler, L., Silveira, M. L., & Bertone-Johnson, E. (2012). Factors associated with Alaska Native fatal and nonfatal suicidal behaviors 2001-2009: Trends and implications for prevention. *Archives of Suicide Research, 16*, 273–286. http://dx.doi.org/10.1080/13811118.2013.722051

Whitbeck, L.B., Adams, G.W., Hoyt, D.R., & Chen, X. (2004). Conceptualizing and measuring historical trauma among American Indian people. *American Journal of Community Psychology, 33*(3–4), 119–130. http://dx.doi.org/10.1023/B:AJCP.0000027000.77357.31

Whitbeck, L., Chen, X., Hoyt, D., & Adams, G. (2004). Discrimination, historical loss and enculturation: Culturally specific risk and resilience factors for alcohol abuse and American Indians. *Journal of Studies on Alcohol, 65*, 409–418. http://dx.doi.org/10.15288/jsa.2004 .65.409

Yuan, N. P., Bartgis, J., & Demers, D. (2014). Promoting ethical research with American Indian and Alaska Native people living in urban areas. *American Journal of Public Health, 104*(11), 2085–2091. http://dx.doi.org/10.2105/AJPH.2014.302027

Yuan, N. P., Belcourt-Dittloff, A., Schultz, K., Packard, G., & Duran, B. M. (2015). Research agenda for violence against American Indian and Alaska Native women: Toward the development of strength-based and resilience interventions. *Psychology of Violence, 5*(4), 367–373. http://dx.doi.org/10.1037/a0038507

Rumors and Realities: Making Sense of HIV/AIDS Conspiracy Narratives and Contemporary Legends

by Jacob Heller, PhD

The social context of the early HIV/AIDS epidemic in the United States provided fertile ground for rumors about transmission. Today, however, rumors about HIV/AIDS persist only within the African American public. Focus group and public discourse data reveal the content and distribution of HIV/AIDS origin and conspiracy rumors. Rumor and contemporary legend theory allows reinterpretation of rumors as a measure of trust between the African American public and health professionals, not as evidence of ignorance or of historical racial oppression. To improve public health results in the African American community, HIV/AIDS efforts must acknowledge the sources and meanings of rumors, include rumors as a measure of trust, and address the underlying distrust that the rumors signify. (*Am J Public Health.* 2015;105:e43–e50. doi:10.2105/AJPH.2014.302284)

Despite major advances in knowledge about the HIV virus, modes of transmission, and treatments that can reduce viral load and extend life, the spread of HIV among African Americans, especially African American men who have sex with men, has remained stubbornly resistant to interventions. As of 2006, 48.1% of new HIV infections in the United States were attributable to male-to-male sexual contact; African Americans had an HIV prevalence rate of 1715.1 per 100 000 (2388 per 100 000 for men and 1122 per 100 000 for women), whereas the rate for Whites was 224.3 per 100,000 (394 per 100 000 for men and 62.7 per 100 000 for women).[1] These persistent high rates among African Americans run counter to the experience of most populations in the United States, for whom better knowledge about HIV/AIDS has led to reductions in morbidity and mortality, as shown in the following diagram:

scientific knowledge → education → behavior changes → reduced infection rates

These relationships, however, work only if people trust the sources of official information. This applies equally to prevention and treatment: no HIV/AIDS program that requires action by the public—however valid or well-originated—can succeed when people distrust the program's sponsors or the sources of information about the disease. Understanding the forces that cause and sustain distrust among African Americans is essential to reducing rates of HIV infection, and this requires recognition of the role of HIV/AIDS rumors—their origins, spread, and capacity to resist contrary information.

Initially, AIDS rumors were widespread, because the social context provided what rumor theorists have identified as fertile ground for the growth and persistence of rumors: a dearth of trusted information in conjunction with high levels of social anxiety.[2,3] Furthermore, the trust and knowledge networks that support rumors are typically bound by the same elements of social stratification that constitute racial and ethnic identities and sub-groups; people circulate stories to people they know and trust, and only retell stories with meaning or resonance.[3,4] Rumors about HIV/AIDS proliferated throughout US society: only gay people can get AIDS[5]; you can catch it from a doorknob, a toilet seat, or a swimming pool; flying insects can transmit it; women are tricking men into having sex with them so they can give them AIDS[4]; AIDS was developed by the Central Intelligence Agency (CIA) to kill off African Americans and gays[6]; it's not caused by a virus at all.[7] As the emerging HIV/AIDS crisis forced scientists and health professionals to change their habits and practices, partly because of the science of the virus but largely because of effective social activism by AIDS-affected lay groups,[8] those same groups invested their faith in the health professions community. They demanded action commensurate with the health crisis: scientific knowledge to replace fears, ignorance, and uninformed suppositions. And they succeeded; as solid, official information developed, general anxiety about HIV/AIDS slowly receded, and so did the stories—most HIV/AIDS rumors have disappeared.[9] Within the African American community, however, specific rumors continue to persist, rumors that understand HIV/AIDS as a genocidal government plot against African Americans. Moreover, these HIV/AIDS rumors do more than indicate distrust, they reinforce distrust by positing an explanation that assigns responsibility so explicitly: an illness that can be traced to an intentional (and familiar) actor, instead of a social and health problem that is part of an impersonal modernity with complex causes that can leave the individual feeling helpless and hopeless.[10]

I collected data from a systematic survey of public discourse and from a series of 6 focus group interviews that I conducted, organized by race/ethnicity among members of a college community, to examine the ways in which HIV/AIDS rumors distribute themselves in some groups—but not others—and serve to sustain distrust. My goals were (1) to establish the uniqueness and pervasiveness of HIV/AIDS rumors within the African American public, (2) to connect those rumors to the distrust that contributes to continued high HIV infection rates, and with that knowledge, (3) to inform best practices to contend with the distrust and possibly destabilize the rumors.

Experts no longer dispute the facts about the causes and modes of transmission for AIDS; as a direct result, we know how to stop HIV from spreading: through such measures as safe sex, clean needles, regular testing, and a screened blood supply, although not everyone follows these practices. People who live with HIV (i.e., who

are HIV positive) can have productive, long, and relatively normal lives. The scientific consensus about the origins of HIV/AIDS has fewer practical applications, but that consensus carries profound consequences for how information about best practices will be received. Persistent HIV/AIDS rumors and contemporary legends that center on a government-led conspiracy or on genocide theory to explain its origins undermine the acceptance of behaviors that can prevent infection.

Rumors may encourage behaviors that appear ignorant, but the source of conspiracy theory rumors about the origins of HIV/AIDS within the African American community, as with any rumors, is not ignorance, but distrust combined with high social anxiety. To understand the meaning and importance of genocide–conspiracy rumors, one must answer the question of why there are different levels of trust across racial/ethnic groups. The sources of the trust gap may be connected to the lack of sustained and effective funding for and attention to the general health of African Americans, the history of health professions' abuses against African Americans, and the persistence of HIV/AIDS among African Americans (as the focus group data suggest, some African Americans see the very mention of high infection rates among African Americans as "blaming," which reinforces the sense of distrust). These rumors are simultaneously evidence of a local situation (the level of distrust by one group in the context of one issue) and indicators of the larger social context in which that distrust occurs. The content of rumors about HIV/AIDS is related to the fraught historical relationship between African Americans and mainstream (White) society, and the perceptions of the health professions as agents of White power. Understanding the rumors (and perhaps dispelling them) first requires an understanding of the different roles that collective memory and rumors play in the creation of distrust.

Collective memory research looks at how groups "know" things and sustain memories of traditions and historical events from generation to generation without formal histories or institutional education.[11–13] Part of the explanation for distrust of health professions and health initiatives stems from the collective memory of racism and discriminatory abuse in US society, a heritage regularly reaffirmed in everyday experience. Collective memory studies fail, however, when it comes to the question of how alternative stories (such as HIV/AIDS conspiracy accounts) might be conveyed. Rumors are not collective memory; they thrive in the absence of commemorative events, memorials, and rituals. There is no evidentiary foundation for the story of the disease as part of a US government or CIA plan to exterminate African Americans.

Although HIV/AIDS transmission rates continue to fall among many demographic groups,[14] rates of new cases within the African American community remain at tragically high levels. The present study found a similar pattern for rumors—declining rapidly among Whites while stubbornly persisting within the African American public. Just as HIV/AIDS has followed different epidemiological courses within different subpopulations, rumors and stories woven around HIV have also covaried by subpopulation with a correlation across group identity, rumors, and HIV prevalence.

Methods of Data Collection

This analysis relies on 2 sources of data. (1) I performed a qualitative review of the public discourse about HIV/AIDS in the "Black Press," on the Internet, and in other public arenas. (The Black Press, which dates to 1827 in the United States, continues to be a media sector that originates in, caters to, and represents the ideas and issues of the African American community.[15–17] African Americans invest higher levels of trust and research in the Black Press than in the mainstream press; despite large overlap between the two,[18] this suggests that African Americans and Whites in the United States constitute separate audiences.[19]) (2) I conducted a series of 6 race/ethnicity-segregated focus group interviews populated according to the self-identified race/ethnicity of participants: 2 each for Whites, Hispanics, and African Americans. I identified the public discourse on rumors regarding HIV/AIDS by tracking down such stories wherever they appeared. This "discursive snowball sampling" led from large searchable databases, newspaper articles, and magazines to advertisements, television shows, and standup comedy routines—any kind of public reference to HIV/AIDS rumors or conspiracy stories. Once new sources began reliably referring back to ones already located, it became clear that the search had reached an important level of closure.

I collected focus group data in a series of 6 focus group interviews over a 2-year period with members of a college community in the northeastern United States. Participants ranged in age from 18 to 53 years and skewed heavily toward women, reflecting the population from which they were drawn; 29 individuals participated, and focus groups ranged in size from 3 to 9 participants. I solicited participants by using posters, social networks, and in-class announcements; I organized the individual groups on the basis of sign-ups by prospective participants into 1 of the 3 race/ethnicity groups: African American, Hispanic/Latino, or White. At the conclusion of each interview, participants had an opportunity to ask questions and make additional comments off the record. They also received my contact information for follow-up questions and a 2-page information sheet detailing the "best knowledge and practices" about such topics as what HIV is, the origins of HIV, the evidence connecting HIV and AIDS, how to prevent transmission, and ways to get tested. I recorded digitally and transcribed the interviews.

Participants were prompted to relate, discuss, mention, or retell stories that they had heard; when the discussion lagged or did not develop rumors, as the focus group moderator I used prods, such as "What have you heard about needle exchange programs?" or "Have you ever heard strange stories about who might have been responsible for HIV/AIDS?" Confidentiality was assured (all participants signed consent forms), and no personal information or medical histories were solicited.

The Contexts for Analyzing Rumors

According to the Centers for Disease Control and Prevention, the most important variables associated with continued high HIV transmission rates are

1. likelihood of having unprotected sex with someone who is either infected with HIV or at high risk for infection,

2. injection drug use,

3. having another sexually transmitted disease,

4. unknown HIV status,

5. social stigma associated with being a man who has sex with men, and

6. socioeconomic factors that contribute to poor health care.[20]

All of these address behaviors, however, not social status or attitudes toward health care. Public health research cites 3 explanations for African American "exceptionalism" to HIV/AIDS prevention efforts. First, the African American community finds itself on the wrong end of a constellation of variables associated with high transmission rates: education, motivation, recognized self-worth, and access to condoms.[21,22] The second stresses aspects of interpersonal, group, and status-based relationships (e.g., "sex on the down low," describing men who identify as heterosexual but secretly engage in sex with men, even while in relationships with women) that interfere with a host of well-established preventive measures.[23,24] The third has to do with deep and abiding distrust for the institutions and intentions of Western (US) medicine and public health.[25–34] Of the 3 explanations, the problem of distrust might seem the easiest to address.

Conventional wisdom posits that education opens the mind, dispels misconceptions, and can change behaviors—a formulation that is generally valid. But to be effective, education efforts require trust. For this reason, using knowledge—"education"—to defeat distrust has been, and is likely to remain, unsuccessful as long as there are high levels of distrust within the African American community.[35,36] Distrust reflected and reinforced by cultural narratives—stories, rumors—cannot easily be displaced by information.[2] Public health efforts to slow the rate of HIV transmission among African Americans cannot succeed without an understanding of how rumors that begin in an environment of distrust develop, persist, and influence behavior.

Distrust based on experience might be addressed by better behavior, promises of future actions, or the simple passage of time. But one of the most problematic features of a distrust based on rumors is that, as narratives, rumors are relatively impervious to falsifiability: you cannot disprove a story told and retold by a "friend of a friend"—it's "just a story." Recent scholarship argues that conspiracy rumors can no longer be dismissed as the result of a "paranoid style,"[37] but should be seen as strategies used by the disempowered to reconceptualize, contend with, or resist mainstream worldviews that contradict lived experiences.[10,38–40] These interpretations validate conspiracy theory rumors as legitimate discourse, and provide a basis for understanding the power of HIV/AIDS rumors within the African American community. Discounting conspiracy rumors, by contrast, is an example of what Paul Farmer described as unilaterally establishing "the underlying rules and conventions that determine whether [an] account is received as true or false, by whom, and with what material consequences."[41(p229)] It is better to interpret the information encoded in HIV/AIDS rumors as a form of meaningful "counter-knowledge."[40] We need to use the knowledge of how narratives and rumors work as discursive forms to inform our understanding of how best to respond to the very real—not at all discursive—situation in which people's beliefs can interfere with public health efforts.

Rumors of Genocide and Distrust in the Data

Evidence of distrust is clearly visible in stories about the origins of HIV/AIDS. The 4 quotations in Table 1 (arranged chronologically) illustrate the range of accounts about the origins of HIV/AIDS and the extent to which different rumors exist among different groups. Two come from the public discourse and 2 from focus group interviews. The first and third quotations, from 1992 and 2012, instantiate the consistent theme found in both public African American discourse and among African American focus group participants. To find a rumor faithfully repeated after 2 decades demonstrates remarkable durability. Substantively, the 2 quotations implicate the government, the main institution responsible for contending with HIV/AIDS, and ascribe intentional, genocidal motives for the creation and epidemiology of the epidemic. Who, finding such stories even mildly plausible, would trust a government agency or program that declares it is working "to help"?

The quotation from 2001 is not a rumor; it is a mainstream press presentation of the consensus scientific findings on the origins of HIV; it contradicts the other 3 quotations. For most people, this explanation is the "authoritative" story of the origins of HIV/AIDS (in some form). White and Hispanic/Latino focus group participants reliably reported it, though sometimes with minor alterations (no one specifically mentioned "the hunting or preparation of meat," for example).

The fourth quotation is an HIV/AIDS rumor that is prevalent among US Whites (it appeared in both White group interviews), and, like many rumors, relates something "I heard"—"a funny story." Like the conspiracy rumors, this story distorts the scientific finding, but it places responsibility for the origins of the epidemic on "somebody who had sex with a monkey"—in Africa. An HIV origin rumor that blames bestiality among Africans comes from a very different relationship to the health professions than one that blames doctors, researchers, and the US government, and also has little effect on the group's status or response to public health advice; it becomes a "funny story."

Dave Chappelle has a comedy routine that satirically calls Africans having sex with monkeys the "scientific explanation" for the origins of HIV/AIDS.[44] Humor can be effective at mentioning and dismissing rumors, as in this quotation from the NBC comedy *30 Rock*, scripted to be uttered by the sole African American character (played by Tracy Morgan):

> Affirmative action was designed to keep women and minorities in competition with each other to distract us while White dudes inject AIDS into our chicken nuggets.[45]

This is a typical mainstream public rendering of the AIDS genocide rumor; it acknowledges and dismisses the genocide rumor in one succinct statement, turning persistent rumors about US efforts at genocide against African Americans into a punch line. Group social position affects community status and power; it also privileges the presentation (and dismissal) of rumors.[41]

The public discourse and focus group findings reveal that an umbrella narrative about HIV/AIDS exists within the African American community: a United States government plot (sometimes spearheaded by the CIA, the military, or health research and public health institutions) to invent, plant (or

release) the virus, cause an epidemic, and thereby complete the racist project to eradicate African Americans.[46] This idea of intentional genocide is the unifying thread running through almost all of these rumors. US celebrities as mainstream as Bill Cosby (in 1991 in the *New York Post*)[47] and Will Smith (in 1999 in *Vanity Fair*)[48] voiced their opinion that the HIV/AIDS epidemic could well be the result of intentional actions, either by the US government or others. The Reverend Jeremiah Wright, who gained national attention as the controversial pastor of Barack Obama's church, railed against the racist power structure in the United States, asserting that "The government lied about inventing the HIV virus as a means of genocide against people of color. Governments lie!"[49] In 1990, *Essence* magazine ran an article entitled "Is It Genocide?" that described the widespread genocide stories about HIV/AIDS and attempted to debunk them, although it also acknowledged that "our whole relationship to [Whites] has been that of [their] practicing genocidal conspiratorial behavior on us . . . from the whole slave encounter up to the Tuskegee study."[50(p78)] This is a version of the collective memory explanation, but researchers have not found that distrust is correlated with knowledge about the Tuskegee syphilis experiment[51]; in focus group interviews, only 1 African American participant was aware of Tuskegee, whereas all were familiar with the genocide rumors.

The genocide rumors have a long history within the African American public. Some of the earliest reports of HIV/AIDS-as-genocide conspiracy rumors appear to have been disseminated by associates of the Nation of Islam (which also sold an alternative AIDS therapy called Kemron, since dismissed by mainstream scientists as useless).[52] In the early 1980s, rumors circulated within the African American community in Atlanta, Georgia blaming health researchers for the disappearances and killings of young African American boys, purportedly used in experimentation; James Baldwin published a book on the case.[53] In 1988, Steve Cokely, then Chicago's coordinator for special projects, pronounced that Jewish doctors were infecting African American infants with HIV.[54] The mainstream press eventually picked up on the circulating rumors; in 1990, a *New York Times* article

Table 1. Excerpts Regarding the Origins of HIV/AIDS From Public Discourse and Focus Group Interviews

Year	Quotation	Source
1992	"I'm convinced AIDS is a government-engineered disease. They got one thing wrong, they never realized It couldn't Just be contained to the groups it was intended to wipe out. So now it's a national priority. Exactly like drugs became when they escaped the urban centers into White suburbia."	Spike Lee, in an advertisement for Benetton, in *Rolling Stone* magazine[42]
2001	"People eat chimpanzees," Dr. Hahn said, "We expect that transmissions occurred through the exposure to blood through hunting or preparation of meat."	Excerpt from a *New York Times* article by Gina Kolata[43]
2012	"I heard that [the government] took people, Black people, gay people, and made them do research . . . experiments, and said, 'You guys will get paid for this' and actually they're given the virus."	A woman in a focus group interview with African American participants
2014	"This is probably not true, but when I was young I heard that somebody had sex with a monkey who had it, yeah—not that I believe it, just a funny story."	A man in a focus group interview with White participants

Note. The 6 focus group interviews were conducted by the author in 2012–2014, with members of a college community in the northeastern United States. The interviews were segregated according to the self-identified race/ethnicity of the participants: 2 interviews each for Whites, Hispanics, and African Americans.

reported the comments of a rap musician on the Arsenio Hall Show that

> AIDS was part of a "clean-up America campaign" intended to hit "target markets" of homosexuals and racial minorities: "I think they definitely have the cure already and I think it was definitely created by some sick person."[55]

These conspiracy rumors have made only rare appearances in the public health literature on HIV/AIDS. A 1991 study examining HIV/AIDS rumors about transmission vectors (whether it is possible to catch AIDS from a swimming pool, for example) found—and then dismissed as too obscure—a rumor that the AIDS virus had been invented at a US military laboratory; they felt it was too "esoteric" for college students to have heard of it.[5] The rare studies that have focused on genocide rumors among African Americans have found their impact to be meaningful.[34,36] Other origin rumors that implicated health professionals enjoyed brief popularity in mainstream discourse (e.g., the *Rolling Stone* article asserting that AIDS was the

accidental result of vaccine testing in Africa[56]) and received widespread attention and careful refutation in the professional literature.[57,58] The audience (and source) for these rumors was the mainstream US population, however.

The data in the present study show the strong connection between distrust, rumors, and behaviors. We know that initiatives that might be uncontroversial with other populations (needle exchange programs, condom availability, sex education) have been met with higher levels of distrust and suspicion among African Americans, and therefore with greater resistance.[59–62] In public discourse, programs to slow the spread of HIV have been seen as the equivalent of a "genocidal campaign,"[59] or, as Calvin O. Butts, III, pastor of the Abyssinian Baptist Church in Harlem, put it, as "cooperating with the devil."[52(p26)] Here, the conspiracy narrative interprets the stated goal of reducing HIV transmission as a blind designed to do active harm by encouraging injection drug use. Part of this discourse is that drug dealing, generally, is a conspiracy against the African American community's young people—a modified genocide conspiracy.[63,64] One African American focus group participant (woman #5) commented about drug users getting brand-new, clean needles:

> How do you know? You see, it goes back to the whole idea of they're purposely spreading this. How do you know they didn't drop some HIV into those needles?

Nearly the same thought came from a participant in a Hispanic group interview (woman #3), who identified herself as African American during the course of the conversation:

> I wouldn't trust it. The government has a history of, like, using people as "subjects," in their little experiments. I would think there was something wrong with the needle.

HIV/AIDS genocide stories of this kind both reflect and perpetuate distrust, and that distrust has clear implications for the success of needle exchange programs. Free condom distribution programs don't fare much better. In a discussion among African American participants, the following exchange took place, in response to the prompt "how about free condoms?":

> It goes back to the government. . . . They hand out "NYC" condoms, and how many people believe in those, use those? None. (man #1)
>
> [The condoms] could be faulty. (woman #1)
>
> People might poke holes in them. . . . I was in high school and people were like, "You don't know if somebody poked holes in them." . . . You hear stories about them, I know speaking to my male friends, that's something that would be their last resort. Plus they say that the condom is not as strong, it may pop easily, and just off basic instinct, people don't trust. (woman #3)

This level of distrust envisions a government that pokes holes in condoms distributed for "safe sex campaigns" and maybe puts HIV into syringes for a "clean needle exchange program." In response to the same prompt, members of a White focus group had a radically different response:

> More people will use them if they get them for free. (woman #2)
>
> People feel "a condom is a condom." (man #1)

This contrast reflects a massive difference in trust.

A related thread that appears in the rumors concerns differential treatments and cures. Following Fine's notion of the "Goliath Effect,"[65] many of the differential treatment rumors focus on the most prominent living African American who is HIV positive, the basketball star Earvin "Magic" Johnson. Here, however, these participants in an African American group interview focused on class rather than race:

> I feel [Magic Johnson] has a whole team of people to keep him alive, and when it comes to your, like, average person, they go to the hospital. . . . This is not taken as seriously. (woman #5)
>
> His private doctors are probably recommending different things from what we could do because we can't afford them. Why am I giving you $200,000 pills when you can't afford $200,000 pills? (man #3)

As the discussion of Magic Johnson continued, the notion of an existing cure became inseparable from a conspiracy rumor (albeit cynically profit-driven rather than racist):

> I feel like they have the cure, and don't want to give it out. (woman #3)
> I definitely do think they have the cure. (woman #2)
> They're making so much money like. . . . (woman #1)
> It's big business. . . . (woman #2)
> [Does anyone get the cure? (moderator)]
> Probably the ones that can afford it. (woman #2)
> [What do you think about Magic Johnson? (moderator)]
> I want to say that he got the cure, but he says he has a low viral count. . . . That's basically saying you got the cure, but you're saying it in a good way. (woman #1)
> I feel that money talks . . . because he's still alive. (woman #2)

He beat the statistics. (woman #1)
[And that's because of the money?
(moderator)]
Yeah| (chorus—all participants)

White focus group participants also expressed some skepticism about health professionals and their cynical financial motivations, but they accorded AIDS researchers high status. The prompt "What motivates doctors?" produced the following brief exchange:

Money! (chorus—all participants)

I think some of them got into it for the right reasons. . . . I think [AIDS] doctors are more highly regarded. . . . That doctor in that situation would be something that you would . . . want to help. (man #1)

Focus group interview conversations among self-identified Hispanic/Latino participants exhibited a more complicated set of stories, partly because some participants self-identified as Hispanic but explained in the course of the discussion that they were of Afro-Latino of Afro-Caribbean background, or African American. This appeared to correlate with exposure to some of the same stories that are common among African Americans. The context of comments, however, helps reveal the perspective from which participants were speaking. (For example, one woman in a Hispanic interview, who self-identified as Hispanic, at one point said, "as a Black woman . . . .") One participant in a Hispanic group interview did report the genocide rumor:

What I remember? . . . They're trying to get rid of African Americans, mainly starting in Africa, which is why they say it started in Africa but from what I heard it was apparently a manmade disease by the Whites, trying to get rid of the African race. (woman #2)

Interestingly, in the Hispanic groups, the main thrust of discussion was not about conspiracies, genocide, or trust, but about the central importance of education as an explanation of why HIV infection rates were high among racial and ethnic minorities; as the same participant said:

A lot of people that are minorities are not educated, and they should be educated. They don't take the time to teach people, in a lot of places—not in New York. We are, for the most part, educated in sex education. But in other parts of the United States, it's, they don't give them the same education. (woman #2)

By asserting her faith in the ability of education to matter, this participant contextualizes her account of the conspiracy rumor: she trusts education, and the institutions that educate, to be working for the benefit of the people they serve. With this one equivocal exception, the genocide rumors were nonexistent in the White and Hispanic group interviews. HIV/AIDS rumors that were typical in the general population during the early 1990s (e.g., the rumor in which an anonymous malefactor places infected needles in gasoline pumps to prick the hands of unsuspecting motorists), and which reflect general fears of contracting the disease through everyday activities, also appeared only among the African American groups.[64]

Understanding the Distrust as History or Experienced Culture

In different and sometimes overlapping ways, the rumors described here can be understood as (1) the result of historical experiences that have engendered distrust, (2) a result of continuing distrust, and (3) an indication of social anxieties associated with the HIV/AIDS epidemic, drug use (as a source of HIV and as an arm of the genocide attempt), and African Americans' place in American society. Establishing a genuinely trusting relationship between the public health professions and the African American community may be the only way to put rumors on the same road to extinction as rumors about mosquitos transmitting HIV.

Establishing trust poses real challenges, however; whether it is a consequence of collective memory or lived experience, African Americans are less likely than nearly any other ethnic or racial group in the United States to trust mainstream institutions.[66–68] Specific distrust for health professions adds another multiplier. Fine and Turner cite the example of HIV-positive men who refused azidothymidine (AZT) treatments because they feared "sometimes it accelerates the rate at which full-blown AIDS develops in Black men."[69(p63)] In 2004, reports circulated that a local health clinic in upper Manhattan was engaged in experimentation on and torture of African American children as part of "hideous experiments by a cabal of plotters including the National Institutes of Health (NIH), the Catholic Archdiocese, GlaxoSmithKline, Columbia-Presbyterian Medical Center."[40] Rumors of genocide reinforce and express the other factors that interfere with public health efforts.[70]

The historical origins of African Americans' distrust of health institutions, from the Tuskegee syphilis experiment[71] to myriad cases of egregious exploitation and mistreatment dating back to slavery, are not unimportant for trust.[32] Turner argues that HIV/AIDS rumors and contemporary legends are not only based on history, but that they serve as tools of resistance against a genuine sense of threat to the group, including the actual bodies of its members.[6] On the basis of the historical relationship alone, however, one would expect to find distrust throughout the African American public—which does not appear to be the case, as individuals usually trust their own doctors, something evident both in the literature on trust[12] and in the focus group interviews. Research has found no racial differences with respect to acceptance of an HIV vaccine,[72] for example, and has found that African Americans were more supportive than the general population of volunteering for HIV vaccine trials.[73]

The connection between conspiracy rumors and so-called "straightforward historical evidence" is problematic, however. A wide variety of scholarly attempts to understand this distrust cite the Tuskegee syphilis experiment as the archetype of racial exploitation in medical research and the basis for the distrust.[25,50,74–77] Among African American focus group participants in this study, only one referred to the Tuskegee syphilis experiment or even recognized it when queried, and she conflated it with the Tuskegee Airmen. Historical events do not appear to be driving the distrust.

Treatment disparities may play a role in the persistence of distrust, and this was reflected in the focus group data on cures and treatments. Effective antiretroviral therapies are nominally available to everyone in the United States through a variety of federal and state programs, yet access to these drugs varies widely across geographic, political, and demographic boundaries in the United States.[78] Disproportionately lower spending on HIV/AIDS prevention in African American communities[79] also contributes to the trust gap. Even statements identifying at-risk groups can trigger anger, because of the implicit implication that there is fault associated with infection, as this excerpt from a focus group interview suggests:

> [L]ook at everybody else who has AIDS, it's not mostly Black women who have AIDS, it's ridiculous. . . . So many people have it, but they're trying to say, "Oh, it's mostly Black women spreading it," it's really offensive to me. (African American woman, 2014)

Understanding such distrust as part of a reasonable response to underfunded and poorly designed programs is neither a complete nor a satisfying explanation, however: when funding is low, it makes sense to ask for more funding, not to reject efforts that are already funded. As with the legacy of historical abuses, underfunding may contribute to African Americans distrust of medical institutions,[32] but until we understand the full range of causes and mechanisms for the distrust, health professionals will continue to confront difficulties irrespective of objective measures of validity. People who distrust can't be reassured by evidence they deem untrustworthy.

Conclusions

As the HIV/AIDS crisis begins its fourth decade, with ambiguities about origins, transmission, and treatments resolved in most sectors of society, there is some concern that the general population has become complacent about HIV/AIDS.[80] The persistence of genocide rumors within the African American public found in this research, however, demonstrates that for African Americans, social anxieties have not been addressed; high HIV infection rates don't appear to be the result of complacency. Changing behaviors will change infection rates, but behavior changes ultimately rely on trust. The nature of the rumors that developed in the African American public was never the same as those in the general population. One thing that is challenging about their existence and persistence is not their agreement or disagreement with views of historical events but their apparent independence of history.

Misunderstanding distrust can compound distrust. In terms of epidemiology, US health professionals typically respond to the HIV/AIDS origin conspiracy stories both correctly and counterproductively. When health professionals see conspiracy rumors as evidence of ignorance that interferes with efforts to change behaviors, they risk reifying the trust gap, by labeling the person (the nonexpert) who has concerns as "ignorant." To dismiss or ignore genuine concerns about racial health disparities because they express themselves through distrust of logical, salient, and valid health professions initiatives confuses cause and effect. Thus, the conversation can become a struggle about who gets to control the tone and content of the discourse, and the side that suffers the depredations of the disease is also expected to surrender the discursive disputation about meaning—about the lived experience of a social group burdened with racism.

There are 3 important approaches to understanding the rumors about HIV/AIDS in the African American community. For folklorists—and for a deeper understanding of the social and cognitive dynamics that underlie the rumors—understanding the origins, meanings, and methods of propagation is inherently important. Addressing the causes of rumors about the origins and transmission of HIV/AIDS forms the basis of the research presented here, because their genealogy is inextricably linked to their meaning to the people who hear them, tell them, (sometimes) believe them, and engage in associated behaviors. Second, there is the information that rumors reveal about the anxieties and concerns of the communities where they persist. Clearly, the segments of the African American public (which may be among the most educated segments) that have sustained HIV/AIDS genocide rumors for decades continue to experience substantial social anxiety about extermination, particularly of the type identified in the United Nations resolution of 1949: threats to bodies, unique culture, and social identity.[81] Finally, by understanding what rumors are and the legitimate anxieties they represent, it becomes possible to reframe "ignorance" as "counter-knowledge,"

and move beyond "education" toward the kind of co-operation (albeit contentious and at times combative) that raised the level of mutual trust between the US gay (White) community and research and public health institutions. Having suspicions of public institutions and an abiding distrust for official sources of knowledge about HIV/AIDS is not illegitimate. The question facing public health professionals is how to contend with the situation that the analysis of these rumors reveals.

Of course, there are no easy solutions. Distrust that is woven into the fabric of a society stratified by race cannot easily be undone. As stories, however, rumors are mutable and can fade—they are more symptom than cause. More effective public health interventions will require a reconceptualization of HIV/AIDS rumors and narratives not as "mistakes," or evidence of ignorance or errors of cognition. Rather, genocide conspiracy rumors and narratives within the African American public make more sense as what Waters called examples of "ethnosociology," with the understanding that "believers will be better acquainted with the social facts that are explained by conspiracy theories."[82(p117)] A measure as simple as ascertaining the prevalence of rumors in a particular community where an HIV/AIDS initiative will be undertaken—through focus groups with a cross-section of community members—can alert public health workers to the level of distrust (detecting rumors as a measure of distrust). Even providing a forum where rumors can be openly spoken about may also help displace them. In this research, off-the-record comments by participants expressed relief and pleasure at having had a chance to participate in discussions where they could speak freely and without judgment about the stories they recounted.

No magic bullet can defeat rumors, but acknowledging the social facts about their origins and effects, and tracking changes in rumors, are necessary first steps to contending with them as part of the real social landscape in which public health education and other measures take place; rumors are neither static or epiphenomenal. Ultimately, only greater trust within the community can reduce the underlying function that rumors serve. Until that happens, awareness of the role, implications, and prevalence of rumors must inform and assist efforts by health professionals to contend with the preventable spread of HIV/AIDS. ∎

About the Author

Jacob Heller is with the Sociology Department, SUNY College at Old Westbury, Old Westbury, NY.

Correspondence should be sent to Jacob Heller, Rm 2031, Sociology Department, SUNY College at Old Westbury, Old Westbury, NY 11568-0120 (e-mail: hellerj@oldwestbury.edu). Reprints can be ordered at http://www.ajph.org by clicking the "Reprints" link.

This article was accepted August 6, 2014.

Acknowledgments

Earlier versions of this research were presented at the annual meeting of the American Sociological Association; August 14–17, 2010; Atlanta, GA; and the 2012 annual meeting of the Eastern Sociological Society; February 23–26; New York, NY.

Thanks to the anonymous reviewers' helpful and constructive comments, and to Amanda Frisken for her detailed and diligent reading and feedback of numerous versions of this article.

Human Participant Protection

This research activity was approved by the Old Westbury College institutional review board.

References

1. Centers for Disease Control and Prevention. HIV Prevalence Estimates—United States 2006. *MMWR Morb Mortal Wkly Rep.* 2008;57(39):1073–1076.

2. Allport GW, Postman L. *The Psychology of Rumor.* New York, NY: Henry Holt & Co; 1947.

3. Shibutani T. *Improvised News: A Sociological Study of Rumor.* Indianapolis, IN: Bobbs-Merrill Educational Publishing; 1966.

4. Kimmel AJ, Keefer R. Psychological correlates of the transmission and acceptance of rumors about AIDS. *J Appl Soc Psychol.* 1991;21(19):1608–1628.

5. Fumento M. *The Myth of Heterosexual AIDS.* New York, NY: Basic Books; 1990.

6. Turner P. *I Heard It Through the Grapevine: Rumor in African American Culture.* Berkeley, CA: University of California Press; 1993.

7. Duesberg P. *Inventing the AIDS Virus.* Washington, DC: Regnery; 1996.

8. Shilts R. *And the Band Played On.* New York, NY: St Martin's Press; 1987.

9. Osmond DH. Epidemiology of HIV/AIDS in the United States. HIV In site knowledge base chapter. 2003. Available at: http://hivinsite.ucsf.edu/InSite?page=kb-01-03. Accessed February 2, 2010.

10. Knight P. Introduction: a nation of conspiracy theorists. In: Knight P. ed. *Conspiracy Nation.* New York, NY: New York University Press; 2002:1–20.

11. Foucault M. *Language, Counter-Memory, Practice: Selected Essays and Interviews.* Ithaca, NY: Cornell University Press; 1977.

12. Halbwachs M. *On Collective Memory.* Chicago, IL: University of Chicago Press; 1992.

13. Zelizer B. Reading the past against the grain: the shape of memory studies. *Crit Stud Mass Commun.* 1995;12(2):214–239.

14. Chicago Dept of Public Health. *STI/HIV Surveillance Report, 2011.* Chicago, IL: City of Chicago; 2011.

15. Wolseley RE. *The Black Press.* Ames: Iowa State University Press; 1990.

16. Pride A, Wilson CC II. *A History of the Black Press.* Washington, DC: Howard University Press; 1997.

17. Washburn PS. *The African American Newspaper: Voice of Freedom.* Evanston, IL: Northwestern University Press; 2006.

18. Gandy OH. Audience construction: race, ethnicity and segmentation in popular media. Paper presented at: 50th Annual Conference of the International Communication Association; June 7, 2000; Acapulco, Mexico.

19. Gibbons RA, Ulloth D. The role of the *Amsterdam News* in New York City's media environment. *Journal Mass Commun Q.* 1982;59:451–455.

20. Centers for Disease Control and Prevention. 2009. HIV and AIDS among gay and bisexual men. CDC fact sheet. December 2013. Available at: http://www.cdc.gov/nchhstp/newsroom/docs/CDC-MSM-508.pdf. Accessed February 2014.

21. Holtgrave DR, Crosby RA. Social capital, poverty, and income inequality as predictors of gonorrhea,

syphilis, chlamydia and AIDS case rates in the United States. *Sex Transm Infect.* 2003;79(1):62–64.

22. Gebbie KM. Policy watch. Vaccines don't work without people, where do you go for information? *AIDS Read.* 2007;17(9):465–466.

23. Airhihenbuwa CO, Webster JD, Titilayo OO, Shine R, Smith-Bankhead N. HIV/AIDS and the African-American community: disparities of policy and identity. *Phylon.* 2002;50:23–46.

24. Millett G, Malebranche D, Mason B, Spikes P. Focusing "down low": bisexual black men, HIV risk and heterosexual transmission. *J Natl Med Assoc.* 2005;97(7 suppl):52S–59S.

25. Gamble VN. Under the shadow of Tuskegee: African Americans and health care. *Am J Public Health.* 1997;87(11):1773–1778.

26. Sengupta S, Strauss RP, DeVellis R, Quinn SC, DeVellis B, Ware WB. Factors affecting African-American participation in AIDS research. *J Acquir Immune Defic Syndr.* 2000;24(3):275–284.

27. Pickle K, Quinn SC, Brown JD. HIV/AIDS coverage in black newspapers, 1991–1996: implications for health communication and health education. *J Health Commun.* 2002;7(5):427–444.

28. Corbie-Smith G. The continuing legacy of the Tuskegee syphilis study. *Am J Med Sci.* 1999;317(1):5–8.

29. Jacobs EA, Rolle I, Ferrans CE, Whitaker EE, Warnecke RB. Understanding African Americans' views of the trustworthiness of physicians. *J Gen Intern Med.* 2006;21(6):642–647.

30. Mokwunye NO. African Americans, trust, and the medical research community. *Online J Health Ethics.* 2006;3(1). Available at: http://aquila.usm.edu/ojhe/vol3/iss1/3. Accessed September 21, 2014.

31. Chambre SM. *Fighting for Our Lives: New York's AIDS Community and the Politics of Disease.* New Brunswick, NJ: Rutgers University Press; 2006.

32. Washington HA. *Medical Apartheid: The Dark History of Medical Experimentation on Black Americans From Colonial Times to the Present.* New York, NY: Doubleday; 2006.

33. Petersen LA. Racial differences in trust: what have we sown? *Med Care.* 2002;40(2):81–84.

34. Bogart LM, Thorburn S. Are HIV/AIDS conspiracy beliefs a barrier to HIV prevention among African Americans? *J Acquir Immune Defic Syndr.* 2005;38(2):213–218.

35. Thomas SB, Quinn SC. The Tuskegee Syphilis Study, 1932 to 1972: implications for HIV education and AIDS risk education programs in the black community. *Am J Public Health.* 1991;81(11):1498–1505.

36. Herek GM, Capitano JP. Conspiracies, contagion, and compassion: trust and public reactions to AIDS. *AIDS Educ Prev.* 1994;6(4):365–375.

37. Hofstadter R. *The Paranoid Style in American Politics and Other Essays.* New York, NY: Vintage Books; 1964.

38. Mason F. A poor person's cognitive mapping. In: Knight P, ed. *Conspiracy Nation.* New York, NY: New York University Press; 2002:40–56.

39. Fenster M. *Conspiracy Theories.* Minneapolis, MN: University of Minnesota Press; 1999.

40. Drugs, disease, denial, June 29, 2005. Available at: http://nypress.com/drugs-disease-denial. Accessed September 21, 2014.

41. Farmer P. *AIDS and Accusation: Haiti and the Geography of Blame.* Berkeley, CA: University of California Press; 1992.

42. Lee S. Benetton advertisement. *Rolling Stone.* 1992;12:2.

43. Kolata G. The genesis of an epidemic: humans, chimps and a virus. *New York Times.* September 4, 2001:F1.

44. Chappelle D. AIDS monkey. Available at: http://www.youtube.com/watch?v=A-IEzYZMo1k. Accessed September 21, 2014.

45. Pilot (first aired episode) of *30 Rock*, NBC television, October 10, 2006.

46. Fiske J. *Media Matters.* Minneapolis, MN: University of Minnesota Press; 1996.

47. Editorial. Bill Cosby's AIDS conspiracy. *New York Post.* December 4, 1991:26.

48. Zeman N. Will Smith rides high. *Vanity Fair.* July 1999:88.

49. Dobbs M. Wright's wild charges. *Washington Post.* May 5, 2008. Available at: http://voices.washingtonpost.com/fact-checker/2008/05/wrights_wild_charges.html. Accessed September 21, 2014.

50. Bates KG. Is it genocide? *Essence.* September 1990:76–78, 116, 118.

51. Brandon DT, Isaac LA, LaVeist TA. The legacy of Tuskegee and trust in medical care: is Tuskegee

responsible for race differences in mistrust in medical care? *J Natl Med Assoc.* 2005;97(7):951–956.

52. Rosin H. The homecoming: paranoia and plague in black America. *New Republic,* June 5, 1995:21–31.

53. Baldwin J. *The Evidence of Things Not Seen.* New York, NY: Holt, Reinhart & Winston; 1985.

54. Whitfield SJ. An anatomy of black anti-Semitism. *Judaism.* 1994;43(4):341–359.

55. DeParle J. Talk of government being out to get blacks falls on more attentive ears. *New York Times.* October 29, 1990:A12.

56. Curtis T. The origin of AIDS: a startling new theory attempts to answer the question "was it an act of God or an act of man?" *Rolling Stone.* March 19, 1992:54–59, 61, 106.

57. Cohen J. Debate on AIDS origin: *Rolling Stone* weighs in. *Science.* 1992;255(5150):1505.

58. Holden C. *Rolling Stone* rolls over for Koprowski. *Science.* 1993;262(5138):1369.

59. Marriott M. Needle exchange angers many minorities. *New York Times.* November 7, 1988:B8.

60. A strong endorsement for clean needles [editorial]. *New York Times.* September 25, 1995:A14.

61. Schwartzman P. Clergy fears needle exchange plan; proposal to limit HIV spread could encourage drug abuse, pastors say. *Washington Post.* March 1, 2000:M3.

62. Klonoff EA, Landrine H. 1997 Distrust of whites, acculturation, and AIDS knowledge among African Americans. *J Black Psychol.* 1997;23(1):50–57.

63. Sasson T. African American conspiracy theories and the social construction of crime. *Sociol Inq.* 1995; 65(3–4):265–285.

64. Gas trick upset. Available at: http://www.snopes.com/horrors/mayhem/gaspump.asp. Accessed September 21, 2014.

65. Fine GA. The Goliath effect: corporate dominance and mercantile legends. *J Am Folklore.* 1985;98(387):63–84.

66. Demaris A, Yang R. Race relations and interpersonal mistrust. *Sociol Spectr.* 1994;14(4):327–349.

67. Boulware LE, Cooper LA, Ratner LE, LaVeist TA, Powe NR. Race and trust in the health care system. *Public Health Rep.* 2003;118(14):358–365.

68. Simpson B, McGrimmon T, Irwin J. Are blacks really less trusting than whites? Revisiting the race and trust question. *Soc Forces.* 2007;86(2): 525–552.

69. Fine GA, Turner PA. *Whispers on the Color Line: Rumor and Race in America.* Berkeley, CA: University of California Press; 2001.

70. Quinn SC. Belief in AIDS as a form of genocide: implications for HIV prevention programs for African Americans. *J Health Educ.* 1997;28(suppl 1):S6–S12.

71. Jones JH. *Bad Blood.* New York, NY: Free Press; 1993.

72. Zimet GD, Liau A, Fortenberry VD. Health beliefs and intention to get immunized for HIV. *J Adolesc Health.* 1997;20(5):354–359.

73. Allen MA, Liang TS, La Salvia T, et al. Assessing the attitudes, knowledge and awareness of HIV vaccine research among adults in the Unites States. *J Acquir Immune Defic Syndr.* 2005;40(5):617–624.

74. Reverby S. *Tuskegee's Truths: Rethinking the Tuskegee Syphilis Study.* Chapel Hill, CA: University of North Carolina Press; 2000.

75. Maddox AH. The anthrax scare: the Tuskegee Study revisited. *Amsterdam News.* November 1, 2001:13.

76. Zanoni C. The deadly disease: African American men battle HIV/AIDS epidemic. *Amsterdam News.* November 11, 2004;1:31.

77. Zook KB. Special report: the New York City AIDS experiment. *Essence.* February 2007:196–201.

78. Pund B, Lefert A. *National ADAP Monitoring Project Annual Report.* Washington, DC: National Alliance of State & Territorial AIDS Directors; May 2011.

79. Kaiser Family Foundation. AIDS drug assistance programs. February 2014. Available at: http://kff.org/hivaids/fact-sheet/aids-drug-assistance-programs. Accessed February 27, 2014.

80. Balán IC, Carballo-Diéguez A, Ventuneac A, Remien HR, Dolezal C, Ford J. Are HIV-negative men who have sex with men and who bareback concerned about HIV infection? Implications for HIV risk reduction interventions. *Arch Sex Behav.* 2013;42(2):279–289.

81. Civil Rights Congress. *We Charge Genocide: The Historic Petition to the United Nations for Relief From a Crime of the United States Government Against the Negro People.* New York, NY: Emergency Conference Committee; 1951.

82. Waters AM. Conspiracy theories as enthosociologies: explanation and intention in African American political culture. *J Black Stud.* 1997;28(1):112–125.

Improving Nursing Care for Lesbian, Bisexual, and Transgender Women

by Patti Rager Zuzelo

Abstract Health care needs of lesbian, bisexual, and transgender (LBT) women are inadequately addressed in nursing education and practice, which may contribute to heterosexism and homophobia on the part of health care providers. Nurses have an obligation to use available tools and resources to assess and positively transform health care environments to ensure high-quality care for LBT women. The context within which care for LBT women is learned, practiced, and experienced requires radical improvement.

Health needs of lesbian, bisexual, and transgender (LBT) women are often not purposefully discussed and explored during nursing education. This learning gap is not unique to nursing education, as other health care providers, including physicians, are insufficiently prepared by medical and health science curricula to meet the needs of LBT women. It seems likely that this inadequate approach to teaching LBT health contributes in part to the heterosexism and homophobia experienced by LBT women from providers and agencies during care encounters (DeHart, 2008; Harcourt, 2006; Keepnews, 2011; Lim, Brown, & Jones, 2013).

It may be that nurses and other health professionals do not know or consider the unique and shared health needs of LBT women in part because of curricular inattentiveness toward sexually marginalized groups that is experienced during formative years of professional education. Health topics that are important to LBT women may only be encountered during clinical practice if a LBT patient, significant other, or family member chooses to share relationship status or sexual identity. It is important to consider LBT care and educational inattention within the larger context of nursing as a profession. Nursing education is informed by nursing practice, and practice is influenced by credentialing and licensure. These components, education, practice, certification, and licensure, provide the context of nursing care.

Within this larger context, LBT health is often inadequately addressed.

As gay and LBT (GLBT) individuals have become more socially visible, health care expectations have slowly followed suit; this is demonstrated by the GLBT objectives of Healthy People 2020 (U.S. Department of Health and Human Services [USDHSS], 2013). The national health care agenda is slowly moving in a more inclusive direction to begin the necessary work of improving health outcomes of sexually marginalized people. Gay health issues are often included with LBT given the typical consolidation of nonheterosexual orientation and nontraditional gender identities in discussions and published research. The term *gay* in this particular discussion refers to men who are sexually attracted to other men whereas *lesbian* refers to women who are sexually attracted to other women. The acronyms *LGBT* and *GLBT* are used interchangeably in this article and are kept consistent with the version used by a particular cited organization, agency, or author(s).

The LGBT national healthcare agenda, along with increasingly positive shifts in LGBT legalities and social issues, illustrate the need for women's health nurses to increase attention to health parity for LBT clients. Nurses, including those providing care to women, child-bearing families, and newborns, must be comfortable with and experts in meeting LBT health needs that may be influenced by sexual behaviors or associated with anatomic sex, demographics, genetics, or environment. Recognizing that many nurses have completed educational programs with inadequate consideration of LBT-specific topics, the purpose of this project was to explore the larger context of LBT health as related to nursing education, practice, and credentialing. Recommendations for improvements in these areas are offered.

Common Meanings of LBT-Related Terminology

Nurses must understand the terms related to LBT issues for accurate communication and assessment. The Joint Commission (TJC; 2011) published an extensive glossary of GLBT-related terms that offers nurses commonly accepted definitions. Johnson, Mimiaga, and Bradford (2008) also provided an overview of key terms specific to GLBT individuals. *Gender* is described as a "construct of psychological, social and cultural factors used to classify individuals as male, female, both or neither" (p. 215). *Transgender* signifies people who "have gender identities, expressions or behaviors not traditionally associated with their birth sex" (p. 216). Transgender individuals express their genders differently than what is "culturally expected of them" (National LGBT Education Center, 2013, p. 3).

Individuals who pursue medical therapies to establish congruency between their physical bodies and intrinsic, sexual self-knowledge are termed "transsexuals" (Johnson et al., 2008). Other important terms include *gender variant*, which describes individuals who are sexually nonconforming compared to societal norms and *intersex*, which describes transgender individuals as well as those born with atypical genitalia or procreative structures (Johnson et al., 2008). The publications and resources of the National LGBT Health Education Center (2013) include guidance on appropriate terminology and language and terms that should be avoided when working with transgender individuals, including "real" woman or "real" man (p. 3).

Sexual orientation has been inconsistently described and measured in the absence of standardized definitions or failure to request this information in survey demographics. Sexual orientation consists of "three components: behavior, identity, and desire" (Ard & Makadon, 2012, p. 1). Harcourt (2006) indicated that poor data result from a variety of factors, including the significant diversity within the rather small LGBT population. Researchers that collect sexual identifiers do so in a variety of ways: some use self-identification of sexual orientation and others rely on reports of the sex of participants' partners or the preferred gender of attraction. Inconsistency between individuals' sexual activity and self-identification may occur, and because of this variation researchers and care providers may elect to categorize behaviors as men who have sex with men (MSM) or women who have sex with women (WSW) (Ard & Makadon, 2012).

Another compounding issue is that the failure to consistently collect demographic data describing sexual orientation has made it difficult to provide quantitative data on LBT issues and health outcomes. Lack of data influences funding access and program support. In response, Healthy People 2020 includes two new developmental objectives. The first calls for an increase in the number of population-based data systems monitoring Healthy People 2020 objectives to include in their core a standardized set of questions that identify lesbian, gay, and bisexual populations. A second objective calls for similar attention to transgender populations (USDHHS 2013). To advance the knowledge and care provided to GLBT individuals, common consistent terminology is needed.

Heterosexism in Nursing Education and Practice

The term *heterosexism* is widely used to describe an "underlying belief that heterosexuality is the natural/normal/acceptable or superior form of sexuality" (Williamson, 2000, p. 98). This particular worldview contributes to prejudice and biases across a number of important societal interactions and institutions, including systems of health care, education, and research. Nurse educators and clinical preceptors must increase students' and clinicians' awareness of health care injustices based on sexual orientation. These injustices are supported by commonly held and typically unquestioned notions concerning LBT females that may be erroneous. These notions may be influenced by an incorrect belief that same-sex couple relationships are not common or that same sex couples generally do not raise children.

To the contrary, Gates (2013) demonstrated the increasing number of same-sex couples and the increasing frequency of child-rearing within these families. Gates summarized key demographic characteristics of same sex couples from 2005 through 2011 based on the U.S. Census Bureau's American Community Survey (ACS). Gates contrasted these findings to those of heterosexual couples and identified trends and anomalies.

> When nursing students are not educated about the needs of lesbian, bisexual, and transgender individuals, stereotypes may persist that perpetuate homophobic perspectives.

Key points included the shift from a majority of male same-sex couples to a greater number of female same-sex couples. A significant number of these couples were raising children younger than age 18 years. Of note, 13% of same sex couples included a Veteran. Particularly relevant to health and insurability, Gates noted that approximately 75% of individuals in same-sex couples hold private-sector employment, 15% work in public-sector jobs, and approximately 1% is self-employed (2013). These comparative data are critically important for nurses to consider because they illustrate shifting demographics that must be fairly and fully addressed to ensure a system of care that is responsive to the current health needs of its citizenry.

Considering Gates' (2013) findings, it was concerning that a cursory review of accessible, popular nursing textbooks related to health assessment and medical-surgical nursing revealed no practical discussion about LBT status and no consideration during subjective data collection about clients' living circumstances and relationship patterns. More recent textbooks and journal articles may offer information describing LGBT discrimination and health disparities, but this content is sparse. Eliason, Dibble, and DeJoseph (2010) reviewed the top 10 nursing journals as ascertained by impact factor between 2005 and 2009 and found that only 0.16% (8/5000) of published articles in these journals addressed LGBT issues.

Textbooks and educational resources that include content on LBT topics may not adequately or accurately represent these issues. For example, general discussions pertaining to the collection of biographical data during a health history consistently include marital status rather than relationship status. Assessment questions typically categorize relationship status as never married, married, widowed, separated, or divorced. These questions appear to presume a heterosexual orientation. Although in the classroom, students may be instructed to query about relationship status during health histories, standardized assessment forms often query about marital status. Ideally, providers should first establish sexual orientation, then query women about partners, civil unions, or same-sex marriages.

The notion of heterosexuality in a traditional form inclusive of marriage and children is ubiquitous in nursing textbooks and resources. This common theme reinforces the predominant heterosexism of nursing students rather than challenging them to consider the true essence of individualized care planning. When textbooks and classroom experiences ignore or misrepresent LBT women, students' negative attitudes or misperceptions are reinforced rather than challenged. In addition, lack of discussion, inclusion, and evidence-based information pertaining to LBT identity likely supports the premise that LBT orientation is not healthy but rather pathological. These concerns are relevant to undergraduate and graduate educational resources and experiences.

Binary categorization of gender predominates throughout nursing assessment literature and health care records, and gender is presented as male or female. This categorization provides additional barriers to relationship building when used with people who are transgender or seeking/considering gender reassignment. In fact, little information is available in textbooks regarding the provision of nursing care specific to transgender individuals or those considering such possibilities.

Education provides an excellent opportunity for transformation. Textbooks facilitate development of professional identity. Pictures, figures, narratives, and case studies represent the culture of nursing. When textbooks, videos, didactic, and online learning fail to normalize LBT women, students' stereotypes likely persist that perpetuate homophobic perspectives. Additionally, the lack of respectful inclusiveness may contribute to serious and adverse effects on LBT health outcomes.

Positive and Incremental Changes in Health Care for LBT Women

Nursing organizations have called for recognition of LGBT health disparities. Lim, Brown, and Jones (2013) noted that the codes of ethics for the American Nurses Association (ANA) and the International Council of Nurses (ICN) acknowledge the importance of valuing individuality and respecting individuals regardless of demographics and attributes, including sexual orientation. The authors observed that LGBT elders are particularly under-served given the poor health outcomes associated with aging compounded by the marginalization occurring as a sexual minority (Lim et al., 2013). This marginalization of LGBT seniors is particularly noteworthy given that, "the proportion of same-sex couples that include at least one senior aged 65 or older has risen from 7.5% in 2005 to nearly one in 10 (9.7%) in 2011" (Gates, 2013, p. 1).

Calling for education and inclusiveness in practice, Lim et al. (2013) asserted the need for faculty development specific to LGBT health. Recommendations for culturally sensitive and responsive care for LGBT persons are supported by TJC (2011) in its field guide for inclusive and culturally sensitive care and advocated for by the USDHHS (2013) through equitable policies, including mandates to provide equal visitation and representation during hospitalization.

Keepnews (2011) recognized the efforts of nursing to address the needs of LGBT persons and offered opportunities for crafting purposeful agendas to promote LGBT equality in four broad areas: policy, practice, education, and research. Keep-news acknowledged nurses as advocates related to HIV/AIDS but called for nursing organizations to move LGBT issues to the forefront in organized and committed strategies. Recognizing the importance of addressing LGBT health needs as a matter of justice and equity, the National Student Nurses' Association (NSNA; 2012) adopted a 2012 resolution in support of TJC's (2011) LGBT field guide.

Incremental changes in LBT health care practices and education are advancing in positive and powerful ways although more work must be done. The Human Rights Campaign (HRC; 2013) conducts an online health care equality index (HEI) designed to ascertain the equity and accessibility of LGBT health care services provided by those institutions that voluntarily participate in the survey. Facilities have the potential to be recognized as Leaders in LGBT Healthcare Equality based on responses to four core leadership criteria, including non-discrimination, equal visitation, employment non-discrimination, and training in LGBT patient-centered care (Snowden, 2013).

Participation in the HRC HEI is free and provides participants with HEI staff support to more fully develop LGBT patient-centered care inclusive of more than 30 best practices (HRC, 2013). The HEI has been available since 2007, and the most recent annual survey in 2013 included 718 institutional respondents. The HEI website provides users with the ability to search by state for the HEI ratings of health care institutions and resources regarding an individual's rights as a health care consumer or employee. Participant institutions represent all states and include most Veterans' hospitals. In addition, as a benefit of survey participation, thousands of hours of continuing education and training are provided to the employees of representative institutions. Interested nurses may consider encouraging their employers to participate in the HEI, particularly given the need for interprofessional educational and collaborative efforts to improve patient-centered care (Snowden, 2013).

> The lack of respectful inclusiveness may contribute to serious and adverse effects on health outcomes for lesbian, bisexual, and transgender women.

The HEI's four core leadership criteria are congruent with TJC's expectations of compliance with LGBT-focused standards of care effective July 2012 (Lim et al., 2013). Although cultural competence and patient-centered communication standards, specifically including LGBT people, were published in 2011, accreditation survey findings did not contribute toward institution accreditation decisions until July 2012 (TJC, 2011, p. 3). The LGBT Field Guide (TJC, 2011) may serve as an excellent tool for organizational self-assessment and as an educational resource for health care providers and staff.

Given the paucity of demographic data collected on sexual orientation or gender identity, the determination of the percent of self-identified LGBT people in the United States is challenging. However, current estimates range from 5% to 10% of the total population (Lim et al., 2013). Partnered with the HEI, nurses have powerful strategies to buttress efforts to transform care environments for LGBT people, including LGBT employees who may or may not have disclosed their sexual orientations. Nurses should consider the ramifications of sexual discrimination and disenfranchisement on LGBT patients and the possible ripple effect that such prejudicial care practices may have on the work and practice environments for health care colleagues who may or may not have disclosed their sexual orientations.

Responses to Disclosure and Relevance to Health Care Quality

The International Gay and Lesbian Human Rights Commission (IGLHRC; 2013a) advocates for human rights across the globe on behalf of people who are discriminated against or mistreated based on actual or perceived sexual orientation, gender identity, or representation. Nurses caring for international patients need to be aware of the stigmatization and potential physical and emotional trauma experienced by people from diverse, international cultures, as these experiences will likely influence the decision to disclose sexual orientation to the health care team (IGLHRC, 2013b). Disclosure of sexual orientation to health professionals may be as difficult for the LBT woman as coming out to family and loved ones. Therefore, it may be helpful for nurses to understand the issues associated with sexual orientation disclosure as they consider strategies to encourage disclosure and recognize disclosure-associated risks and fears.

Martin, Hutson, Kazyak, and Scherrer (2010) conducted an interpretive content analysis of help books to gauge the cultural context of tools available for parents seeking guidance or understanding after their gay or lesbian children disclosed their sexual identities. Books were categorized as one of three types: accepting, accommodating, or disapproving. Only the accepting and accommodating books provided the possibility of a life of normalcy. Disapproving books focused on changing gay or lesbian children into heterosexuals. Particularly striking, the authors found that none of the books proposed happiness or indifference as possible reactions to disclosure. In fact, the response to disclosure was often related to a grief response experienced with news of a death. When considered in a broader fashion, it is likely that health providers and educators may be similarly influenced by this cultural context, which may in turn influence their responses to LBT disclosure or the advice they offer the parents of LBT women.

Hinchliff, Gott, and Galena (2005) used detailed interviews to explore the perspectives of general practitioners (GPs) on the difficulties faced when discussing sexual health concerns with lesbian and gay patients. Their findings indicated that GPs were uninformed regarding gay and lesbian lifestyles and sexual practices although they recognized the need for managing patients' sexual health. They were uncomfortable with language use and uncertain of how to raise questions specific to sexual activities. A few had negative attitudes, and some expressed antipathy toward homosexual acts. Participants believed that training was important to develop the skill set needed to effectively address sexual health. However, the need for educational does not always ensure participation in continuing education, even when that education is readily available and relevant (Hinchliff et al., 2005).

Lambda Legal's (2010a) health care discrimination survey provides recent data to demonstrate that LGBT people are treated in a profoundly unjust fashion by many health care institutions and providers. *When Health Care Isn't Caring* depicts a hostile, uncaring, and unsafe health care environment that provides prejudicial and discriminatory care (Lambda Legal, 2010b). Respondents who were transgender and gender nonconforming, living with human immunodeficiency virus (HIV), and gay, lesbian, and bisexual reported that health care workers refused to provide physical contact or did so in rough and abusive fashion, spoke in a harsh and accusatory style, or used disproportionate precautions (Flemmer, Doutrich, Dekker, & Rondeau, 2012; Lambda Legal, 2010b). Survey data demonstrated that 70% of transgender and gender nonconforming participants experienced negative health care encounters (Lambda Legal,

2010b). Those respondents who were transgender or gender nonconforming and were "respondents of color or those in low-income groups (defined in this survey as having a household income under $20,000) in nearly every category experienced higher rates of discrimination and substandard care" (Lambda Legal, 2010b, p. 11).

The health care discrimination survey (Lambda Legal, 2010b) illustrates an important quandary for LBT women. The disclosure of sexual orientation is necessary for appropriate and best care. However, this necessary disclosure can make LBT women more vulnerable to hostile healthcare encounters. Transgender individuals may find that insurance companies will refuse to cover essential prostate examinations or Papanicolaou (PAP) test screenings after gender identity is disclosed (Lambda Legal, 2010b). Respondents noted insufficient numbers of adequately prepared or expert clinicians available to address LBT health needs (Lambda Legal, 2010b). This finding is not surprising given the inadequate nursing and medical education regarding LBT topics.

Assurance of Professional Expertise

Content regarding LBT issues is lacking in the nursing literature. Lim et al. (2013) noted that the American Association of Colleges of Nursing's (AACN) *Essentials of Baccalaureate Education for Professional Nursing Practice* "offers no specific language that directly addresses LGBT health inclusion into the curriculum" (p. 201). They expressed similar concerns about exclusion of LGBT material from the Quality and Safety Education for Nurses (QSEN) initiative. The exclusion of language regarding LGBT issues in these two important documents suggests that inadequate attention to LGBT health concerns in undergraduate baccalaureate education will continue (Lim et al., 2013), a striking concern given disparate LBT health outcomes.

The consensus model for Advanced Practice Registered Nurse (APRN) Regulation: Licensure, Accreditation, Certification & Education (APRN consensus model) includes six populations for APRN licensure: adult-gerontology, pediatric, neonatal, family/individual across the life span,

psychiatric mental health, and women's health/gender-related (APRN Joint Dialogue Group, 2008). Specialty practice areas are separate from these populations and are not included in licensure requirements. To date, no specialty examinations are available to nurses who may be interested in acquiring expertise related to nonconforming gender identity or LGBT concerns for a particular population. As a consequence, APRN content on this topic may not be sufficiently addressed to meet societal needs, although arguably, LGBT information is relevant to each of these population areas.

A number of examples suggest a gap in deliberate, comprehensive, LBT health education for APRNs. The American Nurses Credentialing Center (ANCC; 2012a) test content outline for the Adult-Gerontology Primary Care Nurse Practitioner examination does not include specific references to LGBT health. Rather, only the term *sexual* is found in the category, "managing disease/health status over time" (p. 8) and *sexuality* is included in "life transitions" (p. 7). Similarly, the Adult-Gerontology Acute Care Nurse Practitioner examination test content outline (ANCC, 2012b) includes only one reference to sexual needs, "Assessing cultural, spiritual, ethnic, gender, sexual orientation and/or age differences in patients with acute, critical, and chronic health conditions" (p. 2). The Adult-Gerontology Clinical Nurse Specialist (CNS) examination content outline (ANCC, 2012c) fails to address sexuality in any explicit form. Genitourinary/reproductive health is noted as a testable body system; however, this very broad area addresses direct care and pharmacologic needs and may not specifically address LBT women. The Adult-Gerontology CNS competencies (AACN, 2010) do not include this content, which is particularly worrisome given the numbers of LBT senior women.

The online test content outline for the Adult Psychiatric Mental-Health Nurse Practitioner (ANCC, 2009) does not make explicit referral to LGBT concerns or general sexuality issues. This particular test refers only "gender differences" (ANCC, 2009, p. 3) as an explicit example of an assessment area falling within biologic considerations. Family Nurse Practitioner test content outline (ANCC, 2012d) requires "Family systems theory and sexuality across the life-span" (p. 5). Specific mention is not made to LGBT individuals, unique care needs of same-sex couples, or pregnancy/parenting for these couples; however, care of "diverse populations" (p. 3) could be interpreted to include LGBT needs.

The Pediatric Primary Care Nurse Practitioner examination content (ANCC, 2012e) is similarly nonspecific related to sexual development, gender identity, or other LGBT concerns. This potentially significant shortcoming can be particularly problematic for adolescents dealing with sexual identity and activity. The case could be made that sexual identity content falls under the broad umbrella topics of patient-centered care or the "care of diverse populations" (ANCC, 2012e, p. 4); however, because no explicit sexual or gender-related care needs are mentioned, insensitive health care may be provided.

Many nurse practitioners focused on women's health concerns have been educated to address the unique needs of lesbian clients and have provided exemplary care to this population (Flemmer, Doutrich, Dekker, & Rondeau, 2012). The Women's Health Care Practitioner examination content map (National Certification Corporation, 2013) does not specifically mention *lesbian, bisexual, transgender*, or *sexual orientation* content items. However, the Population-Focused Nurse Practitioner Competencies (National Organization Nurse Practitioner Faculties, 2013) does include content on Gay-Bisexual-Lesbian-Transgender/Transsexual orientation for the Psychiatric-Mental Health Nurse Practitioner and the Women's Health/Gender-Related Nurse Practitioner roles.

Health needs of LBT women should be consistently and comprehensively addressed in graduate and undergraduate nursing education. Expertise should be assured by credentialing efforts that include certification examinations with content addressing LBT concerns. The Joint Commission has recognized the need for explicit LGBT-specific accreditation standards rather than implicit inclusion under suggestive verbiage. It may be important for certifiers to consider this same strategy so that test content maps consistent with explicit competencies can guide faculty during curriculum design in overt ways that relate to the real-world of practice, a world that includes LBT stakeholders.

Self-Awareness and the Therapeutic Use of Self

Before nurses can authentically interact with LBT patients, they should first reflect on their personal views, including biases and stereotypes. Self-awareness is an important component of the nurse-patient relationship (Campbell, 1980), and reflective practice provides an opportunity to address the tension that exists between what nurses aspire to create in practice versus current realities (Johns, 2004). Some subject matter may challenge nurses to step outside their usual boundaries to explore topics with patients that may be personally uncomfortable, including sexuality or sexual activity. This discomfort should be rectified or at least recognized in order to provide effective patient-centered care.

First Steps in Improving Nursing Care for LBT Women

Women's health clinicians should develop an evidence-based action plan to change practice and improve care outcomes for LBT women. Nurses working at the point of care can begin this effort by more fully developing expertise specific to LBT health and including strategies that support patient-centered care. Women's health clinicians may find it useful to establish an interprofessional team to assess the current health care environment and respond using evidence-based remedies or best-practice recommendations to enhance delivery processes. Tools and resources are available that can be useful as strategic roadmaps.

Developing Clinical Expertise and Improving Outcomes. The resource guide section of the LGBT field guide (TJC, 2011) offers a rich listing of resources including websites, toolkits, and reports that are applicable to addressing a variety of LBT needs. Women's health nurses will likely benefit from reviewing the introductory materials that highlight high-frequency LBT health concerns, including less access to insurance, health promotion, and disease prevention services and higher risks for smoking, substance abuse, and alcohol abuse (TJC, 2011). The LGBT field guide is recommended as an organizational tool for assessment and education. Women's health nurses will likely find many practical uses for this guide that are adaptable in a variety of health care settings. For example, nurses may carefully examine the patient safety content to ascertain whether policies and practices require revision.

Lambda Legal (n.d.) is an organization dedicated to achieving full recognition of the civil rights of LGBT people as well as those with HIV. The organization's website offers practice advice, primarily legal, that pertains to workplace concerns, life planning, marriage-law, and other critical concerns for LGBT individuals. Available web-based publications and resources cover a range of topics and include toolkits, fact sheets, and the organization's journal, *Impact*. Lambda Legal provides information pertaining to legal concerns associated with HIV, including discrimination tactics. Posted videos address a number of topics, including health care proxies and living wills, the Federal Nursing Home Reform Act, wills, and visitation rights.

Nurses and other health professionals may benefit from reviewing Lambda Legal's website to gather information and obtain an accurate sense of the many issues confronting LBT women and their families. Given the complexity of the health care system, it may be wise to recommend this website to patients as they plan for health care experiences or end of life. Although women's health nurses may not frequently require legal information, it is an excellent resource to recommend to LBT women in need of such support. The information is also interesting and provides a broad sense of the social complexities often confronted by LBT women as they navigate difficult health care experiences.

The Institute of Medicine (IOM; 2011a) report *The Health of Lesbian, Gay, Bisexual, and Transgender People: Building a Foundation for Better Understanding* provides a detailed description of LGBT health concerns and concludes with policy recommendations. A research agenda is proposed that identifies realistic opportunities to eliminate gaps in knowledge to insure parity of care. Given the influence of IOM reports on policy decisions, women's health nurses need to become familiar with these findings and recommendations. The report brief is an excellent vehicle for summarizing key points of the full report (IOM, 2011b).

Nurses will also benefit from exploring the diverse resources offered by Fenway Health (2013). Dedicated to "enhance the wellbeing of the lesbian, gay, bisexual and transgender community and all people in our neighborhoods and beyond through access to the highest quality health care, education, research and advocacy" (p. 1), Fenway Health (2013) is operationalized via The Fenway Institute. This institute leads and supports a variety of initiatives including the National LGBT Education Center (2013). The Fenway Institute website (n.d.) provides many evidence-based tools and publications that can be freely downloaded, including an extensive repository of publications and presentations. Nurses practicing in settings that provide Internet access to patients and employees may want to consider highlighting this particular website to LBT clients and to interested staff given the excellent resource repository available at no cost.

> Nurses should employ evidence-based tools to improve health care systems and ensure equitable and excellent outcomes for lesbian, bisexual, and transgender women.

The National Coalition for LGBT Health (n.d.) is an advocacy organization with a commitment to improving health and well-being of LGBT individuals and communities. This coalition sponsors an annual LGBT health awareness week with events offered across the nation. Many resources are available on the coalition's website providing opportunities for self-growth and professional engagement that occur during the health awareness week activities.

Assessing Work Environment Factors. Nurses may want to consider the practice environment beyond the patient–client care encounters to include work environment factors related to sexual orientation and inclusiveness. Nurses who identify as lesbian, bisexual, or transgender may find the *LBGT Individuals and Communities* webpage (ANA, 2013) of the ANA website useful. Nurses must consider that barriers to effective LBT patient-centered care may also adversely affect the practice environment for LBT employees. To date, a unique organization for LBT nurses has not been created; however, GMLA, previously known as

Table 1. Available Resources Regarding Lesbian, Gay, Bisexual, Transgender (LGBT) Issues

Reports	
Title	**Web address**
Healthcare Equality Index (HEI) 2013 Report	http://www.hrc.org/files/assets/resources/HEI_2013_final.pdf
Standards of Care for the Health of Transsexual, Transgender, and Gender-Nonconforming People (Version 7)	http://www.wpath.org/documents/IJT
When Health Care Isn't Caring. Lambda Legal's Survey on Discrimination Against LGBT People and People Living with HIV	http://data.lambdalegal.org/publications/downloads/whcic-report_when-health-care-isnt-caring.pdf
Advancing Effective Communication, Cultural Competence, and Patient- and Family-Centered Care for the Lesbian, Gay, Bisexual, and Transgender (LGBT) Community: A Field Guide	http://www.jointcommission.org/assets/1/18/LGBTFieldGuide.pdf
The Health of Lesbian, Gay, Bisexual, and Transgender People: Building a Foundation for Better Understanding	http://www.iom.edu/Reports/2011/The-Health-of-Lesbian-Gay-Bisexual-and-Transgender-People.aspx
National Healthcare Disparities Report 2011	http://www.ahrq.gov/research/findings/nhqrdr/nhdr11/nhdr11.pdf
Lesbian, Gay, Bisexual, and Transgender Populations in the 2011 National Healthcare Disparities Report	http://www.ahrq.gov/research/findings/nhqrdr/nhqrdr11/lgbt.pdf
Websites	
Title	**Web address**
Healthy People 2020 Webinar on Transgender Health (10 parts)	http://www.youtube.com/playlist?list=PLAF2B68EE4115E13C
The National LGBT Health Education Center	http://www.lgbthealtheducation.org/publications/lgbt-health-resources/
Healthy People 2020. Lesbian, Gay, Bisexual, and Transgender Health.	http://healthypeople.gov/2020/topicsobjectives2020/overview.aspx?topicId=25
National Guideline Clearinghouse. Practice Parameter on Gay, Lesbian or Bisexual Sexual Orientation, Gender Nonconformity, and Gender Discordance in Children and Adolescents.	http://www.guideline.gov/content.aspx?id=38417

the Gay and Lesbian Medical Association (2013), provides opportunities for health professionals to work for GLBT health equality.

Enhancing Learning Experiences for Nursing Students. Staff nurses are often engaged in nursing education by serving as preceptors, clinical instructors, and content experts during practicum experiences. Women's health nurses need to reflect on strategies that support students' consideration of sexual orientation and gender identity beyond heterosexuality and gender conforming expression. Nurses may be interested in leading postconference

discussions that address LBT women's health care needs or unique aspects of health that are influenced by sexual orientation. These discussions can help students to develop patient-centered plans of care. Nurses may also encourage students to avoid word choices during patient admission history taking that suggest heterosexism. There may also be opportunities to connect with students regarding transgender health care concerns. As previously mentioned, NSNA has been active in supporting TJC's field guide for LGBT health care. Encouraging student involvement in NSNA and LBT women's health issues would be an ideal learning opportunity.

Conclusion

Americans consistently recognize nurses for their honesty and ethical standards and recently ranked nurses as the most trustworthy profession (Gallup, 2013). Nurses are morally obliged to plan and provide care in partnership with women and their families using strategies based on a respect for human dignity and self-determination (Fowler, 2010). LBT patients need nurses and other health professionals to actively advocate for improvements in the health care system that will support their rights to dignified, patient-centered care and autonomous decision making. Nurses have a responsibility to examine their contributions to the status quo and remedy those influences that detract from quality care for LBT women. Educators must intentionally revise nursing curricula to conscientiously and accurately describe and plan for LBT health needs using evidence-based strategies for change and expert recommendations. Nurses at the point of care are professionally obliged to improve encounters and transform systems of care to meet the unique and common health needs of LBT women. Many resources are available to inform these changes (see Table 1) that provide tremendous opportunities for interprofessional collaboration.

References

American Association of Colleges of Nursing. (2010). *Adult-gerontology clinical nurse specialist competencies.* Retrieved from http://www.aacn.nche.edu/geriatric-nursing/adultgerocnscomp.pdf

American Nurses Association. (2013). *LGBT individuals & communities.* Retrieved from http://nursingworld. org/Main Menu Categories/The Practiceof Professional Nursing/Improving-Your-Practice/Diversity-Awareness/ LGBT

American Nurses Credentialing Center. (2009). *Adult psychiatricmental health nurse Practitioner test content outline.* Retrieved from http://www.nursecredential-ing.org/Documents/Certification/TestContentOutlines/ AdultPsychNP-TCO-April2011.pdf

American Nurses Credentialing Center. (2012a). *Adult gerontology primary care nurse Practitioner test content outline.* Retrieved from http://www.nursecredentialing.

org/Documents/Certification/TestContentOutlines/ AdultGeroPCNP-TCO.aspx

American Nurses Credentialing Center. (2012b). *Adult gerontology acute care nurse Practitioner test content outline.* Retrieved from http://www.nursecredential-ing.org/Documents/Certification/TestContentOutlines/ AdultGeroAcuteCareNP-TCO.aspx

American Nurses Credentialing Center. (2012c). *Adult gerontology clinical nurse specialist test content out-line.* Retrieved from http://www.nursecredentialing.org/ AdultGeroCNS-TCO

American Nurses Credentialing Center. (2012d). *Family nurse practitioner test content outline.* Retrieved from http://www.nursecredentialing.org/FamilyNP-TCO

American Nurses Credentialing Center. (2012e). *Pediatric primary care nurse practitioner test content outline.* Retrieved from http://www.nursecredentialing. org/Documents/Certification/TestContentOutlines/Pedi-atricNPTCO-Aug2013.aspx

APRN Joint Dialogue Group. (2008). *Consensus model for APRN regulation: Licensure, accreditation, certification & education.* Retrieved from http://www.nursecre-dentialing.org/APRN-ConsensusModelReport.aspx

Ard, K., & Makadon, H. (2012). *Improving the health care of lesbian, gay, bisexual and transgender (LGBT) people: Understanding and eliminating health dispari-ties.* The Fenway Institute, Fenway Health. Retrieved from http://www.lgbthealtheducation.org/wp-content/ uploads/12--054_LGBTHealtharticle_v3_07--09--12.pdf

Campbell, J. (1980). The relationship of nursing and self-awareness. *Advances in Nursing Science, 2*(4), 15–25.

DeHart, D. (2008). Breast health behavior among les-bians: The role of health beliefs, heterosexism, and homophobia. *Women & Health, 48,* 409–427.

Eliason, M., Dibble, S., & DeJoseph, J. (2010). Nursing's silence on lesbian, gay, bisexual, and transgender issues: The need for emancipatory efforts. *Advances in Nursing Science, 33,* 206–218.

Fenway Health. (2013). *2014 Fenway Health. Fenway at a glance. Our mission.* Retrieved from http://www. fenwayhealth.org/site/DocServer/13.160_FenwayAtA-Glance_v3_08.19.2013.pdf? docID=11281

Fenway Institute. (n.d.). *Publications and presenta-tions.* Retrieved from http://www.fenwayhealth.org/site/ PageServer?pagename=FCHC_ins_fenway_Publications

Fenway Institute. (n.d.). *Publications and presenta-tions.* Retrieved from http://thefenwayinstitute.org/ publications-presentations/

Flemmer, N., Doutrich, D., Dekker, L., & Rondeau, D. (2012). Creating a safe and caring health care context for women who have sex with women. *Journal for Nurse Practitioners, 8*, 464–469, 481.

Fowler, M. (Ed.). (2010). *Guide to code of ethics for nurses: Interpretation and application.* Silver Spring, MD: Nursesbooks. org.

Gallup. (2013). *Gallup politics. Congress retains low honesty rating. Nurses have highest honesty rating; car salespeople, lowest.* Retrieved from http://www.gallup.com/poll/159035/congress-retains-low-honesty-rating.aspx

Gates, G. (2013). *Same sex and different sex couples in the American Community Survey: 2005-2011.* Los Angeles, CA: Williams Institute. Retrieved from http://williamsinstitute.law.ucla.edu/research/census-lgbt-demographics-studies/ss-and-ds-couples-in-acs-2005--2011/

GMLA: Health Professionals Advancing LGBT Equality. (2013). *About GMLA.* Retrieved from http://www.glma.org/index.cfm?fuseaction=Page.viewPage&pageId=532

Harcourt, J. (2006). Current issues in lesbian, gay, bisexual, and transgender (LGBT) health; introduction. *Journal of Homosexuality, 51*(1), 1–11.

Hinchliff, S., Gott, M., & Galena, E. (2005). 'I daresay I might find it embarrassing': General practitioners' perspectives on discussing sexual health issues with lesbian and gay patients. *Health and Social Care in the Community, 13*, 345–353.

Human Rights Campaign. (2013). *Healthcare equality index.* Retrieved from http://www.hrc.org/hei/#.UoOVDOKO7zM.

Institute of Medicine. (2011a). *The health of lesbian, gay, bisexual, and transgender people: Building a foundation for better understanding.* Washington, DC: National Academies Press.

Institute of Medicine. (2011b). *Report brief. The health of lesbian, gay, bisexual, and transgender people: Building a foundation for better understanding.* Retrieved from http://www.iom.edu/~/media/Files/Report%20Files/2011/The-Health-of-Lesbian-Gay-Bisexual-and-Transgender-People/LGBT%20Health%202011%20Report%20Brief.pdf

International Gay and Lesbian Human Rights Commission. (2013a). *Home.* Retrieved from http://www.iglhrc.org/

International Gay and Lesbian Human Rights Commission. (2013b). *Information by country.* Retrieved from http://www.iglhrc.org/content/information-country

Johns, C. (2004). *Becoming a reflective practitioner* (2nd ed.). Malden, MA: Blackwell.

Johnson, C., Mimiaga, M., & Bradford, J. (2008). Health care issues among lesbian, gay, bisexual, transgender and intersex (LGBTI) populations in the United States: Introduction. *Journal of Homosexuality, 54*, 213–224.

The Joint Commission. (2011). *Advancing effective communication, cultural competence, and patient- and family-centered care for the lesbian, gay, bisexual, and transgender (LGBT) community: A field guide.* Oakbrook Terrace, IL: Author. Retrieved from http://www.jointcommission.org/assets/1/18/LGBTFieldGuide.pdf

Keepnews, D. (2011). Lesbian, gay, bisexual, and transgender health Issues and nursing: Moving toward an agenda. *Advances in Nursing Science, 34*, 163–170.

Lambda Legal. (n.d.). *About us. Who we are.* Retrieved from http://www.lambdalegal.org/about-us

Lambda Legal. (2010a). *Lambda Legal releases health care discrimination survey results: More than half of LGBT and HIV positive respondents report discrimination.* Retrieved from http://www.lambdalegal.org/news/ny_20100204_lambda-releases-health

Lambda Legal. (2010b). *When health care isn't caring: Lambda Legal's survey of discrimination against LGBT people and people with HIV.* Retrieved from http://www.lambdalegal.org/publications/when-health-care-isnt-caring

Lim, F., Brown, D., & Jones, H. (2013). Lesbian, gay, bisexual, and transgender health: Fundamentals for nursing education. *Journal of Nursing Education, 52*, 198–203.

Martin, K., Hutson, D., Kazyak, E., &Scherrer, K. (2010). Advice when children come out: The cultural "tool kits" of parents. *Journal of Family Issues, 31*, 960–991.

National Certification Corporation. (2013). *2014 candidate guide women's health care practitioner.* Retrieved from http://www.nccwebsite.org/resources/docs/2013-whnp-candidate_guide.pdf

National Coalition for LGBT Health. (n.d.). About us. Retrieved from http://lgbthealth.webolutionary.com/about

National LGBT Education Center. (2013). *Affirmative care for transgender and gender non-conforming people: Best practices for front-line health care staff.* Boston, MA: Author.

National Organization Nurse Practitioner Faculties. (2013). *Population focused nurse practitioner competencies.* Retrieved from http://c.ymcdn.com/sites/www.nonpf.org/resource/resmgr/competencies/populationfocusnpcomps2013.pdf

National Student Nurses Association. (2012). *In support of implementing practices suggested in The Joint Commission report, "Advancing effective communication, cultural competence, and patient and family centered care for the lesbian, gay, bisexual, and transgender (LGBT) community: A field guide."* Retrieved from http://www.nsna.org/Portals/O/Skins/NSNA/pdf/20.pdf

Snowden, S. (2013). *Healthcare equality index 2013: Promoting equitable & inclusive care for lesbian, gay, bisexual and transgender patients and their families.*

Retrieved from http://www.hrc.org/files/assets/resources/HEI_2013_final.pdf

U.S. Department of Health and Human Services. (2013). Healthy people 2020. *Lesbian, gay, bisexual, and transgender health.* Rockville, MD: Author. Retrieved from http://www.healthypeople.gov/2020/topicsobjectives2020/overview.aspx?topicid=25

Williamson, I. (2000). Internalized homophobia and health issues affecting lesbians and gay men. *Health Education Research, 15,* 97–107.

Community Participation for Transformative Action on Women's, Children's, and Adolescents' Health

by Cicely Marston[a], Rachael Hinton[b], Stuart Kean[c], Sushil Baral[d], Arti Ahuja[e], Anthony Costello[f] & Anayda Portela[f]

Abstract *The Global strategy for women's, children's and adolescents' health (2016–2030)* recognizes that people have a central role in improving their own health. We propose that community participation, particularly communities working together with health services (co-production in health care), will be central for achieving the objectives of the global strategy. Community participation specifically addresses the third of the key objectives: to transform societies so that women, children and adolescents can realize their rights to the highest attainable standards of health and well-being. In this paper, we examine what this implies in practice. We discuss three interdependent areas for action towards greater participation of the public in health: improving capabilities for individual and group participation; developing and sustaining people-centred health services; and social accountability. We outline challenges for implementation, and provide policy-makers, programme managers and practitioners with illustrative examples of the types of participatory approaches needed in each area to help achieve the health and development goals.

[a] London School of Hygiene & Tropical Medicine, London, England.
[b] Partnership for Maternal, Newborn & Child Health, Geneva, Switzerland.
[c] World Vision International, Milton Keynes, England.
[d] Health Research and Social Development Forum (HERD), Kathmandu, Nepal.
[e] Department of Health and Family Welfare, Government of Odisha, Bhubaneswar, India.
[f] World Health Organization, Avenue Appia 20, 1211 Geneva 27, Switzerland.
Correspondence to Anayda Portela (email: portelaa@who.int). *(Submitted: 26 December 2015 – Revised version received: 18 February 2016 – Accepted: 18 February 2016)*

Introduction

The *Global strategy for women's, children's and adolescents' health (2016–2030)* calls for action towards three objectives for health: survive (end preventable deaths), thrive (ensure health and well-being) and transform (expand enabling environments).[1] The strategy recognizes that "women, children and adolescents are potentially the most powerful agents for improving their own health and achieving prosperous and sustainable societies". Global, national and sub-national development policies have until now been largely orientated towards addressing the objectives of helping people to survive and thrive. However, to accomplish the overall objectives of the strategy we need to address the third objective: "to transform societies so that women, children and adolescents everywhere can realize their rights to the highest attainable standards of health and well-being". Transforming societies requires participation, including communities working together with health services to reach health goals (what is termed co-production). In this paper, we examine what this implies in practice.

Community participation is promoted in global dialogue as a vital element of a human rights-based approach to health. This means not just ensuring the provision of health services and their use by the public but also tackling the underlying social determinants of health.[2] While proven clinical and health service interventions could save numerous lives by 2030, if they were made available to all, those people most in need of health care are often not reached.[3,4] Many factors – wealth, environment, gender, education, geography, culture and other structural determinants – affect health outcomes directly through health services uptake, and indirectly via relationships and behaviours outside the clinic setting.[5,6] Community participation that is inclusive of underserved groups and is tailored to context is a fundamental principle of equitable primary health care as well as a way of optimizing interventions to improve health.

Participatory approaches

In this paper we examine the concepts of participation and co-production in health care with a focus on health services and communities working together to achieve health goals. Here we define communities as groups of people who share common interests, concerns or identities in settings that are defined by geography, culture, administrative boundaries or geopolitical region or that are identified with joint activities, such as work or recreation.[7,8]

Participatory approaches and the characteristics of participation have been defined in different ways.[9] Some authors[10] distinguish between organic participation such as community-organized actions, contrasting this with induced participation that is externally stimulated. Members of the community may be involved in the latter type to a greater or lesser extent, with participation ranging from outreach and consultation at one end of the spectrum of participation to collaboration and shared leadership at the other end.[11] Countries or programmes may move along the spectrum as they gain experience or according to their objectives.

In this paper we discuss externally-stimulated community participation that falls at the collaboration and shared leadership end of the participation spectrum. This is not to say the burden of resolving health issues is placed on communities. To be transformative, participatory approaches in health require power-sharing with health-service users. This is likely to mean new relationships, including a new culture in health-care institutions that supports participation.[9,12]

Participation does not usually operate as a linear intervention to improve health; rather participatory approaches form a set of complex processes and interactions.[10,11,13] An approach that is based on systems theory is useful to understand participation processes, whereby interdependencies between different parts of a system are explicitly recognized and nonlinear effects are expected to occur and are taken into account.[14]

Issues of power and control should be considered, both to understand systems better and to ensure that participatory interventions do not unintentionally reinforce potentially harmful social structures.[2,8] This means looking at who is engaged, why and in what way. For example, including only men as participants in a programme might reinforce pre-existing gender inequities. Failing to seek out underserved groups may further entrench inequities.

> **Box 1. The four phases of participatory learning and action cycles**
>
> Facilitated participatory learning and action cycles with women's groups involve a four-phase participatory process with a trained facilitator, in which women's groups collectively decide on priority actions, and try to organize activities accordingly. The cycle is structured as follows: (i) identify and prioritize problems that may occur during pregnancy, childbirth and after birth; (ii) plan activities; (iii) implement strategies to address the priority problems; (iv) assess the activities and plan changes as needed.[17]

> **Box 2. Example of a participatory approach to strengthen community support for pregnant women**
>
> In Andhra Pradesh state, India, a participatory intervention attempted to increase demand for quality care through meetings to raise awareness and increase community support for pregnant women; involving families (particularly husbands) in pregnancy-related care; and bi-monthly home visits by a community organizer who helped families access care and create birth preparedness plans. Local elected leaders also held regular meetings to review performance of public health providers and facilities. Afterwards, women reported changes in support received from family members during pregnancy and childbirth and decreased workload during their pregnancy.[21]

Areas for action

To achieve social transformation, participatory approaches in health need to work alongside each other at different levels. We identify three areas for action: (i) individual and community capabilities to participate; (ii) people-centred health services; and (iii) social accountability. These areas align with existing frameworks such as the capabilities approach[15] and health promotion charters[16] that highlight the need to attend to factors outside the traditional realm of health services, including the role of different participants in the production of health.

The three areas are interrelated and should be addressed in parallel. For instance, without improved capabilities for participation on all sides, it will be a challenge to introduce community participation in quality improvement efforts in support of a more people-centred health service. A supportive policy environment that identifies social accountability mechanisms will legitimize and support participatory processes at all levels.

Improving capabilities

For individuals to develop as agents of change and for participatory processes to work well, individuals and groups need the capabilities to achieve the health goals they value.[15]

Facilitated participatory learning and action cycles with women's groups have been identified as an effective way to build individual and group capabilities, to identify and prioritize problems and to develop a plan for implementing locally feasible strategies to address these (Box 1).[17] Freire's concept of critical consciousness (a deepened awareness of the social, political and economic situation, including health, that leads one to understand that one can intervene and that these realities can be transformed) has also been emphasized in participatory learning.[18] Others have proposed that all humans need to feel competent, autonomous and related to others.[19,20] A positive social environment can yield better psychological, developmental and behavioural outcomes by helping meet these three key needs, that is, by supporting people in their activities and giving them a sense of volition and choice.[19,20] When supported to develop their own skills, individuals may voluntarily support others, for example by sharing breastfeeding techniques or setting up support groups, thereby introducing a layer of sustainability independent of the original intervention.

Supportive environments, therefore, are also key determinants of good health and healthy practices (Box 2).[22] Unsupportive environments in society may, for example, deter young people from obtaining condoms or women from breastfeeding in public. Participatory interventions encourage dialogue and can help identify socially-and culturally-acceptable solutions.[23] For instance, strategies to promote men's involvement during pregnancy, childbirth and after birth are recommended to improve care practices for women and newborns. However, these interventions should be designed in dialogue with women to avoid undermining women's choices, autonomy and decision-making.[24]

People-centred services

A key goal in global health is creating people-centred health services, that is, services orientated around the needs and preferences of users rather than around diseases.[25] Achieving this requires participatory approaches. Participation of service users in planning, governance and quality improvement processes, as well as community partnerships with services, can help to make health services and health professionals more responsive to the needs of their clients and the wider community.[11,24–26] The World Health Organization recommends community participation in quality

improvement processes for maternity care services and in programme planning and implementation to improve maternal and newborn health.[24] Others have emphasized the importance of community empowerment for improving care services for women after an abortion.[27]

Participation by members of under-served groups may stimulate services towards more equitable provision of care.[25,28] Attempts to address the needs of excluded groups have included engaging community members as mediators or employing health staff from the relevant culture, for example, to develop culturally-appropriate maternity care services. Another approach is strengthening efforts to build stronger relationships and dialogue between communities, institutions and service providers about the care required.

Box 3. Example of patient participation and co-production in health services quality improvement

In the National Health Service in England, long-term ethnographic study has shown how projects involving patients, clinicians and researchers working together in non-hierarchical teams have helped empower patient participants to collaborate with clinicians to devise healthcare improvements.[30] For example, a patient-held record called My Medication Passport was developed by and for patients, particularly those using multiple services. It is a patient-completed aide memoire containing information about the patient's clinical history and medication. Patients can carry this to appointments to facilitate communication with clinicians, as well as between clinical teams.[31] Patient participants have also played a key role in linking up clinical and non-clinical services.[14]

Box 4. Example of improving service delivery with participatory monitoring

In a randomized field experiment of community-based monitoring of primary health-care providers in the public health system in Uganda, community perceptions of health facilities were summarized into report cards. A community meeting was held to present the reports to the community and share information about health rights. Community members and health staff developed action plans including details of how the community would monitor agreed actions. Service uptake and quality of services improved. After one year, for instance, 36% of treatment facilities had a suggestion box, compared with none in the control facilities. The treatment facilities posted more information on free services and patient rights and obligations, were kept in better condition, had higher uptake of vaccinations and better indicators of service use than the control facilities. The study also reported a 33% reduction in under-five mortality.[39]

Social transformation requires the people who are in control to share their power.[18] This principle has been taken up in the National Health Service in England, which aims to create a culture of shared decision-making, aspiring to create equal partnerships between clinicians, patients and carers and with patients involved in co-design, co-commissioning and, overall, co-production of health care.[29] Converting the aspirations into reality is not easy, although there have been successes (Box 3).[12]

Participatory health interventions require an interactive approach by health-care providers that changes the usual patient–provider dynamic. The skills of health-care providers may need to be developed to help them collaborate with service users or community members[32,33] and to move from solving problems for patients, to solving problems with patients. Health facility leadership that supports this type of collaboration is also essential for people-centred care.[25] A better work environment and greater job satisfaction can improve health-care workers' sense of autonomy and their motivation to engage in respectful care and quality improvement processes.[34,35] If health-care workers appear reluctant to engage in dialogue with patients, the overall work environment needs to be examined to help understand why this is and to address any institutional barriers to health-care workers' autonomy and motivation.

Social accountability

Accountability is central for progress in women's, children's and adolescents' health.[1] Citizens' voices are important to build equitable health systems and to provide quality health services, particularly in settings with poor governance.[36]

The World Bank identifies four factors vital for any social accountability programme: (i) the opportunities for information exchange, dialogue and negotiation between citizens and the state; (ii) the willingness and ability of citizens and civil society to seek government accountability; (iii) the willingness and ability of service providers and policymakers to support constructive engagement with citizens; and (iv) the broader environment that enables increased civic engagement (such as the policy, legal and regulatory environment; the type of political system, the values and norms of society).[37]

Members of the community need to recognize their entitlement to health but also understand the constraints of health systems. This enables them to play an integral role in planning, implementing, monitoring and evaluating policies and services, and identifying workable solutions. Common strategies for participation in accountability processes include community representation in health facility management committees,[26] village health committees, community taskforces or citizens' hearings,[38] as part of community-monitoring processes (Box 4).[11] These processes are dynamic: skills are needed to achieve dialogue and to build the trust required for the different participants to plan and work together.[24] Implementation efforts should raise awareness among individuals and communities (for example, by providing information about health services or promoting awareness of entitlements) and address aspects of the social

context that might affect participation (such as fear of speaking out). Health-service managers can take first steps to gain confidence in participatory processes, such as setting up complaints or comments boxes for patients to use, or publishing health-services statistics to inform and prompt discussion between health, development and community stakeholders. Once they gain experience they can move on to more sophisticated engagement processes.[39,40]

Challenges

Participation is frequently emphasized in global, regional and national health policies, yet we lack examples of large-scale, transformative action in practice. Some challenges to implementation of participatory approaches are outlined below.

Not all approaches described as community or participatory successfully achieve participation or transformation. Our experience suggests this may be because these concepts are often too broadly applied. There may be little open, ongoing dialogue, or no attempt to achieve the collaborative styles of working that are essential for co-production in health care. Selecting and training community health workers, for example, is often classified as a community participation approach. While many community health workers deliver information or services outside clinics or provide a link between communities and health services, they do not necessarily represent the views of the community nor do their tasks necessarily require them to consult with the community. Similarly, nongovernmental organizations (NGOs) are sometimes seen to reflect the voice of the community, despite not having consulted with members of communities or been nominated as their representatives.[41]

Community members may become more committed, engaged and motivated if they see positive results from participatory activities.[12] Conversely, communities may become disengaged from the process if there is no obvious positive effect of engagement or, for instance, if workings of committees are not transparent.[41] A study in Malawi found that attempts by NGOs to foster participation can create expectations that cannot be maintained and can potentially undermine other ways for the community to participate.[42]

> **Box 5. Example of scaling up participatory interventions**
>
> Facilitated participatory learning and action cycles with women's groups (see Box 1) to address maternal and newborn health in poor rural communities were shown to improve newborn health outcomes.[44] A meta-analysis of studies from Bangladesh, India, Malawi and Nepal showed newborn deaths decreased by one third in settings where groups with at least 30% of pregnant women came together to address issues around the health of the mother and the baby.[17]
>
>   Scale-up of women's groups has been undertaken in Odisha state, India. Local experience of greater equity after an intervention involving women's groups, combined with a state-level emphasis on evidence-based policy, prompted a new community dialogue intervention called Shakti Varta. Launched in 2013, Shakti Varta was intended to cover a population of 20 million people across 15 districts (half of the state) who have many health and nutrition challenges.[45] Challenges common to scale-up efforts have been encountered; for instance how to ensure fidelity to the important elements of the intervention across the project districts, and how to ensure high-quality training and implementation.

Hierarchies within health care may make adopting and integrating participatory approaches especially difficult to achieve. For example, if there is no open dialogue about quality improvement within the health service, engaging the users of the service in the discussion will also be difficult. A participatory, respectful management philosophy in the system as a whole provides a foundation for transforming relations with communities.[12,35] It is not enough simply to tell others to use these approaches with community members. For example, if central- or regional-level managers do not communicate with district-level staff, or if different service providers (such as doctors, midwives) do not feel respected by one another and do not work as a team, they are less likely to have the empathy or motivation required for positive, transformative encounters with the community. Health-care workers may also resist the processes of accountability for fear of reprimand or punishment.

Good intentions about participatory approaches may not always be accompanied by the support needed for implementation. The Government of India has promoted a system for women to register complaints with health facility managers or through patient welfare committees. Reports, however, suggest that the procedures may not be clear and that women are not always aware they can make a complaint against a doctor or nurse or they fear reprisals if they do so.[43]

How to scale up participatory approaches is not always clear from the literature, despite the case studies and success stories that exist at district level.

The level of ambition demonstrated by the initiative in Odisha state of India remains rare (Box 5).

Finally, the existing literature reveals little agreement on how to evaluate the impact of participatory approaches. The existence of participatory activities can be demonstrated but it is often difficult to link them to health outcomes. There are several reasons for this: (i) because of the complexities of linking social change directly to health outcomes; (ii) because participatory activities often take place within a package of interventions and so the effects of participation cannot be separated out; and (iii) because health outcomes are so strongly influenced by the performance of the health sector and other social determinants. Furthermore, health improvements and uptake of services are only part of the story; measurement of participatory approaches should also account for any resulting social change, such as changes in equitable use of services, changes in social and gender dynamics, and issues relating to sustainability.[10,11]

Discussion

Achieving transformative action towards improving the health of women, children and adolescents will depend on deploying locally appropriate participatory approaches at community, health service and policy level across the three action areas described in this paper. These contributions will influence whether proven biomedical health interventions reach the intended populations and whether the global goals for sustainable development are met.

The challenge is that to be transformative, power must be shared with health service users. To do this entails building new relationships and fostering a new culture in health-care institutions that is supportive of participatory approaches.[9,12] Participatory approaches need to be embedded throughout the health system: internally (within healthcare teams and between levels of the health system), as well as externally (between services and communities).

Participatory approaches are particularly important in decentralized health systems where local leadership is promoted, because there is more opportunity for bottom-up partnership between communities and health services, including in decision-making processes and community accountability mechanisms.[46]

Interventions can fail because of poor design and implementation. Programme managers and practitioners need to pay attention to detail in implementing participatory approaches, just as an immunization campaign needs to pay attention to the cold-chain supply or to staff training. For example, to build awareness and mobilize the community around a specific issue, attention should be paid to how facilitators are selected and trained, who is participating in the meetings and why, whether training manuals for participants are appropriate to their experience and education, whether meetings are held at convenient times and places, whether there is adequate coverage and frequency of those meetings and how information is shared among peers.

Although participation may be regarded as desirable in itself, participatory approaches are neither widely practised nor well documented. There is a growing evidence base supporting the use of participatory approaches to improve health, but concerted effort is needed to develop better and more relevant measures of participatory interventions and to gain agreement on what is to be measured and how. Factors that are difficult to measure, such as social change, may often be ignored. To understand the mechanisms and dimensions of participation and transformative action, it will be important to measure such factors more adequately.

More guidance on specific community-oriented interventions is required to help inform country and donor investments. We need to understand what works, how different approaches can work in different contexts and what factors need to be taken into account for future scaling up and sustainability of interventions.[47]

All three objectives of the global strategy – survive, thrive and transform – will benefit from participatory approaches in the areas we have described. Indeed, to some extent, progress towards the sustainable development goals could be measured by the presence of mechanisms to enable participatory approaches and co-production in health care to develop in practice.

We know much already about the power of participation. In a sense it is no longer a technical issue, but one of civil rights and political will. For transformative action on women's, children's and adolescents' health, participatory approaches are essential, at all levels: district, national, regional and global. Without these, we face the risk of stalled progress and persisting inequities in health. ∎

Acknowledgements

We thank Alicia Renedo.

Competing interests: None declared.

References

1. Global Strategy for Women's, Children's and Adolescents' health (2016–2030). New York: Every Woman Every Child; 2015. Available from: http://globalstrategy.everywomaneverychild.org/pdf/EWEC_ globalstrategyreport_200915_FINAL_WEB.pdf [cited 2015 July 23].

2. Rifkin SB. Examining the links between community participation and health outcomes: a review of the literature. Health Policy Plan. 2014 Sep;29 Suppl 2:ii98–106. doi: http://dx.doi.org/10.1093/heapol/czu076 PMID: 25274645

3. O'Connell T, Sharkey A. Reaching universal health coverage through district health system strengthening: using a modified Tanahashi model subnationally to attain equitable and effective coverage. Geneva: United Nations Children's Fund; 2013.

4. Requejo J, Bryce J, Victora CG. Fulfilling the health agenda for women and children: the 2014 report. Geneva: United Nations Children's Fund and World Health Organization; 2014.

5. Bohren MA, Hunter EC, Munthe-Kaas HM, Souza JP, Vogel JP, Gülmezoglu AM. Facilitators and barriers to facility-based delivery in low- and middle-income countries: a qualitative evidence synthesis. Reprod Health. 2014;11(1):71. doi: http://dx.doi.org/10.1186/1742-4755-11-71 PMID: 25238684

6. Victora CG, Barros AJ, Axelson H, Bhutta ZA, Chopra M, França GV, et al. How changes in coverage affect equity in maternal and child health interventions in 35 countdown to 2015 countries: an analysis of national surveys. Lancet. 2012 Sep 29;380(9848):1149–56. doi: http://dx.doi.org/10.1016/S0140-6736(12)61427-5 PMID: 22999433

7. Goodman RA, Bunnell R, Posner SF. What is "community health"? Examining the meaning of an evolving field in public health. Prev Med. 2014 Oct;67 Suppl 1:S58–61. doi: http://dx.doi.org/10.1016/j.ypmed.2014.07.028 PMID: 25069043

8. George AS, Mehra V, Scott K, Sriram V. Community participation in health systems research: a systematic review assessing the state of research, the nature of interventions involved and the features of engagement with communities. PLoS ONE. 2015;10(10):e0141091. doi: http://dx.doi.org/10.1371/journal.pone.0141091 PMID: 26496124

9. Aveling EL, Jovchelovitch S. Partnerships as knowledge encounters: a psychosocial theory of partnerships for health and community development. J Health Psychol. 2014 Jan;19(1):34–45. doi: http://dx.doi.org/10.1177/1359105313509733 PMID: 24195915

10. Mansuri G, Rao V. Localizing development: does participation work? Washington: World Bank; 2013.

11. Marston C, Renedo A, McGowan CR, Portela A. Effects of community participation on improving uptake of skilled care for maternal and newborn health: a systematic review. PLoS ONE. 2013;8(2):e55012. doi: http://dx.doi.org/10.1371/journal.pone.0055012 PMID: 23390509

12. Renedo A, Marston CA, Spyridonidis D, Barlow J. Patient and public involvement in healthcare quality improvement: how organizations can help patients and professionals to collaborate. Public Manage Rev. 2015;17(1):17–34. doi: http://dx.doi.org/10.1080/14719037.2014.881535

13. Rifkin SB, Muller F, Bichmann W. Primary health care: on measuring participation. Soc Sci Med. 1988;26(9):931–40. doi: http://dx.doi.org/10.1016/0277-9536(88)90413-3 PMID: 3388072

14. Renedo A, Marston C. Spaces for citizen involvement in healthcare: an ethnographic study. Sociology. 2015 Jun;49(3):488–504. doi: http://dx.doi.org/10.1177/0038038514544208 PMID: 26038612

15. Ruger JP. Health capability: conceptualization and operationalization. Am J Public Health. 2010 Jan;100(1):41–9. doi: http://dx.doi.org/10.2105/AJPH.2008.143651 PMID: 19965570

16. The Ottawa charter for health promotion. In: First International Conference on Health Promotion; 1986 Nov 21; Ottawa, Canada. Geneva: World Health Organization; 1986.

17. Prost A, Colbourn T, Seward N, Azad K, Coomarasamy A, Copas A, et al. Women's groups practising participatory learning and action to improve maternal and newborn health in low-resource settings: a systematic review and meta-analysis. Lancet. 2013 May 18;381(9879):1736–46. doi: http://dx.doi.org/10.1016/S0140-6736(13)60685-6 PMID: 23683640

18. Friere P. Pedagogy of the oppressed. New York: Herder and Herder; 1970.

19. Ryan RM, Deci EL. Self-determination theory and the facilitation of intrinsic motivation, social development, and well-being. Am Psychol. 2000 Jan;55(1):68–78. doi: http://dx.doi.org/10.1037/0003-066X.55.1.68 PMID: 11392867

20. Deci EL, Ryan RM. Facilitating optimal motivation and psychological well-being across life's domains. Can Psychol. 2008;49(1):14–23. doi: http://dx.doi.org/10.1037/0708-5591.49.1.14

21. Sinha D. Empowering communities to make pregnancy safer: an intervention in rural Andhra Pradesh. [Health and Population Innovation Fellowship Programme Working Paper No. 5]. New Delhi: Population Council; 2008.

22. Marston C, King E. Factors that shape young people's sexual behaviour: a systematic review. Lancet. 2006 Nov 4;368(9547):1581–6. doi: http://dx.doi.org/10.1016/S0140-6736(06)69662-1 PMID: 17084758

23. Figueroa ME, Kincaid DL, Rani M, Lewis G. Communication for social change: an integrated model for measuring the process and its outcomes. New York: Rockefeller Foundation; 2002.

24. WHO recommendations on health promotion interventions for maternal and newborn health. Geneva: World Health Organization; 2015.

25. WHO global strategy on people-centred and integrated health services [interim report]. Geneva: World Health Organization; 2015.

26. McCoy DC, Hall JA, Ridge M. A systematic review of the literature for evidence on health facility committees in low- and middle-income countries. Health Policy Plan. 2012 Sep;27(6):449–66. doi: http://dx.doi. org/10.1093/heapol/czr077 PMID: 22155589

27. Solo J, Curtis C, Malarcher S, Leonard A. Post abortion care. Washington: United States Agency for International Development; 2004.

28. Coast E, Jones E, Portela A, Lattof SR. Maternity care services and culture: a systematic global mapping of interventions. PLoS ONE. 2014;9(9):e108130. doi: http://dx.doi.org/10.1371/ journal.pone.0108130 PMID: 25268940

29. Liberating the NHS: no decision about me without me [Internet]. London: National Health Service England. Available from: http://www.england.nhs. uk/ourwork/pe/sdm/ [cited 2016 Feb 10].

30. Renedo A, Marston C. Healthcare professionals' representations of 'patient and public involvement' and creation of 'public participant' identities: implications for the development of inclusive and bottom-up community participation initiatives. J Community Appl Soc Psychol. 2011;21(3):268–80. doi: http://dx.doi.org/10.1002/casp.1092

31. Barber S, Thakkar K, Marvin V, Franklin BD, Bell D. Evaluation of My Medication Passport: a patient-completed aide-memoire designed by patients, for patients, to help towards medicines optimisation. BMJ Open. 2014;4(8):e005608. doi: http:// dx.doi.org/10.1136/bmjopen-2014-005608 PMID: 25138809

32. Baatiema L, Skovdal M, Rifkin S, Campbell C. Assessing participation in a community-based health planning and services programme in Ghana. BMC Health Serv Res. 2013;13(1):233. doi: http:// dx.doi.org/10.1186/1472-6963-13-233 PMID: 23803140

33. Realpe A, Wallace L. What is co-production? London: The Health Foundation; 2010.

34. Alhassan RK, Spieker N, van Ostenberg P, Ogink A, Nketiah-Amponsah E, de Wit TF. Association between health worker motivation and healthcare quality efforts in Ghana. Hum Resour Health. 2013;11(1):37. doi: http://dx.doi.org/10.1186/1478-4491-11-37 PMID: 23945073

35. Weston MJ. Strategies for enhancing autonomy and control over nursing practice. Online J Issues Nurs. 2010;15(1). Manuscript 2. doi: http://dx.doi. org/10.3912/OJIN.Vol15No01Man02

36. Lodenstein E, Dieleman M, Gerretsen B, Broerse JE. A realist synthesis of the effect of social accountability interventions on health service providers' and policymakers' responsiveness. Syst Rev. 2013;2(1):98. doi: http://dx.doi.org/10.1186/2046-4053-2-98 PMID: 24199936

37. Social accountability in the health sector. In: Social accountability sourcebook. Washington: World Bank; 2002. Available from: http://www.worldbank. org/socialaccountability_sourcebook/PrintVersions/ Health%20 06.22.07.pdf [cited 2016 Mar 21].

38. Green C. Nothing about us, without us: citizens' voices for women's, children's and adolescents' health. Washington: White Ribbon Alliance; 2015.

39. Björkman M, Svensson J. Power to the people: evidence from a randomized field experiment on community-based monitoring in Uganda. Q J Econ. 2009;124(2):735–69. doi: http://dx.doi.org/10.1162/ qjec.2009.124.2.735

40. Kaseje D, Olayo R, Musita C, Oindo CO, Wafula C, Muga R. Evidence-based dialogue with communities for district health systems' performance improvement. Glob Public Health. 2010;5(6):595–610. doi: http://dx.doi. org/10.1080/17441690903418969 PMID: 20162482

41. George A, Scott K, Garimella S, Mondal S, Ved R, Sheikh K. Anchoring contextual analysis in health policy and systems research: a narrative review of contextual factors influencing health committees in low and middle income countries. Soc Sci Med. 2015 May;133:159–67. doi: http://dx.doi.org/10.1016/j. socscimed.2015.03.049 PMID: 25875322

42. A framework for analysing participation in development. Oxford: Oxford Policy Management; 2013.

43. Bowser D, Hill K. Exploring evidence for disrespect and abuse in facility-based childbirth: report of a landscape analysis. Washington: United States Agency for International Development; 2010.

44. WHO recommendation on community mobilization through facilitated participatory learning and action cycles with women's groups for maternal and newborn health. Geneva: World Health Organization; 2014.

45. Mission shakti [Internet]. Bhubaneswar: Government of Odisha, Women and Child Development Department; 2001. Available from: http://wcdodisha. gov.in/node/52 [cited 2016 Mar 21].

46. Health systems: decentralization [Internet]. Washington: World Bank; 2011. Available from:

http://web.worldbank.org/WBSITE/EXTERNAL/TOPICS/EXTHEALTHNUTRITIONAND-POPULATION/EXTHSD/0,,contentMDK:2019 0818~menuPK:438810~pagePK:148956~piPK: 216618~theSitePK:376793,00. html [cited 2015 Dec 6].

47. Katz AS, Cheff RM, O'Campo P. Bringing stakeholders together for urban health equity: hallmarks of a compromised process. Int J Equity Health. 2015;14(1):138. doi: http:// dx.doi.org/10.1186/s12939-015-0252-1 PMID: 26590020

Cultural Humility versus Cultural Competence: A Critical Distinction in Defining Physician Training Outcomes in Multicultural Education

by Melanie Tervalon and Jann Murray-García

Abstract Researchers and program developers in medical education presently face the challenge of implementing and evaluating curricula that teach medical students and house staff how to effectively and respectfully deliver healthcare to the increasingly diverse populations of the United States. Inherent in this challenge is clearly defining educational and training outcomes consistent with this imperative. The traditional notion of competence in clinical training as a detached mastery of a theoretically finite body of knowledge may not be appropriate for this area of physician education. Cultural humility is proposed as a more suitable goal in multicultural medical education. Cultural humility incorporates a lifelong commitment to self-evaluation and self-critique, to redressing the power imbalances in the patient-physician dynamic, and to developing mutually beneficial and nonpaternalistic clinical and advocacy partnerships with communities on behalf of individuals and defined populations.

The increasing cultural, racial, and ethnic diversity of the United States compels medical educators to train physicians who will skillfully and respectfully negotiate the implications of this diversity in their clinical practice.

Simultaneously, increasing attention is being paid to nonfinancial barriers that operate at the level of the physician/patient dynamic. This dynamic is often compromised by various sociocultural mismatches between patients and providers, including

"Cultural Humility versus Cultural Competence: A Critical Distinction in Defining Physician Training Outcomes in Multicultural Education," by Melanie Tervalon and Jann Murray-Garcia, *Journal of Health Care for the Poor & Underserved*, 9:2 (1998), 117–125. Reprinted by permission of The Johns Hopkins University Press.

providers' lack of knowledge regarding patients' health beliefs and life experiences, and providers' unintentional and intentional processes of racism, classism, homophobia, and sexism.

Several recent national mandates calling for innovative approaches to multicultural training of physicians have emerged from various sources. The Pew Health Professions Commission, specifically seeking to give direction to health professions education for the twenty-first century, stated that "cultural sensitivity must be a part of the educational experiences that touches the life of every student." The Institute of Medicine defines *optimal primary care* as including "an understanding of the cultural, nutritional and belief systems of patients and communities that may assist or hinder effective healthcare delivery."

The necessity for multicultural medical education provides researchers and program developers with the challenge of defining and measuring training outcomes and proving that chosen instructional strategies do indeed produce these outcomes. However, in the laudable urgency to implement and evaluate programs that aim to produce cultural competence, one dimension to be avoided is the pitfall of narrowly defining competence in medical training and practice in its traditional sense: an easily demonstrable mastery of a finite body of knowledge, an endpoint evidenced largely by comparative quantitative assessments (i.e., MCATs, pre- and post-exams, board certification exams).

Rather, cultural competence in clinical practice is best defined not by a discrete endpoint but as a commitment and active engagement in a lifelong process that individuals enter into on an ongoing basis with patients, communities, colleagues, and with themselves (L. Brown, MPH, Oakland health advocate, personal communication, March 18, 1994). This training outcome, perhaps better described as cultural humility versus cultural competence, actually dovetails several educational initiatives in U.S. physician workforce training as we approach the twenty-first century. It is a process that requires humility as individuals continually engage in self-reflection and self-critique as lifelong learners and reflective practitioners. It is a process that requires humility in how physicians bring into check the power imbalances that exist in the dynamics of physician-patient communication by

using patient-focused interviewing and care. And it is a process that requires humility to develop and maintain mutually respectful and dynamic partnerships with communities on behalf of individual patients and communities in the context of community-based clinical and advocacy training models.

Self-reflection and the Lifelong Learner Model

Increasing trainees' knowledge of health beliefs and practices is critically important. For instance, the Cambodian child who comes in with the linear marks of "coining," a Southeast Asian healing practice, should not be mistaken for the victim of parental child abuse.

To be avoided, however, is the false sense of security in one's training evidenced by the following actual case from our experience: An African American nurse is caring for a middle-aged Latina woman several hours after the patient had undergone surgery. A Latino physician on a consult service approached the bedside and, noting the moaning patient, commented to the nurse that the patient appeared to be in a great deal of postoperative pain. The nurse summarily dismissed his perception, informing him that she took a course in nursing school in cross-cultural medicine and "knew" that Hispanic patients overexpress "the pain they are feeling." The Latino physician had a difficult time influencing the perspective of this nurse, who focused on her self-proclaimed cultural expertise.

This nurse's notion of her own expertise actually stereotyped the patient's experience, ignored clues (the moaning) to the patient's present reality, and disregarded the potential resource of a colleague who might (albeit not necessarily) be able to contribute some relevant cultural insight. The equating of cultural competence with simply having completed a past series of training sessions is an inadequate and potentially harmful model of professional development, as evidenced by this case.

In no way are we discounting the value of knowing as much as possible about the healthcare practices of the communities we serve. Rather, it is imperative that there be a simultaneous process of self-reflection (realistic and ongoing self-appraisal) and commitment to a lifelong learning process. In this way, trainees are ideally flexible and humble enough to let go of the false sense of security that stereotyping brings. They are flexible and humble enough to assess anew the cultural dimensions of the experiences of each patient. And finally, they are flexible and humble enough *to say that they do not know when they truly do not know* and to search for and access resources that might enhance immeasurably the care of the patient as well as their future clinical practice.

In a related manner, an isolated increase in knowledge without a consequent change in attitude and behavior is of questionable value. In fact, existing literature documenting a lack of cultural competence in clinical practice most reflects not a lack of knowledge but rather the need for a change in practitioners' self-awareness and a change in their attitudes toward diverse patients. These data indicate that the prescription of clinical resources from prevention services to potentially life-saving procedures is often differential, dependent on the race or ethnicity of the patient. For example, a study in a university emergency department showed that Latinos were half as likely as white patients to receive analgesia for the same, usually very painful, long-bone fractures, regardless of the linguistic capability or insurance status of the patient. A follow-up study in the same institution showed no difference in physicians' assessment of the level of pain experienced by white and Latino patients experiencing the same, isolated injury. Another study showed that while African Americans are twice as likely to go blind from progressive ophthalmologic diseases such as glaucoma, they are half as likely to receive sight-saving procedures. Such disturbing evidence from the medical profession is a sobering reflection of the parallel reality and tragic costs of racism that persist in American society and that potentially influence every physician.

Clearly, program developers and researchers cannot, in our cultural competency training, simply stimulate a detached, intellectual practice of describing "the other" in the tradition of descriptive medical anthropology. At the heart of this education process should be the provision of intellectual and practical leadership that engages physician trainees in an ongoing, courageous, and honest process of self-critique and self-awareness.

Guiding trainees to identify and examine their own patterns of unintentional and intentional racism, classism, and homophobia is essential.

One way to initiate such a constructive process is to have trainees think consciously about their own, often ill-defined and multidimensional cultural identities and backgrounds. In leading trainees into this process of cultivating self-awareness and awareness of the perspectives of others, trainers and program planners have used the following pedagogical approaches with success: small-group discussions; personal journals; availability of constructive professional role models from cultural groups and from the trainee's groups; and videotaping and feedback, including directed introspection of residents' interactions with patients. Recognition and respect for others' cultural priorities and practices is facilitated by such initial and ongoing processes that engender self-knowledge.

At the same time and by the same process of self-reflection, awakening trainees to the incredible position of power physicians potentially hold over all patients, particularly the poor, is critical. Especially in the context of race, ethnicity, class, linguistic capability, and sexual orientation, physicians must be taught to repeatedly identify and remedy the inappropriate exploitation of this power imbalance in the establishment of treatment priorities and health promotion activities.

Again, humility, and not so much the discrete mastery traditionally implied by the static notion of competence, captures most accurately what researchers need to model and hold programs accountable for evaluating in trainees under the broad scope of multicultural training in medical education.

Patient-focused Interviewing and Care

Embodied in the physician who practices cultural humility is the patient-focused or language-focused interviewing process. Studies of patient-physician communication have shown a strong bias on the part of physicians against patient-initiated questions and agendas, with physicians in one study initiating over 90 percent of the questions. Another study demonstrated that although poor and minority patients wanted as much information regarding their conditions as did other patients, they received less information regarding their conditions, less positive or reinforcing speech, and less talk overall.

Patient-focused interviewing uses a less controlling, less authoritative style that signals to the patient that the practitioner values what the patient's agenda and perspectives are, both biomedical and nonbiomedical. With these communication skills, perhaps along with other specifically cross-cultural interaction techniques, physicians potentially create an atmosphere that enables and does not obstruct the patient's telling of his or her own illness or wellness story. This eliminates the need for a complete mastery of every group's health beliefs and other concerns because the patient in the ideal scenario is encouraged to communicate how little or how much culture has to do with that particular clinical encounter.

For example, Ridley describes the uniqueness of a patient by detailing the patient's "conjoint membership in eight cultural roles:" as a Mexican American, male, father, husband, Catholic, mechanic, night-school student, and resident of East Los Angeles. Only the patient is uniquely qualified to help the physician understand the intersection of race, ethnicity, religion, class, and so on in forming his (the patient's) identity and to clarify the relevance and impact of this intersection on the present illness or wellness experience. Relevant and effective prevention, health promotion, and therapeutic strategies can then be developed that take into account the patient's life priorities, health beliefs, and life stressors. Humility is a prerequisite in this process, as the physician relinquishes the role of *expert* to the patient, becoming the *student* of the patient with a conviction and explicit expression of the patient's potential to be a capable and full partner in the therapeutic alliance.

Community-based Care and Advocacy

There is increasing consensus that a substantial portion of physicians' clinical training needs to occur in community sites. It is argued that training needs to happen in arenas where most physicians will eventually practice, away from the university-based, largely tertiary medical center. Part of this training directive includes a population-based

approach to health promotion and disease prevention that works toward the optimal health of communities; that is, health in its broadest sense of physical, mental, and social wellbeing. Evans states that "surely a small part of each physician's responsibility should extend beyond the care of individual patients to the advocacy for changes in the community's policies and practices that influence determinants of health, causes of disease, and the effectiveness of health services."

Competency in advocacy is actually mandated by the American Academy of Pediatrics as a skill to be acquired during pediatric residency. This professional skill is to be taught by way of "structured educational experiences that prepare residents for their future role as advocates for the health of all children . . . with particular attention to underserved populations."

It is hoped that community-based care and advocacy training would go beyond working with community physicians and even beyond training in legislative advocacy to include systematically and methodically immersing trainees in mutually beneficial, nonpaternalistic, and respectful working relationships with community members and organizations. Experiencing with the community the factors at play in defining health priorities, research activities, and community-informed advocacy activities requires that the physician trainee recognize that foci of expertise with regard to health can indeed reside outside of the academic medical center and even outside of the practice of Western medicine. Competence, thus, again becomes best illustrated by humility, as physician trainees learn to identify, believe in, and build on the assets and adaptive strengths of communities and their often disenfranchised members. Requiring ongoing self-reflection and a parallel notion of patient- (community-) focused interactions, the possibility then exists for planning, practice, and advocacy in community health work in which physicians and physician trainees are both effective students of and partners with the community.

Institutional Consistency

The same processes expected to affect change in physician trainees should simultaneously exist in the institutions whose agenda is to develop cultural competence through educational programs. Self-reflection and self-critique at the institutional level is required, encompassing honest, thorough, and ongoing responses to the following questions: What is the demographic profile of the faculty? Is the faculty composition inclusive of members from diverse cultural, racial, ethnic, and sexual orientation backgrounds? Are faculty members required to undergo multicultural training as are the youngest students of the profession? Does the institutional ethos support inclusion and respectful, substantive discussions of the clinical implications of difference? What institutional processes contradict or obstruct the lessons taught and learned in a multicultural curriculum (i.e., if it is taught that practitioners should not use children or other family members as translators, does the institution provide an accessible alternative?)? What is the history of the healthcare institution with the surrounding community? And what present model of relationship between the institution and the community is seen by trainees?

Time-limited and explicit educational goals are one dimension of demonstrated institutional cultural competence. For instance, developing a written plan of faculty recruitment and/or curricular development to be in place by a designated date could be a point to which the community and/or other external entities hold the institution publicly accountable with regard to issues of race, ethnicity, language, culture, sexual orientation, and class in healthcare.

Summary of the Challenge to Medical Education Researchers

The emphasis on demonstration of process as opposed to endpoint is not meant to imply that training outcomes in cultural competence programs cannot be measured or monitored. Capturing the characteristic of cultural humility in individuals and institutions is possible, especially with mixed methodologies that use qualitative methods (including participant observation, key informant interviews, trainees' journals, and mechanisms for community feedback) and action research models to complement traditional quantitative assessments

(pre- and postknowledge tests, patient and trainee surveys) of program effectiveness. A potentially valuable measure is the documentation of an active, ongoing institutional process that includes training, established recruitment and retention processes, identifiable and funded personnel to facilitate the meeting of program goals, and dynamic feedback loops between the institution and its employees and between the institution and patients and/or other members from the surrounding community.

This is not to say that the measurement of individuals' or institutions' cultural competence is a well-developed area of research. Witness this present discussion on defining training outcomes. Indeed, the definition and measurement of program effectiveness in producing cultural competence is a relatively new arena of inquiry in need of careful and attentive intellectual leadership. Nonetheless, acknowledging the necessity for creativity in a program's development and evaluation stages will help avoid the pitfall of adopting the status quo in documenting clinical competence.

Conclusion

In this critically important dialogue of defining training outcomes, it is proposed that the notion of cultural humility be distinguished from that of cultural competence. Cultural humility incorporates a lifelong commitment to self-evaluation and critique, to redressing the power imbalances in the physician-patient dynamic, and to developing mutually beneficial and non-paternalistic partnerships with communities on behalf of individuals and defined populations.

Acknowledgments

This work was supported by grants from the California Wellness Foundation, the Federal Office of Minority Health (DHHS), the East Bay Neonatology Foundation, and the Bay Area Physicians for Human Rights.

References

A list of references is available in the original source.

Inequalities and Health

1. Culturally competency models have been defined in many ways and cultural competency has become the standard training requirement for service providers to better understand and interact with their patients/clients. Self-assessment is an important step in cultural competency training. Self-assessment begins with how one identifies their self—racially, culturally, languages spoken, sexual orientation, and the place one grew up. These are all important factors in how one thinks about health in general and the healthcare system. Conduct your own self-assessment by describing your background. Describe the ways your background and where you live may influence your experience(s) with and access to the healthcare system.

2. Joe Feagin and Zinobia Bennefield outline how racism continues to play a significant role in persistent disparities and barriers in healthcare. Describe the barriers to healthcare in today's society and who is most affected. In what ways do these barriers impact the broader society? What measures would you employ to reduce barriers?

3. What is the legacy and lessons that today's healthcare practitioners need to understand from Vanessa Northington Gamble's article on the Tuskegee syphilis study?

4. Develop a culturally relevant model to address disparities in the Lesbian, Gay, Bisexual, Transgender, Queer, plus (LBGTQ+) community. What best practices would you recommend to improve the interactions between healthcare practitioners and the LGBTQ+ community?

5. Describe the differences between Cultural Humility by Tevalon and Murray-Garcia and Cultural Competency outlined by the Office of Minority Health (see Resource List in the back of the book). Develop your own model to assist practitioners in delivering quality healthcare services.

6. How does historical trauma affect one's health, the healthcare system, and ability to develop culturally relevant protocols for communities of color to improve their interactions with healthcare practitioners?

Sex, Gender Roles, and Image

3

Many inequalities in our society are reinforced through the perpetuation of gendered and sexed norms, including the notion that sex and gender are biologically determined and defined by binaries (men/women; male/female). Sex and gender are in fact socially and culturally constructed; yet, they dictate acceptable roles, behaviors, as well as body images. This chapter introduces important terms, explores what is at stake when sex and gender are narrowly defined, and addresses body image issues.

This chapter begins with *Sexing the X: How the X Became the "Female Chromosome"* by Sarah Richardson, in which she traces how the human X chromosome has become associated with femaleness. Despite the fact that both males and females have X chromosomes, scientists have utilized the X chromosome to justify male supremacy and explain female "quirks and weaknesses." Richardson argues that the ways in which the X chromosome has been sexed female signifies "a case of gender-ideological bias in science, both historically and in the present day." She suggests that scientists redefine the relationship between sex and the X chromosome and develop new explanatory models.

Next, *Transgender Youth: Providing Medical Treatment for a Misunderstood Population* by Stephanie Brill and Jennifer Hastings offers medical providers a very much needed overview of the transgender youth population. The article provides comprehensive information about what it means to be transgender, an understanding of how one comes to know they are transgender, and the steps taken in transitioning. While there is limited information on how many children and teens are transgender, the medical community across

the United States, Netherlands, United Kingdom, and other places across Europe all agree that early treatment for transgender youth "can change—and even save—lives." *Transmen's Health is a "Women's Health" Issue: Expanding the Boundaries of Sexual and Reproductive Health Care* by E. Cameron Hartofelis and Anu Gómez is another article published by the National Women's Health Network. It addresses specific barriers that trans men face when seeking sexual and reproductive healthcare. While this article could belong in a number of chapters, we place it here because it explicitly defines "transgender" and "trans man" as well as emphasizes how trans men face discrimination due to their transgression of sex and gender norms. Health practitioners need to be aware of the specific health needs of trans men and be willing to administer compassionate care, regardless of a person's gender identity and presentation.

The second half of the chapter focuses on body image issues from the perspective of women. These articles explore how gender, race, age, and sociocultural factors impact basic physiological processes and how women feel about their bodies.

Is Fat a Feminist Issue? Exploring the Gendered Nature of Weight Bias by Janna Fikkan and Esther Rothblum reviews literature on weight bias experienced by fat women. Touching on a range of disciplines and domains, the authors outline research that documents discrimination faced by women in healthcare settings, as well as the workforce, romantic relationships, educational institutions, and the media. The authors state that, in terms of health and the present *war on obesity*, "fat women's health care is actually being compromised because of the bias of various healthcare professionals." The authors propose that feminist scholars begin to recognize weight-based discrimination and how it impacts women in specific localities, such as medical institutions.

Sonya Satinsky and Natalie Ingraham's *At the Intersection of Public Health and Fat Studies: Critical Perspectives on the Measurement of Body Size* interrogates the documentation of body size in the fields of public health and fat studies. The authors argue that scholars and practitioners need to measure body size and use techniques that are decoupled from "health and judgment" and are "not created for the purpose of further stigmatizing fat bodies." Although this article does not specifically focus on the experiences of women, it is useful for scholars and practitioners who work with diverse body types.

Christina Capodilupo and Jessica Forsyth, in their article, *Consistently Inconsistent: A Review of the Literature on Eating Disorders and Body Image among Women of Color* focus on the lived experiences of women of color. As many studies center on White women, the authors argue that the dominant understandings of eating disorders "are not meaningful for particular groups of women of

color." "Cultural and social group contexts differently ascribe meanings to both the physical body and eating/food." Researchers and practitioners need to acquire cultural competence and continue to examine the specific experiences of women of color with an intersectional lens.

The final article in this chapter, *Still Sucked into the Body Image Thing: The Impact of Anti-Aging and Health Discourses on Women's Gendered Identities* by Claire Carter explores how gendered health norms impact aging and older women. After interviewing a group of women about their body practices, she argues that "anti-aging and healthism reinforce normative femininity and limit the potential selves women can become." Anti-aging and health discourses have a disciplinary effect, influencing women to construct their gendered subjectivity and engage in particular practices that reify feminine norms. The discourses also produce anxiety and inner conflict for the study participants. Ultimately, Carter calls for alternative definitions and embodiments of femininity that open up greater possibilities of "who women can become."

Sexing the X: How the X Became the "Female Chromosome"

by Sarah S. Richardson

"**U**nexpected." "Counterintuitive." "Intellectually surprising." These were among the exclamations of researchers upon the 2001 discovery that the human X chromosome carries a large collection of male sperm genes (Wang et al. 2001). Although both males and females possess an X chromosome, the X is frequently typed as the "female chromosome" and researchers assume it carries the genes for femaleness. This essay traces the origins of this long-standing and infrequently questioned association of the X with femaleness and examines the influence of this assumption on historical and contemporary genetic theories of sex and gender difference.

Humans possess twenty-two pairs of autosomal chromosomes and one pair of sex chromosomes— X and Y for males, X and X for females. Today it is well established that the Y carries a critical genetic switch for male sex determination. The X, however, has no parallel relationship to femaleness. Female sexual development is directed by hormones acting in concert with genes carried by many chromosomes and is not localized to the X. Indeed, the X is arguably more important to male biology, given the large number of X-linked diseases to which men are uniquely exposed. Despite this, researchers attribute feminine behavior to the

X itself and assume that female genes and traits are located on it. Researchers look to the X to explain sex differences and female quirks and weaknesses and have argued that men are superior because they possess one fewer X than females.

The X chromosome offers a poignant example of how the gendering of objects of biological study can shape scientific knowledge. Moving freely between stereotypical conceptions of femininity and models of the X chromosome, X-chromosomal theories of sex differences reveal a circular form of reasoning that is familiar in gender analysis of biology. As Evelyn Fox Keller writes: "A basic form common to many [feminist analyses of science] revolves around the identification of synecdochic (or part for whole) errors of the following sort: (a) the world of human bodies is divided into two kinds, male and female (i.e., by sex); (b) additional (extraphysical) properties are culturally attributed to these bodies (e.g., active/passive, independent/dependent, primary/secondary: read *gender*); and (c) the same properties that have been ascribed to the whole are then attributed to the subcategories of, or processes associated with, these bodies" (1995, 87). A classic historical example of this phenomenon is the gendering of the egg and sperm in mid-twentieth-century medical textbooks, documented by Emily Martin (1991). A second example is the gendering of the sex steroids estrogen and testosterone, as told by Nelly Oudshoorn (1994) and Anne Fausto-Sterling (2000).

Rooted in history and philosophy of science, and drawing on the interdisciplinary methods and questions of feminist science studies forged by scholars such as Fausto-Sterling, Keller, Donna Haraway, and Martin, this essay investigates the sexing of the X in a variety of scientific materials both internal and external to the biosciences. The sexing of the X, I argue, represents a case of gender-ideological bias in science, both historically and in the present day. More generally, it demonstrates how biological objects and concepts may take on a gendered valence as they circulate between popular and scientific realms.

The female X has its roots in early sex chromosome science, which assumed for half a century—until the 1950s, when the Y was confirmed as the carrier of the sex-determining locus—that the X was female determining in humans. In the first part of

what follows, I document the contingent technical, material, and ideological factors that led to the feminization of the X during the first decades of sex chromosome research and track the introduction of the "female chromosome" into human genetics at midcentury. In the second part, I demonstrate the continuing influence of the historical feminization of the X on genetic research, exemplified by "X chromosome mosaicism" theories of female biology, behavior, and disease. Focusing on the case of X-mosaicism theories of the higher incidence of autoimmunity in women, I show how the assumption that the X is the female chromosome operates to sustain and cohere hypotheses of dubious empirical merit in research areas urgently relevant to women's health.

The feminine chromosome

Scientific and popular literature on the sex chromosomes is rich with examples of the gendering of the X and Y. The X is dubbed the "female chromosome," takes the feminine pronoun "she," and has been described as the "big sister" to "her derelict brother that is the Y" (Vallender, Pearson, and Lahn 2005, 343) and as the "sexy" chromosome (Graves, Gecz, and Hameister 2002). The X is frequently associated with the mysteriousness and variability of the feminine, as in a 2005 *Science* article headlined "She Moves in Mysterious Ways" and beginning, "The human X chromosome is a study in contradictions" (Gunter 2005, 279). The X is also described in traditionally gendered terms as the more sociable, controlling, conservative, monotonous, and motherly of the two sex chromosomes. Similarly, the Y is a "he" and ascribed traditional masculine qualities—macho, active, clever, wily, dominant, as well as degenerate, lazy, and hyperactive.[1]

There are three common gendered tropes in popular and scientific writing on the sex chromosomes. The first is the portrayal of the X and Y as a heterosexual couple with traditionally gendered opposite or complementary roles and behaviors. For instance, MIT geneticist David Page says, "The Y married up, the X married down. . . . The Y wants to maintain himself but doesn't know how. . . . He's falling apart, like the guy who can't manage to get a doctor's appointment or can't clean

---

[1] See, e.g., Burgoyne (1998), Angier (1999, 2007), Graves (2000), and Bainbridge (2003).

up the house or apartment unless his wife does it" (Dowd 2005). Biologist and science writer David Bainbridge (2003) describes the evolutionary history of the X and Y as a "sad divorce" (56) set in motion when the "couple first stopped dancing," after which "they almost stopped communicating completely" (58). The X is now an "estranged partner" of the Y, he writes, "having to resort to complex tricks" (145). Oxford University geneticist Brian Sykes (2003) similarly describes the X and Y as having a "once happy marriage" (283–84) full of "intimate exchanges" (42–43) now reduced to only an occasional "kiss on the cheek" (44). A 2006 article on X-X pairing in females in *Science* by Pennsylvania State University geneticist Laura Carrel is headlined "'X'-Rated Chromosomal Rendezvous" (2006).

Second, sex chromosome biology is often conceptualized as a war of the sexes. In Matt Ridley's *Genome: The Autobiography of a Species in 23 Chapters* (1999), the chapter on the X and Y chromosomes is titled "Conflict" and relates a story, straight from *Men Are from Mars, Women Are from Venus* (Gray 1992), of two chromosomes locked in antagonism and never able to understand each other (Ridley 1999, 107). A 2007 *ScienceNOW Daily News* article similarly insists on describing a finding about the Z chromosome in male birds (the equivalent of the X in humans) as demonstrating "A Genetic Battle of the Sexes" (Pain 2007), while Bainbridge (2003) describes the lack of a second X in males as a "divisive . . . discrepancy between boys and girls" (83), a genetic basis for the supposed war of the sexes.

Third, sex chromosome researchers promote the X and Y as symbols of maleness and femaleness with which individuals are expected to identify and in which they might take pride. Sykes offers the Y chromosome as a totem of male bonding, urges males to celebrate their unique Y chromosomes, and calls for them to join together to save the Y from extinction in his 2003 *Adam's Curse: A Future without Men*. Females are also encouraged to identify with their Xs. Natalie Angier (1999) urges that women "must take pride in our X chromosomes. . . . They define femaleness" (26). The "XX Factor" is a widely syndicated column about women's work/life issues on Slate.com, with the slogan "What Women Really Think"; it is also the name of an

annual competition for female video gamers.[2] The promotional video for the Society for Women's Health Research, designed to convince the viewer of how very different men and women really are, is titled "What a Difference an X Makes!" (Society for Women's Health Research 2008).

How the X became the female chromosome

The notion of the X as the female chromosome arises from its history as an object of research and its ensuing gendered valence within biological and popular theories of sex. It was originally assumed that the X, not the Y, was the sex-determining chromosome in humans. Theophilus S. Painter, the American cytogeneticist who in 1924 first described the human sex chromosomes, dubbed XX "the female chromosome complex" (1924, 509), the X the "female-producing chromosome" (509), and males as "heterozygous for sex" (522), as they possess only one X. This founding idea, that the X is "female-producing" (509) or female tending, focused theories of the biological determination of femaleness exclusively on the X well into the twentieth century.

Historically contingent technical and material factors also helped to brand the X as female. The dominance of studies of the fruit fly *Drosophila* in the first half-century of genetic research played a central role. Unlike in mammals, in *Drosophila* the X is female determining. This is a threshold effect, in which sex is determined by the ratio of autosomes to X chromosomes, with more Xs producing femaleness. In textbook explanations of sex chromosomes from the first quarter of the century, an ink drawing of *Drosophila* chromosomes was ubiquitously used to illustrate the section on the chromosomal theory of sex (Morgan 1915, 7; Wilson 1925). So pervasive were *Drosophila's* X and Y as the model for the sex chromosomes that the leading American geneticist, Thomas H. Morgan, dubbed the XX/XY chromosome constitution the "Drosophila type," writing that "The genetic evidence so far gained has placed in the Drosophila type the following animal forms: Drosophila, man, cat; and the plants, *Lychnis* and

---

[2] See *Slate's* "The XX Factor: What Women Really Think" blog at http://www.slate.com/blogs/xx_factor.html.

Bryonia" (1915, 78–79). The *Drosophila* model suggested that in humans, as in flies, the X should be expected to determine femaleness.

In the early days chromosomes were also studied almost exclusively in male gametes—the sperm. Looking at sperm, which as reproductive cells possess only one member of each chromosome set, a perfect dichotomy appeared: half the sperm cells had the X, and half did not. This led to a hyperbinary view of the X and Y. The sperm with an X always produces a female, and the X in the males' sperm is always inherited from the female parent. Failing to distinguish between the "sex" of the gamete and the sex of the organism, this distorted perspective helped to prematurely assign the X to femaleness.

Cytologists were originally "spermatologists" (Voeller 1968, 78–80), and spermatology played a large role in setting the research agenda, context, and motivation for sex chromosome studies. Sperm are plentiful, accessible, and easier to study than eggs or other human tissue. Thus, there are good reasons that male gametes were early chromosome researchers' tissue of choice. Nonetheless, the focus on sperm introduced a bias into early sex chromosome research. The centrality of maleness and male tissue to this research led scientists to the conclusion that the X is female and the Y is male. Had researchers looked at somatic tissue, the dichotomy would have been far less clear-cut: both males and females possess at least one X.

The human cytogenetic research revolution of the late 1950s and 1960s, which revealed that it is the Y that determines sex, marked the demise of the X-chromosomal model of human femaleness. After World War II, human genetics research reemerged in the wake of massive US investments in education, life science research, and medicine. Charged with the task of assessing the long-term health and biological consequences of nuclear fallout, human cytogenetics—the study of the structure, behavior, and function of human chromosomes—burst onto the scene in the 1950s with a series of profound and triumphant discoveries. These included confirmation that humans possess forty-six chromosomes (rather than forty-eight, as had been universally believed); the revelation that an extra chromosome 21 causes Down syndrome; the understanding that the Y, not the X, is sex determining; and the identification, through population screening, of a host of surprisingly common human sex chromosome anomalies (see de Chadarevian 2006; Harper 2006).

The first significant breakthrough for human sex chromosome research was the identification of a condensed body present only in female cells. Discovered in 1949, the Barr body, an artifact of the presence of two X chromosomes, suddenly allowed nuclear sexing of any human cell (Barr and Bertram 1949). Murray Barr described the revelation that the "nuclei bear a clear imprint of sex" (Barr 1959, 681) as the "principle of nuclear sexual dimorphism" (682). The notion that every cell has a sex shifted the terms of human sex research and ushered sex difference into the genetic age. Screening for the presence of a Barr body allowed sex chromosome aneuploidies (numerical errors), such as Turner syndrome (XO) and Klinefelter syndrome (XXY), as well as a host of exotics, such as XXXs, XXXYs, XYYs, to be detected well before more detailed chromosome analysis and visualization techniques became available.

By the 1960s, human sex chromosome aneuploidies and other chromosomal anomalies had become potent symbols of the fascinating and exciting new genetics. The historian of midcentury genetics Soraya de Chadarevian (2006, 724–25) argues that this chromosome symbolism, along with the representational schema of the human karyotype, was the public icon of modern genetics in the 1950s and 1960s, before the double helix took its place. It was through this imagery, and the novelty of sex chromosome aneuploidies, that the public first became widely conscious of the X and Y as the molecular pillars of biological femaleness and maleness.

The official findings of human cytogenetics of the 1950s and 1960s were as follows: Human males and females possess twenty-two pairs of autosomes and a pair of sex chromosomes. Males have an X and a Y, and females have two X chromosomes. In females one X in each cell is inactivated early in development, equalizing dosage of X-chromosomal genes in males and females. Subsequent research revealed that the Y chromosome primarily carries a gene that initiates male sexual development and bears few other genes. In contrast, the X chromosome is similar to an autosome, with more than a thousand genes. The X plays no special role in female development, which is controlled by a variety of genes on several different chromosomes.

The idea that the X was female determining was promptly discarded in light of these new findings. The female or feminine resonance that had accumulated around the X chromosome, however, did not fall away. As Fiona Alice Miller (2003) notes with respect to the term "Mongolism" for trisomy 21 (Down syndrome), "Contrary to conventional beliefs about new, breakthrough technologies, the introduction of chromosome analysis in the late 1960s did not displace existing standards of interpretation and practice" (76). Old habits and the force of the idea of a molecular gender binary revealed in the X and Y were irresistible. As the Y would be the male chromosome, the X would continue to be the female one.

Researchers did not give up the search for a relationship between the double X and femaleness in the wake of the 1959 finding that the Y is sex determining. They would continue to ask: What does the extra X do for females? What does an exposed, single X do for males? Elaborated in human genetics over the coming decades, the X and Y became sites for the enactment and rediscovery of traditional gender roles and stereotypes.

X-chromosomal theories of human sex differences

The question of whether the second X bestows human females with something extra, or whether it is more advantageous to have a single X chromosome, a question charged with gender politics, stalked the X from its earliest appearance in the public and scientific consciousness. Though human chromosome research was sporadic prior to the 1950s, the notion that human females carry an extra chromosome found its way into the scientific and social discourse around gender, a discourse that seems to have widely accepted the idea that the facts of biology would help to settle the sex wars and that we should expect to find definitive proof in the X of a sexual hierarchy.

On one side was the idea that double-X females are superior, advantaged, or special as a result of their extra X. This was appropriated by women's advocates: "The ancient idea that the female is essentially an undeveloped male seems to be finally disproved by the fact that it requires more determiners—usually one more chromosome, or a larger sex chromosome—to produce a female than a male," pronounced the feminist psychologist Helen Thompson Woolley (1914, 354). Even the notorious antifeminist Louis Berman conceded in his 1921 *The Glands Regulating Personality* that biologists could no longer seek the source of female inferiority in the chromosomes: "For the time being, let the feminists glory in the fact that they have two more chromosomes to each cell than their opponents. Certainly there can be no talk here of a natural inferiority of women" (1921, 136).[3] The anthropologist and public intellectual Ashley Montagu marshaled the notion of female X chromosome advantage in his 1953 text *The Natural Superiority of Women*. In a chapter titled "'X' Doesn't Equal 'Y,'" Montagu argued that it is "to the presence of two well appointed, well furnished X-chromosomes that the female owes her biological superiority" (1953, 76). Males, with their "X-chromosomal deficiency" (76), fall prey to such diseases as hemophilia and colorblindness, and countless other speculated weaknesses, while females, owing to an extra X, are "constitutionally stronger than the male" (81). Montagu asserted that females' extra X "lies at the base of practically all the differences between the sexes and the biological superiority of the female to the male" (74).

The discourse of female X-chromosomal superiority persisted in the second half of the twentieth century and even continues today. The size of the X and its large number of genes is frequently celebrated, and great emphasis is placed on the notion that, due to the second X, females have more genetic material than males. For example, *Time* magazine reported in 1963: "Because the X chromosome is so much bigger than the Y, women with two X's have 4 percent more genetic material—the vital deoxyribonucleic acid, or DNA—than men. Geneticists have speculated that this might explain women's longer life span. . . . [This] definitely gives women an inherent advantage over men" ("Research Makes It Official," 1963). Johns

---

[3] Berman's assertion that females possess "two more chromosomes" reflects the understanding of female-determining gametes as carrying an "extra" X chromosome. If females receive an extra chromosome from each parent, then in the full chromosome complement, females would be expected to have two more chromosomes than males.

Hopkins geneticist Barbara R. Migeon argues that the second X means that "females have a little extra determinant" compared with males, which "bestows a remarkable biological advantage" (2007, 208). "When it comes to the battle of the sexes," writes E. J. Mundell (2007), reporting on Migeon's work, "nature hands women extra ammunition right from the start. The reason, according to geneticists: Females are gifted with two copies of the powerful X chromosome, while males are born with only one X, plus the relatively weak Y chromosome." Migeon, whose research I will return to below, even argues that the extra genetic material might account for why females and males have a different sense of humor and could explain why "from the first days of school, girls outperform boys, are more attentive, and are more persistent at tasks" (2006, 1432–33).[4]

Countering claims of female X-chromosome superiority has been the far more influential notion that females are the weaker sex precisely because they carry an extra X chromosome. In the early twentieth century, prominent scientists asserted that the single X provided the biological mechanism for superior male cognition. They argued that while the single X may subject males to damaged genes on the X, it also exposes them more wholly to advantageous genes. The risks that males take with their sole X are countered by rich potential rewards. While females enjoy the security of a second X, it dulls their potential for extraordinariness. Males are superior where it counts: intelligence.

Highly influential in sex difference research, the "greater male variability" theory of male intellectual superiority framed research on cognitive differences between males and females from the 1870s to the 1930s. It was subsequently discredited with the rise of new experimental techniques, greater statistical sophistication, and large-scale empirical psychological testing. These studies showed no significant differences between males and females in overall intelligence and demonstrated that, while men were more likely to be at the very low end of the IQ scale, they were not equally likely to be at the high end.

Charles Darwin was among the most prominent adherents of the concept of greater male variability. In *The Descent of Man* ([1871] 1897), he argued that males are the engine of evolution, accumulating variations that lead to species divergence and evolution. For this reason, he wrote, "Man is more courageous, pugnacious, and energetic than woman, and has a more inventive genius" (557). In the nineteenth and early twentieth centuries, the principal evidence for the greater male variability hypothesis was the long-observed predominance of males among residents of what were then known as institutions for the "feeble-minded" and, conversely, among the ranks of genius and the socially eminent. Early twentieth-century observations of an excess of males among the intellectually disabled and documentation of a large number of mentally impairing X-linked conditions exclusive to males led to speculations that the single X was a mechanism for the observed "greater variability" in male intellect—and that the double X was a source of female dullness (Stevenson et al. 1994, 538).

The earliest geneticist to attach the X to male variability and female conservatism was Clarence E. McClung (1899, 1902), who first discovered the link between the X and sex. McClung later wrote of the X chromosome, "It is possible that we have here the explanation of the greater variability of the male" (1918, 162). He continued, "There is a possibility that in the male, the sex [X] chromosome being unmated, or opposed by an inactive element, may be more free to react with the other chromosomes and in this way change their constitution, being in turn affected by the reaction. By the nature of its transmission it must, after this experience, pass into the female line where its relation to the complex is necessarily different. The contrast in these two conditions is obvious and the interpretation strongly suggested" (162). The X-chromosomal theory of male intellectual superiority cyclically resurfaced in sex difference research throughout the twentieth century, and continues to lurk in X chromosome studies today. As the BBC reported in 2005: "Men also have another reason for feeling upbeat about their genetic lot. *New Scientist* reports that although men are more likely to be mentally retarded, they are also more likely to be geniuses. Although the average IQ of men and women is equal, men are more frequently

---

[4] While it is certainly true that a second X shields females from many X-linked diseases, the presence of "extra" genetic material cannot be said to establish any of these claims to female superiority. After all, chimpanzees and corn have more DNA than humans.

found at both extremes of intelligence. This is because, if you have very good intelligence genes on your X chromosome, it pays not to have them muffled by more average genes on another X chromosome" (Kettlewell 2005). Robert Lehrke's *Sex Linkage of Intelligence* (1997) exhumes and reasserts, in near entirety, the greater male variability theory of the late nineteenth and early twentieth centuries. Ongoing research programs at the Medical Research Council in London and University of California–Los Angeles in the United States continue to engage in X chromosome research on the subject—a pursuit that has only been heightened in the wake of the sequencing of the human X in 2005. As a *Nature* article puts it, today "the 'feminine' X chromosome is a prime hunting ground for geneticists interested in the evolution of the cognitive and cultural sophistication that defines the human species" (Check 2005, 266).

Tracking the female X into human genetics

The cases of Turner and Klinefelter syndromes demonstrate how the idea of the female-engendering X was carried forward into the human genetics era and how the notion of the female chromosome continued to inflect reasoning about human health and biology even after the X was found not to determine femaleness in humans. Both Turner and Klinefelter were well-documented syndromes of gonadal dysgenesis prior to human chromosome research. Physicians in the United States identified Turner syndrome in 1938 as a syndromic—meaning characterized by a complex of symptoms not localized to any single organ system—phenotype found exclusively in women. Traits included short stature, infertility, and neck webbing (Turner 1938). A Massachusetts General Hospital physician described Klinefelter syndrome in 1942 as a disorder of gonadal underdevelopment in males, resulting in hormonal deficiencies causing infertility and limited body hair (Klinefelter, Reifenstein, and Albright 1942).

Barr body screening in the 1950s revealed that Turner females lack a second X and that Klinefelter males carry an extra X. Once associated with sex chromosome aneuploidy in the 1950s, the disorders were redescribed in more strongly sexed and

gendered terms. The infertility of the XO Turner woman was portrayed as evidence of her masculinity rather than a disorder of female sexual development and of development in general. Turner women were claimed to have masculine cognitive traits such as facility with spatiality, discomfort with female gender roles, and defeminized body shape. XXY Klinefelter males were portrayed as feminine, with much emphasis on their purportedly unmuscular body frame, female body-fat distribution, lack of body hair, and infertility. The eminent British geneticist Michael Polanyi even proposed that XO females were "sex-reversed males" (Harper 2006, 79). Patricia A. Jacobs and John Anderson Strong (1959) described an XXY individual as "an apparent male . . . with poor facial hair-growth and a high-pitched voice" (302). They continued, "There are strong grounds, both observational and genetic, for believing that human beings with chromatin-positive nuclei are *genetic females* having two X chromosomes. The possibility cannot be excluded, however, that the additional chromosome is an autosome carrying feminizing genes" (302). A 1967 *New York Times* article similarly captures this mode of reasoning. With the headline "If her chromosomes add up, a woman is sure to be woman," it describes XXY males as having "a few female traits" (Brody 1967, 28). Studies were even undertaken to determine whether Turner women show a tendency toward lesbianism or Klinefelter men incline toward homosexuality or cross-dressing.[5]

These assumptions about the X as feminizing distorted understanding of these disorders, stigmatized individuals carrying them, and misdirected research and clinical care. Today, clinicians specializing in Klinefelter and Turner management emphasize that these are not diseases of gender confusion. Klinefelter patients are phenotypic males, and Klinefelter is not a syndrome of feminization. We now know that Klinefelter is one of the most common genetic abnormalities and often has so few manifestations that men live out their lives never knowing of their extra X. Writes Robert Bock (1993), "For this reason, the term 'Klinefelter syndrome' has fallen out of favor with medical

---

[5] See also Miller (2006) on the deliberations over the true gender of Turner and Klinefelter individuals in the decade after the discovery of the Barr body.

researchers. Most prefer to describe men and boys having the extra chromosome as 'XXY males.'" Similarly, XOs are phenotypic females. Turner syndrome, which has more profound and systemic phenotypic effects than XXY, is emphatically not a masculinizing condition. Physical deformities, heart trouble, infertility, and, occasionally, social and cognitive difficulties are the principal concerns for Turner females.

Throughout the history of twentieth-century genetics, gendered conceptions of the X chromosome fueled ideological conceptions of femaleness and maleness. Today the conception of the X as the female chromosome is not obsolete. It remains a common assumption in twenty-first-century genomics and a source of distortion and bias in genetic reasoning. We have already visited, briefly, some of the areas in which the female chromosome appears in contemporary biomedical research: the surprise over the finding of spermatogenesis genes on the X chromosome and X-linked theories of sex differences in intelligence. Perhaps the most prominent case of how the sexing of the X as female continues to operate today, however, is found in "X mosaicism" theories of female biology, health, and behavior.

Female X mosaicism

Mammalian females are genetic mosaics for the X chromosome. In order to equalize the expression of X-linked gene products in males and females, one of the Xs in each somatic cell is randomly inactivated early in female development. Approximately half of a female's cells will express the maternal X chromosome and half the paternal X chromosome. Thus, females have two populations of cells, identical with respect to the twenty-two pairs of autosomes but variable in X-chromosomal gene expression when females carry functionally different versions of an X-chromosomal allele.

X mosaicism has some implications for human female biology. Random X inactivation early in development leaves most women with a 50 : 50 ratio of cells expressing either their paternal or maternal Xs. As a result, females carrying a disease allele on one of their X chromosomes will generally not develop the disease, since cells carrying the other X usually produce adequate amounts of the needed gene product to compensate for any

dysfunction. For this reason, X mosaicism shields females from X-linked diseases. Classic X-linked diseases such as Duchenne muscular dystrophy or hemophilia are infrequent in women and generally affect only men.

In rare cases, X mosaicism will begin to skew, resulting in tissues biased toward the maternal or paternal X chromosome. Tissues grow clonally, so skewing can happen randomly as a result of a bias in the cells from which the tissue grows. As we age, chromosomes fray, whither, and disappear due to the erosion of genetic repair mechanisms, making skewing more common. Usually, skewed X mosaicism has no phenotypic consequence and goes unnoticed. If a woman carries an X chromosome disease allele, however, extreme skewed X inactivation leading to dominance of the chromosome carrying the disease-causing allele can, in rare cases, cause women to exhibit classic X-linked diseases generally restricted to men. Thus, the primary clinical implication of skewed X mosaicism for females is that it may leave them functionally monosomic for the X—like males—making them vulnerable to male-typical X-linked diseases.

Developed in the 1960s by British cytogeneticist Mary Lyon, the X inactivation hypothesis began as a theory of an evolutionary fix that could equalize the X gene product between males and females (Lyon 1992). It was transformed in the 1980s and 1990s into a theory of genetic difference between males and females, and among females. Today, X chromosome mosaicism, the consequence of random X inactivation, is strongly identified with femaleness and used loosely and flexibly, often without any gesture toward experimental validation, to explain biological sex differences. The identification of the X with females, the cultural association of females with chimerism, and the assumption that the sex binary observed in the world will eventually be revealed at the molecular level help to fill in the gaps in the X mosaicism theory of sex differences, veil its empirical deficiencies, and glue its premises together.

Gender in X mosaicism research

From its inception, the hypothesis that females are cellular mosaics for X-chromosomal genes was received as confirmation of dominant cultural assumptions about gender difference. The characterization of females as mosaics or chime-ras resonated with conceptions of women as more mysterious, contradictory, complicated, emotional, or changeable.[6] The future Nobel laureate molecular biologist Joshua Lederberg wrote in 1966, "The chimerical nature of woman has been a preoccupation of poets since the dawn of literature. Recent medical research has given unexpected scientific weight to this concept of femininity" (1966, E7).[7] Reporting on the new finding in 1963, *Time* magazine asserted that "the cocktail-party bore who laces his chatter with the tiresome cliché about 'crazy, mixed-up women' has more medical science on his side than he knows. . . . Even normal women, it appears, are mixtures of two different types of cells, or what the researchers call 'genetic mosaics'" ("Research Makes It Official," 1963).

Today, the notion of X mosaicism as scientific confirmation of traditional ideological conceptions of female instability, contradiction, mystery, complexity, and emotionality is thoroughly entrenched. As science writer Nicholas Wade told the *New York Times* in 2005, "Women are mosaics, one could even say chimeras, in the sense that they are made up of two different kinds of cell. Whereas men are pure and uncomplicated, being made up of just a single kind of cell throughout" (Dowd 2005). A 2005 Pennsylvania State University press release similarly announced, "For every man who thinks women are complex, there's new evidence they're correct; at least when it comes to their genes" ("Men and Women," 2005).

These metaphors and gender assumptions are widely shared by presentday sex chromosome researchers. Duke University geneticist Huntington Willard, for instance, is quoted saying, "Genetically speaking, if you've met one man, you've met them all. We are, I hate to say it, predictable. You can't say that about women," and Massachusetts Institute of Technology geneticist David Page says, "Women's chromosomes have more complexity, which men view as unpredictability" (Dowd 2005). British geneticist Robin Lovell-Badge has

similarly said that "10% [of genes on the X] are sometimes inactivated and sometimes not, giving a mechanism to make women much more genetically variable than men. I always thought they were more interesting!" (Kettlewell 2005).

Barbara Migeon, the Johns Hopkins X chromosome geneticist mentioned above and author of the book *Females Are Mosaics* (2007), is a leading promoter of the theory that X mosaicism is a fundamental mechanism of sex differences and a hallmark of female biology and behavior. Migeon claims that "somatic cellular mosaicism . . . has a profound influence on the phenotype of mammalian females" (1994, 230). According to Migeon, X mosaicism "creates biological differences between the sexes that affect every aspect of their lives, not just the sexual ones" (2007, 211). Migeon proposes that "cellular mosaicism . . . is likely to contribute to some of the gender differences in behavior" (209), including females' response to humor and differences in aggression, emotionality, and educational performance between males and females (2006, 1432–33). Molecular research on X chromosome mosaicism, Migeon argues, offers a promising platform for uncovering sex differences in the brain that studies of brain anatomy have not, thus far, revealed: "Despite dramatically different behavior between the sexes, surprisingly few anatomical differences have been identified," she writes, "[Perhaps] mosaicism for X-linked genes . . . may contribute to some of these sex differences in behavior" (2007, 211).

These speculative scientific conceptions of X mosaicism and femaleness are present in popular discourse around gender differences. Science reporter Natalie Angier, in *Woman: An Intimate Geography* (1999), celebrates female X chromosome mosaicism as a privilege of womanhood and a source of special womanly qualities. "Every daughter," she writes, "is a walking mosaic of clamorous and quiet chromosomes, of fatherly sermons and maternal advice, while every son has but his mother's voice to guide him" (25). She posits what she calls "the mystical X" as a source of "female intuition" and asserts that women "have . . . with the mosaicism of our chromosomes, a potential for considerable brain complexity" (25). Angier imagines a woman's X chromosomes as animating her brain with conflicting voices: "a woman's

---

[6] In biology, a genetic mosaic is distinct from a genetic chimera. Mosaics carry two different types of cells, whereas chimeras are made up of fused cells of two individuals or species. "Mosaic" and "chimera" are used interchangeably and with the same connotations in the literature on X mosaicism, however, and I follow suit here.

[7] Lederberg also notes, however, that the case of XXY males "complicates the myth that chimerism is femininity" (1966, E7).

mind is truly a syncopated pulse of mother and father voices, each speaking through whichever X, maternal or paternal, happens to be active in a given brain cell" (25).

Female X mosaicism is also invoked to bring the authoritative veneer of molecular science to traditional and pejorative views of femininity. Bainbridge's *The X in Sex: How the X Chromosome Controls Our Lives* (2003), for instance, asserts that X chromosome mosaicism confirms that "women are mixed creatures and men are not . . . in a way far deeper" than previously thought (130). Citing the roots of this notion in the Christian vision of Mary as "both virgin and mother" (129), Bainbridge claims that women "represent some intermediate hybrid state" (128), revealed in their "unpredictable, capricious nature" (127). X mosaicism is a "natural reminder of just how deeply ingrained the mixed nature of women actually is" (148), writes Bainbridge. He continues: "So women's bodies truly are mixed—in a very real way. . . . Each woman is one creature and yet two intermingled" (151).

Case study: X mosaicism theories of female autoimmunity

The case of X mosaicism theories of female autoimmunity shows clearly how contemporary biomedicine continues to find resources in the mercurial links between the X chromosome and femaleness. Autoimmune disorders are more prevalent in women than men.[8] The current medical model holds that autoimmunity occurs when the immune system mis-recognizes the body's own tissues as invaders, leading the system, finely tuned to eliminate foreign agents, to continually attack the body's tissues with all of its resources. Some researchers, noting the female prevalence of autoimmune diseases and seeing a parallel between the self-on-self attacks of autoimmunity and mosaic female tissues made up of cells expressing the maternal or paternal X chromosome, have sought a mechanism for autoimmunity in X mosaicism. These theories draw on the notion that the X chromosome mediates female biology and health, as

well as gender-inscribed conceptions of the female body as fundamentally chimeric, to link female autoimmunity to X mosaicism.[9]

The most basic version of the X mosaicism hypothesis of female autoimmunity is that simple mosaicism of the X chromosome, in cases in which the X produces two conflicting immune products, leads to auto-immunity. There is also a more sophisticated version, which holds that if mosaicism is skewed so that an immunologically relevant organ, such as the thymus gland, contains a majority of one X, the immune system may misrecognize tissues that carry the other X, leading to an autoimmune reaction (Kast 1977; Stewart 1998). Evidence for X mosaicism hypotheses of female autoimmunity has been sought in studies of skewed X mosaicism in women with autoimmune disorders. In these studies, researchers look at the percentage of cells carrying the maternal or paternal X chromosome (typically in a blood sample). When one predominates, if it is above a threshold of either 80 or 90 percent, the woman is deemed to have skewed X mosaicism.

These studies provide little evidence that X mosaicism is implicated in female predominance in autoimmunity. A higher rate of skewed X mosaicism than the general population has been demonstrated in just two cases: scleroderma (Ozbalkan et al. 2005) and autoimmune thyroid disorders (Ozcelik et al. 2006). It has not been found in the cases of lupus (Invernizzi et al. 2007), multiple sclerosis (Accelerated Cure Project 2006; Knudsen et al. 2007; Knudsen 2009), type 1 diabetes (Chitnis et al. 2000), or juvenile rheumatoid arthritis (Seldin et al. 1999), nor has it been found in the female-predominant and potentially autoimmune disorders of simple goiter (Brix et al. 2009) and recurrent pregnancy loss (Pasquier et al. 2007). There is conflicting, weak, or ambiguous evidence of an association with skewed X mosaicism in the case of primary biliary cirrhosis (Invernizzi 2007;

---

[8] For statistics on male and female incidence and prevalence of autoimmune diseases, see Jacobson et al. (1997), Walsh and Rau (2000), Lockshin (2006), Eaton et al. (2007), Cooper, Bynum, and Somers (2009), and McCombe, Greer, and Mackay (2009).

[9] Feminist science studies scholars Donna Haraway (1991), Emily Martin (1999), and Lisa H. Weasel (2001) are among those who have explored the relationship between immunity discourse and gendered metaphors and imagery, unpacking the parallels between "horror autotoxis" (medical researcher Paul Ehrlich's 1957 term for autoimmunity) and traditional conceptions of femininity. As Martin (1999) notes, the greater susceptibility of females to autoimmune disease, leading to suggestions that females are biologically "hybrid" (101) and "mixed-up" (103), aligns with ideological notions of females as double, divided against themselves, contradictory, unstable, and lacking in unitary selfhood.

Svyryd et al. 2010) and adult onset rheumatoid arthritis (Svyryd et al. 2010).

Even if studies were to document high rates of X skewing in women with certain autoimmune disorders, this would not, in any case, constitute sufficient evidence that skewed X mosaicism predisposes women to those disorders or that women are more inclined, in general, to autoimmunity. First, almost all X mosaicism studies use blood samples, looking at peripheral lymphocytes rather than cell types within the immune reaction pathways or organ systems of interest. This limits their significance. For example, women with the skin disease scleroderma show skewed mosaicism in their blood, but this skewing was not also found in the skin cells—the tissue of interest for the disorder in question. Second, these studies do not rigorously account for the confounding effect of age. Rates of both autoimmunity and X skewing increase with age in women (Russell et al. 2007), and to date studies of X mosaicism pattern variation do not persuasively disambiguate aging and autoimmunity.[10] Third, the X mosaicism hypothesis does not explain enough specific features of female predominance in autoimmunity to stand as a candidate for an explanation of the greater prevalence of autoimmunity in females. For example, the theory cannot explain the following: why the incidence of autoimmunity, but not the severity of the disease, differs between males and females; why female predominance is much more pronounced among the cohort diagnosed with autoimmune disorders under age 40, with rates becoming more equal between the sexes as they age; why some autoimmune disorders are female predominant, some are male predominant, and others are sex neutral; how X mosaicism interacts with the significant and well-documented role of environmental factors involved in sex differences in autoimmunity (such as chemicals in cosmetics or the workplace); and finally, why there is wide variability in sex ratios of autoimmune diseases between different ethnicities, nations, and in developed versus less-developed regions of the world (see Lockshin 2006, 2010; Oliver and Silman 2009).

In sum, although research is ongoing, the evidence for the X mosaicism hypothesis of female autoimmunity is weak. Degree of X skewing has not been found to be a predictive biomarker of autoimmunity, nor of response to therapy, and it has not been demonstratively linked to autoimmunity in animal models or in humans. Yet researchers confidently assert that X mosaicism mediates female autoimmunity: "autoimmune diseases revolve around the sex chromosomes," writes Carlo Selmi (2008, 913). Zoltan Spolarics (2007) claims that "X-chromosome mosaicism represents an adaptive cellular system" (599) bestowing females with "potentially two distinct regulatory and response arsenals" (598) and predisposing them to autoimmunity.

Such assertions by biomedical researchers that the XX chromosome complement inclines women to autoimmunity are clearly unwarranted. Studies of associations between X mosaicism patterns and autoimmunity do not substantiate a causal link between the two phenomena, nor do they show precisely how the presence of two populations of cells might contribute to autoimmune reactions. The evidence suggests, rather, that X mosaicism is far from a general theory of, or a major factor in, higher rates of autoimmune disorders in females.

The notion that X mosaicism underlies female autoimmunity has become so commonplace that it now regularly appears as authoritative medical knowledge in health news reports and is considered a leading viable hypothesis in much of the literature on autoimmunity.[11] The immediate credibility given by molecular biologists to X mosaicism theories of female autoimmunity, and the theory's widespread uncritical repetition in a variety of research, clinical, and health media contexts, requires explanation given the theory's weak empirical basis. The credulous reception of the theory is driven in part by the stubborn and commonplace belief, documented in this essay, that the gender binary of male and female is present, writ molecular, in the sex chromosomes. Just as the Y is putatively the male chromosome, the X chromosome must, it is

---

[10] The background picture of diversity of X mosaicism patterns in the general female population is also, on the whole, not well understood. James Amos-Landgraf et al. (2006), in the most credible study of its kind, looked at patterns in 1,005 phenotypically unaffected females, finding that skewing was relatively common. The study reported that fully 25 percent of females had patterns skewed at least to 70:30 and concluded that "with advancing age, there is greater variation in X inactivation-ratio distribution" (497).

[11] See, e.g., *Nature Genetics* (2000), Kruszelnicki (2004), Davies (2005), McCoy (2009), and Tingen (2009).

assumed, be a fundamental mediator of femaleness. Rooted in notions of the X as female, and chimerism as feminine, X mosaicism theories of female autoimmunity, I argue, present a contemporary case of synecdochic gendered conceptions of sex in biology leading to flawed scientific reasoning.

Conclusion

Currently, there is a broad popular, scientific, and medical conception of the X chromosome as the mediator of the differences between males and females, as the carrier of female-specific traits, or otherwise as a substrate of femaleness. As this essay has documented, associations between the X and femaleness are the accumulated product of contingent historical and material processes and events, and they are inflected by beliefs rooted in gender ideology. The still very contemporary view that the double X makes females unpredictable, mysterious, chimeric, and conservative, while the single X allows men to learn, evolve, and have bigger brains but also makes them the more risk taking of the two sexes, shows how conceptions of X chromosome structure and function often reflect and support traditional gender stereotypes.

In light of the empirical and conceptual weaknesses of these theories, scientists must work to develop alternative models of the relationship between the X and sex. They must cultivate an active practice of gender criticality, exposing their theories to rigorous examination from all perspectives. While the presence of a single X in males and a double X in females does have different implications for male and female biology, historical and contemporary speculations over the relation between the X and femaleness show that this assumption has consistently contributed to erroneous biological reasoning and that the X has been overburdened with explaining female biology and sex differences. As this essay has shown, the X chromosome has not only become female identified as an object of biological research, but has, more broadly, become a highly gendered screen upon which cultural theories of sex and gender difference have been projected throughout the twentieth century and up to the present day. The case of how the X became the female chromosome presents a prominent example of how unquestioned gender assumptions can distort and mislead, not only within the biological sciences but more generally in the production of knowledge.

Department of the History of Science and Committee on Degrees in Sudies of Women, Gender, and Sexuality Harvard University

References

Accelerated Cure Project. 2006. "Analysis of Genetic Mutations or Alleles on the X or Y Chromosome as Possible Causes of Multiple Sclerosis." Cure Map Document. Accelerated Cure Project for Multiple Sclerosis, Waltham, MA. http://www.acceleratedcure.org/downloads/phase2-genetics-xy-chromosomes.pdf.

Amos-Landgraf, James M., Amy Cottle, Robert M. Plenge, Mike Friez, Charles E. Schwartz, John Longshore, and Huntington F. Willard. 2006. "X Chromosome-Inactivation Patterns of 1,005 Phenotypically Unaffected Females." *American Journal of Human Genetics* 79(3):493–99.

Angier, Natalie. 1999. *Woman: An Intimate Geography.* Boston: Houghton Mifflin.

_____. 2007. "For Motherly X Chromosome, Gender Is Only the Beginning." *New York Times*, May 1, F1, F6.

Bainbridge, David. 2003. *The X in Sex: How the X Chromosome Controls Our Lives.* Cambridge, MA: Harvard University Press.

Barr, Murray L. 1959. "Sex Chromatin and Phenotype in Man." *Science* 130(3377):679–85.

Barr, Murray L., and Ewart G. Bertram. 1949. "A Morphological Distinction between Neurones of the Male and Female, and the Behaviour of the Nucleolar Satellite during Accelerated Nucleoprotein Synthesis." *Nature* 163(4148):676–77.

Berman, Louis. 1921. *The Glands Regulating Personality: A Study of the Glands of Internal Secretion in Relation to the Types of Human Nature.* New York: Macmillan.

Bock, Robert. 1993. *Understanding Klinefelter Syndrome: A Guide for XXY Males and Their Families.* NIH Pub. No. 93-3202. Office of Research Reporting, National Institute of Child Health and Human Development, Bethesda, MD. http://www.nichd.nih.gov/publications/pubs/klinefelter.cfm.

Brix, Thomas Heiberg, Pia Skov Hansen, Gun Peggy S. Knudsen, Marianne K. Kringen, Kirsten Ohm Kyvik, Karen Helene Orstavik, and Laszlo Hegedüs. 2009. "No Link between X Chromosome Inactivation Pattern and Simple Goiter in Females: Evidence from a Twin Study." *Thyroid* 19(2):165–69.

Brody, Jane. 1967. "If Her Chromosomes Add Up, a Woman Is Sure to Be a Woman." *New York Times,* September 16, 28.

Burgoyne, Paul S. 1998. "The Mammalian Y Chromosome: A New Perspective." *Bioessays* 20(5):363–36.

Carrel, Laura. 2006. "'X'-Rated Chromosomal Rendezvous." *Science* 311(5764): 1107–9.

Check, Erika. 2005. "The X Factor." *Nature* 434(7031):266–67.

Chitnis, Smita, Joanita Monteiro, David Glass, Brian Apatoff, Jane Salmon, Patrick Concannon, and Peter K. Gregersen. 2000. "The Role of X-Chromosome Inactivation in Female Predisposition to Autoimmunity." *Arthritis Research and Therapy* 2(5):399–406.

Cooper, Glinda S., Milele L. Bynum, and Emily C. Somers. 2009. "Recent Insights in the Epidemiology of Autoimmune Diseases: Improved Prevalence Estimates and Understanding of Clustering of Diseases." *Journal of Autoimmunity* 33(3–4):197–207.

Darwin, Charles. (1871) 1897. *The Descent of Man and Selection in Relation to Sex.* 2nd ed. New York: Appleton.

Davies, Terry F. 2005. "Editorial: X *versus* X—the Fight for Function within the Female Cell and the Development of Autoimmune Thyroid Disease." *Journal of Clinical Endocrinology and Metabolism* 90(11):6332–33.

de Chadarevian, Soraya. 2006. "Mice and the Reactor: The 'Genetics Experiment' in 1950s Britain." *Journal of the History of Biology* 39(4):707–35.

Dowd, Maureen. 2005. "X-celling over Men." *New York Times,* March 20, C13.

Eaton, William W., Noel R. Rose, Amanda Kalaydjian, Marianne G. Pedersen, and Preben Bo Mortensen. 2007. "Epidemiology of Autoimmune Diseases in Denmark." *Journal of Autoimmunity* 29(1):1–9.

Fausto-Sterling, Anne. 2000. *Sexing the Body: Gender Politics and the Construction of Sexuality.* New York: Basic.

Graves, Jennifer A. M. 2000. "Human Y Chromosome, Sex Determination, and Spermatogenesis— a Feminist View." *Biology of Reproduction* 63(3): 667–76.

Graves, Jennifer A. M., Jozef Gecz, and Horst Hameister. 2002. "Evolution of the Human X—a Smart and Sexy Chromosome That Controls Speciation and Development." *Cytogenetic and Genome Research* 99(1–4):141–45.

Gray, John. 1992. *Men Are from Mars, Women Are from Venus: A Practical Guide for Improving Communication and Getting What You Want in Your Relationships.* New York: HarperCollins.

Gunter, Chris. 2005. "She Moves in Mysterious Ways." *Nature* 434(7031):279–80.

Haraway, Donna J. 1991. The Biopolitics of Postmodern Bodies: Constitutions of Self in Immune System Discourse. In *Simians, Cyborgs, and Women: The Reinvention of Nature,* 203–30. New York: Routledge.

Harper, Peter S. 2006. *First Years of Human Chromosomes: The Beginnings of Human Cytogenetics.* Bloxham: Scion.

Invernizzi, Pietro. 2007. "The X Chromosome in Female-Predominant Autoimmune Diseases." *Annals of the New York Academy of Sciences* 1110(1):57–64.

Invernizzi, Pietro, Monica Miozzo, Sabine Oertelt-Prigione, Pier Luigi Meroni, Luca Persani, Carlo Selmi, Pier Maria Battezzati, et al. 2007. "X Monosomy in Female Systemic Lupus Erythematosus." *Annals of the New York Academy of Sciences* 1110(1):84–91.

Jacobs, Patricia A., and John Anderson Strong. 1959. "A Case of Human Intersexuality Having a Possible XXY Sex-Determining Mechanism." *Nature* 183(4657): 302–3.

Jacobson, Denise L., Stephen J. Gange, Noel R. Rose, and Neil M. H. Graham. 1997. "Epidemiology and Estimated Population Burden of Selected Autoimmune Diseases in the United States." *Clinical Immunology and Immunopathology* 84(3):223–43.

Kast, Richard E. 1977. "Predominance of Autoimmune and Rheumatic Diseases in Females." *Journal of Rheumatology* 4(3):288–92.

Keller, Evelyn Fox. 1995. "The Origin, History, and Politics of the Subject Called 'Gender and Science.'" In *Handbook of Science and Technology Studies,* ed. Sheila Jasanoff, Gerald E. Markle, James C. Petersen, and Trevor J. Pinch, 80–94. Thousand Oaks, CA: Sage.

Kettlewell, Julianna. 2005. "Female Chromosome Has X Factor." *BBC News Online,* March 16. http://news.bbc.co.uk/2/hi/science/nature/4355355.stm.

Klinefelter, Harry F., Edward C. Reifenstein, and Fuller Albright. 1942. "Syndrome Characterized by Gynecomastia, Aspermatogenesis without A-Leydigism, and Increased Excretion of Follicle-Stimulating Hormone." *Journal of Clinical Endocrinology and Metabolism* 2(11):615–27.

Knudsen, Gun Peggy. 2009. "Gender Bias in Autoimmune Diseases: X Chromosome Inactivation in Women with Multiple Sclerosis." *Journal of the Neurological Sciences* 286(1–2):43–46.

Knudsen, Gun Peggy, Hanne F. Harbo, Cathrine Smestad, Elisabeth G. Celius, Elisabet Akesson, Annette Oturai, Lars P. Ryder, Anne Spurkland, and Karen Helene Orstavik. 2007. "X Chromosome Inactivation in Females with Multiple Sclerosis." *European Journal of Neurology* 14(12):1392–96.

Kruszelnicki, Karl S. 2004. "Hybrid Auto-Immune Women 3." *ABC Science In Depth*. http://www.abc.net.au/science/articles/2004/02/12/1002754.htm.

Lederberg, Joshua. 1966. "Poets Knew It All Along: Science Finally Finds Out That Girls Are Chimerical; You Know, Xn/Xa." *Washington Post*, December 18, E7.

Lehrke, Robert. 1997. *Sex Linkage of Intelligence: The X-Factor*. Westport, CT: Praeger.

Lockshin, Michael D. 2006. "Sex Differences in Autoimmune Disease." *Lupus* 15(11):753–56.

_____. 2010. "Nonhormonal Explanations for Sex Discrepancy in Human Illness." *Annals of the New York Academy of Sciences* 1193(1):22–24.

Lyon, Mary. 1992. "Some Milestones in the History of X-Chromosome Inactivation." *Annual Review of Genetics* 26:17–28.

Martin, Emily. 1991. "The Egg and the Sperm: How Science Has Constructed a Romance Based on Stereotypical Male-Female Roles." *Signs: Journal of Women in Culture and Society* 16(3):485–501.

_____. 1999. "The Woman in the Flexible Body." In *Revisioning Women, Health, and Healing: Feminist, Cultural, and Technoscience Perspectives*, ed. Adele E. Clarke and Virginia L. Olesen, 97–115. New York: Routledge.

McClung, Clarence E. 1899. "A Peculiar Nuclear Element in the Male Reproductive Cells of Insects." *Zoological Bulletin* 2(4):187–97.

_____. 1902. "The Accessory Chromosome—Sex Determinant?" *Biological Bulletin* 3(1–2):43–84.

_____. 1918. "Possible Action of the Sex-Determining Mechanism." *Proceedings of the National Academy of Sciences* 4(6):160–63.

McCombe, Pamela A., Judith M. Greer, and Ian R. Mackay. 2009. "Sexual Dimorphism in Autoimmune Disease." *Current Molecular Medicine* 9(9):1058–79.

McCoy, Krisha. 2009. "Women and Autoimmune Disorders." Everydayhealth.com, December 2. http://www.everydayhealth.com/autoimmune-disorders/understanding/women-and-autoimmune-diseases.aspx.

"Men and Women: The Differences Are in the Genes." 2005. *ScienceDaily*, March 25. http://www.sciencedaily.com/releases/2005/03/050323124659.htm.

Migeon, Barbara R. 1994. "X-Chromosome Inactivation: Molecular Mechanisms and Genetic Consequences." *Trends in Genetics* 10(7):230–35.

_____. 2006. "The Role of X Inactivation and Cellular Mosaicism in Women's Health and Sex-Specific Diseases." *JAMA* 295(12):1428–33.

_____. 2007. *Females Are Mosaics: X Inactivation and Sex Differences in Disease*. New York: Oxford University Press.

Miller, Fiona Alice. 2003. "Dermatoglyphics and the Persistence of 'Mongolism': Networks of Technology, Disease and Discipline." *Social Studies of Science* 33(1):75–94.

_____. 2006. "'Your True and Proper Gender': The Barr Body as a Good Enough Science of Sex." *Studies in History and Philosophy of Biological and Biomedical Sciences* 37(3):459–83.

Montagu, Ashley. 1953. *The Natural Superiority of Women*. New York: Macmillan.

Morgan, Thomas Hunt. 1915. *The Mechanism of Mendelian Heredity*. New York: Holt.

Mundell, E. J. 2007. "'X' Factor Boosts Women's Health, Longevity." *Women's Health Issues*, December 11. http://www.womenshealthissues/net/ms/news/531674/main.html.

Nature Genetics. 2000. "Sex, Genes and Women's Health." *Nature Genetics* 25(1):1–2.

Oliver, Jacqueline E., and Alan J. Silman. 2009. "Why Are Women Predisposed to Autoimmune Rheumatic Diseases?" *Arthritis Research and Therapy* 11(5): 252.

Oudshoorn, Nelly. 1994. *Beyond the Natural Body: An Archaeology of Sex Hormones*. New York: Routledge.

Ozbalkan, Zeynep, Sevgi Bagişlar, Sedat Kiraz, Cemaliye Boylu Akyerli, Hüseyin T. E. Ozer, Sule Yavuz, A. Merih Birlik, Meral Calgüneri, and Tayfun Ozçelik. 2005. "Skewed X Chromosome Inactivation in Blood Cells of Women with Scleroderma." *Arthritis and Rheumatism* 52(5):1564–70.

Ozcelik, Tayfun, Elif Uz, Cemaliye B. Akyerli, Sevgi Bagislar, Chigdem A. Mustafa, Alptekin Gursoy, Nurten Akarsu, Gokce Toruner, Nuri Kamel, and Sevim Gullu. 2006. "Evidence from Autoimmune Thyroiditis of Skewed X-Chromosome Inactivation in Female Predisposition to Autoimmunity." *European Journal of Human Genetics* 14(6):791–97.

Pain, Elisabeth. 2007. "A Genetic Battle of the Sexes." *ScienceNOW Daily News*, March 22. http://news.sciencemag.org/sciencenow/2007/03/22-04.html.

Painter, Theophilus S. 1924. "The Sex Chromosomes of Man." *American Naturalist* 58(659):506–24.

Pasquier, Elizabeth, Caroline Bohec, Luc De Saint Martin, Cédric Le Marechal, Marie-Thérèse Le Martelot, Sylvie Roche, Yves Laurent, Claude Ferec, Michel Collet, and Dominique Mottier. 2007. "Strong Evidence that Skewed X-Chromosome Inactivation Is Not Associated with Recurrent Pregnancy Loss: An Incident Paired Case Control Study." *Human Reprodroduction* 22(11):2829–33.

"Research Makes It Official: Women Are Genetic Mosaics." 1963. *Time*, January 4. http://www.time.com/time/magazine/article/0,9171,829719,00.html.

Ridley, Matt. 1999. *Genome: The Autobiography of a Species in 23 Chapters*. New York: HarperCollins.

Russell, Louisa M., Paul Strike, Caroline E. Browne, and Patricia A. Jacobs. 2007. "X Chromosome Loss and Ageing." *Cytogenetic and Genome Research* 116(3): 181–85.

Seldin, Michael F., Christopher I. Amos, Ryk Ward, and Peter K. Gregersen. 1999. "The Genetics Revolution and the Assault on Rheumatoid Arthritis." *Arthritis and Rheumatism* 42(6):1071–79.

Selmi, Carlo. 2008. "The X in Sex: How Autoimmune Diseases Revolve around Sex Chromosomes." *Best Practice and Research Clinical Rheumatology* 22(5): 913–22.

Shields, Stephanie A. 1982. "The Variability Hypothesis: The History of a Biological Model of Sex Differences in Intelligence." *Signs* 7(4):769–97.

Society for Women's Health Research. 2008. "What a Difference an X Makes." Video. Society for Women's Health Research, Washington, DC. http://www.youtube.com/watch?v=u43EciTz-H4.

Spolarics, Zoltan. 2007. "The X-Files of Inflammation: Cellular Mosaicism of X-Linked Polymorphic Genes and the Female Advantage in the Host Response to Injury and Infection." *Shock* 27(6):597–604.

Stevenson, Roger E., Charles E. Schwartz, J. Fernando Arena, and Herbert A. Lubs. 1994. "X-Linked Mental Retardation: The Early Era from 1943 to 1969." *American Journal of Medical Genetics* 51(4):538–41.

Stewart, Jeffrey J. 1998. "The Female X-Inactivation Mosaic in Systemic Lupus Erythematosus." *Immunology Today* 19(8):352–57.

Svyryd, Yevgeniya, Gabriela Hernández-Molina, Florencia Vargas, Jorge Sánchez-Guerrero, Donato Alarcón Segovia, and Osvaldo M. Mutchinick. 2010. "X Chromosome Monosomy in Primary and Overlapping Autoimmune Diseases." *Autoimmunity Review*, March 15.

Sykes, Bryan. 2003. *Adam's Curse: A Future without Men*. New York: Bantam.

Tingen, Candace. 2009. "Science Mini-Lesson: X Chromosome Inactivation." *Institute for Women's Health Research at Northwestern University* blog, October 21. http://blog.womenshealth.northwestern.edu/2009/10/science-mini-lesson-x-chromosome-inactivation/.

Turner, Henry H. 1938. "A Syndrome of Infantilism, Congenital Webbed Neck, and Cubitus Valgus." *Endocrinology* 23(5):566–74.

Vallender, Eric J., Nathaniel M. Pearson, and Bruce T. Lahn. 2005. "The X Chromosome: Not Just Her Brother's Keeper." *Nature Genetics* 37(4):343–45.

Voeller, Bruce R., ed. 1968. *The Chromosome Theory of Inheritance: Classic Papers in Development and Heredity*. New York: Appleton-Century-Crofts.

Walsh, Stephen J., and Laurie M. Rau. 2000. "Autoimmune Diseases: A Leading Cause of Death among Young and Middle-Aged Women in the United States." *American Journal of Public Health* 90(9):1463–66.

Wang, P. Jeremy, John R. McCarrey, Fang Yang, and David C. Page. 2001. "An Abundance of X-Linked Genes Expressed in Spermatogonia." *Nature Genetics* 27(4):422–26.

Weasel, Lisa H. 2001. "Dismantling the Self/Other Dichotomy in Science: Towards a Feminist Model of the Immune System." *Hypatia* 16(1):27–44.

Wilson, Edmund B. 1925. *The Cell in Development and Heredity*. 3rd ed. New York: Macmillan.

Woolley, Helen Thompson. 1914. "The Psychology of Sex." *Psychological Bulletin* 11(10):353–79.

Transgender Youth: Providing Medical Treatment for a Misunderstood Population

by Stephanie Brill and Jennifer Hastings

It is another one of those times in the history of progressive health care. Time to embrace another group of individuals who deserve health care and yet have been marginalized up until this point. An underserved, unrecognized, and much deserving segment of the population. This time it is children—transgender children and teens.

Because of society's lack of awareness of a simple, yet complex part of human identity—gender—transgender children and teens are deeply misunderstood. This lack of understanding feeds family and societal rejection and stigmatization, which unfortunately too often leads to sexual and physical violence directed towards transgender children. A known, or recognizably transgender person is frequently a target for discrimination and violence. The shame and rejection felt by these children in turn leads to self-harming behaviors, increased drug use, homelessness, HIV/AIDS infection, depression, and suicide. One-third (33.2%) of transgender youth have attempted suicide.[1]

Although it is unknown how many children and teens are truly transgender, medical professionals and others who care for children are finally paying attention to this minority group. Doctors in the United States, the Netherlands, the United Kingdom and elsewhere in Europe now agree that early treatment of transgender children can change—and even save—lives. In order to understand what kinds of treatments are needed for transgender children and youth, it is important to understand what a transgender child is, what treatments are available, and how these treatments can help.

What is Transgender?

Transgender people have existed throughout all times and in all cultures. Being transgender is not a mental illness but is, rather, a normal variation of human development. There is nothing wrong with transgender children—the problem lies with the way we understand gender.

Common understanding of gender is based on the premises that there are two genders. and that gender and biological anatomy are synonymous. Each of these premises is incorrect. In fact, a minority of the population experience themselves as either a blend of genders or no gender at all. For most people, gender is static. For some, however, it is fluid or changes over time. Likewise, one's biological anatomy determines one's biological sex. One's internal sense of gender, however, is not determined by biological anatomy but is a different spectra of formative identity altogether. Taken together, biological sex and gender identity create a person's sense of "self". Because it is most common for biological sex and gender identity to align in a predictable pattern, the two separate aspects of "self" have become conflated. In order to understand and serve transgender people, however, it is essential to recognize and distinguish these separate parts of self.

In other words, although it is most common that people with female anatomy identity as girls, a small percentage do not. Of those who do not feel they are girls, some identify as a blend of genders, some as neither gender, and some identify as boys. A female-bodied person who identifies consistently and persistently over time as a boy is a transgender boy. Likewise, although most male-bodied people identify as boys, a small percentage do not. A male-bodied person who identifies consistently and persistently over time as a girl is a transgender girl.

We do not have accurate statistics to reflect how frequently transgenderism or significant gender variance occurs. There have always been transgender children, but in the past the family was likely to deny what was happening, to allow their child to transition but hide this fact from others, or prevent the child from living as their true self until they left home. Awareness of this population is just coming to light, and more parents are openly supporting their children at younger ages. An indicator of this rapid societal shift is the fact that five years ago, Gender Spectrum was called to do trainings in support of transgender children one to three times a year. In 2009, Gender Spectrum was called to support transgender children 10-15 times a week.

How can you know for sure that a child is transgender?

There are many children who are gender-nonconforming in their appearance or interests who still have a gender identity that is congruous with their anatomy. These gender-variant children are usually gender-nonconforming in their self-expression, but still feel that they are in the right-gendered body. For example, Gender Spectrum frequently provides school trainings for anatomical boys who identify as boys but want to wear dresses to school. These boys are perceived to be girls, due to their appearance.

As children and teens, these youth often experience a tremendous amount of ridicule and shame for being "different". Yet, it is important to note that the majority of gender-nonconforming children are not transgender. While they require support and understanding for their gender variance, they do not require medical intervention. Medical providers are uniquely poised to assist transgender children who want their bodies to be perceived as congruous with their inner gender. Medical providers can guide these youth and their families through the process of deciding which medical treatments, if any, are appropriate for the specific child. Likewise, medical providers can provide all gender-nonconforming youth and their families with effective tools and guidance to encourage self-esteem and the courage to continue being themselves.

One of the challenges for parents and caregivers alike there is no way to be 100 percent sure that a child is truly transgender. There is no test to determine if a child who insists over time that he or she is not the gender assigned to them at birth is going to feel the same way as an adult. But, the overwhelming majority of transgender adults report that they knew that they were transgender from the time they were children. The longer a cross-gender identification "phase" persists, the less likely it is to be a phase. So, parents and clinicians alike rely on a combination of the child's experience, the parents' perspectives, the longevity of the gender variance, and psychological assessment to determine if, and when, it is time to validate a child's experience of their own gender with medical intervention. One California parent describes their experience, saying: "We had always allowed our daughter to express herself in the ways that felt right for her. When she was young—two years old—and told us she was a boy, we naturally assumed this was a phase. At first we neither encouraged it nor discouraged it. We essentially ignored it. However, this phase has yet to end! It has been eight years now. After a while, we no longer ignored it and, with the help of a therapist, we allowed our child to change pronouns and live as a boy starting in kindergarten. He is now half way through fifth grade. Our son has always been our son- it just took us a few years to understand this. We fully support him and will whatever it takes for him to live a happy and successful life."

Because of the difficulty in determining if a child is transgender, it is vital that health care providers familiarize themselves with the current literature regarding gender variance and children. This will help them provide sensitive care to their patients and help support families in parenting these children. Studies have shown that acceptance and support from parents and other caregivers are very important to long-term positive outcomes for transgender children. An informed medical professional can help parents and children address transgender feelings and ensure the best possible future for the child.

Social transitioning

When a family feels certain that their child is transgender, they should be encouraged to allow their child to socially transition. This means that the family allows the child to live as the gender the child feels himself or herself to be, rather than insisting that they live according to the gender assigned to them at birth. Seeing the devastating impact on their children of living as the wrong gender, more and more parents are allowing their child to socially transition genders at younger ages. Some children go through a social transition prior to kindergarten, while other children (or their families) are not ready to do so until middle or high school. Ideally, this process occurs with the support of a therapist, pediatrician, and with appropriate training for staff and teachers at the child's school.

Puberty for the transgender child

For many transgender children, the arrival of puberty brings with it a crisis. In puberty, the body enters into changes that mark the individual as male or female. For transgender people, this process means that they will permanently be a member of the sex opposite to the one they experience themselves to be. The suicide rate for transgender teens is exorbitantly high due, in part, to these body changes.

Medical suspension of puberty

Some of puberty's changes are later reversible through surgery and medication. Others are not, however, and may permanently mark the transgender individual. For this reason, hormone blockers are now being used to suspend the natural development of puberty by inhibiting the pituitary's release of gonadatropins. The medications are called "GnRh agonists" and are fully reversible. Within six months of discontinuing GnRh agonists, the patient's body resumes puberty at the point it left off.

One of such a suspension's great advantages is that a child, family, and gender team can effectively press a "pause" button on puberty and gain the time necessary to determine if the individual would benefit from administration of cross-sex hormones. Suspending puberty is especially helpful for a pubertal or pre-pubertal teen who has recently revealed to their family that he or she is transgender. The suspension allows the family time to come to terms with what the child is saying and establish whether he or she is truly transgender before committing the child to unwanted physical changes. It also decreases the likelihood that the child will resort to street hormones or suicide to cope with the agony caused by living in the wrong physical body. These fully reversible medicines are lifesavers, and all medical providers working with older children and adolescents should become familiar with their purpose and function.

When followed by cross-sex hormones (described below), GnRh agonists are a powerful tool that can be used to permanently prevent development of the "wrong" puberty in a transgender child, thereby eliminating the need for future surgeries and reducing societal stigmatization. Some practitioners have ethical concerns about administering these medicines because they fear they are interfering with destiny or are afraid of legal concerns stemming from suppression or redirection of puberty in a minor. In gender clinics in the U.S. and around the world, however, puberty-blocking medications are being used without any adverse effects being reported, and with full reversibility of their effects. Because these medicines may save lives and reduce trauma, some feel the medical provider has an ethical mandate to provide them.

Cross-hormone administration

Testosterone and estrogen are the hormones responsible for puberty. These hormones stimulate the development of physical characteristics we associate with men and women. These natural hormones can be administered as cross-hormonal medicines to a body that desires physical changes that would not normally occur. Administration of estrogen to a male body causes the skin to soften, fat to be redistributed to the hips and thighs, and breasts to develop. Estrogen also suppresses development of secondary male characteristics such as deepening of the voice and hair growth. Administration of testosterone to a female body causes the voice to deepen, development of male hair growth patterns, muscle mass to increase, and fat to be redistributed to the abdomen. Testosterone also suppresses the menstrual cycle and breast development. These medicines are well-researched and have been used in youth to treat delayed puberty for many years; protocols for administration and follow-up care are established, as well.

The decision to administer cross-sex hormones to a transgender child or youth is often more complex than the decision to administer puberty-blocking medications. This is because some of the changes from cross-sex hormones are irreversible (i.e., hair growth patterns, lowering the voice), while others can only be reversed through surgery (i.e., breast growth). For this reason, it is essential that cross-sex hormones only be administered when the individual is ready to begin the transition to the correct gender. Written communication from the child's primary care provider, therapist, or another experienced mental health professional can help document and confirm the patient's clear transgenderism and readiness to transition medically.

The ideal age at which to administer these cross-sex hormones is not firmly established A child can stay on the puberty-blocking medication for years, if needed, before receiving cross-sex hormones. However, the benefits to a transgender youth of being able to go through the "right" puberty at the 'right' time are tremendous. For this reason, once transgenderism has been established, and the youth is of pubertal age, many gender specialists believe that it is appropriate to administer cross-sex medicines. In other words, it is best to slowly initiate cross-sex hormones at the same time that the patient's peers are entering puberty, typically around age 12–14.

Support for Parents and Family of Transgender Children

Parents, other family members, and friends of transgender children need support as much as the transgender child does. It can be very challenging to come to terms with having a transgender child and become an advocate for their health–but doing so is it immensely rewarding and essential for the child's health. Supportive parents may suffer rejection from friends, family members, or co-workers who do not understand why they are embracing their child's transition. In addition, it can be hard to find qualified mental and physical health providers, and to gain the support of the school system.

Parents often find themselves forced to educate their child's doctor and school staff. The parent of a transgender youth also faces daily challenges that include remembering to use the appropriate gender pronoun, coping with unexpected "outings", and addressing both their own and their child's emotions. Luckily, a growing number support groups now exist throughout the country, and the Internet, on-line support groups, and books offer vital support for families.

Outcomes

Relative little research exists on outcomes for gender non-conforming youth. But, individuals from the fields of medicine, mental health, social work, and education consistently report the same findings: when supported by their families, schools, and care providers, transgender youth have the opportunity to thrive and develop strong self-esteem. According to groundbreaking research from the Family Acceptance Project, the way that parents and caregivers respond to their child's gender variance is the most significant marker of long-term health and well-being.[2] We cannot change a child's gender identity, but we can directly impact how a child feels about their gender identity.

Resources

Gender *Spectrum Education* and *Training*, 1 Camino Sobrante, #216, Orinda CA 94563. (925) 254-3907www.genderspectrum.org (http://www.genderspectrum.org/), info@gendespectrum.org (mailto:info@gendespectrum.org)

Brill S and C Ryan, *Early Childhood Development–Your Options–How Do I Know If My Child Is Transgender?* National Association of Social Workers website: http://www.helpstartshere.org/Default.aspx?PageID=1114 (http://www.helpstartshere.org/Default.aspx?PageID=1114)

Reed BWD, Cohen-Kettenis PT, T Reed et al., *Medical care for gender variant young people: Dealing with the practical problems*, Sexologies 2008; 17(4): 258-264.

The following materials and other resources can be found at:http://www.hawaii.edu/hivandaids/links_transgenderYouth.htm (http://www.hawaii.edu/hivandaids/links_transgenderYouth.htm)

This article was written by: Stephanie Brill and Jennifer Hastings, MD

Stephanie Brill is the co-author of The Transgender Child: A Handbook for Families and Professionals. She is also the founding director of Gender Spectrum, which provides support and training to families, medical and mental health care providers, and educators about gender in children and youth. She is the co-founder of MAIA Midwifery and Preconception Services, and the Oakland Children's Hospital's support group for parents of gender variant and transgender children. She speaks and trains on the developmental stages of gender variance in children for medical and lay audiences and can be reached at www.genderspectrum.org (http://www.genderspectrum.org/).

Jennifer Hastings, MD is a family physician working at Planned Parenthood Mar Monte in Santa Cruz, CA. She started a Transgender Healthcare Program in 2005, and works closely with Shane Hill, PhD and the Santa Cruz Trans Therapists Team, providing comprehensive Transgender Care. She is working to expand Transcare Services to other Planned Parenthood clinics.

Notes

1. Clements-Nolle K, Marx R, Katz M, "Attempted suicide among transgender persons: The influence of gender-based discrimination and victimization," Journal of Homosexuality 2006; 51(3):53–69.

2. Ryan C, Huebner H, Diaz R, et al. "Family Rejection as a Predictor of Negative Health Outcomes in White and Latino Lesbian, Gay, and Bisexual Young Adults," Pediatrics 2009; 123(1):346–352.

Trans Men's Health is a "Women's Health" Issue: Expanding the Boundaries of Sexual and Reproductive Health Care

by Cameron Hartofeis and Anu Manchikanti Gomez

During the 2012 elections, Vice President Joe Biden called transgender discrimination, "the civil rights issue of our time." While this is a sign that transgender rights are garnering national attention, the population continues to face many obstacles in accessing needed health care. In particular, transgender men (or "trans men") face significant barriers to accessing sexual and reproductive health care.

Trans men are individuals who were assigned a female sex at birth but who identify as male. Many people have heard of Thomas Beatie, a trans man who self-identified as the world's first "Pregnant Man" after he decided to become pregnant when his wife was found to be infertile. Beatie and his then-wife have described the painful and extended process of seeking care during Beatie's pregnancy, and how some providers refused to treat the couple.[i]

In 1999 another trans man, Robert Eads, died of complications from metastasized ovarian cancer.[1] In his 40s, Eads had sexual reassignment surgery to physically transition from female to male. As a post-menopausal woman prior to transition, Eads was told that it was unnecessary to remove his uterus and ovaries as part of the reassignment.[ii]

Unaware of his need for regular gynecological cancer screenings, Eads suffered from an unidentified illness for over a year, until the Medical College of Georgia accepted him as a patient in 1997 and diagnosed his cancer. While ovarian cancer is notoriously deadly and hard to diagnose and treat, the year-long delay in diagnosis hampered Eads' chance of survival and negatively affected his quality of life.

Regrettably, Beatie's and Eads' stories both illustrate providers' discrimination and the pervasive lack of knowledge about trans men's needs for routine sexual and reproductive health care. Their experiences highlight the need for comprehensive education on trans men's sexual and reproductive health for health care providers and the general public. In particular, women's health care providers must support the needs of transgender men and gender non-conforming female-bodied individuals—or this population will continue to be underserved and at-risk for poor health outcomes.

Who Are Transmen?

First, some background. According to the World Health Organization, *sex* refers to the "biological and physiological characteristics that define men and women," while *gender* describes the "socially constructed roles, behaviors, activities, and attributes that a given society considers appropriate for men and women."[iii] The American Psychological Association defines "transgender" as "an umbrella term for persons whose gender identity, gender expression, and/or behavior does not conform to that typically associated with the sex to which they were assigned at birth."[iv] (In contrast, a *cisgender* individual's gender identity aligns with the sex assigned at birth.)

Trans men were assigned a female sex at birth but have a male gender identity. These individuals may describe themselves as trans men, female-to-male transgender individuals, males, or a range of other identifiers. Trans men are *not* a homogenous group and are *not* defined by what medical procedures they have or haven't had. Trans men may seek a variety of medical procedures if they decide to undergo sexual reassignment surgery, including hormone therapy (e.g., androgen therapy) and reconstructive surgery (e.g., double mastectomy with nipple and areola reconstruction).[v] But, some

who identify as trans men do not use hormones, have surgery, or seek other physical changes to their appearance as part of their transition, and only shift clothing and/or pronouns to signify their transition.

Transmen's Health Needs

Regardless of the medical procedures they have, most trans men are at-risk for women's health problems, such as ovarian, cervical and uterine cancers – before, during and after transition. The American College of Obstetricians and Gynecologists (ACOG) has stated that basic preventative services, such as sexually transmitted infection (STI) tests, comprehensive contraceptive counseling, and cancer screening, does not require "specific expertise in transgender care." *Medical Therapy and Health Maintenance for Transgender Men: A Guide For Health Care Providers* clearly describes trans men's need for comprehensive services before, during, and after transition. It recommends that, in general, "screening *should continue until the patient no longer has the screened organ*" (emphasis added).[v]

The *Guide* stresses the importance of educating trans men who retain their uterus about the signs of endometrial cancers, and notes, "any patient with a uterus/cervix should ideally have yearly pelvic exams with Pap smears. . .even if a Pap smear is not required ACOG still recommends yearly pelvic exams for any adult female-bodied person. This need for screening should be emphasized to trans men who have historically been reticent to seek out appropriate gynecologic care."[v] The *Guide* notes that long-term androgen treatment and testosterone therapy—which aid the physical transition from one sex to another—are linked with high rates of Polycystic Ovarian Syndrome (PCOS), which is associated with an increased risk of endometrial and breast cancers as well as decreased fertility.[v] Similar guidance about screening mammograms should be followed when treating trans men who have not had bilateral mastectomies.

Family planning is another potential area of need, since many trans men have cisgender male sexual partners. Trans men who have not had a hysterectomy can become pregnant and will benefit from access to stigma-free contraception and abortion services.[vi] Yet, clinical guidance on this population's health care needs is usually silent about family planning and abortion counseling and services.

Addressing Barriers to Care

Barriers to sexual and reproductive health services for transgender individuals are created when there is a disconnect between what providers and health care workers *perceive* the individual's needs to be, and the individual's *actual* needs. One way to address this barrier is to ensure providers have the resources needed to provide quality, respectful services to transgender-spectrum and gender-nonconforming patients. And, providers must ensure that all patients' needs are *heard* and *addressed*. Too many trans men and other gender-nonconforming individuals face overwhelming levels of discrimination and marginalization throughout their lives, including discrimination when seeking health care.

The National Gay and Lesbian Task Force and the National Center for Transgender Equality's *National Transgender Discrimination Survey* (NTDS) describes this population's appalling health outcomes, including "much higher rates of HIV infection, smoking, drug and alcohol use[,] and suicide attempts than the general population."[vii] The survey found that 63 percent of "participants had experienced a serious act of discrimination—events that would have a major impact on a person's quality of life and ability to sustain themselves financially or emotionally."[vii]

In a ground-breaking report on lesbian, gay, bisexual and transgender (LGBT) health issues, the Institute of Medicine (IOM) noted the significant barriers to care faced by transgender individuals, which include providers refusing treatment and verbally abusing their patients.[viii] The NTDS found that 28 percent of the respondents had experienced harassment in a doctor's office; 19 percent had been denied medical care; and 2 percent had been physically attacked in a doctor's office.[vii] Respondents were most likely to be refused care in doctor's offices and hospitals (24 percent), followed by Emergency Departments (13 percent), and mental health clinics (11 percent).[vii] Those whose gender presentation closely matched their assigned sex were less likely to report having been refused care. Dishearteningly, the likelihood of

discrimination increased when medical providers were aware of the patient's transgender status."[vii]

Providers need to be better informed about, and more accepting of, transgender patients' sexual and reproductive health care needs. About 62 percent of trans men NTDS respondents reported "having to teach their medical care providers about transgender care."[vii] Most trans men who have sex with men (95 percent) reported getting inadequate information from providers about their overall sexual health.[vii] Providers need to communicate with their female-born transgender patients about the full range of preventative screenings, tests, and precautions needed to maintain their sexual and reproductive health.

Transgender individuals also face economic barriers that hamper their ability to get needed health care. Trans men have high rates of unemployment and, when employed, report workplace abuse and harassment, being forced to present as the wrong gender, and physical assault. Respondents reported being less likely to be covered by private or employer-based insurance; 19 percent had no insurance coverage.[vii]

Further, even in cases where trans men are insured, complications may arise for gender-specific services. For example, a trans man who takes hormones and has legally changed gender from female to male might be denied coverage for a Pap smear, which is covered only as part of a *woman's* wellness visit. Although the Affordable Care Act prevents discrimination based on transgender or gender-nonconforming status by Federally funded programs and organizations, it does not fundamentally ensure that all needed services are covered and/or offered to these individuals.

Where do we go from here?

In 2011 ACOG's Committee on Health Care for Underserved Women published an opinion noting that, "Lack of awareness, knowledge, and sensitivity in health care communities eventually leads to inadequate access to, underutilization of, and disparities within the health care system for this population.[ix] The fact that transgender issues are being discussed by key officials, health care associations, and policy-making entities demonstrates a significant cultural sea change on this issue. Much more must be done, however, to ensure that health care providers and insurance companies are able and willing to provide necessary health care services to all who need them, regardless of their gender expression and identity. Doctor's offices, Emergency Departments, labor and delivery rooms, and clinics *must* be safe spaces for individuals of anygender presentation,

and services must be offered based on a person's need rather than their appearance.

This article was written by: E. Cameron Hartofelis, MA(c), MPH(c) and Anu Manchikanti Gomez, PhD, MSc

Is Fat a Feminist Issue? Exploring the Gendered Nature of Weight Bias

by Janna L. Fikkan and Esther D. Rothblum

Abstract Although research and scholarship on weight-based stigma have increased substantially in recent years, the disproportionate degree of bias experienced by fat women has received considerably less attention. This paper reviews the literature on the weight-based stigma experienced by women in North America in multiple domains, including employment, education settings, romantic relationships, health care and mental health treatment, and portrayals in the media. We also explore the research examining the intersection of gender and ethnicity related to weight stigma. Across numerous settings, fat women fare worse than thinner women and worse than men, whether the men are fat or thin. Women experience multiple deleterious outcomes as a result of weight bias that have a significant impact on health, quality of life, and socioeconomic outcomes. Because of this gender disparity, we argue that feminist scholars need to devote as much attention to the lived experiences of fat women as they have to the "fear of fat" experienced by thin women.

Introduction

In the late 1970s and early 1980s, feminists began to draw increasing attention to the gendered nature of weight preoccupation and disordered eating, with Orbach's self-help book, *Fat is a Feminist*

Issue (1978), perhaps the best known of this genre. Helping women to see their private struggles with compulsive eating and hatred of their bodies as rooted in the social constraints placed on women's autonomy and patriarchal devaluation of all things feminine (including fat bodies) had a major impact on the field of psychotherapy and has spawned subsequent generations of feminist writing on the topic of women and weight. However, as critics noted then (e.g., Diamond 1985), the assumption that "fat" was indicative of pathology and, in Orbach's formulation, unconscious drives to defend against unwanted experiences (such as intimacy), was left largely intact. Additionally, the resolution of these psychological issues was seen as the pathway to permanent weight loss, thus also leaving unquestioned the assumption that thinness should still be a woman's goal.

By contrast, other writers at this time (e.g., Wooley et al. 1979) were starting to question the assumptions about fat as a medical or psychological problem to be solved. Wooley et al. (1979), followed by others (e.g., Brown 1985, 1989; Chrisler 1989), asserted that fat is a feminist issue because the culture at large allows for much less deviation from aesthetic ideals for women than it does for men, meaning that many more women than men end up feeling badly about their (normal and healthy) bodies, and thus engage their energies in all manner of corrective action, from restrictive dieting to eating disorders. Wooley et al. (1979) also noted that the "price paid" by women for having deviant bodies is more than psychological and emotional, and went on to cite some of the early research on weight bias. It is this "price," in the form of discrimination experienced by women due to weight, which is the point of departure for the current article.

The purpose of our review is to pool evidence from several disciplines and across multiple domains that demonstrates the disparate impact of weight bias on women. We conducted an internet search on gender and weight stigma, and also found additional references within those articles. We focus our review on studies of women or studies in which gender is examined as an independent variable. In so doing, we had to eliminate a number of studies that do not mention gender of the sample, especially in the health arena, where the focus is largely on how "obese people" (gender unspecified) are perceived by health care professionals (e.g., Berryman et al. 2006; Klein et al. 1982). We have limited the scope of our review to research conducted on samples of adults and older adolescents in North America, although a number of investigators are also examining the intersection of weight bias and gender in other countries (e.g., Sargent and Blanchflower 1994, and Viner and Cole 2005, in Great Britain; Sarlio-Lähteenkorva and Lahelma 1999; and Sarlio-Lähteenkorva et al. 2004, in Finland; Lundborg et al. 2007, across 10 European countries; Schorb 2009, in Germany) and among children (Tang-Péronard and Heitmann 2008). We also emphasize more recent studies, to avoid replication of earlier reviews of the weight bias literature (Rothblum 1992). When possible, we prefer to use the term "fat," as it is descriptive, whereas the term "overweight" implies unfavorable comparison to a normative standard and "obese" is a medical term with its own negative connotations. However, so that we may most accurately represent the work of others, we at times use the terms (bracketed in quotes) used by the authors themselves in our review of the literature.

We end the paper with our own thoughts on the relative scarcity of feminist writing and scholarship that directly deals with the social meanings and consequences of the fat female body. Though

a significant amount has been written from a feminist perspective on eating disorders, self-starvation, and the "normative discontent" that is rooted in the hatred and fear of fat (cf. Bordo 1993; Fallon et al. 1994; Guille and Chrisler 1999; Hesse-Bieber 2007; Rodin et al. 1984), much less has been written to date that documents and explores the experience for women in this culture of actually *being* fat.

Employment and Income

As we will review in this section, the literature on weight-based employment discrimination spans several disciplines and includes both experimental studies and analyses of trends in occupational attainment and compensation within large data sets. Common to most of the studies exploring this phenomenon is that fat women are more adversely impacted by weight-based employment discrimination than are men in a number of ways (Fikkan and Rothblum 2005; Griffin 2007) and are over 16 times more likely than men to perceive such discrimination, according to results from a large U.S. sample (Roehling et al. 2007). As detailed below, discrimination against fat women in the employment sphere occurs at multiple levels, including hiring, promotion, performance evaluation, and compensation.

Experimental Studies

In the experimental investigations of weight-based discrimination reviewed below, research participants are generally asked to rate hypothetical job candidates on their desirability. With other relevant variables being held constant, experimenters can vary the candidate's weight (either through manipulating photographs or video or through verbal descriptions) to assess the impact of weight on desirability.

Rothblum et al. (1988) assessed the impact of weight on job candidate desirability in an all-female college student sample and found that when raters read written descriptions of candidates' appearance, fat women were rated more negatively than non-fat women on supervisory potential, self-discipline, professional appearance, personal hygiene, and ability to perform a physically strenuous job. When level of attractiveness was controlled, however, the negative stereotyping of fat applicants was considerably reduced, indicating that the bias against fat women may be mostly due to the presumed negative effect on physical attractiveness.

When participants are asked to rate both male and female job candidates, the disparate impact of weight stigma on women can more easily be observed. Two studies by Jasper and Klassen (1990a; 1990b) using a college student sample found participant raters were significantly less likely to report a desire to work with a fat person than with a non-fat person. In the first of these studies (1990a) males reported significantly less desire to work with a fat woman, whereas there was no comparable gender difference in desire to work with a fat man. In the second study (1990b), both male and female participants reported less interest in working with the fat female employee than with the fat male employee. Pingitore et al. (1994) also found that fat female applicants were less likely than fat male applicants to be recommended for hiring, especially by raters who were satisfied with their own bodies and for whom body satisfaction was central to their self-concept.

A recent study by Miller and Lundgren (2010), which also used a college student sample, examined whether a double standard existed for female political candidates based on weight. Consistent with the investigators' hypotheses, "obese" female candidates were evaluated more negatively overall and assessed more negatively in terms of reliability, dependability, honesty, ability to inspire, and ability to perform a strenuous job than were non-obese female applicants. Strikingly, not only was there an absence of the same penalty for obese male candidates, obese men were actually rated *more* positively than non-obese male candidates.

The stigma of being a fat woman is so pronounced that, in one study sample, non-fat men who were merely associated with a fat woman appeared to experience stigmatizing effects. Hebl and Mannix (2003) found in a sample of adult raters that non-fat male job applicants were judged more harshly when seen with a fat woman prior to being interviewed than were men seated next to a non-fat woman.

Once on the job, fat women also appear to face harsher treatment. In studies using samples of actual sales managers recruited from the community, Bellizzi and colleagues (Bellizzi and Hasty 1998; Bellizzi et al. 1989) asked participants to assess treatment of hypothetical employees in "role play" scenarios. They found that employees described as "extremely overweight" were more likely to be assigned by sales managers to undesirable sales territories or to no territory within the manger's region and less likely to be assigned an important or desirable region. This discrimination was stronger for fat women than for fat men (Bellizzi et al. 1989).

Additionally, when managers were presented with scenarios in which they needed to discipline the unethical sales behaviors of hypothetical employees, fat women fared worse than non-fat women (Bellizzi and Hasty 1998). Although a general finding in the sales and marketing literature has been that saleswomen are less harshly punished than salesmen for unethical sales behavior, this leniency seems to disappear when the saleswoman is fat.

Large-Scale Studies

Given the differential treatment of fat women in the job market, it is not surprising that evidence continues to accumulate about the long-term effects of this discrimination. Longitudinal studies using large national data sets, which we review below, have demonstrated trends of lower occupational attainment and lower hourly and lifetime earnings for fat women, even after controlling for other relevant variables, such as education and family socioeconomic status. Investigators have generally used data from the National Longitudinal Survey of Youth (NLSY) and the Panel Study of Income Dynamics (PSID) to analyze these trends.

Some earlier analyses of NLSY data (Averett and Korenman 1996; Gortmaker et al. 1993), have clearly demonstrated that fat women have lower household incomes than non-fat women, while this was not the case for fat men. However, since this is likely confounded with the lower probability of marriage for fat women (discussed later), investigations of the impact of women's weight on their own wages are more relevant to the current review. Register and Williams (1990) found, after controlling for conventional variables associated with income (e.g., years of education, ethnicity, geographic region, etc.) that fat women (defined as those 20% in excess of standard weight for height) in the NLSY sample earned an average of 12% less than non-fat women, whereas this finding did not extend to fat men. Pagán and Dávila (1997) also reported lower occupational attainment and earnings for "obese" women using data from the NLSY and found that men appeared able to offset any weight-related penalty by sorting themselves into jobs in which weight did not impact wages. Women, by contrast, may only be able to offset the wage penalty for being fat by being above average in skill level (Mitra 2001).

Cawley (2004) pooled data from 13 years of the NLSY to examine the relationship between weight and wages and found that the negative relationship between body weight and wages is most consistently found for "significantly overweight" White women, whom he estimates are paid on average 9% less than women of median weight. He proposes this wage difference is equal to that associated with roughly 3 years of prior work experience, 2 years of job tenure, or 1 year of education.

Baum and Ford (2004) also used multiple years of NLSY data to examine the impact of weight on wages over time. Though they did not examine ethnicity, they did control for a number of other socioeconomic and familial variables and also found a weight penalty for both men and women, with that for women roughly twice as large as that for men. Additionally, they found that being "overweight or obese" has a significant impact on women's wages, while only "obesity" negatively impacts the wages of men.

Finally, analysis of NLSY data by Han and colleagues (Han, Norton and Stearns 2009) also found that "obesity" reduces the likelihood of employment among White women and reduces hourly wages for both White and Black women, whereas no effect is observed for men when other variables are controlled. They found this wage effect for women to increase with age (particularly after age 30) and to be larger in occupations requiring more social interactions than in other occupations. A second investigation by these authors (Han, Norton and Powell 2009) was conducted to examine both the direct effect of weight on wages and indirect effects through educational attainment and occupational sorting. Specifically, the authors hypothesized that a higher body mass index (BMI) in the late teen years may predict lower educational

attainment and/or choice of lower-paying occupations. Findings were consistent with hypotheses for both genders, although the findings for women were larger. The authors concluded, in fact, that the total wage penalty for women's BMI is underestimated in other samples by approximately 19% without the inclusion of these indirect effects.

A couple of investigators have more recently extended this work by examining relationships between weight and economic outcomes for men and women using data from the PSID. The PSID is also a national survey of U.S. adults who are, on average, much older than respondents from the NLSY samples described previously. Conley and Glauber (2007) found that "obesity" is associated with a 17.51% reduction on women's wages, with no economic penalty observed for men's weight (except for a small wage penalty experienced by obese Black men). Consistent with previous research, when including examination of race, they also found that the financial penalties for excess weight are experienced by White women. Because of the expanded age range in the PSID sample, they were also able to examine age differences in the weight penalties on earnings and found that differences in earnings by weight are significant for young women (ages 25–34) but not for older women (ages 35–44). They estimate that the difference between the predicted wages of a non-obese White woman and an obese White woman is roughly equivalent to the difference due to 2 years of education.

Gregory and Ruhm (2009) also used PSID sample data to examine these relationships and found that the wage penalty for White women begins well below conventional thresholds for "overweight" or "obese," with wages for this group peaking at a BMI of 21.8, whereas wages peaked at higher BMI values for Black women. Results for men were somewhat dependent on the modeling technique used but main estimates suggested that wages peaked at higher BMI levels (26.7). When other factors were controlled in subsequent modeling, however, wages also appeared to peak at lower values for men.

Given these collective findings of lower occupational attainment and lower earnings among fat women, we should also expect their lifetime earnings to reflect such discrimination. A study by

Fonda and colleagues (Fonda et al. 2004), which used data from the Health and Retirement Study of men and women in their 50s, indeed showed that "overweight" and "obese" women have a lower logged net worth at retirement-age than do their non-fat counterparts. This difference was attenuated to a non-significant level once potential covariates were controlled (e.g., sociodemographics, health, work, and marital status). For men, however, "overweight" and "obesity" were associated with *higher* logged net worth at retirement.

At What Weight Do Women Experience This Wage penalty?

In addition to the main findings of employment-related discrimination against fat women, a few notable trends are worth highlighting. The first is that women, predominantly White women, tend to experience decreasing wages at much lower weights than do men, as found in the aforementioned analysis by Gregory and Ruhm (2009). For example, Maranto and Stenoien (2000), using data from the NLSY, found the negative effect of weight on salaries to be highly significant for White women in the "overweight" range and only marginally significant for Black women. White and Black men, on the other hand, experienced wage *premiums* for being "overweight" or "mildly obese" and only experienced wage penalties at the very highest weight levels (100% above standard weight for their height). In fact, White women in this sample were found to suffer a greater wage penalty for "mild obesity" (20% over standard weight for their height) than Black men did for weight that is 100% over standard weight.

A recent study by Judge and Cable (2011) also explored this phenomenon of women being financially penalized for much lesser deviations from what is considered "ideal" in terms of weight. In their analysis of NLSY data, men experienced increased pay with increased weight. These returns only began to diminish at above-average levels of weight. For women, by contrast, increases in weight had negative linear effects on pay and the negative effect was much stronger at the lower end of the weight spectrum. In other words, it was the point at which women moved from the "thin" category into the "average weight" category that they experienced the most severe punishment, and

decrements in pay for further weight increases were actually less severe. To put this in concrete financial terms, the authors calculate that. . ."all else equal, a woman who is average weight earns $389,300 less across a 25-year career than a woman who is 25 lb below average weight" (p.15).

At What Occupational Level Do Women Experience the Most discrimination?

Another consistent finding is that the penalties for fatness in women vary by occupational level and appear to most significantly impact a women attempting to move into higher prestige (and more highly compensated) occupations. A study by Haskins and Ransford (1999) of female employees in the aerospace industry found that, whereas weight was an important and significant predictor of occupational attainment in the entire sample, it only significantly impacted wages for those women in entry-level professional and managerial strata. The authors suggest that this finding could reflect the fact that women may undergo the most intense "screening" (of both job-relevant and irrelevant factors) at this occupational level, when they are, in essence, moving from lower-paying blue-collar positions into upper-level professional and managerial positions. Moreover, thinness or being at an "ideal weight" was especially related to high occupational status in the male-dominated cluster of professions (e.g., research scientist, senior engineer, physicist, etc.).

If such intense scrutiny is, in fact, being applied to women moving up the ranks, then it could explain the absence of fat women among these ranks. Saporta and Halpern (2002) surveyed male and female lawyers to determine the relationships between weight and compensation. Male lawyers were found to experience a penalty for deviating in either direction from the "ideal" physique whereas women were only penalized for being above the "ideal" weight. Perhaps most interesting, however, is that the relationships between weight and pay did not reach statistical significance among fat female lawyers, most likely due to the fact that there were so few fat female lawyers in the sample at all.

A similar absence of fat women was found by Roehling et al. (2009) in their study of top U.S. CEOs at Fortune 1000 companies. Women in general are underrepresented in this stratum of the corporate world, but fat women remarkably so. Whereas roughly two thirds of adult women in the U.S. are classified as "overweight" or "obese," only 10% of top US female CEOs fall into these weight categories. And though obese men are also quite rare among top CEOs, overweight men are actually overrepresented among them (61% of top US male CEOs are overweight, compared to 31% of an age-matched population sample).

Griffin (2007) has suggested that subjective evaluation systems of a potential employee's disposition, ambition or attitude are more likely to be employed in supervisory or professional jobs (as opposed to blue-collar occupations). This suggests that fat women, who managers tend to view as lacking in self-discipline and overall competence, may face even larger barriers in their efforts to move into these more prestigious positions. Alternatively, it may be that the stigma fat women face is more likely to negatively impact their performance in certain environments. For example, research has demonstrated that fat women's self-esteem is negatively impacted in situations emphasizing achievement, whereas the same is not true for thin women (Jambekar et al. 2001), and that women with a stigmatized appearance perform worse than those without a stigmatized appearance when they are the only woman in a group of men (Kiefer et al. 2006).

In summary, there is ample evidence that weight-based employment discrimination is disproportionately experienced by women and that such discriminatory practices have a significant impact on their work experiences, occupational attainment and financial compensation. Recent findings that women may be experiencing the greatest wage penalty when they move from "below-average" in weight to just slightly over "ideal weight" highlights the extremely narrow range of body weights deemed acceptable for women and the pervasive emphasis placed on appearance in the evaluation of women in professional settings. Additionally, it appears that a woman's weight is even more of a liability as she attempts to move into higher-ranking professions.

Education

Given the disparities that have been documented between fat and non-fat women in the labor market, researchers have also examined whether these differences begin to emerge prior to entering the workforce. There is cross-sectional evidence that body weight and educational attainment are inversely related among White women, whereas the relationship is less consistent among men and women of color (Leigh et al. 1992). Although the direction of effect has often been presumed to be that lower levels of education lead to increases in weight, evidence from longitudinal studies has demonstrated that the educational outcomes of young women are also negatively impacted by prior weight status (Glass et al. 2010; Gortmaker et al. 1993).

Studies highlighting the impact of weight on educational outcomes began nearly 40 years ago with work by Canning and Mayer (1966) demonstrating that, among elite universities in the Northeastern U.S., students classified as "obese" were significantly more likely to be denied acceptance, and this was especially true for women. Based on additional research by these investigators (Canning and Mayer 1967) showing that, among high school students, there were no significant differences between those classified as obese and non-obese on standardized intelligence scores, grades, involvement in extracurricular activities, or interest and intent in pursuing higher education, they concluded that obese students were being discriminated against during in-person interviews by college admission boards primarily based on their weight status. This seminal work has since inspired additional research on how body weight plays a role in both the high school experiences of adolescents and college enrollment rates.

Falkner et al. (2001) conducted a cross-sectional study in a population-based sample of public school students in 7th, 9th, and 11th grades. They found that "obese" status was associated with adverse social and educational outcomes for both boys and girls, but that these associations were both greater in number and worse in severity for girls. After adjusting for the possible influence of confounding variables, they found that "obese" girls, in addition to having greater odds of reporting adverse social and emotional outcomes, were over two times as likely to perceive themselves as being below-average students and one-and-a-half times more likely to report having been held back a year in school. Despite this, these girls did not report lower educational aspirations or less confidence in expecting to be professionally successful in adulthood.

A series of more recent longitudinal studies by Crosnoe and colleagues (Crosnoe 2007; Crosnoe and Muller 2004; Crosnoe et al. 2008) found that the negative impact of body weight on educational outcomes for girls may be partly attributable to the social stigma they experience and the emotional consequences of this stigma. Using data from the National Longitudinal Study of Adolescent Health (Add Health), a nationally representative study of U.S. adolescents in grades 7–12, these researchers found that adolescents of both genders who were "at risk of obesity" (those in the 85th percentile or above in BMI for their age group and gender) had lower academic achievement than other students. This was particularly true in schools where the average BMI of the student body was lower and where there were higher rates of dating, contexts in which a heavier body might be both more noticeable and more of a social liability in the context of romantic activity. This led the authors to conclude that the impact of body weight on achievement may be mediated through lower self-appraisals in the context of higher stigma (Crosnoe and Muller 2004).

These pathways appear to be especially potent in the case of adolescent females. In subsequent research using a subset of Add Health, (Crosnoe et al. 2008) they found that as BMI increased among high school students the likelihood of being nominated by peers as "friends" decreased, especially among girls. Additionally, both boys and girls tended to organize themselves into friendship networks by body size, meaning that girls who were already stigmatized for their own weight were also more likely to be socially segregated from their non-stigmatized peers.

The hypothesis that the social consequences of weight for young women are, at least in part, what determines their academic outcomes was tested in a third study using data from Add Health. In this investigation, Crosnoe (2007) found that adolescent girls classified as "obese" (at or above the 95th percentile of BMI for their age-gender group) were less likely to enter college after high school than their non-obese peers, especially when they attended schools in which obesity was relatively uncommon and even when controlling for numerous other factors (e.g., parental education, academic ability, etc.) that could conceivably be related to both obesity and educational attainment. Obesity was not related to boys' rates of college matriculation. Additionally, body weight for young women predicted an increase in internalizing symptoms, more alcohol and drug use, and academic disengagement. These psychosocial factors explained about one third of obese girls' lower odds of enrolling in college.

A series of studies reported by Crandall (1991; 1995) demonstrated that young women may face additional hurdles rooted in weight-based discrimination even if they do manage to enroll in college. Specifically, he found that college students with higher body weight received less financial support from their parents (and, thus, relied more heavily on jobs, savings and financial aid) to pay for the expense of college. This finding was more reliable for women than it was for men across three different studies in two separate universities and after controlling for parental education level, income, race, family size and number of children attending college (Crandall 1991). In a second set of studies, Crandall (1995) replicated these findings in other college samples and also found evidence consistent with the hypothesis that it was parental attitudes (rather than parental financial means) that most likely explained these discriminatory practices toward fat daughters.

Finally, several other recent studies have replicated the general findings of the negative impact of women's weight on educational outcomes while also considering the role of race. Merten et al. (2008) examined the relationships between weight status during Wave 1 data collection in the Add Health study (average participant age=15) and depressive symptoms and status attainment (indexed by college enrollment, employment and job satisfaction) at Wave 3 (average participant age=22). They found that "obesity" among adolescent girls was associated with more depressive symptoms and lower status attainment in young adulthood when compared with girls with weight in the normative range, whereas obesity status among males was not associated with either outcome. These researchers found no difference in these relationships between White and Black adolescents.

However, two other studies did find that the impact of adolescent girls' weight on academic outcomes differs by race. In cross-sectional analysis of Add Health data, Sabia (2007) found evidence of a significant negative relationship between BMI and grade point average for White females between the ages of 14 and 17. He also found, while controlling for other relevant variables, that White females who *perceived* themselves to be overweight had lower grade point averages than those who did not perceive themselves to be overweight. The results for White females were consistent across statistical estimates, whereas evidence for a significant relationship between weight and academic achievement for nonwhite females and males was not consistent.

Finally, Okunade et al. (2009) examined the longitudinal relationship between weight status among students in grades 7–10 and on-time high school graduation rates. Whereas they found no significant adverse impact of weight on timely high school completion for males, there were significant negative effects for females. In particular, Asian girls appeared to suffer the largest penalty for higher weight status (significant at both the "obese" and "overweight" levels). There was also a strong negative effect of being "overweight" (but not "obese") on White girls and a negative effect for "obesity" (but not "overweight") among Hispanic girls. No adverse impact was found for either overweight or obese status among Black girls.

Collectively, these data point to yet another domain in which a higher body weight is more of a liability for females than for males, perhaps particularly so for certain ethnic groups. Additionally, understanding the discrepancies between fat and non-fat women in the labor market may be better understood by an appreciation for the different trajectories that begin in earlier stages of development and impact employment prospects.

Romantic Relationships

Another area in which females are more heavily penalized for their weight than males is in the context of romantic relationships. The vast majority of this research has been conducted on heterosexual relationships, which we will review first, followed by a discussion about what is known about women's weight in same-sex relationships.

Starting in early adolescence, young women who are at the higher end of the weight spectrum report fewer opportunities to date and less involvement in romantic relationships, relative to their thinner peers. A longitudinal study of seventh and eight-grade girls by Halpern et al. (1999) demonstrated that girls with higher levels of body fat were significantly less likely to report dating activity over the past 6 months, and this was particularly true for White girls and for Black girls whose mothers were college graduates. Heavier girls were also less likely to be engaged in sexual activity, although this was mostly mediated by their reduced opportunities to date. A second study by this group (Halpern et al. 2005) using a large, nationally-representative sample of slightly older girls (mean age=15.7 years) found that, after controlling for potential confounding variables (e.g., physical maturity, demographic characteristics, and prior relationship history), for each one-point increase in BMI, the likelihood of being in a romantic relationship decreased by 6–7%. Widerman and Hurst (1998) found a similar pattern among college-aged women, where being heavier was related to lower probability of being involved in a romantic relationship and less sexual experience, despite the women having similarly positive attitudes toward, and interest in, sexual relationships.

Whereas the preceding three studies only examined these relationships among females, studies that compare the experiences of males and females consistently find that having a heavier body weight is not as detrimental to the dating and sexual relationships of young men. Pearce et al. (2002), for example, found that, among students in grades 9–12, 50% of girls classified as "obese" reported having never dated, compared to only 20% of their average-weight peers. For boys, however, the percentage reporting no dating experience was virtually identical between "obese" boys (29%) and average-weight boys (30%).

A similar pattern of results is found for college students. In a study by Sheets and Ajmere (2005), women who were a standard deviation or more above the mean BMI for the women in their sample were half as likely to be dating as women one standard deviation or more below the mean BMI, with no significant differences in dating status observed between men in various weight categories. Among those in the sample who were coupled, weight was also inversely related to relationship satisfaction among women, but positively correlated with relationships satisfaction among men, indicating that the negative feedback women receive about their weight may both determine the likelihood of being in a relationship and the quality of relationships.

The negative experiences of fat women reported above map on to the perceptions of fat women examined in experimental studies. Regan (1996) found that college students receiving information about a male and female target presumed than an "obese" man's sexual experiences and level of sexual desire would be virtually identical to that of a "normal-weight" man. When the target was a woman, however, her weight status made a significant difference in how participants perceived her. Specifically, the fat female target was not only rated as less sexually desirable and experienced but also as less skilled, warm and responsive as a sexual partner and less likely to feel sexual desire for others. Chen and Brown (2005) asked college students to rate the attractiveness of prospective partners and found that men were more likely to choose sexual partners on the basis of weight than were women. Male study participants rated "obese" women as less attractive than women who were missing a limb, in a wheelchair, mentally ill or had a sexually transmitted disease.

The importance placed on women's weight in the dating sphere is also confirmed by two studies examining personal advertisements. In the first (Smith et al. 1990), significantly more males than females requested partners with a low body weight (primarily using the descriptors "thin," "slim," or "petite"). In a second study, male respondents to a personal advertisement were significantly more likely to respond to an ad in which the woman was described as being in recovery from drug addiction than one who was described as 50 lb "overweight" (Sitton and Blanchard 1995). Not surprisingly, research on self-presentation in online dating profiles finds that women are more likely than men to lie about their weight (Toma et al. 2008).

The finding that women's weight is more of a liability than men's in the sphere of romantic relationships has probably received the most attention in studies of so-called "marriage market" outcomes. This research has largely been done by economists using data from the National Longitudinal Study of Youth (NLSY) and the Panel Study on Income Dynamics (PSID). Findings consistently show that women who are fat have lower rates of both cohabitation (Mukhopadhyay 2008) and marriage (Averett and Korenman 1996; Averett et al. 2008; Conley and Glauber 2007; Fu and Goldman 1996) than thinner women and that, when they do marry, tend to marry partners with lower levels of education (Garn et al. 1989a; b), lower earnings (Averett and Korenman 1996; Conley and Glauber 2007;), of shorter stature (Oreffice and Quintana-Domeque 2010) and less physical attractiveness (Carmalt et al. 2008) than do thinner women, whereas these effects are either less or not observed at all for men's weight.

Thus, for fat women, heterosexual romantic relationships are yet another domain in which they fare worse, primarily because men are both more focused on, and critical of, the weight of their female partners, which may stem, in part, from the negative social judgment leveled at men who are associated with fat women (Hebl and Mannix 2003). The potential outcomes for fat women range from being excluded entirely from desired relationships, to forming relationships with less desirable partners, to the extreme case of being targeted as "easy marks" for sexual conquest (Gailey and Prohaska 2006; Prohaska and Gailey 2009).

There has been no research to date on the impact of body weight on the frequency or quality of relationships among lesbians. Yet this would be an interesting area to investigate, since studies have found lesbians to be feel more satisfied with their bodies, diet less, and score lower on measures related to eating disorders than heterosexual women (Bergeron and Senn 1998; Gettelman and Thompson 1993; Herzog et al. 1992; Moore and Keel 2003; Owens et al. 2003; Share and Mintz 2002; Schneider et al. 1995; Siever 1994). This is despite the fact that some studies have found lesbians to weigh more than heterosexual women (e.g., Boehmer et al. 2007; Guille and Chrisler 1999; Herzog et al. 1992; Owens et al. 2003), even when compared with their heterosexual sisters (Rothblum and Factor 2001). In contrast, gay men are usually found to be less satisfied with their bodies, diet more, and score higher on measures related to eating disorders than heterosexual men (Beren et al. 1996; French et al. 1996; Gettelman and Thompson 1993; Herzog et al. 1991; Schneider et al. 1995; Silberstein et al. 1989; Strong et al. 2000). Based on the above-reported findings that men place more importance on body weight as a factor in selecting romantic partners, we would hypothesize that weight stigma may be much less of a factor in lesbian relationships than in relationships between gay men.

Health and Mental Health

There have been many studies examining attitudes of health and mental health professionals and trainees about weight in their clients and patients (cf., Puhl and Brownell 2001, for a review), but the majority have not examined the role of gender. As will be reviewed below, a few studies have examined the association between weight stigma and gender of health care provider, gender of patient, or gender of case vignette. Other studies have used exclusively female samples.

The Health Care Setting

In a study on attitudes of medical students, student participants watched videos of a female "patient" who appeared either average weight or "overweight" via padding and make-up (Breytspraak et al. 1977). Subsequently students rated the heavier woman more negatively on 14 of 21 variables, such as defensive, cold, nervous, incompetent, depressed, and not likeable. The students also rated the heavier woman as less educated, less in need of help, less likely to benefit from help, more likely to have continuing problems, but also reported that they had more desire to help the heavier woman. More recently, Puhl et al. (2009) asked dietetic students (92% of whom were female) to view a hypothetical patient profile who was either male or female and either "obese" or "non-obese." Students who viewed the profile of an obese patient generally rated him/her as less healthy, as having a poorer diet, and as less likely to comply with treatment recommendations, despite the fact that the health and nutritional habits attributed to these patients were identical across conditions. Although the profile of the obese male patient was given less favorable ratings on energy intake by the overall sample, students with higher levels of fat phobia rated the obese female patient's diet quality as being poorer.

Anderson et al. (2001) sent physicians three hypothetical case vignettes that differed in BMI (25, 28 and 32, respectively), which were either all of women or all of men. Physicians were more likely to recommend weight loss for heavier case vignettes regardless of gender. But for those case vignettes with a BMI of 25, physicians were more likely to recommend weight loss, Weight Watchers, or a reduction in calories when the vignette was female, and more likely to discourage dieting and encourage accepting appearance when the vignette was male. There were no significant effects for physicians' gender.

Schwartz et al. (2003) gave the Implicit Attitudes Test (IAT) to researchers and clinicians attending an international obesity conference. There was significant anti-fat bias on variables of bad/good, lazy/motivated, stupid/smart, and worthless/valuable. In addition, on self-report measures, participants also rated fat people as lazy, stupid and worthless. Women and younger participants showed more anti-fat bias; participants who worked with fat people, had fat friends, or provided clinical care to fat patients had less anti-fat bias. In contrast, Foster et al. (2003) found over half of physicians to regard fat patients as noncompliant, ugly, and awkward, but female physicians had more positive attitudes about fat patients, such as greater empathy.

In a study designed to videotape and analyze how primary care physicians interact with their patients, Bertakis and Azari (2005) used a coding system and trained coders to note the occurrence of a number of practice-related variables. Physicians were twice as likely to diagnose "obesity" in female patients as in male patients. Physicians were more likely to discuss exercise with obese patients and less likely to discuss health education.

Given these results, it is not surprising that women perceive their body weight to be a factor in their interactions with health care providers. Amy et al. (2006) used community samples to survey Black and White women with BMIs of 25 or higher about barriers to gynecological care. BMI was not correlated with education, employment, or access to health insurance, yet there was a strong association between the women's BMI and their decisions to delay seeking health care or cancer-screening tests because of weight. Close to three-quarters of the women reported one or more specific barriers to health care such as disrespectful treatment, embarrassment about being weighed, negative attitudes by health care providers, unsolicited advice to lose weight, or the use of gowns, medical equipment, or exam tables that were too small. Women with higher BMIs were significantly more likely to report each barrier. Adams et al. (1993) recruited women via newspaper advertisements and found a significant difference between "average weight," "moderately overweight," and "very overweight" women (based on Metropolitan Life Tables for weight and height) on self-reported frequency of pelvic exams and reluctance to obtain pelvic exams, with heavier women reporting more reluctance and lower frequency of pelvic exams. They also surveyed physicians and found that 83% did not like performing pelvic exams on "very reluctant" patients, 17% did not like examining the "very obese," and male physicians, especially if they were older, were more averse to examining "reluctant" patients than were female physicians and younger physicians. Fontaine et al. (1998) used data from women in the 1992 National Health Interview Survey. After they controlled for age, race, education, income, smoking, and health insurance status, higher BMI was related to women delaying gynecological exams, Papp smears, and clinical breast exams, though not mammograms. In a study of female nurses (Olson et al. 1994), those who were heavier were more likely to have delayed medical care because they were embarrassed about their weight, did not want a lecture about their weight, or were trying to lose weight before their medical appointment.

In a study that asked male and female patients about the quality of their medical care, Hebl and Mason (2003) found that "overweight" male patients reported that physicians spent less time with them than did average weight male patients; there was no effect for weight among female patients. Physicians were more likely to discuss weight-related issues with heavier female than male patients, including nutrition counseling and stress. At the same time, heavier female patients reported more positive care by physicians than did average weight female patients; there was no weight effect for men.

Exercise

Wee et al. (1999) used data from the National Health Interview Survey to examine factors that are associated with physicians counseling patients to exercise. Physicians were more likely to recommend exercise for patients who were female, had higher BMIs, were in their forties, had health insurance, had higher incomes, and had higher levels of education. However, the gender difference disappeared when the results were adjusted for current weight loss attempts.

Even though exercise for health and/or weight loss is frequently suggested by health care professionals, gyms and fitness clubs may be uncomfortable settings for heavier people. A study of college women by Vartanian and Shaprow (2008) found that a higher frequency of weight stigmatizing experiences was positively correlated with motivation to avoid exercise behavior.

The Mental Health Setting

Young and Powell (1985) asked mental health professionals to evaluate a case history of a middle-aged, White female client accompanied by a photograph that was altered to appear average weight or 20% or 40% over "best weight." The heaviest photograph received significantly higher ratings of psychological dysfunction. Additionally, female mental health professionals as well as mental health professionals who were younger and those who were average weight assigned more negative psychological ratings to the heavier photographs.

Two studies have focused specifically on attitudes toward weight among psychologists. Agell and Rothblum (1991) mailed a case vignette to psychologists who were members of Division 29 (psychotherapy) of the American Psychological Association (APA), which depicted a client as either male or female, average weight or heavy. Psychologists rated the heavier case vignette as more physically unattractive and embarrassed, but also softer and kinder than the average-weight case. Female clients were evaluated as more motivated and less severely impaired than male clients, but there were no significant gender or weight effects on recommendations for therapy. Davis-Coelho et al. (2000) mailed a self-description of a hypothetical Caucasian female client accompanied by a fat or thin photograph to psychologists who were members of APA Division 12 (clinical psychology), 17 (counseling psychology), 29 (psychotherapy) and 42 (independent practice). Psychologists who received the fat photograph were more likely to diagnose an eating disorder, and to suggest "improve body image" and "increase sexual satisfaction" as treatment goals. Younger psychologists who received the fat photograph were more likely to predict that fat clients needed to make more effort, and female psychologists gave the fat "client" a worse prognosis.

In sum, there has been limited research focusing on weight bias and gender in health and mental health settings. Existing research finds strong evidence of bias against fat women among health care providers, who are both more likely to diagnose women as "obese" and to treat fat women as having more negative personal qualities. The fact that fat women report delaying medical care and avoiding exercise facilities because of weight-based stigma, and the subsequent impact on their health, is of considerable concern.

Media

Although a sizable body of research in the field of eating disorders has examined the impact of the ever-present *thin* female body in the media on both standards of attractiveness and eating disorder symptoms (see Greenberg and Worrell 2005, for a review), far fewer studies have explored the roles assigned to fat women in mass media. Indeed, one of the main challenges in analyzing the characterization of fat women in the media is that they are largely absent. One of the first studies examining prevalence of body types in prime time television was conducted by Kaufman in 1980, who found that 88% of the individuals shown in prime time television programming had thin or average body types and only 12% were "overweight or obese." Men with larger body sizes were depicted roughly twice as frequently (15% of the sample) as were women with larger bodies (8% of the sample).

More recent studies have replicated both the under-representation of all fat bodies, as compared with statistics from the general population, and the discrepancy between men and women. Analysis by Spitzer et al. (1999) of the "ideal" body types

portrayed for men and women over the last four decades found that, while the average BMI of Miss America Pageant contestants and centerfold models in *Playboy* has decreased significantly, the BMI of male models featured as centerfolds in *Playgirl* magazine has *increased*. The average body weight for both men and women has increased during this time period; thus, the discrepancy between the BMIs of female bodies portrayed in these media and women in the general population has increased at the same time as the discrepancy between the BMIs of idealized male bodies and those of men in the general population has actually decreased. (The authors do note, however, that the increase in the BMI of male centerfolds likely reflects an increase in muscularity, which is not necessarily accounted for in BMI measurement).

A study analyzing both primetime network television and daytime soap opera characters found that female body types were more slender on average than male body types, with 72.5% and 29.2% of females and males, respectively, in the underweight category. Conversely, 12.8% of female body types were classified as "overweight," compared with 32.9% of male body types (White et al. 1999). Interestingly, thin women even outnumber heavier women on weight loss infomercials, where they are depicted as the "satisfied customers" of products and men (who appear less often overall) are depicted as the "scientific experts" (Blaine and McElroy 2002).

Finally, a study that examined both the distribution and associated characteristics of various body types on prime-time television found that only 14% of females and 24% of males were in the "overweight or obese" category, less than half the percentages in the general population. Although a number of unfavorable characteristics were associated with large body size for both genders (e.g., reduced likelihood of interacting with romantic partners), fat women were also less likely than their thinner counterparts to be judged as attractive, less likely to show physical affection, and more likely to be the object of humor, whereas these differences were not significant between weight categories for male characters (Greenberg et al. 2003).

The tendency for fat women, when they are included in mass media, to be cast primarily as foils for thinner characters has also been studied. Fouts and colleagues (Fouts and Burggraf 1999; 2000; Fouts and Vaughan 2002) have shown in studies of situation comedies shown on prime time television in the late 1990s that below-average weight women are over-represented, compared with the general population, and receive significantly more positive verbal comments from male characters with regards to body weight and shape than do heavier women (Fouts and Burggraf 1999). Conversely, heavier female characters receive significantly more derogatory comments from male characters and the majority of the time these comments are followed by audience reactions of laughter, "oohs," or giggles, implying that male commentary on fat female bodies is a socially acceptable behavior (Fouts and Burggraf 2000).

When they explored whether the same would be true for heavy male characters they found that, while fat men were also underrepresented compared to the population, there was a smaller discrepancy than that for women, and that it was the heavy male characters themselves who made comments about their own weight (again, followed by audience laughter) rather than a dynamic in which either females or other males made reference to their weight (Fouts and Vaughan 2002). Similar findings were also reported by Himes and Thompson (2007), who examined fat stigmatization messages presented in both television shows and movies between 1984 and 2004 and found that, although men and women were almost equally likely to be the targets of fat stigmatization, men were about three times more likely to make comments about someone's weight than were women.

In addition to often being the butt of jokes, as noted above, fat women are less likely to be portrayed as being the object of romantic interest. In a more in-depth analysis of two particular television situation comedies that featured fat female characters, Giovanelli and Ostertag (2009) found that the fat women characters, although often present during discussions of the romantic or sexual adventures of other (thin) characters, either did not participate in these conversations by referring to their own sexual or romantic interests, or were depicted as pursuing love interests who had already been judged by others as clearly flawed and/or who were also the butt of jokes. Analysis of other media (i.e., popular movies and so-called "Chick Lit," a genre of fiction written by and for women) find that even when a fat woman *is* portrayed as a romantic lead, her weight is often as much of interest (comically, or otherwise) as any other aspect of the plot line (Frater 2009; Mendoza 2009).

Indeed, fat women celebrities in general are often discussed as much for their weight and size as anything else, and this is especially true when these women have public "battles" with their weight that become the topic of tabloid news. In their essay on how fat women are sometimes "betrayed" by these celebrity icons, Bernstein and St. John (2009) focus on four women in particular (Ricky Lake, Carnie Wilson, Oprah Winfrey and Roseanne Barr), and their public weight losses (and/or continuing weight loss efforts). The general theme noted by the authors is of women who begin by appearing to defy expectations to apologize for their size who then, subsequent to their own weight loss, distance themselves from this stance by participating in the denigration of fat bodies.

In summary, the media contribute to the marginalization of fat woman either by rendering them invisible when presenting a "norm" of predominantly underweight women and/or by making fat women's weight the most salient characteristic about them as people and a target for remedy (through weight loss), pity, or comedy. Aside from the deleterious effect on consumers of the media, it can also be inferred that, given their scarcity in the industry, fat women likely face steep challenges to obtaining employment in this domain.

Race and Ethnicity

Research has generally found some racial and ethnic minority groups in the U.S. to weigh more than White people but also to be more satisfied with their weight and body size. Carr et al. (2008) found Black participants to self-report higher weights than White participants in the National Survey of Midlife Development in the United States (MIDUS). Winkleby et al. (1996), using data from the Stanford Five-City Project, found that Hispanic participants had higher BMIs than White participants matched on relevant demographic variables, and also had higher desired weights than White counterparts. Rand and Kuldau

(1990) interviewed over 2,000 adults in Florida from a community probability sample; White women had lower BMIs than Black women yet were more likely to state that they had a "weight problem." It is important to note that weight in the U.S. is inversely correlated with income, particularly for women (e.g., Sobal and Stunkard 1989), and that people of color in the U.S. have lower mean incomes than do White people.

These differences in both absolute body weights and in perception of "overweight" among people of color have led researchers to examine how weight-related discrimination is influenced by race or ethnicity. Puhl et al. (2008) used data from MIDUS, which asked participants about daily or lifetime discrimination in interpersonal relationships based on age, gender, race, height or weight, ethnicity or nationality, physical disability, appearance other than height or weight, sexual orientation, religion, or other reason. Women (10.3%) were twice as likely as men (4.9%) to report weight-based discrimination, and weight discrimination was reported more frequently by Black women (23.9%) and Black men (12.7%), who also weighed more. In regression analyses, being younger, female, and having high BMI were predictors of weight discrimination, but there was no effect for race.

Carr et al. (2008) similarly used the discrimination variables in the MIDUS data set to examine the relationship between race, socioeconomic status (SES), gender and weight. Their factor analysis of items of perceived daily interpersonal discrimination yielded three subscales: lack of respect (e.g., being treated with discourtesy, receiving poor service), blemish of character (e.g., being treated as dishonest or frightening to others) and harassment/teasing (e.g., being called names, insulted, or teased). Black participants and those with lower SES had higher BMIs, and people with higher BMIs reported more instances of all three subtypes of discrimination. Women reported greater lack of respect but lower blemish of character and harassment/teasing than did men. White men in the highest BMI category reported higher levels on all three subscales of discrimination than thinner men, whereas Black men in the highest BMI category reported lower levels of discrimination than men who were average weight. There was no significant effect for race among women.

Wade and DiMaria (2003) found an interaction of race and weight when White college students were asked to rate vignettes of women that were accompanied by a photograph depicting the woman as either Black or White, and either fat or thin. The thinner White woman was rated more positively than the fatter White woman on attractiveness, friendliness, enthusiasm, occupational success, and mate potential, whereas there was no difference on trustworthiness or parenting skills. In contrast, the heavier Black woman was rated more positively than the thinner Black woman on friendliness, trustworthiness, parenting skills, and mate potential, while there was no difference on attractiveness, enthusiasm, or occupational success.

Hebl and Heatherton (1998) asked Black and White college students to rate magazine photographs of nine Black and nine White female fashion models; one-third were thin, one-third average weight, and one-third larger than average. White women rated heavier Black and White women in photographs as less attractive, intelligent, good at her job, successful in her relationships, happy with her life, and popular. In contrast, Black women did not rate Black and White women in photographs differently according to weight, except for rating heavier Black women as less attractive. When the participants were asked to select suitable jobs for each target woman, White women assigned jobs much lower in status to heavier women in photographs, whereas there was no such systematic bias in the ratings by Black participants.

Using the same methodology as Hebl and Heatherton (1998), Hebl et al. (2009) also found that White participants rated heavier Black and White targets more negatively than thin or average-weight targets, whereas there was no target weight effect for Black raters. In a second experiment, participants were first asked to read an article that was either neutral or that stated that Black women were thinner than White women (given to Black participants) or the reverse (given to White participants). Reading the article did not change the results for White female participants (who continued to rate heavier Black and White targets more negatively) but Black female participants who read the article stating that Black women have lower weights than White women engaged in more negative stereotyping of heavier Black and White targets. The authors concluded (p. 1168) that "individuals tend to self-affirm in domains in which they succeed."

Latner et al. (2005) asked male and female college students to rate figure drawings of adults (men rated male targets and women rated female targets) who were depicted as average weight with no visible disability, holding crutches with braces on one leg, sitting in a wheelchair, missing a hand, having a facial disfigurement, or fat. Overall the fat figure drawing received the second-to-lowest rating, above the drawing of the adult missing a hand, and men gave the fat drawing lower ratings than did women. Black and Asian students rated the fat drawing more positively than did White students; there was no difference between Hispanic students and White students. In a gender by race/ethnicity interaction, Black women rated the fat drawing more positively than did White women.

A study by Hebl and Turchin (2005) examined differences in weight stigma between White and Black male college students by having them rate targets on seven dimensions. In addition to the male students stigmatizing heavy White men more than heavy Black men, there were also ethnic differences in the ratings given to female targets. Specifically, White men appeared to have a narrower range of acceptable weight for White women, rating both heavy and medium-sized women more negatively than thin women whereas Black men gave more positive ratings to both thin and medium-sized Black women than they gave to heavy Black women. Interestingly, body size did not influence men's evaluations of women of a different race, only their ratings of women within their own racial group.

This greater latitude of body sizes perceived as attractive among Black men may help explain differences in the dating experiences of White and Black women of different sizes. Harris et al. (1991) found that self-reported frequency of dating was negatively correlated with BMI for White female college students, whereas there was no significant relationship between BMI and dating frequency for White male students or for Black female or male students. White male students were significantly more likely than Black male students to have refused to date someone because of her weight. Similarly, Powell and Kahn (1995) found Black male college students to express less desire for dating thin women than did White male students.

In sum, Black and Hispanic women may weigh more than White women and in that regard be subjected more often to weight-related discrimination. On the other hand, research on Black and White women and men shows Black people to be more accepting of heavier weight. Reasons for this could include the greater prevalence of large body size among these groups, or a tendency among people of color to reject mainstream White values, including White standards of bodily attractiveness. Moreover, even if lower body weight is preferred for the sake of attractiveness, fatness is not necessarily associated with negative personal qualities. As Hebl and Heatherton write (1998, p. 424): "This stigma of obesity may condemn large White women to downward socioeconomic mobility because of widespread discrimination.....Although Black women may have an aesthetic preference for thin body shapes, they tend not to generalize this preference to non-weight-relevant domains, such as occupational ability or social status."

We caution against an overly optimistic reading of this phenomenon for two reasons. The first is that other sources of discrimination against Black women may simply overshadow those attributable to body size. The venues in which fat White women are most likely to be discriminated against, namely high status jobs and marriage to earners of high income, may be venues from which many women of color have been excluded due to other factors, making additional effects due to weight impossible to detect (Averett and Korenman 1999).

Second, some scholars have interpreted the apparent lack of size discrimination against Black women in particular as fitting with the racial stereotype of Black women as being large, strong, independent and nurturing of others (Beauboeuf-Lafontant 2003; Bowen et al. 1991). Such a stereotype, however, often masks the very real powerlessness and marginalization of Black women, as well as potentially invalidating the experiences of Black women who do experience body image distress, as well as discrimination due to body size (Neumark-Sztainer et al. 1998).

Conclusion

The price paid by women as a result of weight-based discrimination is significant, cuts across multiple domains, and yet has received relatively little attention by feminist scholars when compared with other topics relating to weight (e.g., eating disorders and body image disturbance) or with other sources of discrimination impacting women. Although research on weight stigma has increased significantly in recent years, few researchers have addressed or attempted to assess the gendered nature of this bias (Griffin 2007 being a notable exception). As can be surmised from this review, however, there is substantial and consistent evidence that women suffer disproportionately from weight bias in a number of domains.

In employment settings, fat women are less likely to be hired, receive worse treatment on the job and earn less than their non-fat peers. Whereas there is some evidence of bias against fat men in employment settings, it is generally of a lower magnitude and/or occurs only at the highest levels of weight. Women also appear to suffer a penalty for being fat when it comes to both their functioning within educational settings and their accumulation of education, whereas men experience this penalty much less frequently, if at all. In romantic relationships and in the so-called "marriage market" women also fare worse if they are fat, with both lower probabilities of marriage and marriage to partners of lower status. Again, evidence for men suffering penalties for weight in this domain is either totally absent or inconsistent across samples.

A reduction of opportunities in the domains of employment, education and marital relationships has a substantial impact on a woman's economic opportunities in life. While there has long been recognition of the inverse relationships between women's weight and socioeconomic status (most particularly in the Western part of the world, but increasingly elsewhere; McLaren 2007), this relationship has often been interpreted as one in which poor women become fat due to lack of resources and education. Given the findings from longitudinal studies reviewed here, however, we agree with the conclusion of Ernsberger (2009) who has argued that "although there is some evidence that poverty is fattening, a stronger case can be made for the converse: fatness is impoverishing" (p. 26). This is especially true for women, who suffer from multiple sources of weight-based discrimination and thus, experience the impact of cumulative disadvantage (Clarke et al. 2010).

At a time when the declared "war on obesity" has brought more attention than ever to the presumed health risks associated with body weight, fat women's health care is actually being compromised because of the bias of various health care professionals. There is evidence that fat women delay care or avoid certain types of facilities entirely in order to avoid these stigmatizing experiences and yet *this* impact on the health of fat women has received very little attention. Moreover, the direct impact of the stress associated with stigmatizing experiences has been proposed to operate as an independent risk factor for adverse health outcomes (Muennig 2008). As women experience more weight bias, they are also likely to shoulder a disproportionate share of this risk.

Lastly, there are very few opportunities for fat women (or, for that matter, any woman who is not exceedingly slender) to view favorable reflections of herself in mass media. Instead, various media outlets display and legitimize the view of fat women as targets of humor or pity. In the rare case of the fat female celebrity, often her size is given more attention than any other aspect of her professional life, and speculations about weight loss or regain predominate any coverage of her activities.

In much of this research, it appears that it is white women who most often experience weight bias (and white men who most often perpetuate anti-fat bias), although this is not universally true and likely depends on other factors, such as socioeconomic status and peer group (Ofusu et al. 1998). It may be that people of color, who tend to weigh more, perceive less "deviance" in a fat body and thus do not stigmatize fatness. Alternatively, the lack of engagement with the thin ideal may reflect a more general disengagement with a mainstream media that largely excludes people of color.

To our knowledge, this is the first systematic review of the ways in which weight bias disproportionately impacts fat women in multiple domains. This is despite research demonstrating the downward social mobility of fat women dating back nearly 50 years (Goldblatt et al. 1965). This is also despite recent research conducted in a large sample of U.S. adults showing that discrimination based on weight ranked as *the third most prevalent cause of perceived discrimination among women* (after gender and age discrimination) and was reported more frequently than discrimination based on race, sexual orientation, religion or physical disability (Puhl et al. 2008).

Given how extensively anti-fat bias impacts the lives of women, we question why feminist scholars have not paid more attention, why, as Hartley (2001) writes, ". . .the fat body has largely been ignored in feminist studies that attempt to theorize the female body" (p. 61). Whereas anorexic bodies have been conceptualized as a metaphor for cultural proscriptions on women, fat bodies too often get interpreted in terms of poor health, with blame placed squarely on the individual (LeBesco 2009). This discrepant treatment in the feminist literature parallels the treatment of eating disorders and fatness in the popular media. Saguy and Gruys (2010) have examined how news media (specifically, the *New York Times* and *Newsweek*) described anorexia versus "overweight" in the years 1995–2005. They state: ". . . the news media treats anorexics as *victims* of a terrible illness beyond their and their parents' control, while obesity is caused by bad individual behavior, including, in the case of children, parental neglect" (p. 232). They also point out that girls with anorexia are portrayed as White and from affluent families whereas fatness is associated with poor girls of color.

Since the publication of *Fat is a Feminist Issue* in the late 1970s, much of the writing by feminists on the subject of women's weight has concerned itself primarily with the question of whether fatness (often conflated with disordered eating or other forms of psychopathology) should be "treated" by feminist therapists (e.g., Chrisler 1989) and, much more often, with the subject of how thinness came to be prized as highly as it is in a patriarchal culture (e.g., Bordo 1993). We propose that it is not enough to note that the ever thinner cultural ideal means that practically every woman will feel badly about her body. Feminists also need to turn our collective attention to the reality that, because of the pervasiveness and gendered nature of weight-based stigma, a majority of women stand to *suffer significant discrimination* because they do not conform to this ever-narrower standard.

Although the feminist movement has mobilized women to organize in opposition to other forms of discrimination that disproportionately impact women, there seems to be an exception when it comes to weight-based discrimination (Rothblum 1994). That a fat woman's experience would not receive the same level of attention, critique, and organized action only serves to further devalue her.

Acknowledgments   The authors would like to thank Kris Willcox for her editorial assistance with an earlier draft of this manuscript.

References

Adams, C. H., Smith, N. J., Wilbur, D. C., & Grady, K. E. (1993). The relationship of obesity to the frequency of pelvic examinations: Do physician and patient attitudes make a difference? *Women & Health, 20*(2), 45–57. doi:10.1300/J013v20n02_04.

Agell, G., & Rothblum, E. D. (1991). Effects of clients' obesity and gender on the therapy judgments of psychologists. *Professional Psychology: Theory and Practice, 22*, 223–229. doi:10.1037/0735-7028.22.3.223.

Amy, N. K., Aalborg, A., Lyons, P., & Keranen, L. (2006). Barriers to routine gynecological cancer screening for White and African-American obese women. *International Journal of Obesity, 30*, 147–155. doi:10.1038/sj.ijo.0803105.

Anderson, C., Peterson, C. B., Fletcher, L., Mitchell, J. E., Thuras, P., & Crow, S. J. (2001). Weight loss and gender: An examination of physician attitudes. *Obesity Research, 9*, 257–263. doi:10.1038/oby.2001.30.

Averett, S., & Korenman, S. (1996). The economic reality of the beauty myth. *Journal of Human Resources, 31*, 304–330. doi:10.2307/146065.

Averett, S., & Korenman, S. (1999). Black–white differences in social and economic consequences of obesity. *International Journal of Obesity, 23*, 166–173. doi:10.1038/sj.ijo.0800805.

Averett, S. L., Sikora, A., & Argys, L. M. (2008). For better or worse: Relationship status and body mass index. *Economics and Human Biology, 6*, 330–349. doi:10.1016/j.ehb.2008.07.003.

Baum, C. L., & Ford, W. F. (2004). The wage effects of obesity: A longitudinal study. *Health Economics, 13*, 885–899. doi:10.1002/hec.881.

Beauboeuf-Lafontant, T. (2003). Strong and large black women? Exploring relationships between deviant womanhood and weight. *Gender and Society, 17*, 111–121. doi:10.1177/0891243202238981.

Bellizzi, J. A., & Hasty, R. W. (1998). Territory assignment decisions and supervising unethical selling behavior: The effects of obesity and gender as moderated by job-related factors. *Journal of Personal Selling & Sales Management, 18*(2), 35–49.

Bellizzi, J. A., Klassen, M. L., & Belonax, J. J. (1989). Stereotypical beliefs about overweight and smoking and decision-making in assignments to sales territories. *Perceptual and Motor Skills, 69*, 419–429.

Beren, S. E., Hayden, H. A., Wilfley, D. E., & Grilo, C. M. (1996). The influence of sexual orientation on body dissatisfaction in adult men and women. *International Journal of Eating Disorders, 20*, 135–141. doi:10.1002/(SICI)1098-108X(199609)20:2<135::AID-EAT3>3.3.CO;2-1.

Bergeron, S. M., & Senn, C. Y. (1998). Body image and sociocultural norms. *Psychology of Women Quarterly, 22*, 385–401. doi:10.1111/j.1471-6402.1998.tb00164.

Bernstein, B., & St. John, M. (2009). The Roseanne Benedict Arnolds: How fat women are betrayed by their celebrity icons. In E. Rothblum & S. Solovay (Eds.), *The fat studies reader* (pp. 263–270). New York: New York University Press.

Berryman, D. E., Dubale, G. M., Manchester, D. S., & Mittelstaedt, R. (2006). Dietetics students possess negative attitudes toward obesity similar to nondietetics students. *Journal of the American Dietetic Association, 106*, 1678–1682. doi:10.1016/j.jada.2006.07.016.

Bertakis, K. D., & Azari, R. (2005). The impact of obesity on primary care visits. *Obesity Research, 13*, 1615–1623. doi:10.1038/oby.2005.198.

Blaine, B., & McElroy, J. (2002). Selling stereotypes: Weight loss infomercials, sexism and weightism. *Sex Roles, 46*, 351–357. doi:10.1023/A:1020284731543.

Boehmer, U., Bowen, D. J., & Bauer, G. R. (2007). Overweight and obesity in sexual-minority women: Evidence from population-based data. *American Journal of Public Health, 97*, 1134–1140. doi:10.2105/AJPH.2006.

Bordo, S. (1993). *Unbearable weight: Feminism, Western culture, and the body.* Berkeley: University of California Press.

Bowen, D., Tomoyasu, N., & Cauce, A. (1991). The triple threat: A discussion of gender, class and race differences in weight. *Women & Health, 17*(4), 123–143. doi:10.1300/J013v17n04_06.

Breytspraak, L. M., McGee, J., Conger, J. C., Whatly, J. L., & Moore, J. T. (1977). Sensitizing medical students to impression formation processes in the patient interview. *Journal of Medical Education, 52*, 47–54. doi:10.1097/00001888-197701000-00007.

Brown, L. S. (1985). Women, weight, and power: Feminist theoretical and therapeutic issues. *Women & Therapy, 4*, 61–71.

Brown, L. S. (1989). Fat-oppressive attitudes and the feminist therapist: Directions for change. *Women & Therapy, 8*, 19–29.

Canning, H., & Mayer, J. (1966). Obesity—its possible effect on college acceptance. *The New England Journal of Medicine, 275*, 1172–1174. doi:10.1056/NEJM196611242752107.

Canning, H., & Mayer, J. (1967). Obesity: An influence on high school performance? *American Journal of Clinical Nutrition, 20*, 352–354.

Carmalt, J. H., Cawley, J., Joyner, K., & Sobal, J. (2008). Body weight and matching with a physically attractive romantic partner. *Journal of Marriage and Family, 70*, 1287–1296. doi:10.1111/j.1741-3737.2008.00566.x.

Carr, D., Jaffe, K. J., & Friedman, M. A. (2008). Perceived interpersonal mistreatment among obese Americans: Do race, class, and gender matter? *Obesity, 16*(Supplement 2), S60–S68. doi:10.1038/oby.2008.453.

Cawley, J. (2004). The impact of obesity on wages. *Journal of Human Resources, 39*, 451–474. doi:10.2307/3559022.

Chen, E. Y., & Brown, M. (2005). Obesity stigma in sexual relationships. *Obesity Research, 13*, 1393–1397. doi:10.1038/oby.2005.168.

Chrisler, J. C. (1989). Should feminist therapists do weight loss counseling? *Women & Therapy, 8*(3), 31–37. doi:10.1300/J015V08N03_05.

Clarke, P. J., O'Malley, P. M., Schulenberg, J. E., & Johnston, L. D. (2010). Midlife health and socioeconomic consequences of persistent overweight across early adulthood: Findings from a national survey of American adults (1986-2008). *American Journal of Epidemiology, 172*, 540–548. doi:10.1093/aje/kwq156.

Conley, D., & Glauber, R. (2007). Gender, body mass, and socioeconomic status: New evidence from the PSID. *Advances in Health Economics and Health Services Research, 17*, 253–275. doi: 10.1016/S0731-2199(06)17010-7.

Crandall, C. S. (1991). Do heavy-weight students have more difficulty paying for college? *Personality and Social Psychology Bulletin, 17*, 606–611. doi:10.1177/0146167291176002.

Crandall, C. S. (1995). Do parents discriminate against their heavyweight daughters? *Personality and Social Psychology Bulletin, 21*, 724–735. doi:10.1177/0146167295217007.

Crosnoe, R. (2007). Gender, obesity, and education. *Sociology of Education, 80*, 241–260. doi:10.1177/003804070708000303.

Crosnoe, R., Mueller, A. S., & Frank, K. (2008). Gender, body size and social relations in American high schools. *Social Forces, 86*, 1189–1216.

Crosnoe, R., & Muller, C. (2004). Body mass index, academic achievement, and school context: Examining the educational experiences of adolescents at risk of obesity. *Journal of Health and Social Behavior, 45,* 393–407. doi:10.1177/002214650404500403.

Davis-Coelho, K., Waltz, J., & Davis-Coelho, B. (2000). Awareness and prevention of bias against fat clients in psychotherapy. *Professional Psychology: Research and Practice, 31,* 682–684. doi:10.1037/0735-7028.31.6.682.

Diamond, N. (1985). Thin is the feminist issue. *Feminist Review, 19,* 45–64.

Ernsberger, P. (2009). Does social class explain the connection between weight and health? In E. Rothblum & S. Solovay (Eds.), *The fat studies reader* (pp. 25–36). New York: New York University Press.

Falkner, N. H., Neumark-Sztainer, D., Story, M., Jeffery, R. W., Beuhring, T., & Resnick, M. D. (2001). Social, educational, and psychological correlates of weight status in adolescents. *Obesity Research, 9,* 32–42. doi:10.1038/oby.2001.5.

Fallon, P., Katzman, M. A., & Wooley, S. C. (1994). *Feminist perspectives on eating disorders.* New York: The Guilford Press.

Fikkan, J., & Rothblum, E. (2005). Weight bias in employment. In K. D. Brownell, R. M. Puhl, M. B. Schwartz, & L. Rudd (Eds.), *Weight bias: Nature, consequences and remedies* (pp. 15–28). New York: Guilford.

Fonda, S. J., Fultz, N. H., Jenkins, K. R., Wheeler, L. M., & Wray, L. A. (2004). Relationship of body mass and net worth for retirement-aged men and women. *Research on Aging, 26,* 153–176. doi:10.1177/0164027503258739.

Fontaine, K. R., Faith, M. S., Allison, D. B., & Cheskin, L. J. (1998). Body weight and health care among women in the general population. *Archives of Family Medicine, 7,* 381–384. doi:10.1001/archfami.7.4.381.

Foster, G. D., Wadden, T. A., Makris, A. P., Davidson, D., Sanderson, R. S., Allison, D. B., et al. (2003). Primary care physicians' attitudes about obesity and its treatment. *Obesity Research, 11,* 1168–1177. doi: 10.1038/oby.2003.161.

Fouts, G., & Burggraf, K. (1999). Television situation comedies: Female body images and verbal reinforcements. *Sex Roles, 40,* 473–481. doi:10.1023/A:1018875711082.

Fouts, G., & Burggraf, K. (2000). Television situation comedies: Female weight, male negative comments, and audience reactions. *Sex Roles, 42,* 925–932. doi:10.1023/A:1007054618340.

Fouts, G., & Vaughan, K. (2002). Television situation comedies: Male weight, negative references, and audience reactions. *Sex Roles, 46,* 439–442. doi:10.1023/A:1020469715532.

Frater, L. (2009). Fat heroines in Chick-Lit: Gateway to acceptance in the mainstream? In E. Rothblum & S. Solovay (Eds.), *The fat studies reader* (pp. 235–240). New York: New York University Press.

French, S. A., Story, M., Remafedi, G., Resnick, M. D., & Blum, R. W. (1996). Sexual orientation and prevalence of body dissatisfaction and eating disordered behaviors: A population-based study of adolescents. *International Journal of Eating Disorders, 19,* 119–126. doi:10.1002/(SICI)1098-108X(199603)19:2<119:: AID-EAT2>3.3.CO;2-B.

Fu, H., & Goldman, N. (1996). Incorporating health into models of marriage choice: Demographic and sociological perspectives. *Journal of Marriage and the Family, 58,* 740–758. doi:10.2307/353733.

Gailey, J. A., & Prohaska, A. (2006). "Knocking off a fat girl": An exploration of hogging, male sexuality and neutralizations. *Deviant Behavior, 27,* 31–49. doi:10.1080/016396290968353.

Garn, S. M., Sullivan, T. V., & Hawthorne, V. M. (1989a). Educational level, fatness and fatness differences between husband and wives. *American Journal of Clinical Nutrition, 50,* 740–745.

Garn, S. M., Sullivan, T. V., & Hawthorne, V. M. (1989b). The education of one spouse and the fatness of the other spouse. *American Journal of Human Biology, 1,* 233–238. doi:10.1002/ajhb.1310010302.

Gettelman, T. E., & Thompson, J. K. (1993). Actual difference and stereotypical perceptions in body image and eating disturbances: A comparison of male and female heterosexual and homosexual samples. *Sex Roles, 29,* 545–562. doi:10.1007/BF00289327.

Giovanelli, D., & Ostertag, S. (2009). Controlling the body: Media representations, body size, and self-discipline. In E. Rothblum & S. Solovay (Eds.), *The fat studies reader* (pp. 289–296). New York: New York University Press.

Glass, C. M., Haas, S. A., & Reither, E. N. (2010). The skinny on success: Body mass, gender and occupational standing across the life course. *Social Forces, 88,* 1777–1806.

Goldblatt, P. B., Moore, M. E., & Stunkard, A. J. (1965). Social factors in obesity. *Journal of the American Medical Association, 192,* 97–102.

Gortmaker, S. L., Must, A., Perrin, J. M., Sobol, A. M., & Dietz, W. H. (1993). Social and economic consequences of overweight in adolescence and young adulthood. *The New England Journal of Medicine, 329,* 1008–1012. doi:10.1056/NEJM199309303291406.

Gregory, C. A., & Ruhm, C. J. (2009). Where does the wage penalty bite? NBER Working Paper Series (Vol. w14984). Retrieved from http://www.nber.org/papers/w14894, May.

Greenberg, B. S., Eastin, M., Hofschire, L., Lachlan, K., & Brownell, K. D. (2003). Portrayals of overweight and obese individuals on commercial television. *American Journal of Public Health, 93*, 1342–1348. doi:10.2105/AJPH.93.8.1342.

Greenberg, B. S., & Worrell, T. R. (2005). The portrayal of weight in the media and its social impact. In K. D. Brownell, R. M. Puhl, M. B. Schwartz, & L. Rudd (Eds.), *Weight bias: Nature, consequences, and remedies* (pp. 42–53). New York: Guilford.

Griffin, A. W. (2007). Women and weight-based employment discrimination. *Cardozo Journal of Law and Gender, 13*, 631–662.

Guille, C., & Chrisler, J. C. (1999). Does feminism serve a protective function against eating disorders? *Journal of Lesbian Studies, 3* (4), 141–148. doi:10.1300/J155v03n04_18.

Halpern, C. T., Udry, J. R., Campbell, B., & Suchindran, C. (1999). Effects of body fat on weight concerns, dating and sexual activity: A longitudinal analysis of Black and White adolescent girls. *Developmental Psychology, 35*, 721–736. doi:10.1037//0012-1649.35.3.721.

Halpern, C. T., King, R. B., Oslak, S. G., & Udry, J. R. (2005). Body mass index, dieting, romance, and sexual activity in adolescent girls: Relationships over time. *Journal of Research on Adolescence, 15*, 535–559. doi:10.1111/j.1532-7795.2005.00110.x.

Han, E., Norton, E. C., & Powell, L. (2009). Direct and indirect effects of teenage body weight on adult wages. NBER Working Paper Series (Vol. w15027). Retrieved from http://ssrn.come/abstracts=1413591, June.

Han, E., Norton, E. C., & Stearns, S. C. (2009). Weight and wages: Fat versus lean paychecks. *Health Economics, 18*, 535–548. doi:10.1002/hec.1386.

Harris, M. B., Walters, L. C., & Waschull, S. (1991). Gender and ethnic differences in obesity-related behaviors and attitudes in a college sample. *Journal of Applied Social Psychology, 21*, 1545–1566. doi:10.1111/j.1559-1816.1991.tb00487.x.

Hartley, C. (2001). Letting ourselves go: Making room for the fat body in feminist scholarship. In J. E. Braziel & K. LeBesco (Eds.), *Bodies out of bounds: Fatness and transgression* (pp. 60–73). Berkeley: University of California Press.

Haskins, K. M., & Ransford, H. E. (1999). The relationship between weight and career payoffs among women. *Sociological Forum, 14*, 295–318. doi:10.1023/A:1021470813182.

Hebl, M. R., & Heatherton, T. E. (1998). The stigma of obesity in women: The difference in black and white. *Personality and Social Psychology Bulletin, 24*, 417–426. doi:10.1177/0146167298244008.

Hebl, M. R., King, E. B., & Perkins, A. (2009). Ethnic differences in the stigma of obesity: Identification and engagement with a thin ideal. *Journal of Experimental Social Psychology, 45*, 1165–1172. doi:10.1016/j.jesp.2009.04.017.

Hebl, M. R., & Mason, M. F. (2003). Weighing the care: Patients' perceptions of physician care as a function of gender and weight. *International Journal of Obesity, 27*, 269–275. doi:10.1038/sj.ijo.802231.

Hebl, M. R., & Mannix, L. M. (2003). The weight of obesity in evaluating others: A mere proximity effect. *Personality and Social Psychology Bulletin, 29*, 28–38. doi:10.1177/0146167202238369.

Hebl, M. R., & Turchin, J. M. (2005). The stigma of obesity: What about men? *Basic and Applied Social Psychology, 27*, 267–275. doi:10.1207/s15324834basp2703_8.

Herzog, D. B., Newman, K. L., & Warshaw, M. (1991). Body image dissatisfaction in homosexual and heterosexual males. *The Journal of Nervous and Mental Disease, 179*, 356–359. doi:10.1097/00005053-199106000-00009.

Herzog, D. B., Newman, K. L., Yeh, C. J., & Warshaw, M. (1992). Body image satisfaction in homosexual and heterosexual women. *International Journal of Eating Disorders, 11*, 391–396. doi:10.1002/1098-108X(199205)11:4<391::AID-EAT2260110413>3.0.CO;2-F.

Hesse-Bieber, S. N. (2007). *The cult of thinness* (2nd ed.). New York: Oxford University Press.

Himes, S. M., & Thompson, J. K. (2007). Fat stigmatization in television shows and movies: A content analysis. *Obesity, 15*, 712–718. doi:10.1038/oby.2007.635.

Jambekar, S., Quinn, D. M., & Crocker, J. (2001). The effects of weight and achievement messages on the self-esteem of women. *Psychology of Women Quarterly, 25*, 48–56. doi: 10.1111/1471-6402.00006.

Jasper, C. R., & Klassen, M. L. (1990a). Perceptions of salespersons' appearance and evaluation of job performance. *Perceptual and Motor Skills, 71*, 563–566. doi:10.2466/PMS.71.5.563–566.

Jasper, C. R., & Klassen, M. L. (1990b). Stereotypical beliefs about appearance: Implications for retailing and consumer issues. *Perceptual and Motor Skills, 71*, 519–528. doi:10.2466/PMS.71.5.519-528.

Judge, T. A., & Cable, D. M. (2011). When it comes to pay, do the thin win? The effect of weight on pay for men and women. *Journal of Applied Psychology, 96*, 95–112. doi:10.1037/a0020860.

Kaufman, L. (1980). Prime-time nutrition. *Journal of Communication, 30*, 37–46. doi:10.1111/j.1460-2466.1980.tb01989.x.

Kiefer, A., Sekaquaptewa, D., & Barczyk, A. (2006). When appearance concerns make women look bad: Solo status and body image concerns diminish women's academic performance. *Journal of Experimental Social Psychology, 42*, 78–86. doi: 10.1016/j. jesp.2004.12.004.

Klein, D., Najman, J., Kohrman, A. F., & Munro, C. (1982). Patient characteristics that elicit negative responses from family physicians. *Journal of Family Practice, 14*, 881–888.

Latner, J. D., Stunkard, A. J., & Wilson, G. T. (2005). Stigmatized students: Age, sex, and ethnicity effects in the stigmatization of obesity. *Obesity Research, 13*, 1226–1231. doi:10.1038/oby.2005.145.

LeBesco, K. (2009). Weight management, good health and the will to normality. In H. Malson & M. Burns (Eds.), *Critical feminist approaches to eating dis/orders* (pp. 147–155). London: Routledge.

Leigh, J. P., Fries, J. F., & Hubert, H. B. (1992). Gender and race differences in the correlation between body mass and education in the 1971-1975 NHANES I. *Journal of Epidemiology and Community Health, 46*, 191–196. doi:10.1136/jech.46.3.191.

Lundborg, P., Bolin, K., Höjgård, S., & Lindren, B. (2007). Obesity and occupational attainment among the 50+ of Europe. *Economics and Human Biology, 5*, 1–19. doi:10.1016/j.ehb.2006.11.002.

Maranto, C. L., & Stenoien, A. F. (2000). Weight discrimination: A multidisciplinary analysis. *Employee Responsibilities and Rights Journal, 12*, 9–24. doi:10.1023/A:1007712500496.

McLaren, L. (2007). Socioeconomic status and obesity. *Epidemiological Reviews, 29*, 29–48. doi:10.1093/epirev/mxm001.

Mendoza, K. R. (2009). Seeing through the layers: Fat suits and thin bodies in *The Nutty Professor* and *Shallow Hal*. In E. Rothblum & S. Solovay (Eds.), *The fat studies reader* (pp. 280–288). New York: New York University Press.

Merten, M. J., Wickrama, K. A. S., & Williams, A. L. (2008). Adolescent obesity and young adult psychosocial outcomes: Gender and racial differences. *Journal of Youth and Adolescence, 37*, 1111–1122. doi:10.1007/s10964-008-9281-z.

Mitra, A. (2001). Effects of physical attributes on the wages of males and females. *Applied Economics Letters, 8*, 731–735. doi:10.1080/13504850110047605.

Miller, B. J., & Lundgren, J. D. (2010). An experimental study of the role of weight bias in candidate evaluation. *Obesity, 18*, 712–718. doi:10.1038/oby.2009.492.

Moore, F., & Keel, P. K. (2003). Influence of sexual orientation and age on disordered eating attitudes and behaviors in women. *International Journal of Eating Disorders, 34*, 370–374. doi:10.1002/eat.10198.

Muennig, P. (2008). The body politic: The relationship between stigma and obesity-associated disease. *British Medical Journal, 8*, 128. doi:10.1186/1471-2458-8-128.

Mukhopadhyay, S. (2008). Do women value marriage more? The effect of obesity on cohabitation and marriage in the USA. *Review of Economics of the Household, 6*, 111–126. doi:10.1007/s11150-007-9025-y.

Neumark-Sztainer, D., Story, M., & Faibisch, L. (1998). Perceived stigmatization among overweight African American and Caucasian adolescent girls. *Journal of Adolescent Health, 23*, 264–270.

Ofusu, H. B., Lafreniere, K. D., & Senn, C. Y. (1998). Body image perception among women of African descent: A normative context? *Feminism & Psychology, 8*, 303–323. doi:10.1177/0959353598083005.

Okunade, A. A., Hussey, A. J., & Karakus, M. C. (2009). Overweight adolescents and on-time high school graduation: Racial and gender disparities. *Atlantic Economic Journal, 37*, 225–242. doi:10.1007/s11293-009-9181-y.

Olson, C. L., Schumaker, H. D., & Yawn, B. P. (1994). Overweight women delay medical care. *Archives of Family Medicine, 3*, 888–892. doi:10.1001/archfami.3.10.888.

Orbach, S. (1978). *Fat is a feminist issue*. New York: Berkeley Books.

Oreffice, S., & Quintana-Domeque, C. (2010). Anthropometry and socioeconomics among couples: Evidence in the United States. *Economics and Human Biology, 8*, 373–384. doi:10.1016/j.ehb.2010.05.001.

Owens, L. K., Hughes, T. L., & Owens-Nicholson, D. (2003). The effects of sexual orientation on body image and attitudes about eating and weight. *Journal of Lesbian Studies, 7*(1), 15–33. doi:10.1300/J155v07n01_02.

Pagán, J. A., & Dávila, A. (1997). Obesity, occupational attainment and earnings. *Social Science Quarterly, 78*, 757–770.

Pearce, M. J., Boergers, J., & Prinstein, M. J. (2002). Adolescent obesity, overt and relational peer victimization, and romantic relationships. *Obesity Research, 10,* 386–393. doi:10.1038/oby.2002.53.

Pingitore, R., Dugoni, B. L., Tindale, R. S., & Spring, B. (1994). Bias against overweight job applicants in a simulated employment interview. *Journal of Applied Psychology, 74,* 909–917. doi:10.1037/0021-9010.79.6.909.

Powell, A. D., & Kahn, A. S. (1995). Racial differences in women's desires to be thin. *International Journal of Eating Disorders, 17,* 191–195. doi:10.1002/1098-108X(199503).

Prohaska, A., & Gailey, J. (2009). Fat women as "easy targets": Achieving masculinity through hogging. In E. D. Rothblum & S. Solovay (Eds.), *The fat studies reader* (pp. 158–166). New York: New York University Press.

Puhl, R. M., Andreyeva, T., & Brownell, K. D. (2008). Perceptions of weight discrimination: Prevalence and comparison to race and gender discrimination in America. *International Journal of Obesity, 32,* 1–9. doi:10.1038/ijo.2008.22.

Puhl, R., & Brownell, K. D. (2001). Bias, discrimination, and obesity. *Obesity Research, 9,* 788–805. doi:10.1038/oby.2001.108.

Puhl, R., Wharton, C., & Heuer, C. (2009). Weight bias among dietetics students: Implications for treatment practices. *Journal of the American Dietetic Association, 109,* 438–444. doi:10.1016/j.jada.2008.11.034.

Rand, C. S. W., & Kuldau, J. M. (1990). The epidemiology of obesity and self-defined weight problem in the general population: Gender, race, age, and social class. *International Journal of Eating Disorders, 9,* 329–343. doi:10.1002/1098-108X(199005).

Regan, P. C. (1996). Sexual outcasts: The perceived impact of body weight and gender on sexuality. *Journal of Applied Social Psychology, 26,* 1803–1815. doi:10.1111/j.1559-1816.1996.tb00099.x.

Register, C. A., & Williams, D. R. (1990). Wage effects of obesity among young workers. *Social Science Quarterly, 71,* 131–141.

Rodin, J., Silberstein, L., & Striegel-Moore, R. (1984). Women and weight: A normative discontent. *Nebraska Symposium on Motivation, 32,* 267–307.

Roehling, P. V., Roehling, M. V., Vandlen, J. D., Blazek, J., & Guy, W. C. (2009). Weight discrimination and glass ceiling effect among top US CEOs. *Equal Opportunities International, 28,* 179–196. doi:10.1108/02610150910937916.

Roehling, M. V., Roehling, P. V., & Pichler, S. (2007). The relationship between body weight and perceived weight-related employment discrimination: The role of sex and race. *Journal of Vocational Behavior, 71,* 300–318. doi:10.1016/j.jvb.2007.04.008.

Rothblum, E. D. (1992). The stigma of women's weight: Social and economic realities. *Feminism & Psychology, 2,* 61–73. doi:10.1177/0959353592021005.

Rothblum, E. D. (1994). "I'll die for the revolution, but don't ask me not to diet": Feminism and the continuing stigmatization of obesity. In P. Fallon, M. A. Katzman, & S. C. Wooley (Eds.), *Feminist perspectives on eating disorders* (pp. 53–76). New York: Guilford.

Rothblum, E. D., & Factor, R. (2001). Lesbians and their sisters as a control group: Demographic and mental health factors. *Psychological Science, 12,* 63–69. doi:10.1111/1467-9280.00311.

Rothblum, E. D., Miller, C. T., & Garbutt, B. (1988). Stereotypes of obese female job applicants. *International Journal of Eating Disorders, 7,* 277–283. doi:10.1002/1098-108X(198803)7:2<277::AID-EAT2260070213>3.0.CO;2-2.

Sabia, J. J. (2007). The effect of body weight on adolescent academic performance. *Southern Economic Journal, 73,* 871–900.

Saguy, A. C., & Gruys, K. (2010). Morality and health: News media constructions of "overweight" versus eating disorders. *Social Problems, 57,* 231–250. doi:10.1525/sp.2010.57.2.231.

Saporta, I., & Halpern, J. J. (2002). Being different can hurt: Effects of deviation from physical norms on lawyers' salaries. *Industrial Relations, 41,* 442–466. doi:10.1111/1468-232X.00256.

Sargent, J. D., & Blanchflower, D. G. (1994). Obesity and stature in adolescence and earnings in young adulthood: Analysis of a British birth cohort. *Archives of Pediatric Adolescent Medicine, 148,* 681–687.

Sarlio-Lähteenkorva, S., & Lahelma, E. (1999). The association of body mass index with social and economic disadvantage in women and men. *International Journal of Epidemiology, 28,* 445–449. doi:10.1093/ije/28.3.445.

Sarlio-Lähteenkorva, S., Silventoinen, K., & Lahelma, E. (2004). Relative weight and income at different levels of socioeconomic status. *American Journal of Public Health, 94,* 468–472. doi:10.2105/AJPH.94.3.468.

Schneider, J. A., O'Leary, A., & Jenkins, S. R. (1995). Gender, sexual orientation, and disordered eating. *Psychology and Health, 10,* 113–128. doi:10.1080/08870449508401942.

Schorb, F. (2009). *Dick doof und arm? Die große Lüge vom Übergewicht und wer von ihr profitiert.* Munich: Droemer Verlag.

Schwartz, M. B., Chambliss, H. O., Brownell, K. D., Blair, S. N., & Billington, C. (2003). Weight bias among health professionals specializing in obesity. *Obesity Research, 11,* 1033–1039. doi:10.1038/oby.2003.142.

Share, T., & Mintz, L. B. (2002). Differences between lesbians and heterosexual women in disordered eating and related attitudes. *Journal of Homosexuality,* 42(4), 89–106. doi:10.1300/J082v42n04_06.

Sheets, V., & Ajmere, K. (2005). Are romantic partners a source of college students' weight concern? *Eating Behaviors, 6,* 1–9. doi:10.1016/j.eatbeh.2004.08.008.

Siever, M. D. (1994). Sexual orientation and gender as factors in socioculturally acquired vulnerability to body dissatisfaction and eating disorders. *Journal of Consulting and Clinical Psychology, 62,* 252–260. doi:10.1037/0022-006X.62.2.252.

Silberstein, L. R., Mishkind, M. E., Striegel-Moore, R. H., Timko, C., & Rodin, J. (1989). Men and their bodies: A comparison of homosexual and heterosexual men. *Psychosomatic Medicine, 51,* 337–346.

Sitton, S., & Blanchard, S. (1995). Men's preferences in romantic partners: Obesity vs. addiction. *Psychological Reports, 77,* 1185–1186.

Smith, J. E., Waldorf, V. A., & Trembath, D. L. (1990). Single white male looking for thin, very attractive. . . . *Sex Roles, 23,* 675–685. doi:10.1007/BF00289255.

Sobal, J., & Stunkard, A. J. (1989). Socioeconomic status and obesity: A review of the literature. *Psychological Bulletin, 105,* 260–275. doi:10.1037/0033-2909.105.2.260.

Spitzer, B. L., Henderson, K. A., & Zivian, M. T. (1999). Gender differences in population versus media body sizes: A comparison over four decades. *Sex Roles, 40,* 545–565. doi:10.1023/A:1018836029738.

Strong, S. M., Singh, D., & Randall, P. K. (2000). Childhood gender nonconformity and body dissatisfaction in gay and heterosexual men. *Sex Roles, 43,* 427–439. doi:10.1023/A:1007126814910.

Tang-Péronard, J. L., & Heitmann, B. L. (2008). Stigmatization of obese children and adolescents: The importance of gender. *Obesity Reviews, 9,* 522–534. doi:10.1111/j.1467-789X.2008.00509.x.

Toma, C. L., Hancock, J. T., & Ellison, N. B. (2008). Separating fact from fiction: An examination of deceptive self-presentation in online dating profiles. *Personality and Social Psychology Bulletin, 34,* 1023–1036. doi:10.1177/0146167208318067.

Vartanian, L. R., & Shaprow, J. G. (2008). Effects of weight stigma on exercise motivation and behavior: A preliminary investigation among college-aged females. *Journal of Health Psychology, 13,* 131–138. doi:10.1177/1359105307084318.

Viner, R. M., & Cole, T. J. (2005). Adult socioeconomic, educational, social, and psychological outcomes of childhood obesity: A national birth cohort study. *BMJ, 330,* 1354. doi:10.1136/bmj.38453.422049.E0.

Wade, T. J., & DiMaria, C. (2003). Weight halo effects: Individual differences in perceived life success as a function of women's race and weight. *Sex Roles, 48,* 461–465. doi:10.1023/A:1023582629538.

Wee, C. C., McCarthy, E. P., Davis, R. B., & Phillips, R. S. (1999). Physician counseling about exercise. *Journal of the American Medical Association, 282,* 1583–1588. doi:10.1001/jama.282.16.1583.

White, S. E., Brown, N. J., & Ginsburg, S. L. (1999). Diversity of body types in network television programming: A content analysis. *Communication Research Reports, 16,* 386–392. doi:10.1080/08824099909388740.

Widerman, M. W., & Hurst, S. R. (1998). Body size, physical attractiveness, and body image among young adult women: Relationships to sexual experience and sexual esteem. *Journal of Sex Research, 35,* 272–281. doi:10.1080/00224499809551943.

Winkleby, M. A., Gardner, C. D., & Taylor, C. B. (1996). The influence of gender and socioeconomic factors on Hispanic/White differences in body mass index. *Preventive Medicine, 25,* 203–211. doi:10.1006/pmed.1996.0047.

Wooley, O. W., Wooley, S. C., & Dyrenforth, S. R. (1979). Obesity and women II: A neglected feminist topic. *Women's Studies International Quarterly, 2,* 81–92. doi:10.1016/S0148-0685(79) 93096-3|.

Young, L. M., & Powell, B. (1985). The effects of obesity on the clinical judgments of mental health professionals. *Journal of Health and Social Behavior, 26,* 233–246. doi:10.2307/2136755.

At the Intersection of Public Health and Fat Studies: Critical Perspectives on the Measurement of Body Size

by Sonya Satinsky and Natalie Ingraham

Department of Health, Sport, and Exercise Sciences, University of Kansas, Lawrence, Kansas, USA

Natalie Ingraham

Department of Social & Behavioral Sciences, University of California, San Francisco, San Francisco, California, USA

Public health and fat studies intersect around documenting varied body sizes, and both disciplines claim that body size is relevant to their research. However, current body size measures are problematic, and nonstigmatizing measures of body size are needed. In particular, means of documenting lived body size that are decoupled from health are desirable for both disciplines. This commentary aims to begin conversations about social justice–oriented means of documenting body diversity, to critically discuss how these measures are used, and potential next steps for body size measurement.

The disciplines of public health and fat studies intersect and overlap around the measurement and experiences of varied body sizes. Both fields document body size diversity among individuals, although generally for quite disparate reasons. Public health measures body size to assess, describe, and predict the health of populations while fat studies tends to document body size as a framework for understanding the lived experience of fat individuals and the cultural meanings around the fat body. At this point in the trajectories of both fat studies and public health as disciplines, we currently still need body size measurement, for two pragmatic reasons.

First, we need to be able to make the case that fat people face significant discrimination and oppression, which we may not be able to do without also documenting that it is fat people who are making these claims. There is the need to document the bodies of people of size, for practical concerns like buying clothing or furniture, or planning travel, as well as the need to work

within existing weight-based paradigms to bring about social change. Additionally, people whose bodies are in the highest weight ranges are likely to experience differential and potentially more severe forms of weight stigma (Gruys, 2012; Lewis, Thomas, Blood, Hyde, Castle, & Komesaroff, 2010). The degree and type of experiences of very fat individuals and communities should be distinguished from the social consequences for those whose body size places them closer to societal norms for body size. However, there is little to no research on these differences; we would argue that a social justice–informed measurement of actual body size would potentially be useful for this purpose. Pragmatically, without some form of body size measurement, we would not be able to make the case that living in a fatter body in our culture carries the potential for socially mediated negative outcomes.

Secondly, the current paradigm in public health calls for increased quantification and measurement in epidemiological surveillance. Given this movement toward large-scale measurement, if we cannot remove the focus on quantification, we can try to temper the means by which bodies are being quantified.

However, existing means of documenting body size are problematic and in need of reconceptualization. Using both the examples of existing imperfect and possible means of capturing body size, this commentary aims to critically discuss how these measures are used both to indicate resistance or reification of body-related claims across disciplines and contexts, and to open up conversations about social justice–oriented means of documenting body diversity. We will also address the potential for digital technologies to move both fields forward in meeting their disciplinary aims.

Despite some potential for synergy, differential approaches to "the body" have forged somewhat divergent paths between the fat studies and public health disciplines that could be more closely aligned. Public health as a discipline attempts to make claims about the health of communities at the population level, and often has a vested interest in "anti-obesity" rhetoric. Fat studies, on the other hand, endeavors as a discipline to uncover and make visible lived experiences of individuals of size and critique population-level claims about the meanings and import of large bodies. Both disciplines make explicit that body size is relevant to their research.

Fat studies, as a discipline, endeavors to "critically examine societal attitudes about body weight and appearance" (Rothblum, 2012, p. 3), with the goal of exploring body diversity and equity from a social justice perspective. Wann (2009) asserts that a key part of engagement in fat studies is the willingness to examine one's personal involvement with the larger social structures that surround body size such as assumptions of fat as inherently unhealthy, fatness as a disease or the belief that fat people can and should lose weight. This also includes personal examination of both external and internal beliefs about fatness that are a result of our interactions with others, society and the beliefs individuals impose on themselves and others about the meaning of fatness.

An important tenet of fat studies as a discipline, in contrast to the field of public health, is the word

choice around the description of larger bodies. Terms like "obesity," "overweight," or "obese" are based on medical definitions of acceptable or "normal" weights rather than terms that merely describe bodies as we do with height (Wann, 2009). For this reason, many involved in fat studies put the term "obesity" inside quotation marks to denote the assumptions and discriminatory consequences it represents. Fat studies scholars use the term "fat" purposively, as a way to reclaim it from the pejorative as well as carve out a political identity.

Fat studies scholars have explicitly focused on critiquing the desire for social control of the fat body. Discussion of the need to control and contain fat bodies is echoed throughout Braziel and LeBesco's (2001) critical text, *Bodies Out of Bounds*. Braziel and LeBesco (2001) consider fatness to be a "subject-marking experience" over which individuals are supposed to have control, unlike race or gender that are "mistakenly" seen as fixed qualities that are not questioned in terms of their cultural, historical, political and economic properties. While both fat studies and public health recognize that bodies change over time and across social characteristics like gender, race, age or class, the key difference may be the motivation for observation and measurement of bodies. Fat studies may observe the malleability of bodies as human difference without expectation of bodily boundaries or containment, while public health observes the changing human body with specific boundaries in mind within the accepted definitions of "healthy."

Public health disciplinarily prioritizes measurement, surveillance, and prediction of human health, which translates to measurement and surveillance of embodied subjects. However, the body has long acted an absent referent (Adams, 2010) in the field of public health. Therefore, though public health is primarily concerned with the health of populations, there is a level of detachment between the rhetorical messages proffered by the field with regard to what constitutes "health" and how to achieve it, and the embodied lived experience of those that are the targets of those messages (Lewis et al., 2010). The proclamations emanating from the field of public health, especially around the management and control of body sizes has not addressed the "someones" but rather has posited body fat as a "something" unconnected from a human shape or envelope. As Broom (2001) notes, public health has not fully explored and resolved the debate about to what degree bodies are biologically determined, socially constructed, or somewhere in between. Therefore, focus on the fat corporeal subjects who experience their bodies both somatically and psychologically is generally absent from public health discourse.

According to Lupton (1995), public health and the focus on "healthiness" is a way to produce certain types of bodies and judge those bodies associated with a lack of health, marginalizing them in the process. Public health tends to individualize health and illness while often removing broader social context (Lupton, 1995). Both public health and medicine privilege individual responsibility, where "placing oneself at risk of disease, or developing a medical condition related to lifestyle factors denotes a certain laxness toward one's body" (Lupton, 1995: 71). When public health does point to the environmental or "upstream" causes of "obesity," as is the case or method for social epidemiologists who study "obesity" (e.g. Gary-Webb, Suglia, & Tehranifar, 2013; Rand & Kuldau, 1990), this perspective is not always taken up by policy makers or intervention developers. Kirkland (2011) argues that this environmental account of "obesity" is not likely to promote structural change because of its problematic assumptions about the relationship between health and fat and about the efficacy of intervention strategies. Kirkland further states that the environmental approach to "obesity" masks moralism, like Lupton's (1995) concept of "healthiness," and legitimizes punitive, ineffective, and patronizing interventions.

The expectation of personal control of body size or fatness is clearly reflected in the individual-based weight loss programs or interventions within public health. Individuals are tasked with rigid control and documentation of all activities related to the body including detailed food and calorie logs (Lieffers & Hanning, 2012), physical activity logs or increasingly technological interventions like pedometers (Acharya, Elci, Sereika, Styn, & Burke, 2011) or accelerometers. These are

all common aspects of public health interventions to "fight against the obesity epidemic" (Chodosh et al., 2005). These interventions focus on weight loss in varying stages of the intervention and often short follow-up terms (6 months to 1 year) or, increasingly, on changes in waist circumference or waist-to-hip ratio. It is due to the sharp rise in interest in "obesity" in the last 30 years that body size measurement is now crucial to support of the public health agenda.

For public health, measuring bodies is a matter of exploring the risk of various body sizes and their associated chronic illnesses. Public health researchers have also explored fat peoples' associated experiences with weight stigma and negative health outcomes associated with it, although some of this research seeks to lessen weight stigma in order to encourage weight loss rather than reducing weight stigma based on its negative affects alone (e.g., Schvey, Puhl, & Brownell, 2011). While others within public health have discussed weight stigma as a social justice issue (e.g. Drury & Louis, 2002), the framing of many articles on weight stigma still upholds the ultimate goal of eliminating "obesity" and, by extension, fat bodies as a public health goal.

Body Size Measurements: Current (Problematic) Techniques

Current measures of body size used in research contexts leave much to be desired; most frequently used are the notoriously inaccurate body mass index (BMI) and body line drawings, originally developed by Stunkard, Sørensen, and Schulsinger (1983) and modified in various ways. BMI has been widely critiqued (e.g., Burkhauser & Cawley, 2008), due to its lack of specificity as a simple height-to-weight ratio, being undifferentiated across genders, lack of explanatory value for body *shape*, poor predictive value as a measure of actual health, and standardization based on a White male body. Despite these critiques, BMI continues to be privileged as a general practice in the measurement and categorization of bodies (Anderson, 2012).

Body line drawings are popular among body image researchers who use silhouette matching tests (SMT) to measure both body image satisfaction or dissatisfaction in concert with a measurement of current body size (Peterson, Ellenberg, & Crossan, 2003). Participants are asked to indicate which silhouette looks most like them right now; usually this question is followed by asking which silhouette the participant would most like to look like (Bulik et al., 2001; Fallon & Rozin, 1985; Gipson et al., 2005; Stunkard et al., 1983; Thompson, 1996). The difference between their choices is considered to represent body dissatisfaction. Recent studies have used SMT to measure body satisfaction differences between Black and White girls, finding that Black girls are less dissatisfied with their bodies, which also tended to be larger (as measured by BMI; Sherwood et al., 2003). According to many public health researchers, this discrepancy between having a larger body and being more satisfied with its shape needs to be "corrected" via intervention. This indicates that "obesity prevention" programs must "combat" this acceptance of larger bodies, even from the perspective of certain social scientists from disciplines like gender studies that might usually be more aligned with the size acceptance framework of fat studies (e.g. Lovejoy, 2001). We should note that many scholars within gender studies are more closely aligned with a size acceptance framework (e.g., see *Sex Roles* volume 66, issues 9/10 for multiple articles on the theme of "fat as a feminist issue.")

Body line drawings are often used to describe and define body image issues in addition to measuring cultural values around "acceptable" body size and shape, especially among women (Swami et al., 2010). However, there are a number of critiques around the accuracy and cultural sensitivity of these measures. Not only are these silhouettes not standardized to distinguish between one drawing and the next, the visual choices they offer to female participants are uniformly white, feminine-presenting, and hourglass-shaped. Therefore, they provide no visible representation for people of color, various gender presentations, or a fuller variety of body shapes. Methodological critiques of existing figural measures have been offered by multiple researchers. Some of these critiques rest on the problems with existing measures, including the limited range of sizes and ethnic identities these measures offer as choices and the lack of size

difference standardization between figures; others profess problems with the idea of figural measures as a practice. Therefore, even within those that use SMT, there are conflicts about how they should be employed and how many and what type of figures are adequate for assessment (Ambrosi-Randić, Pokrajac-Bulian, & Taksić, 2005; Gardner, Jappe, & Gardner, 2009; Peterson et al., 2003).

Each of these varied measures offers its own ranges of reliability and validity estimates, which are enumerated by Gardner and Brown (2010). Concerns remain, however, that methodologists of recording actual body size are still not paying enough attention to the presence of White ethnic facial and body features, which could greatly affect the validity of these measures with populations of color (Gipson et al., 2005). Removing all details that indicate ethnicity is further recommended by Gardner and Brown (2010); however, this assumes that the absence of ethnic identification leaves the figures open to being identifiable by diverse ethnic groups, where the absence may instead indicate a default White ethnicity to the figures.

Finally, most of the figural measures in current use are limited in the upper and lower ranges of size that their measures depict. Gardner et al.'s (2009) scale, the body image assessment scale-body dimension (BIAS-BD), only goes up to 140% of "average body weight," and Peterson et al.'s (2003) 27-item interval silhouette measure only depicts figures up to a BMI of 40. In order to capture the full range of actual body sizes and to make the voices and perspectives of fat subjects visible and included, the range of body sizes must be widened. Virtually all of the measures also base their figures on an hourglass silhouette for women and a fairly "straight" figure for men, and simply widen or contract the image from that basic shape. Given that bodies come in all shapes as well as sizes—for example, a woman may carry most of her weight in her abdomen, and have thinner arms and legs—better measures that take alternate body shapes into account would ultimately end up being more descriptive.

There has been a recent shift in the "obesity" literature to a focus on *where* the fat is located on the body. A number of studies have attempted to categorize and delineate the most "dangerous" type of fat by breaking the body down into regions and analyzing whether trunk (middle of the body) or limb/arm/leg fat, as measured by body scans, is more dangerous. Fat around the middle of the body, called trunk fat, is considered the highest risk, based on epidemiological data connecting trunk fat with heart disease and cancers (Saunders et al., 2009). Fat around the hips, especially in women, is considered a healthier type of fat by those in medicine and public health because a slightly higher body fat concentration in that area has been found to be health-protective (Mason, Craig, & Katzmarzyk, 2008). Through the technology of body scans, individuals with certain types of body fat are segregated into fat diagnostic classifications (healthy/protective vs. unhealthy/harmful fat). Medical-based interventions have been tailored to those classifications in order to work toward the "ideal" levels of body fat. Ultimately, this shift is problematic both numerically and ethically: humans are unable to "spot reduce" fat on specific areas of our bodies or change our body fat distribution, and our current measurements don't take variations in fat distribution into account anyway. The increasing specificity with which public health and medicine are able to measure and quantify bodies demands a renewed effort on the part of health and social justice oriented theorists and researchers to actively contribute and steer the conversation about body measurement toward a more value-neutral stance on body size.

Philosophically, embodied experiences should be important to public health (Broom, 2001) if we are invested in both holistic and somatic means of health promotion. At the very least, there should be little argument that BMI is wholly inadequate. Critiques of the body line measurements listed above should also give researchers in public health and other social sciences grounds to question their use or, at the very least, their limitations in accurately measuring and describing bodies. As argued by Jutel and Buetow (2007), recognizing the cultural norms laden in assessments of health based on appearance should be considered by clinicians and others relying on visual inspections for assessing health.

Body Size Measurement: a Necessary Evil, for the Time Being?

Utilization of digital technologies such as avatar development or digital portraiture may be a way to improve body size measurement in both fields. Digital avatars could be both useful and fun for participants, as well as a means of representation that includes different shapes and sizes, ethnicities and gender presentations. Research is currently being conducted into the use of electronic avatars to represent the self in online 3D worlds, and what connection those avatars have with the lived body size of their creators. For example, Bardzell and Odom (2008) make the case that bodily avatars created by gamers in the online world Second Life are prime sites for social inscription, including the axes of race, gender, and sexual preference. Further research could be conducted on the use of avatar technology, given its flexibility, to assess the actual body size and shape of research participants, as well as being able to better capture and acknowledge intersectional concerns, such as ethnicity, gender presentation, and dis/ability. As discussed by Jutel and Buetow (2007), visual assessment and representation can be useful in clinical encounters in particular, but appearance norms that are raced, classed, and gendered need to be decoupled from assessments of health. At the very least, we should attempt to reduce the over-reliance on inadequate measurements such as BMI, which has been particularly closely (and falsely) tied to health.

New flexible digital measures can both inform public health practice without being tied to health-related claims, as well as offer a means of measuring and documenting the myriad ways humans vary by size and shape, as is among the goals of fat studies scholars. New media gives us the chance to better visually replicate our data, including the digital avatars that participants create. Interactive research methods can create spaces where the symbols of avatars are passed back and forth between researchers and participants, giving more meaning to the interaction, especially in fat studies, where the body size and appearance of the researcher may be of interest to the participant.

There are other fields and disciplines concerned with body size that have created value-neutral means of body size assessment that offer potential for our disciplines. Specifically, we can look to the field of ergonomics, whose goals include creating built environments that can accommodate bodies of all sizes and shapes, often termed "universal design." Ergonomics scholars have created digital human modeling programs to be used for design purposes (Jung, Kwon, & You, 2009; Lin & Wang, 2012; Park & Park, 2013) rather than to make judgments about those bodies. These digital simulations of human bodies are malleable in multiple dimensions and offer an alternative to existing measurements that are inherently tied to health-related claims.

At the same time that we propose that new forms of body size measurement are warranted for both disciplines, it is also important to note that changes in technologies designed to monitor and regulate bodies might also represent transformations in how bodies are understood, "touched, managed and visually displayed, not only from the perspective of professionals operating in the medical or public health field, but also for those who are their subject" (Lupton, 2013: 396). While public health or even fat studies could view these tools as more accurate body measurements or as emancipatory instruments for fat identification, this technology could find itself, like other mobile technologies of the body, engaged in the larger project of problematic self-tracking or self-monitoring. As Lupton (2012, 2013) points out, mobile measurement tools produce numbers that "are not neutral, despite the accepted concept of them as devoid of value judgments, assumptions and meanings" but rather these measurements are always interpreted by humans, giving them implicit power dynamics (Lupton, 2012, 2013: 399). The ways in which phenomena are quantified and interpreted, and the purposes to which these measurements are put, are always implicated in social relationships, power dynamics and ways of seeing (Adkins & Lury, 2011; Ruppert, 2012; Savage & Burrows, 2007). It is these power dynamics and implicated social relationships behind technologies of body measurement that must be taken into consideration by researchers and theorists in both fields when determining the nature and role of body measurement in their work (Jutel, 2001). We hope to problematize current body size measurement tactics based on their tendency to flatten, reduce and essentialize the lived experience of fat people. We proffer that a weight-neutral disciplinary utopia is not a world without body size measurement, but rather a place and time where body size measurement is used for practical purposes without using it as a way

to reify existing problematic systems, including those within public health. Therefore if it's a necessary evil, how do we do it best?

As we stated earlier, we do not have all the answers to the questions we've raised. Rather, we hope to broach the issue of equitable and ethical means of body size measurement from an interdisciplinary perspective, with the goal of continuing the conversation in our fields of expertise.

Regardless of where the future of body size measurement lies, ultimately and unfortunately, size- and fat-positive academics and activists cannot fully control the use of any new body measurement tools. However, we can at least attempt to decouple them from health and judgment and make clear that they were not created for the purpose of further stigmatizing fat bodies. We hope that others will take up the challenge of advancing and improving our means of documenting body diversity, and that this commentary is only the beginning of future conversations about how to best and most ethically represent body diversity across disciplines and perspectives.

References

Acharya, S. D., Elci, O. U., Sereika, S. M., Styn, M. A., & Burke, L. E. (2011). Using a personal digital assistant for self-monitoring influences diet quality in comparison to a standard paper record among overweight/obese adults. *Journal of the American Dietetic Association, 111*(4), 583–588. doi:10.1016/j.jada.2011.01.009

Adams, C. J. (2010). *Sexual politics of meat: A feminist-vegetarian critical theory*. New York, NY: Continuum. Retrieved from http://site.ebrary.com/id/10422448

Adkins, L., & Lury, C. (2011). Introduction: Special measures. *The Sociological Review, 59*, 5–23. doi:10.1111/j.1467-954X.2012.02051.x

Ambrosi-Randić, N., Pokrajac-Bulian, A., & Taksić, V. (2005). Nine, seven, five, or three: How many figures do we need for assessing body image? *Perceptual and Motor Skills, 100*(2), 488–492.

Anderson, J. (2012). Whose voice counts? A critical examination of discourses surrounding the body mass index. *Fat Studies, 1*(2), 195–207. doi: 10.1080/21604851.2012.656500

Bardzell, S., & Odom, W. (2008). The experience of embodied space in virtual worlds: An ethnography of a Second Life community. *Space and Culture, 11*(3), 239–259. doi:10.1177/1206331208319148

Braziel, J. E., & LeBesco, K. (2001). *Bodies out of bounds: Fatness and transgression.* Berkeley, CA: University of California Press.

Broom, D. (2001). Public health, private body. *Australian and New Zealand Journal of Public Health, 25*(1), 5–8.

Bulik, C. M., Wade, T. D., Heath, A. C., Martin, N. G., Stunkard, A. J., & Eaves, L. J. (2001). Relating body mass index to figural stimuli: population-based normative data for Caucasians. *International Journal of Obesity and Related Metabolic Disorders, 25*(10), 1517–1524. doi:10.1038/sj.ijo.0801742

Burkhauser, R. V., & Cawley, J. (2008). Beyond BMI: the value of more accurate measures of fatness and obesity in social science research. *Journal of Health Economics, 27*(2), 519–529. doi:10.1016/j.jhealeco.2007.05.005

Chodosh, J., Morton, S. C., Mojica, W., Maglione, M., Suttorp, M. J., Hilton, L.,. . . Shekelle, P. (2005). Meta-analysis: chronic disease self-management programs for older adults. *Annals of Internal Medicine, 143*(6), 427–438.

Drury, C. A. A., & Louis, M. (2002). Exploring the association between body weight, stigma of obesity, and health care avoidance. *Journal of the American Academy of Nurse Practitioners, 14*(12), 554–561.

Fallon, A. E., & Rozin, P. (1985). Sex differences in perceptions of desirable body shape. *Journal of Abnormal Psychology, 94*(1), 102–105.

Gardner, R. M., & Brown, D. L. (2010). Body image assessment: A review of figural drawing scales. *Personality and Individual Differences, 48*(2), 107–111. doi:10.1016/j.paid.2009.08.017

Gardner, R. M., Jappe, L. M., & Gardner, L. (2009). Development and validation of a new figural drawing scale for body-image assessment: The BIAS-BD. *Journal of Clinical Psychology, 65*(1), 113–122. doi:10.1002/jclp.20526

Gary-Webb, T. L., Suglia, S. F., & Tehranifar, P. (2013). Social epidemiology of diabetes and associated conditions. *Current Diabetes Reports, 13*(6), 850–859. doi:10.1007/s11892-013-0427-3

Gipson, G. W., Reese, S., Vieweg, W. V. R., Anum, E. A., Pandurangi, A. K., Olbrisch, M. E.,. . . Silverman, J. J. (2005). Body image and attitude toward obesity in an historically black university. *Journal of the National Medical Association, 97(2)*, 225–236.

Gruys, K. (2012). Does this make me look fat? Aesthetic labor and fat talk as emotional labor in a women's plus-size clothing store. *Social Problems, 59*(4), 481–500. doi:10.1525/sp.2012.59.4.481

Jung, K., Kwon, O., & You, H. (2009). Development of a digital human model generation method for ergonomic design in virtual environment. *International Journal of Industrial Ergonomics, 39*(5), 744–748. doi: 10.1016/j.ergon.2009.04.001

Jutel, A. (2001). Does size really matter? Weight and values in public health. *Perspectives in Biology and Medicine, 44*(2), 283–296. doi: 10.1353/pbm.2001.0027

Jutel, A., & Buetow, S. (2007). A picture of health? Unmasking the role of appearance in health. *Perspectives in Biology and Medicine, 50*(3), 421–434.

Kirkland, A. (2011). The environmental account of obesity: A case for feminist skepticism. *Signs, 36*(2), 463–486.

Lewis, S., Thomas, S. L., Blood, R. W., Hyde, J., Castle, D. J., & Komesaroff, P. A. (2010). Do health beliefs and behaviors differ according to severity of obesity? A qualitative study of Australian adults. *International Journal of Environmental Research and Public Health, 7*(2), 443–459. doi:10.3390/ijerph7020443

Lieffers, J. R. L., & Hanning, R. M. (2012). Dietary assessment and self-monitoring with nutrition applications for mobile devices. *Canadian Journal of Dietetic Practice and Research, 73*(3), e253–e260. doi:10.3148/73.3.2012.e253

Lin, Y. L., & Wang, M. J. (2012). Constructing 3D human model from front and side images. *Expert Systems with Applications, 39*(5), 5012–5018. doi:10.1016/j.eswa.2011.10.011

Lovejoy, M. (2001). Disturbances in the social body: Differences in body image and eating problems among African American and White women. *Gender & Society, 15*(2), 239–261. doi:10.1177/089124301015002005

Lupton, D. (1995). *The imperative of health: Public health and the regulated body.* Thousand Oaks, CA: Sage.

Lupton, D. (2012). M-health and health promotion: The digital cyborg and surveillance society. *Social Theory & Health, 10*(3), 229–244. doi:10.1057/sth.2012.6

Lupton, D. (2013). Quantifying the body: monitoring and measuring health in the age of mHealth technologies. *Critical Public Health, 23*(4) 393–403. doi:10.1080/09581596.2013.794931

Mason, C., Craig, C. L., & Katzmarzyk, P. T. (2008). Influence of central and extremity circumferences on all-cause mortality in men and women. *Obesity, 16*(12), 2690–2695. doi:10.1038/oby.2008.438

Park, W., & Park, S. (2013). Body shape analyses of large persons in South Korea. *Ergonomics, 56*(4), 692–706. doi:10.1080/00140139.2012.752529

Peterson, M., Ellenberg, D., & Crossan, S. (2003). Body-image perceptions: Reliability of a BMI-based silhouette matching test. *American Journal of Health Behavior, 27*(4), 355–363. doi:10.5993/AJHB.27.4.7

Rand, C. S. W., & Kuldau, J. M. (1990). The epidemiology of obesity and self-defined weight problem in the general population: Gender, race, age, and social class. *International Journal of Eating Disorders, 9*(3), 329–343. doi:10.1002/1098-108X(199005)9:3<329::AID-EAT2260090311>3.0.CO;2-B

Rothblum, E. D. (2012). Why a journal on fat studies? *Fat Studies, 1*(1), 3–5. doi:10.1080/21604851.2012.633469

Ruppert, E. (2012). The governmental topologies of database devices. *Theory, Culture & Society, 29*(4–5), 116–136. doi:10.1177/0263276412439428

Saunders, T. J., Davidson, L. E., Janiszewski, P. M., Despres, J.-P., Hudson, R., & Ross, R. (2009). Associations of the limb fat to trunk fat ratio with markers of cardiometabolic risk in elderly men and women. *The Journals of Gerontology Series A: Biological Sciences and Medical Sciences, 64A*(10), 1066–1070. doi:10.1093/gerona/glp079

Savage, M., & Burrows, R. (2007). The coming crisis of empirical sociology. *Sociology, 41*(5), 885–899. doi:10.1177/0038038507080443

Schvey, N. A., Puhl, R. M., & Brownell, K. D. (2011). The impact of weight stigma on caloric consumption. *Obesity, 19*(10), 1957–1962. doi:10.1038/oby.2011.204

Sherwood, N. E., Story, M., Beech, B., Klesges, L., Mellin, A., Neumark-Sztainer, D., & Davis, M. (2003). Body image perceptions and dieting among African-American pre-adolescent girls and parents/caregivers. *Ethnicity & Disease, 13*(2), 200–207.

Stunkard, A. J., Sørensen, T., & Schulsinger, F. (1983). Use of the Danish Adoption Register for the study of obesity and thinness. *Research Publications: Association for Research in Nervous and Mental Disease, 60,* 115–120.

Swami, V., Frederick, D. A., Aavik, T., Alcalay, L., Allik, J., Anderson, D.,. . . Cunningham, J. (2010). The attractive female body weight and female body dissatisfaction in 26 countries across 10 world regions: Results of the International Body Project I. *Personality and Social Psychology Bulletin, 36*(3), 309–325. doi:10.1177/0146167209359702

Thompson, J. K. (1996). *Body image, eating disorders, and obesity: an integrative guide for assessment and treatment.* Washington, DC: American Psychological Association.

Wann, M. (2009). Foreword: Fat studies: An invitation to revolution. In E. Rothblum & S. Solovay (Eds.), *The fat studies reader* (pp. xi–xxv). New York: New York University Press.

Consistently Inconsistent: A Review of the Literature on Eating Disorders and Body Image among Women of Color

by Christina M. Capodilupo and Jessica M. Forsyth

Over the last decade, there has been growing recognition that the eating disorders literature has largely omitted the experiences of women of color and instead presumed these to be "golden girl" disorders which only affect White girls and women (Mastria, 2002; Smolak & Striegel-Moore, 2001). Though an increasing awareness of the importance of racial and ethnic differences among women has led more researchers to include women of color in their studies, the majority of this work focuses on comparison studies between White women and women of color (with a higher representation of Black women than other racial groups). Comparison studies with White women can obfuscate important aspects of women of color's experiences and can, inadvertently, render the White female experience as the "norm" by which we compare others. Furthermore, women of color's experiences tend to be compared to White women's experiences by applying concepts such as the thin ideal as if they were universal. Very little effort has been made to attempt to understand women of color's lived experiences of body image and eating issues outside and apart from existing theories validated with White women (Bordo, 2009).

Findings across the major areas of eating disorders and body image among women of color are mixed and largely inconclusive. This inconsistency suggests potential methodological issues, but also likely speaks to the fact that women of color represent multiple races, ethnicities, ages, social classes, and immigration statuses. The existing research suggests that the etiology of eating disorders for women of color is distinct from current DSM understanding, varies by racial and ethnic group, and is impacted by age, immigration status, ethnicity, and acculturation. Furthermore, a growing body of research suggests that the constructs that are widely used in mainstream eating disorder research are not meaningful for particular groups of women of color, given that cultural and social group contexts differentially ascribe meaning to both the physical body and eating/food (Crago & Shisslak, 2003). Studies have only recently begun to look at specific groups (e.g., South Asian women, Iyer & Haslam, 2003) and to examine within-group differences, as well as intersections with gender identity, sexual orientation and identity, and social class. As such, research on eating disorders among women of color remains in nascent stages.

Eating Disorders

The DSM-IV-TR (APA, 2000) classifies three types of eating disorders: bulimia nervosa, anorexia nervosa, and eating disorder not otherwise specified. Bulimia nervosa involves recurrent episodes of binge eating which is defined as eating an unusually large amount of food accompanied by a loss of control over eating. The person must also utilize inappropriate compensatory methods to prevent weight gain, such as self-induced vomiting, laxative or diuretic use, or excessive exercising. To meet full criteria for the disorder, these behaviors must occur at least twice weekly for a minimum of 3 consecutive months. The person must also be unduly influenced by weight and shape.

The specific weight and shape criterion may be problematic when attempting to assess some women of color's eating pathology, because research suggests that weight and shape are not always salient aspects of appearance satisfaction for women of color. For example, Black women tend to place importance on the length, texture, and color of their hair (Greene, White, & Whitten, 2000), and Asian-American women tend to report dissatisfaction with specific body parts and physical features that are unrelated to weight and cannot be altered through dieting (Yokoyama, 2007). In one study, over 73 % of a sample of 230 Black women identified hair as the most important body ideal both personally and culturally (Capodilupo, 2007). Skin tone (i.e., how light or dark one is) and complexion also tend to be an important part of appearance for Black women, South Asian women, East Asian women, and Latinas. However, there is virtually no empirical work that makes these appearance characteristics central (if they are included at all), as most questionnaires were created based on the idea that weight, shape, and a thin ideal are the crucial components of body image (Altabe, 1996; Root, 2001).

Anorexia nervosa (AN) involves a refusal to maintain body weight at or above a minimally normal weight for age and height. The defining characteristic is a body weight less than 85 % of what is expected. The person must also experience an intense fear of fatness or gaining weight, be unduly influenced by weight and shape, and/or deny the seriousness of the low weight. Finally, in girls and women, there needs to be a loss of menstruation for 3 consecutive months. There is a large body of work that has explored how AN manifests for White girls and women. In fact, the earliest data and case studies of AN are those of White, upper middle-class women, and as such, this pattern of extreme thinness, refusing to eat, and fearing weight gain became the standard by which diagnoses and theories were formed (Bordo, 2009).

Thus, studies, theories, and measures of eating disorders tend to emphasize the importance of the thin ideal and a drive for weight loss: the major eating disorders require a preoccupation with weight and shape, and the majority of items on body image questionnaires assess the importance of being thin. However, disproportionate numbers of Black and Latina women are overweight and obese (Crago & Shisslak, 2003; Davis, Clance, & Gailis, 1999). The emphasis on the thin ideal is problematic given that the thin ideal is not necessarily salient to women of color and body ideal studies have consistently supported that larger ideals are more relevant to these populations (see Lovejoy, 2001 for a review).

Eating disorder not otherwise specified serves as a catchall for those who do not meet full criteria for bulimia or anorexia, or who exhibit single symptoms of disordered eating which do not fit any specific diagnosis (i.e., someone who chews food and spits it out). This category also includes binge eating disorder, which involves recurrent episodes of binge eating without use of inappropriate compensatory behaviors. Eating disorder not otherwise specified is more common than both anorexia and bulimia, and research suggests that between 50 and 70 % of those who seek treatment for an eating disorder fall into this category (Turner & Bryant-Waugh, 2004).

Obesity (consistently correlated with binge eating or overeating) is a major health epidemic in society at large and among women of color in particular. According to the Office of Minority Health, non-Hispanic Black women have the highest rates of overweight or obesity as compared to all other groups in the USA. Approximately four out of five of these women are overweight or obese (DHHS, 2010). Intersections seem to be particularly important when considering obesity: poor women and lesbians have significantly higher rates of obesity than other groups (Yancey, Leslie, & Abel, 2006), yet these populations receive little if any attention in the eating disorder literature. Given these statistics, it becomes increasingly problematic that the majority of research on eating disorders tends to focus on the diagnoses of bulimia and anorexia, which centralize thinness and a low body weight.

Body Image

Body image has been defined as "a multidimensional construct that refers to subjective perceptual and attitudinal experiences about one's body, particularly one's physical appearance" (Cash, Melnyk, & Hrabosky, 2004, p. 305). The perceptual experience of one's body refers to the way women perceive their bodies, regardless of actual shape and size, whereas the attitudinal experience refers to how they feel about their body shape and size. Traditionally (and in the vast majority of research), body ideals and body discrepancy represent perceptual body image. Body discrepancy is the difference between the ideal (weight or body shape/size) and the actual (weight or shape/size) and is typically measured by asking participants to choose from a set of female silhouettes (in the case of body shape/size). Body dissatisfaction (i.e., dissatisfied feelings about one's body) represents the most widely measured attitudinal body image construct, as it has been consistently implicated as a risk factor in the development of an eating disorder (Thompson, Heinberg, Altabe, & Tantleff-Dunn, 1999). It should be noted here that the term "body dissatisfaction" tends to be synonymous with a dissatisfaction with one's weight. This limitation reflects methodological issues in the research due to the fact that the majority of body image measures ask questions about one's desire to be thin and/or have thinner body parts.

Ethnic/Racial Group Comparisons

Body Dissatisfaction

A large body of research compares the body shape and size ideals, body satisfaction, eating attitudes, and disordered eating symptomology of women of various racial and ethnic groups. Across a majority of studies, Black women are found to be more satisfied with their bodies and to prefer a larger body size (Roberts, Cash, Feingold, & Johnson, 2006) than other groups. Differences between Latina, Asian, and White groups have been less conclusive and studies have tended to yield mixed findings (Grabe & Hyde, 2006). Of note, most research in this area examines participants' personal ideal body shape, but only one known study examined perceived *ethnic* body size ideals (Gordon, Castro, Sitnikov, & Holm-Denoma, 2010). They found that

Black women endorsed an ethnic body size ideal that was significantly larger than that endorsed by both Latina and White women, and Latina women endorsed an ethnic body size ideal that was significantly larger than that endorsed by White women.

In an effort to synthesize mixed findings, authors have conducted large-scale metaanalyses as a means of understanding body satisfaction differences among racial and ethnic groups of women. In their meta-analysis of 55 studies that investigated body dissatisfaction among Black and White female participants, Roberts et al. (2006) found that Black females were significantly more satisfied with their bodies than White females. These findings were supported in Grabe and Hyde's (2006) meta-analysis of 98 studies. Interestingly, Roberts and colleagues found that these results were only true for questionnaires that assess body satisfaction, but not for discrepancy measures that ask participants to compare their actual body to an ideal body. This finding supports the idea that body satisfaction is comprised of multiple aspects of appearance for Black women and is not solely about one's weight or shape. Both studies also reported age effects such that the greatest differences between the racial groups were among women in adolescence and young adulthood, while the differences practically disappeared in women older than 25. This finding suggests that the aging process has a significant effect on body satisfaction for both White and Black women; however, the effect is not well understood as the majority of eating disorder studies include women in their teens and early twenties.

Grabe and Hyde (2006) also found no significant differences between White and Asian-American or White and Hispanic American women's body dissatisfaction and no differences between Asian-American and Black women. However, more body dissatisfaction was found among Hispanic than Black women. There were no significant differences found between Asian and Hispanic females across studies, but age also played an important role in levels of body dissatisfaction in these populations. During adolescence and adulthood, Hispanic women were more dissatisfied, but during young adulthood, Asian women were more dissatisfied. The authors posit that for Asian females, the college experience may heighten their awareness of the disparity between mainstream ideals and their minority status.

Such meta-analyses, while important in summarizing existing research and revealing racial and ethnic differences among set variables (i.e., body dissatisfaction), do not provide an understanding of why these differences exist. For example, with regard to the finding that Black women experience more body satisfaction than women of other races, Collins (1990) suggests that Afrocentric ideals of beauty involve uniqueness and creativity (harmony of diversity, a unity of mind, body, and spirit) that may serve to liberate African-American women from conforming to a rigid, single standard of beauty. There is some evidence that Asian and Asian-American women may espouse a beauty ideal that values a slight built, long limbs, and large breasts and is more similar to the traditional White beauty ideal than that espoused by other women of color (Koff & Benavage, 1998; Yokoyama, 2007). Research has also indicated that body dissatisfaction among both Asian and Asian-American women is often focused on specific racialized body parts such as the nose and eyes that deviate from Western standards of beauty (Kaw, 1993; Sanders & Heiss, 1998). In their qualitative study of Black and Latina women's body aesthetic ideals, Rubin and colleagues (2003) found that Latina women embraced a diverse, multifaceted body ideal that emphasized hygiene, grooming, style, health, and spiritual influences on acceptance of one's body as it is over rigid beauty ideals.

This notion received empirical support in a study examining body image and beauty ideals among African-American and White adolescents. Whereas White adolescents used a fixed set of physical attributes (i.e., tall, blonde, thin) to describe their beauty ideal, African-American adolescents described ideal beauty in terms of internal attributes (e.g., style, attitude, confidence) and deemphasized external characteristics (Parker, Nichter, Vuckovic, Sims, & Ritenbaugh, 1995). A similar finding emerged in a qualitative investigation of Black and Latina females, such that which found that "subjects both contested ideologies defining thinness and Whiteness as inherently beautiful and espoused a body ethic of self-acceptance and nurturance that rejects mainstream cultural pressures to reshape bodies to ideals [presented by the media]" (Rubin, Fitts, & Becker, 2003, p. 49). Therefore, some women of color may have a more flexible and holistic understanding of what constitutes beauty, which would undoubtedly cause them to rate themselves more positively on measures that focus on the thin ideal.

It is also important to note that there are methodological concerns with the existing research on body image among women of color. Kashubeck-West, Mintz, and Saunders (2001) reviewed the most commonly used measures in eating disorder and body image research and practice and found that little or no effort has been made to validate the use of these measures with women of color in the USA. Looking at a specific measure helps bring meaning to this finding.

The Body Esteem Scale (BES) (Franzoi, 1994) is a widely used measure of body image and one of a few that actually includes physical appearance aspects that are of particular relevance to women of color such as facial features, complexion, and hair. In the original study, principal component factor analysis was performed with data from 633 female and 331 male undergraduate students for whom racial and ethnic group membership was not reported. Results revealed a three-factor structure for women (Sexual Attractiveness, $\alpha=.78$; Weight Concern, $\alpha=.87$; and Physical Condition, $\alpha=.82$).

Several studies that include African-American women have used the BES in their design. One (Wade, 2003) included African-American males and females and reported on alpha coefficients for the three subscales. One had a sample of both Black and White women (87 Black and 584 White women) (Schooler et al., 2004) and the authors did not report alpha coefficients by race but did report entire sample subscale alpha coefficients, and one (Frisby, 2004) provided a total score alpha coefficient for the measure in a sample of female African-American college students.

A third more recent investigation of 230 Black women (Capodilupo, 2009) suggested a two-factor solution for this scale. While Sexual Attractiveness remained a distinct factor with items loading in accordance with previous studies, the items that had loaded distinctly onto Weight Concern and Physical Condition in other studies combined to create a unified factor in this study. This finding suggests that women in the study may not distinguish between aspects of their weight and their physical fitness. The finding gives one pause with regard to methodological practices in the field. What might happen if researchers took the extra step of conducting exploratory and confirmatory factor analyses with scales that have been normed with White populations? Would we learn that the factor structure and therefore potentially the construct itself are not as we presumed it to be?

Eating Disorder Symptoms

The majority of studies that examine racial/ethnic differences in eating disorder diagnoses and symptoms include samples of college populations, and findings are not consistent across studies. For example, in a sample of over 700 college students, White females were more likely to meet criteria for binge eating disorder and have greater binge eating severity than African-American students (Napolitano & Himes, 2011). However, in a large-scale study of over 5,000 college students (Franko, Becker, Thomas, & Herzog, 2006) no significant differences were found in the prevalence of binge eating, restrictive eating, vomiting, loss of menstruation, or excessive exercising among White, African-American, Latino, Asian, or Native Americans. Significant differences did emerge with regard to diuretic use such that fewer Asian participants reported use than other groups. Also, Native Americans reported significantly more laxative use than those in other groups, were more likely to use multiple methods of purging, and indicated that exercise interfered with other activities more than those in other groups. Older research supports this finding: Of 85 Chippewa girls and women surveyed, 74 % were attempting to lose weight, and 75 % of these were using a weight control/loss method such as restrictive eating or dieting (Rosen et al., 1988).

A meta-analysis of 35 studies which investigated eating pathology among White, Black, Asian, and non-White women (i.e., participants who did not identify as White, Black, or Asian) concluded that White samples reported greater eating disturbance and body dissatisfaction than non-White samples in more than 75 % of the recorded outcomes included (Wildes, Emery, & Simons, 2001). When the results were examined for specific ethnic group comparisons (as opposed to grouping all ethnic minorities into a non-White category), a different picture emerged. Whereas the significant differences between body dissatisfaction and eating disturbance became stronger between White and Black participants, Asian samples reported more eating disturbance and body dissatisfaction than White counterparts across the majority of studies. When the authors assessed for the influence of age, they found that body dissatisfaction and eating disturbance differences between White and Black women were largest for college age samples and nonsignificant for older (past college), community-based samples (nonclinical). Further, effect sizes between White and non-White samples were greatest for measures of subclinical symptoms such as drive for thinness and fears of fatness and weakest for measures of eating disorder diagnoses (i.e., anorexia and bulimia), especially for bulimia nervosa. Taken together with a number of more recent studies that have found no significant differences in eating disorder symptoms between White women and women of color (e.g., Forbes & Frederick, 2008; Shaw, Ramirez, Trost, Randall, & Stice, 2004), these results seem to suggest that while in certain cases White women and women of color may have somewhat similar rates of eating disorder diagnosis, the etiology and symptom profile of the disorders might be different for these populations.

With respect to bulimia, more recent investigations reveal a similar trend to those reported in Wildes and colleagues' meta-analysis. In a sample of 510 college-aged women, Black women evidenced significantly fewer bulimic symptoms and higher body satisfaction than their White counterparts (Lokken, Worthy, Ferraro, & Atman, 2008). Similarly, among college students, White women endorsed significantly more bulimic symptoms than Latina women, who endorsed significantly more bulimic symptoms than Black women (Gordon et al., 2010). In a college sample of Mexican-American women (Pepper & Ruiz, 2007), viewing oneself as fat positively predicted both bulimic symptoms and binge eating. It is interesting to note that feeling fat was associated positively with binge eating, which is not a weight loss behavior. It is possible that women were using food as a

way to deal with their emotions about feeling fat. Interviews with Black, White, and Latina women suggest that overeating can be comforting and a means to alleviate negative feelings about one's appearance (Thompson, 1994).

Studies that include women in midlife and community-based samples are less frequent in the literature. A community sample of 589 women (mean age: 45) revealed significant racial and ethnic differences among Black, White, and Hispanic women (Marcus, Bromberger, Wei, Brown, & Kravitz, 2007) such that Black women reported greater use of compensatory measures (i.e., laxative use, fasting) than White or Hispanic females. Black and White females endorsed higher rates of binge eating and preoccupation with weight, shape, and eating than Hispanic counterparts.

Conversely, a study of 351 Black, Hispanic, and White women (mean age: 37) (Fitzgibbon et al., 1998) found that Hispanic participants reported a greater severity of binge eating symptoms than either the White or Black participants. There was also a higher proportion of binge eating disorder among Hispanics than the other participants. The authors do not report on the ethnic breakdown or immigration status of their Hispanic participants, which could partially account for the discrepant findings. For example, women of Mexican descent have been shown to subscribe to a larger, more curvaceous body ideal (Chamorro & Flores-Ortiz, 2000), thereby possibly affecting their binge eating behavior (i.e., a desire to be bigger). With regard to immigration status, Latina women who were born and raised in the USA (compared to women who came to the USA at age 11 or older) were more likely to experience body shame and engage in more negative appearance evaluations (Breitkopf, Littleton, & Berenson, 2007) and shame has been shown to be positively related to binge eating behavior (Denious, Russo, & Rubin, 2004).

Research has also found that predictors of binge eating varied across racial groups (Fitzgibbon et al., 1998). For Hispanic females, body mass index (BMI) and depression scores were significant predictors, whereas only depression scores were predictive for White females, and neither was predictive for Black females. Of note, greater obesity was associated with more severe binge eating across all three ethnic groups, suggesting that the heavier a woman was (regardless of race), the more food she consumed and more frequently she engaged in binge eating behavior.

In a study comparing women with eating disorder diagnoses to non-eating disordered controls (matched based on ethnicity), no significant differences in symptom presentation emerged among White, Asian, Hispanic, and Black females for bulimia nervosa, anorexia nervosa, or binge eating disorder (Cachelin, Veisel, Barzegarnazari, & Striegel-Moore, 2002). A similar study of 150 women with binge eating disorder found that White and Black women differed significantly on a number of symptoms (Pike, Dohm, Striegel-Moore, Wilfley, & Fairburn, 2001). Namely, Black women endorsed significantly less eating concern, weight and shape concern, and dietary restraint than White participants and also reported significantly more frequent binge episodes. White women in the sample also weighed significantly less th[an Black] women and were eight times more likely [to have] had a history of bulimia nervosa. Among 3[0 bar]iatric candidates (mean age: 39), no diffe[rences] in rates or severity of binge eating were f[ou]nd among African-American and White women. Although African-American women in the study reported higher self-esteem and lower depression scores overall than their White counterparts, both depression and self-esteem were significantly associated with binge eating in both racial groups (Mazzeo, Saunders, & Mitchell, 2005).

As with the various meta-analyses examining body image differences among White women and women of color, studies that report differences among eating disorder diagnoses and symptom presentations tell us little about why said differences actually exist. Furthermore, these studies also tend to group women of color into a singular category, failing to account for important within-group differences such as age, ethnicity, immigration status, social class, and sexuality. In recent years a growing body of eating disorder and body image research has begun to look at the experiences of distinct ethnic groups (i.e., Mexican-American women as opposed to Latinas) and to address issues of race and culture beyond simple demographic analysis.

Ethnicity, Acculturation, and Internalization of the White Beauty Ideal

Feminist scholars have long argued that White beauty ideals (i.e., thin physique, light skin and hair) are detrimental to women of color due to the pressure to conform to an aesthetic ideal whose physical attributes diverge significantly from their own physical traits (e.g., Collins, 1990; Hooks, 1994). Although comparative studies elucidate differences in body image between racial groups, they provide only limited inferences about the extent to which White aesthetic body ideals impact women of color's body image and eating behaviors.

Much of the research focusing on body image and disordered eating [among wo]men of color tests the applica[bility of the socio-cultu]ral model of eating [disorders which posits that] exposure to the [thin a]nd fit physique [ideal produces body dis]satisfaction, thereby making [women especiall]y vulnerable to the development [of dis]ordered eating (Stice, 1994). Therefore, [an i]mportant factor that influences body dissatisfaction and disordered eating among women of color is the degree to which they internalize White standards of beauty (Gilbert, Crump, Madhere, & Schutz, 2009; Warren, Castillo, & Gleaves, 2010). Researchers in this area posit that to the extent that level of acculturation reflects acceptance of White cultural beauty standards, acculturation should influence eating disorder presentations and body dissatisfaction among women of color.

A number of studies have examined the relationships between various proxy measures of acculturation and body dissatisfaction or eating behaviors. The results of these studies have been mixed. In a meta-analysis of 11 studies, no significant effect was found for the role of acculturation in the development of eating pathology or body dissatisfaction (Wildes et al., 2001) and the researchers posit that variability with regard to how researchers operationalize and measure acculturation (i.e., some use generational status as a sole indicator, and others use multidimensional questionnaires) may account for the mixed findings in this area. For example, among Asian, Hispanic, and White women from a community sample, it was found that more acculturated women (as measured by language choice and parents' country of origin) were more likely to suffer from eating problems (Cachelin et al., 2002). Further, across the three ethnic groups, women who were less acculturated were significantly less likely to seek treatment for their eating disorder than their more acculturated counterparts.

A study of 66 Mexican-American college women (mean age: 24) (Stein, Corte, & Ronis, 2010) used generational status as its measure of acculturation (i.e., the longer one lived in the USA, the more likely she was to be acculturated). They did not find a significant relationship between viewing oneself as fat and acculturation. Generational status did, however, have a direct (albeit small) significant effect on body dissatisfaction, leading the authors to conclude that less acculturated women are more satisfied with their bodies, regardless of whether they view themselves as thin or fat.

Acculturation is complex process involving more than simply the number of years one lives in a country. Berry (1980) argues that acculturation reflects not only one's adoption of the cultural values, beliefs, attitudes, and behaviors of White American culture, but also the extent to which one maintains the values, beliefs, attitudes, and behaviors of one's culture of heritage. Researchers have identified that there are both attitudinal and behavioral dimensions of acculturation and that individuals can acculturate at different rates across these dimensions (Berry, 1980). For example, a study of Mexican-American college students revealed that there could be behavioral acceptance of White culture (i.e., adoption of clothes, language) without attitudinal acceptance (i.e., White values such as individualism were not embraced) (Castillo, Conoley, & Brossart, 2004).

Recent research has more explicitly examined the relationship between internalization of White American body ideals and acculturation using multidimensional measures of acculturation. In a study of 94 Mexican-American college females (mean age: 19.69) (Warren, Castillo, & Gleaves, 2010), it was found that those who were more strongly behaviorally acculturated to White American culture (i.e., wears Western dress, eats Western foods, watches Western media) were more likely to be aware of and internalize White American values of appearance (i.e., the thin ideal) than those who

were less behaviorally acculturated and less aware, providing support for the notion that greater acculturation is associated with increased internalization of White beauty ideals among Mexican-American women. However, regardless of acculturation level, the more aware a woman was of White American values of appearance, the more likely she was to internalize them.

It is important to note that while internalization of White body size ideals is an important area of research that has yielded interesting findings, very few studies have sought to elucidate the influence of immigrant and immigrant-descended women's home culture, customs, and gender roles on their body image and disordered eating. For example, at least two cross-cultural studies have found that although South Asian women in Great Britain had higher rates of maladaptive eating and body dissatisfaction than White British women, the rates of both variables were equally high among the women's peers in Pakistan (Mujtaba & Furnham, 2001; Mumford, Whitehouse, & Choudry, 1992). In addition, another study of Pakistani schoolgirls in Great Britain found that less acculturated girls (as measured by traditional cultural dress and language use) had greater maladaptive eating attitudes than more acculturated girls (Mumford, Whitehouse, & Platts, 1991). Although as argued by the authors, cultural conflict likely played a role in this finding, in light of the similar findings in Pakistan, it seems plausible that at least some of the influence on the more traditional girls' maladaptive eating attitudes might have been influenced by traditional values, customs, attitudes, beliefs, and gender roles of Pakistani culture that were retained by their families.

A study of African-American, Afro-Caribbean, and African students at a historically Black college found that internalization of the White body ideal did not mediate the relationship between awareness of the White ideal and disordered eating (drive for thinness and bulimia) for African and Afro-Caribbean women (Gilbert et al., 2009). Although it is unclear whether these women were international students, immigrants, or the American-born descendents of immigrant parents, these results suggest that African and Afro-Caribbean women may be influenced more by the standards of beauty in their predominantly Black home countries than by White American standards. Of note, the same study also found that African women had the highest rates of bulimia, a result that replicated similar findings from previous studies in continental African populations.

Although somewhat speculative, these studies highlight the fact that the emphasis on internalization of White ideals of thinness may be less relevant to some populations and that the potential influence of non-Western cultures and contexts on the development of disordered eating among women of color of immigrant descent should be considered. For example, women in many countries face significant gender oppression and inequality which is expressed on a spectrum of cultural practices from rigid gender role expectations to tacit acceptance of and lack of legal protection from sexual abuse and violence. To the extent that cultural values and practices are retained among immigrants, they likely also influence the etiology of eating disorders among women of color. Thus, it is possible, and perhaps likely, that while cultural beauty ideals derived from sending countries may protect certain women of color from internalizing White body ideals, there are other factors in the context of both the sending and receiving (American) culture that may influence the development of disordered eating.

The Role of Stress, Trauma, and Racism

Despite the implication of stress and trauma in the development of eating disorders, much of the research on disordered eating among women of color has focused primarily on examining the sociocultural model. A number of scholars have argued that theoretical models that were developed to explain eating pathology among White women do not adequately explain the etiological pathways for women of color (e.g., Harrington, Crowther, Henrickson, & Mickelson, 2006; Root, 2001). An alternate conceptualization that has begun to receive some attention posits that women of color develop eating disorders in response not only to experiences of stress and trauma that result from poverty, abuse, and sexism, but particularly those such as discrimination, racism, and acculturative stress that result from the unique intersection of multiple oppressions (e.g., Root, 1990; Thompson, 1996). A growing body of research has sought to examine this conceptualization.

Acculturative Stress

Counterintuitive results of research linking low acculturation with increases in disordered eating have led researchers to test the hypothesis that acculturative stress or cultural conflict may be an important mechanism underlying the etiology of eating disorders among women of color. For example, Warren and colleagues (2010) found that the relationship between internalization of the thin ideal and body satisfaction was stronger for Mexican-American women who have difficulty accepting White American cultural values than those who have less difficulty. Interestingly, women who had high degrees of difficulty accepting White cultural standards and low internalization had the lowest body dissatisfaction scores, while those with high internalization had the highest body dissatisfaction scores. The authors posited that acculturative stress could explain this relationship, such that a woman who simultaneously rejects White American culture but has internalized White appearance standards could be experiencing cognitive conflict and distress (Warren et al., 2010).

Very few studies have explicitly investigated the effects of acculturative stress on eating disorder symptoms. One study of 118 undergraduate women (51 % White, 30 % Black, 19 % Hispanic) (Perez, Voelz, Pettit, & Joiner, 2002) found significant relationships between acculturative stress, body dissatisfaction, and bulimic symptoms. Specifically, Black and Latina women who were high in acculturative stress had higher body dissatisfaction and more bulimic symptoms. Conversely, Black and Latina women who were low in acculturative stress did not evidence a significant relationship between body dissatisfaction and bulimic symptoms. Similarly, another relationship was significant for those who were high in acculturative stress (but not for those low in acculturative stress): the greater the discrepancy between one's perceived body shape and the ideal body shape, the greater the incidence of bulimic symptoms (Perez et al., 2002).

A more recent study with similar demographics (122 Black, 79 White, 77 Latina women, mean age 18) (Gordon et al., 2010) found that Black participants with higher levels of acculturative stress endorsed greater rates of bulimic symptoms. For Latinas, higher acculturative stress was predictive of a greater drive for thinness. Acculturation did not predict eating disorder symptoms or related cognitions in either group. Similar results have been attained for South Asian women. One study of 74 women (mean age: 24) (Reddy & Crowther, 2007) found that acculturation was not significantly related to body dissatisfaction or maladaptive eating habits. However, women who were higher in cultural conflict (i.e., the degree to which they felt their South Asian cultural values conflicted with mainstream American values) were more likely to experience higher body dissatisfaction and greater rates of maladaptive eating attitudes.

Racism

Just as few studies have included variables of acculturative stress, there is a dearth of research that examines the role of ethnic discrimination and racism in the development of eating pathology or body dissatisfaction. Qualitative research consistently points to the importance of the role of racism in the embodied lives of women of color. While conducting in-depth interviews with Latina, Black, and White women who were recovering from eating problems, Thompson (1994) learned that many of them traced the onset of their disordered eating to stressful or traumatic experiences and that food often served as a means of comfort and a coping mechanism for dealing with experiences of oppression related to racism and sexism. Results from focus groups of Latina and Black women (Rubin et al., 2003) indicate that the majority of participants were upset and discouraged by both negative and stereotypic depictions as well as an exclusion of their race in the media. Further, they discussed a constant pressure to conform to mainstream beauty ideals in order to be accepted by society. Similarly, focus groups of Black women from the community (Capodilupo, 2007) found that women's body image was negatively impacted by the media's representation of Black women, namely that lighter skin and straight hair were prized over more Afrocentric features.

There are a few quantitative studies that have included measures of racism or discrimination. A recent investigation of White ($n=85$) and Black ($N=93$) women (mean age: 21) revealed significant relationships between trauma, stress, and binge eating for both groups. However, a significant relationship emerged between discriminatory stress (measured by scales of racist and sexist events)

and binge eating for the Black participants only (Harrington, Crowther, Henrickson, & Mickelson, 2006). A study of 122 South Asian undergraduate women found that racial teasing was significantly associated with both disturbed body image and eating behaviors, even when controlling for weight, self-esteem, and socioeconomic status (Iyer & Haslam, 2003). In this study, racial teasing was assessed through questions that were specific to South Asians. For example, "People have made fun of you because of your Indian accent or way of dressing." A community sample of South Asian women (mean age: 24) yielded slightly different findings: while greater ethnic teasing was significantly associated with lower body esteem and greater maladaptive eating attitudes, the significance decreased when teasing related to weight and shape was included in the analysis (Reddy & Crowther, 2007).

In a community sample of Black and White women (meeting a binge eating disorder diagnosis and matched with both psychiatric and non-psychiatric controls) childhood bullying was found to be significantly associated with binge eating for both groups. However, racial discrimination was not found to be a specific or general risk factor for binge eating among Black women (Striegel-Moore, Dohm, Pike, Wifley, & Fairburn, 2002). The authors note that women were asked to self-report racially based discrimination experiences before the age of onset of binge eating disorder or aged 18 years. Also, a single question asking participants if they were ever racially discriminated against served as the measure of racism in this study; therefore, a more nuanced understanding of discrimination experiences was not assessed (i.e., major overt racist incident versus daily racial hassles). In a recent study of over 400 Black women from the community (mean age: 37) (Capodilupo & Smith, 2010), greater frequency of daily racial hassles was positively predictive of emotional overeating, regardless of participants' actual weight. Greater reporting of daily racist incidents was also significantly associated with lower appearance satisfaction and higher rates of uncontrolled eating in this sample.

Though research on the relationship between stress, trauma, and racism is in its infancy, the majority of these results provide support for the conceptualization that disordered eating among women of color may be caused at least in part by stress related to their experience as members of racial/ethnic minority groups.

Directions for Future Research

Eating disorder and body image research with women of color is still in its nascent stages and the majority of work in the area has focused on comparison studies between White women and women of color. Future researchers should critically examine their hypotheses to determine if their study's aim is to see how similar or dissimilar women of color are to White women. If the true goal is to better understand what leads and contributes to eating and body image disturbance in different groups of women of color, it is unlikely that such a comparison will be very helpful. For example, the existing eating disorder literature is saturated with the centrality of the thin ideal. Given that the thin ideal may not be central to women of color, what do results of studies that focus on thinness (overtly or otherwise) really tell us? Some researchers conclude that ethnicity buffers these groups from body dissatisfaction and eating pathology; however, could it be that when the question is framed around variables other than the thin ideal, struggles related to appearance and weight do emerge? It would behoove researchers to work to include culturally relevant variables into their study designs.

Racism and discrimination represent one such variable that has received minimal inclusion in quantitative eating disorder studies. Yet, a substantial body of theoretical and qualitative work consistently underscores its importance in the lives of women of color (e.g., Crago & Shisslak, 2003; Thompson, 1994). It is entirely possible that there are still other variables of interest which remain undiscovered. Qualitative inquiries are necessary to assist researchers in identifying variables that are salient and meaningful to their populations of interest.

Not only may some constructs have been left out, but entire groups of women have been left out of this literature as well. Native American women's experiences are largely missing from investigations of body image and eating disorders. When these girls and women have been included

in studies, results suggest that they experience a significant amount of body dissatisfaction and eating pathology. Women who identify as biracial and multiethnic are another underrepresented group in the literature. Future studies are needed in particular with biracial and Native American women to understand these group's unique experiences with eating and body image.

The APA Multicultural Guidelines (APA, 2002) explicitly caution against applying concepts and theory as if they were universal. Yet, much of the research on eating disorders among women of color applies theories that were developed based on White women's experiences, and many of the existing measures of eating pathology and body image have not been validated for use with women of color. Many researchers skip the step of conducting an exploratory factor analysis with established scales; however, it is important to question: Who has this scale been established for? Might it measure a different construct when used with a population of color? As Parham (1993) suggests, "a European-American perspective cannot be appropriately used to understand populations whose cultural traditions, values, and perceptions of reality and life experience are radically different" (p. 255). Researchers should, therefore, take the necessary steps to (a) use measures that have either been normed and validated with the population of interest; (b) assess for the reliability and validity of the measure with the given population (e.g., run a principal component factor analysis on a scale even if it has a preexisting factor solution); or (c) create new measures that accurately capture the construct for that population.

Finally, there is great variability between and among women of color that is drastically underrepresented in the literature on eating disorders and body image. It is possible that findings are consistently inconsistent because the heterogeneity within groups is not being appreciated. Take for example that some findings suggest that Latinas have higher body dissatisfaction and others the opposite. It is likely that samples of "Latinas" include many countries of origin. Therefore, women who identify as Chicana may relate to their bodies differently than those who are Puerto Rican based on their distinct ethnic contexts and cultures. Future investigations that query within-group differences are sorely needed. In addition to country of origin, other distinguishing variables such as racial identity, sexual orientation, and social class should also be considered in research design.

Clinical Implications

Clinicians who adhere strictly to a DSM-IV definition of eating disorders, focusing on ideals of thinness and issues related to weight and shape, may be unaware of body and eating concerns in their clients of color. Consider that Black women are less likely to receive treatment for binge eating disorder (BED) than White women, even when presenting with the same symptoms (Pike et al., 2001). Similarly, undergraduate psychology majors were more likely to recognize an eating disorder in a peer when that peer was White than African American (even when the same symptoms were presented) (Gordon, Perez, & Joiner, 2002). One study found that Asian women who used laxatives were significantly less likely to be referred for additional evaluation than other women (Franko et al., 2006). Empirical findings may be mixed, but as was previously discussed, there is ample support for the idea that women of color experience eating pathology in rates that are similar to or, in some cases, higher than White women. Native American and Asian-American women, in particular, seem to be equally affected by a drive for thinness, restrictive eating, and purging. Latina and African-American women seem to experience significant rates of binge eating, and obesity represents a major health issue in each of these communities. The following case example is helpful in considering the clinical implications of working with a woman of color who experiences body dissatisfaction and eating disturbance.

Case Example

Monica was a 34-year-old biracial female who presented for treatment with a history of depression. Monica's father was a Jamaican immigrant, and her mother was Korean American. She was raised with a greater emphasis on Korean culture, as the majority of her father's family resided in Jamaica, though she phenotypically appeared Black and felt that most people she came into contact with perceived her to be a Black female. Monica was of average weight, approximately five foot four,

140 pounds (BMI = 24.0). In sessions, Monica primarily discussed a disturbed sleep pattern (she had difficulty staying asleep at night), as well as feelings of being lonely and a desire for a significant romantic relationship. She was a musician who sang and played the cello in a small band and she very much enjoyed her job. However, she felt somewhat overshadowed by the lead singer in their group, a "waify White woman" who seemed to get the majority of attention from fans whenever they performed live. In fact, Monica described feeling somewhat "invisible" on the stage due to her lead singer's presence.

Monica's therapist focused his attention on her depressed mood and feelings of loneliness. He felt that she was experiencing envy toward the lead singer in her band, both because she was the lead singer and because her look seemed to attract more people. He shared with Monica that these envious feelings were likely to be exacerbating her depressed mood and potentially causing her to isolate herself and miss out on potential romantic connections. When he inquired with Monica about her use of the word "waify" to describe the singer, and if she herself had a desire to lose weight or have a thinner figure, Monica quickly retorted that she had no such interest. Hearing this, the clinician felt that body image and eating habits were not relevant to the case and he did not explore these topics.

Clinicians such as Monica's need to look beyond the established eating disorder diagnoses and assess their female clients of color for maladaptive eating habits and body disturbance, even when a drive for thinness does not appear to be present. In accordance with the APA Multicultural Guidelines (APA, 2002), clinicians should reflect upon their own biases and assumptions with regard to different groups of women of color. If a client of color appears normal weight or overweight and does not talk at all about weight or shape concerns, does the clinician rule out eating problems and/or body dissatisfaction as Monica's did and assume that there is no issue? Is the clinician aware that there are other roads that can lead to negative self-appraisals and eating problems? Had Monica's clinician taken time to assess her eating habits, he would have learned that she tended to binge eat late at night in an effort to cope with her lonely feelings. Similar to what has been described by other Black women (Capodilupo & Smith, 2010), Monica would sometimes overeat in an effort to gain the attention of Black men, and to purposefully reflect a thicker and more curvy physique than the one her lead singer possessed. Monica resented the notion that being thin and White was received as beautiful and ideal during their performances while her aesthetic was relegated to "back stage." Further, she had a host of complicated feelings related to a conflict which she personally felt between what her father's culture deemed as attractive (i.e., a thicker, curvier shape) and her mother's culture idealized (i.e., more petite, delicate, and thin physique). However, the clinician assumed that because Monica was normal weight and did not express a desire to be thinner that her body image and eating habits were insignificant. The idea that there are risk factors for disturbed eating that are unique to different ethnicities is documented such that acculturative stress, ethnic teasing, and racism have all been linked to eating pathology and body dissatisfaction.

It is a mistake to assume that women of color are immune to negative feelings about their appearance and bodies if they prefer a larger body ideal or score higher on body image measures that assess for the importance of the thin ideal. There is ample evidence to suggest that features beyond weight and shape, such as facial features, skin color, and hair, comprise important aspects of body image for women of color (e.g., Hall, 1995; Solomon, 2005). This underscores the importance of including physical appearance attributes such as hair length and texture and skin color in conversations about body image. Clinicians such as Monica's should make these characteristics explicit in the therapeutic work, specifically talking about both the therapist's and the client's hair, skin tone, face, and body (Parmer, Arnold, Natt, & Janson, 2004). Being that Monica's clinician was a White male, it would have been important to discuss Monica's reactions to him. Did she perceive him, like many of their fans, to see her as belonging "back stage"? Also, how did the therapist perceive Monica racially? Did he receive her as a Black female, as Monica felt so many other people did? Had he asked Monica about important characteristics, he would have learned that her hair was extremely

important to her. She had shorter, kinky hair, and had always pined for longer, straighter hair, closer to how her mother's hair appeared. In fact, when she was feeling badly about her hair, it negatively impacted her self-worth and self-concept.

It is important to find out what aspects of a woman's appearance are most salient to her, and what in her life affects her feelings about her appearance. As was the case with Monica, Black men's aesthetic preferences have been found to play an important role in Black women's appearance satisfaction (Poran, 2006). Black women have reported binge eating in an effort to gain the attention of Black men (Mulholland & Mintz, 2001) and to increase sex appeal (Capodilupo & Smith, 2010). Monica's biracial status was also very important in understanding her body image and appearance satisfaction. She was experiencing conflict between the aesthetic ideals that were valued in her father's and her mother's cultures. In many ways, clinicians and researchers face a similar predicament: there are likely to be several variables that are yet to be discovered but are very important in understanding women of color's eating patterns and body image. At this point, mixed empirical findings may raise more questions than answers with regard to women of color and eating disorders; however, cultural competence requires that we continue to ask these questions until we know as much about women of color as we do about White women and eating disorders.

Resource List

Movies

For Colored Girls (2010), adapted from Ntozake Shange's play "For Colored Girls Who Have Considered Suicide When the Rainbow Is Enuf." A thought-provoking commentary on what it means to be a female of color in the world.

The Souls of Black Girls (2008), a news documentary that questions if women of colors' self-image are negatively affected by the media.

Frybread Babes (2008), a documentary about Native women, body image, and identity.

Asian American Beauty: A Discourse on Female Body Image (2007), a short documentary on body image and eating disorder symptoms among Asian Americans.

Real Women Have Curves (2002), the fictional story of a first generational Mexican-American teenager on the verge of becoming a woman.

Books

Hijas Americanas: Beauty, Body Image, and Growing Up Latina
> Rosie Molinary
> *Body Outlaws: Rewriting the Rules of Beauty and Body Image*
> Ophira Edut Edut
> *Naked: Black Women Bare All About Their Skin, Hair, Hips, Lips, and Other Parts*
> Akiba Solomon & Ayana Byrd

The following are national resources that provide information about eating-related problems and issues including links to counseling centers and individual therapists:

National Eating Disorders Association:
http://www.nationaleatingdisorders.org/

Overeaters Anonymous:
http://www.oa.org/index.htm

References

Altabe, M. (1996). Issues in the assessment and treatment of body image disturbance in culturally diverse populations. In J. K. Thompson (Ed.), *Body image, eating disorders, and obesity: An integrative guide for assessment and treatment* (pp. 129–147). Washington, DC: American Psychological Association.

American Psychiatric Association. (2000). *Diagnostic and statistical manual for mental disorders* (4th ed.). Washington, DC: Author.

American Psychological Association. (2002). *Guidelines on multicultural education, training, research, practice, and organizational change for psychologists.* Washington, DC: Author.

Berry, J. (1980). Acculturation as varieties of adaptation. In A. M. Padilla (Ed.), *Acculturation: Theory, models, and some new findings* (pp. 9–25). Boulder, CO: Westview Press.

Breitkopf, C. R., Littleton, H., & Berenson, A. (2007). Body image: A study in a tri-ethnic sample of low income women. *Sex Roles, 56,* 373–380.

Cachelin, F. M., Veisel, C., Barzegarnazari, E., & Striegel-Moore, R. H. (2002). Disordered eating, acculturation, and treatment-seeking in a community sample of Hispanic, Asian, Black, and White women. *Psychology of Women Quarterly, 24,* 244–253.

C. M. Capodilupo (2007, February). *Rethinking the body image construct: African American women's experiences.* Poster presentation at the Winter Roundtable on Cultural Psychology and Education, New York.

C. M. Capodilupo (2009). *The effects of idealized media images on the body esteem and appearance satisfaction of African American women.* Unpublished doctoral dissertation, Teachers College, Columbia University.

C. M. Capodilupo & K. Smith (2010, October). *Associations between racism, BMI, perceived invisibility, and appearance satisfaction in Black women.* Poster presentation at the Diversity Challenge, Boston College.

Cash, T. F., Melnyk, S. E., & Hrabosky, J. I. (2004). The assessment of body image investment: An extensive revision of the Appearance Schemas Inventory. *International Journal of Eating Disorders, 35*(3), 305–316.

Castillo, L. G., Conoley, C. W., & Brossart, D. F. (2004). Acculturation, white marginalization, and family support as predictors of perceived distress in Mexican American female college students. *Journal of Counseling Psychology, 51*(2), 151.

Chamorro, R., & Flores-Ortiz, Y. (2000). Acculturation and disordered eating patterns among Mexican American women. *International Journal of Eating Disorders, 28,* 125–129.

Collins, P. H. (1990). *Black feminist thought.* London: HarperCollins Academic.

Crago, M., & Shisslak, C. M. (2003). Ethnic differences in dieting, binge eating, and purging behaviors among American females: A review. *Eating Disorders, 11*(4), 289–304.

Davis, N. L., Clance, P. R., & Gailis, A. T. (1999). Treatment approaches for obese and overweight African American women: A consideration of cultural dimensions. *Psychotherapy, 36,* 27–35.

Denious, J. E., Russo, N. F., & Rubin, L. R. (2004). The role of shame in socio- and subcultural influences on disordered eating. In M. Paludi (Ed.), *Praeger guide to the psychology of gender* (pp. 219–237). Westport, CT: Praeger.

Fitzgibbon, M. L., Spring, B., Avellone, M. E., Blackman, L. R., Pingitore, R., & Stolley, M. R. (1998). Correlates of binge eating in Hispanic, Black, and White women. *International Journal of Eating Disorders, 24,* 43–52.

Forbes, G. B., & Frederick, D. A. (2008). The UCLA Body Project II: Breast and body dissatisfaction among African, Asian, European, and Hispanic American college women. *Sex Roles, 58,* 449–457.

Franko, D. L., Becker, A. E., Thomas, J. T., & Herzog, D. B. (2006). Cross-ethnic differences in eating disorder symptoms and related distress. *International Journal of Eating Disorders, 40*, 156–164.

Franzoi, S. L. (1994). Further evidence of the reliability and validity of the Body Esteem Scale. *Journal of Clinical Psychology, 50*(2), 237–239.

Frisby, C. M. (2004). Does race matter? Effects of idealized images on African American women's perceptions of body esteem. *Journal of Black Studies, 34*(3), 323–347.

Gilbert, S. C., Crump, S., Madhere, S., & Schutz, W. (2009). Internalization of the thin ideal as a predictor of body dissatisfaction and disordered eating in African, African-American, and Afro-Caribbean female college students. *Journal of College Student Psychotherapy, 23*, 196–211.

Gordon, K. H., Castro, Y., Sitnikov, L., & Holm-Denoma, J. M. (2010). Cultural body shape ideals and eating disorder symptoms among White, Latina, and Black college women. *Cultural Diversity and Ethnic Minority Psychology, 16*, 135–143.

Gordon, K. H., Perez, M., & Joiner, T. E., Jr. (2002). The impact of racial stereotypes on eating disorder recognition. *International Journal of Eating Disorders, 32*, 219–224.

Grabe, S., & Hyde, J. S. (2006). Ethnicity and body dissatisfaction among women in the United States: A meta-analysis. *Psychological Bulletin, 132*, 622–640.

Greene, B., White, J. C., & Whitten, L. (2000). Hair texture, length, and style as a metaphor in the African American mother-daughter relationship: Considerations in psychodynamic psychotherapy. In L. C. Jackson & B. Greene (Eds.), *Psychotherapy with African American women: Innovations in psychodynamic perspective and practice* (pp. 166–193). New York: Guilford Press.

Hall, C. C. (1995). Asian eyes: Body image and eating disorders of Asian and Asian American women. *Eating Disorders, 3*, 8–19.

Harrington, E. F., Crowther, J. H., Henrickson, H. C. P., & Mickelson, K. D. (2006). The relationships among trauma, stress, ethnicity, and binge eating. *Cultural Diversity and Ethnic Minority Psychology, 12*, 212–229.

Hooks, B. (1994). *Black looks: Race and representation.* Boston: South End Press.

Iyer, D. S., & Haslam, N. (2003). Body image and eating disturbance among South Asian-American women: The role of racial teasing. *The International Journal of Eating Disorders, 34*, 142–147.

Kashubeck-West, S., Mintz, L. B., & Saunders, K. J. (2001). Assessment of eating disorders in women. *Counseling Psychology, 29*(5), 662–694.

Kaw, E. (1993). Medicalization of racial features: Asian American women and cosmetic surgery. *Medical Anthropology Quarterly, 7*(1), 74–89.

Koff, E., & Benavage, A. (1998). Breast size perception and satisfaction, body image, and psychological functioning in Caucasian and Asian American college women. *Sex Roles, 38*, 655–673.

Lokken, K. L., Worthy, S. L., Ferraro, F. R., & Atman, J. (2008). Bulimic symptoms and body image dissatisfaction in college women: More affected by climate or race? *Journal of Psychology, 142*, 386–394.

Lovejoy, M. (2001). Disturbances in the social body: Difference in body image and eating problems among African American and White women. *Gender and Society, 15*(2),239–261. doi:10.1177/08912430101500200.

Marcus, M. D., Bromberger, J. T., Wei, H. L., Brown, C., & Kravitz, H. M. (2007). Prevalence and selected correlates of eating disorder symptoms among a multiethnic community sample of midlife women. *Annals of Behavioral Medicine, 33*, 269–277.

Mastria, M. (2002). Ethnicity and eating disorders. *Psychoanalysis and Psychotherapy, 19*, 59–77.

Mazzeo, S. E., Saunders, R., & Mitchell, K. S. (2005). Binge eating among African American and Caucasian bariatric surgery candidates. *Eating Behaviors, 6*, 189–196.

Mujtaba, T., & Furnham, A. (2001). A cross-cultural study of parental conflict and eating disorders in a non-clinical sample. *International Jounral of Social Psychiatry, 47*, 24–35.

Mulholland, A. M., & Mintz, L. B. (2001). Prevalence of eating disorders among African American women. *Journal of Counseling Psychology, 48*, 111–116.

Mumford, D. B., Whitehouse, A. M., & Choudry, I. Y. (1992). Survey of eating disorders in English-medium schools in Lahore Pakistan. *International Journal of Eating Disorders, 11*, 173–184.

Mumford, D. B., Whitehouse, A. M., & Platts, M. (1991). Sociocultural correlates of eating disorders among Asian schoolgirls in Bradford. *British Journal of Psychiatry, 158*, 222–228.

Napolitano, M. A., & Himes, S. (2011). Race, weight, and correlates of binge eating in female college students. *Eating Behaviors, 12*(1), 29–36.

Parham, T. A. (1993). White researchers conducting multicultural counseling research: Can their efforts be "mo betta"? *Counseling Psychologist, 21*(2), 250–256.

Parker, S., Nichter, M., Vuckovic, N., Sims, C., & Ritenbaugh, C. (1995). Body image and weight concerns among African American and white adolescent females: Differences that make a difference. *Human Organization, 54*, 103–114.

Parmer, T., Arnold, M. S., Natt, T., & Janson, C. (2004). Physical attractiveness as a process of internalized oppression and multigenerational transmission in African American families. *Family Journal, 12*(3), 230–242.

Pepper, A. C., & Ruiz, S. Y. (2007). Acculturation's influence on antifat attitudes, body image and eating behaviors. *Eating Disorders, 15*, 427–447.

Perez, M., Voelz, Z., Pettit, J., & Joiner, T. (2002). The role of acculturative stress and body dissatisfaction in predicting bulimic symptomatology across ethnic groups. *The International Journal of Eating Disorders, 31*, 442–454.

Pike, K. M., Dohm, F., Striegel-Moore, R. H., Wilfley, D. E., & Fairburn, C. (2001). A comparison of Black and White women with binge eating disorder. *American Journal of Psychiatry, 158*, 1455–1460.

Poran, M. A. (2006). The politics of protection: Body image, social pressures, and the misrepresentation of young Black women. *Sex Roles, 55*(11–12), 739–755.

Reddy, S. D., & Crowther, J. H. (2007). Teasing, acculturation, and cultural conflict: Psychosocial correlates of body image and eating attitudes among South Asian women. *Cultural Diversity and Ethnic Minority Psychology, 13*, 45–53.

Roberts, A., Cash, T. F., Feingold, A., & Johnson, B. T. (2006). Are Black-White Differences in females' body dissatisfaction decreasing? A meta-analytic review. *Journal of Consulting and Clinical Psychology, 74*, 1121–1131.

Root, M. P. (1990). Disordered eating in women of color. *Sex Roles, 22*, 525–536.

Root, M. P. (2001). Future considerations in research on eating disorders. *Counseling Psychologist, 29*(5), 754–762.

Rosen, L. W., Shafer, C. L., Dummer, G. M., Cross, L. K., Deuman, G. W., & Malmberg, S. R. (1988). Prevalence of pathogenic weight-control behaviors among Native American women and girls. *The International Journal of Eating Disorders, 7*, 807–811.

Rubin, L. R., Fitts, M. L., & Becker, A. E. (2003). "Whatever feels good in my soul": Body ethics and aesthetics among African American and Latina women. *Culture, Medicine and Psychiatry, 27*(1), 49–75.

Sanders, N. M., & Heiss, C. J. (1998). Eating attitudes and body image of Asian and Caucasian college women. *Eating Disorders, 6*, 15–27.

Schooler, D., Ward, M., Merriwether, A., & Caruthers, A. (2004). Who's that girl: Television's role in the body image development of young White and Black women. *Psychology of Women Quarterly, 28*, 38–47.

Shaw, H., Ramirez, L., Trost, A., Randall, P., & Stice, E. (2004). Body image and eating disturbances across ethnic groups: More similarities than differences. *Psychology of Addictive Behaviors, 18*, 12–18.

Smolak, L., & Striegel-Moore, R. H. (2001). Challenging the myth of the golden girl: Ethnicity and eating disorders. In R. H. Striegel-Moore & L. Smolak (Eds.), *Eating disorders: Innovative directions in research and practice* (pp. 111–132). Washington, DC: American Psychological Association.

Solomon, A. (2005). *Naked: Black women bare all about their skin, hair, hips, lips, and other parts.* New York: Penguin.

Stein, K. F., Corte, C., & Ronis, D. L. (2010). Personal identities and disordered eating behaviors in Mexican American women. *Eating Behaviors, 11*, 197–200.

Stice, E. (1994). Review of the evidence for a sociocultural model of bulimia nervosa and an exploration of the mechanisms of action. *Clinical Psychology Review, 14*, 633–661.

Striegel-Moore, R. H., Dohm, F. A., Pike, K. M., Wifley, D. E., & Fairburn, C. G. (2002). Abuse, bullying, and discrimination as risk factors for binge eating. *American Journal of Psychiatry, 159*, 1902–1907.

Thompson, B. W. (1994). *A hunger so wide and so deep: A multiracial view of women's eating problems.* Minneapolis: University of Minnesota Press.

Thompson, B. (1996). Multiracial feminist theorizing about eating problems: refusing to rank oppressions. *Eating Disorders, 4*, 104–114.

Thompson, J. K., Heinberg, L. J., Altabe, M., & Tantleff-Dunn, S. (1999). Future directions: Integrative theories, multidimensional assessments, and multicomponent interventions. In J. K. Thompson, L. J. Heinberg, M. Altabe, & S. Tantleff-Dunn (Eds.), *Theory, assessment, and treatment of body image disturbance* (pp. 311–332). Washington, DC: American Psychological Association.

Turner, H., & Bryant-Waugh, R. (2004). Eating disorder not otherwise specified (EDNOS): Profiles of clients presenting at a community eating disorder service. *European Eating Disorder Review, 12*, 18–26.

United States. Department of Health and Human Services (DHHS). National Center for Health Statistics (2010). *Health, United States, 2009: With Special Feature on Medical Technology*. Hyattsville, MD. Retrieved May 28, 2011 from the Office of Minority Health website: http://www.cdc.gov/nchs/data/hus/hus09.pdf

Wade, T. J. (2003). Evolutionary theory and African American self-perception: Sex differences in body-esteem predictors of self-perceived physical and sexual attractiveness, and self-esteem. *Journal of Black Psychology, 29*(2), 123–141.

Warren, C. S., Castillo, L. G., & Gleaves, D. H. (2010). The sociocultural model of eating disorders in Mexican American women: Behavioral acculturation and cognitive marginalization as moderators. *Eating Disorders, 18*, 43–57.

Wildes, J. E., Emery, R. E., & Simons, A. D. (2001). The roles of ethnicity and culture in the development of eating disturbance and body dissatisfaction: A meta-analytic review. *Clinical Psychology Review, 21*, 521–551.

Yancey, A. K., Leslie, J., & Abel, E. K. (2006). Obesity at the crossroads: Feminist and public health perspectives. *Signs: Journal of Women in Culture and Society, 31*(2), 425–443.

Yokoyama, K. (2007). The double binds of our bodies: Multiculturally-informed feminist therapy considerations for body image and eating disorders among Asian American women. *Women and Therapy, 30*, 177–192.

Still Sucked into the Body Image Thing: The Impact of Anti-aging and Health Discourses on Women's Gendered Identities

by Claire Carter*

Women's and Gender Studies, University of Regina, 3737 Wascana Parkway, Regina, SK, Canada S4S 0A2

(Received 15 January 2014; accepted 16 May 2014)

Health norms have changed over the past three decades, imposing more responsibility for health onto the individual. There are gendered implications of these changes which, when combined with increasing anti-aging pressures, have the potential to intensify the disciplinary relationship women have with their bodies. This paper, based upon interviews with 14 women, examines the impact of dominant health and anti-aging discourses on women's body practices, including exercise, makeup, clothing and diet, and ongoing construction of gendered subjectivity. Findings suggest that the women in this study are motivated to do particular body practices because of their concern with having a healthy and youthful 'looking' body. The women's stories reveal that anti-aging and health discourses function to reinforce normative bodily demands of femininity and consequently to intensify disciplinary control of their bodies. While the pressure to fight the appearance of aging is not new, the increasing association of aging with ill health, even illness, in conjunction with the promotion of health has implications for women's relationship with their bodies and sense of self.

Keywords: body image; gender; health; aging; subjectivity

Introduction

I recently gave birth and my labour, as I believe is fairly common, did not go as planned. I had been hoping for a water birth at home but due to complications, I ended up having a c-section. Because of this, my partner and I had to spend several days in the hospital. Nurses would come in every so often to check on us, and on every visit, a nurse would need to check my c-section scar to see how it was healing. On one of these visits, a nurse told me was that my scar was healing well and that I would definitely be able to wear a bikini again. This comment surprised me as I had not considered the fact that having an emergency c-section might affect my bikini wearing ability. But this comment was made with kindness; there was a sense that relaying this information would be seen as positive and uplifting to me, the patient. That comment reflected an interplay of discourses on body image, aging, health and femininity; my body was going to recover and return to a state of good health and youthfulness (such that my body would not show signs of wear from birth), and the indication of this was the assertion of bikini possibility. Reflecting on this experience brought to mind stories from my doctoral research, which highlighted the intersection of health and aging norms with (heterosexual) femininity. The women I interviewed struggled to make sense of their identities through their changing bodies and drew on dominant ideals of gender, sexuality and health.

This paper examines women's body practices and the complex role aging and being healthy have on their body image and sense of self. This work is part of a larger project based on 14 interviews with women aged 30–45 in Toronto and Ottawa, which analyses the relationship between women's body practices and gendered subjectivity. Recently, feminist theorists have drawn attention to the gendered nature of health promotion arguing that they reinforce bodily demands of normative femininity, which favour a thin and fit *looking* body (Malson 2008, Moore 2008). In particular, Malson (2008, p. 29) argues that under the guise of health promotion and fears about obesity, weight management practices, such as dieting, have been reformulated as positive, even necessary *health* practices. Feminist critiques of weight management practices as 'patriarchally oppressive and potentially physically and psychologically damaging' (Malson 2008, p. 29) have been marginalized and instead these practices are increasing characterized as 'health maximising' within global health initiatives (Malson 2008, p. 29).

Building upon this work, I draw attention to the reconfiguration of beauty and body management practices as health practices and highlight how, in comparative ways, the medicalization of aging has led to the reframing of youthfulness and anti-aging as tied to good health. Concerns about health and aging provide women with legitimate reasons to control and regulate their bodies – both in the present, and increasingly as they age. Aging represents a loss of control and a potential loss of health and feminine identity for many women. Consequently several women here spoke about needing to do more, be more active and be more conscious of their bodies. This legitimacy of needing to 'ward off aging' and be healthy masks social dynamics of racism, classism, sexism, fat phobia and heterosexism, which compound women's efforts to have self-control and 'feminine' enough bodies. Drawing on women's accounts of their body practices, this paper argues that anti-aging and healthism reinforce normative femininity and limit the potential selves women can become. However, this paper also seeks to demonstrate that women's body practices reflect multiple meanings and to highlight the tension and complexity at play in the negotiation of health and aging norms. As ideal femininity demands of women a bodily size, shape and youthful appearance that few can sustain, women's health and well-being may be at risk as a result of overzealous promotion of body practices purported to promote fitness and youthfulness.

Theoretical frame: feminist post-structuralism

The body is recognized as a site of struggle through which women learn and attempt to emulate what being feminine means within the current socio-historical moment. Bodies are also the site and source of social identities, they are 'physical sites where the relations of class, gender, race, sexuality and age come together and are embodied and practised' (Skeggs 1997, p. 82). As many feminist theorists (Bartky 1997, Bordo 1997, Rice 2006) have argued, the demands of femininity are virtually impossible for women to achieve, as they require unlimited material resources and a transcendence of bodily constraints. This produces a sense of bodily deficiency and failure, which is compounded by the social dynamics of class, race, age and sexuality. As a result, the attempt to recognize oneself as feminine means 'an enormous amount of regulation is faced' (Skeggs 1997, p. 82); women learn that their bodies are something that needs to be controlled in the service of normative femininity.

Foucault (1977) argues that power has come to function on and through bodies at the minute and everyday level, through techniques and practices designed to maximize bodily efficiency and performance in service of subjection to societal and disciplinary demands. Therefore, bodies became the site of individual control and subjected to norms, through 'the primacy of practice over belief' (Bordo 1993, p. 165). Butler's (1990) theory of performativity proposes that gendered subjectivity is not natural or fixed; rather its seemingly natural status is dependent on the continual repetition of acts, movements and gestures that construct and shape the body to meet demands of heterosexuality. Therefore, everyday, 'common sense' body practices are important to improving our understanding of how gender is performed and reproduced. Weedon (1997, p. 72) suggests that 'common sense has an important constitutive role to play in maintaining the centrality of gender difference as a focus of power in society.' For example, gender 'appropriate' child rearing appears to be 'common sense' parenting practice, when in fact it represents 'quite specific values and interests' (Weedon 1997, p. 72). Applying this idea to performativity and women's efforts at being recognizable as feminine, practices that women engage in may seem to be common sense or so routine that the values they serve may not be apparent. To understand how 'discourses impinge on us as fleshy bodies', Bordo argues that analyses need to 'get down and dirty with the body at the level of its practices', to consider 'what people are doing to their bodies in the more mundane service of the "normal"' (1993, pp. 183–184). Several of the women here remarked that they are not 'girly girls' and questioned whether they were good subjects for my study because they do not really do a lot of 'feminine' things. Their stories, however, reveal 'common sense' practices of femininity taken for granted and part of how they negotiate their identities.

Societal changes such as the growth of anti-aging technologies and state policies of health promotion have a significant influence on gendered subjectivity, with particular implications for women. Aging and life course scholars (Featherstone and Hepworth 1996, Gilleard and Higgs 2000, Calsanti and Slevin 2006) argue that the relationship between age identity and the body has been affected by the theoretical, and to a lesser degree societal, shift from modern life stages to the postmodern life course. Featherstone and Hepworth (1996) state that the change from industrialization and modernization to consumerism and/or capitalism has nearly reversed how life development is organized and related to identity; from the institutionalization of life stages to de-institutionalization. As a result, Featherstone and Hepworth (1996, p. 372) argue there is 'less emphasis . . . being placed upon age-specific role transitions and scheduled identity development, leading to the blurring of hitherto clearly distinct life stages, as well as the experiences and characteristic behaviours associated with those stages.' Biggs (1999, p. 5) suggests that the impact of these changes is that notions of 'personal continuity and a sense of embeddedness in the life course may have become outmoded concepts' within theorizing of the postmodern society, as there are 'continuous enticements' and possibilities for changing the self and identity inherent in consumerism. The shift to consumerism has been 'centered upon personal leisure and pleasure' thereby 'amplify[ing] the body's significance to a point where it is increasingly seen as a "central paradigm" for the self' (Biggs 1999, p. 5). Thus, the body in postmodern society 'assumes a new significance as a focus of personal identity and control' (Twigg 2000, p. 39). The body is no longer seen as necessarily illustrative of an individual's life stage or age, but as controllable and changeable, in accordance with desired self-representation and identity. Twigg (2000, p. 42) argues that 'in the contemporary West, identity and selfhood are dependent upon the possession of a physically bounded body.'

As a result, aging is increasingly perceived as something to be avoided, controlled, even cured, with advances in medicine and biotechnology and the success of anti-aging industries seemingly providing the means to achieve this ideal. Woodward (1991) argues that aging is now often equated with illness, although no illness in particular. The medicalization of old age effectively means that aging is not perceived as a normal human process, it is 'the opposite of health', challenging conceptions of bodily processes and transitions (Woodward 1991, p. 89).

The impact of changes on life course transitions and the increasing centrality of the body for identity have gendered implications. While the body and bodily appearance have long been identified as central to gendered identity and femininity, the necessity to control the impact of aging on the body has intensified this relation. In order for women to continue to be recognizable as women, they need to 'maintain a feminine/gendered body', which requires that they 'maintain an *unchanging* body' throughout the aging process (Dillaway 2005, p. 4). Bordo (1997, p. 47) argues that as a result women will develop a different relationship with their bodies; rather than accepting gradual bodily changes that come with aging, women are now expected to react and make every effort to 'correct' any slight change. Their bodies will come to be viewed as an object in need of control and constant management, rather than recognizing that their bodies (and selves) change over time. This has implications, she argues, in terms of doing important psychological work, such as reflecting on one's life, mortality and place in the world (Bordo 1997, p. 47).

Hurd-Clarke's (2002, p. 430) qualitative study on older women's perceptions of body image found that 'aging and the perceived loss of beauty constitute a threat to an older woman's sense of social currency, self-esteem, and identity.' In a similar study on older lesbian women's body image, Slevin (2006, p. 259) found that 'talking about good health, fitness, and activity allows . . . women to perform "active" aging'; their class privilege allowed them the 'means to work on their bodies.' Using the language of health and being health conscious enabled women in her study to 'justif[y] their disciplinary activities' (Slevin 2006, p. 259). Her research makes evident the extent to which femininity is inextricably tied to a youthful, healthy and fit looking body.

Crawford (2006), Blackman (2008) and Moore (2008) all suggest that another development that has occurred in last three decades is the increasing importance of health in everyday life. The concept of healthism, coined by Crawford (2006), draws attention to changes in how health and health care are conceptualized and promoted. Crawford (2006) and Blackman (2008) both argue that despite formal obligation of the state to provide some level of health care, more and more onus for health is placed upon the individual. This is in part the result of political restructuring, whereby social services, such as healthcare, are being cut back in response to neoliberalist economic policies. Crawford (2006) suggests that being healthy has become the moral compass of citizenship, central to the expression of self and one's individual responsibility. Blackman (2008) states that some social theorists view the growth of healthism as a strategy of self and social regulation. Blackman (2008, p. 99) notes that healthisms' rise has coincided with increasing cultures of risk: 'the global spread of HIV/AIDS, concerns with food manufacturing and production, threats of pandemic viruses, and threats of terrorism or global warfare.' Governments around the world respond to these potential risks through the micro-surveillance of their populations. Consequently, the focus moves from macro-practices, such as state sponsored health care/health spending, to the micro-practices of the individual. Being healthy and engaging in practices of self-health have become central to citizenship and individual autonomy; individuals are judged by how well they adopt healthy practices. Moore (2008, p. 96) provides a gendered analysis of these health trends, and argues that 'the very idea of what constitutes healthiness . . . has changed along gendered lines.' Central to Moore's (2008, p. 111) argument is the comparative processes of objectification associated with healthism and hegemonic femininity, wherein the body becomes an object and/or project that is to be worked on and maintained. Critically, she suggests that '"doing health" may become a means of "doing gender"', such that disciplinary body practices could be reinterpreted as health practices even if they are lacking in actual health benefits (Moore 2008, p. 112).

Perhaps not surprisingly, healthism has influenced constructions of the ideal feminine body. The sociocultural change in 'social symbolism of body weight and size' has strong class, race and gendered dimensions (Bordo 1993, p. 191). Bordo (1993, p. 191) articulates that the prevailing norm of thinness was complemented by the promotion of the new, strong and athletic ideal; 'these two ideals, though superficially very different are united in battle against a common enemy: the soft, the loose; un-solid, excess flesh.' The athletic body is no longer read as symbolic of working-class and immigrant labourers, but has become a cultural icon–a glamourized and sexualized yuppie body (Bordo 1993, p. 191). Furthermore, having a toned and fit body is reflective of the 'correct attitude; it means that one cares about oneself and how one appears to others, suggesting willpower, energy, control over impulses, the ability to shape your life' and in turn excess flesh reflects the opposite, a 'lack of discipline, unwillingness to conform' (Bordo 1993, p. 191). The image of health, of a healthy looking body, has become a way of gaining recognition and social acceptance. Both Choi (2000) and Malson (2008) illustrate how contemporary health discourses reinforce dominant constructions of femininity. Choi (2000) argues that healthy and/or exercise activities are presented as, and have become synonymous with, beauty activity; women undertake healthy activity in order to achieve a 'beautiful', slim and toned body. Similarly, Malson (2008) argues that the pursuit of slenderness has been 're-presented' as health promotion and that the pursuit of exercise and health practices is done in the hopes of having a body that *appears* healthy.

Put together, anti-aging and health discourses provide a new language that women draw upon to talk about and act on their bodily anxiety and insecurities. Bartky (1997) states that women are often characterized as trivial and/or immature for their concerns about appearance, which denies the centrality of body image to feminine identity and harsh social sanctions if one does not adhere to social gender norms of appearance. Women may engage in, or not resist, normative gendered body practices, Bartky (1997, p. 145) argues, because of questions of 'identity and internalization'; doing particular body practices is intimately tied to and

affirms women's sense of self. However, in addition to Bartky's recognition of the role of 'identity and internalization', we also need to consider the complex and multiple meanings informing women's body practices. Third Wave feminists (Heywood and Drake 1997, Steenbergen 2001, Edut 2003) reject the notion that body/beauty practices can only, and/or always, be interpreted as oppressive and disciplinary. They seek to reclaim experiences of pleasure and creativity in women's beauty and body practices while also critiquing binary gender norms and beauty culture. In short, Third Wave feminists acknowledge the inherent 'lived messiness' of gendered embodiment and the ways women 'are compelled and constructed by the very things that undermine [them]' (Heywood and Drake 1997, p. 3). This paper primarily focuses on the limiting and regulatory effects of dominant health and aging discourses, but also recognizes the various meanings body practices hold for women.

Anti-aging has become inter-twined with notions of health and the demands of femininity to the extent that the body must continue to appear 'youthful' well into midlife. In order to achieve a feminine, healthy and youthful looking body, women must undertake extensive efforts to discipline and attempt to control their bodies. This can involve monitoring food intake, engaging in exercise routines and being conscious of how their bodies appear–practices which are part and parcel of numerous health campaigns in the contemporary moment (Malson 2008, Moore 2008). But engaging in the so-called health practices is socially accepted and validated, thus offering women a means to discipline their bodies without facing judgement or dismissal. How do women experience and negotiate the changing meanings of health and contradictions of the equation of healthy, anti-aging and beauty practices? And what are the implications for differently positioned women–for women of colour, women of different ages and queer women?

Method

As part of a wider study, 14 women aged 30–45 from Toronto and Ottawa were interviewed. Participants were recruited through flyers posted in community centres and organizations as well as through email listservs and personal contacts. Of the 14 women, eight are White, including three who identify as Italian and one woman as Jewish. Six are women of colour, and identify as East Indian Canadian, South Asian Canadian, mixed race, Middle Eastern, Iranian Canadian and Black. Two women identified as having disabilities, three women as queer/lesbian, one as fat and one as a single parent.[1]

Interviews[2] began with questions about the women's daily body practices from the moment they woke up until they went to bed, including eating and exercise, clothing, hygiene, and makeup practices. Of interest was the range of practices the women engaged in, individually as well as collectively, and how they spoke about their routines. As the interviews progressed, the questions moved from bodily routines to questions about how and why their practices changed over the course of their lives. This was done to get a sense of the how particular life experiences informed the take up of new, or changes to old, practices. After obtaining a general overview of body practices, the focus of the interviews moved to examine particular influences on choice of practices, for example: various media, families, friends, or peer networks, intimate relationships, work situations, and political and spiritual beliefs. Moving from descriptive accounts of their daily routines into discussions of what influenced them facilitated consideration of what was involved in the doing of their practices and why they mattered.[3]

This research is based upon a feminist qualitative methodology and draws on principles of narrative analysis. Chase (2002, p. 85) states that 'the principles of narrative analysis recommend that we ask people about their life experiences rather than ask them sociological questions–questions about cultural ideologies or questions that ask them to generalize about others' experiences.' My interview questions drew out women's everyday experiences, including how their practices have changed and what has influenced their bodily routines. Chase (2002, p. 86) believes that 'the stories a woman tells about her specific experiences and her feelings about her experiences will provide much deeper and more nuanced examples of how she has internalized or rejected or transformed ideologies.' Similarly, Onoufriou's

(2009, p. 16) interpretation of narratives of sexuality was rooted in participants' choice of what to disclose and meaning given to individual narratives by narrators; revealing that the narrative was 'at once already an interpretation and also in need of interpretation'. Starting interviews with an introduction to daily routines enabled participants to tell me about body practices that were significant to them and how they present themselves. Interpretation proved challenging on many occasions. For example, reading about women's struggles with eating and then having to go and make lunch brought the material I was studying into my own daily routines. I closely identify with Skegg's (1997, p. 34) articulation that 'reluctant as I was to become interested in my self, questions of who are "they" informed who "I" was'. The interpretation and analysis of the women's stories involved a reanalysis of *my* body practices and sense of self.

I was interested in what women learnt or were told about their bodies and how they responded to this information, what purpose certain practices held for them, what they represented and how they were connected to social norms of gender, race, age, class and body size. My interpretation of the women's body practices drew upon Scott's (1992) theorizing on women's experience, whereby it is not individuals who *have* experiences, but rather they are constituted *through* experiences. Scott (1992, p. 26) argues that by theorizing experience as constructed and as that which constitutes subjects, the role of experience shifts from being 'the origin of our explanation' to 'that which we seek to explain, that about which knowledge is produced'. My approach utilizes experience in much the same way, as informative of the processes within which women are engaged and embedded and which involve negotiations with multiple and competing norms and discourses in relation to their diverse social identities.

Findings: gendered dynamics of healthy aging bodies
Bodily comparisons of aging

Women receive instructions on femininity through their interactions and bodily comparisons to other women, whether friends or strangers. The role of other women on subjectivity is significant; women learn how to *do* femininity from other women (Smith 1988, p. 38). Several women spoke about interactions they had with other women about their appearance, specifically about aging. Bronwyn was advised to buy anti-aging creams by a beautician instead of her usual moisturizer to ward off 'the first signs of aging'.

> She pointed out that I had dehydration lines on my forehead which I hadn't really noticed so yeah I was a bit surprised . . . I started to think gee I'd better start really taking care of my skin. (Bronwyn early 30s White Italian Canadian)

> When I turned 30 I bought a whole bunch of [anti-aging] products, people were like you have to take care of your skin and wrinkles are going to start showing so I did, I bought eye cream and night cream and that kind of thing, that I use daily. (Ava 32 Trinidad/Pakistan Muslim Canadian)

Despite being told by her dermatologist that anti-aging creams did not work, Bronwyn continues to use them in the hopes that the impact of aging 'won't be as bad'. Similarly, around her 30th birthday, Ava was advised on how to slow the impact of aging from work colleagues as well as beauticians at a local department store. Bronwyn does not notice that her skin has changed, but trusts the advice of the skin care expert at the cosmetic counter over a health professional. Ava defers to the advice of her colleagues concerning the inherent association of age and skin care treatment. While societal messages for women to maintain a youthful appearing body as they age are not new, the intersection of anti-aging with health provides new impetus and validation for women's efforts. If, as Woodward (1991) argues, aging has become synonymous with illness or lack of health, and as Moore (2008) suggests, current health discourses promote viewing one's body as a project or object in need of constant monitoring and maintenance, then the adoption of anti-aging practices might be reinterpreted as adoption of *health* practices.

Women involved in my study also negotiated their femininity through visual comparison with other women's bodies. Simone talks about her growing anxiety; she compares herself and her body with other women to assess how she is aging:

> Simone: Yeah my hair and you know I've noticed some more lines around the eye, and I notice it on other people, like I check the things that I'm self-conscious about I look for other people's grey hair.

> Interviewer: If you know you're in the same age category.

> Simone: Yeah, totally, I look, how old is she and then if she's got a few little wrinkles or lines around the eye I'm like, she's in her 30s . . . I look for things that I'm self-conscious about in other people. (Simone 33 Jewish Canadian)

Changes to appearance are not as easy to monitor, as we like to think they are; there are sociocultural discourses informing changing notions of age and the significance of these for the body. Hockey and James (2004, p. 160) question how we know we are aging, as they suggest that the aging process is 'occurring too slowly for us to catch it in motion—no matter how watchful we might be in front of the bathroom mirror'. In socially constructed accounts, 'the body itself is not seen to *initiate* the aging process' (Hockey and James 2004, p. 160). Rather, aging 'has to be stamped upon the body by society, in order for us to "know" or "experience" it through the symbolic marking out of differences between "then" and "now"' (Hockey and James 2004, p. 160). Therefore, while the body clearly changes, and this has a material reality, these changes and materialities can only be expressed through social means as 'there can be no pure human "aging"' (Gilleard and Higgs 2000, p. 142). Discourses of aging promote particular meanings of aging within a sociohistorical period, and therefore function to shape and construct potential subjectivities women can embody in conjunction with gender, sexuality, race and class.

Simone's analysis of her body's aging process is accomplished through comparative reading of other women's bodies in relation to key social markers of aging, such as wrinkles and grey hair. What age means or looks like to Simone is determined through comparison with other women's bodies and is connected to normative ideals of aging and femininity; her sense of her own aging process is deferred to these external sources. Her concern about whether she is aging on par with women of her age reinforces the notion that to maintain their gendered status, women must 'maintain an unchanging body' (Dillaway 2005, p. 4). While Simone does not specifically talk about her body practices in relation to health, I include her story here because within contemporary culture aging has become synonymous with ill health. Therefore, like Ava and Bronwyn, Simone's concern about her appearance may be more socially supported, even encouraged under the guise of health in addition to more common concerns about appearance or femininity. Bordo (1993) and Moore (2008) argue that bodily appearance in Western society is thought to be reflective of one's attitude and an overall sense of self; self-control, responsibility and self-care or lack thereof. Health may be increasingly providing sociocultural validation for bodily comparisons—and corresponding practices aimed at disciplining and regulating the body—that traditionally were deemed trivialities associated with being a woman (Bartky 1997). As mentioned earlier, it is also important to acknowledge that there can be pleasure and social validation (often, also pleasurable) gained from participation in particular body practices, such as fitness or beauty regimes. While I have noted the disciplinary effects of anti-aging practices, these same practices can be related to a variety of feelings or experiences, including: bodily shame if one does not look one's age or younger; pleasure and security in being a part of a cultural and collegial practice as is evidenced by Ava's experience as well as ambiguity or uncertainty about whether or not to engage in anti-aging practices or if they will make a difference as reflected in Bronwyn's decision to use anti aging creams.

For some of the women interviewed, aging symbolizes a loss of control over their bodies. Some speak of the need to do more, to make a greater effort to look after and maintain their bodies:

> I do find now that I'm older it's harder to kind of maintain yourself so I feel like I have to you know kind of keep at it whereas before when I was younger I didn't have such a kind of an exercise routine, I was still always active but . . . I wasn't so

structured with it whereas now I really get out for my runs. (Elizabeth 36 White British Canadian)

Elizabeth's comments express a heightened awareness of bodily changes and the need to respond to them. She has an inherent expectation or assumption that aging/her body must be controlled if she wishes to maintain her sense of self; this requires an increased level of discipline and structure in her life:

> I think one thing is just starting to notice changes in your body, I'm just becoming more aware of it because maybe they are just happening faster too, and, you know in your 20s, you're not even like paying attention really, so I think that's one thing, you're just kind of really aware of just different changes, more hairs are growing on my face and I've found a couple grey hairs, and the pudge kind of manifests itself in different ways now . . . so I think probably the past like three years or so I've really started to feel like my body . . . just responds differently and that I need to just take care of it more, I need to be more conscious of that. (Elizabeth 36 White British Canadian)

Janet also expresses the need to be more conscientious and take better care of her body in relation to her eating habits:

> I wasn't eating properly, I wasn't eating the right things and, it shows, it shows in skin, it shows in your health, how you feel about yourself and you think, you know as you're getting older you have to start taking better care of yourself. (Janet Heterosexual 43 Black Canadian)

Elizabeth and Janet's comments suggest that aging, by its very nature, requires more bodily regulation and is equated with a decrease in health status. They feel responsible for improving their health and maintaining their bodies, which is reflective of discourses of individualism inherent in healthism and anti-aging. The new paradigm of health requires, Moore (2008) argues, individuals to negotiate a bodily contradiction. On the one hand, we are told that our bodies are 'susceptible to illness' by their very nature, and yet on the other hand, we are expected to do everything we can to ensure we do not get ill; to maintain our healthy status by changing our 'unhealthy behaviours' (Moore 2008, p. 109). In their efforts to be healthy, both Janet and Elizabeth highlight the need for behavioural modifications–getting out for runs or eating a better diet–that are simultaneously focused on bodily *appearance*, such as 'pudge' on the body and unhealthy looking skin. Their comments illustrate a connection between health and appearance, such that needing to look healthy can be equated with being healthy. The seeming insignificance of the fact that the body can–and does–become ill despite any or all changes to bodily behaviours, and that restrictive or disciplinary practices can be unhealthy, is perhaps demonstrative of the moralistic and gendered imperative informing body practices. Societal affirmation is granted not only with respect to doing what one can to be healthy (which inherently involves the fight against aging), but in addition for women, to endlessly pursue the ideal feminine body.

Aging is a concern for many women, as it represents several potential losses; loss of control over their bodies, loss of health and a loss of their gendered identity. It is perceived by some women as a legitimate reason to employ new body practices or begin a more structured and disciplined life style to endeavour to maintain feminine bodies. In addition, I have argued that engaging in anti-aging body practices may also be characterized as health practices. Contemporary discourses of health promote self-discipline and behaviour modification all in the name of well-being, or to put another way, to prevent ill health. With aging increasingly seen as a threat to good health, as it involves the breakdown and/or malfunction of the body over time, efforts to fight aging–through anti-aging practices–can be reimagined as taking care of oneself and one's body.[4]

Doing it for health

Being healthy is conceived as a 'good' thing; therefore, engaging in practices of self-health should be understood as positive. But what does being healthy mean and what informs dominant notions of health? How does the intersection of health with other social dynamics influence women's body practices and the negotiation of their

gendered subjectivities? And what does it mean for an individual to be and/or identify as healthy? Examination of what being healthy means must involve consideration of other discourses and/or social norms reinforced by popular conceptions of health, such as anti-aging, normative femininity, and fat phobias, as well as the effect on women's subjectivity. Consider, for example, my discussion with Janet:

> Janet: . . . I just now, recently started walking three times a week after work with a friend of mine.
>
> Interviewer: Anything inspire that or just . . .?
>
> Janet: Bathing suit season. [laughs] It's coming up, looking at the jiggly legs and I thought you know, got to get out there and firm up a bit, but mainly, mainly for health, mainly for health. (Janet Heterosexual 43 Black Canadian)

Janet's initial assertion and then clarification of her motivations for exercising are important as they represent competing influences on her knowledge of what it means to be a good woman. Hurd-Clarke (2002) and Slevin (2006) both argue that health is often viewed as a more acceptable reason for controlling the body through diet and exercise than are women's insecurities around their physical appearance as they age. Janet's assertion that she started walking to be healthier reinforces the argument that there is a hierarchy of legitimate reasons for women to be active and control their bodies. However, 'bathing suit season', as noted by Janet, is a popular culture phenomenon marked by fashion magazine displays of thin and toned women in bikinis, and the magazine articles and television shows that instruct everyday women how to get 'bikini ready'. Therefore, Janet's assertion that her decision to take up walking for her health does not undo or replace her concern about her 'jiggly bits'; rather, the two operate simultaneously, as she is subjected to both health and normative feminine discourses. An additional dimension at play in Janet's story is the positive impact of social activity that walking provides. At the time of the interview, Janet was working full time and was the primary caregiver for her mother. Therefore, going walking provided a means through which to carve out personal time with a friend that was fun and emotionally healthy. Her decision to begin walking was appearance and 'health' motivated, but equally significant is the potential benefits to her overall emotional well-being. Janet's subjectivity results from the inter-action of dominant social norms with her attempts to know herself as feminine and healthy.

When asked to think ahead 10 years or so and whether or not she might do different body practices, Elizabeth says, 'I always think I would like to do more exercise, to kind of incorporate even more into my, my routine.' This is important because earlier in her interview she alludes to the many ways she structures her life to be active: biking to work, running several times a week and gardening. She defends this comment by saying:

> I need to keep myself agile to you know keep the joints kind of lubricated and everything, yeah so for sure, and it does make me feel better about myself, I'll admit I feel better about myself if I look at myself in the mirror and I feel I look healthy, I don't want to be a toothpick but I want to look like I'm athletic or you know not completely toned, but I do feel better just knowing that I'm moving my body, taking care of it . . . I mean I'm not the make up kind of girl but I'm still sucked into the body image thing even if it's just a little bit of fat. (Elizabeth 36 White British Canadian)

Elizabeth negotiates between intersecting–and competing–motivations; she wants to take care of her body and be healthy, but she also wants to appear thin, toned and good for her age. In the interview, Elizabeth identifies as an active person and an environmentalist, and these facets of her identity–alongside body image and aging concerns–inform her choice of body practices. For example, moving her body is a pleasurable experience and not simply a means of completing a workout and it also fulfils her desire to be sustainable through her decision to commute via bicycle.

A tension between health and appearance was evident in many of the women's stories; they want to be healthy, but they also want to ease their body image anxiety and maintain control over how their (aging) bodies appeared. Both Elizabeth and Janet talk about their desire to be healthy as a legitimate reason for controlling their bodies by increasing their physical activity, but they do so in conjunction with discussing the pressure to discipline their bodies to maintain a feminine and youthful appearance. The impact of healthism is critical to understanding women's motivations for becoming more active and health conscious. The women I interviewed spoke of their desire to be healthier, and it seems that discourses of health have become a venue through which subjectivity is constructed in contemporary society. 'Appearing fit', according to Slevin (2006, p. 248), 'is a modern virtue that has, in the space of a few decades, become highly valued currency'. Women want to identify as healthy which signifies changes in the meanings of health from predominantly a physiological feeling or state (I am in good health or I am in poor health) to an attribute or characteristic informing how we know our self and identify. Aging combined with health concerns give women acceptable reasons to regulate their bodies–both in the present and as they age. Knowing themselves through discourses of health, femininity and anti-aging 'produce subject positions and embodied forms of subjectivity which govern the [women's] behaviour . . . in the interests of broader strategies of power' (Weedon 1997, p. 117).

Being healthy for some of the women I spoke to is a more legitimate reason to regulate their bodies than improving their appearance. However, for Ruby, practicing self-health is in opposition to her experiences as a child and teenager of disciplining of her body and weight control. Her story focuses on her efforts to change her relationship with exercise; from weight loss, she wants to turn her attention to good health and fun. Part of Ruby's challenge is having her body and health status policed in places of exercise, such as gyms, because these are highly gendered and fat phobic spaces. She mentions trying to change her relationship with exercise by taking up a new sport, women's boxing, partly because the gym is queer positive:

> Boxing is a sport where bodies and weight are a big deal so sometimes it gets really like weird and uncomfortable and I don't like it so the instructor, who is generally really cool, I like her a lot but sometimes

she'll say something . . . in a way that she is trying to be nice in that sports way, she's like you move your weight really well, you move like you're 100 pounds and I'm supposed to be like thanks! But instead it's like oh you're talking about my weight that is so unacceptable. (Ruby 30 Lesbian White Canadian)

Despite the gym's queer and feminist politics, Ruby faces familiar bodily discourses whereby thin bodies are celebrated and being compared to them is meant as 'high praise'. Slevin's (2006) analysis of body image among aging lesbians finds that (hetero)feminine norms of anti-aging have a stronger influence than any potential alternative the lesbian community might offer. Ruby's experience with the gym instructor supports Slevin's (2006) findings; the queer gym reinforces rather than disrupts norms of feminine body size and fat phobia. Ruby also took fitness classes at a university gym, where a male instructor jokingly commented to female clients about chocolate consumption and guilt; reinforcing corelation between exercise and weight control. The underlying message that gyms promote is that health equals weight loss and that ability and/or strength are less important than appearance by their seeming absence in gym dialogue. Moving like a thin person or restricting caloric intake were thought to be more validating by her instructors than commenting on endurance, strength or physical ability.

> It's hard right to disassociate [physical activity] from weight loss, it's really hard, I don't think I have yet, no I know I haven't but it's hard to think of it more as something you do to be healthy, but riding my bike has been good . . . because it's transportation and exercise but I don't think of it like exercise in that typical way that I generally do, so that's good. (Ruby 30 Lesbian White Canadian)

In her efforts to disassociate being healthy and active from losing weight, Ruby is constantly made aware of how discourses of health are interwoven with fat phobia and ideal femininity. Rice (2006, p. 413) argues that women in the West 'have been raised in a culture where body size is of paramount importance, where thinness is equated with health,

attractiveness, morality and sexuality'. In the above account, we see that Ruby's ability to critically reflect on sociocultural norms of health and gender informing gym spaces is affected by experiences of constantly having her body monitored and defined by others, especially fitness instructors. Being healthy for Ruby stands in opposition to the control and regulation required to be feminine; she enjoys moving her body but resists the imposition of dominant fitness discourses that are fat/body oppressive.

Conclusion

This article has traced some of the ways anti-aging and health discourses reinforce dominant constructions of femininity and what the implications are for different women. Women's stories about their body practices reveal a sense of anxiety about their changing bodies as well as the complexities they face in the negotiation of their gendered identities. In several accounts, efforts to control aging and be healthy coincide with normative demands of femininity; rather than enhancing well-being, for many of the women, 'health' practices involved increased monitoring and disciplining of their bodies. Efforts at being healthy offered an acceptable way to reduce the impact of aging and endeavour to embody feminine norms. Engaging in the so-called healthy activities and/or looking healthy are increasingly interchangeable with practices aimed at achieving a feminine persona; whether it be to control signs of aging or size and shape of their bodies.

The equation of health with gendered ideal, which is itself ageist, has implications for our conception of both health and gender/femininity. In terms of the former, equating health with normative femininity entails a shift away from what is needed to support or achieve a state of well-being, to a focus on how to manage or control your body in order to *appear* healthy. There are several potential consequences of this stream, notably eating disorders/disordered eating, loss of self-confidence/esteem, obsessive exercise and depression. The consequences of dominant health discourses on our understanding of femininity involve a reassertion of a slim and fit body type as *the* body type for women because of the discursive weight health carries. Further, under healthism, responsibility for health is downloaded onto individuals from the state, which has strong ties in the West to the reality of an increasing aging population. This has particular gendered dynamics because the promotion of health practices mirror those traditionally used to promote the ideal female body (Moore 2008). The increased surveillance of bodies–to ensure they are keeping healthy–also functions to reinforce the regulation of bodies along gender lines; to ensure bodies are conforming to dominant gendered codes. Part and parcel with performing femininity correctly is adhering to anti-aging directives and attempting as much as possible to limit's the body's aging process (or at least so much as is visible).

The anxiety women in my study feel about their bodies was predominantly spoken about through the language of health and anti-aging. Their stories reveal tension and/or conflict over how to embody aging and be healthy while still wanting–and needing–to be recognizable as feminine. While this paper primarily focuses on the limitations of health and anti aging discourses, it also draw attention to the complex meanings of body practices including pleasure in bodily movement, and collegiality and affirmation obtained by participation in gender norms. Through their own experiences and social positions, women negotiate their body struggles in conjunction with sexism, healthism, ageism, as well as fat phobia, racism, and heterosexism. In this paper, I use the women's stories to inform what I see as an increasing trend among women, namely that anxiety about their bodies and efforts to control them can be justified and validated through the language of health and anti-aging. This represents a shift in how we talk about and conceptualize what being feminine means in the current moment, and is an intensification of the discipline and control of women's bodies as well as what it means to be 'feminine' and thus who women can become.

Notes

1. At the start of each interview, I asked women how they identify and/or how they would like to be identified in the research. As a result, some women identified with various, different personal identifiers, including fat, parental status and racial identities. I opted for this approach as opposed to asking participants to fill out checkboxes corresponding to dominant identity categories because I wanted a sense of how women identify, including stories and/or struggles around identity. Using or deferring to standard identity categories would miss out on some of this personal and critical detail.

2. The interviews were audio-taped (using a digital recorder) and then transcribed. Questions were formulated by the author to move from an account of what body practices the women did on a regular basis (questions began with daily, then weekly, finally monthly body practices–including the so-called beauty practices, exercise, eating, etc.) to consideration of what motivated them–from family, peers, media, etc. Pseudonyms were used for all of the participants and data were stored on a password-protected computer and hard copies kept in a locked filing cabinet. Ethical clearance for the research was obtained from York University (Ontario)–each participant signed and was given a copy of a consent form before the interview began.

3. As mentioned, this article is drawn from my doctoral dissertation. My original plan was to interview 25 women. However, after doing about 10 interviews, my supervisor and I agreed that between 10 and 15 interviews would be sufficient; given the richness of stories women were sharing and because I was using narrative analysis. It was agreed that fewer interviews would mean that I could focus more on the complexities–the intersecting meanings and motivations framing various body practices–within stories.

4. To be clear, I am not stating that anti-aging practices are good for one's health (some may be, others not), but rather that increasingly, anti-aging practices may be constructed and promoted as such. An example of this is a store in Toronto (in the Yorkville neighbourhood) called the Anti-Aging Clinic; adopting the term of 'clinic' to the store promotes the sense that well-being and health will be achieved once inside the doors.

References

Bartky, S., 1997. Foucault, femininity, and the modernization of patriarchal power. *In:* K. Conboy, N. Medina and S. Stanbury, eds. *Writing on the body: female embodiment and feminist theory.* New York: Columbia University Press, 129–154.

Biggs, S., 1999. *The mature imagination: dynamics of identity in midlife and beyond.* Buckingham: Open University Press.

Blackman, L., 2008. *The body: the key concepts.* Oxford: Berg.

Bordo, S., 1993. *Unbearable weight: feminism, Western culture, and the body.* Berkeley, CA: University of California Press.

Bordo, S., 1997. *Twilight zones: The hidden life of cultural images from Plato to O.J.* Berkeley, CA: University of California Press.

Butler, J., 1990. *Gender trouble: feminism and the subversion of identity.* New York: Routledge.

Calsanti, T. and Slevin, K., eds, 2006. *Age matters: realigning feminist thinking.* London: Routledge.

Chase, S., 2002. Learning to listen: narrative principles in a qualitative research methods course. *In:* R. Josselson, A. Lieblich and D.P. McAdams, eds. *Up close and personal: the teaching and learning of narrative research.* Washington, DC: American Psychological Association, 79–99.

Choi, P., 2000. *Femininity and the physically active woman.* London: Routledge.

Crawford, R., 2006. Health as a meaningful social practice. *Health: an interdisciplinary journal for the social study of heath, illness and medicine,* 10, 401–420. doi:10.1177/1363459306067310.

Dillaway, H., 2005. (Un)changing menopausal bodies: how women think and act in the face of a reproductive transition and gendered beauty ideals. *Sex roles,* 53, 1–17. doi:10.1007/s11199-005-4269-6.

Edut, O., ed. 2003. *Body outlaws: young women write about body image and identity.* 2nd ed. Emeryville, CA: Seal Press.

Featherstone, M. and Hepworth, M., 1996. The mask of ageing and the postmodern life course. *In:* M. Featherstone, M. Hepworth and B. Turner, eds. *The body: social process and cultural theory.* London: Sage Publication, 371–389.

Foucault, M., 1977. *Discipline and punish: the birth of the prison.* New York: Vintage Books.

Gilleard, C. and Higgs, P., 2000. *Cultures of ageing: self, citizen and the body.* Harlow: Prentice Hall.

Heywood, L. and Drake, J., eds., 1997. *Third wave agenda: being feminist, doing feminism.* Minneapolis, MN: University of Minnesota Press.

Hockey, J. and James, A., 2004. How do we know that we are aging? Embodiment, agency and later life. *In:* E. Tulle, ed. *Old age and agency.* New York: Nova, 157–172.

Hurd-Clarke, L., 2002. Older women's perceptions of ideal body weights: the tensions between health and appearance motivations for weight loss. *Ageing and society,* 22, 751–773. doi:10.1017/S0144686X02008905.

Malson, H., 2008. Deconstructing un/healthy body-weight and weight management. *In:* S. Riley, *et al.* eds. *Critical bodies: representations, identities and practices of weight and body management.* Basingstoke, Hampshire: Palgrave MacMillan, 27–42.

Moore, S., 2008. Gender and the new paradigm of health. *Sociology compass,* 2, 268–280. doi:10.1111/j.1751-9020.2007.00060.x.

Onoufriou, A., 2009. 'Falling in love with someone from your own sex is like going against Cyprus itself . . .' Discourses towards heterosexual and female-to-female subjectivities at the University of Cyprus. *Journal of Gender Studies,* 18, 13–23.

Rice, C., 2006. Out from under occupation: transforming our relationships with our bodies. *In:* A. Medovarsi and B. Cranney, eds. *Canadian woman studies: an introductory reader.* 2nd ed. Toronto: Inanna Publications, 411–423.

Scott, J., 1992. Experience. *In:* J. Butler and J. Scott, eds. *Feminists theorize the political.* New York: Routledge, 22–40.

Skeggs, B., 1997. *Formations of class and gender: becoming respectable.* London: Sage Publications.

Slevin, K., 2006. The embodied experiences of old lesbians. *In:* T.M. Calsanti and K. Slevin, eds. *Age matters: realigning feminist thinking.* New York: Routledge, 247–268.

Smith, D., 1988. Femininity as discourse. *In:* L.G. Roman, L.K. Christian-Smith and E. Ellsworth, eds. *Becoming feminine: the politics of popular culture.* London: The Falmer Press, 37–59.

Steenbergen, C., 2001. Feminism and young women: alive and well and still kicking. *Canadian women's studies,* 20/21. Available from: http://pi.library.yorku.ca/ojs/index.php/cws/article/view/6898/6082

Twigg, J., 2000. *Bathing, the body and community care.* London: Routledge.

Weedon, C., 1997. *Feminist practice and poststructuralist theory.* 2nd ed. London: Blackwell Publishing.

Woodward, K., 1991. *Aging and its discontents: Freud and other fictions.* Indianapolis: Indiana University Press.

Sex, Gender Roles, and Image

1. Demonstrate that you have an understanding of the differences between biologically determined sex differences and socially/culturally constructed gender differences by filling in one or more examples in the table below.

	Female/Feminine	**Male/Masculine**
Biologically identified sex differences		
Socially/Culturally constructed gender differences		
What is missing?		

2. The chart below lists characteristics that society often associates with being a woman and a man.
   A. Identify whether these characteristics are more associated (accepted or expected) with being a woman or a man.
   B. Identify whether the characteristics associated with gender are valued or devalued in society.
   C. Identify how these characteristics influence women's healthcare experiences for both providers and patient/clients.
   D. What is missing?

	Women more than Men	**Men more than Women**	**Valued**	**Devalued**	**Comments**
Passive					
Aggressive					
Independent					
Dependent					
Stable					
Easily excitable					
Strong					
Weak					
Competitive					
Non-Competitive					

	Women more than Men	Men more than Women	Valued	Devalued	Comments
Passive					
Aggressive					
Independent					
Dependent					
Always knows the answer					
Ok not to know the answer					
Cares about things more than people					
Cares about people more than things					
Hides emotions					
Shows emotions					
Other					

3. As future health practitioners, educators, or advocates, how can you discuss bodies without reinforcing the sex and gender binaries?

4. How are people who fall outside of the sex and gender binaries erased or marginalized within the healthcare system?

5. After reading the articles on body image, how do discussions of eating disorders impact women of color?

6. How do fat studies contribute to a broader understanding of women's bodies and the obesity "epidemic?"

Medicalization, Marketing, and the Politics of Information

4

The politics of information is having access to scientifically accurate and personally empowering information, which also makes certain that good information is available and accessible to all women. The availability of accurate, scientific, and good information continues to be a key issue for women's health movements now and in the future. Thus, consumer literacy involves having access to good information and knowing how to use it, and is essential to women's health decision-making and activism. However, because the amount of information available continues to increase, it is important for us to be able to evaluate which perspectives, products, and procedures will actually help us be healthier, as opposed to selling us solutions to perceived problems. This chapter specifically highlights key themes about medicalization, marketing, and the politics of information that are core throughout this book.

The medicalization of women's health refers to normal healthy physiological events in women's lives being defined as medical conditions to be "fixed" by a particular medical product or procedure. Such "medical answers" are often presented to women in a "one size fits all" protocol. Modern medicine, medical knowledge, and products have the ability to save, lengthen, and improve the quality of women's lives. Women's health activism; however, requires us also to explore the "downsides" of medicalization of women's bodies. Normal, healthy physiological events are not researched if there is no profit to be gained from that research. In addition, these normal events are not likely to be the focus of much attention outside medical research. Contrarily, diseases are invented,

as is the case with hypoactive sexual desire disorder. In this case, there was no scientific evidence supporting the claim that women unknowingly suffer from hypoactive sexual desire disorder.

Women's bodies, health, and the health system are subject to pressures of a capitalist economy. For example, whenever there is a profit to be made, profit-making "solutions" will be pushed on people who do not really need them but have the money or health insurance to pay for them. On the other side of the economic divide, those who do not have insurance or resources are denied access to the medical interventions they actually need. Consumer literacy is essential for people to evaluate whether the "solutions" being promoted to them are appropriate. Activism is also essential to ensure that good medical solutions are equally available to all the people who would benefit from them.

Many of these topics can be seen in *How the Pill Became a Lifestyle Drug: The Pharmaceutical Industry and Birth Control in the United States Since 1960* by Elizabeth Siegel Watkins. Rather than invent a disease, pharmaceutical companies created a type of medication, "lifestyle drugs," which consumers use for entire lifespans. This provides long-term profits for the company. The long-term effects of the pill are not entirely known, which prevents women from making fully informed decisions.

The problem with medicalization of many of women's health issues is the unknown and known side effects from medicines and medical procedures. When making medical decisions that will or could save one's life, mild or even serious side effects are a small price to pay. However, safety studies, ethics, and high standards should establish best practices for products or procedures being used by healthy women. This can be seen with the unknown risks of taking hormones across a lifespan. In *Hormone Risk Throughout the Lifespan*, the known risks are addressed so readers can make informed decisions about taking hormones either for birth control or menopause.

The unhealthy narrow definition of health itself is also examined in *The Picture of Health* by Mariamne Whatley. This classic article by Whatley provides a critical examination of how health is represented in photographs in health textbooks. In images, similar to those seen in advertising, those portrayed as "healthy" exclude large segments of the population, leaving a group that is young, white, thin, and physically able to represent health. Health is presented in these images as a commodity that many will not be able to attain; in other words, it is a privilege, not a right.

The Marketing and Politics Behind the Promotion of Female Sexual Dysfunction and its "Pink Viagra" by the National Women's Network shows capitalism's impact on women's health by shifting the drug Viagra, which has been profitable for male impotence, to women without investigation or consideration that women's bodies are different than men's. This article shows the myths and facts about women's sexual function and how the drug company was driven more by profit and less by women's sexual needs and/or wants.

A final consideration in the politics of information is how culture affects our understanding of science. In *The Egg and the Sperm: How Science Has Constructed a Romance Based on Stereotypical Male-Female Roles*, Emily Martin discusses the gendering of science. Biological processes are stereotyped according to cultural definitions of male and female. These cultural definitions value male biological functions over female ones, which naturalizes them.

The articles in this chapter provide a counterweight to the pressures that the health industry applies to women. They are examples of how information and activism attempt to empower consumers to critically examine the ways in which medicalization and marketing are influencing their lives, from individual choices about drugs to societal definitions of biological processes.

How the Pill Became a Lifestyle Drug: The Pharmaceutical Industry and Birth Control in the United States Since 1960

by Elizabeth Siegel Watkins, PhD

Marketing decisions, rather than scientific innovations, have guided the development and positioning of contraceptive products in recent years. I review the stalled progress in contraceptive development in the decades following the advent of the Pill in 1960 and then examine the fine-tuning of the market for oral contraceptives in the 1990s and 2000s. Although birth control has been pitched in the United States as an individual solution, rather than a public health strategy, the purpose of oral contraceptives was understood by manufacturers, physicians, and consumers to be the prevention of pregnancy, a basic health care need for women. Since 1990, the content of that message has changed, reflecting a shift in the drug industry's view of the contraception business. Two factors contributed to bring about this change: first, the industry's move away from research and development in birth control and second, the growth of the class of medications known as lifestyle drugs. (*Am J Public Health.* 2012;102:1462–1472. doi:10.2105/AJPH.2012.300706)

In March 2011, the *San*

*F*rancisco Chronicle ran a front-page story on contraceptives. It began, "These days, choosing a form of birth control can seem as daunting as shopping for a new laptop computer —the technology is constantly changing and there are just so many options."[1] Even though scores of different brand-name and generic products are available on the American market, a closer inspection of the contraceptive landscape reveals a menu of birth control options that relies on science that is more than 50 years old. Since the Pill was first approved in 1960, birth control continues to work in only one of two ways: by preventing fertilization or by preventing ovulation. The barrier methods— condoms, diaphragms, cervical caps, and chemical spermicides—have existed for the better part of a century (and in the case of condoms, for centuries). The modern intrauterine devices (IUDs) became available in the early 1960s, but they merely improved on a method first introduced in the 1920s. Hormonal contraception—in which synthetic hormones, either progesterone alone or in combination with estrogen, prevent ovulation— was the truly innovative contribution made by the Pill. The newer methods that have come onto the market since 1990—the implant, the shot, the skin patch, and the vaginal ring—simply provide different delivery systems for the hormones to enter the bloodstream.[2] Even the technologies behind these delivery systems (e.g., silastic capsules for the implant, transdermal materials for the patch) were developed in the 1960s and 1970s. In the world of contraception, scientific and technological innovation has been moribund for decades.

Why might women need new methods of contraception? A few statistics from 1990 confirm the inadequacy of available methods. An Institute of Medicine study[3] of contraception that year reported that almost 3 million unintended pregnancies

occurred annually in the United States as the result of contraceptive failure. Half of the 1.5 million abortions in the United States every year were performed to deal with pregnancies resulting from contraceptive failure. One million adolescent girls get pregnant each year. Of women younger than 50 years, 20% had been sterilized, with another 15% married to men who had vasectomies; these people chose to end their fertility rather than deal with contraceptive alternatives, but up to 10% of the women regretted their decision after remarriage or the death of a child.[4] Although issues of affordability; cultural constraints; and access to health education, information sources, and contraceptives all influence the effective use of birth control, the physical aspects of existing contraceptive technologies also play a role in women's decisions about whether to use them.

Carl Djerassi, the chemist who first synthesized an orally active progesterone (which made oral hormonal contraception possible), predicted this static state of affairs 40 years ago in a prescient article in *Science* titled "Birth Control after 1984."[5] In 1989, he revisited the topic of contraceptive research and development in "The Bitter Pill" published in *Science.*[6] He attributed the dearth of innovation to the withdrawal of American pharmaceutical companies from the field. In 1970, 13 major drug firms were actively pursuing birth control research and development (of which nine were American); by 1987, there were only four (with just one located in the United States). Little has changed since then, despite the continued success of the pharmaceutical industry and the expansion of small biotechnology enterprises. Djerassi identified three reasons for "Big Pharma's" flight from contraceptive research: (1) two decades of stringent and burdensome animal toxicology tests required by the US Food and Drug Administration (FDA), which greatly increased the time and expense of developing new products; (2) a negative portrayal of the industry by the media in the wake of Senator Gaylord Nelson's congressional inquiry into the safety of the Pill in 1970 and the Dalkon Shield IUD disaster a few years later; and (3) the increasingly litigious nature of American society, as the courts became the place to seek restitution for injuries or diseases attributed to drugs, medical devices, or other toxic substances. Twenty-two years later, the conclusion Djerassi wrote reads as an accurate reflection of our birth control landscape today:

> All we can expect well into the beginning of the 21st century are minor modifications of existing methods: different delivery systems for steroids, possible improvements in sterilization techniques and barrier methods, more precise indications of the safe interval, and possibly a more realistic reconsideration of the IUD option. Such modest developments will extend contraceptive use patterns, but they will not affect our total dependence on conventional 19th and 20th century approaches to birth control.[7]

What has changed over the past several decades is how contraceptives—specifically, birth control pills—have been marketed. From the 1960s to the 1980s, pharmaceutical companies advertised birth control pills expressly for the purpose of birth control. Initial advertisements to physicians in medical journals (direct-to-consumer advertising was not allowed until the mid-1980s) promoted the novelty of hormonal control of fertility and the newly enlarged role of physicians in family planning; later advertisements focused on the benefits to women in planning when to have children. Pharmaceutical companies never marketed oral contraceptive products as beneficial to public health in the United States; their sales targets were individual physicians who catered to private patients. However, organizations such as the World Health Organization clearly recognized that the Pill was an "essential medicine," one that met "the priority health care needs of the population" because of its "public health relevance, evidence on efficacy and safety, and comparative cost-effectiveness."[8] Indeed, birth control continued (and continues) to be a basic health care need for women of

reproductive age, but pharmaceutical companies have found little incentive for investing in the innovation of new methods.

After largely abandoning these avenues of research, pharmaceutical companies moved their marketing of existing contraceptive products away from the function of fertility control. In the 1990s, manufacturers began to promote their new brands of oral contraceptives to both physicians and consumers explicitly as so-called lifestyle drugs. *Lifestyle drugs*—the term was coined in 1978—generally describe medications that are designed to improve a person's quality of life by treating less serious conditions; they also have been called cosmetic, life-enhancing, recreational, or discretionary.[9] These new advertising campaigns emphasized the secondary effects of oral contraceptives—to treat less-serious conditions such as acne and premenstrual dysphoric disorder and to reduce the frequency of menstruation—rather than the primary indication for the prevention of pregnancy. This shift from control of fertility to control of pimples, moods, and the menstrual cycle indicates that pharmaceutical manufacturers chose to emphasize lifestyle options more than contraception for its own sake. Marketing decisions, rather than scientific innovations, have guided the development and positioning of next-generation contraceptive products in recent years.

I review the stalled progress in contraceptive development in the decades following the advent of the Pill and then examine more closely the fine-tuning of the market for oral contraceptives in the 1990s and 2000s. Although birth control has always been pitched in the United States as an individual solution rather than as a public health strategy, the purpose of oral contraceptives was understood by manufacturers, physicians, and consumers to be the prevention of pregnancy, a basic health care need for women of reproductive age. Since 1990, the content of that message has changed, reflecting a shift in the drug industry's perception of the contraception business. This change was brought about by the industry's move away from research and development in birth control and by the growth of the class of medications known as lifestyle drugs; these two trends were influenced by economic, political, and cultural factors, which I discuss later in this article. In the final analysis, the status of contraceptive research and marketing today results from decisions made by the pharmaceutical industry to maximize profits and to minimize risks, decisions that have left women with birth control options that differ little from those available to their grandmothers in the previous century.

The Primacy of the Pill

Margaret Sanger recognized the importance of reliable birth control for public health 100 years ago. Fifty years later, her dream of a "magic pill" became a reality when the FDA approved Enovid, the first progestin-estrogen oral contraceptive.[10] The birth of the Pill in 1960 dramatically altered the contraceptive landscape for women during its first decades. In 1955, more than half of the American women who used birth control relied on either condoms or a diaphragm. Twenty-seven percent reported using a condom most recently, and 25% reported using a diaphragm. Ten years later, those figures had changed radically. In 1965, five years after the Pill was approved, 27% of American women reported use of the Pill, 18% used condoms, and just 10% relied on a diaphragm. By 1973, more than a third of American women (36%) used the Pill for birth control; only 13.5% reported using condoms, and a mere 3.4% used a diaphragm.[11]

The first advertisement for the first oral contraceptive, G. D. Searle's Enovid, showed the image of the mythical persona Andromeda breaking free from manacles around her wrist to symbolize the liberation of women from the threat of pregnancy. The copy read,

> From the beginning, woman has been a vassal to the temporal demands—and frequently the aberrations—of the cyclic mechanism of her reproductive system. Now to a degree heretofore unknown, she is permitted normalization, enhancement, or suspension of cyclic function and procreative potential. This new physiologic control is symbolized in an illustration borrowed from Greek mythology—Andromeda freed from her chains.[12]

This advertisement appeared frequently in medical journals such as *Obstetrics and Gynecology* and *JAMA: The Journal of the American Medical Association*. Another advertisement for Enovid emphasized the novelty of the use of synthetic progesterone to alter the menstrual cycle: "the first fully feminine molecule for cyclic control of ovulation."[13] These advertisements made clear the revolutionary nature of oral hormonal contraception.

G.D. Searle had waited more than a year after receiving FDA approval to advertise Enovid in the pages of medical journals. The company worried about negative publicity and possible boycotts of its other products because of Roman Catholic opposition to contraception. Its fears were unfounded. When the success of G.D. Searle's Enovid became apparent, other pharmaceutical companies rushed to bring their own oral contraceptive brands to market. By 1970, Ortho, Syntex, Parke-Davis, Eli Lilly, Upjohn, Wyeth, and Mead Johnson had received FDA approval for birth control pills.[14] The advertisements for these new pills became lengthier and glossier. Parke-Davis introduced Norlestrin with a three-page spread; Syntex's announcement of its product, Norinyl, occupied a full eight pages in *Obstetrics and Gynecology*.[15] The Ortho Pharmaceutical Company touted the superiority of Ortho-Novum's package design; the "Dialpak" helped remind patients to take the pills daily.[16] As the market became more crowded, each company sought to promote distinctive aspects of what were essentially similar products. These tactics were not unique to the realm of oral contraceptives; they were characteristic of the whole pharmaceutical enterprise, as companies increasingly produced slight variations on one another's products, what would later be described as "me-too" drugs.

Although oral contraceptives were technically marketed only to physicians, consumers were deluged with information about the new pills in newspaper and magazine articles. As Jeremy Greene and David Herzberg have shown, drug companies employed public relations firms to ensure popular coverage of the latest prescription-only medications.[17] In the decades before direct-to-consumer advertising, American women received ample exposure to news about this contraceptive breakthrough, and they went to their physicians to ask for prescriptions for the Pill. By the late 1960s, almost nine million American women were taking oral contraceptives to prevent pregnancy.

Eager to capitalize on the success of hormonal contraception, researchers and birth control advocates sought other ways to deliver the hormones into women's bodies. The subdermal implant was one such adaptation. It was designed for users who could not or would not remember to take a daily pill, who did not want to be permanently sterilized, and who were unsuitable candidates for the IUD. Although the implant was not formally approved for use in the United States until 1990, research on this method began in the 1960s in the laboratories of the Population Council, a private nonprofit organization with an international focus on population and related concerns. The contraceptive shot was another new delivery form that was first developed by Schering AG. One injection provided three months of protection against pregnancy. In the United States, Upjohn applied for approval of its version, Depo-Provera, in the late 1960s. Like Norplant, which was marketed by Wyeth, Depo did not receive FDA approval until many years later, in 1992. However, in the 1960s, these developments, together with the IUD, which had been reintroduced into the American market earlier in the decade, seemed to promise further innovation in the realm of reversible contraception.

By the late 1980s, however, it was clear that this promise had not been realized. Along with Djerassi's "Bitter Pill" article came several other publications lamenting the deceleration in contraceptive innovation. A 1988 article in *Family Planning Perspectives* asked, "Whatever Happened to the Contraceptive Revolution?"[18] A series of meetings held by the National Academy of Science resulted in a 1990 book called *Developing New Contraceptives: Obstacles and Opportunities*, which focused more on obstacles than on opportunities.[19] In 1995, the editor of *Family Planning Perspectives*, Michael Klitsch, summarized the stasis in contraceptive research in an article titled "Still Waiting for the Contraceptive Revolution."[20]

Klitsch reviewed the factors that others had identified as contributing causes of the slowdown. First, he noted the chilling effect of product liability costs, resulting from both individual and class action lawsuits against contraceptive manufacturers. Second, he pointed to the financial burden of increased government regulation of contraceptive products because the FDA required more stringent

testing of experimental methods in animals and humans. Third, he enumerated several reasons for changes in public opinions about contraceptives. The enthusiasm over the Pill in the early 1960s had given way to concern about its side effects by the end of that decade, intensified by media coverage of these adverse health effects. Klitsch attributed greater public scrutiny of and skepticism toward contraceptives in the 1970s (especially those pharmaceuticals and devices available by prescription only) to the growing influence of the consumer movement and the women's movement. Although other drug classes also encountered these challenges, contraceptives faced the additional burden of morally freighted debates over their use. The political dimension of American attitudes toward contraception was further complicated in the 1980s by the emergence of HIV and AIDS, against which only barrier methods offered any protection, and by the increasingly acrimonious abortion conflict, which swept contraceptives into its maelstrom. Collectively, these factors thwarted enthusiasm for exploring novel approaches to preventing pregnancy. Finally, Klitsch reported that the pharmaceutical industry saw limited opportunities for growth (and profits) in the contraceptive sector of developed countries because the market was already saturated with existing products. Companies feared that new contraceptives would not attract enough new users to be profitable or that they might eat into the profits of their products already on the market. The safer bet was to stick with current product lines, tinkering here and there with the formulations but not making any major innovations.

Thus, tinkering is precisely what the major manufacturers did in the 1970s and 1980s. The progestin component had already been lowered in the 1960s from the initial strength of 10 milligrams to one milligram per pill. In response to studies that showed the risk of blood clotting in women who took oral contraceptives could be reduced with a lower dose of estrogen, manufacturers decreased the estrogen component from 80 to 100 micrograms to 50 micrograms and then even further to 35 micrograms. In the mid-1960s, several companies introduced sequential oral contraceptives, which required women to take estrogen-only pills for 14 days and then estrogen-progestin combination pills for six to seven days (followed, as usual, by seven days of placebo or no pills, to allow for a menstrual period). Within a few years, this regimen was found to increase the risk of uterine cancer, and these formulations were taken off the American market in the mid-1970s.[21] In the 1980s, the multiphasics were introduced; with these brands, women took a series of two or three different estrogen-progestin combination pills (e.g., Ortho-Novum 7/7/7 was taken as follows: seven days of 0.5 mg progestin and 35 μg estrogen, then seven days of 0.75 mg progestin and 35 μg estrogen, then seven days of 1.0 mg progestin and 35 μg estrogen) to more closely mimic the cyclical fluctuations of sex hormones in a woman's body. All of these formulations were variations on the original birth control pill introduced in 1960: 21 days of oral tablets containing one of a half-dozen different synthetic progestins in combination with one of two synthetic estrogens.

Meanwhile, nonprofit organizations undertook much of the research, development, and testing of alternative delivery systems for hormonal contraception. The Population Council experimented with a vaginal ring for sustained release of hormones. It also managed the testing of implants in countries such as Chile, Finland, Denmark, Brazil, Jamaica, and the Dominican Republic prior to FDA approval. Only after the testing was complete and the Population Council's application for FDA approval was successful did Wyeth-Ayerst agree to market Norplant in the United States. Similarly, the World Health Organization coordinated multicenter studies of Depo-Provera, which then formed the basis for Upjohn's renewed appeal for FDA approval, awarded in 1992.

The World Health Organization also took the lead in pursuing a hormonal contraceptive for men. Beginning in the 1970s, the World Health Organization sponsored a worldwide network of chemical laboratories, located mainly in developing nations, to research male methods and later organized large multisite clinical trials to test the most promising of these methods. Pharmaceutical companies stayed away from male hormonal contraception until the late 1990s, when a few—most notably, the Dutch firm Organon—began to express interest.[22] As we know, however, no male pill has yet come to fruition; one researcher noted recently, "The joke

in the field is: The male pill's been five to 10 years away for the last 30 years."[23]

In the case of Norplant, and perhaps the other long-acting contraceptive methods, the Population Council applied for FDA approval not to market Norplant in the United States but rather so that the State Department's Agency for International Development could make it available to population control programs in developing nations. Wyeth was licensed as the American distributor of Norplant, hoping to broaden its presence in the domestic contraceptive marketplace. Wyeth was already in the business of selling birth control, with several different Pill formulations, but it had relatively low expectations for Norplant in 1990, predicting that the implant would capture an additional one to two percent of the private sector and three to five percent of the public sector in total contraceptive sales.[24]

Indeed, Norplant never attracted more than two percent of American contraceptive users and for various reasons was taken off the market after just one decade. The other delivery methods also did not garner a significant segment of those using contraceptives.[25] By 2008, just 3.2% used the injectable Depo-Provera (sold by Pfizer), 2.4% used a vaginal ring (Merck's Nuvaring), and a total of 1.1% used the patch (Ortho-McNeil's Ortho Evra) or the implant (Schering-Plough introduced Implanon in the United States in 2006). IUDs are used by 5.5%, just a fraction higher than the 5.2% who report relying on withdrawal as their primary means of contraception. The top of the contraceptive chart continues to be dominated by sterilization (27% of women had undergone tubal ligation, and 10% of their male partners had undergone vasectomies) and the Pill (28%), with condoms well behind in third place (16%).[26]

Condoms have become more popular since the advent of AIDS and HIV in the 1980s as the most effective way to prevent the transmission of disease, but they remain less effective than hormonal methods in preventing pregnancy. Some 13.5% of women reported using condoms in combination with another method to ensure against both pregnancy and sexually transmitted infections. Sterilization as a form of irreversible contraception began to rise in popularity in the 1970s in the wake of concerns about the safety of both oral contraceptives and IUDs and since the 1980s has remained the most common form of birth control in America.[27] However, the Pill still reigns as the most widely used reversible type of contraception.

Promoting the Pill Anew

In recent decades, one trend in the marketing of birth control pills was the great expansion of the oral contraceptive marketplace. A dramatic increase in the number of different birth control pills available in the United States resulted from the Drug Price Competition and Patent Term Restoration Act of 1984, also known as the "Hatch-Waxman Act," which set up the modern system of generic drug approval and regulation. By 2007, more than 90 brand-name and generic oral contraceptive products were on the market in the United States.[28] Physicians, pharmacists, and women could choose pills based on price because the action of these contraceptives, or their therapeutic equivalence, was essentially the same.[29] Brand-name manufacturers had to find a way to make their products stand out from the generic crowd.

One tactic was to develop alternative forms of synthetic progesterone. A so-called third generation was developed in the early 1980s. Following the first-generation molecules, nor-ethynodrel (used in G. D. Searle's Enovid) and norethindrone (used in Syntex's Norinyl and Ortho's Ortho-Novum), and the second-generation molecules, such as levonorgestrel (used in Norplant as well as in oral contraceptives), these compounds had high progestational activity and lower androgenic activity. The high progestational activity meant that lower doses could be used; the lower androgenic activity meant fewer side effects, such as hirsutism and acne, that sometimes accompanied the older synthetic progestins. Desogestrel, for example, was tested and approved for use in Europe in the 1980s; it became available in the United States in 1992, in the form of Organon's Desogen and Ortho-McNeil's Ortho-Cept.[30] That same year, Ortho-McNeil also released Ortho Tri-Cyclen, which used norgestimate. Like desogestrel, norgestimate was described as a third-generation progestin, and, like desogestrel, it had lower androgenic activity than other progestins. Ortho used this lower androgenic activity as the basis for its application to

the FDA for approval of Ortho Tri-Cyclen for the treatment of acne. Although physicians had been prescribing oral contraceptives off-label for acne treatment since the 1960s, Ortho Tri-Cyclen was the first to get formal FDA approval for this indication, in addition to its approved use in pregnancy prevention. Thus, a second tactic used by brand-name manufacturers was to expand the approved indications for certain oral contraceptives.

A third tactic rebranded oral contraceptives as drugs to suppress monthly menstruation. In 2003, DuraMed, a subsidiary of Barr Pharmaceuticals, received FDA approval to market Seasonale, the first extended-cycle oral contraceptive. Seasonale was designed to be taken in three-month cycles, instead of the usual three-week cycles of other formulations, thus reducing the number of bleeding periods from 12 to four per year.[31] As in the case of acne, the knowledge that taking oral contraceptives continually would eliminate monthly periods was not new. In fact, the first advertisement for Enovid in 1960 promoted it not for contraceptive purposes but rather to postpone menstruation "for convenience, for peace of mind, for full efficiency on critical occasions."[32] Even the advertisements that finally did promote Enovid for contraception also made mention of menstrual suppression. Consider the text of the Andromeda advertisement referenced earlier:

> From the beginning, woman has been a vassal to the temporal demands—and frequently the aberrations—of the cyclic mechanism of her reproductive system. Now to a degree heretofore unknown, she is permitted normalization, enhancement, or *suspension of cyclic function* [emphasis added] and procreative potential.[33]

In 2003, Barr formalized this indication. After receiving FDA approval, the company created specialized packaging for Seasonale that incorporated three months' worth of pills into a single dispenser. It developed a promotional campaign that targeted physicians with sales visits, educational materials, and sample kits and a parallel campaign that targeted women with direct-to-consumer advertising in magazines and on television and the Internet.[34]

The most recent expansion in indications for oral contraceptives has been Bayer's successful petition in 2006 to market its Yaz brand as a treatment for premenstrual dysphoric disorder and acne. Yaz has yet another synthetic form of progesterone, drosperinone, which was initially approved in 2001 for Bayer's Yasmin brand. Bayer's brands have been extraordinarily successful; in 2006, Yasmin owned 17% of the global sales of oral contraceptives.[35] In 2009, Yaz was the best-selling oral contraceptive on the American market. Moreover, it was the 21st bestseller among all prescription drugs in terms of number of prescriptions filled (almost 10 million), and it ranked 50 overall in terms of retail sales ($700 million).[36]

Manufacturers aggressively marketed these new uses for oral contraceptives (acne treatment, premenstrual dysphoric disorder treatment, and menstrual suppression) directly to consumers, thanks to the permission granted for pharmaceutical advertising in print media in the mid-1980s and the extension of that advertising to television in 1997. Of course, direct-to-consumer advertising only expanded the ways in which consumers could get information about prescription drugs. Indeed, consumers have been actively engaged in selecting their own medications for centuries. In the modern era—after the Durham-Humphrey Amendment to the Food, Drug, and Cosmetic Act established the category of prescription-only drugs in the United States in 1951—access to drugs became more restricted. Nevertheless, public relations efforts, as discussed earlier, ensured that consumers were made aware of the latest pharmaceutical products available from the local pharmacy with a prescription from a physician. The oral contraceptive is an excellent example of such a prescription drug, and the practice of women going to their physicians and asking for the Pill to prevent pregnancy dates to the early 1960s.

The advertising of oral contraceptives for their secondary effects that began in the 1990s raises the question of whether the pharmaceutical industry is now marketing birth control pills as lifestyle drugs, a term that became a full-fledged member of the scientific and popular lexicon in 1998. A study of English-language uses of the terms lifestyle drugs and lifestyle medicines found only a few dozen mentions per year in the scientific literature (as indexed by MEDLINE, Embase, and PubMed) and the popular literature (as indexed by LexisNexis) before 1998; that year, the number shot up to more

than 400. From 1998 to August 2003, the terms appeared some 2600 times.[37]

It seems inaccurate, and anachronistic, to describe the birth control pill as the first lifestyle drug, as some historians have suggested.[38] Although it was the first prescription medication meant to be taken by healthy people, this categorization diminishes the significance of oral contraceptives in meeting a critical and basic health need for both individuals and populations—namely, the need for a reliable and effective method for preventing pregnancy. However, in the more recent marketing of oral contraceptives, do these new indications fit the description of a lifestyle drug?

Part of the problem in making this assessment is the vagueness of the concept of lifestyle drugs. No single definition exists, although there seems to be some consensus on the broad contours of the category, if not on the specific drugs and indications within that classification. The authors of a piece in the *British Medical Journal* in 2000 provided this working description:

> a lifestyle drug is one used for 'non-health' problems or for problems that lie at the margins of health and well-being. . . . A wider definition would include drugs that are used for health problems that might be better treated by a change in lifestyle.[39]

Joel Lexchin, an associate professor in family and community medicine at the University of Toronto, concurred in a commentary in the *Canadian Medical Association Journal*. He proposed that lifestyle drugs fell into two groups: "any drug intended or used for a problem that falls into the border zone between the medical and social definitions of health" and "those intended to treat diseases that result from a person's lifestyle choices."[40] A *Nature Medicine* writer offered a vague description illustrated with examples: lifestyle drugs were "medicines that treat conditions associated with lifestyle such as weight-loss tablets, anti-smoking agents, impotence therapies and hair restorers."[41] Most commentators agree that the definition is variable, depending on the patient and the context in which he or she is experiencing a given condition for which a drug product might be prescribed. In the 2000s, most also agreed that the issue was not merely one of semantics but also associated with serious financial implications as managed care and third-party payers debated whether to pay for certain drug classes.

Given these definitions, it would be hard to argue that oral contraceptives taken solely for the purpose of controlling fertility should be considered lifestyle drugs. Birth control pills are not cosmetic, enhancing, recreational, or discretionary but confer a significant health benefit (the avoidance of pregnancy) on their users. However, the secondary effects for which some brands are promoted can fit the lifestyle characterization. Acne, periodic moodiness, and monthly bleeding are common conditions that constitute inconveniences, unpleasantness, and varying degrees of suffering, but they are not life threatening or wholly debilitating.

The newest brands of birth control pills are not being marketed solely for the primary indication of family planning. For example, advertisements for Seasonale and its more recent iteration, Seasonique, promote freedom from menstruation, not freedom from pregnancy.[42] Yaz's slogan, "Beyond Birth Control," signaled that its real purpose was to deal with the miseries resulting from menstruation, such as headaches, irritability, and pimples.[43] Pharmaceutical manufacturers are not selling contraception per se as a lifestyle option; rather, they pitch menstruation as an annoying condition to be ameliorated by their products. The emphasis on secondary effects instead of the primary indication in advertisements represents an attempt to differentiate products in a crowded field because no one brand can claim superior efficacy in the prevention of pregnancy.[44] When the contraceptive aspect takes a back seat, the Pill appears to be a veritable lifestyle drug.

As a result, oral contraceptives have found themselves on lists of lifestyle drugs, along with antidepressants and treatments for erectile dysfunction, smoking addiction, obesity, wrinkles, and male pattern balding.[45] This shift in image has economic implications: for example, BlueChoice HealthPlan of South Carolina included several brands of oral contraceptives on its "2011 Lifestyle Medication List" of drugs not covered under the plan's pharmacy benefit.[46]

Note that Bayer's "beyond birth control" claims for Yaz have not gone unchallenged. In 2009, the FDA objected to the misleading nature of Yaz television commercials and forced Bayer to run a revised $20 million advertising campaign as a corrective.[47] Yaz is also the subject of thousands of lawsuits filed by women who experienced adverse health effects. Its synthetic progesterone and its indications may be different from those of earlier oral contraceptives, but this kind of litigation is not new. Since the 1960s, women have turned to the courts to seek restitution for injuries or diseases they believed were caused by hormonal contraceptives, including not only the oral pills but also the subdermal implants, skin patches, and vaginal rings. Recall that the increasingly litigious nature of American society was one of the reasons cited by Carl Djerassi to explain why the pharmaceutical industry moved away from contraceptive research and development in the 1980s.

The trend to sue for damages in courts of law has not been limited to hormonal contraceptives. More than 4000 lawsuits were brought against A. H. Robins, the manufacturer of the Dalkon Shield IUD, which led that company to file for bankruptcy in 1985 and three other companies to take their IUDs off the American market.[47] In 1986, a woman won a $5.1 million lawsuit against Ortho Pharmaceutical for her claim that its contraceptive jelly product caused deformities in her infant.[49] In the 1990s, some 50 000 women had joined class action lawsuits against Norplant.[50] American Home Products, Wyeth's parent company, eventually settled the largest suit for a modest $54 million, but just two months later, it cost the same company $3.75 billion to settle the lawsuits over fenfluramine/phentermine, the diet pill combination that caused heart valve damage in users.[51] Around the same time, more than 19 000 individuals filed lawsuits against Dow Corning and other manufacturers of silicone breast implants. A class action suit resulted in a settlement that set aside $4.25 billion for claimants around the world.[52] Pharmaceuticals and medical devices designed for long-term use, such as contraceptives, or for cosmetic purposes, such as breast implants, are particularly susceptible to consumer lawsuits.

Today, women looking to join suits against Yaz as potential claimants can easily find information at Web sites such as http://www.yaz-side-effects-lawyer.com, http://www.yaz-yasmin-lawsuit.com, and http://yazlawsuit-info.com. Similar sites exist for those women seeking to file claims against the birth control patch, Ortho-Evra. These lawsuits represent women's dissatisfaction with existing methods of contraception. This dissatisfaction suggests that birth control might have something in common with another "feminine technology": brassieres. According to historian of technology Judith McGaw, when women are asked about their bra decisions, they "talk in terms of making the best of a limited array of choices or finding something less unsatisfactory than their previous choice."[53] In similar fashion, women make the best of the limited array of contraceptives and choose the one that is least unsatisfactory. Pharmaceutical companies have been content with this status quo, offering women small lifestyle add-ons to basically the same old oral contraceptives, seeking to maximize profits and minimize losses rather than to develop true innovations in birth control. Therefore, for the past 50 years, the Pill has retained the dubious honor of being the least unsatisfactory choice in contraception for American women.

About the Author

At the time of the writing, Elizabeth Siegel Watkins was with the Department of Anthropology, History, and Social Medicine at the University of California, San Francisco.

Correspondence should be sent to Elizabeth Siegel Watkins, PhD, Graduate Division, UCSF, 1675 Owens St, Suite CC310, San Francisco, CA 94143-0523 (e-mail: elizabeth.watkins@ucsf.edu). Reprints can be ordered at http://www.ajph.org by clicking the "Reprints" link.

This article was accepted January 18, 2012.

Acknowledgments

I thank Carl Djerassi, Jeremy Greene, Lara Marks, and the three anonymous reviewers from the *American Journal of Public Health* for their comments on previous drafts of this article.

Endnotes

1. Erin Allday, "Shots, Patches among Alternatives to the Pill," *San Francisco Chronicle*, March 15, 2011.

2. The implant initially consisted of six silicone rods implanted in a woman's arm that slowly released a synthetic form of the hormone progesterone over a five-year period; the versions currently available consist of one or two rods. The shot is an intramuscular injection of synthetic progesterone administered every 90 days. The patch is a transdermal patch applied to the skin that gradually releases synthetic progesterone and estrogen; a new patch is applied weekly for three of every four weeks. The ring is a flexible plastic ring that slowly releases synthetic progesterone and estrogen; it is inserted into the vagina and left in place for three weeks. For historical studies of the implant and the shot, see Elizabeth Siegel Watkins, "From Breakthrough to Bust: The Brief Life of Norplant, the Contraceptive Implant," *Journal of Women's History* 22 (Fall 2010): 88–111; Elizabeth Siegel Watkins, "The Social Construction of a Contraceptive Technology: An Investigation of the Meanings of Norplant," *Science, Technology, and Human Values* 36 (2011): 33–54; and Wendy Kline, "Bodies of Evidence: Activists, Patients, and the FDA Regulation of Depo-Provera," *Journal of Women's History* 22 (Fall 2010): 64–87. To date, there have been no historical studies of the patch or the ring; however, scores of articles are available in the medical literature on these two methods (and hundreds of articles on contraceptive implants and shots, the two older methods). For recent news articles on the patch and the ring, see "FDA Panel Backs Benefit of Birth Control Patch Despite Risks," *USA Today*, December 9, 2011, http://your-life.usatoday.com/health/medical/womenshealth/story/2011-12-09/FDA-panel-backs-benefit-of-birth-control-patch-despite-risks/51769232/1 (accessed January 4, 2012); and Jim Edwards, "At Merck, an Undercover Video and 40 Deaths Plague Nuvaring Birth Control Brand," CBS News, April 19, 2011, http://www.cbsnews.com/8301-505123_162-42848006/at-merck-an-undercover-video-and-40-deaths-plague-nuvaring-birth-control-brand/?tag=bnetdomain (accessed January 4, 2012).

3. Luigi Mastroianni Jr, Peter J. Donaldson, and Thomas T. Kane, eds., *Developing New Contraceptives: Obstacles and Opportunities* (Washington, DC: National Academy Press, 1990).

4. Teri Randall, "United States Loses Lead in Contraceptive Choices, R&D; Changes in Tort Liability, FDA Review Urged," *JAMA: The Journal of the American Medical Association* 268 (1992): 176–7.

5. Carl Djerassi, "Birth Control after 1984," *Science* 169 (1970): 941–51.

6. Carl Djerassi, "The Bitter Pill," *Science* 245 (1989): 356–61.

7. Ibid., 360.

8. World Health Organization, "Essential Medicines," http://www.who.int/topics/essential_medicines/en (accessed September 19, 2011).

9. Claus Møldrup, "The Use of the Terms 'Lifestyle Medicines' or 'Lifestyle Drugs,' " *Pharmacy World & Science: PWS* 26, no. 4 (2004): 193–6.

10. Elizabeth Siegel Watkins, *On the Pill: A Social History of Oral Contraceptives, 1950-1970* (Baltimore, MD: Johns Hopkins University Press, 1998), 14, 141.

11. Ibid., 61–2; Leslie Aldredge Westoff and Charles F. Westoff, *From Now to Zero: Fertility, Contraception and Abortion in America* (Boston, MA: Little, Brown, 1968), 64; Christine A. Bachrach, "Contraceptive Practice among American Women, 1973-1982," *Family Planning Perspectives* 16, no. 6 (1984): 253–9.

12. *Obstetrics and Gynecology* 18 (1961): 62–3.

13. *Obstetrics and Gynecology* 19 (1962): 114–5.

14. Suzanne White Junod, "Women Over 35 Who Smoke: A Case Study in Risk Management and Risk Communications, 1960-1989," in *Medicating Modern America: Prescription Drugs in History*, eds. Andrea Tone and Elizabeth Siegel Watkins. (New York: NYU Press, 2007), 117–9.

15. *Obstetrics and Gynecology* 23 (1964).

16. *Obstetrics and Gynecology* 21 (February 1963). For more on the Dialpak, see Patricia Peck Gossel, "Packaging the Pill," in *Manifesting Medicine: Bodies and Machines*, ed. Robert Bud. (New York: Taylor & Francis, 1999), 105–21.

17. Jeremy A. Greene and David Herzberg, "Hidden in Plain Sight: Marketing Prescription Drugs to Consumers in the Twentieth Century," *American Journal of Public Health* 100 (2010): 793–803.

18. Richard Lincoln and Lisa Kaeser, "Whatever Happened to the Contraceptive Revolution?," *Family Planning Perspectives* 20 (1988): 20–4.

19. Mastroianni Jr, *Developing New Contraceptives.*

20. Michael Klitsch, "Still Waiting for the Contraceptive Revolution," *Family Planning Perspectives* 27 (1995): 246–53.

21. Junod, "Women Over 35 Who Smoke," 106.

22. Nelly Oudshoorn, *The Male Pill: A Biography of a Technology in the Making* (Durham, NC: Duke University Press, 2003).

23. Dr. John Amory, quoted in Elizabeth Landau, "Where's the Male Birth Control Pill?" *CNN Health*, May 7, 2010, http://articles.cnn.com/2010-05-07/health/future.contraceptives.male. pill_1_sperm-production-male-birth-control-pill-progestin?_s=PM:HEALTH (accessed May 18, 2011).

24. Watkins, "From Breakthrough to Bust," 91–2.

25. Watkins, "From Breakthrough to Bust," and Watkins, "The Social Construction of a Contraceptive Technology."

26. Guttmacher Institute, "Facts on Contraceptive Use in the United States" (June 2010), http://www.guttmacher.org/pubs/fb_contr_use.html (accessed May 18, 2011). Historian Lara Marks reports that there were 430 brands of oral contraceptives worldwide in 1992. See Lara V. Marks, *Sexual Chemistry: A History of the Contraceptive Pill* (New Haven, CT: Yale University Press, 2001), 77.

27. Rebecca M. Kluchin, *Fit to Be Tied: Sterilization and Reproductive Rights in America, 1950-1980* (New Brunswick, NJ: Rutgers University Press, 2009).

28. American College of Obstetricians and Gynecologists, "ACOG Committee Opinion No. 375: Brand Versus Generic Oral Contraceptives," *Obstetrics and Gynecology* 110 (2007): 447–8.

29. Daniel Carpenter and Dominique A. Tobbell, "Bioequivalence: The Regulatory Career of a Pharmaceutical Concept," *Bulletin of the History of Medicine* 85, no. 1 (2011): 93–131.

30. Information about drug formulations and FDA approval dates for new drugs can be found at the Drugs@FDA Web site, http://www.accessdata.fda.gov/scripts/cder/drugsatfda (accessed May 18, 2011).

31. Laura Mamo and Jennifer Ruth Fosket, "Scripting the Body: Pharmaceuticals and the (Re)Making of Menstruation," *Signs: Journal of Women in Culture and Society* 34 (2009): 925–49.

32. Watkins, *On the Pill*, 37.

33. *Obstetrics and Gynecology* 18 (1961): 62–3.

34. Barr Pharmaceuticals Inc, "Annual Report" (June 30, 2004), 13, http://www.secinfo.com/dsvr4.19rf.htm (accessed May 18, 2011). For an interesting discussion of the "naturalness" of menstrual suppression, see Lara Marks, "Preface to the Paperback Edition," in *Sexual Chemistry: A History of the Contraceptive Pill* (New Haven, CT: Yale University Press, 2010), xxiv.

35. Business Insights, "Lifestyle Drugs Market Outlook" (December 2007), http://www.hcmarketplace.com/supplemental/6392_sampleissue.pdf (accessed May 18, 2011).

36. "Top 200 Drugs for 2009 by Units Sold," http://www.drugs.com/top200_units.html (accessed May 18, 2011); "Top 200 Drugs for 2009 by Sales," http://www.drugs.com/top200.html (accessed May 18, 2011).

37. Møldrup, "The Use of the Terms 'Lifestyle Medicines' or 'Lifestyle Drugs,' " 193–6.

38. See, for example, Suzanne White Junod and Lara Marks, "Women's Trials: The Approval of the First Oral Contraceptive Pill in the United States and Great Britain," *Journal of the History of Medicine and Allied Sciences* 57, no. 2 (2002): 117–60.

39. David Gilbert, Tom Walley, and Bill New, "Lifestyle Medicines," *British Medical Journal* 321 (2000): 1341–4, quote on 1341.

40. Joel Lexchin, "Lifestyle Drugs: Issues for Debate," *Canadian Medical Association Journal* 164 (2001): 1449–51, quote on 1449.

41. Tim Atkinson, "Lifestyle Drug Market Booming," *Nature Medicine* 8, no. 9 (2002): 909.

42. Mamo and Fosket, "Scripting the Body," 937.

43. Natasha Singer, "A Birth Control Pill that Promised Too Much," *New York Times*, February 11, 2009.

44. I am grateful to Jeremy A. Greene for sharing his insight on primary versus secondary effects in the marketing of the Pill.

45. Johns Hopkins Medicine, "Health Alerts: What Is a Lifestyle Drug?," http://www.johnshopkinshealthalerts.com/alerts/prescription_drugs/Johns HopkinsPrescriptionDrugsHealthAlert_3241-1.html (accessed May 18, 2011).

46. BlueChoice HealthPlan, "2011 Lifestyle Medication List." BlueChoice HealthPlan, South Carolina, http://www. bluechoicesc.com/ . . . /bluechoice/ . . . / lifestyle-medications.pdf (accessed May 9, 2012).

47. Singer, "A Birth Control Pill that Promised Too Much."

48. Randall, "United States Loses Lead in Contraceptive Choices," 176–8.

49. Ibid., 178.

50. "Citizen's Petition Before the FDA Requesting Withdrawal for Sale of Nor-plant" (June 27, 1996). Docket #96P-0215, Records of the US Food and Drug Administration, Rockville, MD. See also Cynthia M. Klaisle and Philip D. Darney, "From Launch to Litigation: Norplant in America," *Contraception* 11 (2000): 595.

51. David J. Morrow, "Fen-Phen Maker to Pay Billions in Settlement of Diet-Injury Cases," *New York Times*, October 8, 1999, A1.

52. For a scholarly analysis of the effect and meaning of the breast implant litigation, see Sheila Jasanoff, "Science and the Statistical Victim: Modernizing Knowledge in Breast Implant Litigation," *Social Studies of Science* 32 (2002): 37–69. For a more popular treatment, see Marcia Angell, *Science on Trial: The Clash of Medical Evidence and the Law in the Breast Implant Case* (New York: WW Norton, 1997).

53. Judith A. McGaw, "Why Feminine Technologies Matter," in *Gender & Technology: A Reader*, eds. N.E. Lerman, R. Oldenziel, and A.P. Mohun (Baltimore, MD: Johns Hopkins University Press, 2003), 13–36, quote on 19.

Hormone Risk Throughout the Lifespan

by Christina Cherel

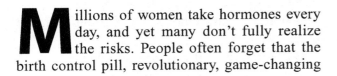

(https://www.nwhn.org/author/c_cherel/)

Millions of women take hormones every day, and yet many don't fully realize the risks. People often forget that the birth control pill, revolutionary, game-changing medicine, is in fact, a drug. In its early form, "the Pill" had such high hormone levels and negative side effects that women, and the women's health community, protested—and succeeded in making it safer. Thirty years ago, women going through the menopausal transition were liberally prescribed hormone therapy not only to help with menopause's unwanted symptoms but also as preventive care. Doctors prescribed and women took menopause hormone therapy without knowing the serious consequences of long-term hormone use, including increased risks of breast cancer and endometrial cancer, and stroke.

Today, we know that both hormonal contraception (like the Pill) and menopause hormone therapy **do** carry risks—and must not be exempted from the scrutiny we conduct on other drugs. In this article, we discuss hormone use over a woman's lifetime, the risks from hormonal birth control and menopause hormone therapy, and how you can decide if taking hormones is right for you.

Hormone Use Throughout Women's Lifetime

Many drugs that women use are indicated for a certain time in their lives. As women age and experience different stages of life, they may be more likely to use different medications and less likely to use others. For example, women in their teens and twenties may be more likely to use prescription acne medication. Bisphosphonates, which treat osteoporosis, are used primarily by women over age 60.

Hormones, however, are an exception. Many women are prescribed hormones like synthetic estrogen and progestin starting in their teens (in the form of hormone-based contraceptives), continuing through the menopausal transition (in the form of menopause hormone therapy), and even later years (in the form of estrogen therapy). It is worth noting that the formulation of estrogen in oral contraceptives and hormone therapy is different.

Some women may take hormone-containing medications for decades at a time without any breaks *or* without questioning these drugs' risks. Drug manufacturers are notorious for "creating" diseases that warrant pharmaceutical intervention to encourage people to take more drugs for longer periods of time (and, ultimately, fill their own pockets). And yet, despite women's common and often extended use of hormone-containing medications, many people often don't consider hormones

to be a drug the way that blood pressure medication or antibiotics are.

But hormones *are* drugs and, because they are prescribed and used by women throughout their entire life, it is especially important to know and understand their significant and sometimes life-threatening risks. While hormones are safe for the majority of people, women need information in order to make the best decision for their own unique health circumstances and preferences.

Regardless of the form or dosage of estrogen, or when hormones are taken over the lifespan, common side effects are similar: nausea, headaches, breast tenderness, and irregular uterine bleeding. Other serious side effects, like certain cancers, vary depending on how the estrogen is administered (orally or through the skin) and when and how long a person takes the hormones.

Hormonal Birth Control

Many women begin using a hormonal birth control method—like the Pill, patch, vaginal ring, or intrauterine device (IUD)—in their teens or twenties and may continue using it for decades to prevent or delay pregnancy.[1] Many women also use hormonal birth control for reasons unrelated to pregnancy prevention, including relief from menstrual pain and excessive menstrual bleeding.[2] The Pill is the most commonly used form of birth control internationally.[3] Of the 62 percent of U.S. women of reproductive age currently using contraception, over a quarter of them (10.6 million) use the Pill.[4]

Many of us don't think twice about using the Pill; it's a symbol of revolution and freedom, for good reason. Hormonal contraception like the Pill has allowed women to take control of their reproductive lives in a revolutionary way, and has helped improve women's social and economic standing immeasurably. This can sometimes mask hormone birth control's negative side effects, and speaking out against the Pill can feel anti-feminist or anti-woman.[5]

But, when the Pill was first introduced, its high estrogen levels carried large health risks, which women's health advocates helped expose (the NWHN was founded out of these advocacy efforts). As a result, today's hormonal contraception is much safer, but there are still risks. Newer formulations of the Pill that contain drosperinone, like Yaz and Yasmin, carry even greater risks, and the NWHN asked the FDA in 2011 to take these versions of the Pill off the market. And, because hormonal birth control is so popular, even statistically small risks can affect a significant number of people in the general population.

Combined hormonal contraceptives (containing both estrogen and progestin) increase the risk of developing a blood clot. As a result of increased blood clot risk, hormones also increase the risk of heart attack and strokes. Some people with a blood clot don't experience any symptoms, while others may experience swelling, pain, tenderness, skin redness, depending on the clot's location. It's important to seek *immediate* medical care if you experience any of these symptoms.

In fact, grassroots movements are increasingly springing up to warn young women about the often overlooked or dismissed risks of hormonal contraceptives (see: *hormonesmatter.com*, and *birthcontrolwisdom.com*). Prompted by the deaths of their own daughters, these activists have made it their mission to make women more informed about hormonal contraception and its risks.

Similarly, Holly Grigg-Spall and Ricki Lake are currently working on a documentary called *Sweetening the Pill* (based on Grigg-Spall's book of the same name), which investigates how women got "hooked" on hormonal birth control and discusses non-hormonal family planning methods. Hormonal contraception is a vital part of many women's reproductive health care, but they deserve to know that certain hormonal contraceptives have higher-potency hormones, and therefore carry slightly more risk.

Menopause Hormone Therapy

For many years, slick pharmaceutical ads marketed hormones to women as a "fountain of youth," promising that taking estrogen would prevent wrinkles, reduce moodiness, and improve sexual responsiveness among menopausal or post-menopausal women. These claims were unfounded, misleading, and dangerous for women's health.

Thanks to the federally-sponsored Women's Health Initiative (WHI)—the largest long-term study of women's health ever conducted—we now know that menopause hormone therapy carries serious risks. The WHI revealed that menopause hormone therapy isn't as safe or effective as researchers, doctors, and drug manufacturers claimed. We also learned that, although menopause hormone therapy does help reduce the risk of bone fractures as long as you're taking it, it *doesn't* help prevent heart attacks and it *does* significantly increase the risk of developing breast cancer, blood clots, or stroke. As a result of women stopping hormone therapy, breast cancer rates have declined significantly in recent years. Using hormones for preventive care has decreased, but many women continue to use hormones to treat symptoms of menopause like vaginal dryness and hot flashes.

When used for the right length of time (less than two years) and at the right dose (the lowest possible), hormones can be an effective treatment for troublesome symptoms of the menopausal transition. But, we have learned that these benefits are not without risk. Thanks to the WHI, we now know that hormones *don't* preserve or restore youth, improve memory, or prevent Alzheimer's disease or heart disease. In fact, otherwise healthy women are more likely to experience heart attacks, blood clot, and stroke while taking combined estrogen/progestin hormones. Women's bodies are not deficient during or after menopause and using menopause hormone therapy as preventive medicine rather than to treat symptoms will not help you stay healthy.

Managing Risks and Making the Best Decisions

Unfortunately, no one knows in advance whether a drug or device will cause an adverse reaction in her body. And there is no simple yes or no when it comes to the question, "Are hormones right for me?" We do know, however, that people may have certain predispositions that increase their risk of blood clots, such as genetic clotting disorders, overweight/obesity, smoking, and prolonged inactivity. We also understand that many people choose to use hormones despite these risks because of the many benefits they offer. It's important to know the risks of any drug or medical device you're using and work with your doctor to make the health care decision that best fits your unique circumstances. Knowledge is power — and hormone use is not an exception to the rule this time.

For more information on hormone use, check out (http://www.nwhn.org/health-information/fact-sheets) the NWHN's Fact Sheet.

Christina S. Cherel, MPH is the NWHN Program Coordinator.

References

1. Based on an average 2 children per woman and reproductive capacity 15-44 years of age; https://www.guttmacher.org/media/presskits/contraception-US/statsandfacts.html

2. https://www.guttmacher.org/media/presskits/contraception-US/statsandfacts.html

3. http://www.guttmacher.org/pubs/fb_contr_use.htm (http://www.guttmacher.org/pubs/fb_contr_use.html)

4. http://www.cdc.gov/nchs/data/nhsr/nhsr060.pdf

The Picture of Health: How Textbook Photographs Construct Health

by Mariamne H. Whatley

Photographs in textbooks may serve the roles of breaking up a long text, emphasizing or clarifying information in the text, attracting the buyer (the professor, teacher, or administrator who selects texts), and engaging the reader. But photographs cannot be dismissed merely as either decorative additions or straightforward illustrations of the text. Photographs are often far more memorable than the passages they illustrate and, because they are seen as objective representations of reality, rather than artists' constructions (Barthes, 1977), may have more impact than drawings or other forms of artwork. In textbooks, photographs can carry connotations, intentional or not, never stated in the text. The selection of photographs for a text is not a neutral process that simply involves being "realistic" or "objective"; selection must take into account issues such as audience expectations and dominant meanings in a given cultural/historical context (Whatley, 1988). In order to understand the ideological work of a textbook, a critique of the photographs is as crucial as a critique of the text itself.

Using ideological analysis to identify patterns of inclusion and exclusion, I examined photographs in the seven best-selling, college-level personal health textbooks. This chapter presents the results of that research. In the first part of the analysis, I examined the photographs that represent "health," describing who and what is "healthy," according to these representations. In the second part of the analysis, I determined where those excluded from the definition of health are represented in the approximately 1,100 remaining photographs in the texts.

Selling Health in Textbooks

Generally, textbook authors do not select specific photographs but may give publishers general descriptions of the type of photographs they wish to have included (for example, a scene showing urban crowding, a woman in a nontraditional job). Due to the great expense involved, new photographs are not usually taken specifically for texts. Instead publishers hire photo researchers to find appropriate photographs, drawing on already existing photographic collections. The result is that the choice of photographs depends on what is already available, and what is available depends to some extent on what has been requested in the past. In fact, because the same sources of photographs may be used by a number of different publishers, identical photographs may appear in competing books. Although authors may have visions of their books' "artwork," the reality may be limited by the selection already on the market. In addition, editors and publishers make decisions about what "artwork" will sell or is considered appropriate, sometimes overruling the authors' choices.

Photographs, especially cover-photos and special color sections, are considered features that sell textbooks, but they also can work as part of another selling process. Textbooks, in many cases, sell the reader a system of belief. An economics text, for example, may "sell" capitalism, and a science text may "sell" the scientific method, both of which help support dominant ideologies. Health textbooks may be even more invested in this selling process because, in addition to convincing readers to "believe" in health, their "success" depends on the readers' adoption of very specific personal behavioral programs to attain health. Health textbooks hold up the ideals of "total wellness" or "holistic fitness" as goals we can attain by exercising, eating right, reducing stress, and avoiding drugs. The readers' belief in health and their ability to attain it by specific behaviors is seen by many health educators as necessary to relevant educational goals; the belief in a clearly marked pathway to health is also part of a process of the commodification of health.

In North America and Western Europe, health is currently a very marketable commodity. This can be seen in its most exaggerated form in the United States in the proliferation of "health" clubs, in the trend among hospitals and clinics to attract a healthy clientele by advertising their abilities to make healthy people healthier (Worcester & Whatley, 1988), and in the advertisements that link a wide range of products, such as high fiber cereals and calcium rich antacids, to health. In a recent article in a medical journal, a physician examined this commercialization of health:

> Health is industrialized and commercialized in a fashion that enhances many people's dissatisfaction with their health. Advertisers, manufacturers, advocacy groups, and proprietary healthcare corporations promote the myth that good health can be purchased; they market products and services that purport to deliver the consumer into the promised land of wellness. (Barsky, 1988, p. 415)

Photographs in health textbooks can play a role in this selling of health similar to that played by visual images in advertising a product in the popular media. According to Berger (1972), the role of advertising or publicity is to

> make the spectator marginally dissatisfied with his present way of life. Not with the way of life of society, but with his own place within it. It suggests that if he buys what it is offering, his life will become better. It offers him an improved alternative to what he is. (p. 142)

The ideal of the healthy person and the healthy lifestyle can be seen as the "improved alternative" to what we are. It can be assumed that most of us will be dissatisfied with ourselves when measured against that ideal, just as most women are dissatisfied with their body shapes and sizes when compared with ideal media representations.

In effective advertising campaigns the visual image is designed to provoke powerful audience responses. In health textbooks the visual representation of "health" is calculated to sell, and it is likely to have a greater impact on the reader than discussions about lengthened life expectancy, reduction in chronic illness, or enhanced cardiovascular fitness. The image of health, not health itself, may be what most people strive for. In the attempt to look healthy, many sacrifice health. For example, people go through very unhealthy practices to lose "extra" weight that is in itself not unhealthy; being slim, however, is a basic component of the *appearance* of health. A recent survey found that people who eat healthy foods do so for their appearance and *not* for their health. "Tanning parlors" have become common features of health and fitness centers, though tanning in itself is unhealthy. As with being slim, having a good tan contributes to the appearance of what is currently defined as health.

The use of color photographs is particularly effective in selling the healthy image, for, as Berger (1972) points out, both oil painting and color photography "use similar highly tactile means to play upon the spectator's sense of acquiring the *real* thing which the image shows" (p. 141). The recent improvement in quality and the increase in number of color photographs in textbooks provide an opportunity to sell the image of health even more effectively than black and white photographs could.

Selection of Textbooks

Rather than trying to examine all college-level personal health (as opposed to community health) textbooks, I selected the best-selling ones, since those would have the widest impact. Based on the sales figures provided by the publisher of one popular text, I selected seven texts published from 1985 to 1988. Sales of these textbooks ranged from approximately 15,000 to 50,000 for each edition. (Complete bibliographic information on these textbooks is provided in the Appendix. Author-date information for these textbooks refer to the Appendix, rather than the chapter references.) Obviously, the sales figures depend on the number of years a specific edition has been in print. For one text (Insel & Roth, 1988), I examined the newest edition (for which there could be no sales figures), based on the fact that its previous editions had high sales. A paper on the readability of personal health textbooks (Overman, Mimms, & Harris, 1987), using a similar selection process, examined the seven top-selling textbooks for the 1984–85 school year, plus three other random titles. Their list has an overlap with mine of only four texts,

which may be due to a number of factors, including differences in editions and changing sales figures.

Analysis I: Healthy-Image Photographs

The first step in my analysis was a close examination of the photographs that I saw as representing "health," the images intended to show who is healthy and illustrate the healthy lifestyle. These included photographs used on covers, opposite title pages, and as openers to units or chapters on wellness or health (as opposed to specific topics such as nutrition, drugs, and mental health). While other pictures throughout the texts may represent healthy individuals, the ones selected, by their placement in conjunction with the book title or chapter title, can be seen as clearly connoting "health." I will refer to these as healthy-image photographs. I included in this analysis only photographs in which there were people. While an apple on a cover conveys a message about health, I was interested only in the question of who is healthy.

A total of 18 different photographs fit my criteria for representing health. I have eliminated three of these from discussion: the cover from Insel and Roth (1988) showing flowers and, from Dintiman and Greenberg (1986), both the cover photograph of apples and the health unit opener of a movie still from the *Wizard of Oz*. (This textbook uses movie stills as openers for all chapters; this moves the photograph away from its perceived "objective" status toward that of an obvious construction.)

There are a number of points of similarity in the 15 remaining photographs. In several photographs (windsurfing, hang gliding), it is hard to determine race, but all individuals whose faces can clearly be seen are white. Except for those who cannot be seen clearly and for several of the eight skydivers in a health unit opener, all are young. No one in these photographs is fat or has any identifiable physical disability. Sports dominate the activities, which, with the exception of rhythmic gymnastics and volleyball played in a gym, are outdoor activities in nonurban settings. Five of these involve beaches or open water. All the activities are leisure activities, with no evidence of work. While it is impossible to say anything definitive about class from these photographs, several of the activities are expensive (hang gliding, skydiving, windsurfing), and others may take money and/or sufficient time off from work to get to places where they can be done (beaches, biking in countryside); these suggest middle-class activities, whether the actual individuals are middle class or not. In several photographs (windsurfing, hang gliding, swimming) it is hard to determine gender. However, excluding these and the large group of male runners in a cross-country race, the overall balance is 23 males to 18 females, so it does seem that there is an attempt to show women both as healthy individuals and in active roles.

How Health Is Portrayed

A detailed analysis of three photographs can provide insight into how these text photographs construct health. The first is a color photograph of a volleyball game on a beach from the back cover of *Understanding Your Health* (Payne & Hahn, 1986). As with most of these images of health, the setting is outdoors, clearly at a distance from urban life. The steep rock walls that serve as a backdrop to the volleyball game additionally isolate the natural beach setting from the invasion of cars[1] and other symbols of "man-made" environmental destruction and ill health. The volleyball players appear to have escaped into a protected idyllic setting of sun, sand, and, we assume, water. They also have clearly escaped from work, since they are engaged in a common leisure activity associated with picnics and holidays. None of them appears to be contemplating the beauty of the natural setting, but merely using it as a location for a game that could go on anywhere in which there is room to set up a net.

The photograph is framed in such a way that the whole net and area of the "court" are not included, so that some players may also not be visible. On one side of the net are three women and a man, on the other two women and a man. While this is not necessarily a representation of heterosexual interactions, it can be read that way. Two players are the focus of the picture, with the other five essentially out of the action. The woman who has just hit the ball, with her back toward the camera, has her arms outstretched, her legs slightly spread, and one foot partly off the ground. The man who is waiting for the ball is crouched slightly, looking

expectantly upward. Her body is partially superimposed on his, her leg crossed over his. This is essentially an interaction between one man and one woman. It would not work the same way if the key players were both female or both male, since part of the "healthiness" of this image appears to be the heterosexual interaction. For heterosexual men, this scene might be viewed as ideal—a great male-female ratio on an isolated beach; perhaps this is their reward for having arrived at the end of this book—this photograph is on the *back* cover—attaining their goal of health.

All the volleyball players are white, young, and slim. The woman farthest left in the frame appears slightly heavier than the others; she is the only woman wearing a shirt, rather than a bikini top, and is also wearing shorts. Besides being an outsider in terms of weight, dress, and location in the frame, she is the only woman who clearly has short hair (three have long hair tied back in ponytails, one cannot be seen completely). Perhaps she can move "inside" by losing weight and changing her image. As viewers, we are just a few steps beyond the end of the court and are also outsiders. As with pickup games, there is room for observers to enter the game—if they are deemed acceptable by the other players. By achieving health, perhaps the observer can step into the game, among the young, white, slim, heterosexual, and physically active. But if the definition of health includes young, white, slim, heterosexual, and physically active, many observers are relegated permanently to the outside.

If this photograph serves as an invitation to join in the lifestyle of the young and healthy, the second photograph, facing the title page of another book, serves the same function, with the additional written message provided by the title of the book—*An Invitation to Health* (Hales & Williams, 1986). The photograph is of six bicycle riders, three women and three men, resting astride their bicycles. This photograph is in black and white, so it is perhaps not as seductive as the sunny color of the first cover. However, the people in this photograph are all smiling directly at the viewer (rather than just leaving a space in back where the viewer could join in). Two of the women, in the middle and the right, have poses and smiles that could be described as flirtatious. They are taking a break from their riding, so it is an opportune moment to join the fun of being healthy.

As with the volleyball players, all the bicycle riders are young, slim, white, and apparently fit. Another similarity is the amount of skin that is exposed. Playing volleyball on the beach and riding bikes in warm weather are activities for which shorts and short-sleeved shirts are preferable to sweatpants and sweatshirts. The choice of these types of activities to represent health results in photographs in which legs and arms are not covered. Appearing healthy apparently involves no need to cover up unsightly flab, "cellulite," or stretch marks. A healthy body is a body that can be revealed.

The bikers are in a fairly isolated, rural setting. While they are clearly on the road, it appears to be a rural, relatively untraveled road. Two cars can be seen far in the distance, and there may also be a house in the distance on the right side of the frame. Otherwise, the landscape is dominated by hills, trees, and grass, the setting and the activity clearly distance the bike riders both from urban life and from work.

In a third photograph, a health unit chapter opener (Levy, Dignan, & Shirreffs, 1987), we can see a possible beginning to alternative images of health. The players in this volleyball game are still slim, young, and apparently white. However, the setting is a gym, which could be urban, suburban, or rural. While four players are wearing shorts, one woman is wearing sweatpants; there are T-shirts rather than bikini tops, and gym socks rather than bare legs. The impression is that they are there to play a hard game of volleyball rather than to bask in the sun and each other's gaze. Two men are going for the ball from opposite sides, while a woman facing the net is clearly ready to move. Compared with the other volleyball scene, this photograph gives more of a sense of action, of actual physical exertion, as well as a sense of real people, rather than models.

It is interesting to imagine how healthy the volleyball players and bike riders actually are, underneath the appearance of health. The outdoor groups, especially the beach group, are susceptible to skin cancer from overexposure to the sun. Cycling is a healthy aerobic sport, though it can be hard on the knees and back. It is particularly surprising, however, to find that the bikers represented in a health text are not wearing helmets, thus modeling behavior that is considered very risky. Compared with biking, volleyball is the kind of weekend activity that sends the enthusiastic untrained player home with pulled muscles, jammed fingers, and not much of a useful workout. The question also arises as to how the particularly thin women on the beach achieved their weight— by unhealthy weight-loss diets, by anorexia, by purging? The glowing image of health may have little to do with the reality.

Similarities to Advertising

Shortly after I began the research for this chapter, I was startled, while waiting for a movie to begin, to see a soft drink advertisement from which almost any still could have been substituted for a healthy-image photograph I had examined. There were the same thin, young, white men and women frolicking on the beach, playing volleyball, and windsurfing. They were clearly occupying the same territory: a never-never land of eternal sunshine, eternal youth, and eternal leisure. Given my argument that these textbook photographs are selling health, the similarities between soft drink advertising images and textbook healthy images are not surprising. They are appealing to the same groups of people, and they are both attempting to create an association between a desirable lifestyle and their product. You can enjoy this fun in the sun if you are part of the "Pepsi generation" or think "Coke is it" or follow the textbook's path to health. These can be considered one variant of the lifestyle format in advertising, as described by Leiss, Kline, and Jhally (1986).

> Here the activity invoked in text or image becomes the central cue for relating the person, product, and setting codes. Lifestyle ads commonly depict a variety of leisure activities (entertaining, going out, holidaying, relaxing). Implicit in each of these activities, however, is the placing of the product within a consumption style by its link to an activity. (p. 210)

Even a naive critic of advertising could point out that drinking a carbonated beverage could not possibly help anyone attain this lifestyle; on the other hand, it might be easier to accept that the same lifestyle is a result of achieving health. However, the association between health and this leisure lifestyle is as much a construction as that created in the soft drink ads. Following all the advice in these textbooks as to diet, exercise, coping with stress, and attaining a healthy sexuality will not help anyone achieve this sun-and-fun fantasy lifestyle any more than drinking Coke or Pepsi would.

These healthy-image photographs borrow directly from popular images of ideal lifestyles already very familiar to viewers through advertising[2] and clearly reflect the current marketing of health. The result is that health is being sold with as much connection to real life and real people's needs as liquor ads that suggest major lifestyle changes associated with changing one's brand of scotch.

Analysis II: Where Are the Excluded?

For each textbook, the next step was to write brief descriptions of all other photographs in the books, totaling approximately 1,100. The results of the analysis of the healthy image photographs suggested a focus on specific aspects of the description of the individuals and activities in examining the remaining 1,100 photographs. The areas I selected for discussion are those in which "health" is linked to specific lifestyles or factors that determine social position/power in our society. I described the setting, the activity, and a number of observable points about the people, including gender, race, age, physical ability/disability, and weight. These photographs were all listed by chapter and when appropriate, by particular topic in that chapter. For example, a chapter on mental health might have images of positive mental health and also images representing problems such as severe depression or stress. These descriptions of photographs were used to establish whether there were images with characteristics not found in the healthy images and, if so, the context in which these characteristics were present. For example, finding no urban representations among the healthy images, I identified topic headings under which I did find photographs of urban settings.

White, young, thin, physically abled, middle-class people in the healthy images represent the

mythical norm with whom the audience is supposed to identify. This not only creates difficulties in identification for whose who do not meet these criteria, but also creates a limiting and limited definition of health. I examined the photographs that did not fit the healthy-image definition to find the invisible—those absent from the healthy images: people of color, people with physical disabilities, fat people, and old people. I also attempted to identify two other absences—the urban setting and work environment. Because there were no obvious gender discrepancies in the healthy images, I did not examine gender as a separate category.

People of Color

After going through the remaining photographs, it was clear that there had been an attempt to include photographs of people of color in a variety of settings, but no obvious patterns emerged. In a previous paper, I examined representations of African-Americans in sexuality texts, finding that positive attempts at being nonracist could be undermined by the patterns of photographs in textbooks that, for example, draw on stereotypes and myths of "dangerous" black sexuality (Whatley, 1988). Rather than reviewing all the representations of people of color in these health textbooks, I will simply repeat what I pointed out earlier—that there is a strong and clear *absence* of photographs of people of color in the healthy-images category. People of color may appear as healthy people elsewhere in the text, but not on covers, title pages, and chapter openers. If publishers wanted to correct this situation, they could simply substitute group photographs that show some diversity for the current all-white covers and title pages.

People with Disabilities

From the healthy-image photographs, it is apparent that people with visible physical disabilities are excluded from the definition of healthy. Therefore, I examined the contexts in which people with disabilities appear in the other photographs. Out of the approximately 1,100 photos, only 9 show people with physical disabilities, with 2 of these showing isolated body parts only (arthritic hands and knees). One shows an old woman being pushed in a wheelchair, while the six remaining photographs all are "positive" images: a number of men playing wheelchair basketball, a man in a wheelchair doing carpentry, a woman walking with her arm around a man in a wheelchair, a man with an amputated leg walking across Canada, children with cancer (which can be seen both as a disease and a disability) at a camp (these last two both in a cancer chapter), and a wheelchair racer. However, three of these six are from one textbook (Payne & Hahn, 1986), and two are from another (Levy, Dignan, & Shirreffs, 1987), so the inclusion of these few positive images is over-shadowed by the fact that three books show absolutely none. In addition, none of these positive images are of women, and the only disabilities represented are those in which an individual uses a wheelchair or has cancer.

This absence of representation of disabled people, particularly women, clearly reflects the invisibility of the physically disabled in our society.

> It would be easy to blame the media for creating and maintaining many of the stereotypes with which the disabled still have to live. But the media only reflect attitudes that already exist in a body-beautiful society that tends to either ignore or ostracize people who don't measure up to the norm. This state of "invisibility" is particularly true for disabled women. (Israel & McPherson, 1983, pp. 4–15)

In a society that values the constructed image of health over health itself, a person with a disability does not fit the definition of healthy. In addition, since the person with a disability may be seen as representing a "failure" of modern medicine and healthcare (Matthews, 1983), there is no place for her or him in a book that promises people that they can attain health. The common attitude that disability and health are incompatible was expressed in its extreme by a faculty member who questioned the affirmative action statement in a position description for a health education faculty member; he wanted to know if encouraging "handicapped" people to apply was appropriate for a *health* education position.

Looking at the issue of health education and disabilities, it should be clear that it is easier for able-bodied people to be healthy, so more energy should be put into helping people with disabilities

maximize their health. Able-bodied people often have more access to exercise, to rewarding work (economically[3] as well as emotionally), to leisure activities, and to healthcare facilities. Healthcare practitioners receive very little training about health issues relating to disability (self-care, sexual health), though they may receive information about specific pathologies, such as multiple sclerosis or muscular dystrophy. The inability to see, hear, or walk need not be the impairments to health they often are considered in our society. Health education is an obvious place to begin to change the societal attitudes toward disability that can help lead to poor physical and emotional health for disabled people. Health textbooks could present possibilities for change by showing ways that both disabled and able-bodied people can maximize health, and this could be done in both the text and the photographs. For example, one of those color chapter openers could include people with disabilities as healthy people. This might mean changing some of the representative "healthy" activities, such as windsurfing. While there are people with disabilities who participate in challenging and risky physical activities, there is no need for pressure to achieve *beyond* what would be expected of the able-bodied.[4] Showing a range of healthy activities that might be more accessible to both the physically disabled and the less physically active able-bodied would be appropriate.

Fat People

There are no fat people in the healthy-image photographs. Some people who agree with the rest of my analysis may respond here, "Of course not!" because there is a common assumption in our society that being thin is healthy and that any weight gain reduces health. In fact, evidence shows that being overweight (but not obese) is *not unhealthy.* In many cases, being very fat is a lot healthier than the ways people are encouraged to attempt to reduce weight—from extreme low-calorie diets, some of which are fatal, to stomach stapling and other surgeries (Norsigian, 1986). In addition, dieting does not work for 99 percent of dieters, with 95 percent ending up heavier than before they started. Repeated dieting stresses the heart, as well as other organs (Norsigian, 1986). Our national obsession with thinness is certainly one factor leading to an unhealthy range of eating behaviors, including, but not limited to, bulimia and anorexia. While health textbooks warn against dangerous diets and "eating disorders," and encourage safe, sensible weight-loss diets, they do nothing to counter the image of thin as healthy.

Defining which people are "fat" in photographs is obviously problematic. In doing so, I am giving my subjective interpretation of what I see as society's definition of ideal weight. The photographs I have identified as "fat" are of people who by common societal definitions would be seen as "needing to lose weight." In the United States most women are dissatisfied with their own body weight, so are more likely to place themselves in the "need to lose weight" category than to give that label to someone else of the same size.

Not counting people who were part of a crowd scene, I found 14 photographs that clearly showed people who were fat. One appeared in a chapter on the healthcare system with a caption referring to "lack of preventive maintenance leading to medical problems" (Carroll & Miller, 1986, p. 471), one in a chapter on drinking, and one under cardiovascular problems. The remaining 11 appeared in chapters on weight control or diet and nutrition. Of the 11, one was the "before" of "before and after" weight-loss photographs. One showed a woman walking briskly as part of a "fat-management program" (Mullen, Gold, Belcastro, & McDermott, 1986, p. 125); that was the most positive of the images. Most of the photographs were of people doing nothing but being fat or adding to that fat (eating or cooking). Three of the photographs showed women with children, referring by caption or topic heading to causes of obesity, either genetic or environmental. Only 3 of the 11 photographs were of men. In these photographs, it seems we are not being shown a person or an activity, but a disease—a disease called obesity that we all might "catch" if we don't carefully follow the prescriptions for health. Fat people's excess weight is seen as their fault for not following these prescriptions. This failure results from a lack of either willpower or restraint, as implied by the photographs that show fat people eating and thus both draw on and lend support to the myth that fat people eat too much. The only health problem of fat people is seen as their weight; if that

were changed, all other problems would presumably disappear. As pointed out earlier, the health problems of losing excess weight, particularly in the yo-yo pattern of weight loss/gain, may be greater than those created by the extra weight. In addition, the emotional and mental health problems caused by our society's fatphobia may be more serious than the physical problems (Worcester, 1988). These texts strongly reinforce fatphobia by validating it with health "science."

Health educators who consciously work against racism and sexism should carefully reevaluate how our attitudes help perpetuate discrimination against all groups. As Nancy Worcester (1988) points out,

> The animosity towards fat people is such a fundamental part of our society, that people who have consciously worked on their other prejudices have not questioned their attitude towards body weight. People who would not think of laughing at a sexist or racist joke ridicule and make comments about fat people without recognizing that they are simply perpetuating another set of attitudes which negatively affect a whole group of people. (p. 234)

An alternative approach would be to recognize that people would be healthier if less pressure were put on them to lose weight. Fat people can benefit from exercise, if it is accessible and appropriate (low impact aerobics, for example), without the goal needing to be weight loss (Sternhell, 1985). Photographs of "not thin" people, involved in a variety of activities, could be scattered throughout the text, and the pictures of those labeled obese could be eliminated completely. We all know what an obese person looks like; we do not need to have that person held up as a symbol of both unhealthiness and lack of moral character.

Old People

The healthy-image photographs show people who appeared to be predominantly in their teens and twenties, which is the age group toward which these college texts would be geared. Rather subjectively, as with the issue of weight, I will describe as old[5] those who appear to be about 65 or older. Obviously I probably judged incorrectly on some photographs, but since the representations seem to be skewed toward the young or the old, with the middle-aged not so prominent, my task was relatively easy. I identified 84 photographs that contained people I classified as old. Of these, 52 appeared in chapters specifically on aging or growing older, 10 appeared in chapters on death and dying, and the remaining 22 were distributed in a wide range of topics. Of these 22, several still focused on the issue of age. For example, a photograph of an old heterosexual couple in a chapter entitled "Courtship and Marriage" is captioned, "While some people change partners repeatedly, many others spend their lifetime with a single spouse" (Carroll & Miller, 1986, p. 271). One text showed a similar photo and caption of a heterosexual couple, but also included an old gay male couple on the next page (Levy, Dignan, & Shirreffs, 1987). This represents an important step in terms of deghettoization of gay and lesbian images, and a broadening of views about sexuality and aging. Two photos showed old people as "non-traditional students;" another depicted a man running after recovering from a stroke; and yet another featured George Burns as a representative of someone who has lived a long life. In others of the 22, the age is incidental, as in a man painting (mental health), people shopping in an open market (nutrition), people walking (fitness), a man smoking.

As the societally stereotyped *appearance* of health diminishes, as occurs with aging, it is assumed that health unavoidably diminishes. In fact, while there is some inevitable biological decline with age, many health problems can be averted by good nutrition, exercise, and preventive healthcare. Many of the health problems of aging have economic, rather than biological, causes, such as lack of appropriate health insurance coverage (Sidel, 1986). In a society that is afraid to face aging, people may not be able to accept that they will experience the effects of aging that they so carefully avoid (if they are lucky enough to live that long). In addition, as with disability, the people who may need to do more to maintain health are those being most ignored.

It is significant that these texts have sections on aging, which contain many positive images, but it is also crucial that health be seen as something that can be attained and maintained by people of all ages. The attempt to include representations of aging in these books must be expanded so that people of all ages are seen to be able to be healthy—a state now seemingly, in those images of health, to be enjoyed only by the young.

Urban Setting

The healthy-image photographs showing outdoor scenes are situated at the beach or in other nonurban settings; it is possible some were set in city parks, but there are no urban markers in the photographs. Bike riding, running, kicking a soccer ball, playing volleyball can all be done in urban settings, though the hang gliding and sky diving would obviously be difficult. Considering the high percentage of the U.S. population that lives in cities (and the numbers of those that cannot easily get out), it seems that urban settings should be represented in the texts. Of the 28 other photographs I identified as clearly having urban settings, I could see only 4 as positive. Two of these showed outdoor vegetable/fruit markets, one showed bike riding as a way of both reducing pollution and getting exercise in the city, and one showed a family playing ball together. Of the rest, 9 appeared in chapters on the environment, with negative images of urban decay, smog, and crowded streets; 10 were in chapters on mental health or stress, showing scenes representing loneliness, stress, or anger, such as a crowded subway or a potential fight on a street corner. Drinking and drug chapters had two urban scenes: "skid row" alcoholics and an apparently drunk man unconscious on the street. There were also three urban scenes in sexuality chapters—two of streets with marquees for sex shows and one showing a "man 'flashing' Central Park" (Payne & Hahn, 1986, p. 348).

There is a clear message that it is unhealthy to live in the city. While this is partly true—that is, the city may have increased pollution of various kinds, specific stresses, less access to certain forms of exercise, and other problems—there are healthy ways to live in a city. One of the roles of health education should be to help us recognize healthier options within the limits imposed on us by economic or other factors. Rather than conveying the message that urban dwelling inevitably condemns people to ill health (unless they can afford to get away periodically to the beach or the mountains), scenes showing health within the city could be presented.

Options for positive images include scenes of outdoor activities in what are clearly city parks, people enjoying cultural events found more easily in cities, gardening in a vacant lot, or a neighborhood block party. Urban settings are excellent for representing walking as a healthy activity. City dwellers are more likely to walk to work, to shopping, and to social activities than are suburbanites, many of whom habitually drive. Urban walking can be presented as free, accessible, and healthy in terms of exercise, stress reduction, and reducing pollution. More indoor activities could be shown so that the external environment is not seen as a determinant of "healthy" activity. These might give a sense of the possibilities for health within what otherwise might appear to be a very dirty, dangerous, stressful place to be.

Work and Leisure

The healthy-image photographs I analyzed were all associated with leisure activities, so I tried to establish how these texts represent work in relationship to health. For this analysis, all photographs of healthcare workers were excluded, since these are used predominantly to illustrate health or medical issues. Of the 16 other photographs showing people at work, 4 were related to discussions of sex roles and women doing nontraditional work (phone "lineman," lawyer). This seems part of a positive trend in textbooks to reduce sexism. An obvious next step would be to show women in nontraditional work roles without commenting on them, as is done with a number of photographs of women as doctors. Six of the photographs of work accompany discussions of stress. Besides stress, there are no illustrations of health hazards at work except for one photograph of a farm worker being sprayed with pesticides. Three positive references to work show someone working at a computer (illustrating self-development), a man in a wheelchair doing carpentry, and an old man continuing to work.

Overall, the number of photographs representing work seems low, considering the amount of time we put into work during our lifetime. Blue-collar work is represented by trash collectors in an environmental health section, police officers in a weight control chapter, firefighters under stress, a construction worker in the opener for a stress chapter, the farm worker mentioned above, and women in nontraditional work. Blue-collar work is seen in terms of neither potential health hazards beyond stress nor the positive health aspects of working. The strongest connection between health and work presented involves the stress of white-collar jobs (symbolized by a man at a desk talking on the phone). The message seems to be that health is not affected by work, unless it is emotionally stressful.

The photographs in this book seem to be aimed at middle-class students who assume they will become white-collar workers or professionals who can afford leisure activities, both in terms of time and money. Those who work in obviously physically dangerous jobs, such as construction work, or in jobs that have stress as only one of many health hazards, are rarely portrayed. These people are also likely not to be able to afford recreation such as hang gliding (and also might not need the stimulus of physical risk taking if their job is physically risky in itself). These photographs serve to compartmentalize work as if it were not part of life and not relevant to health.

Rather than selecting photographs that reinforce the work-leisure split and the alienation of the worker from work, editors could include photographs that show the health rewards of work and the real health risks of a wide variety of work. For example, a photograph of a group of workers talking on a lunch break could be captioned, "Many people find strong support networks among their co-workers." Another photograph could be of a union meeting, illustrating that work-related stress is reduced when we have more control over the conditions of our work. In addition the mental health benefits of a rewarding job might be emphasized, perhaps in contrast with the stress of unemployment. Health risks, and ways to minimize them, could be illustrated with photographs ranging from typists using video display terminals to mine workers. A very important addition would be inclusion in the healthy-image photographs of some representation of work.

Conclusion

The definition of health that emerges from an examination of the healthy-image photographs is very narrow. The healthy person is young, slim, white, physically abled, physically active, and, apparently, comfortable financially. Since these books are trying to "sell" their image of health to college students, the photographs presumably can be seen as representing people whom the students would wish to become. Some students, however, cannot or may not wish to become part of this vision of the healthy person. For example, students of color may feel alienated by this all-white vision. What may be most problematic is that in defining the healthy person, these photographs also define *who can become healthy*. By this definition many are excluded from the potential for health: people who are physically disabled, no longer young, not slim (unless they can lose weight, even if in unhealthy ways), urban dwellers, poor people, and people of color. For various social, economic, and political reasons, these may be among the least healthy groups in the United States, but the potential for health is there if the healthcare and health education systems do not disenfranchise them.

The healthy-image photographs represent the healthy lifestyle, not in the sense of the lifestyle that will help someone attain health, but the white, middle-class, heterosexual, leisure, active lifestyle that is the reward of attaining health. These glowing images imitate common advertising representations. An ice chest of beer would not be out of place next to the volleyball players on the beach, and a soft drink slogan would fit well with the windsurfers or sky divers. It must be remembered, however, that while college students may be the market for beer, soft drinks, and "health," they are not the market for textbooks. Obviously, the biggest single factor affecting a student's purchase of a text is whether it is required. The decision may also be based on how much reading in the book is assigned, whether exam questions will be drawn from the text, its potential future usefulness, or its resale value.

The market for textbooks is the faculty who make text selections for courses (Coser, Kadushin, &

Powell, 1982). While the photographs may be designed to create in students a desire for health, they are also there to sell health educators the book. Therefore, health educators should take some time examining the representations in these texts, while questioning their own definitions of who is healthy and who can become healthy. Do they actually wish to imply that access to health is limited to young, white, slim, middle-class, physically abled, and physically active people? If health educators are committed to increasing the potential for health for *all* people, then the focus should not be directed primarily at those for whom health is most easily attained and maintained. Rethinking the images that represent health may help restructure health educators' goals.

It is an interesting exercise to try to envision alternative healthy-image photographs. Here is one of my choices for a cover photograph: An old woman of color, sitting on a chair with a book in her lap, is looking out at a small garden that has been reclaimed from an urban backlot.

Acknowledgments

I would like to thank Nancy Worcester, Julie D'Acci, Sally Lesher, and Elizabeth Ellsworth for their critical readings of this chapter and their valuable suggestions.

Notes

1. Cars appear in health textbook photographs primarily in the context of either environmental concerns or the stresses of modern life.

2. Occasionally, photographs used were actually taken for advertising purposes. For example, in a chapter on exercise there is a full-page color photograph of a runner with the credit "Photo by Jerry LaRocca for Nike" (Insel & Roth, 1988, p. 316).

3. Examining the wages of disabled women can give a sense of the potential economic problems: "The 1981 Census revealed that disabled women earn less than 24 cents for each dollar earned by nondisabled men; black disabled women earn 12 cents for each dollar. Disabled women earn approximately 52 percent of what nondisabled women earn" (Saxton & Howe, 1987, p xii).

4. "Supercrip" is a term sometimes used among people with disabilities to describe people with disabilities who go beyond what would be expected of those with no disabilities. It should not be necessary to be a one-legged ski champion or a blind physician to prove that people with disabilities deserve the opportunities available to the able-bodied. By emphasizing the individual "heroes," the focus shifts away from societal barriers and obstacles to individual responsibility to excel.

5. I am using "old" rather than "older" for two reasons that have been identified by many writing about ageism. "Older" seems a euphemism that attempts to lessen the impact of discussing someone's age, along with such terms as senior citizen or golden ager. The second point is the simple question: "Older than whom?"

References

A list of references is available in the original source.

Appendix: Textbooks Examined for This Chapter

Carroll, C., & Miller, D. (1986). *Health: The science of human adaptation* (4th ed.). Dubuque, IA: Wm. C. Brown.

Dintiman, G. B., & Greenberg, J. (1986). *Health through discovery* (3rd ed.). New York: Random House.

Hales, D. R., & Williams, B. K. (1986). *An invitation to health: Your personal responsibility* (3rd ed.). Menlo Park, CA: Benjamin/Cummings Publishing Company.

Insel, P. M., & Roth, W. T. (1988). *Core concepts in health* (5th ed.). Mountain View, CA: Mayfield Publishing.

Levy, M. R., Dignan, M., & Shirreffs, J. H. (1987). *Life and health*. (5th ed.). New York: Random House.

Mullen, K. D., Gold, R. S., Belcastro, P. A., & McDermott, R. J. (1986). *Connections for health.* Dubuque, IA: Wm. C. Brown.

Payne, W. A., & Hahn, D. B. (1986). *Understanding your health*, St. Louis: Times Mirror/Mosby.

 # The Marketing and Politics Behind the Promotion of Female Sexual Dysfunction and its "Pink Viagra"

by National Women's Health Network

Female Sexual Dysfunction

The cultural impact and multi-billion dollar profitability of male impotence drugs has accelerated the race to develop and market a parallel drug treatment for women. The overnight success of Viagra, which was developed quite incidentally in an English lab in 1998 when clinical trial volunteers testing a high blood pressure medication reported a suspicious number of erections, prompted drug manufacturers to wonder if Viagra would have a similar effect on women.[1] It didn't. However, drug companies immediately attempted to create and market an expectation for a "pink Viagra." Soon thereafter, a new disease category called "Female Sexual Dysfunction" was created. Despite over a decade of research and millions of dollars spent on drug development, the U.S. Food and Drug Agency (FDA) has yet to approve a single drug treatment for women dealing with sexual problems.

This reality has promoted the pharmaceutical industry to launch a campaign headlined by many prominent women's health advocates in an effort to persuade the FDA to approve of a female sexual dysfunction drug for women. Members of the campaign called "Even the Score" are challenging the FDA on what they claim is a perpetuation of a gender bias by virtue of the claim that the FDA is holding drugs that treat women's sexual problem to a higher standard than those for erectile dysfunction. Even the Score has engaged prominent women's rights organizations, health care providers, the media and members of Congress in a public relations misinformation campaign to criticize the FDA. There are Female Sexual Dysfunction drugs currently under FDA review, and Even the Score is attempting to move the discussion away from the safety and effectiveness of these drugs and towards controversy about gender bias.[2]

The reality is that no amount of public relations or slick marketing can get around the fact that the drugs currently being proposed for Female Sexual Dysfunction simply don't work and may be quite dangerous. Poor efficacy, a strong placebo effect, and valid safety concerns have plagued all of the drugs that have been tested so far.[3] There are many reasons why the proposed drugs may not have been effective in increasing women's sexual enjoyment; chief among them is the heterogeneity of female sexuality and, of course, research demonstrating that sexual problems are mostly shaped by interpersonal, psychological, and social factors. Nevertheless, pharmaceutical executives will continue to drum up hype over the possibility of a "pink Viagra" because the profit market for this type of drug is estimated to be over $2 billion a year.[4]

Even the Score's petition and attempts to make this a conversation about gender equality is misleading and dangerous; while the FDA should be held accountable for gender equality, it should not compromise the safety of women's health by approving a drug that is not effective and not safe.

The FDA should continue to balance a serious and respectful incorporation of patient input while maintaining a rigorous, uncompromised science-based review standard for drugs and devices they approve for women.

Below are some myths and facts to know about Female Sexual Dysfunction (FSD) and the Even the Score Campaign

Myth: There is a norm of female sexual function.

- **Fact:** The implied parallel between female sexual dysfunction and male impotence is actually very deceptive. The word "dysfunction" — medical jargon for anything that doesn't work the way it should — suggests that there is an acknowledged norm for female sexual function. That norm has never been established. Unlike erection, which is a quantifiable physical event, a woman's sexual response is qualitative. It reflects desire, arousal, and gratification — which are utterly subjective and rather difficult to quantify in objective clinical terms. As we all already know, sexual desire differs over time and between people for a range of reasons largely related to relationships, life situations, past experiences and personal and social expectations.

Myth: FSD is a defined disease category.

- **Fact:** Without an empirical standard by which to assess female sexual function, it is extremely difficult, if not impossible, to come up with criteria for female sexual dysfunction. But that hasn't stopped drug manufactures from trying. Insidiously, every time a new drug sponsor touts a solution for women's sexual concerns, the purported cause of female sexual dysfunction changes. For example, when drugs affecting blood flow were being tested, the notion that women had an "insufficiency of vaginal engorgement" had scientific currency. When testosterone was proposed, claims were made that a vast number of women were suffering of a hormone deficiency. Most recently, as drugs that affect the neurotransmitters are being tested for female sexual dysfunction—we are being told that low libido is due to a chemical problem inside a woman's brain.

Myth: Drug developers are searching for a solution for women's sexual concerns.

- **Fact:** The pharmaceutical industry is driven by profit, and as such, if a solution is not found at the bottom of a pill bottle, they are simply not interested. If product-development-driven research was happening in a balanced context with proportionate attention being paid to the myriad of causes of women's sexual concerns, the focus on biomedical causes might not be so damaging. The focus on pharmaceutical rather than emotional solutions has serious limitations. The way the industry has shaped the FSD discussion threatens to make women's sexual experience, no less than men's, a performance issue. Also, without downplaying the significance of any women's pain or distress, there can be real danger in defining difference as "dysfunction". There are many provocative research questions that don't attract pharmaceutical industry funding but yet would hold very important answers for women facing problems with sex, some of these include: What are the effective strategies for couples who are dealing with the impact of a major life crisis and how that affects sexual desire. What's the effect of exercise on sexual desire and does it differ by gender? How does a history of physical and sexual and gender based trauma impact women's sexual satisfaction through the course of their lives.

Myth: 43% of women suffer from FSD.

- **Fact:** There is a perception that Even the Score is trying to advance which suggests that up to 43 percent of women suffer from FSD. The disorder is so widespread that American women are breaking down drug manufacturers' doors desperately pleading for solutions for their sexual problems. The making and marketing of FSD as a distinct disease category was amplified by a 1999 Journal of American Medical Association piece which claimed that 43 percent of American women suffer from a sexual dysfunction. As should come as no surprise, the authors of the paper had financial ties to pharmaceutical companies. The 43 percent figure emerged from an analysis of responses

by 1,749 women to a set of questions. Women who reported any of the following "symptoms" within the last two months—lack of sexual desire, difficulty in becoming aroused, inability to achieve orgasm, anxiety about sexual performance etc.—were considered to have sexual dysfunction. The study also found that women were more likely to suffer from sexual dysfunction if they were single, had less education, had physical or mental health problems, had undergone recent social or economic setbacks, or were dissatisfied with their relationship with a sexual partner.[5] In the years since the report's publication, researchers have revisited it and rightly challenged its conclusions.

Myth: The standard for FDA review of male impotence drugs should be the same for FSD drugs.

- **Fact:** Even the Score's gender equity argument ignores the real safety difference between FSD drugs that are currently being tested and the drugs approved for men: a different indication for use, specifically the dosage and administration. All but one of the drugs approved for men are taken on an as-needed basis, whereas the most recent drug being tested for women is a central nervous system serotonergic agent with effects on adrenaline and dopamine in the brain; it requires chronic—daily, long-term—administration. This raises toxicological concerns that make it appropriate for the FDA to subject that type of drug to an elevated safety scrutiny. Substantial adverse events reports and drop-out rates in the latest FSD trials also rightly require serious consideration.

Myth: There are 24 drugs approved for men, and none approved for women.

- **Fact:** Because several drugs have been approved for male sexual dysfunction, groups have asked whether the FDA is holding women's sexual satisfaction to a different standard. A recent blog titled "The FDA, Sexual Dysfunction and Gender inequality" inaccurately claimed that there are 24 drugs approved for men, and zero for women.[6] This claim perpetuates a miscalculation. It counts each brand name drug and its identical generic counterparts or different formulations as unique treatment options, which artificially inflates the number of drugs available for men. In fact, there are only six different FDA-approved drugs available for male sexual dysfunction, including erectile dysfunction.[7] Nevertheless, the inflammatory claim of gender bias produced press and political attention.

1. CNN Website, *Viagra: The little blue pill that could*, New York, NY: CNN, 2013. Retrieved on June 22, 2015 from: http://www.cnn.com/2013/03/27/health/viagra-anniversary-timeline/index.html.

2. Even the Score Website, The Problem: Even the Score, no date. Retrieved on June 22, 2015 from: http://eventhescore.org/the-problem/.

3. Food and Drug Administration Website, *Summary Minutes of the Advisory Committee for Reproductive Health Drugs Meeting*, Silver Spring, MD: Center for Drug Evaluation and Research, 2010. Retrieved on June 22, 2015 from www.fda.gov/downloads/Advisory-Committees/CommitteesMeetingMaterials/Drugs/ReproductiveHealthDrugsAdvisory-Committee/UCM248751.pdf.

4. ABC News Website, *"Pink Viagra?" Drug Promises to Boost Female Sex Drive*, New York, NY: ABC News, 2010. Retrieved on June 22, 2015 from: http://abcnews.go.com/GMA/OnCall/female-viagra-pill-promises-enhance-female-libido/story?id=10731882.

5. Laumann EO, Paik A, Rosen RC, "Sexual Dysfunction in the United States: Prevalence and Predictors," JAMA 1999; 281(6):537-544. doi:10.1001/jama.281.6.537. Retrieved on June 22, 2015 from: http://jama.jamanetwork.com/article.aspx?articleid=188762.

6. Clayton, Anita, HuffPost Website, The FDA, *Sexual Dysfunction, and Gender INequality*, New York, NY: HuffPost, 2014. Retrieved on June 22, 2015 from: http://www.huffingtonpost.com/anita-h-clayton-md/the-fda-sexual-dysfunctio_b_4724459.html.

7. Bloom J, Is The FDA Really Sexist?: Science 2.0, 2014. Retrieved on June 22, 2015 from: www.science20.com/pfired_still_kicking/fda_really_sexist-130694.

The Egg and the Sperm: How Science Has Constructed a Romance Based on Stereotypical Male-Female Roles

by Emily Martin

The theory of the human body is always a part of a world-picture. . . . The theory of the human body is always a part of a *fantasy*. [JAMES HILLMAN, *The Myth of Analysis*][1]

[1] James Hillman, *The Myth of Analysis* (Evanston, Ill.: Northwestern University Press, 1972), 220.

As an anthropologist, I am intrigued by the possibility that culture shapes how biological scientists describe what they discover about the natural world. If this were so, we would be learning about more than the natural world in high school biology class; we would be learning about cultural beliefs and practices as if they were part of nature. In the course of my research I realized that the picture of egg and sperm drawn in popular as well as scientific accounts of reproductive biology relies on stereotypes central to our cultural definitions of male and female. The stereotypes imply not only that female biological processes are less worthy than their male counterparts but also that women are less worthy than men. Part of my goal in writing this article is to shine a bright light on the gender stereotypes hidden within the scientific language of biology. Exposed in such a light, I hope they will lose much of their power to harm us.

> Portions of this article were presented as the 1987 Becker Lecture, Cornell University. I am grateful for the many suggestions and ideas I received on this occasion. For especially pertinent help with my arguments and data I thank Richard Cone, Kevin Whaley, Sharon Stephens, Barbara Duden, Susanne Kuechler, Lorna Rhodes, and Scott Gilbert. The article was strengthened and clarified by the comments of the anonymous *Signs* reviewers as well as the superb editorial skills of Amy Gage.

Egg and Sperm: A Scientific Fairy Tale

At a fundamental level, all major scientific textbooks depict male and female reproductive organs as systems for the production of valuable substances, such as eggs and sperm.[2] In the case of women, the monthly cycle is described as being designed to produce eggs and prepare a suitable place for them to be fertilized and grown—all to the end of making babies. But the enthusiasm ends there. By extolling the female cycle as a productive enterprise, menstruation must necessarily be viewed as a failure. Medical texts describe menstruation as the "debris" of the uterine lining, the result of necrosis, or death of tissue. The descriptions imply that a system has gone awry, making products of no use, not to specification, unsalable, wasted, scrap. An illustration in a widely used medical text shows menstruation as a chaotic disintegration of form, complementing the many

texts that describe it as "ceasing," "dying," "losing," "denuding," "expelling."[3]

Male reproductive physiology is evaluated quite differently. One of the texts that sees menstruation as failed production employs a sort of breathless prose when it describes the maturation of sperm: "The mechanisms which guide the remarkable cellular transformation from spermatid to mature sperm remain uncertain. . . . Perhaps the most amazing characteristic of spermatogenesis is its sheer magnitude: the normal human male may manufacture several hundred million sperm per day."[4] In the classic text *Medical Physiology*, edited by Vernon Mountcastle, the male/female, productive/destructive comparison is more explicit: "Whereas the female *sheds* only a single gamete each month, the seminiferous tubules *produce* hundreds of millions of sperm each day" (emphasis mine).[5] The female author of another text marvels at the length of the microscopic seminiferous tubules, which, if uncoiled and placed end to end, "would span almost one-third of a mile!" She writes, "In an adult male these structures produce millions of sperm cells each day." Later she asks, "How is this feat accomplished?"[6] None of these texts expresses such intense enthusiasm for any female processes. It is surely no accident that the "remarkable" process of making sperm involves precisely what, in the medical view, menstruation does not: production of something deemed valuable.[7]

One could argue that menstruation and spermatogenesis are not analogous processes and, therefore, should not be expected to elicit the same kind of response. The proper female analogy to spermatogenesis, biologically, is ovulation. Yet ovulation does not merit enthusiasm in these texts either. Textbook descriptions stress that all of the ovarian follicles containing ova are already present at birth. Far from being *produced*, as sperm are,

---

[2] The textbooks I consulted are the main ones used in classes for undergraduate premedical students or medical students (or those held on reserve in the library for these classes) during the past few years at Johns Hopkins University. These texts are widely used at other universities in the country as well.

[3] Arthur C. Guyton, *Physiology* of the Human Body, 6th ed. (Philadelphia: Saunders College Publishing, 1984), 624.

[4] Arthur J. Vander, James H. Sherman, and Dorothy S. Luciano, *Human Physiology: The Mechanisms of Body Function,* 3d ed. (New York: McGraw Hill, 1980), 483–84.

[5] Vernon B. Mountcastle, *Medical Physiology,* 14th ed. (London: Mosby, 1980), 2:1624.

[6] Eldra Pearl Solomon, *Human Anatomy and Physiology* (New York: CBS College Publishing, 1983), 678.

[7] For elaboration, see Emily Martin, *The Woman in the Body: A Cultural Analysis of Reproduction* (Boston: Beacon, 1987), 27–53.

they merely sit on the shelf, slowly degenerating and aging like overstocked inventory: "At birth, normal human ovaries contain an estimated one million follicles [each], and no new ones appear after birth. Thus, in marked contrast to the male, the newborn female already has all the germ cells she will ever have. Only a few, perhaps 400, are destined to reach full maturity during her active productive life. All the others degenerate at some point in their development so that few, if any, remain by the time she reaches menopause at approximately 50 years of age."[8] Note the "marked contrast" that this description sets up between male and female: the male, who continuously produces fresh germ cells, and the female, who has stockpiled germ cells by birth and is faced with their degeneration.

Nor are the female organs spared such vivid descriptions. One scientist writes in a newspaper article that a woman's ovaries become old and worn out from ripening eggs every month, even though the woman herself is still relatively young: "When you look through a laparoscope . . . at an ovary that has been through hundreds of cycles, even in a superbly healthy American female, you see a scarred, battered organ."[9]

To avoid the negative connotations that some people associate with the female reproductive system, scientists could begin to describe male and female processes as homologous. They might credit females with "producing" mature ova one at a time, as they're needed each month, and describe males as having to face problems of degenerating germ cells. This degeneration would occur throughout life among spermatogonia, the undifferentiated germ cells in the testes that are the long-lived, dormant precursors of sperm.

But the texts have an almost dogged insistence on casting female processes in a negative light. The texts celebrate sperm production because it is continuous from puberty to senescence, while they portray egg production as inferior because it is finished at birth. This makes the female seem unproductive, but some texts will also insist that it is she who is wasteful.[10] In a section heading for *Molecular Biology of the Cell*, a best-selling text, we are told that "Oogenesis is wasteful." The text goes on to emphasize that of the seven million oogonia, or egg germ cells, in the female embryo, most degenerate in the ovary. Of those that do go on to become oocytes, or eggs, many also degenerate, so that at birth only two million eggs remain in the ovaries. Degeneration continues throughout a woman's life: by puberty 300,000 eggs remain, and only a few are present by menopause. "During the 40 or so years of a woman's reproductive life, only 400 to 500 eggs will have been released," the authors write. "All the rest will have degenerated. It is still a mystery why so many eggs are formed only to die in the ovaries."[11]

The real mystery is why the male's vast production of sperm is not seen as wasteful.[12] Assuming that a man "produces" 100 million (10^8) sperm per day (a conservative estimate) during an average reproductive life of sixty years, he would produce well over two trillion sperm in his lifetime. Assuming that a woman "ripens" one egg per lunar month, or thirteen per year, over the course of her forty-year reproductive life, she would total five hundred eggs in her lifetime. But the word "waste" implies an excess, too much produced. Assuming two or three offspring, for every baby a woman produces, she wastes only around two hundred eggs. For every baby a man produces, he wastes more than one trillion (10^{12}) sperm.

---

nature to have designed antibody molecules with combining sites that specifically recognize the epitopes on smallpox virus. Nature differs from technology, however: it thinks nothing of wastefulness. (For example, rather than improving the chance that a spermatozoon will meet an egg cell, nature finds it easier to produce millions of spermatozoa.)" (Niels Kaj Jerne, "The Immune System," *Scientific American* 229, no. 1 [July 1973]: 53). Thanks to a *Signs* reviewer for bringing this reference to my attention.

[11] Bruce Alberts et al., *Molecular Biology of the Cell* (New York: Garland, 1983), 795.

[12] In her essay "Have Only Men Evolved?" (in *Discovering Reality: Feminist Perspectives on Epistemology, Metaphysics, Methodology, and Philosophy of Science,* ed. Sandra Harding and Merrill B. Hintikka [Dordrecht: Reidel, 1983], 45–69, esp. 60–61), Ruth Hubbard points out that sociobiologists have said the female invests more energy than the male in the production of her large gametes, claiming that this explains why the female provides parental care. Hubbard questions whether it "really takes more 'energy' to generate the one or relatively few eggs than the large excess of sperms required to achieve fertilization." For further critique of how the greater size of eggs is interpreted in sociobiology, see Donna Haraway, "Investment Strategies for the Evolving Portfolio of Primate Females," in *Body/Politics,* ed. Mary Jacobus, Evelyn Fox Keller, and Sally Shuttleworth (New York: Routledge, 1990), 155–56.

---

[8] Vander, Sherman, and Luciano, 568.

[9] Melvin Konner, "Childbearing and Age," *New York Times Magazine* (December 27, 1987), 22–23, esp. 22.

[10] I have found but one exception to the opinion that the female is wasteful: "Smallpox being the nasty disease it is, one might expect

How is it that positive images are denied to the bodies of women? A look at language—in this case, scientific language—provides the first clue. Take the egg and the sperm.[13] It is remarkable how "femininely" the egg behaves and how "masculinely" the sperm.[14] The egg is seen as large and passive.[15] It does not *move* or *journey*, but passively "is transported," "is swept,"[16] or even "drifts"[17] along the fallopian tube. In utter contrast, sperm are small, "streamlined,"[18] and invariably active. They "deliver" their genes to the egg, "activate the developmental program of the egg,"[19] and have a "velocity" that is often remarked upon.[20] Their tails are "strong" and efficiently powered.[21] Together with the forces of ejaculation, they can "propel the semen into the deepest recesses of the vagina."[22] For this they need "energy," "fuel,"[23] so that with a "whiplash-like motion and strong lurches"[24] they can "burrow through the egg coat"[25] and "penetrate" it.[26]

At its extreme, the age-old relationship of the egg and the sperm takes on a royal or religious patina. The egg coat, its protective barrier, is sometimes called its "vestments," a term usually reserved for sacred, religious dress. The egg is said to have a "corona,"[27] a crown, and to be accompanied by "attendant cells."[28] It is holy, set apart and above, the queen to the sperm's king. The egg is also passive, which means it must depend on sperm for rescue. Gerald Schatten and Helen Schatten liken the egg's role to that of Sleeping Beauty: "a dormant bride awaiting her mate's magic kiss, which instills the spirit that brings her to life."[29] Sperm, by contrast, have a "mission,"[30] which is to "move through the female genital tract in quest of the ovum."[31] One popular account has it that the sperm carry out a "perilous journey" into the "warm darkness," where some fall away "exhausted." "Survivors" "assault" the egg, the successful candidates "surrounding the prize."[32] Part of the urgency of this journey, in more scientific terms, is that "once released from the supportive environment of the ovary, an egg will die within hours unless rescued by a sperm."[33] The wording stresses the fragility and dependency of the egg, even though the same text acknowledges elsewhere that sperm also live for only a few hours.[34]

In 1948, in a book remarkable for its early insights into these matters, Ruth Herschberger argued that female reproductive organs are seen as biologically interdependent, while male organs are viewed as autonomous, operating independently and in isolation:

> At present the functional is stressed only in connection with women: it is in them that ovaries, tubes, uterus, and vagina have endless interdependence. In the male, reproduction would seem to involve "organs" only.

> Yet the sperm, just as much as the egg, is dependent on a great many related processes. There are secretions which mitigate the urine in the urethra before ejaculation, to protect the sperm. There is the reflex

[13] The sources I used for this article provide compelling information on interactions among sperm. Lack of space prevents me from taking up this theme here, but the elements include competition, hierarchy, and sacrifice. For a newspaper report, see Malcolm W. Browne, "Some Thoughts on Self Sacrifice," *New York Times* (July 5, 1988), C6. For a literary rendition, see John Barth, "Night-Sea Journey," in his *Lost in the Funhouse* (Garden City, N.Y.: Doubleday, 1968), 3–13.

[14] See Carol Delaney, "The Meaning of Paternity and the Virgin Birth Debate," *Man* 21, no. 3 (September 1986): 494–513. She discusses the difference between this scientific view that women contribute genetic material to the fetus and the claim of long-standing Western folk theories that the origin and identity of the fetus comes from the male, as in the metaphor of planting a seed in soil.

[15] For a suggested direct link between human behavior and purportedly passive eggs and active sperm, see Erik H. Erikson, "Inner and Outer Space: Reflections on Womanhood," *Daedalus* 93, no. 2 (Spring 1964): 582–606, esp. 591.

[16] Guyton (n. 3 above), 619; and Mountcastle (n. 5 above), 1609.

[17] Jonathan Miller and David Pelham, *The Facts of Life* (New York: Viking Penguin, 1984), 5.

[18] Alberts et al., 796.

[19] Ibid., 796.

[20] See, e.g., William F. Ganong, *Review of Medical Physiology*, 7th ed. (Los Altos, Calif.: Lange Medical Publications, 1975), 322.

[21] Alberts et al. (n. 11 above), 796.

[22] Guyton, 615.

[23] Solomon (n. 6 above), 683.

[24] Vander, Sherman, and Luciano (n. 4 above), 4th ed. (1985), 580.

[25] Alberts et al., 796.

[26] All biology texts quoted above use the word "penetrate."

[27] Solomon, 700.

[28] A. Beldecos et al., "The Importance of Feminist Critique for Contemporary Cell Biology," *Hypatia* 3, no. 1 (Spring 1988): 61–76.

[29] Gerald Schatten and Helen Schatten, "The Energetic Egg," *Medical World News* 23 (January 23, 1984): 51–53, esp. 51.

[30] Alberts et al., 796.

[31] Guyton (n. 3 above), 613.

[32] Miller and Pelham (n. 17 above), 7.

[33] Alberts et al. (n. 11 above), 804.

[34] Ibid., 801.

shutting off of the bladder connection, the provision of prostatic secretions, and various types of muscular propulsion. The sperm is no more independent of its milieu than the egg, and yet from a wish that it were, biologists have lent their support to the notion that the human female, beginning with the egg, is congenitally more dependent than the male.[35]

Bringing out another aspect of the sperm's autonomy, an article in the journal *Cell* has the sperm making an "existential decision" to penetrate the egg: "Sperm are cells with a limited behavioral repertoire, one that is directed toward fertilizing eggs. To execute the decision to abandon the haploid state, sperm swim to an egg and there acquire the ability to effect membrane fusion."[36] Is this a corporate manager's version of the sperm's activities—"executing decisions" while fraught with dismay over difficult options that bring with them very high risk?

There is another way that sperm, despite their small size, can be made to loom in importance over the egg. In a collection of scientific papers, an electron micrograph of an enormous egg and tiny sperm is titled "A Portrait of the Sperm."[37] This is a little like showing a photo of a dog and calling it a picture of the fleas. Granted, microscopic sperm are harder to photograph than eggs, which are just large enough to see with the naked eye. But surely the use of the term "portrait," a word associated with the powerful and wealthy, is significant. Eggs have only micrographs or pictures, not portraits.

One depiction of sperm as weak and timid, instead of strong and powerful—the only such representation in western civilization, so far as I know—occurs in Woody Allen's movie *Everything You Always Wanted To Know About Sex* *But Were Afraid to Ask*. Allen, playing the part of an apprehensive sperm inside a man's testicles, is scared of the man's approaching orgasm. He is reluctant to

launch himself into the darkness, afraid of contraceptive devices, afraid of winding up on the ceiling if the man masturbates.

The more common picture—egg as damsel in distress, shielded only by her sacred garments; sperm as heroic warrior to the rescue—cannot be proved to be dictated by the biology of these events. While the "facts" of biology may not *always* be constructed in cultural terms, I would argue that in this case they are. The degree of metaphorical content in these descriptions, the extent to which differences between egg and sperm are emphasized, and the parallels between cultural stereotypes of male and female behavior and the character of egg and sperm all point to this conclusion.

New Research, Old Imagery

As new understandings of egg and sperm emerge, textbook gender imagery is being revised. But the new research, far from escaping the stereotypical representations of egg and sperm, simply replicates elements of textbook gender imagery in a different form. The persistence of this imagery calls to mind what Ludwik Fleck termed "the self-contained" nature of scientific thought. As he described it, "the interaction between what is already known, what remains to be learned, and those who are to apprehend it, go to ensure harmony within the system. But at the same time they also preserve the harmony of illusions, which is quite secure within the confines of a given thought style."[38] We need to understand the way in which the cultural content in scientific descriptions changes as biological discoveries unfold, and whether that cultural content is solidly entrenched or easily changed.

In all of the texts quoted above, sperm are described as penetrating the egg, and specific substances on a sperm's head are described as binding to the egg. Recently, this description of events was rewritten in a biophysics lab at Johns Hopkins University—transforming the egg from the passive to the active party.[39]

Prior to this research, it was thought that the zona, the inner vestments of the egg, formed an

---

[35] Ruth Herschberger, *Adam's Rib* (New York: Pelligrini & Cudahy, 1948), esp. 84. I am indebted to Ruth Hubbard for telling me about Herschberger's work, although at a point when this paper was already in draft form.

[36] Bennett M. Shapiro. "The Existential Decision of a Sperm," *Cell* 49, no. 3 (May 1987): 293–94, esp. 293.

[37] Lennart Nilsson, "A Portrait of the Sperm," in *The Functional Anatomy of the Spermatozoan*, ed. Bjorn A. Afzelius (New York: Pergamon, 1975), 79–82.

[38] Ludwik Fleck, *Genesis and Development of a Scientific Fact*, ed. Thaddeus J. Trenn and Robert K. Merton (Chicago: University of Chicago Press, 1979), 38.

[39] Jay M. Baltz carried out the research I describe when he was a graduate student in the Thomas C. Jenkins Department of Biophysics at Johns Hopkins University.

impenetrable barrier. Sperm overcame the barrier by mechanically burrowing through, thrashing their tails and slowly working their way along. Later research showed that the sperm released digestive enzymes that chemically broke down the zona; thus, scientists presumed that the sperm used mechanical *and* chemical means to get through to the egg.

In this recent investigation, the researchers began to ask questions about the mechanical force of the sperm's tail. (The lab's goal was to develop a contraceptive that worked topically on sperm.) They discovered, to their great surprise, that the forward thrust of sperm is extremely weak, which contradicts the assumption that sperm are forceful penetrators.[40] Rather than thrusting forward, the sperm's head was now seen to move mostly back and forth. The sideways motion of the sperm's tail makes the head move sideways with a force that is ten times stronger than its forward movement. So even if the overall force of the sperm were strong enough to mechanically break the zona, most of its force would be directed sideways rather than forward. In fact, its strongest tendency, by tenfold, is to escape by attempting to pry itself off the egg. Sperm, then, must be exceptionally efficient at *escaping* from any cell surface they contact. And the surface of the egg must be designed to trap the sperm and prevent their escape. Otherwise, few if any sperm would reach the egg.

The researchers at Johns Hopkins concluded that the sperm and egg stick together because of adhesive molecules on the surfaces of each. The egg traps the sperm and adheres to it so tightly that the sperm's head is forced to lie flat against the surface of the zona, a little bit, they told me, "like Br'er Rabbit getting more and more stuck to tar baby the more he wriggles." The trapped sperm continues to wiggle ineffectually side to side. The mechanical force of its tail is so weak that a sperm cannot break even one chemical bond.

This is where the digestive enzymes released by the sperm come in. If they start to soften the zona just at the tip of the sperm and the sides remain stuck, then the weak, flailing sperm can get oriented in the right direction and make it through the zona—provided that its bonds to the zona dissolve as it moves in.

Although this new version of the saga of the egg and the sperm broke through cultural expectations, the researchers who made the discovery continued to write papers and abstracts as if the sperm were the active party who attacks, binds, penetrates, and enters the egg. The only difference was that sperm were now seen as performing these actions weakly.[41] Not until August 1987, more than three years after the findings described above, did these researchers re-conceptualize the process to give the egg a more active role. They began to describe the zona as an aggressive sperm catcher, covered with adhesive molecules that can capture a sperm with a single bond and clasp it to the zona's surface.[42] In the words of their published account: "The innermost vestment, the *zona pellucida*, is a glycoprotein shell, which captures and tethers the sperm before they penetrate it. . . . The sperm is captured at the initial contact between the sperm tip and the *zona*. . . . Since the thrust [of the sperm] is much smaller than the force needed to break a single affinity bond, the first bond made upon the tip-first meeting of the sperm and *zona* can result in the capture of the sperm."[43]

Experiments in another lab reveal similar patterns of data interpretation. Gerald Schatten and Helen Schatten set out to show that, contrary to conventional wisdom, the "egg is not merely a

---

[40] Far less is known about the physiology of sperm than comparable female substances, which some feminists claim is no accident. Greater scientific scrutiny of female reproduction has long enabled the burden of birth control to be placed on women. In this case, the researchers' discovery did not depend on development of any new technology. The experiments made use of glass pipettes, a manometer, and a simple microscope, all of which have been available for more than one hundred years.

[41] Jay Baltz and Richard A. Cone, "What Force Is Needed to Tether a Sperm?" (abstract for Society for the Study of Reproduction, 1985), and "Flagellar Torque on the Head Determines the Force Needed to Tether a Sperm" (abstract for Biophysical Society, 1986).

[42] Jay M. Baltz, David F. Katz, and Richard A. Cone, "The Mechanics of the Sperm-Egg Interaction at the Zona Pellucida," *Biophysical Journal* 54, no. 4 (October 1988): 643–54. Lab members were somewhat familiar with work on metaphors in the biology of female reproduction. Richard Cone, who runs the lab, is my husband, and he talked with them about my earlier research on the subject from time to time. Even though my current research focuses on biological imagery and I heard about the lab's work from my husband every day, I myself did not recognize the role of imagery in the sperm research until many weeks after the period of research and writing I describe. Therefore, I assume that any awareness the lab members may have had about how underlying metaphor might be guiding this particular research was fairly inchoate.

[43] Ibid., 643, 650.

large, yolk-filled sphere into which the sperm burrows to endow new life. Rather, recent research suggests the almost heretical view that sperm and egg are mutually active partners."[44] This sounds like a departure from the stereotypical textbook view, but further reading reveals Schatten and Schatten's conformity to the aggressive-sperm metaphor. They describe how "the sperm and egg first touch when, from the tip of the sperm's triangular head, a long, thin filament shoots out and harpoons the egg." Then we learn that "remarkably, the harpoon is not so much fired as assembled at great speed, molecule by molecule, from a pool of protein stored in a specialized region called the acrosome. The filament may grow as much as twenty times longer than the sperm head itself before its tip reaches the egg and sticks."[45] Why not call this "making a bridge" or "throwing out a line" rather than firing a harpoon? Harpoons pierce prey and injure or kill them, while this filament only sticks. And why not focus, as the Hopkins lab did, on the stickiness of the egg, rather than the stickiness of the sperm?[46] Later in the article, the Schattens replicate the common view of the sperm's perilous journey into the warm darkness of the vagina, this time for the purpose of explaining its journey into the egg itself: "[The sperm] still has an arduous journey ahead. It must penetrate farther into the egg's huge sphere of cytoplasm and somehow locate the nucleus, so that the two cells' chromosomes can fuse. The sperm dives down into the cytoplasm, its tail beating. But it is soon interrupted by the sudden and swift migration of the egg nucleus, which rushes toward the sperm with a velocity triple that of the movement of chromosomes during cell division, crossing the entire egg in about a minute."[47]

Like Schatten and Schatten and the biophysicists at Johns Hopkins, another researcher has recently made discoveries that seem to point to a more interactive view of the relationship of egg and sperm. This work, which Paul Wassarman conducted on the sperm and eggs of mice, focuses on identifying the specific molecules in the egg coat (the zona pellucida) that are involved in egg-sperm interaction. At first glance, his descriptions seem to fit the model of an egalitarian relationship. Male and female gametes "recognize one another," and "interactions . . . take place between sperm and egg."[48] But the article in *Scientific American* in which those descriptions appear begins with a vignette that presages the dominant motif of their presentation: "It has been more than a century since Hermann Fol, a Swiss zoologist, peered into his microscope and became the first person to see a sperm penetrate an egg, fertilize it and form the first cell of a new embryo."[49] This portrayal of the sperm as the active party—the one that *penetrates* and *fertilizes* the egg and *produces* the embryo—is not cited as an example of an earlier, now outmoded view. In fact, the author reiterates the point later in the article: "Many sperm can bind to and penetrate the zona pellucida, or outer coat, of an unfertilized mouse egg, but only one sperm will eventually fuse with the thin plasma membrane surrounding the egg proper (*inner sphere*), fertilizing the egg and giving rise to a new embryo."[50]

The imagery of sperm as aggressor is particularly startling in this case: the main discovery being reported is isolation of a particular molecule *on the egg coat* that plays an important role in fertilization! Wassarman's choice of language sustains the picture. He calls the molecule that has been isolated, ZP3, a "sperm receptor." By allocating the passive, waiting role to the egg, Wassarman can continue to describe the sperm as the actor, the one that makes it all happen: "The basic process begins when many sperm first attach loosely and then bind tenaciously to receptors on the surface of the egg's thick outer coat, the zona pellucida. Each sperm, which has a large number of egg-binding proteins on its surface, binds to many sperm receptors on the egg. More specifically, a site on each of the egg-binding proteins fits a complementary site on a sperm receptor, much as a key fits a lock."[51] With the sperm designated as the "key" and the egg the "lock," it is obvious which one acts and

---

[44] Schatten and Schatten (n. 29 above), 51.

[45] Ibid., 52.

[46] Surprisingly, in an article intended for a general audience, the authors do not point out that these are sea urchin sperm and note that human sperm do not shoot out filaments at all.

[47] Schatten and Schatten, 53.

[48] Paul M. Wassarman, "Fertilization in Mammals," *Scientific American* 259, no. 6 (December 1988): 78–84, esp. 78, 84.

[49] Ibid., 78.

[50] Ibid., 79.

[51] Ibid., 78.

which one is acted upon. Could this imagery not be reversed, letting the sperm (the lock) wait until the egg produces the key? Or could we speak of two halves of a locket matching, and regard the matching itself as the action that initiates the fertilization?

It is as if Wassarman were determined to make the egg the receiving partner. Usually in biological research, the *protein* member of the pair of binding molecules is called the receptor, and physically it has a pocket in it rather like a lock. As the diagrams that illustrate Wassarman's article show, the molecules on the sperm are proteins and have "pockets." The small, mobile molecules that fit into these pockets are called ligands. As shown in the diagrams, ZP3 on the egg is a polymer of "keys"; many small knobs stick out. Typically, molecules on the sperm would be called receptors and molecules on the egg would be called ligands. But Wassarman chose to name ZP3 on the egg the receptor and to create a new term, "the egg-binding protein," for the molecule on the sperm that otherwise would have been called the receptor.[52]

Wassarman does credit the egg coat with having more functions than those of a sperm receptor. While he notes that "the zona pellucida has at times been viewed by investigators as a nuisance, a barrier to sperm and hence an impediment to fertilization," his new research reveals that the egg coat "serves as a sophisticated biological security system that screens incoming sperm, selects only those compatible with fertilization and development, prepares sperm for fusion with the egg and later protects the resulting embryo from polyspermy [a lethal condition caused by fusion of more than one sperm with a single egg]."[53] Although this description gives the egg an active role, that role is drawn in stereotypically feminine terms. The egg *selects* an appropriate mate, *prepares* him for fusion, and then *protects* the resulting offspring from harm. This is courtship and mating behavior as seen through the eyes of a sociobiologist: woman as the hard-to-get prize, who, following union with

the chosen one, becomes woman as servant and mother.

And Wassarman does not quit there. In a review article for *Science*, he outlines the "chronology of fertilization."[54] Near the end of the article are two subject headings. One is "Sperm Penetration," in which Wassarman describes how the chemical dissolving of the zona pellucida combines with the "substantial propulsive force generated by sperm." The next heading is "Sperm-Egg Fusion." This section details what happens inside the zona after a sperm "penetrates" it. Sperm "can make contact with, adhere to, and fuse with (that is, fertilize) an egg."[55] Wassarman's word choice, again, is astonishingly skewed in favor of the sperm's activity, for in the next breath he says that sperm *lose* all motility upon fusion with the egg's surface. In mouse and sea urchin eggs, the sperm enters at the *egg's* volition, according to Wassarman's description: "Once fused with egg plasma membrane [the surface of the egg], how does a sperm enter the egg? The surface of both mouse and sea urchin eggs is covered with thousands of plasma membrane-bound projections, called microvilli [tiny "hairs"]. Evidence in sea urchins suggests that, after membrane fusion, a group of elongated microvilli cluster tightly around and interdigitate over the sperm head. As these microvilli are resorbed, the sperm is drawn into the egg. Therefore, sperm motility, which ceases at the time of fusion in both sea urchins and mice, is not required for sperm entry."[56] The section called "Sperm Penetration" more logically would be followed by a section called "The Egg Envelops," rather than "Sperm-Egg Fusion." This would give a parallel—and more accurate—sense that both the egg and the sperm initiate action.

Another way that Wassarman makes less of the egg's activity is by describing components of the egg but referring to the sperm as a whole entity. Deborah Gordon has described such an approach as "atomism" ("the part is independent of and primordial to the whole") and identified it as one

---

[52] Since receptor molecules are relatively *immotile* and the ligands that bind to them relatively *motile*, one might imagine the egg being called the receptor and the sperm the ligand. But the molecules in question on egg and sperm are immotile molecules. It is the sperm as a cell that has motility, and the egg as a *cell* that has relative immotility.

[53] Wassarman, 78–79.

[54] Paul M. Wassarman, "The Biology and Chemistry of Fertilization," *Science* 235, no. 4788 (January 30, 1987): 553–60, esp. 554.

[55] Ibid., 557.

[56] Ibid., 557–58. This finding throws into question Schatten and Schatten's description (n. 29 above) of the sperm, its tail beating, diving down into the egg.

of the "tenacious assumptions" of Western science and medicine.[57] Wassarman employs atomism to his advantage. When he refers to processes going on within sperm, he consistently returns to descriptions that remind us from whence these activities came: they are part of sperm that penetrate an egg or generate propulsive force. When he refers to processes going on within eggs, he stops there. As a result, any active role he grants them appears to be assigned to the parts of the egg, and not to the egg itself. In the quote above, it is the microvilli that actively cluster around the sperm. In another example, "the driving force for engulfment of a fused sperm comes from a region of cytoplasm just beneath an egg's plasma membrane."[58]

Social Implications: Thinking Beyond

All three of these revisionist accounts of egg and sperm cannot seem to escape the hierarchical imagery of older accounts. Even though each new account gives the egg a larger and more active role, taken together they bring into play another cultural stereotype: woman as a dangerous and aggressive threat. In the Johns Hopkins lab's revised model, the egg ends up as the female aggressor who "captures and tethers" the sperm with her sticky zona, rather like a spider lying in wait in her web.[59] The Schatten lab has the egg's nucleus "interrupt" the sperm's dive with a "sudden and swift" rush by which she "clasps the sperm and guides its nucleus to the center."[60] Wassarman's description of the surface of the egg "covered with thousands of plasma membrane-bound projections, called microvilli" that reach out and clasp the sperm adds to the spiderlike imagery.[61]

These images grant the egg an active role but at the cost of appearing disturbingly aggressive. Images of woman as dangerous and aggressive, the femme fatale who victimizes men, are widespread in Western literature and culture.[62] More specific is the connection of spider imagery with the idea of an engulfing, devouring mother.[63] New data did not lead scientists to eliminate gender stereotypes in their descriptions of egg and sperm. Instead, scientists simply began to describe egg and sperm in different, but no less damaging, terms.

Can we envision a less stereotypical view? Biology itself provides another model that could be applied to the egg and the sperm. The cybernetic model—with its feedback loops, flexible adaptation to change, coordination of the parts within a whole, evolution over time, and changing response to the environment—is common in genetics, endocrinology, and ecology and has a growing influence in medicine in general.[64] This model has the potential to shift our imagery from the negative, in which the female reproductive system is castigated both for not producing eggs after birth and for producing (and thus wasting) too many eggs overall, to something more positive. The female reproductive system could be seen as responding to the environment (pregnancy or menopause), adjusting to monthly changes (menstruation), and flexibly changing from reproductivity after puberty to nonreproductivity later in life. The sperm and egg's interaction could also be described in cybernetic terms. J. F. Hartman's research in reproductive biology demonstrated fifteen years ago that if an egg is killed by being pricked with a needle, live sperm cannot get through the zona.[65] Clearly, this evidence shows that the egg and sperm *do* interact on more mutual terms, making biology's refusal to portray them that way all the more disturbing.

We would do well to be aware, however, that cybernetic imagery is hardly neutral. In the past, cybernetic models have played an important part in the imposition of social control. These models

---

[57] Deborah R. Gordon, "Tenacious Assumptions in Western Medicine," in *Biomedicine Examined,* ed. Margaret Lock and Deborah Gordon (Dordrecht: Kluwer, 1988), 19–56, esp. 26.

[58] Wassarman, "The Biology and Chemistry of Fertilization," 558.

[59] Baltz, Katz, and Cone (n. 42 above), 643, 650.

[60] Schatten and Schatten, 53.

[61] Wassarman, "The Biology and Chemistry of Fertilization," 557.

[62] Mary Ellman, *Thinking about Women* (New York: Harcourt Brace Jovanovich, 1968), 140; Nina Auerbach, *Woman and the Demon* (Cambridge, Mass.: Harvard University Press, 1982), esp. 186.

[63] Kenneth Alan Adams, "Arachnophobia: Love American Style," *Journal of Psychoanalytic Anthropology* 4, no. 2 (1981): 157–97.

[64] William Ray Arney and Bernard Bergen, *Medicine and the Management of Living* (Chicago: University of Chicago Press, 1984).

[65] J. F. Hartman, R. B. Gwatkin, and C. F. Hutchison, "Early Contact Interactions between Mammalian Gametes *In Vitro,*" *Proceedings of the National Academy of Sciences (U.S.)* 69, no. 10 (1972): 2767–69.

inherently provide a way of thinking about a "field" of interacting components. Once the field can be seen, it can become the object of new forms of knowledge, which in turn can allow new forms of social control to be exerted over the components of the field. During the 1950s, for example, medicine began to recognize the psychosocial *environment* of the patient: the patient's family and its psychodynamics. Professions such as social work began to focus on this new environment, and the resulting knowledge became one way to further control the patient. Patients began to be seen not as isolated, individual bodies, but as psychosocial entities located in an "ecological" system: management of "the patient's psychology was a new entrée to patient control."[66]

The models that biologists use to describe their data can have important social effects. During the nineteenth century, the social and natural sciences strongly influenced each other: the social ideas of Malthus about how to avoid the natural increase of the poor inspired Darwin's *Origin of Species*.[67] Once the *Origin* stood as a description of the natural world, complete with competition and market struggles, it could be reimported into social science as social Darwinism, in order to justify the social order of the time. What we are seeing now is similar: the importation of cultural ideas about passive females and heroic males into the "personalities" of gametes. This amounts to the "implanting of social imagery on representations of nature so as to lay a firm basis for reimporting exactly that same imagery as natural explanations of social phenomena."[68]

Further research would show us exactly what social effects are being wrought from the biological imagery of egg and sperm. At the very least, the imagery keeps alive some of the hoariest old stereotypes about weak damsels in distress and their strong male rescuers. That these stereotypes are now being written in at the level of the *cell* constitutes a powerful move to make them seem so natural as to be beyond alteration.

The stereotypical imagery might also encourage people to imagine that what results from

the interaction of egg and sperm—a fertilized egg—is the result of deliberate "human" action at the cellular level. Whatever the intentions of the human couple, in this microscopic "culture" a cellular "bride" (or femme fatale) and a cellular "groom" (her victim) make a cellular baby. Rosalind Petchesky points out that through visual representations such as sonograms, we are given "*images* of younger and younger, and tinier and tinier, fetuses being 'saved.' " This leads to "the point of visibility being 'pushed back' *indefinitely*."[69] Endowing egg and sperm with intentional action, a key aspect of personhood in our culture, lays the foundation for the point of viability being pushed back to the moment of fertilization. This will likely lead to greater acceptance of technological developments and new forms of scrutiny and manipulation, for the benefit of these inner "persons": court-ordered restrictions on a pregnant woman's activities in order to protect her fetus, fetal surgery, amniocentesis, and rescinding of abortion rights, to name but a few examples.[70]

Even if we succeed in substituting more egalitarian, interactive metaphors to describe the activities of egg and sperm, and manage to avoid the pitfalls of cybernetic models, we would still be guilty of endowing cellular entities with personhood. More crucial, then, than what *kinds* of personalities we bestow on cells is the very fact that we are doing it at all. This process could ultimately have the most disturbing social consequences.

One clear feminist challenge is to wake up sleeping metaphors in science, particularly those involved in descriptions of the egg and the sperm. Although the literary convention is to call such metaphors "dead," they are not so much dead as sleeping, hidden within the scientific content of texts—and all the more powerful for it.[71] Waking

---

[66] Arney and Bergen, 68.

[67] Ruth Hubbard, "Have Only Men Evolved?" (n. 12 above), 51–52.

[68] David Harvey, personal communication, November 1989.

[69] Rosalind Petchesky, "Fetal Images: The Power of Visual Culture in the Politics of Reproduction," *Feminist Studies* 13, no. 2 (Summer 1987): 263–92, esp. 272.

[70] Rita Arditti, Renate Klein, and Shelley Minden, *Test-Tube Women* (London: Pandora, 1984); Ellen Goodman, "Whose Right to Life?" *Baltimore Sun* (November 17, 1987); Tamar Lewin, "Courts Acting to Force Care of the Unborn," *New York Times* (November 23, 1987), A1 and B10; Susan Irwin and Brigitte Jordan, "Knowledge, Practice, and Power: Court Ordered Cesarean Sections," *Medical Anthropology Quarterly* 1, no. 3 (September 1987): 319–34.

[71] Thanks to Elizabeth Fee and David Spain, who in February 1989 and April 1989, respectively, made points related to this.

up such metaphors, by becoming aware of when we are projecting cultural imagery onto what we study, will improve our ability to investigate and understand nature. Waking up such metaphors, by becoming aware of their implications, will rob them of their power to naturalize our social conventions about gender.

Department of Anthropology
Johns Hopkins University

Medicalization, Marketing, and the Politics of Information

1. Describe your definition and image of a healthy woman. What does she look like and what is she doing? How did you arrive at this definition and image? What is missing from the image? How does your image reflect women in our society?

2. After reading "The Picture of Health," research the images of people and descriptions of their environments in a number of health textbooks, medical journals, and healthcare professional publications. Describe who is and who is not included in the images and how those images influence the definition of health. Does the image in the textbook relate to the images you described in the above question? Describe any alternative images you might have and what is missing from the textbooks.

3. Collect drug and medical advertisements that are promoted directly to the consumer through television, the internet, and other media vehicles. What is the benefit of direct advertisement to consumers? How are these ads similar or different compared to the images presented in medical professional publications?

4. How is women's sexuality medicalized in the media by drug companies? Are they appealing and why?

5. What are the effects of the pharmaceutical industry's involvement in medical research?

6. In what ways are gender, racial, cultural, and able-bodied stereotypes reproduced in scientific textbooks and by drug advertisement? What are the implications for women's health needs and social status in society?

Menstruation and the Politics of Sex Education

Women's sexuality and sex education are often challenging topics to discuss; however, they are important aspects of women's identities and well-being. This chapter explores how social and cultural definitions of sexuality can be either supportive of or detrimental to emotional and physical health. The male-centered emphasis on vaginal intercourse limits or invalidates the experiences and preferences of many women. The question of who defines sexuality and whether those definitions encourage or limit women's enjoyment of sexuality and ability to be sexually healthy will be central to this chapter.

The chapter begins with two articles on sex education. *Not Your Mother's Meatloaf: An Inclusive Sex Education Resource,* an original piece by Mary Morrissey, Marissa Knaack, and Dawna Marie Thomas, traces the history of abstinence-only and comprehensive sex education and demonstrates how they fail to encompass the experiences of marginalized groups, including women, queer people, and people of color. They offer *Not Your Mother's Meatloaf: A Sex Education Comic Book* as an inclusive, pedagogical resource that allows high school and college-aged students to see themselves reflected within sex education curricula. *Not Your Mother's Meatloaf* displaces sex and gender binaries, introduces diverse desires and sexual behaviors, and humanizes sexual knowledge.

The Use and Misuse of Pleasure in Sex Education Curricula by Sharon Lam, Kara Lustig, and Kelly Graling expands on Michelle Fine's argument regarding the absence of pleasure and desire in sex education curricula. Through a qualitative analysis of sex education curricula, the authors found that the discourse of pleasurable sex was associated with danger and negative consequences, including pregnancy and STDs. The discourse further "took a medicalized, scientific tone." They conclude that the discourse of desire exists, but maintains that pleasure is dangerous.

The following articles emphasize sexual health and women's sexual pleasure. Emily Impett, Deborah Schooler, and Deborah Tolman's *To Be Seen and Not Heard: Femininity Ideology and Adolescent Girls' Sexual Health* explores the impact of gender norms on the sexual health of adolescent girls. Focusing on "inauthenticity in relationships and body objectification," the authors administered a survey to 116 girls and found that these two domains were linked to "poorer sexual self-efficacy." The adoption of traditional femininity may then diminish girls' ability to vocalize and act on their sexual desires.

The provocative article *Exposed at Last: The Truth about Your Clitoris* by Jennifer Johnson adds to the discussion of the clitoris and women's sexual pleasure. Although textbooks have often defined the clitoris as the "key" to female sexuality (the term "clitoris" is derived from the Greek word for key), they have also hidden it and presented it as small or pea-sized. The clitoris has been largely misrepresented and neglected by the scientific community. Johnson's article raises the question of who has the power to decide what is considered "scientifically interesting" and what information is erased or minimized in order to maintain the patriarchy.

In *Notes from the Back Room: Gender, Power, and (In)Visibility in Women's Experiences of Masturbation,* Breanne Fahs and Elena Frank take up the social taboo of women's masturbation. Through a qualitative study of twenty women, the authors discover five themes related to women's subjectivities and masturbation. Women characterized masturbation as (1) clitoral stimulation instead of self-penetration; (2) sexual labor and frustration; (3) a threat to their male partner's power and control; (4) an emotionless, daily activity geared toward tension release; and (5) a source of fun and pleasure. Taken together, these findings show that women both incorporate and reject gendered scripts that prioritize male pleasure and penetrative sex.

Virginia Braun's *In Search of (Better) Sexual Pleasure: Female Genital "Cosmetic" Surgery* studies the relationship between women's sexual pleasure and genital cosmetic surgery in the media. Various media outlets depict female genital cosmetic surgery as pleasure-enhancing as a means of promoting the procedure. While the media messages importantly suggest that women are "entitled to sexual pleasure," the practice reproduces heterosexuality and normatively sexed bodies. The authors' examination of the discourse surrounding surgical procedures calls into question "the assumptions on which such surgery rests, and the models of sexuality, bodies, and practices it promotes."

A woman's menstruation is another taboo topic, which is not discussed in our society. The normal physiological process of menstruation has been defined and redefined by male experts throughout history. It has been a barrier to higher education for women, labeled as a disability or illness, and characterized as a weakness, keeping women from working outside the home. Later, menstrual cramps were identified as psychogenic in origin, brought on by the fear of femininity and sexuality. Now hormonal fluctuations are blamed for a wide range of premenstrual symptoms, from acne and water retention to depression, homicidal behavior, and self-mutilation.

If Men Could Menstruate by Gloria Steinem demonstrates that feminists do have a sense of humor. This enjoyable, popular article discusses how women's social status is often controlled and censored because she menstruates on a regular basis. Indeed, it is often the first article discussed in women's health courses because it so perfectly sets

a theme to be addressed throughout the semester: when there are inequalities in a society, everything associated with the valued group will be valued and anything connected with the less valued group will be less valued.

In *The Menstrual Mark: Menstruation as Social Stigma*, Ingrid Johnston-Robledo and Joan Chrisler explore menstruation as a source of social stigma. This theoretical piece builds off of the work of sociologist Erving Goffman. Goffman defines stigma as "any stain or mark that sets some people apart from others." Stigmas are either "abominations of the body," "blemishes of individual character," or "tribal" identities or "social markers associated with marginalized groups." Johnston-Robledo and Chrisler argue that menstruation falls under all three types of stigma; therefore, it negatively affects women's health, sexuality, and self-esteem. In face of social stigma, women can challenge the dominant discourse by openly talking about menstruation, creating countercultural artifacts, social activism, and other means. *Riding the Crimson Wave* by Ariela Schnyer introduces ways in which a young feminist can feel empowered by menstruation. It provides a first-hand account of how one manages the stigma and confronts the misogyny that produces it.

Laura Mamo and Jennifer Ruth Fosket's *Scripting the Body: Pharmaceuticals and the (Re)making of Menstruation* analyzes Seasonale, a birth control pill and menstrual suppressant. The authors examine how Seasonale influences the embodiment and subjectivity of women. They find that the discourse and practice surrounding Seasonale produces "meanings and ways for women to be in and experience their bodies." Bodies and culture, however, both influence each other, opening up space for resistance against dominant discourses of femininity.

This chapter ends with *Menstrual Suppression* from the National Women's Health Network. This article offers another perspective on the safety of medications to suppress women's periods. Menstrual suppression products such as Seasonale or Lybrel are used by women for a variety of reasons including relief from pain and discomfort and the regulation of periods. The National Women's Health Network recognizes menstrual suppression products as an option for women, but raises concerns regarding the marketing strategies. Their laundry list of issues range from the misrepresentations and unsupported claims regarding the

products, to incomplete information, to marketing to young teens. "Women need truthful and complete information about these products to make informed decisions."

Not Your Mother's Meatloaf: An Inclusive Sex Education Resource

by Mary Morrissey, Marissa Knaak, Dawna M. Thomas

Abstract Abstinence-only and comprehensive sex education programs have been implemented in public schools to address the issues of sexually transmitted infections (STI) and teen pregnancy. Although they seek to protect young people, they often silence the experiences of marginalized groups, such as women, queer people, and people of color. *Not Your Mother's Meatloaf*, a sex education comic book, alternatively represents an inclusive resource for students, educators, parents, and sex health practitioners. This article suggests that *Not Your Mother's Meatloaf* opens up opportunities for high school and college-aged students to see themselves within sex education curricula, by disrupting sex/gender binaries, positing diverse desires and sexual behaviors, and humanizing sexual knowledge. It further highlights anti-oppressive sex education as an inclusive framework to be used in public schools.

Introduction

In public schools, sex education programs have been designed to prevent sexually transmitted infections (STIs) and unwanted pregnancy. Although these programs aspire to protect students, historically they have been controversial. The controversy surrounds (1) who should be teaching young people about sex—public schools or parents, (2) age appropriateness, and (3) the type of information that should be taught. As a result, sex education curricula are often limited and overly scientific, reinforcing a heterosexual and gender normative ideal and excluding content related to marginalized populations (e.g., queer persons, people of color, and people with

disabilities). In contrast, *Not Your Mother's Meatloaf* by Saiya Miller and Liza Bley is a sex education comic book that represents marginalized students, particularly women and the queer community. This article argues that *Not Your Mother's Meatloaf* represents an inclusive, pedagogical tool that combats traditional sex education curricula, which are often oppressive and problematic, by disrupting the sex/gender binaries, demonstrating diverse desires and sexual activities, and humanizing sexual knowledge. *Not Your Mother's Meatloaf* opens up critical opportunities for high school and college-aged students to see themselves within sex education curricula and access sexual knowledge. Sexual health educators and practitioners can use the text as a resource to resist the systematic silencing of diverse populations' experiences of sex, love, bodies, health, and other related topics.

This article begins by discussing the history of sex education and scholarly responses to abstinence-only and comprehensive frameworks. Second, the concepts of inclusion and inclusive education are defined. Third, the article traces how the comics presented in *Not Your Mother's Meatloaf* include many populations who are often omitted and marginalized from traditional sex education programs. The comic book's materials reach beyond the sex/gender binary, scientific sexual knowledge, and heterosexual relationships and address many normative assumptions within abstinence-only and comprehensive sex education programs. Finally, we recommend anti-oppressive sex education programming to ensure an inclusive curriculum for all students.

A Brief Overview of Sex Education in the United States

The history of sex education is a part of "long-standing efforts to regulate sexual morality" (Irving, 2002, p. 6). Before the 1960s' cultural and sexual revolutions, sex was socially understood as a romanticized function that occurred between married heterosexual men and women (Irving, 2002). Strict religious norms, public laws, and cultural ideals defined sex in relation to procreation rather than pleasure. Women had more children, which caused economic challenges, health problems for birthing mothers, and high infant mortality rates. For these reasons, women expressed a need for birth control. However, many conservatives feared that birth control would promote sexual promiscuity, increase the number of children born out of wedlock, facilitate the spread of STIs, and, most of all, result in a lowering of "American" values. This conservative paradigm resulted in legislation such as the Comstock Laws. The Comstock Act of 1873 prohibited the distribution of birth control methods and literature regarding contraception and abortion. Early feminists, such as Margaret Sanger, risked prison and public censure in order to combat the Act and offer women birth control and information on how to keep themselves safe. Court decisions, such as *People v. Sanger* (1918) and *United States v. One Package of Japanese*

Pessaries (1936), loosened the Comstock regulations. They led to greater acceptance of birth control and circulation of sex educational information among the American public.

As birth control became more accessible during the sexual revolution in the 1960s, women experienced new and greater sexual freedom. The U.S. Supreme Court decision *Griswold v. Connecticut* (1965) lifted the ban on birth control use by married couples. *Eisenstadt v. Baird* (1972) expanded the Griswold decision to unmarried couples. Women could have sex for pleasure, while reducing their risk of unwanted pregnancy. Yet, by the mid-1980s, the HIV/AIDS epidemic and a rise in STIs provoked fear and anxiety among the American public. According to the U.S. Centers for Disease Control and Prevention, from 1981 to 2013, approximately "1,194,039 people in the United States had been diagnosed with AIDS, of those, 658,507 have died" (as cited by The Foundation for AIDS Research, 2016). The catastrophic effects of HIV/AIDS caused many people to "reevaluate the nature of sex" and "unprotected sexual activity" (Andersen & Taylor, 2008, p. 548). Particularly in the case of gay men and female sex workers, HIV/AIDS and other STIs were discursively linked to sexual promiscuity, which allowed the right wing to implement conservative policies and sway attitudes about sexuality (Irving, 2002). In addition to concerns about STIs, teen pregnancy reenergized "traditional moral arguments against sex outside of marriage" (Stossel, 1997). Characterized as an epidemic, teen pregnancy rates increased in the 1970s and "remained steady through the 1980s" (Boonstra, 2002, p. 7; Guttmacher Institute, 2016). Governmental and philanthropic organizations named teen pregnancy as a serious, high priority issue in the United States, establishing new offices, task forces, public service announcements, and funding initiatives to address it.

Both liberal and conservative groups have advocated for sex education in order to ensure safer sex and protect young people from unwanted pregnancies and STIs. In the United States, sex education is most often abstinence-only or what is defined as comprehensive sex education programs. Championed by conservatives, abstinence-only programs focus on abstaining from premarital sex and on the risks associated with sexual activity. As stated in Title V of the Social Security Act of 1935, these programs generally teach students that sex ought to occur within the context of mutually faithful monogamous marriages (Irving, 2002). Abstinence becomes a protective mechanism against STIs, teen pregnancy, physical health issues, and psychological consequences. Proponents of abstinence-only sex education have also argued that (1) "sex education makes kids go out and have sex" and (2) "speaking about sex is sex" (Irving, 2002, p. 132). This logic equates talking and learning about sex with being sexually abused or violated. Sexuality is then constructed as "an unwelcome and disruptive guest," an entity "foreign to the self," and a threat "to the self and the social order" (Gilbert, 2010, p. 233). For abstinence-only proponents, sex education ultimately protects children and youth from harm. It preserves childhood innocence, the sanctity of marriage, and bodily purity, particularly in the case of young women.

Abstinence-only programs rose to prominence in the 1980s in response to the HIV/AIDS epidemic and the passage of the Adolescent and Family Life Act (AFLA) of 1981. In 1981, Senators Jeremiah Denton and Orrin Hatch championed the AFLA as a means of reducing teen pregnancy, creating family centered programming, and promoting "chastity and self-discipline" (as cited by Saul, 1998). The senators believed that the AFLA would counter the nation's "contraceptive mentality" and funding of alternative family planning organizations, namely Planned Parenthood (as cited by Saul, 1998). In a suit originally filed in 1983, the constitutionality of the AFLA was challenged by Chan Kendrick, an ACLU attorney representing a group of federal taxpayers, clergymen, and the American Jewish Congress. Kendrick's challenge focused on the benefits received by religiously affiliated organizations and the First Amendment's Establishment Clause. The Court ultimately ruled in favor of AFLA because "the 'advancement of religion' was not AFLA's primary effect" *(Bowen v. Kendrick,* 1988). Despite the opinion of the majority, Justice Blackmun wrote in the dissent:

> The AFLA, without a doubt, endorses religion. Because of its expressed solicitude for the participation of religious organizations in all AFLA programs in one form or another, the statute creates a symbolic and real partnership between the clergy and the [state] in

addressing a problem with substantial religious overtones *(Bowen v. Kendrick,* 1988).

Paired with some religious institutions, during this time, conservatives such as Denton and Hatch fought to reinforce "American" values and establish the chastity of young people through the implementation of AFLA and abstinence-only sex education.

Under President Clinton, the 1996 Personal Responsibility and Work Reconciliation Act provided millions of dollars of funding for abstinence-only programs (Connell & Elliott, 2009; Kantor, Santelli, Teitler, & Balmer, 2008). Title I of the Act includes Congress' research findings on the topic of sex education, which purport to show "(1) marriage is the foundation of a successful society" and "(2) marriage is an essential institution of a successful society which promotes the interests of children" (Personal Responsibility and Work Reconciliation Act of 1996). In effect, these findings legally endorse and sanction monogamous, procreative, and heterosexual relationships. The other findings include rates of teen pregnancy and the number of children receiving AFDC benefits (Aid to Families with Dependent Children). The Personal Responsibility and Work Reconciliation Act was aimed at lowering teen and out-of-wedlock pregnancies.

Yet, Section 912 of the Act includes an amendment to Title V of the Social Security Act that specifically focuses on abstinence-only sex education. States are provided with an

> "allotment" to "enable the State to provide abstinence education, and at the option of the State, where appropriate, mentoring, counseling, and adult supervision to promote abstinence from sexual activity, with a focus on those groups which are most likely to bear children out-of-wedlock"

(Personal Responsibility and Work Reconciliation Act of 1996). This abstinence education teaches what is "expected" of children without regard for what those children actually think or do. These expectations show an almost complete disregard for the lived experiences of children and adolescents.

Despite its traction and widespread use, studies have demonstrated the unethical nature and ineffectiveness of abstinence-only sex education. Abstinence-only education often fails to reduce teen pregnancy and the spread of sexual transmitted infections (Kantor et al., 2008). It also lacks medical accuracy and violates human rights through withholding or misrepresenting health information (Kantor et al., 2008). In conjunction with scientific studies, health and education scholars have exposed the detrimental effects of abstinence-only education. First, abstinence-only privileges the "medicalization of adolescent sexuality" and the biological aspects of sex (Nakkula & Toshalis, 2010, p. 190). Students primarily learn about the anatomy of the sexed body, STIs, and pregnancy prevention. While it includes useful information, this framework both ignores the diverse desires, preferences, and orientations that influence sexual behaviors as well as reinforces compulsory heterosexuality (Nakkula & Toshalis, 2010; Rich, 1980). It assumes that all students have a heterosexual orientation and fit neatly into normalized categories of gender, sex, and sexuality. This assumption particularly alienates and marginalizes queer students (Cahill, 2002; Elia & Eliason, 2010). With an emphasis on heterosexual relationships, the institution of marriage, and male/female sexed bodies, abstinence-only sex education "reifies hetero-normativity through active silence" and leads queer students "to feelings of being less than human" (Fisher, 2009, p. 75).

Second, abstinence-only sex education denies young people, particularly women, the opportunity to develop their sexual subjectivity. In her foundational works, Fine (1988) argues that desire has been and still is "missing" from sex education curricula (Fine & McClellan, 2006). In an abstinence-only sex education framework, female sexual desire is suppressed in favor of a "discourse of female sexual victimization" (Fine, 1988, p. 30). Through an emphasis on fear and self-defense, abstinence-only curricula deny young women access to sexual knowledge and skills that empower them to explore their own desires and critique conventional gender norms.

In addition, abstinence-only sex education reinforces hegemonic sexual scripts. According to Wiederman (2015), individuals learn and incorporate "metaphorical scripts" as "a function of their involvement in the social groups" (p. 7). Sexual scripts then enforce the norm by providing meaning and instructions for sexual interactions between men and women (Wiederman, 2005). In the case of young women, they are socialized to become sexual "gatekeepers" in their relationships with men (Jozkowski & Peterson, 2013; Wiederman, 2005; Wiederman, 2015). While men actively pursue sexual interactions, women feel compelled to be defensive to initial activities. They interpret sex in terms of risk, often associating sexual experiences with pregnancy or "damage to . . . social reputation" (Wiederman, 2005, p. 498). In conjunction with sexual scripts, abstinence-only sex education programs primarily place the responsibility for abstinence and sexual purity onto young women. While men and boys are expected to explore their sexualities, women and girls are expected to be virgin-like: "without their virginity, girls are just used up and dirty" (Shaley & Earp, 2011). Abstinence-only sex educators, such as Pam Stenzel, enforce the gatekeeping role, believing that young women have "everything to lose" when they have sex (Andersen, 2013).

For these reasons and various others, many states have opted out of the abstinence-only sex education framework and Title V federal funding resources. Yet, according to the Guttmacher Institute (2016), nineteen states "require that instruction on the importance of engaging in sexuality activity only within marriage be provided" as of March 2016. Similarly, twenty-seven states stress abstinence and only two states prohibit the promotion of religion in sexuality education (Guttmacher Institute, 2016). Abstinence-only sex education curricula continue to be a primary source of sexual knowledge for young people across the United States.

In opposition to abstinence-only, comprehensive sex education programming represents the second dominant model in the United States. The comprehensive sex education model emphasizes "developmentally appropriate education" and a "wide range of topics related to sexuality" (Elias & Eliason, 2010, p. 40). These topics include pregnancy, STIs, risks and pleasures of sex, gender identity, sexual orientation, and abstinence as a personal choice. Comprehensive sex education programs range between "abstinence-plus" and LGBT-inclusive. This range is partly due to debates about "when children are developmentally 'ready' to discuss LGBTQ issues" and sex (Elias & Eliason, 2010, p. 40).

In conjunction with a loosening of sexual norms, comprehensive sex education emerged in the 1960s and 1970s. One of the most notable proponents of comprehensive sexuality education has been the Sexuality Information and Education Council of the United States (SIECUS). Founded in 1964 by Dr. Mary Calderone, SIECUS offers evidence-based, comprehensive sex education to students, parents, teachers, healthcare providers, and policymakers on issues related to sexual and reproductive health.

Since its inception, SIECUS has made significant contributions to the fields of sex education and sexual health. According to Irving (2002), SIECUS redefined the concepts of sex and sexuality. For SIECUS activists, sex and sexuality moved beyond genitalia and physical acts, but signified integral components of one's identity and health. By rearticulating sex and sexuality as fundamental rights and aspects of the humanity, SIECUS seeks to "normalize and legitimate sex" (Irving, 2002, p. 24). In addition, their publications, such as The SIECUS Report, *The Guidelines for Comprehensive Sexuality Education,* and literature on HIV/AIDS, have addressed areas of health that have been systematically silenced. However, SIECUS has been criticized for positing a politics of respectability in face of conservative, Christian-right opposition. Rather than challenging prevailing sex norms, they operate as "another mechanism by which sex is policed through the speech and silences of discourses," along with "schools, psychiatry, religions, and the law" (Irving, 2002, p. 32). For Irving (2002), their paradoxical approach to sex education articulates how SIECUS both became a social agent in the regulation of sexuality and was subject to demonizing tactics from right-wing conservatives.

More recently, the Comprehensive National Sexuality Education Standards were created by a group of organizations (i.e., Advocates for Youth, Answer, and the Sexuality Information and Education Council of the United States) as part of a project called the Future of Sex Education. The Standards outline basic guidelines for comprehensive sexuality education for K-12 public school students. They present content and skills that are theory- and evidence-based and designed to support healthy development, age-appropriate

knowledge, and students' specific experiences related to sex and sexuality. Overall, the National Sexuality Education Standards seek to combat "the inconsistent implementation of sexuality education" and the limited time and resources that are devoted to teaching sexual health (Future of Sex Education Initiative, 2012, p. 12).

The National Sexuality Education Standards introduce skills and content that students ought to be able to master by the end of each grade level. Performance indicators fall under one of the following standards: Core Concepts, Analyzing Influences, Accessing Information, Interpersonal Communication, Decision-Making, Goal-Setting, Self-Management, and Advocacy (Future of Sex Education Initiative, 2012, p. 11). The indicators are then further divided by topic:

Anatomy and Physiology, Identity, Pregnancy and Reproduction, Healthy Relationships, Personal Safety, Sexually Transmitted Diseases and HIV, and Puberty and Adolescent Development. For example, at the conclusion of fifth grade, students should be able to "describe the characteristics of healthy relationships" (Future of Sex Education Initiative, 2012, p. 15). By focusing on these specific indicators, the Standards seek to address the high teen pregnancy rate, bullying and harassment of queer students, teen relationship violence, and the correlation between poor health and academic achievement (Future of Sex Education Initiative, 2012). They also require students to learn about gender identity, same-sex attraction, sexual violence, HIV/AIDS, and other essential health-related issues. However, the Standards fail to account for the lived experiences of students. According to their rationale, they exclusively present the "minimum" and "essential content and skills" given the current conditions of the public school system (Future of Sex Education Initiative, 2012, p. 6). Sexual health educators and practitioners are not provided with resources, strategies for implementation, or insight into needs of students who may fall outside of the white, male, heterosexual, cisgender, able-bodied child standard. They are instead expected to build upon the Standards and translate them into practice.

Comprehensive sex education programs overall have proven to be effective in addressing the specific health needs of many young people (Advocates For Youth, 2009; Kirby, 2007;

Sexuality Information and Education Council of the United States [SIECUS], 2009). According to SIECUS, many these programs delay or reduce sexual activity as well as improve condom use among teenagers (Advocates for Youth, 2009; Kirby, 2007; SIECUS, 2009). Comprehensive sex education programs also can be replicated and are accessible to a range of populations (Kirby, 2007). Despite the positive features of programs such as the National Standards, comprehensive sex education programs potentially reproduce some of the same problems as abstinence-only sex education programs. As Connell and Elliott (2009) point out, both "abstinence-only and comprehensive sexuality education programs rely on fear-based and oppressive conceptualizations of sexuality that perpetuate inequality" (Connell & Elliott, 2009, p. 97). While abstinence-only sex education proponents often use the figure of the pregnant teenager, comprehensive sexuality supporters employ the vulnerable queer youth subject (Connell & Elliott, 2009, p. 86). They perpetuate the notion that queer youth need sex education to protect them from suicide and bullying. Even though comprehensive sex education efforts may recognize queer identities as "viable and legitimate," they do not account for the ways in which queer youth can feel empowered by their sexualities and sexual practices (Elia & Eliason, 2010, p. 34). Comprehensive sex education's reliance on the suicidal queer youth subject limits queer subjectivity and offers a universalized approach to queerness.

The needs of queer students, students of color, women, and other marginalized persons continue to be silenced and erased from the curricula. Comprehensive sexuality education typically rewards "White middle- and upper-class heterosexuality" and uses it "as a reference point to determine how to distribute privilege and power" (García, 2009, p. 523). Educators and practitioners cannot simply teach about heterosexual relations, because heterosexuality does not function the same way for all persons (Cohen, 1997). For example, Black women and men have historically been hypersexualized, while persons with disabilities are often infantilized and seemingly incapable of possessing sexual desire (Abdur-Rahman, 2012; Collins, 2000; Erickson, 2013; Gerschick, 2011; Hobson,

2003). Overall, comprehensive sex education does not address the systematic realities that influence students' access to sexual knowledge. Educators and practitioners thus require tangible materials that will broaden students' access to sex education and allow them to see themselves reflected in the curricula.

Defining Inclusion

In order to determine whether *Not Your Mother's Meatloaf* is an inclusive resource, it is important to define the concepts of inclusion and inclusive education. Inclusion and inclusive education originated from the 1960s' disability rights movement. Disability scholars and activists have challenged the ableist values embedded in the educational system (e.g., classrooms, pedagogies, curricula, and policy), which limit students with disabilities from full participation. According to Baglieri, Baglieri, Bejoian, Broderick, Connor, and Valle (2011), schools are designed to operate around the "mythical normal child" (p. 4). The "normal" child possesses qualities or characteristics that are often taken for granted, such as whiteness, heterosexuality, cisgender identity, and able-bodied privilege. Thus, students who fall outside of the normative center often feel alienated within their school community and experience exclusion at the individual and systemic levels. For disability scholars and activists, inclusive education then attempts to look beyond the "normal" child and create an educational environment free of "barriers to learning for all children" (Baglieri et al., 2011, p. 2). It also "seeks to resist and redress the many ways in which students experience marginalization and exclusion," such as ableism, racism, classism, sexism, and other forms of oppression (Baglieri et al., 2011, p. 3). Inclusion education thus does not only work to meet the needs of all students, but also "necessitates serious changes, both in terms of society and its economic, social conditions and relations and in the schools of which they are a part" (Barton, 1998, p. 60). Truly inclusive environments require the (re)construction of institutions so that they accommodate all learners, regardless of their race, disabilities, and other differences.

Although today's public education institutions may outwardly appear committed to addressing inclusion, they often continue to exclude marginalized students. According to Dyson (2001), there are competing definitions surrounding inclusion. The term often remains vague and takes on various meanings for those "who have a vested interest in how it is constructed and interpreted" (Dunne, 2009, p. 43). Sex educators, for example, can include LGBT content, but simultaneously erase the multitude of ways in which queer students can be marginalized. Representations of difference continue to be limited or "bleak" (Dunne, 2009, p. 52). Obscured definitions of inclusion allow for structural conditions and inequality to remain static, unchanged, and unquestioned. *Not Your Mother's Meatloaf*, however, is a critical resource for educators, practitioners, and young people due to its inclusion of diverse experiences and sexual knowledge.

Not Your Mother's Meatloaf

Not Your Mother's Meatloaf (2013) is a sex education comic book compiled by Saiya Miller and Liza Bley. The comics that are collected in the book were created by various young people, activists, and scholars, and cover a range of topics such as heterosexual and queer sex, bodies, pleasure, violence, and romantic relationships. Young people's narratives are a core element of the comics. According to an interview with Miller, *Not Your Mother's Meatloaf* represents the experiences and perspectives of those who "are often silenced," including youth, women, people of color, and queer people (Comic Nurse, 2013). Miller and Bley intentionally choose comics that disrupt heterosexual mandates and gender norms in sex education. While many young people continue to receive abstinence-only or limited sex education, the text offers a "frank and honest look at sex and sexuality" (Kirkus Reviews, 2013). Readers are intended to feel "comforted by knowing" that they are "not alone" (Farmer, 2013, p. 7). The Do-It-Yourself, zine-like project allows *Not Your Mother's Meatloaf* to feel accessible and relevant.

Not Your Mother's Meatloaf is divided into the following seven chapters: Beginnings, Bodies, Health, Identity, Age, Endings, and Personal Best. Each chapter begins with short vignettes from Miller and Bley, detailing their personal experiences with the topic and the ways in which they developed their own sexual knowledge. As Farmer (2013) expresses in the book's Foreword, the comics offer a multiplicity of perspectives that "are beyond honest" and broaden one's understanding of sex education (p. 7). They do not always pertain to everyone, but account for many experiences that are systematically excluded in public schools.

Beyond the Sex/Gender System

Throughout *Not Your Mother's Meatloaf*, comics reflect the experiences of both normative and non-normative gendered and sexed persons. For example, in "She Smiled Back" by Timothy Sinaguglia, the main subject explores their gender identity. Although they appear as a young man in public, they dress up in women's clothing while at home. They experience "a curious division" and pleasure, creating their own "imaginary mind movie" where they embody a "woman's form" (Sinaguglia, 2013, pp. 34–35). Another example is in "My Body, Myself" by Sparky Taylor. Taylor demonstrates a subject's struggle with body image and gender presentation. Although the subject's body and aesthetic appears boyish and stocky, they also desire to be recognized for "all of the gorgeous woman parts of me" (Taylor, 2013, p. 48). The subject waits for a society that acknowledges gender beyond the binary and embraces contradictory embodiments of gender. Other comics refrain from labeling gender and sex altogether.

While some comprehensive sex education programs introduce gender and gender identity in their curricula, *Not Your Mother's Meatloaf* explicitly calls into question the gender binary and essentialist thinking. The United States, like all other societies, maintains the sex/gender system. Coined by theorist Rubin (1997), the sex/gender system is "set of arrangements by which a society transforms biological sexuality into products of human activity" (p. 28). Sex and gender are understood as natural or biologically determined and there is an assumed and institutionally mandated division of sexes. Sex is mapped onto gender, necessitating the coherence between sexed bodies and gender identities, as well as the differentiation between boys and girls or male and female.

Gender and queer theorists, however, argue that sex and gender "are in fact socially constructed systems of classification" (Westbrook, 2016, p. 33). Lorber (1996) notes that gender is "an overarching category," "a major social status that organizes almost all areas of social life" (p. 146). Alternatively, sex is a biological or physiological category. While sex is socially understood to be "clear-cut" or natural, all individuals are "mixed bags" depending on "genes, genitalia, and hormonal input" (Lorber, 1996, p. 148). These definitions ultimately demonstrate that "'women' and 'men' are not equated with 'females' and 'males'" (Lorber, 1994, p. ix). Within social situations, however, individuals reinforce the sex/gender system through processes of categorization. They sort others into the "category of 'male' or 'female'" based on "visual information cues" (e.g., breasts and facial hair). Individuals are expected to abide by "implicit rules" that assign "characteristics to particular genders" (e.g., women are passive) (Westbrook & Schilt, 2014, p. 35). The disruption or transversal of categories can result in panic or even violence.

Comics such as "My Body, Myself" and "She Smiled Back" demonstrate lived experiences of gender variance and the indeterminacy of sexed bodies. The subjects explore and question the ways in which their sex and gender have been defined by society, pushing back against hegemonic norms. The authors Taylor and Sugaglia (2013) teach students that sex and gender are not always linked, but fluctuate depending on age, culture, personal preference, and a range of other factors. They fail to participate in the coercive sex/gender system, which often is reproduced in comprehensive and abstinence-only sex education programs. Not only is it possible for young people (particularly queer people) to see themselves included within *Not Your Mother's Meat-loaf,* but also their embodiments of sex and gender are validated and normalized in the text.

Diversity of Desire and Sexual Activity

Not Your Mother's Meatloaf represents various forms of sexual orientation, pleasure, and love. Comics include masturbation, queer sex, kink and sexual play, casual and committed relationships, healthy and violent partnerships, and other experiences. In the comic "Gray Sex," a queer subject confronts their ageist assumptions about sexual activity. While working in a geriatrics department,

the subject realizes how sexual interest and ability do not "decline with old age" (Defiler, 2013, p. 124). The subject's experience with elder patients exposes them to the ways in which elders are systematically denied the ability to act upon their sexual orientations and pleasures. While older persons are socially constructed as being asexual, the comic articulates a marginalized perspective.

The authors in *Not Your Mother's Meatloaf* do not shy away from complex or unintelligible experiences of desire and love. The untitled comic by Sylvie le Sylvie (2013) articulates the experience of an individual who regains their sex life after overcoming "damage" and "bad memories" (p. 162). A panel reads: "I took my sex back. My body. I claimed myself and remade my life . . . capable of giving myself to another, of finding joy in desire, pleasure in love, power in this body no one else owns" (le Sylvie, 2013, p. 162). In this comic alone, the subject demonstrates resilience in face of past sexual trauma or violence, self-love, bodily integrity, and trust in relationships. The subject's complicated mixture of emotions and desires would fall through the cracks of the educational materials provided by the abstinence-only and comprehensive programs.

In terms of desire and sexual activity, each comic's portrayals appear individualistic; however, taken together, they shatter compulsory heterosexuality. Rather than assuming that all readers are heterosexual, they demonstrate a range of perspectives. Readers have the opportunity to explore their own preferences or become exposed to alternative ones that often do not get taught in public schools.

Humanizing Sexual Knowledge

Although in the form of a comic book, *Not Your Mother's Meatloaf* provides useful information about sex education topics. While missing explicitly scientific knowledge, it presents sexual and health knowledge that is rooted in experience and sociocultural context. These topics include physical anatomy, gynecological examinations, relationship health, and the social stigma surrounding STIs.

In light of present social movements on college campuses, one important topic of discussion is sexual consent and violence. "Drunken Hookups" by Alex Barrett demonstrates how consent is socially constructed within hookup cultures. During a drunken hookup, the subject recalls how a partner had sex with her even though she was unresponsive and petrified. Although she "had trouble saying NO outright," she realizes that, "drunk or not," her sexual partner should have asked for consent (Barrett, 2013, p. 83). "Drunken Hookups" provides critical insight into hookup culture, which is prevalent across college campuses and high schools. Hookups are typically detached from emotional commitment, occur on a one-time basis, involve the consumption of alcohol, and encourage rigid sexual scripts. For these reasons, there can be an absence of consent or confusion over what constitutes consent, as in Barrett's story.

"Sex Talk" by Maisha highlights definitions regarding consent, including informed consent and a no-means-no philosophy. It specifically articulates how to talk about consent, metaphors for better understanding of consent, and the ways in which consent is sexy. "Sex Talk" allows reader to see consent within a social context and learn how to practice consent through Maisha's accessible dialogue and imaginative panels.

The various sex and health related topics in *Not Your Mother's Meatloaf* importantly humanize sexual knowledge. The text provides young people with a social context in which to understand sexual relationships, STIs, pregnancy, and other aspects of sex education curricula. *Not Your Mother's Meatloaf* supplements sanitized, scientific information with imaginative and experiential content that teaches young people about neglected or silenced areas of sex education.

Beyond *Not Your Mother's Meatloaf:* Antioppressive Sex Education

While *Not Your Mother's Meatloaf* represents a pedagogical tool, sex education ultimately requires a systematic transformation in the United States. In order to address the needs of young women, men, and other marginalized groups, an inclusive sex education framework must be woven throughout the curriculum. Many sexuality scholars argue for antioppressive sex education (Elia & Eliason, 2010; Kumashiro, 2001). Like *Not Your Mother's Meatloaf,* antioppressive sex education is interdisciplinary, social constructionist, and acknowledges

the fluidity of "human sexual desires, fantasies, thoughts, and behaviors" (Elia & Eliason, 2010, p. 40). Moreover, antioppressive sex education programs are transparent, student-centered, and social justice-oriented, specifically addressing the various forms of oppression that students may encounter (Elia & Eliason, 2010). Within educational institutions, antioppressive sex education challenges hidden agendas, heteronormative mandates, and other systematic barriers that privilege white, cis, straight, and able-bodied men.

Conclusion

The use of *Not Your Mother's Meatloaf* will likely be met with resistance. As Irving (2002) writes, "talk about sex in the public realm is consistently met with ambivalence and outright efforts to contain and silence it" (p. 4). Based on its imagery, content, and language, conservative camps can discursively transform the text into something that is dangerous or even pornographic. However, for educators, practitioners, parents, and young people, *Not Your Mother's Meatloaf* is an accessible, inclusive resource that confronts the systematic silencing of diverse sexual experiences. It deconstructs the sex/gender binary, incorporates various desires and orientations, and humanizes sexual knowledge, providing high school and college-aged students with essential content knowledge outside of traditional sex education programs. Without willingly resisting the norms surrounding sex education, young women, men, queer students, students of color, and other groups will continually be excluded and restricted from developing their sexual subjectivities.

Bibliography

Abdur-Rahman, A. I. (2012). *Against the closet: Black political longing and the erotics of race.* Durham, NC: Duke University Press.

Advocates For Youth. (2009). *Comprehensive sex education: Research and results* [Fact sheet]. Retrieved from http://www.advocatesforyouth.org/publications/1487.

Andersen, K. (2013, April 13). 'I never said that.' Pro-abstinence speaker accused of 'slut-shaming' speaks out (LSN exclusive). *LifeSite.* Retrieved from https://www.lifesitenews.com/news/i-never-said-that.-pro-abstinence-speaker-accused-ofslut-shaming-speaks-ou.

Andersen, M. L. & Taylor, H. F. (2008). *Sociology: Understanding a diverse society* (4th ed.). Belmont, CA: Thomson Learning Inc.

Baglieri, S., Bejoian, L. M., Broderick, A. A., Connor, D. J., & Valle, J. (2011). [Re]claiming 'inclusive education' toward cohesion in educational reform: Disability studies unravels the myth of the normal child. *Teachers College Record, 113*(10), 2122–2154. Retrieved from http://www.tcrecrod.org.

Barrett, A. (2013). Drunken hookups. In S. Miller & L. Bley (Eds.), *Not your mother's meatloaf: A sex education comic book* (pp. 81–83). Berkeley, CA: Soft Skull Press.

Boonstra, H. D. (2002). Teen pregnancy: Trends and lessons learned. *Guttmacher Policy Review, 5*(1), 7–10. Retrieved from https://www.guttmacher.org/sites/default/files/article_files/ gr050107.pdf.

Bowen v. Kendrick, 487 U.S. 589 (1988).

Cohen, C. (1997). Punks, bulldaggers, and welfare queens: The radical potential of queer politics. *GLQ: A Journal of Lesbian and Gay Studies, 3*(4), 437–465. doi: 10.1215/10642684-3-4-437.

Comic Nurse. (2013, August 28). Not your mother's meatloaf interview. Retrieved from http://www.graphicmedicine.org/not-your-mothers-meatloaf-interview/.

Comstock Act, 18 USCS §334 (1873).

Connell, C. & Elliott, S. (2009). Beyond the birds and the bees: Learning inequality through sexuality education. *American Journal of Sexuality Education, 4*(2), 83–102. doi: 10.1080/15546120903001332.

Defiler, M. (2013). Gray sex. In S. Miller & L. Bley (Eds.), *Not your mother's meatloaf: A sex education comic book* (pp. 123–125). Berkeley, CA: Soft Skull Press.

Dunne, L. (2009). Discourses of inclusion: A critique. *Power and Education, 1*(1), 42–56. doi: 10.2304/power.2009.1.1.42

Dyson, A. (2001) Special needs education as the way forward to equity: An alternative approach. *Support for Learning, 16*(3), 99–104. doi: 10.1111/1467-9604.00199.

Eisenstadt v. Baird, 405 U.S. 438 (1972).

Elias, J. P. & Eliason, M. (2010). Discourses of exclusion: Sexuality education's silencing of sexual others. *Journal of LGBT Youth, 7*(1), 29–48. doi:10.1080/19361650903507791.

Engel, A. (2007). Challenging the heteronormativity of tolerance pluralism. Articulations of nonnormative sexualities. *Redescriptions: Political Thought, Conceptual History and Feminist Theory, 11*(1), 78–98. Retrieved from http://www.jyu.fi/yhtfil/redescriptions/ Yearbook%202007/Engel_2007.pdf.

Erickson, L. (2013). Out of line: The sexy femmegimp politics of flaunting it! In M. Stombler, D. M. Baunach, W. Simonds, E. J. Windsor, & E. O. Burgess (Eds.), *Sex matters: The sexuality and society reader* (4th ed., pp. 135–140). New York, NY: W. W. Norton.

Farmer, J. (2013). Foreword. In S. Miller & L. Bley (Eds.), *Not your mother's meatloaf: A sex education comic book* (p. 7). Berkeley, CA: Soft Skull Press.

Fisher, C. M. (2009). Queer youth experiences with abstinence-only-until-marriage sexuality education: "I can't get married so where does that leave me?" *Journal of LGBT Youth, 6*(1), 61–79. doi: 10.1080/19361650802396775.

Fine, M. (1988). Sexuality, schooling, and adolescent females: The missing discourse of desire. *Harvard Educational Review, 55*(1), 29–51. doi: 10.17763/haer.58.1.u0468k1v2n2n8242.

Fine, M. & McClelland, S. I. (2006). Sexuality education and desire: Still missing after all these years. *Harvard Educational Review, 76*(3), 297–338. doi: 10.1177/0959-353505049702.

Future of Sex Education Initiative. (2012). *National sexuality education standards: Core content and skills, K-12* [a special publication of the *Journal of School Health*]. Retrieved from http://www.futureofsexeducation.org/documents/josh-fose-standards-web.pdf.

Garcia, L. (2009). "Now why do you want to know about that?": Heteronormativity, sexism, and racism in the sexual (mis)education of Latina youth. *Gender & Society, 23*(4), 520–541. doi: 10.1177/0891243209339498.

Gerschick, T.J. (2011). The body, disability, and sexuality. In S. Seidman, N. Fischer, & C. Meeks (Eds.), *Introducing the new sexuality studies* (2nd ed., pp. 75–83). New York, NY: Routledge.

Gilbert, J. (2010). Ambivalence only? Sex education in the age of abstinence. *Sex Education, 10*(3), 233–237. doi: 10.1080/14681811.2010.491631.

Griswold v. Connecticut, 381 U.S. 479 (1965).

Guttmacher Institute. (2016). *State policies in brief: Sex and HIV education* [Fact sheet]. Retrieved from https://www.guttmacher.org/sites/default/files/article_files/gr050107.pdf.

Hale, C. J. (1998). Consuming the living, dis(re)membering the dead in the butch/FTM borderlands. *GLQ:*

A Journal of Lesbian and Gay Studies, 4(2), 311–448. doi: 10.1215/10642684-4-2-311.

Hobson, J. (2003). The 'batty' politic: Toward an aesthetic of the Black female body. *Hypatia, 15*(4), 87–105. doi:10.1111/j.1527-2001.2003.tb01414.x.

Irvine, J. M. (2004). *Talk about sex: The battles over sex education in the United States.* Berkeley, CA: University of California Press.

Jozkowski, K. N. & Peterson, Z. D. (2013). College students and sexual consent: Unique insights. *The Journal of Sex Research, 50*(6), 517–523. doi: 10.1080/00224499.2012.700739.

Kantor, L. M., Santelli, J. S., Teitler, J., & Balmer, R. (2008). Abstinence-only policies and programs: An overview. *Sexuality Research and Social Policy: Journal of NSRC, 5*(3), 6–17. doi: 10.1525/srsp.2008.5.3.6.

Kirby, D. (2007). *Emerging answers 2007: Research findings on programs to reduce teen pregnancy and sexually transmitted diseases.* Washington, DC: National Campaign to Prevent Teen and Unplanned Pregnancy.

Kirkus Reviews. (2013, July 15). Not your mother's meatloaf: A sex education comic book. [Review of the book *Not your mother's meatloaf: A sex education comic book* by S. Miller & L. Bley] *Kirkus Review, 57*(14). Retrieved from https://www.kirkusreviews.com/book-reviews/saiya-miller/not-your-mothers-meatloaf/.

Kumashiro, K. K. (2001). Queer students of color and antiracist, antiheterosexist education: Paradoxes of identity and activism. In K. K. Kumashiro (Ed.), *Troubling intersections of race and sexuality* (pp. 1–26). New York: Rowman & Littlefield.

le Sylvie, S. (2013). Untitled. In S. Miller & L. Bley (Eds.), *Not your mother's meatloaf: A sex education comic book* (pp. 162–163). Berkeley, CA: Soft Skull Press.

Lorber, J. (1994). *Paradoxes of gender.* New Haven, CT: Yale University Press.

Lorber, J. (1996). Beyond the Binaries: Depolarizing the categories of sex, sexuality, and gender. *Sociological Inquiry, 66*(2), 143–160. doi: 10.1111/j.1475-682X.1996.tb00214.x.

Maisha. (2013). Sex talk. In S. Miller & L. Bley (Eds.), *Not your mother's meatloaf: A sex education comic book* (pp. 73–75). Berkeley, CA: Soft Skull Press.

Miller, S. & Bley, L. (2013). *Not your mother's meatloaf: A sex education comic book.* Berkeley, CA: Soft Skull Press.

Nakkula, M. J. & Toshalis, E. (2010). *Understanding youth: Adolescent development for educators.* Cambridge, MA: Harvard Education Press.

People v. Sanger, 222 N.Y. 192 (1918).

Personal Responsibility and Work Opportunity Reconciliation Act of 1996, Pub. L. No. 104–193, §912, 110 Stat. 2353–2354 (1997).

Regales, J. (2008). My identity is fluid as fuck: Transgender zine writers constructing themselves. In S. Driver (Ed.), *Queer youth cultures* (pp. 87–104). Albany, NY: State University of New York Press.

Rich, A. (1980). Compulsory heterosexuality and lesbian existence. *Signs, 5*(4), 631–660. Retrieved from http://www.jstor.org.

Rubin, G. (1997). Traffic in women. In L. Nicholson (Ed.), *The second wave: A reader in feminist theory* (pp. 27–62). New York, NY: Routledge.

Saul, R. (1998). Whatever happened to the Adolescent Family Life Act? *Guttmacher Policy Review, 7*(2). Retrieved from https://www.guttmacher.org/about/gpr/1998/04/whatever-happened-adolescent-family-life-act.

Sexuality Information and Education Council of the United States. (2009). *What the research says...Comprehensive sex education* [Fact sheet]. Retrieved from http://www.siecus.org/ index.cfm?fuseaction=Page.ViewPage&PageID=1193#_edn1.

Shaley, S. (Producer), & Earp, J. (Director). (2011). The *purity myth: The virginity movement's war against women* [Documentary]. United States: Media Education Foundation.

Sinagulia, T. (2013). She smiled back. In S. Miller & L. Bley (Eds.), *Not your mother's meatloaf: A sex education comic book* (pp. 28–35). Berkeley, CA: Soft Skull Press.

Stossel, S. (1997, July–August). The sexual counterrevolution. *The American Prospect.* Retrieved from http://prospect.org/article/sexual-counterrevolution.

Taylor, S. (2013). My body, myself. In S. Miller & L. Bley (Eds.), *Not your mother's meatloaf: A sex education comic book* (pp. 47–48). Berkeley, CA: Soft Skull Press.

The Foundation of AIDS Research. (2016). *Statistics: United States* [Fact sheet]. Retrieved from http://www.amfar.org/About-HIV-and-AIDS/Facts-and-Stats/Statistics--United-States.

Westbrook, L. (2016). Transforming the sex/gender/sexuality system: The construction of trans categories in the United States. In N. L. Fischer & S.

Seidman (Eds.), *Introducing the new sexuality studies* (3rd ed.). New York, NY: Routledge. Retrieved from https://books.google.com.

Westbrook, L. & Schilt, K. (2014). Doing gender, determining gender: Transgender people, gender panics, and the maintenance of the sex/gender/sexuality system. *Gender & Society, 25*(1), 32–57. doi:10.1177/0891243213503203.

Wiederman, M. W. (2005). The gendered nature of sexual scripts. *The Family Journal: Counseling and Therapy for Couples and Families, 73*(4), 496–502. doi:10.1177/1066480705278729.

Wiederman, M.W. (2015). Sexual script theory: Past, present, and future. In J. DeLamater & R. F. Plante (Eds.), *Handbook of the sociology of sexualities* (pp. 7–22). Switzerland: Spring International Publishing.

The Use and Misuse of Pleasure in Sex Education Curricula

by Sharon Lamb, Kara Lustig and
Kelly Graling

Since Michelle Fine's writing on the missing discourse of desire in sex education, there has been considerable prompting among sexuality educators and feminist scholars to incorporate talk of pleasure into sex education curricula. While the calls for inclusion continue, few have actually examined the curricula for a pleasure discourse or explored how it is contextualised within sex education curricula. In this paper, we analysed curricula used in the USA in the past decade. A qualitative thematic analysis revealed that the discourse around pleasurable sex was often linked to a range of dangerous or negative outcomes including not using condoms, rushing into sex without thinking, regretted sex, and pregnancy or STDs. When the discourse around pleasure was included in sections on 'knowing one's body', this discourse took a medicalised, scientific tone. Pleasurable sex was also presented in more positive ways, either linked to marriage in Abstinence Only Until Marriage curricula, or

within a more feminist discourse about female pleasure in comprehensive sex education curricula. Our research indicates that a discourse of desire is not missing, but that this discourse was often situated as part of a discourse on safe practice and there, continues to equate pleasure with danger.

There has been a tremendous response to Fine's (1988) article pointing to the missing discourse of desire in sex education. In the article, Fine connected desire to female sexual subjectivity and argued that sex education's tendency to emphasise female sexual victimisation results in the suppression of a discourse about female desire and pleasure. More recently, researchers note that while pleasure is now a part of the conversation about female adolescent sexuality and is commodified in popular culture, little change has occurred within sex education since the article was published (Fine and McClelland 2006), in part due to the dominant presence of Abstinence Only Until Marriage

(AOUM) curricula in the USA. Although AOUM curricula was the primary type of sex education funded in the USA over the past two decades, Comprehensive and Evidence-Based curricula were taught in schools in states that turned down funding and by religious and community organisations. Unfortunately, little research has examined whether a discourse of pleasure now exists and if it does, when and where this discourse is contextualised within sex education curricula. The current study examines a variety of these curricula for discourses about pleasure and attempts to understand how authors use pleasure to persuade and educate in these teaching texts.

The call for the inclusion of pleasure into sex education has continued since Fine's article (Allen 2004; APA 2007; Bay-Cheng 2003; Fine and McClelland 2006; Lamb 1997; Thompson 1990; Tolman 2002) and has extended to a discussion that includes both boys and girls. Rasmussen (2004) writes that, 'Sex and pleasure are fundamental aspects of students' lives and school cultures . . . integral to students' sense of well-being' (446). Nevertheless, researchers have noted that school-based curricula are saturated with fear-based, rather than pleasure-based or other sex-positive messages (Bay-Cheng 2003), and continue to be replete with sexual stereotypes (Lamb, Graling, and Lustig 2011). Recent critiques of both abstinence and comprehensive sex education (CSE) demonstrate that these curricula continue to focus on the danger of sex instead of pleasure for both boys and girls (Fields 2008; Kendall 2008; Lamb, Graling, and Lustig 2011). When sex educators teach to address this danger (e.g. by teaching refusal skills), sexual desire and entitlement, for girls especially, become associated with being 'bad' or 'slutty' (Tannenbaum 2000) and negatively affect the development of female sexual subjectivity. This is particularly problematic for Black, low-income girls, for whom exploring or expressing desire makes them further vulnerable to the stereotype of being a 'ho' (Froyum 2009; Lamb 2010b). In practice, more open discussions may take place that address such stereotypes, as curricula often provide discussion questions that do (as Fine 1988 showed), but the focus of lessons limits peer classroom discussion to topics related to the dangers of sex.

The discourse of pleasure in sex curricula is not always absent. In her research on New Zealand curricula, Allen (2007a) noted that pleasure is discussed: however, only within a focus on danger prevention. Kiely (2005) argues that in Irish Sexuality and Relationships curricula, the narrowing of sex to mean one act, coitus, means that other pleasurable, and even safer acts are not considered. In these curricula, information about masturbation, sexual positions, fantasy, non-genital activities, and oral–genital contact are not mentioned, suggesting that these behaviours are preliminary to the 'real thing' (Kiely 2005, 259).

Students and teachers have voiced reactions to the missing discourse of pleasure in sex education. Although students have been critical when pleasure is missing in the curricula (Measor, Tiffin, and Miller 2000), they also express worries that sex is something too personal to teach and should happen naturally (Allen 2007a, 2007b). Teachers also express worry about *how* pleasure can be incorporated into sex education and difficulty talking about pleasure outside of the stereotypes of heterosexual relationships (Harrison, Hillier, and Walsh 1996). In one study, when pleasure was used in a way to bolster talk about safety, teachers expressed feeling more comfortable (Harrison, Hillier, and Walsh 1996).

The inclusion of pleasure in sex education curricula could improve education for both girls and boys. Teaching an 'ethics of pleasure' (Allen 2007a, 2007b; Carmody 2005; Lamb 2010a; Rasmussen 2004) could open up 'new possibilities for understanding sexual subjects' (Allen 2007a, 583–4), including non-heterosexual identities. Consideration of non-heterosexual sexual activity is typically absent from sex education curricula (Fine and McClelland 2006). Teaching lesbian, gay, bisexual, and transgender (LGBT) sexuality from a positive and pleasure-oriented perspective in the classroom has almost been 'unthinkable' (Mayo 2011, 70). Rasmussen (2004) argues that sex education should include teaching about pleasure for pleasure's sake and not be used in an attempt to fight 'homophobia, misogyny, or patriarchy' (455). But teaching about pleasure inclusive of LGBT-identified young people can provide a counter-narrative to the 'it gets better' project (www.itgetsbetter.org) and 'wounded identity' discourse (Rasmussen 2004), a discourse that positions all LGBT youth as always harmed by homophobia. Without specific reference to LGBT pleasures, talk about pleasure can re-inscribe harmful stereotypes.

In this paper, we examine discourses of desire and pleasure with consideration of past critiques of sex education, including the framing of discussions of sexual desire in lessons on danger, focus on coitus, and exclusion of LGBT sexuality. We do this in the context of recent school-based sex education in the USA where the federal government has provided more than $1 billion for abstinence-only programming since 1996 (Kendall 2008; Santelli et al. 2006). While President Barack Obama and congressional leaders have called for an end of funding for programmes that do not have evidence to support their effectiveness and have recommended increasing funding to states for teenage pregnancy prevention programmes (Guttmacher Institute 2009), in 2010 the US Congress elected to maintain $50 million of funding for states that wanted to continue to use AOUM curricula. The new focus on evidence-based and health-oriented sex education may mean that goals such as the development of sexual agency and entitlement are again pushed to the side (Lamb 2011, 2012). Although sexual health and sexual pleasure are connected (Tolman 2002), it is unlikely that, given the current political climate, a fully comprehensive sexuality curriculum that addresses pleasure will emerge for use in schools.

The current study examined curricula from the last decade to explore how talk of pleasure was integrated into curricula and in what context it arose. We decided to examine three types of curricula: AOUM curricula, curricula that were written by those who advocate comprehensive or evidence-based sex education (including those comprehensive curricula revised to fit into an abstinence-plus framework—abstinence plus comprehensive information about birth control), and a comprehensive curriculum that is taught outside of the schools but that is considered by liberal sex education advocates to be the gold standard of comprehensive curricula (Estrella 2012). Choosing a range of curricula that represented various political agendas enabled us to see how discourses around pleasure are put to different uses.

Discourse always functions to assert some ideologies over others and our title, the use and misuse of pleasure, is meant to invite reflection over ways in which pleasure might be included in curricula to support more ethical sexual practices in addition to student health and well-being. This paper does not lay out a framework by which pleasure can be put to better use, as previous theoretical writings address this issue (Allen and Carmody 2012; Carmody 2005; Lamb 1997, 2010a; Lamb and Peterson 2011).

The discourse approach stems from Foucault's (1979) writings regarding sexuality as a social construction that is discursively constituted through 'a plethora of social institutions whose meanings are historically and culturally located' (Allen 2007b, 249). If individuals' sexualities are forged through such discourses, then an examination of the pleasure discourse within sex education curricula can inform with regard to what kinds of pleasures are permitted, when, where, and how.

Methods

This research arose as part of a broader study of ethical issues in current sex education curricula for young people in which an array of curricula were analysed. For the current paper, we selected primarily school-based curricula from both AOUM and CSE sources. We reviewed only those curricula that are in wide use today in the USA, were published in the last decade, and were used to teach sex education to adolescents in middle school and high school. Despite substantial efforts, we were unable to obtain accurate statistics about the frequency with which any curriculum is used. The determination of 'popular' curricula was made by looking at the Abstinence Clearinghouse website, talking to leaders in the field at two sex education conferences (individuals in leadership positions of two national organisations), and noting which curricula have been included in previous evaluations of curricula (Administration for Children and Families and the Department for HHS 2007; Committee on Government Reform 2004; Kirby 2007; LeCroy and Milligan Associates 2003; Trenholm et al. 2007). Informed by this information, we created a sample of convenience. This sample included four AOUM curricula, six CSE curricula, and one nonschool-based CSE curriculum (see Table 1). AOUM curricula were self-classified in their titles and by their primary focus on encouraging abstinence from sexual intercourse versus how to engage in sexual intercourse safely. Two of these curricula have new versions that came out recently, but to ensure that we were comparing a similar sample of curricula, we chose to analyse the older versions of these curricula that were written under the same administration's legislation when AOUM curricula were fully supported. We also analysed six CSE curricula, four of which were included in lists of evidence-based, effective curricula (Kirby 2007). The fifth, *Making Sense of Abstinence*, is a group of lessons written by a CSE advocate to conform to AOUM expectations (Taverner and Montfort 2005). We included a sixth truly CSE curriculum, *Our Whole Lives* (OWL 2000), which was written for delivery in Unitarian churches, because OWL has not been edited to conform to legislation around sex education as it is not school-based. We included it with the expectation that it would provide us with examples of what *can* be said about pleasure in sexuality when not confined by legislation and school restrictions. CSE curricula were classified by a central focus on how a student who chooses to engage in sexual intercourse can do so safely.

To analyse sex education curricula, we used a thematic analysis methodology described by Braun and Clarke (2006) conducive to the exploration of discourse. Although we concentrate on themes, our analysis follows discursive psychology's practice of examining language with regard to how it works to construct subjects, in this case sexual subjects, and knowledge, in this case sexual knowledge (Potter and Wetherell 1994; Willig 2008). Following the authors' general guidelines, two to three members of the research team independently read through curricula and identified on note cards salient quotations and comments that were relevant to the theme of pleasure. The team then met and sorted the cards into categories representing overarching themes. One person sorted the quotations. Then the second and third members of this research team re-sorted the first person's categories until all three coders agreed that a quotation or topic fit under a particular category. Quotes were permitted to lie under different themes. Initial

reliability statistics were not attempted as the process was collaborative and first codings were not meant to form lasting categories. Temporary theme titles were assigned to each group.

Members next defined and developed each theme (Braun and Clarke 2006). At the end of this process, we narrowed the categories down to three broad themes with sub-themes. After identifying themes, we used quotes to develop a description of themes and then proceeded to analyse the theme and any problems that might arise in shaping the pleasure discourse for students. The three authors also worked with other research group members, who were consulted on quotes that were difficult to place.

Findings

Pleasure discourse fell into three themes with sub-themes: health and knowing your body; problematic pleasure; and positive pleasure. Themes and sub-themes are identified below.

Health and knowing your body

There is a long history of US sex education including information about body parts, reproduction, and the mechanics of sex. In the past, this information has narrowly represented heterosexual sexual intercourse (Moran 2000). We found that there were still lessons that presented this information and that some of these lessons referenced pleasure and arousal (MSA, PI, SWSW, and OWL).

How the body works: knowing oneself versus pleasing another

Pleasure was sometimes included in larger discussions of physical health and knowledge of the body. In some of these discussions it was presented in a scientific, expert tone that differed from the tone of many of the other chapters, which took on a more casual or conversational tone. This discourse described arousal in a way that suggested that by providing such information, students would better understand how their bodies work.

For example, in PI's sections on negotiating sexual relationships, the authors refer to sexual arousal with slang expressions such as 'feeling very horny' or 'getting very "hot"' (Brick and Taverner 2001, 19). However, when presenting

Table 1. Name, abbreviation, and type of curricula utilised.

Curriculum	Abbreviation	Type	Age group	Citation
WAIT training (Why am I so tempted)	WAIT	AOUM	Middle and high school	Krauth (2003)
Aspire	Aspire	AOUM	High school	Phelps (2006)
Choosing the best journey	Journey	AOUM	9th and 10th	Cook (2006)
Game plan	GP	AOUM	7th grade	Green (2007)
Becoming a responsible teen	BART	CSE	High school	St. Lawrence (2005)
Be proud! Be responsible! Strategies to empower youth to reduce their risk for HIV/AIDS	BPBR	CSE	High school	Jemmott, Jemmott, and McCaffree (2004)
Positive images: Teaching about abstinence, contraception, and sexual health	PI	CSE	High school	Brick and Taverner (2001)
Reducing the risk: Building skills to prevent pregnancy, STDs and HIV	RR	CSE	9th and 10th	Barth (2004)
Streetwise to sexwise: Sexuality education for high-risk youth	SWSW	CSE	High school	Brown and Taverner (2001)
Making sense of abstinence: Lessons for comprehensive sex education	MSA	CSE	High school	Taverner and Montfort (2005)
Our whole lives	OWL	CSE	10th–12th	Goldfarb and Casparian (2000)

pleasure information in lessons on knowing one's body, the authors use a more neutral, expert, and regulating tone, common to the discursive shift from a values emphasis to a science emphasis in sex education (Carlson 2011). For example, PI uses the following language to describe sexual excitement for girls: 'hav[ing] wetness in the vaginal area when sexually aroused' (Brick and Taverner 2012, 142). By presenting the biological bases of arousal and pleasure separately from other chapters and using language and tone that is more medical and expert, the authors take pleasure out of the realm of the emotional and relational experience of sex. While this may imply that pleasure ought to be domesticated through integration into discussions of relationship, we merely mean to point out that most pleasure occurs in relation to another person whether in actuality or in fantasy, and to take it out of a relational context may support a more self-focused, neoliberal project

of self-management (Rose 1996). This language also suggests to students that pleasure is achieved through focus on their own sexual responses rather than the sexual responsiveness and arousal of others, which has been discussed as a problem in sex education (Lamb 2010a, 2011).

While discussion of arousal in medicalised language may have drawbacks, it may also have benefits. Specifically, normalising discourse about pleasure may undermine feelings of shame. MSA, SWSW, and PI provide information that normalises arousal. After including a description of puberty changes (e.g. wet dreams, vaginal lubrication, etc.), SWSW's authors add that students may also 'desire to masturbate more' (Brown and Taverner 2001, 197), thus normalising masturbation. In the past, the discourse of science and medicine has problematically been used to control and discipline those who do not fall under the narrow version of 'normal' and so such a discourse should be critiqued. However, in these curricula, it may be a strategy for those CSE authors who would like to more freely teach about pleasure to insert information about pleasure in an acceptable format. It is also possible, however, that this 'expert normalisation' creates more problems than it solves by creating hegemonic norms that might alienate individuals experiencing different forms of pleasure and arousal, or who may even be asexual or pre-sexual. Sexual experiences, such as masturbation or the sexual arousal response, are not universal and often vary (Tiefer 2004).

Despite past research pointing to heterosexism in the way sexual education presents sex, this was not apparent in the manner in which CSE curricula presented biological information on desire and arousal. In fact, in almost all cases there was no sexual partner within these discussions, which made the sexual response or behaviour being described more applicable to a variety of relationships. The one exception to this is when SWSW describes the vagina as the 'place that holds the penis during sexual intercourse'.

Although the presentation of this information in these curricula was largely not heterosexist in its language, there was one interesting omission that may be related to homophobia. In the curricula's discussion of pleasure and desire in the body, none discuss the anus or perineum as a potential source of pleasure. This omission is particularly noticeable when these curricula discuss the other points of pleasure in the body (clitoris, penis, vagina, G-spot, and skin). While several of these curricula include the anus on a diagram (SWSW), include anal intercourse in their lessons on sexual decision-making (OWL), or mention anal intercourse in passing (MSA), curricula do not explore these regions of the body as pleasure areas. This omission could be related to the stigma against gay men and anal sex among heterosexuals.

Making healthy sexual choices

Talk about pleasure also occurred in the context of making healthy choices and was used as a way to increase the attractiveness of safe sexual behaviours. For example, in BPBR, the authors write that, 'some people focus on how to make sex feel really good and be fun for both people. They also need to think about being safe. . . . Openly communicating needs and concerns can increase

enjoyment of the experience' (Jemmott, Jemmott, and McCaffree 2004, 127). Readers should note that pleasure is fully acknowledged and integrated with a message that also speaks to safety.

Condom use is also an area in which both pleasure and safety are integrated. BART's authors attack the idea that condoms decrease pleasure with the response from one student to another in a vignette, 'It will feel good to know we're keeping each other safe' (St. Lawrence 2005, 174). In this way, the pleasure of sex is matched with the pleasure of taking care of the other person. PI asks, 'which part in the process feels the same whether or not a condom is used?' (Brick and Taverner 2001, 103), in order, it would seem, to show that there is still sexual pleasure to be experienced with a condom even if, during intercourse, it may be lessened. SWSW even makes a suggestion to further increase the pleasure of safe sex, 'A bit of lubricant inside the condom gives many guys more feeling during intercourse' (Brown and Taverner 2001, 79).

Several curricula also focus on non-coital pleasure as a way to keep sex safe. For example, SWSW suggests that there are 'things that two people could do with each other if they want to be sexual' but not have intercourse, and asks students if these activities 'feel good' (2001, 219). OWL (Goldfarb and Casparian 2000, 91–2) asks students to think up a safe sex fantasy: 'sexually exciting and fulfilling behaviors that do not involve penetration'. These curricula may be countering the common cultural assumption that intercourse, especially unprotected intercourse, feels the best. This assumption is not presented directly as a myth or a cultural belief, but is addressed indirectly through the promotion of other practices, including what some call 'outercourse' (MSA; Taverner and Montfort 2005, 61).

AOUM curricula reviewed in this study did not include pleasure information from a 'know your body' or 'safe practices' perspective. The restriction regarding teaching about contraception derives from the belief that teaching about a subject leads to experimentation with that subject. When contraception is mentioned in AOUM curricula, as in the case of *Journey*, it is with the purpose of reinforcing the message that only abstinence is 100% effective against pregnancy and STIs. Discussion of arousal and pleasure may also be seen by these authors as too evocative.

Problematic pleasure

Talk of pleasure was also included in discussions of risk, self-control, regrettable sex, and peer pressure. However, in this context, pleasure is not typically discussed in a way that is meant to enhance self-knowledge, fun, getting to know someone else, or developing sexual subjectivity. Instead, pleasure is presented as a problem in that it is an obstacle to restraint, abstinence, and health.

Pleasure makes it hard to control oneself

In our analyses of AOUM curricula, we found that several AOUM curricula present sexual pleasure as an impediment to self-control. However, when AOUM curricula teach that any sexual activity is dangerous because, once started, a student might not be able to stop, they imply that sex feels good. Several of these curricula use metaphors for desire that tie pleasure to uncontrollability. *Journey* includes a lesson about 'chemistry' and 'attraction' and compares them to lighting a match. When one lights a match, the fire is not contained and it can burn out quickly or burn down the house. But when one lights a log in a fireplace (meant to symbolise marriage or commitment), the fire burns over time and in a 'safe space' (Cook 2006, 37).

This message of desire being uncontrollable was also found in a CSE curriculum. RR presents students with a list of pleasurable activities and asks them to say whether the activities, including massages, fantasising, masturbation, mutual masturbation, and oral sex, are risky or not. In 'red alert' situations (Barth 2004, 161), pleasure is identified as a red alert sign, thus only presented in relation to danger. The uncontrollability of sex is not questioned or explored as an aspect that might make sex enjoyable. Moreover, in some sense the argument that sex is overwhelming and uncontrollable implies a biological, even animal model of sex, which is problematic. Choice is available as an option to students, but only at a certain point in the progression towards sexual intercourse, after which point choice is more difficult or even impossible. In this discourse, having a choice and being able to make a choice is the

focus supporting, once again, a discourse of self-management of the neoliberal subject (Bay-Cheng 2012; Lamb 2012).

Pleasure in relation to STDs and pregnancy

Several of the curricula, both CSE and AOUM, implicitly and explicitly link pleasure and desire to the negative consequences of STDs and pregnancy. For example, in RR, instructors are told to ask the students to identify some of the consequences of having sex: 'Students may include some positive outcomes (e.g. it's fun or it makes us feel close) and these should be acknowledged as reasons that millions of teenagers risk getting pregnant, or infected with HIV and other STD each year' (Barth 2004, 40). The immediate and dizzying jump from fun and intimacy to infection is reminiscent of AOUM curricula, although RR is not identified with that ideology. In MSA, students are given five scenarios in which someone is aroused but needs to make the decision to remain abstinent from sexual intercourse. As with the discourse on sexual arousal inevitably leading to intercourse because it is hard to control, here arousal is presented as leading to disease or pregnancy. While it is true that these are serious risks that are attached with intercourse, the linking of pleasure to these risks raises questions with regard to authors' intended message to students about pleasure.

Pleasure and regret

AOUM curricula also make the case that there are emotional risks linked to pleasure. In several AOUM curricula, desire or pleasure was linked with regret. For example, one vignette presents a couple who had decided to wait to have sex, and, in the 'heat of the moment, they ended up having sex' and then regretted it and broke up (*Journey*; Cook 2006, 54). Other curricula do not explicitly mention the pleasure in the 'heat of the moment', but still introduce the idea of regret. For example, in GP (Green 2007, 45), students are warned, 'many are surprised at the shame and guilt they may experience after engaging in intimate sexual behaviour. They may also feel that they were being used in a relationship for sexual gratification alone'.

Pleasure and pressure

Another very common use of desire and pleasure appeared when curricula presented examples or vignettes of one person pressuring another to have sexual intercourse. This occurred in both CSE and AOUM curricula, although less so in AOUM curricula. In many of these instances, examples were used to help students prepare to deal with these situations. For example in one vignette, a male says to a female, 'we can take things slow I promise. But I think you might change your mind . . . you don't know how good it could be' (*Journey*; Cook 2006, 62). Another example from BART demonstrates one young person pressuring another to have sex by saying, 'come on, baby, I'm going to make your earth move' (St. Lawrence 2005, 217). In this manner, pleasure is again presented as uncontrollable and linked to potentially regrettable or unwanted sex.

Positive pleasure

In addition to discussions about the negative consequences of having sex, we also looked for discourse that acknowledges pleasure in a positive way. We found many positive references to the pleasure of sex, surprisingly in both AOUM and CSE curricula, as well as in OWL. True to their aims, the AOUM curricula emphasised how pleasurable sex can be in marriage. Other curricula emphasised the pleasure of sex in reference to mutuality or female sexuality.

Pleasure in marriage

The aim of many AOUM curricula is to encourage students to wait until they are married to have any form of sex, especially sexual intercourse. One of the promises made to students is that if they wait, they will less likely encounter the negative consequences from sexual activity. But these curricula also advertise better (presumably more pleasurable) sex when a student waits: 'A study done by the University of Chicago shows that married people are having the best and the most sex' (WAIT; Krauth 2003, 58). These curricula also emphasise the role of fidelity and trust in creating more pleasurable sex. GP relates that, 'couples who are faithfully married report better satisfaction with their sex lives than couples who aren't

married' because 'their trust, love, and respect for each other make their physical relationship more enjoyable' (Green 2007, 60). Thus, positive pleasure is mentioned in some AOUM curricula, but only in the context of marriage.

Pleasure together/mutual pleasure

We found that OWL and one CSE curriculum also talked about pleasure within the context of relationships, although not specifically marriage. In SWSW the authors write, 'Sexually healthy people feel positive about sexuality, like their own bodies, can talk openly about sexuality, and see sex as mutual, loving, pleasurable, fun and safe for both partners' (Brown and Taverner 2001, 26). On the very first page of OWL, the authors write that people, 'engage in healthy sexual behavior for a variety of reasons, including to express caring and love, to experience intimacy and connection with another, to share pleasure, to bring new life into the world, and to experience fun and relaxation'. Contextualising pleasure within relationships may be a way in which pleasure was 'tamed' in an era where safety is the primary purpose of sex education. Surprisingly, this was not a tack taken by the majority of CSE curricula which included very few messages about mutual pleasure. There was also very little discussion in CSE curricula that counteracted the 'regret' discourse and pointed out the positive benefits to a relationship once a couple has sex. This may have been a taboo topic in the era of AOUM sex education.

Female pleasure/female pain

Several curricula made special attempts to discuss both female pleasure *and* sexual abuse and victimisation. This may have been an attempt to address some of the concerns expressed over the past two decades with regard to sex education and the lack of a discourse around female pleasure and subjectivity (Fine 1988). Many CSE curricula included information about the female body and female arousal. BPBR gave explicit information with regard to how many women receive pleasure:

> Most women need to have their clitoris (the arousal organ in their vulvas) touched, directly or indirectly in order to have an orgasm . . . sexual intercourse is not the only

way for couples to express feelings, to feel good, or to have fun . . . Using a condom can become part of the touching and stroking that happens prior to intercourse . . . The lubrication will make it more comfortable for her and more slippery and exciting for him. . . . (Jemmott, Jemmott, and McCaffree 2004, 128)

Note that the message of condom use and safety (although combining talk of pleasure with talk of risk) emphasises both male and female pleasure. SWSW authors also discuss 'false scripts', which include beliefs that are deterrents to female pleasure. False scripts include: 'Orgasm is the primary goal of sexual intercourse'; 'Intimacy or a feeling of relationship with a partner is less important'; and 'A sexual encounter is over once the male has had his orgasm' (Brown and Taverner 2001, 12). OWL also explicitly includes information that tells male students to think of one's partner after orgasm. Teachers are told to, 'tell the group that once the condom is removed, the man may relax with and hold his partner, or continue to pleasure his partner without further penetration with the penis' (Goldfarb and Casparian 2000, 87). Although the authors do not specify the gender of the partner, the mention of the man as the main actor suggests it is an antidote to the stereotype of men forgetting about their female partners.

Another way that curricula now seem to address female concerns is by including information about victimisation. Sometimes information about victimisation contains information about pleasure and sex in that pleasure is introduced as an impetus for date rape in several vignettes. In SWSW, Larry gets turned on and tries to go further with Diane and she pushes his hand away and says no. He later insists, 'I'm so turned on let's do it' (Brown and Taverner 2001, 140). These vignettes possibly suggest the problematic idea that pleasure is no indication that someone is safe and that pleasure is linked to female exploitation. The man is pictured as overwhelmed by his own arousal, whereas a different presentation of this scene might have presented him as predatory or very much in control with regard to wanting to have sex independent of the girl's consent.

The message that sex should be pleasurable may be important to combat victimisation. Some

feminist theorists purport that young women's experiences of desire increase their ability to assert themselves against coercive or unwanted sex (Fine 1988; Tolman 2002). Today pleasure is synonymous with sexual subjectivity and agency (Gill 2008) and research shows that sexually agentic women are more able to assert their needs and say no (Impett, Schooler, and Tolman 2006). However, it is unclear how messages about pleasure convey information to boys about assertiveness and violence. Curricula do not say enough about how and why pleasurable sexual experiences are sometimes linked with exploitation and what boys can do about it.

Conclusion

Pleasure is not merely a biological experience; it is defined, controlled, and evoked through context. In this paper, we were interested in examining desire and pleasure as they were represented in sex education curricula in the USA during a historical period during which the mention of pleasure most likely needed to be circumscribed, whereas sex is over-represented in the media young people use. This perspective led us to ask several questions: is pleasure included in curricula at all? If it is, in what context and to what use?

Overall, we found that pleasure is no longer ignored and this was true for both AOUM and CSE sex curricula, and that the discourse around pleasure had various functions. Pleasure and desire were included in medicalised, expert CSE discussions about the body. Many curricula were heterosexist and failed to discuss anal or non-heterosexual pleasures. In many of the curricula, discourses of desire and pleasure are linked with messages about danger and risk, including desire being uncontrollable, desire carrying emotional and health risks, desire used in peer pressure, and desire in relation to victimisation. Positive references to pleasure and desire took place in the context of discussions about the pleasures of safe sex, marital sex, mutual relationships, and being female.

One might argue that students do not need to know that sex is pleasurable, that they will find that out soon enough, or that messages of pleasure are infused within popular media already. However, as noted in the introduction, research suggests that the manner in which girls are socialised interferes with the development of sexual subjectivity (Tolman 2000, 2002; Tolman et al. 2006), that students themselves want to know what feels good (Allen 2007b), and that lack of discussion about the pleasure of sex makes curricula seem to students less relevant (Allen 2007b). Moreover, representations of sexuality in popular media more often than not tend to be heterosexist, sexist, and derivations from pornography (Dines 2010).

The discourse of desire is no longer missing, but is often situated as part of a discourse on safe practice and thus equates pleasure with danger. In a climate where AOUM curricula were federally funded and the authors of CSE curricula were attempting to show CSE's effectiveness in preventing pregnancy and STD reduction, it is no surprise that pleasure and risk were deeply connected. While the acknowledgement of the 'fun', 'good feelings', and pleasure of sex goes far to undermine the link between shame and sex that has been present in a number of eras of sex education (see Carlson 2011), this emphasis on prevention practice largely overshadowed any discussion of issues relating to mutuality and the importance of developing pleasurable sexual practices for both male and female students, though there were exceptions.

How was pleasure defined in these curricula? There were no overarching definitions or detailed descriptions of sexual pleasure *per se*, none similar to those suggested by researchers like Fine (1988), Tolman (2002), or Allen and Carmody (2012). Perhaps that was why we as researchers were limited to teasing out a discourse of pleasure by examining phrasing regarding 'getting horny', getting carried away, and the mechanics of arousal. There are a variety of pleasures that could have been described. Authors pursue a discourse of restraint around desire and instructors are told that if students ask for permission to list the positive consequences of sex (after exercises in which they list negative consequences), then they are to respond with reminders that sex is dangerous.

Although sexual safety is a laudable goal, the juxtaposition of pleasure with danger reinforces old messages about sex and shame; that if one gets carried away, enjoys sex with abandon, or seeks out sexual pleasure, harm will come.

Largely missing in discourse on sexual pleasure is a discourse that connects pleasure to mutuality in non-marital relationships (Lamb 2010a, 2012). Focusing on prevention and danger, educators miss the opportunity to talk to adolescents about pleasure in the context of a good relationship, one in which the adolescent can take care of both her/himself as well as her/his partner. When the young person is positioned as reckless, easily pressured, unknowledgeable, or unwise to consequences, rather than as a human being who seeks relationship and pleasure within it, discussions of sexuality will be as superficial as the kind of sex these curricula are trying to prevent. As the OWL curriculum reminds us, talk of pleasure ought to be embedded in discourse about negotiating relationship, communication, and mutuality. In so doing, the goal of prevention may be reached while higher and more positive goals are also attempted.

References

Administration for Children and Families and the Department for HHS. 2007. http://www.acf.hhs.gov/

Allen, L. 2004. Beyond the birds and the bees: Constituting a discourse of erotics in sexuality education. *Gender and Education* 16, no. 2: 151–67.

Allen, L. 2007a. Doing 'it' differently: Relinquishing the disease and pregnancy prevention focus in sexuality education. *British Journal of Sociology of Education* 28, no. 5: 575–88.

Allen, L. 2007b. 'Pleasurable pedagogy': Young people's ideas about teaching 'pleasure' in sexuality education. *Twenty-First Century Society* 2, no. 3: 249–64.

Allen, L., and M. Carmody. 2012. 'Pleasure has no passport': Re-visiting the potential of pleasure in sexuality education. *Sex Education* 12, no. 4: 455–68.

APA (American Psychological Association). 2007. *Report of the APA task force on the sexualization of girls.* Washington, DC: APA. http://www.apa.org/PI/women/programs/girls/report.aspx (accessed November 20, 2012).

Barth, R.P. 2004. *Reducing the risk: Building skills to prevent pregnancy, STD and HIV.* Scotts Valley, CA: ETR Associates.

Bay-Cheng, L. 2003. The trouble of teen sex: The construction of adolescent sexuality through school-based sexuality education. *Sex Education* 3, no. 1: 61–74.

Bay-Cheng, L. 2012. Recovering empowerment: De-personalizing and re-politicizing adolescent female sexuality. *Sex Roles* 66, nos. 11–12: 758–63.

Braun, V., and V. Clarke. 2006. Using thematic analysis in psychology. *Qualitative Research in Psychology* 3, no. 2: 77–101.

Brick, P., and B. Taverner. 2001. *Positive images: Teaching abstinence, contraception, and sexual health.* Morristown: Planned Parenthood of Greater Northern New Jersey.

Brown, S., and B. Taverner. 2001. *Streetwise to sexwise: Sexuality education for high-risk youth.* 2nd ed. Morristown: Planned Parenthood of Northern New Jersey.

Carlson, D. 2011. Constructing the adolescent body: Cultural studies and sexuality education. In *The sexuality curriculum and youth culture,* ed. D. Carlson and D. Roseboro, 3–28. New York: Peter Lang.

Carmody, M. 2005. Ethical erotics: Reconceptualizing anti-rape education. *Sexualities* 8, no. 4: 465–80.

Committee on Government Reform, Minority Staff. 2004. *The content of federally funded abstinence-only education programs.* Washington, DC: US House of Representatives.

Cook, B. 2006. *Choosing the best journey.* Atlanta, GA: Choosing the Best Publishing.

Dines, G. 2010. *Pornland: How pornography has hijacked our sexuality.* Boston, MA: Beacon Press.

Estrella, S. 2012. Health coalition releases first ever National Sexuality Education Standards. http://www. examiner.com/article/health-coalition-releases-first-ever-national-sexuality-education-standards (accessed November 20, 2012).

Fields, J. 2008. *Risky lessons: Sex education and social inequality.* Piscataway, NJ: Rutgers University Press.

Fine, M. 1988. Sexuality, schooling, and adolescent females: The missing discourse of desire. *Harvard Educational Review* 58, no. 1: 29–53.

Fine, M., and S. McClelland. 2006. Sexuality education and desire: Still missing after all these years. *Harvard Educational Review* 76, no. 3: 297–338.

Foucault, M. 1979. *The history of sexuality.* London: Allen Lane.

Froyum, C.M. 2009. Making 'good girls': Sexual agency in the sexuality education of low income black girls. *Culture, Health & Sexuality* 12, no. 1: 59–82.

Gill, R. 2008. Empowerment/sexism: Figuring female sexual agency in contemporary advertising. *Feminism & Psychology* 18, no. 1: 35–60.

Goldfarb, E.S., and E.M. Casparian. 2000. *Our whole lives: Sexuality education for grades 10–12.* Boston, MA: Unitarian Universalist Association.

Green, A.C. 2007. *Game plan abstinence program.* Golf, IL: Project Reality.

Guttmacher Institute. 2009. The Obama administration's first budget proposal prioritizes sex education and family planning but not abortion access. *Guttmacher Policy Review* 12, no. 2. http://www.guttmacher.org/pubs/gpr/12/2/gpr120223.html (accessed November 20, 2012).

Harrison, L., L. Hillier, and J. Walsh. 1996. Teaching for a positive sexuality: Sounds good, but what about fear, embarrassment, risk and the 'forbidden' discourse of desire? In *Schooling and sexualities: Teaching for a positive sexuality,* ed. L. Lasky and C. Beavis, 69–82. Geelong: Deakin University Press.

Impett, E.A., D. Schooler, and D.L. Tolman. 2006. To be seen and not heard: Femininity ideology and adolescent girls' sexual health. *Archives of Sexual Behavior* 35, no. 2: 129–42.

Jemmott, L.S., J.B. Jemmott, and K.A. McCaffree. 1994. *Be proud! Be responsible!: Strategies to empower youth to reduce their risk for HIV infection. Curriculum manual.* New York: Columbia University School of Nursing, Columbia University, American Foundation of AIDS Research, National Institute of Child Health and Human Development (US), and Centers for Disease Control and Prevention (US).

Kendall, N. 2008. Sexuality education in an abstinence-only era: A comparative case study of two U.S. states. *Sexuality Research & Social Policy* 5, no. 2: 23–44.

Kiely, E. 2005. Where is the discourse of desire? Deconstructing the Irish relationships and sexuality education (RSE) resource materials. *Irish Educational Studies* 24, nos. 2–3: 253–66.

Kirby, D. 2007. *Emerging answers 2007: Research finding on programs to reduce teen pregnancy and sexually transmitted diseases.* Washington, DC: The National Campaign to Prevent Teen and Unplanned Pregnancy.

Krauth, J. 2003. *WAIT training.* Greenwood Village, CO: Abstinence and Relationships Training Center.

Lamb, S. 1997. Sex education as moral education: Teaching for pleasure, about fantasy, and against abuse. *Journal of Moral Education* 26, no. 3: 301–6.

Lamb, S. 2010a. Towards a sexual ethics curriculum: Bringing philosophy and society to bear on individual development. *Harvard Educational Review* 80, no. 1: 81–105.

Lamb, S. 2010b. Feminist ideals of healthy female adolescent sexuality: A critique. *Sex Roles* 62, nos. 5–6: 294–306.

Lamb, S. 2011. The place of mutuality and care in democratic sexuality education: Incorporating the other person. In *The sexuality curriculum and youth culture*, ed. D. Carlson and D. Roseboro, 29–43. New York: Peter Lang.

Lamb, S. 2012. The future of sex education: Just the facts? Paper presented at the Educational Theory Summer Institute, August 20–22, in Urbana-Champaign, IL.

Lamb, S., K. Graling, and K. Lustig. 2011. Stereotypes in four current AOUM curricula: Good girls, good boys, and the new gender equality. *American Journal of Sexuality Education* 6, no. 4: 360–80.

Lamb, S., and Z. Peterson. 2011. Adolescent girls' sexual empowerment: Two feminists explore the concept. *Sex Roles* 66, nos. 11–12: 703–12.

LeCroy and Milligan Associates. 2003. *Final report: Arizona abstinence-only education program evaluation, 1998–2003*. Phoenix: Arizona Department of Health Services, Office of Women's and Children's Health.

Mayo, C. 2011. Philosophy of education is bent. *Studies in Philosophy and Education* 30, no. 5: 471–6.

Measor, L., C. Tiffin, and K. Miller. 2000. *Young people's views on sex education: Education, attitudes, and behavior*. London: Routledge/Falmer.

Moran, J. 2000. *Teaching sex: The shaping of adolescence in the 20th century*. Cambridge, MA: Harvard University Press.

Phelps, S. 2006. *Aspire: Live your life. Be free*. Arlington Heights, IL: A & M Resources.

Potter, J., and M. Wetherell. 1994. Analyzing discourse. In *Analyzing qualitative data*, ed. A. Bryman and R.G. Burgess, 47–68. London: Routledge.

Rasmussen, M.L. 2004. Wounded identities, sex and pleasure: 'Doing it' at school. NOT! *Discourse: Studies in the Cultural Politics of Education* 25, no. 4: 445–58.

Rose, N. 1996. *Inventing ourselves: Psychology, power, and personhood*. Cambridge: Cambridge University Press.

Santelli, J., M. Ott, M. Lyon, J. Rogers, D. Summers, and R. Schleifer. 2006. Abstinence and abstinence-only education: A review of US policies and programs. *Journal of Adolescent Health* 38, no. 1: 72–81.

St. Lawrence, J.S. 2005. *BART = becoming a responsible teen: An HIV risk reduction program for adolescents*. Santa Cruz, CA: ETR Associates.

Tannenbaum, L. 2000. *Slut!: Growing up female with a bad reputation*. New York: Harper Collins Books.

Taverner, B., and S. Montfort. 2005. *Making sense of abstinence: Lessons for comprehensive sex education*. Morristown: Planned Parenthood of Greater Northern New Jersey.

Thompson, S. 1990. Putting a big thing into a little hole: Teenage girls' accounts of sexual initiation. *Journal of Sex Research* 27, no. 3: 341–61.

Tiefer, L. 2004. *Sex is not a natural act and other essays*. 2nd ed. Boulder, CO: Westview Press.

Tolman, D.L. 2000. Object lessons: Romance, violence and female adolescent sexual desire. *Journal of Sex Education and Therapy* 25, no. 1: 70–9.

Tolman, D.L. 2002. *Dilemmas of desire: Teenage girls talk about sexuality*. Cambridge, MA: Harvard University Press.

Tolman, D.L., E.A. Impett, A.J. Tracy, and A. Michael. 2006. Looking good, sounding good: Feminist ideology and adolescent girls' mental health. *Psychology of Women Quarterly* 30, no. 1: 85–95.

Trenholm, C., B. Devaney, K. Fortson, L. Quay, J. Wheeler, and M. Clark. 2007. *Impacts of four Title V, Section 510 abstinence education programs: Final report*. Washington, DC: Mathematica.

Willig, C. 2008. *Introducing qualitative research in psychology*. 2nd ed. Maidenhead/New York: Open University Press.

To Be Seen and Not Heard: Femininity Ideology and Adolescent Girls' Sexual Health

by Emily A. Impett, Ph.D.,[1,2] Deborah Schooler, Ph.D.,[1] and Deborah L. Tolman, Ed.D.[1]

Received March 31, 2005; revision received August 16, 2005; accepted August 24, 2005 Published online: 26 April 2006

This study used a feminist developmental framework to test the hypothesis that internalizing conventional ideas about femininity in two domains—inauthenticity in relationships and body objectification—is associated with diminished sexual health among adolescent girls. In this study, sexual health was conceptualized as feelings of sexual self-efficacy (i.e., a girl's conviction that she can act upon her own sexual needs in a relationship) and protection behavior (i.e., from both STIs and unwanted pregnancy). A total of 116 girls (aged 16–19) completed measures of femininity ideology, sexual self-efficacy, sexual experiences, and protection behavior. Results revealed that inauthenticity in relationships and body objectification were associated with poorer sexual self-efficacy and sexual self-efficacy, in turn, predicted less sexual experience and less use of protection. Further, the two components of femininity ideology were associated with different forms of protection. The importance of a feminist developmental framework for identifying and understanding salient dimensions of sexual health for female adolescents is discussed.

Introduction

A bad thing about guys is sometimes they, they like don't want to talk to you on the phone or something, or if they do want to talk to you on the phone, they don't want to talk to you in front of their guy friends because they're like "I have a girlfriend, girlfriend's there to look nice, shut up don't say anything, girls should be seen, not heard," you know?

—Kim, a study participant

Adolescent girls come of age in a patriarchal society in which they are under pressure to be seen and not heard. Girls experience immense pressures to behave in feminine ways, both in their relationships with other people (i.e., by suppressing their own authentic thoughts and feelings) and in their relationships with their own bodies (i.e., by suppressing bodily hungers and desires to conform to

prevailing images of beauty and attractiveness). At the same time that girls are learning to navigate the demands of femininity, they are exploring their sexuality and becoming adult sexual beings (Tolman, 2002). The development of healthy sexuality is a critical developmental task (Ehrhardt, 1996), much of which takes place during adolescence (Christopher, 2001; Tolman, 2002).

Sexuality Development in Adolescence

From a developmental perspective that acknowledges the normative expectation of girls' developing sexuality in adolescence, a conceptualization of adolescent sexual health must include, among other things, the ability to acknowledge one's own sexual feelings, the freedom and comfort to explore wanted sexual behavior and refuse unwanted behavior, and the requisite knowledge and ability to protect oneself from sexually

[1] Center for Research on Gender and Sexuality, San Francisco State University, San Francisco, California.
[2] To whom correspondence should be addressed at Center for Research on Gender and Sexuality, San Francisco State University, 2017 Mission Street, Suite 300, San Francisco, California 94110; e-mail: eimpett@sfsu.edu.

transmitted infections (STIs) and unwanted pregnancy (Tolman, Striepe, & Harmon, 2003). In the current study, we chose to focus on three specific aspects of this broad definition of sexual health. First, we considered girls' overall level of accumulated sexual experience. Although much of the previous research on girls' sexuality has focused exclusively on sexual intercourse, this approach ignores the much broader family of sexual experiences that many girls explore during adolescence. Accordingly, we incorporated a range of noncoital sexual behaviors in addition to sexual intercourse including kissing, genital touching, and oral sex (SIECUS, 1995; Tolman, 1999).

Second, we considered girls' conviction that they can act upon their own sexual needs in a relationship (i.e., sexual self-efficacy). Sexual decisions concerning the choice of activity or use of contraception often involve negotiation between partners; being able to voice and enact one's own desires, interests, and needs is necessarily central to our conceptualization of sexual health. Third, we consider girls' use of protection during sexual interactions (i.e., protection behavior). In the United States, young people and adolescent girls in particular are at heightened risk for contracting STIs such as HIV, chlamydia, and gonorrhea (CDC, 2003a, 2003b). Further, 10% of all girls and young women aged 15–19 become pregnant each year (Alan Guttmacher Institute, 1999) and 78% of these pregnancies are unplanned (Henshaw, 1998). Because of the effectiveness of condoms and hormonal contraception at preventing these outcomes (Davis & Weller, 1999; Walsh et al., 2004), girls' protection behaviors constitute an important aspect of their sexual health.

A Feminist Developmental Framework

The current study used a feminist developmental framework to explore the extent to which adolescent girls' internalization of conventional ideas about femininity was associated with their sexual health. This framework refers to a set of theories that assume a feminist standpoint (e.g., Jagger, 1983) and describe the ways in which girls' development is shaped by, and is responsive to, the sociocultural context of patriarchy. A feminist

developmental framework calls for attention to how girls develop an internalized recognition of themselves as women in their behavior, thoughts, and feelings and through others' responses to them. In particular, girls enter a patriarchal world in which they experience pressure to behave in "feminine" ways in their relationships with other people (i.e., by avoiding conflict, suppressing anger, being "nice") and through their relationships with their own bodies (i.e., by managing their own bodies and habits to conform with prevailing images of beauty and attractiveness) (Tolman, Impett, Tracy, & Michael, in press). Below, we describe these two specific aspects of femininity ideology, namely inauthenticity in relationships and body objectification, and their possible implications for adolescent girls' sexual health.

Inauthenticity in Relationships and Sexual Health

Traditional theories of human development have described the key tasks of adolescence as achieving separation and autonomy (Erikson, 1968). In contrast, a feminist psychodynamic developmental perspective suggests that, for women in particular, the importance of relationships is central to adolescent development. Anchored in self-in-relation theory (e.g., Jordan, Kaplan, Miller, Stiver, & Surrey, 1991), this perspective describes how the experience and development of a sense of self is intimately bound to relationships and that a woman's (and a developing girl's) sense of self is based, in large part, on her ability to maintain important close relationships (see also review by Cross & Madson, 1997). Qualitative research that has focused on girls' own perspectives has shown that the negotiation of, and the desire to maintain, changing relationships is a primary struggle in adolescence (e.g., Brown, 1998; Brown & Gilligan, 1992). One way in which girls and women maintain important relationships is to silence their own needs and desires as a strategy to reduce conflict. This tendency has been described as "inauthenticity in relationships" (e.g., Tolman & Porche, 2000), "loss of voice" (e.g., Brown & Gilligan, 1992; Gilligan, 1982), "false-self behavior" (e.g., Harter, Waters, & Whitesell, 1997), or "silencing the self" (e.g.,

Jack & Dill, 1992) and is enacted when girls hide their true thoughts and feelings, especially those that are deemed unfeminine, such as anger.

Girls who silence their own needs and desires may be more likely to struggle with making their *sexual* needs and desires known as well. This disregard for the self in the ostensible service of relationships may be especially true in a culture that defines sex in terms of men's desires and denies women's sexual desire and agency (Holland, Ramanzanoglu, Sharpe, & Thomson, 1998; Tolman, 2002; Tolman, Spencer, Rosen-Reynoso, & Porche, 2003). That is, girls and women may be particularly vulnerable to making their own sexual needs and desires including the need for protection against STIs and unwanted pregnancy secondary to the desires of their partners (Amaro, 1995; Wingood & DiClemente, 1998). While no quantitative research has explicitly examined the possible link between girls' ability to be authentic in relationships and sexual decision making, research on sexual communication has shown that women who do not communicate with their sexual partners about sexual issues use condoms less consistently than women who feel comfortable communicating with their partners (e.g., Quina, Harlow, Morokoff, Burkholder, & Dieter, 2000; Wingood & DiClemente, 1998). These findings suggest that girls who find it difficult to assert and communicate their own authentic desires may sacrifice their sexual health in the service of preserving relationships and engage in more sexually risky behavior.

Body Objectification and Sexual Health

A feminist developmental perspective also positions the negotiation of learning to live in a woman's body as a critical developmental task in adolescence. The meaning and experience of being in one's own body (i.e., experiencing one's physical and concomitant emotional feelings) changes as girls undergo puberty in a society that objectifies and commodifies women's physical appearance (Bordo, 1993; Brumberg, 1997; de Beauvoir, 1961). In response to societal objectification, girls learn to internalize and eventually embody objectified constructs of femininity (Fredrickson

& Roberts, 1997; McKinley & Hyde, 1996). The embodiment of femininity includes dissociating from one's body, that is, losing awareness of one's own desires and hungers (i.e., for food, for sex) as well as training the body how to move (and not move) appropriately to conform to "ladylike" norms of physicality (Bartky, 1990; Tolman & Debold, 1993). As de Beauvoir (1961) articulated, this process involves internalizing a "male gaze" and turning it upon oneself and learning to evaluate and assess rather than to feel and experience one's own body. Thus, as girls begin to develop physically mature bodies in adolescence, many of them, to some degree or other, dissociate from their own bodily hungers and engage in the behaviors of constantly controlling and surveilling their own bodies (Fredrickson & Roberts, 1997).

Both of these aspects of body objectification—dissociating from one's own desire and constantly surveilling one's own body from another's perspective—may have negative consequences for female sexuality. A woman who is separated from her own feelings may find it difficult to assert (or even know) her own desires and instead act based on her partner's desires and interests (Tolman, 2002). In a study of college women, body image self-consciousness (i.e., being concerned with how one's body looks to a partner during sex) was negatively associated with sexual self-esteem and sexual assertiveness (Wiederman, 2000; see also Dove & Wiederman, 2000). In another study, college student women who reported feeling more body image self-consciousness and less comfort with their bodies had less overall sexual experience, but when they did engage in sexual intercourse, used condoms and contraception less frequently (Schooler, Ward, Merriwether, & Caruthers, 2005). Other research has shown that adolescent girls who are less satisfied with their body image were less likely to negotiate condom use because they feared abandonment by their partners (Wingood, DiClemente, Harrington, & Davies, 2002). In short, girls who objectify their own bodies may not be able to act in accordance with, or even know their own desires and, as a result, may avoid wanted sexual activity or engage in risky behaviors that pose a serious threat to their sexual well-being.

The Mediating Role of Sexual Self-Efficacy

Both theory and preliminary empirical evidence suggest that inauthenticity in relationships and body objectification may be associated with diminished sexual health among adolescent girls. The mechanisms of this association, however, remain to be established. We suggest that femininity may primarily inhibit girls' sexual self-efficacy, which we define as a girl's conviction that she can act upon her own sexual needs in a relationship, such as enjoying sex, refusing unwanted sex, and insisting on the use of protection (Levinson, 1986). The resulting decreased sexual self-efficacy may interfere with girls' abilities to engage in wanted sexual activity and to enact safer sex practices when they do (Schooler et al., 2005).

Previous empirical work supports such a premise. Girls who find it difficult to assert and communicate their own authentic desires and who objectify their own bodies may be less able to communicate their desires in sexual situations (Impett & Peplau, 2003). Further, research has also shown that sexual self-efficacy is associated with an increased likelihood of practicing safer sex (e.g., Goldman & Harlow, 1993; Parsons, Halkitis, Bimbi, & Borkowski, 2000). Taken together, these results suggest that sexual self-efficacy may mediate the associations between both inauthenticity in relationships and body objectification and sexual health.

Hypotheses and Overview of the Current Research

In the current study, we tested the central hypothesis that the extent to which girls espouse traditional ideas about femininity (i.e., femininity ideology) would be associated with their sexual self-efficacy, and, in turn, with the extent to which they engage in sexual activity and protect themselves from STIs and unwanted pregnancy. This main hypothesis was composed of three specific predictions: First, we predicted that both components of femininity ideology (i.e., relationship inauthenticity and body objectification) will be associated with lower sexual self-efficacy, less sexual experience, and less protection behavior (i.e., less use of condoms and contraception). Second,

we predicted that lower sexual self-efficacy will be associated with less sexual experience and less protection behavior. Third, we expected that sexual self-efficacy will mediate the association between femininity ideology and both sexual experience and protection behavior. So, for example, one reason why girls who have internalized more conventional ideas about femininity may engage in more sexually risky behaviors is because buying into ideas about what it means to be appropriately feminine is at odds with sexual self-efficacy and thus may undermine girls' ability to negotiate and enact protection behaviors. Taken together, these specific predictions are depicted in a conceptual model (see Fig. 1).

Furthermore, because we conceptualized girls' protection behavior as multifaceted, additional questions guided our investigation. First, we considered the use of hormonal contraception (i.e., the pill or Depo), which protects against pregnancy, as potentially different from the use of condoms, which protects against both pregnancy and STIs. In addition to this difference in function, hormonal contraception and condoms also differ in their method of use. Specifically, the use of hormonal contraception often involves extensive advanced planning in expectation of sexual activity; an adolescent girl wishing to "go on the pill" might need to consult with her parents, or at the very least, obtain a prescription from a physician. Condom use, on the other hand, requires less advanced planning, but requires more negotiation with a partner once sexual activity is initiated. As such, although both require asserting oneself, the behaviors involved can look quite different. Because of the somewhat different functions and methods of these two forms of protection, we chose to evaluate whether femininity ideology was differentially associated with the use of hormonal contraception and condoms. Second, because the use and meaning of contraception may change as girls develop and as their relationships become more committed and long lasting (e.g., Reisen & Poppen, 1995; Rosenthal & Shepherd, 1993), we chose to distinguish between protection behaviors at first intercourse, protection behaviors at last intercourse, and the general frequency of protection behaviors across all sexual encounters.

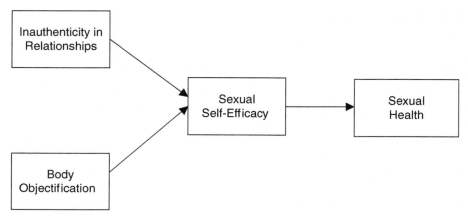

Figure 1. Conceptual model of femininity ideology and sexual health.

In addition, we assessed two demographic factors that have been associated with sexual behaviors and sexual risk taking in adolescence: socioeconomic status (e.g., Crosby, Holtgrave, DiClemente, Wingood, & Gayle, 2003) and religiosity (e.g., McCree, Wingood, DiClemente, Davies, & Harrington, 2003). We controlled for these two demographic factors in the analyses if appropriate.

Method
Participants

The entire 12th grade in a northeastern urban school district was recruited as part of a longitudinal study of adolescent sexual health (our collaboration with administrators and teachers produced 93% compliance for the district; see Tolman & Porche, 2000). A total of 116 girls aged 16–19 ($M = 17.3$) participated in this panel of data collection. The sample was ethnically diverse: 59.5% were white, 27.6% were Latina, 6.9% were multiethnic, 2.6% were African-American, 1.7% were Asian or Pacific Islander, and 1.7% did not provide a description of their ethnicity. The sample was also diverse in terms of socioeconomic status: 23% reported that their mothers did not finish high school, 30% reported that their mothers finished high school, and 47% reported their mother's education as college or better. Sixteen (14%) of the girls reported that Spanish was the primary language used at home. A substantial number of girls (21.6%) were born outside of the United States. Sixty-nine percent of the girls identified their religious affiliation as Catholic; a little more than a quarter of the girls (28.5%) described

religion as "important" or "very important" in their lives.

Procedure

Participants completed a survey that included questions about femininity ideology, sexual experiences, sexual self-efficacy, protection behavior, and demographic characteristics. Written permission was obtained from each child's parent or guardian. Bilingual students and mainstreamed Latinas were offered the option of completing the survey in Spanish (translated and back-translated) with a Spanish-speaking researcher present. Permission slips were translated into Spanish for this group. Students completed the surveys in school either in health education or in physical education class.

Measures
Femininity Ideology

The 20-item version of the Adolescent Femininity Ideology Scale (AFIS; Tolman & Porche, 2000) measured the extent to which girls have internalized two negative conventions of femininity: inauthenticity in relationships with others and objectification of one's own body (see Table I). The AFIS was developed with and for girls of varied ages in adolescence, anchored largely in items constructed out of focus groups.

Based on the results of confirmatory factor analyses of data provided by early adolescent girls in another study (Tolman et al., in press), we dropped 3 of the 20 original items to increase the reliability of each subscale. Girls responded to such statements

Table I. Mean and SDs for Items in the Adolescent Femininity Ideology Scale

Item	M	SD
Inauthentic Self in Relationships Subscale.		
1. I would tell a friend I think she looks nice, even if I think she shouldn't go out of the house dressed like that.	2.33	1.16
2. I worry that I make others feel bad if I am successful.	2.25	1.21
3. I would not change the way I do things in order to please someone else.[a]	4.41	1.26
4. I tell my friends what I honestly think even when it is an unpopular idea.[a]	4.66	0.99
5. Often I look happy on the outside in order to please others, even if I don't feel happy on the inside.	3.25	1.40
6. I wish I could say what I feel more often than I do.	3.48	1.48
7. I feel like it's my fault when I have disagreements with my friends.	2.65	1.18
8. When my friends ignore my feelings, I think that my feelings weren't very important anyway.	2.44	1.41
9. I usually tell my friends when they hurt my feelings.[a]	4.10	1.28
Objectified Relationship with Body Subscale.		
1. The way I can tell that I am at a good weight is when I fit into a small size.	3.09	1.58
2. I often wish my body were different.	3.67	1.51
3. I think that a girl has to be thin to feel beautiful.	2.25	1.32
4. I think a girl has to have a light complexion and delicate features to be thought of as beautiful.	2.07	1.28
5. I am more concerned about how my body looks than how my body feels.	2.73	1.36
6. I often feel uncomfortable in my body.	3.18	1.46
7. There are times when I have really good feelings in my body.[a]	4.66	1.09
8. The way I decide I am at a good weight is when I feel healthy.[a]	4.46	1.23

[a]Item is reversed for coding.

Note. n = 116.

as "I wish I could say what I feel more often than I do" (Inauthentic Self in Relationships Subscale, ISR) and "I am more concerned about how my body looks than how my body feels" (Objectified Relationship with Body Subscale, ORB) on 6-point scales (1 = *strongly disagree* to 6 = *strongly agree*). Several items were reverse-scored and mean scores for each subscale were computed, with higher scores reflecting greater conventionality (i.e., more inauthentic in relationships, more self-objectifying). The Cronbach alphas for the two subscales were adequate ($\alpha_{ISR} = 0.77$, $\alpha_{ORB} = 0.81$).

Sexual Experiences

Participants indicated whether or not they had engaged in each of the following sexual activities: (1) kissing on the mouth, (2) touching another person under their clothing or with no clothes on, (3) being touched under their clothing or with no clothes on, (4) performing oral sex, (5) receiving oral sex, and (6) engaging in sexual intercourse. We summed their responses to each of these questions to create an index of sexual experiences (0 = *none of these behaviors* to 6 = *all of these behaviors*). Those girls who had engaged in sexual intercourse also indicated the number of partners with whom they had engaged in sexual intercourse on a 6-point scale (1 = *1 person*, 2 = *2 people*, etc., to 6 = *6 or more people*).

Sexual Self-Efficacy

A modified version of Levinson's (1986) Contraceptive Self-Efficacy Scale assessed the strength of a girl's conviction that she can act upon her own sexual needs in a relationship, such as enjoying sex, refusing unwanted sex, and insisting on the use of protection. Girls responded to 16 statements such as "When I am with a partner, I feel that I can always be responsible for what happens sexually" and "I could stop things before intercourse if I couldn't bring up the subject of protection" on 5-point scales (1 = *not at all true* to 5 = *completely true*). Because we were interested in girls' use of condoms in addition to contraception, items that originally referred only to contraception were reworded to refer to protection more generally. For example, in one item, the original statement "even if I wasn't using a form of birth control" was changed to "even if I weren't protected." Several items were reverse-scored and a mean scale was computed with higher scores reflecting stronger beliefs that a girl could protect herself from pregnancy and STIs. The Cronbach alpha for this measure was adequate ($\alpha = 0.73$).

Protection Behavior

Girls who reported that they had engaged in sexual intercourse answered questions adopted from the National Longitudinal Study of Adolescent Health about: (1) *general frequency of protection*, (2) *protection at first intercourse*, and (3) *protection at last intercourse*. The first measure, general frequency of protection, was assessed with two questions. Girls indicated (1) how often they used protection to prevent pregnancy and (2) how often they used protection to prevent STIs on 4-point scales (0 = *never*, 1 = *sometimes*, 2 = *usually*, 3 = *always*). For the second and third measures, girls indicated whether or not they used each of the following forms of protection the first time and the last time they engaged in sexual intercourse: condoms, the pill, "the shot" (Depo), a diaphragm, or other. From their responses to these questions, girls were assigned a hormonal contraception score (i.e., protection from pregnancy; 0 = *no*, 1 = *yes*) and a condom score (i.e., protection from pregnancy and STDs; 0 = *no*, 1 = *yes*) for both first and last intercourse.

Socioeconomic Status

Each girl's mother/mother figure's education was included as a proxy for socioeconomic status. Girls reported to the best of their ability the highest level of formal education achieved by their mother or female guardian (1 = *did not finish high school*, 2 = *finished high school/obtained GED*, 3 = *completed some college*, 4 = *finished college*, 5 = *attended school beyond college*). Maternal education has been shown to be an adequate general index of socioeconomic status (Entwisle & Astone, 1994).

Religiosity

Religiosity was measured with a single item: "How important is religion in your life?" (1 = *not at all* to 4 = *very*).

Data Analyses

In this article, we tested three separate models in which sexual self-efficacy mediated the association between both components of femininity ideology and sexual health. First, we tested a model linking femininity ideology with girls' overall level of sexual experience. Second, we tested a model linking femininity ideology with frequency of protection. Third, we tested a model linking femininity ideology with protection at first and last intercourse.

Structural equation modeling estimated with the EQS computer program (Bentler, 1995) was used to test the models linking femininity ideology to sexual experience and frequency of protection. For the first model linking femininity ideology to sexual experience, we assess the significance of the relevant paths and present information regarding model fit. Model fit was assessed with three different indices. First, we report the likelihood ratio chi-square statistic, an index that quantifies the degree of "model misfit" (i.e., a composite of the discrepancies between the obtained data and their model-implied values). Second, because the chi-square is dependent on the assumption of multivariate normality and can be inflated in models with strong associations (Kline, 2005), we report three other fit indices. We will report the Comparative Fit Index (CFI; Bentler, 1990), a common model fit index that is forced to vary between 0 and 1. The root mean square error of approximation (RMSEA) is an index which represents a population-based assessment of the amount of model misfit (less dependent on the sample size and distributional properties of

Table 2. Intercorrelations, Means, and *SD*s for all Measured Variables

Measured variable	1	2	3	4	5	6	7	8	9
1. ISR	—								
2. ORB	0.45**	—							
3. Sexual self-efficacy	−0.49**	−0.49**	—						
4. Sexual experience	−0.15*	−0.17*	0.30*	—					
5. Number of partners	0.08	0.19	−0.34**	0.23	—				
6. Contraception frequency	−0.29*	−0.17	0.35**	0.20	0.02	—			
7. Condom use frequency	−0.18	−0.26*	0.15	0.08	−0.14	0.65**	—		
8. Religiosity	−0.01	−0.05	0.08	−0.12	−0.06	−0.10	−0.02	—	
9. Socioeconomic status	−0.02	−0.19	0.11	0.04	−0.05	0.21	0.20	0.14	—
Mean	2.62	2.60	4.23	4.36	2.52	2.39	2.07	1.93	2.65
SD	0.77	0.79	0.50	1.97	1.75	0.95	1.11	0.96	1.28

Note. $n = 70–116$.
*$p < .05$.
**$p < .01$.

the sample) and which compensates for the effect of model complexity. Browne and Cudeck (1993) recommended that an RMSEA of 0.05 or lower indicates that the model provides a good fit to the data. Finally, we will report the standardized root mean square residual (SRMR), a standardized measure of the average difference between the observed and the modeled covariances among the variables. Hu and Bentler (1999) recommended that an SRMR of 0.08 or lower indicates good fit.

The second set of models linking femininity ideology to frequency of protection (hormonal contraception and condoms) was "just identified" (i.e., we estimated as many paths as there were unique elements in the variance/covariance matrix). In these models, all possible paths were included, resulting in a perfect fit, and, accordingly, the purpose of model testing was to evaluate the significance of the paths between variables. Finally, the third models linking femininity ideology to protection at first and last intercourse were tested using logistic regression because the protection variables were dichotomous.

Results

We present three models, those pertaining to sexual experience, those pertaining to frequency of protection, and those pertaining to protection at first and last intercourse. Table II lists the intercorrelations

among all variables to be included in the models. Because neither socioeconomic status nor religiosity was significantly associated with any of the other variables to be included in the models, they were dropped from the analyses.

Before we test the models, we present descriptive data regarding girls' sexual experiences and protection behavior.

Sexual Experiences and Protection Behavior

Girls reported engaging in a range of sexual experiences from kissing to sexual intercourse. Ninety-two percent of girls had kissed on the mouth, 85% reported touching someone or being touched under their clothing, 66% had either performed or received oral sex, and 60% reported that they had engaged in sexual intercourse. Among girls who had engaged in sexual intercourse, 41% had engaged in sex with one partner, 17% had two partners, 20% had three partners, 3% had four partners, 6% had five partners, and 13% had six or more partners.

Table III lists the percentages of participants who used hormonal contraception and condoms at varying frequencies. Table IV depicts the percentages of girls who used different forms of protection at first and last intercourse.

On the whole, the girls in this sample used a great deal of protection, especially at first intercourse.

Table 3. Descriptive Statistics for Hormonal Contraception and Condom Use Frequency

	Hormonal contraception frequency (%)	Condom use frequency (%)
Never	9	14
Sometimes	7	14
Usually	21	21
Always	63	50

Note. n = 70.

Table 4. Descriptive Statistics for Hormonal Contraception and Condom Use at First and Most Recent Intercourse

	First intercourse (%)	Most recent intercourse (%)
Nothing	12.7	21.4
Hormonal contraception only	1.4	17.1
Condoms only	77.5	52.9
Dual methods	8.5	8.6

Note. n = 70.

For example, less than 13% of girls used no form of protection at first intercourse, and 86% used either condoms only or dual methods of protection. Only one girl reported the use of hormonal contraception only. By most recent intercourse, fewer girls reported the use of condoms or dual methods of protection (62%) whereas more girls reported using hormonal contraception only (17%).

Femininity Ideology and Sexual Experience

Our first model tested predictions linking femininity ideology to girls' overall level of sexual experience. As shown in Table IV, both ISR and ORB were associated with girls' overall level of sexual experience, but not with the number of partners that she reported over her lifetime. Accordingly, we tested one model that included both components of femininity ideology predicting sexual experience (see Fig. 2). This model provided a good fit to the data, $\chi^2(2) = 0.46$, $p = .80$, CFI = 1.00, RMSEA < 0.001, SRMR = 0.02. The Lagrange Multiplier test indicated that no additional paths could be added to improve the fit of the model. All of the hypothesized paths in the model were significant. As hypothesized, both ISR and ORB predicted sexual self-efficacy. Together, these two components of femininity ideology accounted for 26% of the variance in sexual self-efficacy. In turn, sexual self-efficacy predicted overall sexual experience, accounting for 10% of the variance in this variable. Finally, the indirect effect (equivalent to a Sobel [1982] test) of ISR on sexual experience was significant ($z = -2.71$, $p < .05$), providing evidence for mediation. However, the indirect effect of ORB on sexual experience was not significant ($z = -1.73$, $p > .05$). Thus, the association between femininity ideology and sexual experience may be partially explained by the fact that girls who were less authentic in relationships were also lower in sexual self-efficacy.

Femininity Ideology and Frequency of Protection

Our second model tested predictions linking femininity ideology with the frequency with which girls used hormonal contraception and condoms. These analyses were conducted with the subsample of girls who had engaged in sexual intercourse ($N = 70$). As seen in Table IV, whereas inauthenticity in relationships (ISR) was associated with less frequent use of hormonal contraception, body objectification (ORB) was associated with less frequent use of condoms. Results of multiple regression analyses in which ISR and ORB were entered simultaneously further support these differential findings. Whereas ISR ($\beta = -0.27$, $p < .05$) but not ORB ($\beta = -0.04$, $p = .74$) predicted frequency of hormonal contraception, ORB ($\beta = -0.22$, $p = .09$) but not ISR ($\beta = -0.08$, $p = .56$) marginally predicted frequency of condom use. Because ISR and ORB were associated with different outcomes, we tested two separate mediational models, one linking ISR with contraception frequency and one linking ORB with condom use frequency. As explained above, because both of these models were saturated, we only report the significance of

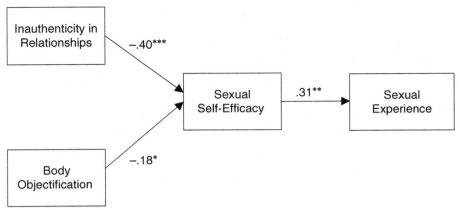

Figure 2. Model with sexual self-efficacy mediating the association between femininity ideology and sexual experience. Note. $n = 70$. $\chi^2(2) = .46$, $p = .80$, CFI $= 1.00$, RMSEA $< .001$, SRMR $= .02$. $*p < .05$, $**p < .01$, $***p < .001$.

paths rather than the fit of the models. Further, tests for mediation were conducted according to the principles of Baron and Kenny (1986).

ISR and Hormonal Contraception Frequency

The first requirement in demonstrating mediation is that the predictor variable be associated with the outcome variable. As shown above, ISR was significantly associated with frequency of hormonal contraception. The second requirement is to show that the predictor variable is associated with the putative mediator, sexual self-efficacy. As shown in Table IV, ISR was significantly associated with sexual self-efficacy. The final requirement is that the mediator predicts the outcome variable and that these effects account for the direct effect between the predictor and the outcome variable. Results showed that sexual self-efficacy significantly predicted hormonal contraception frequency ($\beta = 0.27$, $p < .05$), and the direct effect from ISR to hormonal contraception frequency dropped to nonsignificance ($\beta = -0.17$, $p = .21$). The Sobel (1982) test indicated that the drop in the value of the betas was marginally significant ($z = 1.89$, $p = .06$), suggesting possible, but not strong mediation. Figure 3 depicts this mediational model.

ORB and Condom Use Frequency

As shown in Table IV, sexual self-efficacy was not associated with condom use frequency. Because the mediator (in this case, sexual self-efficacy) was not associated with the outcome variable (condom

use frequency), one of the crucial requirements for mediation was not met. In short, the direct association between ORB and condom use was not mediated by sexual self-efficacy.

Femininity Ideology and Protection at First and Last Intercourse

The analyses concerning frequency of protection suggested that ISR and ORB may be associated with different aspects of protection (i.e., protection from pregnancy vs. protection from STIs). Accordingly, we conducted analyses to see whether ISR and ORB predicted different aspects of protection at first and last intercourse. Because condom use and hormonal contraception use at first and last intercourse were dichotomous variables ($0 = no$, $1 = yes$), we used logistic regression. ISR and ORB were entered into separate logistic regression equations to aid in interpretation, although we should point out that all effects remain significant when the two predictors are entered simultaneously.

Starting with first intercourse, ISR was marginally associated with the use of hormonal contraception (odds ratio [OR] $= 2.89$, 95% CI $= 0.89$, 9.42, $p = .08$), but was not associated with the use of condoms (OR $= 1.60$, 95% CI $= 0.67$, 3.81, $p = .29$). Specifically, for each unit increase in ISR, participants were almost three times as likely to fail to use hormonal contraception. For first intercourse, ORB was associated with the use of condoms (OR $= 3.56$, 95% CI $= 1.36$, 9.31,

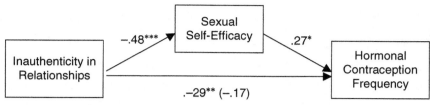

Figure 3. Model with sexual self-efficacy mediating the association between inauthenticity in relationships and hormonal contraception frequency. Note. *p* < .05, **p* < .01, ***p* < .001. All paths are standardized regression coefficients.

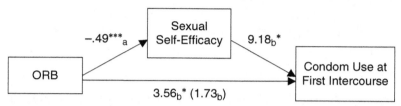

Figure 4. Model with sexual self-efficacy mediating the link between body objectification and condom use at first intercourse. Note. Path coefficients with an "a" subscript are standardized betas; path coefficients with a "b" subscript are exponentiated betas from logistic regression (condom use has been recoded so that all exponentiated betas are greater than one). *p* < .05, ***p* < .001.

p = .01), but was not associated with the use of hormonal contraception (OR = 1.32, 95% CI = 0.46, 3.77, *p* = .61). Specifically, for each unit increase in ORB, participants were more than three times as likely to fail to use condoms. Thus, consistent with the findings regarding frequency of protection, different aspects of femininity ideology were associated with different aspects of protection at first intercourse.

Because ISR was only marginally associated with the use of hormonal contraception at first intercourse, we did not test the full model with sexual self-efficacy as the mediator. Instead, we present only the results for the model linking ORB with condom use at first intercourse. As shown above, ORB was associated with condom use at first intercourse and with sexual self-efficacy. Further, sexual self-efficacy predicted condom use at first intercourse (OR = 9.18, 95% CI = 1.46, 57.76, *p* < .05), and the direct effect from ORB to condom use dropped to nonsignificance (OR dropped to 1.73, 95% CI = 0.54, 5.53, *p* = .36). A significant

Sobel test indicated that the drop in value of the path coefficient from ORB to condom use was significant (*z* = 2.05, *p* < .05), providing evidence for mediation. This model is depicted in Fig. 4. In short, ORB may influence a girl's use of condoms at first intercourse in part through its association with sexual self-efficacy.

Finally, turning to last intercourse, we found that neither ISR nor ORB was associated with the use of hormonal contraception or the use of condoms (all *p*s > .05); therefore we could determine whether sexual self-efficacy mediated any of these associations.

Discussion

In this study, we investigated the role of femininity ideology in understanding late adolescent girls' abilities to make healthy sexual choices. In particular, both inauthenticity in relationships and body objectification were associated with poorer sexual self-efficacy. That is, girls who internalized messages that they should "be seen" (rather than feel their own embodied feelings) and "not heard" (by taking their own thoughts and desires out of relationships) had a diminished ability to act on their own desires in sexual relationships (i.e., enjoy sex, refuse unwanted sex, and insist on the use of protection). In turn, lower feelings of sexual self-efficacy predicted less sexual experience and less protection behavior. The negative associations between femininity ideology and sexual experience suggest that girls who internalize norms of traditional femininity may find it difficult to voice their sexual desires and engage in wanted sexual behavior. Although we cannot determine from these data whether girls' sexual experiences indeed represent *wanted* experiences, the mediating role of sexual self-efficacy supports this interpretation. The finding that sexual self-efficacy mediated associations between femininity ideology and protection behavior points to the specific importance of self-efficacy for adolescent girls' sexuality. Being able to assert one's sexual desires and needs may be a critical prerequisite for enacting safer sex practices. Consequently, the extent to which conventional femininity ideology inhibits this ability may present a threat to the sexual health of adolescent girls.

Our findings further indicate that femininity ideology was a complex and multifaceted construct. Inauthenticity in relationships and body objectification predicted different types of protection behavior. Specifically, whereas inauthenticity was associated with less frequent use of contraception, body objectification was associated with less frequent use of condoms. The results for protection behavior at first intercourse were similar, namely that inauthenticity in relationships predicted less use of the pill and body objectification predicted less use of condoms. Although both of these forms of protection prevent pregnancy, condom use has the added benefit of providing protection from STIs. Given the different processes involved in condom and contraceptive use, such differences are not surprising. Specifically, contraceptive use requires advanced planning and expectation of sexual activity but does not require further action once sexual activity is initiated. Conversely, condom use requires less advanced planning but involves enacting safer sex practices while in the midst of sexual activity. Girls who objectify their bodies

may find it especially difficult to assert themselves *during* ongoing sexual activity, when bodies are exposed and vulnerable to evaluation. This heightened focus on the body may induce shame for girls prone to objectification (Fredrickson & Roberts, 1997), which may stall efforts to enact safer sex practices. Use of hormonal contraceptives is more removed from the immediate context of sexual activity, and, accordingly, may not present the same challenge for girls high in body objectification. Use of oral contraceptives does require that participants are planning for and expecting to engage in sexual activity and that they acknowledge these intentions to a parent or physician. Girls who silence their own thoughts and desires may be less likely to negotiate the initiation of intercourse with a partner or discuss it with an adult. Indeed, a common theme among adolescent girls' stories of first intercourse is that of "it just happened" (Tolman, 2002). Girls who silence their true thoughts and desires may be less likely to experience sexuality with conscious intentions and may therefore be less likely to use hormonal contraception.

We should also note that neither of the femininity ideology factors predicted use of protection during the most recent intercourse experience. It is possible that girls' beliefs about femininity may play a greater role in the beginning of relationships when people rely on gender stereotypes and others' expectations to guide their actions. This explanation is consistent with research on stereotyping processes that shows that increasing familiarity decreases the use of stereotypes (e.g., Fiske, 1998). That is, in the beginning of a relationship, girls' beliefs about gender may influence their use of protection; later on, other concerns may take precedence. Indeed, previous research indicates that as relationships progress, the choice to use condoms as opposed to hormonal contraception becomes conflated with questions of trust and, consequently, many girls elect not to use condoms (e.g., Reisen & Poppen, 1995). Our data were consistent with this pattern; from first to last intercourse, there was a substantial drop in the number of participants who used only condoms (approximately 25%), and a roughly equivalent increase in the number of participants who used hormonal contraception only or no protection at all. For these girls, the lack of condom use may be predicated on other factors of their relationships, such as trust or familiarity. Even outside the context of a relationship, girls' increasing experience and familiarity with sexual activity may function to lessen the importance of gender ideology in sexual decision making. Internalizing ideas about femininity may be especially disadvantageous to adolescent girls who are just beginning to explore sexual activity, who, due to their lack of experience, may rely more heavily on gendered scripts.

Several limitations of this research deserve comment. First, although the sample included moderate numbers of both white and Latina (mostly Dominican) girls, girls from other ethnic groups (e.g., Asian-American, African-American) were underrepresented. Further, there were not sufficient numbers of Latina girls to permit comparisons among ethnic groups. In some ethnic groups, women and girls are actively discouraged from asserting themselves sexually, particularly from initiating discussions about condom use (e.g., Gómez & Marín, 1996). In addition, this sample included a much higher proportion of Catholic girls than are included in the general population. Future research is needed to examine the potential ways in which ethnicity, race, class, religion, and other factors interact with femininity ideology during adolescence. A further limitation of this study is that it was restricted to heterosexual adolescent girls. Future studies should examine the ways in which femininity ideology is linked with sexual health for lesbian adolescent girls.

Second, the direction of causal relations remains to be determined. Feminist developmental theory predicts that lower sexual self-efficacy and riskier sex are liabilities of internalizing conventional aspects of femininity ideology, implying directionality. That is, if a girl suppresses her own wishes and desires and objectifies her own body, she will be more likely to engage in risky sex. It could also be, however, that the extent to which a girl suppresses her desires and objectifies her body is influenced and shaped by her sexual experiences. It is also possible that such a relationship eventually becomes reciprocal, in that internalizing conventional norms of femininity may lead to poorer sexual self-efficacy and more risky sex; subsequently, girls in their abilities to say no to unwanted sexual interactions or protect themselves

in sexual situations, the more they may suppress their own bodily feelings and authentic voices.

Third, the measure of inauthenticity in relationships was not specific to romantic relationships, but instead, assessed a girl's tendency to silence her thoughts and feelings in relationships in general (i.e., with peers). It is not clear the extent to which a girl silences herself in peer relationships overlaps with the degree to which she silences her voice in romantic relationships (particularly in heterosexual relationships in which power differentials are embedded). We believe that had we measured inauthenticity in dating or sexual relationships more specifically, we may have found stronger associations between relationship inauthenticity and actual sexual behavior. Thus, the development of a comparable measure of inauthenticity in romantic relationships that can be used in adolescent samples may make a useful contribution to this line of investigation. Qualitative research would be an important first step in identifying which aspects of relationship authenticity are most salient for adolescent girls in romantic relationships.

Finally, questions can be raised about the validity of self-reports of sexual behavior (Catania, Gibson, Chitwood, & Coates, 1990). One barrier to valid reporting is that participants may have provided socially desirable responses, such as by underreporting instances of sex or unprotected sex. While social desirability may have limited honest reporting, it is not clear how it would have specifically affected the theoretical link between femininity ideology and sexual risk taking. Another barrier concerns the retrospective nature of the data collection, as participants may have experienced difficulties in recalling events fully and accurately. Previous research suggests that first and most recent sexual experiences are highly memorable and salient (Hearn, O'Sullivan, & Dudley, 2003; Kauth, St. Lawrence, & Kelly, 1991). Nonetheless, future research could employ daily experience methods to collect sexual behavior data that minimizes retrospective bias (e.g., Impett, Peplau, & Gable, 2005).

This study suggests several important directions for future research. Our study provides a snapshot of girls at one time point in late adolescence. One future direction concerns the developmental trajectories of girls as they mature throughout adolescence and young adulthood. Do girls tend to internalize or become more resistant to femininity ideologies as they mature? Are possible changes in femininity ideology associated with changes in sexual health over time? Are such trajectories influenced by a girl's race, class, or social status? These questions seem especially important given our findings of differences between first and last intercourse. Longitudinal research designs that utilize latent growth curve methods would be ideal to answer such developmental questions and would enable us to examine more directly the causal association between femininity ideology and sexual health.

A second fruitful direction for future research would be to focus on the gender ideologies and sexual health of boys (Tolman, Spencer, Harmon, Rosen-Reynoso, & Striepe, 2004). Healthy heterosexual interactions require both girls *and* boys to communicate their desires for protection in clear ways. To what extent does internalizing traditional ideas about masculinity impact boys' sexual health? Such gendered ideas include concerns that boys should present themselves as tough and sexually active as well as hide feelings of vulnerability in relationships (Chu, Porche, & Tolman, 2005). Previous research with adolescent boys found that masculinity ideology defined in terms of social gender roles was associated with using condoms less consistently, viewing condoms as reducing male sexual pleasure, being less concerned with whether a partner wanted him to use a condom, believing that males are less responsible for preventing pregnancy and having greater beliefs that pregnancy validates masculinity (Pleck, Sonenstein, & Ku, 1993). The Pleck et al. study focused primarily on preventing pregnancy. It is possible that while boys high in masculinity ideology may not view it as their responsibility to prevent pregnancy, they may take more seriously concerns about preventing the transmission of STIs. Future research could determine whether there are different dimensions of masculinity ideology that are associated with different forms of protection.

A third useful direction for future research would be to collect data from both partners in a romantic relationship. Previous research on married couples has documented moderate associations between spouses' scores on measures of sex role attitudes, with traditional men partnered with traditional women and less traditional men partnered with less traditional women (Peplau, Hill, & Rubin, 1993). Girls who espouse traditional ideas about femininity with partners who also espouse conventional conceptions of femininity (or masculinity) may be at heightened risk, especially given the unequal power dynamics in such relationships (Amaro, 1995). Future research should explore the ways in which both partners' ideas about gender interact to predict sexual health and risk. Although many adolescent relationships are relatively transient, particularly in early adolescence, relationships in middle to late adolescence tend to be more committed and long lasting (Carver, Joyner, & Udry, 2003) making such a developmental period in adolescents' lives ripe for dyadic research.

Given the noted limitations of this study, we developed and tested theoretical predictions from feminist developmental theory about how internalizing conventional ideologies about femininity is associated with adolescent girls' sexual self-efficacy and sexual protection behavior. This research provides the foundation for more expanded models of gender ideology and sexual health, including the experiences of adolescent boys and the role of masculinity ideology. Future research should examine the ways in which girls' and boys' beliefs about gender interact so that we may more fully understand the ways in which patriarchy as it is operationalized in both femininity and masculinity ideologies shapes the lives and sexual experiences of young people.

Acknowledgments

This research was supported by postdoctoral fellowships awarded to Emily A. Impett and Deborah Schooler from the Center for Research on Gender and Sexuality and by grants from the National Institute of Child Health and Development (Grant No. R29 HD33281-02) and the Ford Foundation awarded to Deborah L. Tolman. The authors would like to thank Celeste Hirschman, Janna Kim, Alice Michael, and Lynn Sorsoli for helpful comments on an earlier draft.

References

Alan Guttmacher Institute (1999). *Teenage pregnancy: Overall trends and state-by-state information.* New York: AGI.

Amaro, H. (1995). Love, sex, and power: Considering women's realities in HIV prevention. *American Psychologist, 50,* 437–447.

Baron, R. M., & Kenny, D. A. (1986). The moderator-mediator variable distinction in social psychological research: Conceptual, strategic and statistical considerations. *Journal of Personality and Social Psychology, 51,* 1173–1182.

Bartky, S. L. (1990). *Femininity and domination: Studies in the phenomenology of oppression.* New York: Routledge.

Bentler, P. M. (1990). Comparative fit indexes in structural models. *Psychological Bulletin, 107,* 238–246.

Bentler, P. M. (1995). *EQS structural equations program manual.* Encino, CA: Multivariate Software, Inc.

Bordo, S. (1993). *Unbearable weight: Feminism, western culture, and the body.* Berkeley, CA: University of California Press.

Brown, L. M. (1998). *Raising their voices: The politics of girls' anger.* Cambridge, MA: Harvard University Press.

Brown, L. M., & Gilligan, C. (1992). *Meeting at the crossroads: Women's psychology and girls' development.* Cambridge, MA: Harvard University Press.

Browne, M. W., & Cudeck, R. (1993). Alternative ways of assessing model fit. In K. Bollen & J. S. Long (Eds.), *Testing structural equation models* (pp. 136–162). Newbury Park, CA: Sage.

Brumberg, J. J. (1997). *The body project: An intimate history of American girls.* New York: Random House.

Carver, K., Joyner, K., & Udry, J. R. (2003). National estimates of adolescent romantic relationships. In P. Florsheim (Ed.), *Adolescent romantic relations and sexual behavior* (pp. 23–56). Mahwah, NJ: Lawrence Erlbaum Associates.

Catania, J. A., Gibson, D. R., Chitwood, D. D., & Coates, T. J. (1990). Methodological problems in AIDS behavioral research: Influences on measurement error and participation bias in studies of sexual behavior. *Psychological Bulletin, 108,* 339–362.

CDC. (2003a). *STD surveillance 2003.* Retrieved July 19, 2005, from http://www.cdc.gov/std/stats/adol.htm.

CDC. (2003b). *HIV/AIDS surveillance in adolescents.* Retrieved July 19, 2005, from http://www.cdc.gov/hiv/graphics/adolesnt.htm.

Christopher, F. S. (2001). *To dance the dance: A symbolic interactional exploration of premarital sexuality.* Mahwah, NJ: Lawrence Erlbaum Associates.

Chu, J. Y., Porche, M. V., & Tolman, D. L. (2005). The Adolescent Masculinity Ideology in Relationships Scale: Development and validation of a new measure for boys. *Men and Masculinities, 8,* 93–115.

Crosby, R. A., Holtgrave, D. R., DiClemente, R. J., Wingood, G. M., & Gayle, J. A. (2003). Social capital as a predictor of adolescents' sexual risk behavior: A state-level exploratory study. *AIDS and Behavior, 7,* 245–252.

Cross, S. E., & Madson, L. (1997). Models of the self: Self-construals and gender. *Psychological Bulletin, 122,* 5–37.

Davis, K. R., & Weller, S. G. (1999). The effectiveness of condoms in reducing heterosexual transmission of HIV. *Family Planning Perspectives, 31,* 272–279.

de Beauvoir, S. (1961). *The second sex.* New York: Bantam Books.

Dove, N. L., & Wiederman, M. W. (2000). Cognitive distraction and women's sexual functioning. *Journal of Sex and Marital Therapy, 26,* 67–78.

Ehrhardt, A. A. (1996). Our view of adolescent sexuality: A focus on risk behavior without the developmental context [Editorial]. *American Journal of Public Health, 86,* 1523–1525.

Entwisle, D. R., & Astone, N. M. (1994). Some practical guidelines for measuring youth's race/ethnicity and socioeconomic status. *Child Development, 65,* 1521–1540.

Erikson, E. (1968). *Identity, youth and crisis.* New York: W. W. Norton.

Fiske, S. T. (1998). Stereotyping, prejudice and discrimination. In D. T. Gilbert, S. T. Fiske, & G. Lindzey (Eds.), *Handbook of social psychology* (4th ed., Vol. 2, pp. 357–411). Boston, MA: McGraw Hill.

Fredrickson, B. L., & Roberts, T. A. (1997). Objectification theory: Toward understanding women's lived experiences and mental health risks. *Psychology of Women Quarterly, 21,* 173–206.

Gilligan, C. (1982). *In a different voice: Psychological theory and women's development.* Cambridge, MA: Harvard University Press.

Goldman, J. A., & Harlow, L. L. (1993). Self-perception variables that mediate AIDS-preventive behavior in college students. *Health Psychology, 12,* 489–498.

Gómez, C. A., & Marín, B. V. (1996). Gender, culture, and power: Barriers to HIV prevention strategies for women. *Journal of Sex Research, 33,* 355–362.

Harter, S., Waters, P. L., & Whitesell, N. R. (1997). Lack of voice as a manifestation of false self-behavior among adolescents: The school setting as a stage upon which the drama of authenticity is enacted. *Educational Psychologist, 32*, 153–173.

Hearn, K. D., O'Sullivan, L. F., & Dudley, C. D. (2003). Assessing reliability of early adolescent girls' reports of romantic and sexual behavior. *Archives of Sexual Behavior, 32*, 513–521.

Henshaw, S. K. (1998). Unintended pregnancy in the United States. *Family Planning Perspectives, 30*, 24–29, 46.

Holland, J., Ramazanoglu, C., Sharpe, S., & Thomson, R. (1998). *The male in the head: Young people, heterosexuality, and power.* London: Tufnell Press.

Hu, L. T., & Bentler, P. M. (1999). Cutoff criteria for fit indices in covariance structure analysis: Conventional criteria versus new alternatives. *Structural Equation Modeling, 6*, 1–55.

Impett, E. A., & Peplau, L. A. (2003). Sexual compliance: Gender, motivational, and relationship perspectives. *Journal of Sex Research, 40*, 87–100.

Impett, E. A., Peplau, L. A., & Gable, S. L. (2005). Approach and avoidance sexual motivation: Implications for personal and interpersonal well-being. *Personal Relationships, 12*, 465–482.

Jack, D. C., & Dill, D. (1992). The silencing the self scale: Schemas of intimacy associated with depression in women. *Psychology of Women Quarterly, 16*, 97–106.

Jagger, A. M. (1983). *Feminist politics and human nature.* Totowa, NJ: Rowman and Allanheld.

Jordan, J. V., Kaplan, A. G., Miller, J. B., Stiver, I. P., & Surrey, J. L. (1991). *Women's growth in connection: Writings from the Stone Center.* New York: Guilford.

Kauth, M. R., St. Lawrence, J. S., & Kelly, J. A. (1991). Reliability of retrospective assessments of sexual HIV risk behavior: A comparison of biweekly, three-month, and twelve-month self-reports. *AIDS Education and Prevention, 3*, 207–214.

Kline, R. B. (2005). *Principles and practice of structural equation modeling* (2nd ed.). New York: Guilford Press.

Levinson, R. A. (1986). Contraceptive self-efficacy: A perspective on teenage girls' contraceptive behavior. *Journal of Sex Research, 22*, 347–369.

Manlove, J., Ryan, S., & Franzetta, K. (2003). Patterns of contraceptive use within teenagers' first sexual relationships. *Perspectives on Sexual and Reproductive Health, 35*, 246–255.

McCree, D. H., Wingood, G. M., DiClemente, R., Davies, S., & Harrington, K. F. (2003). Religiosity and risky sexual behavior in African-American adolescent females. *Journal of Adolescent Health, 33*, 2–8.

McKinley, N. M., & Hyde, J. S. (1996). The objectified body consciousness scale: Development and validation. *Psychology of Women Quarterly, 20*, 181–215.

Parsons, J. T., Halkitis, P. N., Bimbi, D., & Borkowski, T. (2000). Perceptions of the benefits and costs associated with condom use and unprotected sex among late adolescent college students. *Journal of Adolescence, 23*, 377–391.

Peplau, L. A., Hill, C. T., & Rubin, Z. (1993). Sex-role attitudes in dating and marriage: A 15-year follow-up of the Boston Couples Study. *Journal of Social Issues, 49*, 31–52.

Pleck, J. H., Sonenstein, F. L., & Ku, L. C. (1993). Masculinity ideology: Its impact on adolescent males' heterosexual relationships. *Journal of Social Issues, 49*, 11–29.

Quina, K., Harlow, L. L., Morokoff, P. J., Burkholder, G., & Deiter, P. J. (2000). Sexual communication in relationships: When words speak louder than actions. *Sex Roles, 42*, 523–549.

Reisen, C. A., & Poppen, P. J. (1995). College women and condom use: Importance of partner relationship. *Journal of Applied Social Psychology, 25*, 1485–1498.

Rosenthal, D. A., & Shepherd, H. (1993). A six-month follow-up of adolescents' sexual risk-taking, HIV/AIDS knowledge, and attitudes to condoms. *Journal of Community and Applied Social Psychology, 3*, 53–65.

Schooler, D., & Ward, L. M., Merriwether, A., & Caruthers, A. (2005). Cycles of shame: Menstrual shame, body shame, and sexual decision-making. *Journal of Sex Research, 42*, 324–334.

SIECUS. (1995). *Consensus statement from the National Commission on Adolescent Sexual Health.* New York: SIECUS.

Sobel, M. E. (1982). Asymptotic confidence intervals for indirect effects in structural equation models. In S. Leinhardt (Ed.), *Sociological methodology* (pp. 290–312). Washington, DC: American Sociological Association.

Tolman, D. L. (1999). Femininity as a barrier to positive sexual health for adolescent girls. *Journal of the American Medical Women's Association, 54*, 133–138.

Tolman, D. L. (2002). *Dilemmas of desire: Teenage girls talk about sexuality.* Cambridge, MA: Harvard University Press.

Tolman, D. L., & Debold, E. (1993). Conflicts of body and image: Female adolescents, desire, and the no-body body. In P. Fallon, M. Katzman, & S. Wooley (Eds.), *Feminist perspectives on eating disorders* (pp. 301–317). New York: Guilford Press.

Tolman, D. L., Impett, E. A., Tracy, A. J., & Michael, A. (in press). Looking good, sounding good: Femininity ideology and adolescent girls' mental health. *Psychology of Women Quarterly.*

Tolman, D. L., & Porche, M. V. (2000). The Adolescent Femininity Ideology Scale: Development and validation of a new measure for girls. *Psychology of Women Quarterly, 24,* 365–376.

Tolman, D. L., Spencer, R., Harmon, T., Rosen-Reynoso, M., & Striepe, M. (2004). Getting close, staying cool: Early adolescent boys' experiences with romantic relationships. In N. Way & J. Y. Chu (Eds.), *Adolescent boys: Exploring diverse cultures of boyhood* (pp. 236–255). New York: New York University Press.

Tolman, D. L., Spencer, R., Rosen-Reynoso, M., & Porche, M. (2003). Sowing the seeds of violence in heterosexual relationships: Early adolescents narrate compulsory heterosexuality. *Journal of Social Issues, 59,* 159–178.

Tolman, D. L., Striepe, M. I., & Harmon, T. (2003). Gender matters: Constructing a model of adolescent sexual health. *Journal of Sex Research, 40,* 4–12.

Walsh, T. L., Frezieres, R. G., Peacock, K., Nelson, A. L., Clark, V. A., Berstein, L., et al. (2004). Effectiveness of the male latex condom: Combined results for three popular condom brands used as controls in randomized clinical trials. *Contraception, 70,* 407–413.

Wiederman, M. W. (2000). Women's body image self-consciousness during physical intimacy with a partner. *Journal of Sex Research, 37,* 60–68.

Wingood, G. M., & DiClemente, R. J. (1998). Partner influences and gender-related factors associated with noncondom use among young adult African American women. *American Journal of Community Psychology, 26,* 29–51.

Wingood, G. M., DiClemente, R. J., Harrington, K., & Davies, S. (2002). Body image and African American females' sexual health. *Journal of Women's Health and Gender-Based Medicine, 11,* 433–439.

Exposed at Last:
The Truth about Your
Clitoris

by Jennifer Johnson

"At a witch trial in 1593, the investigating lawyer (a married man) apparently discovered a clitoris for the first time; he identified it as a devil's teat, sure proof of the witch's guilt. It was 'a little lump of flesh, in a manner sticking out as if it had been a teat, to the length of half an inch,' which the gaoler, 'perceiving at the first sight there of, meant not to disclose, because it was adjoining to so secret a place which was not decent to be seen. Yet in the end, not willing to conceal so strange a matter,' he showed it to various bystanders. The witch was convicted."

from The Vagina Monologues *by Eve Ensler [Villard].*

Pick up almost any medical, anatomy or biology text and you'll find something missing: the greater part of the clitoris.

The clitoris is like an iceberg; only the tip is visible on the outside, its larger mass is under the surface. The visible tip is the glans, or head of the organ. While modern medical science books stop there, the clitoris actually continues under the pelvic bone, then turns down to surround the vagina from above and on either side. The structure forms a dense pyramid of tissue, well-supplied with nerve and vascular network, and is comparable in size to

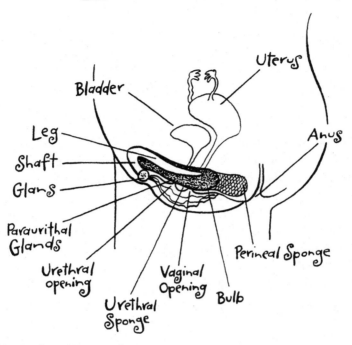

Cross Section of the Non-Erect Clitoris

Illustration: Noreen Stevens

the penis. Like the male organ, the clitoris is flaccid when unaroused and erect when aroused.

And yet, even in the most ponderous, detailed texts, the clitoris is described as a "vestigial organ," or "peasized." The diagrams typically show a diagram of a spread-legged female, with a little bulb arrowed "clitoris." The internal diagrams show her reproductive organs, but the bulk of the clitoris—the shaft (body), legs (crura), and bulbs—are missing. Next to the illustration showing the female sex organ as a bump usually appears a drawing of the male sex organ on an extremely well-hung man. Even *Gray's Anatomy*—the authoritative text of biologists—doesn't accurately depict the clitoris.

As a biologist, I first discovered this while doing an anatomical study (dissection) on a human subject. I was shocked to discover that the clitoris was far larger than I had been taught. I could not understand how such a basic—not to mention crucial—piece of biological information had been neglected. I searched textbooks, consulted doctors and professors and found all of them unaware of the actual size of the clitoris.

Of course, I was not the only student of science to discover this. When Helen O'Connell became curious about why the female sex organ was "glossed over" in the texts, she made it her business to take a closer look when she became a doctor. Now a surgeon at the Royal Melbourne Hospital in Australia, she and her colleagues have been dissecting and measuring the clitoris; her findings were reported in a recent article in *New Scientist*. "Sometimes the whole structure is drawn as a dot," says Dr. O'Connell. In fact, the legs of the clitoris, called the crura, are five to nine centimeters long, extending from the body (shaft) of the clitoris and filling the space between its legs are two bulbs, one on either side of the vaginal cavity. Contrary to the belief that the urethra and clitoris are entirely separate, the clitoris actually encompasses the urethra. Dr. O'Connell believes the clitoris squeezes the urethra shut during sex, reducing the entry of bacteria.

Drawing a more accurate picture of the female sexual anatomy explains a few things. It helps explain why some women are not having orgasms, since women must first be erect before they can reach orgasm. It may also explain why Viagra appears to work for women even though it's not supposed to—suggesting that women may be impotent for the same physiological reasons as men. It also explains why women frequently report that their sex lives were damaged following some types of pelvic surgery—the nerves to the clitoris, and sometimes the organ itself, can be damaged or severed during surgery. It also sheds light on the controversy of the clitoral vs. vaginal orgasm that was debated a few years ago.

When seen as an entire complex organ, there is room for a wide range of experiences. Some women experience orgasm through stimulation of the outer glans of the clitoris; at other times they may experience a different orgasm when combined with penetration. An orgasm reached through external stimulation may feel quite different. For many women, orgasm is intense and relatively easy to reach with digital or oral contact because this is the most direct way to stimulate the large pudendal nerve which runs straight down into the tip of the clitoris (the glans). What has been referred to as "the vaginal orgasm" is a vaginal-induced orgasm, brought on by stimulating the clitoris indirectly through the vaginal walls. (Of course, it's common to add some direct pudendal stimulation on the outside.)

Then there is the G-spot. Part of the vaginal wall clinically known as the urethral sponge, the G-spot can be found by exploring the roof of the vagina. It's about a knuckle-length in—from one and a half to three inches inside. The easiest way to find it is to have your partner crook a finger or two and reach toward the belly button. The size varies from half an inch to 1.5 inches. When unaroused, it feels like the back of the roof of your mouth. If your partner presses up on this spot and you feel like you have to urinate, they've found it. When it is stroked, it will puff out and feel like a marshmallow.

While there are many differences between male and female sexual responses, there are unmistakably many similarities. When the clitoris is engorged and erect, endorphins are released and induce a 'high.' The long bands of the crura become hard and flare out along the pubic bones. Vaginal blood vessels widen and fill with blood and the perineal sponge thickens. The uterus balloons forward, the tubes and ovaries swell. The broad ligament tightens, pulling up the uterus and causing the vagina to enlarge. The neck of the cervix is flexible, like an accordion, and during orgasm, the cervix moves forward and down, dipping its head in the seminal pool if a male partner has ejaculated. As well, ejaculation fluid squirts from the woman's paraurithal glands, located on either side of the urethra. This may come as news to women who haven't had a female sexual partner and therefore may not have experienced a female ejaculation first hand. The ejaculate may be a small amount and not noticeable, or it may be a copious amount that 'soaks the sheets.'

The size of the clitoris is actually not a new 'discovery' but the revealing of a secret. The clitoris was more accurately described in some 19th century anatomy texts, but then it was mysteriously shrunk into a mere speck on the anatomical map. The French, however, have been more accurately depicting the clitoris since before the turn of the century.

While doing research for this article, I contacted many sex-related organizations, including the famous Kinsey Institute, the British Association for Sexual and Marital Therapy, even the German Society for Sex Research. None had accurate information on the clitoris, and most did not believe that the clitoris is larger and more complex than medical texts indicate. In bookstores, I found current sexology books that didn't have more than a paragraph on the clitoris, some only a few lines,

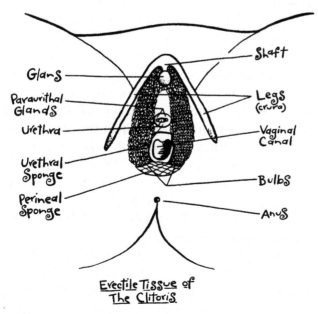

Glans
Paraurithal Glands
Urethra
Urethral Sponge
Perineal Sponge

Shaft
Legs (crura)
Vaginal Canal
Bulbs
Anus

Erectile Tissue of The Clitoris

Illustration: Noreen Stevens

many did not have "clitoris" indexed at all! Even the famous British 'feminist' scientist Desmond Morris's new book, *The Human Sexes*, contains no indexed references for clitoris. Without exception, every sex book gave 'penis' all kinds of room—entire sections, chapters and references.

What does it all mean? Dr. Jennifer Berman, director of the Women's Sexual Health Clinic at Boston University, predicts that knowing the proper female anatomy will lead to research in this area of female function and dysfunction, which she says has been "grossly neglected."

In an article published with her colleagues in *The Journal of Urology* in June 1998, Dr. O'Connell and her colleagues wrote, "Since the studies of Masters and Johnson, there has been surprisingly little investigation of basic female sexual anatomy or physiology." The article describes the intricate connection between the urethra and the clitoris and says that surgeons should be made aware of

the damage that can be done to the organ during urethral surgery. O'Connell says anatomy texts should be changed to accurately depict the clitoris and perineal anatomy. She is now mapping the nerves to the pelvic region innervating the female sex organ.

"They were mapped in men a decade ago," says O'Connell, "but they've never been mapped in women."

It does beg the question doesn't it? Why not? One anthropologist I spoke to explained that the size of the clitoris may have been overlooked because "the size of the male phallus" is a symbol of power; admitting women have the same size organ would be like admitting they are equally powerful. Indeed.

Sex psychologist Dr. Micheal Bailey doesn't buy into the patriarchal conspiracy theory. "There's been very little scientific interest in female sexuality," he insists. Then adds, "It's possible *we* didn't look."

Notes from the Back Room: Gender, Power, and (In)Visibility in Women's Experiences of Masturbation

by Breanne Fahs and Elena Frank
Women and Gender Studies Program, Arizona State University

While popular culture has more frequently depicted women's masturbation in recent years, scholarly attention to women's own meaning making about masturbation remains largely absent. Existing research that emphasizes women's masturbation frequency, health correlates, masturbation as a factor in couples therapy, and masturbation as a substitute for partnered sexual behaviors have dominated the research, largely neglecting social identity correlates and women's subjectivities about masturbation. This study drew upon qualitative interviews with 20 women (mean age = 34, SD = 13.35) from diverse backgrounds to illuminate five themes in women's experiences with masturbation: a) assumptions that most women self-penetrate during masturbation even when primarily using clitoral stimulation; b) masturbation as sexual labor; c) masturbation as a threat to male dominance; d) masturbation as routine tension release; and e) masturbation as a source of joy, fun, and pleasure. Because women revealed such a diverse set of experiences, we explored the advantages and disadvantages of the invisibility of women's masturbation. As a result of the internalization of stereotypically masculine scripts about sexuality—including an imagined penetrative focus, goal-oriented drive toward orgasm, sex as labor, and masturbation as nonemotional—women's masturbation experiences, regardless of sexual orientation, revealed the power imbalances often present in partnered (hetero)sexual dynamics.

Despite the ever-present media fixation on women's sexuality—particularly the exploitation of imagery surrounding women's bodies and attractiveness—minimal scholarly attention has addressed women's experiences of masturbation as a relevant and visible aspect of their sexual expression. While representations or discussions of women's masturbation on popular television programs such as *Sex and the City* and *Oprah*, or feminist-minded online news outlets or blogs such as *Jezebel* or dodsonandross.com clearly provide a challenge to a cultural silence regarding women and masturbation, they stand in stark contrast to the plethora of long-standing depictions, representations, and discussions of men's masturbation as a valid, humorous, deviant, or important part of men's lives, particularly for adolescent boys as they "come of age" (Hall, 1992; Halpern, Udry, Suchindran, & Campbell, 2000; Laqueur, 2003; Stein & Reiser, 1994). For example, while men have a fairly extensive lexicon to draw from when talking about and discussing their genitals and masturbation (e.g., "spanking the monkey," "jacking off," and "choking the chicken"), the cultural lexicon seems to have relatively few terms applicable to women's genitals and masturbation (e.g., "jilling off" and "double-clicking the mouse"). In fact, girls are often not even taught the terms or provided with representations of the details of their genitalia, such as *vulva, clitoris,* or *labia* (De Marneffe, 1997; Fields, 2008; Lerner, 1976), resulting in a "missing discourse of desire" for young women (Fine, 1988). Consequently, the relative *invisibility* of women's masturbation infects women's consciousness about how they *talk about, think about,* and *engage in* masturbation. Further, this invisibility often arrives in tandem with other power-laden assumptions about gender, power, and bodies. We argue that deeper examinations of women's own meaning making

surrounding masturbation can reveal both cultural biases about gender and power that manifest in women's "private" lives, while also highlighting different interpretations women have about entitlement to pleasure, techniques for managing their own and others' sexual needs, and, ultimately, their deeply entrenched feelings about the "sexually normal" body.

Literature on Women's Masturbation
Historical Aspects of Research on Women and Masturbation

Academic cultural histories on the topic of masturbation tend to focus primarily on men, as there is little historical information available on women and masturbation (Bennett & Vernon, 1995; Brenot, 2005; Laqueur, 2003). While women's masturbation has appeared in both art and literature, including analyses of paintings of witches and prostitutes as autonomous agents of sexual pleasure (Weigerl, 1995), Jane Austen's "masturbating girl" (Sedgwick, 1995), historical accounts of masturbating women as "polluting" (Rosario, 1995), and late-19th-century poetry that referenced masturbating women (Bennett, 1995), far more historical attention has focused on men's masturbation.

Most of the information we do have on women comes largely from the records of medical practitioners. In the Victorian period, doctors treated "compulsive" masturbating women as mad and sent them to mental hospitals for treatment and cure (Maines, 2001). Furthermore, though some debate has ensued about the histories of these practices (King, 2011), doctors may have used vibrators in medical settings to "cure" women of hysteria and other bodily and psychological ailments, though these "treatments" did not constitute *sexual* exchanges but rather medical ones (Maines,

2001). Though Freud suggested (quite controversially and several decades later) that both men and women had sexual urges and that "mature" women could orgasm vaginally, little scientific attention was paid to women's masturbatory behavior or experiences.

Research conducted by Kinsey, Pomeroy, Martin, and Gebhard (1953), Masters and Johnson (1966), and Hite (1976) sought to extend the realm of knowledge regarding women's sexuality. These three game-changing studies provided the basis for research on women's sexuality and masturbation worldwide. Kinsey and colleagues (1953) published their landmark study of female sexual behavior in which almost half of the women interviewed ($N = 2,800$) described masturbating at some time during their lives. Kinsey examined such variables as women's "first source" of orgasm, as well as frequency, techniques, attitudes, and sources of information about women's masturbation. In doing so, he helped debunk the notion that penises (or phallic objects) were necessary for women's sexual pleasure, as only 20% of Kinsey's subjects used vaginal insertion in connection with masturbation (Kinsey et al., 1953).

Masters and Johnson's (1966) subsequent research on orgasmic women also dispelled myths regarding the necessity of a phallus for women's sexual pleasure, finding that women's "inability" to orgasm generally corresponded with engaging in penile-vaginal intercourse. Masturbation served as a more effective and efficient means to orgasm, just as it functioned as pain relief for menstruating women and as a method for curing "sexual frustrations" when men were absent (Masters & Johnson, 1966). The following decade, activist and artist Betty Dodson (1974) established masturbation as an important women's liberation issue. Correspondingly, Hite (1976) injected feminism into the science of sex, finding that the conditions of sexuality mirrored the unequal conditions of the culture at large. Divorcing masturbation from partnered sex, Hite (1976) critiqued the way masturbation seemed to function as "replacement sex." Hite's open-ended survey encouraged women to express their individual experiences and perceptions of masturbation, illuminating various ways that masturbation may teach women about their bodies, pleasures, and sexual self-reliance.

Psychological Correlates of Masturbation

In the wake of these groundbreaking studies, a pool of small-scale psychological research emerged that examined women's masturbation practices. The findings of these studies tended to associate women's masturbation with perceived negative characteristics such as guilt (Greenberg & Archambault, 1973; Kelley, 1985), depression (Arafat & Cotton, 1974), pathological deviance (Clower, 1975), unattractiveness (Durham & Grossnickle, 1982), partnered sexual experience or promiscuity (Davidson & Moore, 1994; Herold & Way, 1983), and use of pornography or erotic literature (Clark & Wiederman, 2000). Focusing on the relationship between masturbation (or masturbation guilt) and public health outcomes, other studies specifically examined correlations between masturbation attitudes and behaviors, and attitudes about contraceptive methods (Davidson & Moore, 1994; Mosher & Vonderheide, 1985), and abortion attitudes (Kelley, 1979). Notably, few studies have assessed women's techniques for masturbation (e.g., breast self-stimulation), while far more studies have addressed techniques during partnered sexual activities (Basson, 2000; Levin & Meston, 2006).

In the first nationally representative study to address the topic for decades, Laumann, Gagnon, Michael, and Michaels (1994) gathered data on masturbation in adulthood, including frequency, whether orgasm occurred, and whether participants reported masturbation guilt, concluding that such social factors as education, ethnicity, sexual identity, religion, and marital status all influenced attitudes and behaviors about women's masturbation (Laumann et al., 1994).

That said, some more recent studies have linked women's masturbation and orgasms during masturbation with other positive aspects of women's lives, particularly sexual satisfaction (Phillippsohn & Hartmann, 2009), improvement of mood (Escajadillo-Vargas et al., 2011), reduction in menopausal symptoms (Avis et al., 2009), emotional intelligence (Burri, Cherkas,

& Spector, 2009), and better genital self-image (Herbenick, Schick, et al., 2011), suggesting that research from the past several years yields a more positive appraisal of women's masturbation.

Gender, Sexuality, and Racial Differences in Masturbation

Much of the existing research on masturbation has focused on gender differences between men and women, with consistent findings that men masturbated more often than women (Arafat & Cotton, 1974; Oliver & Hyde, 1993; Petersen & Hyde, 2011), women felt more stigma about masturbating than did men (Kaestle & Allen, 2011), women relied more on (male) partners' approval and comfort with masturbation than did men (Kaestle & Allen, 2011), and women possessed a more negative attitude toward masturbation compared to men (Clark & Wiederman, 2000). In addition, in a study where male masturbators showed higher levels of "neuroticism" than did female masturbators, the author suggested that men "get sex" from women while women do not rely on "getting sex" from men (and therefore men without sex are more neurotic and need to masturbate) (Abramson, 1973).

When examining differences between lesbian and heterosexual women, another early study found that lesbians reported more frequent orgasms during masturbation and partnered sex, and were more sexually satisfied than heterosexual women (Coleman, Hoon, & Hoon, 1983), suggesting that lesbian women's more frequent reliance on clitoral stimulation may lead to higher satisfaction and orgasm compared to heterosexual women (Bressler & Lavender, 1986; Iasenza, 2002; Schreurs & Buunk, 1996) and more frequent masturbation compared to heterosexual women (Laumann et al., 1994). With regard to racial differences in masturbation, researchers have typically studied differences between White women's and Black women's masturbation experiences, with the results generally indicating higher rates of masturbation among White women (Bancroft, Long, & McCabe, 2011; Fisher, 1980; Robinson, Bockting, & Harrell, 2002; Shulman & Horne, 2003; Wyatt, Peters, & Guthrie, 1988). Another study found that both Asian/Pacific Islander women and Black women masturbated less often than White women (Das, 2007).

Vibrators and Masturbation

Researchers have found positive benefits of both vibrator use and masturbation in general, though controversy surrounds the promotion of masturbation as a public health priority (Coleman, 2002). While a few studies have explored how women use vibrators and what health behaviors correspond with vibrator use (Herbenick et al., 2009; Herbenick et al., 2010), other research has demonstrated links between masturbation (sometimes with vibrators) and improvements in women's self-awareness, body image, self-esteem, and overall sexual pleasure (Coleman, 2002; Herbenick et al., 2009; Hurlbert & Whittaker, 1991; Shulman & Horne, 2003). In a study of American women, participants reported primarily using vibrators for clitoral stimulation and to enhance sexual pleasure (Davis, Blank, Lin, & Bonillas, 1996). Nearly two-thirds of women used vibrators during partnered sexual activities and during masturbation; women described vibrators as contributing to intense orgasms and high levels of satisfaction whether alone or with partners (Davis et al., 1996). In the most comprehensive study of American women's vibrator use to date, researchers found that 52.5% of women used vibrators and 46.% used them during masturbation (many also used them in partnered sex). Vibrator users described greater likelihood of engaging in other healthy behaviors like getting regular gynecological exams and performing genital self-examinations during the previous month (Herbenick et al., 2009), and vibrator use also correlated with increased sexual desire, arousal, lubrication, orgasm, absence of sexual pain, and overall sexual functioning (Herbenick et al., 2009; Herbenick, Reece, et al., 2011).

Global Studies on Women's Masturbation

While most masturbation research has studied women from the United States, some studies have examined populations from Europe and Asia. One British study found that women with same-sex partners and higher levels of education masturbated more frequently and that White women masturbated more often than women of color (Gerressu, Mercer, Graham, Wellings, & Johnson, 2008). Women who masturbated typically had more frequent vaginal sex, a greater repertoire of sexual activity, and more sexual partners in the past year compared to women who did not masturbate (Gerressu et al., 2008). Further, for men only, the likelihood of masturbation decreased with higher frequency of partnered sex and increased among those who reported less enjoyment of sex with a current partner (Gerressu et al., 2008).

Consistent with most U.S. studies and large-scale studies on masturbation, Nordic researchers studying women's masturbation found that, compared to men, women reported less frequent masturbation (Bergström-Walan & Nielsen, 1990). That said, in a public health study based in Norway, lesbian women reported higher frequencies of masturbation compared to heterosexual and bisexual women, while bisexual women masturbated more often compared to heterosexual women (Træen, Stigum, & Sørensen, 2002). Looking at intergenerational differences, Finnish researchers found that each new generation engaged in more masturbatory behavior than previous generations (Kontula & Haavio-Mannila, 2003).

In India, researchers studying first-year college women who self-identified as virgins found that 30% of those who masturbated described feelings of guilt, anxiety, and shame associated with masturbation (Sharma & Sharma, 1998). Further, those who masturbated typically had more educated mothers, possessed more knowledge about human sexuality, and did not live at home compared to nonmasturbators (Sharma & Sharma, 1998). In China, women who masturbated did so both to compensate for a lack of partner and, for some women, as an expression of high sexual interest in general. Liberal sexual values and more sexual knowledge correlated with more frequent masturbation (Das, Parish, & Laumann, 2009).

Adolescent Girls and Masturbation

While some studies have targeted younger children and the normativity surrounding genital self-touching (DeLamater & Friedrich, 2002; Friedrich, Fisher, Broughton, Houston, & Shafran, 1998), a larger proportion of recent research on women's masturbation has targeted adolescent girls. One study found that adolescent girls masturbated less frequently than adolescent boys and that masturbation represented the most reliable source of orgasm

for both sexes (Smith, Rosenthal, & Reichler, 1996). In addition, based on a nationally representative sample of 14- to 17-year-olds, Robbins and colleagues (2011) found a relationship between female masturbation and a number of partnered sexual activities, such as mutual masturbation, giving and receiving oral sex, and penile-vaginal and anal intercourse. When examining the phenomenology of girls' sexual desires and experiences, Lamb (2001) and Tolman (2002) also touched upon the complexity of girls' feelings and behaviors regarding masturbation. Hogarth and Ingham (2009) studied masturbation attitudes among a small sample of adolescent girls in the United Kingdom, finding that those with positive attitudes toward masturbation typically felt more comfortable talking about sex, communicated more with parents about sex, and discussed desire and pleasure in their narratives about sex. By contrast, girls who expressed indifference toward masturbation more often mentioned their boyfriends' sexual needs and pleasures and did not express enjoyment or excitement when talking about sex. Girls with negative attitudes toward masturbation spoke of their bodies as "property" of boys and did not mention desire or pleasure in their narratives. This study suggested that attitudes toward masturbation link up with girls' attitudes about their bodies, relationships, and the "purpose" of sex.

Taking this literature into account, this study draws upon qualitative interviews with 20 women to illuminate several previously understudied aspects of women's masturbation experiences. We explored women's techniques when masturbating, as few previous studies have actually asked women *how* they masturbate (notable exceptions: Kinsey et al., 1953; Hite, 1976; Leff & Israel, 1983), and we examine, from a feminist and gender theory framework, women's feelings and ideas about masturbation. Together, these narratives reveal how women's masturbation—in part because of the relative cultural secrecy that surrounds it—remains beholden to patriarchal scripts that women internalize in their private sexual lives. Further, because women so rarely discuss masturbation with others (e.g., mothers, friends, and partners), and because all women in our sample reported masturbating at least once, we explored the implications (both positive and negative) of women imagining their own cultural stories about how *other* women masturbate and what so-called normal masturbation might look like. In doing so, we contribute to a much-needed gap in the literature about women's sexual subjectivities and women's tangible experiences with masturbation.

In particular, this study asked: What kinds of themes appeared in women's descriptions of their feelings, attitudes, and behaviors associated with masturbation, particularly across race, sexual identity, age, and socioeconomic class lines? How do gender and power inform women's masturbation stories, and how might women's techniques for masturbating suggest adherence to, or resistance to, patriarchal norms and social scripts? Finally, what insights do women provide when giving voice to something as culturally taboo, hidden, and invisible as women's masturbation?

Method

This study utilized qualitative data from a sample of 20 adult women (mean age = 34, *SD* = 13.35) recruited in 2011 in a large metropolitan Southwestern U.S. city. Participants were recruited through local entertainment and arts listings as well as the volunteers section of the local online section of Craigslist. Both outlets reached wide audiences and were freely available to community residents. The advertisements asked for women ages 18 to 59 (similar to Laumann et al., 1994) to participate in an interview study about their sexual behaviors, practices, and attitudes that would last for approximately two hours. Participants were screened only for their gender, racial/ethnic background, sexual identity, and age; no other prescreening questions were asked. A purposive sample was selected to provide greater demographic diversity in the sample: sexual-minority women and racial/ethnic minority women were intentionally oversampled, and a diverse range of ages was represented (11 women ages 18 to 31; five women ages 32 to 45; and four women ages 46 to 59). The sample included 11 White women and nine women of color, including three African American women, four Mexican American women, and two Asian American women. For self-reported sexual identity, the sample included 12 heterosexual women, six bisexual women, and two lesbian women (though women's reported sexual behavior often indicated

far more same-sex eroticism than these self-categorized labels suggest). All participants consented to have their interviews audiotaped and fully transcribed, and all received USD$20 compensation. Identifying data were removed, and each participant received a pseudonym to ensure anonymity. Participants directly reported a range of socioeconomic and educational backgrounds, employment histories, and parental and relationship statuses. In addition, participants reported that they volunteered for a range of reasons: they wanted to break silences about sexuality; they needed the money; they felt curious about the study; they felt they had "boring" or "exciting" sexual lives; and they wanted to assist the university.

These 20 participants were interviewed using a semistructured interview protocol that lasted for 1.5 to 2 hours, during which they responded to 36 questions about their sexual histories, sexual practices, and feelings and attitudes about sexuality. Questions included aspects of their best and worst sexual experiences, feelings about contemporary sexual culture and media, personal experiences with orgasm and other sexual events, negotiations of power with partner(s), and reflections on their bodies. The questions about masturbation were asked as part of this series of 36 questions about women's sexuality; many questions targeted short and precise narratives (e.g., "friends with benefits" relationships, feelings about "female Viagra"), while others (e.g., masturbation, body image) targeted women's broader narratives about aspects of their sexual lives. Several of the prompts addressed issues relevant to this study on women's masturbation. For example, women were asked, "Many women describe masturbation as a pleasurable experience. Can you describe your experiences with masturbation, including your process for masturbating, emotional feelings about masturbating, and a particularly pleasurable experience you've had with masturbation?" with the follow-up question: "What kind of relationship do you have with sex toys or props during masturbation or during partnered sex?" These 36 questions were scripted but served to open up other conversations and dialogue about related topics, as follow-up questions were free-flowing and conversational. As the questions were broad and open ended, participants could set the terms of how they would discuss masturbation and what information they wanted to share. The original questions served as sensitizing concepts that allowed previous research to lay the groundwork for topics and themes to look for (Charmaz, 2006).

Responses were analyzed qualitatively using thematic analysis, which relies heavily on feminist theory and gender theory (Braun & Clarke, 2006). This type of analysis was considered the most effective and useful because it allowed for groupings of responses based on women's attitudes and feelings (e.g., significance of nonpenetrative pleasure, beliefs that masturbation is efficient and part of a daily routine). This method of analysis also supported an examination of the intersection between masturbation and other components of women's sexual lives (e.g., body shame). To conduct the analysis, we familiarized ourselves with the data by reading all of the transcripts thoroughly, and we then identified patterns for common interpretations posed by participants. In doing so, we reviewed lines, sentences, and paragraphs of the transcripts looking for patterns in their ways of discussing their masturbation (Braun & Clarke, 2006). We selected and generated themes through the process of identifying logical links and overlaps among participants. After creating these themes, we compared them to previous themes expressed by other participants to identify similarities, differences, and general patterns. This type of thematic analysis relied on a data-driven inductive approach in which themes were generated prior to the interpretation of those themes (Boyatzis, 1998). As such, initial themes were identified, codes were applied and then connected back to the themes, and these themes were then corroborated and legitimized using inductive thematic analysis (Fereday & Muir-Cochrane, 2006). While some interpretation of subtextual meaning is inevitable when using a thematic analysis approach, we nevertheless worked to value and emphasize women's explicit narratives rather than prioritizing covert and implicit narratives.

Results

All 20 women in the sample reported that they had masturbated at least once in their lifetimes, with a range between two to three times ever to at least once a day. Most women (13 out of 20) reported

masturbating at least once per week. Overall, 18 out of 20 described using sex toys either during masturbation or during partnered sex, while two said that they had never used sex toys. This high rate of sex toy use may stem from participants living in an urban center, where sex toys are readily available, or from the fact that these women chose to do a study on sexuality. From these responses about masturbation, five themes were generated. As noted in the descriptions that follow, some participants' responses overlapped among themes in that one participant's responses fit into multiple themes. The five themes included (a) assumptions that most women self-penetrate during masturbation even when primarily using clitoral stimulation; (b) masturbation as sexual labor; (c) masturbation as a threat to male dominance; (d) masturbation as routine tension release; and (e) masturbation as a source of joy, fun, and pleasure.

Theme 1: Assumptions That Most Women Self-Penetrate during Masturbation

When discussing their processes and techniques for masturbating, many women reported that they did not self-penetrate with sex toys or fingers during masturbation but instead relied on fingers and clitoral stimulation. Interestingly, many women believed that *most* women self-penetrate during masturbation and that they were unique or abnormal for relying primarily on clitoral stimulation during masturbation. For example, Tania, a 25-year-old White heterosexual woman, gave a detailed description of how she masturbated, stopping halfway through to ask whether her method was normal:

> I am usually in bed. I have a certain position that I always have to maintain. My legs have to be a certain way, and I have to be relaxed and comfortable. Then I just turn myself on. I actually—it's not inside, just clitoral stimulation for me. It takes about fifteen minutes, and I try to focus with my sex toy on the right spot. I don't touch myself with my fingers, just the sex toy. I actually have never been able to get myself to orgasm with just fingers. I might spread the lips of the vagina out a little so I can get in there. I don't insert though. Is that normal?

This lengthy description suggests that, even though her process felt intuitive to her, when narrating it aloud, she stopped to assess whether she masturbated in a "normal" way.

As another example of women feeling abnormal for relying on clitoral stimulation rather than self-penetration, Keisha, a 34-year-old African American bisexual woman, said that she routinely masturbated without penetration while also hiding her masturbation behaviors from her husband:

> What I use is a vibrator and it's not—to tell you the truth on that, I don't penetrate while masturbating. I just use it on—I go around it, I go around the clitoris and that's it. I don't even penetrate when I use the vibrator. . . . I'm embarrassed to tell my husband about masturbating. If he's on the computer I would even sneak to the back room and take the time just for myself to masturbate while he's in the front room, without even asking for help, or "hey babe, come watch." For some reason, I am embarrassed to masturbate in front of him.

Keisha's notion that she has violated *two* norms of masturbation—that women penetrate and that women allow their male partners to watch—suggests uncertainty about how other women masturbate along with shame about her imagined differences from other women. If women rarely discuss masturbation with partners, family, and friends, they have a less clear and established norm for how women "typically" masturbate and thus have to generate their own understanding of this norm.

Theme 2: Masturbation as Sexual Labor

Though women overwhelmingly described positive and affirming experiences with masturbation, they also said that masturbation sometimes felt frustrating as they "quested" after an orgasm (or two). Leticia, a 41-year-old Latina bisexual, described putting notable labor and effort into masturbation and mentioned that it felt highly goal oriented: "Masturbation is generally really pleasurable but I know there have been times when it wouldn't happen. It happened the other day, and I was getting really frustrated. I don't know why—maybe

because I was in a hurry—but it just didn't happen. I hate it when I can't have an orgasm."

Other women described masturbating as sexual labor they invested in themselves after their partners did not satisfy them or help them orgasm. Leticia admitted that she used masturbation primarily to make up for a male partner's inadequacies: "There are times when I do have a sex partner and he hasn't made me have an orgasm, so I'll go make myself have one." Similarly, Shantele, a 30-year-old African American heterosexual woman, recalled that she masturbated to compensate for her partner's lack of attention after *his* orgasm: "The sex was amazing, but I didn't get off. It was just him having sex and, when we're done, he left. I was still really aroused, but I had to finish myself off. . . . Normally I don't really enjoy masturbating." The juxtaposition of Shantele saying that she had great sex when a partner left and she masturbated, combined with her general belief that masturbating does not please her, suggests a variety of possible interpretations: perhaps her standards for "good sex" may prioritize her partner's pleasure over her own (Nicolson & Burr, 2003) or she may have framed masturbation as an instrumental means to "get off."

Some women also envisioned masturbation as labor devoted to fulfilling sexual needs in an easier and less performative way than partnered sex allowed. For example, Mei, a 22-year-old Asian American heterosexual woman, described her orgasms from masturbation as easier to obtain than orgasms from partnered sex:

> Maybe I'm in the mood and he's not around, or maybe I just feel like doing it. I think it started one time when I was washing down there with a showerhead and it seemed to feel really nice. It became an easy way for me to orgasm. Compared to other girls I don't orgasm easily, so that's why I can't say I orgasm from oral sex or using fingers. It's just easier when I masturbate.

This suggests that Mei and other women may masturbate to avoid the labor they invest with partners to visibly, audibly, and tangibly have pleasure; in other words, masturbation provides a space where women can orgasm without any associated forms of labor (e.g., moaning, groaning, mutual "getting off"), shame, or guilt about their pace and speed of orgasm.

Theme 3: Masturbation as a Threat to Male Dominance

In line with women believing that most women self-penetrate and that working toward orgasm represents sexual labor, other women reported, frankly, that masturbating threatened their male partners' assumed dominance and power. For example, Patricia, a 28-year-old African American heterosexual woman, said that she rarely masturbated because she feared that it would teach her to derive pleasure from sensations other than penile-vaginal intercourse:

> I've tried masturbating, and it doesn't do anything for me. I don't know if it's because I'm afraid that I'm not going to get the same satisfaction that I would from having a penis in me. What I did, I just got some K-Y and just rubbed it on my hand and put my hand down there and started to rub. You know, I was visualizing porno flicks and people I would like to have sex with, and it just didn't happen for me, so I was like, "Oh well."

Women also sometimes transformed their private experiences with masturbation into an action that serviced men's sexual pleasure. Jean, a 57-year-old White heterosexual woman, explained that she masturbated to please her male partners rather than to please herself: "Usually when [masturbation] comes up, it's because, you know, guys like it. When it happens that I do it, it may be because the person I'm having sex with wasn't achieving satisfaction so—so in order to push him along, I would engage in that act, for him." This transfer of pleasure from something devoted to the self to something directed toward stimulating men visually suggests that, in some contexts, masturbation can easily be appropriated from a (rebellious) act of autonomous pleasure to yet another act in service of men's desires.

A few women also upheld the notion that only men masturbated regularly and that only "unlady-like" or "deviant" women masturbated. Rhoda, a 57-year-old White heterosexual woman, recounted the differences between her and her boyfriend disclosing masturbation to others: "I never really talked about it, but I know with my last boyfriend, he would always say it was a big thing for him to do. I didn't get it, I guess. I just think guys are made up differently and they can do it at the drop of a hat, so to speak, but for me it didn't work like that. It's not like I had to do it or not. I'm just blasé about it. I need that human contact." This description highlighted Rhoda's depiction of sexual desire as masculine and masturbation as nonemotional.

Theme 4: Masturbation as Routine Tension Release

Several women talked about masturbation as a no-emotional, routine, and efficient part of their daily routine. For example, Cris, a 22-year-old White lesbian, likened her masturbation (and her partner's disclosure of masturbation) to brushing her teeth:

> It's just kind of quick, whatever, kind of efficient, yeah. It's just kind of quick, like brushing your teeth, like something fast, like, that you don't really even think about. . . . Like if I'm gone, if I'm out at work and stuff, and [my partner and I] haven't done anything for a couple of days, she'll be like "Oh, I whacked it this afternoon," and I'm like, "Okay, that's cool."

Cris expressed no threat in her partner's disclosure of masturbating while also suggesting that her own masturbation signified a casual and guilt-free part of her routines. The predictable tension release aspects of masturbation allowed Cris to strip masturbation from stories and narratives of cultural shame and secrecy.

Other women also detached shame, guilt, and anxiety from masturbation, instead seeing it as a predictable and satisfying part of their daily routines. Dessa, a 19-year-old Mexican American heterosexual woman, reported masturbating every morning:

> Masturbation is pretty freakin' cool. Usually I shower in the morning, and then I have a vibrator so I use that. I put music on and then I'll do whatever feels good that

day so I'll lay down or stand up or lean over. Usually it's my vibrator in the morning and my hands at night. I masturbate about five times out of a week to maybe seven times a week, almost every day. Sometimes I skip days, and I'm fine with that. I guess I've, like, incorporated it into my schedule, so I'm just like, "Okay, time to do that," you know? It's just like a daily routine to me now so it's just like, "Okay, cool, boom, my day has started."

Notably, Dessa's implied ease with masturbation and her shame-free discussions about masturbation as a daily event contrasted sharply with her later stories about not feeling comfortable disclosing masturbation to girlfriends, male friends, or partners. This implies that even when she explicitly debunked notions that women do not masturbate (as Dessa clearly masturbated without shame every day), she often still could not comfortably disclose her masturbatory habits to others.

As a more celebratory example of women incorporating masturbation into their daily routines, Zhang, a 36-year-old Asian American bisexual woman, talked about masturbating as a routine form of self-affirmation and pleasure:

> It's only pleasurable when absolutely private, no one bothering you, and there's a nice sound atmosphere, like nice music on the radio. I like masturbating in the fall or winter every day because it warms up your body. You can stay in the comforter for a little bit longer than usual before you go to work or after work. I honestly have lost count of how many times I masturbate. I do it all the time because it makes me feel better about myself.

Theme 5: Masturbation as a Source of Joy, Fun, and Pleasure

For many women, masturbation allowed them to express positive feelings toward their bodies, and it served as a nurturing and affirming mode of self-acceptance. Whether feeling joy or pleasure, having fun, or relieving stress, masturbation enhanced many women's lives in positive ways. Angelica, a 32-year-old Mexican American heterosexual woman, described masturbation as a mode

to relieve stress and relax during her pregnancy: "I've been under a lot of stress with my school and my other children, so when I feel like that I masturbate a lot and I feel better. I can't drink, I can't smoke, I can't do anything, so it's my stress reliever. Masturbating is something I do *for me*." Because Angelica faced numerous other pressures and stresses related to traditional gender-role expectations, masturbation helped her escape not only her life stressors but also the expectations placed on her as a mother and wife.

Other women masturbated to rebel against conservative, repressive, or sex-negative attitudes they encountered within their families, partnerships, or the culture at large. For example, Inga, a 24-year-old White bisexual woman, recalled growing up with religious parents who forbid her to masturbate:

> We lived in a one-bedroom apartment and we had a bunk bed. [My mother] would tell me not to masturbate because it was gross and disgusting and I shouldn't be doing it. She was religious at the time and God frowned upon it. I was traumatized for a little bit about it, and then after I was raped, my whole relationship with religion kind of got shot so I didn't care and I started masturbating again. I loved it!

This narrative suggests that Inga herself internalized anti-masturbation religious attitudes as well, though a forced confrontation with religious beliefs following sexual violence dislodged her association between shame and masturbation. While certainly a disheartening way to return to masturbating, her self-pleasure nevertheless has its roots in the shame and taboo of her childhood years.

As a final example of masturbation as joyful, some women felt notable pleasure and self-affirmation from masturbation, even while expressing some reluctance to narrate those experiences. For example, when I first asked Florence, a 38-year-old White bisexual woman, about masturbation, she immediately responded, "Wow, well, this is kind of a strange question. I don't know if I would even want to go into this." She then followed up with a lengthy description of how masturbation lets her give back to herself:

It's so pleasurable. I just got out of a relationship, so I needed to learn how to please myself right now. I'm experimenting with a lot of different things, and it feels good. It feels relaxing, like I'm giving something to me. It relieves stress, helps me to feel comfortable with where I am right now in my life.

For Florence, masturbation served not only as a physical way of relaxing but also as a symbolic tool of self-affirmation, agency, and autonomy following the loss of a partner. In this way, masturbation transcended the physical and became a way to emotionally connect to herself and her sexual needs.

Discussion

Women's narratives about masturbation collectively point to the advantages and disadvantages of the cultural silences surrounding women's masturbation. As one advantage of the invisibility of women's masturbation, no single precise norm dictates to women how often they should masturbate and what method they should use to masturbate. Women routinely said they *did not* converse with partners, friends, and family members about masturbation, even for women (like Dessa) who felt relatively shameless about masturbation in their private lives. This lack of communication may indeed allow women to explore their own pleasures without precise norms about the scripts they should use during masturbation.

That said, a clear disadvantage of not having scripted norms about women's masturbation is that women easily and readily internalize easily accessible, traditional patriarchal scripts, particularly the imperative for penetrative intercourse (manifested here as women's belief that most women self-penetrate), concern about men feeling inadequate or undermined (leading women to masturbate either for a partner's pleasure or in secrecy), and goal-oriented and outcome-oriented labor directed toward orgasm as a product. This does not preclude women finding these aspects pleasurable—indeed, many women enjoy penetration and a drive toward orgasm—but it does suggest that women's masturbation experiences link up with traditional understandings of gender, power, and pleasure. When

no clear scripts exist for how women should masturbate, other baggage from the culture at large seeps into women's consciousness, leading to clear gender imbalances about the purpose and meaning they assign to sexual self-pleasure.

Because the cultural lexicon largely ignores women's masturbation, and because the legacy of thinking about, studying, and theorizing masturbation often derives from the context of deviance (e.g., masturbation as "immature," associated with sex guilt, and driven only by the lack of a readily available penis), women have had to script their own stories about masturbation and its meaning. This has resulted in wide diversity of interpretations. While the majority of women incorporated traditional gendered scripts about sexuality in their descriptions of masturbation, particularly the idea that goal-oriented, penetrative sex guides women's sexual pleasure, many women also had different interpretations for how they wanted to engage in masturbation. Some built masturbation into their lives as a routine and nonemotional experience; they brushed their teeth, masturbated, and went to work. This, too, could mimic the "detached sex" model of hegemonic masculinity (i.e., that men only need to "get off" rather than feel emotions during sex, or that men masturbate for simple physical release), or it could signal (as mentioned frequently in these narratives) that women, too, have fairly straightforward goals when masturbating: they want stress relief, physical relaxation, and a sleep aid.

In terms of social identities, while no clear patterns emerged for race, age, or class, some patterns did emerge for sexual identity, as heterosexual women far more often described masturbation as a threat to male dominance in comparison with lesbian or bisexual women. This finding that there may be a link between heterosexuality and the belief that men feel threatened by women's self-pleasure clearly warrants further research. As masturbation (and its focus on clitoral stimulation) has historically threatened men's dominance over women—as women no longer needed the penis for sexual satisfaction—it makes sense that heterosexual women (particularly partnered heterosexual women) might feel more concerned about their masturbating signaling a threat to a male partner's sexual prowess and sexual skills. Heterosexual women also seemed particularly invested in narratives of self-penetration (even when they prioritized clitoral stimulation), again reinforcing the heterosexist notion that "normal" sex—even during masturbation—required penetration.

Further, given the way women discussed orgasm, perhaps the goal-oriented focus of many (hetero) scripts has infected women's masturbation activities as well, as orgasms become the "product" women seek (often with great frustration) while masturbating. Several scholars have expressed concern that traditional sexual scripts often require men to invest labor into women's bodies, while women produce orgasm (real or fake) as a kind of product (Hyde & DeLamater, 1997; Roberts, Kippax, Waldby, & Crawford, 1995), a process that may now appear in women's sexual exchanges with other women (Fahs, 2011b) and in their own masturbation scripts.

Nevertheless, looking broadly at women's stories about masturbation, we argue that the work of making women's masturbation more visible could become a double-edged sword. While women have, to some degree, scripted masturbation norms for themselves, remarkable diversity appeared in women's stories about how they masturbated and what it meant for them. For some, masturbation allowed them to rebel against conservative childhoods (with the taboo and prohibition against masturbation possibly fueling the eroticism); for others, masturbation stimulated their (male) partners even if it did not yield personal orgasms. For still others, masturbation triggered feelings of ambivalence and nervousness, while other women embraced masturbation as an effortless inclusion in their morning routine. For some, the silences surrounding masturbation have allowed (patriarchal) norms to infiltrate their masturbatory experiences, while for others these silences have generated room for resistance and creativity.

Additional qualitative research on men's masturbation may serve as an interesting counterpoint to this diversity; perhaps men would discuss masturbation more similarly to one another (e.g., a physical release and nothing more) or may show similar variability to women. Future research comparing men's and women's subjective narratives could provide useful insights about the different interpretations people have, depending on the cultural visibility or silence around masturbation. The rupturing of norms of silence can make visible all sorts of "inner workings" of how social and cultural scripts trickle down into women's lives, just as the direct confrontation of visible norms for men could prove useful.

The study of women's masturbation also has direct links to other areas of sexuality and body research. The study of sex toys, for example, has also received far too little attention, particularly outside of theorizing the phallic role of dildos in lesbian sex play (Bolsø, 2007; Findlay, 1992) and linking vibrators to health behaviors (Herbenick et al., 2009; Herbenick et al., 2010); only recently have researchers addressed women's subjective narratives about using sex toys in masturbation and partnered sex (Fahs & Swank, 2013). Women's narratives about masturbation may also link up with their stories about other "taboo" bodily experiences, such as growing body hair (Fahs, 2011a; Toerien & Wilkinson, 2004), menstruation and menstrual sex (Allen & Goldberg, 2009; Fahs, 2011c), genital self-image (Berman, Berman, Miles, Pollets, & Powell, 2003), and feelings about childbirth (Martin, 2001). Of these, the question of how women feel about their genitals seems particularly relevant. If women learn that their genitals compare unfavorably to men's, that their genitals "smell" or seem "dirty," and that touching their genitals and (autonomously) providing themselves with pleasure is an inherently negative experience, how can women then associate positive feelings with masturbation? In an age when plastic surgeons target women's genitals for "rejuvenation," "trimming," and "enhancement" via "G-shots," labiaplasties, tightenings, and fresh hymens (Braun & Tiefer, 2010), women may feel ever more concerned about the normality of their genitals even during private experiences with masturbation (Herbenick & Reece, 2010).

Limitations and Future Directions

As with all sexuality research involving self-selected community samples, our study had some limitations worth noting. Women who participated in the study self-selected for a variety of reasons, but all shared a willingness to disclose personal information about their sexual behaviors, feelings, and attitudes. This study likely excluded more conservative and reserved women and emphasized women whose openness to sexuality stood at the forefront of their decision to participate. In addition, while the wording of questions was designed to provide maximum comfort to participants, this may have biased participants' perceptions of comfort with masturbation and encouraged them to consider the more positive aspects of their masturbation experiences. Lack of geographical diversity may also have impacted the findings, as all participants in this study resided in a large Southwestern city; differences between urban and rural women may prove paramount when discussing sensitive subjects like masturbation and sexual pleasure.

Moving forward, this study helps debunk some of the common mythologies surrounding masturbation: women do masturbate whether partnered or single; some women view masturbation as highly practical rather than shameful and guilt laden; women largely do not self-penetrate (even though they believe others do) and largely do not quest for penises in their private masturbatory experiences; and many women feel joy, pleasure, and comfort from masturbation, seeing it as a tool for self-reliance and autonomy. That said, women still tend to construct masturbation in relationship to patriarchal and gendered norms and values, as their private sexual experiences often still perpetuate the notion of masturbation as threatening to men, in service of men's pleasures and desires, or as uneasy and ambivalent. By confronting stereotypes and mythologies about women's masturbation and giving voice to women's experiences of their bodies, we hope future studies will continue to create new spaces for critical inquiry and embodied resistance.

References

Abramson, P. R. (1973). The relationship of the frequency of masturbation to several aspects of personality and behavior. *Journal of Sex Research, 9,* 132–142.

Allen, K. R., & Goldberg, A. E. (2009). Sexual activity during menstruation: A qualitative study. *Journal of Sex Research, 46,* 535–545.

Arafat, I. S., & Cotton, W. L. (1974). Masturbation practices of males and females. *Journal of Sex Research, 10,* 293–307.

Avis, N. E., Brockwell, S., Randolph, J. F. Jr., Shen, S., Cain, V. S., Ory, M., et al (2009). Longitudinal changes in sexual functioning as women transition through menopause: Results from the Study of Women's Health Across the Nation (SWAN). *Menopause, 16,* 442–452.

Bancroft, J., Long, J. S., & McCabe, J. (2011). Sexual well-being: A comparison of U.S. Black and White women in heterosexual relationships. *Archives of Sexual Behavior, 40,* 725–740.

Basson, R. (2000). The female sexual response: A different model. *Journal of Sex and Marital Therapy, 26*(1), 51–65.

Bennett, P. (1995). "Pomegranate-flowers": The phantasmic productions of late-nineteenth-century Anglo-American women poets. In P. Bennett & A. R. Vernon (Eds.), *Solitary pleasures: The historical, literary, and artistic discourses of autoeroticism* (pp. 189–214). New York: Routledge.

Bennett, P., & Vernon, A. R. (Eds.). (1995). *Solitary pleasures: The historical, literary, and artistic discourses of autoeroticism.* New York: Routledge.

Bergström-Walan, M. B., & Nielsen, H. H. (1990). Sexual expression among 60–80-year-old men and women: A sample from Stockholm. *Journal of Sex Research, 27,* 289–295.

Berman, L. A., Berman, J., Miles, M., Pollets, D., & Powell, J. A. (2003). Genital self-image as a component of sexual health: Relationship between genital self-image, female sexual function, and quality of life measures. *Journal of Sex and Marital Therapy, 29,* 11–21.

Bolsø, A. (2007). Approaches to penetration—Theoretical difference in practice. *Sexualities, 10,* 559–581.

Boyatzis, R. E. (1998). *Transforming qualitative information: Thematic analysis and code development.* Thousand Oaks, CA: Sage.

Braun, V., & Clarke, V. (2006). Using thematic analysis in psychology. *Qualitative Research in Psychology, 3,* 77–101.

Braun, V., & Tiefer, L. (2010). The "designer vagina" and the pathologisation of female genital diversity: Interventions for change. *Radical Psychology, 8*(1). Retrieved from http://www.radicalpsychology.org/vol8-1/brauntiefer.html

Brenot, P. (2005). *In praise of masturbation* (P. Buck & C. Petit, Trans.). London: Marion Boyars.

Bressler, L. C., & Lavender, A. D. (1986). Sexual fulfillment of heterosexual, bisexual, and homosexual women. In M. Kehoe (Ed.), *Historical, literary, and erotic aspects of lesbianism* (pp. 109–122). Binghamton, NY: Haworth Press.

Burri, A. V., Cherkas, L. M., & Spector, T. D. (2009). Emotional intelligence and its association with orgasmic frequency in women. *Journal of Sexual Medicine, 6,* 1930–1937.

Charmaz, C. (2006). *Constructing grounded theory.* London: Sage.

Clark, C. A., & Wiederman, M. W. (2000). Gender and reactions to a hypothetical relationship partner's masturbation and use of sexually explicit media. *Journal of Sex Research, 37,* 133–141.

Clower, V. (1975). Significance of masturbation in female sexual development and function. In I. M. Marcus & J. J. Francis (Eds.), *Masturbation: From infancy to senescence* (pp. 104–143). Oxford, England: International Universities Press.

Coleman, E. (2002). Masturbation as a means of achieving sexual health. *Journal of Psychology and Human Sexuality, 14,* 5–16.

Coleman, E. M., Hoon, P. W., & Hoon, E. F. (1983). Arousability and sexual satisfaction in lesbian and heterosexual women. *Journal of Sex Research, 19,* 58–73.

Das, A. (2007). Masturbation in the United States. *Journal of Sex and Marital Therapy, 33,* 301–317.

Das, A, Parish, W. L., & Laumann, E. O. (2009). Masturbation in urban China. *Archives of Sexual Behavior, 38,* 108–120.

Davidson, K. J. Sr., & Moore, N. B. (1994). Masturbation and premarital sexual intercourse among college women: Making choices for sexual fulfillment. *Journal of Sex and Marital Therapy, 20,* 178–199.

Davis, C. M., Blank, J., Lin, H., & Bonillas, C. (1996). Characteristics of vibrator use among women. *Journal of Sex Research, 33,* 313–320.

DeLamater, J., & Friedrich, W. N. (2002). Human sexual development. *Journal of Sex Research, 39*(1), 10–14.

De Marneffe, D. (1997). Bodies and words: A study of young children's genital and gender knowledge. *Gender and Psycho-analysis: An Interdisciplinary Journal, 2,* 3–33.

Dodson, B. (1974). *Sex for one: The joy of selfloving.* New York: Crown Trade.

Durham, T. W., & Grossnickle, W. F. (1982). Attitudes toward masturbation. *Psychological Reports, 51,* 932–934.

Escajadillo-Vargas, N., Mezones-Holguín, E., Castro-Castro, J., Córdova-Marcelo, W., Blümel, J. E., Pérez-López, F. R., et al. (2011). Sexual dysfunction risk and associated factors in young Peruvian university women. *Journal of Sexual Medicine, 8,* 1701–1709.

Fahs, B. (2011a). Dreaded "otherness": Heteronormative patrolling in women's body hair rebellions. *Gender and Society, 25,* 451–472.

Fahs, B. (2011b). *Performing sex: The making and unmaking of women's erotic lives.* Albany: State University of New York Press.

Fahs, B. (2011c). Sex during menstruation: Race, sexual identity, and women's qualitative accounts of pleasure and disgust. *Feminism and Psychology, 21,* 155–178.

Fahs, B., & Swank, E. (2013). Adventures with the "plastic man": Sex toys, compulsory heterosexuality, and the politics of women's sexual pleasure. *Society and Culture.* Advance online publication. doi:10.1007/s12119-013-9167-4

Fereday, J., & Muir-Cochrane, E. (2006). Demonstrating rigor using thematic analysis: A hybrid approach of inductive and deductive coding and theme development. *International Journal of Qualitative Methods, 5,* 1–11.

Fields, J. (2008). *Risky lessons: Sexual education and social inequality.* New Brunswick, NJ: Rutgers University Press.

Findlay, H. (1992). Freud's "fetishism" and the lesbian dildo debates. *Feminist Studies, 18,* 563–580.

Fine, M. (1988). Sexuality, schooling, and adolescent females: The missing discourse of desire. *Harvard Educational Review, 58,* 29–53.

Fisher, S. (1980). Personality correlates of sexual behavior in Black women. *Archives of Sexual Behavior, 9,* 27–35.

Friedrich, W. N., Fisher, J., Broughton, D., Houston, M., & Shafran, C. R. (1998). Normative sexual behavior in children: A contemporary sample. *Pediatrics, 101*(4), 1–8.

Gerressu, M., Mercer, C. H., Graham, C. A., Wellings, K., & Johnson, A. M. (2008). Prevalence of masturbation and associated factors in a British national probability survey. *Archives of Sexual Behavior, 37,* 266–278.

Greenberg, J. S., & Archambault, F. X. (1973). Masturbation, self-esteem, and other variables. *Journal of Sex Research, 9,* 41–51.

Hall, L. A. (1992). Forbidden by God, despised by men: Masturbation, medical warnings, moral panic, and manhood in Great Britain, 1850–1950. *Journal of the History of Sexuality, 2,* 365–387.

Halpern, C. J. T., Udry, R. J., Suchindran, C., & Campbell, B. (2000). Adolescent males' willingness to report masturbation. *Journal of Sex Research, 37,* 327–332.

Herbenick, D. D., & Reece, M. (2010). Development and validation of the Female Genital Self-Image Scale. *Journal of Sexual Medicine, 7*, 1822–1830.

Herbenick, D. D., Reece, M., Sanders, S. A., Dodge, B. S., Ghassemi, A., & Fortenberry, J. D. (2009). Prevalence and characteristics of vibrator use by women in the United States: Results from a nationally representative study. *Journal of Sexual Medicine, 6*, 1857–1867.

Herbenick, D. D., Reece, M., Sanders, S. A., Dodge, B. S., Ghassemi, A., & Fortenberry, J. D. (2010). Women's vibrator use in sexual partnerships: Results from a nationally representative survey in the United States. *Journal of Sex and Marital Therapy, 36*, 49–65.

Herbenick, D. D., Reece, M., Schick, V., Jozkowski, K. N., Middlestadt, S. E., Sanders, S. A., et al (2011). Beliefs about women's vibrator use: Results from a nationally representative probability survey in the United States. *Journal of Sex and Marital Therapy, 37*, 329–345.

Herbenick, D. D., Schick, V., Reece, M., Sanders, S. A., Dodge, B. S., & Fortenberry, J. D. (2011). The Female Genital Self-Image Scale (FGSIS): Results from a nationally representative probability sample of women in the United States. *Journal of Sexual Medicine, 8*, 158–166.

Herold, E. S., & Way, L. (1983). Oral-genital sexual behavior in a sample of university females. *Journal of Sex Research, 19*, 327–338.

Hite, S. (1976). *The Hite report: A nationwide study of female sexuality*. New York: Macmillan.

Hogarth, H., & Ingham, R. (2009). Masturbation among young women and associations with sexual health: An exploratory study. *Journal of Sex Research, 46*, 558–567.

Hurlbert, D. F., & Whittaker, K. E. (1991). The role of masturbation in marital and sexual satisfaction: A comparative study of female masturbators and nonmasturbators. *Journal of Sex Education and Therapy, 17*, 272–282.

Hyde, J. S., & DeLamater, J. D. (1997). *Understanding human sexuality*. New York: McGraw-Hill.

Iasenza, S. (2002). Beyond "lesbian bed death": The passion and play in lesbian relationships. *Journal of Lesbian Studies, 6*, 111–120.

Kaestle, C. E., & Allen, K. R. (2011). The role of masturbation in healthy sexual development: Perceptions of young adults. *Archives of Sexual Behavior, 40*, 983–994.

Kelley, K. (1979). Socialization factors in contraceptive attitudes: Roles of affective responses, parental attitudes, and sexual experiences. *Journal of Sex Research, 15*, 6–20.

Kelley, K. (1985). Sex, sex guilt, and authoritarianism: Differences in responses to explicit heterosexual and masturbatory slides. *Journal of Sex Research, 21*, 68–85.

King, H. (2011). Galen and the widow: Towards a history of therapeutic masturbation in ancient gynaecology. *EuGeStA, 1*, 205–235.

Kinsey, A. C., Pomeroy, W. B., Martin, C. E., & Gebhard, P. H. (1953). *Sexual behavior in the human female*. Philadelphia: W.B. Saunders.

Kontula, O., & Haavio-Mannila, E. (2003). Masturbation in a generational perspective. *Journal of Psychology and Human Sexuality, 14*, 49–83.

Lamb, S. (2001). *The secret lives of girls: What good girls really do—Sex play, aggression, and their guilt*. New York: Free Press.

Laqueur, T. W. (2003). *Solitary sex: A cultural history of masturbation*. New York: Zone Books.

Laumann, E. O., Gagnon, J. H., Michael, R. T., & Michaels, S. (1994). *The social organization of sexuality: Sexual practices in the United States*. Chicago: University of Chicago Press.

Leff, J. J., & Israel, M. (1983). The relationship between mode of female masturbation and achievement in coitus. *Archives of Sexual Behavior, 12*, 227–236.

Lerner, H. E. (1976). Parental mislabeling of female genitals as a determinant of penis envy and learning inhibitions in women. *Journal of the American Psychoanalytic Association, 24*, 269–283.

Levin, R., & Meston, C. (2006). Nipple/breast stimulation and sexual arousal in young men and women. *Journal of Sexual Medicine, 3*(3), 450–454.

Maines, R. (2001). *The technology of orgasm: "Hysteria," the vibrator, and women's sexual satisfaction*. Baltimore, MD: Johns Hopkins University Press.

Martin, E. (2001). *The woman in the body: A cultural analysis of reproduction*. Boston: Beacon Press.

Masters, W. H., & Johnson, V. E. (1966). *Human sexual response*. New York: Bantam Books.

Mosher, D. L., & Vonderheide, S. G. (1985). Contributions of sex guilt and masturbation guilt to women's contraceptive attitudes and use. *Journal of Sex Research, 21*, 24–39.

Nicolson, P., & Burr, J. (2003). What is "normal" about women's (hetero)sexual desire and orgasm? A report of an in-depth interview study. *Social Science and Medicine, 57*, 1735–1745.

Oliver, M. B., & Hyde, J. S. (1993). Gender differences in sexuality: A meta-analysis. *Psychological Bulletin, 114,* 29–51.

Petersen, J. L., & Hyde, J. S. (2011). Gender differences in sexual attitudes and behaviors: A review of meta-analytic results and large datasets. *Journal of Sex Research, 48,* 149–165.

Phillippsohn, S., & Hartmann, U. (2009). Determinants of sexual satisfaction in a sample of German women. *Journal of Sexual Medicine, 6,* 1001–1010.

Robbins, C. L., Schick, V., Reece, M., Herbenick, D., Sanders, S. A., Dodge, B., et al. (2011). Prevalence, frequency, and associations of masturbation with partnered sexual behavior among US adolescents. *Archives of Pediatrics and Adolescent Medicine, 165,* 1087–1093.

Roberts, C., Kippax, S., Waldby, C., & Crawford, J. (1995). Faking it: The story of "Ohh!" *Women's Studies International Forum, 18,* 523–532.

Robinson, B. B. E., Bockting, W. O., & Harrell, T. (2002). Masturbation and sexual health: An exploratory study of low income African American women. *Journal of Psychology and Human Sexuality, 14,* 85–102.

Rosario, V. A. III. (1995). Phantastical pollutions: The public threat of private vice in France. In P. Bennett & A. R. Vernon (Eds.), *Solitary pleasures: The historical, literary, and artistic discourses of autoeroticism* (pp. 101–132). New York: Routledge.

Schreurs, K. M. G., & Buunk, B. P. (1996). Intimacy, autonomy, and relationship satisfaction in Dutch lesbian couples and heterosexual couples. *Journal of Psychology and Human Sexuality, 4,* 41–57.

Sedgwick, E. K. (1995). Jane Austen and the masturbating girl. In P. Bennett & A. R. Vernon (Eds.), *Solitary pleasures: The historical, literary, and artistic discourses of autoeroticism* (pp. 133–154). New York: Routledge.

Sharma, V., & Sharma, A. (1998). The guilt and pleasure of masturbation: A study of college girls in Gujarat, India. *Sexual and Marital Therapy, 13,* 63–70.

Shulman, J. L., & Horne, S. G. (2003). The use of self-pleasure: Masturbation and body image among African American and European American women. *Psychology of Women Quarterly, 27,* 262–269.

Smith, A. M. A., Rosenthal, D. A., & Reichler, H. (1996). High schoolers' masturbatory practices: Their relationship to sexual intercourse and personal characteristics. *Psychological Reports, 79,* 499–509.

Stein, J. H., & Reiser, L. W. (1994). A study of White middle-class adolescent boys' responses to "semenarche" (the first ejaculation). *Journal of Youth and Adolescence, 23,* 373–384.

Toerien, M., & Wilkinson, S. (2004). Exploring the depilation norm: A qualitative questionnaire study of women's body hair removal. *Qualitative Research in Psychology, 1,* 69–92.

Tolman, D. L. (2002). *Dilemmas of desire: Teenage girls talk about sexuality.* Cambridge, MA: Harvard University Press.

Træen, B., Stigum, H., & Sørensen, D. (2002). Sexual diversity in urban Norwegians. *Journal of Sex Research, 39,* 249–258.

Weigerl, L. (1995). Autonomy as deviance: Sixteenth-century images of witches and prostitutes. In P. Bennett & A. R. Vernon (Eds.), *Solitary pleasures: The historical, literary, and artistic discourses of autoeroticism* (pp. 19–48). New York: Routledge.

Wyatt, G., Peters, S., & Guthrie, D. (1988). Kinsey revisited, part II: Comparisons of the sexual socialization and sexual behavior of Black women over 33 years. *Archives of Sexual Behavior, 17,* 289–332.

In Search of (Better) Sexual Pleasure: Female Genital 'Cosmetic' Surgery

by Virginia Braun

In this article, I explore the role of 'sexual pleasure' in accounts of female genital 'cosmetic'[1] surgery (FGCS). FGCS procedures are some of the newest to become popularized in the arsenal of surgical and other cosmetic procedures aimed at transforming the (female)[2] body in some way. My classification of genital surgery as FGCS does not include surgery for transsexual or

Virginia Braun, *Sexualities, Vol 8, No 4,* pp 407–424. Copyright © 2005 by SAGE Publications Ltd. Reprinted by permission of SAGE Publications Ltd.

intersex people,[3] nor is it 'female genital mutilation' (FGM).[4] Procedures for (cosmetic) genital alteration include: labiaplasty/labioplasty (labia minora reductions), labia majora 'augmentations' (tissue removal, fat injections), liposuction (mons pubis, labia majora), vaginal tightening (fat injections, surgical tightening), clitoral hood reductions, clitoral repositioning, G-spot 'amplification' (collagen injected into the 'G-spot,' which swells it significantly), and hymen reconstruction (to restore the *appearance* of 'virginity').

Like cosmetic surgery generally, FGCS can be seen as both *surgical* practice and *cultural* product (see Adams, 1997; Fraser, 2003b) and practice (Haiken, 2000). Dubbed the 'designer vagina', FGCS has received considerable media attention in recent years. Headlines range from the sensational – 'I've saved my sex life' (M30)[5] – to the serious – 'Designer vagina service a first for NZ' (N10). There is an apparent increase in the popularity of FGCS. One magazine reported that 'the operation is not new, he's been doing it for 20 years, but back then he was getting a couple of requests a year. Now he performs the operations once or twice a month' (M23), while another clinic performs '40 operations each month' (M23). Apparently, 'there is no question there's a big trend, . . . it's sort of coming out of the closet. It's basically where breast augmentation was 30 years ago' (M24). By some accounts, this increasing popularity is due, at least in part, to media coverage.

The material practice of FGCS, and women's participation in it, are enabled within particular socio-cultural (and technological) contexts which render certain choices possible, and locate cosmetic surgery as a solution (K. Davis, 2003). The contexts of women's ongoing, widespread, and increasingly specific, body dissatisfactions (Bordo, 1997; Sullivan, 2001), ongoing negative meanings around women's genitalia (Braun and Wilkinson, 2001, 2003), and women's engagement in a wide range of body modification practices – such as hair removal (Toerien and Wilkinson, 2004) – cohere to render women's genitalia a viable site for surgical enhancement. FGCS can thus be theorized as an extension of other currently more culturally normative bodily subjectivities, desires and practices, for women:

> Logically, [labioplasty] operations are merely an extension of other procedures designed either to draw attention to female genitals . . . or to render invisible signs of secondary sexual development . . . In this context, the 'trimming' of visible labia minora . . . is part of a continuum. While labia reduction is not a well-known procedure, hair removal products and procedures are common. (Allotey et al., 2001: 197)

In this article, I focus specifically on the issue of (female) sexual pleasure in accounts of FGCS. Female sexual pleasure appears as a central concern, mirroring a broader socio-cultural shift towards the 'eroticization of female sexuality' (Seidman, 1991: 124) with women's sexual pleasure located as central in (hetero)sex (e.g. Braun et al., 2003; Gordon, 1971) and beyond. A 1996 article in *Flare* magazine ('The Sex Files') identified that 'female pleasure is officially a trend' (M27). More generally, for men *and* women, sex has become highly important (Weeks, 1985: 7), with 'frequent, pleasurable, varied, and ecstatically satisfying sex . . . a preeminent sign of personal happiness' (D'Emilio and Freedman, 1997: 340; Weeks, 1985), and even identity (Heath, 1982). This increased attention to pleasure has also resulted in an increased attention to the body and sexual technique (Seidman, 1991), with possible concurrent increases in feelings of sexual inadequacy (Hart and Wellings, 2002). I will show that the story of FGCS is, at least in part, a story of the (legitimate) search for (better) female sexual pleasure, and argue that this functions not only to legitimate, and promote, FGCS, but also to reaffirm particular models of desirable sexual bodies and practices.

Theorizing and researching FGCS

This article is part of a broader project on FGCS which analyses data drawn from two datasets: media accounts and surgeon interviews.[6] The research is situated with a (feminist) social constructionist framework (Burr, 1995; Tiefer, 1995, 2000; White et al., 2000), which theorizes language and social representations as an integral part of the production of social (and material) realities for individuals, as well as producing possibilities for individual practices. Sexuality is thus a material, but always social, practice (Connell, 1997; Jackson and Scott, 2001).

Media data consist of 106 English-language items from print (newspaper, magazine) and electronic (television, radio, Internet) mass-media sources. My convenience sample was located primarily through Google searches using terms like 'designer vagina' and 'labiaplasty', and through surgeon websites. The sample comprises: 31 print magazine items; 24 Internet-based magazine items; 23 other Internet items; 13 news media items; and 15 other related items. My analysis in this article focuses on the print magazine data.

While the media have various potential uses for consumers at an individual level (Berger, 1998), my primary interest is in the media's roles in contributing to the social construction of FGCS. The media have a range of influences on health (Brown and Wash-Childers, 2002), and are significant contributors to the social construction of ideas about appearance, health, illness, and sexuality (Carpiano, 2001; Sullivan, 2001). They have been theorized as influential in women's decisions and 'choices' about cosmetic surgery (Blum, 2003; Gagne and McGaughey, 2002; Goodman, 1996), their feelings about the appearance of their vulva (Bramwell, 2002; see also Reinholtz and Muehlenhard, 1995), and their 'body image' more generally (Bordo, 1993; Grogan, 1999). Women's magazines, in particular, have been identified as 'a significant cultural source of ideas about appearance as a medical problem' (Sullivan, 2001: 159), and are seen to work 'in tandem with surgeons to promote cosmetic surgery' (Fraser, 2003b: 125). Surgeons consider them to be one of the most important sources of public ideas about cosmetic surgery (Sullivan, 2001).

Surgeons were primarily located via the media (except two, who were located via word of mouth). In total, 24 surgeons were contacted and invited to take part in semi-structured interviews, with 15 agreeing. The sample of surgeons varied in terms of the following.

(a) Geographical location: surgeons were practising in the USA (5), UK (4), Canada (2), Australia (2) and New Zealand (2).

(b) Surgical speciality: nine were plastic surgeons (one was also an urologist), six were gynaecologists.
(c) Type of practice: all but three surgeons who worked on the UK's National Health Service did these surgeries privately, at direct cost to the patient.
(d) Experience: the average time of doing 'cosmetic' genital procedures was more than 11 years (range 25 to 2 years). The estimated total number of FGCS procedures performed ranged from over 1000 to fewer than 50.
(e) Sex: twelve were male, three female.
(f) Ethnicity: one identified as black, one as Jewish, and 11 as white/Caucasian/Anglo-Saxon (two provided no ethnicity information).

Fourteen of the interviews, which lasted between 15 and 70 minutes, were conducted in person (one was via telephone), and all except one were tape recorded. Participants were told that 'the research focuses on ideas about female genital cosmetic surgery, and on the reasons for such procedures' and that I was 'interested in how ideas about women, women's bodies, and women's sexuality relate to these procedures'.

FGCS and female sexual pleasure

Women's sex lives or their sexuality was often reported to be impeded in some way, with pre-operative genitalia:

Extract 1: Woman's Day Magazine, *NZ, 2004*

Amanda was utterly miserable. She no longer enjoyed sex with Russell, the husband she adored, and on those rare occasions when they made love, Amanda would insist they switch off the lights. (M30)

In this and other extracts, general pre-surgical sexual 'impediments' were noted. In addition, specific causes of such sexual impediments were identified in many accounts:

Extract 2: male plastic surgeon, UK

S1: what comes in more and in my practice it is not – quite often it's not purely cosmetic but there are functional complaints with the labia the size of the labia too (Int: mhm) for example . . . it can be painful during intercourse because the labium keeps going in and out with every thrust.

Although physical pain was often discussed, the *psychological* response to genital morphology was frequently highlighted as the crux of the problem which 'hampered' or 'ruined' their sex life:

Extract 3: male plastic surgeon, NZ

S6: I think most w– of the women that I've dealt with have thought that this was a real impediment to sexual enjoyment (Int: mhm) not so much from *their* point of view but from their partner's point of view (Int: oh okay) if they were worried about their *partner* not liking whatever they could see or or touch or whatever then they felt tense themselves (Int: mhm) and so the enjoyment of everything goes (spiralling) (Int: mnn) down.

Int: Yeah so sort of sex was an area of difficulty (S6: yeah) for most of them (S6: yeah) or for (S6: yeah) all of them.

S6: Abso– oh absolutely.

Extract 4: Cosmopolitan Magazine, *AUS/NZ, 1998*

Sarah, a 27-year-old secretary is a case in point. Throughout puberty, she thought her vaginal lips were too long and was embarrassed by one that hung lower than the other.

'They ruined my sex life', she recalls. 'I never felt confident during sex – I felt like a freak. I'd never let anyone see me naked'. (M1)

Extract 5: New Woman Magazine, *AUS, 2003*

. . . the biggest problem was sex. I've been with my boyfriend since I was 15 but I always felt self-conscious when we made love. I'd engineer positions so that he'd always be behind me and couldn't see my

vagina, and I'd never have oral sex because I couldn't bear him seeing me up close. (M20)

The psychological problems invoked to explain a (pre-surgery) sexual impediment included embarrassment, self-consciousness, lack of confidence, and shame. The inclusion of such concepts fits with Frank's (2003) observation of an 'inflation of the language of pain' around medicine to include such psychological concepts.[7] In my data, this negative psychological response to *appearance* often resulted, via other psychological responses like anxiety or self-consciousness, in an inability to 'receive' oral sex from a male partner, an account which fits with women's reports of various genital anxieties, particularly around oral sex (Braun and Wilkinson, 2003; Reinholtz and Muehlenhard, 1995; Roberts et al., 1996). Women's reports of genital anxiety reflect a range of negative sociocultural representations of women's genitalia (Braun and Wilkinson, 2001), and it seems some women 'live these [negative] cultural meanings in their embodiment' (Roberts et al., 1996: 119). However, my concern is not just about women's embodiment, as psychology here provides the 'moral justification' (Frank, 2003) for cosmetic surgery to alleviate this distress.

While *impeded* sexual possibilities and pleasures were central in media and surgeon accounts of why women might choose to have FGCS, *increased* sexual pleasure as an outcome of surgery was the main area in which sexual pleasure was discussed. FGCS, in a variety of forms, was represented as increasing sexual pleasure. The *aim* of sexual enhancement was often explicitly stated in the titles of magazine articles about FGCS – 'THE G-SHOT . . . plastic surgery for your orgasm' (M22) – and in the setting up of media stories:

Extract 6: New Woman Magazine, *UK, date unknown*

Would you go under the knife to improve your sex life? These four women did. (M29)

Extract 7: Marie Claire Magazine, *UK, 2000*

What are the reasons for surgery? Firstly, to improve their sex lives. (M4)

Extract 8: Marie Claire Magazine, *US, 2000*

Some women are going under the knife to change the appearance of their genitals, while others are having surgery in the hopes of better orgasms. (M3)

In some, the possibility of increased sexual pleasure was initially framed with mild scepticism:

Extract 9: Cosmopolitan Magazine, *AUS/ NZ, 1998*

Doctors [in the US] claim to be able to boost women's sexual pleasure, taking them to previously uncharted erotic heights. And their secret weapon in the quest for sexual ecstasy? The scalpel. (M1)

Extract 10: Marie Claire Magazine, *UK, 2000*

The sales pitch being that sexual gratification of the female is diminished if friction is lost because of a slack vagina, so this procedure tightens up your bits and helps you reach orgasm. (M4)

Extract 11: FQ Magazine, *NZ, 2004*

Will sex be mind-blowing once you've been trimmed or tightened? Well, the jury is still out. (M31)

Any initial scepticism in reporting the doctors' 'claim' that the operations 'supposedly increase sexual pleasure' (M3) was typically not reiterated in most media accounts of surgical results and patient experiences, or in surgeon accounts. Instead, overwhelmingly, increased pleasure was noted:

Extract 12: Cleo Magazine, *NZ, 2001*

Feedback from patients suggests their sex lives have improved enormously. (M7)

Extract 13: male urologist, AUS

S7: I've known women who are mono-orgasmic to become multiply orgasmic as a result.

All procedures, even ostensibly cosmetic ones such as labiaplasty, were frequently framed as being 'successful' in terms of increased sexual pleasure:

Extract 14: Cosmopolitan Magazine, *AUS/ NZ, 2004*

I am no longer embarrassed to be naked and my sex life has improved because I'm more confident. (M23)

Extract 15: Company Magazine, *UK, 2003*

I was so thrilled with my new vagina, Dan and I 'tried it out' after just four weeks. What a difference – it was like my whole sex life was beginning again. Suddenly I discovered how amazing oral sex could be, because I could finally relax and be myself during sex. I didn't have to worry about my boyfriend seeing me naked. (M18)

In these extracts, improved sexual function was identified as a key outcome of 'cosmetic' procedures. In Extract 15, psychological changes post-surgery allowed the woman to experience cunnilingus. Surgery reportedly expanded women's sexual repertoires. However, such reports continue to situate heterosex within the bounds of normative heterosexuality, through the suggestion that certain sexual acts (cunnilingus) can only be engaged in, and enjoyed, by either or both partners, within a very limited range of female genital aesthetics. This aesthetic is one where the labia minora do not protrude beyond the labia majora – a youthful, almost pre-pubescent aesthetic, and one often associated with, and derived from, the 'unreal' vulvas displayed in heterosexual male-oriented pornography (see Adams, 1997; S. W. Davis, 2002). This was explicitly noted:

Extract 16: Shine Magazine, *AUS/NZ, 2001*

A lot of women bring in *Playboy*, show me pictures of vaginas and say, 'I want to look like this'. (M5)

The genital produced is one in which diversity is replaced with conformity to this particular aesthetic, a 'cookie cutter' (I25) genital. FGCS becomes a practice of changing women's diverse bodies to fit a certain (male-oriented) aesthetic of what women's genitals *should look like*, if they are to engage in cunnilingus (or other sexual activities). With male (hetero)sexuality continuing to be constructed as *visual* (e.g. Moghaddam and

Braun, 2004), with desire based on the aesthetic, such accounts reinforce a traditional model of male sexuality, and female sexuality alongside it. FGCS effectively becomes surgery to change bodies to fit, and to enable certain sexual practices, through psychological/emotional changes enabled by bodily transformation. A pathologization of 'large' labia minora has a long history, and a long association with perceived sexual 'deviance' (S. Gilman, 1985; Terry, 1995). FGCS appears to offer a surgical process for subsequently passing – to oneself, as well as others – as 'sexy' or just as 'normal' (see K. Davis, 2003).

In these accounts, sexual pleasure occupies a status of almost unquestioned good, which mirrors liberal sexual rhetoric, arguably the dominant form of sexual discourse currently available in western countries. With sex constructed as a 'domain of pleasure' (Seidman, 1991: 124), the pursuit of (more and better) sexual pleasure is situated as a legitimate, or even obligatory (Hawkes, 1996; Heath, 1982), pursuit for the 'liberated' (sexual) subject. There are 'cultural expectations that each individual has a right and a duty to achieve and give maximum satisfaction in their sexual relationships' (Nicolson, 1993: 56). FGCS is framed as a viable means to achieve this. A key question to consider, however, is what (female) sexual pleasure is being offered:

Extract 17: Cosmopolitan Magazine, *AUS/ NZ, 1998*

Four months after the operation, Kate claims to be enjoying the best sex of her life . . . 'removing the excess fat has made me much more easily aroused. Now I achieve orgasm easily and often'. (M1)

Extract 18: New Woman Magazine, *AUS, 2003*

'The G-Shot procedure is all about maximising sexual pleasure for women. By injecting a fluid made up partly of collagen we can increase the G spot to three or four times its normal size, so it's easier to stimulate.

'The effects last about four months and my patients tell me how even something as gentle as yoga is giving them orgasms!' (M20)

Extract 19: New Woman Magazine, *UK, date unknown*

What a result though! All I have to do is think about sex and I can feel my G spot react. Even during my spinning class I can feel the bike seat pressing on it – and I have to pretend I'm just enjoying the workout! I've also had my first ever multiple orgasm and it was great. (M29)

The conception of 'sexual pleasure' for women was typically synonymous with orgasm – or multiple-orgasm. By prioritizing orgasm over other forms of sexual pleasure, such accounts work to reaffirm an orgasm imperative (Heath, 1982; Potts, 2000). Orgasm was framed, a-contextually, as positive – the possibility of orgasm in non-sexual situations was identified not negatively (as, for instance, impeding the woman's ability to partake in exercise without fear of orgasm), but rather positively. Typically, orgasm was framed in unequivocally positive ways:

Extract 20: Cleo Magazine, *NZ, 2003*

Rosemary is promised about four months of orgasmic delights . . . having heard about the G-Shot through a friend who raved about her endless climaxes, Rosemary had no hesitation in handing over US$1850 [NZ$3000] for a dose of heightened pleasure. (M22)

Therefore, the accounts of pleasure in heterosex – and it typically *was* heterosex – presented in the data failed to offer any radical questioning of orgasm as the pinnacle of sexual pleasure and achievement (Jackson and Scott, 2001; Potts, 2000). 'Better' sex typically meant orgasmic sex (or, sometimes, simply more sex), and more (and better) sex was inherently framed as good. By locating orgasm as so central to women's sexual pleasure, other ways in which sex could be more pleasurable – e.g. more fun, more intense, more relaxed, more intimate – were relegated to second place, if any, behind orgasm. This affirms what Seidman (1992: 7) has identified as a 'new tyranny of orgasmic pleasure'.

Although physical changes, such as an enlarged G-spot or tighter vagina, were often identified as resulting in increased pleasure, *psychological* elements were also highlighted as key in explanations for increased sexual pleasure, post-surgery:

Extract 21: male plastic surgeon, UK

S1: when you feel better about what you look like down there if you feel happier with the cosmetic aspect of (Int: mhm) yourself of your genitalia then you are more relaxed in the bedroom (Int: mhm) and a lot of patients report back to me that they *do* feel better and therefore have better sex because (Int: mhm) they're less embarrassed.

Int: 'cos they're more relaxed.

S1: yeah.

Extract 22: Flare Magazine, *CA, 1998*

What does work, according to Angela, is the boost in self-esteem that stems from feeling sexually confident. 'I spent years not feeling good about myself and my sexuality,' she says. 'I started to retreat from my husband. I tried to avoid him sexually because every time we tried, it was disastrous'.

It all gets back to the psychosexual response, says Dr Stubbs. (M26)

Extract 23: Shine Magazine, *AUS/NZ, 2001*

My sex life has improved so much since the operation – we have more sex now than we've ever had. I'm much more into my boyfriend and now that I'm tighter, I'm much more confident about initiating sex. Even better, my boyfriend is enjoying sex with me more, as there's much more stimulation for him, too. (M5)

In these extracts, the psychological was invoked as an essential ingredient in the production of female pleasure, and, indeed, situated as a primary reason this surgery was effective in producing increased sexual pleasure for women. The account was one of (psychological) transformation, from a state of impeded sexuality, to one of liberated, (multi) orgasmic sexuality (transformation is a key theme in accounts of cosmetic surgery, see Blum, 2003; K. Davis, 1995, 2003; Frank, 2003;

Gagne and McGaughey, 2002; Gimlin, 2002; Haiken, 1997; Sullivan, 2001). In such accounts, the psychological was framed as a reason why surgery was necessary, and, in the form of psychological *change*, an explanation of why the surgery was successful. The mind was implicitly constructed as impervious to change *without* surgery, but then as changing once surgical alteration was completed. Cosmetic surgery is thus about changing the body to change the mind (Blum, 2003), and becomes the 'best or most effective means of attaining satisfaction' about bodily distress (Fraser, 2003a: 39).[8] Thus, the body is situated as ontologically prior to the mind, but the mind is located as the crucial variable, in sexual pleasure terms. The idea of cosmetic surgery as 'psychotherapy' can be found in Gilman's (1998; 1999) analyses (see also Fraser, 2003a, 2003b).[9]

Extract 23 is relatively unusual in that increased male sexual pleasure was noted. Women were the primary focus in accounts of sexual pleasure, with comparatively little discussion of male sexual pleasure. This is not surprising, as cosmetic surgery is necessarily often framed as 'for oneself' rather than for others (see Fraser, 2003b). Where male sexual pleasure was referred to, it was often positioned as secondary to, or less important than, female sexual pleasure. For instance, Extract 23 situates her boyfriend's increased sexual pleasure as secondary to her pleasure, as an added bonus, something that makes it 'even better'. The prioritizing of *female* sexual pleasure in accounts of FGCS can be seen in Extract 24:

Extract 24: male gynaecological surgeon, USA

Int: [Vaginal tightening] . . . is talked about as being for sexual gratification um is that um for female sexual gratification or is that um for if they're in a a relationship with a male for male sexual gratification or some combination of both um.

S5: The purpose is for the female (Int: mhm) my objective is for the female I'm a gynaecologist my ah ah I've dedicated my career my life to the healthcare of women and treating women (Int: mhm) damn the man (pause) there's plenty of things (if) I had a problem (clicks fingers) plenty of things (but we're) (Int: mhm) involved with women (Int: mhm) we're involved with women so *my* philosophy there's plenty of things out there *this* is for her I'm happy to say that women come in on their own volition and want to have these procedures *I find* women want to enjoy sex, women want to have the best sexual experience possible that's it (pause) men have got everything okay but women want to have the best sexual experience possible.

Int: And vaginal tightening's important to that I'm just thinking about how . . .

S5: Important to (unclear)

Int: how a tightened vagina *is* necessarily more . . .

S5: Ah it's important to them.

Int: sexually preferable for women.

S5: It's important to them it's important now I've treated patients from all 50 states (Int: mhm) and it's over 30 (unclear) countries it's important to the people (Int: mhm) it's important to the people to the women (pause) *obviously* if I'm enhancing sexual gratification for a female I can enhance sexual gratification for the male (Int: mhm) yeah (Int: mn) but again if a man is *pushing* her I won't do it.

While this extract could be extensively analysed, for the purposes of this article, it is important to note how hard S5 has to work to undermine the suggestion (implicit in my question) that the surgery might 'really' be about male sexual pleasure. Instead he situates male sexual pleasure as a peripheral concern. Such accounts exist in contrast to reports of other genital procedures, such as the 'husband stitch' (Kitzinger, 1994) after childbirth/episiotomy, which tightens a woman's vagina, where *male* sexual pleasure has been emphasized (e.g. Jahoda, 1995).

Overall, the prioritizing of female sexual pleasure and general lack of discussion of male sexual pleasure, work to construct FGCS as something that is in the (sexual) interests of women, rather

than in the sexual interests of (heterosexual) men. Through current accounts, FGCS is effectively constructed as a liberatory action for women – it produces sexual pleasure, which is, socioculturally, almost mandatory for women – rather than a capitulation to unreasonable patriarchal demands on women's bodies. However, while FGCS offers (apparent) empowerment to individuals who have it, albeit within a limited range of options, it simultaneously reinforces oppressive social norms for women (see Gagne and McGaughey, 2002; Gillespie, 1996; Negrin, 2002).

FGCS: normative heterosexuality, generic bodies, and generic pleasures

The central role that (female) pleasure plays in accounts of FGCS is revealing in terms of contemporary discourses of (hetero)sexuality and what it could/should mean to be a woman in the West today. Women's sexual pleasure – or ability to orgasm – appears as a central concern for women, and indeed for society. The account is almost exclusively one where, sexually, women should be comfortable in their bodies and should be able to enjoy sex – and the more sex, and sexual pleasure, the better. Women are represented as (inherently) entitled to sexual pleasure, and indeed, inherently (hetero)sexual. That *these* women are not sexually 'liberated', sexually 'satisfied', or, even, as sexually satisfied as other people appear to be, is, at least in part, what is 'wrong' with their preoperative genitalia. In this sense, accounts of FGCS and women's sexual pleasure fit squarely within a discourse of liberal sexuality (Hollway, 1989), and even, within some feminist discourse around the importance of equality in sex (see Braun et al., 2003). It also affirms an imperative for 'more and better sexual gratification' (Hart and Wellings, 2002: 899), by whatever means possible.

However, the construction of female sexual pleasure in relation to this surgery fails to challenge the bounds of normative heterosexuality. First, sexual pleasure was often (although not exclusively) framed as being derived through coitus, particularly in the case of vaginal tightening, and the sexual pleasure that is derived was typically orgasmic. In this sense, it can be seen to be (at least in part) a practice of designing bodies to fit certain sexual practices, rather than designing sexual practices to fit bodies. We then have to ask whether it is so different from the 'love surgery' of the now disgraced Dr James Burt, who surgically altered women's genitalia to make them more amenable to stimulation during coitus (Adams, 1997). As Adams (1997: 64) noted, such surgeries 'make women conform to traditional heterosexual values'. The same criticism applies to FGCS: the sexual 'freedom' that is being produced is a freedom to enjoy sex within a very limited frame of reference.

Moreover, at the same time as it constructs the legitimate female body as an orgasmic one, it reinforces this 'ideal' as something not all women necessarily (easily) achieve (without surgery). So sexual pleasure, through orgasm, is simultaneously situated both as what most women can/should do and as a current impossibility for some women. The very construction of FGCS as surgery to enhance or enable orgasm fits with an ongoing construction of a woman's orgasm as difficult to achieve, in contrast to a man's inevitable one (Jackson and Scott, 2001; Moghaddam and Braun, 2004). Moreover, although couched in terms of liberation of women (to a 'full' enjoyment of sex), rather than pathology, the framing of FGCS as a solution to 'sub-par' sexual pleasure on the woman's part decontextualizes sex, locating any deficiency in the woman's body/mind, and offering an individualized solution. In this way, FGCS fits within a broadening medicalization of sexual behaviour (Hart and Wellings, 2002; Tiefer, 1997), which, Tiefer (1997: 112) has argued, has 'only reinforced a limited script for heterosexual sexual life'.

These points raise the question of the generic versus the particular. The idea of a surgical 'fix' or enhancement of (lack of) sexual pleasure locates sexual pleasure at the level of the *individual* body, rather than in relation to a 'fit' between bodies/people and the practices they are engaged in. In this sense, the sexual enhancement of the body is framed as generic sexual enhancement, regardless of with whom, and how, one might be having sex. This framing disregards the particularities of sex, with different partners, with different practices, for different purposes, and, indeed, in different moods, modes, and venues. Sex, sexual pleasure, and even sexual desires vary hugely according to this range of contextualizing variables. Accounts of FGCS not only fail to account for this, but actually work to promote the idea of generic sexual pleasure as possible.

The context of consumer culture provides another angle from which to examine public discourse around FGCS. Bordo's (1997: 42) analysis identifies that a consumer system 'depends on our perceiving ourselves as defective and that will continually find new ways to do this'. Media accounts that demonstrate a 'cure' to some problem for women can be seen to also contribute to the creation of that problem in the first place. FGCS, and media coverage of it, have the potential to produce consumer anxiety (S. W. Davis, 2002). One item commented that media coverage had 'taken a very unusual phenomena and concocted a new "embarrassing problem" that could get readers squinting nervously at the privates' (M28). In the case of labiaplasty, then, there is the potential that 'a brand-new worry is being created' (S. W. Davis, 2002: 8). In these accounts, the appearance and sexual function of women's genitalia are rendered *legitimately* problematic and sub-optimal; this part of the body is legitimately commodified, and positioned as 'upgradeable' (see Negrin, 2002). More than this, these media have the potential to construct the very nature of problems and their *solutions*, simultaneously. Both the problem of aesthetically 'unappealing' genitalia and the desire for better sex have a ready worked-up solution – surgery.

While FGCS might seem relatively arcane, a form of cosmetic surgery very few women would access, and one that is unlikely to become popular, the surgeons I interviewed indicated that media coverage seems to increase demand for their services. This fits with Kathy Davis' (2003: 134) observation that media coverage of new surgical interventions 'seduc[es] more individuals to place their bodies under the surgeon's knife' (see also Wolf, 1990). The history of other cosmetic procedures does nothing to dispute this concern. Indeed, as Haiken has commented in her history of cosmetic surgery, individual change can often be 'easier' than social change.

Americans, most of them women, found it easier to alter their own faces than to alter the cultural norms and expectations about aging that confronted them. Together, surgeons and their patients forged a new image of the face-lift as a sensible, practical and relatively simple solution to the social problem of aging. In doing so, they both became producers and products of the modern 'culture of narcissism' and created powerful incentives toward cosmetic surgery that are still in place today. (Haiken, 1997: 135–6)

The appearance of FGCS raises important questions about the alteration of the body in the pursuit of pleasure, which I have only started to address. If media coverage can contribute to the nature of, and legitimate, a 'new' problem for women, with a ready-made surgical solution, we need to continue to act as 'cultural critics' (Bordo, 1993), and question the assumptions on which such surgery rests, and the models of sexuality, bodies, and practices it promotes.

Acknowledgements

Thanks to Tim Kurz, Victoria Clarke and Nicola Gavey for useful feedback on an earlier draft of this article.

Notes

1. My classification of these surgeries as 'cosmetic' is not necessarily the way surgeons or the women themselves would classify them. Some of these surgeries are primarily (or exclusively) done for functional reasons, and even where cosmesis is prioritized, the notion that surgery is purely cosmetic is challenged through diverse accounts of 'functionality'.

2. Although cosmetic surgery is increasingly popular among men, it is important to retain some sense of the gendered context in which cosmetic procedures originated and became popularized, such that women were (and continue to be) the primary consumers of cosmetic surgery (see K. Davis, 2003, for a discussion of the limitations of 'equality' analyses in relation to cosmetic surgery).

3. The techniques might be the same or similar in some instances. At a more theoretical level, the practices around the construction of 'normal'

genitalia through FGCS are, like other genital surgeries, part of the ongoing social, and material, construction of (gendered) genital meaning and appearance. Moreover, an inappropriately 'masculine' appearance/perception of their genitalia was one of the reported reasons some women desired FGCS. The constructed genitalia tend to display *more* gendered genital difference (bigger penises, tighter vaginas, smaller labia minora). So while much cosmetic surgery can be seen to produce the surgical 'erasure of embodied difference' (K. Davis, 2003: 133), the one difference that is promoted, rather than erased, in FGCS is 'gendered' (genital) difference.

4. A comparison between these western practices and FGM was rarely mentioned in the data, and a focus on notions of 'free choice', purported low risk to health, and likely increased sexual pleasure, all rhetorically constructed FGCS as inherently different to FGM. However, Manderson and colleagues (Allotey et al., 2001; Manderson, 1999) point to contradictions between how FGM and FGCS are treated in the West (see also S.W. Davis, 2002; Essen and Johnsdotter, 2004; Sheldon and Wilkinson, 1998).

5. Quotations from data are coded by letter and number: S = surgeon; M = magazine; N = news media; I = Internet material other than 'Internet magazines'. Numbers were applied sequentially across each data source, starting from 1. In the surgeon extracts, material in parentheses (like this) indicates a best guess as to what was said at that point on the tape.

6. Although there are differences between the datasets (e.g. see K. Davis' (1998) comments about media accounts of cosmetic surgery), my analysis treats all data in the same way – as cultural texts.

7. This point is demonstrated by Blum's (2003: 287) observation that 'the surgical patient's shame is intolerable.'

8. Breast surgery has been identified as 'a means of establishing congruency between the body and mind, or developing an embodied self that was comfortable' (Gagne and McGaughey, 2002: 822).

9. This dualistic construction of mind and body is questioned in Budgeon's (2003) work on young women talking about the possibilities of bodies, identity and practice around cosmetic surgery.

References

Adams, A. (1997) 'Moulding Women's Bodies: The Surgeon as Sculptor', in D. S. Wilson and C. M. Laennec (eds) *Bodily Discursions: Gender, Representations, Technologies*, pp. 59–80. New York: State University of New York Press.

Allotey, P., Manderson, L. and Grover, S. (2001) 'The Politics of Female Genital Surgery in Displaced Communities', *Critical Public Health* 11: 189–201.

Berger, A. A. (1998) *Media Analysis Techniques* (2nd edn). Thousand Oaks, CA: Sage.

Blum, V. L. (2003) *Flesh Wounds: The Culture of Cosmetic Surgery*. Berkeley: University of California Press.

Bordo, S. (1993) *Unbearable Weight: Feminism, Western Culture, and the Body*. Berkeley: University of California Press.

Bordo, S. (1997) *Twilight Zones: The Hidden Life of Cultural Images from Plato to O.J.* Berkeley: University of California Press.

Bramwell, R. (2002) 'Invisible Labia: The Representation of Female External Genitals in Women's Magazines', *Journal of Sexual and Relationship Therapy* 17: 187–90.

Braun, V., Gavey, N. and McPhillips, K. (2003) 'The "Fair Deal"? Unpacking Accounts of Reciprocity in Heterosex', *Sexualities* 6(2): 237–61.

Braun, V. and Wilkinson, S. (2001) 'Socio-cultural Representations of the Vagina', *Journal of Reproductive and Infant Psychology* 19: 17–32.

Braun, V. and Wilkinson, S. (2003) 'Liability or Asset? Women Talk about the Vagina', *Psychology of Women Section Review* 5(2): 28–42.

Brown, J. D. and Walsh-Childers, K. (2002) 'Effects of Media on Personal and Public Health', in J. Bryant and D. Zillmann (eds) *Media Effects: Advances in Theory and Research*, 2nd edn, pp. 453–88. Mahwah, NJ: Lawrence Erlbaum Associates.

Budgeon, S. (2003) 'Identity as Embodied Event', *Body and Society* 9: 35–55.

Burr, V. (1995) *An Introduction to Social Constructionism*. London: Routledge.

Carpiano, R. M. (2001) 'Passive Medicalization: The Case of Viagra and Erectile Dysfunction', *Sociological Spectrum* 21: 441–50.

Connell, R. W. (1997) 'Sexual Revolution', in L. Segal (ed.) *New Sexual Agendas*, pp. 60–76. New York: New York University Press.

Davis, K. (1995) *Reshaping the Female Body: The Dilemma of Cosmetic Surgery*. New York: Routledge.

Davis, K. (1998) 'Facing the Dilemma', in P. D. Hopkins (ed.) *Sex/Machine: Readings in Culture, Gender and Technology*, pp. 286–305. Bloomington: Indiana University Press.

Davis, K. (2003) *Dubious Equalities and Embodied Differences: Cultural Studies on Cosmetic Surgery*. Lanham, MD: Rowman and Littlefield.

Davis, S. W. (2002) 'Loose Lips Sink Ships', *Feminist Studies* 28: 7–35.

D'Emilio, J. and Freedman, E. B. (1997) *Intimate Matters: A History of Sexuality in America*, 2nd edn. Chicago, IL: The University of Chicago Press.

Essen, B. and Johnsdotter, S. (2004) 'Female Genital Mutilation in the West: Traditional Circumcision versus Genital Cosmetic Surgery', *Acta Obstetricia et Gynecologica Scandinavica* 83: 611–13.

Frank, A. W. (2003) 'Connecting Body Parts: Technoluxe, Surgical Shapings, and Bioethics'. Paper presented at the *Vital Politics* Conference, London.

Fraser, S. (2003a) 'The Agent Within: Agency Repertoires in Medical Discourse on Cosmetic Surgery', *Australian Feminist Studies* 18: 27–44.

Fraser, S. (2003b) *Cosmetic Surgery, Gender and Culture*. Houndmills: Palgrave Macmillan.

Gagne, P. and McGaughey, D. (2002) 'Designing Women – Cultural Hegemony and the Exercise of Power Among Women Who Have Undergone Elective Mammoplasty', *Gender and Society* 16: 814–38.

Gillespie, R. (1996) 'Women, the Body and Brand Extension in Medicine: Cosmetic Surgery and the Paradox of Choice', *Women and Health* 24(4): 69–85.

Gilman, S. (1985) *Difference and Pathology: Stereotypes of Sexuality, Race and Madness*. Ithaca, NY: Cornell University Press.

Gilman, S. L. (1998) *Creating Beauty to Cure the Soul*. Durham, NC: Duke University Press.

Gilman, S. L. (1999) *Making the Body Beautiful: A Cultural History of Aesthetic Surgery*. Princeton, NJ: Princeton University Press.

Gimlin, D. L. (2002) *Body Work: Beauty and Self-Image in American Culture*. Berkeley, CA: University of California Press.

Goodman, M. (1996) 'Culture, Cohort, and Cosmetic Surgery', *Journal of Women and Aging* 8(2): 55–73.

Gordon, M. (1971) 'From an Unfortunate Necessity to a Cult of Mutual Orgasm: Sex in American Marital Education Literature 1830–1940', in J. M. Henslin (ed.) *Studies in the Sociology of Sex*, pp. 53–77. New York: Appleton-Century-Crofts.

Grogan, S. (1999) *Body Image: Understanding Body Dissatisfaction in Men, Women and Children*. London: Routledge.

Haiken, E. (1997) *Venus Envy: A History of Cosmetic Surgery*. Baltimore, MD: The Johns Hopkins University Press.

Haiken, E. (2000) 'The Making of the Modern Face: Cosmetic Surgery', *Social Research* 67: 81–93.

Hart, G. and Wellings, K. (2002) 'Sexual Behaviour and its Medicalisation: in Sickness and Health', *British Medical Journal* 324: 896–900.

Hawkes, G. (1996) *The Sociology of Sex and Sexuality*. Buckingham: Open University Press.

Heath, S. (1982) *The Sexual Fix*. New York: Schocken Books.

Hollway, W. (1989) *Subjectivity and Method in Psychology: Gender, Meaning and Science*. London: Sage.

Jackson, S. and Scott, S. (2001) 'Embodying Orgasm: Gendered Power Relations and Sexual Pleasure', in E. Kaschak and L. Tiefer (eds) *A New View of Women's Sexual Problems*, pp. 99–110. New York: The Haworth Press.

Jahoda, S. (1995) 'Theatres of Madness', in J. Terry and J. Urla (eds) *Deviant Bodies: Critical Perspectives on Difference in Science and Popular Culture*, pp. 251–76. Bloomington: Indiana University Press.

Kitzinger, S. (1994) *The Year after Childbirth: Surviving and Enjoying the First Year of Motherhood*. Toronto: HarperCollins Publishers.

Manderson, L. (1999) 'Local Rites and the Body Politic: Tensions Between Cultural Diversity and Universal Rites', paper presented at the *Sexual Diversity and Human Rights: Beyond Boundaries* conference, Manchester, July.

Moghaddam, P. and Braun, V. (2004) '"Most of us Guys are Raring to go Anytime, Anyplace, Anywhere": Male (and Female) Sexuality in *Cosmopolitan* and *Cleo*', Manuscript under submission.

Negrin, L. (2002) 'Cosmetic Surgery and the Eclipse of Identity', *Body and Society* 8: 21–42.

Nicolson, P. (1993) 'Public Values and Private Beliefs: Why do some Women Refer Themselves for Sex Therapy?' in J. M. Ussher and C. D. Baker (eds) *Psychological Perspectives on Sexual Problems: New Directions in Theory and Practice*, pp. 56–76. London: Routledge.

Potts, A. (2000) 'Coming, Coming, Gone: A Feminist Deconstruction of Heterosexual Orgasm', *Sexualities* 3: 55–76.

Reinholtz, R. K. and Muehlenhard, C. L. (1995) 'Genital Perceptions and Sexual Activity in a College Population' *Journal of Sex Research* 32: 155–65.

Roberts, C., Kippax, S., Spongberg, M. and Crawford, J. (1996) '"Going Down": Oral Sex, Imaginary Bodies and HIV', *Body and Society* 2(3): 107–24.

Seidman, S. (1991) *Romantic Longings: Love in America, 1830–1980*. New York: Routledge.

Seidman, S. (1992) *Embattled Eros: Sexual Politics and Ethics in Contemporary America*. New York: Routledge.

Sheldon, S. and Wilkinson, S. (1998) 'Female Genital Mutilation and Cosmetic Surgery: Regulating Non-therapeutic Body Modification', *Bioethics* 12: 263–85.

Sullivan, D. A. (2001) *Cosmetic Surgery: The Cutting Edge of Commercial Medicine in America*. New Brunswick, NJ: Rutgers University Press.

Terry, J. (1995) 'Anxious Slippages Between "Us" and "Them": A Brief History of the Scientific Search for Homosexual Bodies', in J. Terry and J. Urla (eds) *Deviant Bodies: Critical Perspectives on Difference in Science and Popular Culture*, pp. 129–69. Bloomington: Indiana University Press.

Tiefer, L. (1995) *Sex is Not a Natural Act and Other Essays*. Boulder, CO: Westview Press.

Tiefer, L. (1997) 'Medicine, Morality, and the Public Management of Sexual Matters', in L. Segal (ed.) *New Sexual Agendas*, pp. 103–12. New York: New York University Press.

Tiefer, L. (2000) 'The Social Construction and Social Effects of Sex Research: The Sexological Model of Sexuality', in C. B. Travis and J. W. White (eds) *Sexuality, Society, and Feminism*, pp. 79–107. Washington, DC: American Psychological Association.

Toerien, M. and Wilkinson, S. (2004) 'Exploring the Depilation Norm: a Qualitative Questionnaire Study of Women's Body Hair Removal', *Qualitative Research in Psychology* 1: 69–92.

Weeks, J. (1985) *Sexuality and Its Discontents: Meanings, Myths and Modern Sexualities*. London: Routledge & Kegan Paul.

White, J. W., Bondurant, B. and Travis, C. B. (2000) 'Social Constructions of Sexuality: Unpacking Hidden Meanings', in C. B. Travis and J. W. White (eds) *Sexuality, Society, and Feminism*, pp. 11–33. Washington, DC: American Psychological Association.

Wolf, N. (1990) *The Beauty Myth*. London: Vintage.

If Men Could Menstruate: A Political Fantasy

by Gloria Steinem

Awhite minority of the world has spent centuries conning us into thinking that a white skin makes people superior—even though the only thing it really does is make them more subject to ultraviolet rays and to wrinkles. Male human beings have built whole cultures around the idea that penis-envy is "natural" to women—though having such an unprotected organ might be said to make men vulnerable, and the power to give birth makes womb-envy at least as logical.

In short, the characteristics of the powerful, whatever they may be, are thought to be better than the characteristics of the powerless—and logic has nothing to do with it.

What would happen, for instance, if suddenly, magically, men could menstruate and women could not?

The answer is clear—menstruation would become an enviable, boast-worthy, masculine event:

Men would brag about how long and how much.

Boys would mark the onset of menses, that longed for proof of manhood, with religious ritual and stag parties.

Congress would fund a National Institute of Dysmenorrhea to help stamp out monthly discomforts.

Sanitary supplies would be federally funded and free. (Of course, some men would still pay for the prestige of commercial brands such as John Wayne Tampons, Muhammad Ali's Rope-a-dope Pads, Joe Namath Jock Shields—"For Those Light Bachelor Days," and Robert "Baretta" Blake Maxi-Pads.) Military men, right-wing politicians, and religious fundamentalists would cite menstruation ("*menstruation*") as proof that only men could serve in the Army ("you have to give blood to take blood"), occupy political office ("can women be aggressive without that steadfast cycle governed by the planet

Mars?"), be priests and ministers ("how could a woman give her blood for our sins?"), or rabbis ("without the monthly loss of impurities, women remain unclean").

Male radicals, left wing politicians, mystics, however, would insist that women are equal, just different, and that any woman could enter their ranks if only she were willing to self-inflict a major wound every month ("you *must* give blood for the revolution"), recognize the preeminence of menstrual issues, or subordinate her selfness to all men in their Cycle of Enlightenment.

Street guys would brag ("I'm a three-pad man") or answer praise from a buddy ("Man, you lookin good!") by giving fives and saying, "Yeah, man, I'm on the rag!"

TV shows would treat the subject at length. ("Happy Days": Richie and Potsie try to convince Fonzie that he is still "The Fonz," though he has missed two periods in a row.) So would newspapers. (SHARK SCARE THREATENS MENSTRUATING MEN. JUDGE CITES MONTHLY STRESS IN PARDONING RAPIST.) And movies. (Newman and Redford in "Blood Brothers"!)

Men would convince women that intercourse was *more* pleasurable at "that time of the month." Lesbians would be said to fear blood and therefore life itself—though probably only because they needed a good menstruating man.

Of course, male intellectuals would offer the most moral and logical arguments. How could a woman master any discipline that demanded a sense of time, space, mathematics, or measurement, for instance, without that in-built gift for measuring the cycles of the moon and planets—and thus for measuring anything at all? In the rarefied fields of philosophy and religion, could women compensate for missing the rhythm of the universe? Or for their lack of symbolic death-and-resurrection every month?

Liberal males in every field would try to be kind: the fact that "these people" have no gift for measuring life or connecting to the universe, the liberals would explain, should be punishment enough.

And how would women be trained to react? One can imagine traditional women agreeing to all these arguments with a staunch and smiling masochism. ("The ERA would force housewives to wound themselves every month": Phyllis Schlafly. "Your husband's blood is as sacred as that of Jesus—and so sexy, too!": Marabel Morgan.) Reformers and Queen Bees would try to imitate men, and *pretend*

to have a monthly cycle. All feminists would explain endlessly that men, too, needed to be liberated from the false idea of Martian aggressiveness, just as women needed to escape the bonds of menses-envy. Radical feminists would add that the oppression of the nonmenstrual was the pattern for all other oppressions ("Vampires were our first freedom fighters!") Cultural feminists would develop a bloodless imagery in art and literature. Socialist feminists would insist that only under capitalism would men be able to monopolize menstrual blood. . . .

In fact, if men could menstruate, the power justifications could probably go on forever.

If we let them.

The Menstrual Mark: Menstruation as Social Stigma

by Ingrid Johnston-Robledo and Joan C. Chrisler

Abstract In this theoretical paper, we argue that menstruation is a source of social stigma for women. The word stigma refers to any stain or mark that renders the individual's body or character defective. This stigma is transmitted through powerful socialization agents in popular culture such as advertisements and educational materials. We demonstrate, in our review of the psychological literature concerning attitudes and experiences of predominantly American girls and women, that the stigmatized status of menstruation has important consequences for their health, sexuality, and well-being. We argue that the stigma of menstruation both reflects and contributes to women's lower social status and conclude with suggestions for ways to resist the stigma.

Introduction

The American artist Vanessa Tiegs (http://menstrala.blogspot.com) and the German artist Petra Paul (http://mum.org/armenpau.htm) are known for collecting their menstrual flow. When they have collected enough, they sprinkle, splash, and brush their blood across their canvases to create beautiful, and intriguing, works of art.

Reactions to their work include shock at their audacity, amazement at their creativity, and disgust at their willingness to exhibit one of nature's most stigmatized fluids (www.truenuff.com/forums/showthread.php?135-Menstrual-Art-by-Vanessa-Tiegs&p=1371&viewfull=1). One journalist (Heath 2007) wondered whether Tiegs' work should more properly be called art or a biohazard.

Contemporary artists often aim to shock viewers (Stallabrass 2006), but these artists have a greater goal in mind (Chesler 2006; Cochrane 2009). They seem to want us to ask ourselves why a mundane product of nature is so shocking, given that most women experience the menses and manage their own menstrual flow for decades of their lives. They want us to consider why menstruation, a benign process essential to the production of human life, evokes fear, disgust, and comparison to toxic waste. We believe that viewers of Tiegs' and Paul's art react the way they do because menstrual blood is a stigmatized substance. In this theoretical paper, we review feminist scholarship regarding the attitudes and experiences of predominantly American girls and women to build the argument that menstruation is a source of social stigma for women. All studies cited in this article were conducted with American samples unless otherwise stated.

What is Stigma?

According to Goffman (1963), the word *stigma* refers to any stain or mark that sets some people apart from others; it conveys the information that those people have a defect of body or of character that spoils their appearance or identity. The word derives from a practice of the ancient Greeks, who branded criminals and slaves to mark their status. People reacted with disgust when they saw the brands associated with thieves or traitors, and citizens avoided interacting socially with criminals and slaves (Goffman 1963). Goffman (1963, p. 4) categorized stigmas into three types: "abominations of the body" (e.g., burns, scars, deformities), "blemishes of individual character" (e.g., criminality, addictions), and "tribal" identities or social markers associated with marginalized groups (e.g., gender, race, sexual orientation, nationality). Social psychologists have conducted empirical studies of stigmatized conditions to determine which aspects of those conditions are most abhorrent to other people. The key dimensions are: peril (i.e., the perceived danger to others; e.g., HIV+ individuals), visibility (i.e., the obviousness of the mark; e.g., facial disfigurement), and controllability (i.e., how responsible the individual is for the condition, such as whether the mark is congenital, accidental, or intentional; e.g., obesity due to a

medical condition or treatment vs. obesity due to "letting oneself go") (Crocker et al. 1998; Deaux et al. 1995; Frable 1993). People's beliefs about the controllability of a stigmatized condition (e.g., homosexuality) are important because they affect how much stigmatized people are disliked and rejected (Dovidio et al. 2000). For example, lesbians and gay men are better liked and more accepted by people who believe that sexual orientation is biologically-based rather than freely chosen (Herek 2009).

Menstruation as a Stigmatized Condition

We argue that menstrual blood is a stigmatizing mark that fits all three of Goffman's categories. Menstrual rituals and hygiene practices imply that, like other bodily fluids (Rozin and Fallon 1987), menstrual blood is considered an abomination. Some have argued that menstrual blood is viewed as more disgusting or aversive than other bodily fluids such as breastmilk (Bramwell 2001) and semen (Goldenberg and Roberts 2004). In some cultures women are believed to be unclean during their menstrual periods, and they must take a ritual bath (e.g., the Jewish Mikvah) to purify themselves before they can be intimate with a man (Cicurel 2000; Goldenberg and Roberts 2004). Given aversions to menstrual blood, a stain may be viewed as a blemish on one's character. From a content analysis of advertisements in Australian magazines, Raftos et al. (1998) concluded that a powerful message these ads send to readers is that leaks of menstrual blood taint women's femininity because, through the proper choice of products, she *should* have kept the evidence of her menses out of sight. Lee (1994) found that 75% of the young women she interviewed had experienced or were afraid of experiencing leaks during menstruation. She concluded that visible signs of menstruation represent emblems of girls' contamination (Lee 1994). Roberts et al. (2002) were able to demonstrate empirically that even reminders of menstrual blood (e.g., tampons) can lead to avoidance and social distancing, which suggests that menstrual blood may serve as a blemish on women's character. Because only girls and women menstruate, menstrual blood also marks a tribal identity of femaleness.

When girls reach menarche (i.e., experience their first menstruation), parents and others treat them differently than they did before (Lee and Sasser-Coen 1996). Post-menarcheal girls are cautioned about sexuality, told that they are now "grown-up," and urged to act "ladylike" in ways that restrict the freedom of behavior they had enjoyed in the past (Lee and Sasser-Coen 1996). Thus menstruation marks girls and women as different from the normative and privileged male body (Young 2005). Furthermore, if people hold cultural beliefs that the menstrual cycle causes women to be physically (menstrual phase) or mentally (premenstrual phase) disordered, then the stigma of menstruation also marks women as ill, disabled, out-ofcontrol, unfeminine, or even crazy (Chrisler 2008; Chrisler and Caplan 2002).

Menstrual blood also reflects several of the key dimensions of a stigmatized condition. For example, it has been considered perilous—both magical and poisonous (Golub 1992). Many anthropologists have theorized about the origins and purposes of this symbolism, but, according to Buckley and Gottlieb (1988), there are few firmly established anthropological theories about why menstrual blood may have been viewed that way. Perhaps menstruation seemed magical because, before the physiology of the menstrual cycle was understood, individuals did not understand how women who were not wounded could bleed for 5 days without being seriously weakened or killed. Because men did not experience menses themselves, they must have been afraid of it, perhaps worried that close contact with menstrual blood might do them some physical damage or pollute them by its association with the mysterious female body. Thus, menstruation may have seemed poisonous.

These ideas are not to be dismissed as naïve or primitive; remnants of them persisted into modern times and remain present today. Cultural feminists (e.g., Owen 1993; Stepanich 1992; Wind 1995) who advocate the celebration of menstruation with praise to the Moon Goddess continue the idea that menses and magic are connected. As late as the 1920s and 1930s, scientists (see Delaney et al. 1987) were attempting to demonstrate that menstruating women exuded what were called menotoxins (i.e., poisonous elements) in their menstrual blood, perspiration, saliva, urine, and tears. Images

in popular culture of premenstrual women as out-of-control and likely at any moment to be verbally abusive or violent reinforce the ancient notion that menstruation constitutes a peril. In the 1990s, in his infamous "giraffe hunting" speech, Congressman Newt Gingrich commented that female soldiers do not belong in the trenches during times when they are highly susceptible to infections. His remarks imply that menstruating women somehow poison themselves and weaken their immune systems, but perhaps what really worried him is the idea that premenstrual American female soldiers might be even more dangerous than the enemy to their male comrades (Chrisler and Caplan 2002).

We assert that menstruation is more like a hidden than a visible stigma, but that is because women go to a great deal of effort to conceal it (Oxley 1998). Menstrual hygiene products (e.g., tampons, pads) are designed to absorb fluid and odors, not to be visible through one's clothes, to be small enough to carry unobtrusively in one's purse, and to be discretely discarded in a bathroom container (Kissling 2006). It is usually not possible to know for certain that a woman is menstruating unless she says so. . .or unless menstrual blood leaks through her clothes and exposes her then stigmatized condition.

Until recently, menstruation was not controllable. The menstrual cycle is a force of nature; hormone levels ebb and flow in a regular (or irregular) rhythm. Unless women had an illness (e.g., anorexia nervosa, polycystic ovary syndrome) or a temporary condition (e.g., pregnancy, lactation, the low level of body fat frequently seen in long-distance runners) that halted the menstrual cycle, they could expect to menstruate at a time determined by their particular cycle. With the advent of oral contraceptives in the 1960s, however, scientists proved that menstruation could be controlled. Women have traditionally taken oral contraceptives daily for 3 weeks, then not taken pills for 1 week in order to allow for a form of "break-through bleeding" that resembles normal menstruation. However, in recent years continuous oral contraceptives have been marketed to women as a way to avoid menstruation altogether (Johnston-Robledo et al. 2006). The ads suggest that women have the "freedom" to make a "choice" about whether to menstruate (Johnston-Robledo et al. 2003). However, against a back-drop of cultural messages that women should always be available (e.g., to the men and children in their lives) and should avoid, if at all possible, anything that might discomfit others (Chrisler 2008), we might soon reach the point where most people believe that women *should* eliminate their menstrual cycles unless they are actively trying to become pregnant. This may increase the stigma attached to those who continue to menstruate regularly.

Transmission of Stigma of Menstruation

Most of the people who react with shock to Tiegs' and Paul's art have probably never been told that menstruation is a stigmatized condition, but their reactions suggest that they "know" it. The stigma of menstruation is conveyed to us everyday through a variety of sociocultural routes. For example, negative attitudes toward menstruation and cultural beliefs about menstruating and premenstrual women are transmitted through products and media (e.g., advertisements, magazine articles, books, television) we see everyday (Chrisler 2008; Erchull 2010).

Advertisements are cultural artifacts that play an important role in the social construction of meaning (Merskin 1999). Ads for menstrual products have contributed to the communication taboo by emphasizing secrecy, avoidance of embarrassment, and freshness (Coutts and Berg 1993; Delaney et al. 1987; Houppert 1999; Merskin 1999). Allegorical images, such as flowers and hearts, and blue rather than reddish liquid, have been used euphemistically to promote secrecy and delicacy (Merskin 1999). Ads play on women's fear of being discovered as menstruating because discovery means stigma (Coutts and Berg 1993). With the invention of panty-liners, advertisers began to tell women to use their products every day so that they can feel "confident" that they will always be "fresh" and untainted (Berg and Coutts 1994). When Oxley (1998) questioned 55 British women about their experiences with menstruation, she found that they echoed many of the themes in the ads. They felt self-conscious during the menses, preferred tampons because they are "less noticeable" than pads, believed that menstrual blood is distasteful to self and others, and supported the sex taboo.

Advertisements are not the only form of public discourse about menstruation. Attitudes are also conveyed through books, magazine and newspaper articles, jokes, and other cultural artifacts, such as "humorous" products like greeting cards and refrigerator magnets (Chrisler 2007, 2008). Most of the attitudes these media convey are negative, and together they have constructed a stereotype of menstruating women, especially premenstrual women, as violent, irrational, emotionally labile, out-of-control, and physically or mentally ill. We have seen bumper stickers (e.g., "A woman with PMS and ESP is a bitch who knows everything"), buttons (e.g., "It's not PMS, I'm always psychotic"), magnets (e.g., "Be very careful: I have PMS and a gun"), cartoons, greeting cards, and books (e.g., *Raging Hormones: The Unofficial PMS Survival Guide*, the cover of which pictures actress Joan Crawford as an axe murderer; Chrisler 2002). If this is what people think about women who are menstruating (or about to menstruate), it's no surprise that women try to conceal this stigmatized condition.

The stigmatized status of menstruation may also be transmitted through the educational booklets produced by sanitary napkin and tampon manufacturers; these booklets typically are written by nurses or health educators employed by the companies. We (Erchull et al. 2002) conducted a content analysis of 28 of these booklets, which were published between 1932 and 1997, and we found that the booklets placed much more emphasis on negative than on positive aspects of menstruation. Cramps, moodiness, and leaks were all mentioned frequently, but growing up was the only positive aspect mentioned. Descriptions of the menstrual cycle were kept vague for the most part. Estrogen and progesterone were mentioned in fewer than one-half of the booklets. Even the terms menstruation and ovulation were not used in every booklet, and only one booklet (produced by Planned Parenthood, not by a manufacturer) actually included the word menarche (the term for a girl's first menstrual period). The illustrations were also problematic. A few of the booklets did not show any external genitalia, and the diagrams of the female reproductive organs often were presented separately from any bodily reference or body outline, which makes it difficult for a girl to imagine the scale of the system if she does not know where it is located. These booklets are used to educate, but girls who read them might learn more about stigma than about their physiology. One booklet stated out-right that "your main concern will probably be *avoiding accidents* with an appropriately absorbent pad, *avoiding a wet feeling*, and using a pad that *doesn't show*." The emphasis on secrecy and the potential for embarrassment is present in all of the booklets, and this emphasis may contribute to negative attitudes toward menstruation (Hoerster et al. 2003).

Finally, menstrual stigma is perpetuated indirectly through silence. Menstruation is typically avoided in conversation (Kissling 1996), except under certain circumstances (e.g., in private with female friends and relatives, in a health education or biology class, in a doctor's office). The majority of American adults surveyed for *The Tampax Report* (1981) agreed that menstruation should not be discussed in "mixed company," and many thought that it should not be discussed with the family at home. Williams (1983) found that 33% of the adolescent girls she surveyed would not talk about menstruation with their fathers, and nearly all of her participants agreed that girls should not discuss menstruation around boys. Even psychotherapists have reported experiencing discomfort when their clients want to discuss some aspect of menstruation (Rhinehart 1989). When teachers separate girls and boys to view films about puberty, and when mothers arrange one-to-one, private, "facts of life" talks with their daughters, they are conveying not only facts but guidelines for communication; they are marking menstruation "as a special topic, not one for ordinary conversation" (Kissling 1996, p. 495). Exclusive talks held in private convey the notion that menstruation is an embarrassing event that must be concealed from others and never discussed openly.

The communication taboo is supported by the existence of dozens of euphemisms for menstruation (Ernster 1975; Golub 1992), and these euphemisms can be found in cultures around the world. Ernster (1975) examined a collection of American expressions in the Folklore Archives at UC-Berkeley, and she grouped them into categories. For example, some refer to female visitors

(e. g., "My friend is here," p.6), others to cyclicity (e.g., "It's that time again," "my time of the month/moon," "my period," p. 6), illness or distress (e.g., "the curse," "the misery," "I'm under the weather," p. 6), nature (e.g., "flowers," "Mother Nature's gift," p. 7), redness or blood (e.g., "I'm wearing red shoes today," "red plague," "red moon," "bloody scourge," p. 6–7), or menstrual products (e.g., "on the rag," "riding the cotton pony," "using mouse mattresses," p. 6). Some of these euphemisms are still in common use today (Chrisler 2011), and new ones have no doubt been invented. If menstrual blood were not stigmatized, there would be no reason to call it anything other than its formal name: menstruation or the menses.

Although feminist scholars and activists (e.g., Owen 1993; Stepanich 1992; Taylor 2003; Wind 1995; see also Bobel 2006, 2010) have tried to promote the celebration of menarche and menstruation, their positive messages may be overshadowed by the stigmatizing messages. Even those women and girls who do internalize the positive messages may find themselves confused about how to celebrate something that is supposed to be hidden. Their concerns about the consequences of doing so may be well-founded.

Consequences of Stigma of Menstruation

The stigma of menstruation has negative consequences for women's health, sexuality, well-being, and social status. One of the consequences most frequently noted in the literature is self-consciousness and hypervigilence associated with concerns about the revelation of one's menstrual status. Oxley (1998) found that both undergraduate women and women employed in the medical professions reported high levels of self-consciousness during menstruation. The behaviors they engaged in, and activities they avoided, reflected their determination to hide their menstrual status from others. For example, they wore baggy clothes and preferred tampons over pads. They avoided swimming and sexual activities during menstruation, often because of their concern about how others would respond to their menstrual blood. The researcher concluded that women might feel unattractive during their menses because menstrual cycle effects (e.g., bloating, acne) indicate that they have been betrayed by their bodies. She argued that, in order for women to accept themselves every day of the month, cultures must change the way menstruation is viewed, and women themselves must take more control over the way they experience and feel about menstruation. In other words, women must resist, and cultures must reduce, the stigma.

The self-monitoring that women do to be sure that they look their best and that their menstrual status is hidden is related to the Foucauldian concept of self-policing (Foucault 1979). In a study of women who met criteria for severe PMS, Ussher (2004) found that women understood, experienced, and interpreted PMS symptoms as violations of the norms for "appropriate" femininity (e.g., resisting the need to nurture others at one's own expense, displaying anger or annoyance one would usually conceal, experiencing one's body as unruly or out-of-control). Ussher argued that women's tendency to pathologize premenstrual experiences and to apply the PMS label to themselves represents a form of behavioral self-policing that allows them to distance themselves from their embodied selves in an effort to retain their femininity. Lapses in self-policing such as choosing to say "no" to others can then be blamed on the body rather than on the woman's own desires.

Objectification theory (Fredrickson and Roberts 1997) may help to explain why certain women are self-conscious about menstruation and go to unusual lengths to hide or eliminate their periods. Sexual objectification occurs when a woman feels that she is separate from, or represented by, parts of her body that are deemed sexual, such as her breasts and buttocks (Bartky 1990). In a culture where women's bodies routinely are sexually objectified, women themselves can internalize the sexual objectification of their bodies and view themselves through the lens of a critical male gaze. This self-objectification may lead women to monitor themselves constantly and to alter their self-presentation accordingly. Looking at the self this way has negative implications for psychological and sexual well-being (Muehlenkamp and Saris-Baglama 2002; Szymanski and Henning 2007; Tylka and Hill 2004). Goldenberg and Roberts (2004) have applied principles of terror management theory (Greenberg et al. 1986) to explain

pervasive negative attitudes toward menstruation. They argued that menstruation and other reproductive functions serves as reminders of the creaturely and therefore mortal nature of humans and women's proximity to nature. In an effort to allay existential angst about mortality, women may distance themselves from menstruation by adhering to cultural beauty standards. Both of these theories shed light on explanations for women's self-consciousness during menstruation and the social stigma attached to menstruation.

Feminist researchers have begun to consider the impact of self-objectification on attitudes toward menstruation, a bodily function that is incompatible with the view of the body as a sex object or as sexually available to others. Women who tend to self-objectify have been found to have particularly negative attitudes toward menstruation (Johnston-Robledo et al. 2007; Roberts 2004). Undergraduate women with higher self-objectification tendencies also have said that they would prefer not to have menstrual cycles (Johnston-Robledo et al. 2003) and reported positive attitudes toward the elimination of menstruation through the use of continuous oral contraception (i.e., menstrual suppression; Johnston-Robledo et al. 2007). Thus, self-objectification may lead women to maintain a sense of global shame about multiple reproductive events, including menstruation, birthing, and breastfeeding (Johnston-Robledo et al. 2007). The shame and lowered self-esteem is psychologically damaging and may lead women to make reproductive decisions (e.g., menstrual suppression, elective cesarean section, high-risk sexual behavior) that could have negative ramifications for their physical health (Andrist 2008; Johnston-Robledo et al. 2007; Kowalski and Chapple 2000; Schooler et al. 2005).

Another consequence of menstrual stigma is observance of the sex taboo, that is, avoidance of intimate sexual relations during the menses. In a study of Latinas/os' sexual behavior during menstruation, the vast majority of women sampled reported that they avoided genital touching, oral sex, and sexual intercourse during menstrual bleeding; the men also reported that they avoided such activities with menstruating sexual partners (Davis et al. 2002). Why should women be bound by ancient fears about the uncleanliness of menstrual blood? Menstruation is a good time to have sex if the partners want to avoid pregnancy, and orgasm is said to relieve menstrual cramps (Boston Women's Health Book Collective 2005). Tanfer and Aral (1996) reported that women who had more lifetime sexual partners and more frequent sex were more likely to have sex during their menses than were women with fewer partners or less frequent sexual encounters. European American women were more likely than African American and Latin American women to say that they had had sex during their menses. Rempel and Baumgartner (2003) found that women who viewed menstruation as a normal and publicly acceptable event scored higher on a measure of personal comfort with sexuality and were more likely to have sexual relations during their periods than women who did not have such positive attitudes toward menstruation. On the contrary, Schooler et al. (2005) found that female undergraduate students who had feelings of shame regarding menstruation reported less sexual experience and more sexual risk-taking than did those who scored low on a measure of menstrual shame.

Finally, we believe that the stigma and taboo of menstruation both reflects and contributes to women's lower social status. In her classic, playful essay Gloria Steinem (1978) imagined that, if men could menstruate, menstruation would become an enviable, boastworthy, masculine event. She suggested, for example, that "sanitary supplies would be federally funded and free" (p. 110). Her essay helps readers to understand that menstruation, as a biological, cultural, and political phenomenon, is only a "problem" because women do it.

Forbes et al. (2003) found that both male and female college students rated a menstruating woman as less sexy, more impure, and more irritable than women in general. Marván et al. (2008) asked college students in the U.S. and Mexico to list words that came to mind when they read the statements "A menstruating woman is . . ." and "A premenstrual woman is . . ." Only words that were mentioned by at least 50% of the 349 students were included in the analysis. Participants listed 92 negative words, which were grouped into the following categories: negative affect (e.g., sad, frustrated), inactivity (e.g., tired, weak), annoyance (e.g., desperate, whining), instability (e.g., unpredictable, moody), limitation/rejection (e.g.,

incapable, unlovable), and physical symptoms (e.g., crampy, bloated). In contrast, they could think of only 55 neutral words (e.g., cyclical, using pads) and 33 positive words (e.g., active, beautiful). Despite the stigma, 50% of the participants thought that women are active and beautiful even at "that time of the month."

Kowalski and Chapple (2000) investigated the consequences of the social stigma of menstruation on women's impression management behavior. They assigned young undergraduate women to be "interviewed" by a male confederate. Fifty percent of these women were menstruating at the time; the others were not. The male "interviewer" was aware of the menstrual status of 50% of the women in each group, and unaware of the menstrual status of the others. The menstruating participants interviewed by the man who was aware of their menstrual status believed that they had made a more negative impression on him than the women in the other three groups thought they had. They were also less concerned about making a positive impression on him than were the women in the other groups.

Roberts et al. (2002) primed menstrual status by manipulating whether their research assistant dropped a tampon or a hairclip where the participants in the study could see her do it. Both male and female undergraduate participants in the tampon condition later rated the research assistant as less competent and likeable than did the participants in the hairclip condition. Those who saw her drop the tampon also exhibited a tendency to sit farther away from her during the data collection than did those who saw her drop the hairclip. Results of this research show that the old ideas about stigma, taboo, and pollution are still operative. This work suggests that ruptures in women's concealment of their menstrual status lead to both social distancing and negative perceptions.

Clearly, more research is needed on how women's menstrual status may impact the way other people interact with and perceive them. However, it appears that women's desire and efforts to conceal their menstrual status may be well-founded. It would be interesting to study how people respond to women who actively subvert the cultural norm that menstruation should be hidden (e.g., by discussing it openly or by washing out an alternative menstrual product, such as "the keeper," in a public restroom).

The self-monitoring for leaks and odors and the self-policing of behavioral or emotional clues to menstrual status is a waste of women's time and psychic energy that could be spent on more important or interesting pursuits. Young (2005) argued that menstruation is a source of oppression for women because of the shame attached to monthly bleeding and the challenges women face as menstruators in public spaces (such as work and school), and she argued that menstruation renders women "queer" in a society that identifies the male non-menstruator as the "normal" human. She suggested that menstruating women are, in effect, "in the closet" about their stigmatized menstrual status. "Social relations of somatophobia and misogyny continue to hold over women, in some circumstances, the threat of being 'outed' as menstruators, sometimes with serious consequences to their self-esteem or opportunities for benefits" (Young 2005, p. 113). Menstrual etiquette requires women to conceal their menstrual flow and to remain in the menstrual closet if they want to occupy public spaces along with men and nonmenstruating women (Laws 1990; Young 2005). But etiquette, like stigmatized conditions, depends on social, cultural, and historical context, and contexts can change.

Challenging/Resisting the Stigma of Menstruation

What would happen if more women like Vanessa Tiegs and Petra Paul were willing to violate cultural norms? We are not suggesting that the menstrual cycle should be romanticized, that all women should celebrate every menses they experience, or that menstruation is central to womanhood or femininity. However, we do believe that the stigma of menstruation limits women's behavior and compromises their well-being. There are many different ways to eliminate the stigma, an important step toward "menstrual justice" (Kissling 2006, p. 126).

Culpepper (1992) suggested that simply talking about menstruation can create more positive attitudes, and she designed workshops aimed at raising women's "menstrual consciousness" to facilitate these conversations. Issues girls and women

discussed in her workshops included names for menstruation, attitudes toward and stories about menstruation, and customs surrounding menstruation. If menstruation were discussed more openly, it might be easier for girls and women to acknowledge the positive aspects of menstruation and to challenge others when they make assumptions that all women hate and want to eliminate their periods. When researchers bother to ask, women are forthcoming about positive aspects of menstruation (Chrisler et al. 1994; Johnston-Robledo et al. 2003) and express concerns about eliminating monthly bleeding through continuous oral contraceptive use (Johnston-Robledo et al. 2003; Rose et al. 2008).

There is some evidence to suggest that adolescent girls are attempting to resist and challenge traditional norms about menstruation through social interactions that take place online among peers. Polak (2006) explored chat rooms, message boards, websites, and individual girls' homepages to learn more about the ways adolescent girls, or "gURLs," are constructing and experiencing menstruation. Her observations indicate that girls are "rewriting" the dominant negative menstruation narrative that was transmitted by both the feminine hygiene product industry and adults in their lives, such as their mothers and grandmothers.

Polak found that American adolescent girls use on-line spaces to talk frankly and openly about menstruation. For example, they answered each other's questions, validated each other's experiences, and encouraged one another to talk to their boyfriends about menstruation. Polak noted an absence of euphemisms and even some open dialogue about extremely stigmatized aspects of menstruation, such as the various colors and consistency of menstrual blood. She argued that these new on-line conversations about menstruation could facilitate girls' identity development and healthy embodiment. Although Polak acknowledged that this forum may leave out girls who do not have immediate access to computers, she did not consider how ethnicity, social class, or sexual orientation might have influenced girls' ideas, dialogue, or posts. It is interesting to consider that the relative anonymity of chat rooms can make it easier to discuss topics that are taboo in face-to-face conversations.

However, face-to-face conversations about menstruation are also more common than they once were, especially among adolescent peers. Fingerson (2006) conducted a series of single-gender group interviews with predominantly European American adolescent boys and girls to explore their "menstrual talk." She concluded that some girls derived agency and empowerment from their menses. Themes that reflected this conclusion include girls' tendencies to embrace the challenge of managing their menstrual flow, to use and enjoy the privilege of having knowledge about their bodies that boys did not have, and to challenge the dominant and often negative social norms about menstruation. Although open talk about taboo topics is an important way to resist stigma, some of the girls attributed the empowerment derived from menstruation to their ability to embarrass boys with the mere mention of tampons or menstrual blood. Like the artists Tiegs and Paul, these girls are using shock to subvert the rule that menstruation must be hidden from the public square, but it is the stigma that allows them the power to embarrass boys at will. In a new print advertisement campaign for UKotex, consumers are encouraged to break the cycle of discomfort with tampons by being more open about them (Newman 2010). This goal is an admirable one, but the slogans for some ads (e.g., "I tied a tampon to my keyring so my brother wouldn't take my car. It worked.") both challenge and reinforce the stigma of menstruation.

Girls living in the U.S. learn simultaneously that menstruation is important and natural and that they should hide and ignore it (Charlesworth 2001). How would this change if we celebrated menarche? Unlike Americans, individuals from countries around the world acknowledge this important rite of passage through various rituals such as a special gathering or party (Chrisler and Zittel 1998). The guest of honor may feel embarrassed initially, but a party could help her to realize that she, like other girls and women in her life, can overcome her embarrassment and have positive, even playful, attitudes toward menstruation. There are many organizations on the Internet, such as the Red Web Foundation (www.redwebfoundation.org) and First Moon (www.celebrategirls.org) that provide special kits to celebrate menarche and many other resources for raising menstrual consciousness.

The social stigma of menstruation can be challenged through the analysis of menstruation in popular culture. For example, social scientists have found that the popular press is rife with articles about menstruation that reinforce and perpetuate stigmatizing messages and provide inaccurate information about menstruation and premenstrual changes (Chrisler and Levy 1990; Johnston-Robledo et al. 2006). Clearly, readers of popular magazines and newspapers should be encouraged to question and discuss what they read about menstruation in this material.

Others have resisted and challenged the stigma of menstruation through the creation of a menstrual counterculture. In his virtual museum, Harry Finley has collected women's stories about their experiences with menstruation as well as many images of advertisements, hygiene products, and other artifacts, which he displays on his website (www.mum.org). In her work on menstrual counterculture, Kissling (2006) noted that Finley's collection has a lot of educational potential because it challenges widely shared ideas about what is considered public and private. Artist/poet Geneva Kachman and several of her friends designated the Monday before Mother's Day as *Menstrual Monday*, a holiday to celebrate menstruation. She designs and distributes kits for this celebration including party blowouts made out of tampon applicators (www.moltx.org). Ani DiFranco's song, *Blood in the Boardroom*, is a rare example of popular music about menstruation. In her book *Cunt*, third wave feminist Inga Muscio (2002) wrote about many different aspects of menstruation in a candid, humorous, and revolutionary way. Her writing on alternative menstrual products is especially compelling. Maybe it will inspire women to try an alternative to pads or tampons.

An important way to reduce stigma is social activism. Bobel (2006, 2008, 2010) has written extensively about the history of menstrual activism as well as the myriad ways contemporary menstrual activists are drawing attention to the health and environmental hazards of menstrual hygiene products through organizations, political action, zines, and other publications. This kind of work could help people to appreciate the extent to which the social stigma of menstruation fuels and is perpetuated by consumerism. Finally, health care providers are beginning to recognize and promote menstruation as an important indicator, even a vital sign, of girls' and women's overall health (Diaz et al. 2006; Stubbs 2008). The mission of the Project Vital Sign (www.projectvitalsign.org) campaign is to raise awareness about the role of menstruation in women's psychological and physical health with the ultimate goal of encouraging an open dialogue about menstruation between health care providers and their female patients. Efforts to politicize and/or normalize menstruation could go a long way toward reducing its stigmatized status.

Conclusion

The consideration of menstruation as a source of social stigma has promising implications for theory, research, and practice. We have demonstrated that menstruation fits all three of Goffman's (1963) categories and reviewed a significant body of literature that supports the stigmatized status of menstruation, the means through which the stigma is transmitted, and the consequences of the stigma. All of these areas are worthy of continued theoretical development and empirical investigation. Clearly, the stigmatized status of menstruation has detrimental consequences for girls' and women's self-esteem, body image, self-presentation, and sexual health. Feminist therapists, educators, and healthcare providers can consider ways to alleviate these negative consequences and to assist girls and women in their efforts to resist the stigma of menstruation. Equally important is the evidence that suggests that menstrual status, both actual and symbolic, primes and elicits negative attitudes toward women. Challenging the stigma of menstruation and learning to appreciate, or at least not loathe, menstruation may have a positive impact on girls' and women's wellbeing as well as their social status.

References

Andrist, L. C. (2008). The implications of objectification theory for women's health: Menstrual suppression and "maternal request" cesarean delivery. *Health Care for Women International, 29*, 551–565. doi:10.1080/07399330801949616.

Bartky, S. L. (1990). *Femininity and domination: Studies in the phenomenology of oppression.* New York: Routledge.

Berg, D. H., & Coutts, L. B. (1994). The extended curse: Being a woman every day. *Health Care for Women International, 15*, 11–22. doi:10.1080/07399339409516090.

Bobel, C. (2006). Our revolution has style: Contemporary menstrual product activists "doing feminism" in the third wave. *Sex Roles, 56*, 331–345. doi:10.1007/s11199-006-9001-7.

Bobel, C. (2008). From convenience to hazard: A short history of the emergence of the menstrual activism movement, 1971–1992. *Health Care for Women International, 29*, 738–754. doi:10.1080/07399330802188909.

Bobel, C. (2010). *New blood: Third-wave feminism and the politics of menstruation.* New Brunswick: Rutgers University Press.

Boston Women's Health Book Collective. (2005). *Our bodies, ourselves: A new edition for a new era.* New York: Simon & Schuster.

Bramwell, R. (2001). Blood and milk: Constructions of female bodily fluids in Western society. *Women & Health, 34*(4), 85–96. doi:10.1300/J013v34n04_06.

Buckley, T., & Gottlieb, A. (1988). *Blood magic: The anthropology of menstruation.* Berkeley, CA: University of California Press.

Charlesworth, D. (2001). Paradoxical constructions of self: Educating young women about menstruation. *Women and Language, 24*, 13–20.

Chesler, G. (Producer & director). (2006). *Period: The end of menstruation* [Motion picture]. New York: Cinema Guild.

Chrisler, J. C. (2002). Hormone hostages: The cultural legacy of PMS as a legal defense. In L. H. Collins, M. R. Dunlap, & J. C. Chrisler (Eds.), *Charting a new course for feminist psychology* (pp. 238–252). Westport: Praeger.

Chrisler, J. C. (2007). PMS as a culture-bound syndrome. In J. C. Chrisler, C. Golden, & P. D. Rozee (Eds.), *Lectures on the psychology of women* (pp. 154–171). Boston: McGraw Hill.

Chrisler, J. C. (2008). 2007 Presidential address: Fear of losing control: Power, perfectionism, and the psychology of women. *Psychology of Women Quarterly, 32*, 1–12. doi:10.1111/j.1471-6402.2007.00402.x.

Chrisler, J. C. (2011). Leaks, lumps, and lines: Stigma and women's bodies. *Psychology of Women Quarterly, 35*, 202–214. doi:10.1177/0361684310397698.

Chrisler, J. C., & Caplan, P. J. (2002). The strange case of Dr. Jekyll and Ms. Hyde: How PMS became a cultural phenomenon and a psychiatric disorder. *Annual Review of Sex Research, 13*, 274–306.

Chrisler, J. C., & Levy, K. B. (1990). The media construct a menstrual monster: A content analysis of PMS articles in the popular press. *Women & Health, 16,* 89–104. doi:10.1300/J013v16n0207.

Chrisler, J. C., & Zittel, C. B. (1998). Menarche stories: Reminiscences of college students from Lithuania, Malaysia, Sudan, and The United States. *Health Care for Women International, 19,* 303–312. doi:10.1080/073993398246287.

Chrisler, J. C., Johnston, I. K., Champagne, N. M., & Preston, K. E. (1994). Menstrual joy: The construct and its consequences. *Psychology of Women Quarterly, 18,* 375–387. doi:10.1111/j.1471-6402.1994.tb00461.x.

Cicurel, I. E. (2000). The Rabbinate versus Israeli (Jewish) women: The Mikvah as a contested domain. *Nashim: A Journal of Jewish Women's Studies, 3,* 164–190.

Cochrane, K. (2009, October). It's in the blood. *The Guardian.* Retrieved from http://www.guardian.co.uk/lifeandstyle/2009/oct/02/menstruation-feminist-activists.

Coutts, L. B., & Berg, D. H. (1993). The portrayal of the menstruating woman in menstrual product advertisements. *Health Care for Women International, 14,* 179–191. doi:10.1080/07399339309516039.

Crocker, J., Major, B., & Steele, C. (1998). Social stigma. In D. T. Gilbert, S. T. Fiske, & G. Lindzey (Eds.), *Handbook of social psychology* (4th ed., Vol. 2, pp. 504–553). Boston: McGraw-Hill.

Culpepper, E. E. (1992). Menstrual consciousness raising: A personal and pedagogical process. In A. J. Dan & L. L. Lewis (Eds.), *Menstrual health in women's lives* (pp. 274–284). Chicago: University of Illinois Press.

Davis, A. R., Nowygrod, S., Shabsigh, R., & Westhoff, C. (2002). The influence of vaginal bleeding on the sexual behavior of urban, Hispanic women and men. *Contraception, 65,* 351–355. doi:10.1016/S0010-7824(02)00279-2.

Deaux, K., Reid, A., Mizrahi, K., & Ethier, K. A. (1995). Parameters of social identity. *Journal of Personality and Social Psychology, 68,* 280–291. doi:10.1037/0022-3514.68.2.280.

Delaney, J., Lupton, M. J., & Toth, E. (1987). *The curse: A cultural history of menstruation* (rev. ed.). Urbana: University of Illinois Press.

Diaz, A., Laufer, M., & Breech, L. (2006). Menstruation in girls and adolescents: Using the menstrual cycle as a vital sign. *Pediatrics, 118*(5), 2245–2250.

Dovidio, J. F., Major, B., & Crocker, J. (2000). Stigma: Introduction and overview. In T. F. Heatherton, R. E. Kleck, M. R. Hebl, & J. G. Hull (Eds.), *The social psychology of stigma* (pp. 1–28). New York: Guilford.

Erchull, M. J. (2010). Distancing through objectification? Depictions of women's bodies in menstrual product advertisements. *Sex Roles.* Advance online publication. doi:10.1007/s11199-011-0004-7.

Erchull, M. J., Chrisler, J. C., Gorman, J. A., & Johnston-Robledo, I. (2002). Education and advertising: A content analysis of commercially produced booklets about menstruation. *Journal of Early Adolescence, 22,* 455–474. doi:10.1111/1471-6402.t01-2-00007.

Ernster, V. L. (1975). American menstrual expressions. *Sex Roles, 1,* 3–13. doi:10.1007/BF00287209.

Fingerson, L. (2006). *Girls in power: Gender, body, and menstruation in adolescence.* Albany: State University of New York Press.

Forbes, G. B., Adams-Curtis, L. E., White, K. B., & Holmgren, K. M. (2003). The role of hostile and benevolent sexism in women's and men's perceptions of the menstruating woman. *Psychology of Women Quarterly, 27,* 58–63. doi:10.1111/1471-6402.t01-2-00007.

Foucault, M. (1979). *Discipline and punish: The birth of the prison.* London: Penguin.

Frable, D. E. (1993). Dimensions of marginality: Distinctions among those who are different. *Personality and Social Psychology Bulletin, 19,* 370–380. doi:10.1177/0146167293194002.

Fredrickson, B. L., & Roberts, T.-A. (1997). Objectification theory: Toward understanding women's lived experiences and mental health risks. *Psychology of Women Quarterly, 21,* 173–206. doi:10.1111/j.1471-6402.1997.tb00108.x.

Goffman, E. (1963). *Stigma: Notes on the management of spoiled identity.* New York: Simon & Schuster.

Goldenberg, J. L., & Roberts, T.-A. (2004). The beast within the beauty: An existential perspective on the objectification and condemnation of women. In J. Greenberg, S. L. Koole, & T. Pyszczynski (Eds.), *Handbook of experimental existential psychology* (pp. 71–85). New York: Guildford.

Golub, S. (1992). *Periods: From menarche to menopause.* Newbury Park: Sage.

Greenberg, J., Pyszczynski, T., & Solomon, S. (1986). The causes and consequences of a need for self-esteem: A terror management theory. In R. F. Baumeister (Ed.), *Public and private self* (pp. 189–212). New York: Springer.

Heath, T. M. (2007). Vanessa Tiegs' menstrual blood painting journal: Art or biohazard? Retrieved from http://www.associatedcontent.com/article/280931/vanessa_tiegs_menstrual_blood_painting.html

Herek, G. M. (2009). Sexual stigma and sexual prejudice in the U.S.: A conceptual framework. In D. A. Hope (Ed.), *Contemporary perspectives on lesbian, gay, and bisexual identities* (pp. 65–111). New York: Springer.

Hoerster, K. D., Chrisler, J. C., & Gorman, J. A. (2003). Attitudes toward and experiences with menstruation in the U.S. and India. *Women & Health, 38*(3), 77–95. doi:10-1300/J013v38n03_06.

Houppert, K. (1999). *The curse: Confronting the last unmentionable taboo.* New York: Farrar, Straus, & Giroux.

Johnston-Robledo, I., Ball, M., Lauta, K., & Zekoll, A. (2003). To bleed or not to bleed: Young women's attitudes toward menstrual suppression. *Women & Health, 38*(3), 59–75. doi:10.1300/J013v38n03_05.

Johnston-Robledo, I., Barnack, J., & Wares, S. (2006). "Kiss your period good-bye": Menstrual suppression in the popular press. *Sex Roles, 54,* 353–360. doi:10.1007/s11199-006-9007-1.

Johnston-Robledo, I., Sheffield, K., Voigt, J., & Wilcox-Constantine, J. (2007). Reproductive shame: Self-objectification and young women's attitudes toward their bodies. *Women & Health, 46*(1), 25–39. doi:10.1300/J013v46n01_03.

Kissling, E. A. (1996). Bleeding out loud: Communication about menstruation. *Feminism & Psychology, 6,* 481–504. doi:10.1177/0959353596064002.

Kissling, E. A. (2006). *Capitalizing on the curse: The business of menstruation.* Boulder: Rienner.

Kowalski, R. M., & Chapple, T. (2000). The social stigma of menstruation: Fact or fiction? *Psychology of Women Quarterly, 24,* 74–80. doi:10.1111/j.1471-6402.2000.tb01023.x.

Laws, S. (1990). *Issues of blood: The politics of menstruation.* London: Macmillan.

Lee, J. (1994). Menarche and the (hetero)sexualization of the female body. *Gender and Society, 8,* 343–362. doi:10.1177/089124394008003004.

Lee, J., & Sasser-Coen, J. (1996). *Blood stories: Menarche and the politics of the female body in contemporary U.S. society.* New York: Routledge.

Marván, M. L., Islas, M., Vela, L., Chrisler, J. C., & Warren, E. A. (2008). Stereotypes of women in different stages of reproductive life: Data from Mexico and the U.S. *Health Care for Women International, 29,* 673–687. doi:10.1080/07399330802188982.

Merskin, D. (1999). Adolescence, advertising, and the idea of menstruation. *Sex Roles, 40,* 941–957. doi:10.1023/A:1018881206965.

Muehlenkamp, J. L., & Saris-Baglama, R. N. (2002). Self-objectification and its psychological outcomes for college women. *Psychology of Women Quarterly, 26,* 371–379. doi:10.1111/1471-6402.t01-1-00076.

Muscio, I. (2002). *Cunt: A declaration of independence.* Emeryville: Seal Press.

Newman, A. A. (2010, March 16). Rebelling against the commonly evasive feminine care ad. *New York Times,* p. B3.

Owen, L. (1993). *Her blood is gold: Celebrating the power and mystery of menstruation.* San Francisco: Harper.

Oxley, T. (1998). Menstrual management: An exploratory study. *Feminism & Psychology, 8,* 185–191.

Polak, M. (2006). From the curse to the rag: Online gURLs rewrite the menstruation narrative. In Y. Jiwani, C. Steenbergen, & C. Mitchell (Eds.), *Girlhood: Redefining the limits* (pp. 191–207). New York: Black Rose Books.

Raftos, M., Jackson, D., & Mannix, J. (1998). Idealised versus tainted femininity: Discourses of the menstrual experience in Australian magazines that target young women. *Nursing Inquiry, 5,* 174–186. doi:10.1046/j.1440-1800.1998.530174.x.

Rempel, J. K., & Baumgartner, B. (2003). The relationship between attitudes toward menstruation and sexual attitudes, desires, and behavior in women. *Archives of Sexual Behavior, 32,* 155–163. doi:10.1023/A:1022404609700.

Rhinehart, E. D. (1989, June). *Psychotherapists' responses to the topic of menstruation in psychotherapy.* Paper presented at the meeting of the Society for Menstrual Cycle Research, Salt Lake City, UT.

Roberts, T.-A. (2004). Female trouble: The Menstrual Self-evaluation Scale and women's self-objectification. *Psychology of Women Quarterly, 28,* 22–26. doi:10.1111/j.1471-6402.2004.00119.x.

Roberts, T.-A., Goldenberg, J. L., Power, C., & Pyszczynski. (2002). "Feminine protection:" The effects of menstruation on attitudes toward women. *Psychology of Women Quarterly, 26,* 131–139. doi:10.1111/1471-6402.00051.

Rose, J. G., Chrisler, J. C., & Couture, S. (2008). Young women's attitudes toward continuous use of oral contraceptives: The effects of priming positive attitudes toward menstruation on women's willingness to suppress menstruation. *Health Care for Women International, 29,* 688–701. doi:10.1080/07399330802188925.

Rozin, P., & Fallon, A. E. (1987). A perspective on disgust. *Psychological Review, 94*, 23–41. doi:10.1037/0033-295X.94.1.23.

Schooler, D., Ward, M. L., Merriwether, A., & Caruthers, A. S. (2005). Cycles of shame: Menstrual shame, body shame, and sexual decision-making. *Journal of Sex Research, 42*, 324–334. doi:10.1080/00224490509552288.

Stallabrass, J. (2006). *Contemporary art: A very short introduction*. Oxford: Oxford University Press.

Steinem, G. (1978, October). If men could menstruate: A political fantasy. *Ms.*, p. 110.

Stepanich, K. K. (1992). *Sister moon lodge: The power and mystery of menstruation*. Woodbury: Llewellyn.

Stubbs, M. L. (2008). Cultural perceptions and practices around menarche and adolescent menstruation in the United States. *Annals of the New York Academy of Science, 1135*, 58–66. doi:10.1196/annals.1429.008.

Szymanski, D. M., & Henning, S. L. (2007). The role of self-objectification in women's depression: A test of objectification theory. *Sex Roles, 56*, 45–53. doi:10.1007/s11199-006-9147-3.

Tampax report, The. (1981). New York: Ruder, Finn, & Rotman.

Tanfer, K., & Aral, S. O. (1996). Sexual intercourse during menstruation and self-reported sexually transmitted disease history among women. *Sexually Transmitted Diseases, 23*, 395–401.

Taylor, D. (2003). *Red flower: Rethinking menstruation*. Caldwell: Blackburn Press.

Tylka, T. L., & Hill, M. S. (2004). Objectification theory as it relates to disordered eating among college women. *Sex Roles, 51*, 719–730. doi:10.1007/s11199-004-0721-2.

Ussher, J. M. (2004). Premenstrual syndrome and self-policing: Ruptures in self-silencing leading to increased self-surveillance and blaming of the body. *Social Theory & Health, 2*, 254–272. doi:10.1057/palgrave.sth.8700032.

Williams, L. R. (1983). Beliefs and attitudes of young girls regarding menstruation. In S. Golub (Ed.), *Menarche: The transition from girl to woman* (pp. 139–148). Lexington: Lexington Books.

Wind, L. H. (1995). *New moon rising: Reclaiming the sacred rites of menstruation*. Chicago: Delphi Press.

Young, I. M. (2005). *On female body experience: "Throwing like a girl" and other essays*. New York: Oxford University Press.

Young Feminist: Riding the Crimson Wave

by Ariela Schnyer

As a biological process, the onset of menstruation is one of the most conventional markers of adulthood for people who have a uterus. Yet, even though approximately half of the people in the world menstruate, the process remains stigmatized and unmentionable in most parts of the world — including in developed countries like the United States.

As a cultural event, menarche and menstruation have social implications that vary wildly by community. In some places, girls and women are confined to isolated huts during their cycles or are not allowed to tend animals, go to school, use community water sources or observe their religion. Still others are completely unaware of what menstruation is when it starts. They often have no access to good menstrual hygiene, and must use things like animal hides, feathers, dirt, and paper to absorb the blood. Stigmas and silence surrounding menstruation inflict harm on women's images of ourselves, and our ability to interact with our communities.

I began menstruating at the end of 6th grade, the same way many people do: pretty unobtrusively. Sure, there were the few unfortunate and inevitable bleed-through-all-clothing incidents, but I remember being fairly informed about what was going on—although tampons would continue to completely stump me for years. My mom was really big on the idea of being in tune with my body and celebrating my "coming into womanhood" and tried to throw me a first moon party, complete with candles and poems about the Mother Goddess. I requested laser tag instead.

Despite all the positive messages from my mother about menstruation, my relationship with my period was much more complicated than expected. I generally felt uncomfortable in my body during my periods and, since I had an extremely irregular cycle, I never knew when it was going to start or how painful it would be. I joined the thousands of women around the world who view menstruation as a curse upon our bodies.

We are conditioned to think of our periods as gross and our bodies as dirty and shameful while we are menstruating. We are inundated with messages that revolve around ensuring we are being "discreet" and "clean," and advertisements for menstrual products focus on how they help us avoid our periods being noticed. Most tampons have plastic applicators and are designed and advertised as a way to limit our contact with our bodies, as if to avoid "contaminating" ourselves and, by extension, everyone around us. These messages are framed as if the *only* way to feel feminine, to be a woman, is to be "fresh and clean" and utterly in control of our bodies 100 percent of the time. When they are paired with the societal ideas that women are uncontrollable and emotional when they are menstruating (or that if a woman is emotional she must be menstruating), they feed our need to hide our periods in order to be viewed as strong and capable.

How many of us have been asked derisively whether we are "on the rag" when we express ourselves, especially with anger or frustration? Or had it used to discredit our opinions or side of an argument? Girls are shamed by their families, teachers, and peers for failing to adequately protect the rest of the world from the "effects" of their menstruation. Feeling confident during our periods is presented as being dependent on concealing the blood and gore, which impacts the already tenuous self-esteem of many young women. I spent plenty of time in middle and high school trying to sneak my pads and tampons from my backpack into my pockets without anyone seeing them on the way to the bathroom. Those days quickly became something to be ashamed of and to conceal as completely as possible.

Two things happened to change my perspective on my menstrual cycle. First, after six years of irregular periods and one particularly concerning three-month gap between cycles, I was diagnosed with polycystic ovarian syndrome (PCOS). Not long after, I started using a menstrual cup. Both of these forced me to become much more aware of my menstrual cycle: the signs that something might be wrong, what ovulation felt like, how much I usually bled each day. Both helped me push back against the silence and shame I had internalized about my period, as I began to feel more connected to the changes my body went through from week to week. How could I be ashamed of something that was irrevocably mine? My cycle can still be painful and my skin still breaks out; none of that changed. But, I no longer feel demeaned by my body for menstruating.

Reclaiming the power of our menstruation doesn't mean we have to pretend we don't sometimes feel uncomfortable during our cycles. It's not about forcing women with endometriosis or painful and heavy periods to experience these conditions without the help of treatments (including hormonal contraception). We just need to recognize that there is nothing wrong with the process that many of our bodies go through. We need to combat the misogyny that tells us that our bodies are less worthy when we are menstruating, and that women are less worthy *because* they menstruate!

Yes, periods can be uncomfortable for a variety of reasons. But encouraging silence and shame about our menstruation doesn't acknowledge these uncomfortable aspects of menstruation in a healthy or validating way. It doesn't help women identify activities and treatments that can help them manage the discomfort. Instead, it perpetuates misconceptions about women's capacities, and undermines the incredible diversity in people's experiences of menstruation. Many people suffer without contacting their doctors or realizing that something could be done to regulate their cycles, because they have internalized that menstruation is a punishment. Many more women don't know the patterns of their menstrual cycles or that there are options besides pads or tampons, because we refuse to talk frankly about this normal, biological process.

For me, menstruation is part of my womanhood; having the opportunity to explore and be comfortable with my menstrual cycle has been important in personally feeling empowered in my body. But not everyone's definition of womanhood even involves menstruation. Some women do not menstruate, including some trans women, post-menopausal women, breastfeeding women, and women on hormonal birth control. This does not make their womanhood any less legitimate. Nor does everyone want to menstruate, including some trans men and those with extremely painful or heavy periods. Pushing back against the shame

we are expected to feel towards menstruation does not mean forcing everyone to be in love with their periods.

We deserve to be able to engage in our complicated relationships with menstruation without being shamed for something our body does naturally. May 28, 2014 marked the first Menstrual Hygiene Management Day. It was organized by a coalition of Non-governmental Organizations that believe threats to girls' safety, health, and ability to go to school or participate in their communities simply because they menstruate are unacceptable. We deserve access to education, bathrooms with clean water, and hygienic forms of menstrual management without stigmas that women's bodies are unclean because of menstruation. We deserve the opportunity to live in our bodies without feeling ashamed of them. So, let's take back ownership of our cycles, and of what happens to our bodies every month—whether that means curling up with a heating pad and some chocolate or throwing a moon party. Sit back, relax and, if you feel so inclined, ride that crimson wave!

Scripting the Body: Pharmaceuticals and the (Re)making of Menstruation

by Laura Mamo Jennifer Ruth Fosket

Seasonale, the first extended-cycle oral contraceptive drug marketed to suppress women's and girls' monthly menstruation, hit the U.S. consumer market in 2003. Designed to be taken daily in three-month cycles, instead of three-week cycles, Seasonale offers girls and women the possibility of having four rather than twelve periods a year. Seasonale is part of a new

class of pharmaceuticals that we group under the rubric of *lifestyle drugs*, relatively new pharmacological therapies (along with others for the treatment of baldness, sleep difficulties, excessive weight, mild depression, sexual performance, general aging, allergies, and so on) that promise a refashioning of the material body with transformative, life-enhancing results.

From *Signs: Journal of Women in Culture and Society, Vol 34, No 4, Summer 2009* by Laura Mamo and Jennifer Ruth Fosket. Copyright © 2009 The University of Chicago Press. Reprinted by permission.

The emergence of Seasonale, along with other drugs aimed at regulating and minimizing menstruation, is part of ongoing biomedicalization processes that emphasize risk reduction and management and the transformation of health itself. Such pharmaceuticals, like other technologies of the body, work from the inside out; they are taken orally and ingested through the material body. The changes they produce are culturally and socially meaningful in their aim to improve life in general—relationships, pleasures, comfort, and so on. Such assumed improvements directly implicate the boundaries of health and illness and, we argue, often do so in particularly gendered ways. With Seasonale, for example, gendered subjectivities and gendered forms of embodiment are produced; they are truth effects of pharmaceutical interventions.

This article presents an analysis of the advertising campaigns for Seasonale that appeared in print, on television, and on the drug's Web site (http://www.seasonale.com) in 2003 and 2004. Our analysis pivots around three questions: What kinds of gendered cultural scripts are transmitted in the marketing of this new form of birth control? In what ways are bodies and feminine embodiments produced through Seasonale? And in what ways does Seasonale shape and constrain feminist health discourse? We pose these questions as a means to understand the complex ways in which the advertising campaign for Seasonale troubles biological facts and cultural meanings of femininity, reshaping cultural assumptions about menstruating (and non-menstruating) bodies and, by extension, reshaping women's experiences of lived embodiment.

As a lifestyle drug marketed for every woman's presumed menstrual suppressant needs, Seasonale not only prevents natural menstruation but also produces natural femininity itself. To provide a discursive comparison of the ways in which earlier mechanical interventions into women's bodies differ from and are similar to contemporary chemical and ingestible interventions, we examine Del-Em, a menstrual extraction tool pioneered in the 1970s. Such a comparison, we believe, highlights the conditions under which contemporary processes of biomedicalization work to reshape embodiment itself.

Biomedicalization and feminist technoscience

Medicalization cannot fully account for the transformations in, and the expansion of, medicine. Innovations such as digitalization, computerization, molecularization, and geneticization, for example, are more often organized through corporate economic entities than through medical or health care institutions. The concept of biomedicalization captures "the increasingly complex, multisited, multidirectional processes of medicalization that today are being both extended and reconstituted through the emergent social forms and practices of a highly and increasingly technoscientific biomedicine" (Clarke et al. 2003, 162). Biomedicalization involves a set of rationalized, disciplining processes through which medical technologies produce bodies while also producing transformative possibilities for corporeality and subjectivity (Clarke et al. 2003).[1] The concept signals a shift "from enhanced control over external nature (i.e., the world around us) to the harnessing and transformation of internal nature (i.e., biological processes of human and nonhuman life forms), often transforming 'life itself'" (164). As a discourse, biomedicalization travels culturally and increasingly shapes people's conceptions of health and illness, social identities, and ways of being in the body. It expands professional medical jurisdiction in the context of a technoscientific revolution in which increased classification and jurisdiction over people's bodies often falls under the purview of pharmaceutical and diagnostic companies rather than health care services, professional organizations, or physicians themselves. Moreover, this process increasingly frames natural experiences less as diseases than as causes of future diseases. In this framework, female corporeality and subjectivity are understood as constituted in and through (cultural) practices of (techno)science: bodies are both objects and effects of technoscientific and biomedical discourse. As such, bodies are not born; bodies are made. Within the works

---

[1] Theorizing biomedicalization processes builds on analyses of qualitative studies of sexual function technologies such as Viagra (Fishman and Mamo 2001; Mamo and Fishman 2001; Fishman 2004), lesbian practices of assisted reproduction (Mamo 2007), breast cancer prevention technologies (Fosket 2004), and cardiovascular health discourse (Shim 2002).

of feminist science studies scholars, material bodies are theorized as being shaped by and, in turn, shaping technoscientific discourse and practices. Donna Haraway's cyborg theory (1991), for example, argues that nature itself is a cultural construct produced among humans and nonhumans. It is an "achievement among many actors, not all of them human, not all of them organic, not all of them technological" (Haraway 1992, 297). As material-semiotic actors, scientific bodies are not ideological constructions; they are objects of knowledge produced, structured, and elaborated in and through discourse/knowledge. As Anne Balsamo (1996b) has noted, these reinterpretations of embodiment do not factor out the material body. Instead, they emphasize the complex ways that bodies are constituted through technological and scientific practices that are part of, rather than outside of, culture and power (see also Balsamo 1996a).[2]

Feminist approaches to biomedicalization also examine the subjectivities and practices of those who use medical technologies (Mamo 2007). Biomedical services, technologies, and knowledges are taken up, used, and given meaning in complicated ways by various actors. Women not only respond to biomedical knowledge and practice but also reshape the very contours and meanings of these practices through "selective resistance and selective compliance" (Lock and Kaufert 1998, 2; see also Root and Browner 2001). As patients, actors, and users of technologies are shaped by technoscience, both uses and users are "pliant to power" (Grosz 1993, 199; see also Foucault 1979) and, at times, able to negotiate power itself.

In this article, we examine the drug Seasonale—both as medical discourse and practice and as a technocultural intervention into biological processes—to demonstrate its corporeal and discursive effects on femininity and experiences of embodiment. Specifically, we argue that, by effacing the intended use of traditional, first-generation pills—to prevent pregnancy—Seasonale produces the nonmenstrual woman as both embodiment and subjectivity.

Biomedicalization and Seasonale: Lifestyle pills for healthy bodies

The first-generation birth control pill entered the market in 1960. Its drug formula is today viewed as a problematically high dose of estrogen that came with several safety concerns, which the women's health movement successfully organized around in the 1970s (Seaman 1969). Developed to allow women to control the number and spacing of births, the birth control pill brought about cultural changes far exceeding expectations.[3]

More than thirty-five years since its initial approval, the birth control pill remains one of the clearest examples of a culturally significant biomedical technotherapy. It has vastly expanded in form and function. While the basic formula remains the same (a lower dose of synthetic estrogen and/or progesterone, both of which inhibit ovulation and uterine implantation), its form includes over forty types of pills, patches, and injectable devices. As a result, the pill not only survived as a (conception) preventive technology but is now another consumer product saturating the market with advertisements promising choice and an array of possibilities.

Seasonale is a daily, oral birth control pill developed by Barr Pharmaceuticals and approved by the Food and Drug Administration (FDA) in September 2003. The drug uses synthetic estrogen and progestin (a synthetic compound that produces effects similar to those of progesterone), effectively the same hormones as earlier birth control pills; has similar side effects; and is just as effective in preventing pregnancy when used properly. The main difference is in delivery method:

---

[2] Balsamo's work draws on Michel Foucault's (1979, 1980) argument that subjectivities in general (and, we can add, gendered subjectivities in particular) are produced within power relations. A biopolitics of populations relies on the discipline of bodies for its accomplishment. Balsamo and others bring forward assertions that subjectivities are intimately connected with the material, lived realities of gender, race, class, and other systems of privilege and inequality. As long as race, class, and gender stratifications are part of social life, individuals are constrained in the ways in which they can shape their bodies and identities. Disciplinary power, as well as choice and freedom, is not universally applied, available, or meaningful. People are variously constrained and/or enabled to imagine and create their selves anew. As a result, poststructuralists like Balsamo are suspicious of claims of agency that do not account for structural constraints of power relations.

[3] See, e.g., Seaman 1969; Merkin 1976; Gordon 1990; Asbell 1995; Marks 2001; Tone 2001. For an examination of the early history of research on hormones, which gave rise to contraceptives like the pill, see Oudshoorn (1994), Clarke (1998), and Angier (1999). For cultural histories and implications of menstruation, see also Olesen and Woods (1986), Delaney, Lupton, and Toth (1988), and Laws (1990). For an analysis of the yet-to-be-realized development of the male pill, see Oudshoorn (2003).

traditional birth control pills are taken for three weeks followed by a week of placebo (sugar pills) that allow for menstruation. Seasonale's pills are taken daily for three months, or eighty-four days consecutively, followed by seven days of placebo pills. The intended biophysical result is four menstrual periods each year.[4]

The idea of taking birth control pills to prevent periods is not new, nor are other attempts to reduce or limit menstruation altogether. For women taking the pill, it has always been possible to skip the week's placebo pills that traditionally follow the three-week birth control pill regimen and continuously take the active pills in order to skip a menstrual period. This off-label usage has been suggested by doctors and known among women for years. For example, advocating for menstrual suppression in an article in the British medical journal *The Lancet*, Sarah Thomas and Charlotte Ellertson state:

> Using oral contraceptives in this way [reducing menstruation] safely lets women control their hormonal profiles as well as whether and when they choose to bleed. Suppression of bleeding by this means is in fact already practiced in "special" circumstances where the inconvenience and disruption of menstruation is especially consequential, such as for healthy women competing in athletic competitions or going on their honeymoons, as well as for women for whom bleeding poses a severe sanitary problem, such as for individuals with severe mental disabilities. Unfortunately however, for most women, the fact that they can suppress their periods on an ongoing basis remains one of medicine's best-kept secrets. (Thomas and Ellerston 2000, 922)

In this passage, the authors draw on familiar cultural scripts about menstruation as being fundamentally at odds with women's ability to function normally: engaging in sports or having heterosexual intercourse are both implied to be hindered by menstruation. Further, menstruation is depicted as

potentially posing a "severe sanitary problem" for women living with "mental disabilities." However, though the kinds of problems menstruation may pose to women with severe mental disabilities are undoubtedly as diverse and complicated as the women themselves, the idea that menstrual blood in and of itself poses a threat is far-fetched. By drawing on scripts about menstruation that resonate with North American ideals of femininity, the authors first produce women's bodies as messy and requiring intervention and then produce menstrual suppression as a seemingly natural solution to an age-old problem. Menstrual suppression becomes a common, necessary, and frequently used practice. Indeed, within this narrative, researchers at Barr simply capitalize on and patent this presumed "best-kept secret."

The release and rapid adoption of the first-generation birth control pill marked the first time healthy people were prescribed a prescription drug in an effort to prevent unwanted outcomes—in this case pregnancy—instead of to treat existing problems (Marks 2001). In this way, the pill ushered in a new era of prevention medications and expanded the ranks of legitimate users of prescription pharmaceuticals from only people diagnosed with medical conditions to healthy people at risk of becoming ill (or pregnant).[5] In doing so, women's menstrual and reproductive bodies were medicalized as (heterosexual) women increasingly turned to the medical profession for assistance in controlling their reproductive lives.

Moreover, with the emergence of Seasonale, the birth control pill once again participates in a significant transformation in how we think about the role of pharmaceuticals in everyday life. With Seasonale, the possibility emerges for bodies and practices to be reshaped; like other lifestyle pharmaceuticals, the drug is aimed at producing a new and improved body rather than merely restoring health or preventing future problems. The goal of Seasonale is not to help maintain order or return the body to a normal or healthy state—or even, as with other oral contraceptives, to sustain a non-pregnant state. Instead, Seasonale is being marketed for something more subtle. As a menstrual

---

[4] It is the case in nearly all oral contraceptive birth control pills that menstruation occurs while women take the placebo pills. One menstrual suppression oral contraceptive, Lybrel, uses the same hormones but without any placebo pills. The designed result is no periods at all.

[5] For an analysis of how this shift turned pregnancy into a disease, see Merkin (1976).

suppressor, it reconfigures bodies in the absence of either pathology or an at-risk state. This is achieved by indirectly playing on cultural scripts that associate menstruation with disorder and impediment and, more directly, by reconfiguring these scripts from narratives of disorder to narratives of inconvenience. Seasonale is depicted as a way to achieve an even better, more convenient body. As we demonstrate below, Seasonale and its marketing discourses produce associations between cleanliness and femininity, between freedom of movement and women's bodies, and between limited menstrual flow and natural embodiment.

As a result, the discourses surrounding Seasonale extend biomedicalization processes to include everyday living more generally.[6] While past examples of biomedicalization have similarly tended to emphasize lifestyle, such emphasis relied on early articulations of bodies and bodily attributes or desires as pathology to garner legitimacy. Examples include the shift from marketing Viagra for erectile dysfunction to marketing it for erectile difficulties. In this case, a disease classification was a necessary first step in the shift toward lifestyle medication (Mamo and Fishman 2001; Fishman 2007). In another example, a classification of breast cancer risk was necessary to market Tamoxifen as a risk-treatment drug used in breast cancer prevention (Fosket 2004). With Seasonale, this early classification and pathologization no longer takes place, and, significantly, previous legitimacy moves concerning disease classification and risk classification are revealed as being an unnecessary first step in the biomedicalization process. Menstruation is depicted as problematic and undesirable, even unnatural, but it is not transformed into a state of disease or risk. Yet it must be noted that, while Seasonale seemingly bypasses the initial need to pathologize women's bodies, bodies do not escape such tendencies: discursive pathologizing remains a subtext in these constructions (for an analysis of the blurred distinction between pathology and wellness, see Pitts-Taylor [2007]). In addition, with the medicalization of women's bodies (see Riessman 1983), women's reproductive bodies in particular had already undergone

significant pathologization prior to the introduction of Seasonale.

Menstruation as a social experience is the contemporary object of medical intervention here. While this positioning of menstruation is not couched in terms of an illness-health binary, Seasonale does have possible health indications and implications.[7] Women with endometriosis, for example, have long used menstruation suppression via birth control pills to manage their unwanted symptoms. However, this possible health-related intervention is absent in the Seasonale advertising we analyzed, as is the intervention of pregnancy prevention. It seems that Seasonale does not want to appeal to the relatively smaller market of those with endometriosis or the large, but still limited, market of women engaging in heterosexual sex who do not want to get pregnant or to use other forms of birth control methods.

Rather, by packaging itself as a menstrual-managing device, Seasonale targets every woman who is imagined as desiring or benefiting from fewer menstrual periods.[8] As we discuss below, the focus in the 2003–4 advertising campaigns for Seasonale is on preventing natural menstruation instead of preventing pregnancy. Here, drugs are being promoted not for any kind of a medical condition whatsoever.

Pharmaceuticals work from the inside out: they are taken internally, through the material body, in order to produce desired changes in that body. Of course, this is the intended purpose of drugs. In the case of Seasonale, synthetic chemicals not only alter bodies and their menstrual flows; these bodily changes are also given social and cultural meaning. As they reconfigure the natural body, these drugs reveal the significance of its cultural makeup.

---

[6] For a discussion of neomedicalization and menstrual suppression drugs, see Lippman (2004).

[7] This kind of pathologization of menstruation as a health risk is occurring elsewhere. See Fosket (2002) and Fosket and Mamo (in preparation) for discussions of menstruation as future disease risk.

[8] The marketing of Seasonale as a lifestyle management technique is understood by scholar and activist Giovanna Chesler as paving the way for other medical devices targeting healthy young women's bodies. For example, hormonal birth control pills may serve as gateway drugs for the human papillomavirus (HPV) vaccine, Gardasil, due to the ubiquity of oral contraceptive pills that often reduce condom use and thereby increase HPV risk. In addition, hormonal birth control pills are known to produce physiological changes to the mucus of the cervix (i.e., thinning), increasing one's susceptibility to the contraction of sexually transmitted infections (see Angier 1999, 113). Personal communication between Mamo and Chesler on September 26, 2008.

Marketing a lifestyle pharmatherapy: Changing thoughts, changing behaviors, changing bodies

The Seasonale advertising campaign begins by emphasizing the need to shift the way we think about the birth control pill and monthly menstruation. Thoughts are targeted as the initial object of intervention. As Seasonale is the first menstrual suppression drug marketed for mass use, a necessary first step is to create a market: to create a group of women for whom fewer periods seems plausible, reasonable, and even desirable. The campaign, thus, is fundamentally aimed at rewriting dominant biomedical and cultural narratives about what is and is not presumed to be natural when it comes to menstruation and birth control. To put it simply, the Seasonale campaign begins by disrupting the taken-for-grantedness of monthly menstruation.

The Seasonale campaign also opens with the visual image of an active, smiling young white woman with a clenched fist. She is dressed all in white against a white backdrop. The advertisement's text reads "Welcome to just four periods a year. . . . The way you take the pill has changed." Several things are apparent in the opening image and accompanying statement. The advertising campaign centers around the number 4, signaling that the possibility of menstruating only four times per year is a desirable outcome. The visual highlight is on the number 4, with four dots (grammatical periods) serving as a double colon and with text imposed upon a large number 4, effectively problematizing the idea that menstruating monthly is natural and that natural female embodiment includes monthly menstruation (more on this below). A new body is produced: a natural body conceptually defined as menstruating four times per year.

The second page of the brochure reads "Introducing Seasonale®: The way you think about the pill has changed 4ever. . . . Fewer periods. More possibilities." This page informs the reader that we need to change not only the way we take the pill but also our thinking about the pill. Of significance is that such rethinking requires us to change how we think about our own bodies, natural bodies,

and normal female embodiment. The implication here is that, as we change our thinking, we will also be changing the very ontological, embodied experience of being in our bodies whether or not we take Seasonale. What we may have previously always experienced as natural—our monthly menstruation—will now be problematic and rendered unnatural. Suddenly, those of us who do menstruate monthly are neither ill nor well but are awaiting definition. What lies ahead? Who will we become?

Our thoughts must change, we are told. We seem to believe that women should menstruate monthly, when according to the advertising, "in reality, there's no medical reason to have one [a period] when you are on the pill." In what we interpret as a strategic move to claim legitimacy by defining the object of their intervention, the marketers of Seasonale separate menstruation into two forms: menstrual periods and pill periods. Menstrual periods occur after the body prepares for the possibility of being pregnant; when one does not become pregnant, one has a menstrual period. In contrast, a pill period occurs when a woman takes the hormones in birth control pills and does not ovulate. The object of the marketers' intervention, however, is not illness or prevention: the object is the suppression of the pill period.

We argue that this reclassification of menstruation is a legitimacy move. By framing the menstrual periods that occur when women take oral contraceptives as pill periods, the marketers of Seasonale frame menstruation itself, in essence, as a side effect of medication. Taking a drug to suppress what is considered to be a normal, natural, unproblematic bodily process is one thing; taking a drug to suppress a pill period, which is not real anyway, which is in fact an artifact of the drug in the first place, is quite another. Once conceptualized in this way, eliminating these unnatural periods seems perfectly reasonable, and thus Seasonale is normalized. Indeed, changing cultural ideas about menstruation was an important first step in the marketing of Seasonale. These changing ideas reconfigure our experiences of our bodies and can then, theoretically, be turned into changing practices—taking pharmaceuticals—that will reshape the body in congruence with the new ideas. The ways in which embodiment, constructed by and therefore part of culture, is produced by Seasonale are revealed, but so too are the ways in which bodies themselves are produced through cultural practices. The continuous loop between culture and embodiment is therefore already apparent.

Body projects: Suturing self-feeling(s) and interior process(es)

If the first step of the 2003–4 advertising campaign is to disrupt the taken-for-grantedness of monthly menstruation, the rest of the campaign produces the non-monthly-menstruating woman. Remember, the image on page 1 of the printed brochure depicts a seemingly happy, young, able-bodied white woman in motion. She is dressed in youthful professional attire that exposes her mid-section, her fists are clenched, her head is thrown back and slightly tilted, her long hair sways with her movement, she wears lipstick and earrings, and she smiles energetically. The image is one of flexibility, femininity, happiness, self-confidence. The fact that she is dressed all in white against a white backdrop connotes cleanliness and purity. Her clenched fists and professional attire position her as strong and empowered, yet her exposed midriff, tilted head, and blowing hair depict her as sexy, fun, and able. The dominance of white in the image provides an explicit juxtaposition to the reds and browns of menstrual blood. The wearing of white is often seen as a bad idea during menstruation, and by dressing this woman all in white the advertisers signal the absence of blood, leaks, and the possible mess associated with menstruation. This woman can risk wearing white because she is confident that the stigma of breakthrough bleeding will not occur. The dominance of white is also a symbolic move to signal purity. As we demonstrate below, purity as a feminine characteristic of Seasonale is produced by limited menstrual flows and not by limited sexual behaviors.

This biomedical script produces meaning and ways for women to be in and experience their bodies. Accordingly, the advertising campaign for Seasonale can be viewed as a body-technology project (Brumberg 1997) that produces subjects and notions of cleanliness, purity, and sexiness.[9] Women in their natural "raw" form are clean and pure and able to be in motion. Their bodies are flexible sites for self-perfection: they not only can achieve beauty, fitness, and freedom from inconvenient menstruation, but they are "naturally" beautiful, free, able-bodied, and nonmenstrual. The campaign, we argue, is not only targeting ideal bodies but also targeting and producing everyday bodily behaviors and experiences of being in the body, including the regimen of taking the pill and doing so as prescribed. Instead, presenting pregnancy prevention as a route to upward mobility and happiness, it is suppressing the presumed constraints imposed by monthly menstruation—women are now free to wear white and, by extension, to run, jump, swim, and twirl their hair. While an implicit assumption exists that women are also free to engage in (heterosexual) sex, this effect is secondary to a broader bodily freedom. Furthermore, another implicit assumption is that, with Seasonale, women are free to engage (or compete) in the professional world with bodies more similar to those of men. Menstruation is produced as a constraining process that, with Seasonale, becomes something to be overcome: a part of every woman's and girl's wellness.

Yet this body-technology project is another site of contradiction, at once signaling a way for women to assert control or agency via the body and also signaling women's bodies and femininity as being targeted by biomedical interventions. The printed brochure states that what has not changed in Seasonale are the same kind of "trusted hormones" and "reliable effectiveness" found in current birth control pills. We are told that it is 99 percent effective when taken as directed. We are not told, however, what the pill is effective for. It is only at the bottom of this page in small print that we are told: "Seasonale tablets are indicated for the prevention of pregnancy." This trend is repeated throughout the brochure, though usually without the small print explanation. As a lifestyle technology, Seasonale effaces effectiveness (a means to an end) in favor of self-transformation (a process of becoming and a future possibility). Instead of emphasizing pregnancy prevention, this narrative promises a seemingly radical change in thinking and, as the campaign asserts, an opening up of possibilities, a lifestyle shift. One wonders, however, more possibilities for what? How must our thoughts change?

---

[9] See also Pitts 2003, 2005.

Lifestyle control or transformation?

Page 3 of the brochure offers another image of an active woman dressed in white. The narrative emphasizes the possibilities brought about by this new pill, but these possibilities are not spelled out. Rather, readers are left to deduce how their lives might improve and to imagine a set of possibilities of their own making if they menstruated just four times a year. While not specified, such possibilities are repeatedly implied in the use of words like *convenience:* Seasonale is described as "letting you have the convenience of only four periods a year." In this way, menstruation is explicated as inconvenient. The possibilities are also implied in the images of the women, who appear to be exuberant, healthy, and active.

In contrast to this lack of specificity, the Seasonale Web site offers an interactive personal planner to "plan events like vacations, business travel, romantic encounters, and family reunions based on your inactive Pill dates." The Web site also offers details and first-person testimonials, providing greater insight into the image Seasonale is representing of women's bodies and lives. One woman on the Web site advertising campaign describes herself as extremely active and says she loves not having to worry about getting a period, especially because she swims a lot. Without explicitly saying it, she implies that swimming during her period is not preferable. Living in a menstruating female body, according to Seasonale, is constructed as living with worry. Seasonale, however, intervenes in daily feminine worries. Women are depicted as in control of their periods and able to live active lives without worrying about a period most of the year. Women have a new choice, and Seasonale's target is the choice to live with fewer periods.

Seasonale produces nonmenstruation as a dynamic process shaped across, not within a particular position in, the life course. External choices shape the interiority of our bodies, but the process does not stop there. The interiority of the nonmenstruating girl and young woman produces a cultural ideal of feminine embodiment itself. Girlhood, a time once marked by menarche, or the beginning of monthly menstruation, is culturally and socially manipulated prior to and without pregnancy, meno-pause, anorexia, or other life-course events and/or illnesses that disrupt menstruation. Female embodiment as developmentally, experientially, and culturally understood is open to revision.

Taking the sex out of sexual liberation: This isn't your mother's pill

In reading the marketing description of this advertising campaign, one thing seems most peculiarly absent: birth control. As described earlier, Seasonale is promoted not as a way to prevent pregnancy but as a way to prevent menstruation. In doing so, Seasonale produces feminine embodiment as free from monthly periods. Pregnancy prevention is relegated to the small print in this campaign's emphasis on convenience and freedom from menstruation.

While this primary emphasis on controlling menstruation effaces the original intended purpose of birth control pills—to prevent pregnancy—it also effaces the (hetero)sexual liberation produced by the first-generation birth control pill of the 1960s. While sexual liberation was the supertext of first-generation birth control pills, it is now relegated to subtext with Seasonale. If liberation remains, what kind of liberation is produced? In our interpretation, it is no longer sexual liberation—freedom from unwanted pregnancy and thus freedom to engage in heterosexual intercourse—but freedom from unwanted menstruation that is produced with Seasonale.

First-generation birth control pills garnered legitimacy in the context of delaying when women would become pregnant and allowing for pregnancy spacing, yet the presumed naturalness of heterosexual reproduction remained intact. Sexual liberation was the unintended consequence of birth control pills. First-generation birth control pills were an early instance of a lifestyle medication: a drug taken by healthy people to prevent a lifestyle problem.

Yet Seasonale garners legitimacy without this kind of repositioning of heterosexual sex. There are no husbands, partners, and couples in this advertising campaign, only empowered women happy to choose their lifestyle and the timing and experience of menstruation itself. Feminine purity (i.e., cleanliness) is produced by effacing pregnancy prevention in favor of menstruation control. Seasonale produces a transformation of female bodies, not a solution to unwanted pregnancy, and therefore also produces a means to (hetero)sexual freedom. (Hetero)sex, however, is not erased completely: normative configurations of heterosexuality weave throughout the Seasonale campaigns as ever-present subtexts. Male sexual partners emerge as implicated actors in the discourses surrounding Seasonale, as in need of protection from menstrual blood during sexual penetration. Seasonale is described as useful for "big events": weddings, anniversaries, and hot dates. Thus, we are to conclude that menstruation is best avoided so that women may be rendered ready and clean for sexual penetration. As a drug aimed at girls and young women, Seasonale produces feminine embodiments of heterosexuality itself.

Feminist health and empowerment? Del-Em and Seasonale

An attempt to reduce or limit menstruation altogether is not new. Self-help menstrual extraction emerged out of the women's health activism of the 1970s (for a review of the movement, see Murphy [2004]). In 1971, Lorraine Rothman and Carol Downer of the Los Angeles Feminist Health Center invented Del-Em, a mechanical self-help kit used to perform menstrual extraction within the context of self-help groups. Once Del-Em had been developed, the inventors embarked on a twenty-three-city U.S. tour to demonstrate and teach the self-help techniques of menstrual extraction and cervical exams.

Within the context of 1970s women's health movements, menstrual extraction emerged as a feminist empowerment tool for manipulating the menstrual body (Bell 1974; Morgen 2002; Bobel 2006) and enhancing women's control over their bodies and bodily processes. In our analysis of a pamphlet for Del-Em distributed at the Women's Community Health Center, we found that Del-Em was described as the "women's liberation method of menstrual extraction" (Women's Community Health Center 1974, 1), as a self-help empowerment tool (Bell 1974) that emerged for "medical reasons" such as debilitating periods and cramps, and as a way to provide women with the choice to control their bodies. Removing menstrual flow was performed for many purposes: as a form of period control, a form of contraception, and a form of

abortion.[10] Whether or not it was used to ameliorate an unwanted bodily experience varied.

In the pamphlet promoting Del-Em that was distributed during a feminist health conference held by Rothman and Downer, the text describing Del-Em stated: "The simple procedure of extracting the menses just after or just before the period begins provides for every woman the choice concerning whether she will have a period this month. Be this for convenience, comfort, or regulation of the menstrual cycle, women using the advanced technology of menstrual suppression are now able to control their lives" (Women's Community Health Center 1974, 1).

The campaign for Seasonale relies on familiar language and imagery of self-help feminist empowerment yet also shift these discourses in significant ways. As in the informational brochures provided for Del-Em, women are described in the advertisements for Seasonale as being empowered by menstrual suppression, as becoming knowledgeable and knowing about their own bodies. The images from the Seasonale campaigns depict women in professional clothing and are aimed to denote confidence and strength. The advertisements for Seasonale utilize language from women's health movements, such as "freedom" and "possibility"; they signal autonomy and self-actualization. The visual imagery in the advertisements depict self-confident, positive, empowered women, but the underlying message is that these women got this way (and you can get there, too) only by virtue of taking a pill to manage (and suppress) their bodily processes.

Seasonale does not represent the first time the language of empowerment has been used in the context of menstrual suppression. On the contrary, the Seasonale campaign echoes the language of control, choice, and convenience used to frame Del-Em. Unlike Seasonale, however, Del-Em was not available as a commercial product. One could not ask one's doctor about menstrual suppression techniques. Del-Em was used within alternative feminist health communities by women who completed training programs (on anatomy and women's

---

[10] While the menstrual extraction performed by the Del-Em technology is the same as the vacuum technique used in self-help abortion, menstrual extraction and abortion are not the same procedure. They have different biophysical attributes, culture meanings, and interpersonal and social effects

bodies, including their own) and who participated in self-help groups. In contrast, Seasonale exists as a heavily marketed commodity, emerging out of the pharmaceutical-industrial complex. While Seasonale relies on the discourse of knowledge of one's own body, it does not actively require the use of such knowledge in the same way that Del-Em, a self-administered technology of greater complexity than a pharmaceutical, did.

Furthermore, in the context of feminist health movements, we found that, while one goal was to challenge dominant American cultural assumptions about menstruation, such challenges often reaffirmed menstruation as a natural part of women's bodies (even in the assertion that all women are different and experience menstruation differently). For example, the Federation of Feminist Women's Health Centers' *A New View of a Woman's Body* asserted that the use of menstrual extraction "should not be viewed as an attempt to avoid menstruation or short-circuit natural functions" (1982, 122). Menstrual extraction was to be used "as a means for a woman to exert influence over changes in her body which she could not control before, in order to eliminate occasional discomfort or inconvenience or an unwanted pregnancy" (122). The 1970s Del-Em menstrual extraction method, therefore, produced menstruation as natural. In contrast, the marketing for Seasonale produces monthly menstruation as not necessarily natural at all.

Like many other examples (see, e.g., Fosket [2004] on Tamoxifen), Seasonale enters the fray of women's health and co-opts the language of empowerment, taps into the desire for freedom, and repackages it into a pharmaceutical. Within commodified, biomedicalized culture, the beneficiaries of these pharmaceuticals are most significantly the pharmaceutical companies themselves. Further, the customization, commodification, and fetishization offered here as health products and services have little actual health value. Rather, it is desires that constitute lifestyle medications—the promise of improvement to one's body and way of being and doing things in the world.

Who benefits from menstrual suppression drugs in the context of biomedicine? Benefits are always context dependent; the meaning of benefit depends on the intentions and experiences of those who use these medical technologies. Particular women's culturally freighted experiences of menstruation influence their decisions about menstrual suppression as well as their experiences with oral contraceptives. Some women for whom menstruation represents a problem for reasons of health, aesthetics, convenience, or otherwise may benefit from these drugs. For women who have pain with their periods, the option of menstrual suppression may be welcome. Menstrual suppression may also be welcomed by women with disabilities who rely on others for body care during menstruation. Others may relish the thought of fewer periods, or no periods, for its convenience. In contrast, others may prefer monthly menstruation to indicate the absence of pregnancy, the presence of a healthy rhythm or cycle, or a celebration of embodied sexed difference as a source of pride and power. Thus, very particular meanings and experiences of menstruation will shape women's choices concerning and experiences with menstrual suppression drugs.

Given the plurality of meanings, these drugs may variously be referred to as "menstrual manipulation," another product in a long line of attempts to medicalize women's bodies, and as "empowerment technology," a means to control pain, messiness, dependency, or embarrassment associated with menstruation. As an empowerment technology, Seasonale allows women to choose when and where to engage in sports, swimming, and sex, and it provides them with a means to schedule travel, wedding dates, and other life events. In shifting toward a discourse of empowerment, Seasonale pushes biomedicalization in new directions. As a discursive technology, Seasonale may succeed because women's bodies have already been extensively pathologized. Biomedicalization not only discursively extends women's bodies beyond pathologization, but with the turn toward lifestyle drugs effaces this move and renders it unnecessary for the drugs' success. As a process, however, this effacement relies on the previous move of pathologization for the present construction of lifestyle drugs targeting social attributes.

Yet our concern lies in the ways in which Seasonale produces femininity itself and in how this construction of femininity signals to girls that menstruation needs to be controlled. We want to maintain the choices available to girls and young women, but we also want to refuse the effacement of the ways in which technoscience participates in shaping girlhood and women's experiences of embodiment. When health becomes the target of intervention, menstruation and, by extension, feminine embodiment are constructed as problematic for some. Like other market-driven pharmaceuticals, commodified menstrual suppression can exacerbate inequalities. In contraceptive markets in which choices are seemingly everywhere, products are strategically aimed at particular niche groups based on social identities as much as on needs and desires. Norplant continues to be prescribed as the best option for urban (read: black, Latina, and Asian) girls and young women, while oral birth control pills (including Seasonale) are marketed to young professional (read: white) girls and women. Young professional women may be the perfect niche market for Seasonale, a product that helps them be "just like" men while also maintaining their feminine sex appeal.

Del-Em provides a useful counterpoint to one-dimensional discussions of the empowerment or disempowerment offered by either technology. Biomedical services, technologies, and knowledges are taken up, used, and given meaning by various women who are able to engage in "selective resistance and selective compliance" (Lock and Kaufert 1998, 2; see also Root and Browner 2001; Mamo 2005, 2007). Within feminist discourses, choice and empowerment are often falsely positioned as opposite to oversimplified notions of objectification and social control. We suggest that questions of empowerment versus control need to be reframed as questions of how and under what circumstances women are able to appropriate technologies to reshape their bodies, minds, and practices as they see fit (Bell 1995). While differences exist between Del-Em and Seasonale and, as we have argued here, meaning is in the hands of users, further research is needed into the various ways women use and give meaning to menstrual suppression drugs with an analytic lens toward the ways women selectively resist and comply with the built-in assumptions and scripts of such technologies.

THE (RE)MAKING OF FEMININITY

What is immediately striking about the discourses around menstrual suppression drugs is that many of the arguments embedded in their marketing emphasize the menstrual body as always already cultural. Seasonale and Del-Em are sites of convergence where technologies and cultural practices have joined forces with an explicit intention to transform menstruating bodies. Here, we can see that bodies and discourses are co-constitutive. The messages about menstruation in the advertising campaigns attempt to reshape the very way in which we think about menstruation, constructing it as an unnaturally frequent event that can safely and easily be lessened or even avoided altogether.[11] When translated into action (taking pharmaceuticals), these messages then transform embodiment by limiting menstruation, among other biological changes that result from daily ingestion of drugs, and by transforming knowledge about bodies themselves.

Through something as simple and familiar as daily birth control pills, women are offered the power to choose how and when to menstruate. What our research does not answer, however, is how these promises are being read and/or taken up. We do know from others' research that they are not being unproblematically embraced. Clusters of women are engaged in reclaiming and redefining menstruation.[12] Interview data suggest that many women actually welcome monthly menstruation and, despite advertising initiatives like those for Seasonale and Del-Em, do not regard it as something to avoid.[13]

Women's health activists are also getting involved in the construction of counterclaims about menstruation. The National Women's Health Network (NWHN) released a fact sheet on menstrual suppression drugs (NWHN 2007) that seeks a more balanced discussion than the one provided by marketing materials. The fact sheet presents a full account of both the health risks and the health benefits associated with menstrual suppression drugs,

---

[11] See also Elsimar Coutinho and Sheldon Segal (1999) and Malcolm Gladwell (2000) for popular attempts to reframe monthly menstruation as disease risk.

[12] See Elson 2002; Fingerson 2005a, 2005b, 2006; Bobel 2006.

[13] See Chrisler et al. 1994; Lee 1994; Lee and Sasser-Coen 1996a, 1996b; Lee 2002.

as well as an in-depth discussion of the choices these drugs offer to women and girls. While the fact sheet supports women's increased options and freedom to choose, the NWHN is primarily concerned about the shaping of what is normal and healthy for girls and young women.

In her film documentary on menstrual suppression, *Period: The End of Menstruation?* (2007), Giovanna Chesler provides a multisided analysis of the feminist choice and freedom discourse by placing pro-menses and menstrual suppression arguments within the context of the medical histories of, for example, premenstrual syndrome, postpartum depression, and hormone replacement therapies. The film presents views of a variety of medical practitioners—several gynecologists, psychologists, nurses, natural healers, and endocrinology researchers, along with conversations between women and girls discussing perspectives that are both pro- and anti-menses views depending on personal stories and understanding of their body. In doing so, Chesler, a feminist critic, activist, and scholar, works against medical discourses that teach girls to feel ashamed, embarrassed, or scared of their bodies. For Chesler, negative associations with menstruation help to maintain women's subordinate position in this world (see Chesler 2005). Similarly, the Canadian Women's Health Network launched a campaign in 2006, "We're not sick—we're women" (see fig. 1), which challenges menstrual suppression drugs' conflation of menstruation with sickness and questions claims that women should be on a daily drug regimen to treat menstruation. The campaign also points out that Seasonale exposes women to nine more weeks of estrogen and progesterone annually than a regular birth control regimen yet no studies have examined the potential long-term effects of this exposure on women's fertility or health. As a form of radical menstrual activism, this campaign pursues a politics designed to trouble depictions of menstruation as a debilitating thing to be managed away. It also uses menstruation itself to trouble deeper dichotomies of sex/gender (see Bobel 2006). Drawing attention to the fact that not all women menstruate and that some people identifying as men do menstruate (e.g., female-to-male transsexuals), radical menstrual activism seeks to upset the essentializing

uses of menstrual discourse. By troubling the tight coupling of menstruation and femininity, these challenges render the cultural specificity of menstruation vivid.

At the same time that menstrual activists disrupt menstrual taboos, they also use performance art, spectacle, writing, and visual images to wrestle menstrual blood from the shameful confines to which it has historically been relegated and to make it visible (Bobel 2006). Rejecting constructions of women as victims of power and coercive co-optation, menstrual activists also employ co-optive tactics—reappropriating the images used in advertisements and messages meant to depict menstruation in shameful and taboo ways to criticize the menstrual products industry and shift power back into the hands of menstruators.

In conclusion, we return to the questions with which we began: Does Seasonale enable bodies to transcend natural constraints, or does it force women back to notions of immanence symbolized by the natural body? Does the tight coupling of menstruation and femininity enable menstrual suppression technologies to reconstitute subjects in ways that alter the very notion of feminine identity, the very substance of what it means to be a woman?

Certainly bodies are not fixed; there is no singular, ahistoric body. As many have argued, then, the dichotomy between a "natural" body and a socially constructed body is not particularly useful. The Seasonale campaign helps to show why "it is time to change how we think" about our bodies.

Technologies emerge and bodies exist in a cultural milieu in which bodies are reconfigured through power relations and discursive constructions. Structured by politics, economics, historicity, and facticity, and haunted by unconscious desire (Clough 2000), bodies are neither limitless nor susceptible to total transformation. Technologies are not neutral. As a pharmatherapeutic technology, Seasonale operates in a cultural context inseparable from the logic of consumption and biomedicalization.[14] Yet the bodies produced with

---

[14] This is especially evident given the limited research available to document the drug's safety. See, e.g., the position paper on menstrual suppression written by the Society for Menstrual Cycle Research (2003), in which the authors assert that there is no evidence that menstrual suppression is either safe or reversible.

Seasonale help shape and reproduce that culture, just as they are shaped by it. Power and domination are not the only dynamics, however. As we have noted, there are alternatives to the dominant interpretation of Seasonale and other pharmaceutical menstrual suppressants. There are multiple possibilities for resistance to emerging discourses of femininity, and there are many women who feel empowered by the choices offered by this medical technology. By seeing that culture and embodiment are thoroughly enmeshed, we can see that there are always other ways to imagine, live, and experience our worlds and bodies.

Department of Sociology University of Maryland (Mamo)

Department of Sociology McGill University (Fosket)

References

Angier, Natalie. 1999. *Woman: An Intimate Geography.* New York: Random House.

Asbell, Bernard. 1995. *The Pill: A Biography of the Drug That Changed the World.* New York: Random House.

Balsamo, Anne. 1996a. "Forms of Technological Embodiment: Reading the Body in Contemporary Culture." In *Cyberspace/Cyberbodies/Cyberpunk: Cultures of Technological Embodiment*, ed. Mike Featherstone and Roger Burrows, 215–37. London: Sage.

———. 1996b. *Technologies of the Gendered Body: Reading Cyborg Women.* Durham, NC: Duke University Press.

Bell, Susan. 1974. "Notes on Self-Help Gynecology and the Women's Health Movement." Unpublished manuscript on file with the author.

———. 1995. "Gendered Medical Science: Producing a Drug for Women." *Feminist Studies* 21(3):469–500.

Bobel, Chris. 2006. "'Our Revolution Has Style': Contemporary Menstrual Product Activists 'Doing Feminism' in the Third Wave." *Sex Roles* 54(5/6):331–45.

Brumberg, Joan Jacobs. 1997. *The Body Project: An Intimate History of American Girls.* New York: Random House.

Chesler, Giovanna. 2005. "Period: The Beginning of a Conversation, or the End of Menstruation?" *vaginaverite.com.* http://www.vaginaverite.com/voice/findingyourvoice/giovannachesler.html.

Chrisler, Joan C., Ingrid K. Johnston, Nicole M. Champagne, and Kathleen E. Preston. 1994. "Menstrual Joy: The Construct and Its Consequences." *Psychology of Women Quarterly* 18(3):375–87.

Clarke, Adele E. 1998. *Disciplining Reproduction: Modernity, American Life Sciences, and the Problems of Sex.* Berkeley: University of California Press.

Clarke, Adele E., Janet K. Shim, Laura Mamo, Jennifer Ruth Fosket, and Jennifer R. Fishman. 2003. "Biomedicalization: Technoscientific Transformations of Health, Illness, and U.S. Biomedicine." *American Sociological Review* 68(2): 161–94.

Clough, Patricia Ticineto. 2000. *Autoaffection: Unconscious Thought in the Age of Teletechnology.* Minneapolis: University of Minnesota Press.

Coutinho, Elsimar M., and Sheldon J. Segal. 1999. *Is Menstruation Obsolete?* New York: Oxford University Press.

de Lauretis, Teresa. 1987. *Technologies of Gender: Essays on Theory, Film, and Fiction.* Bloomington: Indiana University Press.

Delaney, Janice, Mary Jane Lupton, and Emily Toth. 1988. *The Curse: A Cultural History of Menstruation.* Chicago: University of Illinois Press.

Elson, Jean. 2002. "Manipulating Menstruation Is Misguided." *Society for Menstrual Cycle Research Newsletter*, Winter, 4–5.

Federation of Feminist Women's Health Centers. 1982. *A New View of a Woman's Body: A Fully Illustrated Guide.* Los Angeles: Feminist Health.

Fingerson, Laura. 2005a. "Agency and the Body in Adolescent Menstrual Talk." *Childhood* 12(1):91–110.

———. 2005b. "'Yeah, Me Too!' Adolescent Talk Building in Group Interviews." *Sociological Studies of Children and Youth* 11:261–87.

———. 2006. *Girls in Power: Gender, Body, and Menstruation in Adolescence.* Albany, NY: SUNY Press.

Fishman, Jennifer R. 2004. "Manufacturing Desire: The Commodification of Female Sexual Dysfunction." *Social Studies of Science* 34(2):187–218.

———. 2007. "Making Viagra: From Impotence to Erectile Dysfunction." In *Medicating Modern America: Prescription Drugs in History*, ed. Andrea Tone and Elizabeth Siegal Watkins, 229–52. New York: New York University Press.

Fishman, Jennifer R., and Laura Mamo. 2001. "What's in a Disorder: A Cultural Analysis of Medical and Pharmaceutical Constructions of Male and Female Sexual Dysfunction." *Women and Therapy* 24(1/2):179–93.

Fosket, Jennifer Ruth. 2002. "Breast Cancer Risk and the Politics of Prevention: Analysis of a Clinical Trial." PhD dissertation, University of California, San Francisco.

———. 2004. "Constructing 'High-Risk Women': The Development and Standardization of a Breast Cancer Risk Assessment Tool." *Science, Technology and Human Values* 29(3):291–313.

Fosket, Jennifer, and Laura Mamo. In preparation. "Making Menstruation Obsolete: Pharmaceuticals and the Reshaping of Women's Bodies." Unpublished manuscript on file with the authors.

Foucault, Michel. 1979. *Discipline and Punish: The Birth of the Prison*. New York: Vintage.

———. 1980. *The History of Sexuality: An Introduction*. New York: Vintage.

Gladwell, Malcolm. 2000. "John Rock's Error: What the Co-inventor of the Pill Didn't Know; Menstruation Can Endanger Women's Health." *New Yorker*, March 13, 52–63.

Gordon, Linda. 1990. *Woman's Body, Woman's Right: A Social History of Birth Control in America*. New York: Penguin.

Grosz, Elizabeth. 1993. "Bodies and Knowledges: Feminism and the Crisis of Reason." In *Feminist Epistemologies: Thinking Gender*, ed. Linda Alcoff and Elizabeth Potter, 187–216. New York: Routledge.

Haraway, Donna J. 1991. "A Cyborg Manifesto: Science, Technology and Socialist-Feminism in the Late Twentieth Century." In her *Simians, Cyborgs, and Women: The Reinvention of Nature*, 149–82. New York: Routledge.

———. 1992. "The Promises of Monsters: A Regenerative Politics for Inappropriate/d Others." In *Cultural Studies*, ed. Lawrence Grossberg, Cary Nelson, and Paula Treichler, 295–337. New York: Routledge.

Laws, Sophie. 1990. *Issues of Blood: The Politics of Menstruation*. London: Macmillan.

Lee, Janet. 1994. "Menarch and the (Hetero)Sexualization of the Female Body." *Gender and Society* 8(3):343–62.

Lee, Janet, and Jennifer Sasser-Coen. 1996a. *Blood Stories: Menarch and the Politics of the Female Body in Contemporary U.S. Society*. New York: Routledge.

———. 1996b. "Memories of Menarch: Older Women Remember Their First Period." *Journal of Aging Studies* 10(2):83–101.

Lee, Shirley. 2002. "Health and Sickness: The Meaning of Menstruation and Premenstrual Syndrome in Women's Lives." *Sex Roles* 46(1/2):25–35.

Lippman, Abby. 2004. "Women's Cycles up for Sale: Neo-medicalization and Women's Reproductive Health." *Canadian Women's Health Network Magazine* 6/7(4/1). http://www.cwhn.ca/network-reseau/7-1/7-1pg3.html.

Lock, Margaret, and Patricia A. Kaufert, eds. 1998. *Pragmatic Women and Body Politics*. New York: Cambridge University Press.

Mamo, Laura. 2005. "Biomedicalizing Kinship: Sperm Banks and the Creation of Affinity-Ties." *Science as Culture* 14(3):237–64.

———. 2007. *Queering Reproduction: Achieving Pregnancy in the Age of Technoscience*. Durham, NC: Duke University Press.

Mamo, Laura, and Jennifer R. Fishman. 2001. "Potency in All the Right Places: Viagra as a Technology of the Gendered Body." *Body and Society* 7(4):13–35.

Marks, Lara V. 2001. *Sexual Chemistry: A History of the Contraceptive Pill*. New Haven, CT: Yale University Press.

Merkin, Donald H. 1976. *Pregnancy as a Disease: The Pill in Society*. Port Washington, NY: Kennikat.

Morgen, Sandra. 2002. *Into Our Own Hands: The Women's Health Movement in the United States, 1969–1990*. New Brunswick, NJ: Rutgers University Press.

Murphy, Michelle. 2004. "Immodest Witnessing: The Epistemology of Vaginal Self-Examination in the U.S. Feminist Self-Help Movement." *Feminist Studies* 30(1):115–47.

NWHN (National Women's Health Network). 2007. "Fact Sheet: Menstrual Suppression." National Women's Health Network. http://www.nwhn.org/healthinfo/detail.cfm?info_id=14topic=Fact%20Sheets.

Olesen, Virginia L., and Nancy Fugate Woods, eds. 1986. *Culture, Society, and Menstruation*. Washington, DC: Hemisphere.

Oudshoorn, Nelly. 1994. *Beyond the Natural Body: An Archeology of Sex Hormones*. New York: Routledge.

———. 2003. *The Male Pill: A Biography of a Technology in the Making*. Durham, NC: Duke University Press.

Period: The End of Menstruation? 2007. Directed by Giovanna Chesler. New York: Cinema Guild.

Pitts, Victoria. 2003. *In the Flesh: The Cultural Politics of Body Modification*. New York: Palgrave MacMillan.

———. 2005. "Feminism, Technology and Body Projects." *Women's Studies: An Inter-disciplinary Journal* 34(3–4):229–47.

Pitts-Taylor, Victoria. 2007. *Surgery Junkies: Wellness and Pathology in Cosmetic Culture.* New Brunswick, NJ: Rutgers University Press.

Riessman, Catherine Kohler. 1983. "Women and Medicalization: A New Perspective." *Social Policy* 14(1):3–18.

Root, Robin, and C. H. Browner. 2001. "Practices of the Pregnant Self: Compliance with and Resistance to Prenatal Norms." *Culture, Medicine and Psychiatry* 25(2):195–223.

Seaman, Barbara. 1969. *The Doctors' Case against the Pill.* New York: Wyden.

Shim, Janet K. 2002. "Race, Class, and Gender across the Science-Lay Divide: Expertise, Experience, and 'Difference' in Cardiovascular Disease." PhD dissertation, University of California, San Francisco.

Society for Menstrual Cycle Research. 2003. "Menstrual Supression." Paper developed at the Fifteenth Biennial Conference of the Society for Menstrual Cycle Research, Pittsburgh, June 5–7. http://menstruationre-search.org/position/menstrual-supression/.

Thomas, Sarah L., and Charlotte Ellertson. 2000. "Nuisance or Natural and Healthy: Should Monthly Menstruation Be Optional for Women?" *The Lancet* 355(9207):922–24.

Tone, Andrea. 2001. *Devices and Desires: A History of Contraceptives in America.* New York: Hill & Wang.

Women's Community Health Center. 1974. "Statement on Menstrual Extraction." Pamphlet. Cambridge, MA: Women's Community Health Center.

 # Menstrual Suppression

by National Women's Health Network

What woman hasn't at least occasionally wished she could avoid having her period? For decades some women have taken their traditional birth control pills on a non-traditional schedule in order to manipulate the timing of their periods – for example, to avoid menstruating during a vacation, athletic competition or another important personal event. There are now oral contraceptive pills (OCPs) on the market that offer the ability to suppress menstruation. These pills are intended to change a woman's bleeding pattern to produce either no periods (Lybrel) or just four periods a year (Seasonale and Seasonique), instead of a dozen.

Menstrual suppression products are chemically identical to traditional oral contraceptive pills. The active tablets contain a combination of levonorgestrel and ethinyl estradiol. The difference lies in the way a woman takes the pills. The traditional OCP is taken for 21 days, followed by 7 days of placebo pills. Seasonale and Seasonique are taken for 84 days consecutively, followed by 7 days of placebo pills. In both cases, while the woman is taking the placebo pills, she gets her period.* Lybrel uses the same hormones, in a slightly lower dose, with no change in hormone dose throughout the year. Lybrel is designed to produce no periods at all.

Women's individual experiences of, and attitudes about, menstruation play an important role in determining their interest in menstrual suppression and may also affect the level of satisfaction with the method. For women who have pain or other discomforts with their period, the option to suppress menstruation can be a welcome relief. Some women find the thought of fewer periods, or no periods, appealing for its convenience. But others express a preference for monthly menstruation because they rely on it as a signal that they are not pregnant or because they view it as a sign that their bodies are functioning normally. These women may be less likely to choose or be satisfied with a method that reduces the frequency of their periods.

Effectiveness, health risks, and benefits

From a safety perspective, OCPs like Seasonale or Lybrel are options for most women. If your health care provider has determined that you can take birth control pills safely, you can probably take these. It is important to keep in mind that women trying to suppress her period using the pill will take a few dozen more active hormone pills over the course of a year than a woman taking the 21-day version of the pill. However, there does not seem to be a meaningful increase in health risk although no long-term studies have been done. The small risk of stroke or blood clots associated with traditional oral contraceptives – increased in women who smoke, are over 35 years of age, or have high blood pressure – are similarly associated with extended use pills. In addition to the time limitations, another hurdle appears to be the drop-out rate and sample size of the related clinical trials. The FDA approval for Seasonale, for example, was based on a one-year study involving only 809 women.[1] The main study supporting the efficacy of Seasonique began with 1,013 participants but concluded with the data from only 534 due to dropout from adverse event and lost-to-follow-up.[2]

The effectiveness of menstrual suppression products for preventing pregnancy is also very similar to regular OCPs. But their effectiveness for actually suppressing menstruation is not so straightforward. During the first year of use, many women have experienced breakthrough bleeding – instead of ending or reducing their periods, they were bleeding on an irregular, unpredictable schedule. Women using Seasonale or Seasonique had as many days of bleeding as women using traditional oral contraceptives in the first year of use. This fact may have contributed to the high drop-out rate in the trials. It is important to note that most women who experienced breakthrough bleeding and remained in the clinical trials found that the irregular bleeding did eventually subside.

The need for a balanced, accurate discussion of what's normal and what's healthy

The National Women's Health Network supports the availability of menstrual suppression products as an option for women. Our concerns about this method lie with the way these products are being marketed to women by manufacturers and health care providers.

Below are some examples of problematic marketing:

- One doctor brought to a media briefing by the makers of Seasonale asserted that using Seasonale could improve high school girls' test scores because, she said, girls score lower on the SATs when they are menstruating, although she provided no evidence for this claim.[3]

- Several physicians have referred to the experience of women in earlier eras who menstruated less than women today due to more frequent pregnancies and longer periods of amenorrhea (absence of a menstrual period) associated with breastfeeding to support the claim that women weren't intended to menstruate as much as they do today. One gynecologist who conducted research on menstrual suppression said "It's having seven or 10 kids that are natural," explaining that menstrual suppression "gets women to a more natural state."[4] It is accurate to say that women menstruate more today than they have at other times, but the assertion that monthly menstruation is unnatural is unfounded.

- Some scientists have speculated that reducing the frequency of menstruation and ovulation might reduce the risk of breast, endometrial and ovarian cancers and even extend fertility, but these ideas have not been proven by scientific study.[5] The association that has been identified in epidemiological studies between the frequency of menstruation/ovulation and some reproductive cancers does not indicate a causal relationship.

- One manufacturer presented a distorted picture of women's feelings about menstruation by misrepresenting data from a survey that the company commissioned. In a news release about the survey the company wrote that more than half of women feel "messy, fat and unattractive" during their periods; but in fact, only a third of women reported feeling unattractive during their period, and 68 percent of women said they feel healthy.[7]

These misrepresentations and unsupported claims are particularly a concern with respect to young teens or girls who are just beginning to learn about menstruation and are forming a new understanding of the way their bodies work. Telling them that it's unnatural or unhealthy to get a monthly period, or that they'll perform better in school, in sports or socially if they suppress their periods is doing them a real disservice. Introducing menstruation to pre-adolescents and newly menstruating girls as a negative experience to be avoided may affect the girls' body image and relationship to their bodies in negative and lasting ways.

Women need truthful and complete information about these products to make informed decisions. As more products get approved, the marketing competition is likely to increase. Drug companies and clinicians promoting menstrual suppression must not tell women that it's healthier to have fewer periods because this is not supported by evidence. Making menstrual suppression products available will expand women's contraceptive options and increase convenience for some. But this advance should not be undermined by stigmatizing menstruation.

The menstrual period of a woman using hormonal contraception is sometimes called withdrawal bleeding. Instead of a 'natural' menstrual cycle controlled by the body's own hormonal fluctuations, withdrawal bleeding is the body's reaction to the cessation of the hormone dose that the contraceptive has been providing.

Menstruation and the Politics of Sex Education

1. In abstinence-only sex education, what information is lost, misrepresented, or excluded? Does comprehensive sex education include any of the information that abstinence-only sex education excludes?

2. How have women's orgasms and sexual pleasure been misunderstood in medical institutions?

3. How does heterosexual privilege influence medical practices or sex education?

4. In what ways do limited understandings of sexuality affect access to sexual health services?

5. Using Johnston-Robledo and Chrisler's article, how is menstruation constructed as social stigma?

6. What are ways in which women can redefine menstruation as empowering, rather than stigmatizing?

7. In conjunction with the articles from Chapter 4, what role does the pharmaceutical industry play in the social understanding of menstruation?

Disability and Society

The disability rights movement, led by people with disabilities and their families and advocates, fought hard to bring about a profound social change that altered the American landscape. Through legislation and advocacy, our society today is more accessible, includes more job opportunities, and promotes the equality of people with disabilities. In addition, technological and medical advances have improved the quality of life and life expectancy for people with disabilities. Yet, people with disabilities are still one of the largest groups currently living in poverty. The U. S. census estimates that there are 56.7 million people, or nearly 1 in 5, in the United States with some type of disability. Over eighty percent of people with disabilities live in poverty and do not maintain sustainable employment, compared to twelve percent of those without a disability. The Centers for Disease Control (CDC) estimates about 27 million women in the United States have a disability. The majority of these women live in poverty; this includes fifty percent of women older than sixty-five. While technological and medical advances and policies have increased the health of women with disabilities, the social stigma of disability remains. In this chapter, the authors explore the healing powers of spirituality and attempt to understand disability from a variety of cultural and gendered frameworks.

The chapter begins with the article, *A Cape Verdean Perspective on Disability: An Invisible Minority in New England* by Dawna Marie Thomas. Thomas highlights the intersection of race, gender, and culture. The Cape Verdean community serves as a model to explore the intersectionality of race, ethnicity, culture, gender, and disability. The study shows how culture interacts with and often contradicts mainstream disability philosophy and service practices. Cultural competency protocols are often developed with a one-size-fits-all approach, which excludes the needs of most women and particularly those from the Cape Verdean community.

Health Promotion for People with Disabilities: Implications for Empowering the Person and Promoting Disability-Friendly Environments by James H. Rimmer and Jennifer L. Rowland discusses the importance of improving long-term health for people with disabilities. People with disabilities experience poorer health compared to those without disabilities, which puts additional burden on health status. Designing health promotion programs for people with disabilities must consider their chronic conditions as well as personal and environmental factors that may enhance and impede people with disabilities' ability to participate in health promotion activities.

In *Mad Women or Mad Society: Towards a Feminist Practice with Women Survivors of Child Sexual Assault*, Fiona Rummery explores the differences between a feminist counseling practice approach and the more traditional medical model for women dealing with sexual assault. Rummery suggests that the traditional medical model has more of a narrow and rigid structure; whereas the feminist approach is "flexible and evolving, and involves as much an analysis of one's self, as that of the women with whom one is working." The feminist approach is client focused and values a collective versus hierarchical structure. In contrast to the medical model where the professional is the expert, having the scientific tools and language, the feminist perspective allows the client to be a partner in the process and lead it as needed. This truly gives survivors back the control they lost during abuse and the opportunity to lead an empowered life.

In *Preventing Suicide Among Older Adult Asian Women*, K. O. Cao presents findings on a citywide study conducted in New York City on prevention and public awareness about depression, mental illness, and suicide among the Asian population. The article discusses the lack of information and research about Asian women and the various organizations engaged in a community outreach campaign to reach older women in culturally and linguistically diverse Asian communities. The best way to reach community members was through trusted relationships such as family members, caregivers, primary care physicians, and social workers. Community networks such as media outlets and using other video can help raise awareness about depression and provide opportunities for elders to seek assistances. The campaign was seen as being successful for raising awareness about a topic that is so often hidden.

The Paradox of Powerlessness: Gender, Sex, and Power in 12-Step Groups by Sandra L. Herndon explores the basic principles of twelve-step programs that include gender inequality. She encourages alternative features to the programs that support a balance of power, change of language, and that steps be taken to "rid twelve-step groups of destructive gender inequality."

The chapter ends with Donna Marie Cole's article on HIV/AIDS. In *"If They Had a Cure I Would Not Take It": African American Women Living with HIV/AIDS*, Cole shows that healthcare providers must understand how the historical legacy of racism, segregation, and health beliefs impact study participants' choice to use alternative methods over anti-retroviral medication in managing their HIV/AIDS. Healthcare providers must recognize that this alternative approach is not taken lightly, but is an empowered choice.

 # A Cape Verdean Perspective on Disability: An Invisible Minority in New England

by Dawna M. Thomas

Abstract The disability rights movement has brought about broad change in what we see today socially in our imagination and pragmatically within the political landscape. Specifically, it has challenged what it means to be human and what it means to have the right to exist within a social democracy based on principles of equality. Yet the disability rights movement has paid little attention to how disability is understood within culturally diverse communities. Often culturally competent models have a "one-size-fits-all" approach that potentially contributes to disparities. In service delivery. This approach generally ignores ethnic distinctions within broad racial/ethnic categorizations such as black Americans and Latinos. The Cape Verdean Women's Project explores the population of Cape Verdeans in the United States. Findings indicate that they are not only often culturally misidentified but also misunderstood especially as it relates to issues of disability. This study demonstrates how race, gender, and culture interact and often contradict mainstream disability philosophy and service practices.

Introduction

The disability rights movement brought about wide, sweeping social changes. It won hard-fought legislative policies to protect and elevate the rights of those within the disability community, demanding their full inclusion in American society (Berger 2013; Scotch 1998; Smart 2009). It emphasized "culturally competent" service delivery. These are, for example, models of disability service created or adapted to appreciate the values, traditions, and understandings of specific racial and ethnic communities. Yet its impact has not been equitable across groups (Fujiura and Drazen 2010; McDonald et al. 2007; Olney and Kennedy 2002; Smedly et al. 2003; Vernon 2005). In particular, race, ethnicity, gender, and socioeconomic factors (SES) seem to affect service delivery (Fujiura and Drazen 2010; National Council on Disabilities 1993).

Often, culturally competent models have a "one-size-fits-all" approach to service delivery for racially and ethnically marginalized communities such as black Americans and Latinos. Race, ethnicity, and sometimes common histories of slavery and colonialism place many marginalized groups within one or both of these broad demographic categories. Despite the intent, many cultural competency models fail to capture adequately the culture or ethnic variation within these umbrella demographic categories. Consequently, some populations are mazginalized and rendered invisible even among the larger marginal classification.

The Cape Verdean Women's Project explores the relationship between race, gender, culture, and disability within the U.S. Cape Verdean community. Earlier research tells us that, despite the Cape Verdeans' long history of immigration to the United States dating back to the middle 1800s, they continue to be culturally misidentified and misunderstood by the mainstream disability community because of the "one-size-fits-all" approach to understanding their history, traditions, and contemporary circumstances. Current findings take us a step further in understanding the impact of mainstream disability philosophy and practices. Specifically, it seems that the perception of disability in the Cape Verdean community presents contradictions between social stigma and acceptance,

gender roles and functionality, and presents a cultural barrier with the mainstream disability service systems. Overall, findings offer greater understanding of the complexities of ethnicity, gender, and disability among Cape Verdeans in the United States and an opportunity for development of more nuanced support protocols for those with disabilities and their families.

A Western/American Perspective of Disability

Today's disability community celebrates the uniqueness of people with disabilities and their right to choose their own destiny. This includes all the challenges and successes that choice may bring. This Western/American worldview of disability is one that embraces and promotes a philosophy of independent living and a model of self-determination (Hahn 1985; Scotch 1998; Smart 2009). This independent living philosophy is the cornerstone of the disability service system, and it represents the mainstream disability community. It encourages consumer involvement and control and is aimed at empowering a group of people who have, historically, held a subordinate status within society. Yet this mainstream philosophy may, in some ways, contradict practices within racial/ethnic groups, especially those that emphasize privacy and have a more protective view of those with disabilities. From the mainstream view, such approaches are a continuation of the paternalistic and disempowering practices of the past (Rundle and Robinson 2002; Thomas et al. 2010). However, this incongruity is primarily due to how little mainstream researchers and practitioners understand about cultural diversity within racial and ethnic communities and how members within them have been marginalized in society due to racism, sexism, and homophobia.

Historically, disability theories, concepts, and practices have been grounded in defining the differences between what it means to be normal versus abnormal in a society focused on functionality and productivity (Davis 2006; Hahn 1985; Smart 2009). The social model of disability suggests that the problem with having a disability is not with the individual or having a disability; rather, it is the "socially imposed barriers—the inaccessible buildings, limited modes of transportation and communication, the prejudicial attitudes—that construct disability as a subordinate social status, and devalued life experience" (Berger 2013, 27). The social model of disability represents a paradigm shift from the biomedical model and paternalistic perspective that viewed people with disabilities as nature's flaws, mishaps, and abnormal beings. This viewpoint by society either bestowed pity on people with disabilities or demonstrated fear that led to many being institutionalized, sterilized, and/or hidden away from society (Berger 2013; Shakespeare 2006; Smart 2009). Disability studies is a growing field of scholarship with new voices; however, the social model of disability, as well as disability service systems, continues to be centered within Western/American individualism, individual achievement, and meritocracy. Western/American individualism is a grounding prong of policy and service delivery development where self-determination and independence have become the expectation within the disability community and service delivery to those in it (Hahn 1985; Scotch 1998; Smart 2009). It is based on the characteristics that support an ideal that children move away from home and seek individual achievement as soon as they become adults. Harry (1992) suggests that this Western/American ideal contrasts with a collective community environment that not only includes differences in how families live and work with each other, but the realities of being an oppressed member of society. Thus, within the intersection of disability and race, the disability community has become the oppressor as well as the oppressed in American society.

In addition, the disability political platform has largely focused on the idea that having a disability is universal and those with disabilities would have the shared experiences of discrimination based on ableism (Hahn 1985; Hahn and Belt 2004; Scotch 1998; Smart 2009). The disability community has emerged as a cultural group with a social identity redefining what it means to have a disability. "Disability Power" and "Disability Cool" embraces self-determination, a sense of belonging, disability pride, community engagement, political activism, and solidarity (Hahn 1985; Hahn and Belt 2004; Linton 1998; Zola 1993).

Gender, Race, and Disabilities

The disability community (for example, disability studies and service providers) is limited in its investigation of intersecting identities such as gender, race, and sexual orientation. This view is similar to the early feminist movement where sexism was thought to unite all women in the fight for gender equality (Collins 2009; hooks 2000). Both social movements ignored racial and cultural communities' experiences with sexism and racism. In addition, under the umbrella of identity politics, identity was recognized as not standing alone but as being an integral aspect of the "self". Identity is thought to be fluid, often shaping and being shaped by the relationship to others (Groce and Zola 1993). Multiracial, multicultural, and black feminist perspectives recognized the intersectionality and multiplicity of identity, personhood, and oppression. They brought to the forefront the concepts of interlocking systems of oppression with sexism, racism, and homophobia (Collins 2009; books 2000; Thompson 2002).

In addition, Annamma et al. (2013) propose a new theoretical approach within the disability studies field by combining critical-race theory and disability studies. They suggest that racism and ableism are interdependent forces that operate in "neutralized and invisible ways, to uphold the notions of normalcy" (Annamma et al 2013, 11). This multiple layering effect has been described in many ways, such as being a double or triple whammy and/or jeopardy, referring to the disadvantaged position in society where racism, sexism, and ableism overlap and intersect (Annamma et al. 2013; Vernon 2005). These theoretical frameworks point out important realities for people with disabilities from culturally diverse communities, people who are so marginalized by the ableism and racism of the broader society that they become virtually invisible socially even within their own community. As a result, social hierarchy is produced and reinforced between the oppressed and oppressor: abled-bodied and those disabled, white and black, female and male, and straight and gay. Groce (2005) argues that all people are members of a social universe, and this wisdom should be integrated into the disability community rather than be ignored.

The Cape Verdean Women's Project

The framework for the Cape Verdean Women's Project (CVWP) draws on multiracial, multicultural, black feminists, and critical-race theoretical perspectives to examine the disability experience within the U.S. Cape Verdean community. The population provides the setting for a deeper conversation on the intersectionality of race, gender, and disability in the context of multiple levels of oppression that can be seen in other culturally diverse communities.

Brief Research Description

The data for the CVWP grew from the author's community advocacy work, as well as an earlier qualitative study titled "Understanding Disability in the Cape Verdean Community: An Analysis of Disability and Race in Massachusetts."[1] The earlier study was an exploration of how U.S. Cape Verdeans conceptualized "illness" and "disability". It consisted of fifty-nine participants from Cape Verdean families and service providers, some of whom were a part of the disabilities community. Findings suggested that U.S. Cape Verdeans and social service providers perceived considerable obstacles to service delivery because they are often misunderstood. The CVWP[2] was developed from qualitative interviews with fifty Cape Verdean women in New England from the ages of eighteen to eighty. Interview questions were designed to elicit women's perceptions, understandings, and practices with regard to immigration, family life, marriage, domestic violence, healthcare and disability, and concepts of womanhood. The overarching goal of this later project was to gain an in-depth understanding of the experiences of Cape Verdean women, which seemed to be lacking in the earlier research.

Similar to the first project, a variety of disabilities were represented—learning disabilities, multiple sclerosis, and depression. Participants were also drawn from southeastern New England, which has the largest Cape Verdean populations in the United States. Educational levels in both studies range from no high school, high school/GED, some college, college degree, to postgraduate studies (Master's, PhD, MD).

Research procedures adhered to strict protocols with informed consent, and all interviews and focus groups were audio recorded. Data analysis included independent reviews of all transcripts by the principal investigator, followed by ongoing collaboration with research assistants to determine emerging themes, which were coded and categorized (Creswell 2007; DeVault and Gross 2012; Krueger 1997).

In addition to the qualitative research, this article draws on ethnographic data collected during the author's many years of community work as a cofounder of Common Threads (CT), a community-based advocacy group.[3] Common Thread's goal is to link generations of Cape Verdeans in the United States through community conferences that bring service providers and educators together. Past conference themes included health care, disability, cultural identity, immigration, family violence, violence among youth, and economic empowerment. Both immigrants and nonimmigrants participated in this project and attended the conferences.

The themes that emerged from interview and ethnographic data were, in many ways, consistent with data collected in earlier work. That is, culturally competent protocols have been implemented as a standard of care in most, if not all, disability service systems. A lack of understanding about the Cape Verdean culture continues to create barries for effective service delivery, even after the development of research on this particular population. However, the newer data tells us that women seem to experience some issues of disability differently from men. Further, they expressed understandings that further nuanced contradictions embedded in the culturally competent models for marginalized populations.

Brief History of Cape Verdeans in the United States

All too often, mainstream disability service system models and researchers rely on quantitative information that is focused on specific objectives, and service providers typically have little time to invest in establishing a comprehensive history of the people they serve. However, understanding U.S. Cape Verdeans with disabilities and subsequently creating culturally competent models of service, first requires knowledge of the community's homeland

and its location, their complex history of colonialism, the slave trade, independence, and their migration to the United States.

Although Cape Verdeans have been immigrating to the United States since the 1800s, service providers typically do not know where Cape Verde is, how Cape Verdeans came to be in the United States, and/or who Cape Verdeans are—and indication of why this group is so little understood and, therefore, underserved. Once an uninhabited set of islands, Cape Verde's, history begins with the Portuguese settlers and their slave trade in the 1400s (Appiah and Gates 1999; Davidson 1989; Lobban 1995). Cape Verde is a remote set of islands located approxiamately three to four hundred miles off the coast of West Africa near Senegal in the Atlantic Ocean (Lobban 1995; Lobban and Saucier 2007). Twenty-one islands make up Cape Verde, of which ten are inhabited and divided into two regions—Barlavento/Windward Islands and Ilhas Do Sotavento/Leeward Islands. Cape Verde became an independent and free country on July 5, 1975. It has advanced from being categorized as an underdeveloped country with a past shaped by feudalism, slavery, and oppression, to a middle-income country, at least when compared to other sub-Saharan African countries (Lobban 1995; Lobban and Saucier 2007).

Cape Verdean Migration to the United States

An important step in developing tools of cultural competency is being aware of the cultural differences between the most recent immigrants versus those who entered the United States over one hundred years ago. Cape Verdeans' immigration journey to the United States is best understood in three phases: the whaling era of the mid-1800s, the postcolonial era beginning in the 1970s, and the post-9/11 era.

During the whaling era, Cape Verdean men traveling on Portuguese whaling vessels landed on the shores of Massachusetts and Rhode Island. These men were known for their maritime skills and traveled on whaling ships in many capacities from captain to seamen. Women would follow the men to the United States, and together they were some of the earliest migrant laborers in southeastern New England, working in the blueberry fields, cranberry bogs, factories, and homes as housekeepers

(Carling 2003; Halter 1993; Lobban and Saucier 2007). The postcolonial era started in the 1970s shortly before Cape Verde gained its independence from Portugal and continued to more recent times (Lobban and Saucier 2007). Since 9/11, Cape Verdeans immigrating to the United States have been hindered by stricter guidelines and procedures regarding visas and traveling papers. These three discrete phases of immigration have resulted in two Cape Verdean communities; they share one culture but have unique social and political histories that influence their acculturation experiences in the United States, their relationship to Cape Verde, their racial and ethnic identity development, and the perception of others. Knowledge of these social, cultural, and historical elements of this population is important for an appreciation of the critical cross-cultural connections that may support efforts toward culturally competent service provision (Sanchez et al. 2002; Sanchez and Thomas 2000; Thomas et al. 2010).

Cape Verdean Identity: Between Race and Ethnicity

U.S. Cape Verdeans see themselves in diverse ways and this diversity has been confusing to many other Americans. All sorts of factors influence identity development, but most importantly among them are their experiences of acculturation, assimilation, rejection, stigma, race, and racism within the broader society. Halter (1993) notes that Cape Verdean identity development requires its own epistemology, centered within their historical experiences with Portuguese colonialism and immigration to the United States. Thus, how Cape Verdeans identify themselves is, in many ways, related to their immigration experiences and relationships to both Cape Verde and the United States (Halter 1998; Lima 2012; Sánchez-Gibau 2005a, 2005b; Thomas 2001).

For example, immigrants of the whaling era came to the United States under Portuguese colonial rule; therefore, they identified themselves as Portuguese. Their African cultural roots had long been suppressed and overshadowed by racism, fear, and stigma. In addition, they entered the United States in the 1800s, a time of racial strife and tensions over slavery, which conflicted with their Portuguese identity. Later, during the civil rights era, many Cape Verdeans, by contrast, embraced their African heritage and identified as black.

During the postcolonial era, immigrants entered the United States as Cape Verdean people free of Portuguese rule and identified themselves as such. However, Cape Verdeans today, like those in the past, continue to struggle with the black and white binary racial categories used to identify people in the United States (DeAndrade 1997; Halter 1998; Sánchez-Gibau 2005a, 2005b). Cape Verdean immigrants seem reluctant to be defined by strict racial categories. In addition, many seem to not quite comprehend the basis of discrimination based on race as it relates to skin color (Lima 2012; Thomas 2001). Cape Verdeans do not see themselves in terms of skin color or race. In Cape Verde (the islands), the concept of race is not defined by the narrow parameters of black and white, nor is skin color an indicator of group membership. Lima (2012) suggests that skin color is not a determinate to social mobility, success, and/or discrimination, nor are people grouped into or divided by categories based on skin color.

However, Cape Verdeans new to the United States, experience a harsh reality of racialization in American society when they try to fit into a system where race is a prominent factor in identity development and socioeconomic success. For example, a respondent in the earlier project noted, "I am of the same mother and father, yet I am black and my brother is white on paper. On the birth certificate he is white and I am black, society does that" (Thomas 2001, 141). This theme reoccurs in the CVWP study as indicated when a young woman expressed the following: "Why are we always challenged to be a race? When I say I am black, they say, no, you're not; look at your hair, it is straight; look at your mother, she too light. But why can't I be Cape Verdean *and* black? Who says I have to choose?"

These sentiments illustrate the complexities surrounding race in a race- and color-conscious America. Unlike the definitions and racial markers used in the United States, Cape Verdeans (both immigrants and nonimmigrants) are a group with diverse cultural roots with multiethnic, multiracial, and multicultural thoughts and practices. Thus, their physical characteristics vary greatly. They have no single set of common physical markers (for example, hair texture, eye color, skin color). This variation has occurred within families and throughout generations. Yet Cape Verdeans become racialized in the United States and are often misidentified as being members of various groups, such as Latinos, whites, and blacks (Lima 2012; Thomas et al. 2010).

Cape Verdeans also see themselves, in many ways, influenced by their acculturation experiences in America and Cape Verde. Thus, they tend to identify themselves as African, black, Cape Verdean, African American, and other, irrespective of the many common racial and ethnic features used to describe similarity in American society (Halter 1998; Lima 2012; Thomas 2001). Being misidentified within American society continues to be problematic and leads to inaccurate data collection and representation. DeAndrade suggests that "the confusion about Cape Verdean racial identity highlights the fact that race is not simply a single inherited trait, but a collection of physical and social characteristics that are interpreted together" (1997, 25).

Certainly, Cape Verdeans' experiences are similar to other culturally diverse groups whose historical dynamics with slavery, colonialism, inter-racial relationships, and migration all contribute to a cultural identity where physical attributes fall outside the binary racial categories of black and white. For example, Cape Verdeans' experiences may be similar to other culturally diverse groups (such as Latinos) whose population of mixed heritage emerged out of colonization and oppression by whites (Chavez-Dueñas et al. 2014; Chong 2002). However, there is much diversity among the Latino community, for example, in terms of country of origin, language, food, and histories. Nonetheless, they are a community that is widely recognized by the broader American society. In comparison, the Cape Verdean population in the United States is relatively small, and they are often mistakenly categorized as Latinos, which essentially renders their experience invisible and reinforces their marginal status.

Cape Verdeans who live in Cape Verde may experience other social markers, such as class, that divides them internally, but they do not seem to share the problematic issues of skin color or colorism that exists in many Latino cultures. Still, as

Cape Verdeans assimilate more into the American society that is fraught with racist ideology and practices, they experience pressures of racism from the broader community and prejudice from other culturally diverse groups. This may contribute to internalized racism and colorism that can divide those with lighter and darker skin. These challenges that Cape Verdeans, Latinos, and black Americans, and other culturally marginalized racial/ethnic groups experience are typically the results of a system of social hierarchy, domination, oppression, and subordination all based on the socially constructed concept of race, which, in turn, determines "who is who" (Lee 1993; López 1996; Omi and Winant 1994). As a result, Cape Verdeans often become marginalized from even the broader racial/ethnic categories in which they are placed because they do not seem to have a recognizable and accepted group identity. Therefore, they exist under a cloud of "otherness" (Sanchez et al. 2002; Thomas et al. 2010).

Consequently, culturally competent models cannot lump Cape Verdeans into a category with Latino groups just by assuming the groups have similar histories with oppression and racism. A fundamental principle shared among multiracial, multicultural, black feminist theorists is that each group has its own history and experiences with oppression and discrimination that deserve to be recognized (Collins 2009; hooks 2000; Thompson 2002).

The Cape Verdean Culture

The diversity in the Cape Verdean culture, language, and other communication systems is deeply rooted in the social transformation caused by slavery, Portuguese colonialism, independence, and U.S. immigration. Portuguese continues to be the official language of Cape Verde. Creole is a mixture of the various African dialects and Portuguese language that is shaped by each island's cultural nuances and is the language spoken around most dinner tables (Lobban and Saucier 2007). Creole emerged out of the oppressive conditions enforced by the Portuguese, who restricted and suppressed much, if not all, of Cape Verdeans' African heritage. Creole is not just about language and communication, however; it is a vital feature in Cape Verdean identity for both those living in the United States and Cape Verde: "The term Creole embodies the

Cape Verdean identity and defines Cape Verdeans as people" (Lima 2012, 9). Thus, the Cape Verdean population in the United States represents many different generations since the whaling era, and multiple languages are spoken. Therefore, when service providers conduct needs assessment procedures, they must take into account Cape Verdean Creole as a part of identity development as well as language competence with Cape Verdeans.

Another aspect of U.S. Cape Verdean culture is how they communicate. By this, I mean not only spoken and written language but, more broadly, how people interact with one another. In general, research suggests that Cape Verdeans are more reserved and indirect in their communication style compared to the relatively more assertive and direct styles used in American culture (Lima 2012; Lobban and Saucier 2007; Rundle and Robinson 2002). In addition, U.S. Cape Verdeans tend to follow more formal conventions in their social interactions with others, particularly those in authority (for example, using titles to show respect) than do their Anglo U.S. counterparts. For the most part, Cape Verdeans are reserved, expressive, and very private, especially regarding medical and disability issues. Sometimes their need to keep things private is misinterpreted as disinterest and/or resistance by others such as disability service providers (Rundle and Robinson 2002; Thomas 2001, 2009; Thomas et al. 2010).

Gender and Cape Verdean Family Life

The Cape Verdean family is described as being composed of both close blood relatives and extended community members. Family life is centered within deep traditional values, and, for many, this includes close ties to Cape Verde (Lima 2012; Lobban 1995; Rundle and Robinson 2002; Thomas 2001). Extended family members, such as aunts, uncles, cousins, godparents, and grandparents, play a fundamental role in the family. Often, both in the United States and in Cape Verde, extended family members will assist in rearing children and caring for elders or those with illness and disabilities. Strict codes of behavior pervade these family and community groupings, meaning children are expected to respect and obey parents, their elders, and those in authority, including teachers, doctors, and priests.

Migration has had a significant impact on the Cape Verdean family both in the United States and Cape Verde. Lobban (1995) describes Cape Verdean people as Cape Verde's largest export. As a result, historically, many families have been separated due to migration, which, for some families, has lasted for long periods of time. This family separation has been a major factor reinforcing the need for an extended family that provides emotional, spiritual, financial, and physical support in the day-to-day caring for the family.

In terms of gender, for the most part, traditional patriarchal culture is the standard. Male power and authority seem to prevail for families in both Cape Verde and the United States (Lima 2012; Thomas 2009, 2013). In Cape Verde, Lobban noted, women are often considered the "bedrock of Cape Verdean society, especially in terms of preservation of linguistic skills, handicrafts, food preparation, and family solidarity" (1995, 8). They bear the responsibility for the majority of home life, including caring for elders, children, and those with disabilities and illnesses. Male emigration from Cape Verde has had a significant impact on women's roles in the family and community. Women have often assumed both financial and social responsibilities for the home, which gives them a certain level of autonomy and power. Women in both the United States and Cape Verde seem to accept their roles with self-respect and authority. In the past, according to the work of Stephanie Urdang,[4] women in Cape Verde suffered from the triple oppression of colonialism, racism, and male supremacy. In more recent times, it seems women in Cape Verde have made great progress. As Cape Verde has gained economic and social prosperity, women have advanced in education, hold more political offices, and run more businesses.

In the United States, Cape Verdean women have made similar gains with regard to advancements in education and economic prosperity. A participant in the CVWP described Cape Verdean women (in the United States and Cape Verde) in the following way: "A good Cape Verdean woman is like our mothers and grandmothers who take care of the house, husband, children, but she now has a Masters Degree, and she is a lawyer, a doctor." This was also a common theme in earlier data and in ethnographic observations. However, despite women's gains in Cape Verde or the United States, women

share in a social duality. Their emergent leadership and authority coexist with strict patriarchal gender roles; that includes the experience of abuse at the hands of men (Rundle and Robinson 2002; Thomas 2013). These are important features to understanding the intersectionality of disability, culture, and gender, which I discuss in more detail later.

Religion is another important element in the Cape Verdean community; for many, it has a significant influence on their health and disability beliefs and behaviors. U.S. Cape Verdeans are primarily Catholic, and it is not unusual for family members to seek out healing priests, herbs, and other home remedies for illness (Rundle and Robinson 2002; Thomas et al. 2010). Service providers from beyond the Cape Verdean community must, therefore, be open to how their clients use alternative modalities in their healing processes.

Disability in the Cape Verdean Community

The concept of disability is not as well defined, politically and socially in the Cape Verdean community as it seems to be in the broader society. Despite Cape Verdeans' acculturation experiences in the United States, disability remains a private matter not readily or openly discussed (Sanchez and Thomas 1997; Thomas 2001, 2009). The limited knowledge and misinterpretation of Cape Verdean's attitudes and practices with regard to disabilities, on the part of Western/American society and service providers, may lead to disparities in service delivery.

As an example, "disabilities," as both a term and concept, is not well understood by many Cape Verdeans in the United States and even less well in Cape Verde. The term *disability* is not easily translated into Portuguese or Creole; instead, the term *dificiencia* is used, meaning handicap person (Whitlam and Pratt 2008). Another term used is *Quitodo*, meaning "poor thing." Actually, *Quitodo* is an umbrella term symbolizing some great tragedy, catastrophic event, or misfortune (Sanchez and Thomas 1997; Thomas 2001, 2009). Responses from participants in the CVWP study indicate that the concepts and terms regarding disability, for example, "disability", "having a disability", or an "individual with a disability" are not common within the Cape Verdean community in the United States. In fact, many U.S. Cape Verdeans and recent immigrants perceive the term *disability* negatively and as reference to a permanent state of being. One participant noted,

> *Disability* is an American term and it has a dark cloud over the person. I don't say my daughter has a disability; I won't say that.

The concept of "illness" or "being sick" is preferred to "disabled" because it is seen as more positive, expresses hope for recovery and for "normal" function in society (Sanchez and Thomas 1997; Thomas 2001, 2009, 2013). Even those families who are involved with mainstream disability service systems struggled with the term *disability*. As one participant in this study suggested,

> I don't see myself as having a disability. It means something negative to me, like there is no hope, being ill or sick gives me hope.

Another explained, "Those with disabilities are a part of the family, but we don't call them disabled. No, that would be wrong."

The difference between types of disabilities was a theme in the CVWP study that was similar to earlier research. For the most part, physical disabilities, it seems, are easier to understand because they are visible and somewhat explanatory relative to emotional/psychological disabilities. Within this population, it is understood that physical disabilities may present obstacles, but they can be overcome or accommodated by a modification to the environment. Thus, physical disabilities are tangible and fixable. In contrast, emotional/psychological disabilities are explained as relatively unpredictable and as mysteries to respondents. Ethnographic observations suggest that issues surrounding depression and mental illness, like disabilities broadly, are considered a private matter.

Despite a philosophy of privacy, professional assistance—such as psychological, psychiatric, or educational services—is not wholly frowned upon. Instead, it is encouraged because it can provide an opportunity to "fix" the problem. In this study, a participant suggested.

> We don't talk about it, but if there is something, anything, try it; let's see if it works. Maybe you don't talk about it because it may not work, but you still try.

Another participant stated,

> I took my son every place, even to Boston, to get help. I didn't sit with the covers over my head, but my father said to keep it quiet.

Ethnographic observations also suggest that those with disabilities are not to be ridiculed, disrespected, or ignored. Instead, there is a cultural and familial obligation to care for people with disabilities or anyone in need. One participant summarized the perception shared by others in the study:

> You know, women take care of everybody, children, sick, elderly, and even other women's children. That is family, and, when I die, my daughters will take care of her brother like me.

This paternalistic view of those with disabilities is contrary to the independence philosophy championed in the current disability community. Attitudes and practices of privacy and familial obligation, then, may create a cultural divide between Cape Verdeans who experience disabilities and the main-stream disability community in the wider United States.

Disability Stigma in the Cape Verdean Community

The question of stigma and discrimination is complex and has to do with cultural codes of behavior and social activism. In general, research findings suggests that U.S. Cape Verdeans perceive disability to be either a blessing from God or a curse from the devil (Rundle and Robinson 2002; Thomas 2001, 2009; Thomas et al. 2010). Both the Portuguese and Creole terms *dificiência* and *Quitodo* evoke stigma and negative perceptions about those with disabilities (Thomas 2001; Thomas et al. 2010). At the same time, Cape Verdeans manifest a complex understanding of disability. As indicated earlier, those with disabilities are not to be ridiculed or excluded from society; instead, they are loved and cared for—yet this happens in private. For example, the following question was posed to participants: "If you had to install a ramp for a wheelchair, where would you put it, in the back or front [of your home]?" The majority of participants in the earlier and current study reported, "In the back because it is a private matter."

However, the concept of "privacy or disability as a private matter" was not perceived as a stigma or discrimination (Sanchez and Thomas 1997; Thomas 2013). Instead, there is an understanding that one does not discuss personal issues in general. This is not particular to disabilities. Those with disabilities are accepted and loved and participate fully in family and community life. One participant explained, "You interact with them like any other member of the family. We are private people and protective." Another stated, "They are your family. You may not talk about the problem, meaning disability, but you just do what you have to".

Yet "privacy" can potentially be misinterpreted to mean that those with disabilities may be subject to isolation from society, which, in the Western/American perception of disability, would be discriminatory. In this view, disability studies scholars, policy makers, and those with disabilities have pointed out that an inaccessible environment isolates people from society and, therefore, discriminates (Shakespeare 2006; Smart 2009; Berger 2013). However, one could argue that those with disabilities in the U.S. Cape Verdean community experience stigma, discrimination, acceptance, love, and care simultaneously and that one does not necessarily cancel the other.

Gender and Disability within the U.S. Cape Verdean Community

The intersection of gender and disability reveals another level of cultural complexity for both women and men with regard to cultural expectations and responsibilities. As with many other culturally diverse communities, the responsibility for Cape Verdean families' well-being and function falls disproportionately on women (Chong 2002; Lima 2012; Magaña and Smith 2006). They are the primary caregivers for those with disabilities in the family and provide care out of cultural expectation. As one participant in the CVWP suggested,

> The strong values and the strengths that Cape Verdean women have is without a doubt a part of our community. It is who we are. We are very strong women emotionally and physically. And emotionally we get strength from the whole family and can be the caregiver for many people; I think it is a virtue we have.

But the issue of care is especially challenging for women who experience disabilities themselves. What happens to the woman with a disability who is primary caretaker for her family? Who takes care of her? How disability is conceptualized depends on the type of disability and whether it interferes with women's or men's ability to function in the community. For example, many of the participants in the study suggested that having a disability was not a problem for a woman if she could continue to take care of her family, even if she had help from other women. This sentiment was expressed primarily from the older women in the study, and the younger women suggested that there is an intersection of sexuality and disability that people do not talk about. They indicated that a disability would not be a burden if a woman is still sexually appealing and could obtain a husband who would then take care of her and the family. However, the participants were not specific on the "type" of disability. One study participant offered a statement that summarized what was reported by others:

> If she can still take care of the things a woman does in the family, then she won't have a problem, but say she is in a wheelchair and she can't move or if she acts weird—you know, her personality is bad—then maybe her family takes care of her.

Also, participants suggested that a woman's husband would care for her if she had a disability if *he* had help from other women in the family. A respondent offered the following: "It all depends. There are men who don't care about any of that as long as she is a good woman. He will marry her and all the family will help."

Another important theme that emerged out of the study was among women who accepted help from mainstream disability service systems. For them, a major barrier to services for women, and for the family in general, is that mainstream disability service providers do not understand the Cape Verdean culture or how family members interact. A participant noted that

> [t]hey [meaning service provides] just don't understand us. It makes me tired. They don't know about CVs, who we are how we love each other. How we take care of each other, and it is different now. Not

like when I was young when we really stayed together.

All the women in the study agreed that, because women were already socially oppressed, a disability was an additional burden. As one woman explained, "How do we women suffer let me count the ways, there are too many" (Thomas 2001, 2009; Thomas et al. 2010). Women in the study made it clear that they take care of the males in the family and community. According to one respondent, "Men, they do nothing. They are taught not to do anything, so disability does not matter. It is the same, men do nothing."

Therefore, women would take care of the men who have disabilities, or not. Similar to findings from earlier studies, if a man has a disability, it is perceived as being worse than for women, primarily if it impedes his ability to provide for the family. Disability is perceived to emasculate men, who are then relegated to socialize with the women in the household, instead of the traditional male social interactions with other men in both family and social situations. A respondent from the earlier study declared.

> Men are always treated like kings. We do that to them but if he is sick some men don't want to be around because they are afraid [to ask for help]. Men are strong and are afraid, but you need to ask the man. (Thomas 2001, 2009)

These findings demonstrate contradictions between gender and disability. The women all agreed that they are oppressed in many ways and that having a disability would add to their oppression. However, they perceive men with disabilities who could not function in society as being worse off. In general, the complexity of disability in the Cape Verdean community not only includes the concepts that define disability but how gender intersects with oppression and stigma and how all are connected to the way both men and women function and fulfill their cultural roles.

Social Activism in Cape Verde

In Cape Verde, the social activism that surrounds disability political rights is reported in the work of David António Cardoso, the director of the Asso-cição Caboverdiana de Deficientes (Cape Verdean Association of People with Disabilities) (www .acd-cv.org). Cardoso founded the organization and

was largely responsible for the antidiscrimination legislation adopted into the constitution and for developing the legal definitions of disabilities, which are similar to many of those in the United States. The organization is dedicated to disability rights and to raising awareness about disability through Cape Verde's media outlets—radio, television, and the Internet. The association has partnered with a number of organizations throughout Africa, Europe, and the United States to raise awareness of disability and community needs and has been instrumental in changing the perception about what it means to have a disability. In addition, an association for the blind and one for those with cerebral palsy have gained momentum as a result of Cardoso's work.

The U.S. Department of State, Bureau of Democracy, Human Rights and Labor, Country Report on Human Rights Practices (2012) indicated that Cape Verde has adopted antidiscrimination legislation. People with disabilities are protected under section five of Cape Verde's constitution. However, the laws fall short in changing the physical landscape that, some would argue, should include access to public buildings and the provision of other services for people with disabilities. In addition, while the report indicates that there were no cases of discrimination pending in employment or education, at the same time, there was no formalized system in place for complaints to be made. Cape Verde is a young country with only thirty-eight years of independence. In those short years, there has already been great progress in raising awareness about disability and in the development of policies in the midst of major economic, social, and political changes. Cardoso and the Associção Caboverdiana de Deficientes have implemented community-based initiatives that deliver services to families in the cities and in remote locations throughout the islands. Families both in Cape Verde and the United States may consult with *curanderas* or *curlosas*, lay healers, or what we might call shamans. Teas, herbs, salves, and prayer may be used to help those with illness or disability (Rundle and Robinson 2002; Thomas 2001, 2009). For example, one participant reported that her family took her to a healing priest before seeking mainstream disability services. The blend of mainstream services with cultural healing approaches often passed down in the family was not uncommon in the Cape Verdean community during this project (Rundle and Robinson 2002; Thomas 2013). Again, service providers and disability scholars must consider how alternative service approaches, healing methods, and family members' contributions in caring for those with disabilities may play a role in working with both immigrant and nonimmigrant families.

Developing Culturally Competent Concepts

Culturally competent protocols are a fundamental feature necessary to build bridges between underserved populations and mainstream service systems (Balcazar et al. 2010; Lewis and Shamburger 2010; Thomas 2006). It is important for the disability community and service providers to understand the cultural nuances and historical experiences in the Cape Verdean community. Developing culturally competent approaches requires service providers to think outside their comfort zones and make connections with the individual families and clients they serve.

Cultural competency has become a standard of practice for all service providers working in the health and human service industry. Balcazar et al. (2010) points out that cultural competency is important to future service delivery because (1) of the growing cultural diversity in the U.S. population and among those who have disabilities; (2) it addresses disparities and gaps in service delivery; and (3) ignoring cultural differences potentially creates barriers to services and adds to group conflict by reinforcing racism, discrimination, and oppression. While there are many definitions, models, and strategies of cultural competency, the core principles involve linguistically appropriate service delivery, professional development with ongoing training, and hiring staff that reflects the communities being served. In addition, it involves building collaborative relationships with various stakeholders including community leaders, policy makers, and constituents. Organizations are encouraged to engage ongoing research and data collection to assess the things that work and to reevaluate and redesign those that do not. Not only must organizations make a philosophical commitment to being open to such professional development, they must also ensure those commitments have the financial support necessary for success (Jackson 2002; Office of Minority Health 2014; Thomas 2006).

However, Tervalon and Murray-Garcia (1998) note that cultural competency protocols have not addressed the inherent power imbalances in the provider/client relationship. In response, they introduced an alternative model, "Cultural Humility," in which providers "engage in self-reflection and self-critique as lifelong learners and reflective practitioners" (Tervalon and Murray-Garcia 1998, 96). Cultural humility is counterintuitive to much of service provider and disability scholar training, which assumes that education and knowledge lead to expertise. Providers and scholars are encouraged to become experts and share information, but this same training reinforces the inherent power imbalance between client and providers and teacher and student. The golden rule is that those participating in cultural competency training gain knowledge, however, there are no experts in this process (Thomas 2001, 2006; Thomas et al. 2010). Service providers and scholars must relinquish some of their power in order to engage in mutually respectful and collaborative relationships (Tervalon and Murray-Garcia 1998). Therefore, understanding Cape Verdeans' perceptions about disability requires disability scholars and service providers not to dictate concepts and meanings but to evolve with the community to bring about equality for those with disabilities. Cultural humility is a process of transformation for everyone who participates.

Recommendations for Disability Agencies

Working at the Grassroots

Past research, as well as the CVWP suggests that work at the grassroots level in the United States and Cape Verde is essential to achieving real social change and justice. The Western/American sociopolitical concepts of disability have been transported across the globe. There are new legislation, organizations, and changing attitudes in Cape Verde. In the United States, more service delivery agencies are engaged in outreach to the Cape Verdean community. Likewise, in the United States, Cape Verdeans have had long-standing community organizations and groups that provide a wide variety of information on everything from college scholarships, immigration, and housing to employment. These groups fulfill much-needed services for more recent immigrants and nonimmigrants in the Cape Verdean community. Thus, work with grassroots organizations increases awareness of disability and outreach in the Cape Verdean community and benefits both those living in Cape Verde and those in the United States. Not only does it break down barriers and stigma associated with disability, but it educates providers on how to work in and with the Cape Verdean community.

Working with Agencies

Client participation is a core principle for disability service provision. Clients are expected and encouraged to engage fully in their own development. The concept of client participation was developed because people with disabilities often have very little or no control over their own lives. For example, the goal of vocational services is to help clients return to the workforce, which may require education and training programs. Clients are expected to take an active role in developing their Individualized Plan for Employment (IPE).[5] There are similar expectations in education with the Individualized Education Plan (IEP)[6] for children with learning challenges. Both these concepts are important aspects of disability legislation. However, many U.S. Cape Verdeans may not be familiar with the active service participation required in these policies and may misinterpret this more active role in planning. Service providers may be seen as the authority figures in this relationship. Thus, many Cape Verdeans may take a back seat in their development. As a result, the service provider misinterprets this Cape Verdean passive or indirect nature as resistance and disinterest. On the other hand, Cape Verdeans misinterpret the service provider's lack of leadership and authority as discrimination. These misunderstandings not only present barriers to the process but can also cause frustration for both the service provider and the client. Lewis and Shamburger (2010) introduce a three-dimensional model for multicultural rehabilitation counseling that can bridge these cultural gaps between service providers and clients. Their model focuses on (1) cultural identity, (2) state of development with regard to the disability, and (3) adjustment to disability. This model is flexible; encourages counselors to develop a deeper understanding of their clients' race, ethnicity, and culture; and explores what it means to have a disability for that client and how it all might serve the client's best interest. This model provides an opportunity to explore and understand the client being served by building trusting relationships.

Today, there is an ongoing effort to reduce racial and ethnic disparities in health and disability service systems through better data collection. Most in-take and registration forms ask clients to identify both their race and ethnicity. Those who develop such forms recognize that many culturally diverse communities (such as Cape Verdeans) are often not included in much of the data collection procedures. Thus, requesting identity information from the clients themselves ensures accuracy and representation. However, not all health and disability service delivery agencies disaggregate data by ethnicity, and federal census racial categories are the standard commonly used to report consumer/client enrollments. Additionally, Cape Verdeans identify themselves in diverse ways. All these factors contribute to their social invisibility and their marginalized social status. In addition, there is no accurate way to determine the efficacy of disability service delivery systems, and this again reinforces disparities for the Cape Verdean community.

Building Empowerment

Consumer empowerment is another fundamental aspect of disability policy and service delivery. However, empowerment has been associated with the independent living philosophy and model (Smart 2009; Whitney-Thomas et al. 1999), which creates cultural barriers between the mainstream disability community and Cape Verdeans. Empowering Cape Verdeans with disabilities, specifically to become independent, must include a component of interdependence and connection to and work with the community. Disability service providers and scholars need to recognize how marginal communities (such as Cape Verdeans, Latinos, and others) take care of each other not just as a part of their cultural values but because they face discrimination in American society. Culturally diverse communities need culturally appropriate services. Thus, "an interdependence model balances and respects individual needs with the important cultural aspects of family and community" (Thomas et al. 2010, 18) (see table 1). Understanding these differences will lead to more effective community outreach, positive outcomes, and service provisions. Finally, a culturally competent approach in research, community-outreach coalition building, and service delivery involves a lifelong commitment to self-critique and self-evaluation and also recognizes and addresses power differentials between providers and culturally diverse communities including those less well known, such as Cape Verdeans with disabilities and their families.

Table 1. Potential Perceptions regarding Culture and Disabilities Service Delivery System

Service Provision	Cape Verdean Families
Positivistic, scientific basis to assessment/intervention	Spirituality; God's will as a major influence
Nuclear family emphasis	Extended family and community emphasis
Striving toward gender equity	Well-defined gender roles and hierarchical relationships
Monolingual functioning	Bilingual, multilingual functioning
Individualistic achievement	Collective orientation—Family is an extension of community
Personal empowerment	Community/family well-being/love
Disability as diversity	Disability as stigma; misfortune (Quitodo) Deficiência—handicap
Professional as expert	Professionals are experts like parents. Professionals are seen as missionaries of their agency. There must be involvement with community advocates.
General strategies for all children	Culturally specific strategies for all—children, parents, and elders
Open, direct communication	Private, indirect, guarded communication
Disability and special services through formal legal contract	Community assistance through informal relationships
Dependency on agencies	Reliance on family/community supports and connections
Political relationships with societal structures	Beginning of political consciousness around disability issues
Youth-oriented society	Elders as source of wisdom and respect
Formal helping relationships	Relational connections as critical: Becoming a known helper in the Cape Verdean community

Endnotes

I would like to thank the guest editors and reviewers for their helpful comments; the managing editor, Kathryn Vaggalis, for her thoughtful copyediting; and I am especially appreciative of the editor, Jennifer Hamer, who worked with me to edit, refine, and develop the final manuscript.

1. "Understanding Disability in the Cape Verdean Community: An Analysis of Disability and Race in Massachusetts" (CV Disability Study) was a qualitative research project funded by Northeastern University Minority Faculty Development and Massachusetts Developmental Disabilities Council. This project took place in Massachusetts from 1997–2000.

2. "The Cape Verdean Women's Project" (CVWP) was qualitative research project funded by Simmons College Fund for Research. This project took place in Massachusetts and Rhode Island from 2007–10.

3. Common Threads is a grassroots community cultural initiative dedicated to the preservation and celebration of the cultural and historical traditions of the Cape Verdean diaspora in the United States and the transnational Cape Verdean community. Common Threads focuses on linking all Cape Verdean communities in the United States through community conferences that celebrate and preserve Cape Verdean culture. Conferences took place from 1999–2005 in Massachusetts and Rhode Island.

4. See Lobban 1995, 82. See also Lobban 161–45.

5. The Individualized Plan for Employment, an integral component in the Vocational Rehabilitation Act of 1973 and its amendments, is designed to assist clients' return to gainful employment. The plan may

include a wide range of initiatives from vocational training to college education, all focused on gainful employment.

6. The Individual Education Plan, a provision under the individuals with Disabilities Education Act (IDEA) and its amendments, is intended to help children with disabilities reach their educational goals with services designed specifically for the individual's needs.

References

Annamma, Subini Acy, David Connor, and Beth Ferri. "Dis/ability Critical Race Studies (DisCrit): Theorizing at the intersections of Race and Dis/ability." *Race Ethnicity and Education* 16, no. 2 (2013): 1–31.

Appiah, Kwame Anthony, and Henry Louis Gates. *Africana: The Encyclopedia of African and African American Experience.* New York: Basic Books, 1999.

Balcazar, Fabricio, Yolanda Suarez-Balcaza, Celestine Willies, and Francisco Alvarado. "Cultural Competence: A Review of Conceptual Frameworks." In *Race, Culture and Disability: Rehabilitation Science and Practice,* edited by Fabricio E. Balcazar, Yolanda Suarez-Balcazar, Tina Taylor-Ritzier, and Christopher B. Keys, 281–305. Boston: Jones and Bartlett Publishers, 2010.

Berger, Ronald J. *Introducing Disability Studies.* Boulder, CO: Lynne Rienner Publisher Inc., 2013.

Carling, Jørgen. "Cartography of Cape Verdean Transnationalism." *Global Networks* 3, no. 4 (2003): 533–39.

Chavez-Dueñas, Nayeli Y., Hector Y. Adames, and Kurt C. Organista. "Skin-Color Prejudice and Within-Group Racial Discrimination: Historical and Current Impact on Latino/A Populations." *Hispanic Journal Behavioral Sciences* 36, no. 1 (2014): 3–26.

Chong, Nilda. *The Latino Patient: A Cultural Guide for Health Care Providers.* Boston: Intercultural Press, 2002.

Collins, Patricia Hill. *Black Feminist Thought: Knowledge, Consciousness and the Politics of Empowerment.* 2d ed. New York: Routledge, 2009.

Creswell, John W. *Qualitative Inquiry and Research Design: Choosing among Five Approaches.* 2d ed. Thousand Oaks, CA: Sage, 2007.

Davidson, Basil. *The Fortunate Isles: A Study in African Transformation.* Trenton, NJ: Africa World Press, 1989.

Davis, Lennard J. "Constructing Normaicy: The Bell Curve, the Novel, and the invention of Disabled Body in the Nineteenth Century." In *The Disability Reader,* 2d ed., edited by Lennard J. Davis, 3–16. New York: Routledge, 2006.

De Andrade, Lella L. "The Question of Race: Cape Verdean Americans Talk about Their Race and Identity." *Cimboa: A Journal of Letters, Arts and Studies* 4, no. 2 (1997): 23–25.

DeVault, Marjorie L., and Glenda Gross. "Feminist Qualitative Interviewing: Experience, Talk, and Knowledge." *The Handbook of Feminist Research: Theory and Proxis,* 2d ed., edited by Sharlene Nagy Hesse-Biber, 206–36. Thousand Oaks, CA: Sage, 2012.

Fujiura, Glenn T., and Carlos Drazen. "'Ways of Seeing' in Race and Disability Research." In *Race, Culture and Disability: Rehabilitation Science and Practice,* edited by Fabricio E. Balcaza et al., 15–29. Boston: Jones and Bartlett Publishers, 2010.

Groce, Nora. "Immigrants, Disability, and Rehabilitation." In *Culture and Disability: Providing Culturally Competent Service,* edited by John H. Stone, 1–14. Thousand Oaks, CA: Sage, 2005.

Groce, Nora Eilen, and Irving Kenneth Zola. "Multiculturalism, Chronic Illness and Disability." *Pediatrics* 91, no. 5 (1993): 1048–55.

Hahn, Harlan. "Toward a Politics of Disability: Definitions, Disciplines, and Policies." *Social Science Journal* 22, no. 4 (1985): 87–105.

Hahn, Harlan, and Todd L. Belt. "Disability Identity and Attitudes toward Cure in a Sample of Disabled Activists." *Journal of Health and Social Behavior* 45, no. 4 (2004): 453–64.

Halter, Marilyn. *Between Race and Ethnicity: Cape Verdean American Immigrants, 1860–1965.* Chicago: University of Illinois Press, 1993.

———. "Identity Matters: The immigrant Children." In *The Social Construction of Race and Ethnicity in the United States,* edited by Joan Ferrante and Prince Brown, 77–87. New York: Addison-Wesley Educational, 1998.

Harry, Beth. *Cultural Diversity, Families, and the Special Education System: Communication and Empowerment.* New York: Teachers College Press, Columbia University, 1992.

Hooks, bell. *Feminism is for Everybody: Passionate Politics.* Cambridge, MA: South End Press, 2000.

Jackson, Vivan H. "Cultural Competency: The Challenges Posed by a Culturally Diverse Society and Steps toward Meeting Them." *Behavioral Health Management* 22, no. 2 (2002): 20–26.

Krueger, Richard A. *Analyzing and Reporting Focus Group Results.* Thousand Oaks, CA: Sage, 1997.

Lee, Sharon L. "Racial Classifications in the U.S. Census: 1890–1990." *Ethics and Racial Studies* 16, no. 1 (1993): 75–94.

Lewis, Allen N., and Aisha Shamburger. "A Three-Dimensional Model for Multicultural Rehabilitation Counseling." In *Race, Culture and Disability: Rehabilitation Science and Practice*, edited by Fabricio E. Balcazar et al., 229–53. Boston: Jones and Bartlett Publishers, 2010.

Lima, Ambrizeth. *Cape Verdean Immigrants in America: The Socialization of Young Men in an Urban Environment*. El Paso, TX: LFB Scholarly Publishing LLC, 2012.

——. "Creonglish: The New Language Spoken by Capeverdean Creole Speakers in Selected Areas of New England." *Cimboa: A Journal of Letters, Arts and Studies* 2, no. 2 (1997): 22–25.

Linton, Simi. *Claiming Disability: Knowledge and Identity*. New York: New York Press University, 1998.

Lobban, Richard, Jr. *Cape Verde: Crioulo Colony to Independent Nation*. Boulder, CO: Westview, 1995.

——. "A Synthesis of Capeverdean Culture and History." *Cimboa: A Journal of Letters, Arts and Studies* 1, no. 1 (1996): 5–9.

Lobban, Richard A., Jr., and Paul K. Saucier. *Historical Dictionary of the Republic of Cape Verde*. 4th ed. Lanham, MD: Scarecrow Pres, 2007.

Lôpez, Ian Haney F. *White by Law: The Legal Construction of Race*. New York: New York University Press, 1996.

Magaña, Sandra, and Mathew J. Smith. "Psychological Distress and Well-Being of Latina and Non-Latina White Mothers of Youth and Adults with an Autism Spectrum Disorder: Cultural Attitudes towards Coresidence Status." *American Journal of Orthopsychiatry* 76, no. 3 (2006): 346–57.

McDonald, Katherine E., Christopher B. Keys, and Fabricio E. Balcazar. "Disability, Race/Ethnicity and Gender: Themes of Cultural Oppression, Acts of Individual Resistance." *American Journal of Community Psychology* 39, no. 1–2 (2007): 145–61.

Monterio, João, M. "Reflections of Capeverdean Creoleness: Revisiting a Familiar Theme." *Cimboa: A Journal of Letters, Arts and Studies* 4, no. 2 (1997): 19–22.

National Council on Disability. *Meeting the Unique Needs of Minorities with Disabilities: A Report to the President and the Congress*. Report based on a 1990 national conference. "Future Frontiers in the Employment of Minority Persons with Disabilities," March 28–30, 1990. Proceedings of a Conference on Minorities with Disabilities, cosponsored by National Council on Disability and Jackson State University, March 28–30, 1993.

Office of Minority Health. "Assuring Cultural Competence in Health Care: Recommendations for National Standards and an Outcomes-Focused Research Agenda." 2014. http://www.minorityhealth.hhs.gov/templates/browse.aspx?lvl=2&lvllD=15 (accessed April 22, 2014).

Olney, Marjorie F., and Jae Kennedy. "Racial Disparities in VR Use and Job Placement Rates for Adults with Disabilities." *Rehabilitation Counseling Bulletin* 45, no. 3 (2002): 177–85.

Omi, Michael, and Howard Winant. *Racial Formation in the United States: From the 1960s to the 1990s*. New York: Routledge, 1994.

Rundale, Ann, Maria Carvalho, and Mary Robinson M., eds. *Cultural Competency in Health-care: A Practical Guide*. San Francisco: Jossey-Bass, 2002.

Sanchez, William, and Dawna M. Thomas. "Disability and Health Care in the Capeverdean Community: Some Preliminary Findings." *Cimboa: A Journal of Letters, Arts, and Studies* 4, no 2 (1997): 43–47.

——. "Quality World and Capeverdeans: Viewing Basic Needs through a Cultural/Historical Lens." *International Journal of Reality Therapy* 20, no. 1 (2000): 17–21.

Sanchez, William, Dawna M. Thomas, and Ambrizeth Lima, "Special Services and Capeverdean Children: Establishing Culturally Relevant Connections." *Special Services in Schools* 18, no. 1–2 (2002): 21–40.

Sánchez-Gibau, Gina, "Contested Identities: Narratives of Race and Ethnicity in the Cape Verdean Diaspora." *Identities: Global Studies in Culture and Power* 12, (2005a): 405–38.

——. "Disaporic Identity Formation among Cape Verdeans in Boston." *The Western Journal of Black Studies* 29, no. 2 (2005b): 532–39.

Scotch, Richard, K. "Disability as the Basis for a Social Movement: Advocacy and the Politics of Definition." *Journal of Social Issues* 44, no. 1 (1998): 159–72.

Shakespeare, Tom. "The Social Model of Disability." In *The Disability Reader*, 2d ed., edited by Lennard J. Davis, 197–203. New York: Routledge, 2006.

Smart, Julle F. *Disability, Society and the Individual*. 2d ed. Austin, TX: Pro-ED, 2009.

Smedly, Brian D., Adrienne Y. Stith, and Allan R. Nelson, eds. *Unequal Treatment: Confronting Racial and Ethnic Disparities in Healthcare*. Washington, DC: The National Academies Press, 2003.

Tervalon, Melanle, and Jann Murray-Garcia. "Cultural Humility versus Cultural Competence: A Critical Distinction In Defining Physician Training Outcomes in Multicultural Education." *Journal of Health Care for the Poor and Underserved* 9, no. 2 (1998): 117–25.

Thomas, Dawna M. "Culture and Disability: A Cape Verdean Perspective." *Journal of Cultural Diversity* 16, no. 4 (2009): 178–86.

——. "Explorations with Cape Verdean Women: Moving from the Personal to the Political." Unpublished manuscript, last modified September 2013.

——. "Understanding Disability in the Cape Verdean Community: An Analysis of Disability and Race in Massachusetts." PhD diss., Northeastern University, 2001.

——. "Unequal Treatment in Healthcare: Understanding Disparities and What Can We Do." *The Diversity Factor* 14, no. 1 (2006): 5–13.

Thomas, Dawna M., William Sanchez, and M. Joanne Manchle. "Providing Culturally Relevant Vocational Rehabilitation Services to Cape Verdeans with Disabilities." *Journal of Applied Rehabilitation Counseling* 41, no. 4 (2010): 11–20.

Thompson, Becky. "Multiracial Feminism: Recasting the Chronology of Second-Wave Feminism." *Feminist Studies* 2, no. 2 (2002): 337–60.

Vernon, Ayesha. "Multiple Oppression and the Disabled People's Movement." In *The Disability Reader: Social Sciences Perspectives*, edited by Thomas Shakespeare, 201–10, New York: Continuum, 2005.

U.S. Department of the State, Bureau of Democracy, Human Rights, and Labor, 2012 *Human Rights Reports: Cape Verde*. http://www.state.gov/j/drl/rls/hrrpt/2012/af/204100.htm (accessed April 22, 2014).

Whitlam, John, and Lia Correla Raitt. *The Oxford New Portuguese Dictionary*. New York: Penguin Group, 2008.

Whitney-Thomas, J. Jaimie Clulla Timmons, Dana Scott Gllmore, and Dawna M. Thomas. "Expanding Access: Changes in Vocational Rehabilitation Practices since the 1992 Rehabilitation Act Amendments." *Rehabilitation Counseling Bulletin* 43, no. 1 (1999): 30–40.

Zola, Irving K. "Self, Identity and the Naming Question: Reflections on the Language of Disability." *Social Science Medicine* 36, no. 2 (1993): 167–73.

Health Promotion for People With Disabilities: Implications for Empowering the Person and Promoting Disability-Friendly Environments

by James H. Rimmer and Jennifer L. Rowland

Abstract: Developing innovative strategies that promote health among people with disabilities has emerged as an important public health priority. People with disabilities report fewer healthy days than the general population and lower rates of health-promoting behaviors (eg, physical inactivity and poor nutritional intake). One of the major priorities in health promotion for people with disabilities is to prevent secondary conditions. Secondary conditions are health concerns that are not a direct result of the primary disability but rather are acquired at a later time due to lifestyle changes associated with the disability (eg, weight gain, pressure sores, pain, fatigue, depression). It is important for health professionals to recognize that the substantial health disparities that exist between people with and without disabilities requires greater attention to establishing disability-friendly environments that reduce architectural, programmatic, and attitudinal barriers that make it difficult for them to engage in self-initiated health promotion practices. Empowering people with disabilities to self-manage their health requires the full support of community service providers in promoting greater access to all health promotion venues, programs, and services.

Keywords: health promotion; disability; empowerment; environment

James H. Rimmer and Jennifer L. Rowland, *American Journal of Lifestyle Medicine, Vol 2, No 5, Sept-Oct 2008*, pp 409–420. Copyright © 2008 SAGE Publications, Inc. Reprinted by permission of SAGE Publications, Inc.

Many people with disabilities have substantially greater difficulty participating in various types of health-promoting behaviors such as regular physical activity, good nutrition, social activities, regular access to medical care and preventive examinations, smoking cessation classes, and so forth compared with the general population because of limited physical and/or programmatic access to these services and programs.[1-5] Lack of health education and health awareness exacerbates the limited access they have to health care and health care follow-up, creating formidable barriers to effective health promotion practices.[6] The risk to people with disabilities from low participation or adherence to various types of health promotion programs is particularly troublesome, as they report a lower rate of good health[1] and have a higher number of health conditions (eg, spasticity, seizures, pain, fatigue, depression, obesity).[7]

One measure of the importance of this problem is its economic impact. While people with disabilities account for approximately 17% of the non-institutionalized population in the United States, their health care expenditures represent a disproportionately greater percentage of total medical expenditures.[8] Total inpatient and medication costs have also been reported to be higher in people with disabilities compared with the general population,[9] and the lack of accessible health promotion programs and services may contribute to a portion of the differences in health care access and health care utilization.[3,10-17]

There is growing awareness that many health disparities reported among people with disabilities are not necessarily a direct result of having a disability but rather are linked to difficulty accessing community services and programs.[3-18] In the 2005 White House Conference on Aging,[19] experts noted that the lack of appropriately trained health professionals has made it difficult for people with disabilities to self-manage their own health. Physical, programmatic, and attitudinal barriers limit opportunities for participation, thereby increasing health risks among this under-served population.[3,20-22] Compounding the problem is the widely recognized educational achievement gap between people with and without disabilities and the lack of accessible transportation and affordable programs and services, all of which contribute to the ineffectiveness of many health promotion programs offered in most communities to the general public.[23,24]

A critical first step in establishing health promotion programs and services that are accessible to people with disabilities is to understand the dynamic nature between the person and his or her environment.[25] Zola[26] noted that "disabling conditions are not merely the result of some physical or mental impairment, but rather, the fit of such impairments with the social, attitudinal, architectural, and even political environment." A particularly important and distinct area of health promotion directed at people with disabilities is to reduce secondary conditions, improve functional health, and eliminate environmental barriers to community participation.[20,27-32] The recent Institute of Medicine (IOM) report, *The Future of Disability in America*,[22] emphasized the importance of these areas and recommended that Congress fund research on evaluating the effects of secondary conditions that will help guide clinical practice in their prevention and management, and to identify potential environmental contributors to the onset or severity of secondary conditions. The report noted that the environment has a substantial role in facilitating or impeding health among people with disabilities.

Health promotion efforts targeted to people with disabilities can have a substantial impact on improving lifestyle behaviors,[29,33] increasing quality of life,[2,34] and reducing medical costs.[15,16,35] The aim of this article is to make health professionals aware of the growing need to assist people with disabilities in self-managing their own health by creating disability-friendly communities that eliminate the physical, programmatic, and attitudinal barriers that often prevent or limit their participation in many community-based health promotion programs.

Health Disparities in People With Disabilities

People with disabilities, as a group, experience poorer health than the general population. Data from the Centers for Disease Control and Prevention 2001 and 2003 Behavioral Risk Factor Surveillance System (BRFSS) highlight self-reported health status among people with disabilities.[1] As shown in Figure 1, people with disabilities report a substantially lower rate of good health compared with the general population. In Figure 2, people with disabilities report a higher incidence of obesity, smoking, and physical inactivity. The median rate of smoking among people with disabilities is 30.5% compared with 21.7% for those without disabilities. Similarly, people with disabilities are more likely to be obese (median, 31.2%) compared with people without disabilities (median, 19.6%), and people with disabilities are more likely to be physically inactive (median, 22.4%) compared with those without disabilities (median, 11.9%).

Of particular concern is the reportedly higher incidence of obesity observed in people with disabilities.[36,37] As disturbing as the obesity prevalence data are for the general US population, data on persons with disabilities are even more alarming. Two reports on the prevalence of obesity among adults with disabilities show a disproportionately higher prevalence of obesity among adults with disabilities. Weil et al[38] pooled data from the 1994–1995 National Health Interview Survey, the 1994–1995 Disability Supplement, and the 1995 Healthy People 2000 Supplement. Among adults with disabilities, 24.9% were obese compared with 15.1% of people without disabilities. The highest prevalence occurred in adults with lower extremity mobility disabilities. In an analysis by the Centers for Disease Control and Prevention of obesity prevalence data from the 1998 to 1999 BRFSS on people with disabilities,[39] regardless of age, sex, or race/ethnicity, people with disabilities were reported to have higher rates of obesity than people without disabilities.

Although obesity results in significant societal and personal costs for all individuals, among people with disabilities it also reduces or limits opportunities for various types of community participation including employment and leisure activities. Wheelchair transfers, rolling up ramps, walking with a cane or walker, and other essential activities become substantially more difficult in disabled individuals who are also obese. These activities often require greater effort from the caregiver or personal assistant, who must assist the individual with various activities of daily living and instrumental activities of daily living.

Several other reports have noted that people with disabilities have substantially high levels of physical inactivity,[31,40] which predisposes them to a significantly higher incidence and severity of secondary conditions[27,41-44] and, in particular, overweight and obesity.[36,38,45] The environment may also have a substantial negative effect on the health status of people with disabilities. Inaccessibility of the built environment may predispose people with mobility disabilities to remain in their homes for longer periods of the day and subsequently lead to a higher incidence of sedentary behavior and increased caloric intake.

The poorer health status observed among people with disabilities creates an unnecessary burden on the individual, caregiver, and/or other family members.[36] Society is affected by the increased economic costs of supporting health care and community services that may be required, and poor health is known to predict higher rates of unemployment and reduced social participation.[46] These health disparities send a strong message that people with disabilities must be a key target population for broad public health interventions in smoking, obesity, exercise, and other health behaviors.

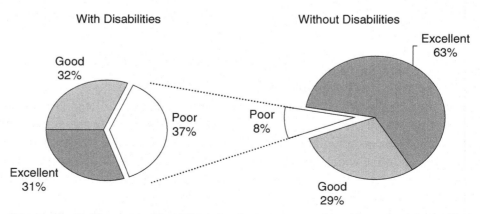

Figure 1. Self-reported health status between people with and without disabilities from the 2001 and 2003 Behavioral Risk Factor Surveillance System.

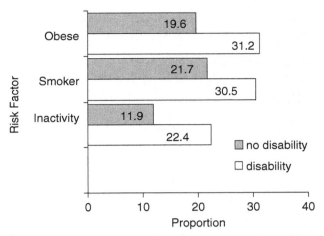

Figure 2. Health risk behaviors and health status between people with and without from the 2001 and 2003 Behavioral Risk Factor Surveillance System.

Barriers to Health Promotion Experienced by People With Disabilities

The creation of universally designed accessible environments that promote independence and community participation among people with disabilities is a critical area of health promotion for this population.[19,22,47,48] Some experts believe that disability is not inherent in the individual but rather the interaction between the individual and his or her environment.[22,25,49] Many different types of inaccessible environments to participating in health-promoting activities by people with disabilities are compounded by architectural, programmatic, and attitudinal barriers.[50] Secondary conditions are exacerbated by environmental barriers that discourage or prevent participation in health promotion activities and present a substantial challenge in altering the built environment for improving access to health-enhancing community activities.[22]

The Americans With Disabilities Act (ADA) provides the legal foundation for ensuring the accessibility of community health promotion programs.[51] Unfortunately, most of these programs are not targeted to the specific needs of people with disabilities, and many people with disabilities do not feel welcome at these facilities.[50] Despite progress in universal design principles and policies, people with disabilities continue to face an enormous array of barriers to participating in self-managed health promotion programs.[34,52] Structures such as parks, recreation and fitness facilities,

grocery stores, and health care facilities are often inaccessible to people with disabilities.[22,48,50,53,54] In the government report *Surgeon General's Call to Action to Improve the Health and Wellness of Persons With Disabilities*,[10] officials noted that more effort must be directed at enhancing the health and wellbeing of people with disabilities by eliminating environmental barriers that make it difficult or impossible for them to have equal access to community activities. The *Healthy People 2010* chapter titled "Disability and Secondary Conditions,"[55] suggests that the significantly lower rate of participation among people with disabilities in health promotion may be related to environmental barriers, including architectural barriers, organizational policies and practices, discrimination, and social attitudes, and recommends that public health agencies begin to evaluate which environmental factors enhance or impede participation.

Despite the enormous health benefits that can be attained from regular physical activity,[56-58] people with mobility disabilities report much lower levels of physical activity compared with the general population,[59] and inaccessibility of the natural and built environments often limits opportunities to participate in various types of recreation, sport, and leisure physical activity in both indoor and outdoor settings. While the general population has access to outdoor physical activity settings such as neighborhood streets, shopping malls, parks, and walking/jogging paths to perform the most common form of physical activity, walking,[60] access to walking for people with mobility disabilities who have difficulty walking (eg, arthritis, extreme obesity, balance impairments, multiple sclerosis, spinal cord injury, limb loss) or cannot walk (eg, some form of paralysis) is often limited by these inaccessible environments.[50] Some streets do not have curb cuts, damaged sidewalks may create a higher risk of falling, walkways or walking paths are too narrow for a wheelchair user and partner to walk side by side, many communities do not have sidewalks, or the terrain's grade or slope is too steep. Other problems with outdoor environments include unsafe neighborhoods, poor weather making sidewalks slippery or impassable, not having enough benches along a trail for people who need frequent rest periods, poorly designated signage, no accessible bathrooms along a trail or path, and no handicapped parking spaces near a trail.[50]

'Health promotion interventions that empower people with disabilities to better manage their health can have a significant impact on health, function, community participation, and quality of life.'

Environmental barriers to nutrition are also commonly observed in people with disabilities. In the United States, obesity and type 2 diabetes follow a socioeconomic gradient, with the highest rates observed among groups with the highest poverty rates and the lowest levels of education.[61-63] Kinne[64] used the term *food deserts* to describe areas in cities where residents without private cars have difficulty accessing supermarkets that have low food prices and wide selections of fresh produce. She found the greatest numbers of food deserts in neighborhoods with the highest concentrations of elderly and disabled individuals. Social isolation, depression, and substance abuse are also associated with poor dietary practices and obesity.[65] These and other characteristics disproportionately affect disabled populations. Weil et al[38] reported that compared with other disabled groups and the general population, individuals with severe lower extremity mobility difficulties had higher percentages of poverty (27% lived in poverty), less education (36% with <12 years), and higher obesity rates and were less likely to attempt weight loss and less frequently counseled by their physicians about weight loss. Other barriers to eating well among individuals with mobility disabilities include being too tired to cook, the higher cost of nutritious foods, difficulty shopping, and not enough time to shop or prepare food.[66-68] Finally, physiologic changes that accompany many types of injuries that cause mobility impairments greatly diminish caloric requirements,[69] although it is common for many individuals to retain preinjury eating habits and calorie intake, leading to excessive weight gain.[68] Collectively, these characteristics and barriers create an environment that predisposes people with disabilities to a higher prevalence of obesity and poor diet quality.

There are several other health promotion domains in addition to physical activity and nutrition that may contain significant participation barriers for people with disabilities. Table 1 lists 15 of these domains and highlights common health behaviors exhibited by many people without disabilities within each domain. The last column lists common personal or environmental barriers that preclude the same level of participation by people with disabilities.

Designing Health Promotion Programs for People With Disabilities: Understanding the Context of Secondary, Associated, and Chronic Conditions

People with disabilities are predisposed to, or at risk for, developing 3 sets of health conditions that must be considered in the design and implementation of health promotion programs. Two of these conditions, secondary and associated, are relevant only to people with disabilities, while the third category, chronic conditions, usually referred to in the medical literature as *comorbidities,* affect the general population. The diversity in health conditions observed in people with various levels (ie, severity) and types (ie, physical, cognitive and sensory) of disabilities requires health professionals to understand the differences between these conditions to develop more effective treatment strategies that consider the effects that one condition (ie, pain) may have on other conditions that the person may be experiencing (ie, obesity, fatigue, type 2 diabetes). Similarly, it is critical to know if a condition such as weakness or fatigue is related to lifestyle factors (ie, physical inactivity) or is directly associated with the disability (ie, multiple sclerosis). Given the importance of various types of health-promoting behaviors in improving health and function, understanding the breadth and scope of each of these conditions is critical for developing successful intervention strategies that complement rather than impede or delay progress.

Secondary Conditions

Since the first definition of *secondary conditions* by the IOM in 1991,[49] several investigators have used the term within a similar framework to describe conditions directly or indirectly associated with a disability and considered preventable.[70-71,73-74] The term grew out of a need to describe conditions that were related to a primary disability or had a substantially higher prevalence in people with disabilities compared with the general population. Since the IOM publication, several federal agencies[28,46] have recommended that one of the major goals of health promotion for people with disabilities is to prevent or minimize secondary conditions. In a report by the IOM,[7]

Workshop on Disability in America, secondary conditions were recognized as a major limiting factor in the promotion of good health, independence, and social integration among people with disabilities. One major recommendation from that report was the need for rehabilitation professionals and health experts to direct more attention toward secondary condition prevention in people with disabilities. This was reemphasized in the new IOM report titled *The Future of Disability in America,*[22] in which recommendations were made to expand the knowledge base about secondary conditions and aging with a disability so that professionals and consumers have a better understanding of how these conditions affect overall health.

There is still some debate as to whether socially related health conditions such as social isolation, lack of access to adequate medical care, or unemployment should be considered secondary conditions. The *Healthy People 2010* report defines secondary conditions more broadly and does recognize that a secondary condition can be physical, psychological, or social: "Secondary conditions are medical, social, emotional, family, or community problems that a person with a primary disabling condition likely experiences." In the same way that more medically related secondary conditions are a direct result of the impairments associated with the primary disability, some professionals suggest that secondary conditions can occur as a result of some barrier or set of barriers in the person's environment (ie, social isolation caused by limitations in access to the built and natural environment).[1,29,31,35,71,74-76] The underlying concept is that secondary conditions are either preventable or can be mitigated by using various types of health-promoting behaviors, using various types of assistive technologies, or providing more enabling environments.

Associated Conditions

Associated conditions are certain aspects or features of the disability and are a direct result of the primary disability.[22] While they are not necessarily preventable, in some cases they can be better controlled or managed to avoid further complications. Examples of associated conditions include seizures, spasticity, incontinence, emotional lability, aphasia, gastrointestinal disorders, visual impairments, autonomic dysfunction, hydrocephalus, and many others. These conditions are often managed with medication, medical devices, cognitive or behavioral therapy, or assistive technologies. Specific examples associated with various disabilities include seizures in persons with cerebral palsy, aphasia in individuals with stroke, autonomic dysfunction in persons with spinal cord injury, hydrocephalus in persons with spina bifida, and visual disturbances in individuals with multiple sclerosis. The primary difference between secondary and associated conditions is the preventable nature of secondary conditions, whereas associated conditions are inextricable from the disease or disablement process.

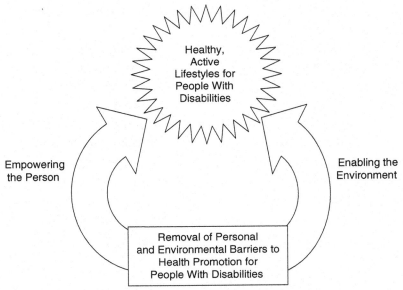

Figure 3. Health promotion program dyad for people with disabilities: empowering the person and enabling the environment.

Table 2. Health Promotion Domains That Can Be Inaccessible to People With Disabilities

Health Domain	General Population	Barriers to People With Disabilities
Exercise	Walking is the most common public health recommendation for physical activity Access to all areas of fitness facility	Inability to walk or difficulty walking because of painful joints (ie, hip pain) Minimal access to certain areas of fitness facility
Nutrition	Choice in eating certain types of foods Obtaining certain nutrients through consumption of vitamins and nutritious types of foods	Lack of dexterity or strength make it difficult to open certain bottles or jars Limited income or gastrointestinal impairment prevent certain foods from being purchased or consumed
Sleep	Regular sleep not affected by secondary conditions associated with a disability	Associated (eg, spasms, incontinence) and secondary conditions (eg, depression, severe obesity) may adversely affect sleep patterns Painful joints may decrease ability to sleep in certain positions and may detract from restful sleep
Social relationships	Accessible and convenient transportation Strong social skills	Lack of accessible transportation Difficulty forming social relationships because of limited social contacts
Relationships with family members	Relationships between family members grow independently	Financial and/or physical dependence on 1 or more family members strains relationships.
Employment	Enjoyable and engaging work Freedom to choose various work settings or change jobs often	Limited opportunities to work Limited work settings available due to functional limitations
Substances	Accessible smoking cessation programs	Materials used in smoking cessation program inaccessible to people with cognitive disabilities or low reading levels
Medications	Limited number of medications used to manage health	Multiple medications lead to further health problems (ie, obesity) and higher risk of overmedication
Hygiene	Simple remedies to maintain good hygiene	Incontinence increases complexity in maintaining good hygiene (ie, odor, skin irritation, increased pressure sore risk)

Table 2. Health Promotion Domains That Can Be Inaccessible to People With Disabilities *(Continued)*

Spirituality	Easy access to materials used in places of worship	No sign language interpreter available during service
Self-efficacy	Opportunities for personal growth enhance self-efficacy	Attitudinal barriers (ie, low expectations) reduce self-efficacy
Sexuality	Common forms of sexual intimacy	Lack of knowledge by health care provider on modifications in sexual intimacy
Stress	Managed through other forms of health behaviors such as exercise and proper nutrition	Limited opportunities to use other forms of health promotion to manage stress
Continued learning throughout the life span	Opportunities to continue lifelong education through various work-related continuing education incentives	Limited opportunities to work results in minimal educational growth
Medical care access	Accessible medical care facilities and affordable health care plans	Limited medical facility access (ie, physician offices, equipment such as examination tables, mammography machines) Low employment rate may reduce quality health insurance

Chronic Conditions

While secondary and associated conditions are a direct consequence of a disability, chronic conditions affect the general population and are usually related to lifestyle and/or environmental factors. Common chronic conditions include hypertension, heart disease, hyperlipidemia, cancer, arthritis, type 2 diabetes, and asthma. People with disabilities may be more susceptible to these conditions because of alterations in lifestyle (eg, increased levels of physical inactivity, weight gain, lack of access to appropriate medical care) related to their disability and/or living arrangement. In some instances, an individual may have been diagnosed with a chronic condition (ie, heart disease, hypertension) before acquiring his or her disability.

A Framework for Improving Health and Reducing Secondary Conditions Among People With Disabilities

A number of short-term studies have demonstrated the beneficial effects of health promotion interventions for people with disabilities.[17,23,29,32,35,77-80] However, most of these interventions were designed in controlled settings to maintain the integrity of the research. A common problem with many health promotion interventions is that their transfer into generic community settings often does not occur because the same level of attention to specific issues associated with the person's disability and/ or inaccessible environment is unavailable.

Figure 3 provides a conceptual framework for designing health promotion programs for people with disabilities emphasizing both personal (empowering the person) and environmental (enabling the environment) factors. The critical nature of this dyad is that both sides must be addressed to achieve optimal health outcomes. For example, a person can be highly responsive to a health promotion intervention (ie, strong personal interest and motivation) but not have an accessible fitness facility near his or her home. Alternatively, an environment may be considered disability friendly, but the person's low exercise self-efficacy or motivational level may reduce his or her participation in the program. To achieve the best outcomes possible, both personal and environmental barriers (illustrated at the bottom of Figure 3) must be eliminated to facilitate higher levels of participation in various types of community-based health promotion programs. Improving one side of the model may have limited or no utility if barriers on the other side are not simultaneously addressed.

Figure 4 presents a contextual model of health promotion for people with disabilities that is composed of 5 key areas. Two primary contributors to the state of health for people with disabilities are (1) personal factors and (2) environmental factors. Personal factors may include the individual's primary impairment and health behaviors such as physical activity and nutrition intake. Environmental factors include built environment accessibility (ie, curb cuts that may impede the ability to travel from one street to the next) or social support and family structures that may be barriers or facilitators to good health. At the bottom of Figure 4 are 3 overlapping circles reflecting the interrelated nature of secondary, associated, and chronic conditions. Although these conditions may be interrelated, they may also represent separate states of health independent of each other.

Empowerment Health

The key feature of empowerment health is to teach individuals with disabilities their rights as a consumer and how they can play an active role in achieving greater access to the health promotion

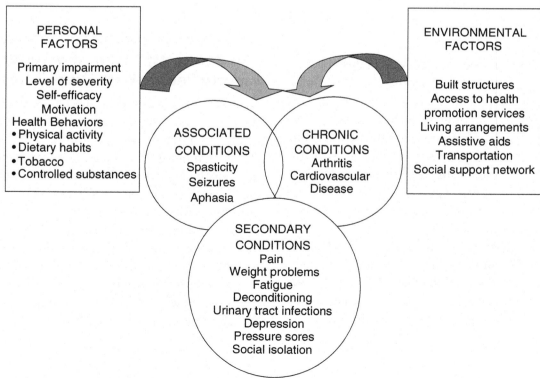

Figure 4. Conceptual delivery model of health promotion for people with disabilities.

programs and services offered in their community.[81-83] Empowerment health for people with disabilities includes 3 general sets of tasks: (1) management of associated conditions (eg, taking medication regularly to control spasticity), (2) reducing or preventing secondary and chronic conditions by engaging in certain health behaviors (eg, increased physical activity), and (3) eliminating environmental barriers that limit access to participation (eg, arranging transportation).[84] These 3 essential features require the collective efforts of the individual, the health provider, and the community at large to ensure that programs and services are accessible to people with disabilities.

Health promotion interventions that empower people with disabilities to better manage their health can have a significant impact on health, function, community participation, and quality of life.[30,35] For example, many individuals with physical disabilities express pain as a major secondary condition.[85] An effective program would provide the person with the knowledge and skills necessary to safely and effectively develop a pain management program that meets his or her needs, possibly through a program that includes medications, appropriate seating and posture, exercise, and relaxation techniques. Table 2 provides examples of possible solutions to health promotion barriers within the context of empowering the person and/or enabling the environment.

A central feature of empowerment health is its basis in individually perceived problems, and it focuses on helping the person overcome barriers by developing problem-solving skills rather than providing formulated solutions or simply offering assistance from a health care provider. By teaching the individual effective strategies for resolving problems or overcoming barriers, empowerment health seeks to increase the person's self-efficacy, which gives the individual a sense of being able to successfully resolve challenges that arise in the course of managing his or her health.[22,34,86-88] It should provide the individual with a sense of assurance that access to health promotion programs are a right and not a privilege and that programs, facilities, and services available and accessible to the general community should be accessible to all persons with disabilities.

Enabling Environments

Throughout history, built social and cultural environments have been created for people without disabilities. It is important for health professionals and public policy makers to recognize that accessible, disability-friendly communities are considered to be part of the ADA. According to Meyers et al,[89] despite passage of the ADA in 1990, access remains an elusive goal and an unkept promise. In addition to the critical need to increase access to the built environment, there is also a tremendous need for more training programs that promote disability awareness and sensitivity, and reduce attitudinal barriers.

The lack of disability-related content in most professional training programs is an enormous problem for providing accessible and effective programs for people with disabilities. One important approach to enabling environments is to include content in health professional training programs that address the needs of people with disabilities. Using person-first terminology, treating all individuals with dignity, and maintaining respect for individual differences are critical for making people with disabilities feel more comfortable in various health promotion settings. Similarly, informing professionals about universally designed products will also help to make facilities structurally more accessible and disability friendly. More and more products are being manufactured using common universal design principles that provide access for a broader group of individuals with disabilities, including accessible medical equipment (ie, examination tables) and exercise products (universally designed exercise equipment). Simpler solutions for enabling environments for people with disabilities include better lighting, larger font sizes on various signage, and rails or steps for hard-to-reach items.

Accessible transportation to get to a fitness or medical facility can be a formidable barrier for many individuals with disabilities.[22,90] Creating accessible transportation options for people with disabilities will result in greater access to health promotion services offered in the community. This access could have a substantial impact on improving health and reducing the risk of secondary and chronic conditions.

Table 2. Empowering the Person and Enabling the Environment: Solutions for Overcoming Health Promotion Barriers

Health Domain	Empowering the Person	Enabling the Environment
Exercise	Seek accessible fitness centers for wheelchair users	Universal design and equipment modifications (ie, adjust height of equipment to accommodate limited range of motion in hips or knees)
Nutrition	Education of acceptable and healthy alternatives to expensive or intolerable food choices Education on availability of assistive devices to perform grocery shopping	Residential facility staff education for healthy food choices when ordering and preparing food Availability of healthy foods in grocery stores; accessibility of these foods both financially and structurally (ie, store shelves and food positioning)
Sleep	Increase understanding of medications to treat symptoms Implement scheduled nighttime bathroom visits or limitation on nighttime beverage intake	Create quiet and comfortable environment (ie, temperature, bedding, ability to transfer independently in and out of bed to toilet at night)
Social relationships	Determine activities of interest and seek participation where others with similar interests may attend	Find accessible public transportation routes or schedule individual pick-up times
Relationships with family members	Self-direct own care through personal assistant Educate person about limitations associated with certain conditions (ie, person with rheumatoid arthritis may have increased pain during the morning, so schedule outings later in the day)	Determine living relationships that minimize conflict and that are convenient for all
Employment	Seek specialized training in field of interest	Determine best fit for accommodating workplace environment based on interests and job skills Design work space to accommodate limitations due to pain or lack of range of motion
Substances	Educate program leaders on ways to make their materials accessible in content and format	Create and distribute accessible materials (ie, large print, audio, Braille) in various community locations

Table 2. Empowering the Person and Enabling the Environment: Solutions for Overcoming Health Promotion Barriers *(Continued)*

Medications	Inform physician of medication side effects	Increased awareness of medication side effects with clear labeling
Hygiene	Set bladder evacuation schedule or coordinate with caregiver to minimize incontinent episodes Use assistive devices (ie, long-handled sponges) to reach difficult areas for washing	Ensure accessible cleansing equipment is available and that individual or caregiver is knowledgeable about use of this equipment/device(s)
Spirituality	Locate accessible places of worship (building entrances, congregation halls)	Educate staff in places of worship on how to make materials more accessible (ie, reading levels, print size)
Self-efficacy	Empowerment through increased access to community and programs of interest	Positive support from staff
Sexuality	Education through social contacts or consumer literature	Access to consumer literature products
Stress	Schedule time in the morning to stretch and meditate using video designed for performing activities in wheelchair	Accessible buildings to healthy services locations (fitness centers, grocery stores, spas)
Continued learning throughout the life span	Seek access to local independent living centers to determine educational opportunities regarding work and health	Improvement in structured/ regular communication with independent living centers
Medical care access	Educate medical office staff on ways to make building and equipment more accessible Investigate health care plan options with independent living centers and disability rights organizations	Improve wheelchair access to health care provider offices Access to adjustable height examination tables and other diagnostic equipment

Conclusion

It is important for health professionals and service providers to recognize the different personal and environmental factors that may enhance or impede participation in health promotion activities among people with disabilities. A truly enabling environment is one in which health promotion programs and services are as accessible to people with disabilities as they are to people without disabilities. Health professionals must also recognize that several personal and environmental barriers not typically reported in the general population (ie, transportation difficulties, inaccessible buildings or structures, lack of staff knowledge on certain accommodations that are needed for managing physical, cognitive, or sensory impairments, etc) are likely to have a negative impact on the person's ability to successfully participate in various kinds of individual and group health promotion activities.

Health promotion for people with disabilities must consist of the following dyad: (1) empowering individuals to self-manage their own health and (2) promoting disability-friendly (enabling) environments that support good health promotion practices in the home, work, and community settings. Within this framework, health promotion programs and services should focus on 3 key areas: (1) reduction or prevention of secondary conditions, (2) improvements in functional health that will allow the person to maintain optimum levels of independence and participation in community activities, and (3) increased access to natural, built, and social environments.

Health promotion has become an important goal in public health and public policy, and reducing health disparities among people with disabilities must be a critical part of this agenda.[10,40] Public health practitioners, health care providers, community organizations, and federal agencies must work together to improve access for people with disasbilities to the tens of thousands of community-based health promotion programs offered throughout the United States and the world.

References

1. Centers for Disease Control and Prevention. *2006 Disability and Health State Chartbook: Profiles of Health for Adults With Disabilities.* Atlanta, GA: US Department of Health and Human Services, Centers for Disease Control and Prevention; 2006.

2. Stuifbergen AK, Becker H. Health promotion practices in women with multiple sclerosis: increasing quality and years of healthy life. *Phys Med Rehabil Clin North Am.* 2001;12(1):9-22.

3. Centers for Disease Control and Prevention. Environmental barriers to health care among persons with disabilities—Los Angeles County, California, 2002-2003. *MMWR Morb Mortal Wkly Rep.* 2006;55:1300-1303.

4. Rimmer JH, Riley B, Wang E, Rauworth A, Jurkowski J. Physical activity participation among persons with disabilities: barriers and facilitators. *Am J Prev Med.* 2004;26(5):419-425.

5. Pierce LL. Barriers to access: frustrations of people who use a wheelchair for full-time mobility. *Rehab Nurs.* 1998;23:120-125.

6. Hughes RB. Achieving effective health promotion for women with disabilities. *Fam Community Health.* 2006;29 (suppl 1):44S-51S.

7. Turk MA. Secondary conditions and disability. In: Field MJ, Jette AM, Martin L, eds. *Workshop on Disability in America.* Washington, DC: National Academies Press; 2006:185-193.

8. Rice MW, Trupin L. Medical expenditures for people with disabilities. *Disability Statistics Abstracts.* 1996;12:1-4.

9. Fried LP, Ferrucci L, Darer J, et al. Untangling the concepts of disability, frailty, and comorbidity: implications for improved targeting and care. *J Gerontol A Biol Sci Med Sci.* 2004:59(3)255-263.

10. US Department of Health and Human Services. *The 2005 Surgeon General's Call to Action to Improve the Health and Wellness of Persons With Disabilities.* Washington, DC: Office of the Surgeon General; 2005.

11. Mitra M, Wilber N, Allen D, et al. Prevalence and correlates of depression as a secondary condition among adults with disabilities. *Am J Orthopsychiatry.* 2005;75:76-85.

12. Becker H, Stuifbergen A. What makes it so hard? Barriers to health promotion experienced by people with multiple sclerosis and polio. *Fam Community Health.* 2004;27:75-85.

13. Scelza WM, Kalpakjian CZ, Zemper ED, Tate DG. Perceived barriers to exercise in people with spinal cord injury. *Am J Phys Med Rehabil.* 2005;84:576-583.

14. Urbina I. In the treatment of diabetes, success often does not pay. *New York Times.* January 11, 2006.

15. Ipsen C, Ravesloot C, Seekins T, et al. A financial cost-benefit analysis of a health promotion program for individuals with mobility impairments. *J Disabil Policy Studies.* 2006;16:220-228.

16. Ravesloot C, Seekins T, White G. Living Well With a Disability health promotion intervention: improved health status for consumers and lower costs for health care policymakers. *Rehab Psych.* 2005;50:239-245.

17. Abdullah N, Horner-Johnson W, Drum C, et al. Healthy lifestyles for people with disabilities. *Californian J Health Promot.* 2004;2:42-54.

18. Harrison T. Health promotion for persons with disabilities. What does the literature reveal? *Fam Community Health.* 2006;29(suppl 1):12S-19S.

19. White House Conference on Aging. Disability and aging: seeking solutions to improve health, productivity, and community living. http://www.whcoa. gov/about/policy/meetings/mini_conf/FINAL%20 REPORT_07_21_05.pdf.

20. Rimmer JH. Health promotion for individuals with disabilities: the need for a transitional model in service delivery. *Disease Manag Health Outcomes.* 2002;10(6):337-343.

21. Lollar D. Public health and disability: emerging opportunities. *Public Health Rep.* 2002;117:131-136.

22. Field M, Jette AM, eds. *The Future of Disability in America.* Washington, DC: National Academies Press; 2007.

23. Rimmer JH, Silverman K, Braunschweig C, Quinn L, Liu Y. Feasibility of a health promotion intervention for a group of predominantly African American women with type 2 diabetes. *Diabetes Educ.* 2002;28(4):571-580.

24. Bell RA, Camacho F, Goonan K, et al. Quality of diabetes care among low-income patients in North Carolina. *Am J Prev Med.* 2001;21(2):124-131.

25. Rimmer JH. Use of the ICF in identifying factors that impact participation in physical activity/rehabilitation among people with disabilities. *Disabil Rehabil.* 2006;28(17):1087-1095.

26. Zola IK. Toward the necessary universalizing of a disability policy. *Milbank Q.* 1989;67(2):2.

27. Coyle CP, Santiago M, Shank JW, Ma GX, Boyd R. Secondary conditions and women with physical disabilities: a descriptive study. *Arch Phys Med Rehabil.* 2000;81:1380-1387.

28. US Department of Education, National Institute on Disability and Rehabilitation Research. *NIDRR Long-Range Plan for Fiscal Years 2005-2009: Executive Summary.* Washington, DC: US Department of Education, National Institute on Disability and Rehabilitation Research; 2007.

29. Seekins T, Traci MA, Szalda-Petree A. Preventing and managing secondary conditions experienced by people with disabilities: roles of personal assistants providers. *J Health Human Serv Admin.* 1999;22:259-269.

30. Rimmer JH, Braddock D. Health promotion for people with physical, cognitive and sensory disabilities: an emerging national priority. *Am J Health Promot.* 2002;16:220-224.

31. US Department of Health and Human Services. *Healthy People 2010: Understanding and Improving Health.* 2nd ed. Washington, DC: Government Printing Office; 2000.

32. Stuifbergen A, Becker H, Blozis S, et al. A randomized clinical trial of a wellness intervention for women with multiple sclerosis. *Arch Phys Med Rehabil.* 2003;84:467-476.

33. Zemper E, Tate DG, Roller S, et al. Assessment of a holistic wellness program for persons with spinal cord injury. *Am J Phys Med Rehabil.* 2003;82:957-968.

34. Nosek MA. Women with disabilities and the delivery of empowerment medicine. *Arch Phys Med Rehabil.* 1997;78(12 suppl 5):S1-S2.

35. Ravesloot C, Seekins T, Cahill T, et al. Health promotion for people with disabilities: development and evaluation of the Living Well With a Disability program. *Health Educ Res.* 2007;22:522-531.

36. Rimmer JH, Wang E. Obesity prevalence among a group of Chicago residents with disabilities. *Arch Phys Med Rehabil.* 2005;86(7):1461-1464.

37. Rimmer JH, Yamaki K. Obesity and intellectual disability. *Ment Retard Dev Disabil Res Rev.* 2006;12(1):22-27.

38. Weil E, Wachterman M, McCarthy EP, et al. Obesity among adults with disabling conditions. *JAMA.* 2002;288(10):1265-1268.

39. Campbell VA, Crews JE, Moriarty DG, Zack MM, Blackman DK. Surveillance for sensory impairment, activity limitation, and health-related quality of life among older adults—United States, 1993-1997. *MMWR CDC Surveill Summ.* 1999;48(8):131-156.

40. Nosek M, Hughes RB, Robinson-Whelen S, et al. Physical activity and nutritional behaviors of women with physical disabilities: physical, psychological, social, and environmental influences. *Womens Health Issues.* 2006;16:323-333.

41. Kinne S, Patrick DL, Doyle DL. Prevalence of secondary conditions among people with disabilities. *Am J Public Health.* 2004; 94:443-445.

42. Nosek MA, Hughes RB, Petersen NJ, et al. Secondary conditions in a community-based sample of women with physical disabilities over a 1-year period. *Arch Phys Med Rehabil.* 2006;87:320-327.

43. Institute of Medicine. *Workshop on Disability in America: A New Look.* Washington, DC: National Academy of Sciences; 2005.

44. Rimmer J, Shenoy SS. Impact of exercise on targeted secondary conditions In: Field M, Jette, AM, Martin L, eds. *Workshop on Disability in America: A New Look*. Washington, DC: National Academies Press; 2006:205-221.

45. Campbell V, Crews J, Sinclair L. State-specific prevalence of obesity among adults with disabilities—eight states and the District of Columbia, 1998-1999. *MMWR CDC Surveill Summ.* 2002;56(36):805-808.

46. Centers for Disease Control and Prevention. *The Imperative of Public Health in the Lives of People With Disabilities*. Atlanta, GA: Centers for Disease Control and Prevention; 2006.

47. World Health Organization. *International Classification of Functioning, Disability and Health (ICF)*. Geneva, Switzerland: World Health Organization; 2002.

48. Kroll T, Jones GC, Kehn M, et al. Barriers and strategies affecting the utilisation of primary preventive services for people with physical disabilities: a qualitative inquiry. *Health Soc Care Community.* 2006;14:284-293.

49. Pope A, Tarlov AR, ed. *Disability in America: Toward a National Agenda for Prevention*. Washington, DC: National Academy Press; 1991.

50. Rimmer JH. The conspicuous absence of people with disabilities in public fitness and recreation facilities: lack of interest or lack of access? *Am J Health Promot.* 2005;19:327-329.

51. US 101st Congress. Americans With Disabilities Act, Public Law 101-336 (1990).

52. North Carolina Office on Disability and Health. *Removing Barriers to Health Clubs and Fitness Facilities*. Chapel Hill, NC: Frank Porter Graham Child Development Center; 2001.

53. Rimmer JH. Building inclusive physical activity communities for people with vision loss. *J Vis Impair Blind.* 2006;100(suppl):863-865.

54. Piotrowski K, Snell L. Health needs of women with disabilities across the lifespan. *J Obstet Gynecol Neonatal Nurs.* 2007;36:79-87.

55. *Healthy People 2010 Disability and Secondary Conditions*. Chapter 6. Atlanta, GA: Centers for Disease Control and Prevention; 2001.

56. Paffenbarger RS Jr, Hyde RT, Wing AL, Hsieh CC. Physical activity, all-cause mortality, and longevity of college alumni. *N Engl J Med.* 1986;314(10):605-613.

57. Blair SN, Kohl HW, Paffenbarger RS, Clark DG, Cooper KH, Gibbons LW. Physical fitness and all-cause mortality: a prospective study of healthy men and women. *JAMA.* 1989;262(17):2395-2401.

58. US Department of Health and Human Services Public Health Service, Centers for Disease Control and Prevention, National Center for Chronic Disease Prevention and Health Promotion. *Promoting Physical Activity: A Guide for Community Action*. Champaign, IL: Human Kinetics; 1999.

59. Centers for Disease Control and Prevention. *Disability and Health Chartbook, 2006. Profiles of Health for Adults With Disabilities*. Atlanta, GA: Centers for Disease Control and Prevention; 2006.

60. Centers for Disease Control and Prevention. Prevalence of physical activity, including lifestyle activities among adults—United States, 2000-2001. *MMWR Morb Mortal Wkly Rep.* 2003;52:764-769.

61. National Institutes of Health. Clinical guidelines on the identification, evaluation and treatment of overweight and obesity in adults—the evidence report. *Obes Res.* 1998;6:1S-209S.

62. Paeratakul S, Lovejoy JC, Ryan DH, Bray GA. The relation of gender, race and socioeconomic status to obesity and obesity comorbidities in a sample of US adults. *Int J Obes.* 2002;26:1205-1210.

63. Flegal KM, Carroll MD, Ogden CL, Johnson CI. Prevalence and trends in obesity among US adults 1999-2000. *JAMA.* 2002;288:1723-1727.

64. Kinne S. Improving access to healthy food: mapping urban food deserts. Paper presented at: American Public Health Association; November 2004; Washington, DC.

65. Hearn MD, Baranowski T, Baranowski J, et al. Environmental influences on dietary behavior among children: availability and accessibility of fruits and vegetables enable consumption. *J Health Educ.* 1998;29(1):26-36.

66. Hall L, Colantonio A, Yoshida K. Barriers to nutrition as a health promotion practice for women with disabilities. *Int J Rehabil Res.* 2003;26:245-247.

67. Rimmer JH. Health promotion for people with disabilities: a new era for managing medical costs and improving quality of life. *Dis Manag Health Outcomes.* 2002;10:337-343.

68. Tomey KM, Chen DM, Wang X, Braunschweig CL. Dietary intake and nutritional status of urban community-dwelling males with paraplegia. *Arch Phys Med Rehabil.* 2005;86(4):664-671.

69. Monroe MB, Tataranni PA, Pratley R, Manore MM, Skinner JS, Ravussin E. Lower daily energy expenditure as measured by a respiratory chamber in subjects with spinal cord injury compared with control subjects. *Am J Clin Nutr.* 1998;68:1233-1237.

70. Seekins T, Clay J, Ravesloot C. A descriptive study of secondary conditions reported by a population of adults with physical disabilities served by three independent living centers in a rural state. *J Rehabil.* 1994;60:47-51.

71. Wilber N, Mitra M, Walker D, et al. Disability as a public health issue: findings and reflections from the Massachusetts survey of secondary conditions. *Milbank Q.* 2002;80:393-421.

72. Kinne S. Correlates of exercise maintenance among people with mobility impairments. *Disabil Rehabil.* 1999;21(1):15-22.

73. White G, Gutierrez RT, Seekins T. Preventing and managing secondary conditions: a proposed role for independent living centers. *J Rehabil.* 1996;62:14-20.

74. Kinne S, Patrick DL, Doyle DL. Prevalence of secondary conditions among people with disabilities. *Am J Public Health.* 2004;94:443-445.

75. Traci MA, Seekins T, Szalda-Petree A, et al. Assessing secondary conditions among adults with developmental disabilities: a preliminary study. *Ment Retard.* 2002;40(2):119-131.

76. Drum C, Krahn G, Culley C, et al. Recognizing and responding to the health disparities of people with disabilities. *Californian J Health Promot.* 2005;3:29-42.

77. Mann J, Zhou H, McDermott S, et al. Healthy behavior change of adults with mental retardation: attendance in a health promotion program. *Am J Mental Retard.* 2006;111:62-73.

78. Eng JJ, Chu KS, Maria Kim C, Dawson AS, Carswell A, Hepburn KE. A community-based group exercise program for persons with chronic stroke. *Med Sci Sports Exerc.* 2003;35(8):1271-1278.

79. Rimmer J, Braunschweig C, Silverman K, et al. Effects of a short-term health promotion intervention for a predominantly African-American group of stroke survivors. *Am J Prev Med.* 2000;18:332-338.

80. Hughes R, Nosek M, Groff J, et al. Health promotion for women with physical disabilities: a pilot study. *Rehabil Psychol.* 2003;48:182-188.

81. Lorig KR, Holman H. Self-management education: history, definition, outcomes, and mechanisms. *Ann Behav Med.* 2003;26(1):1-7.

82. Corbin J, Strauss A. *Unending Work and Care: Managing a Chronic Illness at Home.* San Francisco, CA: Jossey-Bass; 1988.

83. Block P, Everhart Skeels SE, Keys CB, Rimmer JH. Shake-It-Up: health promotion and capacity building for people with spinal cord injuries related to neurological disabilities. *Disabil Rehabil.* 2005;27: 185-190.

84. Lorig K, Holman H. Self-management education: history, definition, outcomes, and mechanisms. *Ann Behav Med.* 2003;26:1-7.

85. Jensen MP, Chodroff MJ, Dworkin RH. The impact of neuropathic pain on health-related quality of life: review and implications. *Neurology.* 2007;68(15):1178.

86. Schrader PG, Lawless KA. The knowledge, attitudes, and behaviors approach: how to evaluate performance and learning in complex environments. *Performance Improvement.* 2004;43(9):8-15.

87. Nosek M, Hughes RB, Robinson-Whelen S, et al. Physical activity and nutritional behaviors of women with physical disabilities: physical, psychological, social, and environmental influences. *Womens Health Issues.* 2006;16:323-333.

88. Stuifbergen AK, Becker H, Sands D. Barriers to health promotion for individuals with disabilities. *Fam Community Health.* 1990;13:11-22.

89. Meyers A, Anderson J, Miller D, et al. Barriers, facilitators, and access for wheelchair users: substantive and methodologic lessons from a pilot study of environmental effects. *Soc Sci Med.* 2002;55(8):1435-1446.

90. Rimmer J, Riley BB, Wang E, Rauworth AE, Jukowksi J. Physical activity participation among persons with disabilities: barriers and facilitators. *Am J Prev Med.* 2004;26(5):419-425.

Mad Women or Mad Society: Towards a Feminist Practice with Women Survivors of Child Sexual Assault

by Fiona Rummery

This chapter examines an aspect of structural violence as embodied in traditional psychiatric labels of mental ill health. Although this discussion revolves around the issues of child sexual assault (which is constituted by physical violation) it does not focus on the interpersonal aspects of such abuse. Rather, it explores the subtler abuse which often informs the framework of societal institutions, such as medicine. When considering violence against women, it is usually overt and direct experiences of violence which are highlighted. It is arguable that women's experiences of systemic violence when seeking assistance are as worthy of detailed assessment. As Irwin and Thorpe argue in the opening chapter in this collection, systemic violence plays a crucial role in allowing interpersonal violence to continue, partly through the processes of silencing and discrediting, as this chapter details.

This chapter considers the question of what it is about a feminist counselling practice that differentiates it from other, more traditional modes of working. It will thus utilise an illustrative discussion of an issue which arose for me whilst working as a sexual assault counsellor. This involved working with an incest survivor who had an extensive history with the psychiatric profession, and my subsequent investigation into this area. As such, this chapter encompasses discussions of the issues involved in child sexual assault generally; women and notions of madness and the way these intersect with constructions of femininity; as well as ideas about working as a feminist practitioner. This is not an exhaustive discussion but rather exists as an exploration of some of the more subtle ways in which we, as workers, must always consider and reconsider the theoretical underpinnings of any practice, as well as constantly analyzing the practical implications of any theoretical formulation.

Child Sexual Assault

Misconceptions, fear and denial surround the issue of child sexual assault, as its existence problematises popular ideas about the fundamental institution of the family. In most cases of child sexual assault the perpetrator is known to the child, and the abuse continues over some time (Waldby 1985). The dominant cultural discourses which attempt to deal with child sexual assault form a powerful and ubiquitous part of the social fabric. More importantly (and confusingly) they are bizarrely contradictory in their nature:

> It doesn't happen; it only happens to poor families; it doesn't happen to THIS family; men do it when their wives are frigid or otherwise unavailable; children are naturally seductive; it doesn't do any harm; it damages for life. (Linnell & Cora 1993, 24)

The sexual assault of children usually involves progressive intrusion over a long period of time, with gradual coercion or co-option of the child, and with disclosure not occurring until some time after the abuse has ended (Cashmore & Bussey 1988). Child sexual assault is a particularly silenced experience; still commonly eliciting responses of disbelief and stigmatisation. It is also a particularly silencing experience in that the intensity and intimacy of violation often leads women to such a state of depression, self-hatred and/or distrust that they are unable or reluctant to talk about it (Stanko 1985; Ward 1984). Much of the early literature on child sexual assault documented the ravages of abuse, focussing on the tragedy of supposedly ruined lives. More recently the focus has shifted towards the process of recovery, with the aid of appropriate intervention. Incest survivors need to be provided with appropriate supportive services that allow them to actively and consciously confront the legacy of their abusive history.

One of the issues that I experienced when I began working with incest survivors, was that a high number had some psychiatric history or diagnosis. Approximately seventy percent of the clients I had seen had been categorised with Borderline Personality Disorder, or as Manic Depressive or as having psychotic episodes and as a result had been hospitalised or prescribed medication. When I questioned these women as to the details of the exact nature of the causes of their depression—or psychotic episodes—I was again surprised by the manner in which the symptoms manifested by these women seemed to me to be normal reactions to abusive situations. This led me to do some reading into women and psychiatry so that I could better understand theoretically the unease I felt intuitively to such psychiatric labelling of women's distress. Moreover, I wanted to incorporate this unease more effectively into my practice.

Women and Madness

The history of the connections between women and madness has been examined by a number of feminist writers in the last twenty years. These have ranged from historians (such as Matthews 1984) through to psychiatrists and social workers (such as Penfold & Walker 1983) and to philosophers (Russell, 1986, 1995). They have examined the manner in which what is defined as "madness" has changed over time according to context. In addition, they have exposed the manner in which the mental health profession has been used as a mechanism of social control, inextricably intertwined with notions of what constitutes "femininity".

The "science" of mental health will be treated in this discussion as an elastic and value-driven social science. Whilst I acknowledge that some women may be genuinely suffering from psychiatric illnesses, there are also many whose emotions, responses and "symptoms" are unnecessarily deemed "sick" within a psychiatric framework. It is this process of pathologising women's behaviour with which this paper is most concerned.

Phyllis Chesler says of her interviews with sixty women aged 17–70 with regard to their experiences in both private therapy and mental asylums: "Most were simply unhappy and self-destructive in typically (and approved) female ways. Their experiences made it very clear to me that help-seeking or help-needing behaviour is not particularly valued or understood in our culture" (Chesler 1973, XXII).

Central to the definition of what constitutes madness then, is the manner in which femininity is socially constructed. Caplan like Chesler, asserts that: "A misogynist society has created a myriad of situations that make women unhappy. And then that same society uses the myth of women's masochism to blame the women themselves for their misery" (Caplan 1985, 9).

The traditional "psychology of women" correlates closely with the "characteristics of oppression" (Penfold & Walker 1983). Women's sane, average, even self-preserving responses to situations of abuse or oppression are often used as evidence of their own lack of mental health.

Debra

I want at this point to introduce a case example in order to highlight some of the issues referred to throughout. Whilst I am loathe to do this in some senses—as it easily becomes voyeuristic and simplistically condenses a woman's struggle and life—it elucidates my point at different stages of this discussion more effectively than any abstract discussion of "women" can.

Debra was a woman whom I saw for counselling after she referred herself to the sexual assault service. It was largely through my contact with her that I undertook this research into women and psychiatry. She was thirty-four at the time and had a nine-year-old daughter. She was chronically and sadistically sexually abused by a male family member from the age of approximately eight until sixteen. She has had extensive contact with the psychiatric profession, has had a variety of diagnoses and been prescribed nearly every type of medication. Her first contact with psychiatrists was at age eight when she attempted suicide. After hospitalisation she was labelled "depressed" and given Valium and sleeping tablets for a number of years.

Her first psychotic episode occurred after the birth of her daughter, at which time she was placed in a psychiatric institution for some months. Since then, intrusive flashbacks of the sexual abuse she had experienced as a child have increased and intensified. She regularly had bouts of depression, suicidal feelings and tendencies as well as repeated psychotic episodes during which time she was hospitalised. She had been prescribed a plethora of drugs, none of which alleviate either the psychotic episodes or her flashbacks. Debra sought counselling at the sexual assault service as her flashbacks had further intensified since the time her daughter turned eight, and she felt strongly that there were things about the sexual assault which she needed to resolve.

Although Debra had a history of extensive contact with health professionals, at no time was she asked about her childhood. Even at age eight, and during her adolescence when Debra was medicated and hospitalised a number of times, the safety and stability of her family life was not questioned. The psychiatrists she saw did not ask her whether she had any ideas about what might be causing her distress. Rather, the manifestations of her emotional distress in response to abuse were treated as symptoms of an illness which could be cured by psychiatric intervention, such as medication.

It became clear to me quite early on that the messages which I was giving Debra directly contradicted those of her psychiatrist, whom she was still seeing. The things that he said to her are best encapsulated in the following examples:

> You have no control over this.

> You don't know what you need, I know what's *best for you.*

> Just do as I say and take the medication.

> The sexual assault is not *particularly relevant.* You must not indulge in self-pity and dwell on it. Put it out of your mind, it is in the past now.

> You are psychotic and manic depressive. There is nothing you can do about it. You must learn to live with your mental illness.

The work that I undertook with Debra, some of which will be described here, focussed upon validating both her feelings and memories, believing her, and giving her control over the counselling relationship. This approach stems from the belief that the core experiences of child sexual assault are disempowerment and disconnection from self and others. Recovery, therefore, is based primarily upon the empowerment of the incest survivor and the creation of new relationships which are non-abusive. "No intervention that takes power away from the Survivor can possibly foster her recovery, regardless of how much it appears to be in her best interest" (Herman 1992, 133).

The way in which Debra's psychotic episodes were dealt with by psychiatrists provides an illuminating illustration of the manner in which women's distress is pathologised rather than validated. When I questioned Debra as to the exact nature of her psychotic episodes, these were revealed (over some time) to be a series of extremely distressing memory flashbacks. To label these "psychotic" effectively removes them from her reality, thereby denying her the opportunity of integration. Whilst these memories were extremely distressing and often bizarre in nature, it was only through exploring them fully that Debra was able to become less afraid of them.

As one survivor of childhood sexual abuse wrote: "I've looked memories in the face and smelled their breath. They can't hurt me any more" (Bass & Davis 1988, 70).

The validation that her terror of flashbacks was an expression of the terror she had felt at the time of the abuse enabled Debra to remove these from the realm of paranoia. By extension, she was then able to turn fear into (justifiable) rage toward a perpetrator who could do such cruel things to a child. This change was in direct contrast to her previous self-blame and confusion about feeling crazy due to her mood hallucinations. The process of remembering and mourning has been well-documented by feminist practitioners as a crucial stage in recovery from childhood trauma of any kind, as it is only through knowing what happened that women can begin to heal and recover from the damage done to them (Herman 1992, 155).

The Problems with Categorisation

A major part of the construction of femininity is the emphasis which is placed upon serving others. This is exemplified in the importance which is accorded to motherhood and women's roles in providing for children. This role, however, has gradually become devalued in western society, so women are ensnared within the paradox of being both glorified and trapped within an oppressive definition of what they should be. At its extreme, some feminist commentators have argued that concepts of femininity and madness are actually interchangeable.

Numerous psychological studies have pointed out that what in the west is generally regarded as the woman's role happens to coincide with what is regarded as mentally unhealthy (Russell 1986, 86; Russell 1995). *The Diagnostic and Statistical Manual of Mental Disorders* (DSM-IIIR), created by the American Psychiatric Association, lists symptoms of all psychiatric disorders and is considered to be the essential reference for those working in Mental Health in the western world. Whilst the length of this chapter prevents greater exposition, it is useful

to compare the set of criteria for certain diagnoses, particularly those which are most often assigned to women.

Kaplan (cited in Russell 1986, 82–90) undertook a comparison of the DSM-III description of Histrionic Personality Disorder (which is far more frequently diagnosed in women than in men) with the findings of Broverman's (1972, in Russell) research into what constitutes a mentally healthy woman. The criteria for a diagnosis of Histrionic Personality Disorder are "self-dramatization, for example exaggerated expression of emotions, overreaction to minor events" (Spitzer & Williams 1987). Remarkably similar is the woman deemed mentally healthy in Broverman's research "being more emotional and more excitable in minor crises" (as cited in Russell 1986, 82–90).

This comparison illustrates the paradox in which women are placed, in that what are described as healthy feminine attributes can equally be seen as symptoms of psychiatric disorders. Thus, through assumptions about appropriate sex roles on the part of practitioners, a woman who is "successfully" fulfilling the feminine role by "revealing emotional responsibility, naivete, dependency and childishness" (Lerner & Wolowitz as cited in Russell 1986, 88) can be very easily diagnosed and labelled. The example used here is by no means the only one. A woman conforming to the female role can also be deemed to have a "dependent personality disorder", or "avoidant personality disorder". These definitions also include a high level of ambiguity, allowing for much interpretation on the part of the practitioner.

Whether women comply with or rebel against traditional precepts of femininity, we risk being labelled "dysfunctional". As the above examples reveal, compliance with femininity is not necessarily the safer option, as it can imply any variety of mental disorders; but rebellion against it can be seen as signifying aggressiveness, lack of gender identity, and social maladjustment. The "catch-22" inherent in this paradox is treacherous for women.

Constructing Reality

> The dominant group in any society controls the meaning of what is valid information. For women and other subordinate groups, the version of the world which has been sanctioned as reality does not address their lived experience . . . (Penfold & Walker 1983, 56)

When there is a disjunction between the world as women experience it and the terms given them to understand the experience, women often have little alternative but to feel "crazy". Labels of mental ill-health thus create and authorise ways in which women can conceptualise their unhappiness and despair, in a societally acceptable manner. In struggling against this, rather than treating Debra's symptoms as hers alone, a feminist approach seeks to normalise these by placing them within a context. Whilst this does not necessarily alter the feelings she experiences, it does alleviate accompanying feelings of isolation and fault. For example, when I pointed out to Debra that many women experience an increase in intensity and number of memory flashbacks after the birth of a child, or when a daughter reaches the age that they were when the abuse began, she was relieved, and we were able to explore what a daughter's vulnerability might mean to her. I would stress again that this does not necessarily relieve the distress experienced during these flashback episodes, but rather that the panic of feeling "crazy" and out of control during and afterwards is alleviated. Thus, Debra was able to view her symptoms as having a cause, rather than being something intrinsic to her as an individual which she needed to "learn to live with". It is important to remember that women's symptoms are real. Although this chapter criticises the fact that these symptoms are seen to constitute an identifiable (or classifiable) mental illness, this does not negate the fact that the symptoms as experienced by individual women can be intense and overpowering. Thus, the theoretical underpinnings of one's practice are revealed in the manner in which one defines women's distress. The psychiatrists who saw Debra acknowledged her distress, as did I. It is the framework in which we interpreted this that differed dramatically.

Mental Illness as Social Control

> The institution of psychiatry presents itself as healing, benign and compassionate while obscuring its function as part of the apparatus through which society is ordered. (Penfold & Walker 1983, 244)

Depressed or subservient women serve a social function in that they are unlikely to question their subordinate gender roles nor challenge broader social structures. This is exemplified by Miles (1988) in her discussion of the role of housewife:

> The stresses inherent in domestic work and the role of the housewife can lead to neurosis which in its turn is likely to make her even more home-centered and thus vulnerable to further stress . . . [T]he home can become . . . a setting which, by its peculiar strains, "drives her mad" yet which provides asylum from the impossible demands of the world outside with which she feels that she can no longer cope. (Miles 1988, 7)

If one accepts the premise that the construction of mental health reflects a social ordering of gender, one must then ask what purpose the pathologising of women's behaviour serves. To medicate Debra meant that she remained socially compliant. To label her as crazy enabled both professionals and her family to dismiss those disclosures she did make about the child sexual assault as imagined or exaggerated. This silenced her more effectively than any terror she may have felt.

Jordanova (1981, 106) expands upon this idea, by examining depression within the paradigm of an "illness". She compares those illnesses from which men most commonly suffer, with those of women, highlighting how rarely women are allowed to take on the "sick role": a role which provides relief from day-to-day burdens of work. This is not to negate the underlying framework which operates to posit the female condition as continuously or innately "sick". Rather, my point is that men are given societal access to a "legitimate" sick role. Jordanova effectively contrasts a woman who is depressed and on medication but still expected to perform familial duties, with the more "serious" illnesses which lead to time spent in bed, relaxation, holidays, and time off work for men. Again, Debra had been medicated and encouraged to "cope". For ten years her ability to care for her child and elderly relatives (including her and her partner's grandparents) domestically was actively rewarded, and the time that she spent in hospital frowned upon as indulgent. At no point was she offered the space, time or care to understand and deal with the cause of her distress.

Strategies for a Feminist Practice

Practicing from a feminist perspective will involve a variety of methodological approaches depending upon the context in which one is working. Thus, I do not intend to discuss method, but rather the underlying ideals informing a feminist approach. The ideal is to empower clients to challenge both external power structures and their own internalised oppression. This is necessary because both external and internal oppression can be equally debilitating and disempowering in the manner in which they are personally experienced (Fook 1990, 30).

A feminist approach cannot be a set of "how-to's" which can be easily adopted. A feminist framework is flexible and evolving, and involves as much an analysis of one's self, as that of the women with whom one is working. This is not to simplify feminism, nor to unify all feminist counsellors into the one category. I acknowledge the diversities within the existing definitions of feminism (and women) and the way in which these manifest in work practices. In order to establish and maintain a feminist practice, the worker must firstly be a feminist. This is in some senses stating the obvious, but I would reiterate that undertaking counselling in a feminist manner is not simply a job or framework which can be utilised and then discarded. Feminist practice is also not merely client-focused. Rather, it extends into all areas of work, examining and analysing the structures in which one is working and in the dynamics between staff members. An example which is pertinent is that of working within a psychiatric institution. In such an environment, one's feminist perspective would be of crucial motivation when interacting with other staff members in the organisation, particularly doctors, and others in positions of power in the hierarchy—in challenging the established frameworks in which they think and label people and which influence their practice.

A feminist approach values collective rather than hierarchical structures and seeks to deconstruct the "expert worker"—"client in need of help" dynamic, favoring instead empowerment of clients. This is particularly pertinent to a discussion on working with incest survivors. Working from a feminist perspective in essence allows women to be the expert of their own lives. This structuring of one's practices, so that the client is more than merely a recipient, allows the space for them to control the relationship. This is crucial as Herman points out, "The first principle of recovery is the empowerment of the Survivor. Others may offer advice, support, assistance, affection and care, but not cure" (Herman 1992, 133).

A feminist focus upon validating women's experiences is paramount—indicating to them that they have been listened to, heard, and believed, as this so rarely occurs elsewhere. This again is particularly pertinent to working with victims of sexual assault whose experiences of abuse may have been denied, trivialised or ignored—as in Debra's situation. The silence surrounding sexual assault makes it incredibly difficult for women to speak of their experiences; thus it is not possible to underestimate the impact on a personal level of a worker hearing and believing a woman's disclosure. Working with Debra involved providing constant reassurance that I did believe her memories and that I did not think that she was lying. At times, her fear of having spoken the abuse was palpable. This again reinforces the transformative power of merely disclosing the abusive experiences. It has been stressed that as workers we should never lose sight of the terror of disclosure, adding that on many occasions it is actually as if the perpetrator were in the room: "The terror is as though the patient and therapist convene in the presence of yet another person. The third image is of the victimiser, who . . . demanded silence and whose command is now being broken" (Herman 1992, 137).

This also highlights the importance of the manner in which the counsellor perceives of change. The worker should not view change simply as a change in behaviour, but rather expand this to create an environment in which it is recognised that change does not have to be structural or large to be of importance. The emphasis is therefore shifted so that an apparently slight change in awareness is valued and its ability to facilitate considerable difference in a woman's life is acknowledged. For Debra this type of change in awareness allowed her to begin to redefine her self and formulate a differing self-image from that previously provided to her. The creation of a new manner in which to perceive her self and her life allowed her to reinterpret her own life experience (Linnell & Cora 1993, 36). This new-found ability to resist the dominant discourse of her experience facilitates the potential for both social and personal empowerment. Goldstein comments that the personal narrative has been the way in which women have attempted (often privately and without recognition) to link up their lived experiences and feelings in the face of social definitions: "The use of this method is most instructive for social work because it reveals how personal and social change may be spurred by the kind of consciousness raising that occurs when people explore their own stories" (Goldstein 1990, 40).

Another essential feature of a feminist practice is that the worker's values are stated, and there is no pretence at objectivity or impartiality: "The consciousness of oppression has implications for alternative approaches such as those developed in self-help groups, women's studies, political action and consciousness raising" (Penfold & Walker 1983, XI).

In my practice, in order to challenge dominant constructions of power and knowledge, I take an overtly non-neutral position. This is achieved through providing the woman with the space, opportunity and information which is necessary for her to begin to consider her own experiences in the light of the broader cultural and social context. An example of this involves providing women with knowledge of the incidence of child sexual assault (as well as common reactions and experiences as detailed previously). This broader context allows the woman's perspective to encompass her own experience as well as the knowledge of a complex social dynamic. It is then possible to provide questions and possibilities which facilitate the reframing of personal experience within the context of this new knowledge (Linnell & Cora 1993, 34). Whilst this mode of working could be accused of not being "impartial" enough by traditional practitioners, it is important to differentiate here between making one's political and social ideologies clear without rupturing the boundaries

of the counselling relationship, and importing the worker's own emotional personal agenda into the working relationship. Herman provides a poignant explanation of the difference between the technical neutrality of the practitioner as opposed to what she calls moral neutrality: "Working with victimised people requires a committed moral stand. The therapist is called upon to bear witness to a crime. She must affirm a position of solidarity with the victim" (Herman 1992, 135).

She further extends this notion to explain that it does not necessitate a simplicity which assumes that the victim can do no wrong and asserts that rather it involves an understanding of the fundamental injustice of the child sexual assault and the victim's subsequent need for "a resolution that restores some sense of social justice" (Herman 1992, 135).

If we see that the depression of women speaks their lived experiences and represents a feminised manner of calling for some kind of understanding, then "a detailed examination is called for which concerns itself not just with which women in the population get depressed, but how and why" (Jordanova 1981, 106–07).

Social analysis does not necessarily help those women who feel unable to cope with their day-to-day existence. Knowledge that their "illness" is part of broader structural problems, and attributable to their social situation does not automatically endow them with feelings of joy and liberation. Whilst this is an important long-term aim, it does little to alleviate the suffering women individually experience. It "highlights the immediacy of the problem for women, and the need to think in terms of immediate action, not just the distant solutions implied in abstract analysis" (Jordanova 1981, 105).

If counselling is about negotiating an adjustment between client and environment (Fook 1990), then the treatment undertaken for women deemed "mentally unhealthy" has largely sought to adapt them to their environment. A feminist approach, however, would necessitate an examination of the societal factors which have led to the level of emotional distress present. Essentially then, public and private struggles are as inextricably linked as are theory and practice. Most importantly, neither partner in either equation should be treated as superior as each is crucial to the other.

Conclusion

It is necessary for a feminist practice to examine the oppression of women in both private and public, individual and institutional, structural contexts. Although this chapter has utilised the example of parts of one woman's story, as stated earlier this is representative of the experiences of many of the women with whom I have worked. The process of labelling these women when they exhibit intense emotional distress as "disordered" or "sick", effectively silences their disclosures of abuse. To accept that there are extremely cruel and sadistic acts perpetrated against children within our society is confronting and difficult. The manner in which social institutions and scientific discourse interact with the ideologies of patriarchy, needs to be exposed, and such interactions condemned for the manner in which they subjugate women.

Labels of mental illness do not exist in a social vacuum. To deny the importance of an individual's abusive childhood is to abdicate the responsibility that we all have for the impact of our actions on others. Such denial contributes to the continuation of such abuse. Links between madness as a social construction, and madness as a subjective experience (or as a "sane" response to abusive or oppressive experiences) need to be explored. Further, the label of "madness" when applied to women needs to be viewed with utter skepticism before being accepted as an appropriate diagnosis.

References

A list of references is available in original source.

 # Preventing Suicide Among Older Adult Asian Women
by Cao K. O.
Lessons learned in a New York City
suicide prevention public awareness
and education campaign.

In January 2010, the Asian American Federation in New York City initiated a citywide suicide prevention public awareness and education campaign to increase community attention to the high rate of suicides among older adult Asian American women. Working in coordination with Hamilton-Madison House, Filipino American Human Services, Inc., the New York Coalition for Asian American Mental Health, and the South Asian Council for Social Services, this campaign targeted older adult Asian women, as well as people who would likely have frequent contact with them, including caregivers and family members, frontline health and human service workers, religious leaders, staff at major healthcare institutions and long-term-care facilities, plus physicians in private practice.

Genesis of the Campaign

On December 7, 2006, the New York State Assembly Committee on Mental Health, Mental Retardation and Developmental Disabilities, the Puerto Rican/Hispanic Task Force, and the Task Force on Women's Issues (a task force of the New York State Assembly) conducted a joint public hearing on the high rate of suicide attempts by Asian and Hispanic women. Public health experts have had a poor understanding of these women's experiences with depression and other mental illnesses because little research has been done in this area.

Nationally, as well as in New York City, Asian American women had the highest suicide rate among women ages 65 and older, according to data from the Centers for Disease Control and Prevention (2006) and the New York City Department of Health and Mental Hygiene (2006). Knowledge about suicides and mental health needs of Asian American elders has been very limited. A study based on interviews conducted in 2000 of a regionally representative sample of Asian elders, ages 65 and older, in New York City found that Asian elders experienced greater socioeconomic vulnerability and had fewer options for culturally and linguistically appropriate healthcare and social services than the general older adult population in the city. Older Asian Americans endured a lower than average quality of life, marked by higher levels of depression, anxiety, loneliness, physical illness, and social difficulties. Forty percent of the elders interviewed reported depressive symptoms ranging from mild to severe. The risk factors of depression, as identified, included living arrangements, marital status, poor physical health, stressful life changes, as well as experience of a greater cultural gap between themselves and their children (Asian American Federation of New York, 2003a).

Older adult participants in a September 11th–related study complained about post-traumatic stress symptoms, expressed a sense of grief and loss around the attack on the Twin Towers, and suffered from a sense of hopelessness and helplessness about their lives and the future. Most study participants, older adults included, reported low mental health service use. They largely perceived professional mental health services to be unhelpful, inappropriate, or irrelevant. In addition, they preferred culturally embedded means of alleviating physical symptoms of stress, such as the use of herbal medicines and acupuncture instead of Western therapies (Asian American Federation of New York, 2003b).

In April 2008, with funds appropriated by the New York State Assembly following the 2006 public hearing, the New York State Office of Mental Health announced grant awards to seven organizations to implement suicide prevention public awareness and education campaigns separately targeting Latina adolescents and older adult Asian women. Hamilton-Madison House and the Asian American Federation were among these seven

organizations. To help extend the campaign's reach to older women in the culturally and linguistically diverse Asian ethnic communities, the Wallace H. Coulter Foundation provided additional funding to the Federation in 2009, which enabled three more organizations to join in the campaign.

Implementing the Project

For eight months, the campaign conducted intensive grassroots outreach and education in Chinese, Japanese, Korean, Tagalog, Vietnamese, five South Asian languages, and English. Outreach activities included one-on-one contacts and group sessions on Asian American mental health, issues related to elders' isolation, loneliness, and depression, as well as suicide risk factors. Group sessions often started with a presentation of "Healing the Spirit, Treatment of Depression among Asian Americans," a video highlighting the stories of nine Asian individuals, including three older adult women who have struggled with depression. The Asian Pacific Fund in the California Bay Area produced this video in nine Asian languages and in English. Following the presentation, participants were actively engaged in questions and answers, sharing experiences, and discussions about ways to increase awareness and prevention of suicides. Copies of this well-received video were given to all participants and widely distributed to caregivers and community organizations.

The campaign also has compiled and disseminated other helpful information on depression and suicide, suicide warning signs, myths about mental health, and where to go to seek help. To facilitate service access or referrals, the project partners have identified available bilingual, bicultural mental health professionals and their affiliations. And, the Federation developed a website, compiled for easy reference by caregivers and service providers, that houses relevant mental health and suicide prevention information and materials.

The New York Coalition for Asian American Mental Health conducted a community education program through Chinese-language media. The program featured monthly mental health–related live talk shows on four Chinese-language radio stations, articles written in Chinese for the weekly mental health column of a Chinese newspaper, plus scheduled appearances and public service announcements on one Chinese-language television station. Topics have included menopause and depression, elder abuse, domestic violence, anxiety disorder, pathological gambling, and sleep problems. During all of the radio shows, the listening audience was encouraged to call in to ask questions or to discuss their feelings and concerns as they related to the mental health topics being discussed in the broadcasts. Similarly, the South Asian Council for Social Services has prepared articles about depression and suicide for publication in three South Asian newspapers. In-language public service announcements also have been produced for one radio and two television stations.

As a licensed mental health service provider, Hamilton-Madison House made available their clinical services to uninsured older adults with high suicide risk, including victims of elder abuse or domestic violence and individuals with history of substance abuse, compulsive gambling, or Post-Traumatic Stress Disorder.

Lessons Learned and Continuing Challenges

The campaign has demonstrated that the best way to reach the intended target audience of older adult Asian women was through sources and contacts they trust, such as family members, caregivers, primary care doctors, and social workers. Ethnic media could help effectively relay the campaign message.

Because of cultural stigma, depression and suicide are not topics that Asian elders or their family members discuss. This especially is the case among Filipino Americans, a predominantly Catholic community. However, when the subject was introduced to older adults in a group setting with their peers and with linguistically and culturally appropriate materials such as the "Healing the Spirit" DVD, most elders were open to discussing their situations and to learning from one another.

In-language ethnic media have proven to be an effective channel for informing Asian elders about mental health issues.

Mental health programs that serve Asian elders must increase their capacity. As the campaign succeeded in calling the community's attention to the issues of depression, suicide, and mental health care, a major challenge was finding appropriate service referrals for individuals ready to seek help. During the campaign period, Asian LifeNet, a bilingual mental health hotline, experienced an increase in inquiries. But callers often had to wait for more than ten minutes on the phone. Besides, the language capacity of the hotline at the time was limited to Chinese (both Mandarin and Cantonese dialects included). In general, existing licensed Asian American mental health clinics are able to serve primarily Chinese-, Korean-, and Japanese-speaking patients. Access to culturally appropriate mental health services is extremely limited for Filipino and South Asian community members.

By and large, Asian elders do not seek mental health services and would resist going to a mental health clinic for talk therapy. Meanwhile, professionals with mental health training do not staff most programs serving older adults. Therefore, it would make sense to have mental health professionals out-stationed at natural settings such as senior centers, senior housing, shelters for abused women, etc., as a way to better connect mental health care to Asian elders. Engaging older adults who experience loneliness and isolation in therapeutic group activities would be an effective intervention approach.

There also are more systemic challenges to overcome. Medicare and Medicaid reimburse services provided at freestanding mental health outpatient clinics licensed by the New York State Office of Mental Health. Therefore, these mental health clinics could not send their professional staff to engage elders in therapeutic activities off-site, unless other funds were found to cover the costs of those activities. Similarly, mental health programs at community health centers licensed by the New York State Department of Health are restricted to serving only primary care patients of their health centers. While a community health center would be a more conducive setting than a stand-alone mental health clinic for Asian elders to consider mental health care, this would not be an option for older adults whose primary care doctors are in private practice.

Professional training on mental health care for Asian elders and on working with clients with high suicide risk also would enhance the capacity of existing mental health programs to serve Asian older adults.

The suicide prevention public awareness and education campaign ended after nine months due to lack of funding. The Federation, as well as the partner organizations, considered the campaign a successful experiment for raising public awareness of a not-so-hidden but unspoken problem. In the past four years, as reported in the Asian language media, there have been occasional incidents of suicides committed by Asian older adults, male and female, in their late 50s or ages 65 and older. Clearly, sustained public education efforts, as well as improved availability and competency of culturally appropriate mental health care for Asian elders, are needed.

Cao K. O, M.S.W., is a founder and former executive director of the Asian American Federation in New York City.

References

Asian American Federation of New York. 2003a. *Asian American Elders in New York City: A Study of Health, Social Needs, Quality of Life and Quality of Care.* New York, NY: Asian American Federation of New York.

Asian American Federation of New York. 2003b. *Asian American Mental Health: A Post–September 11th Needs Assessment.* New York, NY: Asian American Federation of New York.

Centers for Disease Control and Prevention. 2006. "Death Rates for Suicide by Sex, Race, Hispanic Origin, and Age: United States, Selected Years, 1950–2006." www.cdc.gov/injury/wisqars. Retrieved June 2014.

New York City Department of Health and Mental Hygiene. 2006. "New York City Vital Statistics Summaries, 2000–2006." www.nyc.gov/html/doh/html/data/vs.shtml. Retrieved June 2014.

The Paradox of Powerlessness: Gender, Sex, and Power in 12-Step Groups

by Sandra L. Herndon

Abstract: All 12-step groups rely on a version of Step One from Alcoholics Anonymous which states, "We admitted we were powerless over alcohol–that our lives had become unmanageable." The paradox inherent in this statement is the contradiction of asking group members to admit powerlessness in a group whose purpose is empowerment. This paper explorers the paradox of power and powerlessness in 12-step groups, especially in relation to gender and sex. Power in the western tradition is equated with control, authority, and masculinity while powerlessness suggests the opposite and is associated with femininity. This paper re-envisions the concepts of power and powerlessness from a broader perspective, avoiding a dichotomy and suggesting a framework based on mutuality, flexibility, and inherent strength through which mutually respectful relationships can be developed.

Introduction

The growth of twelve-step groups, part of the larger self-help recovery movement, is a response to personal and social problems in which individuals seek empowerment and transformation. Originating with Alcoholics Anonymous in the 1930s and now international in scope, twelve-step groups address a wide range of problems, including drug addiction (Narcotics Anonymous), gambling (Gamblers Anonymous), food addiction (Overeaters Anonymous), sex and relationship problems (Sex and Love Addicts Anonymous), emotional problems (Emotions Anonymous), families of alcoholics (Al-Anon), children of alcoholics (Alateen, Adult Children of Alcoholics), and families of drug addicts (Nar-Anon). Recovery from these problems into a "normal, useful way of life" is a primary goal of all these groups (AFGH, 1988, p. 233).

All twelve-step groups typically rely on an adaptation of Step One of *Alcoholics Anonymous* (AAWS, 1976): "We admitted we were powerless over alcohol—that our lives had become unmanageable" (p. 59). What exactly is the paradox here? *Webster's Unabridged Dictionary* identifies a paradox as a statement that seems contradictory, unbelievable, or even absurd, but that may indeed be true. In an earlier work (Herndon & Eastland, 1999), I described this paradox as one which asks group members to admit powerlessness in a group whose purpose is empowerment—a seemingly contradictory, if not absurd, idea. The purpose of this paper is to explore the paradox of power and its obverse, powerlessness, in twelve-step groups, especially in relation to gender. To accomplish this goal I will 1) identify some of the fundamental issues in twelve-step groups relating to the idea of powerlessness, 2) discuss briefly the philosophical basis of the paradox of power and powerlessness, 3) explore the gender implications of this paradox, and 4) identify alternative ways of addressing these issues in the context of twelve-step groups.

The paradox of powerlessness inherent in twelve-step groups has generated controversy and critique in part because of the connotations of the term 'power.' Power is defined by *Webster's Unabridged Dictionary* as vigor, force, strength, influence, or ability to control others, while powerlessness is defined as weakness or impotence, without force or energy. Why and how are members expected to admit their powerlessness? To the Western mind such an act is untenable. For members of self-help groups seeking direction and guidance in solving difficult problems to be told, first and foremost, to admit powerlessness appears tantamount to being told to admit defeat. In addition, the relationship between gender and powerlessness is significant. *Webster's* defines masculine as strong (therefore powerful) and feminine as weak (therefore powerless). Hence the meaning of admitting powerlessness must inevitably differ, depending on one's gender and/or sex role.

The matter of gender or sex is rarely acknowledged in twelve-step literature and then principally as a role (e.g., the wife of the alcoholic). However, gender and sex-role issues underlie the groups' histories. Alcoholics Anonymous (AA), the earliest and perhaps most recognizable of these groups, began as a group of white upper-middle-class Protestant alcoholic men in the 1930s (see AFGH, 1989; Rudy & Greil, 1988; AFGH, 1976) although many women now participate in AA. Al-Anon, begun by the wives of AA founders for families and friends of alcoholics, continues to consist predominantly of women. This paper will use Al-Anon as its primary example of a twelve-step group because it evidences issues clearly related to gender and defined sex roles, but many of the issues are similar in all groups modeled on AA.

Power and Powerlessness in Twelve-Step Groups

This section will identify some fundamental tenets related to power and powerlessness in twelve-step groups which are based on a set of twelve steps and twelve traditions (see Appendix A for a list of Al-Anon's twelve steps). The steps provide a guide for personal change and growth based on personal responsibility and a belief in a spiritual force or Higher Power while the twelve traditions guide group process and structure (Herndon, 1992).

Much of the current literature about alcoholism describes family roles, based frequently on the model of the alcoholic husband, codependent or enabling wife, and children who enact a variety of roles. The nature of these interpersonal interactions, regardless of who occupies which role, is addressed in Al-Anon, a program for families and friends of alcoholics. According to *Al-Anon's Twelve Steps and Twelve Traditions* (AFGH, 1981), the twelve steps are the "heart of the program in which the family of an alcoholic can find a new way of life in the fellowship" of the group (p. ix). Several of these steps are related directly to issues of power/powerlessness:

"Step 1: We admitted we were powerless over alcohol—that our lives had become unmanageable." In this and related steps, group members are encouraged to understand that by admitting powerlessness over the "facts of our situation and the other people involved," they will discover that they "are not helpless" (AFGH, 1990, p. 31). Following this step, it is advised, provides a feeling "of release, of yielding or letting go" when it becomes clear that "no change in others can be forced" (AFGH, 1989, p. 8). An Al-Anon member writes, "Many meetings later, I grasped the idea that the only person I have any power over is myself" (AFGH, 1990, pp. 40-41).

"Step 3: We made a decision to turn our will and our lives over to the care of God as we understood Him." Al-Anon guidance suggests a reliance on and relationship with a "benign Power" in which "our part . . . was to learn to recognize, reach out, accept—and act, with the inner awareness of the spiritual presence whose direction we decided to follow when we made a decision to turn over our will and our lives" (AFGH, 1981, p. 21). Commonly referred to as "turning it over," this step acknowledges reliance on a Higher Power, however it is defined. Kasl (1992) calls this the "let go and let god" step, referring to one of the frequently used slogans in twelve-step groups (p. 312).

However, the official language always refers to "God" as "Him," thus reaffirming a patriarchal view of spiritual guidance. While individuals or local groups may be flexible in their own language use, nowhere has the issue of sexist language or its power implications been addressed in conference-approved twelve-step publications (those materials officially sanctioned by Al-Anon Family Group Headquarters, Alcoholics Anonymous World Services, or their counterparts). The equation of God with a male 'Higher Power' reinforces an inherent gender inequality.

Step 8: "We made a list of all persons we had harmed, and became willing to make amends to them all, and Step 10: "We continued to take personal inventory and when we were wrong promptly admitted it." In these and related steps, members are encouraged to confess their mistakes and strive to be more aware of the consequences of their actions in relation to other people. Al-Anon guidance suggests, "Taking Step Ten gave us the opportunity to spare ourselves the consequences of being stubbornly opinionated. It reminded us that we were not all-wise, that the philosophy of our Steps is based on humility, on acknowledging a Power greater than ourselves" (AFGH, 1981, p. 64). Admitting one's failings and making amends can certainly be cleansing and renewing; it may also be a source of shame and reconfirmation of one's worthlessness. Kasl (1992) identifies this problem as a "cultural double bind" where the "victim" may be taking responsibility not only for her own behavior but also for what has been done to her (p. 322). A feminist critique would ask why she should focus on her shortcomings at the expense of her achievements.

The Paradox

How can admitting powerlessness empower someone? How can yielding or surrendering produce strength? Although these ideas may seem contradictory to those of us schooled in the Western tradition, they have a long history in Eastern philosophy. In this section I want to demonstrate very briefly the philosophical roots of this paradox.

A description of the "working principles" of Al-Anon identifies them as the "concepts on which all spiritual philosophies are based," in the "Bible as well as the sacred literature of the Orient" (AFGH, 1988, p. 229). The Al-Anon book of daily meditations, *Courage to Change* (AFGH, 1992), is punctuated with quotations from a variety of sources, including Lao Tzu, Confucius, Kagawa, Helen Keller, Kahlil Gibran, Carl Jung, Soren Kierkegaard, Antoine de Saint-Exupery, Langston Hughes, Meister Eckhart, The Bhagavad Gita, The Bible, The Talmud, and Persian poems, as well as Ojibway, Zen, Turkish, and American proverbs and sayings. The debt to the thinking of many of the world's great writers and traditions is evident.

Writing in the sixth century B.C., Lao Tzu penned *Tao Te Ching* (1972), the basis of Taoism which remains a central part of Chinese culture. The paradox of power and powerlessness is a prominent theme, as evidenced in these excerpts:

Yield and overcome;
Bend and be straight;
Empty and be full;
Wear out and be new;
Have little and gain;
Have much and be confused. (Twenty-Two)

The softest thing in the universe
Overcomes the hardest thing in the universe.
    (Forty-Three)

A man *(sic)* is born gentle and weak.
At his death he is hard and stiff.
Green plants are tender and filled with sap.
At their death they are withered and dry.
Therefore the stiff and unbending is the disciple
  of death.
The gentle and yielding is the disciple of life.
Thus an army without flexibility never wins a battle.
A tree that is unbending is easily broken.
The hard and strong will fall.

The soft and weak will overcome. (Seventy-Six)

The truth is often paradoxical. (Seventy-Eight)

Hassett (1996) writes in an article unrelated to twelve-step programs, "The many paradoxes of the Tao now make sense. When Lao Tzu says 'yield and overcome,' I know what he means because I've pushed against life, trying to make it obey my desires, and have learned that it doesn't work that way." Here we can begin to see how, ironically, admitting powerlessness may result in a sense of power—flexibility may provide strength, yielding may "get" us what we cannot get through force.

The Buddhist tradition also illustrates the paradox of having and turning loose. Mark Epstein (1995), a Western-trained psychiatrist and a practicing Buddhist, explores our Western confusion about the nature of happiness which he describes as "the ability to receive the pleasant without grasping and the unpleasant without condemning." Ultimately, he says, happiness is "release from the attachment to pleasant feelings." Ron Leifer (1997), a Buddhist as well as a psychiatrist, says that from the Buddhist perspective suffering results from our selfish pursuit of happiness. In describing the "way of the Lotus" associated with Buddhism, Herman (1997) suggests that "the Lotus way invites us to engage in action . . . but to do it with unattachment," comparing this principle with the teachings of the Upanishads, Jesus of Nazareth, Islam, the Bhagavad Gita, and Taoism. This paradox is reflected in the Al-Anon principle of detachment: "We let go of our obsession with another's behavior and begin to lead happier and more manageable lives, lives with dignity and rights, lives guided by a Power greater than ourselves" (AFGH, 1992, p. 43).

For many of us steeped in the Western tradition, the idea of being powerless suggests losing, being dominated or defeated. These ideas are based on the assumption of a dichotomy (one wins and one loses) rather than complementarity or mutuality (Berenson, 1991). The paradox is that one may become empowered by accepting one's powerlessness. The gender implications of this paradox will be explored in the next section.

Gender Implications

I begin this section with a brief summary of the obvious. The dichotomous stereotypes of masculine as rational, objective, strong (and therefore powerful) and feminine as emotional, subjective, weak (and therefore less powerful or even powerless) continue with us. Being powerful connotes being successful, in control, in charge, in authority. Inevitably, in a patriarchy, power, being associated with masculinity, gets conflated with being male. Being powerless, however, suggests the opposite and therefore gets conflated with being female, a double-bind ("catch-22"), explicated by Kasl (1992), Jamieson (1995), and others.

It becomes evident that the twelve-step prescription to admit powerlessness carries an implicit challenge, albeit a paradoxical one, to normative expectations, especially of masculine behavior. While accepting powerlessness may be difficult for anyone in a culture which celebrates being in control, it is not surprising that females, having been socialized into expectations of femininity, may have less difficulty acknowledging powerlessness. According to Kasl (1992), AA founder Bill Wilson was "constantly concerned with the need to deflate a rigid, over-blown ego as a prerequisite to admitting one has a problem with alcohol" (p. 17) which worked well for the privileged white men with whom he worked. Kasl points out, however, that such an admission of powerlessness does not necessarily serve the same purpose for most women and many underprivileged people who may already be painfully aware of their powerlessness. Indeed, building up a healthy ego may need to be the goal for those who suffer from oppression as well as problems associated with addiction.

Furthermore, turning over one's will and life to a Higher Power, always referred to as masculine, is also paradoxical. On one hand, the process of letting go can be liberating, hence the slogan "Let Go and Let God" (AFGH, 1988, p. 248). On the other hand, it can increase one's sense of powerlessness. Kasl (1992) argues that the "last thing women and minorities need to do is hand their wills over to others to control. To do so is at the heart of oppression" (p. 313). A feminist critique would argue that people who have had their power and autonomy restricted or even stripped away (e.g., women, racial/ethnic minorities, gays and lesbians) are rightly wary of prescriptions to do anything that might further reduce their strength, power, dignity.

Another major gender implication inherent in Al-Anon practice is the reliance on stereotyped sex roles, perhaps best illustrated by a free pamphlet made available at meetings and identified as a helpful source of information especially for newcomers. Using a theatrical metaphor, *Alcoholism: A Merry-Go-Round Named Denial* (Kellerman, 1969) identifies one of the major characters as the "provoker," a role described in other literature as codependent. This "key person" in the play is "usually the wife or mother," who is "hurt and upset by [the alcoholic's] repeated drinking episodes; but she holds the family together . . . she feeds back . . . her bitterness, resentment, fear and hurt, and so becomes the source of provocation. She controls, she tries to force the changes she wants; she sacrifices, adjusts, never gives up, never gives in, but never forgets" (pp. 5-6). Kellerman explains that "the customs of our society train and condition the wife to play this role" (p. 6). While this pamphlet is sympathetic to the woman's position and its difficulties, it reveals the classic double-bind, or paradox of powerlessness. If she actively tries to change him, she is denying his autonomy; if she passively accepts the situation, she reinforces her own sense of powerlessness. Either way, she loses.

One criticism of Al-Anon is that by privatizing the problems of living with an alcoholic, it implicitly reinforces societal expectations of female passivity in the name of acceptance. The story of one such group member is detailed under the title "I Learned to Love" in *Al-Anon Faces Alcoholism* (AFGH, 1988, 134-139). The "wife of an active alcoholic" recounts that since she learned not to "hand over the money" to him, her husband now "manages to pay the bills." She has allayed her anxiety about his irresponsibility by recognizing her own flaws and determining not to "blame" him for his drinking. No mention is made of the consequences of unpaid bills or any alternatives she might have to this dependency. In describing a similarly unhealthy relationship, Kasl (1992) stated that the woman in this situation needed "some feminist consciousness-raising" (p. 265). Repressing anger, Kasl argues, results in loss of power.

Krestan and Bepko (1991) describe codependency, such as the behavior described above, as the "process of 'losing' one's identity to an overfocus on another person or relationship" (p. 50). Such behavior becomes even more problematic when it is described as a disease. While Al-Anon literature refers to alcoholism as a "family disease" (AFGH, 1988, p. 47), its members often speak of their own "disease" of codependency in meetings. Medicalizing social or political conditions only serves to perpetuate them because the underlying causes are not examined, as Western medicine customarily proceeds from a mechanistic model of the body independent of circumstance. The traditional medical model casts the doctor as a knowledgeable and powerful (usually masculine) authority, the patient as supplicant (usually female) having less power or knowledge. Gender inequality, hardly a medical condition, is certainly a major source of what is described as dysfunctional, codependent behavior (see Berenson, 1991; Krestan & Bepko, 1991). Kasl (1992) reframes the idea of disease by redefining codependency as "a disease of inequality— a predictable set of behavior patterns that people in a subordinate role typically adopt to survive in the dominant culture. Codependency is a euphemism for internalized oppression and includes traits of passivity, compliance, lack of initiative, abandonment of self, and fear of showing power openly" (p. 279). She argues that this behavior is taught and reinforced through our primary cultural institutions in order to maintain patriarchy and capitalism.

Concern over issues relating to gender and powerlessness has spawned some critique and spurred the development of alternatives which will be identified in the next section.

Alternatives

Several authors have revised the twelve steps to address many of the issues described in this paper (see Berenson, 1991; Kasl, 1992). These revisions fall outside the boundary of "conference-approved literature" (AFGH, 1988, p. 258), a limitation which has resulted in material that does not challenge or critique gender inequality. First published in *Ms.*, Kasl's (1990) original revision of the steps (see Appendix B) offers a provocative alternative addressing the fundamental issues of power/powerlessness and gender inequality. Following is her revised version of the steps analyzed earlier in this paper: Steps 1, 3, and 8-10 (pp. 30-31):

"Step 1: We acknowledge we were out of control with–but have the power to take charge of our lives and stop being dependent on others for our self-esteem and security." This formulation moves away from powerlessness as loss of control toward claiming power over one's own life.

"Step 3: I declared myself willing to tune into my inner wisdom, to listen and act based upon these truths." A radical departure from the original, this revision places the primary locus of spirituality inside the individual, rather than in a masculine deity.

"Step 8-9: We took steps to clear out all negative feelings between us and other people by sharing grievances in a respectful way and making amends when appropriate." This revision rights the imbalance of the original one-sided version by emphasizing respect and openness as opposed to an apologetic attitude.

"Step 10: Continued to trust my reality, and when I was right promptly admitted it and refused to back down; we do not take responsibility for, analyze, or cover up the shortcomings of others." A complete inversion of the original, this step now emphasizes the right to stand up for oneself and not to take responsibility for others, rather than focusing solely on one's mistakes.

Another interesting alternative is provided by "J" (1996) who has translated AA's primary text "from the gender-weighted English of the 1930s to an English that treats men and women equally" (p. vii). Arguing that the original version essentially ignored women except in the role of wife, "J," a self-identified sober alcoholic in AA, seeks to rectify this imbalance both by getting rid of the masculine pronouns and by changing the sex of the principals in several examples in the text. To date, this version has not been conference-approved.

In addition to alternatives focusing on changing language, Kasl (1992) identifies three twelve-step programs which have formed as alternatives

to Alcoholics Anonymous: Women for Sobriety (WFS), Rational Recovery (RR), and Secular Organization for Sobriety or Save Our Selves (SOS), which were begun because of dissatisfaction with the treatment in AA of such issues as powerlessness, definition of God, and sexism.

At a fundamental level all these alternatives attempt to restore a balance of power. Berenson (1991) argues for a redefinition or "recovery" of power, to move from power as "technical will" or control toward power as "existential will" or willingness. He suggests that the "process of recovery from addiction is a process of recovering a different, more feminine, sense of power and will" (p. 74). Rather than power as domination over, we can think of power as autonomy, the ability to take responsibility for oneself and act in a caring and respectful way toward others, a conception of power that is mutual and balanced. The revised twelve steps reinforce this view. Autry and Mitchell (1998), in drawing lessons for business from the Tao, argue for just such a redefinition of power.

Conclusion

This paper has attempted to identify and explore a fundamental paradox at the heart of twelve-step programs—the paradox of powerlessness—and to explore its gender implications. It can be well argued that paradox is what makes the program work. However imperfectly, it reflects the wisdom of the ages. Yet equally valid is the need to rid twelve-step groups of destructive gender inequality. Perhaps the Serenity Prayer, written by theologian Reinhold Neibuhr and used in many twelve-step group meetings, reflects the balance needed to manage these paradoxical demands:

God grant me the serenity
To accept the things I cannot change,
Courage to change the things I can,
And the wisdom to know the difference.
(AFGH, 1988, p. 252)

Appendix A

Al-Anon's Twelve Steps (From Al-Anon Family Group Headquarters, Inc. [1981]. *Al-Anon's twelve steps and twelve traditions*. New York: Author.)

1. We admitted we were powerless over alcohol—that our lives had become unmanageable.

2. Came to believe that a Power greater than ourselves could restore us to sanity.

3. Made a decision to turn our will and our lives over to the care of God *as we understood Him* (emphasis in original).

4. Made a searching and fearless moral inventory of ourselves.

5. Admitted to God, to ourselves and to another human being the exact nature of our wrongs.

6. Were entirely ready to have God remove all these defects of character.

7. Humbly asked Him to remove our shortcomings.

8. Made a list of all persons we had harmed, and became willing to make amends to them all.

9. Made direct amends to such people wherever possible, except when to do so would injure them or others.

10. Continued to take personal inventory and when we were wrong promptly admitted it.

11. Sought through prayer and meditation to improve our conscious contact with God *as we understood Him* (emphasis in original), praying only for knowledge of His will for us and the power to carry that out.

12. Having had a spiritual awakening as the result of these Steps, we tried to carry this message to others, and to practice these principles in all our affairs.

Appendix B

Revised Twelve Steps (Kasl, C. D. [1990, Nov.-Dec.]. The twelve-step controversy. *Ms.*, pp. 30-31.)

1. We acknowledge we were out of control with _____ but have the power to take charge of our lives and stop being dependent on others for our self-esteem and security.

2. I came to believe that the Universe/Goddess/Great Spirit would awaken the healing wisdom within me if I opened myself to that power.

3. I declared myself willing to tune into my inner wisdom, to listen and act based upon these truths.

4. We examined our behavior and beliefs in the context of living in a hierarchal, male-dominated culture.

5. We shared with others the ways we have been harmed, harmed ourselves and others, striving to forgive ourselves and to change our behavior.

6. We admitted to our talents, strengths, and accomplishments, agreeing not to hide these qualities to protect others' egos.

7. We became willing to let go of our shame, guilt, and other behavior that prevents us from taking control of our lives and loving ourselves.

8-9. We took steps to clear out all negative feelings between us and other people by sharing grievances in a respectful way and making amends when appropriate.

10. Continued to trust my reality, and when I was right promptly admitted it and refused to back down. We do not take responsibility for, analyze, or cover up the shortcomings of others.

11. Sought through meditation and inner awareness the ability to listen to our inward calling and gain the will and wisdom to follow it.

12. Having had a spiritual awakening as the result of these steps, we tried to carry this message to others, and to practice these principles in all our affairs.

Notes

1. An earlier version of this paper was presented at the annual conference of the Eastern Communication Association in Portland, ME, in April 2001.

2. Special thanks to Anita Taylor for helping me clarify the title of this paper.

References

Al-Anon Family Group Headquarters, Inc. (AFGH) (1988). *Al-Anon faces alcoholism* (2nd ed.). New York: Author.

Al-Anon Family Group Headquarters, Inc. (AFGH) (1981). *Al-Anon's twelve steps and twelve traditions*. New York: Author.

Al-Anon Family Group Headquarters, Inc. (AFGH) (1992). *Courage to change: One day at a time in Al-Anon II.* New York: Author.

Al-Anon Family Group Headquarters, Inc. (AFGH) (1990). *In all our affairs: Making crises work for you.* New York: Author.

Alcoholics Anonymous World Services. Inc. (AAWS) (1976). *Alcoholics Anonymous.* New York: Author.

Autry, J. A., & Mitchell, S. (1995). *Real power: Business lessons from the Tai Te Ching.* NY: Riverhead Books.

Berenson. D. (1991). Powerlessness—liberating or enslaving? Responding to the feminist critique of the twelve steps. In C. Bepko (Ed.), *Feminism and addiction* (pp. 67-84). New York: The Haworth Press.

Epstein, M. (1995). Opening up to happiness. *Psychology today* [On-line], *28*(4). Available: http://web.lexis-nexis.com/univers . . . 5=f99b6e9824f2f89420d63e47b3a7980e

Hassett, B. (1996, Sept. 22). Finding wisdom in ancient philosophy means letting analysis go. *Sacramento Bee* [On-line], D5. Available: http://web.lexis-nexis.com/univers . . . 5=acfd081cf283814e2450c883d214d86a

Herman, A. L. (1997). The way of the lotus: Critical reflections on the ethics of the "Saddharmapundarika Sutra." *Asian Philosophy* [On-line], 7(1). Available: http://web3.searchbank.com/infotra . . . on/411/306/2031 3689w3/7!xrn_11&bkm

Herndon, S. L. (1992, May). *The twelve traditions: A study in group process and organizational structure.* A paper presented at the annual convention of the Eastern Communication Association, Portland, ME.

Herndon, S. L., & Eastland, L. S. (1999). Introduction. In L. S. Eastland, S. L. Herndon, & J. S. Barr (Eds.), *Communication in recovery: Perspectives on twelve-step groups* (pp. 1-10). Cresskill, NJ: Hampton Press.

"J" (1996). *A simple program: A contemporary translation of the book "Alcoholics Anonymous."* New York: Hyperion.

Jamieson, K. H. (1995). *Beyond the double bind: Women and leadership.* NY: Oxford University Press.

Kasl, C. D. (1992). *Many roads, one journey: Moving beyond the twelve steps.* New York: Harper Perennial.

Kasl, C. D. (1990, Nov.-Dec.). The twelve-step controversy,. *Ms.*, 30-31.

Kellerman, J. L. (1969). *A merry-go-round named denial.* New York: Al-Anon Family Group Headquarters, Inc.

Krestan. J. A., & Bepko, C. (1991). Codependency: The social reconstruction of female experience. In C. Bepko (Ed.), *Feminism and addiction* (pp. 49-66). New York: The Haworth Press, Inc.

Lao, Tzu. (1972). *Tao teaching* [G. F. Feng & J. English, Trans.]. New York: Vintage Books.

Leifer, R. (1997). *The happiness project.* Ithaca, NY: Snow Lion Publications.

Rudy, D. R., & Greil, A. L. (1988). Is Alcoholics Anonymous a religious organization?: Meditations on marginality. *Sociological Analysis, 50*(1), 41-51.

Sandra L. Herndon is Professor and Chair of the Graduate Program in Communications at Ithaca College. She has published a volume on "Communication in Recovery: Perspectives on Twelve-Step Groups" and finds the intricacies of paradox to be intriguing.

A Case Study: "If They Had a Cure I Would Not Take It": African American Women Living with HIV/AIDS

by Donna M. Cole

Introduction

African-American women experience a disproportionate prevalence of HIV/AIDS, creating the need to evaluate all factors that may impact adherence to anti-retroviral therapy (ART). The experiences of African-American women living with HIV/AIDS occur within a historical and social context that impacts current perceptions of treatment. African Americans are most adversely impacted by HIV/AIDS disease burden (Centers for Disease Control, 2016). Despite increased access to treatment, medication adherence remains a challenge for many women living with HIV. Practitioners and scholars of health science must be aware of the impact of slavery, segregation, and racism on the health beliefs and practices of African-American women. This case study draws on data collected from "The Role of Illness Representation on ART Adherence among African American Women."[1] The perceptions of anti-retroviral medication and the use of alternative medicine are explored with study participants (Cole, 2014).

HIV and the Importance of Adherence

Human Immunodeficiency Virus (HIV) is a retrovirus that if left untreated causes disease progression that compromises the immune system and leads to acquired immunodeficiency syndrome (AIDS) complications resulting in death. Like all viruses, HIV cannot reproduce itself independent of a host cell. The virus infects a human CD4 (or human T-cell), a key part of the immune system; this infection causes the cells to decline in number and infect other cells in the body, causing immune system depression (Wagner & Hewlett, 2004). As a result, the body is susceptible to invading bacteria and viruses leading to complications that include opportunistic infection, cancer, and tuberculosis. HIV can only be transmitted when one of four bodily fluids has the human immunodeficiency virus in it; these four bodily fluids are blood, semen, vaginal fluids, and breast milk. Contamination must be present in the bloodstream of an infected person and then passed to another through direct contact with their bloodstream. The virus cannot pass through contact with feces or saliva. It cannot pass through contact with unbroken skin, perspiration, or tears. The virus can enter the bloodstream through blood to blood contact by sharing needles or razors. Open cuts, sores or lesions, and vaginal or anal walls are susceptible to transmission.

Women are vulnerable to contracting HIV for various reasons, including the higher viral concentration found in semen. Undetected sexually transmitted infections depress immunity increasing the likelihood of infection for women (Turmen, 2003; Higgins, 2010). In addition, women's social position increases vulnerability in that they are more likely to be economically dependent on men, which makes advocacy for safe sex difficult increasing the likelihood of transmission. Women experiencing intimate partner violence are at advanced risk of contracting HIV and those with lower levels of academic attainment are also at higher risk of HIV disease susceptibility (Turmen, 2003). African-American women experience a disproportionate burden with regard to HIV/AIDS (Brawner, 2014). Because the virus causes immune system dysfunction, adherence to anti-retroviral therapy is extremely important in preventing AIDS progression.

Much of the research on anti-retroviral therapy adherence among African Americans focuses on distrust of the medical system. Most notable is the reflection on the significance of the Tuskegee syphilis study which left African-American men and their families untreated for syphilis over a thirty-year period (Thomas, 1991). Other researchers state that African-Americans' beliefs in conspiracy theories either that HIV/AIDS was created in a laboratory as a form of biological warfare or that it was created specifically to decrease the numbers of African Americans have had an adverse impact on prevention efforts (Bogart, 2005). HIV/AIDS was not created in a laboratory to destroy African Americans. If this were true, researchers would find an increase in disease prevalence among African Americans separate from other forms of illness; however, African-American health is adverse across disease states and HIV/AIDS is no exception.

Theories on the reasons for non-adherence among African Americans should also include an account of the historical influence of non-Western medical practices in the lives of African Americans. Consideration should be given to the practice of intergenerational messages passed from mothers to daughters, from aunts to nieces, and from grandmothers to granddaughters. These patterns of distrust communication have survived as a result of persistent and longstanding patterns of segregation in predominantly African-American communities. This pattern of oral history of storytelling and of sharing distrust of Western medicine began long before the Tuskegee experiment that began in 1932. Nicolaidis' (2010) research found that African-American women did not seek services for depression because of intergenerational messages of distrust of Western medicine passed to them from older African-American women. In my study, the theme of distrust communication stemmed from conversations participants had with neighbors, older family members and friends. This is especially relevant because women in this study were not aware of the Tuskegee experiment, however, intergenerational messages of distrust of Western medicine was relevant to self-care practices.

The Historical Context of West African Influence in Health Beliefs

African-American women have a historical legacy of self-care and the use of non-conventional medical practices. These practices originated in West Africa and are characterized by a strong belief that the physical and spiritual worlds are interconnected. This belief assumes that health is based upon the relationships a woman has with others in her community. There has historically been a strong use of botanical and non-herbal treatments among African-American women. Prayer and spirituality are often seen as forms of healing (Bailey 2002; Covey, 2007; and Dalmida, 2006). Healing practices of placing hands on the body of a sick person and offering a prayer or word of encouragement have become common practices among African-American women. These practices have been used in the absence of or in addition to Western medicine.

In 2014, this study, "The Role of Illness Representation on ART Adherence among African American Women,"[2] consisted of semi-structured interviews with ten women currently managing an HIV diagnosis. The study found that African-American women living with HIV/AIDS used self-care in managing their diagnosis. In addition, the study found that two women in the study had been diagnosed in 1985 and 1987 respectively, prior to the availability of anti-retroviral medication. For the purposes of illustrating the importance of the practice of self-care, the narratives of these two women will be explored in this case study. Both women

reported that they had used alternative and non-conventional treatments in managing the disease.

One of the women diagnosed in 1985 stated that she did not begin receiving anti-retroviral therapy until 1999. She reported:

> There was nothing so they prayed for me, they brought oil and massaged me, prayed, they brought me incense and candles, they cooked for me, made me juice and tea put that in the fridge and told me to change my diet you know eat better fruits and vegetables.

There was a perception among both women in the study that one could survive HIV/AIDS with and without HIV medication. As one of the women suggested: "You see people in the community and you know they are not on meds but they are surviving. We don't know what they put in the medication."

Each of the women reported harsh side effects as a result of taking anti-retroviral medication. They stated that rashes or nausea were common as well as upset stomach. As home remedies, they said that for headaches, putting a lemon on the back of the head provided comfort. For a stomach ache, the use of peppermint or ginger tea was beneficial. Both women said that they had been told about these remedies from older African-American women.

> You know them old women in the church, my grandmother was like that, they get the sheet and pray for people and then we kids get sick and here they come with something that smells bad and tastes bad, but before you know it, you better.

All of the women expressed difficulties in daily functioning as a result of managing an HIV diagnosis. Women with HIV/AIDS manage their disability in a variety of ways. Both women cited prayer on days that were more difficult. "Some days I have plans but I just can't follow through. With this thing, you never know how you are going to feel from one day to the next, I just ask God to help me get through it."

Each woman discussed the challenges of managing their diagnosis, and the importance of prayer and self-care based upon intergenerational messages passed to them from older women in their families. They stressed the importance of the church as a place for them to meet with others even if the others did not know about their diagnosis. However, one of the women stated that after she disclosed her diagnosis to members of her congregation, people in the church who had at one time embraced her, began to ignore her.

> I spoke one day, gave my testimony and told everyone I had it you know. Everyone in my church they hug you, we hug each other, after that they didn't want to hug me. This is church right? I was really hurt by that.

A key aspect of disease management among African-American women is the belief that members of the community play a role in managing illness. Thus, the fact that one of the women was rejected after disclosing her illness is of great significance. African-American churches must recognize their importance in providing a place of worship, fellowship, and acceptance for all of its members. Disease management does not exist in isolation. Community level support is very important for people living with HIV in addition to other chronic illnesses.

When asked if they would consider a vaccine for HIV or a cure if it were to become available, both women said they would not participate in any vaccine trial or adhere to a new drug treatment therapy.

> If they had a cure, I would not take it, they don't know enough about these medications, look at interferon at one time they thought that was a cure then it made people feel like they had the flu so they don't give it to them anymore now on to the next thing. I'm not taking any so called cure, my viral load is good, I'm managing okay they change things up, I end up messed up, dead and then I'll be pissed.

The other woman stated similar distrust beliefs and communication of the healthcare system and said that a second opinion was helpful if she felt unsure about a physician's assessment. She also stated: "No I don't trust these people, I go to the doctor they tell me something, I go home and get on the internet to check you know make sure they know what they are talking about."

Conclusion

African-American women living with HIV are constrained, limited, and oppressed but still have a sense of agency and empowerment. Researchers must find the balance between identification of structural constraints and acknowledging the ability, persistence, sheer will and drive of African American women to exact some level of control over their lives. African-American women managing a diagnosis of HIV/AIDS are not passive in their attempts to direct their lives. They are active agents making decisions based upon a historical legacy of self-awareness and self-care, and a social environment in which HIV/AIDS is a highly-stigmatized illness. Health science professionals and scholars must take into account the ways in which slavery created a need for alternatives to Western medicine as medical care was not always available to slaves working on plantations or in segregated communities. In addition, African-American women have inherited a health system which includes practices and beliefs based in West African traditions. In the midst of persistent racism due to the legacy of slavery and segregated communities, African Americans have survived by creating alternatives to Western medicine. Disease management of African-American women living with HIV/AIDS is complex and multifaceted, but any exploration of adherence to anti-retroviral therapy must take into account the ways in which African-American women's definition of adherence might differ from the models forwarded by those in the health sciences.

References

Bailey, E. J. (2002). *African American alternative medicine: Using alternative medicine to prevent and control chronic diseases*. Westport, CT: Bergin & Garvey.

Bogart, L. M., & Thorburn, S. (2005). Are HIV/AIDS conspiracy beliefs a barrier to HIV prevention among African Americans? *Journal of Acquired Immune Deficiency Syndromes, 38*(2), 213–218 doi: 10.1097/00126334-200502010-00014.

Brawner, B. M. (2014). A multilevel understanding of HIV/AIDS disease burden among African American women. *Journal of Obstetric, Gynecologic & Neonatal Nursing, 43*(5), 633–643 doi:10.111/1552-6909.12480.

Centers for Disease Control and Prevention (n.d.). HIV among African Americans. Retrieved December 15, 2016 from http://www.cdc.gov/hiv/group/racialethnic/africanamericans.

Cole, D. M. (2014). Use of alternative medicine among African Americans: Implications for Art adherence. Retrieved December 23, 2016 from https://apha.confex.com/apha/142am/webprogram/Paper299312.html

Covey, H. C. (2007). *African American slave medicine: Herbal and non-herbal treatments.* Lanham, MD: Lexington Books.

Dalmida, S. G. Holstad, M. M. Dilorio, C., & Laderman, G. (2012). The meaning and use of spirituality among African American women living with HIV/AIDS. *Western Journal of Nursing Research,* 34(6), 736–765. doi:10.1177/0193945912443740.

Higgins, J. A., Hoffman, S., & Dworkin, S.L. (2010). Rethinking gender, heterosexual men, and women's vulnerability to HIV/AIDS. *American Journal of Public Health,* 100(3), 435–445. doi:10.2105/ajph.2009.159723.

Nicolaidis, C., Timmons, V., Thomas, M.J., Waters, A.S., Wahab, S., Mejia, A., & Mitchell, S.R. (2010). "You don't go tell white people nothing": African American women's perspectives on the influence of violence and race on depression and depression care. *American Journal of Public Health,* 100(8), 1470–1476. doi:10.2105/ajph.2009.161950.

Thomas, S. B., & Quinn, S.C. (1991). The Tuskegee syphilis study, 1932–1972: Implications for HIV education and AIDS risk education programs in the black community. *American Journal of Public Health, 81* (11), 1498–1505 doi:10.2105/ajph.81.11.1498.

Turmen, T. (2003). Gender and HIV/AIDS. *International Journal of Gynecology & Obstetrics, 82* (3), 411–418. doi:10.1016/s0020-7292(03)00202-9.

Wagner, E. K. & Hewlett, M. J. (2004). *Basic virology.* Malden, MA: Blackwell Publishing.

Endnotes

[1]Acknowledgments: Funded by the National Institute of Mental Health (R25MH087217 Guthrie and Schensul PIs) Dr. Barbara Guthrie, Dr. Trace Kershaw, Dr. Jean Schensul, REIDS, Yale School of Public Health; Center for Interdisciplinary Research on AIDS (CIRA) Special thanks to Elaine O'Keefe, Salimah Bey, Natalie Massenburg, Sabrina Bradford, and Alderman Cole.

[2]The National Institute of Mental Health and the Yale School of Public Health—this study adhered to strict protocols, procedures, and guidelines outlined by the Institutional Review Board (IRB).

Biography: Donna Marie Cole, Ph.D., M.P.H., M.Ed. is a medical sociologist and Assistant Professor of Sociology and Public Health at Simmons College in Boston, Massachusetts. Her research focuses on infectious disease outbreaks and HIV/AIDS among African American women.

Disability and Society

1. In what ways is disability defined by culture? How has American society defined disability?

2. Stress is defined as the non-specific response of the body to demands made on it. These demands can be physical or emotional. The response is non-specific in the sense that, no matter whether the stressor (cause of stress) is seemingly negative or positive, the body responds the same way physiologically. On the scales that measure stress of life events, marriage, graduation, and promotion get high stress ratings, along with ending a relationship, death in the family, and a jail sentence. There are long-term physical and emotional health consequences for poorly managed stress. Think about what is stress, how we measure stress, and how to reduce stress. Next list the stressors in your life and how you manage them.

   A. List the ways your body responds to stressors.

   B. List the ways you cope or manage stress.

   C. List the ways you want to manage stress, but for some reason cannot.

3. Reviewing the article *Cultural Humility versus Cultural Competence* by Tervalon and Murray-Garcia from Chapter 2, how would you design an outreach program to a specific group of women with disabilities? Identify your approach and why it might be successful.

4. What historical factors contribute to the link between oppression and mental health for women?

5. Search the Internet for alternative substance abuse programs that support women and their families. Identify their program mission, philosophy, and activities.

6. How does Donna Cole's article about African American Women and HIV/AIDS reflect broader social and political issues that impact Black women? How does the role of segregation preserve alternative health narratives? How does history shape the perceptions of certain populations? In what ways can healthcare practitioners reach out to Black women in general and those with illnesses? What lessons are learned from the women in Cole's article?

Violence Against Women

Violence in the home is a major health issue for women and children. The National Coalition Against Domestic Violence estimates that every 9 seconds a woman is assaulted or beaten in the United States. On average, 20 people per minute are physically abused by an intimate partner. On a typical day, domestic violence hotlines nationwide receive approximately 20,800 calls. The terms used to describe this type of violence include: domestic violence, family violence, violence against women, and intimate partner violence, and are all used interchangeably. Regardless of the term, the Centers for Disease Control and Prevention (CDC) describes intimate partner violence (IPV) as a serious preventable public health problem that affects millions of people in the United States. The CDC defines IPV as "physical violence, sexual violence, stalking and psychological aggression (including coercive acts) by a current or former intimate partner."

Violence manifests itself in girls' (and boys') and women's lives in many different forms including child sexual abuse, physical abuse, dating violence, sexual harassment, stalking, pornography, date rape, and elder abuse. It exists among family members and intimate partners. Although each specific form of violence may be unique in its consequences and the knowledge needed to recognize it, respond to it, and prevent it, all forms of violence against women must be understood as issues of power and control where one person or a group takes power and control through both physical and psychological violence over another. While men may experience intimate partner violence, women

and children (girls and boys) are more profoundly impacted by IPV.

Intimate partner violence was once considered to be private family business. However, the women's movement has been at the forefront in changing society's perception. The modern women's movement has tirelessly worked for over three decades raising public awareness about IPV, creating legislation, developing programs for survivors, opening shelters and rape crisis centers, maintaining hotlines, and developing training protocols for those who serve the public such as police officers, educators, and healthcare practitioners. Healthcare practitioners are on the frontlines of IPV as mandatory reporters in cases of child abuse, offering care during crises, as well as safety and intervention when requested. This chapter focuses on a range of topics addressing the complexities of IPV.

The chapter begins with several classic articles that identify the spectrum of violence and provide training tools to combat violence. First, the *Continuum of Family Violence* by the Alaska Department of Public Safety provides a chart demonstrating the relationship of subtle forms of physical, verbal/emotional, and sexual abuse, which society all too often tolerates or condones, to the forms more obviously recognized as serious and deadly. The subtler forms of abuse can themselves have serious consequences and invariably lead to other means of control and violence. It is important to understand that this continuum is an important teaching tool and would look different for different women.

The *Power and Control Wheel* is from the Domestic Abuse Intervention Project. It was developed by battered women and survivors as a key tool for educating people about IPV. The goal is to show that IPV is not just about physical abuse, but is an ongoing pattern where those who are battered are controlled by those perpetuating the abuse. The power and control wheels remind us that IPV is not just about anger management problems or losing control; it is about choosing violence to control another person. Abusers are not always easily recognizable and they do not wear a sign, may never get caught or leave obvious physical evidence on those they abuse, but as the wheels show they use many methods such as controlling finances, the manipulation of children, playing mind games, and, most often, isolating their partner from family and other support systems. Because healthcare practitioners are on the frontlines of IPV, *The Medical Power and Control Wheel and Medical Advocacy* provides the tools to assist practitioners who work with and advocate for women and their families dealing with violence. In contrast, the *Equity Wheel* by the Domestic Abuse Intervention Project serves as an inspiring model as to what creating a healthy relationship looks like by striving to equalize rather than to use or abuse power.

In a post-9/11 world where the talk of terrorism dominates so many national policy decisions, Carole J. Sheffield, in the article *Sexual Terrorism,* powerfully captures the reality of how violence and the fear of violence dominates many women's lives. The article is unique in observing the enormous impact of "the fear of violence" even for women who would never identify themselves as victims of violence. In a statement related to every topic in a women's health course, Sheffield provocatively concludes that "violence against the female body and the perpetuation of fear of violence form the basis of patriarchal power."

In *Breaking the Silence*, Megan Steffer shares her own story of date rape. At the time Steffer wrote this piece, she was a college student. She emphasizes that the "vast majority of rapes (80%) occur between people who know each other and take place in environments that are generally considered to be safe." Steffer urges other survivors to tell their stories and for everyone to "listen and support these women as their stories unfold." She recognizes the power and value in speaking and sees speaking up as a way to take back the power they lost from the violence of rape.

Next, Kathryn M. Ryan, in *The Relationship between Rape Myths and Sexual Scripts: The Social Construction of Rape*, shows through her research of the rape myth how it can influence sexual scripts that determine sexual beliefs, attitudes, and behavior that support sexual violence. Sexual scripts are culturally socialized patterns of behavior that inform desire and influence behavior, which support rape culture in our society. Sexual scripts include hook up culture, seduction, rape, and acquaintance rape. The social construction of rape myths and scripts leads to normalizing behavior which puts women at a greater risk and increases vulnerability to sexual aggression and violence.

The following articles examine barriers to services among diverse communities. For example, Latina(x) communities, same-sex partners, and trans individuals. *Exploring the Challenges Faced by Latinas Experiencing Intimate Partner Violence* by Judy L. Postmus, Sarah McMahon, Elithet Silva-Martinez, and Corinne D. Warrener explores the experiences of Latinas who sought help from IPV services and those who did not. Latina women in the study faced a number of challenges and barriers from their communities, IPV services, and family members when they sought formal services. Challenges included lack of awareness about IPV in Latina communities, a lack of culturally sensitive information among formal service providers, and resistance from the community and some family members. The authors include recommendations on IPV and the specific needs of the Latina population for service providers in both formal and informal networks that work with victims of IPV.

Ruling the Exceptions: Same-Sex Battering and Domestic Violence Theory by Gregory S. Merrill is an excellent classic article that continues to be relevant today. It addresses the important issue of violence in lesbian and gay relationships, but also challenges gender-based domestic violence theory. Merrill explores "the many dimensions of power and explains gender-based domestic violence as it occurs in all relationship configurations." Three conditions for battering are identified: learning to abuse; having the opportunity to abuse; and choosing to abuse. It becomes evident how violence is connected to privilege and oppression when one thinks about how society gives very clear messages about who has "the opportunity to abuse without suffering negative consequences."

This chapter ends with an article by Nancy Worcester, *Women's Use of Force: Complexities and Challenges of Taking the Issue Seriously*. This is a classic article that examines the controversial topic of women's use of force. There has been a steadily growing media attention on "violent women" and "mean girls" but nearly all the information on this topic has been from an anti-woman, backlash perspective or by people inappropriately missing a gender-neutral approach. Worcester's article reflects on work of the Wisconsin Coalition Against Domestic Violence's Education and Emerging Issues Committee. "The challenge is to take violence by women seriously without losing sight of the fact that the patterns of male and female violence within adult intimate relationships are usually very different, often happen within different contexts, and generally have different consequences and that both violence itself and the barriers to ending violence are related to societal inequalities."

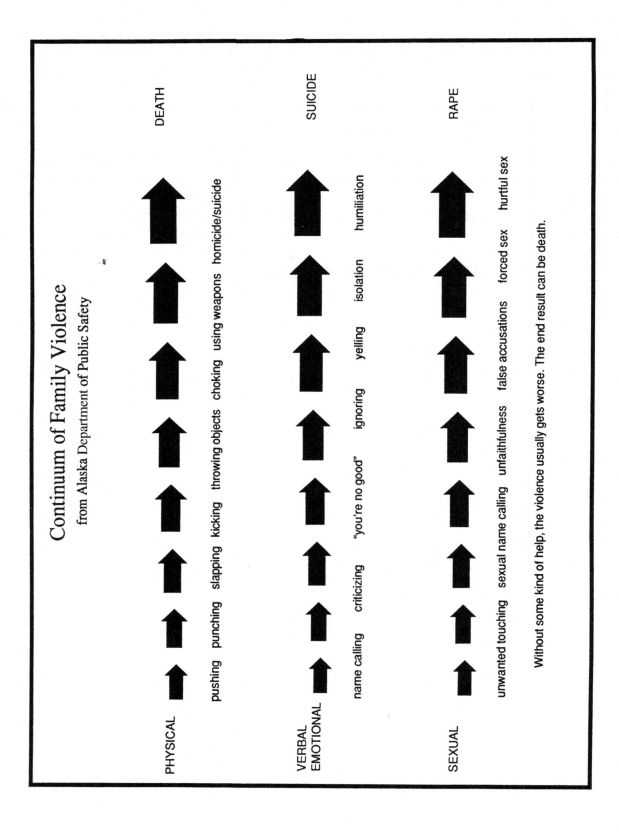

Continuum of Family Violence
from Alaska Department of Public Safety

PHYSICAL — pushing · punching · slapping · kicking · throwing objects · choking · using weapons · homicide/suicide → DEATH

VERBAL EMOTIONAL — name calling · criticizing · "you're no good" · ignoring · yelling · isolation · humiliation → SUICIDE

SEXUAL — unwanted touching · sexual name calling · unfaithfulness · false accusations · forced sex · hurtful sex → RAPE

Without some kind of help, the violence usually gets worse. The end result can be death.

Power and Control Wheel

by the Domestic Abuse Intervention Project, Duluth MN

DOMESTIC ABUSE
INTERVENTION PROJECT
206 West Fourth Street
Duluth, Minnesota 55806
218-722-4134

Medical Power and Control Wheel and Medical Advocacy Wheel

by the Domestic Abuse Intervention Project, Kenosha

ESCALATING DANGER

VIOLATING CONFIDENTIALITY:
Interviewing her in front of family members. Telling colleagues issues discussed in confidence without her consent. Calling the police without her consent.

NORMALIZING VICTIMIZATION:
Failing to respond to her disclosure of abuse. Acceptance of intimidation as normal in relationships. Belief that abuse is the outcome of non-compliance with patriarchy.

TRIVIALIZING AND MINIMIZING THE ABUSE:
Not taking the danger she feels seriously. Expecting tolerance because of the number of years in the relationship.

IGNORING THE NEED FOR SAFETY:
Failing to recognize her sense of danger. Being unwilling to ask, "Is it safe to go home?" or "Do you have a place to go if the abuse escalates?"

Medical Power & Control

BLAMING THE VICTIM:
Asking what she did to provoke the abuse. Focusing on her as the problem and asking, "Why don't you just leave?," "Why do you put up with it?," or "Why do you let him do that to you?"

NOT RESPECTING HER AUTONOMY:
"Prescribing" divorce, sedative medications, going to a shelter, couples counseling, or the involvement of law enforcement. Punishing her for not taking your advice.

INCREASED ENTRAPMENT

Produced and distributed by:

Developed by: The Domestic Violence Project, Kenosha, WI, adapted from the original wheel by the Domestic Abuse Intervention Project
202 East Superior Street
Duluth, MN 558022
18.722.4134

Equality Wheel

by the Domestic Abuse
Intervention Project, Duluth MN

DOMESTIC ABUSE
INTERVENTION PROJECT
206 West Fourth Street
Duluth, Minnesota 55806
218-722-4134

Sexual Terrorism

by Carole J. Sheffield

The right of men to control the female body is a cornerstone of patriarchy. It is expressed by their efforts to control pregnancy and childbirth and to define female healthcare in general. Male opposition to abortion is rooted in opposition to female autonomy. Violence and the threat of violence against females represent the need of patriarchy to deny that a woman's body is her own property and that no one should have access to it without her consent. Violence and its corollary, fear, serve to terrorize females and to maintain the patriarchal definition of woman's place.

The word *terrorism* invokes images of furtive organizations of the far right or left, whose members blow up buildings and cars, hijack airplanes, and murder innocent people in some country other than ours. But there is a different kind of terrorism, one that so pervades our culture that we have learned to live with it as though it were the natural order of things. Its targets are females—of all ages, races, and classes. It is the common characteristic of rape, wife battery, incest, pornography, harassment, and all forms of sexual violence. I call it *sexual terrorism* because it is a system by which males frighten and, by frightening, control and dominate females.

The concept of terrorism captured my attention in an "ordinary" event. One afternoon I collected my laundry and went to a nearby laundromat. The place is located in a small shopping center on a very busy highway. After I had loaded and started the machines, I became acutely aware of my environment. It was just after 6:00 p.m. and dark; the other stores were closed; the laundromat was brightly lit; and my car was the only one in the lot. Anyone passing by could readily see that I was alone and isolated. Knowing that rape is a crime of opportunity, I became terrified. I wanted to leave and find a laundromat that was busier, but my clothes were well into the wash cycle, and besides, I felt I was being "silly," "paranoid." The feeling of terror persisted, so I sat in my car, windows up, and doors locked. When the wash was completed, I dashed in, threw the clothes into the dryer, and ran back out to my car. When the clothes were dry, I tossed them recklessly into the basket and hurriedly drove away to fold them in the security of my home.

Although I was not victimized in a direct, physical way or by objective or measurable standards, I felt victimized. It was, for me, a terrifying experience. I felt controlled by an invisible force. I was angry that something as commonplace as doing laundry after a day's work jeopardized my well-being. Mostly I was angry at being unfree: a hostage of a culture that, for the most part, encourages violence against females, instructs men in the methodology of sexual violence, and provides them with ready justification for their violence. I was angry that I could be victimized by being "in the wrong place at the wrong time." The essence of terrorism is that one never knows when is the wrong time and where is the wrong place.

Following my experience at the laundromat, I talked with my students about terrorization. Women students began to open up and reveal terrors that they had kept secret because of embarrassment: fears of jogging alone, dining alone, going to the movies alone. One woman recalled feelings of terror in her adolescence when she did child care for extra money. Nothing had ever happened and she had not been afraid of anyone in particular, but she had felt a vague terror when being driven home late at night by the man of the house.

The men listened incredulously and then demanded equal time. The harder they tried the more they realized how very different—qualitatively,

"Sexual Terrorism," by Carole J. Sheffield as appeared in *Women and Health: Power, Technology, Inequality, and Conflict in a Gendered World*, edited by Kathryn Strother Ratcliff, 2002, Boston: Allyn & Bacon, pp. 75–77. Reprinted by permission of Carole Sheffield.

Reprinted with permission from bulbul, Feminist Connection, Madison, WI. December, 1984.

quantitatively, and contextually—their fears were. All agreed that, while they experience fear in a violent society, they did not experience terror; nor did they experience fear of rape or sexual mutilation. They felt more in control, either from a psychophysical sense of security that they could defend themselves or from a confidence in being able to determine wrong places and times. All the women admitted fear and anxiety when walking to their cars on the campus, especially after an evening class or activity. None of the men experience fear on campus at any time. The men could be rather specific in describing when they were afraid: in Harlem, for example, or in certain parts of downtown Paterson, New Jersey—places that have a reputation for violence. But these places could either be avoided or, if not, the men felt capable of self-protective action. Above all, male students said that they *never* feared being attacked simply because they were male. They *never* feared going to a movie or to dinner alone. Their daily activities were not characterized by a concern for their physical integrity.

As I read the literature on terrorism it became clear that both sexual violence and nonviolent sexual intimidation could be better understood as terrorism. For example, although an act of rape, an unnecessary hysterectomy, and the publishing of *Playboy* magazine appear to be quite different, they are in fact more similar than dissimilar. Each is based on fear, hostility, and a need to dominate women. Rape is an act of aggression and possession, not of sexuality. Unnecessary hysterectomies are extraordinary abuses of power rooted in man's concept of woman as primarily a reproductive being and in his need to assert power over reproduction. *Playboy*, like all forms of pornography, attempts to control women through the power of definition. Male pornographers define women's sexuality for their male customers. The basis of pornography is men's fantasies about women's sexuality.

Components of Sexual Terrorism

The literature on terrorism does not provide a precise definition.[1] Mine is taken from Hacker, who says that "terrorism aims to frighten, and by frightening, to dominate and control."[2] Writers agree more readily on the characteristics and functions of terrorism than on a definition. This analysis will focus on five components to illuminate the similarities of and distinctions between sexual terrorism and political terrorism. The five components are: ideology, propaganda, indiscriminate and amoral violence, voluntary compliance, and society's perception of the terrorist and the terrorized.

An *ideology* is an integrated set of beliefs about the world that explains the way things are and provides a vision of how they ought to be. Patriarchy, meaning the "rule of the fathers," is the ideological foundation of sexism in our society. It asserts the superiority of males and the inferiority of females. It also provides the rationale for sexual terrorism. The taproot of patriarchy is the masculine/warrior ideal. Masculinity must include not only a proclivity for violence but also all those characteristics necessary for survival: aggression, control, emotional reserve, rationality, sexual potency, etc. Marc Feigen Fasteau, in *The Male Machine*, argues that "men are brought up with the idea that there ought to be some part of them, under control until released by necessity, that thrives on violence. This capacity, even affinity, for violence, lurking beneath the surface of every real man, is supposed to represent the primal untamed base of masculinity."[3]

Propaganda is the methodical dissemination of information for the purpose of promoting a particular ideology. Propaganda, by definition, is biased or even false information. Its purpose is to present one point of view on a subject and to discredit opposing points of view. Propaganda is essential to the conduct of terrorism. According to Francis Watson, in *Political Terrorism: The Threat and the Response*, "Terrorism must not be defined only in terms of violence, but also in terms of propaganda. The two are in operation together. Violence of terrorism is a coercive means for attempting to influence the thinking and actions of people. Propaganda is a persuasive means for doing the same thing."[4] The propaganda of sexual terrorism is found in all expressions of the popular culture: films, television, music, literature, advertising, pornography. The propaganda of sexual terrorism is also found in the ideas of patriarchy expressed in science, medicine, and psychology.

The third component, which is common to all forms of political terrorism, consists of "indiscriminateness, unpredictability, arbitrariness, ruthless destructiveness and amorality."[5] Indiscriminate violence and amorality are also at the heart of sexual terrorism. Every female is a potential target of violence—at any age, at any time, in any place. In her study of rape, Susan Brown-miller argues that rape is "nothing more or less than a conscious process of intimidation by which all men keep all women in a state of fear."[6] Further, as we shall see, amorality pervades sexual violence. Child molesters, incestuous fathers, wife beaters,

and rapists often do not understand that they have done anything wrong. Their views are routinely shared by police officers, lawyers, and judges, and crimes of sexual violence are rarely punished in American society.

The fourth component of the theory of terrorism is "voluntary compliance." The institutionalization of a system of terror requires the development of mechanisms other than sustained violence to achieve its goals. Violence must be employed to maintain terrorism, but sustained violence can be costly and debilitating. Therefore, strategies for ensuring a significant degree of voluntary compliance must be developed. Sexual terrorism is maintained to a great extent by an elaborate system of sex-role socialization that in effect instructs men to be terrorists in the name of masculinity and women to be victims in the name of femininity.

Sexual and political terrorism differ in the final component, perception of the terrorist and the victim. In political terrorism we know who is the terrorist and who is the victim. We may condemn or condone the terrorist depending on our political views, but we sympathize with the victim. In sexual terrorism, however, we blame the victim and excuse the offender. We believe that the offender either is "sick" and therefore in need of our compassion or is acting out normal male impulses. . . .

Conclusion

Sexual terrorism is a system that functions to maintain male supremacy through actual and implied violence. Violence against the female body (rape, battery, incest, and harassment) and the perpetuation of fear of violence form the basis of patriarchal power. Both violence and fear are functional. Without the power to intimidate and to punish, the domination of women in all spheres of society—political, social, and economic—could not exist.

References

A list of references is available in the original source.

Breaking the Silence

by Megan Steffer

Rape and sexual assault are public health issues that most of us would prefer to ignore. In 1987, it was first reported that approximately 27 percent of college-aged women had been rape victims since age 14.[1] Further studies have gone on to specify that anywhere from 15–20 percent of women are raped during their time as an undergraduate student.[2] These numbers rise significantly when statistics also include attempted rape and sexual assault:studies report that as many as 57 percent of college women have been victims of some kind of sexual assault during their college careers.[2] Despite having rape prevention programs in place at almost every major university in the country, current figures still estimate that one in four college women are survivors of rape or attempted rape.[3]

When many people think of rape, they imagine a sinister-looking man sexually assaulting a woman in a dark alley. While these situations do occur, the vast majority of rapes (80%) occur between people who know each other, and take place in environments that are generally considered to be safe.[4] Rapists also do not match most stereotypes: men who commit rape are our friends, co-workers, neighbors, and relatives. In some groups (such as sports teams and fraternities) sexual aggressiveness is seen as a positive trait for men to have. From conversations I've had, it seems that many rapists don't even know what they have committed is rape, assuming that it was okay because a girl was drunk, provocatively dressed, or displaying "suggestive" behavior.

Something clearly needs to be changed in our society when this kind of violence towards women is accepted or ignored by the majority of the population. Even women at the highest risk of becoming victims of rape seem ultimately unconvinced that it could happen to them. Even me.

My story is all too typical. I am the one college woman in four. My experience began on an average Saturday night, partying with my roommates at a co-worker's house outside campus. Not in the mood to drink, I shared a beer with a roommate so

people would stop pestering us about the fact that we weren't holding red cups of beer.

As the night wore on, my roommates grew bored and wanted to go home, but I was having fun with my coworker and his friends. He assured me that he would get me home safely. I bid my roommates adieu, refilled my red cup with water, and returned to the party. Less than 15 minutes later, I had my last memory of the evening.

I opened my eyes the next morning, naked, in a room I had never seen before. Next to me was my co-worker, naked and sound asleep. Large purple bruises covered both of my arms and legs, two parallel lines were burned into my right forearm, and dried blood covered my thighs and the sheets all around me. I saw my clothes nearby. My only thought: "Get out now." As I climbed out of the bed, he opened his eyes and gazed at my bloody, bruised, and burned body. "Good morning, beautiful."

When I asked him what had happened he just laughed. "You had a good time," he told me, after grumbling about how he'd have to wash my blood out of his formerly clean sheets. "Take me home now," I demanded. After assuring him that I did not, in fact, want to stay for breakfast, he got his keys.

The following days were extremely difficult, as I tried to determine what actually happened. To me, it is pretty clear that "date-rape drugs" were involved. These sedatives, which include GHB, Rophynol, and Ketamine, usually are colorless and odorless when added to a drink. The sedatives often make the person who drinks them appear to drunk and makes them lose their memory; for this reason, they have become widely known for their use in conjunction with rape and sexual assault. Although I will never be completely sure that someone gave me such a sedative, the blood and pain clearly tell me I was raped.

Thankfully, although I knew him from work, our interactions there were few and far between. I saw him in the building two or three times after that night, and did my best to avoid him. When I saw him at work, he acted as if nothing had happened, asking: "Why haven't you called?" Some days he would show up in the parking lot or outside my apartment complex, but I refused to talk to him. The last time I saw him was when he showed up at a restaurant where I worked, told me he missed me, and kissed me on the cheek. I almost slapped him. He sat in another server's section, and I avoided that part of the restaurant until he was gone.

It has been a year and a half since that night. At first, I couldn't even think about what had happened, not wanting to face the reality of what I had been through. I did not report the crime. I knew that my lack of memory about the evening would weaken my case. I was also confused because I had once seen this man as a friend and wanted to believe that he had not betrayed my trust.

Eventually, I began talking about my experience. Some friends seemed hesitant to believe my story, suggesting that I could have been drunk and blacked out, or that I had led him on. Others did believe me, but continued to interact with him like nothing had happened.

Similar reactions have been documented across the country. We simply don't want to believe that rape happens. We especially don't want to accept that our friends or family members could be perpetrators or victims of rape. Before this experience, I didn't either.

As difficult as it was, I found that talking about what had happened was the most helpful thing in allowing me to move on with my life. Even after I had shared my story, it seemed as though I was talking about something I had seen in a movie or heard from a friend, not an experience that I had lived through. It wasn't until about three months later, when I was beginning a romantic relationship with another man, that the reality of it all finally hit me.

When he touched me in certain ways, or even cast certain looks at me, it could cause bouts of uncontrolled panic and grief. Fortunately, he was very understanding, talked with me about my experience, and helped me to work through the pain. I was very lucky to have someone who was so patient and supportive of me as I tried to make sense of my feelings and reactions. After accepting the fact that this experience was not something that I could simply block out of my life, I decided to seek counseling at the campus health center. Through the support of some close friends and the counseling sessions, I am finally able to speak openly about my experience, and recognize the value of being able to share it with others.

If one benefit can come from this, it is that I can tell you that rape does happen, it is a problem, and we can make a difference. Please, if you are a victim of sexual violence, start talking about it. Ask your daughters and friends about their experiences. Most importantly, be ready to listen and support these women as their stories unfold.

References

1. Koss MP, Gidycz CA, Wisniewski N. "The scope of rape: incidence and prevalence of sexual aggression and victimization in a national sample of higher education students." *Journal of Consulting and Clinical Psychology* 1987; 55(2): 162–170.

2. Koss MP, Dinero TE, Siebel CA et al. "Stranger and acquaintance rape: are there differences in women's experiences." *Psycholgy of Women Quarterly* 1988; 12: 1–24. Gary JM. "An overview of sexual assault on campus." In: Gary JM (ed). *The Campus Community Confronts Sexual Assault: Institutional Issues and Campus Awareness*, Holmes Beach, FL: Learning Publications, 1994,

1–9, Brener ND, McMahon PM, Warren CW et al. "Forced sexual intercourse and associated health-risk behaviors among female college students in the United States. *Journal of Consulting and Clinical Psychology* 1999; 67(2): 252–9; Fisher B, Cullen F, Turner M. *The Sexual Victimization of College Women.* Washington, DC: U.S. Dept. of Justice, 2000.

3. Fisher, Cullen, and Turner, see above.

4. Tjaden P, Thoennes N. *Full Report of the Prevalence, Incidence, and Consequences of Violence Against Women: Findings from the National Violence Against Women Survey* (Report NCJ 183781). Washington, DC: National Institute of Justice, 2000.

The Relationship Between Rape Myths and Sexual Scripts: The Social Construction of Rape

by Kathryn M. Ryan

Abstract   Rape myths can influence sexual scripts that determine sexual attitudes and behavior. Sexual scripts are culturally determined patterns of behavior that inform desire and influence sexual behavior. Sexual scripts include hook up, seduction, rape, and acquaintance rape scripts (e.g., the too-much-to drink script, the man-is-ready-for-sex script, and the friends-gone-too-far script). However, research shows that many individuals still hold an erroneous real rape script, even when asked to describe acquaintance rape. This may prevent acquaintance rape victims from acknowledging their rape and it may allow acquaintance rapists to engage in sexual aggression while denying it is rape. Rape scripts research supports several of the rape myths reviewed by Edwards and her colleagues (Edwards, Turchik, Dardis, Reynolds, & Gidycz, 2011), but suggests two additional rape myths (i.e., the myth that men cannot stop once they have started to become sexually aroused and the myth that rapists are obviously different from other men). The study of the relationship between rape myths and sexual scripts may help to understand the social construction of rape and consensual sex. Rape myths and sexual scripts may work in conjunction to support rape.

Introduction

Edwards et al. (2011) have presented a compelling argument that rape myths are deeply rooted in US history, law, religion, and media stereotypes. These myths help to foster a climate in which rape is perpetrated and rape victims blamed for their victimization. Edwards and her colleagues suggest that four key rape myths (i.e., husbands cannot rape their wives, women enjoy rape, women ask to be raped, and women lie about being raped) are representative of a number of other contemporary beliefs that arise from a patriarchal system that accepts and fosters rape. The current paper will extend this thesis by proposing that rape myths influence sexual scripts which effect sexual beliefs and behavior.

The concept of myth has (at least) two connotations. One is myth as a story that is imbedded in history, religion, and culture and that guides human behavior and gives it meaning (e.g., Campbell 1988; May 1990). The second is myth as a mistaken belief—a lie. It is this connotation of rape myth that is evoked by Edwards and her colleagues in describing rape myth research. Others also share this view of rape myths. "Rape myths are attitudes and beliefs that are generally false but are widely and persistently held, and that serve to deny and justify male sexual aggression against women" (Lonsway and Fitzgerald 1994, p. 134). Rape myths have been called "the most self-serving justification of sexual coercion ever invented by callous men" (Zillmann and Weaver 1989, p. 101).

Myths can inform our understanding of our lives and give us meaning (e.g., Campbell 1988; May 1990). "A myth is a way of making sense in a senseless world. Myths are narrative patterns that give significance to our existence" (May 1990, p. 15). Myths can provide prototypical stories that guide behavior. "Myth is a form of expression which reveals a process of thought and feeling—man's awareness of and response to the universe, his fellow men, and his separate being. It is a projection in concrete and dramatic form of fears and desires undiscoverable and inexpressible in any other way" (Feder as cited in May 1990, p. 28).

Myths can become scripts that are enacted or avoided. These scripts structure our understanding of our own and others' experience (Schank and Abelson 1977). Rape myths may be part of a cognitive scheme that reflect the belief in a just world and facilitate sexual aggression (Bohner et al. 2009). Rape myths can provide comfort to women and men because they allow them to distance themselves and their own behavior from the possibility of being victims or perpetrators of rape. Bohner and colleagues (2009) found that rape myth acceptance served as a buffer for women who experienced less anxiety when presented with the issue of sexual violence. In contrast, for men, rape myth acceptance served as a "means to rationalize and justify their own tendencies to engage in sexual aggression" (p. 34). Thus, myths that blame women for rape, disbelieve claims of rape, and exonerate the perpetrator operate differently in women and men (Bohner et al. 2009: Lonsway and Fitzgerald 1995). Rape myths can also provide cautionary tales of what could happen when women

are incautious or unguarded (e.g., women invite rape by engaging in overtly sexual behavior or wearing provocative dress; only certain women are raped—those who drink too much, sleep around, or hang out in the wrong places). Finally, rape myths can be used as guidelines or instructions for the perpetration of sexual aggression (e.g., it's okay to rape women who tease men, dress provocatively, or engage in sexual behavior; women mean yes when they say no; and women want to be raped).

Rape Scripts

Scripts are prototypes for how events normally proceed (Schank and Abelson 1977). Schank and Abelson described four conceptualizations that establish a script: precondition (s), elements that depend on other elements (e.g., one must take the subway to go to the restaurant), location(s), and role (s). Scripts may be shared, concealed, competing with other scripts, and/or instrumental (i.e., rigid sequences of behavior in the service of a goal). Sexual scripts are culturally determined, they create sexual meaning and desire, and they enable individuals to interpret their own and their partner's behavior (e.g., Frith 2009; McCormick 2010a; Simon and Gagnon 1984, 1986). Sexual scripts include predictable patterns of behavior (e.g., male persistence), methods of consent (usually clear and direct), and methods of nonconsent (often polite and indirect) (Frith 2009). Script research has been applied to a variety of sexual behaviors including rape and seduction (e.g., Littleton and Axsom 2003), acquaintance rape (e.g., Carroll and Clark 2006), and hook ups (Littleton et al. 2009).

Rape scripts are beliefs about the nature of rape (e.g., the location, weaponry, sex of perpetrators), the roles of the sexes in rape, boundaries of vulnerability to rape, and the disposition of the victims (Crome and McCabe 2001). In an early study of rape scripts, Ryan (1988) asked a small number of participants to describe the *typical rape* and the *typical seduction* "in as much detail as possible, including what led up to, what happened during, and what followed the events" (p. 239). Participants were also asked to describe the characteristics of the individuals, including their thoughts and feelings. Half of the participants described the rape first and half, the seduction first.

Ryan (1988) content analyzed the scripts based on prior rape research and elements that were commonly repeated in the scripts. Common categories included perceived precondition (s), location(s), and role(s). Results showed that the rape and seduction scripts were very different. Rape scripts resembled a *blitz rape.* They involved a stranger who was a crazed male, who attacked a woman outdoors, at night, in a sudden and physically violent attack. In contrast, seduction scripts more closely resembled an acquaintance rape (e.g., they were indoors, involved alcohol, and prior conversation). Complete rape and seduction scripts from two of the participants in the original study follow (the first is from a male, the second is from a female) (Ryan 1986):

> **Rape** A woman is walking down (a) road that is poorly lit. Not that many people go that way so it is empty. As she is walking along, a man comes up from behind she (sic) and knocks her down to the ground. At first the woman doesn't know what's going on, but soon realizes that there's a man on top of her ripping her clothes off. She is so terrified that she can't scream and the man is too strong so she can't get him off of her. The man is probably a loner with a lot of mental problems who is angered very easily and very frustrated with his life. He lurks around barren places hoping women will come by. The woman could (be) an average business woman on her way home from work, she got out late and so decided to take a short cut and save time. When it's over the man is temporarily content but will soon become frustrated. It doesn't bother him on what he did and he wouldn't think twice. The woman would be mentally tormented for many years. Because of the way women are treated in rape cases, she may be afraid to report it. (Male, 19 years old)

> It usually begins with a female who is walking alone at night. No one is around, except a man looking for a victim. He begins to follow her at first keeping at a distance. He waits to see her reactions, does she become nervous, or does she stay calm? If she gets really nervous, she'll practically be running. Then, he'll go for the attack.

He'll grab her putting his hand over her mouth. Depending upon where they are, he may drag her to a more secluded area. He'll hit her a few times for a warning, and to show who is in control. He'll hold her hands back, and begin to remove her clothing. As quickly as he can, he'll force himself into her, as she struggles to prevent the act. She is scared because she does not want to be hurt or killed. He is scared that she'll fight back or he'll be caught. Then, he may beat her more to make her unable to run away and get help quickly. She is left scarred emotionally for life, he lives in fear she will get revenge. (Female, 18 years old)

> **Seduction** A man comes up to a woman at a bar. He buys her a drink and starts a conversation with her. If the woman is responsive then he continues and buys her some more drinks. By the end of the night he asks her back to his place. Takes her back and gives her some more to drink. The majority of the time both people feel it's a "one night stand" and that there is little likelyhood (sic) of them ever meeting again. They probably feel little real emotional attachment and that it is mostly physical. The next morning they say goodbye and the woman leaves, and by the next day may think little about the entire situations. The next weekend, both will do the same thing. Both participants are working people during the week, who are tired, need to get out and have a good time, as well as have some companionship. (Male, 19 years old)

> You see a person who is very attractive. Something about them really interests you. They give you a certain look, and they have a mysterious look in their eyes. They'll walk over to you, and begin to talk to you, introducing themselves. You'll both talk for a while, and then one of the two will make a suggestion to go somewhere where you'll be alone—either to go for a walk another room (sic), back to one's house for a drink, etc. Usually the people do not know much about each other, and seem only interested in a "one night

stand." Infatuation plays a big part. Then, they'll go back to one's house. Drinks will be poured, and the setting is very romantic. Then (usually) the man will grab the woman and give her a passionate kiss. Things get heavier, until the couple go all the way. Then they depart, never to see each other again. (Female, 18 years old)

Subsequent research showed the key features of rape scripts are the assailant's use of physical violence and the victim's resistance (e.g., Krahé et al. 2007; Littleton and Axsom 2003), as well as negative psychological consequences for the victim (e.g., Littleton et al. 2007). This is often called the *real rape script* (e.g., Horvath and Brown 2009). The real rape script involves a sudden and physically violent attack on an unsuspecting woman, usually by a stranger. The woman is alone at the time of the attack. She may physically resist the rape or she may be too afraid to resist. There is no doubt that the victim was raped-her only mistake was being in the wrong place at the wrong time. She is devastated after the rape.

Research also showed that unacknowledged rape victims were more likely than acknowledged rape victims to hold a real-rape script (e.g., Bondurant 2001; Kahn et al. 1994). Thus, their belief that rape involved high levels of violence may have led them to label their personal experience with a relatively non-physically violent sexual assault as something other than rape. It is also possible that this belief makes women more vulnerable to sexual predation (Turchik et al. 2010). Turchik and her colleagues asked college women to write about a hypothetical experience with unwanted sexual advances from an acquaintance. Participants were asked a series of questions to elicit details of the script, including how long they knew the perpetrator. Sexual victimization was assessed at two times, at the time they completed their acquaintance rape scripts and 8 weeks later. Script content significantly correlated with the experience of victimization at time two. Women who experienced severe sexual victimization at time two wrote scripts at time one that described an outdoor setting, non-forceful victim resistance, and a perpetrator who was known for less than 1 month. Turchik and her colleagues suggest that "some women may hold scripts that are less consistent with an acquaintance rape, making it

less likely for them to recognize important risk cues in contexts that do not fit their idea of a real rape" (pp. 81–82). They believe that women who hold a real rape script may be at risk for sexual assault.

Subsequent research showed that people may have a variety of rape scripts. These scripts include several acquaintance rape scripts: the too-much-to drink script, the man-is-ready-for-sex script, and the friends gone-too-far script (Carroll and Clark 2006). However, some individuals write real rape scripts when asked to write about acquaintance rape (Clark and Carroll 2008; Turchik et al. 2010). Still others do not appear to acknowledge the possibility that rape could occur during casual sexual encounters, like a hook up (Littleton et al. 2009). Thus, the real rape script may be strong and powerful even after years of acquaintance rape-education efforts. The belief that rape involves a sudden and extreme physical attack from a stranger may interfere with the ability to recognize a rape in which an acquaintance uses physical restraint to subdue the victim. If it takes longer for a victim to recognize the intent of the perpetrator, it can make it more difficult to avoid rape (Bart and O'Brien 1985). In addition, women show less forceful resistance for lower level sexual coercion than for rape (Fisher et al. 2007) and forceful physical resistance works better than non-forceful verbal resistance in preventing rape (e.g., Ullman 2007; Ullman and Knight 1991). Thus, if a potential victim misreads a situation, she might use less forceful resistance than necessary and risk being raped. Moreover, the belief in a real rape script may also delay the individual's ability to define the experience as rape and make it less likely that assistance will be sought (Warshaw 1988).

The predominance of the real rape script may be related to women's very real fears about rape and the possibility of extreme physical violence and even death (Gordon and Riger 1989). Senn and Dzinas (1996) constructed a Fear of Rape Scale based on prior research. Most of the items dealt with fears of being alone (or in public spaces) late at night and the resultant consequences, including vigilance and behavioral restrictions. Thus, fear of rape is assessed as fear of *real rape*, not fear of acquaintance rape. Moreover, women's fear of real rape acts as a *master offense* heightening their fear of other crimes (Ferraro 1996). Fisher and Sloan (2003) found that college women showed a relatively high fear of rape on campus at night. Fear of rape was associated with constrained behaviors (e.g., carrying keys in a defensive manner, asking someone to walk with them at night, avoiding certain areas on campus). In addition, fear of rape influenced fear of other crimes such as assault and robbery.

Krahé and her colleagues (2007) presented evidence that contemporary adolescents still hold a real rape script, which they called the *"real rape stereotype"* (p. 316). They described the script for non-consensual intercourse as reflecting several key elements, including the threat of physical force, threat with a weapon, and victim resistance. In comparison to a script for a first sexual encounter, the script for non-consensual intercourse was also distinguished by its location (e.g., more chance meetings, outdoors, at a party), the intention for sex, and perceived greater drug or alcohol consumption by the boy. Moreover, girls were more likely than boys to believe in the real rape stereotype.

Clark and Carroll (2008) studied date rape scripts in college students. They found that men's and women's date rape scripts contained many of the same elements (e.g., the man is only interested in sex, the woman is not ready for sex, and the woman is upset). However, women wrote more real rape scripts (which involved physical force, negative victim emotions, and the label of rape) and scripts suggesting consent for early sexual activities (e.g., petting) that were followed by the use of physical force to make the woman do things that made her uncomfortable. In contrast, men wrote more *wrong accusation* scripts, in which a man was falsely accused of rape because coercion and resistance were verbal and the woman gave in, and *party rape scripts*, in which alcohol consumption was a major element. Clark and Carroll believe that these gender differences may be because women tend to focus on the victim and her emotions, whereas men may seek to understand the perpetrator's behavior in the context of mixed signals and the absence of a definitive refusal. Thus, it appears that some date rape scripts are commonly held, whereas others are less commonly held. Moreover, gender differences in date rape scripts may contribute to misunderstanding and sexual coercion (Clark et al. 2009). Very simply, men may believe in a yes/no form of consent, whereas

women may see consent as negotiated through an ongoing process that involves a series of gates, in which they are willing to do some things but not others. However, both men and women expect women to be careful in their refusal of sex in order to preserve the man's face (Frith 2009). Thus, rape scripts can make it more difficult for women to assess an ongoing sexual coercion attempt and to negotiate a tolerable conclusion.

Rape Scripts and Sexual Predation

Most of the research linking rape scripts to participants' interpretations of their own experience as a rape focuses on female victims of sexual aggression (e.g., Bondurant 2001; Kahn et al. 1994). For example, researchers have sought to understand why some women do not label their personal experience as rape when it clearly matches the legal definition of rape. Rape myths and rape scripts can narrow victims' definitions of rape and decrease the likelihood that victims will acknowledge an event is rape (Peterson and Muehlenhard 2004). In addition, the presence of an experience that strongly contradicts the real rape script (e.g., a victim's initial sexual desire) may prevent the application of the rape label to nonconsensual sexual experiences (Peterson and Muehlenhard 2007). It is also possible that victims might resist labeling their experience as rape because of the perceived negative ramifications of being a rape victim, including changes in worldview and view of self (Crome and McCabe 2001). Having a strong real rape script may allow them to escape some of the negative ramifications of being a rape victim. However, belief in the real rape script may also make them more vulnerable to a legally defined rape (Turchik et al. 2010). And, it may not prevent the psychological ramifications of rape victimization (e.g., Koss et al. 1988; McMullin and White 2006). Research shows unacknowledged rape victims experience many of the same negative consequences as those who acknowledged rape.

The role of rape scripts in sexual predation is less well-studied. At the level of culture, rape scripts may become instructional guides, defining the nature and parameters of a just world (Crome and McCabe 2001). I have argued (Ryan 2004) that acquaintance rapists and convicted sex offenders have a common belief system that includes rape myths, other rape-supportive beliefs (e.g., adversarial sex, hyper-sexuality), and sexual scripts. These beliefs encourage sexual narcissism, allow for victim blame, and the minimization and denial of rape. Rape myths may lead to sexual scripts that are reinforced by fantasy and enacted in rape. These sexual scripts may involve a seduction or a rape and they may be an important link in the connection between rape myths and sexual aggression.

However, there is little research on the rape and seduction scripts of sexually aggressive (and non-aggressive) men. As far as I know, researchers have not asked sexually aggressive men for their sexual scripts. Instead, rape script research in men frequently focuses on overt verbalizations and behaviors that imply the presence of scripts. For example, Beauregard et al. (2007b) used a script approach to describe the hunting process engaged in by serial sex offenders. They interviewed convicted sex offenders. They assumed that sex offending is a product of rational choice in which decisions are made about where to search for potential victims, the techniques that can be used to disable victims, and techniques for later victim release. These accounts were characterized by a *hunting model*, an apt metaphor when one considers the amount of time many sex offenders spent prowling for victims.

In later research, using interviews and police records, Beauregard and colleagues (Beauregard et al. 2007a; Deslauriers-Varin and Beauregard 2010) found six scripts among sex offenders (three scripts with two tracks each); however, some of the scripts were primarily for pedophiles (those with younger victims). The location of encounter was an important distinguishing feature in most scripts (i.e., indoors versus outdoors). The four rape scripts were home intrusion, home invasion (using trust to enter the home), coercive-outdoors, and social or recreational onsite attacks. Approximately half of the offenders were willing to use multiple scripts. The offenses of the convicted serial sex offenders often matched a real rape script (e.g., involving a sudden assault, using threats and violence, taking place outside or when a woman was home alone). More importantly, two key script elements, location and role, appeared to be strong indicators of different rape scripts. Is it possible that enacting a real rape script makes offenders at greater risk for detection, conviction, and punishment? The real rape script

might be an important part of the legal and criminal justice systems' responses to an alleged rape.

Kanin (1975) studied men who were not incarcerated for sexual offenses. He interviewed sexually aggressive college men about their experience with sexual aggression. He did not ask for their sexual scripts, but the stories they told held several script elements. For example, sexual aggression was usually preceded by consensual sexual foreplay, while later refusals were ignored. Sexual foreplay may be one precondition for the acceptable use of force in some sexually aggressive men. This may allow the acquaintance rapist to hold the woman to be responsible for her victimization. Do these men believe that men cannot stop once they have become sexually aroused? This rape myth may be part of a personal, instrumental script that results in acquaintance rape. In addition, several men mentioned rape myths such as female provocation and female promiscuity. These myths also suggest potential precursors for sexual aggression. Finally, other men suggested that sexual aggression was an apt punishment for a teasing or exploitative woman, which suggests the possibility that they held a rape script (for a *justifiable rape*).

In a later article, Kanin (1985) described date rapists as sexual predators who employed a variety of techniques to gain sexual access including "drugging, extortion, fraud, and lying" (p. 223). Sexual preoccupation is a major predictor of sexual coercion (e.g., Clark et al. 2009). Kanin found that date rapists were relatively more likely than controls to attempt to intoxicate a female with drugs or alcohol, frequently profess love, promise to further the relationship, and threaten to terminate the relationship. These sexual coercion techniques have been found by many other researchers (e.g., Byers and O'Sullivan 1996) and suggest that some individuals believe that it is acceptable to coerce sex. Moreover, sexually aggressive men may seek peer group support for their behavior (Schwartz and DeKeseredy 1997) and they may obtain a degree of status from coercing sex with an unwilling female (Kanin 1967). Kanin found that sexually coercive men believed that prestige was obtained for coercing sex from *gold diggers* and *teasers*. In addition, a variety of verbal justifications were offered that stigmatized the victim, especially her prior sexual experience. Thus, several rape myths allowed for forceful sex (or *justifiable rape*) scripts in sexually aggressive men. The establishment of certain pre-conditions, the presence of certain locations, and the assumption of certain roles produce a sequence of events that can result in rape.

Sexual script research supports several of the myths reviewed by Edwards and her colleagues (2011) and those present in rape myth measures (e.g., Bohner et al. 2009; Burt 1980; Feild and Bienen 1980; Payne et al. 1999). For example, the presence of the *wrong accusation acquaintance rape script* in men, especially among students at a military academy, may be reflective of the myth that women lie about rape (Carroll and Clark 2006; Clark and Carroll 2008). Embedded in this script is the presumption that the victim did not show sufficient resistance to verbal coercion tactics and eventually consented. This could reflect a myth related to the real rape script (that rape must involve overt physical force and physical resistance). This belies the nature of much date rape, which is often less physically violent than stranger rape and may involve verbal resistance (e.g., Koss et al. 1988; Warshaw 1988). The real rape script might arise from and contribute to the religious, historical, and legal injunctions presented by Edwards and her colleagues.

The presence of a *party acquaintance rape script* indicates the possibility that some may believe that alcohol could be implicated in acquaintance rape and it might reflect the myth that women ask to be raped, because of their own complicity or negligence. Edwards and her colleagues noted research on the role of provocative dress and excessive alcohol or drug use in perceived victim culpability. Alcohol use may make the perpetrator appear to be less responsible and the victim, more responsible for rape (e.g., Richardson and Campbell 1982; Sims et al. 2007). It also may be used by acquaintance rapists to minimize and deny their own rape. The belief that alcohol use reduces rapist culpability is found in several measures of rape myths (e.g., Burt 1980; Payne et al. 1999).

One rape myth not reviewed by Edwards and her colleagues that is suggested by script research is the myth that men cannot stop themselves once they have become sexually aroused (*blue balls*). This is one of the four major types of rape myths (called exonerating the perpetrator) cited by Bohner and his colleagues (2009) and it is a subscale on the Illinois Rape Myth Acceptance Scale (Payne et al. 1999). This myth holds that men are very sexual and they cannot control their sexual behavior. As previously noted, it may be a belief in some sexually aggressive men. It may also be responsible for some victims eventually consenting to unwanted sex (e.g., Gavey 2005).

A second rape myth not reviewed by Edwards and her colleagues that is also present in rape scripts is the myth that rapists are obviously different from other men (e.g., mentally sick, sexually frustrated, not normal) (Feild 1978; Payne et al. 1999). This belief is even stronger in real rape scripts, in which very negative descriptions of rapists are common (e.g., "obviously psychologically disoriented," "a demented weirdo," and "A sick person-usually a druggie or heavy boozer or something (sic) won't be able to have a woman because he is so gross") (Ryan 1986). The socially skilled predator may be able to con himself and potential victims because he does not resemble the myth of the obviously different rapist. This myth may also impact the legal and criminal justice systems' responses to an alleged rapist.

The Role of the Media in Rape Myths and Sexual Scripts

Edwards and her colleagues (2011) note the importance of the media in promoting rape myths. Mass media may also help to structure sexual scripts (McCormick 2010b). These sexual scripts include the beliefs that sex defines masculinity, heterosexual men objectify women, and heterosexual men are sexually preoccupied (Kim et al. 2007). In contrast, women are seen as sexual gatekeepers and negatively judged for their sexual conduct. This is especially true in television sitcoms. Do these media-induced sexual scripts feed upon rape myths that endorse female culpability for sexual aggression and forgive male sexual coercion? Edwards and her colleagues (2011) believe that the media support rape myths. The media may also foster rape through the sexual scripts they provide.

One medium that provides sexual scripts is hardcore pornography. Consuming pornography can influence people's sexual knowledge, attitudes, and behavior, as well as their perceptions of the opposite sex (Hald and Malamuth 2008). Although pornography consumption may provide positive benefits, it might also have negative consequences.

Pornography consumption is associated with sexual coercion in college men (e.g., Bouffard 2010; Carr and VanDeusen 2004). Research has shown that the use of pornography (especially the use of violent pornography) is correlated with sexual coercion and a variety of related measures, including rape myth acceptance (e.g., Hald et al. 2010; Malamuth et al. 2000). However, recent research suggests that, "it may be that the effects of pornography are important for some individuals but not for others and that they may be relatively powerful only as they interact with some other factors" (Malamuth et al. 2000; p 19).

Malamuth and his colleagues (e.g., Kingston et al. 2009; Vega and Malamuth 2007) described a confluence model in which sexual aggression was predicted by the interaction between several factors. These factors include hostile masculinity, the desire for impersonal sex, and general hostility. Hostile masculinity includes several rape-supportive beliefs such as rape myth acceptance, adversarial sexual beliefs, hostility toward women, and dominance motives for sex. Malamuth and his colleagues (e.g., Malamuth et al. 2000; Vega and Malamuth 2007) found that pornography use was associated with sexual aggression only for men who were at high risk as indicated by the confluence model. In addition, bivariate correlations indicated significant relationships between pornography use and rape myth acceptance and between pornography use and sexual aggression (Vega and Malamuth 2007).

Kingston and his colleagues (2009) suggest that pornography may act two ways to increase sexual aggression. It might provide models of behavior that are observed and imitated. It might also prime rape myth attitudes and negative beliefs about certain women (e.g., loose women, whores). This could be especially likely for men at risk in the confluence model: those who hold hostile attitudes toward women and female sexuality, those who desire impersonal sex, and those who have hostile and impulsive personalities. Moreover, the influence may be bi-directional (Kingston et al. 2009; Malamuth et al. 2000). Sexually aggressive men may be more attracted to violent media. Thus, as suggested by Edwards and her colleagues (2011), rape myths do not have to be widely held to impact society negatively. Rape myths in sexually aggressive individuals may allow them to construct sexual scripts that result in rape.

Questions for Future Research

- We need to learn more about the processes underlying rape myths and sexual scripts. Why do rape myths persevere in the face of their untruth? And, how do culture, gender, and age influence rape myths and sexual scripts?

- Are rape myths inevitable in a patriarchal society because they allow for the construction of sexual scripts that facilitate sexual aggression? Will new myths replace old myths? Are some myths more intransigent than others?

- Do acquaintance rapists hold different scripts than non-aggressive individuals or convicted sex offenders? Are there *acknowledged* and *unacknowledged rapists* and do they differ in their rape myths and sexual scripts? Moreover, exactly how do rape myths relate to the sexual and rape scripts that allow for rape? Do rape myths offer protection for sexually licentious people because their behavior does not match their rape scripts? Or, do some sexually aggressive individuals enact rape scripts that are justified by rape myths?

- Can people be influenced by rape myths even if they don't believe them? Research on stereotype threat shows that even disbelieved stereotypes can inhibit the performance of stereotype targets (Steele et al. 2002). Are the priming effects of rape myths and concomitant sexual scripts limited to those who believe them or might they influence non-believers? Can a few people who believe rape myths have an impact greater than their number? And, does the knowledge that others believe rape myths influence the behavior of those who do not hold these myths?

In conclusion, the current paper suggests that rape myths may influence sexual scripts in some individuals. These individuals may be those most vulnerable to victimization and those who are sexually aggressive. It is suggested that future research study rape and seduction scripts in non-aggressive and sexually aggressive individuals, including convicted offenders and those who are undetected acquaintance rapists (both *acknowledged* and *unacknowledged rapists*). The study of rape myths and sexual scripts could help to elucidate the relationship between them and to further describe the social construction of rape. Finally, this research must attend to the influence of culture, gender, and age on rape myths and sexual scripts.

Acknowledgement Thanks to M. Diane Clark for comments on this manuscript.

References

Bart, P. B., & O'Brien, P. H. (1985). *Stopping rape: Successful survival strategies.* Oxford: Pergamon.

Beauregard, E., Proulx, J., Rossmo, K., Leclerc, B., & Allaire, J. (2007a). Script analysis of the hunting process of serial sex offenders. *Criminal Justice and Behavior, 34,* 1069–1084. doi:10.1177/0093854807300851.

Beauregard, E., Rossmo, D. K., & Proulx, J. (2007b). A descriptive model of the hunting process of serial sex offenders: A rational choice perspective. *Journal of Family Violence, 22,* 449–463. doi:10.1007/s10896-007-9101-3.

Bohner, G., Eyssel, F., Pina, A., Siebler, F., & Viki, G. T. (2009). Rape myth acceptance: Cognitive affective and behavioural effects of beliefs that blame the victim and exonerate the perpetrator. In M. Horvath & J. Brown (Eds.), *Rape: Challenging contemporary thinking* (pp. 17–45). Devon: Willan.

Bondurant, B. (2001). University women's acknowledgment of rape: Individual, situational, and social factors. *Violence Against Women, 7,* 294–314. doi:10.1177/1077801201007003004.

Bouffard, L. A. (2010). Exploring the utility of entitlement in understanding sexual aggression. *Journal of Criminal Justice, 38,* 870–879. doi:10.1016/j.jcrimjus.2010.06.002.

Burt, M. R. (1980). Cultural myths and supports for rape. *Journal of Personality and Social Psychology, 38,* 217–230. doi:10.1037/0022-3514.38.2.217.

Byers, E. S., & O'Sullivan, L. F. (1996). *Sexual coercion in dating relationships.* New York: Haworth.

Campbell, J. (1988). *The power of myth with Bill Moyers.* New York: Doubleday.

Carr, J. L., & VanDeusen, K. M. (2004). Risk factors for male sexual aggression on college campuses. *Journal of Family Violence, 19,* 279–289. doi:10.1023/B:JOFV.0000042078.55308.4d.

Carroll, M. H., & Clark, M. D. (2006). Men's acquaintance rape scripts: A comparison between a regional university and a military academy. *Sex Roles, 55,* 469–480. doi:10.1007/s1199-006-9102-3.

Clark, M. D., & Carroll, M. H. (2008). Acquaintance rape scripts of women and men: Similarities and differences. *Sex Roles, 58,* 616–625. doi:10.1007/s11199-007-9373-3.

Clark, M. D., Carroll, M. H., Bartoli, A. M., & Taylor, M. A. (2009). Flirting to rape: The influence of the traditional sexual script. In J. H. Ulrich & B. T. Cosell (Eds.), *Handbook on gender roles* (pp. 1–32). Hauppauge: Nova Science.

Crome, S. A., & McCabe, M. P. (2001). Adult rape scripting within a victimological perspective. *Aggression and Violent Behavior, 6,* 395–413. doi:10.1016/S1359-1789(00)00013-6.

Deslauriers-Varin, N., & Beauregard, E. (2010). Victims' routine activities and sex offenders' target selection scripts: A latent analysis. *Sexual Abuse: A Journal of Research and Treatment, 22,* 315–342. doi:10.1177/1079063210375975.

Edwards, K. M., Turchik, J. A., Dardis, C., Reynolds, N., & Gidycz, C. A. (2011). Rape myths: History, individual and institutional-level presence, and implications for change. Sex Roles, this issue. doi:10.1007/s11199-011-9943-2.

Feild, H. S. (1978). Attitudes toward rape: A comparative analysis of police, rapists, crisis counselors, and citizens. *Journal of Personality and Social Psychology, 36,* 156–179. doi:10.1037/0022-3514.36.2.156.

Feild, H. S., & Bienen, L. B. (1980). *Jurors and rape.* Lexington: Lexington Books.

Ferraro, K. F. (1996). Women's fear of victimization: Shadow of sexual assault? *Social Forces, 75,* 667–690. doi:10.2307/2580418.

Fisher, B. S., & Sloan, J. J. (2003). Unraveling the fear of victimization among college women: Is the "shadow of sexual assault hypothesis" supported? *Justice Quarterly, 20,* 633–659. doi:10.1080/07418820300095641.

Fisher, B. S., Daigle, L. E., Cullen, F. T., & Santana, S. A. (2007). Assessing the efficacy of the protective action-completion nexus for sexual victimizations. *Violence and Victims, 22,* 18–42. doi:10.1891/vv-v22i1a002.

Frith, H. (2009). Sexual scripts, sexual refusals, and rape. In M. Horvath & J. Brown (Eds.), *Rape: Challenging contemporary thinking* (pp. 99–122). Devon: Willan.

Gavey, N. (2005). *Just sex? The cultural scaffolding of rape.* London: Routledge.

Gordon, M. T., & Riger, S. (1989). *The female fear: The social costs of rape.* Urbana: University of Illinois Press.

Hald, G. M., & Malamuth, N. M. (2008). Self-perceived effects of pornography consumption. *Archives of Sexual Behavior, 37,* 614–625. doi:10.1007/s10508-007-9212-1.

Hald, G. M., Malamuth, N. M., & Yuen, C. (2010). Pornography and attitudes supporting violence against women: Revisiting the relationship in nonexperimental studies. *Aggressive Behavior, 36*, 14–20. doi:10.1002/ab.20328.

Horvath, M., & Brown, J. (2009). *Rape: Challenging contemporary thinking.* Devon: Willan.

Kahn, A. S., Mathie, V. A., & Torgler, C. (1994). Rape scripts and rape acknowledgement. *Psychology of Women Quarterly, 18*, 53–66. doi:10.1111/j.1471-6402.1994.tb00296.x.

Kanin, E. J. (1967). Reference groups and sex conduct norm violations. *Sociological Quarterly, 8*, 495–504. doi:10.1111/j.1533-8525.1967.tb01085.x.

Kanin, E. J. (1975). Selected dyadic aspects of male sex aggression. In L. G. Schultz (Ed.), *Rape victimology* (pp. 59–76). Springfield: Charles C. Thomas.

Kanin, E. J. (1985). Date rapists: Differential sexual socialization and relative deprivation. *Archives of Sexual Behavior, 14*, 219–231. doi:10.1007/BF01542105.

Kim, J. L., Sorsoli, C. L., Collins, K., Zylbergold, B. A., Schooler, D., & Tolman, D. L. (2007). From sex to sexuality: Exposing the heterosexual script on primetime network television. *Journal of Sex Research, 44*, 145–157. doi:10.1080/00224490701263660.

Kingston, D. A., Malamuth, N. M., Fedoroff, P., & Marshall, W. L. (2009). The importance of individual differences in pornography use: Theoretical perspectives and implications for treating sex offenders. *Journal of Sex Research, 46*, 216–232. doi:10.1080/00224490902747701.

Koss, M. P., Dinero, T. E., Seibel, C. A., & Cox, S. L. (1988). Stranger and acquaintance rape: Are there differences in the victim's experience? *Psychology of Women Quarterly, 12*, 1–24. doi:10.1111/j.1471-6402.1988.tb00924.x.

Krahé, B., Bieneck, S., & Scheinberger-Olwig, R. (2007). Adolescents' sexual scripts: Schematic representations of consensual and non-consensual heterosexual interactions. *Journal of Sex Research, 4*, 316–327. doi:10.1080/00224490701580923.

Littleton, H. L., & Axsom, D. (2003). Rape and seduction scripts of university students: Implications for rape attributions and unacknowledged rape. *Sex Roles, 49*, 465–475. doi:10.1023/A:1025824505185.

Littleton, H., Breitkopf, C. R., & Berenson, A. B. (2007). Rape scripts of low-income European American and Latina women. *Sex Roles, 56*, 509–516. doi:10.1007/s/11199-007-9189-1.

Littleton, H., Tabernik, H., Canales, E. J., & Backstrom, T. (2009). Risky situation or harmless fun? A qualitative examination of college women's bad hook-up and rape scripts. *Sex Roles, 60*, 793–804. doi:10.1007/s1199-009-9586-8.

Lonsway, K. A., & Fitzgerald, L. F. (1994). Rape myths: In review. *Psychology of Women Quarterly, 18*, 133–164. doi:10.1111/j.1471-6402.1994.tb00448.x.

Lonsway, K. A., & Fitzgerald, L. F. (1995). Attitudinal antecedents of rape myth acceptance: A theoretical and empirical reexamination. *Journal of Personality and Social Psychology, 68*, 704–711. doi:10.1037/0022-3514.68.4.704.

Malamuth, N. M., Addison, T., & Koss, M. (2000). Pornography and sexual aggression: Are there reliable effects and can we understand them? *Annual Review of Sex Research, 11*, 26–91.

May, R. (1990). *The cry for myth.* New York: Norton.

McCormick, N. B. (2010a). Sexual scripts: Social and therapeutic implications. *Sexual and Relationship Therapy, 25*, 96–120. doi:10.1080/14681990903550167.

McCormick, N. B. (2010b). Preface to sexual scripts: Social and therapeutic implications. *Sexual and Relationship Therapy, 25*, 91–95. doi:10.1080/14681990903563707.

McMullin, D., & White, J. W. (2006). Long-term effects of labeling a rape experience. *Psychology of Women Quarterly, 30*, 96–105. doi:10.1111/j.1471-6402.2006.00266.x.

Payne, D. L., Lonsway, K. A., & Fitzgerald, L. F. (1999). Rape myth acceptance: Exploration of its structure and its measurement using the Illinois Rape Myth Acceptance Scale. *Journal of Research in Personality, 33*, 27–68. doi:10.1006/jrpe.1998.2238.

Peterson, Z. D., & Muehlenhard, C. L. (2004). Was it rape? The function of women's rape myth acceptance and definitions of sex in labeling their own experience. *Sex Roles, 51*, 129–144. doi:10.1023/B:SERS.0000037758.95376.00.

Peterson, Z. D., & Muehlenhard, C. L. (2007). Conceptualizing the "wantedness" of women's consensual and nonconsensual sexual experiences: Implications for how women label their experiences with rape. *Journal of Sex Research, 44*, 72–88. doi:10.1080/00224490709336794.

Richardson, D., & Campbell, J. L. (1982). Alcohol and rape: The effect of alcohol on attributions of blame for rape. *Personality and Social Psychology Bulletin, 8*, 468–476. doi:10.1177/0146167282083013.

Ryan, K. (1986). [Rape and seduction scripts]. Unpublished raw data.

Ryan, K. (1988). Rape and seduction scripts. *Psychology of Women Quarterly, 12*, 237–245. doi:10.1111/j.1471-6402.1988. tb00939.x.

Ryan, K. M. (2004). Further evidence for a cognitive component of rape. *Aggression and Violent Behavior, 9,* 579–604. doi:10.1016/j.avb.2003.05.001.

Schank, R. C., & Abelson, R. P. (1977). *Scripts, plans, goals, and understanding.* Hillsdale: Lawrence Erlbaum.

Schwartz, M. D., & DeKeseredy, W. S. (1997). *Sexual assault on the college campus.* Thousand Oaks: Sage.

Senn, C. Y., & Dzinas, K. (1996). Measuring fear of rape: A new scale. *Canadian Journal of Behavioural Science, 28,* 141–144. doi:10.1037/0008-400X.28.2.141.

Simon, W., & Gagnon, J. J. (1984). Sexual scripts. *Society, 22,* 53–60. doi:10.1007/BF02701260.

Simon, W., & Gagnon, J. J. (1986). Sexual scripts: Permanence and change. *Archives of Sexual Behavior, 15,* 97–120. doi:10.1007/BF01542219.

Sims, C. M., Noel, N. E., & Maisto, S. A. (2007). Rape blame as a function of alcohol presence and resistance type. *Addictive Behaviors, 32,* 2766–2775. doi:10.1016/j.addbeh.2007.04.013.

Steele, C. M., Spencer, S. J., & Aronson, J. (2002). Contending with group image: The psychology of stereotype and social identity threat. In M. Zanna (Ed.), *Advances in experimental social psychology* (pp. 379–440). San Diego: Academic.

Turchik, J. A., Probst, D. R., Irvin, C. R., Chau, M., & Gidycz, C. A. (2010). Prediction of sexual assault experiences in college women based on rape scripts: A prospective analysis. *Psychology of Violence, 1,* 76–83. doi:10.1037/2152-0828.1.S.76.

Ullman, S. E. (2007). A 10-year update of "review and critique of empirical studies of rape avoidance." *Criminal Justice and Behavior, 34,* 411–429. doi:10.1177/0093854806297117.

Ullman, S. E., & Knight, R. A. (1991). A multivariate model for predicting rape and physical injury outcomes during sexual assault. *Journal of Consulting and Clinical Psychology, 59,* 724–731. doi:10.1037/0022-006X.59.5.724.

Vega, V., & Malamuth, N. M. (2007). Predicting sexual aggression: The role of pornography in the context of general and specific risk factors. *Aggressive Behavior, 33,* 104–117. doi:10.1002/ab.20172.

Warshaw, R. (1988). *I never called it rape.* New York: HarperPerennial.

Zillmann, D., & Weaver, J. B. (1989). Pornography and men's sexual callousness toward women. In D. Zillmann & J. Bryant (Eds.), *Pornography: Research advances and policy considerations* (pp. 95–125). Hillsdale: Lawrence Erlbaum.

Exploring the Challenges Faced by Latinas Experiencing Intimate Partner Violence

by Judy L. Postmus[1], Sarah McMahon[1], Elithet Silva-Martinez[2], and Corinne D. Warrener[3]

Abstract

This article explores the help-seeking challenges faced by a community sample of 25 Latina intimate partner violence (IPV) survivors. We include the experiences of Latinas who sought help from IPV services and those who did not. Additionally, we utilize an ecological framework to highlight the barriers that are present at multiple levels for Latinas who seek assistance, and we include their recommendations for increasing access. The

[1] Center on Violence Against Women & Children, Rutgers University, School of Social Work, New Brunswick, NJ, USA
[2] Beatriz Lassalle Graduate School of Social Work, University of Puerto Rico, San Juan, PA, USA
[3] Clark Atlanta University, Whitney M. Young School of Social Work, Atlanta, GA, USA

Corresponding Author:
Judy L. Postmus, Sarah McMahon, Elithet Silva-Martinez and Corinne D. Warrener, *Journal of Women and Social Work, Vol 29, No 4,* pp 462–477.

information provided by these Latina survivors afford social workers the opportunity to address the barriers experienced by them as well as the opportunity to take a proactive stance in further enhancing services available in the community.

Intimate partner violence (IPV) affects an estimate of 6.9 million women in the United States each year (Centers for Disease Control and Prevention, 2010). The negative impact of IPV on a number of domains for women has been well documented, including mental and physical health (Cerulli et al., 2011; Lacey, McPherson, Samuel, Sears, & Head, 2013). The negative consequences of IPV reflect a number of issues that represent key concerns for the social work profession. Although many social workers are well equipped to assist IPV survivors, the extant literature demonstrates that most survivors do not seek formal social services (Dichter & Gelles, 2012; Liang, Goodman, Tummala-Narra, & Weintraub, 2005). Instead, most survivors disclose first to informal support systems such as family or friends, and then formal systems such as social workers, advocates, or police (Coker, Derrick, Lumpkin, Aldrich, & Oldendick, 2000; Macy, Nurius, Kernic, & Holt, 2005).

A number of barriers are present for survivors to disclose to informal or formal support networks, such as economic dependency, cultural expectations for women to stay in committed relationships (Marrs Fuchsel, Murphy, & Dufresne, 2012), and lack of access to services (Hien & Ruglass, 2009). In many cases, survivors feel shame, fear, stigma, and concern of losing their children (Rodriguez, Valentine, Son, & Muhammad, 2009). In addition to these barriers, there are a number of obstacles to help-seeking that are faced by women from various ethnic and cultural groups, including Latinas. Research indicates that Latina women experience IPV at rates similar to non-Latinas; however, there may be particular barriers that are faced by Latina survivors in help seeking. These barriers may exist at multiple levels, ranging from family or group norms to organizational obstacles.

This article explores the help-seeking challenges faced by a community sample of Latina IPV survivors. We extend the literature by including the experiences of both Latinas who sought help from IPV services and those who did not. Additionally,

we utilize an ecological framework to highlight the barriers that are present at multiple levels for Latinas who seek assistance, and we include their recommendations for increasing access. We end with a discussion that includes implications for social work practice and policy.

Latinas and IPV

The research literature available on Latina survivors of IPV varies greatly in how the term, Latina, is defined. Although researchers often do not explicitly define Latino/Latina, it is apparent that many use the definition to include anyone born or with ancestors from Central America including Mexico, and any Spanish-speaking countries in South America and the Caribbean (Klevens, 2007). The term Latino/Latina may also include new immigrants, descendants of immigrants, citizens, residents, and undocumented persons, as well as both English and Spanish speakers (Gutiérrez, Yeakley, & Ortega, 2000). Unfortunately, the research presented in this article did not distinguish the variability in the Latina ethnic population studied but instead, defined Latina as any female who is connected through birth or ancestry to countries in Central or South America, or the Caribbean. When reviewing the literature, we use the same descriptor of the population that the authors used.

Latinos/Latinas in general are exposed to health disparities that make them a vulnerable and underserved population. Latinas who experience IPV are even more susceptible to limitations on access to resources (Smedley, Stith, & Nelson, 2003). Although research on IPV among Latinas is limited, it is clear that Latinas (immigrant or U.S.-born) experience similar rates and trends of violence when compared to non-Latinas (Bonami, Anderson, Cannon, Slesnick, & Rodriguez, 2009; Huisman, 1996; Klevens, 2007; Loke, 1997; Raj & Silverman, 2002). Catalano (2005) reported that Latinos/Latinas and non-Latinos/Latinas were equally likely to experience rape and sexual assault; Tjaden and Thoennes (2000) found that there was no significant difference among ethnic groups in reports of physical assault and stalking in an intimate relationship. Acknowledging the presence of IPV in the lives of many Latina women, other studies have documented its effect on their mental health (Hazen, Connelly, Soriano, & Landsverk, 2008). Fedovsky, Higgins, and Paranjape (2008) found that Latinas who survived IPV were 3 times more likely to report having posttraumatic stress disorder, than those who had not. Similarly, Kelly (2010) found that Latinas who needed shelter and other types of services for IPV, experienced more severe mental health issues than Anglo-American or African American women. Even though it is evident that Latinas who experience IPV need support from informal and formal sources, many of them do not seek help or wait long periods of time before doing so (Klevens, 2007). One of the reasons for not seeking help is because of the unique barriers confronted by these women.

Research reveals multiple and interlocking barriers Latinas face when deciding to seek services (Bhuyan & Velagapudi, 2013). These range from barriers at the family, cultural, and organizational levels. An ecological model provides a useful framework for understanding the multiple layers of Latina's lives that may present these barriers. It is common to analyze the experiences of women and violence at the individual level. However, acknowledging factors at all levels that come into play when experiencing IPV is important because it brings awareness to the complexities around this multifaceted issue (Heise, 1998). The interaction of factors at the individual, familial, social, and cultural levels and how they operate in the articulation of the experience around IPV also facilitate understanding help seeking. Another important element to consider when using an ecological perspective is the effect that social and cultural expectations have in patriarchal societies on women, especially when gender inequality is present (Meyers & Post, 2006). The following sections examine the literature on help-seeking and IPV at the family, community or cultural, and organizational levels.

Challenges to Seeking Help at the Family Level

Research focusing on extended family and informal support has found that there are major differences between Anglos and Mexican Americans

in kinship structure as well as the involvement of family members in daily life (West, Kaufman Kantor, & Jasinski, 1998). Studies that focus on extended family and informal support report that among Latino families, the kinship structure and participation of family members in daily life are unique (Keefe, 1979, 1984; Markides, Boldt, & Ray, 1986). On one hand, support from family members is pivotal in seeking help and can be a protective factor (Rodriguez et al., 2010) while on the other, disclosing "intimate issues" such as IPV can be perceived as shameful (Vidales, 2010).

A study on disclosure of IPV and social support comparing African American, Asian and Latina battered women found that the majority of all three groups turned to kin for assistance (Yoshioka, Gilbert, El-Bassel, & Baig-Amin, 2003). One quarter of the Latina participants even sought support from the abuser's family (Yoshioka et al., 2003). Because the in-laws could be more likely to support the abuser in cases of IPV, these types of family support can be quite challenging for battered women. Contradictory values in the Latino/Latina community have an impact on the informal family support available to battered Latinas. Unity in the family and close ties with extended family are anchored in values of *familismo*[1] which should encourage informal support for battered Latinas (Perilla, Bakeman, & Norris, 1994). For example, in their work with Mexican battered women, Fawcett, Heise, Isita-Espejel, and Pick (1999) found that participants perceive family and friends as more accessible to provide support than formal institutions. However, they pointed out that the responses of the participants were not uniform and some of them identified family members and friends as judgmental and blaming, pointing out that informal network support can have a negative side for battered women.

A more recent study found that Latinas were hesitant to disclose to formal sources with only 20% seeking any type of formal help, whereas most Latinas in the same study (58%) disclosed to informal sources such as parents, family, friends, or neighbors (Cuevas & Sabina, 2010). Therefore, using informal support for something as "private and personal" as IPV becomes problematic (Fawcett, Heise, Isita-Espejel, & Pick, 1999). Sharma (2001) explains that although the extended family can be very helpful for child rearing and financial assistance purposes, boundaries between the couple and the rest of the family may be difficult to draw. As a result, battered women may feel pressured to stay in the abusive relationship.

Challenges to Seeking Help at the Community/Cultural Level

Battered Latinas also face barriers to seeking help at the community or cultural level. For example, several cultural beliefs about *machismo* and *marianismo* may dictate how men and women are to behave in a relationship (Marrs Fuchsel et al., 2012). Machismo is a set of beliefs about how Latinos should act and is a term that is frequently used yet poorly understood. Many individuals view machismo as a negative term, associated with characteristics such as having a strong sexual prowess, consuming large quantities of alcohol, or being aggressive (Goldberg-Edelson, Hokoda, & Ramos-Lira, 2007). Indeed, it is often viewed as an exaggeration of the male stereotype that uses power and control over women (Perilla, 1999). However, machismo also includes the honor, pride, responsibility, and obligation of the male to the family. Often, Latinos are taught to be the decision maker and provider for the family and must maintain the honor of the home. Typically, boys who are raised in a traditional manner are taught to be strong in the face of adversity and to maintain their pride at all costs.

In contrast, marianismo is the set of beliefs that direct Latinas in the role women take within the family. Traits such as submissiveness, deference to others, spiritually untainted, and self-sacrificing behaviors mirror the role of the suffering Virgin Mary (Goldberg-Edelson et al., 2007). The maintenance of the family unit is often placed before the well-being of the woman herself. Additionally, Latinas are often socialized to allow someone else to make decisions for them, most often the men in their lives. Women are taught to depend on men financially; they continue this cycle by raising their daughters in the same way (Kasturirangan & Nutt-Williams, 2003).

Hence, machismo and marianismo often direct the gender roles in the families with fathers seen as the sole provider, protector, and authority figure, (Kasturirangan & Nutt-Williams, 2003; Perilla,

1999) and mothers seen as responsible for child rearing and the well-being of the family (Perilla, 1999). As such, some Latinas traditionally do not work out of the home; for those who choose to do so out of desire or necessity, they may be at greater risk of IPV due to the shift in gender roles and perceived threat to their partner's machismo (Erez, Adelman, & Gregory, 2009). For example, in one study, when Latino men who were jailed for IPV were asked about machismo, the majority of them agreed that it was a main element in their culture and a major influence on them. One participant said, "I believed that because I was a man I had the right to offend my partner and to do whatever I wanted to her" (Saez-Betacourt, Lam, & Nguyen, 2008, p. 139).

Additionally, marital problems may stem from a strong belief in machismo and marianismo since problems are to be kept private and not shared with others at all, not even extended family. Such discussion of problems or expressing dissatisfaction with the relationship would cast the marriage and family in a negative light and bring shame to the family (Perilla, 1999). Latina survivors have reported that they were told by family members that if their marriage ended, it would put their children's welfare at risk including damaging future marriage opportunities for female children (ALAS, 2004; Erez et al., 2009). Researchers have reported that many Latina IPV survivors believe that their extended families would not be supportive, would blame them for not being good wives, and would encourage them to stay in the relationship and endure the violence (Kasturirangan & Nutt-Williams, 2003; Klevens, 2007).

Challenges to Seeking Help at the Organizational Level

In addition to seeking help from their family or community, IPV survivors may reach out for help to multiple types of organizations such as law enforcement, human services, and religious organizations. Indeed, faith-based organizations can provide healing and support to survivors whose faith is an important aspect of their lives (Bent-Goodley & Fowler, 2006). Unfortunately, not all survivors report positive experiences but rather may experience negative interactions (Ahrens, 2006; Chen & Ulman, 2010; Humphreys & Thiara, 2003;

Postmus, Severson, Berry, & Yoo, 2009). Hilbert and Krishnan (2000) explain that disallowing, disregarding, and prohibiting people from accessing the services they need have negatively impacted IPV survivors when seeking help. In fact, they define this lack of access as social exclusion. They go further in stating that limited funding and staff and limited services for diverse populations are additional forms of discrimination against IPV survivors of color. In addition, limits to outreach work, including sharing with underserved communities about services available particularly for immigrant survivors of IPV, affect help-seeking (Raj & Silverman, 2002).

Regarding cultural competency and specialized services for Latina survivors of IPV, Erez and Hartley (2003) reviewed the need to consider that many Latinas may not be proficient in English and may not be literate in their own languages. The lack of access to linguistically competent services puts these women in disadvantage allowing for their revictimization and isolation (Sabina, Cuevas, & Schally, 2012; Wrangle, Fisher, & Paranjape, 2008). In order to have a clear conceptualization of the needs of Latina survivors of IPV and their communities, Silva-Martinez and Murty (2011) suggest learning about the culture of these women, which includes their cultural, social, and economic backgrounds in both the home and host countries.

In sum, seeking services for Latina survivors of IPV is a complex process. Factors at the family, community, and organizational levels have an impact on decisions related to seeking help. One gap in the review of the literature includes the lack of suggestions from Latina survivors themselves as to how to address challenges when seeking help. This article addresses this gap by presenting the results of a qualitative study in which Latina survivors, including those who had received IPV services as well as those who had not, were asked about their challenges to seeking help and their recommendations to address those challenges. Specifically, the research questions driving this study include: (1) What are the challenges faced by Latina survivors when getting help for IPV? Specifically, what challenges exist at the family, community, and organizational levels? (2) What recommendations do Latina survivors provide to help those become better connected to IPV service providers?

Method

Participants and Data Collection Procedures

The data for this project come from qualitative interviews with Latina IPV survivors residing in a midsized community in Northeastern United States ($n = 25$). Almost half of the community identify as Hispanic, with the majority of Mexican and Puerto Rican backgrounds (U.S. Census Bureau, 2013). The area is racially diverse and has a mix of urban and suburban environments. Thirteen participants were survivors who had utilized the services of a bilingual, bicultural program provided collaboratively between an IPV service provider and a nonprofit agency specifically providing services to Latinas/Latinos in the community; this group of participants is referred to as the *service group*. The remaining 12 women were survivors who had not utilized these services; this group is referred to as the *community group*. The research protocol was reviewed and approved by an institutional review board, including recruitment, interview guides, consent forms, and compensation for participants.

Participants in the service group were recruited by program staff informing them of the study and inviting them to participate. They were clearly informed that their participation in the study had no impact on their ability to receive services. If the individual was interested in participating, they were given the phone number of the bilingual researcher and contact information was released to the researcher if desired by the participant.

Those in the community group were recruited through referrals from local social service agencies and by posting fliers throughout businesses in the community which Latinas frequent. The flier described the eligibility criteria for the study which included questions about experiencing physical, verbal, or emotional abuse.

All of the women interested in participating (from both the service and community groups) were instructed to contact a bilingual member of the research team by phone to determine whether they qualified and to schedule an interview. All participants were Latina women over the age of 18 who lived in the community and who had experienced IPV since the time the program was initiated. During the screening phone call, eligibility criteria were confirmed.

Interviews typically lasted about 1 hour, were audiotaped, and were conducted at a space that was agreed upon by the researcher and participant, with most being held at either at a local library or space provided by one of the participating agencies. All interviews were conducted in the language of the participant's choosing, either English or Spanish, and were conducted by a bilingual interviewer. Interviewers were trained in qualitative interviewing techniques prior to data collection. Such training focused on improving the consistency among interviewers, establishing rapport with participants, asking questions sensitively, distinguishing between encouraging and feedback, and keeping a participant focused. All interviewers were either students or graduates of a social work master's or PhD program.

Measurements

A semistructured interview guide was created by the researchers based on a review of the literature and in collaboration with the partnering agencies. Interviews consisted of open-ended questions and numerous probes, centering on how Latinas learned of IPV services, the barriers encountered, and thoughts about how to reach other Latina survivors. The questions for those who had or had not used services were similar in content but were tailored to reflect why the participant had or had not utilized services. For those survivors who had not used the bilingual services, referral information was provided at the end of the interview. Demographic questions such as age and immigration status were not asked in order to ensure the confidentiality and safety of participants, given the sensitive nature of the study. Any names used in this article have been changed.

Data Analysis

All interviews were transcribed in Spanish, and translated into English, or transcribed directly into English if conducted in English. The transcripts were imported into Atlas Ti, a software package for qualitative analysis. Data were analyzed using a line-by-line coding and constant comparison methods (Glaser & Strauss, 1967) intended to identify as many codes as possible across the transcripts.

Codes were then merged into groups (called "families") based on their commonalities. Finally, "families" were condensed into themes that captured the essence of the data. To improve the reliability of the findings, investigator triangulation (Patton, 2002) was used in which one reviewer completed coding for all of the interviews, and a second reviewer completed coding on three cases from each group. The reviewers then met to compare codes and themes and found that the majority of codes and themes were similar or the same between reviewers. Those themes that were not the same were discussed between the researchers until consensus was reached.

Results

The results are framed around the two research questions driving this study which included: (1) What are the challenges faced by Latina survivors when getting help for IPV? Specifically, what challenges exist at the family, community, and organizational levels? (2) What recommendations do Latina survivors provide to help those become better connected to IPV service providers?

Challenges and Supports Encountered When Seeking Help

All of the participants in both the services and community groups talked about both challenges and supportive factors they faced when seeking help from a number of levels. Such sources include family and friends, the Latino community, and organizations or service providers. The participants' views on challenges and opportunities presented by each of these levels are outlined below.

Challenges and support from family and friends.
For those women who had received formal IPV services, it was very common for them to report that family members were supportive of leaving the husband to get help. A few women reported that their family did not live close by and the only family they had was the abuser's family. As such, the women reported that these family members were unsupportive of their decision to get help. For example, one survivor explained:

> His friends-his family says that they're angry. They're angry because I involved the police … They're all mad at me. But

the thing is they don't think about the way he is. They just think about him as their brother but they don't think about the way they behave.—Isabel (services)

However, at the same time, these women acknowledged that they thought their families were unaware of the abuse they experienced until they told them about it. Some of these women explained that they themselves didn't know what abuse was until the advocate helped them to understand the different dimensions of IPV.

For the group of women who had not received services (the community group), about half of them did not talk to anybody about the abuse, not even to family members. This was mainly due to shame and a sense of not wanting to burden others with their issues. One survivor explained:

I choose not to talk to my best friend because I love her to death but she's going through her own stuff. And I don't wanna burden you with my crap when you're going through your own stuff. Same thing with my sister. She's going through a lot right now too and it just-I don't feel it would be fair for me to burden anyone that's going through something, but I know it's bad keeping it bottled in because I'm very angry, very edgy, very irritable.—Sabrina (community)

Challenges from the Latino/Latina community. Overall, women from both groups expressed the belief that the Latino/Latina community misunderstands IPV. A few women explained that, as a result of this lack of understanding, community members do not know what to do when someone experiences IPV. Some women reported that they believed the community sees certain forms of IPV, such as jealousy, as being an expression of love and commitment. Two participants illustrated this by stating:

People who don't have an idea about what domestic violence is, who don't live it, they only hear about it, have no idea what it is to go through it. They think that it's an illness like the flu that goes away quickly. That it doesn't matter ... So sometimes people don't understand until they've lived it. And it's hard to make them understand.—Julia (services)

They [the community] see it as your husband is jealous or, you know your husband is being protective or overprotective. They don't see it as domestic violence at all. There's no emotional aspect of it or economical, no. Most people see domestic violence as, like you're almost dead. Or you have to like show up with bruises and cuts and-which a lot of them can be hidden. You can hide your bruises and your cuts and everything just as easy as your emotional.—Flora (services)

Women from the service group also reported that it is not always easy for the Latino community to separate IPV from machismo. Prior to obtaining services, the participants acknowledged that they did not realize that abuse existed because they thought it was just part of machismo. One participant said:

Which is strange because if you're Hispanic-a Latino and you live on machismo, it's not OK for your sister's husband to beat her, but then your-you might not be beating your own wife, as a Latino man, but you're still, you know, taking her money and you're still keeping her from her friends and you're still acting jealous and stalking and having rages and breaking her things. You're still doing the same thing. You're just not accepting that that's part of domestic violence.—Flora (services)

Women in the community group identified this lack of understanding of IPV as a barrier to help seeking. For example:

When a boy is born, they always say, in our culture, you're the man of the house. You're in charge of your sister, tell her bring me this, just ordering around, they shouldn't do anything, don't touch the plates that's for women, don't lift a plate that's for women, and at least that's how it is in our culture. And even the kids need to be educated too so that they help.—Maris (community)

Well there are a lot of people now that don't think it's a problem but that it's part of married life, you get accustomed to it, they don't see it as bad ... I see that that a lot of people think that, they do think it's normal.—Barbara (community)

Challenges and support from organizations or service providers. For those women in the services group, they were asked about their experiences with the IPV provider and how they were connected to those services. The women explained that they did not know about the service provider until the police or hospital gave them the phone number. The participants commented that it was easy to receive services and that many of the services were truly needed (e.g., food, shelter, and English classes).

> I don't think it can get any easier, I mean, they don't require anything. You just have to go and say your story and they'll help you from there.—Irma (services)

Overall, the women were extremely satisfied with the services they received. All of the women were very thankful of all the help given to them and commented on how their life has drastically improved.

> They are attentive to me, seeing if everything is OK or if I need anything. Thank God, they have helped me.—Mary (services)
>
> I feel confident. I feel more confident because I did lose a lot of faith in the justice system. I feel more confident and safe. Since I know my rights, I feel like I'm able to move on or to move forward or to start a new life. I feel like I'm able to do that now, but most of all I feel confident.—Flora (services)

One woman in particular spoke of how appreciative she was that the advocate never told her what she had to do. Instead, the advocate gave her options but always allowed her to make her own decisions.

> When you're ready to take that step, they'll help you all the way through, but until you're ready to make that decision and get to that step, they don't tell you, do this, do that. They tell you, these are your options. This is what you could do, but it's up to you to make that decision and go through that step.—Carmen (services)

All of the participants appreciated the bilingual bicultural legal advocate and especially thankful that she was bilingual. They reported that if the counselor was not bilingual, they would have never called for help, and it scared them to think of what could have happened if they did not get help. For example, one woman said:

> It's scary but she (bilingual advocate) was there the whole time. She was very supportive and she explained step-by-step how to talk to the judge, how-you know, wait for your turn when it's his time to talk you listen and you don't make any comments. You look directly to the judge; you don't look at him and stuff like that so it helped a lot. Cuz it's overwhelming and at the end when you walk in there you kind of forget certain things, but I knew the basics.—Carmen (services)

For the women who had not received services, they explained how they were afraid to ask for help from formal services because of the possible repercussions from their abuser and the possible mistreatment from those organizations. For example, one woman explained:

> Usually you're afraid to talk to somebody. Maybe the person will intervene and do something that you need to do but you're not willing to do because you're scared, you're afraid of the person.—Rosa (community)

Although one woman from the community group spoke to a counselor at her child's school, about half of the women turned to the church for support when they felt they had nobody else to turn to. These women said how their belief in God was helpful to their recovery, but others described how the priest or religious leader was not helpful to them.

> I spoke to the priest (at my church), and I talked to him about my problem, about my situation, and he told me that (I should) get married, that I should look more for God. And then the priest said, I give you such date to get married through church, start fixing your marriage, get married, do things that God will like because all of that (abuse) is due to evil.—Bianca (community)

The main help was my family. After my family, at the organizational level was the church. I'm a Christian. We went to the church to ask for help, to ask for backing and it wasn't until that last time that I had contact with my ex-husband was when I went to the police station. I should be honest; the biggest help apart from the church and my family was a friend who to be a good friend.—Mayra (community)

Although it was clear that women from the community group had been informed of the local IPV service provider by the police, very few of them spoke in detail about their interactions with the police. However, one participant explained in detail how the police had not helped her.

I called the police so that they'd take him away but they didn't take him away. He-because he started to grab the knives and scare the children so I called the police and when he saw that the kids were yelling that the police were coming, quickly he was so calm and the police came in, they looked around and on the couch where he was sitting there was a knife and they said to him, what's with this knife? I have this knife to cut a lemon because I'm having my beer. And the police said to me that nothing was wrong and they left.—Barbara (community)

The women from the community group said that at the time of the abuse, they did not know about the IPV service provider and did not know where to look for services. If they had known about such services when they were experiencing IPV, they would have used it.

I used to cry in the middle of all of that, my children cried, and what did the police say, get help, get help. And I used to say, where, where am I going to look ... Yes that would have helped me; I would have known what to do with my partner a long time ago.—Bianca (community)

Participant Recommendations

All of the women who received services from the bilingual advocate were extremely satisfied with those services received; however, they did have recommendations on further services they wished they had received. Most focused on wanting help to find jobs and housing; others suggested wanting classes to teach children about IPV to break the cycle. Other participants talked about providing more services in Spanish and getting more help with immigration challenges.

I think more organizations or more people who help in Spanish. I say that for us, the language is what often stops us from moving forward.—Mary (services)

Giving like awareness that even though you might have another problem with immigration and those things that we can also help with that, that you can guide us with what to do to become legal and to be OK and so that the person who is abusing you can't continue putting pressure on you with those things and that you can help with that too.—Gloria (services)

Almost all of the women (those receiving services and those from the community) stated that something needs to be done to raise awareness of IPV in the Latino community. They suggested having more fliers posted and billboards about IPV and available services. Others suggested sending home information with children from school because mothers will see it more often than not. Other ways to distribute the fliers included posting them at churches, schools, and Laundromats. Participants also suggested television and radio ads.

Maybe more advertisement because they do need more advertisement ... Possibly TV, during soap operas. That's perfect because every woman watches soap operas. Yeah. That would be the best because that would hit everybody-low-income, high-income, medium-it doesn't matter. Everybody would hear about them—Irma (services)

I think that it would be good, a commercial, an announcement on television as well, it would be good because we all watch television all the time (laughs), it's our main source of entertainment, I think that it would be a way to get to our ears, a little easily—Paula (community)

... the churches is where a lot of desperate women go, looking for help, it's the place where I imagine that the majority of people find a little bit of relief maybe when no one listens to them, they come there. I imagine that would be the best place.—Maris (community)

Discussion

This study provides some information about the help-seeking barriers and supportive factors encountered by Latina survivors of IPV in one setting. While our findings are specific to one particular community, they suggest important next steps for better understanding on how to address IPV among the Latina population. Indeed, some of our findings can also be applied to non-Latina populations, as many obstacles faced by IPV survivors transcend cultural differences. Additionally, our findings support the ecological model as a useful framework for organizing our understanding of help seeking, as the women reported obstacles and support systems occurring at various levels of interactions.

At the family or group level, women reported mixed findings. As found with other research on support-seeking more generally, families and friends were sometimes a source of strength and support while other times presented obstacles for the women (Coker et al., 2000; Macy et al., 2005; Vidales, 2010). As evidenced in the literature, understanding *familismo* as a social construct that can shape disclosing victimization may help in making sense of mixed findings when it comes to informal support (Marrs Fuchsel, 2013). While this may be true for many IPV survivors, for Latinas, this finding may be exacerbated by the obstacles encountered from the broader community or cultural level, where some community norms such as machismo were reported by the women as presenting another layer of barriers to help seeking. Many of the women perceived the Latino/Latina community as often failing to identify abusive behaviors as IPV, especially those that were not physical. Instead, cultural norms around gender framed behaviors as "normal" or acceptable acts within a relationship. Additionally, for those community members who may recognize IPV, the women expressed concern that they would not know how to intervene or where to seek resources. Finding innovative, culturally sensitive ways to

raise awareness within the Latino/Latina community about IPV and resources is a task facing social workers and others who engage in this work.

At the organizational level, the women talked about the utility of IPV service providers as well as other organizations where they turned for assistance. Participants indicated that organizations such as churches were sometimes helpful to survivors and other times were not, which is consistent with the previous research that details the ways in which religious organizations can be both empowering for victims yet also have the potential to perpetuate silence around IPV (Pyles, 2007). This finding reinforces other work that suggests that more attention and training are needed for informal networks within communities, such as churches and schools, where Latinas may turn for support first (Bent-Goodley & Fowler, 2006). Additionally, this finding likely applies to other groups beyond Latinas as well. In order to work effectively with Latinas and other groups that may not seek traditional assistance, social workers should consider partnering with faith-based institutions and other community-based organizations to develop and implement culturally relevant training for clergy and staff to recognize and respond to IPV (Bent-Goodley & Fowler, 2006).

Those women who pursued formal IPV services emphasized the importance of having a bilingual advocate available. Many women suggested that without a bilingual advocate, they would not have pursued seeking services. While the importance of bilingual advocates is not a new finding, this adds to the mounting evidence that it is an essential component for IPV service providers (Silva-Martinez & Murty, 2011). Indeed, such multilingual services are relevant and should be an essential component for most immigrant or non-English speaking survivors.

Those women that did not receive IPV services reported that a lack of awareness of the services was the primary obstacle, which has been found in previous studies (Belknap & VandeVuss, 2010). This clearly suggests that additional outreach about the availability of services is needed. When considering outreach strategies, IPV agencies should include gatekeepers or leaders from the community such as the police or medical personnel as suggested by this sample of Latinas (Silva-Martinez &

Murty, 2011). While many communities and our culture as a whole may lack awareness about IPV, there are specific barriers for various groups that need to be understood through a cultural lens. Within our sample of Latinas, it appears that the concepts of machismo and marianismo seem to complicate individuals' ability to define certain behaviors as abusive or wrong at times.

Educating community members about IPV and its effects on communities might result in better understanding of the issue and also disseminate information about services available. Once gatekeepers and community leaders gain this knowledge, women experiencing IPV in these vulnerable communities can become educated and feel more trusting of organizations that specialize in IPV because it has been suggested by community leaders. Organizations should consider establishing reciprocal relationships with these individuals and have them as allies.

Another contribution of our study was the series of recommendations provided by Latinas themselves about how to better address the issue of IPV in their community. Nearly all of the participants in the study recommended that increased awareness of IPV and services available are needed in their community. Many of the suggestions were for these messages to be disseminated in places where Latinas frequent. Additionally, there were a number of suggestions for increased media messaging through fliers, billboards, television, and advertisements.

In line with the recommendations from the participants, research on effectiveness of social norms media marketing has been emerging in the field of sexual violence and can perhaps be applied to IPV as well (Potter & Stapleton, 2011). This approach uses marketing vehicles such as posters and the media to change perceptions about what attitudes and behaviors are approved and desirable within their community (Paluk & Ball, 2010). One of the tenets of social norms marketing is that the message is relevant to the particular population and is based on feedback and information from the community itself (Potter, Moynihan, & Stapleton, 2011; Potter & Stapleton, 2011). This seems especially important when addressing the needs of Latina/Latino immigrant communities, where community members themselves can address culturally relevant norms such as machismo and marianismo, and provide insight as to the language and definitions used to describe abuse. Identifying the social norms and structures that need to be addressed should be done in conjunction with community members who can speak to the particular norms of their context (Casey & Lindhorst, 2009).

Limitations

There are several limitations to consider when discussing this study. First, the study uses a purposeful sampling technique; hence, it is not random and therefore is limited in applicability to other Latina populations. Given the difficulty in recruiting vulnerable populations such as battered women and Latinas (who may be undocumented), the sample size is small and not necessarily representative of the broader community. Women who had used services were recruited by the community agencies' staff and were easier to recruit. Recruiting women directly from the community who had not used services proved more difficult. Every attempt was made to ensure confidentiality and safety; therefore, some potentially useful data were not collected in order to protect participants' identities. While demographic data such as age, immigration status, and country of origin could have contributed to understanding certain aspects of these groups, it was determined that safety was paramount and superseded the need for these data. Another potential problem area is the use of translated interview transcripts, as the translation process opens up the potential for error in interpreting the participants' words. To minimize problems with interpretation, the translators consulted with each other when there was a question about a word's meaning or intent when translating from Spanish to English.

Conclusion

The information provided by these Latina survivors afford social workers the opportunity to address the barriers experienced by them as well as the opportunity to take a proactive stance in further enhancing services available in the community. Specifically, social workers can provide a greater awareness about IPV in Latina communities with attention given to developing culturally sensitive information that could be widely disseminated, especially when acknowledging the intersection of gender and race when working with Latinas. Part of providing this awareness would include offering training on IPV and the specific needs of the Latina population for those helping systems that come into contact with victims. Churches, law enforcement, schools, community centers, as well as other informal networks should be targeted to receive such training to enhance their awareness of IPV as well as their understanding of how to best respond to Latina survivors. When creating such awareness, social workers must ensure that all information is congruent with the cultural values and beliefs held by different Latino populations living in the United States. Additionally, many of the findings from the current study represent factors influencing IPV survivors in cultures other than Latina. Social workers can use these findings as a framework to engage with diverse cultural groups around the issue of IPV.

Authors' Note

We would like to recognize the important contribution to this project from the Puerto Rican Action Board and Women Aware, both located in New Brunswick, NJ. The authors would also like to acknowledge the work of Jennifer Martinez for her assistance in the data analysis of this project.

Declaration of Conflicting Interests

The author(s) declared no potential conflicts of interest with respect to the research, authorship, and/or publication of this article.

Funding

The author(s) disclosed receipt of the following financial support for the research, authorship, and/or publication of this article: This project was supported by the Puerto Rican Action Board in collaboration with Women Aware, both located in New Brunswick, NJ. Points of view in this document are those of the authors and do not necessarily represent the official position or policies of these agencies.

Note

1. *Familismo* is a value that underlies the strong Latino identification with members of the extended family, attachment and loyalty of individuals to their families, and a sense of community (Hurtado, 1998).

References

Ahrens, C. E. (2006). Being silenced: The impact of negative social reactions on the disclosure of rape. *American Journal of Community Psychology, 38,* 263–274.

Alianza Latina en Contra la Aggresion Sexual. (2004). *Eliminating barriers to services for Latina/o survivors of sexual and intimate partner violence.* Austin, TX: Author (Latina Alliance Against Sexual Aggression).

Belknap, R., & VandeVuss, L. (2010). Listening sessions with Latinas: Documenting life contexts and creating connections. *Public Health Nursing, 27,* 337–346. doi:10.1111/j.1525-1446.2010.00864.x

Bent-Goodley, T. B., & Fowler, D. N. (2006). Spiritual and religious abuse: Expanding what is known about domestic violence. *Affilia, 21,* 292–295.

Bhuyan, R., & Velagapudi, K. (2013). From one "dragon sleigh' to another: Advocating for immigrant women facing violence in Kansas. *Affilia, 28,* 65–78.

Bonami, A., Anderson, M., Cannon, E., Slesnick, N., & Rodriguez, M. (2009). Intimate partner violence in Latina and non-Latina women. *American Journal of Preventive Medicine, 36,* 43–48.

Casey, A. E., & Lindhorst, T. P. (2009). Toward a multi-level, ecological approach to the primary prevention of sexual assault: Prevention in peer and community contexts. *Trauma, Violence, & Abuse, 10,* 91–114.

Catalano, S. M. (2005). *Criminal victimization.* (NCJ210674). Washington, DC: Bureau of Justice Statistics, National Crime Victimization Survey.

Centers for Disease Control and Prevention. (2010). *Intimate partner and sexual violence survey: 2010 summary report.* Atlanta, GA: Centers for Disease Control and Prevention, National Center for Injury Prevention and Control.

Cerulli, C., Gellman, R. A., Nichols, C., Hall, D., Conner, K. R., & Caine, E. D. (2011). Mental and physical health symptoms of family court intimate partner violence petitioners. *International Journal of Law and Psychiatry, 34,* 94–98.

Chen, Y., & Ulman, S. E. (2010). Women's reporting of sexual and physical assaults to police in the National Violence Against Women Survey. *Violence Against Women, 16,* 262–279.

Coker, A. L., Derrick, C., Lumpkin, J. L., Aldrich, T. E., & Oldendick, R. (2000). Help-seeking for intimate partner violence and forced sex in South Carolina. *American Journal of Preventive Medicine, 19,* 316–320.

Cuevas, C. A., & Sabina, C. (2010). *The experience of sexual victimization and help-seeking among Latino women*. Washington, DC: U.S. Department of Justice, Office of Justice Programs, National Criminal Justice Reference Service.

Dichter, M. E., & Gelles, R. J. (2012). Women's perceptions of safety and risk following police intervention for intimate partner violence. *Violence Against Women, 18*, 44–63.

Erez, E., Adelman, M., & Gregory, C. (2009). Intersections of immigration and domestic violence voices of battered immigrant women. *Feminist Criminology, 4*, 32–56.

Erez, E., & Hartley, C. (2003). Battered immigrant women and the legal system: A therapeutic jurisprudence perspective. *Western Criminology Review, 4*, 155–169.

Fawcett, G., Heise, L., Isita-Espejel, L., & Pick, S. (1999). Changing community responses to wife abuse: A research and demonstration project in Iztacalco, Mexico. *American Psychologist, 54*, 41–49.

Fedovsky, K., Higgins, S., & Paranjape, A. (2008). Intimate partner violence: How does it impact major depressive disorder and post traumatic stress disorder among immigrant Latinas? *Journal of Immigrant and Minority Health, 10*, 45–51.

Glaser, B. G., & Strauss, A. L. (1967). *The discovery of grounded theory: Strategies for qualitative research*. Chicago, IL: Aldine.

Goldberg-Edelson, M., Hokoda, A., & Ramos-Lira, L. (2007). Differences in effects of domestic violence between Latina and non-Latina women. *Journal of Family Violence, 22*, 1–10.

Gutiérrez, L., Yeakley, A., & Ortega, R. (2000). Educating students for social work with Latinos: Issues for the new millennium. *Journal of Social Work Education, 36*, 541–557.

Hazen, A. L., Connelly, C. D., Soriano, F. I., & Landsverk, J. A. (2008). Intimate partner violence and psychological functioning in Latina women. *Health Care for Women International, 29*, 282–299.

Heise, L. L. (1998). Violence against women: An integrated, ecological framework. *Violence Against Women, 4*, 262–290.

Hien, D., & Ruglass, L. (2009). Interpersonal partner violence and women in the United States: An overview of prevalence rates, psychiatric correlates and consequences and barriers to help seeking. *International Journal of Law and Psychiatry, 32*, 48–55.

Hilbert, J. C., & Krishnan, S. P. (2000). Addressing barriers to community care of battered women in rural environments: Creating a policy of social inclusion. *Journal of Health Social Policy, 12*, 41–52.

Huisman, K. A. (1996). Wife battering in Asian American communities: Identifying the service needs of an overlooked segment of the U.S. population. *Violence Against Women, 2*, 260–285.

Humphreys, C., & Thiara, R. (2003). Mental health and domestic violence: 'I call it symptoms of abuse'. *British Journal of Social Work, 33*, 209–226.

Hurtado, A. (1998). The politics of sexuality in the gender subordination of Chicanas. In C. M. Trujillo (Ed.), *Living Chicana theory* (pp. 383–428). Berkeley, CA: Third Woman Press.

Kasturirangan, A., & Nutt-Williams, E. (2003). Counseling Latina battered women: A qualitative study of the Latina perspective. *Journal of Multicultural Counseling and Development, 31*, 162–178.

Keefe, S. E. (1979). The Mexican-American extended family as an emotional support system. *Human Organization, 38*, 144–152.

Keefe, S. E. (1984). Real and ideal extended familism among Mexican Americans and Anglo Americans: On the meaning of "close" family ties. *Human Organization, 43*, 65–70.

Kelly, U. (2010). Symptoms of PTSD and major depression in Latinas who have experienced intimate partner violence. *Issues in Mental Health Nursing, 31*, 119–127.

Klevens, J. (2007). An overview of intimate partner violence among Latinos. *Violence Against Women, 13*, 111–122.

Lacey, K. K., McPherson, M. D., Samuel, P. S., Sears, K. P., & Head, D. (2013). The impact of different types of intimate partner violence on the mental and physical health of women in different ethnic groups. *Journal of Interpersonal Violence, 28*, 359–385.

Liang, B., Goodman, L., Tummala-Narra, P., & Weintraub, S. (2005). A theoretical framework for understanding help-seeking processes among survivors of intimate partner violence. *American Journal of Community Psychology, 36*, 71–84.

Loke, T. L. (1997). *Trapped in domestic violence: The impact of United States immigration laws on battered immigrant women*. Retrieved January 11, 2000, from http://web.lexis-nexis.com/universe.373fd75cca7b1dde&taggedDocs=Z1,8Z9

Macy, R. J., Nurius, P. S., Kernic, M. A., & Holt, V. L. (2005). Battered women's profiles associated with service help-seeking efforts: illuminating opportunities for intervention. *Social Work Research, 29*, 137–150.

Markides, K. S., Boldt, J. S., & Ray, L. A. (1986). Sources of helping and intergenerational solidarity: A three-generations study of Mexican Americans. *The Journals of Gerontology, 41*, 506–511.

Marrs Fuchsel, C. L. (2013). Familism, sexual abuse, and domestic violence among immigrant Mexican women. *Affilia, 28*, 379–290.

Marrs Fuchsel, C. L., Murphy, S. B., & Dufresne, R. (2012). Domestic violence, culture, and relationship dynamics among immigrant Mexican women. *Affilia, 27*, 263–274.

Meyers, E., & Post, L. A. (2006). Alone at night: A feminist ecological model of community violence. *Feminist Criminology, 1*, 207–227.

Paluk, E. L., & Ball, L. (2010). *Social norms marketing aimed at gender-based violence: A literature review and critical assessment* New York, NY: International Rescue Committee.

Patton, M. Q. (2002). *Qualitative research & evaluation methods* (3rd ed.). Thousand Oaks, CA: Sage.

Perilla, J. L. (1999). Domestic violence as a human rights issue: The case of immigrant Latinos. *Hispanic Journal of Behavioral Sciences, 21*, 107–133.

Perilla, J. L., Bakeman, R., & Norris, F. H. (1994). Culture and domestic violence: The ecology of abused Latinas. *Violence and Victims, 9*, 325–339.

Postmus, J. L., Severson, M. E., Berry, M., & Yoo, J. A. (2009). Women's experiences of violence and seeking help. *Violence Against Women, 15*, 852–868.

Potter, S. J., Moynihan, M. M., & Stapleton, J. G. (2011). Using social self-identification in social marketing materials aimed at reducing violence agianst women on campus. *Journal of Interpersonal Violence, 26*, 971–990. doi:10.1177/0886260510365870

Potter, S. J., & Stapleton, J. G. (2011). Bringing in the target audience in bystander social marketing materials for communities: Suggestions for practitioners. *Violence Against Women, 17*, 797–812. doi:10.1177/1077801211410364

Pyles, L. (2007). The complexities of the religious response to domestic violence: Implications for faith-based initiatives. *Affilia, 22*, 281–291. doi:10.1177/0886109907302271

Raj, A., & Silverman, J. (2002). Violence against immigrant women: The roles of culture, context, and legal immigrant status on intimate partner violence. *Violence Against Women, 8*, 367–399.

Rodriguez, M. A., Valentine, J., Ahmed, S. R., Eisenman, D. P., Sumner, L. A., Heilemann, M. V., & Liu, H. (2010). Intimate partner violence and maternal depression during the perinatal period: A longitudinal investigation of Latinas. *Violence Against Women, 16*, 543–559.

Rodriguez, M. A., Valentine, J. M., Son, J. B., & Muhammad, M. (2009). Intimate partner violence and

barriers to mental health care for ethnically diverse populations of women. *Trauma, Violence, & Abuse, 10*, 358–374.

Sabina, C., Cuevas, C. A., & Schally, J. L. (2012). Help-seeking in a national sample of victimized Latino women: The influence of victimization types. *Journal of Interpersonal Violence, 27*, 40–61.

Saez-Betacourt, A., Lam, B. T., & Nguyen, T. (2008). The meaning of being incarcerated on a domestic violence charge and its impact on self and family among Latino immigrant batterers. *Journal of Ethnic and Cultural Diversity in Social Work, 17*, 130–156.

Sharma, A. (2001). Healing the wounds of domestic abuse: Improving the effectiveness of feminist therapeutic interventions with immigrant and racially visible women who have been abused. *Violence Against Women, 7*, 1405–1428.

Silva-Martinez, E., & Murty, S. (2011). Ethics and cultural competence in research with battered immigrant Latina women. *Journal of Ethic and Cultural Diversity in Social Work, 20*, 223–239.

Smedley, B. D., Stith, A. Y., & Nelson, A. R. (2003). *Unequal treatment: Confronting racial and ethnic disparities in health care.* Washington, DC: National Academies Press.

Tjaden, P., & Thoennes, N. (2000). *Full report of the prevalence, incidence, and consequences of violence against women: Findings from the National Violence Against Women Survey.* Atlanta, GA: Centers for Disease Control and Prevention, National Center for Injury Prevention and Control.

U.S.Census Bureau. (2013). *State and county quick facts: Middlesex county, New Jersey.* Washington, DC: U.S. Department of Commerce.

Vidales, G. T. (2010). Arrested justice: The multifaceted plight of immigrant Latinas who faced domestic violence. *Journal of Family Violence, 25*, 533–544.

West, C. M., Kaufman Kantor, G., & Jasinski, J. L. (1998). Sociodemographic predictors and cultural barriers to help-seeking behavior by Latina and Anglo American battered women. *Violence and Victims, 13*, 361–375.

Wrangle, J., Fisher, J. W., & Paranjape, A. (2008). Ha sentido sola? Culturally competent screening for intimate partner violence in Latina women. *Journal of Women's Health, 17*, 261–268.

Yoshioka, M. R., Gilbert, L., El-Bassel, N., & Baig-Amin, M. (2003). Social support and disclosure of abuse: Comparing South Asian, African American, and Hispanic battered women. *Journal of Family Violence, 18*, 171–180.

Ruling the Exceptions:
Same-Sex Battering
and Domestic Violence Theory

by Gregory S. Merrill

Summary   This paper examines the challenges presented to current gender-based domestic violence theory by the existence of same-sex domestic violence. Charging that dominant theory is heterosexist and ignores the experience of battered lesbians and gay men, Island and Letellier have argued that domestic violence is not a gender issue and advocate a psychological framework that emphasizes batterer treatment. Examining the theoretical conflicts, this paper attempts to demonstrate that sociopolitical and psychological theories can be successfully integrated into a social-psychological model. Such a model, developed by Zemsky and Gilbert, Poorman, and Simmons, is explored and critiqued as an excellent beginning. By integrating psychological principles and sociological concepts, this theory explores the many dimensions of power and explains the phenomenon of domestic violence as it occurs in all relationship configurations. Suggestions for further theoretical considerations and research are made. *[Article copies available from The Haworth Document Delivery Service: 1-800-342-9678.]*

One would hope that this article could begin without the assertion and lengthy accompanying arguments that same-sex domestic violence is a serious problem. Most of the authors who have written about this phenomenon make explicit reference to the degree of resistance to accepting the frequency and severity of its occurrence. In addition to the outright refusal of the lesbian, gay, and bisexual communities to organize around this issue, current domestic violence theory contributes to denial of the problem by failing to recognize and explain same-sex domestic violence. In this paper, I will explore current theory, particularly the tension between feminist sociopolitical theory and the psychological theory proposed by gay male theorists Island and Letellier. I intend to demonstrate that the two theories are not mutually exclusive and can be meaningfully integrated into a social-psychological theory. This integrated theory, while in its early stage of development, has the potential to explain domestic violence as it occurs in all relationship configurations.

Overview of Current Feminist Sociopolitical Theory

To begin to understand the development of theory about domestic violence, we must examine the social and historical context in which it developed. Prior to the rise of the modern women's movement, the existing research and theories minimized domestic violence and, one way or another, blamed the victim. In the late 1960s and early 1970s, feminism flourishing in this country helped to change this minimization through its primary tenet, the personal is political. This tenet called upon women to examine the conditions of their lives, the roles assigned to them (and also made unavailable to them) in families, the workplace, and society in general, vis-à-vis men. Through consciousness-raising groups and efforts, women began to discover the many insidious ways by which they are made second-class citizens, subordinate to men. In particular, women who had experienced men's emotional, physical, and/or sexual abuse began to share their experiences with one another and, as a result, no longer saw battering as an individual problem. Women organized and politicized around the issue of domestic violence, defining it as a crime against women, and therefore, a women's issue.

Using the feminist lens, activists, researchers, and professionals devoted considerable energy to developing a feminist analysis of domestic violence. They determined that violence, the threat thereof, ascribed family roles, and limited economic opportunity acted together to further gender-based oppression. When looking for the root of domestic violence, feminists saw cultural misogyny and sexism. Del Martin convincingly argued that domestic violence is the logical, if brutal, extreme of sexist gender-role socialization. If a culture socializes its men to be brave, dominant, aggressive, and strong, and its women to be passive, placating, dependent, and obedient, and oppresses any attempts at androgyny or "transgendering," then that culture has effectively trained its men and women for bipolar abuser and victim roles, respectively. Men learn that it is permissible to use violence and that they are expected to be in charge of "their" women and children; women learn to accept that their role is one of a subordinate and a care-taker. According to this analysis, domestic violence is a gender-based phenomenon, a socially-based illness used as a tool of the patriarchy to keep women down.

Despite cultural sexism and the resistance of those who persist in believing that victims have some responsibility for the violence, this gender-based theory has become the most commonly accepted explanation for domestic violence among academicians, the domestic violence movement, and lay people. It has won widespread support because it coherently explains the phenomenon in a way which intuitively makes sense. While there is dissent, a substantial body of research supports feminist contentions. Coleman notes that most studies conducted about battering conclude that it is a significant problem that is almost always perpetrated by men against women.

While this theory is inarguably an important starting place, it leaves many questions unanswered and makes many experiences invisible. For example, as Island and Letellier point out, gender-based

theory fails to explain why some heterosexual men batter their partners and others do not. Feminists of color also have argued legitimately that the theory does not reflect their experiences.[1]

With few exceptions, most authors have not attempted to integrate the phenomenon of same-sex partner abuse into feminist domestic violence theory. Indeed, it is not easy to do so without contributing to one of the four most popular misconceptions about same-sex partner abuse: (1) an outbreak of gay male domestic violence is logical (because all or most men are prone to violence), but lesbian domestic violence does not occur (because women are not); (2) same-sex partner abuse is not as severe as when a woman is battered by a man; (3) because the partners are of the same gender, it is mutual abuse, with each perpetrating and receiving "equally"; and (4) the perpetrator must be the "man" or the "butch" and the victim must be the "woman" or the "femme" in emulation of heterosexual relationships. Although the body of research on same-sex domestic violence is limited, Coleman, Kelly and Warshafsky, and Renzetti effectively confront and refute the above misconceptions.

Robert Geffner, editor of the *Family Violence and Sexual-Assault Bulletin*, expresses a common sentiment when he makes the following statement: "We need to learn more about this [same-sex domestic] violence and be willing to modify our theories and programs to include these 'exceptions to the rule'". Indeed, same-sex domestic violence, if viewed from the feminist lens, does seem like an exception. This is because sociopolitical theory alone does not fully or adequately explain why the same dynamic of abuse in heterosexual relationships occurs with as much frequency and severity in same-sex relationships.

Psychological Theory

Highly critical of the dominant feminist theory, Island and Letellier break with it altogether. First, they assert that it is heterosexist because it fails to acknowledge or explain the existence of same-sex partner abuse. Second, they make the controversial assertion that domestic violence is *not a gender issue.* Island believes that sociopolitical theory has led to ineffective batterer treatment programs and that treatment must be based primarily, if not solely, on the personality and behavioral characteristics of the batterer. Sociopolitical theory, he argues, has over-focused on the experience of battered women and does not focus at all on or explain the source of the problem, that is, the psychology of perpetrators. As a result, Island and Letellier propose a gender-neutral theory of domestic violence which focuses on the psychology of the batterer. They provide batterer diagnostic criteria for the American Psychiatric Association to adopt and support its application to men and women of all sexual orientations. Essentially, Island and Letellier argue that the feminist lens should be replaced by a psychological lens and that batterers should be identified and classified by behavior, not gender.

While their objections are strong and have been controversial in the domestic violence movement, Island and Letellier have more in common with feminists than even they have acknowledged. They agree with the feminist analysis that victims are created by batterers, do not necessarily have pathology that led them to become victims, and are not necessarily in need of treatment (beyond counseling and advocacy to promote safety and to help manage the effects of the abuse). Interestingly, they also devote several pages to the discussion of masculinity as malignant, arguing that male batterers are unclear on the concept of masculinity, having equated it with violence. Finally, Island and Letellier note in the opening of their book that in heterosexual relationships where abuse is occurring, 95% of the perpetrators are male, citing statistics produced by New York's Office for Prevention of Domestic Violence. And yet, if their assertion that domestic violence is not a gender issue were true, one would assume that heterosexual domestic violence would be equally perpetrated by men and women. So, just as feminist theory alone does not fully explain same-sex domestic violence, the strictly psychological theory proposed by Island and Letellier fails to explain the disproportionate number of male perpetrators in heterosexual domestic violence.

Integrating a Social-Psychological Model

What I would like to suggest here is that domestic violence must be understood as both a social *and* a psychological phenomenon and must be examined under both lenses simultaneously in order to be completely understood. Feminist theory and psychological theory are not necessarily mutually exclusive and do not have to negate one another. In fact, if synthesized, they can enhance our vision. Viewing domestic violence through an integrated framework permits us to see that domestic violence is a gender issue; that heterosexual domestic violence is, in fact, primarily perpetrated by men against women. We also see that gender is only one of several determining social and psychological factors and that the absence of gender inequity, as in same-sex relationships, by no means precludes the possibility that battering will occur.

Zemsky, in conjunction with Gilbert, Poorman, and Simmons, proposes a social-psychological theory of lesbian battering which can be applied to heterosexual and gay male relationships as well. They separate the causation of battering into three categories: learning to abuse; having the opportunity to abuse; and choosing to abuse. The individual who abuses has first learned to abuse through a combination of three psychological processes, usually occurring in the family of origin: one, direct instruction; two, modeling or learning through observation; and three, operant conditioning, or learning by reinforcement that violence is effective and "rewarding." They also suggest that men might be especially prone to learning abuse because of sex-role socialization, but agree with Hart that women in our culture also learn and internalize relationship models that are based upon inequity.

According to Zemsky and Gilbert et al., learning to abuse does not necessarily lead individuals to enact abuse. For that to occur, they must also have the opportunity to abuse without suffering negative consequences. In other words, would-be abusive individuals must perceive that they can "get away with it." Because of the pervasiveness of cultural sexism, homophobia, racism, classism, antisemitism, ageism, and ableism, some groups are empowered with privileges at the expense of others. For the battered heterosexual woman, the cultural context of sexism and other oppressions which may affect her (such as racism in the instance of a woman of color), as enforced by friends, family members, hospital workers, mental health providers, and the criminal justice system, contribute to an environment in which her abusive partner can batter her without intervention or consequence. Likewise, homophobia, heterosexism, and other oppressions operate in the same way to isolate the battered person in a same-sex relationship, permitting the violence to continue. While the social phenomenon of prejudice does not cause battering, it does create an opportune environment that supports abusive behavior by its refusal to challenge it.

Zemsky uses an apt example to describe the roles of actual and perceived power relations in creating opportunity. She writes that it is unlikely that individuals who had learned to harass the people with whom they work would harass their supervisors because the potential consequence of being immediately fired would decrease the level of opportunity. To extend Zemsky's analysis, if these same people were the supervisors, they would, in fact, be likely to harass their employees, because they would probably believe they could get away with it. To extend this even further, while these same people may not harass their supervisors, they may harass a colleague, someone at their same level of employment. They would be particularly likely to do so if they believed the victim would be unlikely or unable to report it and/or if they believed such a report would not be taken seriously or responded to. Thus, according to this model, abuse against someone with perceived greater power and/or the perceived power to bring effective, negative consequences is unlikely to be expressed, whereas abuse against someone with perceived equal or lesser power and/or a perceived diminished capacity to bring such consequences would be a more ripe opportunity.

Lastly, Zemsky and Gilbert et al. emphasize that although the learning may have occurred and the opportunity might be present, abusive individuals make a conscious choice to abuse. Although many abusive people may not perceive it this way, they have the ability to make alternative choices (or at least to learn alternative choices) and are solely responsible for their violence.

In formulating this theory, the authors successfully integrate sociopolitical concepts and psychological principles and begin to explore their very complex relationship. For instance, the learning process they propose is explicitly psychological since it involves the individual internalizing beliefs and learning behaviors, and yet, Zemsky and Gilbert et al. acknowledge that what is internalized is most definitely shaped by social mores. Their analysis of opportunity is largely informed by feminism and an analysis of power which expands beyond gender, including racism, sexism, heterosexism, and other oppressions. They argue that the social environment, particularly the relation of power and the ability to bring consequences, impacts how the potentially abusive person behaves. And yet they posit that this is not purely sociological either, because as important as the actual power relation is, the abusers' *perception* of the power relation and their *perception* of the partner's capacity to enact consequences (which can be distorted and different from the actual) are also important in explaining battering. Zemsky and Gilbert et al. close their model by promoting a psychological healing model, emphasizing abusers' complete responsibility for their behavior.

This social-psychological theory adequately explains why men predominantly perpetrate heterosexual domestic violence and why women are less likely to perpetrate. Heterosexual men who have learned to batter live in a culture which systematically devalues, discriminates against, and exploits women. In effect, misogyny and sexism increase the opportunity for heterosexual men to batter their female partners without receiving negative consequences. As a result, it is likely that these men would choose to batter. By contrast, heterosexual women who have learned to batter are not as likely to express abuse toward their male partners because their partners generally have more perceived and actual social power and the accompanying access to punish them. Instead, a heterosexual woman who batters might choose to express her abuse toward her children, siblings, elderly parents, or others whom she perceives to have lesser or equal social power and/or a diminished capacity to enact negative consequences against her.

Social-psychological theory also explains the existence of same-sex domestic violence by acknowledging the role of homophobia and by positing that the opportunity for abuse of power can exist not only when recipients have less social power, but also when they have roughly equal social power. This phenomenon of lateral abuse is especially likely to occur in circumstances in which the potential victim is perceived to be unwilling or unlikely to report, and/or in which the abuser believes reporting will have no effect. Like their heterosexual counterparts, same-sex abusers learn to abuse. Homophobia helps to create the opportunity for abuse without consequences by isolating the victims and preventing them access to resources such as their family, appropriate social services, and the criminal justice and legal systems. As a result, battered lesbians and gay men are unlikely to seek assistance, and even if they do, are not likely to be helped. In such a climate of opportunity, it is not surprising that lesbian and gay abusive persons are as likely to express abuse toward their partners as are their heterosexual male counterparts.

The Explanatory Power of a Social-Psychological Model

One challenge to social-psychological theory is its ability to explain exceptions. How does this theory hold up if asked to explain the existence of domestic violence perpetrated against someone who has more power than the perpetrator? Specifically, how does this theory explain the occasional incidence of men who are battered by their female partners? Although most people know that a small minority of men are battered by women, this question and the challenge it poses to theory is rarely addressed. One answer might be that abusive heterosexual women only batter their partners in instances where they have or perceive themselves as having more social power, either economically, racially, or along other dimensions, and/or perceive their partners as being unwilling or unable to enact negative consequences against them.

While this explanation is plausible and remains within the framework of the theory, I believe we also need to add to our analysis a variable that is primarily psychological, the degree of severity of the batterer.[2] Those of us who work with victims and/or batterers know that some batterers will draw the line at pushing or milder forms of abuse while others will stop at nothing, the difference based largely upon their capacity for impulse control. I posit here that the more severe the degree of severity of the batterer, the more likely the batterers are to choose to abuse, regardless of the level of opportunity. For instance, a heterosexual woman who is a "severe" batterer with little impulse control might be likely to abuse her male partner, even though he has more perceived and actual power and can enact negative consequences against her. Because of the cycle of violence in which the abuse escalates over time, the degree of severity might change across time and situations, making it difficult to measure. Other complex variables which influence degree of severity and make it difficult to measure include batterers' own shifting perceptions of being powerless and of not perceiving themselves as having resolution options other than violence.[3] Future work should develop the concept of degree of batterer severity and an appropriate measure, not only because of its explanatory value, but also for its important to treatment considerstions.[4]

I also believe domestic violence theory could benefit from further analysis of power. To date, the analysis of social power, as endowed or denied on the basis of gender, race, sexual orientation, and so on has been extensively explored and is useful. By contrast, the concept of psychological or personal power, referring to a person's ability to access the social and other resources available to him or her has not been adequately explored. Just as some of my clients are physically stronger than their abusive partners and could overpower them if they chose to, some of my clients are also professional gay men who have significantly more social power, and the access it affords them, than their abusers. However, because they have been manipulated emotionally by guilt, shame, fear, attacks upon their self-esteem, a distorted sense of responsibility and other complex psychological tactics frequently employed by batterers, many have been rendered powerless to use resources that are available to them. These cases demonstrate that individuals with greater physical or social power who do not have, or have been robbed of, their sense of personal power can be dominated by an abusive person with less actual power. In other words, the experiences of same-sex domestic violence victims teach us that domestic violence is not always necessarily about the abuser having more physical or social power, but is also about their willingness to use whatever tools and tactics they may have to subordinate their partner. Further attention to this less evident type of psychological or personal power, which is certainly related to self-esteem, will add a new, psychological dimension, strengthening the theory's ability to account for what otherwise might be considered "exceptions to the rule."

Conclusion

To conclude, this paper argues that in order for domestic violence theory to be comprehensive, it must account for both sociopolitical and psychological dynamics, and their complex, often intertwined relationship. A social-psychological model proposed by Zemsky and Gilbert et al. was discussed as an excellent starting place, and suggestions for future analysis, especially for measuring the degree of severity of the batterer and developing the concept of personal power, were made. As all theories must be tested, researchers are challenged to design tools for assessment and studies which will support or refute a social-psychological model and contribute to our understanding.

For those who strategize to stop domestic violence, the challenge is to devote ourselves to changing the social context so as to reduce the opportunities for abuse, including confronting oppressions, developing culturally-appropriate prevention and early intervention programs, and improving the legal system for all battered individuals, as well as developing a body of knowledge about the psychology of batterers that will aid individual, psychological intervention. If domestic violence is caused by both social and psychological factors, then viable solutions must address both. Finally, researchers are challenged to develop theories based upon behavior rather

than upon social identity, theories which explain phenomena for every group that experiences it, not only the majority group. While these theories should not be identity-based, they also should not be blind to the very real impact of identity-based social oppression. These, indeed, are challenges to us all.

Notes

1. A colleague of mine, Cara Page, instructed me in a feminist of color critique of domestic violence theory for which I am sincerely grateful. As Ms. Page brought to my attention, the feminist theory I have summarized here is predominately white feminist theory and does not reflect the valuable contributions of feminist of color. And yet I chose to represent it this way, exclusionary as it may be, because this is the most dominant form of the theory and the one most commonly subscribed. There is much to be gained from advocates for battered women of color and for battered lesbians and gay men of all colors working together to expand the current theoretical lens. To familiarize yourself with relevant feminist of color writings, see *Home girls: A black feminist anthology*, edited by Barbara Smith; *This bridge called my back*, edited by Cherrie Moraga and Gloria Anzaldua; *Mejor sola que acompanada: Para la mujer golpeada: For the Latina in an abusive relationship* by Myrna Zambrano; *Chain chain change: For black woman dealing with physical and emotional abuse* by Evelyn White and others.

2. The concept *degree of severity of the batterer* assumes that batterers can be placed along a continuum of mild to severe depending upon their capacity for impulse control and the severity of violence used. This concept helps us to distinguish between batterers who have a higher degree of control over their impulses and use "milder" forms of abusive behavior and batterers who have little or no impulse control and regularly use severe, life-threatening forms of violence. I use the words "mild" and "milder" only to provide contrast between degrees of severity, not to suggest that domestic violence in any form, mild or severe, is minor.

3. Thank you to Beth Zemsky for raising this point in her critique of this paper.

4. Further attention to this concept, while crucial, is beyond the scope of this paper and the author's current level of expertise.

References

A list of reference is available in the original source.

Women's Use of Force: Complexities and Challenges of Taking the Issue Seriously

by Nancy Worcester

This article discusses the complexities, challenges, and urgency surrounding addressing women's use of force. The author emphasizes that women's and girls' use of force needs to be analyzed using a framework that keeps power and control central to the definition of domestic violence and identifies that violence by men and women takes place within a social, historical, and economic context in which men's and women's roles, opportunities, and social power differ. The article builds on an understanding of women's use of force in heterosexual relationships; however, a similar contextual analysis is also applied to women's use of force in teen dating relationships, lesbian relationships, and against children.

Many people are paying enormous attention to the issues of girls' and women's violence. More women are being arrested for assaulting their partners. Many domestic violence programs are making difficult decisions about whether to run "abuser" groups for arrested women or whether women arrested for fighting back are more appropriately served by being in support groups for battered women.

The antifeminist backlash picks up on "conflict tactics"-type studies or the anti-domestic violence movement's own work to give visibility to lesbian violence in order to promote the idea that women are as violent as men. In most audiences, someone knows one man who has been hurt by an intimate partner and his story must be told. Many well-meaning professionals who have chosen to devote their lives to humanitarian service work pride themselves on publicly demonstrating that their services are equally available to men and women without the information, training, or professional support to develop an analysis of the limitations and dangers of a gender-neutral approach to antiviolence work.

This article examines some of the complexities, challenges, and urgency of reintegrating a gender analysis into violence work and addressing the issue of women using force[1] in ways that build on more than 25 years of work by some of the best thinkers and organizers addressing difficult issues within the battered women's movement. This article particularly draws on my experiences of working with the Education and Emerging Issues Committee of the Wisconsin Coalition Against Domestic Violence to encourage dialogue on the issue through a series of conference presentations, a 1-day membership meeting, think tanks, a special newsletter on this issue, and hours and hours of discussion. The article also builds on my many years of working within the battered women's movement, collaborating with others to ensure that the movement addresses challenging, cutting edge issues. I welcome the wider readership of this journal and encourage readers to explore how debates around the issue of women and girls using force can help set the agenda for the next decade of antiviolence research and activism.

"Women's Use of Force: Complexities and Challenges of Taking the Issue Seriously" by Nancy Worcester, *Violence Against Women*, Vol. 6, No. 11, November 2002.

Core issues of power and control and the context of violence need to be central to discussions and policies regarding domestic violence and battering and women's use of force. Violence by men or women and violence against men or women take place within a social, historical, and economic context in which men and women, in general, still play different roles, have different opportunities, and have different social power. Thus, it is important that violence is not simplistically "counted" separately from the context of societal inequalities and gender roles violence helps to keep in place. In addressing the issue of women using force, counting the violence should never be the goal so much as looking at the meaning and consequences of violence in people's lives. It is urgent that antiviolence thinkers, researchers, workers, and activists take leadership roles in taking women's use of force seriously so that information on female violence is no longer given from just antiwomen, backlash perspectives. The challenge is to take violence by women seriously without losing sight of the fact that the patterns of male and female violence within adult intimate relationships are usually very different, often happen within different contexts, and generally have very different consequences and that both the violence itself and the barriers to ending violence are related to societal inequalities.

Female violence must be taken very seriously. Female perpetrators must be held accountable. I know there are women who are violent. I have been curious about violent women ever since I read MacDonald's book *Shoot the Women First* ("The first book to tell why women are the most feared terrorists in the world," back cover), the cover of which exclaimed,

> "Shoot the women first" is the advice given to German police teams handling terrorist incidents, but is recognized as valid by anti-terrorist groups the world over. Armed men may hesitate before they shoot, women rarely do. They are more ruthless, more determined and consequently more feared than their male comrades, and make the most deadly adversaries.

I am a firm believer that many women are extremely good at whatever they decide to do, so it makes sense that if a woman "decides" violence is necessary, she might be very good at it. It also makes sense to me that when girls and women are rewarded for paying attention to what other people need and for developing good verbal and emotional skills, they could turn those areas of expertise into something that could very much hurt a loved one. Indeed, unless our society starts to give clearer, more consistent messages that will not reward or ignore violence, I think we should expect that more girls will get the message that violence is acceptable or even glamorous. I am obviously writing this article, however, because I want to inspire readers to take female violence seriously without losing sight of the general patterns in intimate partner violence (i.e., male violence keeps women from maximizing their fullest potential) that need to guide antiviolence work. We need to be careful that our curiosity about female violence, our knowledge that some women are violent and thus that some men get hurt in heterosexual relationships, and our commitment to holding abusers accountable do not get in the way of thinking through the complexities of addressing the issues of female violence.

It is time to reframe a number of issues.

Connecting and Disconnecting: Issues of Girls and Women Using Force

The question, "What about girls and women using force?" is so big. There are many answers and many more questions than answers. When the Wisconsin Coalition Against Domestic Violence Education Committee first initiated discussion on this topic, we did not want to leave out any part of the question, so we tried to address all the following questions in our first short workshop:

1. What are the experiences of domestic abuse programs with girls' and women's use of force?

2. What are the political ramifications of asking this question? How do we frame the issue to make sure we are not compromising the integrity of the battered women's movement? What are the dangers of addressing this issue?

3. Do men and women use violence in different ways? Much on the power and control

wheel may look the same for male and female violence. But what about the "using male privilege" piece that supports violence against women? A lesbian batterer may use homophobia to hurt her partner, but are there similar privilege or social oppression weapons being used if a heterosexual woman is a perpetrator?

4. What are the similarities and differences of batterers' treatment for men and women? Are there different ways to hold men and women accountable for their violence? Will the same types of intervention work for abusive women and abusive men?

5. What are the similarities and differences between women as perpetrators in lesbian versus heterosexual relationships? (What are the similarities and differences between women as victims or survivors in lesbian versus heterosexual relationships?)

6. If we believe that violence against women is related to gender socialization, are we moving toward boys and men being less violent and/or girls and women being more violent? What are we doing right? What are we doing wrong?

7. Should we make these questions more central to the battered women's movement? If so, how?

8. Are there other forms of girls' and women's use of force we should be addressing? What else should we be discussing?

The fact that more than 100 people attended a workshop, which we expected to be very small (it was scheduled at the same time as many workshops by popular national speakers), demonstrated that people are eager for a chance to talk about the issues. Time ran out much too quickly, and it became obvious that each question needs weeks, not minutes, of discussion time. It was clear that one challenge for the antidomestic violence movement is making the time and creating safe spaces so that we can slowly and carefully develop our thinking about the different ways girls and women may use or are accused of using force at different ages and in different contexts.

Many of us who have worked on a range of violence against women issues have felt connected under the widest violence against women "umbrella" but have found times when we needed to specifically work on lesbian violence, sexual assault, gender harassment, elder abuse, or heterosexual domestic violence; we have done that specific work with the bigger picture of analysis of violence against women in mind. In the same way, it will be important to remember the context of sex-role socialization, societal inequalities, and violence as power and control as the questions about girls and women using force are addressed in relation to teen dating violence, gang violence, lesbian battering, child abuse, elder abuse, heterosexual domestic violence, and other issues. Unique aspects of each of these topics merit much in-depth exploration, and simultaneously, each needs to be contextualized within the broader framework of violence against and by females within a violent, patriarchal society. (Key issues related to several of these topics are introduced at the end of this article.)

Strategy: Acknowledge That Men Get Hurt by Violence

Backlash against a movement is always a sign of how successful a movement has been. No one would be talking about whether women are as violent as men if there had not been more than 25 years of organizing against violence against women; establishing shelters, anti-domestic violence programs, and support groups; working to get the criminal justice system to hold perpetrators accountable; and developing coordinated community responses to domestic violence. Quite rightly, violence against women has received much attention.

Who gets left out of attention focused on violence against women? Men and boys as victims of violence.

Acknowledging that men and boys get terribly hurt by violence may be just as important as exploring the issue of women as perpetrators of violence. It certainly helps shift the discussion in more fruitful directions. Acknowledging that men and boys are killed by violence (mostly by other men and boys) more often than are women and girls in this society may be an effective strategy for making a gender analysis more central to violence work.

Male violence not only hurts women but also disproportionately kills men, especially men of color. Of homicide victims from 1976 to 1999 in the United States, 76% were men, as were 88% of those who committed homicide. White men between the ages of 15 and 25 are more likely to be killed than White women, and Black men are more likely to be killed than Black women.[2] Male violence particularly devastates Black communities. Black women aged 15 to 24 are killed at nearly the same rate as are White men in the United States, whereas Black men are killed at a rate 8.5 times higher than are Black women or White men.

Both the battered women's movement and many parts of the wider women's (liberation) movement have done an excellent job of making connections among images of women, the socialization of women and their roles in society, and violence against women. An important next stage of working on violence prevention must be to develop a more thorough gender analysis so that the roots of violence are better understood in relation to definitions of masculinity, the socialization of men and their roles in society. Hiding the prevalence of male violence (against both men and women) contributes to the climate in which it becomes acceptable or even fashionable to ask whether women are as violent as men. For example, despite the fact that almost all the so-called school violence that hit the headlines in the 1990s has been perpetrated by (White) male youths, the media have consistently failed to note that, and one could easily get the idea that school violence is a gender-neutral problem. How many people have any idea about the disproportionate amount of violence committed by men?[3] While identifying that both men and women get hurt or killed by living in a violent society, a gender analysis also helps identify that men and women get hurt by violence in very different contexts. Men mostly get hurt by strangers, whereas women mostly get hurt by people they know and care about.[4] Women are more than five times more likely than men to be victimized by a spouse or partner, ex-partner, boyfriend, or girlfriend.

There is not a hierarchy of violence, but the ramifications for intervention, prevention, and long-term consequences are totally different for someone hurt by a stranger and someone hurt by a loved one. These are important issues to identify

for anyone questioning the necessity of a gender analysis of violence. Many emergency room and criminal justice system personnel have observed that when someone (usually a man) is hurt by a stranger, they are likely to want to report the crime, to want the other person prosecuted, and to hope they will never see that person again. In contrast, a different pattern is observed when someone (usually a woman) has lived with or loved the person who is hurting them. Reporting the abuse has different ramifications when there are shared children, dreams, identities, finances, and futures and where reporting may cause escalation of the violence. Unlike stranger violence in which men are the main victims of what is usually a one-time occurrence, intimate partner violence, with women as the primary victims, tends to be an on-going pattern of abuse of power and control. Consequently, in general, violence disrupts the lives of men and women in quite different ways.

Gender, Race, and Class

Momentarily focusing on the seriousness of how much male violence hurts men may be an effective way to reassure men that we care about anyone getting hurt by violence, it may help us get on with our presentations and our work, and it may help contextualize the fact that violence against women happens within societies that allow and support the widest range of violence. However, it is also important to recognize the limitations and dangers of this tactic.

First, it is vital to acknowledge that gender differences in homicide rates do not reflect the differences in quality of life for men and women. Many women hurt by violence get hurt every day. The woman who says, "I probably only got hurt once a year for 20 years, but I woke up every one of those other 364 days of the year wondering if that would be the day" (quote from a survivor in the video "Any Day Now," WomanReach, Inc. and the Domestic Violence Advocacy Council of Charlotte/Mecklenburg, 1991) reminds us how violence and the fear of violence affect the quality of women's lives.

Also, it is important to be careful not to leave out an analysis of how other inequalities in society are related to violence. Note that in the previous discussion of homicide victimization of Black and White people aged 15 to 24, gender analysis is meaningless unless the impact of race or racism on homicide is also examined. These figures show that Black women and White men are killed at similar rates and that the homicide rate is 4.2 times higher for Black than for White women. Black men are killed at a rate 35 times higher than are White women.

Both race and class analyses are crucial in addressing violence and understanding that the battered women's movement, the criminal justice system, and other systems have particularly failed to adequately address the needs of many battered women of color, poor women, and other women from marginalized communities. Lack of appropriate services and policies may force some women to resort to using force or other unhealthy coping strategies. In *Compelled to Crime: The Gender Entrapment of Battered Black Women*, Richie wrote,

> The extent to which some women experience this predicament [domestic violence] is directly related to the degree of stigma, isolation, and marginalization imposed by their social position. The choices are harder and the consequences are more serious for women with low incomes, women of color, lesbians, women who become pregnant at a young age, and others whose decisions, circumstances, and status violate the dominate culture's expectations or offend hegemonic images of "womanhood."
>
> Studies that have been conducted from the standpoint of battered women have been overwhelmingly concerned with the experiences of White women. . . . The aggregate effect is that while *some* battered women are safer in the 1990s than they were in the 1970s, and while we know more about *general* patterns in the population, we still have very little theoretical or empirical work that speaks to African-American battered women from low-income communities. Consequently, few antiviolence programs, criminal justice policies, or theoretical explanations are sensitive to ethnic differences or address cultural issues that give particular meaning to violence in intimate relationships for African-American or

other women of color. Furthermore, those whose lives are complicated by drug use, prostitution, illegal immigrant status, low literacy, and a criminal record continue to be misunderstood, underserved, isolated, and … in serious physical and emotional danger. (pp. 2–12)

E. Assata Wright gives examples of well-meaning public policy having an adverse effect for women of color because no one thought through how policies like mandatory arrest might have an impact on these women's lives:

> The mandatory arrest policy is particularly problematic for Black women because … they are more likely to fight back and protect themselves when being abused. In cases where a woman hits her abuser, she can be arrested along with the attacker.
>
> Many Black women and Latinas may protect the abuser from jail even if it means risking their own safety. In a 1996 report on police brutality in New York City, Amnesty International found that between 1993 and 1994 there was a "substantial" increase in the number of Blacks and Latinos who were shot or killed while in police custody. Advocates point out that while women want protection from their batterers, they don't want him beaten by cops or worse, killed by them. (pp. 550–551)

Economic issues relate to battering a number of ways, such as in both the relationship between poverty and family violence and the potential loss of employment opportunities for self-sufficiency abused women arrested for assaulting their abusive partners may face. Kurz's research found that the poorest divorced women, those on welfare, experienced higher rates of violence than did any other groups of women and that the poorer the woman, the more serious the violence was that she experienced. She questions the relationship between poverty and abuse as follows:

> What is the reason for the higher levels of violence reported by low income women? Are poor women more forthcoming about the amount of violence they experience, or do more of them report the violence to the police because they have less access

to other kinds of legal assistance? These are possibilities, but at this point no data answer this question. It is also possible that something about the circumstances of those living in poverty contributes to the higher rates of violence among poorer men. For example, men from lower income groups may have a stronger belief in the legitimacy of violence than other men, since they typically hold more traditional gender ideologies than other men. It is not clear, however, that lower income men actually behave in more gendered ways than do other men. Another explanation for the higher rates of violence reported by poorer women could be that lower-income men have fewer ways of controlling their partners than other men. The higher men's social class, the more ability they have to control their female partners through their greater economic resources. (pp. 136–137)

The National Clearinghouse for the Defense of Battered Women has raised awareness of the economic ramifications of battered women being arrested for and convicted of using force against abusive partners and then having a criminal record, which affects their financial situation.

> We know many women, eager to "get the case over with," accept guilty pleas without being fully appraised of the potential consequences of have a record. Might a conviction bar a woman from certain employment opportunities, public housing situations, welfare benefits, or affect her immigration status or a custody determination? We want to work with defense counsel to help them better understand the consequences of a conviction and the disparate impact on women clients (since so many of the jobs barred by convictions are traditionally "women's work," such as child care and healthcare jobs, and because so many women, as primary caretakers for their children, are the ones to apply for public benefits and housing). (p. 8)

It is clear that researchers and practitioners need to more fully understand how gender, race, and class affect battered women's experiences and how and why they may choose to, or need to, use violence.

Domestic Violence = Woman Battering

Domestic violence is certainly not gender exclusive, but the pattern of male perpetrator and female victim reflects and is encouraged by societal power inequalities between women and men and serves to maintain gender inequality. In fact, domestic violence is an extreme example of gender inequality.

The battered women's movement was clearly built on a sophisticated understanding of how violence in intimate relationships relates to and helps perpetuate inequalities between women and men. As the movement grew more visible, as many more players became involved in providing services to victims of intimate violence, and as more funding became available, domestic violence became a hot topic and a very mainstream issue. It was no longer unusual, controversial, or even radical to work to end domestic violence. This was a very exciting phenomenon: Many more people know about and benefited from domestic violence services, and whole communities identified roles different professionals could play in recognizing and responding to domestic violence. This mainstreaming of the battered women's movement coincided with a changing environment where the work of many aspects of the women's movement became less visible and debates about "political correctness" made it much more challenging to figure out how to work on societal inequalities. Although it was no big deal that people involved in this work gradually stopped calling themselves the battered women's movement and became known as people working against domestic violence, symbolically "women" visibly got left out of the name of the movement and out of the analysis of intimate partner violence. (Throughout this article, I use both the terms *battered women's movement and domestic violence movement*). Once an issue has a gender-neutral name, it is easy to forget that it is not a gender-neutral issue.

Renzetti illustrated the dangers of a gender-neutral approach to domestic violence in relation to the criminal justice system as follows:

> The police, attorneys, and judges, like the backlash writers, argue that women, like men, must be held accountable for their behavior. To them, prosecuting women

who have used violence against an intimate partner represents a gender-neutral application of the law. However, by decontextualizing women's violence and scrutinizing it in terms of a male normative standard juxtaposed against stereotypes of respectable femininity, the justice system thereby treats unjustly many women who have used violence. The outcome will be—indeed, it already is—"gendered injustice." Women are increasingly being treated like men by the legal system, even though their circumstances typically are quite different. If these differential circumstances are not taken into account, the outcomes can hardly be fair. (p. 49)

With more women getting arrested for domestic violence in heterosexual relationships, it will be increasingly important to have trustworthy assessment tools that help identify when women use force in self-defense or within the context of long-term battering rather than initiate violence as power and control. The complexities of assessing who are the victims and who are the perpetrators have long been issues for discussion in relation to lesbian violence. Burk (C. Burk, personal communications, May 11, 1999, & July 14, 2000) and others have observed that unlike those working on heterosexual domestic violence, people working on lesbian intimate violence have always had to look at how any behavior can be used as power and control, how any behavior can be used as a survival tactic, and the fact that victims may well identify as abusers. There is also an important "reporting artifact" that is recognized in the violence literature: Studies show that women are more likely than men to admit they are abusive. In an article titled "Violent Women: Fact and Fantasy—Social Service Agencies Have the Responsibility to Know the Difference," Edleson stressed that accurate assessment is vital for providing different effective interventions for women who use force in different ways, for different reasons. He summarized how the Domestic Abuse Project's *Women Who Abuse in Intimate Relationships* treatment manual categorizes women who use force into the following three groups:

One group includes women who use violence in self-defense to escape or protect themselves from their partner's violence.

Saunders (1986) found that this was the most frequently reported motivation for women's use of violence.

In a second group are women who have a long history of victimization at the hands of previous partners as well as during childhood. These women are described as taking a stance in life that "no one is ever going to hurt me that way again," and their violence is interpreted as an effort to decrease their own chances of victimization.

Violent women in a third group are identified as primary aggressors who use their greater physical power to control their partners. (p. 3)

Obviously, it is of the utmost importance to recognize that many women who use force are battered women who are not safe. Breaking their isolation and helping them be safer may be even more important than it is for women who do not use force because battered women's use of violence may make them even more vulnerable to their partner's aggression.

In general, the context and consequences of male and female violence within intimate relationships is different. Although studies often report that women use violence as a conflict tactic as often as men, women are the recipients of more injurious and life-threatening violence committed by intimate partners than are men. Women are also more likely than men to be killed by intimate partners.[5]

For much of the past decade, anti-domestic violence programs have been conscientiously letting their communities know that they are committed to helping both women and men in violent relationships. Although many anti-domestic violence programs do serve a few men, a committed public effort to reach out to male victims has not resulted in anti-domestic violence programs suddenly discovering they need to rethink their emphasis on serving women. In fact, no man has ever stayed in the first shelter for battered men, established in Britain in 1992 by the group Families Need Fathers. Hanusa (D. Hanusa, personal communication, November 10, 1998) and others who lead abuser groups have observed that the services needed by heterosexual men who identify themselves as abused seem to be different from those needed by abused women because safety is less of an issue and leaving the relationship is not usually associated with increased danger as it is for abused women.

In "Counseling Heterosexual Women Arrested for Domestic Violence," Hamberger and Potente concluded that domestic violence by women and men show distinctly different patterns.

> First, although women are domestically violent, often at levels of severity similar to that of men, the impact of their violence is typically less than men's violence. Second, women tend to commit violence less frequently than do men, and for different reasons. Specifically, women tend to initiate physical assault motivated by a need for self-protection or retaliation of a previous assault by their partner. Men, in contrast, tend to identify control or punishment as the primary motivations for assaults on their partners. (p. 59)

Saunders showed that 71% of battered women arrested for domestic violence had used violence in self-defense. Hanusa (D. Hanusa, personal communication, November 10, 1998) observed that there is a functional difference in how men and women use violence in intimate relationships: Women use it to end oppression geared toward them, whereas men use it to control someone. In 32 in-depth interviews with women court-ordered or referred to counseling because they had used violence, Dasgupta found that "the most pervasive and persistent motivation for women's use of violence is ending abuse in their own lives" (p. 217), and "when viewed in terms of motives, intentions, and consequences, these women's use of violence emerges as instrumental; that is, the incidents are directed toward the resolution of conflicts or control of immediate surroundings" (p. 210), including the fact that "many of the women became physically aggressive with their partners when their children were being abused" (p. 208).

In examining the differences between male and female violence, it may be useful to keep in mind the definition of domestic violence as an on-going pattern in which one person controls the other person and one person thus lives in fear for her or his safety. It is crucial to keep asking who is afraid and who is not safe. We need to explore much more about how men and women use emotional control. We know women can be effective at using emotional control, but whether it takes on the same level of threat to safety and whether the other person lives in constant fear may be a major difference between male and female use of emotional control. In Dasgupta's study of 32 women who had used physical violence, it was clear that even the use of violence did not equalize who was in control and who was afraid in these heterosexual relationships.

> Regardless of the degree of physical force women used, none of the interviewees believed that it made their partners fearful. Neither did it control their behaviors. This perception was not without its base in reality. A group of 10 men whose female partners had been arrested on domestic abuse charges and interviewed as a part of this study also denied that their partner's violence resulted in their experiencing prolonged or significant fear for their safety. This finding is supported by studies that indicate that men in violent relationships, compared to their female counterparts, express little fear of their partners and wives. (pp. 209–210)

In addition to the research quoted throughout this article, most of the ideas and analysis in this article have grown out of on-going discussions with domestic violence service providers, abuser group facilitators, and policy makers. Everyone agrees that much better research is needed on women's use of force. Meanwhile, however, many people agree that they have observed the following different patterns in male and female violence in intimate relationships and the different consequences of male and female violence in intimate relationships:

1. Male violence is more apt to be a pattern to be repeated in subsequent relationships rather than situational in particular relationships. Adult women who are perpetrators in one relationship are less likely to become perpetrators in their next relationship. How many domestic violence programs have served several women hurt by the same man? (Talking

about this phenomenon is a good way of reinforcing that most men are not violent. The high percentage of women who get hurt by domestic violence is a reflection of the same men hurting several women rather than a high percentage of men being violent.)

2. Men are more likely to physically injure their partners.

3. Women are more likely than men to be killed by intimate partners and are more likely than men to be punched, hit, burned, thrown out of a window, or strangled by intimate partners (Belluck, 1997).

4. Men have an ability to control women and children by creating an ongoing pattern whereby women and children live in fear. (How much will this situation change when more women have access to guns? In Dasgupta's interviews with women who had used force, she concluded that "only when women picked up weapons, guns, knives, and household objects did their partners become temporarily afraid," p. 210. But the interviewees also said that having used force, including weapons, led to more abusive behaviors in the future by their male partners. What are the dynamics that create an on-going pattern of fear?).

5. A different pattern in ending male and female violence in heterosexual relationships has been observed: If a woman is hurting a man, the violence usually ends when the relationship ends. If a man is hurting a woman, the violence generally escalates and becomes most dangerous when the relationship ends and in subsequent years. Therefore, barriers to ending violence may be fundamentally different for men and women.

In the arena of sexual assault, activists working to end violence against women have been critical of the overemphasis on women learning self-defense when the real issue that needs to be addressed is stopping male violence. Ironically, with domestic violence, the issue of women fighting back is now getting increased negative attention (and more arrests), with too little attention being paid to why women need to resort to violence. Why are other strategies failing to keep women safe within their intimate relationships? Once again, the key issue of how to stop men's abuse of power and control is left out when the discussions focus on whether women should use force to protect themselves.

Violence in Lesbian Relationships

Lesbian battering includes many of the same issues as heterosexual domestic violence (power and control, fear, lack of safety) but is additionally affected by homophobia and a lack of services for victims of lesbian violence. In many communities, neither lesbian organizations nor anti-domestic violence programs have adequately addressed lesbian battering because of the fear that it could rip lesbian communities apart, dilute the issue of male violence against women, draw the "wrong" kind of attention to gay and lesbian issues, or draw the "wrong" kind of attention to a domestic violence program that may need financial support from a conservative community. Unfortunately, it is often the backlash to the violence against women movement that draws attention to lesbian domestic violence in an effort to say that women are as violent as men.

That women tend to be more likely than men to report they are violent must certainly affect studies of lesbian violence. I also wonder whether there is an additional reporting artifact in that women are more likely to identify abuse in a lesbian than in a heterosexual relationship. (Is more equality expected in a lesbian relationship so that an abuse of power and control is more easily identified?). There are extremes related to lesbian violence: It often is ignored or, in contrast, reported at quite high rates (e.g., in surveys at the Michigan Women's Music Festival, although these surveys do not use scientific sampling methods). Why these extremes? Is less known about the prevalence of lesbian violence than about heterosexual violence because of the added complexities of studying it, or are people just more honest about saying that too little is known about the prevalence or consequences of lesbian battering? As someone who teaches women's health topics to 840 university students each year, I have curiously observed that students pay much more attention to the issue of lesbian battering than to other issues, such as legal discrimination against lesbians, lack of partner health insurance for lesbians, lesbian parenting, lesbian alcohol use, or lesbian menopause. Perhaps it is because the battered women's movement has been a major arena for important feminist discussion and debate during the past two decades and the issue rightly belongs here; there have not been similarly effective movements around which to organize other equally urgent lesbian issues. The good news is that because some people have made lesbian battering a visible issue, there are now some very good resources on this topic.[6]

An excellent article, "Ruling, the Exceptions: Same Sex Battering and Domestic Violence Theory" by Merrill, builds on the analysis of power and control in heterosexual domestic violence relationships to look at theoretical frameworks that bring together sociopolitical and psychological theories to include same-sex violence. Merrill identified the following three factors that make someone violent: (a) growing up learning how to be violent (obviously, everyone growing up in the United States learns how to be violent, but many people choose not to act on that); (b) having an opportunity to be violent; and (c) personally choosing to be violent. Merrill said that having the opportunity to be violent can be emphasized as a way to explain same-sex violence because homophobia allows someone to abuse a same-sex partner knowing that homophobia in the outside world will protect abusers from suffering negative consequences for their abusive behavior. Homophobia and heterosexism operate so that battering in same-sex relationships is ignored or not taken seriously; the perpetrators clearly get the message that our society will tolerate it. Potentially violent women in lesbian relationships get the message that they will not be negatively sanctioned for being violent "in that kind of relationship." In contrast, potentially violent women in heterosexual relationships will get strong messages that their violence against male partners would not be socially acceptable or tolerated. Merrill concluded, "While the social phenomenon of prejudice (homophobia) does not cause lesbian or gay battering, it does create an opportune environment that supports this abusive behavior by its refusal to challenge it" (p. 15).

Lesbian battering experts have much to offer the anti-domestic violence field from their years of recognizing the complexities of identifying who are the perpetrators and who may have used force in self-defense. As anti-domestic violence programs work to develop more effective assessment tools for women arrested for using force, this may be an opportunity for activists who have worked on lesbian and heterosexual battering assessment to have more dialogue about what can be learned from each other. Clearly, all communities need to give both men and women consistent messages that violence in any relationship, by either partner, is not tolerated.

Women as Perpetrators of Child Abuse

Of all the areas I work in, child abuse is the area I find the most mother blaming and outright woman hating, and it is the area in which I am most concerned about the increasing levels of woman blaming. Society in general and child protective services in particular assign responsibility for child abuse to mothers, regardless of who assaults the children or the context in which the abuse occurs.

There has now been more than a decade of organizing and education on the effects of domestic violence on children. Ironically, instead of people being better at seeing how child abuse is an extension and predictable component of the ongoing power and control that hurts women in domestic violence, more and more battered women are being charged with child abuse because they "allowed" their children to witness domestic violence or "failed to protect" them from harm, despite the power relations that make it dangerous and impossible for many battered women to keep their children safe.

In their important article "Women and Children at Risk: A Feminist Perspective on Child Abuse," Stark and Flitcraft concluded,

> Representative sample surveys indicate that fathers may be as likely or more likely than mothers to abuse children. . . . More important, there is little doubt that if a man is involved in a relationship, he is many times more likely than a woman to abuse the children. . . . National survey data indicate that men were responsible for two-thirds of the reported incidents of child abuse in which men were present in the relationship. (p. 75)

They are careful to point out that they reach this conclusion despite the obvious fact that women spend many more hours per day, per week with children and that many children are raised by single women.

The issues of child abuse and woman abuse are so clearly interrelated that it feels very intentional that others are not seeing or are choosing to ignore the connection. Years ago, Walker, best know for her important work on battered woman syndrome, noted that if a child is being abused, the most predictable correlation is that the child's mother is also being abused. (That factor—the mother being abused—is more consistent and predictable than is any other variable, including age, income group, and geographic area.) Indeed, if the woman is abusing the child, it is even more predictable that the woman herself is being abused and that her abuse of the child is related to (or a consequence of) the ongoing power, control, and fear in her life. Walker found mothers were eight times more likely to hurt their children when they were battered than when they were safe from violence.

The example of child abuse is a model for how antiviolence activists and researchers can take the issue of women's use of force more seriously, that is, to make sure we take the context of women's violence very seriously. If women are more likely to hurt their children when they themselves are being hurt, it of course reinforces the need for ending violence against women, but it also reinforces our need to find more effective ways to communicate and collaborate with agencies and institutions that have not always seen violence against women as their issue. The Advocacy for Women and Kids in Emergencies Program at Boston Children's Hospital (Schechter & Gary) is a model that takes both child abuse and woman abuse seriously and does not leave anyone pulled between two systems or two victims. Schecter's work at the Advocacy for Women and Kids in Emergencies Program inspired others to work on the premise that if a child is being hurt, the mother may also be getting hurt and that child abuse intervention needs to be consistently done in a way that ensures the violence in a mother's life will be addressed. Different sets of advocates are available to help the child through the child protective service system, and another set of advocates helps the mother end the violence in her life. Instead of seeing a conflict between the interests of abused children and their mothers, a reframing of the issue helped this agency identify that in many cases, helping women to be safe is a very effective way to help children be safe.

Teen Dating Violence

This issue of women getting mixed messages about whether it is acceptable to initiate violence or to fight back for self-protection is particularly crucial in relation to work on girls' use of force in teen dating relationships.

An example of what is happening in teen dating violence is apparent in Molidor and Tolman's article, "Gender and Contextual Factors in Adolescent Dating Violence," which reported a study of 635 students surveyed about dating violence. The study found that male and female adolescents did not differ in overall frequency of violence in dating relationships. However, when researchers went beyond simply counting experiences of violence to looking for the context and consequences of teen intimate violence, they found that adolescent girls experienced significantly higher levels of severe violence and emotional reactions to the violence than did boys.

This is an important example of an article that clarifies the difference between the amount of violence and the consequences of violence for male and female teens. But most observations of teen violence do not make that important distinction. All too often, it is simply stated that girls are pushing and shoving just as much as boys these days. How many of us have been a part of meetings where researchers indicate they know there are limitations to the usefulness of conflict tactics scales but then quickly move on to simply report the interesting data they have that girls say they are using considerable amounts of violence? Once a girl has identified herself as "using violence," how much more difficult will it be for her to identify herself as needing support and safety planning if she is in a pattern of ongoing power and control?

The American Association of University Women Educational Foundation study on sexual harassment at school reported that sexual harassment was an issue for both girls and boys but stressed that the consequences were distinctly different. Boys reported knowing they had been harassed, but they could not remember when it started. In contrast, girls could remember exactly when they were harassed and the serious consequences (i.e., hating school, skipping school, not speaking up in class) that resulted from the harassment.

There is a dangerous trend in the resources designed for teens. Concern has been expressed about the lack of antiviolence resources appropriate for young men. There is a need for resources that are male positive but clearly antiviolence, in contrast to some of the present dating violence materials that some young men feel are anti-male. Unfortunately, in aiming for this newly defined "market," there is a trend toward dating violence resources showing equal levels and consequences of male and female violence. It is crucial that resources and messages are developed and disseminated that appeal to young men but do not hide the different patterns and consequences of male and female violence.

The arena of the middle school is a most urgent one in which to address the question, "What about women or girls as perpetrators?" In many ways, middle school is "no person's land: Everyone is powerless" (D. Hanusa, personal communication, November 10, 1998), but it is also the key opportunity for helping young people learn healthy ways of reclaiming their personal power and setting very high standards for themselves as to how they will perform and what they will expect from future relationships. As more and more dating violence prevention resources and messages are rightly being aimed at this age group, it is important that educators and policy makers find effective messages that do not downplay the seriousness or prevalence of male violence or present violence in intimate relationships as a gender-neutral topic.

Whenever violence in a group is first noticed, attention is wrongly paid to the fact that much of the violence is probably "mutual violence." This is what happened with the initial observations of both adult heterosexual domestic violence and lesbian violence. Then, as people were more careful about understanding the dynamics and consequences, it became apparent that most domestic violence and lesbian battering was the ongoing pattern of one person abusing power and control in all or most aspects of the relationship. Now, middle school violence is increasingly labeled *mutual abuse*. Many well-meaning educators and youth leaders describe middle schools girls as being as violent as middle school boys. What is happening here? Is there a short time in that "no person's land" when girls and boys have not yet learned their "appropriate" social roles regarding who should and should not be violent? Do they grow out of this a couple of years later when gender roles become exaggeratedly defined in high school? Is this another case in which it is dangerous not to be identifying the perpetrators (who are otherwise not held responsible or are sent to mediation)? Substantial resources need to be devoted to studying and preventing the dynamics and consequences of middle school violence.

On the other hand, if there is a real trend toward girls becoming more violent (either as perpetrators or learning that violence is the most effective way to not be controlled by someone else), it is urgent that this trend be recognized and addressed. If girls are learning that it pays to be violent, this raises important issues for the antiviolence movement. After more than 25 years of activism against violence against women, we should be reaching a point where we are starting to notice a decline in male violence. Is it possible that wider societal influences are so strong that instead of decreasing violence against women, we are seeing more young women get the message that their own violence is acceptable?

Conclusion

It is time for antiviolence researchers and activists to take the question "What about girls and women using force?" seriously. The question is useful for reframing the analysis of violence to examine more carefully how male violence hurts both women and men, although in different ways and in different contexts. We also need to find ways to take female violence seriously without taking a gender-neutral approach to violence. It is possible to simultaneously acknowledge individual female violence and show how the pattern of male violence against women reflects and perpetuates societal inequalities between men and women. We also must more carefully examine the intersection of race, class, sexuality, and gender in our antiviolence work.

The battered women's movement has been good at listening to each victim's story. Sometimes people's stories help us see general patterns that help us predict, understand, and interrupt ongoing power and control in relationships; sometimes a person's situation needs to be understood and addressed uniquely. We are fully capable of taking female violence against men seriously and serving individual men hurt by intimate partner violence without losing sight of the societal patterns of male violence hurting both men (usually as strangers) and women (usually within intimate relationships).

We can also use the question "What about female violence?" to explore other difficult issues. The gun industry, video games, and the media have been giving girls and women powerful messages about using violence. After more than 25 years of violence against women activism, is it possible that instead of diminishing or ending violence against women, we are seeing an increase in the number of girls and women who are learning that violence is an effective way to have power in a society that often limits their opportunity for healthy control in their own lives? What are we going to do about this?

Violence is a social issue. There is nothing "natural" about men being violent and women being less violent or passive. Male violence is rooted in the socialization processes our society has consistently imposed on boys and men. If there is an increase in girls and young women (and maybe even women of all ages) using force, it is a reminder that we need to start now to address socialization toward violence in new ways. The antiviolence against women movement, as with women's movements more generally, was never about making girls and women more like men. It was about building a fundamentally different, violence-free society. Asking hard questions about women's possible use of force may be an important way of remembering the social change work that still needs to be accomplished. Much work needs to be done to create a world in which girls and boys learn they can have a healthy amount of control in their own lives without controlling someone else. All communities need to give clearer, more consistent messages that neither male nor female violence is ignored or rewarded. In our work for a violence-free society, what are we doing right and what do we need to do differently? How can we use the question "What about women and girls using force?" to help set the agenda for the next decades of violence research and activism?

Notes

1. Erin House (n.d.) has encouraged the use of the term *force* rather than *violence*, noting that

   according to Webster's Dictionary, violence is defined as "rough or injurious physical force," "an unjust or unwarranted exertion of force and power." Thus, violence can be defined as a type of force, used unjustly, with the intention of causing injury. Force itself is descriptive of the use of physical strength to accomplish a task—but does not imply the same degree of wrong-doing or harmful intent. (p. 2)

2. In 1997, White men aged 15 to 24 were killed at the rate of 13.2 per 100,000 compared with White women aged 15 to 24, who were killed at the rate of 3.2 per 100,000 (Kumanyika, Morssink, & Nestle, 2001). Thus, White men are 4.2 times more likely to be killed than White women. Black women aged 15 to 24 are killed at nearly the same rate (13.3) as are White men in the United States. With a homicide rate of 113.3 per 100,000, Black men are killed at a rate 8.5 times higher than Black women (Kumanyika et al., 2001).

3. For example, men committed 88% of homicides in the United States between 1976 and 1999 (Fox & Zawitz, 2001b).

4. According to the National Crime Victimization Survey, in 2000, 54% of nonfatal violent crime (rape or sexual assault, robbery, and aggravated or simple assault) against men was committed by strangers and 44% was committed by intimates, other relatives, or friends or acquaintances. In contrast, 33% of nonfatal violent crime against women was committed by strangers and 66% was committed by intimates, other relatives, or friends or acquaintances (Rennison, 2001).

5. In 1999, 32.1% of female homicide victims were killed by intimates (in the cases in which the victim-offender relationship was known) compared with 3.6% of male homicide victims (Fox & Zawitz, 2001a).

6. Lesbian resource lists are available from both the Wisconsin Coalition Against Domestic Violence (phone: 608-255-0539).

References

A list of references is available in the original source.

Violence Against Women

1. Societal responsibility for violence against women:

   A. How and where do boys and men get the message "it's ok" or "it's socially acceptable" to be disrespectful and abusive toward women? Give examples from TV, literature, movies, Internet, video games, advertising, etc.

   B. For one day in your life, take notice of all the situations (TV, video games, Internet, cartoons, jokes, lectures, friends, language, etc.) in which violence is allowed or even encouraged.

   C. Identify ways that gender-role socialization (of both girls and boys) may play a part in violence against women.

2. There are many forms and places of violence against women including sexual harassment at school or work, pornography, child sexual abuse, date rape, sexual assault, battering, and elder abuse. Select two of these forms of violence, or two of your own not mentioned here, and illustrate how they are similar. What types of attitudes about women are inherent in these forms of violence and how might they limit women's roles in society?

3. How are children socialized in reference to gender norms? In what ways would these social norms support violence against women?

4. Using the *Continuum of Family Violence*, what other items should be considered when thinking about different groups of women (culturally diverse women, women new to the United States, lesbians, trans women, single women, married women)?

5. How is dating violence experienced by college women similar to and different from intimate partner violence experienced by older women? What resources are there on your campus and in your community for young women who experience intimate partner violence?

6. What specific challenges do LGBTQ individuals experiencing IPV face in accessing resources?

7. How do structural forms (oppression, racism, sexism, ableism, homophobia, transphobia) intersect with intimate partner violence?

8. Identify some of the barriers the following women might face in trying to safely end violence in their lives:

A poor woman	An undocumented woman
A woman who is ill	A woman with disabilities
A woman whose abuser is ill	A very rich woman
A doctor's wife	A minister's wife
A woman who is a minister	A Latina woman
A woman who is pregnant	A woman with children
An older woman	A woman who is a stay-at-home mom

9. The Power & Control Wheel and the Equity Wheel provide an important teaching tool. What other items might you add to the wheel to increase its applicability?

10. Healthcare practitioners play an important role in helping families be safe and they should now routinely screen for intimate partner violence. A health practitioner has screened you; describe the experience. Would you have done anything differently?

11. How can cultural competency be integrated into screening processes, the Power & Control Wheels, and other intervention/prevention forms to raise awareness and assist women dealing with intimate partner violence?

Fertility, Childbirth, and Reproductive Justice

8

Fertility, childbirth, and reproductive justice encompass many aspects of women's health. These topics center on who can access what information about childbearing and reproduction. Additionally, which populations have access to services and the ability of minority women to make their own healthcare decisions are important elements of reproductive justice. This chapter begins with an investigation into the racial disparities in low birthweight in *Role of Stress in Low Birthweight Disparities between Black and White Women: A Population-based Study*. Authors Clay and Andrade discuss how stress affects birthweight across populations. This scientific study shows that societal stressors influence the health of infants.

Next, reproductive justice is not limited to abortion and contraception. Reproductive rights include when, whether, and under what conditions to have children, how many children to have, and the ability to survive and thrive across the lifespan. What kind of health system would truly allow *all* women to have healthy babies, healthy children, and healthy families? What other societal changes need to happen for women to be able to make their own "choices" not to have children or to have the number of children they want? Issues of reproductive justice are addressed in the next three articles in this chapter. Each article focuses on a specific population.

In *Whose Bodies? Black Lives Matter and the Reproductive Justice Imperative* by Sikivu Hutchinson. Hutchinson discusses how rhetoric is used to "smear abortion and demonize black women's bodies." She points out how the rearticulation of Black Lives Matter into the "All Lives Matter Act" in Missouri continues the regulation of Black women's bodies over time. In the classic article *Latina Agenda for Reproductive Justice* by Angela Hooton, she examines the lack of quality and access to healthcare for Latina women, including education and policy initiatives to address these disparities.

In *The Need for Different Voices: Revisiting Reproductive Justice, Health and Rights*, Grace Adofoli shows the differences among reproductive justice, reproductive health, and reproductive rights. This article suggests these terms "are often used interchangeably, but are rooted in 'different analyses, strategies, and constituencies.'" Together they offer an interdisciplinary framework that expands the physical, spiritual, political, economic, and legal lenses to better understand and work on women's health problems that range from sexual violence to pregnancy. These terms emerge from social movements that have been "grounded in specific cultures and respond to issues that are that community's top priority."

Access to contraception is one of the most common elements of reproductive justice. Advancements in technology have changed how women experience contraception and pregnancy. In *Provision of No-Cost, Long-Acting Contraception and Teenage Pregnancy*, the authors study how rates of teenage pregnancy are affected when women are provided with information on long-acting birth control, and then provided with that birth control at no cost. This study showed that when young women are fully informed about their contraception options and can receive healthcare regardless of cost, their rates of pregnancy, abortion, and birth were lower than the national average.

Technological advancements have also led to processes like in vitro fertilization and the possibilities of "designer babies." Tuhus-Dubrow, in

Designer Babies and the Pro-Choice Movement, discusses how the separation between sex and pregnancy has led to the possibility of a "new eugenics movement." Pro-choice language has been appropriated by those who advocate "choosing" specific traits rather than "choosing" whether to be pregnant at all. *A Call to Protect the Health of Women Who Donate Their Eggs* by Judy Norsigian and Timothy R. B. Johnson is another article that shows how the egg market continues to grow as more couples turn to technology for reproductive assistance growing their family. While women are paid for their services, research findings show that they often know too little about the egg donation process and its risks. More research and oversight are warranted to ensure when women donate their eggs their health is not compromised as well.

Reproductive Justice and Childbearing by Rebecca Spence shows how women also have birthing rights that allow them to choose how and where they want to have their babies. "The vision for reproductive rights and birthing rights is to improve outcomes for women and their babies while honoring women's fundamental right to control their bodies." Yet, women's rights and options are compromised in many ways from social structural factors of oppression, racism in healthcare, discrimination, and mistreatment. Many states have outlawed midwifery practices and insurance companies may not cover services that are not medically approved birthing practices. As a result, women's choices are limited, but also medicalized birthing procedures are sanctioned as the appropriate and only way to give birth. The article provides a set of questions as a guide in defending women's child birthing rights.

The last article, by Kate Ryan, addresses women's fears about childbirth. *Why Are Women Afraid of Giving Birth?* offers explanations about how to deliver one's baby either naturally, and what that truly means, via home birth, or in a hospital. The article offers women a brief, but comprehensive, overview of birthing choices, which may help some women ease their fears.

 # Role of Stress in Low Birthweight Disparities Between Black and White Women: A Population-based Study

by Shondra Loggins Clay[1] and Flavia Cristina Drumond Andrade[2]

It has been well documented that Black–White health disparities exist in infant mortality rates. Previous studies have shown that psychological and physiological stress are associated with poor birth outcomes[1–3] such as infant mortality and low birthweight (LBW). In most analyses, researchers utilised one or more of the conventional measures of stress (e.g. negative life events, daily anxieties, psychological distress or perceived stress) to explore the impact on birth outcomes. Even though stress has been associated with several negative birth outcomes, scholars do not always agree

From *Journal of Pediatrics and Child Health, Vol 51, No 4, April 2015* by Shondra Loggins Clay and Flavia Cristina Drummond Andrade. Copyright © 2015 Shondra Loggins Clay and Flavia Cristina Drummond Andrade. Reprinted by permission.

on how to operationalise stress.[4–8] For example, Mutale and colleagues[4] defined stress based on a measure of negative life events,[4] whereas other studies have defined stress as experiencing daily anxieties.[5,6] Others such as Killingsworth-Rini and colleagues[7] operationalise stress as anxiety and/or depression. Nonetheless, one of the most common measures of stress has been perceived stress.[8,9] This methodological approach examines how the individual perceives stress rather than measuring the occurrence of stressful events.

However, we believe that the analyses of complex health issues, such as LBW, require the use of multiple dimensions related to stress. We argue that factors beyond the standard measures of stress offer a more thorough explanation of the reason for racial health disparities. Other authors[7–9] asserted that stress can be perceived differently, and we hypothesised that the factors examined in this study have a unique relationship to health, more particularly health disparities in birth outcomes. From an all-inclusive perspective, factors such as socioeconomic conditions, health-eroding behaviours, cultural experiences, neighbourhood characteristics and lack of emotional/social support are indicators of stress. For example, we hypothesise that religious association uniquely impacts different ethnicities and can serve as a marker of a stressful experience. We believe that this is true for most of our factors explored and the aforementioned stressors differ from perceived stress because they are more antecedent rather than responsive. In particular, a large body of literature on the factors associated with an increased risk of LBW has shown that conventional socio-economic measures such as educational attainment, income levels and employment status are strongly associated with racial disparities in pregnancy outcomes.[10–13]

This study has two purposes: (i) to examine whether several measures of stress (individual and household socio-economic conditions, health-eroding behaviours, cultural experiences, neighbourhood characteristics and lack of emotional/social support) explain the racial disparities in LBW and (ii) to understand the role of stressors on LBW among Black and White women by marital status in the United States.

Data from the Fragile Family and Child Wellbeing Study (FFS), a longitudinal survey of at-risk families and children (beginning at birth), were used to explore the role of stress on racial differences in LBW. The term at-risk refers to unmarried parents, parents who are at greater risk of separating and those who are more likely to live in poverty compared with traditional families. The FFS is unique because it follows almost 5000 children born between the years of 1998 and 2000 and assesses at-risk familial relationships including living conditions, patterns of the relationship, the children's performance within the family and the impact of outside influences (e.g. policy and environmental conditions) on the family. Specifically, the interviews collect information on behaviour, attitudes, demographic characteristics, physical and mental health conditions, and neighbourhood characteristics (http://www.fragilefamilies.princeton.edu/). Data were collected from US cities with populations of at least 200 000 individuals from the longitudinal studies. Our study adds to the current literature by exploring a broader measure of stress to explore racial differences in LBW between Black and White women.

Methods

Participants

We used data from FFS collected from the years 1998–2000 to analyse the role of stress on LBW disparities in Black and White women. Participants in the FFS study have been followed after 1, 3, 5 and 9 years. However, data for this study were based on baseline surveys because the follow-up waves did not contain information on birth outcomes. The participants were Black and White women who reported on their last birth ($n = 3869$) as the unit of analysis, and measures were based on self-reports from the mothers. Even though it is possible for the father of the child to report information on their own stressors, we opted to use information provided by the mothers based on the assumption that their report will yield a more accurate depiction of stressors directly influencing the pregnancy outcomes.

Measures

The dependent variable was LBW. Babies weighing less than 2500 g at birth were defined as LBW babies ($n = 425$), and babies over 2500 g were classified as normal weight ($n = 3444$). The independent variables focused on risk factors and stressors for LBW included individual-level socio-economic status (SES), health-eroding behaviours, household-level SES, access to quality care, cultural experiences, neighbourhood characteristics, and emotional and social support. All analyses included demographic variables maternal age (in years) and marital status (married vs. unmarried).

The individual-level SES factors were educational attainment and employment. A dummy variable was used reflecting whether the mother had less than high school or high school education or higher (reference category). Employment was measured as based on the number of hours worked during the pregnancy ($0 = 40$ h or less; $1 =$ more than 40 h). Health-eroding behaviours during pregnancy refer to smoking, drinking alcohol and using drugs. A dummy variable was included reflecting whether the mother had reported having smoked cigarette during pregnancy (reference category) or never smoked. Response categories for drinking alcohol and use of drugs were every day, several times a week, several times a month, less than once a month and never. Two dummy variables, one for drinking and another for drug use, were constructed to reflect any use (reference category) versus never. Household socio-economic factors included income from earnings, dependence on government assistance and how the individual paid for the birth. A dummy variable was used to reflect whether the mother had any income from earnings (reference category) or not. Three dummy variables ($1 =$ yes; $0 =$ no/none) were used to capture dependence on government assistance (whether government resources were used to pay for birth, whether living in public housing project, receiving housing assistance from government and receiving income assistance from government). Access to adequate prenatal care assesses if the mother received prenatal care in the first trimester. Neighbourhood characteristics examined whether the streets around their homes were safe at night ($0 =$ no; $1 =$ yes). Cultural experiences were based on two religion variables: religious attendance and affiliation. A dummy variable was used to reflect whether the mother attended religious services (reference category which included hardly, several times a year, several times a month, weekly) or

never attended. Religious affiliation was categorised as any (reference category) or none. Emotional and social support was measured based on two characteristics of the romantic relationship. These characteristics are only available for unmarried women in the sample. The first variable refers to whether the boyfriend or romantic partner was not fair or affectionate (reference category) or not. The second refers to whether or not the relationship with boyfriend or romantic partner had ended due to financial reasons, distance, income, relationship reasons, drugs, violence or abuse ($1 =$ yes; $0 =$ no).

Statistical Method

Descriptive statistics were conducted using SPSS STATISTICS (Armonk, NY, IBM Corp) Version 19.0, and logistic regressions were performed using STATA S.E. 11.0. Logistic regression models based on weighted data were estimated for each marital status separately to explore the role of stress on the probability of LBW. Complex samples procedures in STATA (College Station, TX, StataCorp LP.) (svy command) were used in the logistic regression analyses.

Results

Descriptive statistics

Of the 3869 survey participants in our sample, 2389 were Black women and 1480 were White women. Most of the women were unmarried (76.1%) and had educational attainment equivalent to a high school degree or less (63.6%). There were 425 mothers reporting having had babies with LBW (314 Black women and 111 White women).

Important differences were identified between Black and White women (Table 1). A higher percentage of Black women reported being unmarried compared with White women ($P < 0.001$). Black women also reported lower educational attainment than their White counterparts. A higher proportion of White women worked overtime hours (>40 h) during pregnancy compared with Black women (11% for White women and 7.6% for Black women). Black women had a statistically higher prevalence of drug use (8.1% for Black women and 3.7% for White women, $P = 0.029$); however, a higher percentage of White women smoked (23.3%

Table 1. Characteristics of the participants in study, 1998–2000 FFS

	All women		White women		Black women	
	% n = 3869	LBW n = 425	% n = 1480	LBW n = 111	% n = 2389	LBW n = 314
SES individual-level stress						
Marital status						
Unmarried	75.6	86.1	58.5	75.7***	86.9	91.1***
Married	24.4	13.9	41.5	24.3	13.1	8.9
Education level						
Less than HS	34.7	36.9	28.3	32.4	33.4	38.3
HS or more	65.3	63.1	71.7	67.6	60.6	61.7
Work during pregnancy						
>40 h	8.8	11.2	11.0	15.3*	7.6	9.6*
≤40 h	91.2	88.8	89.0	84.7	92.4	90.4
Health-eroding behaviours						
Alcohol						
Yes	10.7	16.8	13.0	16.2	11.0	18.9
No	89.3	83.2	87.0	83.8	89.0	81.1
Smoke						
Yes	19.5	37.3	23.3	46.0	21.2*	36.7*
Never	80.5	62.7	76.7	54.0	78.8	63.3
Drugs						
Yes	5.5	14.7	3.7	9.1	8.1**	17.8**
Never	94.5	85.3	96.3	90.9	91.9	82.2

*$P < 0.10$; **$P < 0.05$; ***$P < 0.001$. FFS, Fragile Family and Child Wellbeing Study; HS, high school; LBW, low birthweight; SES, socio-economic status.

for White women and 21.2% for Black women, $P = 0.088$). Black women had higher rates of dependency on government resources such as paying for the baby's birth with government resources ($P = 0.001$), receiving housing assistance from the government ($P = 0.009$) and no form of income during their pregnancy ($P = 0.007$). Although only marginally significant, White women had higher rates of access to prenatal care in the first trimester ($P = 0.067$). Black women were more exposed to unsafe streets (20.2%) compared with White women (11.5%) ($P = 0.011$). In terms of cultural indicators, a higher percentage of Black women reported attending church than White women ($P = 0.011$). However, a higher percentage of White women reported having a religious affiliation ($P = 0.043$). For emotional and social support, a

higher proportion of unmarried Black women had an unfair or unaffectionate significant other as well as higher rates of the relationship ending because of stress reasons than their White counterparts.

Logistic regression results

Results from the multivariate nested logistic regression model indicate that Blacks were almost three times more likely to have an LBW baby compared with Whites in the baseline model. Being Black remained significant and predicted LBW even after SES individual-level stressors, health-eroding behaviours, SES household stress, access to quality care, cultural experiences, and neighbourhood characteristics were included in the analyses. Model 7 indicates that Black women were 2.7 times more likely to have LBW than White women after controlling for all these factors. Model 8 focuses on unmarried women. Results for model 8 confirm that racial disparities are also relevant for this group in which Black unmarried women were 2.6 times more likely to have an LBW (Table 2).

Next, analyses desegregated by race and marital status were performed to assess differences between Black and White women (Table 3).

Marital status

For married mothers, Black race and maternal age were significant SES individual-level stress predictors of LBW. Black married women were 2.2 times more likely to have an LBW baby compared with White married women. Higher maternal age was positively associated with LBW among married mothers. Married women who smoked were 3.7 times more likely to have an LBW baby. Married women using government funds to pay for baby birth were 2.3 times more likely to have an LBW, and those who depended on the government to pay for housing were 3.4 times more likely to experience an LBW.

For unmarried mothers, significant SES individual-level stress predictors of LBW were Black race and work hours per week. Black unmarried mothers were 1.6 times more likely to have an LBW than their White counterparts. Similarly, unmarried mothers who worked more than 40 h a week were 1.5 times more likely to have an LBW baby. Significant historical health-eroding behaviour stress predictors were smoking and use of drugs. The SES household-level stress predictor of LBW that showed significance was using government funds for support during pregnancy (e.g. pay for baby birth), which increased the likelihood of an LBW by 1.5 times.

Marital status and race

Among married White mothers, the only significant SES individual-level stress predictor of LBW was maternal age (odds ratio (OR) = 1.10, 95% confidence interval (CI) (1.00–1.20)). The only significant health-eroding behaviour stress predictor was smoking (OR = 5.17, 95% CI (1.73–15.49)). The SES household-level stress predictors of LBW that showed significance were using government funds for support during pregnancy (i.e.

pay for baby birth), which increased the likelihood of having an LBW baby by 3.6 times, and for using government funds for housing, which also increased the likelihood of having an LBW by 9.1 times. The only predictor of LBW among unmarried White mothers was smoking, which doubled the likelihood of having an LBW baby.

For married Black mothers, there were no significant predictors of LBW. For unmarried Black mothers, two health-eroding behaviours were associated with higher odds of having an LBW: smoking (OR = 1.65, CI (1.18, 2.32)) and drug use (OR = 1.65, CI (1.03, 2.64)). The SES household-level stress predictor of LBW that showed significance was using government funds for support during pregnancy (i.e. pay for baby's birth) which increased the likelihood of having an LBW by 1.6 times. Religious affiliation was also a marginally significant predictor of LBW and increased the likelihood of an LBW by 1.6 times as well (P = 0.052).

Discussion

The results suggest several predictive stressors for poor pregnancy outcomes for Black and White women, including SES individual-level stressors, SES household-level stressors, access to quality care, health-eroding stressors and cultural experiences. Low-SES White women who were married had more significant predictors of LBW compared with low-SES married Black women. In contrast, Black women who were unmarried had more significant predictors of LBW compared with unmarried White women. The findings have implications for Black women and White women, particularly those 'at risk'. Our findings related to unmarried Black women experiencing more forms of stress, especially those who are of lower SES, are consistent with other studies.[1,14,15] However, for low-SES White women who are married, dependency on the government may cause a higher level of stress.[16,17] Scholars such as Khanani and colleagues and Elliot have hypothesised that this is because White women feel that they should not be in the position where they need to depend on the government for funding, especially as they are married.[16,17]

There were also racial differences in religious affiliation and on the impact of religious affiliation on LBW among unmarried women. In our study,

Table 2. Odd ratios from nested models of stressor that influence LBW for US Blacks and Whites, 1998–2000 FFS

Variables	Model 1 ($n = 3473$)	Model 2 ($n = 3473$)	Model 3 ($n = 3473$)	Model 4 ($n = 3473$)	Model 5 ($n = 3473$)	Model 6 ($n = 3473$)	Model 7 ($n = 3473$)	Model 8† ($n = 2634$)
Black (ref = White)	2.89***	2.83***	3.18***	2.53**	2.53**	2.60**	2.72**	2.63**
Maternal age	0.98	0.99	0.98	0.99	0.99	0.99	1.00	1.00
SES individual-level stress								
Educated (ref = less than HS)	–	0.77	0.86	1.10	1.09	1.08	1.05	1.07
Hours worked per week >40 (ref = hours <40)	–	0.82	0.81	0.84	0.84	0.84	0.84	0.84
Health-eroding behaviours								
Alcohol use (ref = no use)	–	–	2.31	2.38	2.39	2.37	2.35	2.31
Smoke (ref = never)	–	–	2.35**	2.10*	2.10*	2.13*	2.03	2.01
Drugs (ref = never)	–	–	1.11	0.94	0.94	0.97	0.90	0.90
SES household-level stress								
Income (ref = no income)	–	–	–	0.73	0.73	0.73	0.74	0.75
Pay for baby's birth with government resources (ref = none)	–	–	–	2.03	2.03	2.02	1.97	1.92
Housing assistance from government (ref = no assistance)	–	–	–	1.26	1.26	1.28	1.27	1.29
Income from public assistance (ref = none)	–	–	–	0.87	0.87	0.90	0.91	0.94
Access to quality care								
Prenatal care first trimester (ref = no care)	–	–	–	–	1.15	1.07	1.19	1.19
Neighbourhood characteristics								
Streets not safe (ref = safe)	–	–	–	–	–	0.64	0.62	0.62
Culture								
Religion attendance (ref = never)	–	–	–	–	–	–	0.67	0.66
Religious affiliation (ref = none)	–	–	–	–	–	–	1.43	1.46
Emotional and social support								
BF is not fair or affectionate	–	–	–	–	–	–	–	0.37
Relationship ended (stress reasons)	–	–	–	–	–	–	–	0.49

*P < 0.10; **P < 0.05; ***P < 0.01. †Restricted to unmarried women. Source: 1998–2000 Fragile Family and Child Wellbeing Study (FFS). BF, boyfriend; FFS, Fragile Family and Child Wellbeing Study; HS, high school; LBW, low birthweight; ref, reference; SES, socio-economic status.

Table 3. Summary of logistic regression analysis for variables predicting LBW by marital status for the complete sample by race (FFS 1998–2000)

| | Married | | | | | | Unmarried | | | | | |
| | Total (n = 839) | | White (n = 464) | | Black (n = 277) | | Total (n = 2634) | | White (n = 1480) | | Black (n = 1848) | |
	OR	95% CI	OR	95% CI	OR	95% CI	OR	95% CI	OR	95% CI	OR	95% CI
Black (ref = White)	2.2**	(1.2, 4.0)	NA	NA	NA	NA	1.6**	(1.2, 2.1)	NA	NA	NA	NA
Maternal age	1.1**	(1.0, 1.1)	1.1**	(1.0, 1.2)	1.1	(1.0, 1.2)	1.0	(1.0, 1.0)	1.0	(1.0, 1.1)	1.0	(1.0, 1.1)
SES individual-level stress												
HS or higher (ref = less than HS)	2.1	(0.7, 6.2)	NA	NA	0.6	(0.2, 2.0)	1.0	(0.8, 1.3)	1.0	(0.6, 1.7)	1.0	(0.7, 1.3)
Hours worked per week >40 (ref = ≤40)	1.3	(0.5, 3.2)	0.8	(0.2, 3.7)	2.0	(0.6, 6.9)	1.5**	(1.0, 2.2)	1.7	(0.9, 3.4)	1.4	(0.9, 2.3)
Health-eroding behaviours												
Alcohol use (ref = no use)	0.8	(0.3, 2.2)	0.6	(0.2, 2.1)	1.1	(0.2, 6.8)	1.2	(0.9, 1.8)	1.3	(0.6, 2.6)	1.2	(0.8, 1.8)
Smoke (ref = never)	3.7**	(1.7, 8.2)	5.2***	(1.7, 15.5)	2.1	(0.6, 7.6)	1.8**	(1.3, 2.3)	2.0**	(1.2, 3.2)	1.7***	(1.2, 2.3)
Drugs (ref = never)	1.8	(0.2, 20.1)	NA	NA	3.5	(0.2, 69.4)	1.6**	(1.1, 2.5)	1.8	(0.7, 4.5)	1.7**	(1.0, 2.6)
SES household-level stress												
Income (ref = no income)	1.0	(0.5, 2.0)	0.9	(0.3, 2.3)	1.4	(0.5, 4.2)	1.0	(0.8, 1.4)	1.0	(0.5, 1.9)	1.0	(0.8, 1.4)
Pay for baby's birth with government resources (ref = none)	2.3**	(1.1, 5.0)	3.6**	(1.0, 12.4)	2.1	(0.8, 5.5)	1.5**	(1.1, 2.1)	1.2	(0.6, 2.2)	1.6**	(1.1, 2.4)
Housing assistance from government (ref = no assistance)	3.4**	(1.2, 9.7)	9.1***	(2.0, 41.1)	1.1	(0.2, 5.8)	1.1	(0.8, 1.4)	1.6	(0.8, 3.4)	1.0	(0.8, 1.4)
Income from public assistance (ref = none)	1.0	(0.4, 2.5)	0.8	(0.2, 4.5)	1.0	(0.3, 3.6)	0.9	(0.7, 1.1)	1.2	(0.7, 2.0)	0.8*	(0.6, 1.0)
Access to quality care												
Prenatal care first trimester (ref = no care in first trimester)	1.9	(0.5, 6.6)	1.5	(0.2, 13.0)	1.4	(0.3, 7.0)	0.8	(0.6, 1.1)	0.9	(0.5, 1.7)	0.8	(0.6, 1.1)
Neighbourhood characteristics												
Streets not safe (ref = safe)	0.4	(0.1, 1.5)	NA	NA	0.7	(0.2, 2.9)	1.1	(0.8, 1.4)	0.8	(0.4, 1.7)	1.1	(0.8, 1.5)
Culture												
Religion attendance (ref = never)	0.8	(0.4, 1.6)	0.4*	(0.2, 1.1)	1.8	(0.5, 7.2)	0.8*	(0.6, 1.0)	0.7	(0.4, 1.3)	0.8	(0.6, 1.1)
Religious affiliation (ref = none)	0.9	(0.3, 3.0)	1.3	(0.2, 7.5)	0.3	(0.1, 2.3)	1.2	(0.8, 1.7)	0.6	(0.3, 1.2)	1.6	(1.0, 2.5)
Emotional and social support												
BF is not fair or affectionate	NA	NA	NA	NA	NA	NA	0.9	(0.5, 1.9)	1.0	(0.3, 4.0)	0.9	(0.4, 2.2)
Relationship ended (stress)	NA	NA	NA	NA	NA	NA	0.8	(0.4, 1.8)	0.7	(0.2, 3.0)	0.9	(0.3, 2.2)

*P < 0.10; **P < 0.05; ***P < 0.01. BF, boyfriend; CI, confidence interval; FFS, Fragile Family and Child Wellbeing Study; HS, high school; LBW, low birthweight; NA, did not examine the variable or it was omitted because of collinearity; OR, odds ratio; ref, reference; SES, socio-economic status.

Black women reported attendance at religious ceremonies more often than White women; however, White women had higher rates of religious affiliation. In some studies, religion has been shown to be negatively associated to LBW.[18–20] Similar to previous studies,[20–22] our results indicated higher levels of LBW among unmarried Black women with a religious affiliation. However, no effects were found among White unmarried women. Black unmarried women may be unknowingly criticised as unwed childbearing is not condoned in the religious culture.[21] Alternatively, the some religions may encourage divine intervention,[20] which may cause a delay in seeking necessary medical treatment. Mann *et al.* provides an alternative explanation and suggests that women with higher levels of stress may attempt to cope by seeking comfort in religion.[22] Therefore, those under higher levels of stress would be more likely to report being affiliated to a religion.

Past studies have shown that lack of adequate financial resources is associated with anxiety and stress, which can have detrimental effects on pregnancy outcomes, regardless of race.[2,23] Similar results were shown in our study. Financial stress had an impact on White and Black women; however, married women were affected more than unmarried women. Married women, regardless of race who had to pay for the baby's birth with government resources or who received housing assistance from the government, were at a greater risk of LBW. The results exemplify the impact that financial stress has on pregnancy outcomes.

Several limitations of our study need consideration in interpreting the findings. Stress is difficult to operationalise. In this study, we generally used similar instruments that were validated in other research studies. Additional work should integrate other racial groups[24] and also different categories of marital status. In the FFS data set, only a binary option for marital status was provided and coded as 'yes' or 'no' indicating married or unmarried. Nonetheless, it has been shown in research that there is a great deal of difference between women who are single and those who are in a relationship but not married, especially those who are cohabitating. Due to the unavailability of other options for marital status, the exploration of marital differences as forms of stress experiences was limited. Future research should include subcategories of marital status as there is likely to be a great deal of difference in stress experience. The FFS sample consists mostly of 'at-risk' women. Generalising the findings to other groups should be implemented with caution. Finally, the FFS baseline was collected between 1998 and 2000, and some of these findings may reflect processes that may have changed over the last years. However, current indicators of infant mortality and LBW continue to point out to large differences between Whites and Blacks. Therefore, we believe that many of these factors remain largely significant in addressing disparities between these groups. In addition, the wealth of data from FFS can be used to identify trajectories of these children as they grow older.

Conclusion

This study revealed differences in stressors contributing to LBW for 'at-risk' Black and White women. The specific finding in this study that Black women had more stressors compared with White women confirms previous research findings on racial disparities in birth outcomes.[1,8,10,13,15,16] Finally, our results point to the need of additional study given that other variables may help better explain the racial disparities in LBW.

Acknowledgements

This study was supported by the Diversifying Faculty in Illinois (DFI) Fellowship. The authors graciously thank Dr. Reginald Alston, Dr. Susan Farner and Dr. Karin Rosenblatt from the Department of Kinesiology and Community Health in the University of Illinois at Urbana-Champaign for their critical constructive feedback. Additionally, the authors thank Dr. Keera Allendorf from the Department of Sociology and International Studies at Indiana University. The authors also wish to thank the administrative staff at the DFI for their ongoing support. The authors thank the Eunice Kennedy Shriver National Institute of Child Health and Human Development (NICHD) through grants R01HD36916, R01HD39135 and R01HD40421, as well as a consortium of private foundations, for their support of the Fragile Families and Child Wellbeing Study.

References

1. Dominquez TP. Adverse birth outcomes in Black women: the social context of persistent reproductive disadvantage. *Soc. Work Public Health* 2010; **26**: 3–16.

2. Gennaro S, Hennessy MD. Psychological and physiological stress: impact on preterm birth. *J. Obstet. Gynecol. Neonatal Nurs.* 2003; **32**: 668–75.

3. Sawyer PJ, Major B, Casad BJ, Townsend SS, Mendes WB. Discrimination and the stress response: psychological and physiological consequences of anticipating prejudice in interethnic interactions. *Am. J. Public Health* 2012; **102**: 1020–6.

4. Mutale T, Creed F, Maresh M, Hunt L. Life events and low birthweight – analysis by infants preterm and small for gestational age. *Br. J. Obstet. Gynaecol.* 1991; **98**: 166–72.

5. Hobel CJ, Dunkel-Schetter C, Roescho SC, Castro LC, Arora CP. Maternal plasma corticotropin-releasing hormone associated with stress at 20 weeks gestation in pregnancies ending in preterm delivery. *Am. J. Obstet. Gynecol.* 1999; **180**: 257–63.

6. Wadhwa PD, Sandman CA, Porto M, Dunkel-Schetter C, Garite TJ. The association between prenatal stress and infant birth weight and gestational age at birth: a prospective investigation. *Am. J. Obstet. Gynecol.* 1993; **169**: 858–65.

7. Killingsworth-Rini C, Dunkel-Schetter C, Wadwa P, Sandman C. Psychological adaptation and birth outcomes: the role of personal resources, stress, and sociocultural context in pregnancy. *Health Psychol.* 1999; **18**: 333–45.

8. Lobel M, Dunkel-Schetter C, Scrimshaw S. Prenatal maternal stress and prematurity: a prospective study of socioeconomically disadvantaged women. *Health Psychol.* 1992; **11**: 32–40.

9. Cohen S, Kamarck T, Mermelstein R. A global measure of perceived stress. *J. Health Soc. Behav.* 1983; **24**: 385–96.

10. Lu MC, Halfon N. Racial and ethnic disparities in birth outcomes: a life-course perspective. *Matern. Child Health J.* 2003; **7**: 13–30.

11. Taylor HG. Persisting cognitive deficits in survivors of very low birthweight and their implications for adult functioning. *Dev. Med. Child Neurol.* 2010; **52**: 1078–9.

12. Cox RG, Zhang L, Zotti ME, Graham J. Prenatal care utilization in Mississippi: racial disparities and implications for unfavorable birth outcomes. *Matern. Child Health J.* 2009; **15**: 931–42.

13. Dennis EF, Webb DA, Lorch SA, Mathew L, Bloch JR, Culhane JF. Subjective social status and maternal health in a low income urban population. *Matern. Child Health J.* 2012; **16**: 834–43.

14. Kirchengast S, Mayer M, Voigt M. Pregnancy outcome is associated with maternal marital status in Austria-Even at the beginning of the 21st century. *Anthropol. Anz.* 2007; **65**: 415–26.

15. Luo ZC, Wilkins R, Kramer MS. Disparities in pregnancy outcomes according to marital and cohabitation status. *Obstet. Gynecol.* 2004; **103**: 1300–7.

16. Khanani I, Elam J, Hearn R, Jones C, Maseru N. The impact of prenatal WIC participation on infant mortality and racial disparities. *Am. J. Public Health* 2010; **100**: 204–9.

17. Elliot M. Impact of work, family, and welfare receipt on women's self-esteem in young adulthood. *Soc. Psychol. Q.* 1996; **59**: 80–95.

18. Dupre M, Franzese A, Parrado E. Religious attendance and mortality: implications for the Black-White mortality crossover. *Demography* 2006; **43**: 141–64.

19. Jarvis G, Northcott H. Religion and differences in morbidity and mortality. *Soc. Sci. Med.* 1987; **25**: 813–24.

20. Ellison C, Levin J. The religion-health connection: evidence, theory, and future directions. *Health Educ. Behav.* 1998; **25**: 700–20.

21. Lee BY, Newberg AB. Religion and health: a review and critical analysis. *Zygon J. Relig. Sci.* 2005; **40**: 443–68.

22. Mann J, Mannan J, Quinones L, Palmer A, Torres M. Religion, spirituality, social support, and perceived stress in pregnant and postpartum Hispanic women. *J. Obstet. Gynecol. Neonatal Nurs.* 2010; **39**: 645–57.

23. Dole N, Savitz DA, Hertz-Picciotto I, Siega-Riz AM, McMahon MJ, Buekens P. Maternal stress and preterm birth. *Am. J. Epidemiol.* 2003; **157**: 14–24.

24. Reeb KG, Graham AV, Zyzanski SJ, Kitson GC. Predicting low birthweight and complicated labor in urban Black women: a biopsychosocial perspective. *Soc. Sci. Med.* 1987; **25**: 1321–7.

Whose Bodies? Black Lives Matter and the Reproductive Justice Imperative

by Sikivu Hutchinson

Over the past several years toxic canards like "abortion is black genocide" and "the most dangerous place for a black child is the womb," which are often cloaked (https://www.laprogressive.com/personhood-campaign/) in civil rights rhetoric, have been used to smear abortion and demonize black women's bodies. In 2009, when conservative organizations began targeting (http://www.forharriet.com/2014/04/thank-god-for-abortion-whats-at-stake.html#axzz43ZKbkfN1) communities of color with anti-abortion billboard propaganda, black and Latina women's organizations fought back with their own billboards and media campaigns. These unrelenting assaults on the reproductive rights and self-determination of black women are epitomized by the wave of anti-abortion and anti-contraception state laws that have rocked the nation. One of the most egregious recent examples is a Missouri bill (http://www.motherjones.com/politics/2016/01/tone-deaf-missouri-lawmaker-sponsors-all-lives-matter-act-limit-abortions) dubbed the "All Lives Matter Act," which would define a fertilized egg as a person with rights. This blatant appropriation (http://www.thefeminist-wire.com/2016/01/all-lives-matter-act-is-a-blatant-attack-on-black-female-bodies-in-missouri/) of the Black Lives Matter mantle is just another example of the right wing's efforts to undermine black liberation struggle by distorting the language of human rights.

To bolster its claims that abortion is genocide, images of Planned Parenthood founder Margaret Sanger are stamped with Nazi swastikas.

Historically revisionist assessments of Planned Parenthood conveniently omit the connection many early-twentieth-century progressive black activists made between family planning, birth control, abortion, and black liberation. Tellingly, Ida B. Wells, Martin Luther King, Malcolm X, and Mary McLeod Bethune supported Sanger's controversial work with the Birth Control Federation of America.

This past February, in an effort to address this tactic, Black Lives Matter (BLM) activists publicly aligned (http://www.trustblackwomen.org/solidarity-with-black-lives-matter) with reproductive justice activists. Historically, reproductive justice(http://www.trustblackwomen.org/our-work/what-is-reproductive-justice/9-what-is-reproductive-justice) has always been about more than just unrestricted access to abortion and birth control. Under slavery and Jim Crow, black women had little to no control (http://www.amazon.com/Killing-Black-Body-Reproduction-Meaning/dp/0679758690/ref=sr_1_1? s=books&ie=UTF8&qid=1328554814&sr=1-1) over their reproductive destinies. In addition to having the least wealth (http://www.theroot.com/articles/culture/2010/03/closing_the_wealth_gap_between_black_and_white_women.html) of any group in the United States, black women, according to the Center for Disease Control and Prevention statistics, are also more likely(http://www.cdc.gov/mmwr/preview/mmwrhtml/ss5808a1.htm?s_cid=ss5808a1_e) to get abortions—precisely because of wealth and health care disparities. Thus, for black women, reproductive justice is a precondition for mental health, wellness, bodily autonomy, and community enfranchisement. Spearheaded nationally by the Atlanta-based African-American women's organization Sister Song (http://www.trustblackwomen.org/), the concept of reproductive justice draws upon the notion of intersectionality (https://en.wikipedia.org/wiki/Intersectionality), which situates women's right to self-determination within a broader economic justice and human rights framework. As Sister Song notes:

> Reproductive justice is a positive approach that links sexuality, health, and human rights to social justice movements by placing abortion and reproductive health issues in the larger context of the well-being and health of women, families, and communities because reproductive justice seamlessly integrates those individual and group human rights particularly important to marginalized communities. We believe that the ability of any woman to determine her own reproductive destiny is directly linked to the conditions in her community and these conditions are not just a matter of individual choice and access.

Discussing the relationship between Black Lives Matter activism and reproductive justice in a February 9 statement published at the daily news site *Color Lines*, BLM co-founder Alicia Garza maintained (https://www.colorlines.com/articles/black-lives-matter-partners-reproductive-justice-groups-fight-black-women):

> I think from our perspective, reproductive justice is very much situated within the Black Lives Matter movement. And the way we that talk about that is that essentially, it's not just about the right for women to be able to determine when and how and where they want to start families, but it is also very much about our right to be able to raise families, to be able to raise children to become adults…. And that is being hindered by state violence in many different forms. One form being violence by law enforcement or

other state forces, and the other form of crisis through poverty and lack of access to resources and lack of access to health communities that are safe and sustainable. So we certainly understand that BLM and reproductive justice go hand in hand.

This is an important juncture in the BLM movement because it further broadens its scope, making an explicit connection between anti-abortion legislation, reactionary misogynist, anti-black "messaging," and economic justice activism. BLM's embrace also comes at critical moment in the national mobilization over women's rights. As the Supreme Court weighs (http://www.usnews.com/news/blogs/data-mine/2016/01/11/supreme-court-and-abortion-why-whole-womans-health-v-hellerstedt-matters)

HB2, a Texas law requiring that doctors who perform abortions at local health clinics have hospital admitting privileges, the threat to health care for poor and working class women has deepened. If the court upholds this dangerous law, Texas would be left with as few as nine abortion clinics, and other states would have the right to enforce similar laws. The insidious implications of this shift should be a catalyst for further intersectional organizing—bringing together humanist, feminist, and progressive voices against the forces of religious and political fascism.

*Published in the **May / June 2016 Humanist*** (/magazine/may-june-2016)

Tags: BlackLivesMatter(http://thehumanist.com/tag/blacklivesmatter/), reproductive rights (http://thehumanist.com/tag/reproductive-rights/)
Sikivu Hutchinson *is the author of Moral Combat: Black Atheists. Gender Politics, and the Values Wars* (http://www.amazon.com/Moral-Combat-Atheists-Gender-Politics/dp/057807186X/ref=cm_cr_pr_sims_t) and *Godless Americana: Race and Religious Rebels* (http://www.amazon.com/Godless-Americana-Race-Religious-Rebels/dp/0615586104/ref=cm_cr_pr_product_top).

Latina Agenda
for Reproductive Justice

by Angela Hooton

Latinas are facing a reproductive health care crisis in the United States: over 41 percent of Latinas are uninsured and almost one-third lack a regular health care provider. In addition, immigrant Latinas are being systematically shut out of the public health system and, as a result, face even greater barriers to reproductive health care.

Limited access to basic reproductive health care services has forced many Latinas to forgo or delay essential preventative screenings. As a result, Latinas suffer from many preventable conditions. For example, their HIV/AIDS infection rate is six times higher than the rate among non-Hispanic Caucasian women, and Latinas have higher rates of syphilis, gonorrhea, and chlamydia than Caucasian women. As a result of inadequate screening, Mexican-American and Puerto Rican women's cervical cancer rates are approximately twice that of Caucasian women. Although Latinas have lower rates of breast cancer than Caucasian and African American women, breast cancer is the leading cause of cancer-related deaths among Latinas. The five-year survival rate for non-Hispanic Caucasian women with breast cancer is 85 percent, compared to 76 percent for Latinas.

Many of the reproductive health disparities that plague Latinas can be attributed to low health insurance rates. Yet, other barriers, including language and poverty, also inhibit their ability to achieve positive reproductive health outcomes and to exercise their reproductive rights. For example, the poverty rate among Latinos was 22.5 percent in 2003, compared to 8.2 percent for Caucasians. According to recent Census reports, about 28 percent of Latinas speak English either poorly or not at all. It is not surprising, since interpretive services are not always available, that many Latinas report that they have difficulty communicating with their health care providers.

Latinas' high poverty rates, coupled with restrictive reproductive health policies, affect their childbearing decisions and impede their ability to freely choose between parenting and abortion. Increased restrictions on access to abortion and the dearth of public funding for abortion force many low-income Latinas to make serious sacrifices in order to obtain abortions. In fact, Rosie Jimenez, a Latina college student who was unable to pay for a legal abortion, was the first woman documented to have died from an illegal, back-alley abortion after the 1977 Hyde Amendment restricted federal funding of the procedure.

At the same time, Latinas faced barriers—including widespread and coercive sterilization practices—that have restricted them from bearing children. Coercive and punitive policies are proliferating in the U.S. and disproportionately affect women of color, including Latinas. These policies include caps on the amount of welfare support a woman receives when she has additional children, court-mandated use of contraceptives such as Norplant, and cuts in Medicaid-funded services for pregnant immigrants. All of these policies have had a disproportionate impact on low-income women of color, including Latinas. While their tactics vary, these policies seek to remove control of reproductive health decisions from women, thereby violating the fundamental human right

"Latina Agenda for Reproductive Justice," by Angela Hooton, originally published in the *Women's Health Activist*, September/October 2005, pp. 10 & 14, the newsletter of the National Women's Health Network (NWHN). It is reprinted with the permission of the author and the NWHN.

to self-determination and undermining Latinas' health and well-being.

The National Latina Institute for Reproductive Health (NLIRH)'s mission is to address these issues and to safeguard the fundamental human right to reproductive health care for Latinas, their families, and their communities. NLIRH understands that the fight for reproductive health and rights is inextricably linked to the struggle for social justice. There can be no reproductive justice for Latinas without racial equality, without quality health care, without educational opportunities, without immigration reform, and without affordable child care options.

NLIRH has created a model national policy agenda to address the broad range of reproductive health challenges Latinas face today. The *National Latina Agenda for Reproductive Justice* has several priority areas: increasing access to affordable health care; ensuring the availability of culturally and linguistically competent health care services; expanding family planning options; promoting comprehensive sexuality education; protecting reproductive rights; and developing accurate and unbiased research on Latina health status. We hope that the *Agenda* will not only serve as a useful tool for improving Latina reproductive health, but also contribute to national efforts to broaden and diversify the reproductive rights movement.

NLIRH focuses on three specific policy campaigns. First, we work to expand Latinas' access to and knowledge of Emergency Contraception (EC). NLIRH believes that EC can play an important role in reducing Latinas' unwanted pregnancies and enabling them to exercise greater reproductive choice. Latinas who do not have access to a health care provider will benefit greatly if EC is available without prescription—provided it is affordable and women know about the method. We are working with our activists to expand EC access at the state and national levels. We are also supporting state legislation that requires emergency rooms to provide EC to sexual assault survivors and allows pharmacists to dispense EC without an advance prescription. On the national level, we are advocating for the FDA to make EC available over-the-counter (OTC) and for state Medicaid

programs to continue to cover EC if it becomes an OTC product.

Our second campaign is aimed at improving the reproductive health status of Latina immigrants. NLIRH recognizes that many Latina immigrants lack access to prenatal care and other basic reproductive health care services. Further, there is a growing trend to provide health care for pregnant immigrants by covering the fetus rather than the woman. We believe that Latinas have a right to health care regardless of their immigration status. For this reason, NLIRH advocates for state and federal policies to expand health care coverage (especially family planning and prenatal care services) for Latina immigrants. Specifically, we are fighting to pass the 'Immigrant Children's Health Improvement Act', which would allow states to use federal Medicaid and S-CHIP funding to provide health care to legal immigrant children and pregnant women. Under current law, these groups are barred from these programs unless they have lived in the United States for over five years. Although states can choose to cover immigrant women and children through state Medicaid funds, budget constraints and pressure from anti-immigrant legislators has resulted in many states electing not to cover this vulnerable population.

Third, NLIRH is dedicated to ensuring that all Latinas have access to reproductive health care services through viable public funding sources. Through public education and advocacy efforts, we advocate that Congress increase Title X's family planning funds, protect Medicaid funds from threatened budgetary cuts, and eliminate the Hyde Amendment that restricts federal funding of abortions.

NLIRH does not work in a vacuum. We collaborate with Latina leaders across the country and provide a Leadership Training series to ensure that our national policy agenda and grassroots campaigns remain relevant and reflect the reality of Latinas' lives. If you are interested in joining NLIRH in our advocacy and community mobilization efforts, or want a copy of the *National Latina Agenda for Reproductive Justice* please visit our website at www.latinainstitute.org.

Young Feminist: The Need for Different Voices: Revisiting Reproductive Justice, Health and Rights

by Grace Adofoli

As an African woman, I come from a place where sexual and reproductive health is not explicitly discussed or confronted like it is here. I've long struggled to understand the ways that issues and concepts like Reproductive Justice, Reproductive Health, and Reproductive Rights fit together and interact within the women's health movement. So, I was delighted to have the opportunity, as a NWHN intern, to attend the United Nations' 57th session of the Commission on the Status of Women (CSW57), and participate in the dialogues about these issues and women's rights. (CSW57 was held in March 2013, at the United Nations' headquarters in New York City.)

I am very interested in women's health research and advocacy to end sexual violence. My career goal is to help change policies and create global networks that improve women's status around the world, specifically on the African continent. What I learned at CSW57 is that you cannot impact sexual violence without considering Reproductive Justice, reproductive health, and reproductive rights—they are all intertwined.

These terms—"Reproductive Justice," "Reproductive Health," and "Reproductive Rights"—are often used interchangeably, but they are rooted in "different analyses, strategies, and constituencies.[1] Reproductive Justice (often just called "RJ") is defined as the physical, spiritual, political, economic, and social wellbeing of women and girls. It merges the concepts of reproductive health and social justice.[2] RJ "is based on the human right to make personal decisions about one's life, and the obligation of government and society to ensure that the conditions are suitable for implementing one's decisions."[2] Proponents say that it "will be achieved when women and girls have economic, social, and political power and resources to make healthy decisions about our bodies, sexuality, and reproduction for ourselves, our families and our communities in all areas of our lives."[2]

"Reproductive Health" (RH) specifically promotes people's ability to "have a responsible, satisfying and safe sex life and ... the capability to reproduce and the freedom to decide if, when and how often to do so."[3] RH is about helping people access reproductive health information and services—including contraception and childbirth care. Reproductive and sexual health problems (like HIV/AIDS, maternal mortality, lack of contraception access, and teen pregnancy) are much worse in low-income communities and communities of color, due to factors like the high cost of services, lack of transportation, and restrictive laws and policies. RH is about overcoming these barriers to affordable, accessible, and culturally competent services.[1]

"Reproductive Rights" (RR) refers to efforts to ensure people have the legal and political ability to make their own sexual and reproductive choices. The term, coined by the pro-choice movement in the 1980s, focuses on creating the legal protection, laws, and/or enforcement of laws that ensure an individual's (usually women's) "legal right to reproductive health care services" and information.[2, 4]

These frameworks—Reproductive Justice, Reproductive Health, and Reproductive Rights—encompass different aspects of the lives of women from all backgrounds. At CSW57, different organizations and groups connected these frameworks to sexual violence. Sexual violence is costly and harmful to woman, particularly for 16-to-24-year-olds, who are at a greater risk. It limits the woman's ability to manage her life (and her reproductive health) and exposes her to sexually transmitted infections (STIs). According to Future Without Violence, girls who are abused by their boyfriends are five times as likely to be forced into having sex without a condom, and eight times more likely to be pressured to become pregnant.[4]

After participating in CSW57, I've concluded that collaboration between sexual violence prevention and reproductive frameworks is needed to address the issues of violence against women. A broad view is needed because, when it comes to these issues, no one-size-fits-all solution exists; understanding the individual's unique personal situation is imperative when addressing violence against women. The different frameworks of RJ, RH, and RR can impact sexual violence in multiple ways—by addressing oppression, poverty and economic status, lack of social support, negative legal systems, cultural stigma against rape, immigration, and barriers to services. One can focus on one framework or another, but only by affecting all three will real change occur.

I attended CSW57 eager to learn about applying these frameworks in the international context to promote women's health. While attending CSW57, I found myself in conversations that made me uncomfortable, because I realized that not everyone was on the same page about Reproductive Justice, Health, and Rights. For example, an older African woman asked: "Do they want our kids to get pregnant and abort the babies? I need someone to explain to me what 'reproductive' means." This just reminded me that the frameworks have to be clearly expressed and the goals communicated as part of promoting them.

While attending CSW57, I realized that the heterogeneity of these frameworks can be prioritized in different ways in different countries. For example, Africa has 54 countries and countless tribes, traditions, cultures, and languages—but people tend to group Africa into one category and discount its diversity. Hence, in the African context, efforts to advance Reproductive Justice,

Reproductive Health, and Reproductive Rights will vary depending on the specific country. For example, in Sudan and Congo, the major reproductive and sexual health issue might be combating violence against women, protecting women from rape, and providing access to clinics in times of conflict and war. On the other hand, in countries like Zambia and Ghana, which are more stable, the main focus might be reducing the very high rates of maternal mortality.

All of these efforts fit into the larger framework of women's reproductive justice, rights, and health. From a rights perspective, it is important to pass laws that defend women who have been abused and encourage stern prosecution of abusers. In relation to reproductive rights, policies are needed to expand women's access to services (like contraception and abortion) that help them avoid unplanned pregnancies and STIs. Providing reproductive health services that cater to women's needs enables them to act upon the best decisions about their bodies. Each community and country must determine which issues are most significant to them and where they want to put their energies.

The RJ, RR, and RH frameworks all provide a lens through which to understand, and work on, women's health problems that range from sexual violence to pregnancy prevention. In order to be successful, these movements have to be grounded in specific cultures and respond to issues that are that community's top priority.

For more information, follow organizations like Every Mother Counts; Our Bodies, Ourselves; the United Nations; Ipas; Amnesty International; Madre; and NWHN —just to mention a few. They are taking the lead on expanding the work and conversations within Reproductive Justice, Reproductive Health, and Reproductive Rights frameworks internationally.

This article was written by: Grace Adofoli

Grace Adofoli is a graduate from University of Wisconsin-River Falls. She interned at NWHN in the spring of 2013 and plans to pursue her graduate degree in women's health and policy. She also hopes to receive her PhD in Public Health after the completion of her Master's.

References

1. Silliman J M, Undivided Rights: Women of Color Organize for Reproductive Justice, Cambridge MA: South End Press, 2004.

2. Forward Together (formerly Asian Communities for Reproductive Justice), A New Vision for Advancing Our Movement for Reproductive Health, Reproductive Rights and Reproductive Justice, Oakland CA: Forward Together, 2005.

3. World Health Organization (WHO), Health Topics: Reproductive Health, Geneva: WHO, 2013.

Available online at: http://www.who.int/topics/reproductive health/en/(http://www.who.int/topics/reproductive_health/en/)

4. Futures Without Violence, The Facts on Reproductive Health and Partner Abuse. San Francisco: Futures Without Violence, no date. Available online at:http://www.futureswithoutviolence.org/userfiles/file/Children_and_Famili… (http://www.futureswithoutviolence.org/userfiles/file/Children_and_Families/Reproductive.pdf)

Provision of No-Cost, Long-Acting Contraception and Teenage Pregnancy

by Gina M. Secura, Ph.D., M.P.H., Tessa Madden, M.D., M.P.H., Colleen McNicholas, D.O., Jennifer Mullersman, B.S.N., Christina M. Buckel, M.S.W., Qiuhong Zhao, M.S., and Jeffrey F. Peipert, M.D., Ph.D.

Abstract

Background

The rate of teenage pregnancy in the United States is higher than in other developed nations. Teenage births result in substantial costs, including public assistance, health care costs, and income losses due to lower educational attainment and reduced earning potential.

Methods

The Contraceptive CHOICE Project was a large prospective cohort study designed to promote the use of long-acting, reversible contraceptive (LARC) methods to reduce unintended pregnancy in the St. Louis region. Participants were educated about reversible contraception, with an emphasis on the benefits of LARC methods, were provided with their choice of reversible contraception at no cost, and were followed for 2 to 3 years. We analyzed pregnancy, birth, and induced-abortion rates among teenage girls and women 15 to 19 years of age in this cohort and compared them with those observed nationally among U.S. teens in the same age group.

Results

Of the 1404 teenage girls and women enrolled in CHOICE, 72% chose an intrauterine device or implant (LARC methods); the remaining 28% chose another method. During the 2008–2013 period, the mean annual rates of pregnancy, birth, and abortion among CHOICE participants were 34.0, 19.4, and 9.7 per 1000 teens, respectively. In comparison, rates of pregnancy, birth, and abortion among sexually experienced U.S. teens in 2008 were 158.5, 94.0, and 41.5 per 1000, respectively.

From *The New England Journal of Medicine, Vol 371, No 14, October 2, 2014* by Gina M. Secura, Tessa Madden, Colleen McNicholas, Jennifer Mullersman, Christina M. Buckel, Qiuhong Zhao, Jeffrey F. Peipert. Copyright © 2014, Massachusetts Medical Society. Reprinted by permission.

Conclusions

Teenage girls and women who were provided contraception at no cost and educated about reversible contraception and the benefits of LARC methods had rates of pregnancy, birth, and abortion that were much lower than the national rates for sexually experienced teens. (Funded by the Susan Thompson Buffett Foundation and others.)

Although it has declined SUBSTANtially over the past two decades, the pregnancy rate among girls and women 15 to 19 years of age remains a stubborn public health problem. Each year, more than 600,000 teens become pregnant, and 3 in 10 teens will become pregnant before they reach 20 years of age.[1,2] Rates are higher among black and Hispanic teens, with 4 in 10 becoming pregnant by 20 years of age, as compared with 2 in 10 white teens.[2-4] In addition to the negative health and social consequences borne by teenage mothers and their children, the national financial burden is substantial. In 2010, births involving teenage mothers cost the United States nearly $10 billion in increased public assistance and health care and in income lost as a result of lower educational attainment and reduced earnings among children born to teenage mothers.[5]

The President's Teen Pregnancy Prevention Initiative was launched in 2010 to address the high teenage pregnancy rate by replicating evidence-based models and innovative strategies.[6] Teenage pregnancy has also been designated by the Centers for Disease Control and Prevention (CDC) as one of the six Winnable Battles because of the magnitude of the problem and the belief that it can be addressed by strategies that are known to be effective.[7] The Winnable Battle target is to reduce the teenage birth rate by 20%, from 37.9 births per 1000 teens in 2009 to 30.3 per 1000 by 2015.

Long-acting, reversible contraceptive (LARC) methods, which include intrauterine devices (IUDs) and implants, have been shown to be acceptable to teens and young women, with higher continuation rates than shorter-acting methods.[8,9] LARC methods reduce the likelihood of pregnancy and of repeat pregnancy among adolescents,[10,11] yet less than 5% of U.S. teens report using LARC methods.[12]

Lack of information about effective contraception, limited access, and cost remain barriers to the use of LARC methods by teens.[13-15] It is unclear whether removal of these barriers can reduce unintended pregnancy and birth rates among high-risk, sexually active teens. We assessed pregnancy, birth, and abortion rates in a cohort of teens among whom these three barriers to highly effective reversible contraception were removed, and we compared these rates with rates observed nationally among all teens in the United States.

Methods

Study enrollment

The Contraceptive CHOICE Project was a prospective cohort study involving 9256 St. Louis area girls and women 14 to 45 years of age, in which the use of LARC methods was promoted to reduce unintended pregnancy.[16] Participants were recruited through referral from medical providers, word of mouth, and study flyers. The Washington University School of Medicine in St. Louis Human Research Protection Office approved the study protocol before recruitment began, and all participants provided written informed consent. Participants 14 to 17 years of age provided written assent, and a parent or guardian provided written consent. Minors could enroll under a waiver of parental consent if they did not know the whereabouts of their parents or guardians or if they did not want their parents or guardians to know that they were seeking contraception. We enrolled four minors using the waiver.

Women and adolescent girls were eligible to participate in CHOICE if they were English-speaking or Spanish-speaking, resided in the St. Louis region or sought contraceptive services in selected community clinics, had no desire for pregnancy for at least 12 months, were sexually active or planning to be sexually active with a male partner during the next 6 months, and were not using a contraceptive method or were willing to switch to a new, reversible contraceptive method. Women and adolescent girls were ineligible if they had undergone a hysterectomy or sterilization procedure.

Study design

CHOICE provided standardized contraceptive counseling to study participants regarding commonly used reversible contraceptive methods.[17] Methods were presented in order from most to least effective, and the potential side effects, risks, and benefits of each method were reviewed. Participants were provided with their chosen method at their enrollment session in accordance with evidence-based clinical guidelines.[18,19] If medical contraindications did not allow for same-day insertion of a LARC device (e.g., if pregnancy could not be ruled out definitively or if the participant had active cervicitis), participants received a shorter-acting method, such as oral contraceptive pills or depot medroxyprogesterone acetate (DMPA) injection, until their chosen method could be initiated. During the enrollment session, study staff performed a baseline interview, and participants were screened for sexually transmitted infections.

Participants were followed for 2 to 3 years, depending on their enrollment date. Telephone interviews were administered by study staff at 3 and 6 months and every 6 months thereafter. Participants received a $10 gift card after every completed follow-up survey. During the baseline and follow-up surveys, we collected detailed information regarding demographic characteristics and reproductive history, including contraceptive method use and satisfaction, sexual behavior, and pregnancy.

This analysis involves the 1404 adolescents who enrolled in CHOICE between 14 and 19 years of age, from 2007 through 2011; 716 teens were followed for 3 years, and 688 teens were followed for 2 years. At each follow-up survey, we asked participants if they had had a pregnancy. Participants who contacted study staff outside a scheduled survey or came to the clinic with concerns about possible pregnancy completed a urine pregnancy test. We recorded all pregnancies in a pregnancy log and documented the contraceptive method used at the time of conception. If the outcome of the pregnancy was known at the time of the survey (e.g., birth, miscarriage, or abortion), it was documented in the pregnancy log. If a participant was currently pregnant, we subsequently contacted her to record the pregnancy outcome.

Study outcomes

The primary outcomes of the study were the rates of pregnancy, live birth, and induced abortion observed among participants who were 15 to 19 years of age at any time during study participation. We compared the rates in the CHOICE cohort with the most recent available rates among all U.S. teens 15 to 19 years of age, from 2010,[1] and hypothesized that the rates in CHOICE would be lower than the national rates. Because the U.S. rates represent all teenage girls and women 15 to 19 years of age, including those who are and those who are not sexually experienced, we also compared the CHOICE rates with the national rates reported among sexually experienced teenage girls and women in 2008 (the most recent available data).[20] In addition, we examined rates according to age and race as secondary outcomes. All analyses of rates of pregnancy, live birth, and induced abortion; teen-years of use of contraceptive methods; and failure rates of contraceptive methods included data collected when members of the cohort were 15 to 19 years of age.

Statistical analysis

We used frequencies, percentages, medians, and ranges to describe the demographic and reproductive characteristics of the participants at the time of study enrollment. A chi-square test was performed for categorical data, and a Wilcoxon two-sample test was performed for continuous data that was not normally distributed.

For this analysis, we calculated annual means and 95% confidence intervals for rates of pregnancy, live birth, and induced abortion from 2008 through 2013, because the number of pregnancies and pregnancy outcomes that occurred among teenage CHOICE participants each year was small. Each rate represents the total number of events (i.e., pregnancy, birth, or abortion) that occurred among the participants divided by the total amount of time contributed from 2008 through 2013. For a pregnancy to be considered in the analysis, the outcome of the pregnancy (i.e., birth or abortion, for the purposes of this study) had to occur before 20 years of age. This is the same approach used by the National Center for Health Statistics in calculating U.S. rates.[1] We calculated the time contributed by each participant during which she was not pregnant. If at the last survey the participant reported she had not been pregnant since the previous contact, we subtracted 6 weeks of contributed time to account for the possibility of an early-stage and unknown pregnancy. For a participant who had a pregnancy, we subtracted the total time she was pregnant plus 1 month if she delivered, to account for postpartum infecundity. For participants who were lost to follow-up, the last date of contact was the cutoff point for outcomes and contributed time. All analyses were performed with the use of Stata software, version 11 (StataCorp).

Results

Characteristics of the participants

Table 1 gives the baseline demographic and reproductive characteristics of the 1404 teenage participants, stratified by age group at enrollment (14 to 17 years vs. 18 to 19 years). Nearly 500 minors 14 to 17 years of age were enrolled in the study. Nearly half the participants reported a previous unintended pregnancy, and 18% had a history of abortion. As compared with younger teens, those who were 18 to 19 years of age reported more lifetime male sex partners and greater parity and had a higher frequency of previous sexually transmitted infections. The majority of teens in both age groups chose LARC methods, but teens 14 to 17 years of age were more likely than older teens to do so (77.5% vs. 68.4%, P < 0.001). The implant was the most common contraceptive choice for participants 14 to 17 years of age, whereas an IUD was most commonly chosen by older teens (Table 1).

Pregnancy, birth, and abortion rates

The 12-month, 24-month, and 36-month follow-up rates among CHOICE participants were 92%, 82%, and 75%, respectively. During 1738 teen-years of follow-up between 2008 and 2013, teens in the CHOICE cohort reported 56 pregnancies, 32 births, 16 induced abortions, 7 miscarriages, and 1 stillbirth. Reported methods used at the time of conception included the levonorgestrel IUD (2 participants), DMPA injection (1), oral

contraceptive pills (13), the ring (4), the patch (2), condoms (9), and no method (25). The teen-years of use and failure rates of contraceptive methods among the participants using these methods were as follows: 394.2 teen-years and 5.1 failures per 1000 teen-years for the levonorgestrel IUD, 193.8 teen-years and 5.2 failures per 1000 teen-years for DMPA injection, 229.0 teen-years and 56.8 failures per 1000 teen-years for oral contraceptive pills, 77.2 teen-years and 51.8 failures per 1000 teen-years for the contraceptive ring, and 32.9 teen-years and 60.8 failures per 1000 teen-years for the contraceptive patch. No pregnancies occurred with the copper IUD (57.3 teen-years) or the etonogestrel subdermal implant (633.3 teen-years).

Table 2 gives the overall rates of pregnancy, live birth, and induced abortion in the CHOICE teenage cohort; respective rates for teens in the United States in 2010 are provided for comparison. The mean annual rates were 34.0 per 1000 teens (95% confidence interval [CI], 25.7 to 44.1), 19.4 per 1000 (95% CI, 13.3 to 27.4), and 9.7 per 1000 (95% CI, 5.6 to 15.8), respectively. The corresponding 2010 rates among U.S. teens nationally were 57.4, 34.4, and 14.7 per 1000.

Among teenage girls and women enrolled in CHOICE, 97% were sexually experienced at baseline, and 99% were sexually experienced by 12 months of follow-up. Thus, Table 2 also presents a comparison of the mean annual rates in CHOICE as compared with 2008 U.S. rates representing only sexually experienced teens. The pregnancy, birth, and abortion rates per 1000 sexually experienced U.S. teens in 2008 were 158.5, 94.0, and 41.5, respectively.

Figure 1 shows the pregnancy, birth, and abortion rates among CHOICE participants, as compared with the 2010 rates among all U.S. teens. The rates were stratified according to age group and race. For all three outcomes within each stratum, the rates among CHOICE participants were lower than the U.S. rates. The difference between rates in CHOICE and national rates was greater for those 18 to 19 years of age and among black teens. Figure 2 shows the pregnancy rates among

Table 1. Baseline Characteristics of Study Participants Overall and According to Age Group.

Characteristic	Total Cohort (N = 1404)	14–17 Years of Age (N = 484)	18–19 Years of Age (N = 920)	P Value*
Race—no. (%)†				<0.01
Black	877 (62.5)	328 (67.8)	549 (59.7)	
White	416 (29.6)	119 (24.6)	297 (32.3)	
Other	111 (7.9)	37 (7.6)	74 (8.0)	
Low socioeconomic status— no. (%)‡	623 (44.4)	163 (33.7)	460 (50.0)	<0.01
Health insurance—no./total no. (%)				<0.01
None	392/1361 (28.8)	78/453 (17.2)	314/908 (34.6)	
Private	583/1361 (42.8)	218/453 (48.1)	365/908 (40.2)	
Public	386/1361 (28.4)	157/453 (34.7)	229/908 (25.2)	
Lifetime male sex partners— median no. (range)	3.0 (0–175)	2.0 (0–30)	3.0 (0–175)	<0.01
Parity—no. (%)				<0.01
0	1059 (75.4)	397 (82.0)	662 (72.0)	
1	289 (20.6)	79 (16.3)	210 (22.8)	
≥2	56 (4.0)	8 (1.7)	48 (5.2)	
Previous unintended pregnancy— no./total no. (%)	671/1403 (47.8)	219/484 (45.2)	452/919 (49.2)	0.16
History of abortion—no. (%)	259 (18.4)	70 (14.5)	189 (20.5)	<0.01
History of sexually transmitted infection—no. (%)§	331 (23.6)	88 (18.2)	243 (26.4)	<0.01
Baseline chosen contraceptive method—no. (%)¶				<0.01
Hormonal IUD	445 (31.7)	119 (24.6)	326 (35.4)	
Nonhormonal IUD	75 (5.3)	14 (2.9)	61 (6.6)	
Etonogestrel implant	485 (34.5)	242 (50.0)	243 (26.4)	
DMPA injection	127 (9.0)	51 (10.5)	76 (8.3)	
Oral contraceptive pill	175 (12.5)	39 (8.1)	136 (14.8)	
Ring	69 (4.9)	11 (2.3)	58 (6.3)	
Patch	28 (2.0)	8 (1.7)	20 (2.2)	

* P values are for the comparison between the age groups (14 to 17 vs. 18 to 19 years of age).

† Race was self-reported.

‡ Participants were classified as having low socioeconomic status if they reported current receipt of food stamps; vouchers from the Special Supplemental Nutrition Program for Women, Infants, and Children; other welfare benefits; unemployment benefits; or difficulty in paying for transportation, housing, health or medical care, or food.

§ Data are based on a self-reported history of chlamydia infection, gonorrhea, or trichomoniasis.

¶ DMPA denotes depot medroxyprogesterone acetate, and IUD intrauterine device.

Table 2. Pregnancy, Birth, and Abortion Rates among Girls and Women 15 to 19 Years of Age in the CHOICE Cohort as Compared with Those in the U.S. Population.*

Outcome	U.S. Population, All Teens*	U.S. Population, Sexually Experienced Teens†	CHOICE Cohort‡
	no. per 1000 teens		*mean no. per 1000 teens (95% CI)*
Pregnancy	57.4	158.5	34.0 (25.7–44.1)
Birth	34.4	94.0	19.4 (13.3–27.4)
Abortion	14.7	41.5	9.7 (5.6–15.8)

* Data are U.S. rates for the year 2010.[1]
† Data are U.S. rates for the year 2008.[20]
‡ Data are the mean annual rates for the years 2008 through 2013. CI denotes confidence interval.

CHOICE teens, as compared with sexually experienced U.S. teens, according to age group and race. For both age groups and both races, the CHOICE rates were substantially lower than the national rates.

Discussion

We found that pregnancy, birth, and abortion rates were low among teenage girls and women enrolled in a project that removed financial and access barriers to contraception and informed them about the particular efficacy of LARC methods. The observed rates of pregnancy, birth, and abortion were substantially lower than national rates among all U.S. teens, particularly when compared with sexually experienced U.S. teens. Stratification according to factors known to be associated with sexual behavior and pregnancy risk (age and race)[21] showed that this was true among both older teens (18 to 19 years of age) and younger teens, as well as among both white and black teens.

The CDC Winnable Battle 2015 goal for teenage births is 30.3 per 1000 teens. The mean annual teenage birth rate in our cohort was 19.4 per 1000 teens, 36% lower than the 2015 goal. Our teenage pregnancy and birth rates reflect teens using highly effective contraception, with a high rate of LARC use in this cohort (i.e., 72% overall among teens). Although the rate of LARC use among teens 15 to 19 years of age in the United States has increased from less than 1% in 2002 to almost 5% in 2009, our study suggests that it is possible to achieve a much greater rate of use.[12] Furthermore, teens in our cohort continued to use LARC methods longer than shorter-acting methods such as the oral contraceptive pill and DMPA injection; two thirds of teens in CHOICE were still using their LARC method at 24 months of follow-up, as compared with only one third of teens using a non-LARC method.[8]

The limitations of our study must be considered. First, information about pregnancy was self-reported by participants, and thus it is possible that the number of teenage pregnancies was underestimated in the CHOICE cohort. The U.S. pregnancy statistics rely on a composite of birth data, the abortion surveillance system, and self-reporting to estimate pregnancy rates. Second, teens were surveyed on a regular basis regarding their contraceptive method use, which may have influenced adherence to their contraceptive method. Third, the generalizability of our results is uncertain. Teens in CHOICE received standardized contraceptive counseling during which methods were presented in order from most to least effective. This counseling approach may differ from the usual counseling that teens receive in the United States but could certainly be applied in routine practice. Fourth, the enrollment of minors in CHOICE required parental consent. Most teens can access confidential contraceptive services without parental notification or consent, regardless of age. Minors who enrolled in CHOICE with the consent of their parent or guardian may represent a group of teens at lower risk for contraceptive nonuse and pregnancy.[22] However, as compared with teens nationally, the teens enrolled in CHOICE are at greater risk for unintended pregnancy; 60% of the participants are black (vs. 16% of female teens 15 to 19 years of age in the United States),[23] and almost all had had sexual intercourse at the time of enrollment, with nearly three quarters reporting sexual intercourse in the previous 30 days (vs. national frequencies of 43% and one quarter, respectively).[21]

A final limitation is that we compared a mean annual rate for the period from 2008 through 2013 with 2010 national rates. From 2008 to 2010, the pregnancy rate declined by 15% among all teens in the United States. The most recent birth data (2012) indicate that the birth rate among teens 15 to 19 years of age dropped to 29.4 per 1000, the lowest rate ever reported for the United States.[24] (Data on national pregnancy and abortion rates are not yet available beyond 2010.) Even with this continued decline, the reductions observed in CHOICE are substantial and of public health importance.

In summary, we found that in a cohort of teenage girls and women for whom barriers to contraception (lack of knowledge, limited access, and cost) are removed and the use of the

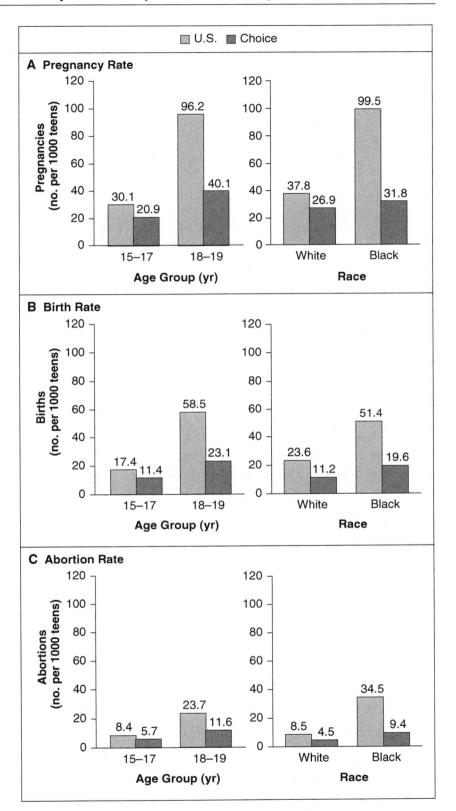

Figure 1. Pregnancy, Birth, and Abortion Rates among U.S. Teenage Girls and Women, as Compared with CHOICE Participants, Stratified According to Age and Race.

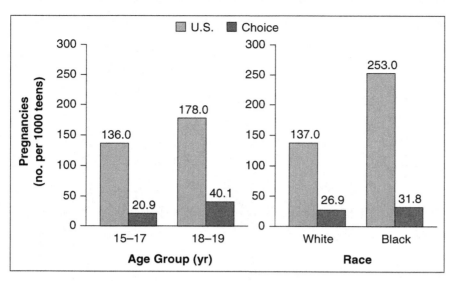

Figure 2. Pregnancy Rates among Sexually Experienced U.S. Teenage Girls and Women, as Compared with CHOICE Participants, Stratified According to Age and Race.

Data for the 2008 U.S. rates stratified according to age and race are from K. Kost, Guttmacher Institute (personal communication).

most effective contraceptive methods is encouraged, a large percentage opted to use LARC methods. The rates of pregnancy, birth, and abortion in our cohort were below both the most recent corresponding national rates and the CDC Winnable Battle 2015 goal.

The content of this article is solely the responsibility of the authors and does not necessarily represent the official views of the Eunice Kennedy Shriver National Institute of Child Health and Human Development or the National Institutes of Health.

Presented in part at the North American Forum on Family Planning, Seattle, October 6 and 7, 2013.

Supported by grants from the Susan Thompson Buffett Foundation, the Eunice Kennedy Shriver National Institute of Child Health and Human Development (K23HD070979), and the National Center for Advancing Translational Sciences, National Institutes of Health (UL1 TR000448 and TL1 TR000449, to Washington University Institute of Clinical and Translational Sciences).

Dr. Madden reports receiving fees for serving on advisory boards from Bayer. Dr. Peipert reports receiving fees for serving on advisory boards from Bayer, Teva, MicroCHIPS, and Watson/Activis and grant support from Bayer, Teva, and Merck. No other potential conflict of interest relevant to this article was reported.

Disclosure forms provided by the authors are available with the full text of this article at NEJM.org.

We thank Dr. Kathryn Kost and the staff of the Guttmacher Institute for providing us with data from unpublished tabulations of sexually experienced U.S. teens and guidance regarding the calculation of teen pregnancy, birth, and abortion rates.

References

1. Kost K, Henshaw SK. U.S. teenage pregnancies, births and abortions 2010: national and state trends by age, race and ethnicity. New York: Guttmacher Institute, 2014 (http://www.guttmacher.org/pubs/ USTPtrends10.pdf).

2. The National Campaign to Prevent Teen and Unplanned Pregnancy. Fast facts: how is the 3 in 10 statistic calculated? February 2011 (http://grist.files. wordpress.com/2011/10/fastfacts_3in10 .pdf).

3. The National Campaign to Prevent Teen and Unplanned Pregnancy. Fast facts: teen pregnancy and childbearing among Latina teens. December 2013 (https://thenationalcampaign.org/sites/default/ files/resource-primary-download/fast_facts_-_teen_ pregnancy_and_child-bearing_among_latino_teens_ decembe.pdf).

4. The National Campaign to Prevent Teen and Unplanned Pregnancy. Fast facts: teen pregnancy and childbearing among non-Hispanic black teens. December 2013 (http://thenationalcampaign.org/ sites/default/files/resource-primary-download/fast_ facts_-_teen_pregnancy_and_childbearing_among_ non-hispanic_black_te.pdf).

5. The National Campaign to Prevent Teen and Unplanned Pregnancy. Counting it up: the public costs of teen childbearing—key data. December 2013 (https://thenationalcampaign.org/sites/default/

files/resource-primary-download/counting-it-up-key-data-2013-update.pdf).

6. Boonstra HD. Key questions for consideration as a new federal teen pregnancy prevention initiative is implemented. Guttmacher policy review. Vol. 13. No. 1. New York: Guttmacher Institute, 2010.

7. Centers for Disease Control and Prevention. Winnable Battles fact sheet. 2012 (http://www.cdc.gov/winnablebattles/pdf/wb_fact_sheet_aug2012.pdf).

8. O'Neil-Callahan M, Peipert JF, Zhao Q, Madden T, Secura G. Twenty-four-month continuation of reversible contraception. Obstet Gynecol 2013;122:1083-91.

9. Rosenstock JR, Peipert JF, Madden T, Zhao Q, Secura GM. Continuation of reversible contraception in teenagers and young women. Obstet Gynecol 2012;120: 1298-305.

10. Winner B, Peipert JF, Zhao Q, et al. Effectiveness of long-acting reversible contraception. N Engl J Med 2012;366: 1998-2007.

11. Tocce KM, Sheeder JL, Teal SB. Rapid repeat pregnancy in adolescents: do immediate postpartum contraceptive implants make a difference? Am J Obstet Gynecol 2012;206(6):481.e1-7.

12. Finer LB, Jerman J, Kavanaugh ML. Changes in use of long-acting contraceptive methods in the United States, 2007-2009. Fertil Steril 2012;98:893-7.

13. Kavanaugh ML, Frohwirth L, Jerman J, Popkin R, Ethier K. Long-acting reversible contraception for adolescents and young adults: patient and provider perspectives. J Pediatr Adolesc Gynecol 2013; 26:86-95.

14. Kavanaugh ML, Jerman J, Ethier K, Moskosky S. Meeting the contraceptive needs of teens and young adults: youth-friendly and long-acting reversible contraceptive services in U.S. family planning facilities. J Adolesc Health 2013;52:284-92.

15. Secura G, McNicholas C. Long-acting reversible contraceptive use among teens prevents unintended

pregnancy: a look at the evidence. Expert Rev Obstet Gynecol 2013;8:297-9.

16. Secura GM, Allsworth JE, Madden T, Mullersman JL, Peipert JF. The Contraceptive CHOICE Project: reducing barriers to long-acting reversible contraception. Am J Obstet Gynecol 2010;203(2):115.e1-7.

17. Madden T, Mullersman JL, Omvig KJ, Secura GM, Peipert JF. Structured contraceptive counseling provided by the Contraceptive CHOICE Project. Contraception 2013;88:243-9.

18. U.S. selected practice recommendations for contraceptive use, 2013: adapted from the World Health Organization selected practice recommendations for contraceptive use, 2nd edition. MMWR Recomm Rep 2013;62(RR-5):1-46.

19. Medical eligibility criteria for contraceptive use. 3rd ed. Geneva: World Health Organization, 2004.

20. Kost K, Henshaw SK. U.S. teenage pregnancies, births and abortions, 2008: national trends by age, race and ethnicity. New York: Guttmacher Institute, February 2012.

21. Martinez G, Copen CE, Abma JC. Teenagers in the United States: sexual activity, contraceptive use, and childbearing, 2006-2010 national survey of family growth. Vital Health Stat 23 2011;31:1-35.

22. Harper C, Callegari L, Raine T, Blum M, Darney P. Adolescent clinic visits for contraception: support from mothers, male partners and friends. Perspect Sex Reprod Health 2004;36:20-6.

23. Annual estimates of the resident population by sex, age, race, and Hispanic origin for the United States and States: April 1, 2010 to July 1, 2012 (http://fact-finder2.census.gov/faces/tableservices/jsf/pages/productview.xhtml?pid=PEP_2012_PEPASR6H&prodType=table).

24. Martin JA, Hamilton BE, Osterman MJK, Curtin SC, Mathews TJ. Births: final data for 2012. Natl Vital Stat Rep 2013;62: 1-87.

Designer Babies and the Pro-Choice Movement

by Rebecca Tuhus-Dubrow

Over the last century, the link between sex and reproduction has weakened. Feminist activism, aided by technological advances, has given middle-class women in the United States widespread access to effective contraception and safe, legal abortion. Although far too many exceptions persist, for large numbers of women, sex today has no necessary relationship to childbearing. Meanwhile, a burgeoning fertility industry has, for thousands, taken baby-making from the bedroom to the laboratory.

In vitro fertilization (IVF) does not merely help the infertile to procreate; increasingly, it allows parents to determine the genetic makeup of their offspring. Initially, preimplantation genetic diagnosis (PGD) targeted severe childhood diseases, such as Tay-Sachs and sickle cell anemia. Now, more parents use it to screen out genes for late-onset, treatable diseases, such as colon cancer; sex selection is also popular. According to a 2006 survey conducted by the Genetics and Public Policy Center at Johns Hopkins University, 42 percent of 137 IVF-PGD clinics allowed parents to select for gender. Scientists predict that parents will be able to choose such characteristics as blue eyes or curly hair. Less certain, but plausible, is that scientists will be able to identify genes for more complex traits, such as intelligence and homosexuality. Genetic engineering, which will enable not merely the selection but the insertion of desired genes, is on the horizon. In the United States, this rapidly advancing technology is unchecked by any regulatory mechanism.

It will emerge as an important political issue, complicated by competing values, such as individual liberty and social equality. Nowhere will this tension be more conspicuous than in the reproductive rights movement. There is a lot of messy overlap between reproductive rights and what could emerge as a neo-eugenics: both benefit from the separation of sex and reproduction and both entail increased "choice." Pro-choice advocates already find themselves associated with advocates of this "reprogenetic" technology, who often appropriate pro-choice language. "It's about Reproductive Rights, Stupid," reads the title of an article on the Web site betterhumans.com, which promotes the use of biotechnologies to improve the human species.

Even without the borrowed buzzwords, the pro-choice movement would be uneasily close to the issue. Historically, pro-choice arguments have focused on the right to privacy and freedom from government interference. Legally, those are the terms that define reproductive rights. The landmark Supreme Court cases *Connecticut* v. *Griswold* (1965) and *Roe* v. *Wade* (1973) recognized the right of individuals to control their reproductive destinies. Legal scholars predict that when the question of selecting the traits of offspring inevitably arrives in court, it will be considered in this framework.

Like it or not, pro-choice groups, then, will be compelled to take a stand. They will have to distinguish their concept of reproductive rights from that advanced by neo-eugenicists and to decide whether and how to endorse regulation of reproductive technologies without jeopardizing already tenuous rights. But along with these challenges come opportunities. By incorporating concerns about the abuse of reproductive technologies into a pro-choice platform, the movement can shift away from an individual-liberties paradigm toward a social justice orientation; move away from a single-issue focus on abortion toward a more comprehensive agenda; and form coalitions with other segments of the left.

The Twentieth Century

The link between reproductive rights and eugenics is not new; in fact, it has dogged the movement since its early days. Margaret Sanger, the tireless pioneer of birth control in the United States, started out in the early twentieth century as a radical socialist and feminist. A nurse with working-class origins, she saw firsthand the travails of poor women drained physically and financially by endless births. Sanger believed that birth control—legally restricted at the time—was all but a panacea for society's ills. She launched a crusade, even subordinating other values to the cause: during World War I, for example, she kept quiet about her pacifist beliefs out of fear that her unpopular opinion would undermine support for birth control.

By 1919, Sanger's far-left political background was a liability in a climate hostile to radicalism. At the same time, the eugenics movement was seen as socially responsible and forward-thinking by the public and many intellectuals. Eugenicists argued that society would benefit if families with "good genes" reproduced prolifically, while the "unfit" refrained from procreating.

To advance the latter goal, some eugenicists advocated sterilization, by force, if necessary. This option was presented as a humane alternative: the "dysgenic" would not have to be permanently institutionalized or even remain celibate to avoid propagating their undesirable genes. Forced sterilization received Supreme Court approval in *Buck* v. *Bell* (1927). Justice Oliver Wendell Holmes, Jr., famously wrote, "It is better for all the world, if instead of waiting to execute degenerate offspring for crime, or to let them starve for their imbecility, society can prevent those who are manifestly unfit from continuing their kind .... Three generations of imbeciles are enough." Numerous state laws were enacted to authorize forced sterilization.

In an attempt to gain the imprimatur of science, and in a move that has since haunted her legacy, Sanger became associated with the eugenics movement. She had promoted birth control for the poor because she saw that they suffered most for the lack of it. The well-off always managed to procure means for controlling their fertility; Sanger's poor patients begged her for the secrets of the rich. When she embraced eugenics, her rhetoric adapted easily to the values of the movement. "While I

personally believe in the sterilization of the feeble-minded, the insane and the syphiletic [sic]," she wrote in 1919, "I have not been able to discover that these measures are more than superficial deterrents when applied to the constantly growing stream of the unfit. ... Birth control, on the other hand, not only opens the way to the eugenist [sic], but it preserves his work."

This early association, along with certain government policies, helped to taint birth control and abortion in the eyes of many minorities. Plenty of poor white people suffered under eugenic policies, but black, Hispanic, and indigenous women were targeted disproportionately. (In the rural South, sterilizations of black women—often performed without their knowledge following childbirth, abortion, or other operations—were known as the "Mississippi appendectomy," a term coined by Fannie Lou Hamer to describe her own.) In the 1960s and 1970s, the Black Panther Party and the Nation of Islam both denounced birth control as genocidal. Other groups, such as the National Association for the Advancement of Colored People and the Student Non-violent Coordinating Committee, also harbored suspicions. When the government funded birth control rather than health care or child care in poor communities, some activists angrily pointed out that reducing the number of poor people was not the same as reducing poverty. Fears ran deep that contraception and abortion, as well as sterilization, were means of controlling, if not eliminating, these communities.

Meanwhile, the mainstream pro-choice movement was operating from a vastly different perspective. Mainstream feminists wanted the choice *not* to have children, to be emancipated from the constraints of the traditional female role. Rarely did white women have to fight to have children; the struggle was to avoid having them. In the 1960s and 1970s, abortion rights activists framed the debate in terms of feminism and sexual liberation. The movement triumphed with *Roe v. Wade*.

In the following decades, some strands of the mainstream pro-choice movement, notably NARAL (then known as the National Abortion Rights Action League), modified their approach in the face of changing political realities. In the aftermath of the *Webster* v. *Reproductive Health*

Services Supreme Court decision (1989), which upheld a Missouri statute prohibiting the use of public facilities for abortions, NARAL launched its successful "Who Decides?" campaign, which toned down the women's liberation language and focused on the right to freedom from government intervention. As Kate Michelman, until recently NARAL's president, recalls in her 2005 book, *With Liberty and Justice for All*, "The issue was not whether abortion was morally right or wrong; that was a matter of individual conscience. The question was, who had the right to decide—women or the government?" On the defensive against a passionately committed (and sometimes murderous) anti-abortion movement, many feminists focused more intensively on abortion, shifting energy away from other goals, such as child care, maternity leave, and support for alternative sexual lifestyles. All of these had once been integral parts of the feminist pro-choice agenda, as Carole Joffe discussed in these pages ("It's Not *Just* Abortion, Stupid," Winter 2005).

Although arguably a political necessity at the time, focusing on abortion and adopting an individual liberties paradigm had its costs. (William Saletan has analyzed the campaign in his book *Bearing Right: How Conservatives Won the Abortion War*.) One was the loss of a compelling moral narrative, which left a vacuum for the anti-abortion side to fill. Another was the alienation of poor minority women. Abortion was less of a priority for women struggling with multiple reproductive challenges: environmental hazards, lack of health care and child care, the fear of coerced sterilization. Some of those who wanted abortions couldn't afford to pay for them, so the freedom from government intervention was inadequate. The racial component of reproductive politics has been analyzed by scholars such as Dorothy Roberts in *Killing the Black Body* and Jennifer Nelson in *Women of Color and the Reproductive Rights Movement*.

Currently, the pro-choice movement is under siege to a greater degree than any time since 1973, a situation that has led it to reassess its strategy. Now, some supporters of abortion rights want to move beyond the stagnant terms of the debate. Efforts to rethink the conventional approach are evident in the work of Frances Kissling, former president of Catholics for a Free Choice;

"reproductive justice" advocates, including Loretta Ross; mainstream players in the Democratic Party, such as George Lakoff, a linguist and consultant; and would-be presidential nominee Hillary Clinton; as well as many other feminists and activists. The term "choice" itself has come under scrutiny, often criticized as a problematic concept and a weak and morally flaccid competitor with "life." Recent documents, such as *Beyond Choice*, a 2004 book by Alexander Sanger, grandson of Margaret and chair of the International Planned Parenthood Council, and *More than a Choice*, a 2006 paper by the Center for American Progress, reflect this attitude.

Choice rhetoric has seeped into other aspects of feminism as well, with mixed results. Linda Hirschman caused a stir in 2005 with an article in the *American Prospect* decrying "choice feminism"—the notion that staying home with the kids is as feminist as working, provided that it's the woman's "choice." Her article focused on the "mommy wars" debate, but the same rationale can apply to other aspects of female life. Some women assert that anything from wearing lipstick to topless dancing can be a feminist act, because a woman is empowered by her choice to perform it. (Ariel Levy discusses this phenomenon in her book *Female Chauvinist Pigs*.) Hirschman argued that women, with the goal of collective advancement in mind, ought to aggressively pursue high-power, high-paying positions.

Although I don't agree with everything Hirschman wrote—for instance, that we should eschew low-paying, socially beneficial work in favor of cutthroat corporate success—I think she was onto something. "Choice feminism" is uncomfortably close to the ethos of consumer culture. A feminism that consecrates individual choices, endorsing them all as equally valid, has lost its mission and its soul. (Indeed, "choice feminism" is Hirschman's term, not a movement with an agenda; but some women do subscribe to the idea.)

And here is where the reprogenetic technologies fit in. What is a "designer baby" but a new consumer choice? When a vague, distorted feminism is conflated with enthusiastic consumerism, when "choice" is the catchword of both, designer babies can easily emerge as the natural, if not inevitable, next step in the evolution of our liberated, capitalist society, in which choices will continue to multiply for consumers—especially for those consumers par excellence, women.

Assessing the "New Eugenics"

Eugenics is a bad word, and "designer baby" is a term the media use to conjure science fiction dystopias, but is it really wrong to use new technologies to improve the human species?

There's no easy answer. Many people instinctively react against the idea of tinkering with genetics. It evokes fears of playing God, of technological experimentation gone horribly awry, even of the end of humanity as we know it. If only, or primarily, out of pure nostalgia, a lot of us bristle at the prospect.

Approached on the level of specifics, however, the questions appear more complicated. A couple profiled in the *New York Times* underwent elective in vitro fertilization—even though they could likely have conceived without it—in order to choose an embryo without a gene that would predispose their child to colon cancer. There are several possible criticisms of their decision. Colon cancer is a late-onset, treatable disease. By the time the child is an adult, a cure may be found. The gene is not even certain to cause the disease. How can they justify the expenditure and the godlike control they've assumed? On the other hand, their family has suffered immensely from this disease, and they want to ensure that their child avoids that suffering. If the technology is available, and they choose to spend their money on it, how can we deprive them of that option?

This example leads us down the slippery slope. Where, and how, do we draw the line between acceptable and unacceptable? Many people condone health-related genetic tinkering, but not a cosmetic kind. Or, we may feel comfortable with treatment, but not enhancement. Yet, in a culture in which health and beauty are increasingly conflated, as are treatments and enhancements (as more natural variation is pathologized), these distinctions are exceedingly difficult to make. It is even more difficult to imagine how they would be regulated.

The "new eugenics" is in many ways the opposite of its predecessor. The original eugenics was largely "negative": its goal was to curtail the population growth of the "unfit," often through involuntary, state-sanctioned, sometimes state-funded sterilization. Today's version is "positive": it allows for the creation of more desirable babies. (Granted, it could be interpreted as negative because, at this stage, it involves discarding "unfit" embryos. And the original eugenics also included a "positive" element: encouraging "fit families" to breed.) The more meaningful distinction is that the original eugenics involved coercion, depriving people of their rights and liberties. Today's variety technically does the opposite: the technologies offer *more* choices. Indeed, some proponents of their use accuse "bio-Luddites" of being the true descendants of eugenicists—for proposing state interference in the arena, for seeking to circumscribe the full range of available "reproductive choices."

But individual choices can have larger social consequences. Princeton professor Lee Silver has outlined a nightmarish scenario in which an essentially new species evolves: "The GenRich class and the Natural class will become entirely separate species with no ability to crossbreed, and with as much romantic interest in each other as a current human would have for a chimpanzee." Others, such as bio-ethicist George Annas, have worried that such a scenario could undermine the notion of human rights, which is based on a concept of our shared humanity. On a less existentially threatening but disturbing note, Annas and others have also predicted an "arms race" among relatively affluent parents: added to pressure to enroll kids in the most prestigious preschools will be pressure to provide them with the best genes. The result could be an increased tendency to see children as commodities and status markers; on the other hand, parents who choose to forgo these measures could be seen as negligent.

Clearly, there is great potential for good as well as harm in these technologies. They shouldn't be left, as they currently are, entirely to the market. It's time for a society-wide conversation about their use and abuse. The United States is lagging in this regard. Many countries, mostly in Europe, but also Canada, Australia, and Trinidad and Tobago have passed laws or regulations restricting or proscribing various kinds of genetic modifications. The United Kingdom has the Human Fertilization and Embryology Authority (HFEA), which licenses and monitors all fertility clinics.

Responses and Political Possibilities

This issue creates strange bedmates. The common political assumption is that conservatives would oppose the potentially radical change promised by reprogenetic technologies, while liberals would embrace the scientific progress they represent. And indeed, the religious right, concerned about the embryo and the blasphemy of playing God, condemns them, while some liberals are more inclined to welcome them on the grounds of "progress"— and, perhaps, in opposition to "culture of life" priorities. At the same time, economic libertarians oppose regulation of this three-billion-dollar-a-year industry, and a fringe of neo-eugenicists wants to create a super race. Qualms on the left include the potential exacerbation of inequalities, the eugenic overtones, and the environmental implications of meddling with nature.

Other progressive contingents have their worries. Disability activists are wary of technologies that essentially aim to eliminate their community. Gay and lesbian people have an especially complex relationship to assisted reproductive technology. I spoke to staff at the GLBT (Gay, Lesbian, Bisexual and Transgendered) Community Center in New York, who said that to the extent that it helps them have genetically related families, they welcome the technology. But if a "gay gene" is ever identified, their communities, too, could be threatened. Many feminists are troubled by sex selection, but fear that regulating any aspect of reproduction could jeopardize abortion rights.

The relevant legal infrastructure adds another complication. The court decisions that uphold rights valued by progressives could also afford protection to the right to design babies. This applies to all of the major cases affirming the right to contraception and abortion: *Griswold* and *Roe*, but also *Eisenstadt* v. *Baird* (1972), which recognized the right of unmarried people to use contraception, and even *Planned Parenthood* v. *Casey* (1992), which allowed some restrictions on abortion but reiterated the essential right of people to make decisions regarding reproduction. Further, *Lawrence* v. *Texas* (2003), hailed by the left for striking down sodomy laws, dramatically limits the ability of government to restrict personal decisions "absent injury to a person or abuse of an institution the law protects." Although progressives welcome these freedoms,

the implications for the unfettered use of reprogenetic technologies are disturbing. (Of course, the recent decision in *Gonzalez v. Carhart* raises questions about the durability of these liberties under the current Supreme Court.)

Legal issues aside, in the court of public opinion reproductive rights may be conflated with a libertarian view on genetic technologies. University of Texas law professor John Robertson has defended the use of reprogenetic technologies on the grounds of "procreative liberty." His argument goes like this: people have the right to procreate; sometimes the choice whether to procreate depends on the qualities of the prospective offspring; therefore, enhancement must be permitted (although he endorses limited restrictions). British author Nicholas Agar, in his recent book *Liberal Eugenics*, writes, "The eugenics defended here [is] primarily concerned with the protection and extension of reproductive freedom." Thus can the concept of reproductive choice be appropriated and abused.

The first and least controversial task for pro-choice activists, then, is to make it very clear that the rights for which they have fought are fundamentally different from the right to determine the genetic makeup of offspring. Whether the latter right is legitimate or not, it is not the same as or an extension of the former. Pro-choice activists have struggled for women's freedom to control their own lives and bodies, not to control the lives and bodies of their children.

Drawing this distinction could lead to another step: emphasizing the morality of abortion rights. Abortion should be legal because women should have the same rights as men to shape their lives; because sometimes bringing a child into the world is the wrong thing to do; because without legal abortion, women suffer and die. Abortion-rights advocates can frame abortion as a matter of social justice, not just of freedom from government interference.

As an alternative to "choice," women of color have created the concept of "reproductive justice." In the literature of SisterSong Women of Color Reproductive Health Collective, the national coordinator, Loretta Ross, defines the term, coined in 1994, as "(1) the right to have a child; (2) the right not to have a child; (3) the right to parent the children we have . . . . We also fight for the necessary enabling conditions to realize these rights." This more comprehensive notion of reproductive justice can be useful in confronting the issue of designer babies. Although not currently one of the main items on the reproductive justice agenda, a position on reprogenetic technologies can easily be added to the list of concerns, which include environmental hazards and health care. In fact, of the reproductive rights activists I've spoken to, Ross was the most sympathetic to the prospect of regulating these technologies.

As Joffe pointed out in the *Dissent* article mentioned earlier, "the logic of seeing abortion as just one part of the mosaic of reproductive and sexual rights and services is not simply that it is persuasive to others. It is also the most authentic position of the reproductive freedom movement itself." Reproductive technologies did not factor into the original movement, because they didn't yet exist. But now that they do, promoting sensible policies on their use should fit into a broader platform. Such a platform could appeal to other factions of the left as well as moderates, who might be turned off by the focus on abortion but who share concerns about related issues, including the abuse of reprogenetic technologies.

The concept of reproductive justice has already made inroads into the mainstream movement. The pro-choice movement eludes generalization, because different organizations have different priorities and approaches, but many parts of it have already begun to shift toward a social justice focus and a broader platform. The literature of Choice USA, a fifteen-year-old organization founded by Gloria Steinem, uses the term reproductive justice, and Planned Parenthood sponsored a conference in 2005 at Smith College titled "Reproductive Justice for All."

Concerns about reprogenetics have also surfaced. The Planned Parenthood conference devoted a quarter of the agenda to reproductive technologies. The Center for Genetics and Society, billed as "a pro-choice organization working for sensible policies on genetic engineering technology," aims to initiate and facilitate conversations about the subject. One effort was a retreat in October 2006 with representatives from various progressive organizations, including Planned Parenthood, Choice USA, the ACLU, the disability rights group

Not Dead Yet, and the LGBT Community Center of New York.

According to Sujatha Jesudason of the Center for Genetics and Society, the groups that attended that retreat were enthusiastic about continuing the conversations within their own organizations and forming coalitions to address the issue. The pro-choice advocates in particular started a process of reflection on the tensions—between individual liberties and social justice—that are especially prominent in their movement.

In contemplating regulation, an example from the past might prove illuminating. In 1975, in New York, a multiracial coalition called the Advisory Committee on Sterilization helped implement guidelines for regulating sterilization, including a mandatory waiting period. The aim was to ensure informed consent, because so many poor minority women had been sterilized without it, in haste. Planned Parenthood and NARAL opposed the restrictions, arguing that they infringed on reproductive freedom. (White women, who frequently could not persuade doctors to sterilize them, did not want to make the process more cumbersome.) This conflict was perhaps the clearest manifestation of the discordant outlooks of different feminists.

The opposition of the mainstream groups was understandable, but it also reflected a degree of myopia. Likewise, Margaret Sanger was so single-minded in the promotion of her cause that she endorsed wrongheaded ideas that she believed would serve it. Now, we who support abortion rights may fear that regulating reproductive technologies could endanger our cause. There is no doubt that maintaining the legality of abortion—and fighting to reverse harmful restrictions of it—is paramount. But it is also important for us to sustain a larger moral vision. We have to find a way to advance that multifaceted program, including views on reproductive technologies, while protecting the right to abortion.

It appears inevitable that genetic technologies of all kinds will become one of the major issues of this century. It appears equally inevitable that the pro-choice movement will become entangled in the debate. In this new challenge, Margaret Sanger provides an instructive example—today's reproductive-rights advocates should emulate her passionate advocacy and avoid repeating her mistakes.

A Call to Protect the Health of Women Who Donate Their Eggs

by Judy Norsigian and Timothy R. B. Johnson

The egg market is growing. As couples and individuals continue to rely on assisted reproductive technology to overcome infertility, to make parenthood possible for gay people, and for other reasons, the demand for eggs is increasing swiftly.[1] Between 2000 and 2010, the number of donor eggs used for *in vitro* fertilization increased about 70 percent, from 10,801 to 18,306, according to a report in the *Journal of the American Medical Association* (JAMA).[2]

And, although there are no exact figures for how many young women engage in egg-retrieval-for-pay, the numbers are at least in the thousands. Many of these women are in their early 20s—and are often university students who need cash to cover their tuition fees.[3] But, most people don't realize that there are no good longterm safety data that would enable these young women to make truly informed choices about selling their eggs.

Now, a number of women's health and public interest advocacy organizations—including Our Bodies Ourselves, the Pro-Choice Alliance for (https://www.nwhn.org/wp-content/uploads/2016/11/Screen-Shot-2016-11-12-at-8.52.00-AM.png)

Responsible Research, and the Center for Genetics and Society—are studying women's knowledge about egg retrieval and calling for more and better research about its risks.[4]

What we are finding is that women often know too little about the egg donation process and potential risks. Here's an example: One drug frequently used to suppress ovarian function is leuprolide acetate (Lupron).[5] The U.S. Food and Drug Administration (FDA) has not given approval for this particular use of the drug (Lupron is approved as a treatment for endometriosis, fibroids, early puberty and prostate cancer). So, it is used during egg retrieval protocols through "off label"

use. In various surveys of younger women who are donating their eggs, it appears that this fact about off-label use is rarely shared. Probably few, if any, of these young women know about the 300-page review of many Lupron studies that Dr. David Redwine submitted to the FDA in 2011. In this report, he documents a plethora of problems, many serious, and some long-term.[6]

These problems include subsequent infertility, a

> ### How Does Egg Donation Work?
>
> The first step in providing eggs involves synchronizing the menstrual cycles of both donor and recipient, so the recipient's uterine lining will be ready for implantation when the donor's eggs are retrieved and fertilized. Donors are given hormones to first "shut down" ovulation. Then donors are given hormones to hyperstimulate their ovaries to produce multiple eggs. (Multiple eggs are needed because some eggs won't fertilize or develop normally after fertilization.) Once the eggs have developed, they are surgically extracted, usually by transvaginal ultrasound aspiration. This process involves a physician inserting a thin needle into an ultrasound guide and guiding it through the vagina and into the follicles to retrieve the eggs. The egg(s) are then fertilized outside the donor or recipient's body.

possible link to certain cancers, and more prevalent short-term problems with Ovarian Hyperstimulation Syndrome (OHSS) than previously reported in the literature. Given the strong anecdotal evidence of such problems, more well-done studies are critically needed.

How can we encourage the collection of adequate long-term data about the extent and severity of egg retrieval risks? There's one independent voluntary national registry in the U.S., the Infertility Family Research Registry (IFRR), based at Dartmouth-Hitchcock Medical Center in New

Hampshire. But, very few large fertility centers are even willing to put out the brochures and placard for the IFRR. (See www.ifrr-registry.org.)

In the absence of prospective clinical trials that follow women over a long time to assess egg donation's risks, the IFRR is one of the few ways we can track women to determine the longer-term dangers. We hope this situation will change soon, but that's only likely if a large number of egg donors start *demanding* this is assessed, and that clinics make young women aware of the registry's existence. Find out what you can do here (http://www.ourbodiesourselves.org/take-action/egg-donation-health-risks-safety-data).

Ironically, many of the fertility centers that don't make those brochures available in their waiting areas are members of the American Society for Reproductive Medicine (ASRM), the professional organization of fertility practitioners that has provided modest grant support to the IFRR.

To address the situation, in early 2013, three young women formed "We Are Egg Donors," the first-ever self-help advocacy group created by women who have provided eggs (www.weareeggdonors.com). These women have been collaborating with Diane Tober, PhD, at the University of California, San Francisco (UCSF) to conduct in-depth interviews with other women who have provided their eggs and systematically collect information about a full range of their experiences, from emotional to physical (see http://eggdonorresearch.org). They join other women's health and public interest advocacy organizations that are studying women's knowledge about egg retrieval, calling for more research, and encouraging greater participation in the IFRR.

Raquel Cool, a founding member of We Are Egg Donors, says that the U.S is "among the only countries in the world where eggs are freely and openly exchanged for uncapped amounts." She continues, "I recall one member's experience, a first-time donor, whose reproductive endocrinologist deemed her at a high risk of Ovarian Hyperstimulation Syndrome. He canceled the cycle. I've seen that happen once in three years. More often, we regularly see cases of OHSS, a fully preventable condition where, in severe cases, the [egg] provider's abdomen swells with fluid and needs to be drained with a needle, or can cause a stroke. Collecting safety data—both of the short- and long-term risks—can only support informed choice."

Dr. Tober, who is also producing "The Perfect Donor (http://perfectdonormovie.com)," a film about egg donation, notes that "there is a great deal of inconsistency in how egg donors are treated, both in their interactions at clinics and agencies and medically." She continues, "While some physicians are more conservative with the medical protocols, others use very aggressive protocols and end up with excessive numbers of eggs in their donors. Even though some women do naturally produce more eggs than others, the number of mature oocytes produced can be somewhat controlled by using more conservative medication dosages. Some insurance companies are also now refusing to insure physicians with high OHSS rates in their donors, but this information is not being made available beyond those in the industry. Doctors are thus far not held accountable when a donor has severe complications."

A 2013 editorial in JAMA noted that "more complete data on both short- and long-term outcomes of donation are needed so donors can make truly informed choices and, once those data are available, mechanisms can be put in place to ensure that the donor recruitment and consent process at clinics is conducted according to the highest ethical standards."[7]

A 2014 statement by the National Perinatal Association recommends that: "State regulatory agencies who license and provide oversight for collection and use of human tissues should provide the same level of oversight for sperm banks, the selling of human eggs and egg 'donation.'"

We agree with the 2007 *New England Journal of Medicine* article that said, "If women are going to donate eggs, we must ensure that their health is not compromised. We need, therefore, to subject egg donation to far more scientific scrutiny than it currently receives. We need more longitudinal studies of the drugs involved in ovarian hyper-stimulation, for example, more long-term follow-up of egg donors, and deeper analyses of the conditions under which dangerous complications occur."[8]

Jennifer Schneider, M.D., a Tucson-based internist whose own daughter was an egg donor and later died of colon cancer, has written: "Right now, egg donors are treated like vendors, not as patients. Patients need to be followed up."[9] As many egg providers will attest, after the first few days of being discharged with no immediate consequences, they are never contacted again.

As current and former women who have provided their eggs increasingly pool their experiences and provide a growing body of anecdotal evidence pointing to significant harms, especially in cases where women provide eggs on multiple occasions, we need to establish a more rigorous system of evaluating the risks. Studies sponsored by independent researchers, the government and other responsible entities can provide the evidence that is currently lacking and finally make truly informed consent possible. Collecting more thorough safety data will allow young women to better assess the pros and cons of exchanging their eggs for cash.

An earlier version of this article first appeared on WBUR's CommonHealth, http://www.wbur.org/commonhealth/2016/03/28/patient-protection-egg-donors.

Article written by: Judy Norsigian and Dr. Timothy R.B. Johnson

Timothy R.B. Johnson, M.D., is chair of obstetrics and gynecology, University of Michigan, Ann Arbor; Judy Norsigian is co-founder and past executive director, Our Bodies Ourselves.

REFERENCES

1. Centers for Disease Control and Prevention (CDC), *Assisted Reproductive Technology*, Atlanta: CDC, no date. Available online at: *http://www.cdc.gov/art/index.html.*

2. Kawwass JF, Monsour M, Crawford S, et al., for the National ART Surveillance System (NASS) Group, "Trends and Outcomes for Donor Oocyte Cycles in the United States, 2000-2010," *JAMA* 2013; 310(22):2426-2434. doi:10.1001/jama.2013.280924.

3. Edwards B, "The High Costs of Giving up Your Eggs," NYU Livewire, no date. Available online at: *http://journalism.nyu.edu/publishing/archives/livewire/archived/high_cost_eggs.*

4. Merritt T, Phillips R, Goldstein M, et al., Position Statement—*Ethical Use of Assisted Reproductive Technologies: A Call for Greater Transparency, Better Counseling of Prospective Parents, and Single Embryo Transfer to Improve Outcomes for Mothers and Babies,* National Perinatal Association, 2014. Available online at: *http://www.nationalperinatal.org/Resources/NT-MAR14-NPA.pdf.*

5. National Cancer Instiiute (NCI), Cancer Drugs: Leuprolide Acetate, Bethesda MD: NCI, September 17, 2014. Available online at: http://www.cancer.gov/about-cancer/treatment/drugs/leuprolideacetate

6. Redwine D, "Laparoscopic Excision of Endometriosis," available online at: https://www.facebook.com/permalink.php?story_fbid=283184988378691&id=195664767130714

7. Myers ER, "Outcomes of Donor Oocyte Cycles in Assisted Reproduction," *JAMA* 2013; 310(22):2403-2404. doi:10.1001/jama.2013.280925.

8. Spar D, "The Egg Trade—Making Sense of the Market for Human Oocytes," *N Engl J Med* 2007; 356:1289-1291. DOI: 10.1056/NEJMp078012.

9. Schneider J, "Fatal colon cancer in a young egg donor: a physician mother's call for follow up and research on the long-term risks of ovarian stimulation," *Fertility and Sterility* 2008; 90(5): 2016e1-e5. doi: 10.1016/j.fertnstert.2007.12.074.

Reproductive Justice and Childbearing Women

by Rebecca Spence

In January, the U.S. women's health movement celebrated the 40th anniversary of Roe v. Wade, which gave women the right to legal abortion. In the decades since Roe, health activists have focused on advocating for reproductive justice, which demands that women have the right to be parents—as well as the right not to parent—and to decide where, with whom, and how we give birth. Reproductive justice includes the rights to accept or refuse any type of maternity care and to access this care from respectful and culturally appropriate providers—which are essential for women to be able to make the best decisions for themselves and their families.

The movement for reproductive justice is far from over, and women's experience during childbirth stands out as a key area for improvement. The vision for reproductive justice and birthing rights is to improve outcomes for women and their babies while honoring women's fundamental right to control their bodies and reproductive lives.

Most people think that the U.S. is a safe place to give birth but—for many women—it's not. American women experience breathtakingly high rates of maternal death and disability: they have a greater risk of dying during pregnancy or childbirth than women in 49 other countries, including Kuwait, Bulgaria, and South Korea.[i] Maternal morbidity is disproportionately suffered by women of color: Black women are nearly four times more likely to die in childbirth than White women.[1] Given the United States' advanced health care system and infrastructure, both survival and dignified care should be the norm.

Most women in the U.S. (82%) give birth at some point, and many have a wide range of values and preferences about how they wish to experience childbirth.[ii] Some women prefer to receive care from a physician, others a midwife, while still others opt not to receive professional assistance at all. Some women's values or culture orient them to giving birth at home or in a birth center. Others need immediate access to high-tech monitoring, intervention, and medical pain management, and need to give birth in a hospital. Still others opt for a hospital-setting birth, but want to avoid interventions unless they are medically necessary. Many women's options are constrained by their insurance coverage: with hospital births averaging between $10,000-$23,000, paying out-of-pocket for childbirth is beyond many women's means.[iii]

Women's rights are undermined by any inability to receive safe care and act on their preferences. Yet, in our society—where medically managed childbirth and women's oppression are the norm, and racism in health care is pervasive—too many women experience discrimination, punishment, or mistreatment in maternity care. In addition to institutionalized discrimination against women,

explicit legal or policy barriers often hamper women's choices.

Seemingly small, incremental restrictions can impose significant roadblocks to women's access to safe and respectful maternity care. For example, many U.S. hospitals restrict women's choices by banning women from having a vaginal birth if they had cesarean surgery for a previous birth.[iv] These bans impact a large proportion of hospital patients, either through explicit prohibitions against vaginal births or a lack of physicians who will attend these deliveries. In 2010, a National Institutes of Health advisory panel noted that women's childbirth preferences should be honored and urged hospitals and professional societies to revisit these bans.[v]

In addition, many states outlaw the practice of midwifery by midwives who do not first train as nurses,[vi] preventing women from using these providers during childbirth. Other states license both nurse-midwives and Certified Professional Midwives, but restrict their scope of practice.[vii] Even in states where midwives practice legally, insurance may fail to cover their services, which just as effectively eliminates the option.[viii] There have been cases where families who used a midwife were charged with child abuse or neglect.[ix] The end result is that many women are forced by legal restrictions and/or insurance company requirements to give birth in a hospital, when they would not otherwise choose to do so and where their only option may be to undergo cesarean surgery.

Other examples of punishment and mistreatment of childbearing women include medical staff threatening to involve child protective services[x] and, in at least one known case, a woman losing parental rights as a consequence of refusing to consent to cesarean surgery[xi]; police visiting the homes of women who planned a home birth and, in several known cases, law enforcement physically restraining a woman and transporting her to a hospital to undergo surgery;[xii] and hospital staff mistreating families who transfer in from a planned home birth.[x] These cases are at the extreme end of the infringement of rights during childbirth that many women experience.

As we celebrate Roe, we also recognize the law's power to revolutionize women's reproductive experiences by empowering their choices or restricting their rights. Further, an enshrined legal right does not alone guarantee a woman's ability to access or enjoy that right. One of the oldest lessons of the women's health advocacy movement rings true: health care rights are meaningless without access to providers and social supports to make choice meaningful.

Legal Advocates for Birth Options & Rights (LABOR) was founded in 2010 to address women's legal rights during childbirth and remove legal barriers to reproductive justice for birthing women. LABOR identifies legal barriers to reproductive justice in birth, and gathers and facilitates a network of attorneys whose legal skills can protect, promote, and defend women's childbirth rights. While we do not offer direct representation, the questions we receive help illustrate women and providers' range of legal concerns. For example:

- I want a home birth but I had a cesarean for my first baby. State law says a licensed midwife can't attend me at home and the closest hospital that will take me is 100 miles away. How can I get the law changed? What risk does my midwife face if she serves me in violation of the law?

- I want to go in to labor naturally but my doctor sent me a letter firing me as a patient because I am 40 weeks pregnant and do not wish to be induced without medical indication. I can't find someone else who will take my insurance. Is this illegal patient abandonment?

- I am a midwife practicing legally. The local hospital makes a report against my license for any and all transfers of my clients, even when I follow medically appropriate protocol. One doctor told me they are determined to "shut me down." What can I do?

- I am an obstetrician and want to back-up our local midwives to provide continuity of care to patients. My practice group said they will fire me if I do, and my hospital is refusing home birth transfers. Is this legal?

- I am an obstetrician and want to offer my patients an opportunity to have a vaginal birth after a prior cesarean. My liability insurance company said I will lose my coverage if I do. How can I change the contract?

As women who had given birth, and as sisters, advocates, and friends, LABOR's founders had often been asked to provide legal support and advice in our own communities. We saw the need for coordinated legal strategies, and for a place to support one another and achieve reproductive justice for birthing women. The problems and solutions we face are as multi-faceted as the system, but we begin with the simple premise that pregnant women have a fundamental right to give birth safely and decide the circumstances of our births. Learn more about LABOR at birthoptionsandrights.org.

This article was written by: Rebecca Spence

Rebecca Spence is an attorney and bioethicist practicing in Northern Virginia. She was a 2011-2012 Law Students for Reproductive Justice Fellow. Rebecca founded LABOR in 2010 with Susan Jenkins, Esq., and it remains her most important pro bono project.

[i] Amnesty International, Deadly Delivery: The Maternal Healthcare Crisis in the USA, New York: Amnesty International, 2010. Available online at: http://www.amnestyusa.org/dignity/pdf/DeadlyDelivery.pdf.

[ii] Livingston G, and Cohn D, Wang W, et al., Childlessness Up Among All Women; Down Among Women with Advanced Degrees, Washington DC: Pew Research Center, 2010. Available online at: http://www.pewsocialtrends.org/2010/06/25/childlessness-up-among-all-women-down-among-women-with-advanced-degrees.

[iii] Childbirth Connection, Average U.S. Facility Charges for Giving Birth 2008-2010, 2013. Available online at: http://transform.childbirthconnection.org/resources/datacenter/chargeschart.

[iv] For example, see: Cohen V, "Mom fights, gets the delivery she wants," CNN Health Website, December 17, 2009. Available online at: http://articles.cnn.com/2009-12-17/health/birth.plan.tips_1_vaginal-delivery-caesareans-vaginal-births?_s=PM:HEALTH

[v] Cunningham FG, Bangdiwala S, Brown SS, et al., "National Institutes of Health Consensus Development Conference Statement: Vaginal Birth After Cesarean: New Insights. March 8—10, 2010," Obstetrics & Gynecology 2010; 115(6): 1279–1295. Available online at: http://consensus.nih.gov/2010/vbacstatement.htm.

[vi] The Big Push for Midwives, Legal Status of CPMs [Certified Professional Midwives] State-by-State Map, no date. Available online at: http://pushformidwives.org/cpms-by-state.

[vii] American College of Nurse Midwives (ACNM), Comparison of Certified Nurse-Midwives, Certified Midwives, and Certified Professional Midwives, Silver Spring MD: ACNM, August 2011. Available online at: http://www.midwife.org/ACNM/files/ccLibraryFiles/Filename/000000001385/CNM% 20CM%20CPM%20ComparisonChart%20082511.pdf

[viii] For example, Vermont recently required insurance coverage: Perez M, "The Cost of Being Born at Home," RH Reality Check Website, March 19, 2009. Available online at: http://rhrealitycheck.org/article/2009/03/19/the-cost-being-born-at-home.

[ix] For example, Bayer A, "Baby born via homebirth taken from parents," Examiner.com, September 2, 2010. Available online at: http://www.examiner.com/article/baby-born-via-homebirth-taken-from-parents.

[x] Declarations on file with the author.

[xi] New Jersey Division of Youth and Family Services v. V.M. and B.G., Defendants-Appellants. In the Matter of J.M.G., A Minor. Argued Nov. 3, 2008.—July 16, 2009. See: http://caselaw.findlaw.com/nj-superior-court-appellate-division/1152604.html

[xii] Pemberton v. Tallahassee Memorial Regional Center. Wests Fed Suppl. 1999;66:1247-57. See: http://www.ncbi.nlm.nih.gov/pubmed/11868571.

Why Women Are Afraid of Giving Birth?

by Kate Ryan

Growing up, I never thought of giving birth as something painful or inherently dangerous. I didn't realize until later in life that my perspective on giving birth, and pregnancy in general, was a bit out of the ordinary. For one thing, I was thinking about the process of giving birth when I was in grade school—which is apparently not typical! And, when I did think about birth, it seemed like a normal part of life, not a potentially life-threatening medical crisis.

As an adult, when my friends and I started to talk about this, I learned that many of them are "terrified" of giving birth... and I don't mean they are nervous, I mean petrified. Several have even said that, although they would like to have children, they may not because they are too scared of giving birth. While other young women seem able to empathize with this position, I have trouble doing so; I just can't identify with birth as they describe it. And, as an advocate working on women's health policy, I worry about what this seemingly common perspective says about quality of the care that mothers-to-be receive in the U.S. today.

My mother had three planned homebirths that were all attended by a lay midwife. Throughout my childhood on each of our birthdays, my mom gathered us together and told us the story of our birth. Again, this wasn't something I realized was uncommon until high school, when I learned that not only did my peers not know the story of their births, but they also weren't born at home—and thought it strange that I was.

But, my siblings and I didn't think it was strange at all. We grew up knowing that my mom made tuna fish for my older brother's lunch while she was in labor with me, and that he ran home from school to be there for my birth. We knew that it was raining the night my younger brother was born and that my mom listened to Frank Sinatra in the car while taking me over to my aunt's house. We knew that my aunt was the midwife's assistant for my younger sister's birth, and I remember being woken up as a four-year-old so I could watch my sister's birth. I know all these things because my mother talked about them with us, thereby normalizing these parts of life for my siblings and me.

She didn't gloss over the physical aspects of birth; she talked about breathing, walking, contractions, dilation, and feeling her baby transitioning into the birth canal. They weren't scary stories to us, they were exciting—we used to ask to hear our birth stories.

Let me be clear: my mom didn't have us at home because she's opposed to modern medical care or because we lived in a remote part of the world. In fact, she's a health care provider who runs a hospital in Philadelphia. She chose homebirth because she believes that birth is a normal part of life. She felt her body was made to give birth and that, for her—a healthy young woman with healthy pregnancies—medical intervention wasn't necessary for safe birth. In 2012, however, this attitude is quite rare and it's not just the apprehension I hear from my friends that makes me say that. Although there are no U.S. data available, surveys of British women show that nearly 87 percent of women report that they are "frightened of giving birth."[1] My question is, why?

The fact is that giving birth in developed countries, in any setting, is incredibly safe for a woman who has access to healthcare. The maternal mortality rate in the U.S. is 12.7 maternal deaths per 100,000 live births[2] compared to 500 per 100,000 in South Asia, and 920 per 100,000 in Sub-Saharan Africa (the highest regional rate).[3] A report on American women's experiences with birth sums up the situation quite well: "In the United States, the great majority of pregnant women are healthy and have good reason to anticipate uncomplicated childbirth."[4] Again I ask, given these facts, why are so many women so scared of birth?

An article in the Journal of Perinatal Education offers one explanation: its negative portrayal in the mainstream media. The author provides examples of births as they are portrayed on TV and explains how such shows "can single-handedly convince most women that their bodies are incapable of birthing without major medical intervention and that they would be crazy not to want all the technology they can get their hands on."[5] On TV, pregnant women are usually shown in a state of panic as they are rushed to the Emergency Room. Once at the hospital, the woman screams about the pain and demands drugs, which usually elicits a laugh in comedies. In dramas, as often as not, some

life-threatening medical emergency arises that requires a team of personnel to rush the woman to the operating room where she, her baby, or both, nearly die but are miraculously saved by some combination of modern medical technology and an attractive doctor. I'd be willing to bet that most people have seen some, if not many, variations of this chain of events on their favorite medical-themed TV show.

With this as the most common exposure women have to the birth process, it is easy to understand both women's fear of childbirth and their discomfort with homebirth. If all births were like those portrayed on TV, maternal mortality rates in the U.S. would be much higher than they actually are, and homebirth would be a pretty dicey prospect. I'm glad I know that's not the case, but I wish more women understood how safe childbirth is in the U.S. today.

In the hospital, even for what doctors describe as a "normal birth" where nothing goes wrong, the medical model relies on technology to manage the birth process. Consequently, most women who give birth in hospitals are connected to machines throughout their labor in order to allow continuous electronic fetal monitoring. Nearly half of all women who experience a hospital birth are given intravenous medication to speed up their labor; many also get an epidural for pain relief. Additionally, in the U.S., nearly one in three pregnant women deliver via a Cesarean section (C-section), although the World Health Organization estimates that C-sections are necessary in only five to ten percent of births.[6] The extremely high rate of C-sections in the U.S. is cause for serious concern; according to a recent study, a national C-section rate of over 15 percent results in more harm than good for women and their babies.[7] While this surgery can be life-saving when needed, current practices are subjecting many, many women to major abdominal surgery that they don't need.

When a woman gives birth at a birthing center or at home, as my mother did, the experience is usually very different. Non-hospital births typically rely on a midwifery model that treats pregnancy and birth as normal life events. This model includes minimizing technological interventions while identifying women who might need obstetrical attention; a model that has been shown to reduce the incidence of birth injury, trauma, and C-section.[8] But, less than one percent of births in the U.S. occur outside a hospital[9] and only a tiny fraction of non-hospital births occur at home.

Women who have homebirths often describe with appreciation the experience of going through labor in the comfort of their own home. At home a woman can eat, drink, go for a walk and if, like my mother, she wants to continue with some of her typical routines, make lunch for her son—all while in labor. Some of these activities aren't allowed in hospitals, such as eating or drinking during labor, and some just aren't possible, like cooking in your own kitchen. But, one of the key differences is that, without the constraints of the hospital setting, a woman's labor can proceed at the pace established by her body, rather than the pace established by institutional policies. This, among other things, makes unnecessary C-sections much less likely.

Homebirth is not an option (or the right option) for every woman, however. Even a woman who has a healthy, uncomplicated pregnancy might encounter a problem during labor. For this reason, it's important that women planning homebirths have the option of a safe, smooth transition to a hospital when necessary.

Recently, I attended a national summit to discuss the status of homebirth in the U.S. maternity care system, convened by a group of health care providers and advocates seeking to ensure safe maternity care. Although the summit attendees held many different views on homebirth—ranging from those who believe it is never a wise choice to those who think maternal and child health outcomes would be vastly improved if the majority of women gave birth at home—the summit focused on how to ensure safe homebirth for the women who choose it. With that shared goal, we developed and agreed on several key elements that can make homebirth a better, safer option for women, including validating midwives within the maternity care system and better integrating the maternity care system to ensure smooth transitions of care between the home and hospitals.[10] (See box.) These steps have the potential to improve maternity care for all women, and are vital to giving every woman the chance to have a happy, healthy and safe birth when, where, and how she chooses.

(To learn more, see: http://homebirthsummit.org/summit-outcomes.html.)

I feel lucky that my mother introduced me to the idea of pregnancy and birth in such a natural way, although I know that homebirth isn't for everyone, I left the summit more convinced than ever that making homebirth safer not only expands women's options for childbirth, but also can improve the whole spectrum of birth experiences and outcomes. Helping more people learn about birth as a normal part of life, not a made-for-TV drama, will change women's expectations dramatically. And, a more integrated maternity care system can make birth in a range of settings, with fewer unnecessary medical interventions, an accessible option for more women. Together, these changes can reduce the fear that is so common today and increase women's chances of having an uncomplicated and healthy birth experience.

BOX: Summary of Key Elements for Safe Homebirth

1. Recognizing the value of women-centered care in all birth settings and the importance of shared decision-making between a women and her provider

2. Integrating the maternity care system to ensure smooth transitions of care between the home and hospitals

3. Ensuring equitable, culturally appropriate maternity care in all birth settings without disparities in access, delivery of care, or outcomes

4. Validating midwives within the maternity care system

5. Increasing participation of consumers in initiatives to improve homebirth services within the maternity care system

6. Improving collaboration among all practitioners in the maternity care system by ensuring all practitioners learn about maternity care in all birth settings

7. Improving the medical liability system as a way to increase choices in pregnancy and birth including access to homebirth

8. Improving the collection of patient level data on pregnancy and birth outcomes in all birth settings

9. Recognizing the value of physiologic birth for women, babies, families and society and the value of appropriate interventions based on the best available evidence

This article was written by: Kate Ryan

Kate Ryan is a NWHN Program Coordinator

REFERENCES

1. UK National Birth and Motherhood Survey, Mother & Baby Magazine, October 2002. Available online at http://news.bbc.co.uk/2/hi/health/667444.stm.

2. U.S. Department of Health and Human Services (HHS), Health Resources and Services Administration, Maternal and Child Health Bureau, Women's Health USA 2010, Rockville, MD: HHS, 2010. http://mchb.hrsa.gov/whusa10/hstat/mh/pages/237mm.html

3. UNICEF, Progress for Children: A Report Card on Maternal Mortality, New York, NY: UNICEF, 2008. http://www.unicef.org/factoftheweek/index_50177.html.

4. Declercq, Eugene R., Carol Sakala, Maureen P. Corry, et al., Listening to Mothers II: Report of the Second National U.S. Survey of Women's Childbearing Experiences, New York, NY: Childbirth Connection and Lamaze International, October 2006.

5. Lothian, J A and A Grauer, " "Reality" Birth: Marketing Fear to Childbearing Women", The Journal of Perinatal Education 2003; 12(2): Pgs. 6-8.

6. Declercq, Eugene R., Carol Sakala, Maureen P. Corry, et al., Listening to Mothers II: Report of the Second National U.S. Survey of Women's Childbearing Experiences, New York, NY: Childbirth Connection and Lamaze International, October 2006.

7. Althabe F and JF Belizan, "Caesarean section: the paradox", The Lancet October 28, 2006; Volume 368, Issue 9546:Pgs. 1472-3.

8. Midwifery Task Force, Midwives Alliance of North America, "Midwives Model of Care", 2011. Available online at: http://mana.org/definitions.html#MMOC

9. MacDorman M, Menacker F, Declercq E. "Trends and characteristics of home and other out-of-hospital births in the United States, 1990–2006." National Vital Statistics r\Reports; Vol 58, No. 11. Hyattsville, MD: National Center for Health Statistics. March 3, 2010.

10. Home Birth Consensus Summit, The Future of Home Birth in the United States: Addressing Shared Responsibility. Common Ground Statements, 2011. Available online at:http://www.homebirthsummit.org/summit-outcomes.html

Fertility, Childbirth, and Reproductive Justice

1. What are the elements of reproductive justice beyond contraception?

2. How does technology affect ideas of childbearing?

3. In which ways do women challenge social constructs of motherhood through alternative childbirth practices?

4. What are the racial implications of babies with low birthweight described in Clay and Andrade's article? What other implications should be considered?

5. What guidelines as described in *Reproductive Justice and Childbearing Women* by the National Women's Health Network might women want to discuss with their medical provider? What elements of reproductive justice and childbirth rights would they want to include in their birth plan? How would one ensure that those elements are followed?

6. How does structural oppression, such as racism, sexism, and ableism, affect maternal healthcare?

7. Locate egg donor ads and the places they appear. Which demographics or personal characteristics are privileged? How many ads did you find and what was most attractive about the ads?

8. What complications and dangers arise with the increase of technology with regards to women's reproductive healthcare?

Aging, Ageism, and Older Women's Issues

A core theme of this book is to remember that women have various health needs and require a range of health services depending on their specific lived experiences. This chapter examines issues for middle-aged and older women. Because women outnumber men in the over-75 age group, health issues of aging are disproportionately women's health issues. Women have very different aging experiences compared to men because they live longer and their social status. For example, men are much more likely to be cared for by a loved one in their dying days; women are more likely to spend their last days or years in nursing homes.

In *Women and Ageing: The Dreaded Old Woman Fights Back*, Madge Sceriha identifies how sexism and society's lack of respect for older people come together in anophobia, the fear of old women. Although she describes this powerful social, economic, and political issue, she also emphasizes how older women are actively organizing and fighting against this oppression. This classic article continues to be relevant today when older women are lost and forgotten if they don't adhere to the immense societal pressure to be, look, and act young at any cost. For Sceriha, all women can work to end ageism, regardless of their age.

Mammography for Black Women by Dr. Tracy A. Weitz discusses the controversy over whether mammograms actually assist women in early detection of breast cancer and save lives. Despite the rise in screening Black women who have cancer, they continue to have worse health outcomes compared to Whites. Weitz suggests ongoing use of mammography "is really two-fold and has little to do with breast cancer and a lot to do with structural racism." While continued use of mammograms may have brought healthcare resources

to communities often overlooked, it is not the solution. She suggests there is more pressing need for universal access to quality primary care, financial support for community health workers, and to acknowledge the impact of structural racism.

Reconceptualizing Successful Aging Among Black Women and the Relevance of the Strong Black Woman Archetype focuses on older Black women and the mechanisms that allow them to age successfully. While the majority of gerontological literature focuses on social challenges, the authors consider the Strong Black Women archetype as a means of empowering older Black women to combat physical and mental health problems. Known for their unwavering strength and self-reliance, the Strong Black Women archetype can help define successful aging for Black women and encourage them to seek the help they deserve.

The following articles examine specific health issues and conditions that affect older women. *HIV/AIDS in Older Women: Unique Challenges, Unmet Needs* by Ramani Durvasula argues that older women are largely excluded from HIV/AIDS discourse and prevention programs. Practitioners often fail to test older women for sexually transmitted infections or acknowledge possible sexual health risks. Due to the fact that they are socially constructed as asexual, older women may feel stigmatized and fail to seek the sexual health services that they need. Durvasula urges researchers to focus on the relationship between older women and HIV/AIDS and identify useful practices for intervention and prevention.

Women and Alzheimer's Disease: A Global Epidemic, produced by The Alzheimer's Association, places women at the center of the Alzheimer's disease epidemic. According to their 2016 Alzheimer's

Disease Facts and Figures report, women are more likely to be affected by Alzheimer's disease than men. They represent approximately two-thirds of all Americans with Alzheimer's and three-fifths of Alzheimer's caregivers. Projects such as My Brain Movement fight to end the Alzheimer's epidemic on a global scale and raise awareness on the ways in which Alzheimer's disproportionately affects women.

KEEPS on Keeping On by Adriane Fugh-Berman introduces the medicalization of menopause and the marketing of hormone replacement drugs. Hormone replacement therapy has been part of a recurring pattern of untested, unneeded products being marketed to healthy women for pharmaceutical-company-inspired "medical conditions." Hormone replacement was originally marketed as a means to prevent heart attack and dementia. However, the Women's Health Initiative (WHI) study revealed the risks of such therapy. Fugh-Berman

fought to provide women with scientifically accurate information so that they could make informed decisions about their bodies. This is the information women need to know when deciding whether to use hormone therapy or alternative medicines for menopausal concerns and disease prevention.

The final article in this chapter, *Proactive Caregiving: Legal, Financial, and Emotional Supports for Family Caregivers* by Jennifer Berger, addresses aging women's caregivers. As the Baby Boomers grow older, there will be a greater demand for family caregivers, who are disproportionately women. Building off of personal experience, Berger outlines the physical, emotional, and financial burdens of caregiving. She recommends specific documents and resources to help prepare potential caregivers for their roles and to alleviate physical and emotional challenges. For her, self-care is critical when caring for older women and loved ones.

 # Women and Aging: The Dreaded Old Woman Fights Back

by Madge Sceriha

Introduction

Ageism is one sociopolitical issue which has been conspicuously absent from the agenda of mainstream feminism over the years since its second wave surged some thirty years ago. For those feminists like myself who are presently facing the challenge of growing old, there is an immediacy to our concern that this omission be addressed. One compelling reason is that, while older women are increasingly evident in demographic data describing our ageing population, they are virtually *invisible* elsewhere in literature about women except as depressed, despairing, demented burdens.

Over the last decade, however, there has been a vocal and determined resistance movement gathering

momentum among older women. To a large extent this represents a grassroots rebellion against the socially invalidating experience of older women's virtual invisibility within white, male-dominated western societies. Many within this movement have brought a feminist consciousness to the analysis of their experience and this has contributed to a more encompassing awareness of the effects of all forms of oppression on women throughout their lives. (Anike & Ariel 1987; Ford & Sinclair 1987; Job 1984; Rosenthal 1990; Scutt 1993; Walker 1985). Pioneers of second-wave feminism and public figures such as Germaine Greer (1991), Betty Friedan (1993) and Robin Morgan, the woman who coined the slogan 'the personal is political' and who is now editor-in-chief of *Ms Magazine,* have joined the ranks too and added strength to the movement.

It is still early days though, and inspiring women who are ageing to challenge the stereotype of the 'old woman' is no easy task. This chapter will highlight the insidiousness of ageism as it affects women: the 'links between the social devaluation of women and their own self deprecating beliefs' (Fook 1993, 15).

Anophobia

> When I am an old woman I shall wear purple . . .' (Jenny Joseph, cited in Martz 1991, 1)

These opening words from Jenny Joseph, in the now familiar poem 'Warning', sound as if they were written especially for feminists growing old. It certainly is a poem of protest against conventional role expectations for women and paints a picture of the old woman as defiant and outrageous. Yet such is the power of ageism that it is more than likely that the woman who emulates this poem's urgings would be ridiculed and her purpose in rebelling ignored or trivialised.

Most older women are not overtly rebellious. Instead they have learned to step out carefully amid the minefields of patriarchal capitalism and ever more so as they negotiate the added dangers of ageism. Were they to look more closely at ageism though, they would see that their experience of it is neither gender neutral nor new. In a different form, which Germaine Greer (1991, 2) has called 'anophobia', it has stalked them throughout their lives as women.

'Anophobia' means 'the irrational fear of old women'. This is the fear that has made being called an 'old woman' one of the most insulting things that can be said by one man about another man. This is the fear which, because it is internalized by women from an early age, complicates their own inevitable ageing experience. This is the fear that is in effect yet another way in which women are systematically oppressed in our white, male supremacist society. Anophobia is the fuel which feeds sexist ageism.

Anophobia is a most effective social control mechanism every time it silences the rage and pain of old women's existence as they struggle to survive against the constraints of economic, social and political marginalisation. It is effective too when it perpetuates divisiveness among women of different ages. Perhaps the worst outcome of all is its effectiveness in reinforcing fear and a sense of helplessness in women as ageing progresses and their capacity to serve others diminishes. For many, all that seems to be left for them is to passively serve out their time till death comes as a welcome release.

Serving and servicing others still characterises the work women do in the home and in the paid workforce and, although this 'women's work' has traditionally been devalued as low status in a male-defined model of work, it has provided many older women with a role identity over their lifetime. Where there is unquestioned commitment to this role, it can drain women physically and emotionally. An example of this is the work older women do in caring for a partner who is dying or who has some lingering illness requiring constant care. This work is all too easily taken for granted because most women in traditional marriages:

> . . . honour their commitment to selfless caregiving in line with religious beliefs as well as sex role expectations . . . [at the cost of] social isolation and problematic return to life outside family relations [when the caring role ends]. (Rosenthal 1990, 4)

The exploitation of women this represents is seldom if ever recognised on a societal basis nor is the work costed and thereby included as contributing to the economy. To have the courage to reject the caring role is not without its costs either, for the woman who fails to fulfil her role in selfless serving is all too often labelled selfish. This negative label is particularly effective as a means of social control when applied to women, especially those who are conditioned to put others' needs before their own.

The women's movement certainly has challenged structural inequalities with respect to work because such inequalities discount the value of what women do and consequently deny women as a social group access to economic power and independence. These structural inequalities have, however, not yet yielded to change fast enough or far enough for this to be reflected in major changes to women's identification with traditional roles. Ageing women therefore face an identity crisis when they contemplate a future in which they are increasingly likely to need the services of others rather than being the ones providing the services.

This identity crisis is exacerbated by the stereotypes which have been perpetuated under anophobic influence; stereotypes which infiltrate our awareness from an early age in fairy tales, legends, books, movies and television. Think about these all too familiar examples:

- the wicked witch with superhuman powers, sharp featured, hunched over her evil brew, cackling to herself or shrieking curses;

- this is not far removed from the feared and reviled matriarch who, with her razor-sharp tongue and control of the purse strings emasculates the males of the household and enslaves the females;

- in contrast there's the pathetic, useless, dried up, shabby shadow of a woman who is the ultimate form of female passivity and powerlessness, huddled in a lonely room waiting to die;

- then there's the old maid who, unfulfilled without a man and children in her life, is portrayed as an object of scorn or pity;

- for a good opportunity to ridicule think of Dame Edna Everage, an image created and exploited by a man which gives it just that extra impact;

- and of course there's Maggie in 'Mother and Son' whose image reminds us of our fears of becoming a burden, of losing our memories and doing outrageous things which shame our families and we're meant to laugh *at* her not *with* her;

- the best that is offered is the idealised grandmother image, but it is an image of a paragon of smiling, ever-available sacrifice whose own needs are always secondary to those of family and community.

Words too which are typically associated with old women are loaded with derision: 'dithering', 'dotty', 'doddering', 'little old lady', 'shrivelled shrew' and 'old bag' are telling examples. Woe betide her too if she's sexual because then she's grotesque or disgusting, especially if her partner is a younger man or, even more unspeakable, a woman.

Then there are the doom and gloom projections about the future sensationalised by the media which tell us that 'by the year 2021, 17% of our population will be over the age of 65' (Cross 1992, 13). We are warned that this will burden the young and strain the health services to say nothing of all the other services which will be clogged with these dependent, decrepit drains on the public purse. Let's face it though, the bulk of the older persons likely to be affected by such messages are women. It is women who are likely to spend most of our years supposedly 'past our prime' for it is suggested that 'women get pushed into the category of nonpersons our society calls older people twenty years or so before men do.' (Cross 1992, 14). Because women also live longer on average than men, we are likely to experience the loss of status associated with ageing as a double burden—it starts earlier and lasts longer. Anophobia ensures also that we are likely to experience it more intensely.

This gender dimension has until recently been largely ignored in the literature on ageing as indeed has race and ethnicity. 'Very few Aboriginal people or Torres Strait Islanders survive to old age' we are reminded in a recent report. This report reminds us also of the 'growing numbers of migrants in the older population who are increasingly . . . from non-English speaking backgrounds,' (Davison, Kendig, Stephens & Merrill 1993, 16–17). These two facts can very easily be ignored when neither of the groups concerned has yet a voice (least of all a female voice) that commands attention in male-dominated, white, English-speaking Australian society.

The dominant societal voice is rather one that sounds out loudly and clearly that to be an old woman is the pits in the destiny stakes. Searching for an identity as an old woman is therefore fraught with anxiety when selfless sacrifice appears to be the only alternative to her more blatantly negative stereotypes. All too often we defend ourselves against this anxiety with denial, and fall back on the belief that age is a state of mind not a matter of chronological years. This belief is reflected in the observation that 'most people perceive themselves as essentially younger than they are' (Greer 1991, 272) and is exploited by advertisers every time they target older people and promote their products with images that evoke fantasies of passing for or emulating youth.

Every time we succumb to such propaganda we reinforce our own internalised anophobia. This is evident with regard to health and self-care products and procedures which are promoted through association with youthful attractiveness and youthful desirability. The success of sales of pills and potions from the health food stores, pins and tucks from cosmetic surgeons, the creams and dyes from the cosmetic houses, to say nothing of weight control regimes, is founded on unrealistic expectations for miracles of repair, restoration, reconstruction and, in terms of weight, reduction. What publicity there has been about the costs in economic terms, emotional anguish and often enough, the traumatising physical consequences of these examples of the pursuit of beauty has not had a marked impact on the thriving beauty industries which benefit from women's fear of growing old.

The Beginning of the End or the End of the Beginning

It hasn't been so easy though to deny the menopause which marks the end of women's reproductive years and, it is suggested, the end of her 'prime time' as well (Cross 1992, 14). Not so easy that is until the advent of the menopause industry. Working on the premise that menopause is an endocrine deficiency disease, the medical profession with quite a little help from the media has effectively promoted the idea that what women need to carry them through the 'dreaded change of life' is a steady dose of medicalisation in the form of hormone replacement therapy (HRT). It'll calm them down, keep them cool, and even allow them to have a bleed once a month if they want.

It's certainly a lot easier for the medical profession to prescribe pills than it is for them to deal with the social reality that this is likely to be a particularly stressful time in many women's lives. One such stressful social reality is the powerful influence of anophobia. Small wonder then that the 'quick fix' promise of HRT is so widely taken up when it is presented as providing the possibility 'of eliminating menopause and keeping all women both appetising and responsive to male demand from puberty to the grave [thereby] driving the dreaded old woman off the face of the earth forever' (Greer 1992, 2).

Women are certainly not expected to think about the fact that HRT is a very lucrative product for the drug companies if they can be assured of a population of consumers with some thirty years of consuming to do from menopause to death. We're not expected to think either about the costs to women (economic, emotional and physical) of a regime

of HRT. Nor perhaps are we expected to remember that, before HRT, a woman at menopause who experienced symptoms which led her to seek out help was likely to be dismissed or trivialised, whereas now, as a potential consumer of HRT, the midlife woman is much sought after.

Nowhere is this more obvious than in the marketing of osteoporosis. In *The Menopause Industry* Sandra Coney cautions us to question the motives of that industry, in particular the pharmaceutical companies, that would have us believe that osteoporosis is a 'silent epidemic' with the potential to leave us all deformed past midlife. 'Osteoporosis sells things' she reminds us, like calcium supplements and HRT and its sales success is based on our fear of the little old lady who may turn out to be even 'littler' than our worst fears could imagine (Coney 1991, 105ff). Fear is the enemy as much as any potentially debilitating condition though, especially if we allow ourselves to be 'persuaded to feel anxious, fragile and prey to a host of unpleasant diseases [thereby] . . . worrying ourselves half to death,' (Coney 1991, 277).

We might otherwise recognise that osteoporosis could have as much to do with chronic dieting and overexercising and the tendency some women have to wear themselves out or starve themselves half to death because of an obsession with slenderness. It appears that there is advantage in the presence of a little padding as we grow older provided we also keep fit. Not only does carrying this weight benefit bone structure, it cushions any falls that could lead to fractures as well. It appears also that this padding is involved in the process of oestrogen production in our bodies after menopause. This process involves the conversion of androgens, which are produced by the ovaries and the adrenal glands, into a form of oestrogen called oestrone and this process takes place primarily in the fat of women's breasts and stomach (Coney 1991, 85, 149).

It is significant too that anophobic obsession with the idea that the young female is the yardstick of what is worthwhile and desirable in a woman is divisive and keeps women in competition with each other between and within age groupings. We must remember though that it is a particular image of the young female which is idealized. An image which, furthermore, is elusive because it is created by the media in collusion with advertisers who have no scruples about using the airbrush and computer technology to shape their models to their whim. Magazines, we are told,

> ignore older women or pretend they don't exist . . . [and] consciously or half consciously, must project the attitude that looking one's age is bad because $650 million of their ad revenue comes from people who would go out of business if visible age looked good. (Wolf 1990, 82–4)

That age is airbrushed off the faces of any older women who do happen to be featured 'has the same political echo that would resound if all positive images of blacks were routinely lightened, . . . that less is more' (Wolf 1990, 82–4).

Even within the covers of those magazines which target an older female population, the emphasis is on the message that 'it's all right to get older as long as you look as young as possible' (Gerike 1990, 42). Thus, although there are many articles featured in these magazines which take up social issues of concern to older women, they appear alongside a proliferation of advertisements in which the models are young, trim and trendy. For good measure there are the occasional accounts of celebrities like Elizabeth Taylor who at sixty still appear ever young and ravishing. It isn't surprising therefore that so many women find comfort and reassurance from being told that they've 'worn well' or they 'don't look their age' and who dread being judged as having 'let themselves go.'

There are limits to what is tolerated in the effort to pass as or emulate the young though, and this has been very clearly demonstrated in the widespread controversy attendant on the news that two postmenopausal women have given birth after undergoing fertility treatment in an Italian clinic. Reports about the international uproar these events have caused focus on concerns for the future welfare of children of an elderly mother who might die or, for some other reason, not be able to care for her children (*Townsville Bulletin*, 31 December 1993). The double standard this represents is ignored, for males past 'their prime' who father a child are more than likely to get a pat on the back because what they've done shows that there's 'life in the old dog yet'.

Within the politics of reproduction, reproductive technology has emerged as a new frontier for the women's movement in its protracted struggle against patriarchal-capitalist power and control. 'Science and commercial enterprises (forms of institutional power) join forces with ideological forms of power (the control myth of woman as mother) in their attempt to control woman's procreative power' (Rowland 1988, 163–64). Reproductive technology stands alongside the medicalisation of childbirth and menopause, the radical invasive surgery of hysterectomy and the castration of women through oophorectomy as sociopolitical issues about which we need to develop a rigorous woman-honouring 'reproductive consciousness' (Rowland 1988, 165).

We certainly need such a consciousness to counteract complacency about the effects of the removal of a woman's uterus, cervix and ovaries when she is close to menopause. The removal of these organs is often justified on the basis of the argument that they are 'useless organs, sources of potential disease and decay' (Schumacher 1990, 58). Yet evidence is accumulating that, far from being useless, these organs have lifelong structural and functional significance for women's health and wellbeing other than that associated with reproduction. Not least of the functional aspects is the part these organs play in woman's sexual pleasure from arousal to orgasm. Women have been too easily persuaded to accept the 'take it all out' technique and then later, when they experience the very real sexual losses this entails, to accept that '[s]ex is all psychological' anyway (Schumacher 1990, 55).

Seldom though have we heard it suggested that we name the indiscriminate use of medical practices and procedures that experiment on, invade, mutilate and manipulate women's bodies for what they are—another form of sexual abuse (Schumacher 1990, 64). Seldom too do we reflect on the marked contrast there is in our attitudes to the prospect of hysterectomy as opposed to mastectomy. "Hysterectomy is trivialised where mastectomy is dramatised; the visible mutilation . . . is dreaded in the same irrational proportion as the internal mutilation is courted' (Greer 1992, 52). Prescriptive body image beliefs and the sexual objectification of women once again triumph when we fail to make such connections.

Women still trust the male-dominated medical profession to give them authoritative advice. Perhaps though we should remind ourselves of the absurdity of such authority about women's reproductive processes as it fuelled nineteenth-century arguments that women should not be admitted to universities. Then it was said that women's monthly bleeding would rob their brains 'of the constant and substantial flow of blood . . . required for intellectual activity' (Scutt 1993, 3). Keeping them out once menopause removed this impediment to participation was then left to other mechanisms of social control, not least of which was anophobic-driven sexist-ageism. Even today when menopause could be perceived as the beginning of another developmental stage in women's lives, prevailing medical authority favours a deficiency-disease diagnosis.

Medical authority is a form of institutionalised power which can influence our beliefs about ourselves. Where that authority influences us to believe the ageing woman's body is deficient and her once valued organs of reproduction are useless, it becomes another source of tacit legitimation for the continued medicalisation of women's lives and the social practices which devalue older women on the basis of their perceived biological inferiority. It is as if '[o]ur society has the idea that the value of women over 40 starts dropping rapidly and makes it a reality by turning the assumptions into facts' (Anike 1987, 26).

The Dreaded Old Women Unmasked

Devaluing is a form of social abuse which is 'so systematic that it . . . is considered normal by the society at large' (Dworkin 1988, 133). Its purpose is to marginalise and disempower and it is most successful when it generates feelings of revulsion and fear of the devalued group. Anophobia is such an abuse. Its obvious expression is in the pathological representation and negative stereotyping of women's ageing. It is much less obvious and therefore more difficult to confront when it takes the form of patronising tolerance. Worst of all though is when women start to feel that they are invisible, as this tends to silence them as well. It is not uncommon for women to remark that they really became aware of feeling old when they were ignored in shops and bumped into in the street as if they weren't there. Experiences of that sort soon erode self-esteem and self-confidence, especially if there were little of either at the outset.

The life expectancy of women in white Australian society has increased by some thirty years over this century and women outnumber men in all age groups after the age of 65 (Parliamentary Report 1992, 18–19). Women are the majority of the aged population and will be into the future and that population is projected to increase dramatically.

Alarmist reports in the media about the consequences of this demographic phenomenon refer to a '. . . "time-bomb" that threatens to blow the economy to pieces' (Parliamentary Report 1992, 52). It isn't difficult to see how the fear this has generated already in our society will attach to women in particular because they live longer. The double standard which persists in granting males as they age greater status and privilege than women accentuates this possibility. It is not that males are immune to ageist oppression but there is no male equivalent of anophobia nor is the image of unattractiveness, asexuality, passivity, dependency and incompetence associated with being old thrust upon them so early nor so destructively.

A 1992 Parliamentary Report observes,

> Demographic change may expose inadequacies in economic and social institutions and practices, but the former is not in itself the problem . . . The debate over how best to run an economic system is not primarily an ageing discussion . . . the ageing of populations may have little to do with the outcome. (Parliamentary Report 1992, 68, 70)

We must therefore maintain a critical consciousness of how easily the aged (and most particularly women) could be scapegoated when politicians blame welfare spending for the country's economic crises. Our society would have more to fear if older women were to withdraw the unpaid caring work they do within family networks and as volunteers in the community which is a contribution they are likely to make as long as they are able. Research indicates that

> older people are more likely to be providers than recipients of any kinds of support . . . [In addition it seems that more than 60% of the over 65 population have no limit on their functional ability and about 30% report only some minor restrictions to their activity. (Edgar 1991, 17)

There is a danger in focusing on 'use value' as a justification for older women's right to more visibility and respect though, especially where it is so closely linked to privatisation of service provision within the family structure. Such a view constrains women who want to 'retire' from such role expectations and venture into other pursuits which interest them and negates those women who are frail or disabled. These issues are among the many which increasing numbers of older women are coming together to confront as part of an older women's movement which has the potential to become as politically significant as any of the radical movements which developed in the 1960s.

Accounts of this movement worldwide are proliferating. The Older Women's League (OWL) in America, The Older Feminist's Network and the Growing Older Disgracefully Collective in the United Kingdom, the Older Women's Network (OWN) in Australia and the Raging Grannies in Canada are examples of action groups that are inspiring older women to be who they are with courage, openness and a commitment to living more fully than they have ever before been allowed to think possible. These groups offer support and encouragement for women to explore their potential without imposing expectations for dramatic change. In such an environment it is more possible to become aware of internalised anophobia and all other forms of oppression which ageist prejudice exacerbates. They are not about establishing new stereotypes for old women for not all women have secret burning desires to abseil or bungee jump or even to join in direct social action. Not all women could, even if they wanted to, because of frailty, disability and/or economic constraints.

Many of these groups are encouraging women to write their own stories, to join in theatre workshops, to learn public speaking, to lead discussions, to learn self-defence, to be involved in environmental and peace issues and to link in with younger women's groups for events like International Women's Day and Reclaim the Night marches and rallies. Through involvement in such activities and action women can break down the barriers isolating them from each other within and between age groups, break the silence about their concerns and discover that the world of the young woman is no utopia nor is the world of the old woman necessarily a hell on earth.

That it is a hell on earth for too many is a fact that all women, both young and old, have a stake in addressing. We know that old women are likely to be victims of socio-economic violence (or what has been more euphemistically labelled the 'feminisation of poverty') because structural inequalities in our society continue to disproportionately disadvantage women throughout their lives. We know from the burgeoning literature on elder abuse that old women are often victims of emotional, physical and sexual violence just as their younger sisters are. We know that many feel isolated, lonely, hopeless and helpless because poverty, prejudice and powerlessness confine them to the margins of societal concerns. There is good reason, therefore, for all women to be actively anti-ageist and, in particular, anti-anophobic for it is an investment in their own future.

For references, see the original.

 # Mammography for Black Women: Why I Won't Be Silent Anymore

by Tracy A. Weitz

Back in February, a new study, this one published in the *British Medical Journal*, again questioned the value of screening mammography in the general population. This is a "gold standard" study with a large randomized sample followed over a significant time period: "Twenty five year follow-up for breast cancer incidence and mortality of the Canadian National Breast Screening Study: randomised screening trial."[1]

This study from Canada found no reduction in mortality among women diagnosed with breast cancer discovered with or without mammography. Breast Cancer Action immediately raised our long-standing concerns about the lack of clear benefit to screening (as opposed to diagnostic) use of mammography in the general population.[2] In responding to the study, the question was rightfully raised about why a study of almost all White women could be extrapolated to say anything about the value of mammography in the African American population.

Had I made that easy slip of assuming that studies about White women can be universalized to all women? Had I spoken for women that I do not represent, or women whose experiences I do not share? Should I temper my comments to say I think this research tells us why White women should think more critically before blindly following their doctors' recommendations that they get regular mammograms? As a White woman, should I stay silent and sit out this fight?

As I contemplated these options, I felt the tears well up in my eyes. I remember all too well what silence bought me before. My silence helped cost me my mom and it cost my mom not only her life but her dream. Diane Olds, my beloved mom, was diagnosed with breast cancer in her early 50's following a routine screening mammogram. At that time, we didn't know much about Ductal Carcinoma in Situ (DCIS) and the recommended treatment was surgery, followed by radiation and chemotherapy, and then hormonal therapy in the form of tamoxifen. Despite being a women's health activist, I didn't know much about breast cancer treatment and we dutifully complied with this recommended regime.

As the years progressed, I studied the breast cancer issue, followed the science, and engaged with leading scholars in the field. I began to question whether the mammogram that led to my mom's diagnosis was necessary and whether the cancer they found really needed to be treated. But I stayed silent. "What good would come from my raising this question?" I asked myself. By this point, my mom had decided not to complete her doctoral degree. She had found it too hard to balance treatment, teaching (she was an elementary school teacher) and data collection for her dissertation. Like many women her age, my mother had already delayed pursuing additional education until after her children were out of the house. She had always wanted to be Dr. Olds, but now, managing her health seemed more important. Furthermore my mom was a proud "breast cancer survivor." She did the walks, the runs, and her house was filled with pink ribbon paraphernalia. She believed the mammogram saved her life and was grateful.

In 2005, ten days after she started complaining of shortness of breath, I lost my mom to an aggressive uterine cancer caused by her breast cancer treatment. By then, the world knew that ten years of tamoxifen put women at risk of a horrible side effect—uterine cancers.

This is why I care so deeply about the over-diagnosis caused by routine screening mammography. While the cause of my mom's death was a very rare side effect, her death is emblematic of a larger set of harms that come when we turn healthy people into cancer patients.

The mantra "early detection saves lives" makes intuitive sense. Find breast cancer before it grows and the outcomes have to be better, right? Wrong. The science just doesn't support this narrative anymore. This latest Canadian study is one more study questioning the assumption that mammography as a screening tool reduces mortality in the general population. Additional analysis, done both in the U.S. and in Europe, finds that **most of the benefit historically attributed to screening mammography is actually the result of improvements in treatments.**

But aren't all of these studies of White women and isn't my mother's story a story of a White woman, and of White women's breast cancer? Yes, yes, and yes. But that doesn't mean that Black women should think the story is different for them.

Yes, Black women aren't included in most of the studies that show harm from mammography. But ironically, adequate numbers of Black women were not present in the studies that showed mammography might be beneficial either. Rather this latter idea was just accepted on faith with the hope that perhaps this tool could stem the higher mortality rate from breast cancer among Black women.

So here is my outrage. Black women, like White women, like all women, got sold a bill of goods. They were told that screening mammography would save their lives. Breast cancer in Black women appears earlier and is more aggressive. So it makes sense that we would think mammograms would be more beneficial in this population, even if they are not helpful in the larger population. But the evidence is just not there. At the population level, the screening rates for Black women have risen dramatically in the last decade. But the mortality rate from breast cancer has not reduced correspondently. And mammography is very bad at detecting cancers in premenopausal women, so more application in younger women doesn't help either.

I am outraged that even after this many years of knowing the limitations of mammography and the reality of higher mortality rates of breast cancer in Black women we still don't have a better screening test and we haven't figured out how to treat the bad breast cancer–the one that appears earlier and presents more aggressively, the one that Black women get more often.

So why do some hold onto mammography as critical to Black women's health with such passion? The answer is really two-fold and has little to do with breast cancer and a lot to do with structural racism. Black women have the worst health outcomes on almost all health indicators. The average life expectancy for a Black woman is five years less than for a White woman. And mammography has been the doorway into healthcare for many Black women, especially for women in their 40s and 50s who have higher rates of being uninsured than their younger counterparts.

The campaign to get Black women mammograms brought health care resources to communities long ignored by the public health sector. Free mammograms were accompanied by visits to the doctor and blood pressure checks—perhaps an even more critical healthcare intervention for this group for whom heart disease and stroke are major causes of disability. And funds were poured into communities to support community health educators who taught women not only about breast health but also about nutrition and exercise, information that contributes to health improvements of all kinds.

So I understand that recommending fewer mammograms is not a neutral issue and that overall health status is at risk when mammograms are under attack. But I don't think the solution is to continue to push mammograms for Black women. We need universal access to quality primary care; we need financial support for community health workers; we need to acknowledge that structural racism gets under the skin and contributes to poor health outcomes. However, these goals just shouldn't be part of a mammography agenda.

And I won't stay silent about mammography in Black women any longer.

There are many amazing Black women in my life who serve as my friends and mentors on all matters in life. I will look to them to tell me if I am making the mistake of speaking on their behalf, rather than what I think I'm doing today, which is speaking on behalf of good science for all women. However, in this case, if I remain silent I would just be exercising a privilege of a different kind.

This article was written by: Tracy A. Weitz, PhD, MPA, Chair of Breast Cancer Action's Board of Directors

Tracy A. Weitz is Chair of Breast Cancer Action's Board of Directors. This article was originally published on April 3, 2014, by Breast Cancer Action at http://bcaction.org/2014/04/03/ mammography-for-black-women-why-i-wont-be-silent-anymore-2 (http://bcaction.org/2014/04/03/ mammography-for-black-women-why-i-wont-be-silent-anymore-2/) and is republished with permission. ©2014, BCAction

References

1. Miller AB, Wall C, Baines CJ et. al., "Twenty five year follow-up for breast cancer incidence and mortality of the Canadian National Breast Screening Study: randomised screening trial," *BMJ* 2014;348:g366. Available online at: http://www.bmj.com/content/348/bmj.g366 (http://www.bmj.com/content/348/bmj.g366)

2. Breast Cancer Action, "Science-based Evidence Demonstrates That "Early Detection Save Lives" Is Wrong Message," Posted on February 12, 2014 at: http://bcaction.org/2014/02/12/ science-based-evidence-demonstrates-that-... (http://bcaction.org/2014/02/12/science-based-evidence-demonstrates-that-early-detection-save-lives-is-the-wrong-message/#sthash. KBUyiW3F.dpuf)

Reconceptualizing Successful Aging Among Black Women and the Relevance of the Strong Black Woman Archetype

by Tamara A. Baker, PhD,[*,1] NiCole T. Buchanan, PhD,[2] Chivon A. Mingo, PhD,[3] Rosalyn Roker, MA,[4] and Candace S. Brown, MAG, MEd[5]

Decision Editor: Barbara J. Bowers, PhD

Although there are multiple pathways to successful aging, little is known of what it means to age successfully among black women. There is a growing body of literature suggesting that black women experience a number of social challenges (sexism and racism) that may present as barriers to aging successfully. Applying aspects of the Strong Black Women ideal, into theoretical concepts of successful aging, may be particularly relevant in understanding which factors impair or promote the ability of black women to age successfully. The Strong Black Women archetype is a culturally salient ideal prescribing that black women render a guise of self-reliance, selflessness, and psychological, emotional, and physical strength. Although this ideal has received considerable attention in the behavioral sciences, it has been largely absent within the gerontology field. Nevertheless, understanding the dynamics of this cultural ideal may enhance our knowledge while developing an appreciation of the black woman's ability to age successfully. Rather than summarize the social, physical, and mental health literature focusing on health outcomes of black women, this conceptual review examines the Strong Black Women archetype and its application to the lived experiences of black women and contributions to current theories of successful aging. Focusing on successful aging exclusively among black women enhances our understanding of this group by considering their identity as women of color while recognizing factors that dictate their ability to age successfully.

Key words: Black women, Strong black women archetype, Mental and physical health, Disparities, Social inequities

There is a kind of strength that is almost frightening in Black women. It's as if a steel rod runs right through the head down to the feet.

Maya Angelou (Interview broadcast, November 21, 1973)

Challenges related to social change, exclusion, violence, discrimination, and cultural alienation impair physical and psychological well-being, and successful aging, particularly among those from underrepresented populations (Baker, Buchanan, & Spencer, 2010).

[1]Department of Psychology, University of Kansas, Lawrence. [2]Department of Psychology, Michigan State University, East Lansing. [3]Gerontology Institute, Georgia State University, Atlanta. [4]School of Aging Studies, University of South Florida, Tampa. [5]Center for Gerontology, Western Kentucky University, Bowling Green.
[*]Address correspondence to Tamara A. Baker, PhD, Department of Psychology, University of Kansas, 1415 Jayhawk Blvd., 426 Fraser Hall, Lawrence, KS 66045. E-mail: tbakerthomas@ku.edu
Received January 7 2014; Accepted October 4 2014.

Black women's marginalized social positioning puts them at an increased risk of such experiences that often results in feelings of powerlessness (Baker, Buchanan, & Corson, 2008). Yet, the buffering effects of adaptive coping behaviors and support systems may mitigate these issues (Baker et al., 2010) and create a foundation by which black women survive, live, and age (Lincoln, Taylor, & Chatters, 2003; van Olphen et al., 2003).

Despite these outcomes, there remains a lack of research identifying and examining factors that enhance (or impair) successful aging among black women. We propose that conceptualizations of successful aging will better reflect the lived experiences of black women by including relevant concepts of the Strong Black Women archetype. The Strong Black Women archetype is a cultural ideal that reflects an expectation that black women be selfless, self-reliant, psychologically and physically strong, and resilient despite the many social challenges (sexism, racism) they encounter (Beauboeuf-Lafontant, 2003 2007; Romero, 2000; Wallace, 1978). Despite its application to theories of health and social well-being, the Strong Black Women ideal has not been adequately considered in aging studies, which may limit the relevance of gerontological theory of successful aging to (older) black women.

Societal Images of Black Women

Black women have been idealized as an embodiment of stoicism and strength, which may be internalized as a positive characteristic of womanhood (Settles, Pratt-Hyatt, & Buchanan, 2008). The historical image of black women acknowledges their struggles juxtaposed against their individual and collective successes. Whether recognized for their contributions as Secretary of State or domestic worker (Allen & Chin-Sang, 1990), black women have made significant contributions to the social tapestry of the United States, with successes associated in their sense of strength (Settles et al., 2008). Yet, it has been argued that the focus on strength and perseverance has an exact affect on physical and psychological well-being, which may influence how these women age.

Showing this level of resilience may ultimately challenge their ability (and resources) to age successfully. Understanding these issues is further complicated by the limitations in being able to apply current theories of successful aging to (older) black women. This, of course, is a limited area of research that suggests the need to develop models not only describing the social, behavioral, and physical constructs by which black women age, but also, recognizing mechanisms by which this group of women age successfully, which has not been adequately addressed in the gerontology literature.

Theories of Successful Aging Across Diverse Populations

Successful aging has been well studied across majority populations; however, the applicability of successful aging concepts across older minority groups remains limited (Thorpe & Angel, 2014). Although there is increased recognition of the influence cultural, social, political, and environmental factors have on aging more generally (Crowther, Parker, Achenbaum, Larimore, & Koenig, 2002; Dillaway & Byrnes, 2009; Fry, 2012; Kelly, Martin, & Poon, 2012; Martin, Kelly, Kahana, Kahana, & Poon, 2012; Romo et al., 2012), current theory has not considered their relationship(s) to aging successfully. Despite this absence, scholars recognize the need for current successful aging criteria to include these concepts (historical, social, and cultural) (Depp & Jeste, 2006; Pruchno, Wilson-Genderson, Rose, & Cartwright, 2010; Rowe & Kahn, 1987, 1997; Strawbridge, Wallhagen, & Cohen, 2002), particularly as they address the experiences of black women.

As defined by Rowe and Kahn (and others), successful aging is more than a distinction between a pathological and nonpathological state, but rather conceded as a threefold criteria: (a) avoiding disease and disability, (b) high cognitive and physical functioning, and (c) remaining productive and actively engaged (Depp & Jeste, 2006; Kelly et al., 2012; Martin et al., 2012; Rowe & Kahn, 1987, 1997). Although regarded as the "gold standard" in how successful aging is defined, these criteria focus primarily on avoidance of disease and disability. This use of terminology implies a win/successful (i.e., healthy aging, free of disease and disability, and longevity) or lose/failure (i.e., poor health, disability, and threat to longevity) concept. Dichotomizing successful aging into such concrete categories may unintentionally isolate groups where aging successfully is an obvious misnomer.

A similar criticism has been recognized, particularly among older (minority) adults, where advanced age may place them at a greater risk for being diagnosed with multiple chronic and debilitating medical conditions (Kelly et al., 2012; Strawbridge et al., 2002). This is an important observation considering that only 12% of the older adult population are able to meet the rigors of the more traditional criteria of successful aging (McLaughlin, Connell, Heeringa, Li, & Roberts, 2010). Strawbridge and colleagues (2002) similarly suggest that when applying these established criteria, less than 20% of older adults would be considered successful agers. Both studies acknowledge that incorporating current theoretical concepts of successful aging excludes many older adults from aging successfully.

Considering the current health outcomes of black Americans (compared with other race groups), the current definition of successful aging, with its emphasis on physical health outcomes, would further marginalize an already oppressed group. Specific to black women, given the disproportionate rates of disability and chronic illness (e.g., cancer, arthritis) compared with white men and women, and black men (Andresen & Brownson, 2000; McKinnon & Bennett, 2005), the narrow definition of successful aging fails to include structural factors that influence the ability to age successfully despite these adverse health outcomes.

A series of studies from the Black Women's Health Study, for example, have shown the influence educational and economic status, discrimination, mortality, cultural background, physical activity, community resources, dietary patterns, and neighborhood characteristics have on the health of black women (Albert et al., 2010; Coogan et al., 2009, 2010; Cozier, Wise, Palmer, & Rosenberg, 2009; Phillips, Wise, Rich-Edwards, Stampfer, & Rosenberg, 2009). In recognizing these influences, a more broad definition of successful aging is needed to understand how aging is defined among this group of women.

Understanding that the more conventional definition of successful aging focuses on the maintenance of physical and cognitive health (Andresen & Brownson, 2000; McKinnon &

Bennett, 2005), scholars have begun to redefine what it means to age successfully, thereby placing less emphasis on health outcomes and more on the social and cultural factors that promote well-being (e.g., independence, spirituality, activity, service to others, and generativity) (Troutman, Nies, & Mavellia, 2011; Versey & Newton, 2013). These areas of interest reconceptualizes the idea of successful aging for black women, particularly as it relates to the critical roles independence and spirituality have in many black communities (Cernin, Lysack, & Lichtenberg, 2011; Parker et al., 2002; Romo et al., 2012; Troutman et al., 2011). Identifying existing theories addressing these constructs is only one step to understanding their influence on how diverse race groups age.

The Preventive and Corrective Proactivity model, for example, offers an inclusive and modern explanation of successful aging that recognizes health promoting behaviors as more appropriate predictors of successful aging, particularly among those with health challenges (e.g., functional impairments, comorbid conditions) (Kahana et al., 2002; Martin et al., 2012). This model attempts to account for social and health-related factors that facilitate and/or hinder successful aging.

Yet, despite attempts to broaden how successful aging is defined, gerontological theory has failed to provide tangible explanations of what is meant to age successfully among dually marginalized groups. As a result, little is known regarding appropriate markers to successful aging among black women. To broaden our understanding of this concept, we need to incorporate constructs that are both culturally relevant and gender specific. The Strong Black Women archetype is an evolving ideal that may begin to address this need, thereby augmenting our understanding of what it means to age successfully among a racially diverse group of women.

Strong Black Woman Archetype

The Strong Black Woman (SBW) archetype is a cultural ideal that portrays black women as strong, self-reliant, nurturing, resilient, and invulnerable to psychological or physical challenges (Woods, 2013). This ideal intersects identities as a woman and as a black person, thereby representing a unique collection of experiences, expectations, and standards that differ from those of either white women or black men (Woods, 2013). Significance of this archetype suggests an internalization as an ideal that many black women strive to achieve, which may promote effective coping despite ensuing hardships. This archetype, however, can also be problematic as it narrowly defines acceptable behavior, where black women not only be self-reliant but also suppress any outward appearance of physical or emotional distress (Jones & Shorter-Gooden, 2003). This may ultimately present as being unrealistic and self-defeating (Mitchell & Herring, 1998). Yet, this is often seen when black women appear to be physically and emotionally strong, and a source of support to others, while fulfilling the responsibilities of homemaker, parent, and partner and simultaneously suppressing any vulnerabilities and denying their own pain, suffering, and emotions (Jackson, 2011). Maintaining this façade may interact with social and economic demands that predispose black women to greater psychological distress and negative health outcomes (Beauboeuf-Lafontant, 2009). This may be especially relevant among older black women who typically experience comorbid health conditions, reduced incomes, and other related stressors of aging.

With this argument, the self-discrepancy theory suggests that when an individual's daily experiences differ from one's perceived ideal, individuals are more prone to experiencing disappointment, a sense of failure, and depression (Higgins, 1987). This definition clearly shows that internalizing the SBW archetype may create such a discrepancy, where the expectation of self-reliance not only facilitates negative outcomes (e.g., depression) but also contributes to the underutilization of needed (mental health) services (Beauboeuf-Lafontant, 2007; Himle, Baser, Taylor, Campbell, & Jackson, 2009; Williams et al., 2007; Wise, Adams-Campbell, Palmer, & Rosenberg, 2006). This may be the case, particularly for black women, who feel both an obligation to family and the community, while attempting to maintain her own well-being (Taylor, Chatters, Woodward, & Brown, 2013).

Recognizing its impact on psychological well-being, internalizing the SBW ideal may similarly promote negative outcomes on physical health (Baker et al., 2010). Studies indicate that the need to maintain an appearance of strength and resilience may contribute to recurrent illnesses (Jackson,

2011). Specifically, the General Adaptation Syndrome (Selye, 1979) suggests that when an individual is presented with a stressful event(s) (e.g., financial strain and familial obligations) over a period of time, his/her resources to effectively cope with the stress(or) become depleted. Moreover, the biological systems that buffer the effects of acute stress may worsen health outcomes, especially when the stress becomes chronic (Gruenewald & Seeman, 2010; Jackson, Knight, & Rafferty, 2010). This is all the more apparent among black women who are at a higher risk for experiencing multiple forms of chronic stressors because of their membership in more than one socially marginalized group (e.g., women and racial minority) (Beal, 1970; Bowleg, 2008; King, 1988).

Positive Aspects of the SBW Ideal and Successful Aging

The SBW archetype can be dually recognized as a mechanism of promotion or as an obstacle to achieving total wellbeing. Yet, as the black woman ages, this ideal takes on the characteristics of yet another described archetype (i.e., the Matriarch), where previous lived events may serve as a source of strength that contextualizes her present day-to-day experiences (Sewell, 2012).

The Matriarch image similarly yields a sense of perseverance, strength, and optimism. Its prescribed ideal has further allowed black women to remain steadfast despite the dual oppressions of racism and sexism (Ladner, 1971; Romero, 2000). As such, from a developmental standpoint, black girls are (often) reared to embrace the SBW archetype (and ultimately the Matriarch ideal) and see their ability to maintain a stance of unwavering strength as an essential component of their identity and connectedness to others (Morgan, 1999). This is all the more important as generations black women maintain a sense of dignity while reflecting on their lives and contributions to their families and communities.

Future Implications of Successful Aging Among Black Women

Few studies have examined successful aging as it applies to black women. The successful aging concept has largely been equated with being physically and psychologically healthy, thereby marginalizing those with less than optimal health. This perspective not only ignores the means by which black women age but more importantly reflects a failure to incorporate culturally relevant constructs into behavioral interventions. Therefore, such, future efforts are needed to determine how social, cultural, and historical factors change the meaning of successful aging, where emphasis is focused more on what a person can do, rather than what s/he cannot do.

Similarly, efforts are needed to define healthy aging among black women who incorporate viewpoints of the SBW archetype into their daily lives. A positive consequence of internalizing the SBW ideal is that black women report less conflict when their multiple roles, as a nurturer and economic provider, are integrated instead of disparate (Littlefield, 2003). Endorsement of this cultural archetype may also promote resilience by providing inspiration and encouragement in increasing one's sense of control and confidence when faced with obstacles (Harrington, 2007; Harris-Lacewell, 2001; Littlefield, 2003).

To move the gerontology field forward, it is important to provide training (to health care providers, therapists, researchers, theorist, etc.) on the relevance of the SBW ideal and the impact it has on healthy living and aging. This level of awareness provides a mechanism by which to understand, rather than pathologize, a woman's endorsement of this ideal and how it may serve as a positive coping resource to aging successfully despite its dual interpretations.

Another area that should be considered is how the SBW archetype is assessed across varying disciplines. Proper measurement of the SBW ideal may determine how strongly a woman endorses this gender role (or certain aspects of it) and how it may predict and/or dictate certain help-seeking and coping behaviors. Knowing this information may allow for more individually tailored interventions that promote healthy living (and aging) among black women.

These efforts should, however, follow extant work of others (e.g., Parks, 2010; Thomas, Witherspoon, Karen, & Speight, 2004; Woods, 2013) who serve as facilitators to understanding the SBW ideal and how these concepts may be applied to defining successful aging among black women. Understanding the application of this ideal may provide black women with the strength to seek (health-related) interventions early while recognizing the more positive aspects of what it means to be "strong" without jeopardizing one's quality of life or well-being.

Conclusion

Despite the dual context of the SBW archetype, the implications of this ideal are generally positive (Beauboeuf-Lafontant, 2007; Harris-Lacewell, 2001) and may serve as a mechanism by which successful aging is defined among black women. This cultural image encourages independence of black women (Littlefield, 2003) and provides a mechanism to cope with race- and gender-based victimization (Etowa, Keddy, Egbeyemi, & Eghan, 2007).

Given black women's current social positioning, it is important that those focusing on the needs of older adults actively incorporate theories of successful aging that are grounded in black women's identities both as a woman and as a person of color. Such an approach will augment our understanding on their day-to-day experiences and more accurately reflect the raced and gendered context of their lives. Toward this goal, it is necessary that gerontological theory include understanding how social, cultural, behavioral, and environmental constructs affect physical health and psychological well-being while guiding policy, health care services, and research among diverse race and gendered populations. Including concepts of the SBW archetype into current theories of successful aging may begin to address questions of how socialization patterns characterize the experiences of older black women while promoting the confidence and ability to age successfully among current and future generations of women.

Funding

Dr. Baker was however, supported by the National Cancer Institute (K01CA131722-01A1, PI) at the time that the manuscript was written and accepted.

Acknowledgment

The authors declare no financial or nonfinancial competing interests.

References

Albert, M. A., Cozier, Y. C., Ridker, P. M., Glynn, R. J., Rose, L., & Rosenberg, L. (2010). Perceptions of race/ethnic discrimination in relation to mortality among Black women: Results from the Black Women's Health Study. *Archives of Internal Medicine*, **170**, 896–904. doi:10.1001/archinternmed.2010.116

Allen, K. R., & Chin-Sang, V. (1990). A lifetime of work: The context and meanings of leisure for aging black women. *The Gerontologist*, **30**, 734–740. doi:10.1093/geront/30.6.734

Andresen, E. M., & Brownson, R. C. (2000). Disability and health status: Ethnic differences among women in the United States. *Journal of Epidemiology and Community Health*, **54**, 200–206. doi:10.1136/jech.54.3.200

Baker, T. A., Buchanan, N. T., & Corson, N. (2008). Factors influencing chronic pain intensity in older black women: Examining depression, locus of control, and physical health. *Journal of Women's Health*, **17**, 869–878. doi:10.1089/jwh.2007.0452

Baker, T. A., Buchanan, N. T., & Spencer, T. R. (2010). Disparities and social inequities: Is the health of African American women still in peril? *Ethnicity & Disease*, **20**, 304–309. ISSN:1049-510X.

Beal, F. M. (1970). Double jeopardy: To be Black and female. In T. Cade (Ed.), *The Black woman: An anthology* (pp. 90–100). New York: Signet.

Beauboeuf-Lafontant, T. (2003). Strong and large Black women? Exploring relationships between deviant womanhood and weight. *Gender & Society*, **17**, 111–121. doi:10.1177/0891243202238981

Beauboeuf-Lafontant, T. (2007). You have to show strength: An exploration of gender, race, and depression. *Gender & Society*, **21**, 28–51. doi:10.1177/0891243206294108

Beauboeuf-Lafontant, T. (2009). *Behind the mask of the strong black women: Voice and the embodiment of a costly performance*. Philadelphia: Temple University Press.

Bowleg, L. (2008). When black + lesbian + woman ≠ black lesbian woman: The methodological challenges of qualitative and quantitative intersectionality research. *Sex Roles*, **59**, 312–325. doi:10.1007/s11199-008-9400-z

Cernin, P. A., Lysack, C., & Lichtenberg, P. A. (2011). A comparison of self-rated and objectively measured successful aging constructs in an urban sample of African American older adults. *Clinical Gerontologist*, **34**, 89–102. doi:10.1080/07317115.20 11.539525

Coogan, P. F., Cozier, Y. C., Krishnan, S., Wise, L. A., Adams-Campbell, L. L., Rosenberg, L., & Palmer, J. R. (2010). Neighborhood socioeconomic status in relation to 10-year weight gain in the Black Women's Health Study. *Obesity (Silver Spring, Md.)*, **18**, 1105–1117. doi:10.1038/oby.2010.69

Coogan, P. F., White, L. F., Adler, T. J., Hathaway, K. M., Palmer, J. R., & Rosenberg, L. (2009). Prospective study of urban form and physical activity in the Black Women's Health Study. *American Journal of Epidemiology*, **17**, 1105–1117. doi:10.1093/aje/kwp264

Cozier, Y. C., Wise, L. A., Palmer, J. R., & Rosenberg, L. (2009). Perceived racism in relation to weight change in the Black Women's Health Study. *Annals of Epidemiology*, **19**, 379–387. doi:10.1016/j.annepidem.2009.01.008

Crowther, M. R., Parker, M. W., Achenbaum, W. A., Larimore, W. L., & Koenig, H. G. (2002). Rowe and Kahn's model of successful aging revisited: Positive spirituality—The forgotten factor. *The Gerontologist*, **42**, 613–620. doi:10.1093/geront/42.5.613

Depp, C. A., & Jeste, D. V. (2006). Definitions and predictors of successful aging: A comprehensive review of larger quantitative studies. *The American Journal of Geriatric Psychiatry*, **14**, 6–20. doi:10.1097/01.JGP.0000192501.03069.bc

Dillaway, H. E., & Byrnes, M. (2009). Reconsidering successful aging: A call for renewed and expanded academic critiques and conceptualizations. *Journal of Applied Gerontology*, **28**, 702–722. doi:10.1177/0733464809333882

Etowa, J., Keddy, B., Egbeyemi, J., & Eghan, F. (2007). Depression: The 'invisible grey fog' influencing the midlife health of African Canadian women. *International Journal of Mental Health Nursing*, **16**, 203–213. doi:10.1111/j.1447-0349.2007.00469.x

Fry, C. L. (2012). *Paper 4: Social structure and successful aging*. Athens, GA: University of Georgia Healthy & Successful Aging Clearinghouse. Retrieved from http://healthyandsucces sfulaging.wordpress.com/2012/11/12/paper-4-social-structure-and-successful-aging/

Gruenewald, T. L., & Seeman, T. E. (2010). Stress and aging: A biological double jeopardy? *Annual Review of Gerontology & Geriatrics*, **30**, 155–177. doi:10.1891/0198-8794.30.155

Harrington, E. F. (2007). Binge eating and the "Strong Black Woman": An explanatory model of binge eating in African American women. Unpublished dissertation, Kent State University, Ohio.

Harris-Lacewell, M. (2001). No place to rest: African American political attitudes and the myth of Black women's strength. *Women & Politics*, 23, 1–33. doi:10.1300/J014v23n03_01

Higgins, E. T. (1987). Self-discrepancy: A theory relating self and affect. *Psychological Review*, **3**, 319–340. doi:10.1037/0033-295X.94.3.319

Himle, J. A., Baser, R. E., Taylor, R. J., Campbell, R. D., & Jackson, J. S. (2009). Anxiety disorders among African Americans, blacks of Caribbean descent, and non-Hispanic whites in the United States. *Journal of Anxiety Disorders*, **23**, 578–590. doi:10.1016/j. janxdis.2009.01.002

Jackson, J. S., Knight, K. M., & Rafferty, J. A. (2010). Race and unhealthy behaviors: Chronic stress, the HPA axis, and physical and mental health disparities over the life course. *American Journal of Public Health*, **100**, 933–939. doi:10.2105/AJPH.2008.143446

Jackson, O. (2011). From strong Black women to womanist: An Afrocentric approach to understanding perspectives of strengths, life experiences, and coping mechanisms of single, African American custodial grandmothers (Doctoral dissertation). Retrieved from ProQuest Dissertation and Theses database. (UMI No. 3452837).

Jones, C., & Shorter-Gooden, K. (2003). *Shifting: The double lives of Black women in America*. New York: Harper Collins.

Kahana, E., Lawrence, R. H., Kahana, B., Kercher, K., Wisniewski, A., Stoller, E., . . . Stange, K. (2002). Long-term impact of preventive proactivity on quality of life of the old-old. *Psychosomatic Medicine*, **64**, 382–394. ISSN:0033-3174.

Kelly, N., Martin, P., & Poon, L. (2012). *Paper 2: Future directions in successful aging—Realized or remaining?* Athens, GA: University of Georgia Healthy & Successful Aging Clearinghouse. Retrieved from http://healthyand-successfulaging.wordpress.com/2012/11/12/future-directions-in-successful-aging-realized-or-remaining/

King, D. K. (1988). Multiple jeopardy, multiple consciousness: The context of Black feminist ideology. *Signs*, **14**, 42–72. doi:10.1086/494491

Ladner, J. A. (1971). *Tomorrow's tomorrow: The Black woman*. Garden City, NY: Doubleday & Co.

Lincoln, K. D., Taylor, R. J., & Chatters, L. M. (2003). Correlates of emotional support and negative interaction among older Black Americans. *The Journals of Gerontology. Series B: Psychological Sciences and Social Sciences*, **58**, S225–S233. doi:10.1093/geronb/58.4.S225

Littlefield, M. B. (2003). A womanist perspective for social work with African American women. *Social Thought*, **22**, 3–17. doi:10.1080/15426432.2003.9960354

Martin, P., Kelly, N., Kahana, E., Kahana, B., & Poon L. W. (2012). *Paper 1: Defining successful aging: A tangible or elusive concept?* Athens, GA: University of Georgia Healthy & Successful Aging Clearinghouse. Retrieved from http://healthyandsuccessfulaging.word-press.com/2012/11/12/paper-1-defining-successful-aging-a-tangible-or-elusive-concept/

McKinnon, J. D., & Bennett, C. E. (2005). *We the people: Black in the United States. US Census Bureau 2000 Special Reports*. Retrieved from http://www.census.gov/prod/2005pubs/censr-25.pdf

McLaughlin, S. J., Connell, C. M., Heeringa, S. G., Li, L. W., & Roberts, J. S. (2010). Successful aging in the United States: Prevalence estimates from a national sample of older adults. *The Journals of Gerontology. Series B: Psychological Sciences and Social Sciences*, **65**, 216–226. doi:10.1093/geronb/gbp101

Mitchell, A., & Herring, K. (1998). *What the blues is all about: Black women overcoming stress and depression*. New York: Perigee.

Morgan, J. (1999). *When chickenheads come home to roost: My life as a hip-hop feminist*. New York: Touchstone.

Parker, M. W., Bellis, J. M., Bishop, P., Harper, M., Allman, R. M., Moore, C., & Thompson, P. (2002). A multidisciplinary model of health promotion incorporating spirituality into a successful aging intervention with African American and white elderly groups. *The Gerontologist*, **42**, 406–415. doi:10.1093/geront/42.3.406

Parks, S. (2010). *Fierce angels: The strong black women in America life and culture*. New York: One World/Ballantine Books.

Phillips, G. S., Wise, L. A., Rich-Edwards, J. W., Stampfer, M. J., & Rosenberg, L. (2009). Income incongruity, relative household income, and preterm birth in the Black Women's Health Study. *Social Science & Medicine*, **68**, 2122–2128. doi:10.1016/j. socscimed.2009.03.039

Pruchno, R. A., Wilson-Genderson, M., Rose, M., & Cartwright, F. (2010). Successful aging: Early influences and contemporary characteristics. *The Gerontologist*, **50**, 821–833. doi:10.1093/geront/gnq041

Romero, R. E. (2000). The icon of the strong Black woman: The paradox of strength. In L. C. Jackson & B. Greene (Eds.), *Psychotherapy with African American women: Innovations in psychodynamic perspective and practice*. New York: Guilford Press.

Romo, R. D., Wallhagen, M. I., Yourman, L., Yeung, C. C., Eng, C., Micco, G., . . . Smith, A. K. (2012). Perceptions of successful aging among diverse elders with late-life disability. *The Gerontologist*, **53**, 939–949. doi:10.1093/geront/gns160

Rowe, J. W., & Kahn, R. L. (1987). Human aging: Usual and successful. *Science (New York, N.Y.)*, **237**, 143–149. doi:10.1126/science.3299702

Rowe, J. W., & Kahn, R. L. (1997). Successful aging. *The Gerontologist*, **37**, 433–440. doi:10.1093/geront/37.4.433

Selye, H. (1979). Stress and the reduction of distress. *Journal of the South Carolina Medical Association*, **75**, 562–566. doi:10.1093/geront/37.4.433

Settles, I. H., Pratt-Hyatt, J. S., & Buchanan, N. T. (2008). Through the lens of race: Black and White women's perceptions of womanhood. *Psychology of Women Quarterly*, **32**, 454–468. doi:10.1111/j.1471-6402.2008.00458.x

Sewell, C. J. P. (2012). Mammies and matriarchs: Tracing images of the black female in popular culture 1950s to present. *Journal of African American Studies*, **17**, 308–326. doi:10.1007/s12111-012-9238-x

Strawbridge, W. J., Wallhagen, M. I., & Cohen, R. D. (2002). Successful aging and well-being: Self-rated compared with Rowe and Kahn. *The Gerontologist*, **42**, 727–733. doi:10.1093/geront/42.6.727

Taylor, R. J., Chatters, L. M., Woodward, A. T., & Brown, E. (2013). Racial and ethnic differences in extended family, friendship, fictive kin and congregational informal support networks. *Family Relations*, **62**, 609–624. doi:10.1111/fare.12030

Thomas, A. J., Witherspoon, K. M., Karen, M., & Speight, S. L. (2004). Toward the development of the stereotypic roles for Black Women Scale. *Journal of Black Psychology*, **30**, 426–442. doi:10.1177/0095798404266061

Thorpe, R., & Angel, J. (2014). Introduction: Sociology of minority aging. In K. Whitfield & T. Baker (Eds.), *Handbook of minority aging* (pp. 381–385). New York: Springer.

Troutman, M., Nies, M. A., & Mavellia, H. (2011). Perceptions of successful aging in Black older adults.

Journal of Psychosocial Nursing and Mental Health Services, **49**, 28–34. doi:10.3928/02793695-20101201-01

van Olphen, J., Schulz, A., Israel, B., Chatters, L., Klem, L., Parker, E., & Williams, D. (2003). Religious involvement, social support, and health among African-American women on the east side of Detroit. *Journal of General Internal Medicine*, **18**, 549–557. doi:10.1046/j.1525-1497.2003.21031.x

Versey, H. S., & Newton, N. J. (2013). Generativity and productive pursuits: Pathways to successful aging in late midlife African American and White women. *Journal of Adult Development*, **20**, 185–196. doi:10.1007/s10804-013-9170-x

Wallace, M. ([1978] 1990). *Black macho and the myth of the superwoman*. New York: Verso.

Williams, D. R., González, H. M., Neighbors, H., Neese, R., Ableson, J. M., Sweetman, J., & Jackson, J. S. (2007). Prevalence and distribution of major depressive disorder in African Americans, Caribbean Blacks, and non-Hispanic Whites. *Archives of General Psychiatry*, **64**, 305–315. doi:10.1001/archpsyc.64.3.305

Wise, L. A., Adams-Campbell, L. L., Palmer, J. R., & Rosenberg, L. (2006). Leisure time physical activity in relation to depressive symptoms in the Black Women's Health Study. *Annals of Behavioral Medicine*, **32**, 68–76. doi:10.1207/s15324796abm3201_8

Woods, K. C. (2013). The strong Black woman archetype and intentions to seek therapy for depression: A cultural application of the theory of planned behavior. Unpublished doctoral dissertation, Michigan State University, East Lansing, MI.

HIV/AIDS in Older Women: Unique Challenges, Unmet Needs

by Ramani Durvasula

California State University Los Angeles

As persons living with HIV/AIDS live longer, both the prevalence and incidence of HIV infection in older women is expected to increase, and this review presents a model and review of the extant literature on older women with HIV/AIDS in the United States. Older women are rarely addressed in the discourse about HIV risk and prevention, and their concerns are often missed by risk-reduction programs that typically target men and younger adults. Societal biases around aging can compound factors such as stigma and disclosure for older women. Primary care providers are often not recommending routine HIV testing to older women, or addressing the impact of age-related physiological changes on risk and sexual health. Many older women may be starting new relationships, so it is important that providers understand the relational variables specific to this group of women. Empirical research focused on the needs of older women, and recognition of the diverse composition and needs of this group, are needed to inform prevention, intervention, and best practices with this population of women.

Yolanda Diaz, 50, is experiencing a joy she never expected: menopause. When she first received her AIDS diagnosis in 1989, she had no interest in treatment—instead she smoked more crack and heroin, bounced in and out of prison, and let the father of her children raise them. But age and the disease have mellowed her. Now she follows her regimen and works for an AIDS organization called Iris House, performing interventions for women with addictions. AIDS has given her life meaning and community. "Man, I'm going to be 51," she said, lingering over the number like a fresh miracle. "I don't think I'm going to die from HIV and AIDS. But in the long run, I am going to die from O.I.'s, from opportunistic infections. I just don't think about it on a daily basis."[1]

As Ms. Diaz's story illustrates, HIV infection and AIDS in older women represents a longer story; typically, these women's stories are nuanced narratives of relationships, families, children, stigma, illness, substance use, and the evolution of the illness as a person ages. The clinical snapshots often generated of women living with HIV/AIDS miss the myriad factors that can change over a lifetime and impact health, wellness, and life. Older adults with HIV have been termed the "unserved, unseen, and unheard,"[2] a characterization that is even more pronounced for older women with HIV. The relative dearth of literature addressing women is notable, and remains a major knowledge gap, particularly as the current population of HIV-seropositive women ages, and we observe more incident infections in women over 50.

The shifting demographic of HIV/AIDS is best manifested in older adults. It is predicted that by 2015, 50% of all cases of HIV/AIDS in the United States will be in persons over the age of 50. At the end of 2009, over 50,000 women over the age of 50 are HIV seropositive.[3] These shifts are being evidenced differentially in men and women. Since the beginning of the HIV epidemic, women have manifested lower rates of infection, and this has resulted in a relative dearth of research and targeted clinical care for women. The pocketed disproportionalities of the distribution of infection (eg, the proportion of African American women represented in the

overall epidemiology of the disease), as well as the disparate types of stressors, treatments, and experiences of HIV-infected women (eg, care-giving duties, implications for reproduction, stigma related issues) call for more research not only on women, but with a specific focus on older women who bring variegated experiences.[4]

In older adults (for purposes of this article, older adults will be defined as those adults over the age of 50), the shifts in epidemiology are notable. Rates of infection in women age 50 and over remained stable from 2007–2010, with incidence rates during that time period for women of approximately 4.2/100,000, with incidence rates for men at 13.6/100,000[5] and a similar trend is observed for prevalence rates at the end of 2009 in this population (women 113.2/100,000; men 476.3/100,000). Women over the age of 50 are largely contracting HIV through heterosexual contact, and in incident infections in the period of 2007–2010, 82% were attributed to heterosexual infection, while prevalence rates reveal that 66% of infections were due to heterosexual infection. Older women evidenced a higher percentage increase in deaths due to HIV compared to men (32% increase for women, 18% for men).

These prevalence statistics suggest that while older men are still disproportionately represented in the epidemiological data on HIV/AIDS in older adults, the ground is shifting for women, who may also fare more poorly with the illness, and bring different types of psychosocial and psychological burdens. However, little research exists that focuses solely on older women living with HIV/AIDS or on risk behaviors in older women. The advent and evolution of better treatments for HIV implies that as survival times for all individuals with HIV increase, the confluence of health problems due to HIV/AIDS as well as normal aging is going to be an issue for both men and women. As the issue of older adults, and particularly older women is addressed via intervention and prevention programs, there must be recognition of two distinct groups—those who became infected at a younger age and are growing old with HIV/AIDS and those who are becoming newly infected over the age of 50.[6] Both groups bring different clinical challenges in terms of prevention, testing, and monitoring, but regardless of age at the time of infection, as the HIV-seropositive population ages—the burden on the health care system will proliferate and models of care delivery tailored to older women will be needed.

Consistently, there has been significantly less empirical literature focusing on the psychological, psychiatric, and psychosocial needs of women, as well as the unique medical and biological vulnerabilities both HIV-infected women and women at risk for HIV face. This has resulted in delays in treatment, as well as tailored prevention and intervention programs for women. In addition, the entire population of men and women with HIV is living longer and getting older. There is an even greater dearth of literature addressing women over 50 living with HIV. This review endeavors to address key issues in understanding key issues in HIV/AIDS in older women: (a) sexual risk; (b) testing; (c) primary care; (d) neuropsychiatric issues; (e) psychosocial factors (f) substance use/abuse; and (g) targeted intervention. These issues are also considered within a contextualized framework of structural variables including ageism, stigma, and power/oppression. The initial literature review focused on literature published since 2000 to account for the advent of highly active antiretroviral therapy. Because of the relative paucity of literature on older women, older empirical studies were pulled to round out understanding of key concepts as needed.

The literature review was conducted using multiple search databases to ensure coverage of research deriving from multiple disciplines related to this topic. Specifically, the search databases included AccessMedicine, PILOTS Database, Google Scholar, ProQuest Psychology Database, PsycArticles, PsycINFO, PubMed (includes MEDLINE) and employed keywords and various combinations of search terms as follows: women, older, elderly, HIV, AIDS. The decision to choose articles published in 2000 and later was largely driven by the fact that treatment, health outcomes, and survival times in persons living with HIV/AIDS shifted significantly after the mid-1990s with the advent of highly active antiretroviral therapies, and this choice of publication date was meant to draw from literature that is congruent with the contemporary prevention and intervention environment for HIV/AIDS. Additional and often older literature was then utilized to build upon points raised by studies focusing on older adults, or to highlight issues specific to women, or specific subpopulations of women, and to address the contextual factors listed above. Epidemiology statistics were derived from CDC publications and data. After ruling out studies that were deemed inappropriate for our focus (eg, international samples, younger women, men) we selected roughly 75 articles to use for this review.

Conceptual Model

Based on the extant literature, figure 1 depicts the three key issues to address in older women living with HIV/AIDS (a) care; (b) prevention; and (c) comorbidities. Most importantly, this model also recognizes that these three key elements must always be viewed within the contexts of issues specific to this group of women. Given that intersectionality of multiple statuses, as well as the societal context in which these contexts occur have direct impacts on the experience of older women with HIV/AIDS—each of the issues put forth in the article will address the reciprocal relationship between these individual factors and the larger context.

Flawed Assumptions

The research literature and data from primary care together reveal assumptions that can have deleterious or downright dangerous impacts for the care of older women at risk for HIV/AIDS or who may already be infected. Foremost among these are: (a) older women do not have sex; and (b) older women don't know and don't want to talk about HIV/AIDS. The disconnect between valuing a sex life in a culture that "de-sexualizes" older women and the attendant shame of talking about having sex, compounded by issues of stigma about HIV results in an unfortunate synergy that can make older women reluctant to discuss issues such as sex or HIV/AIDS.[7] There is a robust literature suggesting that among older adults, both men and women still want to have sex, are having sex, and want to talk about sex with their healthcare providers, but often look to healthcare providers to start the discussion.[8–10] In addition, flawed assumptions about the uniformity of older women with HIV/AIDS can be damaging. Older women with HIV/AIDS may not only be ethnic minority group members, but also may be sexual minorities or disabled, and carried these statuses at a time when discrimination and severe societal approbation resulted in a lifetime of oppression, stress, isolation, and in some cases violence and trauma. Attempts at progressive legislation and more open dialogue about equality, acceptance and access were simply often not part of the developmental histories of these women, and continuing to maintain stereotyped assumptions about these women only perpetuates ignorance of their experience.

Older adults with HIV often must face down two chronic sources of stigma: HIV seropositivity and ageist biases.[11,12] Ageism is a pervasive influence in our culture and promulgated through stereotyping, media, and pejorative attitudes toward older adults. Given the overfocus on sexuality and appearance as a salient characteristic in women, ageist beliefs toward women can have deleterious impacts on identity, self esteem, and engagement in health care. In a series of qualitative interviews conducted by Emlet et al[11] with a small sample of older adults living with HIV/AIDS (N = 8), women revealed that rejection, stereotyping, and isolation emerged as intersecting themes of HIV stigma and ageism. Of note, HIV serostatus may be but one of many stigmas that older HIV infected women may struggle with. For example, older lesbian and bisexual women in particular came of age in a time

when criminalization and stigmatization of same-sex relationships were endemic and identities were forced to be closeted from society and family. Such stigmatized identities are often repeated in multiple ways for older women whether as a function of sexual orientation, ethnic minority status, disability status, HIV serostatus and older age. While there may have been greater evolution in societal acceptance of some of these statuses, it is critical to remain mindful of the fact that older women came of age at a time when these statuses placed them more acutely in the crosshairs of stigma and isolation.[13]

HIV Testing in Older Women

While the CDC recommends regular HIV/AIDS testing in persons up to the age of 64,[14] few older adults report being offered testing. Women over the age of 50 may delay HIV testing, even in the face of symptoms, because in older adults, symptoms may be interpreted as indicative of other health conditions.[15] In one community sample of 101 older adults (70% women), 90% reported that their health care providers had never discussed HIV or other sexually transmitted infections (STIs) with them.[16] Overall, research suggests that 15%–30% of women ages 55 and older have previously been tested for HIV.[16] Rates of HIV testing in the population indicate that 44% of adults have been tested during their lifetime, but only 10%–15% of those 45–64 years of age have undergone testing,[17] with some studies reporting rates as low as 3% of older samples receiving a recommendation for testing.[16] When older adults are tested, they are often tested later in the course of HIV, and are more likely to have opportunistic infections, progress more rapidly to AIDS, or die within a year of HIV diagnosis. As such, testing of older adults is essential to manage new infections in older adults and mitigate morbidity and mortality in those who are infected.

Older women themselves may not perceive themselves as being at risk and simply report a lack of interest in being tested. Akers et al[18] found that 71% of women in their sample were not interested in testing despite nearly 50% having moderate to high levels of lifetime risk and exposure. This also intersects with patient reports that less than 25% experienced a provider ever recommending HIV testing.[18] Risk-based screening may not

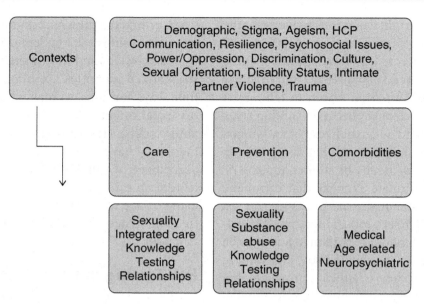

Figure 1 Contextualized Model for HIV/AIDS Care and Prevention for Older Women.

be sufficient in this population as women's perceptions of risk are not always accurate, and older women's motivation for pursuing HIV testing is influenced not only by knowledge about HIV but also perceptions and misperceptions about risk of contracting the virus and actual risk status. When comparing cohorts of older women to younger women, especially when older women evidence patterns of less drug use, fewer sex partners, and lowered likelihood of having an STI, there may be an attendant lowered perception of risk and less opportunities in which testing is offered, which can result in delays in diagnosis and treatment.[19]

Shifts in Relationship Factors

Midlife women are more likely to have had changes in relationship status (eg, divorce, separation, or death of a partner) and as such may be more likely to acquire new partners, but may be doing so after a long period of not seeking new partners.[20] In our data on 71 HIV-positive women, 67% of older women reported that they were not in a committed relationship compared to 38% of younger women.[21] Older women in newer relationships (6 months duration or shorter) were more likely to report having multiple partners.[22] These women may be less efficacious in discussing issues such as HIV serostatus, protection against HIV and STIs, and even in the development of new relationship dynamics that can facilitate or hamper healthy

sexual communication.[20] Relational variables such as trust, dependence on a partner, and taking personal responsibility for obtaining condoms have all been associated with safer sex decisions, and found to be more important than general knowledge about HIV transmission.[23] Sexual communication has been found to be a greater challenge for older women.[24] In general, the literature suggests that older women are less willing to be assertive in asking partners about their sexual risk histories. This is a notable finding as it suggests that useful interventions with this population of women may focus on enhancement of communication within a relationship or even take a dyadic approach with a focus on both partners within a relationship.

Intimate partner violence (IPV) is also a factor to be considered when assessing the role of the relationship in HIV risk. IPV has been associated with greater risk for HIV and overall, women living with HIV/AIDS have a higher likelihood of having experienced IPV.[25–27] In older women, IPV is associated with greater risks for HIV including multiple sexual partners, a history of STIs, and more frequent risk behaviors in partners.[22] Because older women may feel less agentic in their relationships and in cases of IPV, fearful of their partners, ongoing IPV may place older women at risk for multiple deleterious health outcomes including HIV as well as physical injuries from which recovery may be more complicated, and psychological distress for which they may be less likely to seek help.[28] However, reports of fear of reprisal from partners if requests for condom use were made were not reported in all cohorts of older women.[29] As such, interventions with older women may need to account for IPV but also assume that women can also take on the mantle of sexual advocacy around condoms. In addition, assumptions about the likelihood of IPV may mean that certain subpopulations of older women may be overlooked. For example, the misassumption that IPV is only about man on woman violence may mean that women who have female partners are overlooked, and in addition, women with disabilities are particularly vulnerable to IPV.

The traditionally reductionistic approach to risk reduction has been skills development, capacity building, and communications training. However, this ignores the subtext of power and oppression that can characterize heterosexual relationships for women, especially ethnic minority and low income women, and this is likely to be potentiated in older women. Ultimately, behavioral interventions will not be viable without addressing power dynamics. Relationship power has been described as a factor that can impact the ability of women to work with partners to engage in risk protective behavior.[30] Amaro and Raj et al[30] highlight three dynamics of oppression: silencing, violence/fear of violence, and internalized oppression—all of which they suggest must be considered when developing, implementing, and maintaining HIV risk reduction strategies in women. In the absence of such contextualization, behavioral and communication skills are unlikely to be implemented, even if women are able to articulate or demonstrate skills and knowledge in clinical settings. The dynamics of oppression are likely to be magnified in groups who face what could be termed "intersectional oppression"—with etiologies driven by multiple factors including poverty, minority statuses, disability status, and the fact that historically, older women grew up in a time when oppression was culturally mandated against many of the roles and identities they hold.

The relationship between stigma, the negative impact on communication, knowledge, and the potential for subsequent risk behaviors is impacted by relational variables or variables that are brought into starker focus in a relational setting.[7] Variables found to contribute to HIV stigma in older women include self esteem, self silencing, and sexual assertiveness.[7] Societal and relational variables including oppression of women, economic dependence on men, loneliness, discrimination, and the valuation of close relationships by women can foster variables such as self silencing, which may maintain stigma and risk.

Siegel and Scrimshaw[31] examined older women's narratives about sexuality and HIV, and in their sample of 63 older adults found that older HIV-infected women were more likely to choose celibacy (78% of women compared to 36% of men). The reasons for celibacy provided by these women included loss of interest in sex since their diagnosis, aversion to sex, and fear of infecting someone else. They also indicated that pulling back from the time required by a close relationship provided them with the time to focus on their own needs rather than the needs of a partner. This dynamic of time allotment and having to "attend" to a relationship is likely to be more pronounced for women. The narratives accumulated by these authors also reveal strong themes of distrust and anger toward men, and particularly toward the partner that infected them. The choice to abstain from sexual activity and intimate relationships was found to be more emotionally driven for women when compared to the men in this cohort. While celibacy certainly is its own form of "prevention," the authors astutely point out that the psychological fallout of HIV may result in these women becoming isolationist—which could have implications for mental health, social support, and willingness to engage in and access health care relationships. As such, successful interventions would address the feelings of anger, distrust, and betrayal these women may experience within the context of their own sexual drives to ensure that celibacy represents an authentic choice that is not diminishing overall quality of life. In addition, social isolation must also be observed through the viewpoint of policies that do not facilitate committed relationships (eg, lack of support for same-sex marriage, housing discrimination and other types of discrimination facing same-sex couples), as such, lesbian or bisexual women may be at greater risk for social isolation and, by extension, for outcomes such as decrements in physical and mental health, poor adherence, and morbidity and mortality.[13]

Heterosexist assumptions that all women are in intimate relationships with men can be isolating for women, particularly older women, who may have faced lifelong discrimination and isolation for sexual minority status, or for women who may find themselves in non-traditional living arrangements. Awareness and understanding of a diversity of women's relationship statuses, and avoidance of presumption is key in ensuring that those that are providing medical and mental health care services are being maximally responsive to client needs. Fredriksen-Goldsen et al[32] found that in older LGB adults that in the dyadic relationships in their sample, high levels of depressive symptomatology were observed, and also highlighted the function of the caregiving relationship as a protection from the negative impacts of discrimination. Dyadic relationships bring numerous benefits and challenges to older women, but they must be considered within a larger social context. Biased assumptions based on traditional relational structures must be avoided and instead objective assessment of these relationships must be standard in all clinical and research settings.

Relationships between men and women in our culture are frequently characterized by power imbalances that can be magnified in light of economic dependency and abuse, as well as societally concretized gender inequities—all of which may be more pronounced in older women since these characteristics are often lifelong conditions which can magnify in older age. Older women also face a double burden of ageism and sexism, and this can diminish their power in relationships and their ability to successfully interact with health care systems that may leave them feeling misunderstood and ashamed around issues such as later life sexuality.[7] This can be a triple burden or even more pronounced in other groups of older women. For example, older lesbian women are far more likely than men to be living in poverty,[33] and ethnic minority women and disabled women are more likely to be living in poverty than nearly all other groups as well. As such, when examining power imbalances in light of economic inequities, other variables contributing to a greater likelihood of such discrepancies must also be recognized and

considered when establishing treatment, research and policy agendas.

Primary Care Issues

Older adults, both men and women, often present with multiple clinical concerns during primary care visits, and as such, routine HIV testing is often missed or not offered. Acute retroviral syndrome may be missed in women over 50, because they are not considered to be probabilistic candidates for HIV infection, however, this can be a critical error as it may delimit the likelihood that women are detected for early infection and given appropriate treatment. For women at any kind of risk, HIV and acute seroconversion should be a differential for flu-like symptoms. However, because many women are not assessed for or presumed to be at risk, this opportunity may often be missed.

Another primary care issue that frequently arises in the population of older adults, including women, is medication interactions and toxicities. These risks are pronounced because of factors including number of medications, patient age, disease severity, renal and hepatic dysfunction, drug metabolic factors, and drug interactions. HAART has also been associated with elevated LH and FSH which in turn can contribute to menstrual irregularities.[34] Santoro et al's[35] review of menopause in women with HIV suggests that women with HIV evidence earlier menopause, though it is unclear whether this is due to HIV per se or to other risk factors for early menopause that tend to cluster in HIV infected women such as smoking, stress, and drug use.

HIV related symptoms and medication related side effects often mirror age related comorbidities that can be pronounced in older women including anemia, wasting, dyspnea on exertion, rheumatologic disorders, dementia, osteoporosis, lipid abnormalities, insulin resistance, and vulvar and cervical neoplasia.[35,36] Increased cardiovascular disease risk burden is also observed in HIV infected women regardless of whether or not they are receiving HAART.[35] HIV infection has been found to have independent associations with menopause symptoms and in older women, the intersection of HIV and menopause may be observed via greater psychological symptoms from both HIV and menopausal transition.[37]

Even more specific issues can arise for trans and gender-nonconforming older adults who may not only be facing the issues around becoming older with HIV but also the use of hormone related treatments as part of gender transition that can further complicate assessment.[38] In addition, many lesbian women, bisexual women, and trans and gender non-conforming adults find that they are misunderstood by health care delivery systems and that these barriers are magnified in the face of poverty, disability status, and ethnic minority status, with a greater likelihood of avoiding healthcare delivery systems due to these systematic prejudices. Because of biases from within their own racial, ethnic and cultural communities, this isolation can result in having few avenues to consider in the face of significant health crises.

Older women report that not only are they having sex, but that they wish to discuss it with their healthcare providers.[10,39] It has been noted that medications and illnesses, including HIV/AIDS can impact sexual health in myriad ways, yet women are often not informed about this possibility, placing the onus of initiating such communications on the patient.[40] Embarrassment about discussing sex with older adults for fear of offending, especially by younger health care practitioners, can be a barrier to addressing sexual health in older adults.[41]

Obesity and the attendant health risks of obesity are more frequently observed in lesbian women, in certain ethnic minority subgroups, can be pronounced in older women who may have limited mobility, and is often associated with socioeconomic status. The health consequences of obesity including diabetes, musculoskeletal stress, and higher cardiovascular risk are likely to be compounded for older women, and once again, the key issue of multiple vulnerabilities as a function of different role statuses cannot be underestimated in assessing and managing health and primary in older women with HIV/AIDS.[13]

Medication adherence remains an important issue in HIV care, with adherence to HAART regimens predictive of slower disease progression and better health outcomes. While older adults have been characterized as being more adherent, Bianco et al[42] found that only about 50% of older women in their sample were adherent to HAART.

They also observed that psychological factors were not useful predictors of adherence in older women, speculating that other factors such as family and caregiving obligations, pill burden, or self efficacy may be more useful predictors in women.[42] Hinkin et al[43] observed that older adults per se did not have poorer medication adherence, but rather patients evidencing neuropsychological impairment and with more complex regimens were those that had greater difficulties with medication adherence. As such, it is not presumptive that older adults, or older women specifically would have significant problems in adherence, but that other factors such as cognitive functioning and regimen factors should be considered when monitoring adherence. In general, studies of medication adherence in older HIV-infected adults examine both men and women, and do not specifically focus on the needs of HIV-positive women.

Knowledge About HIV

Although knowledge about HIV prevention doesn't necessarily directly translate into behavior, knowledge about transmission, susceptibility, and methods of protection remain an essential ingredient in the arsenal of HIV prevention. In older women who are not infected with HIV, knowledge can be limited, with women maintaining the belief that HIV is not a salient issue for them and perpetuation of HIV-related stigma.[44,45] Knowledge about the utility of condoms, even amongst those using condoms, has been found to be low in older women who reside in urban communities with high rates of HIV incidence and prevalence, with some studies reporting that only 13% of older women were aware that condoms were very effective in preventing HIV.[23,46] Older women have been observed to maintain some consistent general knowledge about HIV and HIV transmission, but will often have far less personal awareness of their own risks.[47,48] Overall, the literature on knowledge suggests that factual knowledge about HIV/AIDS is generally high, however, personal perceptions and assessments of risk tend to be suboptimal in older women.[24]

Risk for HIV

The assumption that older women do not have sex is clearly not supported by the data. Older women do have sex, and value sex as an important part of their lives.[8,9,49,50] As adults live longer, and the advent of medications such as sildenafil make it likely that older men will continue to be able to manage issues such as erectile dysfunction, older adults will continue to want to have sex and will have sex which places them at risk for STIs and HIV. From an infection perspective, incident HIV infections in older women typically occur through heterosexual transmission, but other vectors such as infection through injection drug use are also observed. Mitigation of these risks occurs via safer sex practices or safer injection drug use practices. Older women are less likely to use condoms, with over 90% of women in one national survey reporting no condom use over a 6-month period, and over 90% of those who reported engaging in risky behaviors did not perceive themselves as being at risk.[51] In a sample of sexually active African American and Latina older women (largely HIV-negative), Sormanti et al[22] observed that 80% of the women had sexual intercourse in the prior 90 days, and 86% reported not using condoms, with 10% indicating that their primary partners placed them at risk for HIV. As will be noted, physiological changes in older women can place them at greater risk for infection, and biological changes due to aging such as decreases in antibody production can also increase vulnerability to HIV.[52]

Stigma can be a powerful predictor of risk in women over the age of 50. Compared to gay and bisexual men, older women with HIV are more likely to experience greater stigma across various dimensions including disclosure, negative self-image and public attitudes.[53] Jacobs and Kane[7] found that both personal stigmas about HIV as well as fear of stigma from sexual partners should a woman address safer sex practices can reinforce the likelihood of engaging in risky behaviors (eg, avoiding condom use instead of talking about it). Stigma can also diminish the likelihood of older women discussing HIV/AIDS and this can in turn diminish the likelihood of older women having accurate information or skills to manage risk behaviors.[54] Stigma also acts to distance women from believing they or their partners are at risk by reinforcing an "us/them" mentality and miscalculation of susceptibility and risk.

Neundorfer et al[55] interviewed 24 HIV-positive women between the ages of 45 and 71 years and generated narratives which revealed 5 distinct factors that had placed these women at risk for infection with HIV. These risks included (a) drug and alcohol abuse; (b) being unaware of the risk histories of male partners; (c) mental health issues, physical and sexual trauma, and life stressors; (d) taking risks within a relationship; and (e) lack of HIV-prevention information. These factors are well established in the literature as placing all women at greater risk for infection, and it is also likely that older women may be less likely or less equipped to engage in pointed conversations about partner sexual histories, advocacy for condom use, and seeking out HIV-prevention information, especially since so little of the information and prevention programming is targeted at their experience. The authors observed that for older women, number of partners did decrease, but so too did condom use.

Risk of HIV infection for specific groups such as older lesbian women or trans and gender nonconforming adults occurs within a context not simply of sexual behavior but also of violence, discrimination, and economic instability. Prevention information and education is often predicated on a heterosexist model of disease transmission. In addition, risk is often underestimated in lesbian and bisexual women. Older studies have found that while lesbian and bisexual women may perceive themselves at lower risk, that they were more likely than heterosexual women to report high risk behaviors such as unsafe injection drug use as well as unprotected vaginal and anal sex.[56] In order for risk prevention models to succeed they must develop past presumptive frameworks of sexual risk, and be embedded in contextualized frameworks that account for the intersectionalities facing older women at risk for or living with HIV/AIDS. The stressors associated with sexual minority status have also been associated with not only negative mental and physical health outcomes and distress but also a greater likelihood of high risk sexual behaviors.[57]

It has been suggested that some of the success of condom use programs in younger women may emanate from the implementation of such programs within larger sexual education programs that also focus on issues such as pregnancy prevention. Since older women may no longer perceive pregnancy as a risk, the drive for contraception may drop, and subsequently the motivation to use barrier methods such as condoms becomes less salient. In addition, since health care providers are unlikely to discuss sex with older patients, the systems in place may also contribute to older women's lower perception of risk.

Safe Sex Practices

The use of barrier methods such as condoms remains a first line of prevention among sexually active adults in new relationships or with partners whose HIV status is unknown. However, the use of condoms and other safe sex practices raises some issues specific to older women. Reproductive health changes in midlife due to perimenopause and menopause can render women more physiologically vulnerable to STIs including HIV.[20] Vaginal dryness secondary to decreasing hormone levels in perimenopausal and menopausal women can heighten the importance of condom use given that lack of lubrication and other changes such as atrophic vaginitis can lead to more efficient viral transmission through mucosal transmission and vaginal tearing. Interventions including the use of water-based lubricants and vaginal estrogen preparations should be discussed by primary care and gynecologic health care providers.

Acquiring condoms has also been found to be associated with safer sex practices, and Paranjape et al[23] found that personally acquiring condoms was associated with safe sex decisions, which they believe may be a correlate of greater self efficacy. However, these authors also found that safer sex practices were observed even when older women in their sample depended on men to provide condoms.

Neuropsychiatric Factors and HIV in Older Adults

Overall, HIV-infected older adults are more likely to have more depressive symptoms, suicidal ideation, AIDS related stigma, and comorbid health conditions.[11,58,59] Loneliness and HIV-related stigma are associated with depression in older HIV-positive adults.[59] We found that 67% of older women in our dataset reported a current

Axis I diagnosis, compared to 50% of younger women.[21]

HIV has been well documented to have direct effects on the CNS, and with a range of neurocognitive symptoms ranging from minor cognitive disorder to HIV-associated dementia (for a thorough review of the neuropsychological issues of HIV/AIDS in older adults see Hardy and Vance).[60] Very few studies of the neuropsychology of HIV have focused exclusively on older women, and few take on the issue of women at any age. Those studies that have focused on women, suggest that HIV-seropositive women evidence more impairment than HIV-negative women, with the greatest impairments observed on psychomotor tasks, and that impairment was more frequently observed in those not receiving HAART.[61,62] In general, older age is associated with poorer performance in multiple domains including memory, executive functioning and motor/psychomotor performance when older adults are compared to younger adults.[60,63] Age increases risk for neurocognitive symptoms in women with HIV. In older women with HIV, they may be facing multiple threats to cognition including normal aging, HIV, lifelong issues including substance use or neurological insults, and in a subset of women, low education. Research on the use of post-menopausal hormonal replacement therapies has shown mixed results, and may have some promise for mitigation of symptoms in older women, though further research targeted at HIV-infected older women is needed.[64,65]

An overview of psychiatric, psychological, and cognitive evaluation in older adults reveals that evaluations that encompass all of the following should represent standard of care in evaluation and monitoring of older women with HIV: (a) cognitive impairment; (b) depression; (c) anxiety; (d) PTSD; (e) suicidal ideation; (f) alcohol and substance use; (g) sleep and appetite; (h) psychiatric history and psychiatric medications; (i) psychosocial issues (eg, IPV, housing, supports); and (j) caregiving responsibilities.

Substance Use and Abuse

In the general population of older women, it has been estimated that approximately 10% abuse drugs or alcohol.[66] Older women may also be more physiologically vulnerable to the effects of alcohol and selected drugs.[66] Much like the underassessment of sexual risk because it is assumed that older women don't have sex, substance use is often also missed in older women because they are not believed to be at risk for drug use or because their use is not causing disruption in the lives of others. While the vast majority of older women report being infected via heterosexual transmission, there is still a significant proportion (10%–30%) that were infected via injection drug use. In addition, drug use is often an indirect vector of HIV as it may contribute to risky sexual decision making, and substance dependence may place a woman at risk for exchanging sex for drugs or money.[55,67]

When compared to cohorts of younger women, older women have been found to have lower rates of substance use.[68] However, in lesbian and bisexual women, older age does not confer a protective effect against alcohol and drug use, and that overall lesbian and bisexual women are at greater risk for alcohol and drug-use disorders.[69] In an analysis of the literature on women, substance use, and HIV across women of all ages, Barroso and Sandelowski[67] found that a diagnosis of HIV often motivated women to want to abstain from drug use as part of taking back their health or taking back custody of children. HIV-positive women with substance-use histories typically had histories characterized by sexual and physical abuse, familial substance abuse histories, IPV, and trauma. Over the course of a lifetime, these variables will have impacts on older women, who may still experience difficulties with sexual decision making or ongoing maintenance of sobriety. Narratives of older HIV-seropositive women reveal that large proportions of women reported histories of substance use (71%), but of the 24 women studied in a qualitative study, none reported current alcohol or drug abuse.[55] In our sample of 71 HIV-positive women, 20 of whom were over the age of 50, 85% reported a lifetime history of substance abuse/dependence, while 10% reported a current history of abuse. These rates were comparable to those reported by younger women in our sample (12% current, 70% lifetime).[21] Assumptions that drug or alcohol use may be less prevalent in older women, and the potential augmentation of the impact of drug and alcohol use in older women reveals that assessment of substance use in older women must be conducted in a contextualized manner (and mindful of sexual orientation, ethnic minority status, and trauma history).

Psychosocial Issues in Older Women Living With HIV/AIDS

Regardless of HIV serostatus, caregiving issues represent a unique factor for older women who may be assisting adult children with young children, and may even be caring for elderly parents. In addition, older women may also have partners or spouses who may require assistance. These responsibilities can impede self-care in older women and contribute to fatigue, financial burdens, and overall mental, psychological, emotional and physical burden.[70] These issues are likely to be compounded in older women who are also managing the burdens of HIV. In addition, these ongoing stressors contribute to overall burden and allostatic load in women already burdened by the wear and tear of HIV/AIDS, other comorbid health conditions, and normal aging.

Studies of women living with HIV/AIDS at all ages reveal that psychological stressors are a key factor in women's experience of the illness. Physiological stressors include the infection itself, access to care, gynecologic symptoms, other health conditions, and stigma within the health care system.[71] Psychological stressors are wide ranging and include universal stressors such as finances, employment related stress, and interpersonal relationships, as well as HIV-specific stressors such as fear of disclosure, stigma about HIV, body image issues, fear of infecting others or finding a partner, and end of life issues.[71,72] Social support can be a complex issue for women, and especially HIV-infected women. The various elements of support including emotional, instrumental, and informational support can be key coping tools for women with HIV, and interventions focused on shoring up social support can have utility for coping with HIV- and non-HIV-related stressors.[71] However, virtually no studies focus on social support and stressors in older women with HIV/AIDS. While older women may actually have larger networks than younger women or men living with HIV/AIDS, these networks can also be a source of demand and burden. A large proportion of older women have also been observed to not be prepared for the legal and procedural issues that may arise in later life that are related to management of their health care and decision making (eg, advance directives, power of attorney/conservatorship, probate).

There also remains the issue of caregiving FOR women with HIV/AIDS. A substantial proportion of older women with HIV/AIDS are not married or do not have long term partners that are willing or able to engage in caregiving. Adult children may also not be available for such duties. Literature on caregiving by and for older lesbian women reveals there is often concern about availability of caregiving at the time it would become necessitated,[32] and that prejudice and discrimination can be major impediments to receiving caregiving in older age—factors that would be magnified in sexual minorities, ethnic minority women, disabled women and amongst those with limited financial resources. Intersectional identities and experiences—aging, chronic illness, poverty, disability status, sexual orientation, gender, and HIV—highlight the importance of addressing both discrimination and the additive risk of these intersecting identities on health and disease.[32]

Interventions Targeting Older Women Living With HIV/AIDS

Bringing HIV intervention and prevention programs to older women requires awareness of the cultural variables they bring to the table. Older women may be less likely to use technologically driven programs such as those delivered by the internet, or may be less likely to turn to media that may offer safer sex messages and likely skews to a younger demographic. Targeting accessible and approachable spaces where older women may already come together to foster such prevention programs (eg, churches) may be a useful tool to proliferate safer sex and risk awareness messages,[29] however the content of such communications and programs may still leave women reticent even if they are housed within approachable structures. Curricula that are ethnically responsive, and account for education, skills training, and coping were found to be acceptable by cohorts of older women.[29] In addition, older women may also reside in assisted living settings where they may

feel less able to discuss stigmatized issues such as sex, STIs, and HIV because it is their residential community and they may fear stigmatization. This then becomes a training issue for practitioners in these settings, and a mandate that practitioners in these settings make discussion of these issues a normalized part of care and dialogue within these communities.[7]

While not specifically targeted at older women, Orel et al[12] provide four thematic recommendations to account for when developing prevention materials for older adults. They caution that these recommendations must be contextualized for specific target groups on the basis of sociodemographic factors, cultural variables, and physical/cognitive/psychological functioning.

1. Raise older adults' perceived sense of susceptibility to HIV/AIDS

2. Provide appropriate HIV/AIDS factual information

3. Incorporate HIV/AIDS risk reduction strategies

4. Emphasize early intervention—testing and treatment options[12, pp. 498–499]

When considering the contextualization of these issues into a gendered framework—issues such as awareness of partner characteristics, addressing physiological changes that can impact sexual health in older women, opening up primary care practitioners to being more directive in addressing sex with older women, establishing psychosocial and psychological supports and minimizing testing and treatment delays should remain a key focus in programs for older women.

Age, Culture, Economics, Ethnicity, and Risk

Cornelius et al[29] also highlight the role of ethnicity in considering relational variables. Citing Utz[73] they point out that 74% of older African American women are not in a relationship due to widowhood or divorce. However, this group of women often has less-than-accurate appraisals of risk (eg, believing HIV can be transmitted through coughing), and little regular condom use. Nonetheless, Cornelius et al[29] actually found that older African American women were willing to discuss condom use and sexual behavior with their partners.

Lesbian and bisexual women have received virtually no attention in the research on HIV/AIDS. Because lesbian women may have a current or past history of sex with men, a self-identification as being lesbian may not obviate risk.[74] In addition, in older women who presently self-identify as exclusively lesbian, over the course of a lifetime it is still not known whether a woman has had sex with men, and many health care practitioners may not feel comfortable asking an older woman this question. Informed and responsive health care options are often limited for lesbian, trans and gender-nonconforming older adults, and health care providers are often woefully underinformed about the specific health issues facing trans and gender nonconforming populations in particular.[38] Older women are a diverse group, and it would be erroneous to assume that all older women with HIV/AIDS or those who are not infected will behave in similar ways. By recognizing that older women, by dint of age and life experience, bring more experiences, risks, and expectations and who may be at very variable relationship stages (eg, some who are in long term marriages, others entering new relationships)—interventions with this group must be dynamic and recognize universal factors such as perimenopausal and menopausal changes, but contextualize such issues in a framework of diversity.[74]

The myriad issues facing older women with HIV—sexual health changes due to aging, gaps in knowledge, inaccurate perceptions of risk, ageism, relational factors, and other transitions due to aging make this a group, that while not overrepresented in prevalence statistics, that will continue to grow as the HIV-infected population lives longer and ages. Economic issues are also critical to understand as many of these women may have had lifelong financial hardship, but are also less likely to garner new employment for age related reasons and are facing the limitations of a fixed income despite greater financial need. It will be critical to transform Emlet and Poindexter's[2] characterization of this group as "unserved, unseen and unheard"— and develop interventions, responsive primary health care and integrated treatment programs that serve, see and hear this group of women.

Themes of Resilience and Aspiration

There are some losses and anxieties more specific to older adults, and typically older women with HIV. Murphy et al[75] addressed the issue of "empty nest" issues in older HIV-positive women and described worries including: (a) identity loss; (b) loss of social support; (c) financial insecurity; (d) worsening physical health; and (e) death and dying. Many of these concerns are universal among any older mothers dealing with the transitions of adult children, but the risks of morbidity and mortality and the psychosocial stressors associated with HIV can magnify these empty nest issues in older HIV-seropositive women. The authors also pointed out that the same women also listed hopes including (*a*) self-improvement; (*b*) change of life focus; (*c*) travel; (*d*) romantic partners; and (*e*) familial ties. But again, while these are universal hopes for older women, HIV serostatus can complicate the achievement of these hopes and goals. Many older women living with HIV/AIDS managed caregiver duties while also managing illness related issues, and the shifting identity as well as fears of growing older with a potentially stigmatizing illness raises issues that must be addressed in comprehensive intervention programs designed for older women living with HIV/AIDS.

Emlet et al[76] highlight the finding of resilience in older adults with HIV, drawn from narratives of both older women and men living with HIV. These themes include (*a*) self-acceptance; (*b*) optimism; (*c*) will to live; (*d*) generativity; (*e*) self-management; (*f*) relational living; and (*g*) independence. These themes should be built upon and shored up in any interventions with older women with HIV, as they provide a foundational structure which may result in better self-care, and better quality of life for older women living with HIV/AIDS.

Conclusions

A model for contextualized care, prevention, and research in older women with HIV/AIDS can guide key recommendations based on the small extant literature targeting this population of women. First of all it is essential to recognize that all of the recommendations issued below must be viewed within the context of poverty, race, ethnicity, culture, systems of care, psychosocial variables (social support, coping resources, role strains, environmental stressors), extant structures of power/oppression that differentially impact older women, discrimination, disability status (which is more likely to be observed or pronounced in older women), history of trauma/violence or ongoing violence within the context of a relationship. In addition, accounting for the strengths that older women with HIV/AIDS maintain such as resilience, is key in harnessing their sense of efficacy as partners in care. Best practices call for multidisciplinary teams that provide primary care, psychological services, ongoing assessment of change, and address barriers such as housing, nutrition, transportation, and access.

Care

In the early years of the HIV epidemic, research on women lagged, and rates of infection increased before women were sufficiently targeted by prevention programs, as well as tailored primary care. This resulted in delays in responsive care for women, who often presented with very different issues medically and psychologically. The risk for the same delays may occur again with older women. Even societal stigmas such as our avoidance of talking about sex in older people may contribute to more incident infections, ignorance about intersectionality and risk, less targeted prevention programs, and delays in care for older adults, and particularly women.[20]

Fundamental recommendations for primary care for older women include the following:

Training in Health Care Provider Communication and Awareness

Health care providers must be trained to query older women about sexual behavior and drug use as standard of care. Discomfort with such assessment and misassumptions must be addressed to ensure that older women aren't being missed in terms of HIV testing and early initiation of treatment. HIV testing should be a standard part of comprehensive medical care for older women.

Supporting Adherence

Older women with HIV may face unique barriers to adherence that are magnified by issues including socioeconomic status, stigma, discriminatory health care systems, and a dearth of providers that specifically target the clinical needs of older

women with HIV/AIDS. Identifying and addressing barriers to adherence specific to older women is an essential element of primary care.

Menopause and Treatment Issues

Peri-menopausal and menopausal women may face the added vulnerability to becoming infected due to physiological changes and in addition, the ramifications of the interaction of hormone replacement therapy and HAART is still being determined. Health care providers working with older women must remain mindful of the impact of menopause on sexual risk and of the interactions of other medications with HAART in this group.

Shoring Up Support Networks

Traditional expectations of caregiving and support cannot be maintained with older women with HIV/AIDS. Older women with HIV/AIDS may not have traditional relationship or family structures to provide assistance, may have limited access to financial resources to afford care, and may face discriminatory social structures that limit their ability to access care. Health care providers must carefully assess availability of support and caregiving, especially given the impact that this can have on physical and mental health outcomes.

Neuropsychiatric Changes

Age related cognitive changes, as well as cognitive and psychiatric changes due to menopause must be considered within the context of HIV/AIDS which can also independently contribute to cognitive slowing, apathy, and other neuropsychiatric sequelae. Careful assessment of neuropsychiatric variables in older women with HIV/AIDS is essential for monitoring changes and to make determinations regarding medications and psychiatric care.

Paniagua and O'Boyle[77] suggest that six domains should be consistently addressed in assessment and research with HIV-infected older adults. These recommendations derive from literature as well as their own survey research. They suggest that the domains include (*a*) knowledge of factual information and inaccuracies regarding HIV transmission; (*b*) personal sense of internal versus external control of the cognitive and behavioral factors associated with HIV prevention; (*c*) perceived peer norms about HIV; (*d*) intention to change behaviors when faced with HIV risks; (*e*) communication with partners and family; and (*f*) assessment of behavioral risks for HIV. All of these factors are contributors to understanding HIV risk in older adults, and by applying a systematic framework, the authors are suggesting that we will better understand risk in diverse populations of older adults.

Prevention

Some basic shifts are needed to ensure that older women who are at risk for HIV/AIDS and those living with HIV/AIDS are recipients of appropriate prevention materials. Age appropriate risk reduction materials must be developed that feature images of older women and address issues specific to older women such as menopause, dating in midlife and later life, and discussing sexuality with primary care providers. There are also needs to be an expansion of simplistic risk reduction training to include broader issues such as relationship dynamics, ensuring that prevention programs specifically address subgroups of women who have been traditionally missed by prevention programs and materials (eg, lesbian women, disabled women) power and oppression, ageism, self esteem, interpersonal assertiveness, and sexual communication to allow for more authentic and effective programming. In addition, better training of all care providers is needed to better address and assess risk, and this includes patient education, provision of HIV testing, and early detection and treatment.

Comorbidities

Older women with HIV face other comorbidities and age related transitions that must be considered in assessment and treatment:

- Neuropsychiatric changes

- Health changes due to menopause

- Pain and neuropathy

- Ongoing drug, alcohol, and tobacco use

- Shifts in cardiovascular health

- Age related immune decline

- Musculoskeletal vulnerabilities including osteoporosis

- Caregiver issues and access to psychosocial supports

As both men and women with HIV/AIDS live longer and remain sexually active into later life, remaining aware of these comorbidities and co-occurring issues becomes key to ensure that synergistic progressive conditions are being appropriately managed and that misdiagnosis is not resulting in mismanagement and undertreatment of symptomatology.

Research Agendas

The model used to guide this review can also serve as a roadmap for the areas of empirical investigation that must be pursued with older women with HIV/AIDS. At a minimum, large, longitudinal studies examining the natural history of HIV/AIDS in older women that also examine variables including menopause, hormone replacement therapy, and other age related shifts such as age related cognitive changes are essential. In addition, speculation about older women's sexuality must be replaced with data about sexual choice, behavior, and condom use to address both prevention and quality of life in older women with HIV/AIDS. Finally, there is a profound need for better research on the use of HAART in older women with HIV/AIDS, particularly amongst those who may also be receiving hormone replacement, or simply to determine the impact of HAART on older women. Few clinical trials to date have focused specifically on this subgroup, and this will be essential as more women become infected and live longer with HIV. All research must strive to adequately sample this diverse population of interest. The heterogeneity within the sample of older women living with HIV/AIDS can easily be lost if studies do not attempt to address across the spectrum of women on the basis of economic status, race, ethnicity, sexual orientation, disability status, motherhood, and years since infection.

Finally, extant research highlighting themes of resilience focus the need to also move away from a deficit approach to understanding aging and HIV, and to build upon existing strengths in these women. Narratives from older women highlight their hopes for success, relationships, and health in later life despite, and in some cases because of

HIV/AIDS. As such, ongoing work with this sample of women should not fall prey to an overfocus on disease, but also address shoring up strengths and promulgating better quality of life in older women living with HIV.

Policy Guidelines

While policy guidelines can be developed to ensure that older women receive testing, prevention training, and better primary care, ultimately, shifts in policy that address power/oppression differentials in educational and occupational systems, health care delivery, and intimate relationships must occur in parallel to prevention, care, and research recommendations. For example, legislation such as the Family and Medical Leave Act of 1993 often does not support caregiving that occurs within a same-sex relationship or within networks of friends.[32] The issue of intersectionality may be even more pronounced for older women as primary care, prevention and integrated intervention programs must account for not only HIV serostatus but also ethnicity, disability status, sexual orientation, socioeconomic status, and be mindful of ageism all of which can often complicate information seeking in older women. In addition, groups that face even greater vulnerability due to socioeconomic status, ethnic minority status, sexual orientation, gender orientation, and disability status must be afforded greater access and human rights protections. Societal biases such as HIV-related stigma interact with ageist biases, and attempts to address this via policy shifts, education and training are key in generating systems of care, prevention, and research that can operate more efficiently and responsively to the needs of an aging population of women with HIV/AIDS.

In closing, while the present review was focused on the issues facing older women with HIV/AIDS in the United States, international research focused on older women with HIV/AIDS suggests that key contributors to increased morbidity and mortality for older women with HIV/AIDS include limited health care, lack of resources, caregiving, and omission from research and prevention programs. Similarly, in the United States, there are certain groups of women more vulnerable to these barriers, and ongoing awareness and capacity building to ensure higher standards of care for vulnerable groups of older women living with HIV/AIDS are needed.

Acknowledgments

Dr. Durvasula would like to acknowledge the editorial and literature review assistance provided by Mr. Theodore Miller as well as acknowledging the participants of the Health Adherence Research Project who were willing to share their stories as a part of this research.

Funding

This work was supported in part by NIMH Grant 1SC1MH093181-01A1.

References

1. Leland J. "People think it's over": spared death, aging people with H.I.V. struggle to live. *New York Times.* June 1, 2013. http://www. nytimes. com/2013/06/02/nyregion/spared-death-aging-people-with-hiv-struggle-to-live.html?_r=0. Accessed October 15, 2013.

2. Emlet CA, Poindexter CC. Unserved, unseen, and unheard: integrating programs for HIV-infected and HIV-affected older adults. *Health Soc Work.* 2004;29:86–96.

3. Center For Disease Control and Prevention. HIV/AIDS among persons aged 50 and older. *CDC HIV/AIDS FactS.* 2008.

4. Tabnak F, Sun R. Need for HIV/AIDS early identification and preventive measures among middle-aged and elderly women. *Am J Public Health.* 2000;90:287.

5. Center For Disease Control and Prevention. Diagnoses of HIV infection among adults aged 50 years and older in the united states and dependent areas, 2007–2010. *HIV Surveillance Supplemental.* 2013;18.

6. Mack KA, Ory MG. AIDS and older Americans at the end of the twentieth century. *JAIDS.* 2003;33:S68–S75.

7. Jacobs RJ, Kane MN. HIV-related stigma in midlife and older women. *Soc Work Health Care.* 2010;49:68–89.

8. Lindau ST, Leitsch SA, Lundberg KL, Jerome J. Older women's attitudes, behavior, and communication about sex and HIV: a community-based study. *J Women's Health.* 2006;15:747–753.

9. Lindau ST, Schumm LP, Laumann EO, Levinson W, O'Muircheartaigh CA, Waite LJ. A study of sexuality and health among older adults in the united states. *N Engl J Med.* 2007;357:762–774.

10. Farrell J, Belza B. Are older patients comfortable discussing sexual health with nurses? *Nurs Res.* 2012;61:51–57.

11. Emlet CA. "You're awfully old to have this disease": experiences of stigma and ageism in adults 50 years and older living with HIV/AIDS. *Gerontologist.* 2006;46:781–790.

12. Orel NA, Spence M, Steele J. Getting the message out to older adults: effective HIV health education risk reduction publications. *J Appl Gerontol.* 2005;24:490–508.

13. Fredriksen-Goldsen KI, Kim H, Barkan SE, Muraco A, Hoy-Ellis CP. Health disparities among lesbian, gay, and bisexual older adults: results from a population-based study. *Am J Public Health.* 2013: e1–e8.

14. Branson B, Handsfield H, Lampe M, et al. Revised recommendations for HIV testing of adults, adolescents, and pregnant women in healthcare settings. *MMWR.* 2005;55:1–17.

15. Siegel K, Schrimshaw EW, Dean L. Symptom interpretation: implications for delay in HIV testing and care among HIV-infected late middle-aged and older adults. *AIDS Care.* 1999;11:525–535.

16. Harawa NT, Leng M, Kim J, Cunningham WE. Racial/ethnic and gender differences among older adults in nonmonogamous partnerships, time spent single, and HIV testing. *Sex Transm Dis.* 2011;38:1110.

17. McDavid K, Li J, Lee LM. Racial and ethnic disparities in HIV diagnoses for women in the united states. *JAIDS.* 2006;42:101–107.

18. Akers A, Bernstein L, Henderson S, Doyle J, Corbie-Smith G. Factors associated with lack of interest in HIV testing in older at-risk women. *J Women's Health.* 2007;16:842–858.

19. Schable B, Chu SY, Diaz T. Characteristics of women 50 years of age or older with heterosexually acquired AIDS. *Am J Public Health.* 1996;86:1616–1618.

20. Sherman CA, Harvey SM, Noell J. "Are they still having sex?" STIs and unintended pregnancy among mid-life women. *J Women Aging.* 2005;17:41–55.

21. Durvasula RS. *Progress report: Psychopathology, decision making and sexual risk.* Progress report submitted to the National Institute of Mental Health. Unpublished Report. 2013.

22. Sormanti M, Wu E, El-Bassel N. Considering HIV risk and intimate partner violence among older women of color: a descriptive analysis. *Women Health.* 2004;39:45–63.

23. Paranjape A, Bernstein L, St. George DM, Doyle J, Henderson S, Corbie-Smith G. Effect of relationship factors on safer sex decisions in older inner-city women. *J Women's Health.* 2006;15:90–97.

24. Zablotsky D, Kennedy M. Risk factors and HIV transmission to mid-life and older women: knowledge, options, and the initiation of safer sexual practices. *JAIDS.* 2003;33:S122–S130.

25. Stockman JK, Lucea MB, Campbell JC. Forced sexual initiation, sexual intimate partner violence and HIV risk in women: a global review of the literature. *AIDS Behav.* 2013:17:832–847.

26. Gielen AC, Ghandour RM, Burke JG, Mahoney P, McDonnell KA, O'campo P. HIV/AIDS and intimate partner violence intersecting women's health issues in the united states. *Trauma, Violence Abuse.* 2007;8:178–198.

27. Campbell JC, Baty M, Ghandour RM, Stockman JK, Francisco L, Wagman J. The intersection of intimate partner violence against women and HIV/AIDS: a review. *Int J Injury Control Safety Promotion.* 2008;15:221–231.

28. Wyatt GE, Myers HF, Williams JK, et al. Does a history of trauma contribute to HIV risk for women of color? implications for prevention and policy. *Am J Public Health.* 2002;92:660–665.

29. Cornelius JB, Moneyham L, LeGrand S. Adaptation of an HIV prevention curriculum for use with older African American women. *J Assn Nurses AIDS Care.* 2008;19:16–27.

30. Amaro H, Raj A. On the margin: power and women's HIV risk reduction strategies. *Sex Roles.* 2000;42:723–749.

31. Siegel K, Schrimshaw EW. Reasons for the adoption of celibacy among older men and women living with HIV/AIDS. *J Sex Res.* 2003;40:189–200.

32. Fredriksen-Goldsen KI, Kim H, Muraco A, Mincer S. Chronically ill midlife and older lesbians, gay men, and bisexuals and their informal caregivers: the impact of the social context. *Sex Res Soc Policy J NSRC.* 2009;6:52–64.

33. Sears JT. Introduction: Queering later life. 2008.

34. Santoro N, Lo Y, Moskaleva G, et al. Factors affecting reproductive hormones in HIV-infected, substance-using middle-aged women. *Menopause.* 2007;14:859–865.

35. Santoro N, Fan M, Maslow B, Schoenbaum E. Women and HIV infection: the makings of a midlife crisis. *Maturitas.* 2009;64: 160–164.

36. New York State Department of Health AIDS Institute. Medical care for menopausal and older women with HIV infection. *HIV Guidelines*. March 2008. http://www.hivguidelines.org.

37. Ferreira CE, Pinto-Neto AM, Conde DM, Costa-Paiva L, Morais SS, Magalhaes J. Menopause symptoms in women infected with HIV: Prevalence and associated factors. *Gynecological Endocrinology*. 2007;23:198–205.

38. Finkenauer S, Sherratt J, Marlow J, Brodey A. When injustice gets old: a systematic review of trans aging. *J Gay Lesbian Soc Serv*. 2012;24:311–330.

39. Hinchliff S, Gott M. Seeking medical help for sexual concerns in mid-and later life: A review of the literature. *J Sex Res*. 2011;48:106–117.

40. Lemieux L, Kaiser S, Pereira J, Meadows LM. Sexuality in palliative care: patient perspectives. *Palliat Med*. 2004;18:630–637.

41. Gott M, Hinchliff S, Galena E. General practitioner attitudes to discussing sexual health issues with older people. *Soc Sci Med*. 2004;58:2093–2103.

42. Bianco JA, Heckman TG, Sutton M, Watakakosol R, Lovejoy T. Predicting adherence to antiretroviral therapy in HIV-infected older adults: the moderating role of gender. *AIDS Behav*. 2011;15: 1437–1446.

43. Hinkin C, Castellon S, Durvasula R, et al. Medication adherence among HIV adults effects of cognitive dysfunction and regimen complexity. *Neurology*. 2002;59:1944–1950.

44. Hillman J. Knowledge and attitudes about HIV/AIDS among community-living older women: reexamining issues of age and gender. *J Women Aging*. 2007;19:53–67.

45. Savasta AM. HIV: Associated transmission risks in older adults–an integrative review of the literature. *J Assn Nurses AIDS Care*. 2004;15:50–59.

46. Henderson SJ, Bernstein LB, George DMS, Doyle JP, Paranjape AS, Corbie-Smith G. Older women and HIV: how much do they know and where are they getting their information? *J Am Geriatr Soc*. 2004;52:1549–1553.

47. Winningham A, Richter D, Corwin S, Gore-Felton C. Perceptions of vulnerability to HIV among older african american women: the role of intimate partners. *Journal of HIV/AIDS Soc Serv*. 2004;3:25–42.

48. Williams PB, Ekundayo O, Udezulu IE, Omishakin AM. An ethnically sensitive and gender-specific HIV/AIDS assessment of African American women: a comparative study of urban and rural American communities. *Fam Community Health*. 2003;26:108–123.

49. Robinson JG, Molzahn AE. Sexuality and quality of life. *J Gerontol Nurs*. 2007;33:19–27; quiz 38–39.

50. DeLamater J, Moorman SM. Sexual behavior in later life. *J Aging Health*. 2007;19:921–945.

51. Binson D, Pollack L, Catania JA. Aids-related risk behaviors and safer sex practices of women in midlife and older in the united states: 1990 to 1992. *Health Care Women Int*. 1997;18:343–354.

52. Levy JA. AIDS and injecting drug use in later life. *Res Aging*. 1998;20:776–797.

53. Brennan DJ, Emlet CA, Brennenstuhl S, Rueda S. Sociodemographic profile of older adults with HIV/AIDS: gender and sexual orientation differences. *Canadian J Aging*. 2013;32:31–43.

54. Montoya ID, Whitsett DD. New frontiers and chal. lenges in HIV research among older minority populations. *JAIDS*. 2003;33:S218–S221.

55. Neundorfer MM, Harris PB, Britton PJ, Lynch DA. HIV-risk factors for midlife and older women. *Gerontologist*. 2005;45:617–625.

56. Lemp GF, Jones M, Kellogg TA, et al. HIV seroprevalence and risk behaviors among lesbians and bisexual women in San Francisco and Berkeley, California. *Am J Public Health*. 1995;85:1549–1552.

57. Grossman AH, D'augelli AR, O'connell TS. Being lesbian, gay, bisexual, and 60 or older in North America. *J Gay Lesbian Soc Serv*. 2002;13:23–40.

58. Heckman TG, Heckman B, Kochman A, Sikkema KJ, Suhr J, Goodkin K. Psychological symptoms among persons 50 years of age and older living with HIV disease. *Aging Ment Health*. 2002;6:121–128.

59. Grov C, Golub SA, Parsons JT, Brennan M, Karpiak SE. Loneliness and HIV-related stigma explain depression among older HIV-positive adults. *AIDS Care*. 2010;22:630–639.

60. Hardy DJ, Vance DE. The neuropsychology of HIV/AIDS in older adults. *Neuropsychol Rev*. 2009;19:263–272.

61. Maki PM, Martin-Thormeyer E. HIV, cognition and women. *Neuropsychol Rev*. 2009;19:204–214.

62. Richardson JL, Martin EM, Jimenez N, et al. Neuropsychological functioning in a cohort of HIV infected women: importance of antiretroviral therapy. *J Int Neuropsychol Soc*. 2002;8:781–793.

63. Sacktor N, Skolasky R, Selnes OA, et al. Neuropsychological test profile differences between young and old human immunodeficiency virus-positive individuals. *J Neurovirol*. 2007;13: 203–209.

64. Santoro N, Fan M, Maslow B, Schoenbaum E. Women and HIV infection: the makings of a midlife crisis. *Maturitas.* 2009;64:160–164.

65. Maki PM, Zonderman AB, Resnick SM. Enhanced verbal memory in nondemented elderly women receiving hormone-replacement therapy. *Am J Psychiatry.* 2001;158:227–233.

66. Finfgeld-Connett DL. Treatment of substance misuse in older women: using a brief intervention model. *J Gerontol Nurs.* 2004;30:30–37.

67. Barroso J, Sandelowski M. Substance abuse in HIV-positive women. *J Assn Nurses AIDS Care.* 2004;15:48–59.

68. Schable B, Chu SY, Diaz T. Characteristics of women 50 years of age or older with heterosexually acquired AIDS. *Am J Public Health.* 1996;86:1616–1618.

69. Green KE, Feinstein BA. Substance use in lesbian, gay, and bisexual populations: An update on empirical research and implications for treatment. *Psychol Addict Behav.* 2012;26:265.

70. Chimwaza AF, Watkins SC. *Giving Care to People with Symptoms of AIDS in Rural Sub-Saharan Africa*; 2004.

71. Hudson AL, Lee KA, Miramontes H, Portillo CJ. Social interactions, perceived support, and level of distress in HIV-positive women. *J Assn Nurses AIDS Care.* 2001;12:68–76.

72. Sowell R, Seals B, Moneyham L, Demi A, Cohen L, Brake S. Quality of life in HIV-infected women in the south-eastern united states. *AIDS Care.* 1997;9:501–512.

73. Utz RL. The single older woman: Life after marriage. *Gerontologist.* 2005;45:411–414.

74. Zablotsky D, Kennedy M. Risk factors and HIV transmission to mid-life and older women: knowledge, options, and the initiation of safer sexual practices. *JAIDS.* 2003;33:S122–S130.

75. Murphy DA, Roberts KJ, Herbeck DM. HIV-positive mothers with late adolescent/early adult children: "empty nest" concerns. *Health Care Women Int.* 2012;33:387–402.

76. Emlet CA, Tozay S, Raveis VH. "I'm not going to die from the AIDS": resilience in aging with HIV disease. *Gerontologist.* 2011;51:101–111.

77. Paniagua FA, O'Boyle M. Comprehensively assessing cognitive and behavioral risks for HIV infection among middle-aged and older adults. *Educational Gerontology.* 2008;34:267–281.

Women and Alzheimer's Disease: A Global Epidemic

by The Alzheimer's Association

Worldwide, at least 44 million people are living with Alzheimer's disease and other dementias, with at least 5 million in the United States alone. The number of Americans who have Alzheimer's and other dementias will escalate rapidly in coming years as the Baby Boom generation ages. By 2050, the number of people age 65 and older with Alzheimer's disease may nearly triple, from 5 million to as many as 16 million, barring the development of medical breakthroughs to prevent, slow or stop the disease.

Alzheimer's is the 6th leading cause of death in the United States; however, it may cause even more deaths than official sources recognize. The disease kills more people than prostate cancer and breast cancer combined. Alzheimer's disease is the only cause of death among the top 10 in the nation that cannot be prevented, cured, or even slowed.

Women are at the epicenter of the Alzheimer's epidemic

According to the Alzheimer's Association *2014 Alzheimer's Disease Facts and Figures* report, women account for almost two-thirds of Americans with Alzheimer's disease. A woman's estimated lifetime risk of developing Alzheimer's at age 65 is 1 in 6, compared with nearly 1 in 11 for a man. As real a concern as breast cancer is to women's health, women in their 60s are about twice as likely to develop Alzheimer's over the rest of their lives as they are to develop breast cancer.

Not only are women more likely to have Alzheimer's, they are also more likely to be caregivers of those with the disease. More than 3 in 5 unpaid Alzheimer's caregivers are women—and there are 2.5 times as many women than men who provide intensive "on-duty" care 24 hours a day for someone living with the disease.

Because of caregiving duties, women are likely to experience adverse consequences in the workplace. Among caregivers who have been employed while they were also caregiving:

- 20% of women vs. 3% of men went from working full-time to working part-time while acting as a caregiver.

- 18% of women vs. 11% of men took a leave of absence.

- 11% of women vs. 5% of men gave up work entirely.

- 10% of women vs. 5% of men lost job benefits as a result of their caregiving duties.

Women's brains matter

Women are leaders and influencers in family, community, business and philanthropy. Realizing the impact Alzheimer's has on women—and the impact women can have when they work together–the Alzheimer's Association has launched a national initiative highlighting the power of women in the fight against this disease. The Alzheimer's Association *My Brain Movement* calls on 1 million women to use their amazing brains to help wipe out Alzheimer's disease—one of the greatest threats to women's health.

We believe women have the passion and the strength to make real change. By using our collective brainpower and voices, we can create awareness of the impact Alzheimer's has on our health, our families, and our nation. We can use our voices on Capitol Hill to increase funding for research and care. And, we can make an impact by donating, volunteering, and getting involved in this issue.

We need our collective brainpower to fight Alzheimer's

The *My Brain Movement* is a united commitment to take action and make change for future generations. Be one of the 1 million women using their brains to wipe out Alzheimer's. The time is now. Join the movement. Learn how you can change the numbers for future generations at alz.org/mybrain.

The Alzheimer's Association® is the world's leading voluntary health organization in Alzheimer's care, support and research.

Pull Quotes for use with article:

"My husband has younger-onset Alzheimer's disease. When my children look back, I want them to know that I did everything in my power to release our family from this tragedy. I am a fighter. I am someone that wants to make a difference."–Karen Garner, care partner, working mother, passionate Alzheimer's advocate

"My mother, a teacher for 35 years, can no longer feed herself, dress herself or recognize her loved ones. The more I lose my mom to Alzheimer's, the more I experience how painful it is to miss someone who is sitting right in front of you."–Lauren Miller Rogen, screen writer, actress, funny lady, co-founder of Hilarity for Charity

This article was written by: The Alzheimer's Association®

KEEPS on Keeping On

by Adriane Fugh-Berman, MD

(https://www.nwhn.org/author/a_fughberman/)

The myth that menopausal hormone therapy prevents heart attack and dementia should have died a swift death after the definitive results of the Women's Health Initiative (WHI) a dozen years ago. But the concept that hormones might prevent some disease—in some women, somewhere, sometime, somehow—just keeps rising from the grave.

The Kronos Early Estrogen Prevention Study (KEEPS) is the name of an unnecessary trial that was conducted by hormone enthusiasts after the WHI proved that the harms of menopausal hormone therapy (including increased risks of breast cancer, heart attacks, strokes and dementia) outweighed its only disease prevention benefit–a reduced risk of fractures.

The research question explored in KEEPS was based on the ludicrous "timing hypothesis." This implausible hypothesis posits that, although healthy women given menopausal hormones experienced no disease prevention benefit, a benefit *might* be revealed if hormones were given to women who were close to the menopausal transition rather than to older women who went through menopause many years earlier. This was always a faulty foundation for a study because the average age of menopause is 51 and the WHI had *already* studied more than 5,000 women in their 50s—and found no such benefits. (For background on the claims made by KEEPS researchers, see "Two Years Too Late: Researchers Announce Hoped-For Results. Stall on Revealing Actual Data (https://www.nwhn.org/two-years-too-late-researchers-announce-hoped-for-results-stall-on-revealing-actual-data)."

National Women's Health Network (NWHN) members know that the NWHN has been the most important and effective force for questioning claims for hormone therapy's benefits, and demanding that the right studies be done to assess the impact on women's health. Our efforts helped launch the WHI, a large, longterm, federally-funded, randomized controlled trial that examined the risks and benefits of hormone therapy in more than 26,000 women.

Let's review what the WHI found:

- Starting in 1991, more than 16,000 women took either an estrogen/progestin combination (Prempro) or a placebo. In 2002, this study was stopped early because women taking the combined pills experienced harm, including higher rates of invasive breast cancer and heart attacks.[1]

- Another arm of the WHI study tested an estrogen-only hormone therapy (Premarin) against placebo in more than 10,000 women. All of the women had had hysterectomies, so they did not need a progestin to protect their uterus from estrogen-induced cancers. In 2004, the WHI's estrogen-only arm was stopped because an increased risk of stroke was found among women taking the hormones.[2]

These findings have been verified by other research. A systematic review of WHI and 22 other randomized controlled trials of menopausal hormone therapy use, involving a total of 42,830 women, found that estrogen-progestin combinations increased the risk of a cardiac event; blood clot; stroke; breast cancer; gallbladder disease; death from lung cancer; and, in women over 65, dementia.[3]

Although there was little point in doing a smaller, limited study after the large, comprehensive WHI study showed no benefit, the KEEPs researchers, many of whom had received payments from hormone manufacturers, randomized 727 recently menopausal women (with an average age of 52.6, and 1.4 years past their last menstrual period) to either a placebo or oral or transdermal (skin patch) estrogen with micronized progesterone. Notably, the progestin in this study was different than that used in the WHI—some alternative medicine practitioners have touted micronized progesterone as a better "bioidentical" hormone. These women were followed for four years. Hormone therapy failed to benefit measures of cardiovascular health and—in recent news—failed to have any benefit on cognition in a large substudy that included 693 women.[4]

All of the KEEPS findings are consistent with the results from the WHI and other randomized controlled trials—except that KEEPS found a minor mood-elevating effect in non-depressed women who took oral (but not transdermal) estrogen. There was *no* effect on real depression. (WHI, on the other hand, found no benefit of hormones on symptoms of depression or any other quality-of-life measures.)

When even the most loyal hormone enthusiasts can find no benefit of hormone therapy, it's time to give up searching. The concept that hormones will benefit some woman, somewhere, if we just gave the right dose and mix of at some crucial—but elusive—moment is magical thinking. At this point, anyone who believes that menopause hormone therapy benefits women's hearts or brains believes something that is inconsistent with science.

We've said it before and we'll say it again: The risks of menopause hormone therapy overwhelmingly outweigh benefits for menopausal women—excepting those who have severe hot flashes or vaginal dryness, which estrogen helps.

The KEEPS results should drive the final nail in the coffin of the myth that menopausal hormone therapy has health benefits that outweigh its risks. So, why do we have the lurking sense that someday, the specter of hormone benefit will rise from the dead again to haunt us?

Adriane Fugh-Berman, MD, is an associate professor in the Georgetown University Medical Center; a former chair of the NWHN Board of Directors; and director of PharmedOut, which educates prescribers about pharmaceutical marketing techniques.

References

1. Writing Group for the Women's Health Initiative Investigators, "Risks and benefits of estrogen plus progestin in healthy postmenopausal women: Principal results from the Women's Health Initiative randomized controlled trial," *JAMA* 2002; 288(3):321–33.

2. Hsia J, Langer RD, Manson JE, et al., "Conjugated equine estrogens and coronary heart disease: the Women's Health Initiative," *Arch Intern Med* 2006; 66(3):357-65.

3. Marjoribanks J, Farquhar C, Roberts H, et al., "Long term hormone therapy for perimenopausal and postmenopausal women," *Cochrane Database Syst Rev.* 2012; Jul 11;7:CD004143. doi:10.1002/14651858. CD004143.pub4.

4. Gleason CE, Dowling NM, Wharton W, et al., "Effects of Hormone Therapy on Cognition and Mood in Recently Postmenopausal Women: Findings from the Randomized, Controlled KEEPS-Cognitive and Affective Study," *PLoS Med.* 2015; 12(6):e1001833; discussion e1001833. doi: 10.1371/journal.pmed.1001833. eCollection 2015 Jun.

Related:

- Two Years Too Late? Researchers Announce Hoped-For Results, Stall on Revealing Actual Data (https://www.nwhn.org/two-years-too-late-researchers-announce-hoped-for-results-stall-on-revealing-actual-data/)
- Menopause Hormone Therapy: Timing Doesn't Matter (https://www.nwhn.org/menopause-hormone-therapy-timing-doesnt-matter/)

Proactive Caregiving: Legal, Financial, and Emotional Supports for Family Caregivers

by Jennifer L. Berger

Two years ago, my partner's 77-year-old mother was experiencing weakness in her limbs and unexplained falls. Soon afterward, she was diagnosed with **Amyotrophic Lateral Sclerosis (ALS)**. Her husband, 72 at the time, was resourceful and compassionate as his wife progressively lost the ability to walk, speak clearly and, ultimately, eat. My partner, an only child, flew out to St. Louis frequently to help her parents cope with the realities of ALS' unmitigated harshness. The ALS Association and Muscular Dystrophy Association provided valuable support groups, home health care, hospice care, and durable medical equipment to buffer the journey. In June 2014, my partner's mother died peacefully in the home she had moved into 45 years earlier, thanks to community supports and the compassionate care of her family.

More and more of us are having similar experiences as the U.S. population ages. The youngest Baby Boomers turned 50 last year—the oldest are almost 70—and Boomers now account for about one-quarter of the nation's population.[1] By 2030, people aged 65 and older will make up 19 percent of the population.[2] The aging population increases the demand for family caregivers, most of whom are women.[3]

Caregiving can be very rewarding and much appreciated. Yet, caregivers who are unprepared for their role, or lack support, often pay a huge physical and emotional toll, which is compounded by the absence of proper planning. To meet the needs of our aging population, caregivers have to be prepared financially, legally, and emotionally for this role.

Advance Directives & Protective Arrangements

One of the most stressful parts of caregiving is the need to make health care decisions for a loved one while under pressure and without guidance from the vulnerable adult (it is particularly hard when your loved one lacks the ability to make decisions and/or communicate). Being proactive and creating financial and health care powers of attorney well in advance of any illness can reduce caregiver stress. The documents you'll need are:

- *Financial power of attorney*: prevents financial abuse and exploitation by enabling trusted relatives or friends to make any needed financial decisions. The financial power of attorney can be durable (effective from the moment it is signed) or springing (effective only upon occurrence of a specific event, typically lack of ability to make and/or communicate financial decisions oneself). Financial power of attorney also minimizes the risk a senior will fail to pay rent or mortgage, utilities, and/or taxes, and enables the person with power of attorney to step in for court matters, as needed.

- *Health care power of attorney*: appoints a substitute decision-maker for an individual who lacks the ability to communicate orally or in writing, and/or understand the nature and consequences of health care decisions. Similar to a financial power of attorney, a health care power of attorney, can be designated as either durable or springing.

- *Living will*: clarifies what, if any, medical intervention(s) a person wants when their medical condition is terminal, or they are in a permanent vegetative state or coma. This includes artificial respiration, feeding or hydration, blood transfusion, cardiopulmonary resuscitation, chemotherapy, dialysis, and/or medication that brings physical comfort but hastens death.

- *Will*: directs a person (the executor) to manage the individuals' estate and specifies how assets and property should be distributed.

- *Trusts*: financial arrangements that protect assets by allowing a third party (the trustee) to hold assets for a beneficiary; families can also create a trust to protect assets from Medicaid liens.

- *Burial arrangements*: making pre-paid burial arrangements (or including burial wishes in one's will) is critical to preventing survivors from having to make arrangements during the emotionally difficult time of loss. But, beware of pre-paid burial scams and investigate prospective providers thoroughly.

Being prepared helps caregivers make weighty treatment decisions; removes the stress of wondering if caregivers are following their loved one's wishes; and can help prevent disputes from arising. The danger of not preparing in advance of incapacity is that caregivers then have to deal with the additional stress of filing a guardianship (for health care matters) and/or conservatorship (for financial matters). The alternative—the risk that estranged family members, doctors, or even judges, who do not know the person well will make these decisions—is untenable. State Bar Associations can direct residents to legal services, including organizations offering free services to low-income clients.

Caregiver Resources

Family caregivers are often new to this role and may quickly become overwhelmed. Fortunately, there are many places to find support and useful resources, including AARP's *Caregiving Resource Center*, which is a good place to identify next steps and local assistance.[4] The Center offers several guides and resource lists to help caregivers manage financial, physical, and emotional challenges.[5]

It also has resources to help family members talk with their loved ones about their wishes and planning for the future.

There are a host of public programs focused on helping older adults and individuals with disabilities, which also assist family caregivers, too. Sadly, many people miss out on helpful services because they do not know about benefits they're eligible for, such as home health aide resources provided to Medicaid and Medicare beneficiaries.[6] Websites like the National Council on Aging's Benefitscheckup.org, and Social Security's website (www. SSA.gov (http://www.SSA.gov)) help identify benefits (i.e., food, housing, nutrition, health care, etc.) that can help support individuals and relieve caregiver stress.

Housing is a significant stressor for older people; as income shrinks in retirement, housing affordability is a real challenge—particularly for medically vulnerable adults. In response, many states provide tax benefits for housing costs, as well as Federally subsidized, affordable housing for seniors. It is important to know that Federal laws prohibit housing discrimination based on disability and/or handicap.[7] Local human rights laws also protect individuals with disabilities from discrimination in both housing and the provision of other services.

Community organizations—like your Area Agency on Aging, local non-profits, and local government programs—can help caregivers identify needed services for themselves and their loved ones (like respite care and health services), programs to keep seniors connected with their community (like adult education and day care programs) and legal assistance (to help with accessibility and affordability).

Each state has a Long-Term Care Ombudsman that monitors the quality of care in nursing homes, assisted living facilities and, sometimes, of home health aides. They are important allies to ensure your loved one receives proper care. Many associations provide valuable, illness-specific resources for caregivers (like durable medical equipment, respite care, visiting nurses, and hospice referrals). Examples include the ALS Association, Alzheimer's Association, American Heart Association, American Cancer Society, and MS Society.

Most important is self-care, which is critical to caring for others. Thankfully, an incredible network of caregiver supports exists in this country. Eldercare Locator *(www.eldercare.gov (http://www.eldercare.gov))* helps link caregivers with local resources (including Adult Day Care, Long-term Care, health insurance, housing, and transportation) that can help relieve caregivers' burdens.

Conclusion

Caregiving is a challenging experience, both emotionally and physically. The key is to have difficult conversations with your loved one early, so you can be prepared; get the legal, financial, and emotional supports lined up well before any emergency occurs; and identify and use available supports and benefits. The most important message is to avoid being proud—take advantage of available resources, and take proper care of yourself!

This article was written by: Jennifer L. Berger

Jennifer L. Berger supervises the eviction prevention team at AARP Legal Counsel for the Elderly. She helps elders age in place by enhancing their housing's affordability, accessibility, and habitability, and helps family caregivers obtain protective arrangements. She has degrees in social work and law from S.U.N.Y. Buffalo. She dedicates this article to her partner's mother, Mary Ann Lang, and her devoted caregivers, Joseph and Karen Lang.

References

1. "Baby Boomers" were born between 1946 and 1964. U.S. Census, "U.S. Census Bureau Projections Show a Slower Growing, Older, More Diverse Nation a Half Century from Now," Washington, DC: US Census, 2012; available online at: http://www.census.gov/newsroom/releases/archives/population/cb12-243.html.

2. U.S. Administration on Aging (AoA), "Aging Statistics," Washington, DC: Department of Health and Human Services, 2013. Available online at: http://www.aoa.acl.gov/Aging_Statistics/index.aspx

3. National Alliance for Caregiving (NAC)/AARP, Caregiving in the U.S., Washington, DC: NAC/AARP, 2004; available online at: http://assets.aarp.org/rgcenter/il/us_caregiving_1.pdf.

4. See http://www.aarp.org/home-family/caregiving/?intcmp=HP-LN-CRGVNG-CRC (viewed 8/13/2014). Caregivers can sign up for the AARP Advocates e-newsletter at: http://action.aarp.org/site/PageServer?pagename=Get_Involved&intcmp=HP-LN-sec9-pos1 and connect with their local AARP State Office (http://www.aarp.org/states/AARP) and get telephone assistance by calling 1-877-333-5885 (1-888-971-2013 in Spanish) Monday-Friday: 7 a.m.-11 p.m. ET, Saturday 9 a.m.-5 p.m. ET.

5. "Prepare to Care: A Planning Guide for Families", AARP Caregiving Resource Center (2012); available at: http://www.aarp.org/content/dam/aarp/home-and-family/caregiving/2012-10/prepare-to-care-lores.pdf

6. See http://www.medicare.gov/Pubs/pdf/10969.pdf. (viewed 8/13/2014).

7. Fair Housing Amendment Act of 1988, 42 U.S.C. § 3604(f)(1)-(2); Title III of the Americans with Disabilities Act (ADA) 42 U.S.C. § 12182(a).

Aging, Ageism, and Older Women's Issues

1. How and where do you see yourself at the ages of 30, 40, 50, 60, and 70? How do you think society will have changed? What do you think will have changed in the healthcare system?

2. How does ageism influence women's healthcare?

3. In what ways does race, ethnicity, culture, class, and where you live impact older women and ageism?

4. What are the strategies that older women of color use to counteract ageism in medical institutions?

5. Why are women disproportionately family caregivers?

6. In what ways does gender contribute to health outcomes for older women?

7. Is there a life plan you should be thinking about and what would be in it?

8. In Chapter 6, Donna Cole's article focuses on Black women with HIV/AIDS and in this Chapter 9 Ramani Durvasula describes the challenges and unmet needs of older women with HIV/AIDS. Describe any similarities and differences between the research projects and their demographic groups.

Politics of Disease and Alternative Approaches to Healthcare

10

This chapter not only highlights the impact of politics of disease, but also focuses on the increasing interest in alternative approaches to disease and illness, especially when traditional medical methods fail. The politics of disease can be seen in the decisions made by government agencies, pharmaceutical companies, and the healthcare industry regarding priorities in funding, research, services, and education. Alternative methods in healthcare refer to options outside the biomedical field. As discussed in earlier chapters, health care in general, and women's health care specifically, has been hyper-medicalized, for example, the confining of childbirth to hospitals. This process has received pushback, most noticeable in the realm of pregnancy and childbirth. Women are now choosing to give birth at home either with a midwife or, rarely, alone, and more women are breastfeeding. Alternative medicine, spirituality, and faith-based initiatives all work to promote women's health and wellness in the midst of a highly-politicized environment about health care, especially women's health care. Women interact as both consumers and practitioners within these systems; which populations are studied and how information about disease is distributed are politically motivated. All of these factors combine to influence the lived realities of women, not only in the United States, but also across the world.

This chapter begins with the article *Environmental Toxins Threaten Reproductive Health and Justice* by Sara Alcid and Anseje Miller. Alcid and Miller discuss how air quality and personal care products affect women's reproductive health and the health of families. They show how the Toxic Substances Control Act of 1976 continues to fail to address the public health concerns of widespread toxin use despite mounting evidence that dangerous chemicals are all around us and have long-lasting effects on health. *Breast Cancer Risks & the Environment: So Much We Don't Know* by Rachel Walden reviewed the Institute of Medicine's (IOM) report on *Breast Cancer and the Environment: A Life Course Approach*, which was commissioned by the Susan G. Komen for the Cure organization. The IOM suggested more research is needed and explained the complexity in studying the environmental risk factors that may affect breast cancer risk. Although there were no conclusive answers to be drawn from the IOM report, and a lack of stringent environmental regulations persist, NWHN noted the "most important activity we can engage in is to press for regulations requiring more extensive study and testing before products go to market."

The next set of articles focuses on alternative approaches to illness, healing, and promoting wellness for women. David R. Hodge, Stephanie E. Moser, and Michael S. Shafer focus on the mental health of homeless mothers in *Spirituality and Mental Health among Homeless Mothers*. They point out how mental health issues often lead to homelessness, but they also seek to understand the effects of homelessness over time, and, specifically, how "forgiveness, congregational problems, negative religious coping, and spiritual meaning" are influential to the long-term mental health of homeless women. Homeless mothers are a growing population that continues to be underserved.

The article *Performing Spiritual Healing in the Here and Now: Botánicas and Holistic Health Care* by Angela Casteñeda is an ethnographic study of how Midwestern botánicas in Indiana address immediate and emergent spiritual, financial, and health problems among diverse populations in the community. Botánicas provide an alternative to an often-inaccessible healthcare system, an alternative that takes economic and spiritual factors into account.

In *Developing a Culturally Competent Faith-Based Framework to Promote Breast Cancer Screening among Afghan Immigrant Women* by Mehra Shirazi, Aida Shirazi, and Joan Bloom. The authors stress the need for cultural competency in women's health activism. Cultural competency is especially important within immigrant and Muslim communities that have been historically excluded from the American healthcare system. Creating a space for immigrant women to access information about comprehensive health care, including about breast cancer, is important.

In *Nurse-Curanderas: Las Que Curan at the Heart of Hispanic Culture*, Elaine Luna discusses the emergence of bilingual nurse-curanderas who integrate Hispanic folk healing with allopathic healthcare, showing how they interact with other healthcare providers as well as evaluating the safety and efficacy of a blended service approach. Luna

suggests that this unique set of nurses deliver culturally competent care by balancing cultural features and medical needs, which reduces cultural conflicts, improves patient compliance with treatment regimens, and most of all promotes health and wellness.

How information about health, health hazards, alternative methods for treatment, and care in general is made available to the people who need it reflects our engendered political system and decision-making processes. Too often, however, these decisions are not made based on need, but rather, they are made based on other factors, the foremost of which is profit. Women's health activists not only need to know where to find correct information, but also how to disseminate it. Overall, alternative approaches focus on how women mediate between a hyper-medicalized society and their lived realities, which include religious and cultural traditions. Increased access to information and increased mobility allow women to find healthcare outside the traditional system. In advocating for women's health, it is important to understand how women interact with the various options available to them.

Environmental Toxins Threaten Reproductive Health and Justice

by Sara Alcid and Ansje Miller

Amidst the hard-fought battles to protect and expand access to basic reproductive health care, including abortion care and contraception, we don't often stop to connect the dots between reproductive health and environmental health. This is due partly to the siloed nature of our two movements, and to the historically defensive nature of work to protect environmental and reproductive health and rights. But, it is important to remember that reproductive health includes both access to services to prevent or end a pregnancy *and* the ability to become pregnant, have a healthy pregnancy, and parent one's children. Too often, our everyday environment—from the air we breathe to the personal

care products we use—negatively impacts the health of women, families, and communities.

Most of us would be surprised to learn that the products we use every day, from our sofas to our shampoos, can harm our health. Most of us falsely assume that the products we buy are safe for human consumption and use. After all, how could it be legal to put toxic and untested chemicals into maternity clothes and baby toys?

Yet, mounting scientific evidence indicates that personal care products may be especially dangerous to *reproductive* health because they contain a large number of toxic chemicals. Many of these toxic ingredients are endocrine disruptors that interfere with the body's normal hormone functions, even at low levels of exposure.[1]

The endocrine system is the communication system for the glands, hormones, and cellular receptors that control the body's internal functions. It plays an important role during critical windows of development, including during pregnancy, infancy, and puberty. Endocrine-disrupting chemicals are all around us—in pesticides, wood preservatives, paints, plastics, personal care products, and chemicals used for natural gas extraction and coal mining.

The sad truth is, the Toxic Substance Control Act of 1976—which regulates chemical use in this country—is more than 30 years old and has *never* adequately protected us from the dangers of chemical exposure. The Act was inadequate when it was first signed into law and continues to fail public health today. In fact, our current system for regulating chemicals is so broken that only 200 of the 80,000 *chemicals* in production today have been tested for safety; some uses of only 5 of these toxic chemicals have been restricted.[2]

The result is widespread and ubiquitous exposure to damaging toxins. The evidence is mounting that these dangerous chemicals do significant and lasting damage. A recent study examined the link between fertility and phthalates, which are a common group of endocrine-disrupting chemicals found in personal care products. Researchers followed 501 couples trying to conceive and found that high concentrations of three particular phthalates in male partners were associated with a 20 percent increase in the time it took to achieve pregnancy, compared to couples where the male partner did not have high phthalate concentrations.[3]

Another study revealed that pregnant women with high blood levels of Bisphenol A (BPA, another type of endocrine-disrupting chemical) have a significantly increased risk of experiencing a miscarriage.[4] Of additional concern is the fact that damage from chemical exposure can be passed on to subsequent generations: exposure to certain synthetic chemicals during pregnancy is associated with genital malformation in the *grandsons* of the women who were first exposed.[5]

We need meaningful chemical policy reform to replace our current system for regulating chemicals with one focused on prioritizing public health rather than granting a free pass to the chemical industry. There are currently two bills before Congress that aim to update the Toxic Substance Control Act: the Chemicals in Commerce Act and the Chemical Safety Improvement Act. Sadly, both do more to protect the chemical industry than women, their families, and communities.[6]

Exposure to environmental toxins from products we use is significant, but just one piece of the puzzle. Reproductive and environmental health concerns are also generated from hydraulic fracturing (or "fracking") and coal mining.

Fracking has generated new energy resources, but they come at a severe cost to both environmental and reproductive health. The hundreds of chemicals used in fracking have not been publically disclosed in most states, because they are considered "trade secrets." Of known fracking chemicals, 35 percent are endocrine disruptors linked to infertility, miscarriage, birth defects, impaired learning and brain development, and reproductive cancers.[7] The frightening power of "trade secrets" became crystal clear in June when a North Carolina bill was signed into law, making disclosure of trade secret-protected information about fracking chemicals a misdemeanor.[8]

Communities near fracking sites are exposed to these reproductive toxins through water and air that has been compromised by chemicals. Water treatment facilities are unable to adequately process dirty water generated by fracking, and leave high methane levels in the communities' drinking water. The problem is so bad that the methane makes drinking water *flammable*—yet people in the community are still expected to drink it.[9] While fracking currently occurs in 32 states, federal regulations fail to match this reach. Despite the number of risks that fracking poses for our health and the environment, the gas industry is largely exempt from major federal environmental protection laws.

Coal mining has similar dangers. Coal ash (the waste product of burning coal) contains some of the world's deadliest toxic metals, including arsenic, lead, mercury, cadmium, chromium, and selenium. Prolonged exposure to coal ash has been linked to birth defects, several types of cancer affecting the reproductive system, and infertility. There are more than 1,100 coal ash sites nationwide, yet there are no federal safeguards to protect people's health from coal ash or other coal-related water contamination.

This article was written by: Sara Alcid and Ansje Miller

References

1. Environmental Working Group Website, *Dirty Dozen Endocrine Disruptors*, Washington, DC: Environmental Working Group. October 28, 2013. Retrieved June 2, 2014 fromhttp://www.ewg.org/research/dirty-dozen-list-endocrine-disruptors (http://www.ewg.org/research/dirty-dozen-list-endocrine-disruptors)

2. Reproductive Health Technologies Project Website, *Creating a Climate for Change: THE EARTH KIT*, Washington, DC: Reproductive Health Technologies Project. No date. Retrieved June 2, 2014 fromhttp://www.rhtp.org/fertility/vallombrosa/documents/Toolkit.pdf (http://www.rhtp.org/fertility/vallombrosa/documents/Toolkit.pdf)

3. National Institutes of Health Website, *High plasticizer levels in males linked to delayed pregnancy for female partners*, Washington, DC: National Institutes of Health. March 5, 2014. Retrieved June 2, 2014 from http://www.nichd.nih.gov/news/releases/Pages/030514-phthalates-conception.aspx (http://www.nichd.nih.gov/news/releases/Pages/030514-phthalates-conception.aspx)

4. American Society for Reproductive Medicine Website, *Effects of BPA and Phthalates on Conception and Pregnancy*, Birmingham, AL: American Society for Reproductive Medicine. October 14, 2013. Retrieved June 2, 2014 from http://www.asrm.org/Effects of BPA_and_Phthalates_on_Conception_and_Pregnancy/(http://www.asrm.org/Effects_of_BPA_and_Phthalates_on_Conception_and_Pregnancy/)

5. Program on Reproductive Health and the Environment Website, *Shaping Our Legacy: Reproductive Health and the Environment*, San Francisco, CA: Program on Reproductive Health and the Environment. September 2008. Retrieved June 2, 2014 from http://www.prhe.ucsf.edu/prhe/pubs/shapingourlegacy.pdf (http://www.prhe.ucsf.edu/prhe/pubs/shapingourlegacy.pdf)

6. Safer Chemicals Healthy Families Website, *Legislative Update*, Washington, DC: Safer Chemicals Healthy Families. No date. Retrieved June 2, 2014 from http://saferchemicals.org/legislative-update/ (http://saferchemicals.org/legislative-update/)

7. Center for Environmental Health Website, *Toxic & Dirty Secrets: The truth about fracking & your family's health*, Oakland, CA: Center for Environmental Health. No date. Retrieved June 2, 2014 fromhttp://www.ceh.org/legacy/storage/documents/Fracking/fracking_final-low-1.pdf (http://www.ceh.org/legacy/storage/documents/Fracking/fracking_final-low-1.pdf)

8. ThinkProgress Website, *North Carolina to Lift Ban and Criminalize The Disclosure of Fracking Chemicals*, Washington, DC: ThinkProgress. June 9, 2014. Retrieved June 9, 2014 fromhttp://thinkprogress.org/climate/2014/06/05/3445260/north-carolina-frack... (http://thinkprogress.org/climate/2014/06/05/3445260/north-carolina-fracking-criminalize-chemical-disclosure).

9. Reproductive Health Technologies Project Website, *Creating a Climate for Change: THE EARTH KIT*, Washington, DC: Reproductive Health Technologies Project. No date. Retrieved June 2, 2014 fromhttp://www.rhtp.org/fertility/vallombrosa/documents/Toolkit.pdf (http://www.rhtp.org/fertility/vallombrosa/documents/Toolkit.pdf)

Breast Cancer Risks & the Environment: So Much We Don't Know

by Rachel Walden

In December, the Institute of Medicine (IOM) released a new report, Breast Cancer and the Environment: A Life Course Approach.[1] Commissioned by the Susan G. Komen for the Cure organization, the report reviewed evidence on breast cancer and the environment, explained the difficulties of studying how environmental factors affect breast cancer risk, and recommended both future research needs and ways to reduce breast cancer risk.

The IOM is a well-respected non-profit, non-governmental organization that produces reports on a wide range of health care issues. Komen is more controversial and has been criticized for allowing products to be marketed with its pink ribbon symbol while there are questions about whether those products contribute to breast cancer. One example is Komen's "Promise Me" perfume, which is being reformulated after criticism that it contained a known carcinogen. Komen has also been criticized for focusing on mammography and "the cure" and spending relatively few dollars on prevention or research into breast cancer's causes.[2]

The IOM report took a broad approach to "the environment" and included well-understood risks like smoking, obesity, alcohol consumption, and menopause hormone therapy. It gave somewhat less coverage to exposures women can't readily modify that might require high-level regulatory change, like increasing product safety testing and reducing pollution. The IOM elected not to take a comprehensive approach to environmental issues, but to "focus on a limited selection of various types of environmental factors and potential routes of exposure." The report addresses a number of consumer products components, but is not able to say much that is conclusive. For example, it describes perfume ingredient toluene as being "of concern" as a potential endocrine disrupter. So, although specific consumer products of concern are not addressed, the report may be a good reference for advocates who wish to raise concerns about potentially dangerous products and ingredients.

The IOM also explored the relatively well-documented risks of exposure to "ionizing" radiation, which occurs during medical imaging studies like X-rays, mammograms, and CT scans. It advises women to: "Avoid inappropriate medical radiation exposure" but qualifies the statement by adding that it "is not the committee's intent to dissuade women from routine mammography screening, which aids in detecting early-stage tumors." Routine mammography (especially in low-risk, younger women) has been controversial since the recent U.S. Preventive Services Task Force recommendation to replace routine screening of women in their 40s with individualized decision-making supported by more honest discussion of the very limited usefulness of mammography in pre-menopausal women. Komen rejected these recommendations, and the IOM report does not address this controversy at all. CT scans deliver the highest radiation doses, so women may at least be able

to question the number of these higher-risk scans they receive based on the IOM report.

The IOM notes that more study is needed on several areas. One is shift work involving working at night, which is thought to increase risk. Studies on this issue included very few women of color, which presents a major limitation in understanding this potential risk. A lack of sufficient research is also noted for exposure to nail products, which is of concern both for customers and the largely female salon workforce. The IOM concludes that: "widespread lower level exposure of consumers suggests that this is an area for further inquiry." The IOM also found insufficient evidence about risks from phthalates (found in many plastics, cosmetics, and food products), and states that it's possible that bisphenol A (BPA) could pose a risk, but there is insufficient evidence about this possible toxin. The IOM indirectly addresses environmental pollution with sections on metals, industrial chemicals, and pesticides but provides very little guidance for women who might work in or live near potentially dangerous industries or pollution sources.

The clear thread, beyond well-known risks like smoking and radiation, is the lack of sufficient evidence and the difficulty in studying environmental factors. Women can't readily be assigned to live downwind from a pollution source, or to use a certain consumer product. And, we're exposed to so many different ingredients and substances that it is difficult to determine which, if any, increase our risks or what exposure levels are harmful. We're also only beginning to understand how exposures may affect women differently based on their genetic make-up.

The lack of good data is exacerbated by a lack of regulation to require study before products are brought to market. As the IOM notes, "Premarket testing of chemicals used in consumer products and in industry is rarely undertaken because the federal government has limited authority to require it under the Toxic Substances Control Act. [TSCA]. Carcinogenicity testing is also generally not required before new cosmetics and dietary supplements are marketed. Manufacturers are responsible for identifying ingredients and declaring that they are safe for the intended use."

This means—while there are serious gaps in our understanding of how chemicals affect breast cancer risk—it's unlikely that we will get many clear answers in the short-term. These studies are difficult to conduct, and there is no regulatory reason companies should perform them. Hence, the most important activity we can engage in is to press for regulations requiring more extensive study and testing before products go to market, and ongoing safety studies for things already on the market. For more information, see the coalition of health, environmental and advocacy groups proposing reform of the TSCA at Safer Chemicals, Healthy Families: http://www.saferchemicals.org

This article was written by: Rachel Walden

Rachel R. Walden, MLIS is a medical librarian and blogger for Women's Health News and Our Bodies Our Blog.

References

1. Institute of Medicine, Breast cancer and the environment: A life course approach. Washington, DC: The National Academies Press, 2012

2. Susan G. Komen for the Cure Research Grant Programs, Available online at:http://ww5.komen.org/ResearchGrants/GrantPrograms.html. Accessed: 1/20/2012.

 # Spirituality and Mental Health among Homeless Mothers

by David R. Hodge, Stephanie E. Moser, and Michael S. Shafer

Mothers are one of the fastest growing segments of the homeless population in the United States. Although mental health problems often contribute to homelessness, little is known about the factors that affect mothers' mental health. To help identify protective factors, this longitudinal study examined the relationship between spirituality and mental health among a sample of homeless women with children (*N* = 222). A growth curve analysis was conducted to examine relationships over a 15-month time span. Forgiveness, congregational problems, negative religious coping, and spiritual meaning all variously predicted mental health outcomes. The implications of these findings are discussed as they intersect practice with homeless mothers.

Over the course of the past few decades, homelessness has emerged as a significant social issue (Fertig & Reingold, 2008). Obtaining accurate estimates of the number of homeless individuals is difficult because of the use of different definitions of homelessness and problems counting the homeless (Rollins, Saris, & Johnston-Robledo, 2001). For instance, according to the U.S. Department of Housing and Urban Development's latest Annual Homeless Assessment Report (2010), an estimated 643,067 people lived on the streets or in shelters on a single night, and 1.56 million people used an emergency shelter or a transitional housing program over the course of a 12-month period. Although estimates vary, general agreement exists that the number of homeless people in the United States has increased dramatically since the late 1970s (Wachholz, 2005).

In addition to growing in size, the composition of the homeless population has changed substantially over the past few decades (Averitt, 2003; T. N. Richards, Garland, Bumphus, & Thompson, 2010). Families with children have emerged as a major component of the homeless population (Meadows-Oliver, 2003; Paquette & Bassuk, 2009; Weinreb, Nicholson, Anthes, & Williams, 2007). The majority

David R. Hodge, Stephanie E. Moser, and Michael S. Shafer, "Spirituality and Mental Health Among Homeless Mothers", pp. 245–255, *Social Work Research, Volume 36, Number 4, December 2012*, by permission of Oxford University Press.

of homeless families are headed by single mothers (Goldberg, 1999). Indeed, according to some commentators, women are the fastest growing segment of the homeless population in the United States (Arangua, Andersen, & Gelberg, 2006).

The causes underlying the changing composition of the homeless population are not fully understood (Lehmann, Kass, Drake, & Nichols, 2007). The increase in the number of homeless families is not limited to the United States, but extends to Canada (Schiff, 2007), the United Kingdom (Tischler & Vostanis, 2007), and perhaps other countries as well (Daiski, 2007). Although a small but growing body of research on homeless mothers exists, this area of inquiry is still in its infancy (Cosgrove & Flynn, 2005; Gelberg, Browner, Lejano, & Arangua, 2004; Stainbrook & *Hornik*, 2006).

One relatively established contributor to homelessness among mothers is mental health status (Arangua et al., 2006; Fertig & Reingold, 2008; Lee & Oyserman, 2009; Tischler, Rademeyer, & Vostanis, 2007; Williams & Hall, 2009; Zlotnick, Tam, & Bradley, 2007). The relationship between mental health and homelessness is complex. Poor psychological health can be both an antecedent to, and a consequence of, homelessness (Philippot, Lecocq, Sempoux, Nachtergael, & Galand, 2007). In terms of the former, the onset of a mental disorder can, for example, lead to deteriorating social and economic conditions that eventually result in homelessness (Weinreb et al., 2007).

Many events unrelated to the onset of a mental disorder can result in women becoming homeless, including domestic violence, unaffordable rents, divorce or separation, condemned housing, loss of employment, and so on (Meadows-Oliver, 2003; Rollins et al., 2001; Tischler et al., 2007). On becoming homeless, mothers often report experiencing deep senses of loss, stress, or depression (Meadows-Oliver, 2003). Negative life events, cumulating with the loss of their homes and their struggle to adapt to a homeless lifestyle while parenting children, can overwhelm mothers, resulting in increased depression, anxiety, and other mental health problems (Banyard & Graham-Bermann, 1998; Tischler et al., 2007). In turn, the onset of various forms of psychological distress caused by becoming homeless can hinder women's ability to exit homelessness, causing a downward spiral (Daiski, 2007).

Although it is generally accepted that homelessness is stressful and the mental health of homeless mothers is often poor, relatively little is known about the factors that affect the mental health of these women (Tischler et al., 2007). Given the stigma homeless mothers often face, it is particularly important to focus on the strengths or protective factors that help mothers deal with mental health problems (Cosgrove & Flynn, 2005; Wachholz, 2005). Protective factors can be understood as variables that facilitate positive outcomes by buffering individuals from constructs that place them at risk (Fraser, Richman, & Galinsky, 1999; Smith, 2006). One such factor that may help engender positive mental health among homeless mothers is spirituality (Larkin, Beckos, & Martin, in press).

Spirituality and Mental Health

A growing body of evidence suggests that spirituality is positively associated with women's mental health (Dailey & Stewart, 2007). Similarly, reviews of the extant research on spirituality and mental health have found generally positive associations (Ano & Vasconcelles, 2005; Hackney & Sanders, 2003; H. G. Koenig, 2007; H. G. Koenig, McCullough, & Larson, 2001; Shreve-Neiger & Edelstein, 2004). Although it is important to note that the results are not uniformly positive, in aggregate, higher levels of spirituality tend to be linked to greater psychological well-being in hundreds of studies (H. G. Koenig, 2008).

This emerging body of evidence is consistent with studies exploring coping strategies among homeless women. A number of qualitative studies have found that both women (Bhui, Shanahan, & Harding, 2006; Montgomery, 1994; Washington, Moxley, Garriott, & Weinberger, 2009) and mothers (Cosgrove & Flynn, 2005; Meadows-Oliver, 2003) use spirituality to cope with the stress of being homeless. For instance, a meta-synthesis of qualitative research on homeless mothers revealed that praying was among the most common strategies used to deal with the difficulties resulting from homelessness (Meadows-Oliver, 2003).

At least two longitudinal studies have explored the relationship between spirituality and mental health among homeless mothers, with, at best, mixed results. In the United Kingdom, the relationship between five different coping strategies and mental health outcomes was examined (Tischler

& Vostanis, 2007). Seeking spiritual support was assessed using the Family Crisis Oriented Personal Evaluation Scales. Mental health was assessed using the General Health Questionnaire at baseline ($N = 72$) and at four-month follow-up ($n = 44$). Seeking spiritual support was unrelated to mental health, both at baseline and at follow-up.

In the United States, the relationship between spirituality and mental health was explored among a sample of African American ($n = 88$) and non–African American mothers ($n = 101$) in the Connecticut area (Douglas, Jimenez, Lin, & Frisman, 2008). Spirituality was measured with the Spiritual Well-being Scale, and multiple standardized batteries were used to measure 10 dimensions of mental health. Outcomes were assessed at baseline and three follow-up points over a 15-month period. Although no significant main effects emerged, a moderator analysis was significant. Among African American mothers, higher levels of spiritual wellbeing predicted lower levels of anxiety and post-traumatic stress over time.

Among the possible explanations for the largely nonsignificant findings recorded in these two studies is the operationalization of spirituality. In other words, how spirituality was operationalized may account for the failure of spirituality to predict mental health (Hackney & Sanders, 2003).

Spirituality and Religion as Multidimensional Constructs

Spirituality and religion are increasingly defined as distinct but overlapping constructs (Derezotes, 2006; Miller & Thoresen, 2003). Spirituality is commonly defined in individual, existential, or relational terms, typically incorporating some reference to the sacred or the transcendent (Hill & Pargament, 2003; Hodge, 2005). Conversely, religion tends to be conceptualized in communal, organizational, or structural terms (Canda & Furman, 2010).

As part of the process of distinguishing spirituality from religion, observers have increasingly recognized that these constructs are multidimensional (Miller & Thoresen, 2003). In other words, spirituality and religion, regardless of which is considered to be the more encompassing construct, consist of multiple dimensions in much the same way that mental health consists of multiple dimensions (for example, depression, anxiety) (Berry, 2005).

Examples of various dimensions include forgiveness, spiritual meaning, and positive and negative approaches to spiritual coping (Idler et al., 2003).

Thus, outcomes can vary depending on how spirituality is operationalized (Hackney & Sanders, 2003). In some cases, different dimensions of spirituality can even be inversely related to mental health (Ano & Vasconcelles, 2005). Positive spiritual coping, for example, tends to be positively associated with mental health, whereas negative spiritual coping tends to be inversely associated (Ano & Vasconcelles, 2005; H. G. Koenig et al., 2001; Pargament, 2002).

Recognition of the multifaceted nature of spirituality and religion has sparked calls for the use of multidimensional measures in research exploring the relationship between spirituality and health outcomes (Berry, 2005; H. G. Koenig et al., 2001; Miller & Thoresen, 2003). Using psychometrically sound multidimensional instruments can help clarify which aspects of spirituality and religion are linked to mental health (Shreve-Neiger & Edelstein, 2004).

Accordingly, this study used a multidimensional measure to examine the relationship between spirituality and religion and mental health among a sample of homeless mothers in the United States. As discussed in greater detail in the following sections, a prospective longitudinal design was used to conduct this examination. Specifically, this study explored the degree to which 11 dimensions of spirituality and religion were associated with nine dimensions of mental health over the course of a 15-month time span.

Method

Participants

Participants were women ($N = 222$) enrolled in an emergency homeless shelter program in a large Southwestern city. The program provided up to 120 days of emergency shelter and supportive services (for example, child care; employment education; social skills training; substance abuse treatment, material support in form of transportation assistance, clothing, food boxes, and toiletries) and 12-months of aftercare services to homeless families. To be enrolled in the program, participants had to meet the following criteria: be 18 years of age or older, be homeless (that is, lack a fixed, regular, or adequate nighttime residence), be a female head of household, have at least one child between two and 16 years of age living with the mother at program entry, and have a *Diagnostic and Statistical Manual of Mental Disorders* (4th ed.) (American Psychiatric Asssociation, 1994) Axis I diagnosis for either a mental health or substance use disorder in the past year.

Over the course of 20 months, 423 women were screened, of which 262 met the eligibility criteria for program enrollment. Of these, 84.73% ($N = 222$) agreed to participate in the study. The mean age of the participants was 31.7 years ($SD = 7.9$), and their average number of children was 3.3 ($SD = 1.9$). Twenty-seven percent ($n = 60$) reported living with a partner at baseline. In terms of race/ethnicity, 47.7% ($n = 106$) identified as non-Hispanic white or Caucasian, 14.4% identified as Hispanic/Latina ($n = 32$), and the remaining participants selected alternative descriptors or declined to self-identify.

Twenty-five participants (11.26%) could not be located for the final 15-month interview. An attrition analysis was conducted to see if baseline participants differed from those who completed the study. No significant differences emerged between the two groups on demographic, baseline mental health, and spirituality measures.

Measures

Spirituality and religion were assessed using a slightly modified version of the NIA/Fetzer Short Form for the Measurement of Religion and Spirituality (Fetzer Institute, 1999; Idler et al., 2003). This measure is designed to assess 11 different dimensions of spirituality and religion that are theoretically related to health and well-being among adults of all ages. The instrument was validated with a nationally representative sample of adults (Idler et al., 2003) and has been widely used (Maselko & Kubzansky, 2006; Neff, 2006; Shreve-Neiger & Edelstein, 2004).

The 11 domains, the number of items in each domain, a sample item from the subscale, means and standard deviations for each scale averaged across the four time points, and Cronbach's alpha reliability coefficients for each subscale are listed in Table 1. Reliability coefficients were generally acceptable (Kline, 2000), particularly given the low number of items making up many of the domains (Cortina, 1993), and comparable to the coefficients

recorded among the general population (Idler et al., 2003). The major exception was the beliefs and values domain, which recorded an unacceptable level of error ($\alpha = .46$ in the present study compared with $\alpha = .64$ in the validation study). As is the case with the following dependent measures, all sub-scales were scored so that higher values represent greater degrees of the individual construct assessed.

Mental health was measured using the Brief Symptom Inventory (BSI) (Derogatis & Melisaratos, 1983). The BSI is a widely used measure of mental health status (Ryan, 2007) and has been used previously to assess psychological symptoms among other homeless populations (Solorio, Milburn, Andersen, Trifskin, & Rodgriquez, 2006), including homeless mothers (Douglas et al., 2008). It assesses emotional distress in the past seven days using a five-point scale ("not at all" = 0 to "extremely" = 4) in nine psychological dimensions: (1) somatization, (2) obsessive–compulsive behavior, (3) interpersonal sensitivity, (4) depression, (5) anxiety, (6) hostility, (7) phobic anxiety, (8) paranoid ideation, and (9) psychoticism. Further information about these nine dimensions can be found in Derogatis and Melisaratos (1983).

The BSI was previously validated with a primarily female sample (Derogatis & Melisaratos, 1983). Reliability coefficients for the nine subscales in the validation study ranged from .71 to .85, with similar values obtained in subsequent research with samples of homeless adolescents (Solorio et al., 2006) and mothers (Douglas et al., 2008). In this study, the coefficients for the nine subscales ranged from .73 to .90.

Procedures

Under the supervision of a university institutional review board, participants were interviewed within one month of entering the program (baseline measurement). Subsequent interviews were conducted at three months, nine months, and 15 months post baseline. The interviews were conducted by trained interviewers. Participants were paid for their time. The amount of compensation was increased with each subsequent interview to maximize participant retention. Initial interviews were compensated at $30, three-month follow-up interviews were compensated at $40, and 15-month interviews were compensated at $60.

Data Analytic Approach

To examine the relationship between spirituality and mental health outcomes over the 15-month period, separate multilevel longitudinal growth curve analyses were constructed to predict each of the nine mental health outcomes using the mixed regression procedure in SPSS version 17 (Raudenbush & Bryk, 2002). Within this framework, each mother received an intercept and a slope that defined her personal regression line. The intercept was an indicator of the initial level of mental health for a given mother at the beginning of the study period. The slope represented the individual's rate of change. Additional explanatory variables, such as the 11 spirituality and religion measures, can be added to the model to ascertain their effects on the intercept. Interaction terms, comprising the explanatory variables × time, were used to assess the variables' effect on the slope. This approach allowed us to examine the effect of spirituality on both initial mental health outcomes and the trajectory of mental health outcomes over time.

Table 1: Psychometric Properties of Spirituality and Religion Measures across All Time Points

Measure (Sample Item)	Number of Items	M	SD	α
Private religious practices (How often do you pray privately in places other than at church or synagogue?)	3	4.19	1.70	.77
Public religious practices (How often do you go to religious services?)	2	2.56	1.16	.60
Congregational problems (How often do people in your spiritual group make too many demands on you?)	2	1.43	0.48	.63
Negative spiritual coping (I wonder whether God has abandoned me.)	2	1.55	0.62	.77
Forgiveness (I know that God forgives me.)	3	3.23	0.59	.68
Congregational benefits (If you were ill, how much would the people in your congregation help you out?)	2	2.43	0.93	.91
Intensity (To what extent do you consider yourself to be a spiritual person?)	2	2.53	0.65	.63
Positive spiritual coping (I think about how my life is part of a larger spiritual force.)	3	2.59	0.74	.77
Daily spiritual experiences (I feel God's presence.)	6	3.77	1.21	.89
Beliefs and values (I believe in a God who watches over me.)	3	3.05	0.45	.46
Spiritual meaning (The events in my life unfold according to a divine or greater Plan.)	2	3.77	1.21	.72

Analysis proceeded in a hierarchical manner. As implied in the introduction, mental health is malleable and may be affected affected by homelessness. Examining the linear trend of the nine mental health outcomes provides an understanding of changes in mental health status over time. Toward this end, in level 1 we predicted each mental health outcome for an individual as a function of her intercept (for example, mental health score at baseline), her growth rate (slope), and the residual mental health score at each time point. In these models, the time variable was coded 0 = baseline interview, 1 = three-month interview, 2 = nine-month interview, and 3 = 15-month interview.

Following the examination of the linear trend in mental health outcomes, the following demographic characteristics were included as time-invariant covariates of the intercept and slope in the level 2 model: woman's age at program admission (mean centered at age 31), whether she was living with a partner (0 = no, 1 = yes), whether she identified as Hispanic/Latina (0 = not Hispanic/Latina, 1 = Hispanic/Latina), and whether she identified as white/Caucasian (0 = white/Caucasian, 1 = not white/Caucasian). In addition, the mean centered scores of the 11 spirituality measures were calculated across the four time points and included as time-invariant predictors of intercept and slope. This approach was selected because adult female spirituality tends to be relatively stable over time (Dalby, 2006; Koenig, McGue, & Iacono, 2008).

Thus, in level 2 we specified the intercept for an individual as a function of the average mental health outcome at baseline for 31-year-old, non-Hispanic, Caucasian women, not living with a partner, with average scores on all 11 spirituality measures, and the average effects of each individual covariate/predictor on mental health outcomes at baseline. As implied earlier, the effects of the spirituality measures on the intercepts provides a cross-sectional understanding of the relationship between spirituality and mental health at the beginning of the study.

We further specified the growth rate of an individual as a function of the average growth rate in mental health outcomes for 31-year-old, non-Hispanic, Caucasian women not living with a partner, with average scores on all 11 spirituality measures, and the average individual effects of each individual covariate/predictor on the growth rate of mental health outcomes, controlling for every other predictor/covariate. The effect of the spirituality measures on the slopes provides an understanding of the effects of spirituality on mental health over the 15-month study period.

Model fit was assessed using likelihood ratio tests. Full information maximum likelihood estimation was used to account for missing data (Enders & Bandalos, 2001).

Results

Correlations among Spirituality Measures

The correlations among the 11 spirituality measures, averaged across the four time points, are presented in Table 2. The correlations varied substantially across the measures, reflecting the multidimensional nature of the NIA/Fetzer instrument. Coefficients ranged from .88 to −.29.

Linear Trend of Mental Health Outcomes

Mental health outcome scores over time are depicted in Table 3. With the exception of hostility, the coefficients were all negative, suggesting that mental health decreased over time. This apparent decrease was only significant for interpersonal sensitivity and depression.

Inclusion of Demographic Covariates and Spirituality Measures

After examination of the linear trend of the mental health outcomes over time, the demographic covariates and spirituality measures were incorporated into the model (see Table 4). The inclusion of these predictors significantly improved model fit for each mental health outcome, as evidenced by log likelihood tests [each $\times 2(26 > 54.05, p < .001]$. The effects of the spirituality measures on the intercepts are depicted in the top half of Table 4, and the effects on the slopes are depicted in the bottom half of the table (for example, Private Religious Practices $\times$ Time).

Table 2: Correlation Matrix of Spirituality and Religion Measures											
Measure	**1**	**2**	**3**	**4**	**5**	**6**	**7**	**8**	**9**	**10**	**11**
1. Private religious practices	—										
2. Public religious practices	.68	—									
3. Congregational problems	.21	.26	—								
4. Negative spiritual coping	−.18	−.16	.11	—							
5. Forgiveness	.50	.42	.11	−.28	—						
6. Congregational benefits	.53	.62	.22	−.20	.43	—					
7. Intensity	.58	.47	.20	−.23	.53	.43	—				
8. Positive spiritual coping	.71	.60	.24	−.25	.61	.54	.64	—			
9. Daily spiritual experiences	.74	.57	.16	−.29	.65	.55	.71	.88	—		
10. Beliefs and values	.57	.48	.23	−.21	.52	.41	.62	.73	.73	—	
11. Spiritual meaning	.55	.50	.23	−.28	.52	.42	.58	.70	.74	.66	—
Note: All correlations significant at $p < .001$.											

Table 3: Linear Trend of Mental Health Outcomes								
Model 1	**SOM**	**OCD**	**IS**	**DEP**	**ANX**	**HOS**	**PHOB**	**PAR**	**PSY**
Intercept	0.72	1.19	0.98	1.04	0.84	0.80	0.59	1.04	0.75
Time	−0.03	−0.04	−0.05*	−0.06*	−0.03	0.02	−0.03	−0.04	−0.03
Deviance	1,488.49	1,885.86	1,982.43	1,977.68	1,803.87	1,645.10	1,641.45	1,846.67	1,632.38

Note: SOM = somatization; OCD = obsessive–compulsive behavior; IS = interpersonal sensitivity; DEP = depression; ANX = anxiety; HOS = hostility; PHOB = phobic anxiety; PAR = paranoid ideation; PSY = psychoticism.

* $p < .05$.

Effects on Intercepts. Four spirituality measures were significantly related to mental health outcomes at baseline: (1) forgiveness, (2) negative spiritual coping, (3) beliefs and values, and (4) spiritual meaning. Of these, forgiveness exhibited the strongest and most pervasive relationship. This construct was associated with significantly lower scores on each of the nine mental health outcomes. This indicates that greater overall scores on forgiveness were associated with better mental health outcomes at baseline, controlling for all other spirituality measures and demographics.

Two other spirituality measures also exhibited relatively consistent associations with mental health: negative spiritual coping and spiritual meaning. Greater overall scores on negative spiritual coping were associated with significantly higher levels of interpersonal sensitivity, depression, anxiety, paranoid ideation, and psychoticism at baseline. In other words, with all other spirituality measures and demographics controlled for, negative spiritual coping was linked to worse mental health at baseline.

Spiritual meaning was also linked to five mental health outcomes. More specifically, higher spiritual meaning scores were associated with significantly higher levels of interpersonal sensitivity, hostility, phobic anxiety, paranoid ideation, and psychoticism at baseline. In contrast to the other significant relationships that emerged at baseline, these relationships are inconsistent with previous research. In other words, the existing literature suggests that higher levels of spiritual meaning will be associated with better, rather than worse, mental health (Koenig, 2007; Koenig et al., 2001).

Finally, the beliefs and values measure was associated with one mental health outcome. In keeping with extant theory and research, higher scores on beliefs and values were associated with

significantly lower levels of paranoid ideation at baseline. Interpretation of this result is complicated, however, by the unacceptable level of error associated with the beliefs and values measure (that is, a Cronbach's alpha of .46).

Effects on Slopes. Three spirituality measures demonstrated significant interaction effects with time. The measure with the most pervasive effect on mental health was congregational problems. Higher levels of congregational problems predicted significant increases in somatization, obsessive–compulsive behavior, interpersonal sensitivity, depression, hostility, phobic anxiety, paranoid ideation, and psychoticism over the 15 months.

Spiritual meaning was associated with four mental health outcomes. In contrast to the cross-sectional findings, higher levels of spiritual meaning predicted significant decreases in interpersonal sensitivity, hostility, and phobic anxiety over time. As noted, this finding is consistent with prior theory and research (Idler et al., 2003; Koenig et al., 2001).

The beliefs and values measure predicted two outcomes: Higher levels were associated with significantly higher levels of interpersonal sensitivity and paranoid ideation over time. As is the case with the previous cross-sectional finding, the high level of error associated with the beliefs and values measure implies that this result should be treated cautiously.

Discussion

It is widely recognized that mental health challenges contribute to the onset of homelessness and that the state of being homeless itself can also engender psychological problems (Philippot et al., 2007). As mothers cope with the stress of homelessness, it is all too easy for them to become

Table 4: Effects of Spirituality and Religion on Mental Health at Baseline and Over Time

Model 2	SOM	OCD	IS	DEP	ANX	HOS	PHOB	PAR	PSY
Intercept	0.79	1.26	1.06	1.12	0.97	0.78	0.68	1.11	0.80
Time	-0.02	-0.03	-0.04	-0.04	-0.01	0.03	-0.02	-0.03	-0.02
Private religious practices	-0.02	-0.04	0.02	0.02	0.04	0.01	0.05	0.04	0.00
Public religious practices	0.10	0.14	0.13	0.09	0.12	-0.01	0.07	0.07	0.07
Congregational problems	0.12	0.12	0.11	0.04	0.18	0.14	0.02	0.15	-0.07
Negative spiritual coping	0.14	0.09	0.26**	0.23**	0.20*	0.14	0.15	0.22*	0.22**†
Forgiveness	-0.23*	-0.34**	-0.44***†	-0.43**	-0.35**	-0.27**	-0.27*	-0.51***†	-0.46***†
Congregational benefits	-0.06	-0.04	-0.04	-0.07	-0.01	0.04	-0.03	-0.07	-0.04
Intensity	0.06	0.07	0.002	0.04	0.04	-0.02	0.11	0.11	-0.01
Positive spiritual coping	-0.02	-0.12	-0.11	-0.13	-0.16	-0.23	-0.14	-0.08	-0.09
Daily spiritual experiences	0.003	0.02	0.05	0.14	0.05	0.08	-0.02	0.13	0.07
Beliefs and values	0.10	-0.02	-0.22	0.10	0.04	0.16	-0.05	-0.40*	0.12
Spiritual meaning	0.18	0.31	0.52***†	-0.02	0.20	0.31*	0.30*	0.37*	0.29*
Private Religious Practices × Time	0.02	0.03	0.01	0.01	-0.004	0.01	0.01	-0.02	0.01
Public Religious Practices × Time	-0.001	-0.02	-0.05	-0.01	-0.002	-0.01	-0.001	-0.01	-0.003
Congregational Problems × Time	0.10*	0.17***†	0.20***†	0.18***†	0.09	0.20***	0.12*	0.14**	0.16***
Negative Spiritual Coping × Time	-0.03	0.03	-0.03	0.01	0.0001	0.01	-0.04	-0.01	0.02
Forgiveness × Time	0.03	0.06	0.08	0.09	0.07	0.07	-0.01	0.09	0.08
Congregational Benefits × Time	-0.02	-0.03	-0.05	-0.05	-0.03	-0.04	-0.02	-0.04	-0.04
Intensity × Time	0.01	0.000	0.03	-0.01	0.03	-0.03	0.03	-0.03	0.001
Positive Spiritual Coping × Time	-0.02	-0.06	-0.04	-0.08	0.01	-0.06	0.01	-0.03	-0.04
Daily Spiritual Experiences × Time	-0.01	-0.01	0.02	0.02	0.000	0.07	-0.02	0.01	0.02
Beliefs and Values × Time	0.03	0.07	0.20*	0.07	0.04	0.10	0.12	0.16*	0.01
Spiritual Meaning × Time	-0.07	-0.04	-0.21***	-0.04	-0.11	-0.17**	-0.13*	-0.11	-0.09
Mother's age	0.01	0.00	0.00	0.003	0.002	-0.01	-0.01	0.00	0.00
Living with partner at baseline	-0.12	-0.12	-0.14	-0.23*	-0.16	0.04	-0.21*	-0.19*	-0.23**
Hispanic/Latina	0.14	0.17	0.19	0.19	0.02	0.12	0.04	0.19	0.16
White	-0.22*	-0.29*	-0.32***†	-0.24*	-0.32***†	-0.15	-0.22*	-0.24*	-0.16*
Deviance	1,321.19	1,717.55	1,771.66	1,768.53	1,604.91	1,432.43	1,445.88	1,659.13	1,407.38

Notes: Superscript daggers denote significance at the corrected alpha level. SOM = somatization; OCD = obsessive–compulsive behavior; IS = interpersonal sensitivity; DEP = depression; ANX = anxiety; HOS = hostility; PHOB = phobic anxiety; PAR = paranoid ideation; PSY = psychoticism.

*$p < .05$. **$p < .01$. ***$p < .001$. †$p .0045$.

ensnared in a downward spiral as the increasing severity of psychological distress compromises their ability to escape homelessness. Identifying strengths or protective factors can play a crucial role in helping mothers exit homelessness or avoid its onset.

Toward this end, the present study used a longitudinal design to examine the relationship between spirituality and mental health among homeless mothers over the course of 15 months. Of the 11 dimensions of spirituality examined, the strongest, most pervasive relationship emerged for forgiveness. At baseline, forgiveness was positively associated with all nine dimensions of mental health. No interaction with time occurred, indicating a stable relationship between forgiveness and mental health over time (that is, the slope did not change over time). In other words, mental health outcomes did not improve over time for those with higher levels of forgiveness beyond the relationship identified at baseline.

The second most pervasive relationship occurred with congregational problems. Although this variable was not associated with mental health at baseline, it was associated with eight of the nine mental health dimensions over time. Congregational problems predicted increasingly worse mental health over the course of the 15-month study.

Negative religious coping was positively related to five dimensions of mental distress at baseline. As was the case with forgiveness, the slope did not change over time. Higher levels of negative coping did not predict increasingly worse levels of mental health over time.

Spiritual meaning was positively associated with five dimensions of mental health at baseline. Unlike the other significant relationships that emerged in this study, this finding runs counter to existing theory and research on spirituality and religion (Ano & Vasconcelles, 2005; Idler et al., 2003; Koenig et al., 2001; Pargament, 2002). It is interesting to note that the longitude findings were consistent with prior theory and research. In other words, over time, higher levels of spiritual meaning predicted better mental health.

Although more research is needed to understand this finding, the results may be partially explained by dynamics related to homelessness. At baseline, mothers may have been wrestling with the onset

of homelessness and induction into the program. Women with a strong sense of spiritual meaning, as exemplified by the sample item "The events in my life unfold according to a divine or greater Plan," may have felt abandoned by God (Pargament, 1997; Pargament, 2002). However, over time, as they adjusted to their status and continued to understand life events through a spiritual lens, mental health may have improved.

The results obtained in this study are also consistent with the existing qualitative research on spirituality and homelessness. As noted in the introduction, a number of studies indicate that spirituality is a strength that helps mothers deal with the stress of homelessness (for example, Cosgrove & Flynn, 2005; Meadows-Oliver, 2003). The present research corroborates this prior body of work and expands it by adding a longitudinal perspective.

Conversely, the results differ from those obtained in previous longitudinal studies of spirituality and mental health among homeless mothers, in which largely nonsignificant relationships have emerged (Douglas et al., 2008; Tischler & Vostanis, 2007). Although various explanations may account for the differences, it is notable that previous research used unidimensional spirituality measures, whereas this study used a multidimensional instrument (Idler et al., 2003). The differential results may be attributed to the fact that multiple dimensions of spirituality and religion were assessed in the present study, allowing for a more nuanced understanding of the relationship between spirituality and mental health among homeless mothers (Berry, 2005; Miller & Thoresen, 2003; Shreve-Neiger & Edelstein, 2004).

The results have important implications for practitioners working with homeless mothers. Some qualitative research suggests that homeless mothers recognize the barriers that mental health problems present in terms of escaping homelessness but find it difficult to imagine pathways that might lead to improvement (Lee & Oyserman, 2009). Thus, interventions designed to foster improvement in this area may be particularly important.

Toward this end, practitioners may wish to explore mothers' understanding of forgiveness, perhaps while conducting a spiritual assessment

(Hodge, 2004). The relationship between forgiveness and mental health is relatively well established (McCullough, Paragament & Thoresen, 2000). Interventions designed to foster forgiveness have appeared in the literature (DiBlasio, 1998). Practitioners may assist homeless mothers by tapping clients' spiritual strengths to enhance forgiveness. In a similar manner, exploring clients' sense of spiritual meaning may also help foster mental health. However, as is the case in all work that engages client spirituality, it is important to consider one's degree of cultural competence with the client's spiritual tradition and use collaboration or referral strategies as necessary (Richards & Bergin, 2000).

Practitioners may also wish to ascertain the existence of congregational problems during a spiritual assessment. The collaborative exploration of strategies that alleviate these problems may foster mental health. In addition, resolving tensions between mothers and their congregations, with clients' consent, may have the added, secondary benefit of connecting mothers with social support resources that can help them in their efforts to escape homelessness (Irwin, LaGory, Ritchey, & Fitzptrick, 2008; Zugazaga, 2008).

These implications must be considered tentatively in light of the study's limitations. For example, the low reliabilities obtained with some of the spirituality and religion measures should be noted. One measure had an alpha coefficient of just .46, and four others had coefficients between .60 and .70. Although the small number of items comprised by these subscales helps account for the low reliabilities (Cortina, 1993), those coefficients all fall below the widely accepted .70 value (Kline, 2000).

The lack of generalizability should also be noted. The sample was drawn from one homeless program with a unique set of services. It is possible that the set of services provided by the program affected the results. Results might vary with different programs or samples, particularly in geographic regions in which the background demographics differ. For instance, outcomes might differ with samples of African American mothers, given the salience of spirituality in the black community (Douglas et al., 2008; Stahler, Kirby, & Kerwin, 2007).

Further research is needed with other samples to confirm the findings obtained in this study. Future research should use multidimensional measures to assess both spirituality and mental health (Berry, 2005; Miller & Thoresen, 2003; Shreve-Neiger & Edelstein, 2004). Given the growing number of homeless mothers in the United States, such research should be prioritized (Goldberg, 1999; Paquette & Bassuk, 2009).

Conclusion

Female-headed familie may constitute the fastest growing segment of the homeless population (Arangua et al., 2006; Goldberg, 1999; Paquette & Bassuk, 2009; Richards et al., 2010). Many of these women wrestle with mental health issues that inhibit their escape from homelessness (Lee & Oyserman, 2009). Using a longitudinal design with multidimensional measures of spirituality and mental health, this study identified a number of spiritual and religious variables that may help mitigate mental health problems. In short, the present results clarify some of the pathways that may help mothers exit homelessness or avoid it entirely.

References

Ano, G. G., & Vasconcelles, E. B. (2005). Religious coping and psychological adjustment to stress: A meta-analysis. *Journal of Clinical Psychology, 61*, 461–480.

Arangua, L., Andersen, R., & Gelberg, L. (2005). The health circumstances of homelessness women in the United States. *International Journal of Mental Health, 34*, 62–92.

Averitt, S. S. (2003). "Homelessness is not a choice!" The plight of homeless women with preschool children living in temporary shelters. *Journal of Family Nursing, 9*(1), 79–100.

Banyard, V. L., & Graham-Bermann, S. A. (1998). Surviving poverty: Stress and coping in the lives of housed and homeless mothers. *American Journal of Orthopsychiatry, 68*, 479–489.

Berry, D. (2005). Methodological pitfalls in the study of religiosity and spirituality. *Western Journal of Nursing Research, 27*, 628–647.

Bhui, K., Shanahan, L., & Harding, G. (2006). Homelessness and mental illness: A literature review and a qualitative study of perceptions of the adequacy of care. *International Journal of Social Psychiatry, 52*, 152–165.

Canda, E. R., & Furman, L. D. (2010). *Spiritual diversity in social work practice: The heart of helping* (2nd ed.). New York: Oxford University Press.

Cortina, J. M. (1993). What is coefficient alpha? An examination of theory and applications. *Journal of Applied Psychology, 78,* 98–104.

Cosgrove, L., & Flynn, C. (2005). Marginalized mothers: Parenting without a home. *Analysis of Social Issues and Public Policy, 5,* 127–143.

Dailey, D. E., & Stewart, A. L. (2007). Psychometric characteristics of the spiritual perspectives scale in pregnant African-American women. *Research in Nursing & Health, 30,* 61–71.

Daiski, I. (2007). Perspectives of homeless people on their health and health needs priorities. *Journal of Advanced Nursing, 58,* 273–281.

Dalby, P. (2006). Is there a process of spiritual change or development associated with aging? A critical review of research. *Aging and Mental Health, 10*(1), 4–12.

Derezotes, D. S. (2006). *Spiritually oriented social work practice.* Boston: Pearson.

Derogatis, L. R., & Melisaratos, N. (1983). The Brief Symptom Inventory: An introductory report. *Psychological Medicine, 13,* 595–605.

DiBlasio, F. A. (1998). The use of a decision-based forgiveness intervention within intergenerational family therapy. *Journal of Family Therapy, 20,* 77–94.

Douglas, A. N., Jimenez, S., Lin, H.-J., & Frisman, L. K. (2008). Ethnic differences in the effects of spiritual well-being on long-term psychological and behavioral outcomes within a sample of homeless women. *Cultural Diversity and Ethnic Minority Psychology, 14,* 344–352.

Enders, C. K., & Bandalos, D. L. (2001). The relative performance of full information maximum likelihood estimation for missing data in structural equation modeling. *Structural Equation Modeling: An Interdisciplinary Journal, 8,* 430–457.

Fertig, A. R., & Reingold, D. A. (2008). Homelessness among at-risk families with children in twenty American cities. *Social Service Review, 82,* 485–510.

Fetzer Institute. (1999). *Multidimensional measurement of religiousness/spirituality for use in health research.* Retrieved from http://www.fetzer.org/component/content/article/18-main/248-dses

Fraser, M. W., Richman, J. M., & Galinsky, M. J. (1999). Risk, protection, and resilience: Toward a conceptual framework for social work practice. *Social Work Research, 23,* 131–143.

Gelberg, L., Browner, C. H., Lejano, E., & Arangua, L. (2004). Access to women's health care: A qualitative study of barriers perceived by homeless women. *Women & Health, 40,* 87–100.

Goldberg, J. E. (1999). A short term approach to intervention with homeless mothers: A role for clinicians in homeless shelters. *Families in Society, 80,* 161–168.

Hackney, C. H., & Sanders, G. S. (2003). Religiosity and mental health: A meta-analysis. *Journal for the Scientific Study of Religion, 42,* 43–55.

Hill, P. C., & Pargament, K. I. (2003). Advances in the conceptualization and measurement of religion and spirituality. *American Psychologist, 58,* 64–74.

Hodge, D. R. (2004). Spirituality and people with mental illness: Developing spiritual competency in assessment and intervention. *Families in Society, 85,* 36–44.

Hodge, D. R. (2005). Spiritual ecograms: A new assessment instrument for identifying clients' spiritual strengths in space and across time. *Families in Society, 86,* 287–296.

Idler, E. L., Musick, M. A., Ellison, C. G., George, L. K., Krause, N., Ory, M. G., et al. (2003). Measuring multiple dimensions of religion and spirituality for health research. *Research on Aging, 25,* 327–365.

Irwin, J., LaGory, M., Ritchey, F., & Fitzptrick, K. (2008). Social assets and mental distress among the homeless: Exploring the roles of social support and other forms of social capital on depression. *Social Science & Medicine, 67,* 1935–1943.

Kline, P. (2000). *The handbook of psychology testing* (2nd ed.). New York: Routledge.

Koenig, H. G. (2007). *Spirituality in patient care* (2nd ed.). Philadelphia: Templeton Foundation Press.

Koenig, H. G. (2008). Religion and mental health: What should psychiatrists do? *Psychiatric Bulletin, 32,* 201–203.

Koenig, H. G., McCullough, M. E., & Larson, D. B. (2001). *Handbook of religion and health.* New York: Oxford University Press.

Koenig, L. B., McGue, M., & Iacono, W. G. (2008). Stability and change in religiousness during emerging adulthood. *Developmental Psychology, 44,* 532–543.

Larkin, H., Beckos, B., & Martin, E. (in press). Applied integral methodological pluralism: Designing comprehensive social service program evaluation. In S. Esbjorn-Hargens (Ed.), *Enacting an integral future: New horizons for integral theory.* SUNY Press.

Lee, S. J., & Oyserman, D. (2009). Expecting to work, fearing homelessness: The possible selves of low-income mothers. *Journal of Applied Social Psychology, 39,* 1334–1355.

Lehmann, E. R., Kass, P. H., Drake, C. M., & Nichols, S. B. (2007). Risk factors for first-time homelessness in low-income women. *American Journal of Orthopsychiatry, 77,* 20–28.

Maselko, J., & Kubzansky, L. D. (2006). Gender differences in religious practices, spiritual experiences and health: Results from the US General Social Survey. *Social Science & Medicine, 62,* 2848–2860.

McCullough, M. E., Paragament, K. I., & Thoresen, C. E. (Eds). (2000). *Forgiveness.* New York: Guilford Press.

Meadows-Oliver, M. (2003). Mothering in public: A meta-synthesis of homeless women with children living in shelters. *Journal for Specialists in Pediatric Nursing, 8,* 130–136.

Miller, W. R., & Thoresen, C. E. (2003). Spirituality, religion, and health: An emerging research field. *American Psychologist, 58,* 24–35.

Montgomery, C. (1994). Swimming upstream: The strengths of women who survive homelessness. *Advances in Nursing Science, 16,* 34–45.

Neff, J. A. (2006). Exploring the dimensionality of "religiosity" and "spirituality" in the Fetzer multidimensional measure. *Journal for the Scientific Study of Religion, 45,* 449–459.

Paquette, K., & Bassuk, E. L. (2009). Parenting and homelessness: Overview and introduction to the special issue. *American Journal of Orthopsychiatry, 79,* 292–298.

Pargament, K. I. (1997). *The psychology of religion and coping.* New York: Guilford Press.

Pargament, K. I. (2002). The bitter and the sweet: An evaluation of the costs and benefits of religiousness. *Psychological Inquiry, 13,* 168–181.

Philippot, P., Lecocq, C., Sempoux, F., Nachtergael, H., & Galand, B. (2007). Psychological research on homelessness in Western Europe: A review from 1970–2001. *Journal of Social Issues, 63,* 483–504.

Raudenbush, S. W., & Bryk, A. S. (2002). *Hierarchical linear models: Applications and data analysis methods.* Thousand Oaks, CA: Sage Publications

Richards, P. S., & Bergin, A. E. (Ed.). (2000). *Handbook of psychotherapy and religious diversity.* Washington, DC: American Psychological Association.

Richards, T. N., Garland, T. S., Bumphus, V. W., & Thompson, R. (2010). Personal and political? Exploring the feminization of the American homeless population. *Journal of Poverty, 14,* 97–115.

Rollins, J. H., Saris, R. N., & Johnston-Robledo, I. (2001). Low-income women speak out about housing: A high-stakes game of musical chairs. *Journal of Social Issues, 57,* 277–298.

Ryan, C. (2007). British outpatient norms for the Brief Symptom Inventory. *Psychology and Psychotherapy: Theory, Research and Practice, 80,* 183–191.

Schiff, J. W. (2007). Homeless families in Canada: Discovering total families. *Families in Society, 88,* 131–140.

Shreve-Neiger, A. K., & Edelstein, B. A. (2004). Religion and anxiety: A critical review of the literature. *Clinical Psychology Review, 24,* 379–397.

Smith, E. J. (2006). The strength-based counseling model. *The Counseling Psychologist, 34,* 13–79.

Solorio, M. R., Milburn, N. G., Andersen, R. M., Trifskin, S., & Rodriquez, M. A. (2006). Emotional distress and mental health service use among urban homeless adolescents. *Journal of Behavioral Health Services & Research, 33,* 381–393.

Stahler, G. J., Kirby, K. C., & Kerwin, M. E. (2007). A faith-based intervention for cocaine-dependent black women. *Journal of Psychoactive Drugs, 39,* 183–190.

Stainbrook, K. A., & Homik, J. (2006). Similarities in characteristics and needs of women with children in homeless family and domestic violence shelters. *Families in Society, 87,* 53–62.

Tischler, V., Rademeyer, A., & Vostanis, P. (2007). Mothers experiencing homelessness: Mental health, support and social care needs. *Health and Social Care in the Community, 15,* 246–253.

Tischler, V. A., & Vostanis, P. (2007). Homeless mothers: Is there a relationship between coping strategies, mental health and goal achievement? *Journal of Community & Applied Social Psychology, 17,* 85–102.

U.S. Department of Housing and Urban Development. (2010). *The 2009 annual homeless assessment report to Congress.* Retrieved from http://www.hudhre.info/documents/5thHomelessAssessmentReport.pdf

Wachholz, S. (2005). Hate crimes against the homeless: Warning-out New England style. *Journal of Sociology and Social Welfare, 32,* 141–163.

Washington, O.G.M., Moxley, D. P., Garriott, L., & Weinberger, J. P. (2009). Five dimensions of faith and spirituality of older African American women transitioning out of homelessness. *Journal of Religion & Health, 48,* 431–444.

Weinreb, L., Nicholson, J., Anthes, F., & Williams, V. (2007). Integrating behavioral health services for homeless mothers and children in primary care. *American Journal of Orthopsychiatry, 77,* 142–152.

Williams, J. K., & Hall, J. A. (2009). Stress and traumatic stress: How do past events influence current traumatic stress among mothers experiencing homelessness? *Social Work Research, 33,* 199–207.

Zlotnick, C., Tam, T., & Bradley, K. (2007). Impact of adulthood trauma on homeless mothers. *Community Mental Health Journal, 43*, 13–32.

Zugazaga, C. B. (2008). Understanding social support of the homeless: A comparison of single men, single women, and women with children. *Families in Society, 89*, 447–455.

Performing Spiritual Healing in the Here and Now: Botánicas and Holistic Health Care

by Angela Castañeda*

Department of Sociology and Anthropology, DePauw University, Greencastle, IN, USA

Through ethnographic study of midwestern botánicas in Indiana, this research illustrates the multifunctional nature of these spaces. Research findings point to botánicas as working in the 'here and now', addressing immediate and emergent spiritual, financial, and health problems in a diverse community. Local religious leaders also perform divinations and healing in this space; thus the botánica both symbolizes and acts as a cross-cultural health system. I analyze a therapeutic form of traditional medicine through a focus on one of the main activities that takes place in botánicas – healings or *limpias*. Limpias cleanse a person, place, or object of any bad, evil, or harmful energy or sickness. I also explore the role of botánicas as a form of spiritual/medical diplomacy. Ultimately, this paper demonstrates that botánicas serve as economically and culturally acceptable health care alternatives, offering a means to address otherwise unmet community needs.

Keywords: botánicas; performance; healing; Santería; Afro-Cuban religion

Afro-Cuban introduction

At first glance, botánicas may be easily overlooked in the urban landscape that is often purposefully used to camouflage their existence. However, to those in need, the botánica signifies the potential for ritual healing to be found within its walls. Botánicas are found throughout the USA emerging as 'a pan-Latino phenomenon' Polk (2004a, 31). In the most general of terms, they are stores that sell products used for healing and/or spiritual practice. Botánicas were originally associated with the sale of both dried and fresh medicinal herbs. Today you may find prepackaged herbal baths and teas next to aerosol cans claiming to do what was once the domain of fresh herbs. Botánicas have changed and expanded with the ebb and flow of the many immigrants that constitute their clientele. Recent studies on traditional healing systems have worked to demystify the role

of botánicas by uncovering the multiple functions these stores serve in their communities (Viladrich 2006a, 2006b; Polk 2004b; Gomez-Beloz and Chavez 2001; Long 2001). This chapter furthers this work with ethnographic data from the Midwest United States, which illustrates the integral position botánicas hold as a form of cross-cultural health care in primarily immigrant communities. As such, botánicas serve an unrecognized role in diasporic medical diplomacy.

Medical diplomacy involves collaboration between countries working to build stronger international relations and increase health benefits. Julie Feinsilver writes that medical diplomacy is a form of soft power with its ability to gather 'symbolic capital (prestige, good will, and influence) … and therefore, material capital' (2008, 273, 275).

Since the 1960s, Cuba has engaged in an active form of medical diplomacy by sending an estimated half a million Cuban civilian workers around the world in the past 25 years (Feinsilver 2003). Recent scholarship on medical diplomacy identifies the incorporation of 'traditional' healing approaches, which include the commercialization of ritual knowledge associated with Afro-Cuban Santería practice (Moret 2008). Botánicas extend Cuban medical diplomacy in unanticipated ways through (1) the practice of Afro-Cuban religious traditions sought for healing in the Diaspora; and (2) encouraging clients and devotees to travel to Cuba for religious initiations and therefore contributing to material capital in the form of what scholars have termed 'Santurísmo' (Hagedorn 2001).[1]

Methodology

Ethnographic fieldwork for this study was conducted for a total of 19 months between 2005 and 2012. In addition to participant observation and photo documentation of 12 botánicas, I conducted semi-structured interviews with 7 botánica owners and 30 customers. I identified botánicas via Internet phone listings (i.e., White Pages and Yellow Pages), local advertisements and direct visits to communities with Latino populations. The botánicas included in this study represent a diverse range from rural cities of 15,000 residents to mid-sized cities of 80,000 and metropolitan areas with 800,000 inhabitants. Each of these botánicas claimed a direct link to Cuba either through a religious practice such as *Santería* or a botánica owner of Cuban ancestry. Names of individuals and stores have been changed to protect the confidentiality of research participants.

Each botánica presented similar challenges to research access. For example botánica owners were reticent to participate due to concerns about negative portrayals of their businesses in mainstream media. Suspicion of my possible connection to immigration officials and concern about immigration status also posed a barrier. Botánica owners were also concerned with how my presence in their establishments could negatively impact their business. Class differences and outsider residential status were difficult barriers to overcome. While my identity as a Mexican-American and fluency in Spanish served to ease the discomfort and suspicion for some botánica owners, for others it

was not enough, and I had to reassure participants of the goal of my research while working to build rapport. My previous experience working with religious communities of the African Diaspora in both Mexico and Brazil helped to overcome some of these barriers. The cultural and spiritual competency on Santería practice I had gained in my previous work proved invaluable in these situations. One botánica owner, for example, regularly quizzed me to test my knowledge on Santería. She would gather one of her ceremonial beaded necklaces from around her neck, delicately pass the beads through her fingers and ask me, 'Now remind me again whose necklace is this?' Through my persistence and willingness to learn from others, the doors of these botánicas were opened to my ethnographic gaze.

Botánicas from the outside in

Packed tightly between zapaterías, supermercados, panaderías, and restaurants serving 'autentica' comida or antojitos 'típicos' I found the all too common yet sometimes invisible space known as the botánica. Functioning as sites for spiritual advice, alternative health care, and community building, the visibility of botánicas depended on my gaze and proximity to the space and community. Most importantly for this study was the local perception of the botánica or, as Patrick Polk states, 'in the eyes of believers and seekers, the botánica is a place where gods, saints, and guiding spirits may be encountered first in frozen material form and then harnessed via more actively corporeal modes of symbolic communication' (Polk 2004c, 18–19).

Looking at a botánica from the outside, it was easy to identify the clearly Catholic elements, which were used to represent this space from an external viewpoint. The advertisement on business cards, in storefront windows, and on store signs often depicted Catholic imagery. These symbols included pictures of saints, rosaries, first communion dresses, holy water containers, wedding albums, crucifixes, and a focus on the sale of 'religious articles'. This emphasis on the Catholic belief system functioned as a tool to help these stores become more readily accepted in their particular context – city, state, and region.

While the outward appearance of these botánicas reflected a Catholic influence, upon entrance to these spaces, even a person unfamiliar with African-derived religions found merchandise foreign to a typical Catholic religious store. To the uninitiated, this merchandise took on a mysterious aura as alongside plastic statues of Catholic saints there are a rainbow assortment of candles, beads, herbs and oils, which proudly proclaim their power to make others 'Do as I say', 'Come to me', 'Break up' or simply 'Shut up'. As Hernández and Jones note in their research on botánicas in California:

> Clearly this is much more than a retail establishment dispensing homeopathic remedies. It is in fact a locus of the spiritual, and the abundant assortment of sacramental items so richly displayed reflects the needs of the community as well as the spiritual traditions of the owner. (Hernández and Jones 2004, 46)

Almost always packed with items, the botánicas included in this study overflowed with colorful sights and smells, so much so that to navigate this space with ease signified a level of cultural competency and knowledge of the symbolism and services offered. Research on botánicas finds clear divisions between front and back spaces (Jones et al. 2001). This research suggests the existence of an intermediary space between the front and back, which served to transition individuals from public and private services. Front spaces were for the public and best represent Catholic imagery and material goods: rosaries, candles, and *lazos* for weddings, clothing, and articles for Catholic sacraments like baptism, first communion, and confirmation. Some of the botánicas in this study also used the front space for the sale of secular objects like flags, pins, and lottery cards. This front stage was the principle site of commercial material transactions.

Past the communion dresses on plastic hangers, candles, and Puerto Rican and Cuban flags, there hung a rainbow assortment of dangling beads representing the various African deities worshiped in Santería. In this intermediary space, dolls representing Santería deities or *orichas* (gods) dressed in symbolic colors and holding ritual objects such as mirrors, bows and arrows, or double-axes replaced the images of Catholic saints.[2] Visitors to this section of the botánica entered with the knowledge and experience of African-derived religions. Those purchasing items for a ritual or home altar arrived with lists detailing the candles, perfumes, crockery, or herbs necessary to fulfill their obligations. This intermediary space contained the objects 'para llevar' or for take home use, a form of self-help for issues easily remedied. Yet this space did not mark the end of the botánica.

Farther back, sometimes in a basement or separate room, were areas that brought elements from the public and intermediary spaces together via divination or ritual ceremonies. A majority of the botánicas identified in this study contained these spaces. I found the absence of such spaces in 4 of the 12 botánicas due to space constraints and concerns or complaints from neighbors often due to noise or other privacy issues. One botánica owner explained, 'We used to hold beautiful ceremonies in the basement, but the neighbors started to complain about the noise from the drums and I became scared that they might involve the police. I knew that if the police arrived we would have a real problem.' Yet it was within these private spaces that active healing took place for many who came to the botánica in search of spiritual, emotional, and physical relief. The commercial transactions that occurred at the front stage of the botánica became invested with an additional layer of spirituality as I recorded services, goods, and offerings, both ritual and monetary, exchanged via divine consultation. Examples of the services provided include spiritual advising or ritual ceremonies involving Espiritismo, Santería, or Curanderismo among others (Jones et al. 2001). These services varied depending on the expertise of the botánica owner, and while not all botánica owners identified as 'healers', they all clearly served as intermediaries for customers in search of healing. Therefore, I observed botánicas marked as either direct sites for active healing or indirect sites offering the tools, ingredients, or connections to more direct forms of healing. Indeed, a journey through the botánica from back to front and public to private illustrated the multidimensional nature of the space.

Case study: one woman and many spirits

Reflecting on my own childhood growing-up in this region of the Midwest, I vaguely recall passing similar spaces as blurry memories of doorways tucked in between bakeries and restaurants. Despite these repeated near encounters, I recall that one such botánica stands out, in all honesty because it was located on a busy corner intersection familiar to me while growing-up for the ice cream shop in front. In fact, it was not until my academic initiation to religions of the African Diaspora that I began to question the function and placement of this botánica in my own backyard.

In order to protect the confidentiality of my consultants, I refer to the exact location of this botánica in more general terms. It is, however, important to note its regional location near the southern shore of Lake Michigan; a place with close historical ties to the steel industry, which fostered the growth of immigrant populations in this area. As a consequence, the economic status of many families rose and fell in accordance with the successes and failures of the steel industry. Census data from 2010 recorded this city's population near 30,000 including racial breakdown percentages with over 50% of the population identified as Hispanic, 40% Black, 7% White, and less than 1% Asian. The role of the steel industry in attracting immigrant groups translated to the presence of nearly 60 different religious institutions of various denominations including Catholic, Baptist, Lutheran, Seventh-Day Adventist, Methodist, Jehovah's Witness, Pentecostal, Lutheran, Romanian, and Serbian Orthodox. The presence of botánicas in this city suggests we add to this list the practice of religious traditions of the African Diaspora.

The Botánica San Lazaro and its owner exemplify how botánicas serve as multifunctional, and more specifically cross-cultural, health care systems. Lucia, a Mexican born mother of three whose husband immigrated to the USA from Cuba, owns this botánica. Lucia first opened the doors in 1991, and since then has been busy sharing her spiritual knowledge with the many people that have passed through. Lucia shared with me her reason for opening the botánica:

> When I was a little girl my grandmother used to tell me that I had a gift. I never understood what she meant until I came to this country and found myself alone and scared, searching for a community and a home. Thankfully I met my husband and together we began building our life together. We had our first daughter and when she fell ill I was scared to death but I prayed to my saint and slowly she became better. After this, I promised to thank my saint and learn more about my gift, and with the encouragement of my husband, I opened this botánica.

The role that her husband played in the creation of this botánica extended beyond emotional support. In many ways his Cubanness translated into economic and spiritual capital for Lucia.

Lucia was not alone in her capacity to extend her responsibilities beyond merely botánica owner. In fact, many botánica owners actively engaged in various forms of healing. The work by Hernández and Jones notes that like Lucia, 'many botánica owners are self- or community-designated healers, counselors, or consultants who ascertain the troubles of their clients through various techniques of divination and provide advice, limpias, referrals to doctors and clinics, and herbal or ritual therapies' (2004, 48). The types of ailments most commonly addressed by botánica healers necessitate a more holistic approach to illness and healing. Karen Holliday identifies three primary reasons people seek healing through a botánica, '(1) holistic view of the body; (2) dynamic counseling between health practitioner and client; (3) personal difficulties previously experienced with biomedical treatment obtained through conventional sources' (2008, 403). These reasons necessitate an assessment of the role of 'environmental sources' on an individual's well-being, which leads to stress from 'work or household responsibilities, problems relating to immigration issues, injuries incurred on the job, and emotional distress produced by cultural differences' (Hernández and Jones 2004, 48–49).

One way that healers treat these illnesses is through *limpias* or ritual cleansings, which aims to rid a person of negative energy. Ritual cleansings are not structured and rigid, but instead vary widely based on a client's need and healer's particular spiritual guide. While Lucia prided herself on the simplest of cleansings, she also admitted that some cases called for more complex rituals involving costly preparations. She explained that once a young couple came to her frantic that their young daughter was unable to sleep. For weeks they struggled with the poor exhausted girl. Lucia said she treated her with a quick ritual cleansing, but ultimately the problem required multiple cleansings each more elaborate than the next and requiring more extended family members to step forward and participate. Ultimately Lucia, with the help of her spirits, rid the young girl and family of the negative energy, which Lucia claimed was caused by the envy of a neighbor. For Lucia, the most important part of these ritual cleansings stemmed from her relationship with Saint Lazarus.

Born on 17 December, Lucia shares her birthday with the feast day of Saint Lazarus or *San Lazaro*, which was reflected in the store's name. According to Lucia, 'San Lazaro represents great force and spiritual power.' It is important to note that within the space of the botánica the saint known as Lazarus also occupies a corresponding spiritual connection with the Afro-Cuban deity known as Babaluaye. Historical circumstances during the slave trade led to the forced religious conversion of Africans arriving in the Americas. Slaves brought with them a variety of spiritual deities and ancestors, which were subsequently enmeshed with Catholic saints. For example, Saint Lazarus is known in the Catholic faith for becoming ill and later rising from the dead. Saint Lazarus became syncretized with the oricha Babaluaye based on their shared attributes and associations with healing and sickness.

Of particular interest in this relationship of spirits and healing was the role that Lucia occupied when she channeled San Lazaro's healing powers through her limpias or spiritual cleansings. Lucia stated that she viewed herself 'as

an instrument of God sent to lift up and cleanse people of all the negative energy that they bring with them'. People came from afar to seek her healings, but they also faxed pictures of loved ones unable to come in person. People came to the botánica to be healed by Lucia and to receive a blessing from San Lazaro, which Lucia carried out symbolically through ritual actions. Clients also expressed immediate feelings of relief after sessions with Lucia. These limpias were a therapeutic form of holistic healing, where Lucia served as friend, confidant, and healer. One example of the healings conducted by Lucia involved passing an egg over the entire body of the individual while reciting a prayer in which she invoked various religious entities – God Almighty, Saint Lazarus, and Babaluaye, at times all within the same sentence. Thus, Lucia's spiritual healings reflected multiple traditions, but ultimately were important because they helped resolve the problems of those in need. Indeed, people found Lucia's strength as a healer in her ability to provide symbolic treatments that transferred easily from one culture to another.

Lucia's role in the botánica also symbolizes the need to address problems in the 'here and now' as opposed to a focus on solutions in the afterlife. Her function within this space illustrates the connection between two levels of reality: the harsh events of everyday life and the invisible world of the spirits and ancestors. Lucia believed it was her job to act as a mediator between these two worlds, as she worked with many spirits, invoking the names of various Santería deities or orichas such as Yemanja, Oshun, and Babaluaye. Lucia reported that she incorporated these African elements into her practice as a direct result of her marriage to a Cuban national: 'I learned very early on in our marriage that to love my husband would mean to love all of him and that meant his spiritual family too.' She went on to explain that she saw strong parallels between Catholic saints and Santeria orichas, such that she felt her calling to initiate in Santería was a complement to her Catholic faith. And while not Cuban herself, Lucia was quick to reference her 'Cubanness' via her marriages both spiritual and physical to those from the island. She highlighted this in her decision to travel to Cuba to become initiated in

Santería. In essence, Lucia performs her Cuban-ness in both her everyday speech speckled with Cuban rhythm and slang as well as her ritual cleansings that invoke the powers of Santería orichas. And this connection to Cuba translates to both spiritual and monetary gains for Lucia because for many customers who seek her help, the connection to Cuba serves to further authenticate Lucia's healing abilities. As one client expressed, 'I know that Lucia can help me. She has been home, I mean to the island and she works with a strong family of spirits. They are real and so is she, I mean, I can trust her.' When asked how others perceive her identity, Lucia explained that:

> People come to me in need and I work hard to meet them where they are, so sometimes that means I draw upon my Mexican roots or my Cuban spiritual family or my basic knowledge of Catholic sacraments … Whatever people need I do what I can to give it to them so they leave feeling better than when they came in.

Through her use of spiritual tools, Lucia performed multiple identities in this space. Using Bauman's understanding of performance as verbal exchange (1977) and Turner's 'social drama' (1986), I recognized the work that Lucia and other botánica healers engage in as more than merely one-way speech performed to a passive audience, but instead their performance as conversation or dialogic process. In her limpias, Lucia in essence embodied San Lazaro with audible and visual cues marking a change in identity. While not the type of possession encountered in formal Santería rituals, this embodiment accentuated Lucia's role as a mediator and bridge between spiritual and everyday realities. The spiritual cleansings Lucia performed serve to as Turner notes 'exaggerate' her connection to Cuba and ultimately her Cubanness.

In addition to highlighting the bodily dimensions of cultural performance, the link between power and performance is also essential to this study. The rituals Lucia performed form a powerful force in healing clients in this space and actively create positive change in their lives. Cultural performance as active agents of change also translate into the possession of power:

> Performance, like power, is not a product that can be given, exchanged, or recovered. It always necessarily is a process that is subject to on-the-spot improvisation… Just as power is a diffuse resource accessible—albeit to varying degrees—to everyone, so too is performance engaged in by everyone present (Askew 2002, 291).

Observations of Lucia's ritual cleansings revealed their flexible nature and her ability to comfort her clients by investing confidence in them. As Lucia shared, 'These people come here beaten down and I need to lift them up … I believe in my family of spirits and I know from personal experience that change can happen … I believe in them too [her clients].'

Ultimately, the function of the botánica and Lucia's role in this space stems from an ability to cater to the needs of the clientele on multiple levels including offering immediate and proximal means to resolve their problems. The majority of problems that Lucia encounters stem from issues of love and money, and she points out that in this increasingly complex and fast-paced world, people, especially immigrants, are searching for survival strategies. Lucia commented, 'I've seen many of this before, that look people have when they come in and I can just tell even before they say a word that they are hurting or scared. People come here [to the United States] thinking life will be easy, but it's not.' She believes that saints and spirits help cure the depression caused by the drastic culture shock felt by many immigrants upon arrival in the USA As one client commented, 'I was very sick when I first came here and Lucia helped me. She told me who to pray to and when to make offerings. Before long I began to feel whole again, like I had found a home.' The type of ritual help Lucia offered was calibrated to the socio-economic status of her customers as she prided herself on being humble, and she pointed out that the materials she used to solve problems involved basic elements such as flowers, candles, and fruit. Observation of clientele who utilized the botánica along with Lucia's perceptions demonstrated that people of all ages, ethnicities, and economic status traveled from both near and far to resolve their problems through the Botánica San Lazaro.

Conclusion

This research demonstrates the multifunctional dimensions of botánicas. In-depth analysis of one botánica and its owner illustrates that botánicas are not only much more than alternative healing systems, but also sites for the constitution of identity and community (both secular and sacred). Botánicas work to respond to emergent issues faced by their communities. How will new health care and/or immigration policies impact the use and shape of these botánicas? Will these practices be viewed as a threat to existing health care systems? And how might we use ethnographic research on botánicas to illuminate the effects of these policies? Julie Feinsilver identifies Cuban medical diplomacy as a threat:

> Cuban doctors serve the poor in areas in which no local doctor would work ... Because they do a diagnosis of the community and treat patients as a whole person living and working in a specific environment rather than just clinically ... they get to know their patients better. This more familiar approach is changing expectations as well as the nature of doctor-patient relations in the host country. (2008, 284)

In essence, this description of the work by Cuban doctors parallels the healing practices performed by Lucia and other botánica owners. The form of healing taking place at the botánicas included in this study illustrates a holistic form of healing and approach to health care.

The complexity of botánica space and the different belief systems performed form a bridge between the harsh realities of daily life and the spirits made visible via rituals performed in the 'here and now'. This unique blend of sacred and secular systems is a direct reflection of the community and specific cultural context in which it is found. It symbolizes the diverse composition of the community as well as the particular cultural and historical environment in which these sacred spaces grow. Ultimately, the power found within the space created by botánica owners lies in their ability to craft culturally appropriate recommendations for physical, psychological, and spiritual conditions.

Notes

1. Santurísmo is a tourist industry directed at foreigners with a focus on selling religious experiences, rituals, and initiation into Santería. Following the collapse of the Soviet Union, the Cuban Government sponsored tours to Cuba for foreigners interested in initiating into Santería (see Hagedorn 2001).

2. Orichas are Afro-Cuban deities of Yoruban origin. Santería practitioners recognize a pantheon of orichas with human characteristics who control elements of one's natural environment.

References

Askew, Kelly M. 2002. *Performing the Nation: Swahili Music and Cultural Politics in Tanzania.* Chicago: The University of Chicago Press.

Bauman, Richard. 1977. *Verbal Art as Performance.* Prospect Heights, IL: Waveland Press.

Feinsilver, Julie M. 2003. "Cuban Medical Diplomacy." In *The Cuba Reader: History, Culture, Politics*, edited by A. Chomsky, B. Carr, and P. M. Smorkaloff, 590–598. Durham: Duke University Press.

Feinsilver, Julie M. 2008. "Cuba's Medical Diplomacy." In *Changing Cuba/Changing World*, edited by Mauricio A. Font, 273–286. New York: Bildner Center for Western Hemisphere Studies.

Gomez-Beloz, Alfredo and Noel Chavez. 2001. "The *Botánica* as a Culturally Appropriate Health Care Option for Latinos." *The Journal of Alternative and Complementary Medicine* 7 (5): 537–546. doi:10.1089/10755530152639765.

Hagedorn, Katherine J. 2001. *Divine Utterances: The Performance of Afro-Cuban Santería.* Washington, DC: Smithsonian Institution Press.

Hernández, Claudia J., and Michael Owen Jones. 2004. "Botánicas." In *Botánica Los Angeles: Latino Popular Religious Art in the City of Angels*, edited by Patrick Polk, 46–55. Los Angeles, CA: UCLA Fowler Museum of Cultural History.

Holliday, Karen V. 2008. "'Folk' or 'Traditional' Versus 'Complementary' and 'Alternative' Medicine: Constructing Latino/a Health and Illness through Biomedical Labeling." *Latino Studies* 6 (4): 398–417. doi:10.1057/lst.2008.44.

Jones, Michael Owen, Patrick A. Polk, Ysamur Flores-Peña, and Roberta J. Evanchuk. 2001. "Invisible Hospitals: Botánicas in Ethnic Health Care." In *Healing Logics: Culture and Medicine in Modern Health Belief Systems*, edited by Erika Brady, 39–87. Logan: Utah State University Press.

Long, Carolyn Morrow. 2001. *Spiritual Merchants.* Knoxville, TN: The University of Tennessee Press.

Moret, Erica. 2008. "Afro-Cuban Religion, Ethnobotany and Healthcare in the Context of Global Political and Economic Change." *Bulletin of Latin American Research* 27 (3): 333–350. doi:10.1111/j.1470-9856.2008.00273.x.

Polk, Patrick A. 2004a. "Objects of Devotion." In *Botánica Los Angeles: Latino Popular Religious Art in the City of Angels*, edited by Patrick Polk, 26–45. Los Angeles, CA: UCLA Fowler Museum of Cultural History.

Polk, Patrick A., ed. 2004b. *Botánica Los Angeles: Latino Popular Religious Art in the City of Angels.* Los Angeles, CA: UCLA Fowler Museum of Cultural History.

Polk, Patrick A. 2004c. "Botánica Los Angeles." In *Bótanica Los Angeles: Latino Popular Religious Art in the City of Angels*, edited by Patrick Polk, 14–25. Los Angeles, CA: UCLA Fowler Museum of Cultural History.

Turner, Victor. 1986. *The Anthropology of Performance.* New York: PAJ.

Viladrich, Anahí. 2006a. "Botánicas in America's Backyard: Uncovering the World of Latino Healers' Herb-healing Practices in New York City." *Human Organization* 65 (4): 407–419.

Viladrich, Anahí. 2006b. "Beyond the Supernatural: Latino Healers Treating Latino Immigrants in NYC." *Journal of Latino/Latin American Studies* 2 (1): 134–148.

Developing a Culturally Competent Faith-Based Framework to Promote Breast Cancer Screening Among Afghan Immigrant Women

by Mehra Shirazi, Aida Shirazi and
Joan Bloom

Abstract For the tens of thousands of Afghan immigrant women currently living in the USA, religious and cultural beliefs can act as a barrier to health care access. Islamic frameworks and men's gatekeeping roles often control women's decision-making power about their health care needs. Gatekeepers, however, can be reconceived as facilitators empowered to protect the well-being of the family, and positive messages within Islam can foster collaborative investment in women's health. Drawing upon a pilot study utilizing community-based participatory research involving the largest Afghan community in the USA, this paper documents the need for culturally sensitive faith-based education to promote breast cancer screening among this growing population.

Displaced Afghans represent one of the largest refugee populations in the world. Driven by decades of conflict, the humanitarian crisis in Afghanistan has caused a sharp increase in the number of Afghan immigrants in the USA (Poureslami et al. 2004). According to recent estimates, there are more than 60,000 Afghans now living in the USA (UNHCR 2004). The San Francisco Bay Area is home to the largest US Afghan community, estimated to be above 30,000; two-thirds of this population is female, a significant percent being widowed (Lipson et al. 1996).

Existing studies suggest these women are among those at the highest risk for health problems due to lack of access to health services, lack of education, language barriers, social isolation, cultural and religious barriers, and men's gatekeeping (Poureslami et al. 2004). These women, the majority of them Sunni Muslims, have received limited health care and have little, or no, prior experience with the concepts of early detection and western medicine (UNHCR 2004; Lipson et al. 1996; Khan et al. 1997; Lipson and Omidan 1997). The available literature suggests that Afghan women may have a younger average age for the development of breast cancer, but they are diagnosed at a later stage when treatment options are more limited and outcomes poorer. The few existing studies of this population indicate that the late stage of presentation may be due to inadequate knowledge among the Afghan immigrant community about breast cancer and the need for breast health care (UNHCR 2004; Lipson et al. 1996). In seeking health care, Afghan immigrant women face major barriers of which the rest of the population, particularly health care providers, often is unaware (Anderson et al. 2006).

Islamic Perspectives on Health

Islam is the second largest religion in the world (Kettani 2010). According to a 2010 demographic study, about 1.6 billion people worldwide are Muslims, representing more than 23 % of the global population (Pew Forum on Religion & Public Life 2011). Religion among Muslims is not merely a set of spiritual beliefs; it affects many dimensions of life and directs their cultural, socioeconomic, and even political perspectives (Gunes Murat and Azadarmaki 2008).

Islamic frameworks may lead Muslims to attribute the causes of illness, directly or indirectly, to God's will. For example, a study of African-American, Arab American, and South Asian American Muslims found that participants believed both health and illness to be decreed by God; human agents were thought to play a secondary but complementary role (Padela et al. 2012). In another study of South Asian Muslim women, breast cancer was often seen as a "disease of fate" ordained by God (Johnson et al. 1999). Among Somalis in Minnesota, Deshaw also observed a fatalistic belief that disease expresses the will of God and the authors inferred that this notion may pose a barrier to seeking preventive care (DeShaw 2006). In a study of Arab American immigrants in New York, respondents commented that cancer was a punishment from God for their religious failings (Shah et al. 2008). To the extent that individuals see a particular illness as a result of God's will or from their own spiritual failings, they may decide that the illness is not to be treated. On the other hand, religious beliefs may also provide positive resources in the face of illness, as when faith in God provides psychological strength to a cancer patient undergoing chemotherapy (Powe and Finnie 2003).

In a positively focused, Islamic-centered framework, however, Muslims might turn to Islam itself as a source of healing (Alrawi et al. 2011). Thus, if Muslims believe that health is constituted by, and results from, observance of the teachings and practices of Islam, they may turn to worship practices in order to restore their health. A study of Afghani elders in California found that they believed an individual's health depended upon whether the individual adhered to Islamic guidelines and performed religious rituals, and the elders engaged in worship practices for the purpose of healing (Morioka-Douglas et al. 2004). Other studies have found that Muslim patients experience physical and mental benefits from religious practices such as prayer, fasting, and recitation of the Qur'an (Carroll et al. 2007). Indeed, many Islamic observances, such as sexual monogamy, ritual cleansing, dietary strictures, and avoidance of alcohol and drugs, probably do promote health.

Muslims might also turn to traditional healing practices that are described in the Qur'an and the *hadith*. These may include the use of black seed, herbs, and special foods such as honey. Other practices, such as cupping, are prescribed or conducted by specialized healers (Alrawi et al. 2011). Importantly, individuals may use Islamic healing practices in addition to, or in lieu of, the treatments offered by the professional medical domain. In the latter case, by turning to Islamic healing practices, some Muslims delay or altogether avoid seeking medical attention from which they would benefit. There are few empirical studies to account for how these decisions are made or to document how often such decisions occur.

Pilot Study on Afghan Women's Breast Health Behaviors

In 2007, with funding from University of California's Breast Cancer Research Program, the authors conducted a pilot study known as "Breast Health Behaviors of Afghan Immigrant Women in Northern California." This study provided a preliminary understanding of how Afghan women in Northern California view their breast health.

The specific aims of the study were the following: (1) to identify what Afghan community members believe to be their greatest concerns and barriers to breast health care, including both cultural and religious attitudes that may facilitate or hinder their seeking care; and (2) to identify the women's knowledge about and attitudes toward breast health care (Shirazi et al. 2013). Using community-based participatory research (CBPR), the researchers worked collaboratively with Afghan community members to frame the inquiry and distill the information gathered.

The pilot study conducted in-depth, semi-structured interviews with 53 non-English speaking, first-generation immigrant, Muslim Afghan women, 40 years and older, with no history of breast cancer. Study results indicated a very low level of knowledge about breast cancer in this group, low screening rates, and a lack of awareness of symptoms, risk factors, and screening procedures. Major barriers to screening included: an absence of culturally and linguistically appropriate breast health education information and programs, language difficulties, lack of transportation, low health literacy, embarrassment, and modesty (Shirazi et al. 2013).

In-depth interviews also highlighted the centrality of spiritual and Islamic beliefs in the lives of Afghan women. These women frequently mentioned the notion of faith; they believed health to be a blessing from God (Allah) and understood their bodies to be gifts from God. They considered themselves responsible to do everything in their power to survive or overcome health problems and to seek medical treatment as necessary. The women commented that, in their religious faith, life is sacred and must be respected and protected with care. Another religious matter was the women's perspective of the status of women according to Islam. Contrary to common Western stereotypes, many believed that Islam regards women as independent members of society who are equal to men in basic human rights and the pursuit of education and knowledge. Many expressed interest in reinforcing appropriate Islamic teachings as a way not only to empower women to acquire knowledge about breast health care, but also to improve men's understanding of the issues (Shirazi et al. 2013).

The pilot study's results produced the following recommendations: (1) Training of "grass roots" bilingual members of the community in all aspects of the program including planning, design, implementation, and evaluation; (2) incorporation of male-specific educational sessions led by male health advisors; (3) use of narrative communication consistent with the Afghan oral culture where storytelling is used to relate information and cultural/religious values; and (4) inclusion of Islamic faith components that are inspirational and relevant to the lives of the women and their male gatekeepers (e.g., husbands, brothers) and that will influence these men to understand the women's needs and support them.

Developing a Culturally Competent Framework Using CBPR

The inclusion of community-based Islamic and cultural concepts fits well with the Afghan culture of collective identity and with Islamic views on health and well-being. It also provides valuable guidelines for ensuring that any intervention is culturally specific by placing cultural practices and religious values at the center of the planning process. Adopting CBPR principles, a Community Advisory Board (CAB) was formed, composed of community leaders, health care providers, academic research partners, a cultural consultant, community navigators, and women from the community. The main goal of the CAB is to ensure the development of culturally appropriate cancer intervention programs (Israel et al. 2005). Meetings of the CAB are structured to help to develop a partnership where there is equality of control and participation by the community and research partners.

To ensure a shared understanding of both research and the CBPR approach, training sessions were conducted by research scientists. These scientists trained community leaders on various aspects of research, and the community leaders provided feedback and cultural and religious input emphasizing the key elements of conducting research in the community. Community leaders and CAB members were actively involved, and their views on cultural issues were incorporated into our framework.

In designing a faith-based breast health education framework, we considered the women's preferences for formats and how messages and information should be presented. Most immigrant Afghan women are linguistically isolated in their homes. The women we interviewed were enthusiastic about meeting in small groups, where information could be shared and passed on to other women through word of mouth. Family relationships in the Afghan culture and Muslim religion, however, were understood to be fundamental. In addition, men's gatekeeping roles, together with the traditional understanding and expectation of men as the heads of the household and caretakers of the family, often controlled women's decisions about their health care needs. Many women commented that these factors not only created communication barriers with health care providers, but also decreased the women's ability to make appropriate health care decisions. Therefore, the CAB recommended providing an education program using cultural/ religious values to reach male family members. Because of the sensitive nature of the educational information about women's bodies, and out of respect for conservative Afghan cultural practices, members of the CAB suggested that the educational sessions be conducted in gender-specific groups led by Health Advisors (HAs) of the same gender.

In the discussion of the findings from the interviews, our CAB decided that the small-group educational sessions should be interactive, with question-and-answer sessions and storytelling in which breast cancer survivors might share their personal narratives with hopeful messages and perspectives. The literacy rate, even in their native Farsi/Dari or Pashto, is very low—40 % had no formal education—so participants expressed a strong desire for educational resources, tools, and formats with visual and oral components, these being perceived as most effective for learning about breast health. Videos or programs shown on Afghan TV and Web sites could also be incorporated into educational material.

The CAB felt that, given the many comments from interviewees expressing the centrality of religion, religious ideas including quotes from the Quran and Prophet Mohammed about the importance of preserving one's health should be incorporated in educational curricula for both women and their male family members. Reinforcing Islamic teachings would not only empower the women but also influence their male relatives to understand the women's needs and support them.

Incorporating Islamic Concepts

We identified several Islamic concepts that can facilitate the framing of determinants for health and encourage positive health care behaviors among Afghan community members. The element of *Imaan*, which means belief or faith, is the foundation on which the Islamic lifestyle is built. It highlights the importance of fellowship and community involvement and fosters an environment for social support by encouraging social organization. *Da'waa* literally means "invitation," inviting or calling people to know and learn about practices in real life that are beneficial for their own and their community's well-being. It applies to every Muslim's own family, relatives, and friends. The main objective is to invite people to know about and participate in the provision of basic needs for their community—such as food, shelter, education, and health care—through advocating for social justice, solidarity, a peaceful, and safe environment, and healthy behavior. *Taleem va Ta'alom*, or the promotion of learning and teaching, is highly valued in Islamic culture because Islam considers education to be a sacred duty for both men and women. *Shura*, or collaboration, is a basic Islamic principle that ensures that the views of the community are taken into consideration in all affairs and calls for transparency and accountability. The concept of *Shura* is also used to emphasize gender justice and equality in a variety of situations, such as interpersonal relationships within the family and the community.

These concepts provide a framework for family members and kin, who occupy the center of the Islamic lifestyle. The incorporation of these four Islamic constructs in breast health education can help the majority of community members toward a collaborative understanding of the purpose of community health programs and the roles and responsibilities of both men and women in supporting the well-being of their families and community.

Conclusions

Based on the results of the pilot study, we received strong support from the Afghan community to address barriers to breast cancer screening. Guided by CBPR principles, a multi-component intervention program has been developed by a team of academic and community partners to address unmet needs of the Muslim Afghan community. The Afghan Women's Breast Health Project (AWBHP), a culturally appropriate, faith-based intervention program for Afghan immigrant women, has been awarded a 5-year grant from the National Institute of Health. To the best of our knowledge, the AWBHP is the first study that has used a faith-based CBPR approach to enhance breast cancer knowledge and screening among immigrant Afghan women. This research represents a formative area of study with respect to (1) better understanding of role of community partners and (2) experience in faith-based health promotion research, which has received limited attention in the literature of public health. Specific emphases on cultural competency, community ownership, interdependence, and capacity building will be keys to success (Israel et al. 1998, 2001).

It is important to note that the development and planning of the AWBHP involves much more than just a Farsi/Dari translation of materials and messages. Rather, it consists of collective strategies, culturally tailored for appropriateness and competency. The program recognizes the importance of faith and spirituality in this community and, by incorporating Islamic components that are important and inspirational to the lives of participants, it reframes Islam as a facilitator of women's health. Crucially, the AWBHP is geared toward defining and delivering key Islamic messages that will promote breast health care among Muslim Afghan women.

American Muslims are one minority group for whom a shared religious identity may have important health impacts that are independent of race, ethnicity, and socioeconomic status. Numbering between five and seven million in the USA, Muslims represent a growing minority population that is racially, ethnically, and socioeconomically diverse (Allied Media Corp 2000). A large proportion are immigrants from Islamic countries. Therefore, the framework we propose may provide a template for reaching a wide range of Islamic communities in the USA by treating religious beliefs and their influence on health and health care-seeking behavior as facilitators, and not merely as "cultural barriers." At the conclusion of the 5-year intervention, the AWBHP will be evaluated and best practices and recommendations for a faith-based program to address breast cancer screening will be adopted. We anticipate that if the program is successful, we will have a model for religious and culturally tailored evidenced-based education and breast cancer awareness programs for Muslim immigrant women, whether they speak Farsi/Dari (Afghan and Persian women) or other dialects/languages. The knowledge gained and the guidelines developed will have an impact that reaches far beyond the Afghan community in Northern California.

Acknowledgments This research was funded by the California Breast Cancer Research Program

References

Allied Media Corp (2000). *Muslim American demographic facts.* Retrieved from http://www.allied-media.com/AM/.

Alrawi, S., Fetters, M. D., Killawi, A., Hammad, A., & Padela, A. (2011). Traditional healing practices among American Muslims: Perceptions of community leaders in Southeast Michigan. *Journal of Immigrant and Minority Health, 14*(3), 489–496.

Anderson, B. O., Shyyan, R., Eniu, A., Smith, R. A., Yip, C. H., Bese, N. S., et al. (2006). Breast cancer in limited-resource countries: An overview of the Breast Health Global Initiative 2005 guidelines. *The Breast Journal, 12*(S1), S3–S15.

Carroll, J., Epstein, R., Fiscella, K., Volpe, E., Diaz, K., & Omar, S. (2007). Knowledge and beliefs about health promotion and preventive health care among Somali women in the United States. *Health Care for Women International, 28*(4), 360–380.

DeShaw, P. (2006). Use of the emergency department by Somali immigrants and refugee. *Minnesota Medicine, 89*(8), 42–45.

Gunes Murat, T., & Azadarmaki, T. (2008). Religiosity and Islamic rule in Iran. *Journal for the Scientific Study of Religion, 47*(2), 211–224.

Israel, B. A., Eng, E., Schulz, A. J., Parker, E. A., & Satcher, D. (2005). Methods in community-based participatory research for health. San Francisco, CA: Jossey Bass.

Israel, B. A., Lichtenstein, R., Lantz, P., McGranaghan, R., Allen, A., Guzman, R. J., et al. (2001). The Detroit community-academic urban research center: Development, implementation, and evaluation. *Journal of Pulbic Health Management and Practice, 7*(5), 1–19.

Israel, B. A., Schulz, A. J., Parker, E. A., & Becker, A. B. (1998). Review of community-based research: Assessing partnership approaches to improve public health. *Annual Review of Public Health, 19*, 173–202.

Johnson, J. L., Bottorff, J. L., Balneaves, L. G., Grewal, S., Bhagat, R., Hilton, B., et al. (1999). South Asian womens' views on the causes of breast cancer: Images and explanations. *Patient Education and Counseling, 37*(3), 243–254.

Kettani, H. (2010). *2010 World Muslim Population*. Unpublished paper presented at the Eighth Annual Hawaii International Conference on Arts & Humanities, Honolulu, HI.

Khan, S. M., Gillani, J., Nasreen, S., & Zai, S. (1997). Cancer in north west Pakistan and Afghan refugees. *Journal of the Pakistan Medical Association, 47*(4), 122–124.

Lipson, J. G., Hosseini, M. A., Kabir, S., & Edmonston, F. (1996). Health Issues among Afghan Women in California. *Health Care for Women International, 16*, 279–286.

Lipson, J. G., & Omidan, P. A. (1997). Afghan refugee issues in the U.S. social environment. *Western Journal of Nursing Research, 19*(1), 110–126.

Morioka-Douglas, N., Sacks, T., & Yeo, G. (2004). Issues in caring for Afghan American elders: Insights from literature and a focus group. *Journal of Cross-Cultural Gerontology, 19*(1), 27–40.

Padela, A. I., Gunter, K., Killawi, A., & Heisler, M. (2012). Religious values and healthcare accommodations: Voices from the American Muslim Community. *Journal of General Internal Medicine, 27*(6), 708–715.

Pew Forum on Religion & Public Life. (2011). *The future of the global Muslim population*. Retrieved from http://www.pewforum.org/The-Future-of-the-Global-Muslim-Population.aspx.

Poureslami, I. M., MacLean, D. R., Spiegel, J., & Yassi, A. (2004). Sociocultural, environmental, and health challenges facing women and children living near the borders between Afghanistan, Iran, and Pakistan (AIP Region). *Medscape General Medicine, 6*(3), 51.

Powe, B. D., & Finnie, R. (2003). Cancer fatalism: The state of the science [Review]. *Cancer Nursing, 26*(6), 454–465 (quiz 466–457).

Shah, S. M., Ayash, C., Pharaon, N. A., & Gany, F. M. (2008). Arab American immigrants in New York: Health care and cancer knowledge, attitudes, and beliefs. *Journal of Immigrant and Minority Health, 10*(5), 429–436.

Shirazi, M., Bloom, J., Shirazi, A., & Popal, R. (2013). Muslim Afghan immigrant women's knowledge and behaviors around breast cancer screening. *Journal of Psycho-Oncology, 22*(8), 1679–1917.

UNHCR. (2004). *Background paper on refugees and asylum seekers from Afghanistan*. Geneva: UNHCR Center for Documentation and Research Publications.

Nurse-Curanderas: Las Que Curan at the Heart of Hispanic Culture

by Elaine Luna, R.N., M.S.N.
New Mexico State University

Bilingual nurse-curanderas are an emerging group of health care providers who blend the profession of nursing with Hispanic folk healing, thus providing culturally competent care to one of the largest growing minority groups in the United States. Nurse-curanderas integrate curanderismo (Hispanic folk healing) with allopathic health care, evaluate safety and efficacy, and implement appropriate interventions. This balance reduces cultural conflict and improves outcomes by increasing patient compliance with the treatment regimen. A Spanish-English glossary of terms used is included.

Elaine Luna, *Journal of Holistic Nursing, Vol 21, No 4, December 2003*, pp 326-342. Copyright © 2003 SAGE Publications, Inc. Reprinted by permission of SAGE Publications, Inc.

From the beginning of time, indigenous healers have helped ensure the survival of the human race. As enamored as contemporary health care professionals are with the biomedical model, humans have survived for at least 80,000 years without this model (Stein & Rowe, 1989). One essential link to human survival has been the traditional healer. The advent of the biomedical model has not eliminated such healers. Indeed, some traditional healers and biomedical practitioners are willingly working together. More specifically, nurse-curanderas are an emerging group whose influence is growing in the practice of professional nursing. This article discusses the importance and significance of the unique blend of traditional Hispanic folk healers and bicultural professional nurses.

Las Que Curan

Who are "Las Que Curan"?

Emerging from the womb of our Mestiza Madre

Barely remembering the ways of our antepasados

With vergueza, we do not speak our native tongues.

Did we come into this healing art by chance?

Perhaps suerte placed us on the "camino curandera"?

Some entered through the backdoor of a university school house

Validating our right to exist, to speak, to be different!

Las Que Curan stand in the circle of ritual and ceremony

We watch unseen open wounds bleed and dry teardrops fall

We pray the universal prayers of love, light, hope, and peace

Guided by the souls who bore us.

Las Que Curan will not be lost again

We are here to teach the next generations—no olvides!

When we join the abuelas and abuelos in antepasado heaven

Our legacy will live on, old souls reborn to serve again

—Luna (2001)

Do bicultural nurse-curanderas have a distinctive role in nursing? Elena Avila (1999) describes her role as a nurse and a curandera and how her role evolved over 25 years of practice. With innovative expertise in applying curanderismo in today's health care setting, Avila demonstrates that clients benefit from a synthesis of professional health care and personalized folk medicine.

The limited body of literature focusing on traditional Hispanic folk medicine comes mostly from an etic—or outside observer's—perspective. Information coming from within the Hispanic culture—the emic perspective—is even more limited, especially in academia and biomedicine, where information is compartmentalized. Discussing the debate about the value of etic versus emic perspectives, Fetterman (1989) suggests that "the insider's perception of reality is instrumental to understanding and accurately describing situations and behaviors" (p. 30). As a bicultural nurse and a curandera, this author is synthesizing the essence of Hispanic culture and the culture of professional nursing (see Table 1).

Table 1 Translation and Definition of Terms	
Hispanic, Mexican American	For the purpose of this paper, these terms are used interchangeably
abuelas, abuelos	Grandmothers, grandfathers
antepasados	Ancestors
bruja	A folk practitioner who uses "black magic" to cast evil spells
camino curandera	The road of the healer

(Continued)

Table 1 Translation and Definition of Terms (Continued)	
curandera	Hispanic folk healer who practices in one or more of the following specialties: *huesero* (bone setter), *yerbera* (herbalist), *partera* (midwife), *sobadora* (masseur), *señora* (card reader), or *espiritista* (works in spiritual realm through ritual and prayer, or as a medium)
curanderismo	The art and science of Hispanic folk healing; a quintessential model of holistic healing that addresses the spiritual, physical, social, psychological, and soulful needs of traditional individuals; a diagnostic and treatment regimen specific to Hispanic folk illnesses and conditions that has evolved to include non-Hispanic folk illnesses (Arizaga, 1999)
Hispanic	General term used to describe individuals with ethnic origin from countries where Spanish is the primary language; includes people from Mexico, Puerto Rico, Cuba, the Dominican Republic, some Central and South American countries, and Spain (Mendoza, 1994)
indigenous	Native
Latina, Latino	Individuals of various ethnic origins from a Spanish-speaking country in the Americas; describes the vast majority of people in the United States who originated from a Spanish-speaking country (Mendoza, 1994)
limpia	Spiritual cleansing performed to treat various illnesses; techniques vary depending on the practice of the curandera
No olvides	Do not forget
plática	Informal conversation between curandera and client to discern the needs and concerns of the client; serves as an assessment tool in formulating a plan of care
mestizo	Individuals of Spanish-Indian mixed-blood and cultures; the majority population in Mexico, now known as Mexicans (De Mente, 1998)
Mexican Americans	Individuals of Mexican descent, many of whose families have lived in the United States for extended periods but whose citizenship is not explicitly defined (Mendoza, 1994).
suerte	Luck
susto	Soul or spirit loss resulting from a traumatic event
verguenza	Shame

Historical Influences

The old tradition of curanderismo is both holistic and eclectic, blending New World indigenous beliefs (15th and 16th century) and Old World European medicine and theories (Avila, 1999; Davidow, 1999; Gutiérrez, 1970; Krassner, 1986; Torres, 1984; Trotter & Chavira, 1997). The roots of curanderismo reach as far back as the Kabbalah, the ancient wisdom of Jewish mysticism, according to various texts published in Spain (R. Spector, personal communication, April 14, 2003). Curanderismo can be defined not only as an art but also as a science related to current discoveries in quantum physics, holographic models, and psychoneuroimmunology.

Curanderismo is healing, not magic. Watson (1999) states that "the thinking from quantum physics and holographic models of science evokes new metaphors and a new aesthetic language to reflect some of the metaphysical and human dimensions of transpersonal caring, consciousness and energy" (p. 109). The concepts of universal connectedness, caring-healing consciousness and interdependence are clearly present in curanderismo.

Spanish influences were brought to the New World at the time of the conquest of Mexico in 1519. This influence included a combination of early Greek and Roman practices based on Hippocratic and Galenic medicine, merged with the highly successful Arabic medicine introduced into Spain by the Moors. According to Trotter and Chavira (1997), two important contributions from the Hispano-Arabic medical system included the concept of health as a balanced condition, where a lack of harmony with the social, spiritual, or physical environment produces illness, with the restoration of this balance being the work of the healer, and the Spanish use of Biblical teachings supporting the use of medicinal remedies derived from plants and animals, which in turn led to a zealous search for new herbal medicines in the Old and New World.

The Aztec Empire and earlier civilizations of the Olmec, Toltec, Zapotec, and Maya contributed significantly to the practice of curanderismo as Spanish medicine came into contact with Aztec medicine (Krassner, 1986). According to Gutiérrez (1970), the Aztecs had a far greater knowledge of botany and its application to healing than did the Europeans. The Aztec botanic classification system predated that of Linnaeus by more than two centuries (Gutiérrez, 1970). The first botanical garden in the Aztec empire was started in Padua, half a century before its European counterpart (Gutiérrez, 1970). Records suggest that Aztec medicine was highly spiritual and that spiritual forces were involved in the treatment of ailments.

Contributions of the New World's indigenous medicinal knowledge, beliefs, and practices varied from region to region, depending on which tribe came in contact with the Spaniards. However, it is clear that indigenous knowledge of the curative value of local plants and animals greatly expanded the imported European pharmacology (Trotter & Chavira, 1997; Viesca, 1986).

The influence of African medicine was also part of the emerging eclectic medicine in Mexico, as well as other parts of the continent (Morales, 1998). Avila (1999) states, "Millions of African slaves came to North America and Mexico between 1500 and 1870, bringing spiritual beliefs and medical practices that were incorporated into curanderismo" (p. 22). Africans held some beliefs in common with indigenous populations of the New World, such as the belief that spirit and soul are not disconnected from the physical body (Avila, 1999).

The use of curanderismo over the centuries has been influenced by the Hispanic understanding of disease as having spiritual, social, and personal consequences that go beyond biological significance (Richardson, 1982; Taylor & Skinner, 2000). Curanderismo continues to survive and evolve despite the more recent appearance of allopathic medicine (Avila, 1999; Lopiccolo, 1990; Trotter & Chavira, 1997). Despite many attempts to eliminate the practice of traditional folk medicine, it has clearly not been obliterated by allopathic medicine, especially in Latin America (Pederson & Baruffati, 1989).

Reasons why folk medicine continues to survive, according to Wilkinson (1987), include regional location of users; repeated success with particular plants and herbs; limited economic resources; escalating costs of physicians' services, prescription medicines, and hospitalization; lack of health insurance; distrust of modern medical technology and doctors; intrinsic intrafamily sentiments and traditional help patterns; and lack of immediate access to treatment facilities in rural and isolated communities.

Urdaneta, Livingston, Aguilar, Enciso, and Kaye (2002) acknowledge the above reasons as identified by Wilkinson (1987) and note the following additional factors: no separation of the body from the mind, spirit, or soul; no language barrier, as the curandera is usually a resident of the same barrio; no cryptic medical terminology; involvement of the patient and patient's family in the treatment and healing process, with the family serving as a natural support system; willingness of the curandera to spend adequate time and provide nonthreatening counsel; availability in border communities for people regardless of citizenship; and reinforcement of cultural identification.

Curanderismo as Complementary and Alternative Medicine

The practice of curanderismo falls into the category of alternative medical systems: traditional indigenous systems, as identified by the National Center for Complementary and Alternative Medicine (NCCAM, 2002). Curanderismo is linked to Complementary and Alternative Medicine (CAM) therapies by virtue of its holistic orientation, which does not separate the physical, mental, spiritual, and soulful influences of the illness processes. Hufford (1997) comments, "by definition and by history, folk medicine is one of the basic—probably the most basic—aspects of alternative medicine" (p. 731).

The increased use of CAM therapies has been documented in the literature by Eisenberg et al. (1998). Today's consumers are dissatisfied with the delivery of impersonal health care, as mediated through office staff members, non–health care professionals, and insurance administrators. In response, some consumers seek therapies that incorporate and promote a holistic approach. As Bushy (1992) observes,

> For years, health professionals have adhered to the belief that western medicine with its mechanistic and reductionistic intervention is the only way to treat illness. Now we realize that this model does not have all the answers; in fact, the model has perpetuated a national health care crisis. (p. 16)

Alternative medical systems have not generated a great deal of quantitative research, partly because they rely on well-developed clinical observation skills and experiences consistent with their explanatory frameworks (Fontaine, 2000). Folk medicine has not been supplanted by biomedicine and is not limited to the poor and less educated (Hufford, 1997; Lopiccolo, 1990). Bushy (1992) observed that any health care system would be overwhelmed with clients if there were no self-care practices such as traditional folk medicine.

Curanderas traditionally do not "bill" clients for their services. Payment is often made by unconventional means such as barter for produce or services; when harsh circumstances indicate, there is no compensation. Instances in which "healers" expect large fees for services—usually involving the so-called removal of a "curse"—are not considered legitimate by reputable practitioners (Avila, 1999).

Folk Healers

Hispanics are one of the fastest growing ethnic groups in the United States and are emerging as the largest minority. Hispanics outnumber African Americans and by 2025 will account for 18% of the U.S. population (AmeriStat, 2000). Most Mexican

immigrants live in states that border Mexico: Arizona, California, New Mexico, and Texas. Like other immigrants, many Mexican immigrants, especially the elderly, retain cultural patterns, values, and beliefs brought from their country of origin. This retention is enhanced by the proximity to Mexico and the "fluidity" of the border (Gordon, 1994).

The use of Hispanic folk healers in the United States is probably underreported. According to Higginbotham, Trevino, and Ray (1990) the Hispanic Health and Nutritional Examination Survey reported that as few as 4.2% of respondents between the ages of 18 and 74 reported consulting a curandera, herbalist, or other folk practitioner within the 12 months prior to that survey. Mayers (1989) completed a study on elderly Mexican American women in Dallas, Texas, which revealed that the women used folk remedies and consulted curanderas but concealed these facts from their children and doctors, fearing nonacceptance and ridicule for using the folk therapies.

Keegan (1996) conducted a study on the use of alternative therapies among Mexican Americans in the Texas Rio Grande valley. This study revealed that 44% of participants used an alternative therapy (including herbal medicine, spiritual healing, massage, and curanderas) at least once during the previous year. Sixty-six percent of these participants, however, did not report the visits to their primary health providers. Keegan (2000) conducted another study comparing the use of alternative therapies among Mexican Americans and Anglo-Americans in the Texas Rio Grande valley. The results indicated that twice as many Mexican American participants reported using an alternative therapy (158 visits) once or more during the previous year as their Anglo counterparts (72 visits). Fifty-five percent of the Mexican American participants did not report these practices to their primary care provider, whereas 73% of Anglo-Americans did not report use of alternative practices to their primary health providers (Keegan, 2000).

Urdaneta, Aguilar, Livingston, Gonzales-Bogran, and Kaye (2001) found that approximately 50% of client informants knew about and had used the services of folk healers and/or parteras. Another 45.5% of the sample knew about curanderas and parteras but had not used their services. Thus, over 95% of the client informants knew about curanderos and parteras, with half of the informants using the services while also availing themselves of mainstream medical services (Urdaneta et al., 2001).

Nursing and Healing

Holistic practitioners in general have increased in numbers since the 1970s, and many of these practitioners are nurses (Keegan, 1996). Nursing's holistic and unique participation in the healing process goes well beyond the Cartesian model. Kritek (1997) states, "Nurses embrace the idea of healing readily, and think of themselves as persons engaged in healing the whole person, the family, and indeed, even the communities where they serve" (p. 14). The concepts of holism and humanism are embedded in the nursing profession and are consistent with the importance of the biological, psychological, emotional, and spiritual components of illness and health (Fontaine, 2000).

Nurse-curanderas are not only professional nurses, they are also healers. They acquire their knowledge base from nursing science as well as from many generations of ancestors. The ancestral knowledge has been passed down almost exclusively in oral form. Some nurse-curanderas apprentice with experienced curanderas to learn the folk medicine. Familiarity with the Hispanic culture, language, and folk medicine adds a unique dimension to the practice of the nurse-curandera. The curandera's relationships with clients, families, and the community go beyond the time-restricted and impersonal care often provided by allopathic medicine.

Theoretical Foundation

Culturally competent nursing practice requires a theoretical framework. One such framework that encompasses curanderismo is the holistic health model, a set of highly abstract constructs. Holistic health is a term used to define a state in which the individual is integrated at all levels—body, mind, spirit, and soul. Emphasis is placed on the interdependence and interrelatedness of all systems to each other, to all individuals, and to the universe. Holistic nursing is oriented to the prevention of illness, the maintenance of health, and the healing process (Dossey, Keegan, Guzzetta, & Kolkmeier, 1995).

Assumptions of the holistic model include the interrelatedness of wholes, an emphasis on moral/ethical dimensions of care, the value of nonduality,

and universal bonding (Dossey et al., 1995). The holistic model in nursing incorporates perennial philosophy, humanistic philosophy, natural systems theory, the nursing process framework, Standards of Practice of the American Holistic Nurses Association (AHNA), and the North American Nursing Diagnosis Associations's taxonomy (Dossey et al., 1995).

Application of nursing theorists to the holistic model include the works of Rogers, Watson, Newman, Parse, Leininger, Benner, and Dossey (Chinn & Kramer, 1995), as well as the work of nurse anthropologists DeSantis, Lipson, Tripp-Reimer, Brink, and Barbee (Urdaneta et al., 2001). Because holism encompasses humanistic philosophy, other humanistic, nonnursing theories and philosophies also apply to this model. These include Dewey, Clandinin, Heidegger, Rogers, Connelly, Husserl, Kierkegaard, and Whitehead (Lamont, 1990).

Cultural Relevance

Despite the importance of cultural relevance and competence in the delivery of health care as documented in the literature (Andrews & Boyle, 1999; Giger & Davidhizar, 1995; Leininger, 1995; Spector, 2000; Urdaneta et al., 2001), many nurses continue to ignore or dismiss the evidence. The concept of cultural competence is supported by the AHNA (2000), the American Nurses' Association (ANA, 1996) and the American Association of Colleges of Nursing (AACN, 2000). The AACN has entered into a collaborative agreement with two of the major national Hispanic organizations to increase access to nursing education opportunities (AACN, 2000).

On more than one occasion, this author has encountered an indignant nurse when suggesting that nurses study Hispanic culture and learn some basic Spanish to improve client care and compliance. It is not unreasonable to expect nurses to be culturally sensitive and even culturally competent. Bushy (1992) comments, "Nurses must be astutely sensitive to the fact that when scientific knowledge is presented so that it appears to be incompatible with a client's traditional belief, the traditional way will probably be accepted" (p. 17).

Pacquiao (1995) states that "consumer preference for ethnically congruent health care services has been documented in the literature" (p. 4).

Incorporating traditional practices in the delivery of health care can increase utilization rates of allopathic care, improve client compliance with the treatment regimen, enhance client-provider relationships, and empower the client to take a more active role in his or her care. Reducing conflicts between ethnic and allopathic medicine may conceivably result in cost-effective reductions in length of stay, morbidity, mortality, and number of hospitalizations (Rankin & Kappy, 1993). Delivering culturally competent care also reduces the likelihood of ethnocentrism by the nurse, who will in turn model culturally aware behavior for other health care providers.

Although individualized care is emphasized in nursing education, "lip service" is more often than not paid to this concept in the actual delivery of care to minority clients. Nursing practice and theory are not ethical unless cultural factors are included; this concept is basic to nursing practice and philosophy (Eliason, 1993).

Advanced Practice Role of the Nurse-Curandera

Clients consulting a bilingual nurse-curandera are not likely to feel degraded or ridiculed for their beliefs or for using curanderismo. In contrast to allopathic medicine, no cultural or language issues impede the healing process or interfere with patient compliance of the treatment regimen. Referrals for allopathic care, as well as insight into the educational needs of the client are common. Because the nurse-curandera has a scientific background, she can evaluate the safety of a folk remedy or treatment and refer clients to other health care providers when appropriate.

Ideally, health care providers would include the nurse-curandera in the client's plan of care. In combination, allopathic medicine and curanderismo potentiate a synergistic effect of healing and curing for the client and family. Many consumers seek the services of both a medical doctor and a curandera (Avila, 1999). More referrals occur from curanderos to medical practitioners than the reverse (Krassner, 1986). Avila's (1999) experiences are similar:

> While I refer many of my clients to medical doctors, and/or make myself available to work with them in the context of a team, I rarely hear from a doctor who is interested in working with me for the health of the patient. (p. 308)

There is no currently defined role for the bicultural nurse-curandera within the nursing profession, nor is there a defined role for the advanced practice nurse (APN)-curandera. Fortunately, though, such nurses do exist. Several bicultural APN-curanderas function in this unique role in New Mexico. They include a nurse practitioner who incorporates curanderismo into her practice in a clinic setting, and other nurse-curanderas who work in hospital and hospice settings, where ritual and ceremony provide comfort for terminally ill patients and their families. These nurses creatively blend nursing practice with traditional Hispanic folk healing. They establish a personal relationship with the client that transcends the physical realm of care, creating an intimate and sacred space in which to explore emotional/mental/spiritual/soulful causes of illness, which manifest in physical form and can be linked to cultural identity.

The following scenario demonstrates the application of nursing and curanderismo. In the author's private practice, a 20-year-old woman presented with a complaint of chronic back pain of more than 10 years' duration. She had consulted numerous physicians (internists, general practitioners, and orthopedists) in two states. Her examinations, MRI, CT, and x-rays were all normal. Despite the negative findings, the young woman insisted "something is wrong." Over-the-counter and prescription medications did not relieve the pain that limited her activities and her ability to fully participate in life.

During the course of our work together, the client revealed that she had suffered from traumatic physical abuse at the age of 5 and had witnessed similar violence directed toward her mother. Eventually, she was able to recall that her back pain began shortly after the traumatic events. The memory of this susto had been physically stored in the area of her lower back. With these insights, the client was able to begin her process of deep healing.

Table 2 illustrates how the care of a client with susto translates into practice for the advanced practice holistic nurse-curandera. Comparisons are made between the ANA (1996) standards of advanced practice nursing, AHNA (2000) standards of holistic nursing practice, and the practice domains and competencies, which include the work of Benner (1984), as identified by Fenton and Brykczynski (1993).

Table 2 Comparing Standards of Practice

Nurse-Curandera's Treatment Regimen	American Nursing Association Standards of Advanced Practice Nursing (1996)	American Holistic Nursing Association Standards: Core Values of the Holistic Caring Process (2000)	Practice Domains and Competencies. Benner (1984), Fenton, and Brykczynski (1993)
1. Assessment is conducted during a platica (talk)	The advanced practice nurse (APN) collects comprehensive client health data	Each person is assessed holistically using appropriate traditional and holistic methods while the uniqueness of the person is honored	Diagnostic and patient monitoring function; the consulting role of the nurse; interpreting the role of nursing to others; role modeling assessment, monitoring, coordination, management of patient care over time; developing strategies for dealing with concerns
2. Diagnosis encompasses the biomedical model and the Hispanic folk model	The APN critically analyzes the assessment data in determining diagnoses	Actual and potential patterns, problems, needs, and life processes related to health, wellness, disease, or illness that may or may not facilitate well-being are identified and prioritized	Detecting acute and/or chronic disease while attending to illness
3. Outcomes and planning are based on the needs and willingness voiced by the client	The APN identifies expected outcomes derived from the assessment data and diagnoses and individualized expected outcomes with the client and other health care team members	Each person's actual or potential patterns, problems, and needs have appropriate outcomes specified	The helping role of the nurse; teaching and coaching function, and providing emotional and informational support to patients' families. Health care needs and capacities: teaching self-care, and making health and illness approachable and understandable
4. Client and healer formulate a plan for implementation, timing, and methods to be used	The APN develops a comprehensive plan of care that includes interventions and treatment to attain expected outcomes	Therapeutic Care Plan: Each person engages with the holistic nurse to mutually create an appropriate plan of care that focuses on health promotion, recovery or restoration, or peaceful dying so that the person is as independent as possible	Administering and monitoring therapeutic interventions and regimens Management of patient health status in ambulatory care settings: selecting and recommending diagnostic and therapeutic interventions

(Continued)

Table 2 Comparing Standards of Practice *(Continued)*

5. Implementation of interventions includes additional platicas and one or more limpias (cleansings)	The APN prescribes, orders, or implements interventions and treatments as planned	Each person's plan of holistic care is prioritized, and holistic nursing interventions are implemented accordingly
6. Evaluating effectiveness of the treatment regimen includes client, healer, and often the patient's family	The APN evaluates client's progress in attaining expected outcomes	Each person's responses to holistic care are regularly and systematically evaluated; the continuing holistic nature of the healing process is recognized and honored
7. Referrals are made to appropriate health care professionals as needed	Negotiation when patient and provider priorities conflict	Monitoring and ensuring the quality of health care practices, making the bureaucracy respond to patient and family needs, and giving constructive feedback to ensure safe practices
		Providing consultations to doctors and other staff members on patient management; using physician consultation effectively

Conclusion

Effective and culturally competent care is provided by bicultural nurse-curanderas. This unique group of practitioners serves as a valuable resource not only to their clients but to the nursing profession as well. As nurse-curanderas practice and demonstrate the integration of curanderismo with allopathic medicine, the role will be more clearly defined and understood.

The "melting pot" and its associated myth of assimilation has proven to be elusive; in fact, blending into a melting pot is no longer viewed as desirable by many people of cultural minorities in this country. Clearly, nurses must learn to work with clients from other cultures (Spector, 2000). In the case of Hispanic culture, the benefits of integrating curanderismo into professional nursing practice are apparent. Assimilating the insights of complementary and alternative medicine into advanced nursing practice will provide important and valuable links in the process of rendering truly holistic care in more mainstream biomedical settings.

References

American Association of Colleges of Nursing. (2000). *Media relations: AACN, Hispanic organizations join in pact to boost nursing education opportunities.* Retrieved April 26, 2001, from http://www.aacn.nche.edu/Media/NewsReleases/hspagwb.htm

American Holistic Nurses Association. (2000). *Standards of holistic nursing practice.* Flagstaff, AZ: Author.

American Nurses Association. (1996). *Scope and standards of advanced practice registered nursing.* Washington DC: Author.

AmeriStat. (2000). *The changing American pie, 1999 and 2025.* Retrieved April 23, 2001, from http://www.prb.org/Content/NavigationMenu/Ameristat/Topics1/Estimates__Projections/The_Changing_American_Pie,_1999_and_2025.htm

Andrews, M. M., & Boyle, J. S. (1999). *Transcultural concepts in nursing care* (3rd ed.). Philadelphia: J. B. Lippincott.

Arizaga, G. (1999). Curanderismo as holistic medicine. In G. Cajete (Ed.), *A people's ecology—Explorations in sustainable living: Health, environment, agriculture, native traditions* (pp. 210-223). Santa Fe, NM: Clear Light.

Avila, E. (1999). *Woman who glows in the dark.* New York: J. P. Tarcher.

Benner, P. (1984). *From novice to expert.* Menlo Park, CA: Addison-Wesley.

Bushy, A. (1992). Cultural considerations for primary health care: Where do self-care and folk medicine fit? *Holistic Nursing Practice, 6*(3), 10-18.

Chinn, P., & Kramer, M. (1995). *Theory and nursing: A systematic approach* (4th ed.). St. Louis, MO: Mosby.

Davidow, J. (1999). *Infusions of healing: A treasury of Mexican-American herbal remedies.* New York: Fireside.

De Mente, B. L. (1998). *There's a word for it in Mexico: The complete guide to Mexican thought and culture.* Lincolnwood, IL: Passport Books.

Dossey, B. M., Keegan, L., Guzzetta, C. E., & Kolkmeier, L. G. (1995). *Holistic nursing: A handbook for practice* (2nd ed.). Gaithersburg, MD: Aspen.

Eisenberg, D. M., Davis, R. B., Ettner, S. L., Appel, S., Wilkey, S., Van Romany, M., et al. (1998). Trends in alternative medicine in the United States 1990-1997. *JAMA, 280,* 1569-1575.

Eliason, M. J. (1993). Ethics and transcultural nursing care. *Nursing Outlook, 41,* 225-228.

Fenton, M. V., & Brykczynski, K. A. (1993). Qualitative distinctions and similarities in the practice of clinical nurse specialists and nurse practitioners. *Journal of Professional Nursing, 9,* 313-324.

Fetterman, D. (1989). *Ethnography: Step by step.* Newbury Park, CA: Sage.

Fontaine, K. L. (2000). *Healing practices: Alternative therapies for nursing.* Upper Saddle River, NJ: Prentice Hall.

Giger, J. N., & Davidhizar, R. E. (1995). *Transcultural nursing: Assessment and intervention* (2nd ed.). St. Louis, MO: Mosby.

Gordon, S. M. (1994). Hispanic cultural health beliefs and folk remedies. *Journal of Holistic Nursing, 12,* 307-322.

Gutiérrez, E. D. (1970). *La medicina primitiva en México* [Primitive medicine in Mexico]. Mexico: Artes de Mexico.

Higginbotham, J. C., Trevino, F. M., & Ray, L. A. (1990). Utilization of curanderos by Mexican Americans: Prevalence and predictors findings from HHANES, 1980-1984. *American Journal of Public Health, 80,* 32-35.

Hufford, D. J. (1997). Folk medicine and health culture in contemporary society. *Primary Care, 24,* 723-741.

Keegan, L. (1996). Use of alternative therapies among Mexican Americans in the Texas Rio Grande valley. *Journal of Holistic Nursing, 14,* 277-293.

Keegan, L. (2000). A comparison of the use of alternative therapies among Mexican Americans and Anglo-Americans in the Texas Rio Grande valley. *Journal of Holistic Nursing, 18*, 281-295.

Krassner, M. (1986). Effective features of therapy from the healer's perspective: A study of curanderismo. *Smith College Studies in Social Work, 56*, 157-183.

Kritek, P. B. (Ed.). (1997). *Reflections on healing: A central nursing construct.* New York: NLN.

Lamont, C. (1990). *The philosophy of humanism* (7th ed.). New York: Continuum.

Leininger, M. (1995). *Transcultural nursing: Concepts, theories, research & practice* (2nd ed.). New York: McGraw-Hill.

Lopiccolo, P. (1990). *Curanderismo in the El Paso/Las Cruces/Ciudad Juarez area.* Unpublished master's thesis, New Mexico State University, Las Cruces.

Luna, E. (2001). *Las que curan.* Unpublished manuscript.

Mayers, M. (1989). Use of folk medicine by elderly Mexican-American women. *Journal of Drug Issues, 19*, 283-295.

Mendoza, F. S. (1994). The health of Latino children in the United States. *Critical Health Issues for Children and Youth, 4*(3), 44-72.

Morales, A. L. (1998). *Remedios: Stories of earth and iron from the history of Puertorriqueñas.* Boston: Beacon.

National Center for Complementary and Alternative Medicine. (2002). *What is Complementary and Alternative Medicine (CAM)?* Retrieved March 28, 2003, from http://nccam.nih.gov/health/whatiscam/index.htm

Pacquiao, D. F. (1995). Multicultural issues in nursing practice and education. *Issues, 16*(2), 1, 4-5, 11.

Pederson, D., & Baruffati, V. (1989). Healers, deities, saints, and doctors: Elements for analysis of medical systems. *Social Science Medicine, 29*, 487-496.

Rankin, S. B., & Kappy, M. S. (1993). Developing therapeutic relationships in multicultural settings. *Academic Medicine, 68*, 826-827.

Richardson, L. (1982). Caring through understanding, part II: Folk medicine in the Hispanic population. *Imprint, 29*(21), 72, 75-77.

Spector, R. E. (2000). *Cultural diversity in health and illness* (5th ed.). Upper Saddle River, NJ: Prentice Hall.

Stein, P. L., & Rowe, B. M. (1989). *Physical anthropology.* New York: McGraw-Hill.

Taylor, A., & Skinner, M. L. (2000). La salud y métodos integrales de curación: Diferentes práctivas tradicionales y alternativas para lograr cambios positivos [Health and integrated practices of healing: Different traditional practices and alternatives to achieve positive changes]. In Boston Women's Health Book Collective (Ed.), *Nuestros cuerpos, nuestras vidas* (pp. 89-106). New York: Seven Stories.

Torres, E. (1984). *The folk healer: The Mexican-American tradition of curanderismo.* Kingsville, TX: Nieves.

Trotter, R. T., & Chavira, J. A. (1997). *Curanderismo: Mexican-American folk healing* (2nd ed.). Athens, GA: University of Georgia Press.

Urdaneta, M. L., Aguilar, M. C., Livingston, J., Gonzales-Bogran, S., & Kaye, C. I. (2001). *Understanding Mexican American cultural beliefs and traditional healing practices: A guide for genetic service providers in South Texas.* San Antonio: University of Texas.

Urdaneta, M. L., Livingston, J. E., Aguilar, M. C., Enciso, V. B., & Kaye, C. I. (2002). *Understanding Mexican American cultural beliefs and traditional healing practices: A guide for genetic service providers on the U.S.-Mexican border.* San Antonio: University of Texas.

Viesca, T. C. (1986). *Medicina prehispánica de México: El conocimiento de los nahuas* [Prehispanic medicine of Mexico: The knowledge of the Nahuas]. Mexico City, Mexico: Panorama Editorial.

Watson, J. (1999). *Postmodern nursing and beyond.* New York: Churchill Livingstone.

Wilkinson, D. (1987). Traditional medicine in American families: Reliance on the wisdom of elders. *Marriage and Family Review, 11*(3/4), 65-76.

Elaine Luna, R.N., M.S.N., is a part-time clinical nursing instructor at New Mexico State University in Las Cruces, New Mexico. She completed her master's degree at New Mexico State University and earned a graduate certificate in holistic nursing from Beth-El College of Nursing and Health Sciences, University of Colorado at Colorado Springs. Recent presentations include Curanderismo: The healing ways of Hispanic culture *and* Working with belief systems—A faith-based approach: Curanderismo.

Politics of Disease and Alternative Approaches to Healthcare

1. How do lived environments contribute to women's overall health?

2. Identify blogs or organizations working to address environmental issues that contribute to poor health. What type of policies and/or regulations would you support and advocate for us to have a safer environment?

3. How does race and where a person lives impact the experiences of breast cancer?

4. What role does spirituality play in women's holistic health?

5. Cultural competency has been discussed throughout the textbook; identify policies and procedures that impact access to healthcare.

6. Identify and define ways alternative approaches help women manage their illnesses and health. How do alternative modalities redefine women's understanding of healthcare?

7. What is wellness and how does our society promote and support or not support this concept? How should the healthcare industry promote wellness?

RESOURCES
By Marissa Knaak and Mary Morrissey

General Resources

Center for Health and Gender Equality
www.genderhealth.org

The Guttmacher Institute
www.guttmacher.org

Mayo Clinic
www.mayoclinic.org

National Women's Health Network
www.nwhn.org

The National Women's Health Resource Center
www.healthywomen.org

Our Bodies Ourselves
www.ourbodiesourselves.org

U.S. Department of Health & Human Services,
Source for Women's Health Information
www.womenshealth.gov

Women's Health
Centers for Disease Control and Preventions
www.cdc.gov/women

Women's Health Initiative
U.S. Department of Health and Human Services
National Institutes of Health
www.nhlbi.nih.gov/whi

World Health Organization
http://www.who.int/en

Chapter 1: Women and the Healthcare System

American Medical Women's Association
www.amwa-doc.org

American Nurses Association
www.nursingworld.org

Go Ask Alice
www.goaskalice.columbia.edu

Raising Women's Voices
www.raisingwomensvoices.net

The American Congress of Obstetricians and Gynecologists
www.acog.org

Women Physician Section—American Medical Association
www.ama-assn.org/ama/pub/about-ama/our-people/member-groups-sections/women-physicians-section.page

Chapter 2: Inequalities and Health

Asian and Pacific Islander American Health Forum
www.apiahf.org

Asian American Network for Cancer Awareness, Research and Training
www.aancart.org

Black Women's Health Imperative
www.bwhi.org

Center for Black Women's Wellness
www.cbww.org

Center for Excellence of Transgender Health
www.transhealth.ucsf.edu

Fenway Health
www.fenwayhealth.org

Gay & Lesbian Medical Association
www.glma.org

Indian Health Service
www.ihs.gov

My Trans Health
www.mytranshealth.com

National Alliance for Hispanic Health
www.hispanichealth.org

National Indigenous Women's Resource Center
www.niwrc.org

National Institute on Minority Health and Health Disparities
www.nimhd.nih.gov

National Latina Health Network
www.nlhn.net

Rural Health Information Hub
www.ruralhealthinfo.org

Chapter 3: Sex, Gender Roles, and Image

Fat Studies Journal
www.tandfonline.com/toc/ufts20/current

Gender and Society (journal)
www.gas.sagepub.com

International Journal of Transgenderism
www.tandfonline.com/loi/wijt20

Intersex Society of North America
www.isna.org

Journal of Sex Research
www.sexscience.org/journal_of_sex_research

National Eating Disorders Association
www.nationaleatingdisorders.org

Sex Roles (journal)
www.link.springer.com/journal/11199

The Body Positive
www.thebodypositive.org

Chapter 4: Medicalization, Marketing, and the Politics of Information

Center for Drug Evaluation and Research
www.fda.gov/cder

Center for Medical Consumers
www.medicalconsumers.com

Drug Information Association
www.diaglobal.org

Drug Watch
www.drugwatch.com

The James Lind Library
www.jameslindlibrary.com

The National Institute for Health and Clinical Excellence (UK)
www.nice.org.uk

National Pharmaceutical Council
www.npcnow.com

Chapter 5: Menstruation and the Politics of Sex Education

Advocates for Youth
www.advocatesforyouth.org

American Journal of Sexuality Education
www.tandfonline.com/loi/wajs20

The Centre for Menstrual Cycle and Ovulation Research
www.cembor.ubc.ca

American Sexual Health Association
www.ashasexualhealth.org

Journal of Bisexuality
www.tandfonline.com/loi/wjbi20

Days for Girls
www.daysforgirls.org

Future of Sex Education (FoSE)
www.futureofsexed.org

GLQ: A Journal of Lesbian and Gay Studies
www.dukeupress.edu/glq

The Kinsey Institute
www.kinseyinstitute.org

National Coalition for Sexual Health
www.nationalcoalitionforsexualhealth.org

Scarleteen
www.scarleteen.com

Sexualities (journal)
www.sex.sagepub.com

Sex Education (journal)
www.tandfonline.com/loi/csed20

Sexual Information and Education Council of the United States
www.siecus.org

50 Cents Period
www.50centsperiod.org

National Association for Premenstrual Syndrome (UK)
www.pms.org/uk

Society for Menstrual Cycle Research
www.menstruationresearch.org

Good Vibrations
www.goodvibes.com

Chapter 6: Disability and Society

American Association on Health and Disability
www.aahd.us

AIDS.gov
www.aids.gov

American Foundation for Suicide Prevention
www.afsp.org

CROWD: Center for Research on Women with Disabilities
www.bcm.edu/crowd

Center for Women's Mental Health
Mass General Hospital
www.womensmentalhealth.org

Disability & Society (journal)
www.tandfonline.com/loi/cdso20

ILI: Independent Living Institute
www.independentliving.org

Mental Health America
www.mentalhealthamerica.net

Women's Mental Health (journal)
www.link.springer.com/journal/737

Chapter 7: Violence Against Women

Battered Women's Justice Project
www.bwjp.org

Domestic Abuse Intervention Project
www.theduluthmodel.org

End Rape on Campus
www.endrapeoncampus.org

Institute on Domestic Violence in the African American Community
www.idvaac.org

Jane Doe, Inc.—The Massachusetts Coalition Against Sexual Assault and Domestic Violence
www.janedoe.org

Includes resources for LGBTQ people.

Know Your IX (Title IX)
www.knowyourix.org

Love Is Respect
www.loveisrespect.org

National Coalition Against Domestic Violence
www.ncadv.org

The National Domestic Violence Hotline
www.thehotline.org

U.S. Department of Justice, Office on Violence Against Women

www.justice.gov/ovw

Chapter 8: Fertility, Childbirth, and Reproductive Justice

American College of Nurse-Midwives
www.midwife.org

La Leche League USA
www.lllusa.org

NARAL Pro-Choice America
naral.org

National Latina Institute for Reproductive Health
www.latinainstitute.org

Path2Parenthood (formerly American Fertility Association)
www.path2parenthood.org

Planned Parenthood
www.plannedparenthood.org

Resolve: The National Infertility Association
www.resolve.org

Society for Reproductive Endocrinology and Infertility
www.socrei.org

Unassisted Childbirth
www.unassistedchildbirth.com

Chapter 9: Aging, Ageism, and Older Women's Issues

Alzheimer's Association
www.alz.org

American Society on Aging
www.asaging.org

The Arthritis Association
www.arthritis.org

Caregiver Action Network
www.caregiveraction.org

The Endometriosis Association
www.endometriosis.org

The Gerontological Society of America
www.geron.org

Journal of Women and Aging
www.tandfonline.com/loi/wjwa20

National Alliance for Caregiving
www.caregiving.org

National Institute on Aging
U.S. Department of Health and Human Services
www.nia.nih.gov

National Osteoporosis Foundation
www.nof.org

North American Menopause Society
www.menopause.org

WomenHeart: The National Coalition for Women with Heart Disease
www.womenheart.org

Chapter 10: Politics of Disease and Alternative Approaches to Health Care

Academic Collaborative for Integrative Health
www.integrativehealth.org

American Holistic Health Association
www.ahha.org

Alternative Medicine
www.alternativemedicine.com

Centers for Disease Control and Prevention
www.cdc.gov

American Public Health Association
http://www.apha.org

National Center for Complementary and Integrative Health
www.nccih.nih.gov

Environmental Health (journal)
www.ehjournal.biomedcentral.com

The George Washington Institute for Spirituality and Health
www.smhs.gwu.edu/gwish

Journal of Holistic Nursing
www.jhn.sagepub.com

Journal of Transcultural Nursing
www.tcn.sagepub.com

RealClearPolitics—Healthcare Index
www.realclearpolitics.com/health_care

INDEX

CPSIA information can be obtained
at www.ICGtesting.com
Printed in the USA
LVOW02s2113170817
545323LV00003B/3/P